BIOFEEDBACK

BIOFEEDBACK
A PRACTITIONER'S GUIDE
Second Edition

**Mark S. Schwartz
and Associates**

Foreword by Frank Andrasik

The Guilford Press
New York   London

© 1995 The Mayo Foundation
Published by The Guilford Press
A Division of Guilford Publications, Inc.
72 Spring Street
New York, NY 10012

Printed in the United States of America

This book is printed on acid-free paper.

Last digit is print number: 9   8   7   6   5   4   3   2

Library of Congress Cataloging-in-Publication Data

Biofeedback : a practitioner's guide / edited by Mark S.
   Schwartz—2nd ed.
      p. cm.
     Rev. ed. of: Biofeedback / Mark S. Schwartz and Associates.
     c1987.
     ISBN 0-89862-806-7
     1. Biofeedback training.   I. Schwartz, Mark S.
  II. Schwartz, Mark S. Biofeedback.
     [DNLM: 1. Biofeedback (Psychology)   WL 103 B6145 1995]
     RC49.B484 1995
     615.8'51—dc20
     DNLM/DLC
     for Library of Congress   94-45417
                                   CIP

Memorial Statement
for Susan P. Lowery

I include this memorial to Susan not only because she was a friend and colleague many years ago, but because she was an inspiration and model for how to live with chronic disease, manage life despite physical limitations, care for others, and keep reaching and accomplishing.

On October 27, 1992, Susan died at age 40 after a 2-year struggle against a rare liver disease. Susan was widely known in Baltimore for her work as a volunteer for several social and health-related causes. As a psychotherapist and a person who endured the personal distress and social dilemmas of ulcerative colitis diagnosed when she was age 12, she provided stress management for people faced with this disease.

In her career she held positions at the Mayo Clinic Rochester, the John F. Kennedy Institue (now Kennedy–Krieger Institute), and the Francis Scott Key Medical Center of the John's Hopkins medical institutions. From 1983, she worked in general psychotherapy in private practices in Baltimore. She also participated as a volunteer for several Baltimore-based organizations, including the Crohn's and Colitis Foundation of America.

She married in 1986 and adopted Cristina, a baby from Medellin, Columbia. She wrote to me on January 3, 1992, 10 months before her death. She requested a letter of recommendation to help her get back into graduate school to complete her Ph.D. She already had two master's degrees in psychology and behavior modification from Southern Illinois University. In the letter she shared her excitement about being a mother, and she told me how alert, happy, and outgoing Cristina is.

Friends who supported Susan through the last months of her life were struck, but not surprised, by her will to live as normally as possible despite much pain and exhaustion.

This memorial statement was gleaned from a longer one written by her husband, Michael Mazepink, and from her letter to me.

Contributors

Barbara Bailey, R.N., M.S.N., C.D.E., Diabetes Education Coordinator, St. Vincent Medical Center, Toledo, Ohio

Keith I. Block, M.D., Cancer Treatment Program, Edgewater Medical Center, Chicago, Illinois; University of Illinois College of Medicine, Chicago, Illinois

Eugene Eisman, Ph.D., Private practice, Milwaukee, Wisconsin

Eric R. Fogel, R.P.T., Therapeutic Consultation Associates, Ashland, Oregon

Audrey L. Gemberling, M.A., Psychology, Mayo Clinic, Jacksonville, Florida

Richard N. Gevirtz, Ph.D., Department of Psychology, California School of Professional Psychology, San Diego, California

Alan G. Glaros, Ph.D., Department of Behavioral Sciences, University of Missouri, Kansas City, Missouri

Jack C. Hartje, Ph.D., Hartje Pain and Stress Clinic, and University of North Florida, Jacksonville, Florida

Deborah Hopper, Ph.D., Private practice, San Diego, California

Mark F. Kelly, M.A., St. Augustine, Florida

David E. Krebs, Ph.D., Graduate Program in Physical Therapy, MGH Institute of Health Professions; MGH Biomotion Laboratory, Massachusetts General Hospital, Boston; Harvard Medical School, Boston, Massachusetts; Massachusetts Institute of Technology, Cambridge, Massachusetts

J. Suzanne Kroon, B.A., The Minneapolis Clinic of Neurology, Edina, Minnesota

Susan P. Lowery, M.A., M.S., Private practice, Baltimore, Maryland (deceased)

Joel F. Lubar, Ph.D., Department of Psychology, University of Tennessee, Knoxville

Angele McGrady, Ph.D., Department of Psychiatry, Medical College of Ohio, Toledo

R. Paul Olson, Ph.D., Minnesota School of Professional Psychology, Minneapolis

Charles J. Peek, Ph.D., Group Health Inc., Health Partners, Minneapolis, Minnesota

Mark S. Schwartz, Ph.D., Psychology, Mayo Clinic Jacksonville, Florida

Nancy M. Schwartz, M.A., Associates for Counseling and Biofeedback, Jacksonville, Florida

Sebastian Striefel, Ph.D., Utah State University, Logan, Utah

Jeannette Tries, M.S.O.T.R., Sacred Heart Rehabilitation Hospital, Milwaukee, Wisconsin

Foreword

When first approached about preparing a foreword for this text, I must confess to having cold feet (so cold that thermal biofeedback might not even have been effective). How could I, in the few pages allotted and the brief time frame demanded by publication schedules, do justice to the approximately 1,200 pages of manuscript text that would need to be examined. Two things influenced my decision to accept this assignment. The first is my deep and abiding respect for the editor and lead author for the text, Dr. Mark S. Schwartz. Mark's early entrance into the field of biofeedback; his extensive clinical work at Mayo, beginning in the late 1960's; his wide-ranging participation at all levels in the governance of the Association for Applied Psychophysiology and Biofeedback (AAPB), the only professional society directly dealing with topics that are the focus of this text, and the Biofeedback Certification Institute of America, the only certifying body for biofeedback in the world; and his voracious appetite for keeping up with the published literature combine to allow Mark to stand shoulder to shoulder with the giants in the world of biofeedback. Mark possesses a wealth of information about what to do, how to do, and when to do it. In fact, this is one of the unifying themes for the text, optimizing the fit between the patient and the treatment.

The second influencing factor was that I was already quite familiar with the previous edition, having used it extensively when preparing various lectures for classes and workshops around the country and as a required text in undergraduate and graduate courses on biofeedback and behavioral medicine at my university. I could find no better text overall for these purposes and no better chapters for coverage of most topics. Around the time that Mark's first edition appeared in print, I was approached by another publisher about the possibility of preparing a similar type of text on biofeedback. After examining Mark's text and realizing that there were few if any stones left for me to unturn, I knew the only choice was to decline the offer. I knew then that his text would corner the market. One needs only to quickly page through the present volume to see that the market that was captured previously by the first edition will remain captive by this second edition.

What is so special about this text? It is rare for a text to try to be all things to all readers and almost unheard of to come any where close to this objective. However, this is truly the case for the present text. The academic novice, the neophyte biofeedback clinician, the seasoned veteran contemplating expanding practice domains, and the hardcore researcher seeking tips for meaningful clinical as well as basic science topics to address in future studies will all find something of value within the pages of this text. They may not come away with the same levels of understanding, nor find all chapters to be of equal value, but they will most assuredly come away with a new found appreciation for the field.

In the Foreword to the first edition, Dr. Joel F. Lubar began by claiming that biofeedback had come of age. With this edition, biofeedback enters a new era. We've all seen texts where the revisions, although described as extensive, are more cosmetic than substantial. Not so for the present text. After all, one cannot enter a new era without new knowledge. The first edition of this text was notable in many respects, only a few of which are mentioned here. They are included in this Foreword because these features remain true for the second edition. Those of us who know Mark well knew, even before the book went to print, that clinical procedures would be described in exquisite detail. It has a level of detail you don't realize you need until you have the patient seated in front of you and are asked that first difficult question. Master this book and you will know how to field those questions. Another distinguishing feature was a consistent attempt to stay true to the extant empirical literature, to try to make sense of the conflicting and sometimes downright negative data, and to draw upon his vast storehouse of clinical experience when research was lacking or too confusing to provide helpful guidance. Mark is particularly adept at gleaning the practice implications from what seems at times rather esoteric research. Yet another feature that set this text apart from others was its inclusion of many chapters dealing with important professional topics that one could not find elsewhere (entry requirements, routes to competence, practice models, job descriptions, quality control, communication, and client preparation, to name just some) and with important nonpharmacological adjunctive techniques that must be included in a comprehensive approach (nutrition, allied cognitive-behavioral and relaxation-based strategies, etc.). In fact, when reading both editions, I was struck by the extensive attention given to non-biofeedback approaches. Titling the text, "biofeedback," does not do it justice in many respects. A more apt title might stress the integrationist approach that threads through the text.

Mark's knowledge is wide-ranging, but, as is true of any responsible professional, he knows the boundaries of his competence and when to seek consultation from other, more knowledgeable experts. Enlistment of expert collaborators to cover topics that fell outside his areas of practice served not only to enrich the first edition of the text but to provide a tangible demonstration of his professional approach to his work. A final distinguishing feature to mention here is a steadfast adherence to the stepped-care model to treatment, or attempting the most cost-effective approach with a likely chance of success first. More complex and costly treatments are used only as justified. Proper use of this approach, which has at its heart the goal of patient–treatment matching, demands that one understand the pros and cons of approaches outside of biofeedback, as well as the various ways to approach biofeedback itself. What was seen in this text then was a mature, thoughtful approach to practice; an approach that is embodied in the scientist–practitioner model.

The second edition of this text has thankfully retained all of the aforementioned distinguishing features and all of the original expert collaborators (Eric R. Fogel, David E. Krebs, J. Suzanne Kroon, Susan P. Lowery, R. Paul Olson, and Charles J. Peek). All topics covered in the first edition remain, but most have been substantially revised and updated to reflect advances in research. Advances in knowledge warranted the inclusion of new topics, expertly prepared by several new contributors. Mark continues to have a knack for selecting the right people for the right job. New topics included in this edition are too numerous to identify, but range from those that are quickly becoming accepted targets for biofeedback (such as, attention-deficit/hyperactivity disorder, tinnitus, and phantom-limb pain), to those described as being the next frontier for biofeedback (such as, occupational cramps, hyperhidrosis, fibromyalgia, voice and vision disorders, immune disorders, and dysmenorrhea). I can think of no other text that provides the range and depth of coverage for these emerging topics. Mark continues to emphasize the importance of responsible practice and has recruited a leading expert (Striefel) to prepare a novel chapter on ethical issues and behavior in biofeedback. A particularly welcome addition is the inclusion of chapter glossaries for terms that may be unfamiliar to certain readers.

In my presidential address presented at the silver anniversary meeting of AAPB in Atlanta, March, 1994, I concluded with cautious optimism for the future of biofeedback. Upon reading the second edition of this text, I am prepared to drop the caution and more strongly embrace the optimism.

Once in a great while, a text comes along and captures the richness, complexity, and excitement of a field. For biofeedback, this is that text.

—FRANK ANDRASIK
Center for Behavioral Medicine
University of West Florida
Pensacola, Florida

Preface

This book is for health care practitioners using biofeedback, for researchers, and health care policy-makers and administrators. There is information for providers of reimbursement to consider seriously as well.

I am profoundly thankful for the response to the first edition that motivated this second edition. I still believe that no book can completely cover the diverse and rich field of biofeedback and applied psychophysiology. Yet, it was clear there was much more to include in the second edition. This book intends to fill perceived voids in the published literature.

As with all such volumes, this book has inherent advantages and disadvantages. Despite reflecting and expressing extensive experience, it reflects the judgments and recommendations of individual professionals.

Several new chapters have been added by other authors since the first edition, covering topics such as diabetes, computers, attention-deficit disorder, urinary incontinence, and ethics. I also added chapters discussing applications, which were not included in the first edition.

The chapter on bruxism underwent necessary and appreciated revision by Richard Gevirtz, Alan Glaros, and Deborah Hopper. Angele McGrady assisted in substantial updating and revision of the hypertension chapter. R. Paul Olson and Suzanne Kroon remained involved in this and other chapters. The dietary chapter expansion and updating owes much to the major contributions of Keith Block. A second part to the definitions chapter by Nancy Schwartz is a welcome addition. Nancy also helped revise the relaxation problems chapter. The chapter on breathing, scarcely a chapter in the first edition, received much needed attention and expansion in the current volume. Major revisions and updating also occurred for the chapters covering intake, headache, enuresis, and instrumentation (Charles Peek). Other chapters revised and updated include the Raynaud's chapter, thanks to the help of Mark Kelly, and the chapter on therapist presence is vastly improved due to the help of Audrey Gemberling.

I make special note to point out the revision of the chapter on research. As I reviewed this chapter, I remembered one prestigious researcher's concerns about the first edition version. This motivated me to make changes.

My professional experience with biofeedback began in 1974, at an early point in the development and acceptance of biofeedback in clinical applications. Up until then, I had been on the Mayo Clinic Rochester staff for 7 years. Biofeedback followed logically in the context of behavior therapy, which I introduced there in 1969, but biofeedback was neither in widespread use nor as accepted as it was in 1987 when this book first appeared.

In 1978, the Biofeedback Society of America (BSA) gave me an opportunity for which I am eternally grateful. I became Chair of the Professional Affairs Committee that subsumed the subcommittees of Certification, Applications Standards, Peer Review, Ethics, and Membership. I chaired that committee for 3 years and worked with many fine professionals, with whom I felt privileged to interact and learn from. From 1978 through 1982, we developed the original *Applications Standards and Guidelines for Providers of Biofeedback Services* published in 1982. The initial ethics document was started during that time and reached completion in 1984. The Biofeedback Certification Institute of America (BCIA) was founded in 1981, and I chaired that Board from March 1981 to March 1983. Within the BCIA, I chaired the development of the written exam. These experiences afforded me opportunities to gain a unique perspective on this field.

I will always be thankful for being President of the BSA. Actually, I was the last President of the organization with that name during the year March 1987–March 1988. The name officially evolved from the BSA to the Association of Applied Psychophysiology and Biofeedback (AAPB) in April 1988. I hope that most professionals will view this transition as a positive metamorphosis. Biofeedback and closely associated therapies are major aspects under the broader rubric of *applied psychophysiology*. The second edition of this book acknowledges and reflects both the change and broader concept. However, the focus of the book remains biofeedback.

After 21 years at the Mayo Clinic Rochester, I transferred to the Mayo Clinic Jacksonville in October 1988 to develop psychology services there, among other reasons. My involvement with the AAPB and BCIA are now fond memories. The endurance of this book helps me maintain the freshness of those memories and establish new ones. I sincerely invite readers for their comments. Thank you all.

—MARK S. SCHWARTZ

Acknowledgments

I am very fortunate in my professional and personal life and have always sensed a deep appreciation for those persons who showed confidence in me and provided support, patience, and loyalty. I again express my deep gratitude and love for my parents, Pearl and Sol Schwartz, for providing the foundation, early confidence, encouragement, and support. Thank you for your your persistence in life. Mom is now 85 and Dad is 82, and they still live on their own in Miami. I thank their doctors and nurses who periodically help keep them with me (so mom can keep supplying the best matzo balls).

To Nancy M. Schwartz, my wife and partner: for her brilliant ideas, editing, and willingness to help me in many ways; for her inspiration, respect, and devotion; for her warmth and therapeutic skills; for the way she continues to rise and surmount challenges; for her tenderness and the joy she brings to me and to my children; for her humor and infectious laughter. She helped transform my life immeasurably. Thank you Nancy!

There are many professionals to whom I am indebted and grateful. I again thank Edward Taub and Francine Butler for their confidence, understanding, cooperation, and friendship. I thanked many professionals in the first edition, and my gratitude remains. Over the past few years, a special enduring thanks goes to Wesley Sime, Steven Wolf, Joel Lubar, Richard Gevirtz, and Keith Sedlacek for their friendships and inspirations. To Joel Lubar, for his inspiration and support for the first edition, I extend a special expression of deep gratitude. I remain thankful to my original mentor, Donn Byrne, who inspired me and who provided much support during and after graduate school. He will always be with me.

To the many practitioners, and other professionals who bought the book, thank you. To the many educators who adopted the first edition in their academic courses and training programs, thank you for helping make this book successful. To their students, thank you for your kind words. Your feedback was a large part of the motivation for many of the changes such as adding the glossary.

Many thanks to the Guilford Press, for continued acceptance, support, and patience. Thank you Seymour Weingarten, Editor-in-Chief, and Robert Matloff, President. To the copy-editor, Elissa Schiff, and to Jodi Creditor, the Production Editor, and the entire production and marketing staff, a special thanks for excellence in quality, outstanding efficiency, support, and patience.

To the original authors, for their contributions and friendship, and for making this book a success, thank you. Your contributions, and those of our new authors, are uplifting and respected. To the new authors, thank you for agreeing to join this project and adding your wonderful wisdom and experience.

To T. Carey Merritt, M.D., and Paul A. Fredrickson, M.D., two very close colleagues and friends, thank you for your many years of support, respect, and humor that surpass description.

To my four adult children and granddaughter, my endless love, gratitude, and encouragement. Your struggles and successes continue to make me proud and relieved me of the strain of worry. Thank you Angela Renee, Ian Scott, Cynthia Michelle, and David Israel for your continued patience, your love, and for understanding the idiosyncracies of your father. I am proud of each of you and love you all very much. To my granddaughter, Michaela (Angela), age 9, a special thank you for being so charming and radiating so much joy.

In the first edition, I thanked both my ex-wives, Lora and Marta. Those sentiments are still alive. As the mothers of our beloved children I wish them both well.

To Jesse George, age 17, and Shane George, age 19, my wife Nancy's boys, I applaud their courage, their struggles, their wit, their patience with me, and their love for their mother. To Allyn and Dolores Hankins, Nancy's wonderful parents, for their unconditional acceptance of me into their family, I extend my gratitude.

To Audrey L. Gemberling, for dedication, patience, wisdom, skills, and help with myriad administrative tasks, I am very grateful. For more than 6 years, she has stood at my side and enriched the Section of Psychology at the Mayo Clinic Jacksonville. She is a biofeedback therapist, psychometrist, research assistant, and supervisor at the Mayo Clinic Jacksonville. She often played a vital role in making this second edition a reality.

To the Mayo Clinics and Mayo Foundation that have continued to provide opportunities, confidence, patience, and support for me for over 27 years, my unyielding devotion and thanks. Working in this climate of excellence and cost-efficient health care, infused with devotion to patients and respect for colleagues, is an unsurpassable life experience. My special appreciation to Robert Benassi, past Chair of Medical Illustrations, and his colleagues George DeVinney, John Hagen, and Peter M. McConahey whose talents added so much to the first edition and live on in the second. For this edition I add thanks to David Factor, from Mayo Clinic Rochester Medical Illustrations, and Mark A. Peterson, from Mayo Clinic Jacksonville Visual Communications, who both responded with excellent professionalism and dedication in added illustrations and photographs.

Thank you to Patricia Rollins, a soon to be biofeedback therapist, and to Canoy Roberson, a mental health counselor—both of whom helped considerably in the page proof reading. And, a special thank you to Laura Winters, a secretary with unique talents, wonderful humor, and frequent patience, who helped repeatedly.

—MARK S. SCHWARTZ

Contents

VII. NEUROFEEDBACK APPLICATIONS

VIII. NEUROMUSCULAR APPLICATIONS

IX. ELIMINATION DISORDERS

X. PROFESSIONAL ISSUES, CONSIDERATIONS, AND GUIDELINES

XI. QUALITY CONTROL AND RESEARCH

Introduction and Overview

The clinical use of biofeedback continues as an important part of health care in North America and several foreign countries. Health care professionals from several disciplines in many major medical centers and other settings treat a wide range of disorders using a variety of biofeedback therapies. Research and clinical reports support the therapeutic role of biofeedback and other types of applied psychophysiology in the treatment of many symptoms and disorders.

There are several reasons for the continued acceptance of, confidence in, and growth of biofeedback. These include improvements of research methodology, research results, new application areas, improved clinical procedures, and advances in biomedical instrumentation. Furthermore, more professionals have better education and training in biofeedback than was true several years ago.

The Biofeedback Certification of America (BCIA) added to the credibility of practitioners using biofeedback. Many professionals and institutions accept the BCIA credential as evidence that a practitioner attained and is maintaining a specified and desired level of competence.

Practitioners can often provide therapies with biofeedback at no more cost than other acceptable therapies. Selecting disorders and patients to treat, and when to treat them are among the topics in this book.

There are many advantages for including biofeedback into clinical practice. For patients, there are several advantages.

1. Increased awareness of psychophysiological[1] activity, reactivity, and recovery from arousal.
2. Increased self-efficacy and confidence in their psychophysiological self-regulation ability.
3. Learning to use the relationships between thoughts and behavior and physiologic functioning.
4. Developing psychophysiological self-regulation often unlearnable without this information and these procedures and often learning it faster.
5. Acceptance of therapies for those persons who resist psychotherapies.
6. Increased interest in developing and applying psychophysiological self-regulation with a fresh approach.
7. Provision of safe, effective, and cost efficient nonpharmacological therapies.

[1]For the purpose of this book, a broad use of the term "psychophysiological" subsumes all physiological activity and changes because all physiological functioning requires the brain.

For practitioners, there are advantages.

1. A valuable source of diagnostic and therapeutic information.
2. Assessment and documentation of psychophysiological functioning that affects symptoms, including reactivity to stimulation and recovery after stimulation.
3. Assessment and documentation of psychophysiological changes within and across sessions.
4. Enhanced professional interest in and confidence for providing psychophysiological self-regulatory therapies.

Proper use of biofeedback instrumentation, procedures, and applied psychophysiological therapies are integral parts of good clinical practice and research. However, this requires much more than understanding and using instrumentation. There are obviously many components in these therapies. A partial listing of these elements provides a sense of the scope of the therapies. One needs:

1. Proper, reliable, and safe instrumentation.
2. Immediate and useful feedback information.
3. Competent therapists.
4. Sufficient patient education.
5. Proper use of learning principles.
6. Proper assessment and therapy procedures.
7. Proper interpretation of psychophysiological data.
8. Varied self-regulatory and other therapies.
9. Transfer of training and generalization procedures.
10. Sufficient compliance.

The stepped-care model for providing clinical services is again one major theme throughout much of this book. Stepped care is providing less expensive and less complicated therapeutic recommendations and procedures before more expensive and complicated approaches. It is even more important now than a few years ago.

Part I begins with a historical perspective on biofeedback and applied psychophysiology. This provides an awareness of the richness of the background of this field. Considerations and guidelines for entering this field and maintaining competence are next. We kept the varied historical definitions of biofeedback. Part B of the definitions chapter goes beyond these definitions. It discusses dimensions of biofeedback and the views about specific and nonspecific factors, and it offers a revised definition.

Part II starts with an improved instrumentation chapter providing an understanding of the three most common biofeedback modalities. A new chapter on computers helps readers learn about many of the basics concerning computers.

The theme of Part III is the assessment and treatment process. It starts with an expanded chapter on intake and guidelines. Baselines for symptoms and psychophysiological assessment is in an expanded chapter. The presence or absence of a therapist in the room with a patient during the biofeedback process is the focus of the next chapter. The next chapter focuses on factors influencing patient compliance.

The chapters in Part IV focus on issues and considerations for cultivating lower physiological arousal. First is an updated and expanded chapter on dietary considerations. The expanded breathing chapter is next and followed by the chapter on problems associated with relaxation therapies. Both chapters address expanded discussions of relaxation-induced anxiety and guidelines for managing this and other problems. A discussion of the use of cassette tapes follows in the next chapter.

The next four parts address clinical issues, procedures, and considerations associated with different types of biofeedback applications. In Part V, therapies discussed are the traditional disorders needing cultivated low or lower physiological tension and arousal. The first two of these chapters address headache in two parts. The temporomandibular disorders chapter, formerly bruxism, is updated and mostly new. Also updated is the chapter on Raynaud's disease. The chapter on hypertension also received a significant update.

Part VI contains a nontraditional application area involving applied psychophysiology and biofeedback. We chose diabetes. Part VII opens a new area of application and presentation of a new modality for this book—neurofeedback—the specialized (EEG) feedback for attention-deficit disorder. Part VIII involves two updated chapters focused on therapies for a variety of neuromuscular disorders and conditions and related topics. The three chapters in Part IX involve applications to elimination disorders. First is the new chapter on urinary incontinence and then the updated chapter on fecal incontinence. The third is an updating of the nocturnal enuresis (or bedwetting) chapter.

Professional issues, considerations, and guidelines are the four chapters in Part X. The first chapter is the newly added chapter on ethics. The next three are the chapters on models of practice, interprofessional communications, and job descriptions. The Part XI chapters are quality control and evaluating research in clinical biofeedback.

The seven chapters in Part XII discuss and provide perspective on the status, frontier, and future of applied psychophysiology and biofeedback illustrated by several other applications for many other symptoms and disorders.

This edition added much to the first edition. It covers many topics in ways different from that available elsewhere. However, it cannot cover all topics and all perspectives. It is not my intent to imply, by omission, any disapproval or diminishment of interest, importance, or credibility of these biofeedback modalities or application areas. A topic seriously considered but omitted is the effects of medications on relaxation and biofeedback. This is a very complex topic with scant literature.

Biofeedback continues to make many important contributions to health care. It emerged from its childhood before the first edition, entered its adolescence, and now is in early adulthood. Remember, for many symptoms and disorders, biofeedback does not substitute for proper medical evaluation and care by proper and competent physicians. Also, it does it substitute for other necessary evaluations and treatments by other proper health care practitioners. Biofeedback and other applied psychophysiological therapies are among the preferred treatments for some disorders and patients. However, one reaches this conclusion only concurrent with or after careful considerations by properly educated and trained health care providers with appropriate credentials.

—Mark S. Schwartz

I
HISTORY, ENTERING, AND DEFINITIONS

1

A Historical Perspective on the Field of Biofeedback and Applied Psychophysiology

Mark S. Schwartz
R. Paul Olson

This chapter conveys a rich appreciation of the converging trends that have influenced the development of applied biofeedback. This historical perspective helps to understand not only the origins of biofeedback but also some factors shaping its future. It also helps to illuminate the broader concept of applied psychophysiology and to give perspective to the name changes of the professional organization.

Applied biofeedback began in the United States with the convergence of many disciplines in the late 1950s. The major antecedents and fields from which it developed include the following:

1. *Instrumental conditioning* of autonomic nervous system (ANS) responses
2. *Psychophysiology*
3. Behavior therapy and behavioral medicine
4. Stress research and stress-management strategies
5. Biomedical engineering
6. *Electromyography* (*EMG*), diagnostic EMG, and single *motor unit* control
7. Consciousness, altered states of consciousness, and *electroencephalographic* (*EEG*) feedback
8. *Cybernetics*
9. Cultural factors
10. Professional developments[1]

The order of this list reflects neither historical sequence nor importance. Other classifications and historical perspectives on biofeedback applications are in Gaarder and Montgomery (1977, 1983), Gatchel and Price (1979), Anchor, Beck, Sieviking, and Adkins (1982), and Basmajian (1989).

---

[1]The 25th anniversary meeting of the professional membership organization (Association of Applied Psychophysiology and Biofeedback [AAPB]) was in 1994. The commemorative *AAPB Silver Anniversary Yearbook* published for that meeting contains articles about the history and development of the biofeedback field and the Organization. Reading it is enriching and informative. It is available from the AAPB, 10200 West 44th Ave., Suite 304, Wheatridge, CO 80033; (303)422-8436; FAX (303)422-8894.

INSTRUMENTAL CONDITIONING
OF ANS RESPONSES

Learning theory developed within experimental psychology to help understand, predict, and control variations in animal and human behavior. In contrast with those who emphasize heredity as the major determinant of behavior, learning theorists emphasize the importance of one's environment. Specifically, this means environmental contingencies, including reinforcers, which lead to acquisition and maintenance of learned behavior.

Learning means a change in behavior as the direct result of experience. Reinforcement is necessary for *operant conditioning* or *instrumental* learning to take place. From this perspective, both overt behavior and covert behavior, such as thoughts, feelings, and physiological responses, are functions of the antecedents and consequences of such behaviors. This model describes the learning of responses instrumental to obtaining or avoiding positive or negative consequences.

The prevailing scientific viewpoint for several decades was that only the *voluntary musculoskeletal system*, mediated by the *central nervous system* (CNS), was responsive to operant conditioning. This view held that the autonomic nervous system (ANS) functioned automatically beyond conscious awareness, hence beyond voluntary control. Most scientists thought that the internal, homeostatic controls for such functions as circulation and digestion were innate and unaffected by self-regulatory learning. Most scientists assumed that ANS functioning or visceral learning was modifiable only via classical conditioning, if subject to learning at all. In this view, responses are automatic after conditioning occurs. In classical conditioning, thoughts can even become *conditioned stimuli* and elicit physiological responses.

The strong biases against instrumental conditioning of the ANS and the visceral responses it controls limited the amount of experimental work in this area until less than three decades ago (Miller, 1978). Later studies with humans and animals showed that instrumental training could produce increases and decreases in several body responses. These included vasomotor responses, blood pressure, salivation, galvanic skin response, and cardiac rates and rhythms (see reviews by Kimmel, 1974, and Harris & Brady, 1974).

Research indicated that one could gain volitional control over several different ANS functions without attributing the learning to cognitive factors. Many scientists and professionals were very skeptical of these findings. There was much disagreement concerning whether the research really demonstrated cortical control over ANS activity. As research advanced, it became clear that to show operant learning effects in the ANS researchers needed more sophisticated designs. One had to rule out skeletally mediated mechanical artifacts and visceral reflexes.

By the 1970s, researchers began studying CNS-controlled, integrated skeletal–visceral responses and patterns. They also studied specificity and patterning of learned visceral responses and cognitively mediated strategies for producing visceral changes (Miller, 1978). The curarized animal studies of Miller and his associates (Miller & DiCara, 1967) countered the argument that skeletal muscle activity was mediating some visceral changes. The skeletal muscles were temporarily paralyzed.

Orne (1979), a cautious but supporting conscience of the biofeedback field, reminded us that, in terms of animal studies,

> It would be misleading, however . . . not to point out that the important studies with curarized animals . . . while initially replicated, cannot now be reproduced. Though there is no difficulty in demonstrating statistically significant changes in visceral function as a result of

instrumental conditioning in curarized animals—leaving no doubt about the phenomenon—obtaining effects sufficiently large to be clinically significant eludes the present techniques. (p. 495)

The research with instrumental conditioning of visceral responses mediated by the ANS gave a major impetus to the development of clinical biofeedback. It appeared to resolve the controversy concerning whether such conditioning was a legitimate phenomenon. An assumption of clinical biofeedback is that it can help persons improve the accuracy of their perceptions of their visceral events that include blood pressure, heart rate, and vascular dilation and constriction. These perceptions allow them to gain greater self-regulation of these processes. Indeed, some professionals view some biofeedback as instrumental conditioning of visceral responses.

This operant model of biofeedback has significant heuristic value. One can apply principles of instrumental conditioning to physiological self-regulation. These principles include reinforcement schedules, shaping, extinction, and fading.

Although it is helpful to view biofeedback primarily as instrumental conditioning of visceral responses, this model is seriously limiting. Learning theory has developed far beyond the more traditional views of operant conditioning. Other professionals believe that human learning includes major cognitive dimensions as well as environmental reinforcers. Examples include thinking, expectation, visualization and imagery, foresight and planning, and problem-solving strategies.

One can include cognitive factors within the operant conditioning model. However, professionals adhering to more stringent interpretations of the model consider cognitive factors inadmissible because one cannot observe or objectively measure them. Nevertheless, studies of motor skill learning (Blumenthal, 1977) show that humans develop mental models ("motor programs") of what a skilled movement should be like. Furthermore, research shows that one may acquire behavior without obvious practice or even reinforcement. This evidence comes from latent learning experiments (Harlow & Harlow, 1962), studies of discovery learning (Bruner, 1968), and those of observational learning involving imitation of a model (Rosenthal & Zimmerman, 1978).

Increased acceptance for the role of mental processes in learning led to cognitive-behavioral therapies and studies of cognitively mediated strategies in the changes occurring during biofeedback therapies. The emphasis on cognitive learning also supported the applications of cybernetics to biofeedback.

PSYCHOPHYSIOLOGY

David Shapiro offered the first academic course in psychophysiology at Harvard University in 1965. The *Handbook of Psychophysiology*, a major publication, appeared 7 years later (Greenfield & Sternback, 1972).

Psychophysiology involves the scientific study of the interrelationships of physiological and cognitive processes. Some consider it a special branch of physiology. Some also consider it an offspring of psychobiology, which, in turn, is the child of the marriage between the physical and social sciences (Hassett, 1978). Physiological psychologists often manipulate physiology and observe behavior. In contrast, psychophysiologists often facilitate, manage, guide, hinder, or obstruct human psychological variables and observe the physiological effects.

As a form of *applied psychophysiology*,[2] clinical biofeedback helps people alter their behaviors with feedback from their physiology. These include muscle activity, peripheral blood flow, cardiac activity, sweat gland activity, brain electrical activity, and blood pressure. Some providers of clinical biofeedback call themselves *clinical psychophysiologists*. This name emphasizes the applied nature of their professional activities and their involvement with this scientific specialty.

BEHAVIOR THERAPY AND BEHAVIORAL MEDICINE

Related outgrowths of both learning theory and psychophysiology are the fields of behavior therapy and behavioral medicine. Behavior therapy developed in the 1950s. It was as an alternative to insight-oriented psychodynamic theories and therapies for mental disorders. Early proponents of behavior therapies included Wolpe (1974), Paul (1966), Bandura and Walters (1963), and Ullman and Krasner (1965). The roots of behavior therapy include the notion that one learns maladaptive behaviors. Thus, in most cases, one can unlearn them. The model is largely educational rather than medical as such. It applies the principles of operant and respondent conditioning, and cognitive learning to change a wide range of behaviors. Many professionals view some biofeedback applications as a form of operant learning. Others view biofeedback more cognitively within an information-processing model.

Behavioral medicine is another outgrowth of learning theory, psychophysiology, and behavior therapy. This specialty developed within behavior therapy and psychosomatic medicine. It appeared as a distinct entity in the late 1970s. Behavioral medicine focuses on applications of learning theories to medical disorders and other health-related topics. It does not focus on psychopathology or mental disorders. Schwartz and Weiss (1978) reported a definition of behavioral medicine proposed at the Yale Conference held in 1977:

> Behavioral medicine is the field concerned with the development of behavior science knowledge and techniques relevant to the understanding of physical health and illness and the application of this knowledge and these techniques to diagnosis, prevention, treatment, and rehabilitation. Psychosis, neurosis, and substance abuse are included only insofar as they contribute to physical disorders as an end point.

Behavioral medicine[3] also developed because traditional medical approaches were insufficient for managing and treating many chronic diseases, conditions, and health-damaging or maladaptive behaviors. This new specialty goes beyond the traditional germ theory of the etiology and progression of diseases. It recognizes the important roles of stress, life-style, habits, and environmental variables in the development, maintenance, and treatment of medical and dental diseases and conditions.

Behavioral medicine places much emphasis on the patient's role in prevention and recovery from organic diseases and conditions. The same emphases are clear in applied or

[2]Note that this sentence appeared in the first edition in early 1987. It does not seem to be a coincidence that the Biofeedback Society of America (BSA) went through the process of changing its name to include *applied psychophysiology* during that year while the first author was president of the BSA. However, it is a coincidence! Long after the name change and during a review of this chapter in preparation for its revision, I noted the term here. Its presence in this chapter was never raised or discussed during any of the board meetings or other public or private meetings concerning the name change. The term was written into an early draft of this chapter several years before 1987.

[3]"Health psychology" is a more recent field with similar roots and ties to behavioral medicine. The focus is more on prevention and health enhancement.

clinical biofeedback. In fact, some professionals consider clinical biofeedback to be a major specialty within the broader field of behavioral medicine.

The contributions of behavior therapy and behavioral medicine to the development and applications of applied biofeedback and applied psychophysiology are clear. The interactions among professionals from all of these fields will continue to be enriching.

STRESS RESEARCH, RELAXATION THERAPIES, AND OTHER STRESS MANAGEMENT TECHNIQUES

An important area of behavioral medicine is research on the effects of stress on causing physical symptoms and altering the immune system. However, research on stress began long before the development of behavioral medicine or biofeedback. Both fields have their roots partly in stress research. Selye's (1974) report of more than 130,000 entries on stress showed the extent of stress research.

Pioneering research was by the physicians Claude Bernard and Walter B. Cannon, and by Hans Selye. Bernard (quoted by Pi-Suner, 1955) developed the physiological homeostasis concept as the major process by which the body maintains itself. As Langley (1965) noted, the concept became integral to the discipline of physiology. Physical and mental disease occur because some homeostatic feedback mechanism is malfunctioning. One of the major effects of such homeostatic imbalance is stress.

In his book, *The Wisdom of the Body*, Cannon (1932) indicated the nature, causes, and results of the innate stress response. He named this the "fight-or-flight" response. Selye's (1974, 1976, 1983) extensive research lead to a triphasic conceptualization of the nature of our physiological stress response. It includes stages of alarm, resistance, and exhaustion. One first experiences stressful events as hardship; then one gets used to them; and finally one cannot stand them any longer (Selye, 1971).

The brilliant and pioneering works of Cannon and Selye contributed significantly to the development of the field of psychosomatic medicine. Their work increased awareness of the role of stress in physical and mental diseases. This awareness nurtured applied biofeedback, and many applications focused on stress-related disorders. Furthermore, as noted by Miller (1978), the emphasis of biofeedback on measurement and producing changes in bodily processes contributes to other behavioral techniques for relieving stress effects.

Many stress management systems evolved with the awareness of the effects of stress on health and disease. Included among these are many relaxation therapies. Some perceive biofeedback as a specific treatment modality. In practice, the effects of relaxation have a major role in achieving the therapeutic effects with biofeedback.

A very early form of physical relaxation is *hatha yoga*. It is a technique adopted from the Far East and popularized in Western countries in the 1960s. In the United States in the 1930s, Edmund Jacobson (1938, 1978) developed *progressive relaxation training*. This is a series of muscle activities designed to teach people ways to distinguish degrees of tension and relaxation and to reduce specific and general muscle tension. It also reduces or stops many symptoms and some causes and effects of stress.

> Muscle relaxation has long been noted as an important treatment for a variety of psychophysiological and stress-related disorders. The value of taking time to relax is becoming increasingly recognized in Western society, and we are borrowing techniques from those Eastern cultures where relaxation procedures. . . . have been practiced for centuries. (Tarlar-Benlolo, 1978)

Lehrer and Woolfolk (1984) reviewed the empirical and comparative studies involving progressive relaxation and versions of it. Lichstein (1988) provides one of the most thorough reviews of relaxation strategies and research results. Other very useful resources are by Smith (1989, 1990). Examples of modifications were by Wolpe (1973), Bernstein and Borkovec (1973), and Jacobson and McGuigan (1982). A related technique developed in England by Laura Mitchell (1977, 1987) involved stretch-release procedures.

In addition to the physiological relaxation procedures, there was a proliferation of primarily mental techniques, most of which are some form of meditation. Islamic Sufis, Hindu yogis, Christian contemplatives, and Hasidic Jews have practiced religious meditation for centuries. However, meditation was not a popular practice in the United States except among a very small minority.

Meditation became popularized in the United States in the 1960s as a result of the development of Transcendental Meditation (TM) as practiced and promoted by a teacher from India named Maharishi Mahesh Yogi (Forem, 1974). More Westernized variations of TM were subsequently developed as "Clinically Standardized Meditation" (Carrington, 1977) and the "Relaxation Response" (Benson, 1975). A modification of a meditative-type technique combined with physiological relaxation is Strobel's (1982) "Quieting Reflex."

Another meditation approach is "Open Focus" developed by Fehmi and Fritz (1980). This intends to promote an open, relaxed, and integrated mind–body state. It is closer to Soto Zen meditation in sharing the goal of a content-free and quiet mind in contrast to the focused concentration of yoga and TM meditation. The emigration of Zen Buddhist teachers to the United States beginning in the 1940s was yet another factor contributing to the meditation movement.

There are still other approaches involving relaxation–meditation: Ira Progroff's (1980) "process meditation," Jose Silva's (1977) "Silva Mind Control," and C. Norman Shealy's (1977) "biogenics." Practitioners often use relaxation–meditation techniques with biofeedback instrumentation to enhance learning psychophysiological self-regulation.

Hypnosis is another approach developed to aid persons to control pain and stress. In the 1700s, Franz Mesmer first postulated "animal magnetism" to explain persons' responses to suggestion. Hypnosis developed slowly until the 20th century. Over the past few decades, it has become more sophisticated and empirically grounded as a set of therapeutic techniques. Liebeault, Charcot, and Freud were among the first to apply the techniques to patients (Moss, 1965). Contemporary researchers, such as Barber, Hilgard, Weitzenhoffer, and Erickson, have conducted serious investigations into the parameters of hypnosis.

In Germany, early in the present century, J.H. Schultz developed a form of physiologically directed, self-generated therapy called "Autogenic Training." Wolfgang Luthe (1969) reported the extensive research and therapeutic applications of this popular technique, variations of which are now also in common practice. Some, like Wickramasekara (1976, 1988) reported integration of hypnosis and biofeedback.

There are numerous other stress management techniques with many summarized by Davis, Eshelman, and McKay (1980), McKay, Davis, and Fanning (1981), Charlesworth and Nathan (1985), and Lehrer and Woolfolk (1993).

BIOMEDICAL ENGINEERING

Without high-quality instrumentation for measuring physiological events accurately and reliably, there would be no biofeedback. As Tarlar-Benlolo (1978) reminds us, "prior to World War II, available equipment was not sufficiently sensitive for measuring most of the body's internally generated electric impulses" (p. 728). Progress occurred after the war, and

> technology had advanced far . . . making feasible the task of designing and constructing instruments that could accurately detect and record minute electrical discharges, integrate and amplify these responses, and produce a corresponding signal that could be interpreted by the person being monitored. (p. 728)

Biomedical engineers developed a technology that is both noninvasive and sophisticated. Surface recordings used for biofeedback measurement provide feedback for many different physiological activities. These include sweat gland activity, skin temperature, and muscle activity. One also can measure and feedback cardiovascular parameters such as heart rate, blood volume, and blood pressure, respiration, and brain electrical activity. One also can feedback angles of limbs and the force of muscles and limbs. Instruments continuously monitor, amplify, and transform the electronic and electromechanical signals into audio and visual feedback-understandable information.

Now, multiple and simultaneous recordings of several channels of physiological information are available with instrumentation linked to computers. Computers allow greater storage capabilities, rapid signal and statistical analyses, simultaneous recording and integration of multiple channels, and displays impossible only a few years ago.

ELECTROMYOGRAPHY, DIAGNOSTIC ELECTROMYOGRAPHY, AND SINGLE MOTOR UNIT CONTROL

The workhorse of the biofeedback field is EMG feedback. According to Basmajian (1983) EMG instrumentation grew out of the studies of neuromuscular and spinal cord functions. He reminds us that "it began with the classic paper in 1929 by Adrian and Bronk, who showed that the electrical responses in individual muscles provided an accurate reflection of the actual functional activity of the muscles" (p. 2).

Physicians' use of EMG in diagnosing neuromuscular disorders is many decades old. As early as 1934, reports appeared that voluntary, conscious control of individual motor unit potentials was possible (Smith, 1934). Marinacci and Horande (1960) added case reports of the potential value of displaying EMG signals to assist patients in neuromuscular re-education. Basmajian (1963, 1979) also reported on the control of single motor units.

Several investigators reported EMG feedback in the rehabilitation of stroke patients (Andrews, 1964; Brudny, 1982; Basmajian, Kukulka, Narayan, & Takebe, 1975; Wolf & Binder-MacLeod, 1983; Binder-MacLeod, 1983). Such research was important in the development of applied biofeedback, especially for the field of neuromuscular rehabilitation. Thus, EMG biofeedback gained solid support among researchers and clinicians.

Practitioners also used EMG feedback for treating symptoms and disorders such as tension headaches and tension myalgias, and more recently, incontinence.

CONSCIOUSNESS, ALTERED STATES OF CONSCIOUSNESS, AND ELECTROENCEPHALOGRAPHIC FEEDBACK

Some viewed psychology as a discipline that lost its mind when it stopped studying human consciousness and lost its soul when it discarded a phenomenology of the self. Within the past two decades, these trends reversed. Humanistic psychology re-established the human self as a legitimate source of inquiry. Scientists in transpersonal psychology and neurophysiology renewed the study of human consciousness. Theorists such as Tart (1969), Krippner (1972), Ornstein (1972), Pelletier and Garfield (1976), Schwartz and Beatty (1977), and Jacobson (1982) are among those who made significant contributions to our understanding of human consciousness.

Many studies of altered states of consciousness induced by drugs, hypnosis, or meditation added to our knowledge of the relationships between brain functioning and human behavior. Such research helped stimulate the development of biofeedback, which also focuses on the functional relationships between brain and behavior.

In the early 1960s studies began appearing reporting the relationships among EEG alpha-wave activity, 8–12 Hertz, and emotional states and certain states of consciousness. Alpha biofeedback, commonly reported as associated with a relaxed but alert state, received its most attention in the late 1960s. Clinical applications were mostly for general relaxation.

Kamiya (1969) reported that one could voluntarily control alpha waves previously believed impossible. Support for these and related findings came from Brown (1977), Nowlis and Kamiya (1970), and Hart (1968). "Though these studies tended to lack systematic controls, they nonetheless caught the imagination of many serious scientists as well as the media" (Orne, 1979, p. 493).

Some investigators and practitioners continued to advocate the value of alpha biofeedback (Gaarder & Montgomery, 1981), despite recognizing "there was no clear-cut and concrete rationale to explain why it should help patients" (p. 155). Interested readers can review their informative discussion. In contrast, Basmajian (1983) noted that,

> alpha feedback . . . has virtually dried up as a scientifically defensible clinical tool . . . it has . . . returned to the research laboratory from which it probably should not have emerged prematurely. Through the next generation of scientific investigation, it may return as a useful applied technique. (p. 3)

Other investigators studied specialized learning processes and other EEG parameters such as theta waves, evoked cortical responses, and EEG phase synchrony of multiple areas of the cortex (Beatty, Greenberg, Deibler, & O'Hanlon, 1974; Fehmi & Selzer, 1980; Fox & Rudell, 1968). A few continue this experimental work.

Specialized EEG biofeedback from selected brain areas and selected EEG parameters such as sensorimotor rhythms and 3–8 Hz slow-wave activity became the focus of well-controlled studies. These emerged as effective therapeutic approaches for very carefully selected patients with CNS disorders such as epilepsy (Lubar, 1982, 1983; Sterman, 1982) and other selected patients with attention-deficit/hyperactivity disorder (ADHD; Lubar, 1991; see Chapter 20).

There are recently emerging alpha–theta EEG feedback procedures that proport to be successful in treating patients' addictive behaviors such as alcoholism and other difficult-to-treat disorders (Ochs, 1992; Rosenfeld, 1992; Wuttke, 1992; Peniston & Kulkosky, 1989; Peniston & Kulkosky, 1990; see Chapter 38). Clinical applications occur as the debate and research continues.

CYBERNETICS

The term "biofeedback" is a shorthand term for *external psychophysiological feedback, physiological feedback,* and sometimes *augmented proprioception.* The basic idea is to provide individuals with increased information about what is going on inside their bodies, including their brains.

The field that deals most directly with information processing and feedback is called "cybernetics." A basic principle of cybernetics is that one cannot control a variable unless information about the variable is available to the controller. The information provided is called feedback (Ashby, 1963; Mayr, 1970).

Another principle of cybernetics is that feedback makes learning possible. Annent (1969) reviewed the evidence for this principle. In applied biofeedback, individuals receive direct and clear feedback about their physiology. This helps them learn to control such functions. For example, from an EMG instrument, persons receive information concerning their muscle activity. This helps them learn to reduce, increase, or otherwise regulate the muscle tension.

From a cybernetic perspective, operant conditioning is one form of feedback. It is feedback provided in the form of positive or negative results of a particular behavior. The point is that another significant contribution to the development of applied biofeedback is an information-processing model derived from cybernetic theory and research. Proponents of this model in the field of biofeedback include Brown (1977), Anliker (1977), Mulholland (1977), and Gaarder and Montgomery (1981).

CULTURAL FACTORS

Several cultural factors contributed to the development of applied biofeedback. The gradual merging of the traditions and techniques of the East and West is one major factor. The rise in popularity of schools of meditation was an expression of a cultural change providing a context in which applied biofeedback developed. Yoga and Zen masters reportedly alter their physiological states significantly through meditation. Related phenomena presumably occur in some forms of biofeedback experiences. Therefore, some have referred to biofeedback as the "Yoga of the West" and "electronic Zen."

Within the United States, there is another cultural factor adding to a *Zeitgeist* encouraging biofeedback applications. This is the heightened distress about costs of health care and the need for more efficacious and cost-effective treatments. In addition, there is common recognition that pharmacotherapy, with all its benefits, is of limited value for many patients. Some patients cannot take medications because of untoward side effects. Many patients avoid compliance, and some physicians deemphasize pharmacotherapy.

Perhaps more significant is the current popular public health emphasis on prevention. The movement toward wellness has continued to grow since the 1960s. Practitioners of holistic health also emphasize self-regulation and self-control. The result of the emphases is more people involving themselves in life-style changes to self-regulate their health. These changes include enhancing physical fitness, avoiding caffeine and nicotine, reducing or stopping alcohol use, and better weight control. More people are assuming increased responsibility for their physical, mental, and spiritual well-being. Additionally, more people are accepting responsibility for their health and recovery from illness. Many believe that biofeedback therapies facilitate and fit well into these efforts at greater self-regulation, wellness, and growth.

PROFESSIONAL DEVELOPMENTS

Also adding to the development of applied biofeedback are the organizations of professionals engaged in both research and clinical–educational applications. One organization is notable here. In 1969, a handful of psychophysiology researchers formed the

Biofeedback Research Society. In 1976, that organization renamed itself the Biofeedback Society of America (BSA) with both an experimental and an applied division. This change in name reflected the growth and importance of the applied area.

A measure of the maturity of a field is the existence of and quality of its professional journal. The journal *Biofeedback and Self-Regulation*, published by Plenum, started in 1976. In 1988, the expanding scope of the field transformed the name of the organization to the Association of Applied Psychophysiology and Biofeedback (AAPB). With a membership of about 2000, the AAPB continues to be a productive, intellectually stimulating, clinically useful, scientifically sound, and vibrant organization.

There continues to be disagreement about the most appropriate name for both the membership organization and its journal. Some argue for only Association of Applied Psychophysiology. Others argue for maintaining the terms "Biofeedback" and "Self-regulation." There is good reasoning on both sides and this debate will continue. Those supporting Applied Psychophysiology as sufficient emphasize a broader scope. This is more acceptable conceptually and politically to many psychophysiologically oriented researchers with close ties to biofeedback. Those who advocate keeping the term "Biofeedback" in the names of the organization and journal focus on the established place of this among professionals and the public, its history, its brevity, and ease of communication. Why change horses in midstream, they argue, especially from a familiar one that is doing so well?

One should note that another national membership organization, The American Association of Biofeedback Clinicians, started in 1975 and went out of existence in the late 1980s. This left the then BSA, now AAPB, as the only organization with a major emphasis on biofeedback. Many other professional and scientific societies also devote space in their publications and time at their meetings for biofeedback and applied psychophysiological research.

Another professional organization that influenced the continued development of the field is the Biofeedback Certification Institute of America (BCIA). It maintains a credible credentialing. Before 1979, credentialing was in the hands of a few state biofeedback societies. These credentialing programs, well meaning as they were, suffered from the understandable problems of small groups of professionals who typically had little or no training and experience with the complexities of credentialing. Thus, there was considerable variability in the credentialing across states. In most states, there was no credentialing at all— or the hope of any.

Ed Taub, then president-elect of the BSA, had the foresight and wisdom to inspire the development of an independent, credible, national credentialing program. The BSA sponsored and supported establishing the BCIA, named by Bernard Engel, the first chair of the board in January 1981 when the BCIA officially began. Three months later, he graciously relinquished the chair to his successor. The BCIA evolved with more stringent criteria for education, training, experience, and recertification. Many professionals continue to seek and earn this credential as the only one of its kind.

Educational opportunities exist in many undergraduate and graduate courses in biofeedback. There are private training programs and workshops offered by national, state, and regional professional organizations. There are many companies manufacturing biofeedback instrumentation and several companies selling and servicing a variety of instruments from different manufacturers.

The number of publications is one barometer of the history, growth, and possibly the future of a field. The first bibliography of the biofeedback literature (Butler & Stoyva, 1973) contained about 850 references. The next edition, 5 years later, listed about 2300 references (Butler, 1978). Thousands more have appeared since 1978 (Hatch & Riley, 1985; Hatch & Satoh, 1990). There was a downward trend in journal publications in English from 1985 through 1991 (Hatch & Satoh, 1993). However, about 150 per year continue appearing with no decline between the years 1987 through 1991. (See Chapter 38 for more discussion of publications.)

Note there are dozens of papers published each year in non-English speaking countries. For example, the important Japanese literature was still in its early stages in 1979. That literature rapidly increased in the 1980s (Hatch & Saito, 1990). There is also a rich history of research publications and clinical applications in Russia and other former-USSR countries (Sokhadze & Shtark, 1991). This foreign literature is not well known in the United States. One reason is the use of different terminology. For example, the Russians often use the term "adaptive biocontrol" for biofeedback.

A perspective on the issues of history, publications, and past and current interest, and a full appreciation for roots, research, and applications all require awareness of and access to foreign publication data bases.

SUMMARY

The field of biofeedback has a very rich history with multiple roots. Awareness of this background can be helpful in understanding the beginnings of biofeedback, its status, and salient factors shaping its future. From feedback research and applications of the past, one may find inspiration and momentum for a creative future in this exciting field. The scope and contributions of biofeedback encompass many professional fields. For some professionals, biofeedback is a field in itself. It is still premature to forecast additional metamorphoses. Discussions of the frontiers, the status, and speculations about the future appear at the end of this book. Biofeedback remains a viable and enduring term with a rich and complex history, present status, and future. This is true whether, by implication or design, it is independent, linked to, or subsumed by broader terms and conceptual models.

GLOSSARY

ALPHA WAVE ACTIVITY. Electroencephalographic activity commonly, but not always, thought to be associated with an alert but relaxed state, 8 to 12 Hertz.

AUTONOMIC NERVOUS SYSTEM (ANS). That part of the nervous system that connects to all organs and blood vessels and transmits signals that control their functioning. It consists of two branches, the SNS and PNS, which usually produce opposite responses. Examples include dilations and constrictions, and starting and increasing secretions versus reducing and stopping them. Once thought to be totally involuntary, it is now known to be under some significant voluntary control, although less than the CNS.

CENTRAL NERVOUS SYSTEM (CNS). The part of the nervous system including human thought, sense organs, and control of skeletal muscles. Once believed to be totally separate from the ANS, it is now known to interact with the ANS.

CLASSICAL CONDITIONING. Originating with Pavlov, the type of conditioning or learning that assumes that there are stimuli that naturally (unconditioned stimuli, UCS) evoke uncondi-

*Note.*The glossary in this and other chapters is mostly for students and professionals unfamiliar with the terms. The definitions for each are sometimes very brief, intentionally not always complete, and sometimes more extensive. The intent is to provide enough information to allow the reader to have a reasonable idea of the meaning of the term.

tioned or unlearned responses (UCR) (e.g., acute pain evokes crying, withdrawal, and fear) and that other, previously neutral, stimuli (conditioned stimuli) associated with the pairing of these events develop the capacity to elicit the same or similar responses or conditioned responses (CR). For example, frequent yelling and arguing (UCS) at mealtime (CS) can result in a person becoming emotionally upset, nausea, and loss of appetite (all CRs) at mealtimes and at the thought of and sight of food even when there is no yelling or arguing.

CURARIZED ANIMALS. Animals intentionally paralyzed by the drug curare to control for body movements during visceral conditioning such as biofeedback of heart rate.

CYBERNETICS. The science of internal body control systems in humans and electrical and mechanical systems designed to replace the human systems.

ELECTROENCEPHALOGRAPHY (EEG). The measurement of electrical activity of the brain.

ELECTROMECHANICAL. Devices that measure mechanical aspects of the body such as position of a joint or degree of pressure or weight placed on it rather than a property of it such as its direct electrical activity or temperature. Examples include degrees that a knee bends in a person after knee surgery, steadiness of the head of a child with cerebral palsy, the weight pressure placed on a leg and foot by someone after a stroke. Instruments transform these mechanical forces into electrical signals.

ELECTROMYOGRAPHY (EMG). The use of special instruments to measure the electrical activity of skeletal muscles.

EXTINCTION. The behavioral principle that predicts that abruptly and totally stopping all positive reinforcements after specified behaviors will lead to the behavior no longer occurring.

FADING. Gradually changing a stimulus that controls a person's or animals's performance to another stimulus. As a behavioral procedure, it does not always mean disappearance of a stimulus.

FIGHT OR FLIGHT. Walter Cannon's well-known and well-accepted concept of the body's complex psychophysiological arousal and preparation for fighting or fleeing actual or perceived threatening stimuli.

GALVANIC SKIN RESPONSE (GSR). A form of electrodermal activity: increased resistance of the skin to conducting tiny electrical currents because of reduced sweat and dryness. Older term less often used now but still accepted. Opposite of skin conductance (SC).

INSIGHT-ORIENTED PSYCHODYNAMIC THEORIES AND THERAPIES. A wide range of psychological theories and therapies starting from the time of Sigmund Freud. A basic assumption is that patients need to gain insight into the psychological origins and forces that motivate current psychological problems and behaviors before they can achieve adequate relief of symptoms.

INSTRUMENTAL CONDITIONING. Same as operant conditioning. The behavioral theories and therapies originated by B. F. Skinner. For example, reinforcers are said to be instrumentally linked to the recurrence of behaviors. See *operant conditioning*.

OBSERVATIONAL LEARNING. Learning that takes place by the organism observing another organism doing the task to be learned.

OPERANT CONDITIONING. The same as instrumental conditioning originating with B. F. Skinner. Operant means that a response is identified and understood in terms of its consequences rather than by a stimulus that evokes it. Stimuli and circumstances emit responses rather than evoke them as in classical conditioning.

PROPRIOCEPTION. Perception mediated by sensory nerve terminals within tissues, mostly muscles, tendons, and the labyrinthal system for balance. They give us information concerning movements and position. Examples include the sense of knowing when we are slightly off balance; the process and ability to perceive the difference and approximate weight, even with eyes closed, between weights of 5 oz and 7 oz held in each hand.

PSYCHOPHYSIOLOGY. The science of studying the causal and interactive processes of physiology, behavior, and subjective experience.

REINFORCERS. Events or stimuli that increase the probability of recurrence of behaviors they follow.

SCHEDULES OF REINFORCEMENT. Usually, intermittent reinforcement of an operant behavior. A common schedule in life, and most resistant to extinction, is a variable-ratio schedule. The number of times a reinforcement follows a specific behavior varies randomly so the person or animal never knows when the reinforcer will occur. Contrast with variable-interval, fixed-interval, and fixed-ratio schedules.

SENSORIMOTOR RHYTHM. An EEG rhythm recorded from the central scalp and involving both the sensory and motor parts of the brain, the sensory–motor cortex, 12–14 Hertz. Used in the EEG biofeedback of some persons with seizure disorders.

SHAPING. The behavioral principle primarily from Skinnerian or operant conditioning that refers to procedures designed to help a living organism (e.g., an animal) learn new behaviors, often in very small steps—hence shaping, fashioning, by successive approximations, a new, more complex behavior pattern.

SINGLE MOTOR UNIT. Individual spinal nerves or neurons involved in movement. Single spinal motor neuron biofeedback training was a major advance in the late 1950s and early 1960s. Requires fine-wire EMG electrodes.

SKELETALLY MEDIATED MECHANICAL ARTIFACTS. Intentional body movements that cause artifacts in instrumentation recorded signals. Examples include moving a body part such as the head and neck when recording resting muscle activity, clenching the teeth during EEG recordings.

SLOW-WAVE ACTIVITY (3–8 Hertz). Included in the EEG frequency range often called theta activity, also reported as 4–7 Hertz.

VASOMOTOR. Affecting the caliber (diameter) of a blood vessel.

VISCERAL LEARNING. Refers to learning that takes place by body organs, especially those in the abdominal cavity such as the stomach and bowels.

VISCERAL REFLEXES. Reflexes in which the stimulus is a state of an internal organ.

ZEITGEIST. The spirit or general trend of thought of a time in history. Often used to refer to times in history when new ways of thinking and technologies are more likely to be acceptable by the culture in question.

REFERENCES

Adler, C. S., & Adler, S. M. (1984). Biofeedback. In T. B. Karasu (Ed.), *The psychiatric therapies: The American Psychiatric Association Commission on Psychiatric Therapies*. Washington, DC: American Psychiatric Association.

Anchor, K. N., Beck, S. E., Sieveking, N., & Adkins, J. (1982). A history of clinical biofeedback. *American Journal of Clinical Biofeedback, 5*(1), 3–16.

Andrews, J. M. (1964). Neuromuscular re-education of the hemiplegic with aid of electromyograph. *Archives of Physical Medicine and Rehabilitation, 45*, 530–532.

Anliker, J. (1977). Biofeedback from the perspective of cybernetics and systems science. In J. Beatty & H. Legewis (Eds.), *Biofeedback and behavior.* New York: Plenum Press.

Annert, J. (1969). *Feedback and human behavior.* Baltimore: Penguin Books.

Ashby, W. R. (1963). An introduction to cybernetics. New York: Wiley.

Bandura, A., & Walters, R. (1963). Social learning and personality development. New York: Holt.

Basmajian, J. V. (1963). Conscious control of individual motor units. *Science, 141,* 440–441.

Basmajian, J. V. (1978). *Muscles alive: Their functions revealed by electromyography* (4th ed.). Baltimore: Williams & Wilkins.

Basmajian, J. V. (Ed.). (1989). *Biofeedback: Principles & practice for clinicians* (3rd ed.). Baltimore: Williams & Wilkins.

Basmajian, J. V., Kukulka, C. G., Narayan, M. G., & Takebe, K. (1975). Biofeedback treatment of foot drop after stroke compared with standard rehabilitation technique: Effects on voluntary control and strength. *Archives of Physical Medicine and Rehabilitation, 56,* 231–236.

Beatty, J., Greenberg, A., Deibler, W. P., & O'Hanlon, J. F. (1974). Operant control of occipital theta rhythm affects performance in radar monitoring task. *Science, 183,* 871–873.

Benson, H. (1975). *The relaxation response.* New York: Morrow.

Bernstein, D. A., & Borkovec, T. D. (1973). *Progressive relaxation training: A manual for the helping professionals.* Urbana, IL: Research Press.

Binder-MacLeod, S. A. (1983). Biofeedback in stroke rehabilitation. In J. V. Basmajian (Ed.), *Biofeedback: Principles & practice for clinicians* (2nd ed.). Baltimore: Williams & Wilkins.

Blumenthal, A. L. (1977). *The process of cognition.* Englewood Cliffs, NJ: Prentice-Hall.

Brown, B. (1977). *Stress and the art of biofeedback.* New York: Harper & Row.

Brudny, J. (1982). Biofeedback in chronic neurological cases: Therapeutic electromyography. In L. White & B. Tursky (Eds.), *Clinical biofeedback: Efficacy and mechanisms.* New York: Guilford Press.

Brunar, J. S. (1968). *Toward a theory of instruction.* New York: Norton.

Budzynski, T. H., Stoyva, J. M., Adler, C. S., & Mullaney, D. J. (1973). EMG biofeedback and tension headache: A controlled outcome study. *Psychosomatic Medicine, 35,* 484–496.

Butler, F. (1978). *Biofeedback: A survey of the literature.* New York: Plenum Press.

Butler, F., & Stoyva, J. (1973). *Biofeedback and self-control: A bibliography.* Wheatridge, CO: Biofeedback Society of America.

Cannon, W. B. (1932). *The wisdom of the body.* New York: Norton.

Carrington, P. (1977). *Freedom in meditation.* Garden City, NY: Doubleday/Anchor.

Charlesworth, E. A., & Nathan, R. G. (1985). *Stress management: A comprehensive guide to wellness.* New York: Atheneum.

Davis, M., Eshelman, E., & McKay, M. (1980). *The relaxation and stress reduction workbook.* Richmond, CA: New Harbinger.

Fehmi, L. G., & Fritz, G. (1980, Spring). Open focus: The attentional foundation of health and well being. *Somatics,* 24–30.

Fehmi, L. G., & Selzer, F. (1980). Attention and biofeedback training in psychotherapy and transpersonal growth. In S. Boorstein & K. Speeth (Eds.), *Explorations in transpersonal psychotherapy.* New York: Jason Aronson.

Forem, J. (1974). *Transcendental meditation.* New York: Dutton.

Fox, S. S., & Rudell, A. P. (1968). Operant controlled neural event: Formal and systematic approach to electrical coding of behavior in brain. *Science, 162,* 1299–1302.

Gaarder, K. R., & Montgomery, P. S. (1977). *Clinical biofeedback: A procedural manual for behavioral medicine.* Baltimore: Williams & Wilkins.

Gaarder, K. R., & Montgomery, P. S. (1981). *Clinical biofeedback: A procedural manual for behavioral medicine* (2nd ed.). Baltimore: Williams & Wilkins.

Gatchel, R. J., & Price, K. P. (1979). *Clinical applications of biofeedback: Appraisal & status.* New York: Pergamon Press.

Greenfield, N. S., & Sternback, R. A. (1972). *Handbook of psychophysiology.* New York: Holt, Rinehart & Winston.

Harlow, H. F., & Harlow, M. K. (1962). Social deprivation in monkeys. *Scientific American, 207,* 136–146.

Harris, A. H., & Brady, J. V. (1974). Animal learning—visceral and autonomic conditioning. *Annual Review of Psychology, 25,* 107–133.

Hart, J. T. (1968). Autocontrol of EEG alpha. *Psychophysiology, 4,* 506. (Abstract)

Hassett, J. (1978). *A primer of psychophysiology.* San Francisco: Freeman.

Hatch, J. P. (1993, March 25–30). Declining rates of publication within the field of biofeedback continue: 1988–1991. *Proceedings of the 24th annual meeting of the Association for Applied Psychophysiology and Biofeedback, Los Angeles.* Wheatridge, CO: Association for Applied Psychophysiology and Biofeedback.

Hatch, J. P., & Riley, P. (1985). Growth and development of biofeedback: A bibliographic analysis. *Biofeedback and Self-Regulation, 10*(4), 289–299.

Hatch, J. P., & Saito, I. (1990). Growth and development of biofeedback: A bibliographic update. *Biofeedback and Self-Regulation, 15*(1), 37–46.

Jacobson, E. (1938). *Progressive relaxation.* Chicago: University of Chicago Press.

Jacobson, E. (1978). *You must relax.* New York: McGraw-Hill.

Jacobson, E. (1982). *The human mind: A physiological clarification.* Springfield, IL: Charles C. Thomas.

Jacobson, E., & McGuigan, F. J. (1982). *Principles and practice of progressive relaxation: A teaching primer* (cassette). New York: BMA Audio Cassettes.

Kamiya, J. (1969). Operant control of the EEG alpha rhythm and some of its reported effects on consciousness. In C. T. Tart (Ed.), *Altered states of consciousness.* New York: Wiley.

Kimmel, H. O. (1979). Instrumental conditioning of autonomically mediated responses in human beings. *American Psychologist, 29,* 325–335.

Krippner, S. (1972). Altered states of consciousness. In J. White (Ed.), *The highest state of consciousness.* Garden City, NY: Doubleday.

Langley, L. L. (1965). *Homeostasis.* New York: Van Nostrand Reinhold.

Lehrer, P. M., & Woolfolk, R. L. (1984). Are all stress reduction techniques equivalent, or do they have differential effects: A review of the comparative empirical literature. In R. L. Woolfolk & P. M. Lehrer (Eds.), *Handbook of relaxation and stress management techniques.* New York: Guilford Press.

Lehrer, P. M., & Woolfolk, R. L. (Eds.). (1993). *Principles and practice of stress management* (2nd ed.). New York: Guilford Press.

Lichstein, K. L. (1988). *Clinical relaxation strategies.* New York: Wiley.

Lubar, J. F. (1982). EEG operant conditioning in severe epileptics: Controlled multidimensional studies. In L. White & B. Tursky (Eds.), *Clinical biofeedback: Efficacy and mechanisms.* New York: Guilford Press.

Lubar, J. F. (1983). Electroencephalographic biofeedback and neurological applications. In J. V. Basmajian (Ed.), *Biofeedback: Principles & practice for clinicians.* Baltimore: Williams & Wilkins.

Lubar, J. F. (1991). Discourse on the development of EEG diagnostics and biofeedback treatment for attention-deficit/hyperactivity disorders. *Biofeedback and Self-Regulation, 16,* 201–225.

Luthe, W. (Ed.). (1969). *Autogenic therapy* (Vols. 1–6). New York: Grune & Stratton.

Marinacci, A. A., & Horande, M. (1960). Electromyogram in neuromuscular re-education. *Bulletin of the Los Angeles Neurological Society, 25,* 57–71.

Mayr, O. (1970). *The origins of feedback control.* Cambridge, MA: MIT Press.

McKay, M., Davis, M., & Farming, P. (1981). *Thoughts and feelings: The art of cognitive stress intervention.* Richmond, CA: New Harbinger.

Miller, N. E. (1978). Biofeedback and visceral learning. *Annual Review of Psychology, 29,* 373–404.

Miller, N. E., & DiCara, L. (1967). Instrumental learning of heart rate changes in curarized rats: Shaping and specificity to discriminative stimulus. *Journal of Comparative and Physiological Psychology, 63,* 12–19.

Mitchell, L. (1977). *Simple relaxation: The physiological method for easing tension.* New York: Atheneum.

Mitchell, L. (1987). *Simple relaxation: The Mitchell method for easing tension* (rev. ed.). London: John Murray.

Moss, C. S. (1965). *Hypnosis in perspective.* New York: Macmillan.

Mulholland, T. (1977). Biofeedback as scientific method. In G. E. Schwartz & J. Beatty (Eds.), *Biofeedback: Theory and research.* New York: Academic Press.

Nowlis, D. P., & Kamiya, J. (1970). The control of electroencephalographic alpha rhythms through auditory feedback and the associated mental activity. *Psychophysiology, 6,* 476–484.

Ochs, L. (1992). EEG treatment of addictions. *Biofeedback, 20*(1), 8–16.

Orne, M. T. (1979). The efficacy of biofeedback therapy. *Annual Review of Medicine, 30,* 489–503.

Ornstein, R. E. (1972). *The psychology of consciousness.* San Francisco: Freeman.

Paul, G. L. (1966). *Insight vs. desensitization in psychology.* Stanford, CA: Stanford University Press.

Pelletier, K. R., & Garfield, C. (1976). *Consciousness: East and west.* New York: Harper & Row (Harper Colophon Books).

Peniston, E. G., & Kulkosky, P. J. (1989, March/April). Alpha–theta brainwave training and endorphin levels of alcoholics. *Alcoholism: Clinical and Experimental Research, 13*(2), 271–279.

Peniston, E. G., & Kulkosky, P. J. (1990). Alcoholic personality and alpha–theta brainwave training. *Medical Psychotherapy, 3,* 37–55.

Pi-Suner, A. (1955). *The whole and its parts in biology.* New York: Philosophical Library.

Progoff, I. (1980). *The practice of process meditation.* New York: Dialogue House Library.

Rosenfeld, J. P. (1992). "EEG" treatment of addictions: Commentary on Ochs, Peniston, and Kulkosky. *Biofeedback, 20*(2), 12–17.

Rosenthal, T. L., & Zimmerman, B. J. (1978). *Social learning & cognition.* New York: Academic Press.

Schwartz, G., & Beatty, J. (Eds.). (1977). *Biofeedback: Theory & research.* New York: Academic Press.

Schwartz, G. E., & Weiss, S. M. (1978). What is behavioral medicine? *Psychosomatic Medicine, 39*(6), 377–381.

Selye, H. (1971). The evolution of the stress concept—stress and cardiovascular disease. In L. Levi (Ed.), *Society, stress, and disease* (Vol. 1). New York: Oxford University Press.

Selye, H. (1974). *Stress without distress.* Philadelphia: Lippincott.

Selye, H. (1976). *The stress of life* (rev. ed.). New York: McGraw-Hill.

Shealy, C. N. (1977). *Ninety days to self-health.* New York: Dial Press.

Silva, J. (1977). *Silva mind control method.* New York: Simon & Shuster.

Smith, J. C. (1989). *Relaxation dynamics.* Champaign, IL: Research Press.

Smith, J. C. (1990). *Cognitive behavioral relaxation training.* New York: Springer.

Smith, O. C. (1934). Action potentials from single motor units in voluntary contraction. *American Journal of Physiology, 108,* 629–638.

Sokhadze, E. M., & Shtark, M. B. (1991). Scientific and clinical biofeedback in the USSR. *Biofeedback and Self-Regulation, 16*(3), 253–260.

Sterman, M. B. (1982). EEG biofeedback in the treatment of epilepsy: An overview circa 1980. In L. W. White & B. Tursky (Eds.), *Clinical biofeedback: Efficacy and mechanisms.* New York: Guilford Press.

Stroebel, C. (1982). *The quieting reflex.* New York: Putnam's Sons.

Tarlar-Benlolo, L. (1978). The role of relaxation in biofeedback training: A critical review of the literature. *Psychological Bulletin, 85,* 727–755.

Tart, C. T. (Ed.). (1969). *Altered states of consciousness: A book of readings.* New York: Wiley.

Ullmann, L., & Krasner, L. (Eds.). (1965). *Case studies in behavior modification.* New York: Holt, Rhinehart, & Winston.

Wickramasekera, I. E. (Ed.). (1976). *Biofeedback, behavior therapy and hypnosis: Potentiating the verbal control of behavior for clinicians.* Chicago: Nelson Hall.

Wickramasekera, I. E. (1988). *Clinical behavioral medicine: Some concepts and procedures.* New York: Plenum Press.

Wolf, S. L., & Binder-MacLeod, S. A. (1983). Electromyographic biofeedback in the physical therapy clinic. In J. V. Basmajian (Ed.), *Biofeedback: Principles & practice for clinicians* (2nd ed.). Baltimore: Williams & Wilkins.

Wolpe, J. (1973). *The practice of behavior therapy* (2nd ed.). New York: Pergamon Press.

Wuttke, M. (1992). Addiction, awakening, and EEG biofeedback. *Biofeedback, 20*(2), 18–22.

2

Entering the Field of Applied Psychophysiology and Biofeedback and Assuring Competence

Mark S. Schwartz

Biofeedback and applied psychophysiology constitute a multidisciplinary and heterogenous field of professional disciplines and types of applications. Each year many practitioners start to offer clinical biofeedback and applied psychophysiological services. Others seek to continue to gain more knowledge in the field to help assure their competence.

Education and training in the field ranges from courses at universities and individual workshops to comprehensive biofeedback training programs. The Biofeedback Certification Institute of America (BCIA) provides accreditation for many biofeedback programs independent of universities. For many people, the primary sources of preparation are the annual meetings and workshops of the Association for Applied Psychophysiology and Biofeedback (AAPB). State biofeedback society workshops provide another excellent source of education, and a few private training programs offer multiday programs in varied national locations.

Many of the courses, programs, meetings, and workshops provide important and useful education and training. However, there are problems that limit their impact and usefulness. First, as the field continues to change, those who have already finished their formal education usually can no longer avail themselves of many educational and training opportunities. The schedules of professionals, for example, often do not permit enrollment in university courses and many of such courses thus remain unavailable to established practitioners.

Second, the costs of attending training programs and workshops are well beyond the comfortable reach of many people. Therefore, professionals seeking to enter this field or maintain competence often do not get this education and training.

Third, until recently there were no national and credible criteria for students and professionals to rely upon to select among educational and training offerings. The BCIA accreditation certainly represents a big step toward remedying this problem. However, not all professionals who offer education and training in biofeedback use this accreditation. Furthermore, some professionals do not use this criteria for selecting programs.

Fourth, although BCIA certification has many merits, is important and useful for practitioners and others, and deserves support, it has had limited impact thus far. Most practitioners do not seek this voluntary credential. Additionally, many practitioners certified years ago decided to avoid the recertification process. Furthermore, passing written and practical certification exams and meeting other criteria for certification cannot assess fully a person's knowledge, skills, and competence for all applied practice.

Practitioners and supervisory professionals sometimes do not know what they do not know. The development and maintenance of clinical competence requires active participation in a variety of educational and training experiences. Responsible professionals seek initial and continuing education and training. Supervisors and others with the authority to support education and training of professionals in their setting have the responsibility to support attendance at educational and training programs. Professionals providing clinical services have a responsibility to request time and financial support to attend these programs. They may need to to finance some or all of the expenses needed to attend education and training programs.

I do not have all the answers to the many questions and problems with entering this field and developing and maintaining competence. However, I offer suggestions reflecting my perspective and my biases. These are not in any order of preference. Not all are viable for every person. I only suggest that readers seriously consider them and try as many as are feasible.

GENERAL SUGGESTIONS FOR ENTERING AND MAINTAINING COMPETENCE IN BIOFEEDBACK

1. Would-be practitioners of biofeedback and professionals already in this field should enroll in carefully selected workshops, private programs, and academic courses. They should ask sponsors and presenters for the names of those who have attended in the past and talk to them.

2. Would-be practitioners should read recommended books, journal articles, manuals, and patient-education booklets. They should consider the BCIA references as a resource. Further, they should listen to audiotapes such as those from national meetings and include AAPB publications.

3. When feasible, would-be practitioners should visit with highly credible professionals to discuss and observe their clinical approaches. These opportunities are very limited, as most clinical professionals do not have the time or are unable to provide such services. However, some are able and willing to do this. Some provide such opportunities for a fee.

4. Students and would-be practitioners should study the BCIA Blueprint Tasks and Knowledge Statements.

5. Students and would-be practitioners should prepare for and attain BCIA certification.

6. Students and would-be practitioners should regularly read the principal journal in this field, *Biofeedback and Self-Regulation*, as well as other journals that publish pertinent articles. They should subscribe to abstracting services such as those from the American Psychological Association and the Society of Behavioral Medicine.

7. Every practitioner should attend the annual spring meetings of the AAPB.[1] This meeting is the single best chance to attend a wide variety of symposia, panels, and workshops. It presents an excellent chance to talk with professionals in this field. These meetings are high in caliber and attended by many clinicians and researchers who are very interesting, competent, academically sound, and especially sociable.

8. Practitioners should become involved in a state biofeedback society.

9. Students and would-be practitioners should contact highly credible professionals with much experience with biofeedback. They should ask their advice about treatment of selected

[1]The address of the AAPB is 10200 West 44th Ave., Suite 304, Wheatridge, CO 80033.

patients. State and national meetings are excellent chances to meet other professionals. The BCIA and AAPB directories are good resources. Isolation breeds limited competence.

10. Practitioners should invite to their professional setting highly credible and experienced professionals who are good therapists, educators, and/or researchers. This is especially useful for those professionals who do not regularly attend educational and training workshops or programs elsewhere. Institutions or other groups of professionals can cooperate to absorb the costs. Some larger institutions provide special status to professionals visiting the institution.

11. Beginners should usually limit the number of biofeedback modalities used. They should consider starting with electromyographic and skin temperature feedback. Trying to learn and use several modalities often unduly complicates assessment and therapy sessions.

12. Practitioners should be familiar with a few instrumentation manufacturers before purchasing instruments and discuss instrumentation with a few professionals experienced with at least different manufacturers and models. The AAPB annual meeting and some state and regional meetings usually provide such exposure. There are a number of independent distributors who sell instruments from several manufacturers. Professionals should learn about these companies and discuss needs and questions with them. Some distributors have field representatives who can visit with practitioners individually. It is wise to shop around and get good advice about what will ideally meet one's particular needs and be most cost effective. One should avoid getting more instruments than needed for one's practice. On the other hand, one should avoid getting less than is needed.

13. Practitioners should avoid "stand-alone" instruments without computer connection or at least other integration methods over varying time intervals.

14. EMG instrumentation that allows multiple simultaneous recording sites often enhances assessment and therapy. Clinical practice often requires recording from at least two muscle sites and often four sites or more. I suggest having at least four muscle channels.

15. Professionals should locate a competent biomedical engineer and familiarize him or her with existing instruments. This is crucial unless the practitioner is sufficiently competent in this area. Some companies provide good phone services and can help solve the more common and minor problems. A local competent biomedical engineer could reduce time lost sending instruments away for needless checking.

16. Professionals should consider limiting the number of disorders for which they initially offer services. It is logical to choose among disorders that are more prevalent and those for which the research on effectiveness is more supportive. They should also consider those disorders for which they have the most interest and are more likely to receive referrals.

17. Practitioners should be prepared and willing to accept patients with difficult problems. They may not have much of a choice. Professionals should be prepared and willing to invest more time with these patients and adjust therapeutic goals. Even some improvement can be very satisfying to such patients and to the referral source. Referral sources will probably appreciate a practitioner's willingness to accept such patients.

18. Practitioners should review sample assessment and therapy protocols from highly credible and experienced professionals. This is especially useful when starting a practice or broadening services to include new disorders or new modalities. Standardized assessment and therapy protocols have a place in some practices. However, it is equally true that successful and cost-efficient services benefit from tailoring assessment and treatment to the patient. Practitioners can always alter the protocols of other therapists to fit their own needs, preferences, and situations. Again, isolation breeds limited competence.

19. Providers should review the patient-education documents and presentations of others.

20. Biofeedback providers who employ or supervise other professionals should make every effort to see that such persons attain certification by the BCIA or are seriously working toward certification.

21. For those supervising others and for those supervised, close and frequent communications about the patients and biofeedback services should be maintained. Supervision varies with circumstances, such as competence, type, and complexity of patients, and specific responsibilities or job functions (see Chapter 29). There are some therapists who need supervision yet who practice with little or no supervision. Others practice with supervision by professionals with little or no biofeedback expertise. Some well-meaning professionals do not know what they do not know. Limited or no supervision by qualified professionals is not good for anyone.

Competent use of biofeedback obviously requires an understanding of the symptoms and disorders treated. Interpretation of psychophysiological and clinical data must be proper and responsible. One must provide clear, accurate, and responsible interprofessional communications. Proper interpretation of publications is yet another part of competent practice. All this, and more, is a lot to expect from many biofeedback therapists and similarly titled professionals. Proper supervision by qualified professionals is often necessary to guarantee all of the above. Furthermore, none of us may avoid self-scrutiny and reappraisal. All of us must be willing to update and change our practices.

22. Supervisory professionals should usually provide at least some assessments and therapy sessions with biofeedback. There is no substitute for this type of direct experience, at least periodically. Prudent supervising professionals avoid allowing too much distance from patients. One exception occurs when the person supervised and providing therapy with limited supervision is clearly highly qualified, competent, and highly experienced.

EDUCATION AND TRAINING PROGRAMS

Selecting courses, workshops, and training programs is often difficult. Since the first edition of this book, BCIA has made progress on its national accreditation program. The *BCIA Didactic Education Accreditation Program* was established in January, 1990. Selecting programs is now easier. Would-be practitioners should contact the BCIA office[2] for Institute criteria and the names and addresses of accredited educational and training programs. In addition, they should consider several factors before selecting educational and training programs without the BCIA accreditation. It is essential to:

1. Consider the presenter's reputation as a clinical practitioner.
2. Consider the presenter's experience. This includes years using biofeedback, number of patients directly treated, and the percentage of their time using biofeedback.
3. Select a program sponsored or accredited by a credible organization.
4. Consider the presenter's qualifications and experience to teach about the specific topic as well as the number of workshops, courses, and other presentations provided by the presenter. However, one can attend a program offered for the first time by a specific professional. I recommend attending if the sponsoring or accrediting agency is credible and the presenter is known for high quality presentations in other areas.

---

[2]The address for the BCIA office is 10020 West 44th Ave., Suite 304, Wheatridge, CO 80033; (303) 422-8436, FAX (303) 422-8894.

5. Consider what previous recipients of the specific education and training program have to say about it.

6. Check the time available for the topics listed in the program. A minimum of 1 hour is often necessary to cover very specific topics. One-half and full day workshops are often necessary for covering one or a few topics thoroughly. It would be desirable for presenters to know the needs and preferences of enrollees a few weeks ahead of time.

7. Ask about the meaning of the term "hands-on experience." Will the presenter observe the practitioner preparing a subject, attaching electrodes and thermistors, adjusting the instruments, and providing a few minutes of physiological monitoring and biofeedback? If the professional only needs or wants to observe and briefly become familiar with an instrument, then he or she does not need much hands-on experience. However, if the professional needs or wants to learn more about using the instruments in assessment and therapy, then more time with the instruments is preferable and necessary.

8. Be sure the presenter clearly specifies specific aims.

9. If there will be instrumentation available for demonstration or use and to verify which models.

10. Check for availability of printed educational information.

11. Ask about time for audience questions and discussion.

12. Consider the cost–benefit ratio of attending. Very experienced and talented professionals deserve and have the right to expect reasonable compensation for their educational services. Promotional materials, space, administrative factors, transportation for the presenter and daily expenses are all expensive items. It is also necessary to consider preparation time even if the presenter has presented the same or similar content before. Most professionals presenting workshops are usually underpaid and rarely overly compensated. Registration fees are usually good buys.

13. Check whether the instructor has BCIA certification. This is not necessary. However, it is one piece of useful information about the presenter's broader knowledge and skills, and involvement in the field.

CERTIFICATION OF BIOFEEDBACK PROFESSIONALS

Rationale

There are several advantages for providers of biofeedback attaining BCIA certification. This category includes researchers, practitioners, and presenters of biofeedback educational and training programs. It is especially valuable for supervised and supervisory professionals. There are competent practitioners without certification. Some are as competent as and even more competent than some with certification. Certification is not a guarantee of competence and it was never intended to guarantee a full range of competencies. However, certification provides a useful index of fundamental knowledge and basic instrumentation proficiency.

The reasons vary for avoiding certification. Sometimes, there is a philosophical or economic basis for the avoidance. For example, some professionals oppose any certification for themselves and others. Others say they cannot financially afford it. Sometimes the avoidance serves to evade examination anxiety. One must be sensitive to those who fear they might not successfully fulfill the criterion. Some harbor doubts about their compentencies to practice in this field. However, for many responsible professionals, these are not sufficient justifications to avoid the process. One exception would be those professionals with excellent credentials and extensive experience. For some, there is no doubt they know what they need to know.

However, there are several compelling reasons most practitioners using biofeedback should seriously consider attaining and maintaining BCIA certification.

1. Certification reflects involvement in this field and often increases one's credibility to patients and professionals.

2. It attests that the certified individual meets specified criteria to use biofeedback.

3. It increases "market value" and mobility for many.

4. It gives employers a credible index of a competence.

5. Some reimbursement systems view the BCIA credential as an important criterion when considering reimbursement.

6. A credible certification program is a cornerstone and important sign of the maturation of the field. It improves the image of biofeedback to health care professionals, referral sources, and others outside the field. We should not undervalue the importance of this.

7. Preparing for and maintaining certification involves considerable studying and learning—a benefit for applicants, certificants, and patients.

Choosing a Certification Program

The question of which certification to get and rely upon involved two topics in the first edition of this book. The first was national versus state certification, and the second was choosing between two national certification programs. Neither of these questions requires attention now. There is only national certification, and there is now only one such certification since all state certifications volunteered to cease their programs.

The other national certification, the American Board of Clinical Biofeedback, ceased functioning in the late 1980s. I salute their founders, board, and certificants. They had a vision, and they admirably pursued it. In the complex, demanding, and competitive world of professional and certification organizations, they did not survive.

Even the National Commission for Health Certifying Agencies (NCHCA) suffered from limited support later and required transformation. The NCHCA started in 1977 with strong recommendations from and initial financial support from the federal government. The mission was to provide "certification of certifying agencies." The NCHCA required certifying organizations to fulfill extensive, demanding, and challenging criteria. To the credit of the early BCIA Board, it achieved full membership in 1983. The BCIA later dropped its membership in the NCHCA partly for financial reasons and partly because of the weakened state of the NCHCA. As a small certifying agency, BCIA had concerns about investing thousands of certificants' dollars in a weak and uncertain NCHCA.

The NCHCA deserve our thanks for establishing both a vision and admirable criteria. They were very helpful to the early credibility and success of the BCIA. My own experience with the NCHCA was in multiple roles. I was the representative of BCIA as Chairperson of the Board. I was on the Board of the NCHCA and was Speaker of the General Assembly for nearly 4 years. I miss the NCHCA as it was in those days. I especially miss their early leaders.

The weakening of the NCHCA occurred for at least two major reasons. The criteria for membership were stringent and extensive. It allowed up to 5 years for fulfillment of all the criteria, but many certifying organizations could not or would not do what was necessary. The NCHCA had a dynamic and highly competent executive director who was very successful in getting financial support for projects and keeping the organization together.

A tragic car accident changed all that. The NCHCA continues with a broader certifying mission, but most health certifying organizations are probably not members.

There are lessons to learn from the NCHCA experience. We must not establish credential criteria so extensive and strict that many potential applicants cannot fulfill them in the time frame required. We should apply the basic learning principles of successive approximation or shaping, and use small steps over a long enough time to allow participants to learn, change, and maintain their gains. No organization should rely on a single leader. Accidents happen. Leaders should make every possible effort to acquire and wisely invest enough money to sustain an organization over at least 2 years of hard times. However, they must be realistic about the fees for members and certificants. Is anyone listening?

BCIA Certification

There are more requirements and pathways now for certification than existed in the early years. Requirements include educational degrees, didactic training in a core curriculum, clinical biofeedback training, direct experience with EMG and thermal modalities, clinical biofeedback supervision, and biofeedback case conferences.

The BCIA's *Blueprint Tasks and Knowledge Statements* provide a detailed outline of provider roles and knowledge needed to enter the biofeedback field and prepare for the examinations. The practical exam requires applicants to show their understanding and basic proficiency with selected modalities and instruments. The BCIA completed a revision of the original 1981 blueprint in 1990. It continued to recognize the original edition until at least 1993. The outline below lists the revised topic areas for the knowledge statements.

1. An Introduction to Biofeedback
2. Preparation for Clinical Intervention
3. Neuromuscular Interventions: General
4. Neuromuscular Interventions: Specific
5. Central Nervous System Interventions: General
6. Autonomic Nervous System Interventions: General
7. Autonomic Nervous System Interventions: Specific
8. Biofeedback and Distress
9. Instrumentation
10. Adjunctive Techniques and Cognitive Interventions
11. Professional Conduct

The certification process acts to deter the least competent and is an incentive for increasing competence. It is an objective and acceptable criterion for persons to assess their entry-level competence.

SUMMARY

In summary, this chapter provides ideas and suggestions for persons entering the biofeedback field. For those already in the field, these ideas and suggestions may help them maintain and enhance their competence. Biofeedback is a broad, heterogeneous, and complex field now in its early adulthood. Practitioners need infusions of new knowledge, ideas, and skills. Deciding when, where, and by whom these infusions are to take place is not always easy. In this chapter, I provided some guidance.

The AAPB and the BCIA continue to be the national resources and centers for continued maturation of the field. Those who are not members of the AAPB should join or rejoin. Those who are not certified by the BCIA should consider this credential for themselves. Those currently certified should recertify. Those who were certified in the past but are not currently certified should try and return.

3A

Definitions of Biofeedback and Applied Psychophysiology

R. Paul Olson

A REVIEW OF DEFINITIONS

Several definitions of biofeedback exist. *Operational* definitions emphasize the processes or procedures involved. Definitions that stress the aims or objectives of biofeedback are *teleological* definitions. Other definitions combine elements of both. This chapter includes samples of each type of definition and a synthesis.

Process Definitions

These are examples of process definitions of biofeedback.

1. "Biofeedback is a recently coined term that refers to a group of experimental procedures in which an external sensor is used to provide the organism with an indication of the state of a bodily process, usually in an attempt to effect a change in the measured quantity" (Schwartz & Beatty, 1977, p. 1).

2. "The term biofeedback has come into widespread use to designate the process. A more precise term would be external psychophysiological feedback" (Gaarder & Montgomery, 1977, p. 9).

3. Kamiya suggested three procedural requirements for biofeedback training: "First, the physiological function to be brought under control must be continuously monitored with sufficient sensitivity to detect moment-by-moment changes. Second, changes in the physiological measure must be reflected immediately to the person attempting to control the process. Third, the person must be motivated to learn to effect the physiological changes under study" (Kamiya, 1971, p. 1).

Teleological Definitions

Teleological definitions emphasize the goals of biofeedback. Three examples are:

1. "The primary goal of biofeedback has been to promote the acquisition of self-control of physiological processes" (Ray, Raczynski, Rogers, & Kimball, 1979, p. 1).

2. "A tentative definition is that biofeedback is the process or technique for learning voluntary control over automatically, reflexively regulated body functions" (Brown, 1977, p. 3).

3. "Biofeedback training is a tool for learning psychosomatic self-regulation" (Green & Green, 1977, p. 42).

Combined Definitions

Definitions that combine both process and goals represent steps toward synthesis. The following examples represent attempts at a synthesis:

1. "Biofeedback can be defined as the use of monitoring instruments (usually electrical) to detect and amplify internal physiologic processes within the body, in order to make this ordinarily unavailable internal information available to the individual and literally feed it back to him in some form" (Birk, 1973, p. 2).

2. Biofeedback is a process that "involves making one aware of very subtle changes in physiological states in the hope of bringing those processes under conscious control" (Hassett, 1978, p. 137).

3. "Biofeedback may be defined as the technique of using equipment (usually electronic) to reveal to human beings some of their internal physiological events, normal and abnormal, in the form of visual and auditory signals in order to teach them to manipulate these otherwise involuntary or unfelt events by manipulating and displayed signals" (Basmajian, 1979, p. 1).

4. "Biofeedback involves the use of sensitive (e.g., electronic or electromechanical devices) to measure, process, and indicate (i.e., feedback) the ongoing activity of various body processes or conditions of which the person is usually unaware so that the patient, client, or student may have the opportunity to change and to develop beneficial control over these body processes" (Schwartz & Fehmi, 1982, p. 4).

Theoretical Models

Theoretical models influence all the above definitions. The primary models from which biofeedback definitions derive include a learning theory model, a cybernetics model, and a stress management model. These models differ in emphasis but are not mutually exclusive.

A learning theory model views biofeedback as instrumental conditioning of neuromuscular and autonomic activity. Physiological responses such as muscle tension and heart rate are operant behaviors changed by their consequences or effects. The effects include the feedback signals as positive reinforcers.

In a cybernetics model, biofeedback signals are sources of information that complete an external feedback loop. Adjustment or control of the physiological process occurs because a motivated person receives information about his or her physiology during conditions such as rest and stress.

In a stress management model, biofeedback is one of many noninvasive techniques sharing the goal of enhancing a person's ability to manage stress.

Practitioners need not commit to only one theory. There is heuristic value in each of these and benefit from a synthesis or composite. The following definition of applied biofeedback is an attempt at synthesis.

A PROPOSED DEFINITION OF APPLIED BIOFEEDBACK

A comprehensive definition includes statements of both the process and purpose of biofeedback. As a synthesis, the following includes seven procedural elements (1–7) and three goals (8–10).

As a process, applied biofeedback is (1) a group of therapeutic procedures that (2) utilizes electronic or electromechanical instruments (3) to accurately measure, process, and "feed back" to persons (4) information with reinforcing properties (5) about their neuro-muscular and autonomic activity, both normal and abnormal, (6) in the form of analogue or binary, auditory and/or visual feedback signals. (7) Best achieved with a competent bio-feedback professional, (8) the objectives are to help persons develop greater awareness and voluntary control over their physiological processes that are otherwise outside awareness and/or under less voluntary control, (9) by first controlling the external signal, (10) and then with internal psychophysiological cues.

Here is a discussion of each element of the definition.

1. ". . . a group of therapeutic procedures . . ."—Biofeedback is not one generic thera-peutic modality; it can involve different sites, modalities, and procedures. Even when feed-back is provided through only one modality, as EMG, there are many dimensions and steps. These include verbal instructions, focused attention, relaxation procedures, feedback, stress challenges, and motor skill learning.

2. ". . . utilizes electronic or electromechanical instruments . . ."—Most internal physiological systems involve natural feedback mechanisms to maintain homeostatic bal-ance. The body's internal biofeedback, or "living feedback" systems, have limits and mal-functions that result in impaired functioning and symptoms. Some areas of the body have fewer or less efficient feedback systems. For example, there are fewer sensory and motor nerves connecting most head muscles to the brain compared to the number of nerves con-necting the hands and lips to the brain. Biofeedback therapy does not usually refer to the body's internal biological feedback systems but, rather, to external electronic or electrome-chanical feedback systems.

Biofeedback does not refer to physiological self-regulation that omits external instru-mentation and feedback. The latter includes relaxation, meditation, hypnosis, and imag-ery techniques commonly used independently or with biofeedback instrumentation.

Applied biofeedback typically refers to electronic modalities such as electromyographic (EMG), skin temperature or thermal, electrodermal (ED) or perspiration, heart rate, blood volume, blood pressure (BP), respiration, and electroencephalographic (EEG). In addition, there are various forms of electromechanical instruments such as "pressure transducers" and "goniometers." A detailed discussion of EMG, thermal, and ED modalities is in Chapter 4. Examples of electromechanical instruments are in Chapter 21.

3. ". . . to accurately measure, process, and 'feed back' to persons . . ."—One unique feature of applied biofeedback is to provide accurate and meaningful physiological informa-tion directly to the patient. Regardless of the theoretical model, accuracy of measurement is important. Chapter 5 discusses measurement and electronic processing of the signals.

The signals are fed back to the patient to enable him or her to assume a greater and different role in treatment than with other therapies. "The patient is no longer an object of treatment, he is the treatment" (Brown, 1977, p. 13). There is a shift in the role of the therapist who sometimes also becomes a coach or instructor as well as a therapist.

4. ". . . information with reinforcing properties . . ."—This phrase integrates the perspectives of both cybernetics and learning theory. The biofeedback signals fed back to a person convey information, and this information often contains reinforcing properties. Admittedly, the therapist often needs to explain to the patient the meaning of the informa-tion. From a behavioral perspective, the person learns to self-regulate his or her physio-logical processes with the help of feedback information. Feedback information reinforces, facilitates, augments, and encourages physiological and cognitive learning.

The term "feedback" comes from the mathematician Norbert Weiner who defined it as "a method of controlling the system by reinserting the results of its past performance" (Birk, 1973, p. 3). The physiological information fed back can be with or without awareness. In either case, it is information that is fed back.

5. ". . . about their neuromuscular and autonomic activity, both normal and abnormal . . ."—The somatic processes recorded are both neuromuscular and visceral activities innervated by either central or autonomic nervous systems or both.

6. ". . . in the form of analogue or binary, auditory, and/or visual feedback signals."—Analogue feedback is continuous feedback. For example, a continuous tone of varying pitch may indicate rising or falling muscle activity or skin temperature. Binary feedback is discontinuous, either on or off. For example, one may set a signal to go on or off when the patient lowers his or her respiration rate from 16 cycles per minute (cpm) to 12 cpm or lower. In this example, the threshold is 12 cycles.

Feedback may be visual and/or auditory, and sometimes kinesthetic. Visual feedback may be continuous as in a numerical meter or on a computer display. It may be discrete as in a sound that turns on or off by changing the level of one's physiological activity. One can present both continuous and discrete signals graphically on computer-generated displays.

7. "Best achieved with a competent biofeedback professional . . ."—In the preceding example, a person does not usually learn to reduce respiration rate and make it smooth, effortless, and diaphragmatic by simply listening or watching feedback signals. Attachment to biofeedback instruments without proper cognitive preparation, instructions, and guidance is not appropriate biofeedback therapy.

Some professionals consider biofeedback as a form of education. For many applications, it is psychophysiological education. As with all education, results are partly the result of the teacher's skills, personality, and attention to the student. Other professionals consider biofeedback as therapy. As with all forms of therapy, the therapist's skills, personality, and attention to the patient affect the outcome.

The important point is that the professional conducting biofeedback therapy sessions is an integral part of the intervention. Whether construed as therapy or education, goals are most likely achieved with competent professionals who work well with motivated patients or clients.

8. ". . . the objectives are to help persons develop greater awareness and voluntary control over their physiological processes that are otherwise outside awareness and/or under less voluntary control. . . ."—A basic premise of the biofeedback field is that one can develop or enhance significant self-regulation for any physiological process or activity accurately measured.

One reason for skepticism about biofeedback is the belief that many of the body's systems function without awareness and involuntarily. One original and crucial claim shown by biofeedback research is that this long-held belief is only a partial truth. Humans are much more capable of developing physiological self-regulation than has been previously believed.

It is no longer tenable to assert that humans have little or no capacity for some self-regulation of organs and functions mediated by the autonomic nervous system. Neither can one assume that for muscles and nerves malfunctioning because of injury or disease. However, neither is it tenable to argue there are no limits to the degree of physiological self-regulation. There clearly are such limits but those limits, are less than once believed. Biofeedback is neither a placebo nor a panacea.

9. ". . . by first controlling the external signal . . ."—Finite sensory feedback and control systems of humans limit the development of physiological self-regulation. For example,

most persons are unaware of changes in muscle activity corresponding to a few or several microvolts. Most are unaware of blood pressure changes of a few to several millimeters of mercury (mm Hg) and in the electrical activity of the brain. Minute changes in skin temperature or sweat gland activity are too small for awareness.

Biofeedback instruments detect minute changes in bioelectrical activity that human sensory systems cannot detect or are not detecting. Theoretically, the person first learns to control the external signal and then develops more control over his or her physiological processes.

10. ". . . and then with internal psychophysiologic cues."—The final goal is for persons to maintain physiological self-regulation without feedback from external instruments. People learn to apply self-regulation in their daily lives by learning to identify undesirable internal cues and reproducing desired cues associated with physiological changes learned and reinforced with external feedback. An effective biofeedback program includes methods to help people transfer and generalize the acquired self-regulation responses.

REFERENCES

Basmajian, J. V. (Ed.). (1979). *Biofeedback: Principles and practice for clinicians.* Baltimore: Williams & Wilkins.

Birk, L. (Ed.). (1973). *Biofeedback: Behavioral medicine.* New York: Grune & Stratton.

Brown, B. (1977). *Stress and the art of biofeedback.* New York: Harper & Row.

Gaarder, K. R., & Montgomery, P. S. (1977). *Clinical biofeedback: A procedural manual for behavioral medicine.* Baltimore: Williams & Wilkins.

Green, E., & Green, A. (1977). *Beyond biofeedback.* New York: Delta.

Hassett, J. (1978). *A primer of psychophysiology.* San Francisco: Freeman.

Kamiya, J. (1971). Preface. In T. Barber, L. DiCara, J. Kamiya, N. Miller, D. Shapiro, & J. Stoyva (Eds.), *Biofeedback and self-control.* Chicago: Aldine-Atherton.

Ray, W. J., Raczynski, J. M., Rogers, T., & Kimball, W. H. (1979). *Evaluation of clinical biofeedback.* New York: Plenum Press.

Schwartz, G. E., & Beatty, J. (1977). *Biofeedback: Theory and research.* New York: Academic Press.

Schwartz, M. S., & Fehmi, L. (1982). *Applications standards and guidelines for providers of biofeedback services.* Wheatridge, CO: Biofeedback Society of America.

3B

Definitions of Biofeedback and Applied Psychophysiology

Nancy M. Schwartz
Mark S. Schwartz

BACKGROUND

The following discussion is consistent with Olson's definition of biofeedback and prior models of how it works (Chapter 3, Part A). We propose being more inclusive, however, and broadening the definition. We move toward resolution of disputes about whether biofeedback works and how it works by integrating explanations.

Different opinions exist about whether or not the specific feedback signals, as such, result in changes. However, even the critics of biofeedback agree that many of the feedback procedures are part of something that works. The disagreement focuses on the ingredients and process that result in changed outcome.

The debate between Furedy (1987) and Shellenberger and Green (1987) was a heated and invigorating exchange. Attempts to moderate and create perspective were valuable and appreciated by many (Rosenfeld, 1987). A detailed discussion of these papers is beyond the scope of this chapter. Practitioners, students, and critics of biofeedback should be familiar with these issues and the references. We could not do justice to the debate here. However, it was a major element propelling us to develop this chapter.

Another inspiration for this paper came from Susan Middaugh in her Presidential Address (Middaugh, 1990). She discussed and gave excellent examples for how biofeedback contributes to the therapeutic process. Middaugh focused on patient selection, treatment protocol selection, instrumentation, and patient–therapist interactions, in combination with other techniques.

This fits well with the Aptitude × Treatment × Interaction (A × T × I) model (Holloway & Rogers, 1988; Dance & Neufeld, 1988) of therapy effectiveness which has been gaining more attention recently. This is the interaction of the person and treatment that often accounts for the outcome. It is similar to the still vibrant idea from Paul (1966): Briefly, treatments work for selected patients in selected conditions.

ASSUMPTIONS

Many assumptions form a background for the discussion that follows. We assume all or most practitioners and critics agree with most, perhaps all, of the assumptions. For convenience, we divide the assumptions into three groups labeled Biofeedback, Patient Education, and Integration.

Biofeedback

- Something therapeutic happens in the context in which biofeedback is a part.
- Many patients improve significantly during and after exposure to biofeedback and the therapy context in which it is a part. This is true for many disorders.
- Many patients do not improve with biofeedback treatment packages.
- Similar studies and procedures in different laboratories lead to different results.
- Similar procedures, by the same therapist in the same study or office, lead to different results among different patients or subjects.
- The same treatment delivered by different professionals to the same type of patient and in a similar manner, often yields different results.

Patient Education

- Patients, especially patients with medical disorders, are often skeptical about therapies with psychological features.
- Patients forget most of what they hear.
- Patients often do not understand patient-education information from health professionals.
- The quality and clarity of communications vary across patients and across professionals.
- Expectations affect satisfaction, compliance, mood, motivation, arousal, attention and concentration, and therefore, outcome.
- Patient education and knowledge affect expectations, satisfaction, and compliance.

Integration

- Practitioners differ widely in education, training, and interpersonal skills. They differ widely in the instruments available and knowledge and skills with the instruments. They also differ in their choices of theoretical models.
- Most professionals agree that biofeedback, like other treatments, contains many different elements. They also assume that, for many applications of biofeedback, one needs multiple elements. Many of these are as important as the feedback signal itself. The relationship between the elements is probably synergistic. In gestalt terms, "the whole is greater than the sum of its parts."
- Most professionals further assume that some elements or factors are more important than others in some applications and with some patients. For example, in some cases the feedback signal is more important for the physiological information it conveys to the patient. In some situations, its value is the information for the therapist. In others, the signal helps shape or positively reinforce cognitive changes that, in turn, are a step resulting in symptom changes.

A PATIENT-EDUCATION MODEL: SEVEN LEVELS AND FACETS OF INFORMATION ABOUT BIOFEEDBACK

This model proposes that patient education is an active ingredient of biofeedback regardless of the discipline within which one uses it. In physical therapy, it can help a patient see small changes in muscle activity before the patient can feel it. This can help the patient relearn control of a specific muscle or group of muscles. In psychotherapy, it can be useful to show the relationship between thoughts and physiology. When one uses biofeedback with relaxation, the physiological measurements suggest which techniques work better than others for a specific patient. In these situations, biofeedback provides useful educational information to both the patient and to the therapist.

Instead of asking whether biofeedback is a tool for patient education, we assume that it is. We therefore ask what needs communication and how best to do it. Instead of asking whether biofeedback is necessary, we ask under what circumstances, for which patients, how, and in combination with what else should it be applied (Middaugh, 1990). We refer here to seven levels of information. This helps us gain perspective on biofeedback and its different educational uses.

These levels of information mesh with the seven procedural elements and the three goals that are part of Olson's definition of biofeedback in part A of this chapter. However, to fully include number seven of Olson's procedural elements, one needs more than to merely attach instruments to people, show them feedback, and talk to them briefly about their physiology. One needs a competent therapist who also is a competent patient educator and uses biofeedback to optimize the quality of information relayed to the patient. A patient who can understand the relevance of the signal and who understands and accepts the treatment is more likely to reach treatment goals.

SUMMARY OF THE SEVEN LEVELS OR FACETS OF INFORMATION ABOUT BIOFEEDBACK

We think it is useful to distinguish separate levels or facets of biofeedback. For the present, we distinguish seven levels or facets. Each carries different amounts of information and each is of different value for patient education.

1. The raw signal is basic to biofeedback but lacking useful information.
2. Explanation of the signal.
3. Explanation of the signal in relation to the person's physiology.
4. Explanation of the signal and physiology in relation to symptoms.
5. Therapist suggestions for how to change physiology.
6. Information to therapist and doctor to adjust treatment.
7. Information to patient about progess. This is positive cognitive reinforcement or "feedforward" for the patient that she or he can regulate target physiology.

LEVEL OF INFORMATION AND THERAPIST ACTIONS

Signal Presentation

Although the signal itself is a feature unique to biofeedback, it is only the first level of information. However, therapist input is critical even at this basic level. There is no standardization of signal presentations even with the same instrument. One can use audio and/or visual signals; they are analog or binary.

Furthermore, therapists use various speeds and sensitivities of the signals. The speed is the time it takes for a visual signal to cross the screen. The sensitivity is the size of the physiological change required to show a change in the feedback signal. Thus, one can vary the range displayed. This is comparable to using a microscope with different powers of magnification. You see smaller changes with higher magnification. Computer-based instruments expand the choices for presenting feedback signals. One can now vary colors and the type of feedback displays. Some prefer lines crossing the screen. Others choose bar graphs. Images fade and sharpen. The choices are extensive.

Therapists also use and feed back different numbers of modalities. There also are differences in the number of channels fed back simultaneously within the same modality.

The challenge for the therapist is to choose signal displays that convey necessary and sufficient information to help the patient meet the session and therapy goals. In addition, the challenge is to do this without presenting distracting or anxiety-producing signal information.

By definition (Chapter 3, Part A), the signal should have some reinforcing properties. Therapists should be very familiar with the instruments and patients' needs and limitations. This familiarity facilitates selection of the signals and displays that help ease information processing by the patient. For example, if the range is too large in temperature biofeedback, initial tiny changes in the desired direction go undetected. If a patient is primarily a visual learner, then audio feedback with eyes closed probably is not the ideal choice for presentation of the information.

Standardized program displays are available. However, therapists enhance patient education by selecting feedback signals and displays that tailor these to a patient's needs and therapy goals.

Research and guidelines about tailoring signal presentations and displays to patients and tasks are both scarce. Practitioners need this type of guidance and research. The biofeedback field needs it. Thus, the signal as the basic and lowest level of information is complex. It varies across studies, clinical practitioners, patients, and sessions. By itself, the signal provides limited systematic and reliably useful information. With some displays of one signal, some patients could eventually learn information about their psychophysiological functioning by trial and error. However, it would require more time than would be practical or cost efficient.

Explanation of Signal

The second level of information is the explanation of the signal and display. At this level, the information might be as simple as "the red line is temperature, the blue one is muscle activity, and the green one is perspiration." Another example is "you are getting immediate feedback about changes in your body that are occurring right now."

The patients may only have information that the signals they see or hear connect to specific sensors attached to them. Listening to patients who had biofeedback elsewhere suggests to us that some seem to have no more information than this. This is similar to a child learning how to play a video game without any instruction. Through trial and error they can learn to master the game. Through trial and error patients can learn to control the signal. If patients can control the signals, they control some part of their physiology.

There has been much discussion about what biofeedback is and whether or not it works. Furedy's (1987) focus was on only these first two levels of information. Shellenberger and Green (1987) suggest that these two levels are not biofeedback. Neither are correct. The first two levels are biofeedback, but they usually do not provide enough information to accomplish desired goals in clinical practice.

Explanation of the Signals in Relation to Physiology

The third information level relates the signal to physiology. Examples of some therapist statements[1] are: "When your hand temperature is above 92°F, you are more relaxed." "If you have the blue line below this dotted blue line, then you are below 2.0 microvolts and you are showing that you can relax that muscle group." "If you can keep the blue line above 30 microvolts for 10 seconds, you will show that you have increased your strength."

Again, computer-based instruments expand the potential ability to convey information. One can store measurements and display data with data summary displays such as a "histograph." The ability to freeze the screen allows therapists to review events and discuss the signals in more detail. Therapists discuss the meaning of the signal display at various points in relation to the patient's psychophysiology.

All of this is also biofeedback. It is therapist feedback using stop action and/or summarized and visually displayed psychophysiological data. Starting at this level, from a patient-education viewpoint, some verbal instruction or education about physiology can enhance patient understanding of the signals. This should increase the usefulness of the information provided by the signal.

Explanation of Signal in Relation to Symptoms

The fourth level requires the therapist to inform the patient about how the signal display relates to the patient's symptoms. A therapist might say,

> "Keeping the blue line down means your muscles are more relaxed. Notice that it only takes you a few moments to reach this level. It took much longer when you started. When you relax your muscles like this often enough, you can have fewer headaches. Relaxing often and quickly throughout the day prevents the excess tension that leads to headaches."

Therapist Suggestions

At this information level, the therapist gives suggestions and coaches the patient to help achieve the desired feedback. Examples are instructions in posture, releasing muscle tension, slow and deep abdominal breathing, visualization, or ways to increase muscle strength. A therapist might say,

> "Allow your arms to feel heavy and relaxed. Visualize relaxing at the beach on a warm, bright day. You are in a comfortable recliner chair. No one is close by. All you hear are the waves lapping at the shore and a few sea gulls in the distance. You may feel your hands warming."

Fred keeps his head shifted forward when he works at his computer and often when he is standing. He often clenches his teeth while working. This increases the tension in the muscles in the back of his neck. A therapist might say,

---

[1]The therapist statements in the following sections are only for illustrative purposes.

"Change your posture slightly. Keep your head level and shift your head back slightly. Drop your chin slightly. Let your jaw drop slightly. This can reduce the muscle tension in the back of your neck."

Instructions may be to relax very briefly many times a day. Patients should be encouraged to use this information and their internal cues rather than be dependent on external feedback. A therapist might advise,

"Notice how you feel right now. You can reproduce that feeling in your daily life."

Information to Therapist

Level six is the information available to the therapist. Biofeedback instruments allow therapists to improve their ability to assess psychophysiological baselines, reactivity to stress challenges, and recoveries. Therapists can adjust treatment as needed to meet physiological goals. If the patient is attaining these goals, the therapist informs the patient to attend to the body cues and sensations associated with the desired physiological activity.

The therapist may see that one relaxation procedure is not as helpful as another. For example, releasing muscle tension without first tensing the muscle group might be better than tensing the muscles first. One type or style of autogenic-like or self-generating phrases might lead to lowered arousal more so than other phrases.

Accurately measuring changes in physiology helps the art in these therapies be more scientific. The therapist does not need to guess what exercises or adjunctive techniques are most helpful. The therapist can see from the feedback what helps and what does not. A therapist might say,

"I see that this relaxation procedure is not very helpful for you. There are several others we can try. We will start with this one. . . . "

Informing Patients They Are Successful

The issue of feedback versus *feedforward* also is a subject of discussion and disagreement. This information level underscores the feedforward aspect of treatment. Mary has a panic disorder and feels that her physiology is out of control. She is learning relaxation skills. With the feedback signals she sees that she can control her physiology. She feels more confident about her relaxation skills and less threatened when she notices physiological arousal cues. She learns to use the cues to prompt herself to employ self-regulation procedures. The confidence she gains helps her interrupt the negative self-talk that previously made her symptoms worse.

Fred sees how the changes in posture affect the tension in his neck. He now knows how this affects his neck pain and headaches. He sees that simple adjustments of his posture lower the EMG activity. He *could* make the adjustments without the feedback. However, the feedback serves to show him the result immediately and reinforces his confidence.

There is also disagreement about whether symptom changes result from changes in physiology or changes in thoughts. Both are probably valid views. Both probably occur to varying degrees in different patients at different times in the therapy process. For example, seeing self-generated changes in physiology helps alter thoughts. It increases thoughts of self-efficacy and decreases feelings of helplessness. This can help encourage compliance. Knowledge of results is helpful for achieving treatment goals (Salmoni, Schmidt, & Walter, 1984).

EXPLANATIONS, MODELS, AND MODEL BUILDING

The above discussion of information levels in biofeedback is a step in the direction of model building. We now turn to other models and then return to a synthesis and proposed revised definition.

A detailed discussion of the various explanations or models for how biofeedback works is beyond the intent of this chapter and the space allotted. However, mention of these is germane to give perspective. We also borrow ideas and models from other fields to offer fresh ideas and insights. The list of models is not in any order of preference.

Prior models used in the biofeedback literature include:

Model 1. *Physiological changes result in symptom changes.*
Model 2. *Cognitive changes (beliefs and expectations) lead to symptom changes.*
Model 3. *Placebo/nonspecific effects account for symptom changes.*
Model 4. *Feedforward processes account for symptoms changes.*

Other models that have relevance for biofeedback are:

Model 5. *Banduras' Self-Efficacy Model*
Model 6. *The Patient-Education Model*
Model 7. *The R. Rosenthal Interpersonal Expectancy Model*
Model 8. *The Omer and London Model*
Model 9. *The A × T × I Model*

Prior Models Used in the Biofeedback Literature

Model 1

Physiological changes result in symptom changes. This is the traditional model. It suggests that information from the target physiological system made available to the patient allows the patient to gain control. A common example is reducing muscle tension to reduce tension-type headaches. Another example is increasing muscle awareness and tension in pelvic floor muscles to reduce urinary or fecal incontinence. Reducing peripheral vasoconstriction to reduce vasospastic episodes is a third example.

Some professionals allow for an important revision of this model that proposes that the feedback encourages the person to attend more to the body area and functioning. This heightened awareness of sensations and circumstances that precede the symptoms results in developing other voluntary behaviors to manage and reduce the symptoms. Examples are relaxing more often or remembering to tighten sphincters.

Model 2

Cognitive changes including beliefs and expectations result in symptom changes (Holroyd et al., 1984; Meichenbaum, 1976). This model suggests that the process of biofeedback with its performance feedback and verbal encouragement from a therapist results in cognitive changes. These include positive expectations, perceived success, and reduced anxiety and symptoms associated with a reduced sense of helplessness. These cognitive factors are the mediators and necessary elements in change. The therapeutic value of self-efficacy fits well into this model.

Model 3

Placebo or nonspecific effects account for symptom changes (Furedy, 1987; Roberts, 1985, 1986). Concepts such as expectations, therapist credibility, and therapist–patient relationship are among the concepts interwoven with, and inseparable from, placebo and nonspecific factors. This overlaps with the cognitive model. However, it attributes the changes to unspecified or miscellaneous factors unrelated directly to the active ingredients in the biofeedback. This explanation is no different from that proposed to explain some other therapies. Although the subject of extensive attention for decades, views of placebo and nonspecific factors are now in a major metamorphosis (Critelli & Neumann, 1984; White, Tursky, & Schwartz, 1985, chapter 25; Omer & London, 1989).

Model 4

Feedforward processes account for symptoms changes. In this view (Dunn, Gillig, Ponsor, Weil, & Utz, 1986; LaCroix, 1984), the person already can execute a response and uses the feedback signals as confirmation and reinforcement.

Other Models That Have Relevance for Biofeedback

Model 5

Banduras' self-efficacy model states that performance and mastery experiences are among the most potent in their effects on efficacy expectations and behavior. In other words, what I do and clearly see that I can do has a more significant impact on my beliefs and behavior than what someone else tells me they think I can do.

Model 6

A *patient-education* model encompasses and implies more and different concepts, elements, and processes than other models including those involving cognitive and information processing. The elements and emphases include many components within the rubrics of knowledge, communication, patient, professional, memory, patient satisfaction, competing factors, social support (Schwartz, in press).

Model 7

The R. Rosenthal interpersonal expectancy model focuses on interpersonal expectancy effects and outcome. This research shows that a teacher's expectations about a student changes the teacher's affect concerning the student. This results in a somewhat independent change in the teacher's degree of effort while teaching the student. The belief that a student can learn reinforces the belief that the teacher's efforts are worthwhile. Rosenthal and colleagues (Harris, & Rosenthal, 1985; Rosenthal, 1990; Learman, Avorn, Everitt, & Rosenthal, 1990) extend this model to clinical situations.

Model 8

The Omer and London model represents the metamorphosis of the concepts of placebo and nonspecific effects. "Now . . . nonspecific factors are not noise to be filtered out of 'real' treatment, but are important signal events in it" (Omer & London, 1989, p. 239). They conceptualize these factors into four groups: relationship, expectancy, reorganizing, and impact.

1. Under *relationship*, Rosenthal and colleagues include trust, warmth, understanding, and a secure atmosphere for exploration, learning, and change.

2. They emphasize cognitive factors such as *expectancy* and self-efficacy. Patients' beliefs about their abilities to develop and apply recommended physiological skills and changes affect success. Health professionals who believe in a treatment and the patients' abilities to be successful will probably convey this confidence to the patients.

3. The *reorganizing* element involves health professionals trying to help patients dismantle or "unfreeze" dysfunctional patterns. Treatments, such as biofeedback, give patients new views and new logical versions of their problems—new "conceptual schemes of the change process" (Omer & London, 1989, p. 243). This resembles Wickramasekara's (1988) proposal that practitioners using biofeedback shape the cognitions of patients into accepting a new role and a revised perspective with new vocabulary.

4. *Impact* refers to successful treatments and professionals having enough impact to "overcome . . . [patients'] . . . tendencies to ignore . . . [a problem or] . . . neglect it, habituate to it, or forget it" (Omer & London, 1989, p. 244).

Model 9

An *aptitude × treatment × interaction model* ($A \times T \times I$) adds much to our model building (Holloway, Spivey, Zismer, & Withington, 1988). It permits inclusion of all aptitudes of patients and personal characteristics that might interact with treatments or informational strategies. (See Holloway et al., 1988, for excellent summaries of this model).

This model has the capability to describe better treatments for selected clients (Dance & Neufeld, 1988). One can use this as a framework to subdivide patients on a pertinent attribute. One then assigns patients to different forms of intervention or focuses on certain educational components. The ATI model is a single interaction model. One expects more than one level of interaction. Others include professional variables, competing variables, social support variables, and reinforcers.

Increased information and patient education are common elements in all models. We suggest a conceptualization that includes different levels and types of information received by patients during biofeedback sessions. This discussion acknowledges the contributions of Gary Schwartz (1982, 1983) who emphasized the contextual, organistic, multicategory, and multicausal approach to understanding biofeedback. We also borrow from Middaugh's synthesis. For her, the question is not simply how does biofeedback work. Rather, the question is how it works for different people and under what circumstances?

Toward a More Inclusive Definition

Furedy (1987, p. 180) asks if the information provided by biofeedback is really helpful. If one employs only the first two information levels, it is probable that the limited information provided is not sufficiently helpful. A better question might be, "Is all the information provided by the therapist sufficiently helpful?" By Olson's definition, a competent therapist is an important part of biofeedback therapies. With computerized biofeedback, it is like having a high-tech electronic chalkboard for teaching and a built-in ability to measure progress. It is up to the therapist to be the best teacher and communicator.

In much research, it is difficult to assess if biofeedback, as such, was helpful. It often is not clear how many and which information levels and facets the therapists employed. In future research, it would be helpful to tease apart these levels and facets. The aim would be to see not if the biofeedback has been useful but which levels and facets of information are most helpful and how can we expand and optimize each. The question is not whether the signal is helpful but how can we improve upon the information from the signal?

In essence, biofeedback, used in the broad sense of signals, explanations, and patient education, *provides missing or deficient information in the therapy context. These are for the patient, the therapist, or the interaction.* One does not evaluate a school book or this biofeedback book when presented to students by itself. Some students have:

- Sufficient motivation
- Sufficient capabilities
- No significant interferences
- The time and places to study it
- Other resources to use as references
- An experiential background conducive for self-learning
- Confidence in their ability
- A teacher for help if they reach an impasse

Some students do well with self-study and never need to go to class. Others need classroom instructions and review of the text. Some need text review paragraph by paragraph, page by page, section by section, and chapter by chapter. Some learn it for an average grade. Others seek or need a grade of A. Some never learn it. None of this is news. However, the point is that we do not attribute the problem to the book unless it is written poorly and/or not tailored well to the student.

Thus, we propose slight but important additions to Olson's definition. As a process, applied biofeedback is:

1. A group of therapeutic procedures that . . .
2. uses electronic or electromechanical instruments . . .
3. to accurately measure, process, and feed back, to persons *and their therapists* . . .
4. information with *educational* and reinforcing properties . . .
5. about their neuromuscular and autonomic activity, both normal and abnormal, . . .
6. in the form of analogue or binary, auditory and/or visual feedback signals.
7. Best achieved with a competent biofeedback professional, the objectives are . . .
8. to help persons develop greater awareness *of, confidence in, and an increase in* voluntary control over their physiological processes that are otherwise outside awareness and/or under less voluntary control, . . .
9. by first controlling the external signal, . . .
10. and then with internal psychophysiological *cognitions, and/or by engaging in and applying behaviors to prevent symptom onset, stop it, or reduce it soon after onset.*

REFERENCES

Critelli, J. W., & Neumann, K. F. (1984). The placebo: Conceptual analysis of a construct in transition. *American Psychologist, 39*(1), 32–39.

Dance, K. A., & Neufeld, R. W. (1988). Aptitude-treatment interaction research in the clinical setting: A review of attempts to dispel the "patient uniformity" myth. *Psychological Bulletin, 104*(2), 192–213.

Dunn, T. G., Gillig, S. E., Ponser, S. E., Weil, N., & Utz, S. W. (1986). The learning process in biofeedback: Is it feed-forward or feedback? *Biofeedback and Self-Regulation, 11*(2), 143–156.

Furedy, J. J. (1987). Specific versus placebo effects in biofeedback training: A critical lay perspective. *Biofeedback and Self-Regulation, 12*, 169–184.

Harris, M. J., & Rosenthal, R. (1985). Mediation of interpersonal expectancy effects: Thirty-one meta-analyses. *Psychological Bulletin, 97*, 363–386.

Holloway, R. L., & Rogers, J. C. (1988). Aptitude x treatment x interactions in family medicine research. *Family Medicine, 21*(5), 374–378.

Holloway, R. L., Spivey, R. N., Zismer, D. K., & Withington, A. M. (1988). Aptitude x treatment interactions: Implications for patient education research. *Health Education Quarterly, 15*(3), 241–257.

Holroyd, K. A., Penzien, D. B., Hursey, K. G., Tobin, D. L., Rogers, L., Holm, J. E., Marcille, P. J., Hall, J. R., & Chila, A. G. (1984). Change mechanisms in EMG biofeedback training: Cognitive changes underlying improvements in tension headache. *Journal of Consulting and Clinical Psychology, 52*(6), 1039–1053.

LaCroix, J. M. (1984). *Mechanisms of biofeedback control: On the importance of verbal (conscious) processing.* Manuscript submitted for publication.

Learman, L. A., Avorn, J., Everitt, D. E., & Rosenthal, R. (1990). Pygmalion in the nursing home: The effects of caregiver expectations on patient outcomes. *Journal of the American Geriatric Society, 38*(7), 797–803.

Meichenbaum, D. (1976). Cognitive factors in biofeedback therapy. *Biofeedback and Self-Regulation, 1*, 201–216.

Middaugh, S. J. (1990). On clinical efficacy: Why biofeedback does—and does not—work (Presidential address). *Biofeedback and Self-Regulation, 15*(3), 191–208.

Omer, H., & London, P. (1989). Signal and noise in psychotherapy: The role and control of non-specific factors. *British Journal of Psychiatry, 155*, 239–245.

Paul, G. L. (1966). *Insight vs. desensitization in psychotherapy.* Stanford, CA: Stanford University Press.

Roberts, A. H. (1985). Biofeedback. *American Psychologist, 40*, 938–941.

Roberts, A. H. (1986). Biofeedback, science, and training. *American Psychologist, 41*, 1010.

Rosenfeld, J. P. (1987). Can clinical biofeedback be scientifically validated? A follow-up on the Green–Shellenberger–Furedy–Roberts debates. *Biofeedback and Self-Regulation, 12*(3), 217–222.

Rosenthal, R. (1990). *Experimenter expectancy, covert communication, and meta-analytic methods.* (Donald T. Campbell Award presentation, American Psychological Association Meeting, August 14, 1989) (ERIC Document Reproduction Service No. TMO14556, ED 317551.)

Salmoni, A. W., Schmidt, R. A., & Walter, C. B. (1984). Knowledge of results and motor learning: A review and critical reappraisal. *Psychological Bulletin, 95*(3), 355–386.

Schwartz, G. E. (1982). Testing the biopsychosocial model: The ultimate challenge facing behavioral medicine? *Journal of Consulting and Clinical Psychology, 50*(6), 1040–1053.

Schwartz, G. E. (1983). Social psychophysiology and behavioral medicine: A systems perspective. In J. T. Cacioppo & R. E. Petty (Eds.), *Social psychophysiology: A sourcebook.* New York: Guilford Press.

Schwartz, M. S. (Ed.). (in press). *Patient education: A practitioner's guide.* New York: Guilford Press.

Shellenberger, R., & Green, J. (1987). Specific effects and biofeedback versus biofeedback-assisted self-regulation training. *Biofeedback and Self-Regulation, 12*(3), 185–209.

White, L., Tursky, B., & Schwartz, G. E. (1985). Proposed synthesis of placebo models. In L. White, B. Tursky, & G. E. Schwartz, *Placebo: Theory, Research, and Mechanisms.* New York: Guilford Press.

Wickramasekara, I. E. (1988). *Clinical behavioral medicine: Some concepts and procedures.* New York: Plenum Press.

II
INSTRUMENTATION
AND COMPUTERS

4

A Primer
of Biofeedback
Instrumentation

Charles J. Peek

MONITORING PSYCHOPHYSIOLOGICAL AROUSAL:
THE CENTRAL FOCUS OF BIOFEEDBACK

A major application for biofeedback (and probably the primary impetus for its growth) is as a tool for detecting and managing psychophysiological arousal. As the health fields matured, it became clear that frequent, excessive, and sustained psychophysiological tension and overarousal cause or exacerbate many health problems. Interest in detecting and managing these states intensified. Over the same period, advancing technology had made it practical to monitor heretofore invisible physiological processes associated with overarousal.

The natural combination of these developments in health and technology found expression in the new field of biofeedback in which the languages and concepts of psychology, physiology, and electronics freely intermingle. The terms "stress," "anticipation," "autonomic arousal," and "muscle fibers" are found in the same sentences as "electromyography," "microvolts," "bandwidths," and "filters." Such "hybrid" sentences usually contain at least some mystery to those of us (i.e., most of us) who are not fluent in all these languages. Probably the greatest mystery among biofeedback devotees and beginners is in the language of electronics. Of the three languages spoken in biofeedback, this has the least similarity to ordinary language.

This chapter aims to put into ordinary language the major technical matters of practical importance in biofeedback. Technical concepts are introduced through analogy or heuristic description, such that they can (I hope) become a usable part of the reader's biofeedback language. In addition, this chapter contains many judgments on the practical importance of things encountered in using biofeedback, and therefore to a large extent, it represents the author's views on the subject. This is to be expected, especially in matters where no definitive conceptual, empirical, or practical view holds sway in the field.

This chapter is therefore put forth as a primer. It is practically focused rather than comprehensive and simplified rather than highly technical. It is heuristically presented, with emphasis on principle as well as fact, and contains practical judgments rather than being strictly objective.

CORRELATES OF AROUSAL: THREE PHYSIOLOGICAL PROCESSES OF INTEREST IN BIOFEEDBACK

Three of the physiological processes commonly associated with overarousal are skeletal muscle tension, peripheral vasoconstriction (smooth muscle activity), and electrodermal activity. These three, especially the first two, are the most common biofeedback modalities. There is no surprise in this, since these processes have been recognized all along as intimately involved in anger, fear, excitement, and arousal.

This association can be seen by recalling for a moment common expressions or idioms that have found their way into everyday language. For example, when a person is said to be "braced" for an onslaught, one gets a picture of muscles "at the ready." The person is tense and might have fists "clenched" and jaw "set"; in a word, the person is "uptight." If this tension were unrealistic or simply habitual, commonplace advice would be to "loosen up," "relax," or "let go."

The expression "my blood ran cold" evokes in ordinary language the connection between fear and cold extremities, seen even more clearly in the classic "cold hands– warm heart" image. In both is the recognition that having cold hands is a sign of emotional responsivity. These phrases express common knowledge that peripheral vasoconstriction is a sign of arousal. In referring to electrodermal activity, a person might illustrate fear with the image of "a cold sweat" or of "sweating bullets." A picture of calm and ease is drawn by the term "no sweat."

These examples illustrate that it is not news to people that muscle tension, peripheral vasoconstriction, and electrodermal activity are related to arousal. The systematic study and modification of these processes are relatively new and are in the domain of biofeedback. Biofeedback devices exist to aid in the study and especially in the modification of these processes.

BIOFEEDBACK EQUIPMENT

Terminology

A piece of biofeedback hardware might be referred to as "instrument," "machine," "device," "equipment," "apparatus," "unit," and even "gadget" or "gizmo." Most of these terms are used interchangeably and with little or no uniformity or consistency; often choice is made simply on preference or whim. This is not offered as a criticism, for people often have many terms for things that are interesting to them. It may simply be a case of the ancient Chinese proverb, "A child who is loved has many names."

In any case, it is worthwhile to discuss briefly the connotations of some of the more popular terms for biofeedback hardware. "Instrument," perhaps the most formal of the terms, denotes a measuring device for determining the present value of a quantity under observation. Much biofeedback hardware does not qualify under this definition, since actual measurements are not being made; only changes or relative magnitudes are being monitored. For example, "mood rings" and other simple biofeedback "gadgets" or "gizmos" do not qualify as instruments. The terms "apparatus," "equipment," and "device" leave unspecified whether or not measurement is made and, hence, are safe general terms, although "device" implies the performance of a highly specific function. The term "unit" is even more neutral, claiming nothing more than there is an entity being referred to. The term "machine" denotes a mechanism that transmits forces, action, or energy in a predetermined manner. Those familiar with electronics see electronic equipment transmitting (albeit abstractly) forces, motion, and energy within their circuits, and hence often use the term "machine" in describing biofeedback equipment.

In this chapter, most of these terms are used, and as in common practice, they are used more or less interchangeably. Nothing beyond the ordinary meanings and connotations is intended.

What Biofeedback Instruments Are Supposed to Do

A biofeedback instrument has three tasks:

1. To monitor (in some way) physiological process of interest.
2. To measure (objectify) the monitoring.
3. To present what is monitored or measured as meaningful information.

The following sections briefly discuss how access is gained to three important psychophysiological processes in biofeedback.

Electromyography: An Electrical Correlate of Muscle Contraction

A biofeedback device cannot just "lock onto" muscle contraction and measure it in a simple, direct way. When a muscle contracts, it tries to pull its two anchor points together: that is what is meant by "muscle contraction." It is therefore a kinetic phenomenon involving force and sometimes movement. Practically speaking, this is not easily monitored. One cannot, for example, insert a strain gauge between one end of a muscle and its anchor point to measure grams of pull. (Force and movement gauges, called "goniometers," are used as muscle contraction monitors in physical medicine applications, but these are not sensitive to the levels or locations of muscle contraction involved in relaxation and low-arousal applications of biofeedback.)

Since muscle contraction itself is inaccessible, some aspect or correlate of it will have to do. Biofeedback exploits the electrical aspect of muscle contraction. Muscle contraction results from the more or less synchronous contraction of the many muscle fibers that comprise a muscle. Muscle fibers are actuated by electrical signals carried by cells called "motor units," and muscle contraction corresponds to the aggregate electrical activity in these muscle fibers (see Chapter 22). This electrical activity can be sensed with fine wire or needle electrodes that actually penetrate the skin above the muscle. More commonly, it is sensed with surface electrodes that contact the skin above the muscle, where there exist weakened electrical signals from muscle fibers beneath the skin. This is the preferred biofeedback method for monitoring muscle contraction, because it is practical and corresponds well to the actual muscle contraction. Note that this electrical method (called electromyography [EMG]) does not actually monitor muscle contraction per se, but monitors an electrical aspect of muscle contraction that bears a more or less regular relationship to muscle contraction.

The important point here is this: EMG is the preferred method for monitoring muscle contraction, but it does not literally measure muscle contraction. It measures the electrical correlate of muscle contraction. Therefore, an EMG device does not "read out" in force or movement units. Instead, it reads out in electrical units. This is because it is making an electrical, not a kinetic, measurement. It so happens that the appropriate electrical unit is the volt. A microvolt is one-millionth of a volt. An EMG reading in microvolts is categorically different from a muscle contraction measurement in a kinetic unit such as grams or millimeters. This explains the initial puzzlement that usually comes over the biofeedback novice upon learning that muscle contraction is measured in volts, an electrical unit, which at face value seems to have little to do with muscle contraction.

In summary, muscle contraction is monitored via an electrical method called EMG that measures the electrical energy given off by contracting muscle fibers. An EMG device gives readings in microvolts, a unit of electrical pressure, which corresponds well to muscle contraction.

Peripheral Temperature: A Correlate of Peripheral Vasoconstriction

A biofeedback device cannot simply measure the changing diameter of peripheral blood vessels or the smooth muscle activity that brings about these changes. Therefore, some correlate of vascular diameter will have to do. Dilated vessels pass more warm blood than constricted vessels. Therefore, surrounding tissue tends to warm and cool as vascular diameter increases and decreases, providing a good correlate of vascular diameter. This effect is most pronounced in the extremities such as fingers and toes, where vascular diameter changes are pronounced and where the relatively small amount of surrounding tissue warms and cools rapidly in response to changes in the blood supply.

Here again the physiological process of interest (peripheral vasoconstriction) is inaccessible, but an accessible correlate (peripheral temperature) is a useable indication.

Biofeedback devices typically read out in degrees Fahrenheit as the indirect measure of peripheral vasoconstriction. A temperature unit is categorically different from a unit of vascular diameter. This emphasizes that only indirect access to peripheral vasoconstriction is possible in biofeedback.

Finger Phototransmission: Another Correlate of Peripheral Vasoconstriction

A second indirect way of gaining access to peripheral vasoconstriction takes advantage of the fact that a finger or toe having less blood in its vessels allows more light to pass through than an extremity with more blood. That is, pale skin passes more light than ruddy skin. A small light is shined through the flesh of a finger and is reflected off the bone back to a light sensor. Variation in light intensity at the sensor and resulting electrical signal indicates variation in blood volume.

This device is commonly called a "photoplethysmograph" and is sometimes used in biofeedback. It monitors pulse, and (with appropriate circuitry to average out the pulses) can give an indication of relative blood volume, another correlate of vasoconstriction. Such devices read out only in relative units. That is, they read changes, but they are not anchored to some outside standard reference point. Photoplethysmography is not employed nearly as often as peripheral temperature to indicate peripheral vasoconstriction. Further description of photoplethysmography is beyond the scope of this chapter. For more information, the reader is referred to Jennings, Tahmoush, and Redmond (1980).

Skin Conductance Activity: A Correlate of Sweat Gland Activity

Sweat gland activity is another physiological process not directly accessible. One cannot tell whether a sweat gland is "on," how much sweat is being secreted, or how many such glands are active. However, sweat contains electrically conductive salts that make sweaty skin more conductive to electricity than dry skin. Hence, skin conductance activity (SCA) corresponds well to sweat gland activity. This, along with other electrical phenomena of the skin, is known as electrodermal activity (EDA), historically known as "galvanic skin response" (GSR). A skin conductance device applies a very small electrical pressure (voltage) to the skin, typically on the volar surface of the fingers or the palmar surface of the hand (where there are many sweat glands), and measures the amount of electrical current that the skin will allow to pass. The magnitude of this current is an indication of skin sweatiness and is read out in units of electrical conductance called "micromhos."

Here again, an electrical unit (conductance) serves as the indirect measure of a physiological phenomenon (sweat gland activity). This explains what might initially seem odd: that sweat gland activity is measured in an electrical unit that at face value has nothing to do with sweat gland activity.

Objectification and Measurement

As noted above, direct monitoring of muscle contraction, peripheral vasoconstriction, and sweat gland activity is not feasible. Therefore, biofeedback devices gain access indirectly through monitoring more accessible correlates of these physiological processes. This means that a biofeedback reading should be taken as a convenient indication of a physiological process but understood as separate from the physiological process itself. Practitioners must distinguish the physiological process beneath the skin from the instrumentation schemes outside the skin used to gain access to it. This distinction is important for understanding measurement, objectification, artifact, and the interpretation of biofeedback data.

To compare a person's biofeedback readings from one occasion to another, or to compare readings between different individuals, some objective scale permitting such measurement is advantageous. First, let us establish the difference between "monitoring" and "measuring." Monitoring takes place when an observable signal such as a meter reading is made to correspond to a particular process (e.g., skin temperature or muscle contraction), but the correspondence is not displayed in standardized quantitative units. Measurement takes place when the device is calibrated to and reads out in standardized quantitative units that show how the monitored process is varying.

To illustrate this contrast, consider the two thermometers in Figure 4.1, constructed identically except for the scales. Thermometer A has a scale that permits the user to observe relative levels and changes and correlate these with other events. The user can develop his or her own norms about what levels or changes are meaningful for his or her purposes. Thermometer A is internally consistent over time but is not referenced to an outside temperature standard. Thermometer B, on the other hand, has a scale that reads out in standardized temperature units: degrees Fahrenheit. It measures temperature according to this widely accepted standard temperature scale (assuming that it is properly calibrated to the Fahrenheit standard).

The advantage of measurement over monitoring is, of course, that observers from different locations or perspectives can make direct quantitative comparisons of their observations. With monitoring, they can make only nonquantitative comparisons of relative magnitude or change. Measurement tends to increase replicability of procedures and comparability of results. However, measurement in this sense is often not possible because biofeedback often lacks clearly defined and/or widely accepted standardized scales for measurement.

For example, EMG devices typically have meters or scaled outputs that give readings in microvolts. Because numbers appear on the meters, this appears to give objectivity to the readings and to permit measurement, such as in the case of thermometer B. In fact, however, there is no widely accepted and standardized scale for EMG microvolts. In effect, each model or brand of EMG device becomes its own reference standard. Consequently, different equipment gives different readings for the very same degree of muscle contrac-

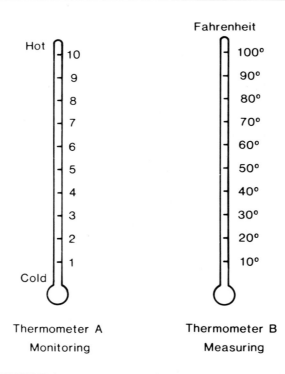

FIGURE 4.1. Monitoring and measuring thermometers.

tion. Therefore, EMG readings can be compared only when using the same (or very similarly designed) equipment for all the readings. Explanations for this will become clear later, when the design of the EMG device is described. The important point to remember now is that EMG readings are better thought of as monitorings (as in thermometer A) than as measurements (as in thermometer B). The same is true for skin conductance readings. Skin temperature readings, however, are measurements (as in thermometer B), assuming that the temperature device is properly calibrated to a standard temperature scale such as degrees Fahrenheit.

OPERATION OF THE EMG INSTRUMENT

The EMG instrument picks up the weak electrical signals generated during muscle action. Each muscle is comprised of many muscle fibers with "motor neurons" or electrical connection to higher levels of the nervous system. Muscle contraction occurs when these motor neurons carry electrical activating signals to the muscle fibers. A small part of this electrical energy leaves the muscle and migrates through surrounding tissue. Some of this energy becomes available for monitoring at the surface of the skin. The tasks of an EMG machine are these:

1. To receive this very small amount of electrical energy from the skin.
2. To separate this EMG energy from other extraneous energy on the skin and greatly magnify the EMG energy.

3. To convert this amplified EMG energy into forms of information or feedback meaningful to the user.

Receiving EMG Energy from the Skin: Electrodes

"Surface electrodes" (usually small metallic discs mounted on plastic or rubber) contact the skin through an electrically conductive cream or gel. Wires complete the electrical pathways from the skin to the EMG machine. Some electrodes are quite small and designed for precise locations such as monitoring small muscles. Some are individually attached with tape or double-stick adhesive washers. Others come on strips or on a headband for simultaneous application of the three electrodes generally required for EMG biofeedback. Some electrodes are permanently attached to electrode cables, whereas others are made to snap onto the cable, permitting changes of electrodes without changing the cable. One advantage of this is ease of changing a suspect electrode without changing the entire cable and ease of changing a suspect cable without taking the electrodes themselves out of service. This may have the disadvantage of being bulkier than permanently wired electrodes.

Many electrodes are made of simple materials, such as nickel-plated brass or stainless steel, whereas others are made of rare materials such as gold or silver chloride over silver (silver/silver chloride). The precious-metal electrodes have historically been the materials of choice for most physiological monitoring because the materials do not interact significantly with skin or other substances with which they are in contact. However, the simpler and cheaper electrodes have been found to be quite satisfactory for biofeedback EMG applications and are now in widespread use. Advances in electronic design have reduced the need for precious-metal electrodes for EMG biofeedback. (Readers will discover later in the chapter that EMG amplifiers are now made with extremely high input impedances, high common-mode rejection ratios, and therefore can well tolerate imperfect electrodes and skin preparation.)

Electrode Cream and Gel

Common to nearly all EMG electrodes is the use of an electrode gel or cream. Because this conductive substance flows into the irregularities of the skin and the electrode, it establishes a stable and highly conductive connection between them (see Figure 4.2). Some electrode preparations are more conductive than others. In principle, higher conductivity is an advantage, because there is less to impede the travel of bioelectric signals from the skin to the electrode. However, in ordinary practice, this difference is negligible, thanks to the advanced electronic characteristics of reputable EMG instruments.

Skin Preparation

A standard part of electrode application is to remove dirt, oil, dead skin cells, and makeup. These impede the travel of bioelectric signals from the skin to the electrode gel. Some manufacturers suggest the use of an abrasive skin cleaner for this purpose, while others suggest wiping the skin with an alcohol swab. The risk in underpreparing the skin is erroneously high EMG readings, but usually the skin must be oily or covered with makeup for this to result. The risk of overpreparing the skin, particularly with the abrasive compounds, is skin (and patient/client) irritation. There is nothing to be gained by actually scrubbing skin unless there remains visible evidence of dirt, oil, or makeup. In fact, some specialized EMG biofeedback equipment (used in neuromuscular rehabilitation) operates not only with simple

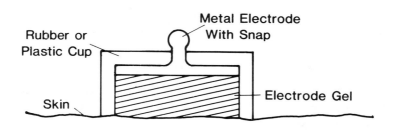

FIGURE 4.2. EMG electrode and gel.

metal electrodes, but with no electrode gel or skin preparation. This is not to say, however, that one can just forget about skin preparation.

In general, the electrodes supplied with any reputable EMG device will work with that device, provided one follows the manufacturer's instructions for electrode application and maintenance.

Separating EMG Energy from Extraneous ("Noise") Energy

"Noise" is the general term for unwanted or extraneous signals. In EMG machines, there are two kinds of noise; electrical interference and internally generated noise.

Electrical Interference and the Differential Amplifier

The environment is continuously saturated with electrical energy transmitted through space from power lines, motors, lights, electrical equipment, and radio stations. Human bodies and EMG electrodes pick up this energy. In this way, the EMG apparatus receives unwanted electrical noise signals in addition to the desired bioelectric signals from the muscles. The EMG unit must therefore find a way to reject the noise so that only EMG signals remain.

Much interference rejection is done in an ingenious way using an electrical subtraction process in a "differential amplifier." The electrodes establish three independent pathways from an area of the skin to the EMG instrument. One pathway, called the "reference," is used by the instrument as a point of reference from which the minute electrical pressure (voltage) exerted from the other two "active" electrodes is gauged. We must remember that any electrical pressure or voltage measurement is defined as a pressure difference between one point and another point. There is no such thing as a voltage measurement without respect to some second point of reference. This results in two "sources" feeding the instrument, each using the reference electrode as the point of reference (see Figure 4.3). Note that the reference electrode can be placed nearly anywhere on the body, but it is shown in Figure 4.3 between the two active electrodes for the sake of illustration, and because it is a common arrangement.

The differential amplifier requires these two sources in order to separate the EMG energy from the extraneous energy. To see why, we must remember that this extraneous energy is the hum or noise transmitted through space from power lines, motors, and appliances that is picked up by the body acting as an antenna. Most of this extraneous electrical noise energy rises and falls rhythmically (60 cycles per second). At any given moment, this energy is in exactly the same place in its rhythm ("in phase") at any point on the body and, therefore, at any point that an electrode can be placed. Hence, it is possible for the differ-

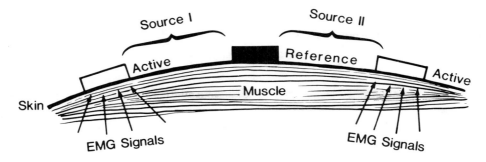

FIGURE 4.3. Active and reference EMG electrodes.

ential amplifier to continuously subtract the voltage at source 1 from that at source 2. This cancels the noise voltage. Only slightly simplified, this is illustrated graphically in Figure 4.4, assuming that the muscle is at rest and giving off no EMG signals. The following steps explain Figure 4.4:

1. Electrical interference is received by the body acting as an antenna.
2. The interference is in the same place in its rhythm for both active electrodes. Therefore,
3. the active inputs (from source 1 and source 2) of the differential amplifier "see" exactly the same interference signal at any given moment (interference is in the "common mode"). Since
4. the output of the differential amplifier is proportional to the difference between the signals at its two active inputs (from sources 1 and 2), and
5. the interference signals are always identical (restatement of point 3). Then
6. the output of the differential amplifier is zero for electrical interference.

But What About EMG Signals? Suppose that motor neurons now signal the resting muscle to contract. Each electrode receives most strongly from the area of muscle directly beneath it. Since electrodes are spaced along the muscle, they each receive a different pattern of EMG signals. An analogy: If two microphones were placed in a room full of speaking people, each one would pick up a different pattern of sounds, even if the overall loudness of sound

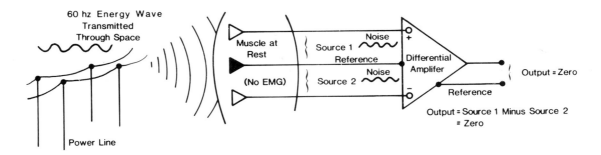

FIGURE 4.4. Differential amplifier eliminating the electrical interference picked up by the body acting as an antenna.

in each microphone were the same. Therefore at any given moment, the electrodes feed the differential amplifier "differential" EMG signals superimposed on the previously discussed identical "common-mode" signals.

Now, as the differential amplifier continuously subtracts the signal at source 2 from that at source 1 (thus amplifying only differences between them), the common-mode noise signals will cancel, while the differential EMG signals will always leave a remainder to be amplified and ultimately displayed on a meter. The operation of the differential EMG amplifier is shown graphically in Figure 4.5 and is summarized below:

1. Different EMG signals arrive at the two electrodes as the muscle beneath them contracts. Therefore,
2. sources 1 and 2 feed differential EMG signals to the inputs of the differential amplifier. At the same time,
3. identical (common-mode) interference signals are superimposed on the differential EMG signals. Thus,
4. the inputs (from sources 1 and 2) "see" composite signals that have an identical component (common-mode noise) and a differing component (differential EMG signals). Since
5. the output of the differential amplifier is proportional to the difference between the signals at its two inputs (from sources 1 and 2), and
6. a portion of the signals are identical (common-mode) and a portion are different (differential-mode) (restatement of point 4), then
7. the output of the differential amplifier is zero for common-mode interference and high for differential-mode EMG signals.

Analogies. The differential amplifier can also be explained through analogy. Consider the following illustrative, although actually unworkable, analogy. Imagine two microphones set up outdoors to measure the loudness of songs from a group of birds in the vicinity (see Figure 4.6). Each microphone receives a slightly different sound, because some birds are closer to one microphone than the other. Therefore, with the mikes fed to a differential amplifier, which simply subtracts one mike signal from the other, there will always be a remainder. The louder the birds sing, the bigger the remainder. This is fed to a sound-level meter that indicates the loudness of the singing. Now suppose there is a thunderstorm in the area that emits a big bolt of lightning and a sharp crack of thunder. This crack of thunder moves outward in all directions as a pressure (sound) wave, and eventually reaches the microphones. Since the thunderclap is from a distant source, it hits the two relatively closely spaced microphones at the same time and with the same intensity. The microphones pick up this clap and feed it to the differ-

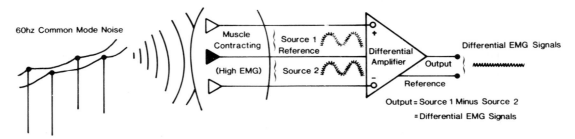

FIGURE 4.5. Differential amplifier eliminating the common-mode interference while amplifying differential EMG signals.

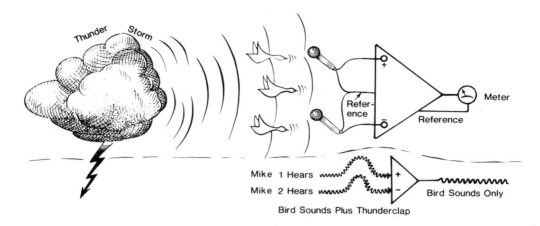

FIGURE 4.6. Analogy illustrating noise subtraction in a differential amplifier.

ential amplifier, along with whatever bird sounds they are picking up at the time. Since the differential amplifier subtracts one mike signal from the other (thus amplifying differences between one mike and the other), the crack of thunder is canceled; yet the bird sounds come through, because they are heard differently by each mike.

Although this particular setup would not work in practice for canceling thunder from bird recordings, it does illustrate the basic principle of cancellation of electrical interference from EMG signals. The bird sounds represent electrical activity in muscle fibers different from the muscles beneath the electrodes. The microphones represent the "sources" described earlier from the two active electrodes and one reference electrode. The thunder represents the distant electrical interference from power lines, which is transmitted through space. The differential amplifier is used in both cases, and the sound-level meter represents the EMG-level meter.

Note that effective noise reduction in the differential amplifier requires that the noise signals be at equal magnitudes and that they rise and fall in exactly the same rhythm. Otherwise, the subtraction process leaves a noise remainder as well as an EMG remainder. This would happen if, in the bird sounds analogy, one of the microphones were less sensitive than the other. Deteriorated electrodes or improper contact with the skin can lead to this condition for EMG recordings. In this event, erroneously high EMG readings are observed because a "less sensitive" electrode unbalances the common mode noise signals fed to the differential amplifier.

A second and more precise analogy further clarifies the operation of the differential amplifier. Imagine a sensitive chemist's balance scale, with its two pans, center fulcrum, and a set of weights (see Figure 4.7). With no weights in the pans, the scale balances. With equal weights in the pans, it also balances. Even if we stretch our imagination to envision the weights constantly changing (but always remaining equal in both pans), the scale will still remain balanced. However, a fly landing on one pan during this process will upset the balance, and the pointer will move off center. Moreover, if two flies of equal weight hop up and down, one on each pan, each with its own idiosyncratic rhythm, the pointer will move from side to side. The deflection indicates, at any given moment, the difference in weight on the two pans. Only differences in total weights can lead to a pointer deflection.

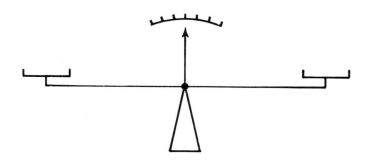

FIGURE 4.7. Chemist's balance analogy for the differential amplifier.

By now, the reader may recognize the differential amplifier as an electronic version of the chemist's balance. Table 4.1 and Figure 4.8 further show the correspondence between the two.

The preceding discussion of the differential amplifier makes it easier to see why deteriorated electrodes or improper (high-resistance) contact with the skin can lead to erroneously high EMG readings. For example, one of the active electrodes making poor contact with the skin feeds a reduced signal to the differential amplifier. Since the other electrode is feeding a full-sized signal to the differential amplifier, the common-mode noise signals applied to the two inputs are of different size. Therefore, when the subtraction process takes place, there is a noise remainder as well as an EMG remainder that artificially elevates the reading. Figure 4.9 shows this graphically. The ratio of differential signal amplification to common-mode signal amplification for a particular differential amplifier is the "common-mode rejection ratio." This is typically quite high for reputable machines.

"Input impedance" is the differential amplifier specification indicating its protection from inaccuracy due to unequal electrode contact. This is quite high for reputable machines. Further discussion of these specifications is beyond the scope of this chapter.

Internal Noise: Filters and Bandwidth

The task of removing extraneous signals is still not complete. Electrical "filters" further reduce interference from power lines and also limit the noise inevitably generated within the circuits of the EMG amplifiers themselves. These filters are comparable to tone controls on a stereo amplifier, except they are usually set in one position at the factory. The purpose of these is to make the EMG amplifier sensitive to some frequencies (or pitches) of incoming signals and less sensitive to others.

Speech or music is comprised of a wide range of frequencies or pitches, all combined to give us the familiar sounds. Tone controls alter these by increasing or decreasing bass and treble, depending on the listener's preference. For example, turning down the treble might improve the sound of a particularly scratchy record by reducing some of the high-frequency scratch and hiss sounds. Turning down the bass might improve the sound of an amplifier that hums. In both cases, a modification of the amplifier's frequency sensitivity or "bandwidth" or "bandshape" is being made.

There are reasons to do something similar with an EMG device. For example, much of the electrical interference or noise from power lines is concentrated in a narrow pitch range around 60 cycles or vibrations per second (Hertz). Anyone with a stereo that hums

TABLE 4.1 Correspondence between Chemist's Balance and Differential Amplifier

Chemist's balance	Differential amplifier
1. Pans	1. Inputs
2. Pointer	2. Output
3. Fulcrum	3. Reference
4. Equal weights in the pans→balance (pointer remains straight)	4. Common-mode signals→zero output
5. Different weights in the pans→imbalance (pointer deflects)	5. Differential signals→nonzero output
6. Two equal weights in the pans *and* Two unequal weights in the pans →imbalance (pointer reflects the difference between the unequal weights only, as equal weights cancel out)	6. Common-mode signals *and* Differential signals →nonzero output (output reflects the difference between the differential signals only, as equal signals cancel out)

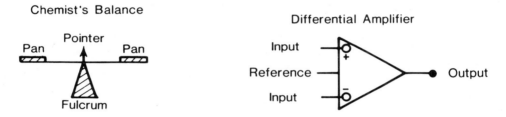

FIGURE 4.8. Graphic representation of data in Table 4.1.

or buzzes knows this sound. To further reduce this noise signal, a special filter can make the EMG amplifier much less sensitive to this pitch. More typically, the entire bass response of the amplifier is "rolled off" to further reduce electrical interference remaining after the differential amplifier. A typical "bass" or low-frequency bandwidth limit is around 100 Hertz.

There is also good reason to limit the EMG amplifier's "treble" frequency sensitivity. All amplifiers unavoidably generate high-pitched noise within their own circuits that sounds

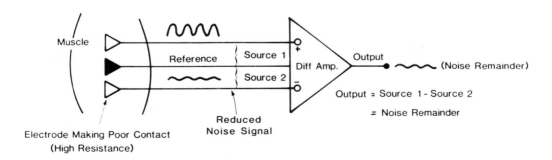

FIGURE 4.9. Unequal common-mode noise inputs leading to a noise remainder.

like hiss (a sound also familiar to users of stereo equipment). The EMG amplifier's treble response is typically "rolled off" (e.g., above 1000 Hertz) to diminish this internal noise. All EMG amplifiers have built-in limits to their frequency sensitivity to reduce noise contributions to EMG readings.

The space between the bass frequency limit and the treble limit is called the "bandwidth." Bandwidth defines the frequency or pitch range within which the amplifier is most sensitive. The amplifier is less and less sensitive to frequencies farther and farther outside this range.

Like speech and music sounds, EMG signals are comprised of a range of frequencies or pitch. They tend to vary from about 10 to a thousand Hertz (cycles per second). Figure 4.10 shows a hypothetical frequency distribution of EMG signals. The graph in Figure 4.11 shows two idealized bandwidths superimposed on the hypothetical EMG frequency distribution. This shows that even with treble and bass limits, an EMG amplifier is sensitive to significant amounts of EMG energy.

In both cases, the amplifier's bandwidth (range of sensitivity) includes a significant area of EMG energy. However, the wide bandwidth includes more EMG energy (and noise) than the narrower bandwidth. This means that (other things being equal) the instrument set with a wider bandwidth will give higher readings than the one with the narrower bandwidth.

A stereo can also illustrate this. Turning the bass and treble controls all the way down narrows the bandwidth and produces not only a different tone, but less volume of sound. The same holds for noise. The wider bandwidth includes more noise as well as EMG. The proportion of the reading that is noise (the "signal-to-noise ratio") might be the same in both cases, but the levels of both EMG and noise will be higher with a wide-bandwidth amplifier.

EMG biofeedback devices are made with different bandwidths, due to differing design philosophies. This means that some read higher than others for both EMG and noise. It cannot be said with assurance that one currently available bandwidth is better than another, as machines with various bandwidths provide useful EMG biofeedback. The most important message here is that *different bandwidths lead to different readings*. This should be taken into account when comparing readings and noise specifications between different models of EMG equipment.

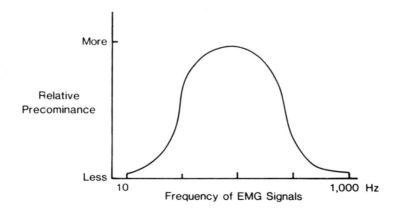

FIGURE 4.10. A hypothetical frequency distribution of EMG signals.

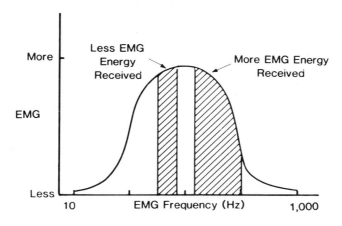

FIGURE 4.11. Two hypothetical bandwidths.

Other things being equal, the wider the bandwidth, the higher the readings for both EMG and noise. This, of course, means that users must evaluate EMG equipment specifications in the context of overall design. For example, an instrument with a lower noise or sensitivity specification may not really be any more sensitive or noise-resistant than another; it may just have a narrower bandwidth. Readers who wish to know more about EMG frequency distribution, filters, and bandwidth are referred to Mathieu and Sullivan (1990).

Converting EMG Energy to Information

Thus far, readers see how EMG energy is taken from the skin and separated from extraneous noise energy. The resulting signal is proportional to the electrical activity of the motor neurons in the muscle being monitored and is often referred to as "raw EMG."

Raw EMG

Raw EMG resembles auditory static or a rushing sound, the loudness of which rises and falls with muscle contraction. This "raw" or "raw filtered" EMG is one form of audio feedback. Commercial EMG units usually do not provide raw EMG audio output. Instead, they generate an audio tone or series of beeps or clicks. The pitch or repetition rate is made proportional to the amplitude or "loudness" of the raw EMG, and therefore to the muscle contraction. Raw EMG amplitude can also be displayed on a meter, although further processing is required.

Smoothing and Integration

"Smoothing" and "integration" refer to two ways of processing the EMG signal. They both permit quantification of EMG energy over time. "Smoothing" is a general term that refers to evening out the peaks and valleys of a changing electrical signal. "Integration" is a mathematical term that refers to measuring the area under a curve.

Rectification and Pulsating Direct Current. Raw EMG is an alternating current (AC) signal (in this case, an alternating voltage). Alternating voltage pushes alternately back and forth or "vibrates" like a reed in the wind or a swinging clock pendulum, as represented graphically in Figure 4.12. The curve represents the change in electrical pressure over time, first in one direction and then in the opposite direction. The "+" represents pressure in one direction, and the "−"represents pressure in the other direction. The center line represents the point of zero voltage, analogous to the position of the reed at rest or the clock pendulum in its straight-down position. The height of a wave represents its peak amplitude or peak voltage. Figure 4.12 shows an electrical signal "vibrating" at a specific frequency (number of oscillations per second, or Hertz).

In addition, the electrical signal is not only oscillating, but the amplitude or magnitude of the oscillations first builds to a high point and then diminishes. It is the measurement of this overall increase and then decrease that is significant for EMG biofeedback. The first step in accomplishing this is to "flip" the negative peaks up above the zero line with the positive peaks, a process called "rectification." Without rectification, the sum of the negative peaks and positive peaks would always equal zero (i.e., they would cancel each other). Without rectification it would be hard to recognize overall trends in magnitude unless one was viewing the oscillations on an oscilloscope screen or listening to the raw EMG over a speaker. Figure 4.13 shows the rectified EMG wave. The negative peaks have been electronically "flipped" up with the positive peaks, so that all the peaks are positive. This means that the electrical signal now pushes in just one direction; hence the term "direct current" (DC). In this case, the signal is "pulsating DC."

Smoothing the EMG Signal for Moment-to-Moment Quantification. If the voltage in Figure 4.13 is applied to a needle-type DC voltmeter, the meter mechanism and attached needle will be driven in the positive direction. However, mechanical inertia will prevent the mechanism from following each rapid voltage pulse. It will, in effect, smooth out the pulses by displaying a voltage value somewhat less than the peak voltages of the successive, positive-going EMG pulses. The value it displays will roughly parallel a line drawn connecting the peak values of each successive EMG pulse. This changing voltage level is called "rectified smoothed" or "filtered" EMG, illustrated in Figure 4.14. Its voltage value is the mathematical average of the rectified EMG voltage for a constant-amplitude EMG signal. For the varying-amplitude EMG signal shown in Figure 4.12, the smoothed signal will be a "time-varying average" whose "tracking time" depends on the inertial "time constant" of the electromechanical meter movement. The voltage value of the time-varying average (expressed in microvolts) gives a moment-by-moment quantification of EMG voltage.

Most mechanical meters respond faster than is optimal for smoothing changes in EMG amplitude, and this inertial time constant is not alterable. Fortunately, electronic smoothing or filtering can be performed on the rectified EMG signal. The outputs of smoothing

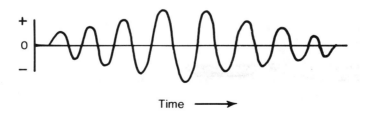

FIGURE 4.12. Gradually increasing, then decreasing alternating voltage.

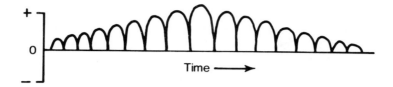

FIGURE 4.13. Rectified alternating voltage.

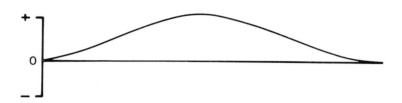

FIGURE 4.14. Rectified filtered or smoothed EMG.

circuits are then used to drive the meter, as well as audio feedback circuitry if included. Electronic smoothing is essential in using digital meters, because they have no mechanical inertia to smooth out the pulses.

An electronic smoothing circuit exaggerates the mechanical smoothing effect of a mechanical meter. The circuit is designed so that its output cannot change faster than a certain rate, analogous to the mechanical sluggishness of a needle-type meter. This is accomplished by a filter and leads to a smoothing effect (see Figure 4.14) on the rectified pulsating EMG signal (see Figure 4.13). A great advantage is that smoothing or filtering circuits are not limited to one time constant or response time, as are mechanical meters. Therefore, the designer has wide choice of how fast the meter responds to momentary changes in EMG level (tracking time).

The most common form of smoothing or filtering found in commercial EMG equipment employs a fixed time constant and therefore a fixed tracking time suitable for general-purpose use. Some EMG machines and computer-based systems have selectable tracking times that require the user to decide how much smoothing of the curve he or she desires. Long tracking time leads to a smoother output that is less responsive to momentary ups and downs in the EMG level. Unsmoothed output may seem too jumpy for relaxation training, and overly smoothed output may cover or delay information. There is no generally agreed-upon optimum tracking time; choice is based on application, technique, and subjective preference. It does not appear to me that any one tracking time is particularly advantageous for relaxation training. This view is apparently shared by the manufacturers, who build their instruments with various fixed or adjustable tracking times.

Integration for Cumulative EMG or Average EMG over a Fixed Time Period. A second quantification scheme involves letting the area under the EMG curve (in microvolt minutes) accumulate over a period of time, such that the reading starts at zero and continually builds until the time period ends.

The accumulated area at the end of the trial indicates the accumulated number of microvolt minutes of EMG received over that time. Dividing the accumulated microvolt minutes of integrated EMG by the accumulated time in minutes yields the average level of EMG (in microvolts) during that time. Then the timer and integrator are reset to zero, and a new time period or trial begins.

Integration establishes relaxation trials of many seconds (e.g., 30, 60, 120 or more seconds). Comparisons can then be made over multiple training trials. Integration is illustrated in Figure 4.15.

Audio Feedback

Audio feedback is very important in biofeedback because it transmits information without the need for visual attention. Audio feedback encodes the EMG level in auditory form. A common way to do this is to use the smoothed EMG signal to vary the pitch of an electronic tone generator. The higher the EMG level, the higher the pitch. The progression from raw EMG to a continuous audio tone feedback is shown in Figure 4.16.

Another form of audio feedback consists of a "pulsed tone." The tone described above is interrupted so it comes in beeps separated by silence. The higher the EMG level, the higher the tone's pitch, and the more frequent the beeps. Small changes in level are very apparent using this form of feedback.

The range of possibilities for audio feedback is virtually limitless, and many forms have appeared on commercial units. There is no one optimum form of audio feedback. Preferences develop on the basis of purely subjective criteria as well as application requirements.

Visual Feedback: Meters

An analog meter that displays the smoothed EMG signal provides visual indication of the strength of muscle contraction at that moment. This is used for making moment-to-moment quantified readings. Most EMG meters are calibrated with scales that show quantified units such as microvolts. Others give only a relative scale without quantification.

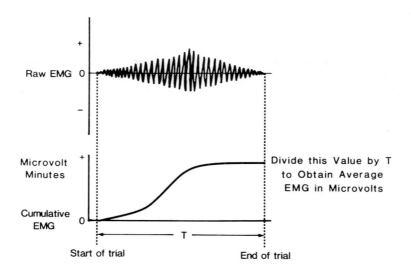

FIGURE 4.15. Integration for cumulative EMG or average EMG over a fixed time period.

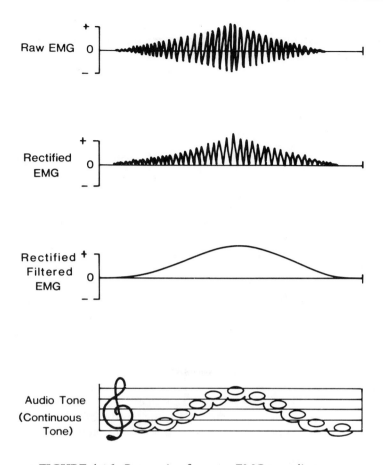

FIGURE 4.16. Progression from raw EMG to audio tone.

Biofeedback devices use analog and digital meters. A digital meter displays information in changing numbers, which are read directly like an automobile odometer. An analog meter has a continuous scale and a moving needle like an auto speedometer. The user reads an analog meter by estimating the quantity to which the needle points. Although digital meters are associated with high technology, analog meters should not be summarily dismissed as obsolete. Each type has its advantages.

For example, digital meters excel at precise quantification of readings over a very wide range. But the user must actually *read* the meter's numbers to get the information. On the other hand, the relative position of the analog meter needle and its motion together communicate a great deal without requiring the user to actually read any figures. Feedback requires minimum effort from the user. Even peripheral vision is sufficient to recognize levels and changes. The swing of a needle on a large meter scale can be a very simple and inherently meaningful way to present information.

In contrast, the changing digits of a digital meter are not as comfortable or instinctively meaningful to some users. Moreover, the analog meter scale implicitly brackets the range of obtainable readings and therefore provides a quantitative context for any given reading. The expression "off the scale" refers to this feature of an analog meter scale. With a digital meter, one may not know whether the reading is in the high or low part of the range unless one remembers the actual numerical range as compared to the digital reading. In summary, digital meters are better for some purposes, and analog meters are better for others.

Computer-generated visual displays similarly differ in how much attention is required to grasp and use the information. Some display numbers or other information that requires more focused attention than simpler displays such as bar or line graphs.

Objective Units of Measurement

There are several factors besides degree of muscle contraction that affect the number of microvolts that an EMG device displays. Briefly reviewing the earlier section on objectification and measurement, the microvolt is the unit of EMG measurement. This is an electrical term used as a measure of muscle contraction. Even so, the microvolt is not literally a measure of muscle contraction; it is a measure of an electrical correlate of muscle contraction. Therefore, microvolt readings involve the characteristics of the electrical apparatus (the EMG unit) that monitors and processes the EMG signals. Because of differences in design philosophy, EMG devices differ from one another, and so do the readings obtained for any given degree of muscle tension at a given site on a given person. Consequently, microvolt readings are only objectively comparable from one model to another if the instruments are known to have the same bandwidth and quantification method.

EMG instruments are AC voltmeters and make objective AC voltage measurements. However, the internal characteristics of bandwidth or bandshape and quantification method affect these measurements. Accuracy, if specified, is only at a given frequency within the bandwidth. Because EMG voltages sensed by surface electrodes are composed of an ever-changing blend of frequencies (see Figure 4.10), the bandwidth or bandshape of any particular unit will affect the readings. (This was discussed in the section, "Internal Noise: Filters and Bandwidth").

Quantification method affects EMG instrument readings. First of all, there is no standardized EMG signal for calibrating EMG instruments. Instead, calibration is done using conveniently available constant-amplitude AC signals called "sine waves." (Figure 4.12 shows a changing-amplitude sine wave.) Accordingly, the use of sine waves rather than actual EMG signals is the basis for the following discussion.

"Peak-to-peak microvolts" refers to the voltage difference between the positive peaks and the negative peaks of the unrectified AC sine wave. Quantification by the "averaging" method usually involves rectification, smoothing, and then moment-to-moment display on a meter or integration and division by time, both described earlier. The "average" voltage of a sine wave after rectification as displayed on a meter is equal to just less than one-third of the "peak-to-peak" value. Conversely, the peak-to-peak value is just over three times the average value. Some of the earliest commercial EMG instruments responded to average EMG amplitude but had meters scaled in peak-to-peak microvolts. For consistency, many EMG instruments still use this method. To convert from peak-to-peak to average, divide by 3.14.

Quantification by the "root mean square" method (RMS) involves electronically making a mathematical computation on either the alternating or rectified version of the filtered EMG signal to arrive at an RMS voltage. RMS quantification is necessary to know the electrical *power,* as contrasted with *voltage,* carried by the signal. This is usually not important in biofeedback. RMS values for EMG are usually within 20% of average values.

There is little practical difference between these quantification methods or in the action of the meter needle—just different scales on its face. In any case, the user of EMG equipment should become familiar with the range of readings obtained under various conditions and should be cautious about comparing microvolt readings between units that are not known to have similar characteristics.

Most important here is that even though EMG instruments are AC voltmeters, EMG readings are not made on standardized scales and are not standardized measurements of muscle contraction. Variability exists between EMG instruments, and there is no standardized scaled correspondence between EMG microvolts and muscle contraction. An analogy may help illustrate this: EMG readings are to muscle contraction as the readings of thermometer A in Figure 4.1 are to temperature. Although EMG readings are measurements of voltage, they are not truly measurements of muscle contraction.

Thresholds

A threshold control allows the user to set a particular EMG level as a criterion for some form of feedback. For example, one might set a threshold such that audio feedback comes on only when EMG exceeds the threshold. Visual feedback, such as lights or computer display line may indicate when EMG exceeds or drops below the chosen threshold level. Thresholds are adjusted over time as training goals change.

Other Feedback Modes

The smoothed EMG level can be used to operate virtually any feedback method including lights, sound, appliances, computers, or tactile feedback devices. All forms of feedback are ways of encoding EMG level as meaningful information or consequences. Choice of feedback mode depends on the requirements of the application and the people using the feedback. Although complex or novel feedback may be interesting, the best feedback modes for a given application are the ones that get the information or consequences across with a minimum of distraction and ambiguity. Simple, well-designed feedback usually fits this criterion. Practitioners often settle on a limited number of practical feedback modes.

Safety

EMG equipment makes direct electrical connection to a person via surface electrodes, thereby establishing a path for bioelectric signals between the person and the instrument. Although this path is intended for bioelectric signals, electricity from other sources also can take this path under some conditions. The presence of other currents in the signal path is a risk. Consequently, great care is taken in the design and manufacture of top-grade biomedical instruments to minimize the possibility of exposing patients to extraneous electrical currents. Despite this, no equipment, no matter how well made and installed, is 100% immune from electrical hazards for all time.

The chance of risky electrical faults developing is small, especially in battery-operated equipment, but the manner in which the equipment user sets up and maintains the equipment is at least as important to patient safety as the soundness of the equipment design. It is therefore the responsibility of each professional using these instruments to be aware of potential electrical hazards and to take standard safety precautions in installing, using, and maintaining the equipment. If there is any question about the safety of a particular installation, the professional must consult the manufacturer of the equipment or a qualified biomedical engineer. *This is particularly important when there are multiple instruments or any connections to powerline-operated equipment or accessories.*

A good rule of thumb is to doubt the safety of all setups involving powerline-operated auxiliary equipment until you positively establish the safety of the installation. This is because the potential consequences of leakage current from the AC power line can be extreme. For example, it takes only 0.009 amperes (9 milliamperes) or less to cause a person to be unable to release his or her grasp on an object through which the leakage current flows. Respiration may be affected at approximately 18 milliamperes, and heart fibrillation (and death) may occur at around 50 milliamperes. This is hundreds of times less than the current required to blow a standard household fuse, so fuses provide no protection. There are several precautions one should take, some of which require the consultation of a biomedical engineer or technician:

1. Each powerline-operated piece of auxiliary equipment should be periodically evaluated technically and certified by a biomedical technician for electrical safety.

2. Keep all patients or subjects out of arm's reach of all metal building parts, such as radiators and plumbing.

3. Ground all equipment properly. Use a "ground fault interrupter," a device that senses a diversion of electricity from the normal pathway established by the two legs of the standard power circuit. This device shuts down power to the equipment if more than about 5 milliamperes of current is "lost" through nonnormal pathways such as leakage current to ground through a person.

Troubleshooting with a "Dummy Subject"

High-grade EMG circuitry is quite reliable, but electrodes, cables, and batteries may need frequent service in heavily used equipment. Diagnosing failure of these parts is usually simple and requires few tools.

Faulty electrodes or electrode contact usually leads to spuriously high readings. The equipment user should carefully follow the electrode maintenance and application instructions supplied with the instrument. If unexpected or suspiciously high readings are observed, it is wise to determine whether the problem is in the electrodes, electrode contact, or in the cable or EMG unit. Use a "dummy subject," which is nothing more than two resistors that can be snapped to the electrode cable in place of the normal electrodes. This simulates a subject with zero EMG (see Figure 4.17).

The dummy subject supplies about the same "input resistance" as actual electrodes on skin, but generates no EMG signals. With the dummy subject in place, the readings should therefore be close to the residual noise level of the instrument as given in its specifications. For a fair test, hold the electrode cable between the fingers at least a foot away from the dummy subject as it dangles toward the floor. This distance prevents excessive noise being coupled from the user's body to the dummy subject. EMG readings with the dummy subject typically vary as you twist the cable between the fingers, much as television reception on "rabbit ears" varies as one rotates the antenna.

High readings are attributable to excessive noise (i.e., too much for the differential amplifier and filters to reject) from nearby electrical equipment, or a fault in the electrode cable or EMG unit. If the dummy subject test in the patient area results in a reading near the instrument's residual noise specification, then it is safe to conclude that electrical noise in the area is not overpowering. This means that the high readings with the real subject are

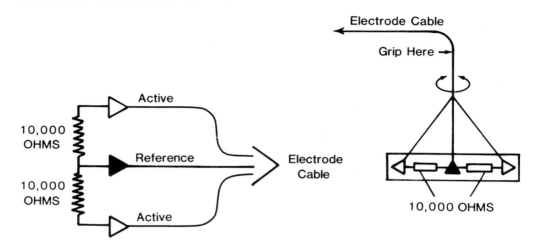

FIGURE 4.17. Dummy subject.

not the result of failure of the EMG unit or electrode cable. In this case, the fault is most likely with the electrodes or electrode contact.

If the reading goes off scale and stays there while the dummy subject is rotated, there is likely a break in the electrode cable. Verify this by substituting another cable. If the repeat test still leads to off-scale or very high readings, then it is likely that the fault is with the EMG unit itself, or that the work area is saturated with electrical noise. Check this by moving the machine to other locations and repeat the dummy subject test.

If the dummy subject test indicates that the instrument and cable are working properly, but abnormally high readings with the real subject remain, consider removing the electrodes, cleaning the skin again, and reapplying them.

It is wise for equipment users to construct dummy subjects if they do not already have them and to experiment with the dummy subjects when they know their machines and cables are working properly. Users will then be in a better position to judge test results with dummy subjects when actual failures occur.

Battery Failure

Abnormally high or low readings may result from battery failure. Most instruments have a built-in battery check. Use it whenever there is doubt about the accuracy of the readings. Units without a battery check usually include battery-checking instructions in the user's manual.

Aging batteries may pass the check and work fine early in a session, deteriorate during the session, and then "self-rejuvenate" after a few idle hours. The usable time after these "self-rejuvenations" gets shorter and shorter, until the batteries are unable to power the equipment at all.

Summary

A summary block diagram of a hypothetical EMG instrument with several outputs is presented in Figure 4.18.

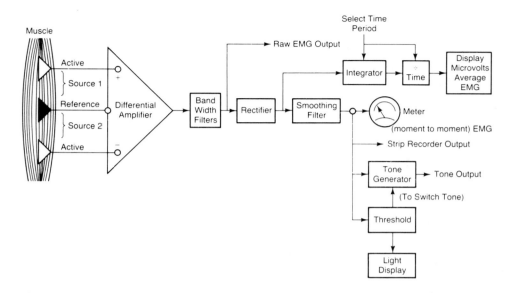

FIGURE 4.18. Block diagram of hypothetical EMG instrument with several outputs.

OPERATION OF THE TEMPERATURE BIOFEEDBACK INSTRUMENT

Temperature biofeedback instruments measure changing skin temperature. Skin temperature is significant because it is linked to sympathetic arousal: Sympathetic arousal affects vasoconstriction. Vasoconstriction affects perfusion of blood, particularly in extremities such as fingers and toes. Perfusion of blood affects skin temperature. Typically, sympathetic arousal leads to increased vasoconstriction, which leads to a reduction in blood volume and hence to a cooling effect at the skin.

Although this neurovascular phenomenon involves the constriction and dilation of vessels, the single term "vasoconstriction" is used here to denote all changes in vascular diameter. For example, "reduced vasoconstriction" is used to express the idea of vasodilation.

The tasks of a temperature biofeedback instrument are:

1. To let the skin heat a temperature-sensitive probe.
2. To make the probe serve as a temperature-sensitive electrical "valve" that modulates an electric sensing current applied to the probe.
3. To convert temperature-dependent variations in electric current flow through the probe into displayed temperature in degrees and provide other feedback or information meaningful to the user.

Letting the Skin Heat a Probe

A typical temperature probe is made of one or more small pieces of heat-sensitive electrical material (called "thermistors") encased in electrically insulating material with wires protruding for connection to the temperature unit. A temperature probe is not an electrode. It is specifically designed to make only *thermal* contact, not *electrical* contact with the skin.

The probe accepts only heat from the skin and remains at nearly the same temperature as the skin immediately beneath it. Typically, the probe tip is taped or strapped to the skin. As the skin warms and cools, the probe warms and cools accordingly, but with a slight delay because the probe temperature takes a little time to "catch up" with the skin temperature.

The probe is attached to either side of any one of the fingers. No single site is standard, nor has any particular site been shown to be superior. However, consistency from session to session is important because temperature or speed of response may vary from site to site. The dorsal surface (back side) of the fingers is a common site. This permits the person to rest the hand on the chair or lap without articially warming the probe between the finger and the chair or body. Furthermore, the dorsal surface has fewer sweat glands, so the chance of evaporative cooling is less. It is no doubt possible to make a case for the use of other sites as well. However, consistency will probably remain more important than the specific choice of finger site.

The Probe as a Temperature-Sensitive Electrical Valve

The heat-sensitive thermistors of the probe act like a "valve" for electricity applied to them from the instrument. This is analogous to a water valve that gradually opens and closes to regulate water flow. But in this case, probe temperature operates the "valve" and regulates the flow of electricity. As the probe heats, its electrical resistance decreases, and more electric current flows. As the probe cools, its resistance increases (the "valve" closes a little), and less electric current flows. In this way, the temperature of the probe is encoded in the electrical flow through the probe.

Displaying Temperature and Other Feedback

The temperature instrument measures the current flow through the probe and displays this quantity (properly scaled) as degrees or as other feedback.

Internal Workings

Temperature feedback instruments can perform the required operations in more than one related way. Intelligent use of temperature biofeedback equipment does not require detailed knowledge of internal workings. However, it is important to understand the basic scheme shared by all temperature devices.

Ohm's Law

Temperature feedback devices operate on one or another form of Ohm's Law. Georg Ohm was the Bavarian scientist who, in 1827, specified the quantitative relationships among three basic elements of an electrical circuit: voltage, resistance, and current. In 1891, the Electrical Congress in Paris agreed that electrical pressure would be measured in volts, after Volta, the Italian; electrical flow volume in amperes, after Ampere, the Frenchman; and resistance in ohms, after Ohm, the German. Since there is a convenient hydraulic analogy to Ohm's Law, the law and the analogy are presented together in Table 4.2.

Ohm's Law and the Temperature Feedback Device

Ohm's Law says that the amount of current flowing in a circuit powered by a constant voltage depends entirely upon the resistance in the circuit. The resistance of a thermistor

TABLE 4.2. Ohm's Law: Voltage, Resistance, and Current

Electrical law	Hydraulic analogy
Units	
Volt: Unit of electrical pressure	Pounds per square inch: Unit of water pressure
Ampere: Unit of electric current flow	Gallons per minute: Unit of water flow
Ohm: Unit of resistance to electric current flow	Unspecified unit of resistance to water flow
Circuit description	
Pressure (in volts) pushes the current (in amperes) through the resistance (in ohms) of the circuit	Pressure (in pounds per square inch) pushes the water flow (in gallons per minute) through the resistance of the pipes
Quantification	
Current = pressure/resistance; that is, Amperes = volts/ohms (Ohm's Law)	
Algebraic formulas	
Volts = amperes × ohms Ohms = volts/amperes	
Conventional abbreviations	
Voltage: V or E Current: I Resistance: R	

(thermal resistor) varies with its temperature. Therefore, when a thermistor is the only resistance element in a constant-voltage circuit, the current flow in the circuit is proportional to the temperature of the thermistor. The quantitative relationship between temperature and thermistor resistance is a property of the thermistor and varies greatly from one model to another. For this reason, probe models are usually not interchangeable. A suitable current-sensing circuit and meter display a reading in degrees. Figure 4.19 shows a hypothetical temperature feedback device.

Parameters of Temperature Feedback Devices: Ways They Differ from One Another

Temperature feedback devices come in a wide range of performance and cost, ranging from those that are properly called "instruments" to those that are more like "gizmos." The following three parameters—response time, absolute accuracy, and resolution—provide a basis for judging or comparing the performance of temperature feedback devices.

Response Time

"Response time" is primarily a property of the probe, indicating how rapidly it responds to a change in skin temperature. If a probe responds quickly, feedback delay is minimal. Small temperature changes are readily apparent. However, quick response time is usually gained at the expense of increased cost and fragility. A very fast-responding probe (e.g., 0.3 sec-

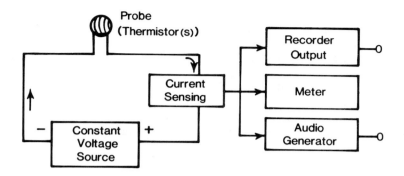

FIGURE 4.19. A hypothetical temperature feedback device.

onds) is very small and light, encased in a material that conducts heat readily so that it gains or loses heat very rapidly in step with skin temperature. Such probes are more delicate and expensive to manufacture. Larger, more bulky probes are cheaper and more durable, but they take more time to heat and cool as skin temperature changes.

A very fast-responding probe is not thought necessary in most applications. To understand why, recall that skin temperature is important because it provides indirect access to peripheral vasoconstriction. There is already considerable time delay between a change in vascular diameter and the resultant change in skin temperature. Probe response time adds a second delay to the overall delay between the vascular event and the resulting temperature event. One could argue that because of these delays, it is important to minimize probe response time so that further delay is kept to a minimum. A counterargument is that skin temperature is a relatively slow-changing phenomenon to which rapid response time does not add value for relaxation applications. Neither view holds obvious sway. Successful thermal biofeedback appears to have been done with temperature devices of widely differing response times. Calculations of "tracking error" based on conditions expected in biofeedback suggests that probe response times on the order of 1 second are probably adequate.

Absolute Accuracy

"Absolute accuracy" refers to how closely the displayed temperature corresponds to the actual probe temperature. Virtually any temperature machine will follow temperature changes (delayed by its particular response time), but there is variation between instruments in the accuracy of the temperature readings. Although a given unit may respond very sensitively to *changes* in temperature, it is unlikely that readings will exactly equal the *true* temperature of the probe. For example, it may read up to a few degrees higher or lower than the true temperature.

Furthermore, two identical units monitoring the same site will probably not give exactly the same readings. This variability in absolute accuracy is to be expected, and the error range for a given unit is usually included in its specifications. Absolute accuracy of ±1°F is considered sufficient. Absolute accuracy is a tradeoff against cost, because a high degree of absolute accuracy tends to be very expensive to assure. Practical advantages of highly accurate temperature equipment for clinical biofeedback are not obvious. Successful biofeedback takes place using units with widely differing degrees of absolute accuracy—including those that are not calibrated to the Fahrenheit standard at all. These devices give only relative indications of warming and cooling.

The question of accuracy arises for temperature feedback equipment because there exist standardized temperature scales (Fahrenheit and Centigrade) that set absolute standards for temperature measurement. In contrast, the question of accuracy is less pertinent for EMG equipment, because there is no standardized EMG scale for reference comparable to the standardized temperature scales. Remember, although *temperature* is measured on a standardized scale, *vasoconstriction* is not. An absolutely accurate temperature reading does not imply an absolutely accurate gauge of vasoconstriction, much less sympathetic arousal.

Resolution

"Resolution" refers to the smallest temperature change that the instrument can discern and display. Resolution affects length of feedback delay. For example, a digital unit that resolves to 1°F will feed back that a temperature change has taken place when a 1°F change has occurred. Since temperature change occurs over time, the feedback will be delayed by however long it takes for the temperature to change 1°F. A resolution of 0.1°F will provide much more rapid feedback, since it takes far less time in a given case for the temperature to move 0.1°F than 1°F. Instruments can be built to resolve 0.01°F, and this reduces feedback delay even further. However, extremely high resolution also increases the risk of mistaking artifact for vasoconstriction-caused temperature change. For example, the effects of movement, a light breeze, and room cooling are much more likely to affect the readings from an instrument with exceedingly fine resolution than from one with more coarse resolution. Furthermore, a high-resolution temperature instrument must be manufactured with much more exacting tolerances and increased expense. Otherwise it may create discernable change in the readings through "drift" in its own circuits. A machine with exceedingly high resolution is more likely to display distracting information or artifacts superimposed on true vasoconstrictive effects. A resolution of 0.1°F is a typical resolution value for temperature instruments and appears to be a suitable general-purpose value.

Digital and analog feedback have different resolving power. For example, a digital meter with three digits (tens, ones, and tenths) can resolve to 0.1°F. However, an audio tone (such as the sensitive pulsed tone feedback described in the EMG section) indicates even finer differences that occur during the interval between changes of the tenths digit on the meter.

Artifacts

Because peripheral temperature is an indirect index of peripheral vasoconstriction, there are several sources of misleading readings. In looking for sources of artifact, the question to ask is: "What conditions lead to temperature changes that are not linked to vasoconstrictive changes?"

Cool Room Temperature

Air temperature in the room where measurements are being made may affect the readings. For a given degree of vasoconstriction, skin temperature may be cooler in a cool room than in a warm room simply because the cool air absorbs more heat from the skin. Cool air may also directly cool the probe.

Breeze

Moving air exaggerates the cooling effect mentioned above in two ways. First, breeze removes heat from the skin more rapidly than still air. Second, breeze evaporates sweat more rapidly than still air.

Warm Room Temperature

Remember that the room temperature sets an approximate lower limit for hand temperature. That is, a hand cannot cool very much below the temperature of the air around it. This is because cooling takes place through the dissipation of heat from the hand to the air. As soon as the hand cools down to the temperature of the air, there is no longer any place for heat to go. The hand remains at about that temperature regardless of further vasoconstriction. However, it is possible that the skin might cool a little further as a result of evaporation of sweat. Warm-air effect is usually not a problem because room temperature is usually around 72°F, close to the low end of the skin temperature range for most persons. However, in the event of a high room temperature, higher skin temperature will be observed than in a cooler room, even with an identical degree of vasoconstriction. For example, using thermal biofeedback in a 90°F room will lead to warmer hands for everyone, regardless of the degree of vasoconstriction. In such a case, even the hand temperature of a cadaver, which has no warm blood at all, would be 90°F!

Room Temperature and the Temperature Feedback Instrument

Even if the temperature of the probe is held constant, temperature readings may change as the temperature unit *itself* is heated and cooled. This is because electronic components are sensitive to temperature. Consequently, the performance of electronic circuitry is vulnerable to change or "drift" as surrounding air temperature changes. This is a well-known phenomenon that designers usually compensate for within the circuits. Such "temperature compensation" is very important for temperature instruments, because they are required to resolve exceedingly small changes in electric current from the probe. If temperature compensation is incomplete, then readings vary somewhat as a function of room temperature as well as skin temperature. This source of artifact is usually not practically significant unless room temperature is known to vary over a wide range.

Probe Contact and "Blanketing"

Changes in probe contact caused by movement also affect temperature readings. If the probe begins to lift from the skin, when pulled by its leads, then lower readings are likely. The opposite occurs when the probe is covered by a hand, clothing, or even materials used to secure the probe to the skin, all of which have the effect of "blanketing" the probe.

Chill

If the person to be monitored comes in chilled from the outside, cold hands are likely. Let the person regain a comfortable hand temperature. Otherwise, the body's natural method for conserving heat through peripheral vasoconstriction will significantly affect the readings observed in a biofeedback session. Even the person who is not chilled but who comes in from the outside with cold hands should be allowed to restabilize skin temperature before training begins. Otherwise, the natural warming of the hands after being exposed to cold may be mistaken for a training effect.

Testing for Absolute Accuracy

Test the accuracy of temperature instruments by immersing the probe in a glass of water along with a lab thermometer of known accuracy and then stirring the water. Compare the readings after they have stabilized. This test is useful when the accuracy of the instrument or probe is questioned or when the actual interchangeability of "identical" probes is assessed. If done carefully, this method can be used to test for temperature drift in the temperature instrument itself. With the probe temperature stabilized in a glass of water, heat and cool the instrument while noting any change in its reading. For this test, hold the temperature of the water constant by using a thermos bottle.

Other Feedback

Audio Feedback

Digital meters are often used for visual feedback because they resolve small differences over a very wide range. Audio tones cannot provide the same resolution over such a wide range. If a usable range of audio pitches is simply distributed over the working range of skin temperature, then persons with very low or high skin temperature will have to listen to feedback in the extremes of the audio range. This will be uncomfortable to listen to for long. Moreover, small changes in temperature will give only slight changes in the pitch of the tone. A good solution to this problem is to let the user move the entire pitch range of audio tones up and down the temperature range, so that high-resolution audio feedback in a comfortable pitch range can be obtained, regardless of the actual skin temperature. This is shown graphically in Figure 4.20. Moving the audio range is accomplished by turning a control that affects the pitch of the audio feedback but not the meter readings. In this way, the user adjusts the audio feedback for a comfortable pitch range around any temperature.

   Some temperature machines have an audio "slope" control that allows the user to select whether the pitch rises or falls with temperature. This encourages the user to fit the audio feedback to his or her warming images. For example, some users feel that pitch increasing with temperature has natural heuristic value, as the image of blood vessels and of blood flowing through the fingertips is visualized. Others find decreasing pitch more natural as relaxation occurs.

Derivative Feedback

"Derivative" or "rate" feedback is sometimes found on temperature instruments. "Derivative" is a mathematical term referring to rate of change. In a temperature machine, this usually takes the form of a light or tone that turns on when skin temperature is changing at

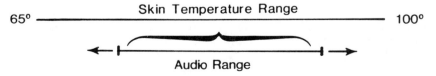

FIGURE 4.20. Audio feedback range adjustable over skin temperature range.

a certain rate. For example, a red light turns on when the person's hand temperature is climbing at 1°F or more per minute. Another light or tone might come on if the person's hand temperature were falling at that rate. This establishes a target hand-warming rate, and permits a summary quantification such as the percentage of time above the target warming rate.

Safety

Because no electrodes are used, temperature biofeedback equipment may not pose the same potential electrical safety challenges as EMG equipment. Since the probe is deliberately electrically insulated from the subject, the chances of a risky electrical fault developing may be lower than with EMG equipment. Nevertheless, temperature equipment should not be considered exempt from the safety precautions discussed earlier for EMG equipment. If, for example, a probe fails (internally or through a break in the insulation of its wires), so that it is no longer insulated from the skin, it becomes in effect an electrode. This increases the potential for electric shock or leakage currents, particularly since the temperature device is probably not specifically designed to operate safely with a direct electrical connection to a person. Therefore, to be as safe as possible, follow the safety guidelines for EMG equipment. Moreover, *safety guidelines are best thought of as applying to entire biofeedback installations, not just the individual units in isolation.*

ELECTRODERMAL BIOFEEDBACK

Early History of Electrodermal Research

The early history of electrodermal research is an interesting story recounted by Neumann and Blanton (1970). They begin the story with Galvani's discovery of the electrical processes in nerve and muscle action, which quickly stimulated research into the medical applications of electricity. By 1840, it was widely believed that electrical processes provided a basis for explaining disease and generating diagnoses and therapies. The authors note that this was strongly consistent with the physicalistic thinking of the day, in reaction to the vitalistic thinking of earlier times. By 1870, then-sophisticated instrumentation and procedures had been developed as part of electrophysiological research methodology. (A fascinating collection of such literature and instrumentation exists at the Bakken Museum of Electricity in Life, in Minneapolis, Minnesota.)

As the field developed, investigators noted that skin resistance varied over the body. Since investigation focused on the physical effects of electrical currents and static fields, the early workers noted that variations in skin resistance introduced variations in current flow through the body, and hence they viewed variations in skin resistance as a source of artifact. Instruments were built that controlled for this artifact. Most researchers continued to regard variations in skin resistance as artifact encountered while applying electric current or static fields for diagnostic or therapeutic purposes.

But in 1879, Romain Vigouroux measured skin resistance as an experimental variable in cases of hysterical anesthesias. This, according to Neumann and Blanton, is generally regarded as the first observation of psychological factors in electrodermal phenomena. In 1888, Vigouroux's colleague, Charles Fere, studied the effect of physical stimulation on skin resistance, noting increases in current flow following stimulation. This, the reviewers say, was the first study of what by 1915 was called galvanic skin response (GSR), and it was probably the first statement of an arousal theory.

It is noteworthy that by Fere's time, the French physicist D'Arsonval had developed silver chloride nonpolarizable electrodes for physiological research, as well as a sophisticated galvanometer (needle-type meter), a forerunner of modern meter movements that still bear his name. The German investigator Hermann linked GSR with sweat gland activity in 1881, thus establishing a physiological basis for the phenomenon. In 1889, the Russian investigator Ivan Tarchanoff, while investigating skin potentials, showed that not only physical stimuli but also mental activity (such as mental arithmetic and the recollection of upsetting events) led to skin potential changes. Moreover, he linked this phenomenon to the distribution of sweat glands and proposed that it was related to the action of "secretory nerves." Neumann and Blanton report that Tarchanoff's and Fere's papers were followed by "several years of oblivion." GSR was rediscovered in 1904.

At that time, a Swiss engineer, E. K. Mueller, noticed that skin resistance changed with psychological events. He showed this to the Swiss neurologist Veraguth, and both believed this to be a newly discovered phenomenon. Mueller went on to assume the role of a psychological expert and to address the technical problems of measurement, reliability of electrode design, and experimentation with the use of AC current. By 1905, Veraguth had finished some preliminary experiments when he embarrassedly discovered the earlier work of Tarchanoff and others.

Veraguth and Carl Jung were friends, and somehow (each claimed to have suggested it to the other) GSR was used in Jung's word association experiments. Jung then provided most of the impetus for further studies in this area. By 1907 he considered GSR, known to Veraguth and Jung as "psychogalvanic reflex," a means to objectify heretofore invisible "emotional tones." Jung embarked on extensive studies and exported this idea to friends in the United States. Neumann and Blanton report that a "flood" of papers in America appeared over the next two decades and established this field as a major research area. Since then, GSR has been recognized as a way to gain objective access to psychophysiological arousal.

This physiological variable has appeared in countless psychological experiments, in clinical practice, in "lie detector" equipment, and even in toys and parlor games. Biofeedback has used it for access to autonomic arousal. Skin resistance is recognized as distinctively sensitive to transitory emotional states and mental events, while often remaining more or less independent of other biofeedback measures such as muscle tension and skin temperature. It is a complex variable, responsive to a wide range of overt and covert activities and external and internal stimulation. Its responsivity to psychological content in actual or laboratory human situations apparently prompted Barbara Brown (1974) to dub GSR "skin talk." This is an apt metaphor that does justice to its psychological responsivity while legitimizing its often complex and seemingly unpredictable variations and individual differences. Just as with actual languages, "skin talk" must be studied and experienced to be understood. EMG and temperature biofeedback are, in comparison, more easily understood by virtue of their less articulated response to mental events. That is, EMG and temperature biofeedback tend not to reflect mental events as quickly or with as much resolution as GSR.

Electrodermal phenomena are often less well conceptualized and more disparagingly discussed than other biofeedback measures because of complexity, individual variability, methodological challenges in measurement, and the multiplicity of technical approaches. The purpose of this section is to conceptualize the skin conductance phenomenon and to describe and critique some of the approaches to skin conductance measurement and instrumentation.

As revealed in the history given above, two forms of EDA have been studied. The most common is the *exosomatically* recorded activity of Fere, Veraguth, and Jung, in which an external electric current is passed through the skin. Activity is indicated by the skin's electrical resistance (or its reciprocal, conductance). The second method, that of Tarchanoff, is *endosomatically* recorded activity (skin potentials), which involves monitoring voltage differences between electrodes at two points on the surface of the skin. The endosomatic method is not covered in this chapter because it is much less common in biofeedback than exosomatically recorded skin conductance. For more on the endosomatic method, see Venables and Christie (1980).

Terms

GSR is no doubt the most universally recognized term for EDA. Perhaps this is because the term has been used for a long time to refer to a variety of exosomatic and endosomatic phenomena, and both electrodermal levels and responses. Although the term GSR will probably continue in widespread use, other, more specific terminology has been suggested that is more descriptive of specific electrodermal phenomena. Adopted from Venables and Christie (1980), the following nomenclature is used in this chapter.

EDA, electrodermal response (EDR), and electrodermal level (EDL) are used as general terms for either exosomatic or endosomatic phenomena: EDL refers to baseline *levels*; EDR refers to *responses* away from baselines; and EDA is the most general term, referring to *levels and/or responses.*

Skin conductance activity (SCA), skin conductance response (SCR), and skin conductance level (SCL) specify the exosomatic method and the conductance (in contrast to resistance) scale. Again, SCL refers to baseline levels, SCR refers to changes from baselines, and SCA refers to either or both.

Parallel terms for skin resistance and skin potentials are used: skin resistance activity (SRA), skin resistance response (SRR), and skin resistance level (SRL); skin potential activity (SPA), skin potential response (SPR), and skin potential level (SPL).

Table 4.3 clarifies the meaning of all these terms and their interrelationships. Although the table contains a dozen terms, this chapter is concerned only with SCA, that is, SCL and SCR. These are clearly prevalent forms of electrodermal biofeedback.

Electrical Model of the Skin

The skin is electrically complex, and despite extensive study, no one claims to have perfect knowledge of the physiology of EDA. But the following electrical model of the skin brings out the essential features of practical importance in biofeedback.

The skin on the palm or volar surface of the hand contains up to 2000 sweat glands per square centimeter. Eccrine rather than apocrine sweat glands are relevant to biofeedback. Each sweat gland when activated can be considered a separate electrical pathway from the surface of the skin, which normally has high resistance, to deeper and more conductive layers of the skin. This is shown in Figure 4.21, adapted from Venables and Christie (1980).

Each resistor represents the conductive pathway of a sweat gland. For illustrative purposes, a sweat gland is considered "on" or "off." When it is "on," it forms a low-resistance path from the skin surface to deeper layers. When it is "off," it makes a very high-resistance pathway. In Figure 4.21, some glands are shown "on" and others are shown "off." Since the inner layers of skin are highly conductive, but the outer layer is highly resistive, the resistors are electrically tied together at the deeper layers within the skin, but are electrically isolated from each other at the surface. This presents an opportunity for monitoring sweat-

TABLE 4.3. Organization of Electrodermal Terms

	Endosomatic or exosomatic	Exosomatic		Endosomatic
		Conductance	Resistance	
Activity	EDA	SCA	SRA	SPA
Response	EDR	SCR	SRR	SPR
Level	EDL	SCL	SRL	SPL

gland activity electrically. If two electrodes are placed over skin laden with sweat glands, and a voltage is applied to the electrodes, a circuit is formed, and an electric current will flow. The size of the current will depend (according to Ohm's Law) on the resistance of the skin, which in turn depends on the number of sweat glands turned "on." See Figure 4.22 for an illustration.

As more and more sweat glands turn "on," more and more conductive pathways switch into the circuit, and (since some current flows through each pathway) more and more total current flows. In this case, Ohm's Law determines current flow, just as it does in temperature instruments. The difference is that the skin instead of a temperature probe, acts as a variable resistor that regulates current flow through the circuit. The meter measures current flow in the circuit, and the reading is proportional to sweat-gland activity. (Review this circuit in the section on temperature biofeedback instruments by substituting "skin resistance" for "probe resistance" in the explanation of Ohm's Law.)

Scales and Measurement: Resistance and Conductance

At this point, we must distinguish resistance from conductance and explain why conductance is the preferred measurement unit. Resistance and conductance are defined as reciprocals of each other, and they represent the same basic electrical property of materials. As discussed earlier, the ohm is the unit of resistance. The unit of conductance is the "mho" ("ohm" spelled backward); it is defined as the reciprocal of resistance (i.e., 1 divided by resistance). Therefore, resistance is also the reciprocal of conductance (1 divided by conductance). These are two scales for measuring the same phenomenon (see Table 4.4).

Although these alternative scales measure the same property, there is a good reason to use the conductance measurement scale. Recall that as sweat glands turn "on," they add conductance pathways within the skin. This means that conductance increases in a linear

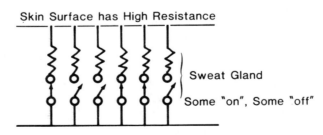

Skin Surface has High Resistance

Sweat Gland
Some "on", Some "off"

Deep Layers of Skin Have Low Resistance

FIGURE 4.21. Electrical model of the skin. (Adapted from Venables & Christie, 1980.)

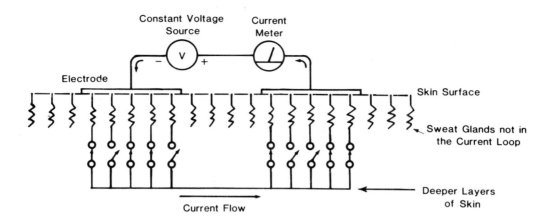

FIGURE 4.22. Basic skin conductance current loop.

relationship to the number of activated sweat glands. Resistance, on the other hand, decreases in a nonlinear fashion as more and more sweat glands are activated. This is shown graphically in Figure 4.23.

The linear relationship between sweat-gland activity and skin conductance is statistically preferable for scaling and quantification. This is why skin conductance is now the standard unit. There are times, such as when using Ohm's Law or when testing electrodes, when it is more convenient to think in terms of resistance rather than conductance. Once you understand the relationship between these two scales, shifting from one scale to the other presents no problem.

TABLE 4.4. Correspondence between Conductance and Resistance

Conductance	Resistance
Units	
Mho	Ohm
Micromho (millionth)	Megohm (million)
Conversion formulas	
Conductance = 1/resistance	Resistance = 1/conductance
Mho = 1/ohm	Ohm = 1/mho
Micromho = 1/megohm	Megohm = 1/micromho
Sample correspondences	
1 micromho ~ 1 megohm	
10 micromhos ~ .1 megohm	
100 micromhos ~ .01 megohm	
Range of skin conductance values	
Approx. 0.5 micromho to 50 micromhos	Approx. 0.02 megohm to 2 megohms

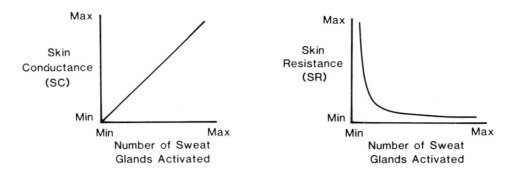

FIGURE 4.23. Comparison of skin conductance (left) and resistance (right) scales.

Speaking of scales and measurement, note that skin conductance is not a *direct* measure of sweat-gland activity. It is not a measure of how many are turned on. Rather, it is an *indirect* measure that, except for artifact, correlates highly with sweat-gland activity. Remember that skin conductance results only when an electrical voltage is imposed from outside. Therefore, the measurement apparatus is inextricably tied into the skin conductance phenomena and contributes heavily to the observations. To repeat, conductance in micromhos is an electrical concept, not a physiological concept. It is not a direct measure of how many sweat glands are in operation. Therefore, always keep in mind that skin conductance readings are only an analogue to the physiological processes of interest and only reflect (not directly measure) these processes.

Skin resistance or skin conductance biofeedback instruments are designed to be ohm-measuring or mho-measuring meters. As such, they objectively measure whatever electrical equivalent network is presented to their inputs. They are characterized in part by the means of applying electrical excitation to the skin—either a steady-state (DC) voltage or current, or an alternating (AC) voltage or current—and by their readout in either ohms or mhos. If a calibrated readout is provided, calibration is usually done by presenting a known value or values of simple electrical resistors and by verifying that the unit displays those values to within the specified accuracy of the instrument.

The problem is that skin presents a far more complex and variable electrical network than simple calibration resistors. Sweat glands are not uniformly distributed in skin tissue, so sensing sites and electrode surface areas affect readings. If DC current loops are used, electrode material may be very important, because the skin–electrode interfaces will tend to "polarize," thereby influencing the readings. The use of silver/silver chloride electrodes will minimize but not eliminate this artifact. If AC current loops are used, polarization effects are minimized, but "reactive" components of the electrical equivalent network of the skin will cause an apparent increase in skin conductance. (These and other artifacts are discussed in a later section.) Finally, the electrical resistance of skin tissue varies with the magnitude of the current in the current loop.

In summary, biofeedback providers should not assume that each other's or published quantified SCA readings are actually comparable. Specification of the conditions outlined above, plus the technical knowledge required to interpret the effects of these conditions, are necessary in order to compare SCA readings from different contexts. Even then, quantitative SCA readings are comparable in form to those of thermometer A (see Figure 4.1) rather than to those of thermometer B.

Parameters of SCA

The hypothetical 20-second SCA record in Figure 4.24 yields three primary and two secondary parameters.

Primary Parameters

SCL or Tonic Level. SCL expressed in micromhos represents a baseline or resting level. Although this level may change, a resting, quiescent person is likely to hover around a value identified as the tonic level. SCL or tonic level is thought to be an index of baseline level of sweat gland activity, an inferred indication of a relative level of sympathetic arousal. For example, conductance values above 5–10 micromhos are thought to be relatively high, whereas those below 1 micromho are thought to be low. Remember that these estimates depend on a number of other variables and should be taken only as a rule of thumb based on the use of $^3/_8$-inch dry electrodes on the volar surface of fingertips.

SCR or Phasic Changes. Phasic changes are noticeable episodes of increased conductance caused by sympathetic arousal generated by a stimulus. For example, in the case of the stimulus introduced after 5 seconds, there is a 1- or 2-second delay and then an increase in conductance that peaks, levels out, and then falls back to the baseline or tonic level. This is a phasic change, and its magnitude (height) is expressed as the number of micromhos reached above baseline. The size of phasic changes is thought to be an indication of the degree of arousal caused by stimuli—for example, a startle or orientation to novel internal or external stimuli.

SCR Half-Recovery Time. "SCR half-recovery time" is defined as the time elapsed from the peak of the phasic change to *one-half* of the way back down to baseline. SCR half-recovery time is thought to be an index of a person's ability to calm down after a transitory excitation. It has been hypothesized that persons with chronic overarousal may have difficulty returning to relaxed baselines after even minor stimulation.

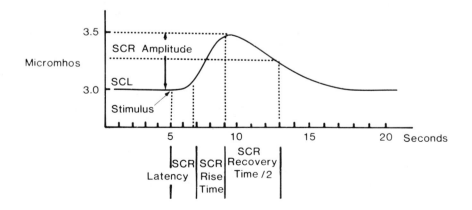

FIGURE 4.24. Parameters of skin conductance. (SCA values shown are taken from Venables & Christie, 1980.)

Secondary Parameters

SCR latency is defined as the time from stimulus onset until the beginning of an SCR. SCR rise time is defined as the time elapsed from the beginning of an SCR to its peak. These parameters have carried little significance in biofeedback, and therefore they are not discussed in detail here.

Normative Values for the Parameters

The hypothetical SCA record in Figure 4.24 shows specific values for the parameters. These values are actual mean values taken from normative samples of SCA records for tropical nonpatients, summarized in Venables and Christie (1980). However, do not assume that these are representative of values obtainable in ordinary biofeedback practice. Since large individual differences in SCL and SCR are common, readings far different from those cited normative values should come as no surprise. Furthermore, potential sources of normative variation include differences between patient and nonpatient groups, the effects of medications on SCL and SCR, differing procedures for establishing baselines and especially SCRs, and the great differences in instruments and electrodes likely to be used. This probable lack of normative consistency seems assured by the lack of a widely standardized measurement scale for both SCL and SCR. Recall that SCA readings are comparable to the readings of thermometer A in Figure 4.1. Imagine the difficulty of establishing consistent norms when using various different forms of thermometer A as data sources.

To increase your confidence in norms, find or build normative samples specific to the instrument scheme employed and to the characteristics of the subjects of the sample. At this time, there is no solid substitute for one's own accumulated experience with one's own patient group, purposes, and equipment. This is not meant to be disparaging, only a reflection of the present state of the art.

Scales and Measurement: The "Percent Increase" Scale for SCR Amplitude

Displaying SCR amplitude as the number of micromhos increase is not the only alternative. SCR amplitude can also be expressed as a percentage change from the tonic level. For example, an SCR consisting of a 1-micromho change from 3 to 4 micromhos is expressed as a 33% change. This has the effect of "relativizing" the SCR to the baseline from which it occurs. Using this method, a change from 6 to 8 micromhos is also a 33% change, and so is a change from 1.5 to 2 micromhos.

The rationale for this scale is the assumption that a given increase in autonomic arousal leads to a given percentage increase in conductance over the baseline level and, further, that this holds for all baseline levels. The following hypothetical examples and the electrical model of the skin illustrate this: Imagine a case in which 200 sweat glands are turned on, giving an SCL of 2 micromhos. Now a stimulus comes along that turns on an additional 100 sweat glands, thus leading to a 1-micromho or a 50% increase. Now imagine another case in which there are 600 sweat glands turned on for an SCL of 6 micromhos. According to the percentage model, a stimulus with the same arousing properties as in the first case will lead again to a 50% increase in conductance by turning on an additional 300 sweat glands for a 3-micromho increase in conductance.

To repeat, the assumption here is that changes in arousal are better gauged as percentage increases in conductance over existing baselines than as absolute increases in conductance with no regard to initial baselines. This is analogous in the economic domain to expressing a year's growth in the gross domestic product as a percentage increase over the previous year's level rather than as an increase in the number of dollars.

Loudness perception also provides an analogy: To achieve a given increase in perceived loudness, it takes larger absolute increases in loudness above noisy background levels than above quiet background levels. If an SCR is some sort of "orienting response," it is plausible that, to be psychophysiologically "noticeable," a stimulus must lead to a significant increase in conductance relative to existing baseline arousal, parallel to what occurs in loudness perception.

Pitch perception supplies a third analogy: It is common knowledge that the difference in pitch between the note C and the note A above it sounds the same in any octave. (It is the musical interval of a sixth.) The difference between middle C (258 Hertz) and the A above it (440 Hertz) is 184 Hertz, a 72% increase in frequency. The difference between the next C (512 Hertz) and the next A (880 Hertz) is 368 Hertz, but it is also a 72% increase in frequency. In this case, the percentage increase in frequency, rather than the number of vibrations per second leads to the perception of equal increases in pitch.

The absolute micromho increase scale for SCR amplitude rests on an assumption opposite to that of the percentage increase scale—that a micromho increase in conductance indicates a given increment in arousal, no matter where it is observed on the continuum of possible initial baselines. Stated again, this assumption says a micromho is a fixed increment of arousal, regardless of initial baseline. This assumption is also plausible.

There are, to my knowledge, no published data or definitive conceptual arguments to support or disconfirm either of the assumptions presented above. Each of these scales has plausibility and appeal, and it is apparently yet to be discovered whether either has distinct practical advantages or greater psychophysiological appropriateness. However, I prefer the assumptions supporting the use of the percentage increase scale for SCR amplitude. This is because the method of relating the magnitude of changes to initial baselines is appropriate and useful in perceptual contexts that to me are analogous to SCR. In addition, my informal observations suggest that persons with low SCL baselines often show fewer micromhos of SCR than persons with average SCL baselines. For me, intrinsic plausibility and these informal observations tip the balance toward the percentage increase scale for SCR amplitude. However, at very high SCLs, the percentage increase scale probably loses appropriateness, because most of the available sweat glands are already turned on to make the high SCLs.

Convenient scaling techniques follow from the percentage increase scale assumption. For example, if you plot the skin conductance continuum along a line, a logarithmic scale conveniently contains all possible SCA values while retaining a useful degree of resolution all along the line. This scale is illustrated in Figure 4.25. It has the advantage of providing adequate resolution at the low end while avoiding excessive resolution at the high end. Recall that the percentage increase scale supposes that the difference between 1 and 2 micromhos is more significant than the difference between 10 and 11 micromhos, and in fact is equivalent to the difference between 10 and 20 micromhos. On the logarithmic scale, equal distances along the line represent equal percentage changes. That is, the distance from 1 to 2

FIGURE 4.25. Logarithmic scale for SCA values.

is the same as that from 10 to 20: Both are 100% changes. This means that an SCR amplitude of any given percentage is represented by the same distance along the line, regardless of initial baseline.

Skin Conductance Record Interpretation

The three primary parameters discussed earlier help describe actual skin conductance records and extract data from them. But because records usually contain compounded changes in both responses and levels, considerable interpretation is often required to specify values for the parameters. Below are paradigmatic descriptions of complex skin conductance records and interpretive hypotheses.

Upward Tonic Level Shift

The sample record in Figure 4.26 reveals a phasic change away from the beginning tonic level and incomplete return to that level. Think of this as an SCR that did not recover and led to a new and higher tonic level from which subsequent phasic changes depart. A hypothesis is that whatever arousal led to the phasic change did not completely "wear off," thereby leaving the person with a new and elevated tonic level. Increase in conductance may be slow like "drift," rather than rapid like a typical SCR.

Downward Tonic Level Shift

The arousal leading to the new or elevated tonic level discussed above may in time "wear off" or be "relaxed away," leading to a downward trend in skin conductance. As shown hypothetically in Figure 4.27, this record has downward slope to it, although SCRs may be superimposed. In this way, a new lower tonic level may eventually be reached.

Stairstepping

With multiple excitatory stimuli, especially with persons who show high-magnitude phasic changes and slow recovery time, a phenomenon called "stairstepping" may occur. As shown in Figure 4.28, this results when an excitatory stimulus occurs before the phasic changes from previous stimuli have had time to return to the prior tonic level. The SCA may then "stairstep" higher and higher. This stairstepping process could theoretically be implicated

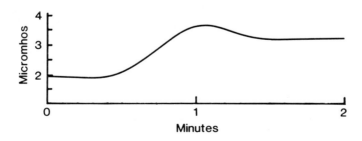

FIGURE 4.26. Upward tonic level shift.

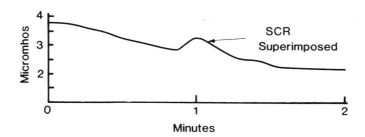

FIGURE 4.27. Downward tonic level shift.

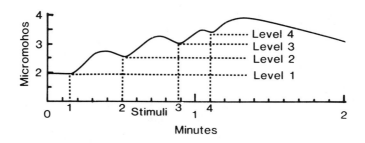

FIGURE 4.28. Stairstepping.

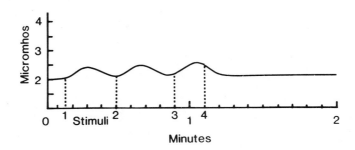

FIGURE 4.29. Rapid return to baseline, reducing stairstepping.

in development of overarousal. Figure 4.29 illustrates how individuals who show lower-magnitude phasic changes and more rapid return to baseline are less susceptible to stairstepping from repeated stimulation.

Nonresponsive Pattern

A "nonresponsive pattern" is an unusually flat conductance level (see Figure 4.30), which does not to respond much to typically arousing stimuli even when there is a reason to believe that strong emotion is or should be present. A hypothesis for this pattern, when ex-

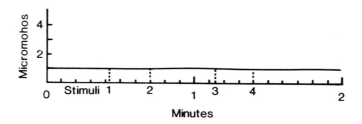

FIGURE 4.30.   Nonresponsive pattern.

treme, is inappropriate detachment, overcontrol, or helplessness, rather than relaxation (Toomin & Toomin, 1975).

Optimal Skin Conductance Patterns

Skin conductance is linked to arousal, but optimal SCA patterns are not necessarily the lowest or flattest patterns. This is because persistent minimal arousal, over-control, or flattened affect is not usually considered desirable. There is a time for minimizing arousal during deep relaxation training, in which a steady, low level of skin conductance may be desired, but uniformly invariant or flat levels are not necessarily desirable.

For example, encountering a novel stimulus calls for recognizing and treating it appropriately. Habitual blunting of the arousal associated with orientation or action is not thought to be healthy or adaptive. However, after a person orients to the novel stimulus and takes appropriate action, arousal should drop to baseline levels, avoiding unnecessary arousal or wasted energy. It is possible for a person to react too vigorously to novel stimuli, such that the reaction is out of proportion, wasting energy in overarousal. In this case, the person is treating stimuli as more alarming, dangerous, or exciting than warranted and is paying a price in energy and physical tension.

SCA is not something to be minimized but something to be optimized, and this requires judgment about what is appropriate for a given person in a given circumstance. At this time, no one claims to know optimum tonic levels and SCRs, or even be able to show that there is any such thing as specifiable optimums. What is clear is that it is possible to have overreaction and underreaction, and that this holds for both the tonic levels and phasic changes. Quick return to baseline after an SCR may be consistently desirable except when rapid return is part of an underresponsive pattern.

Because of large individual differences in SCA patterns and the lack of normative data under various standard paradigms of stimulation and measurement, it is difficult to specify clear and widely accepted procedures for SCA training or even diagnostic use. Useful SCA biofeedback at this time requires experience and judgment on the part of the clinician. The best way to acquire the "feel" of how SCA works under various conditions is to observe it within and between individuals, especially oneself. Those who work regularly with SCA are often quick to point out its ambiguities and uncertainties, but, undiscouraged, are also eager to discuss its unique responsiveness to transitory emotional states and thoughts. Its apparent complexity and ambiguity may conceal a wealth of valuable psychological as well as physiological information to those who have the patience to learn and further describe its patterns.

Operation of the Skin Conductance Instrument

Most Basic Constant DC Voltage Scheme

Figure 4.31 shows the most basic SCA monitoring scheme. A constant voltage is impressed across the two electrodes. The variable resistance of the skin leads to a variable current through the circuit. A current amplifier monitors this current, and, through proper scaling, drives a meter that reads out in micromhos. In this most basic form, it is similar to temperature instruments. However, to be practical, it must be refined.

Adjustable Viewing "Window"

SCL baselines are spread over a wide range, yet it is important to distinguish small SCRs (e.g., a 5% change from any SCL) from all possible baselines. If the entire range of possible SCA values were made to fit on a meter face, SCL values would be discernible, but an SCR would barely deflect the needle. Figure 4.32 illustrates that a 5% SCR from, for example, a 1-micromho SCL would barely show up. It would take a much larger SCR to move the needle enough to accurately gauge SCR amplitude and recovery time. This is the familiar issue of *resolution*, discussed earlier in connection with temperature biofeedback instruments. A digital meter overcomes resolution problems simply by having enough digits (e.g., tenths or even hundredths). However, a digital meter is not suitable for observing SCRs because

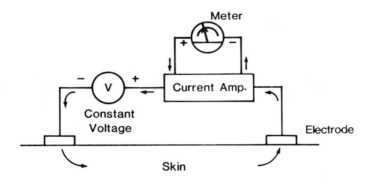

FIGURE 4.31. Most basic SCA monitoring scheme.

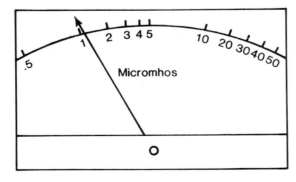

FIGURE 4.32. Lack of resolution when entire SCA range is squeezed onto a meter face.

the changing of digits during an SCR is hard to read and record. In contrast, the swing of a meter needle or light bar up and then back down is much more meaningful for SCRs.

A common solution to this problem is to use an analog meter for SCR display, but to restrict its range to form a "viewing window" that looks on only a portion of the SCA continuum. Of course, this "window" must be movable to any part of the SCA continuum, so an SCR can be monitored regardless of initial baseline SCL. This is shown graphically in Figure 4.33. The "window," which looks upon a small portion of the SCA range, is expanded on the entire meter scale. This way, small SCRs result in significant meter deflections. The center zero point on the meter in the figure represents the center of the "window." The meter scale is calibrated so that the extent of the needle swing indicates the percentage change from a starting baseline.

In the illustration, the meter is calibrated for a +50% or −50% change. The user operates a calibrated control that moves the window up and down the SCA continuum until the SCL of the person being monitored "comes into view." If this level is approached from the left, the needle will remain off scale to the right until the window moves over the SCL. Once the SCL is in view, the needle falls back to the left as the window moves toward the center zero point. With the needle at zero, the window is centered over the person's SCL. The SCL value is read off the digitally calibrated potentiometer that moves the window up and down the SCA continuum. When an SCR occurs, the meter needle moves upward. At maximum deflection, the needle points to the percentage change. The digital control remains in place during SCRs so it "remembers" the starting SCL baseline. If a person's SCL changes a lot or "drifts," the user moves the window along the SCA continuum with the digital control. The SCL is kept "in view," and the digital control indicates the new baseline.

To reduce how often the window must be moved to keep the SCL reading on scale, some instruments have adjustable window "widths" or choice of resolution. A very wide window width, for example, ± 100% change, will cover more of the SCA continuum and hence will require readjustment less often during periods of SCL drift or for very large SCRs. Wider windows also reduce resolution. That is, small SCRs will be less pronounced on the meter scale. When observing a very stable SCL with very small SCRs, switching to a nar-

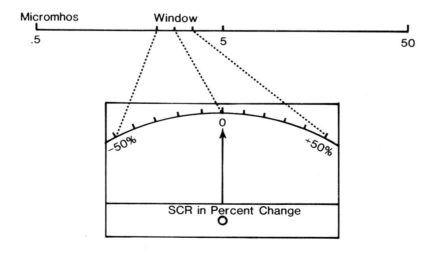

FIGURE 4.33. Movable viewing window.

row window width (e.g., ± 10%) expands small changes on the meter face, thus increasing visual resolution of the response.

Electrical Operation of the Movable Viewing Window

Figure 4.34 graphically presents a skin conductance instrument with a movable viewing window. The constant-voltage source feeds two current loops. First is the familiar loop through the electrodes and skin described earlier. The second loop is identical, except that a calibrated variable resistance (or variable conductance) takes the place of the electrodes and skin. In each loop, a current-to-voltage amplifier produces an output voltage proportional to the current through its loop.

Whenever current flow through the loops is equal, the outputs of the amplifiers are equal. Whenever the current flow through the loops is unequal, the outputs of the loop amplifiers are unequal in proportion to the difference in loop current flow. A meter measures the difference between the two loop amplifier outputs. This meter has a zero center, with the needle normally at rest in the center of the scale, pointing to zero. When current through the loops is equal, the outputs of the amplifiers are equal, and the needle remains at rest in the center, pointing to zero. When current through the loops is unequal, the meter needle will swing left or right, depending on which loop has the greater current. The extent of the deflection indicates the magnitude of the difference in current through the loops and reads out in percentage. The meter measures only *differences* in current flow in the two loops. The reader may notice the similarity between this circuit and the differential amplifier discussed in the EMG section.

The user adjusts the variable conductance (calibrated potentiometer) so that the meter balances at its zero point. This means that current through the loops is equal. This, in turn, means that the micromho value set on the control equals the person's SCL. Now suppose an SCR comes along. Skin conductance increases, but the calibrated control remains at the same position (at a value that equals the previous SCL). Because skin conductance has just increased over the previous level, current flow through the loops is unequal, and the meter deflects to the right. SCR magnitude is proportional to the meter deflection. The needle

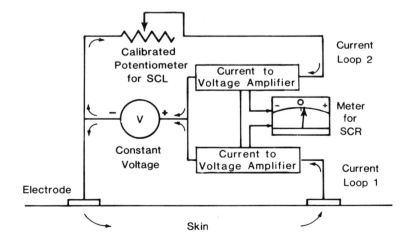

FIGURE 4.34. Skin conductance device with movable viewing window.

points to the percent increase above the SCL shown on the calibrated control. As recovery from the SCR takes place, the needle moves back toward its center balance point, where loop currents are equal.

This is how the viewing window is electrically moved along the SCA continuum to accomodate any person's baseline SCL. Changing window width is accomplished electrically by changing the "gain" or sensitivity of the current-to-voltage amplifiers so that a given difference in loop current leads to greater or lesser meter deflections. This is why the window width switch is usually called a "sensitivity" control, though "resolution" would be a better term for it. Audio feedback follows SCR, shifting along with the viewing window.

Self-Adjusting Baseline

The previous illustration is a classic design. But filtering or smoothing can be used to minimize the need to manually readjust the position of the viewing window as SCA drifts to a much different baseline SCL. (To review smoothing and filtering, refer back to the EMG section.)

To make a self-adjusting baseline, the SCL is filtered (smoothed over time). Any SCRs are also smoothed into this average level. The smoothed average is displayed as SCL on a digital meter. This SCL baseline anchors SCR percentages displayed on an analog meter. As the person's baseline changes or drifts, the filtered baseline reading gradually moves toward the new level, in effect, slowly moving the viewing window along after a drifting SCL. This circuit, in effect, adjusts an internal baseline control.

If SCL suddenly changes, as when a new person is attached, the user pushes a "reset" button to instantly readjust the instrument to the new SCL. This eliminates the need to wait for the filter to gradually "catch up" to a new person's SCL. The self-adjusting system has the convenience of virtually eliminating manual readjustment of the baseline, but it does not keep track of or "remember" the initial starting baseline as does a manual control.

Electrical Operation of a Filtered Self-Adjusting Baseline

Figure 4.35 illustrates the familiar current loop through the skin, but the output of the current amplifier goes to a filter with a long response time, so that SCRs are smoothed out. That is, the output of the filter is a slow-changing level proportional to the average SCA over the preceding period of time (e.g., 60 seconds). This slow-changing output is considered the baseline or SCL and displayed on a digital meter. The level at the *output* of the filter differs from the nonfiltered signal at the *input* of the filter. Since SCRs are "averaged out" in the former but left unchanged in the latter, the difference between these two signals reflects SCRs over a slowly self-adjusting baseline. An analog meter is connected between these two points for viewing SCRs. A "reset" button allows the filter to "catch up" instantly to a new baseline. This quickly establishes the starting SCL at the beginning of a session.

With self-adjusting baseline design, the choice of filter response time affects the SCL reading (and to a lesser extent, the SCR readings and the audio tone as well). Since there is no standardized filter response time, this introduces what amounts to a more or less arbitrary variation in the speed of self-adjustment. Very long filter response times make the baseline catch up to the present reading very slowly, hence approximate the performance of the manual baseline control design discussed earlier. This minimizes the effect of filtering on the readings but leads to more frequent manual readjustment (with the "reset" button). On the other hand, shorter filter response times minimize baseline resetting because

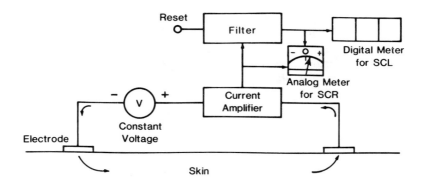

FIGURE 4.35. Filtering scheme for self-adjusting baseline.

the baseline catches up more quickly with the actual SCL. But the baseline changes more quickly and is artificially responsive to large or long-lasting SCRs.

To summarize, short filter response times lead to quicker adaptation of the instrument to a new baseline, but they also lead to gradually changing SCL readings attributable to filter response time as well as to actual SCA phenomenon. On the other hand, long response times minimize this effect, but they may not adjust to new baselines quickly enough to avoid resetting.

Simple SCR Devices

Simple SCR devices use a manual, noncalibrated (or roughly calibrated) baseline adjustment and feed back SCR with an audio tone or noncalibrated meter scale. These devices quantify neither SCL nor SCR and are more susceptible to artifact than full-sized instruments. Even so, they provide very interesting and useful information to a person about patterns of SCR.

For example, the rise and fall of an audio tone communicates a great deal about the person's responsivity in actual situations, even when quantified SCL or SCR is absent. These devices have distinct advantages when it comes to ambulatory use in real life. Pocket-sized miniaturization, dry finger electrodes, and an earplug for private feedback permit a person to conveniently wear the unit while walking, talking, driving, phoning, writing, thinking, reading, or carrying out other real activities. This provides insight into patterns of responsivity in active situations not obtainable in the clinic setting. It is a very good way for a person to discover his or her own patterns of responsivity. In any application, the therapist involved must provide adequate instruction in the use and limitations of the device and in the interpretation of results.

Artifact

There are many ways to process and display SCA, and there is no firm consensus on the most appropriate way to do it. However, the most common method is probably the one shown in Figure 4.34, with a manual calibrated baseline control and an analog zero center meter for SCR. Simple SCR devices certainly have a useful place in clinical biofeedback, even though quantitative measurements are usually not possible. The following points about artifact are important for all SCA devices.

Electrode Size. Different-sized electrodes lead to different readings. A larger electrode covers more skin and therefore places more sweat glands in the previously described current loop. This leads to a higher SCL than does a smaller electrode that places fewer sweat glands in the loop. Therefore, electrode size must be standardized in order to assure comparability of readings, particularly for quantified SCL.

Movement. Because electrode size affects SCA, anything that alters the effective contact area of an electrode also alters SCA. Finger or hand movement causes variations in contact pressure. The electrode may lift slightly and diminish the contact area. The electrode may press harder against the skin, thereby increasing the contact area. These effects are more pronounced for dry electrodes than for precious-metal electrodes with electrode gel. The practitioner should encourage the monitored person to minimize hand movements and arrange the electrodes and cables so that a reasonably stable position can be maintained. When hand movement cannot be avoided (e.g., in a study of a motor task requiring movement of both hands), corresponding sites on the toes could be used. This requires the development of separate norms for SCL and SCR. Fortunately, movement artifact is usually easy to spot, because the resultant patterns are often abrupt and uncharacteristic of true SCA patterns, and because movement can usually be observed.

Skin Condition. Skin condition can affect conductance readings. For example, if a person has a skin abrasion or a fresh cut through the high-resistance skin surface, a high-conductance path may be established from the electrode to deeper layers of the skin, and lead to an increased SCL. If a person has developed a callus, the high-resistance surface layer increases in thickness and dryness, leading to a much lower SCL and diminished SCR amplitude.

Venables and Christie (1980) note that SCL falls markedly after washing with soap and water, as residual salt is removed. Because salt builds up over time since the last wash, they recommend that persons begin sessions with freshly washed hands. It is not clear how important this is to clinical biofeedback, but it is clear that this standardizing procedure is not universally followed.

Room Temperature. There is some evidence (Venables & Christie, 1980) that SCA is affected when individuals feel cold, and that warmer-than-usual office conditions appear to produce what they call more "normal" responsivity. It is also plausible that the temperature-regulating function of sweating in an overly warm room would lead to increases in SCL that are not psychophysiologically significant.

Electrode Polarization Potentials and Electrode Design. The exosomatic method involves the passage of current through the skin via surface electrodes. Polarization potentials develop at the skin–electrode interface as DC current passes, and the polarization effect builds up over time. The size of polarization potential is variable and unknown.

When polarized, the skin–electrode interface is like a tiny battery charged by the passing current. Polarization voltage is thereby added to (or subtracted from) the constant voltage applied by the instrument. Because the polarization potential (voltage) is variable, the voltage in the current loop is no longer constant. Therefore, what appear to be changes in SCL may be due, in part, to variable electrode polarization potentials. Skin conductance level drift due to the buildup of polarization potential causes artifact, but it is not clear how practically significant it is. For this reason, silver/silver chloride electrodes have been used. These electrodes develop minimal polarization potentials and therefore add minimal polarization artifact, but they are more expensive and less convenient than dry electrodes. The gel used with silver/

silver chloride electrodes may prolong the recovery phase of SCRs. A similar prolongation may occur in very humid climates even when dry electrodes are used. Artifactual prolongation of SCR recovery could lead to results mistakenly interpreted as "stairstepping."

Dry electrodes are often secured by Velcro straps that conveniently adjust to different finger sizes. They are made from various materials, including lead, zinc, chrome, stainless steel, gold, or silver-coated fuzz. They are simpler, cheaper, and more convenient than silver/silver chloride electrodes, especially in clinical practice. However, they suffer from polarization potentials to various degrees. For this reason, alternative instrument designs have been evolved to get around the effects of polarization potentials.

The most obvious of these alternatives is to use an AC voltage source rather than the DC voltage source described earlier. Using AC in the current loop helps in two ways. First, the constantly reversing polarity of AC first charges and then discharges the electrode-skin interface "battery," thus reducing the buildup of polarization voltage. Second, whatever remaining polarization voltage exists is blocked by capacitors in the current loop. Capacitors permit only the AC current to pass. This scheme is illustrated in Figure 4.36.

As suggested by its electronic symbol, a capacitor is an electronic component with conductive plates separated by an insulating membrane. Alternating attraction and repulsion of charges across the insulating membrane permits AC current to pass through a capacitor. No current actually flows through the membrane. This is illustrated by analogy. Imagine a fluid-filled cylinder fitted with an elastic diaphragm in the middle and an opening at each end (Figure 4.37). If the fluid pressure at opening A is greater than at B, then fluid flows into the cylinder at A and bulges the membrane, forcing fluid out through opening B. If the pressure diminishes, the membrane begins to move back to its original position as fluid returns to the cylinder through opening B and the same amount of fluid leaves through opening A. If pressure at A continues to drop, then more fluid leaves through opening A; the membrane bulges to the left, drawing fluid into the cylinder through opening B. So long as there is a cycle of pressure changes at A, then there will be a corresponding cycle of changes at B. This is analogous to how a capacitor passes AC.

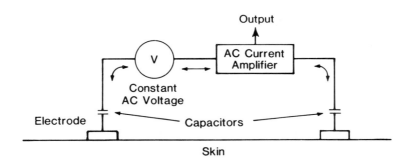

FIGURE 4.36. AC current loop with DC-blocking capacitors.

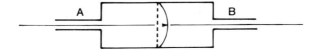

FIGURE 4.37. Fluid analogy to the capacitor.

However, suppose that a modest unchanging pressure is introduced at A. The membrane bulges a little and then stops. There is fluid flow from A only while the pressure is building and the membrane is in motion. After it stops in a bulged position, no more fluid moves at B. This is analogous to how a capacitor blocks DC.

This analogy shows how a capacitor blocks small residual DC polarization potentials in an AC loop while passing the AC unrestricted. This does remove polarization potential artifact. However, it generates another kind of artifact, which is probably more of a problem. It turns out that the skin itself forms a capacitor. Although this fact is of no consequence when one is using a constant DC voltage, as in the designs described earlier, it does become a significant factor when using AC. Figure 4.38 shows the location of this natural capacitor.

Skin capacitance forms a second "reactive" pathway for AC in the loop. If AC is applied to the skin, a portion of the current flows as usual through the diminished resistance of the activated sweat glands. But some additional current flows through the skin capacitance. This means that total current flow is greater, and the readings show greater SCL. This effect can be quite pronounced and cannot be neglected. Note that an AC measurement in which skin capacitance contributes to the reading should be called "skin impedance" (analogous to resistance) or "skin admittance" (analogous to conductance).

To make matters worse, impedance or admittance varies with the frequency of the AC, because higher frequencies pass through a capacitor more easily than lower frequencies. The reader need not worry because there are still other ways to minimize polarization artifact without generating capacitance artifacts. Explanation of these sophisticated systems is beyond the scope of this chapter. Such systems are commercially available and minimize these artifacts even when using simple dry electrodes. A wise buyer who is very concerned about repeatable quantified SCL data inquires about how these artifacts are handled when considering purchase of specific instruments. As for the miniature SCR devices described earlier, their lack of quantification makes polarization artifact much less relevant than for instruments capable of quantification. Skin capacitance artifact is generally not an issue with the miniature devices, because they almost always use simple DC loops.

Safety

Electrical safety precautions for SCA devices are the same as for EMG devices. Both are electrically connected to the person via electrodes, and therefore the same stringent stan-

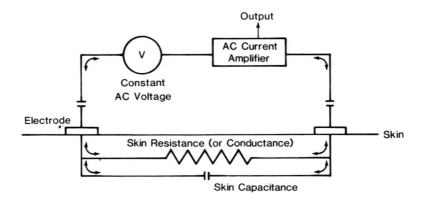

FIGURE 4.38. AC current loop and skin capacitance.

dards for design, manufacture, installation, and maintenance should be followed for SCA and EMG devices, and the entire installation of which any of these instruments is a part.

The passage of DC from an electrode to the skin over a prolonged time leads to the formation of chemical by-products on the skin if the voltage drop across the skin exceeds about 3 DC volts. This effect is normally negligible, but if the current passed is high enough and is passed long enough, then skin irritation could develop. This effect is unlikely to occur in modern skin conductance instruments, but very old units, those that are made as novelties or toys, or those that have developed leakage currents might be more likely to create this effect. As a rule of thumb, any device that passes 10 microamperes or less current per square centimeter of electrode area in its current loop and applies less than 3 DC volts to the skin will not lead to the accumulation of irritating chemicals on the skin, even with prolonged use.

ACKNOWLEDGMENTS

My thanks go to Wallace A. Peek, the late Roland E. Mohr, and John B. Picchiottino, who have acted so generously as my engineering mentors. I give special thanks to John B. Picchiottino, whose suggestions for this manuscript carry forward a long and much-appreciated history of helpfulness with biofeedback projects. Thanks must also go to Mark S. Schwartz, without whose enthusiasm this writing would doubtless have remained on my list of things to do someday.

REFERENCES

Brown, B. (1974). *New mind, new body: New directions for the mind*. New York: Harper & Row.

Jennings, J. R., Tahmoush, A. J., & Redmond, D. D. (1980). Non-invasive measurement of peripheral vascular activity. In I. Martin & P. H. Venables (Eds.), *Techniques in psychophysiology* (pp. 70–131). New York: Wiley.

Mathieu, P. A., & Sullivan, S. J. (1990). Frequency characteristics of signals and instrumentation: Implication for EMG biofeedback studies. *Biofeedback and Self-regulation, 15*(4).

Neumann, E., & Blanton, R. (1970). The early history of electrodermal research. *Psychophysiology, 8*(4), 463–474.

Toomin, M., & Toomin, H. (1975, February). *Psychological dynamic correlates of the paradoxically invariant of the GSR*. Paper presented at the Fifth Annual Convention of the Biofeedback Research Society, Monterey, CA.

Venables, P. H., & Christie, M. J. (1980). Electrodermal activity. In I. Martin & P. H. Venables (Eds.), *Techniques in psychophysiology* (pp. 3–67). New York: Wiley.

5

Computers in Biofeedback: Megabyte Is Not a Dental Problem

Jack C. Hartje

I am on a boat in the middle of the Caribbean Sea. I am sitting in a lounge chair with a 6.8-pound notebook computer in my lap. It is an IBM clone with a 486SX microprocessor. It runs at a clock speed of 66 megahertz. It has a 240-megabyte hard disc. The floppy drive uses a 3.5-inch disc formatted for 1.44 megabytes of information. It has two megabytes of random access memory. It has a video graphics adaptor (VGA) card and can interface with an external 0.29 dot-pitch VGA monitor. I can send a draft of this chapter to Dr. Schwartz with an internal 2400-baud modem. The NiCad battery will last for 2.5 hours. The crew will serve another meal in 45 minutes.

Which of the above statements did you understand? If the clearest sentence discussed the next meal, then this chapter is clearly for you. You could also benefit from this chapter if you already have a computer-based system that is not meeting your needs or if you do not have one and are considering the investment. This chapter reviews computer makes, types of microprocessors, memory considerations, monitors, printers, and other topics that combine to determine whether a particular system is suited for biofeedback. Since price is almost always a factor, the chapter gives several "packages" representing different levels of investments.

THE PROS OF COMPUTERS IN BIOFEEDBACK

Feedback Display

Imagine that you are a patient or client starting therapy with biofeedback. You might be a student learning to use biofeedback with yourself and others. Your therapist or instructor gives you a choice. You may listen to a tone and watch meters for several sessions over several weeks. The other option is to select among many different displays (e.g., 50) on a color computer monitor with many color options (e.g., 256) and perhaps to use simple video games as you learn to develop self-regulation skills to manage your migraine headaches. Let us see . . . which would you choose?

One advantage of computer-based feedback is the versatility of the displays. Although adequate research is still lacking, many practitioners and educators believe that these displays are more informative and motivating for patients and therapists. This variety of displays should be carefully reviewed prior to selection of a system. Some of these displays are in the form of video games that may add to learner motivation. Imagine playing a game with your heart rate instead of a keyboard or joystick! Some professionals believe that biofeedback works because it adds information for the patient or client, and the therapist. To the degree this is valid, then computer-based visual displays are more useful than audio feedback because they convey more information.

Data Storage and Analyses

Do you want to record your data by hand or would you prefer to automate that task? Would you like instant graphs and data analysis? Does the ability to show patients their progress data across sessions sound like it would help you be a better therapist? Computers easily handle all these tasks.

Public Presentations and Continuing Education Presentations

Do you give talks to professional and lay audiences? Demonstrating biofeedback to groups is easier and more informative with computer-based biofeedback. It permits examples and demonstrations of what is possible with biofeedback.

Focusing on the Patient

You may believe that computer-based biofeedback makes the therapy process more difficult. That is not true. Without a computer, you will often be manually adjusting the instruments. There are times when you focus most of your attention on operating the instruments instead of the patient or subject. A computer helps free the therapist to do what you should do—observe, teach, and treat. The computer can display instructions to you and/or the patient as you progress through training stages.

Statistical Analyses

Do you conduct research? Elaborate statistical data analyses require only a few keystrokes after proper programming. A variety of graphs, including three-dimensional graphs, depict data to identify patterns and trends more easily.

Communications to Other Professionals

Would you like to send data to another professional? This is easy with a modem. You can use a modem to send patient information and data to another therapist such as a supervisor; however, proper confidentiality must be insured.

Video Disc Images

Does the notion of incorporating images from a video disc into the feedback display interest you? Consider the potential motivating effects of incorporating real pictures into a display. The patient or client can play realistic games by self-regulating his physiology. Imagine, for example, presenting a display to a headache patient that shows a picture of a throbbing head. As the patient learns to self-regulate, the throbbing noticeably decreases. A patient suffering from right arm paresis could watch a visual image of a person gradually moving his right arm as the patient gains success at movement. The possibilities are endless, and this software is all currently available.

THE CONS OF COMPUTERS FOR BIOFEEDBACK

Are you "computer phobic?" Do you fear that the wrong keystroke will ruin something in the computer? If so, computers may not be for you, or you might need help learning about them and becoming more comfortable. Many professionals are uncomfortable with computers. However, many can learn to be more comfortable with them.

Is your main priority *cost*? If so, you can get noncomputer-based instruments for less cost. The field of biofeedback developed without computer-based instruments. Many practitioners and researchers successfully used noncomputer, free-standing, systems for many years before computer-based systems were available. There is much that you can do with such instruments until you can afford, justify, and become skilled and comfortable with a computer-based system.

Do you need to *move your instruments often*? It is often easier to move free-standing instruments than a computer, monitor, and biofeedback interface. However, laptop and notebook-sized computers that fit in your briefcase are easy to transport. One can use the built-in monitor or attach the smaller computer to a larger monitor.

Do you use only one or two channels of temperature and one channel of electrodermal (ED) feedback? Do you use only two channels of electromyography (EMG)? For example, do you limit your applications to treating Raynaud's disease? Do you limit your use of biofeedback to ED during psychotherapy? Do you focus on muscle strengthening of one agonist muscle and relaxation of one antagonist muscle? If so, then free-standing instruments might well suffice. There *are* advantages for using a computer-based system in these examples. However, one can successfully use free-standing instruments for limited applications.

COMPUTER HARDWARE
OR WHAT YOU CAN TOUCH

Dedicated versus Nondedicated Systems

A dedicated computer-based biofeedback system is one that a therapist can use for biofeedback only. It is "dedicated" to this one function. A "nondedicated" system is usable for any purposes for which a computer is capable. For example, practitioners use nondedicated systems for word processing, scoring psychological measures, and billing. One early decision for the practitioner is deciding between these two options.

The argument presented by companies selling dedicated systems is usually their ease of use. Each button has a function directly related to biofeedback. This reduces the number of buttons (or keys) and makes the instrument more user friendly. Nondedicated systems usually rely on an existing computer system, such as the IBM family or clones.

Attend a national, regional, or large state professional biofeedback meeting where you can operate each type of system. The ease of operation for the nondedicated systems is usually a function of the software. Some software systems are not particularly user friendly, but some are very easy to operate. Some practitioners experienced with both types of systems believe that the easy nondedicated systems can be more user friendly than the dedicated systems.

IBM and IBM-Compatible versus Apple

If you choose to invest in a nondedicated system, then which computer is best? The answer is that there is no *best*. There is only that which best meets *your* needs. If you plan to use the computer for nonbiofeedback purposes primarily related to business goals, then IBM and compatibles allow the widest selection of software. It would be the choice. The IBM compatibles offer the advantages of IBM but usually at lower prices. However, if you are interested in desktop publishing or want the ease of use of the Apple system, then consider an Apple Mac, although it may be more expensive. However, there are still significant limits for biofeedback software. The most popular computer for biofeedback systems is the IBM or its compatibles.

CPU, Clock Speed, RAM, BIOS . . . ?

What are the critical specifications of the computer you plan to use for biofeedback? The answer is whatever specifications your selected software requires. Do *not* make the common mistake of first investing in the computer and then searching for software. It is best to invest in a system that includes the correct computer, internal components, monitor, and printer. Consider getting someone who knows computers and biofeedback to help you coordinate the hardware and software needs to insure proper operation. The next section gives some helpful information.

The central processing unit, or CPU, is the heart of the computer. There are older IBM-XT versions with a 8088 CPU chip which are still available at very cheap prices. Do not buy one. They are very slow compared to later versions and have serious limitations for biofeedback. The next version of the CPU, the 80286, commonly referred to by the last three numbers (286), first appeared in the IBM-AT in 1984. This was the most popular computer for biofeedback systems for many years. It still is acceptable for biofeedback software from only a few years ago and an option for getting started, especially if cost is a major concern. However, it is relatively slow for other purposes compared to newer computers of the last few years.

However, there are advantages to the faster 386 and very recent software developments that require the most powerful of the the 486 CPUs (486DX266) to use the latest and most sophisticated software. You probably do not need a 486 unless you are considering the latest software. Before buying a 486, be sure that it meets all the requirements of the latest software.

Clock speed refers to how fast the computer can process information. If the computer is too slow, the biofeedback display will be in short abrupt movements instead of being smooth. The minimum clock speed recommended by biofeedback software developers for past versions of the software is 12 megahertz. That is the fastest speed of the 286 CPU without a special modification. Sixteen megahertz is better and 20 megahertz is even better. The latest software recommends 66 megahertz. The faster clock speed affects all biofeedback operations, including updating the visual displays, accessing the hard disc, retrieving and saving data, printing, and statistical calculations.

Adding a math coprocessor can enhance the overall operating speed for procedures requiring calculations. A math coprocessor is an additional piece of hardware (a "chip") that fits into a socket in the computer. This significantly improves the speed of operation for software applications requiring many calculations. An example is fast Fourier transformations (FFT) analysis in electroencephalographic (EEG) feedback. The latest biofeedback software requires a math coprocessor. There are very rapid screen updates, complex graphics, and rapid calculations that underlie EEG and EMG feedback displays.

Speed also is a function of the "wait state." This is an index of how long it takes for the computer to route information from various sources to the CPU for processing. All else being equal, (as it never is!), a "zero wait state" is desirable. The speed of the hard drive finding information also affects the overall speed of the software. One measures this speed in milliseconds. Fewer is better. A typical range is 12 to 28 milliseconds. With larger numbers, you wait longer as the computer searches for information stored on the hard drive.

You pay a lot more as you approach 12 milliseconds. As the capacity or size of the hard drive increases, you must also increase the access speed to avoid irritatingly long delays.

Random access memory (RAM) refers to the memory used to process information; RAM is only used while the computer is operating. Do not confuse this with the memory used to permanently *store* information. When the computer is off, everything in RAM disappears. The units of RAM capacity are kilobytes (KB) or thousands of bytes. The minimum needed for biofeedback software is 640 KB. Find out how much RAM the software requires *before* you purchase any software. Be sure your computer has enough. The cost of adding RAM is low, so get at least 2 megabytes (MB) or million bytes. Capacity of 4 MB is better, and 8 MB is best but not usually needed. Remember, everything on the screen needs memory.

Some software systems provide a menu of programs from which to select what you want to do. This is the shell. It uses memory even when you do not see it. With 640 KB of RAM, it is not possible to use a shell menu and still operate one of the popular muscle-scanning programs. As software becomes more user-friendly, memory resident space gets very crowded. There is a definite movement in biofeedback software toward user-friendly software, so programs will need more RAM. In addition to the 640 KB of RAM, there is more temporary memory available for software that can use it. This is "extended memory" and often used by programs called "memory resident" programs. The advantage is that anything stored in an extended memory location does not use your precious 640 KB of RAM. For example, some biofeedback programs store all information related to printing in extended memory. Incidentally, if your computer ever freezes during operation and ignores your keyboard input, it may be because you have used up all your RAM.

A Port with No Ships?

Computers must have a way, or ways, to communicate with other devices—the world outside the computer. These devices connect by cables to special receptacles called *ports* into which you plug the cables. A keyboard is one way to communicate with a computer. The keyboard cable connects to one of the ports. Biofeedback instruments and printers need two other ports to connect to the computer. The printer port is a *parallel* port. Another designation for this is line printer 1 (LPTI). Parallel means that it permits sending information in two directions at the same time. The printer tells the computer when it is ready to receive information, and the computer sends the information. Virtually all computers have at least one parallel port, but ask anyway.

Biofeedback instruments most commonly connect to a serial port. A serial port sends or receives information in one direction at a time. Not all computers have a serial port, so be sure to ask. Other names for a serial port are "com port" or an "RS-232 port." Here, com stands for communication. Its designation may be com1, com2, etc., depending upon how many com ports you have. The term RS-232 is not in common use, but I include it for the reader's information. If you use an external mouse (a pointer device) *and* a modem *and* a biofeedback instrument that requires a serial port, then you will need three ports. Some new biofeedback software is mouse-driven, and you should, therefore, get the number of required ports.

The speed of transfer through the port is important and the index of speed is the baud rate. A relatively slow com port transfers information at 1200 baud. A fast com port operates at 9600 baud and is better for biofeedback.

This port may be a 9-pin or a 25-pin port. The cable between the biofeedback device and this port must have the matching number of pins (or holes). There are cable adapters that allow a 25-pin cable to connect to 9-pin port.

VIDEO

The most common way to get information out of the computer is through a monitor, or cathode ray tube (CRT). Laptop- and notebook-sized computers use liquid crystal display (LCD) or gas displays to save space. The CRT resembles a television set except the computer generates the signal inside your computer with the help of a video board.

A video board is a circuit board that determines the quality of the display that is available to the monitor. One must therefore match the quality of the video board with the quality of the monitor. Here is a sample description of a very good video board, "16 bit, color, super VGA video card with 1 MB [megabyte] of VRAM." This means that various lines of resolution are available (640 × 480, 800 × 600, and 1024 × 768). These choices allow you to match your monitor and software capabilities to the video card. With the right software, monitor, and video card, you can display up to 32,000 different colors! As biofeedback software advances, the displays are becoming much more realistic, and proper shading and hues are part of the reality. The megabytes of volatile random access memory (VRAM) translate into speed. Graphs appear very quickly if the memory is on the video card instead of in the circuity of the computer. The three major considerations are: (1) lines of resolution, (2) type of display, and (3) dot pitch.

Lines of Resolution

"Lines of resolution" refers to the screen image that is being made with horizontal lines. (Although the image does not appear that way, it is made by lines). More lines mean better resolution and sharper images. As noted above, 1024 × 768 represents high resolution. Low resolution would be 640 × 480. Be sure that you match the monitor you select with the lines of resolution generated by the video card. Read the specifications of the monitor you are considering and of the video card. High resolution requires *both* a high-resolution video card *and* a high-resolution monitor with matching lines of resolution. The choices depend upon the next consideration, type of display.

Displays

There are four basic types of display—monochrome and three color graphics: color graphics adaptor (CGA), enhanced graphics adaptor (EGA), and video graphics array (VGA). Get VGA, although EGA is acceptable. The least expensive is monochrome. These monitors do not display color but are fine for many applications, such as word processing. They are not for most biofeedback applications. One might use a monochrome notebook with 64 shades of gray if the notebook computer output is linked to a separate color monitor. Monochrome displays compromise the quality of the displays.

A color display is more interesting, and the colors make it easier to discriminate among different display features. One type of color monitor is the CGA. These older monitors can only display up to four colors and with poor resolution. Much better monitors are available for only a little more expense, so do not consider CGA for biofeedback.

The third type of monitor to consider is EGA. These monitors can display 16 colors with very good resolution. They are acceptable for biofeedback, but not ideal. Higher quality monitors are the same price; so get the best.

The next type of monitor to consider is the VGA. The VGA monitors can display 16 colors with high resolution. This is the minimum you want. You must have a VGA video card to use a VGA monitor. There are differences among VGA monitors. Some of them are super VGA, permitting 256 colors and much finer resolution. This relates to our final variable, "dot pitch."

Dot Pitch

A computer image is made from thousands of tiny colored dots called "pixels." Resolution or image crispness increases with reduced space between the dots. This relates to eye strain, and it is why I suggest a low dot pitch such as 0.28. This means the dots are 28/100th of a millimeter apart. The difference is very similar to the difference between a 9-pin dot-matrix printout and a 24-pin letter-quality printout. The dots that make up the letters on the paper are evident with the 9-pin printout. The dots virtually disappear with a 24-pin printout.

PRICE

Price is, of course, an important consideration. However, this should not be the main priority. You should make a decision based on the comparison of specifications to price. Thus, invest in the system that has the best specifications for the cost. Ask those who have been in the field for a while what they prefer. If you are planning to attend a training program, wait until after the training to make your investment. This gives you a chance to learn how to read specifications before you make your selection. Here are sample systems with price estimates.

1. $6000. An IBM clone 486 computer with VGA monitor operating with 0.28 dot pitch combined with a 1024 × 768 video card and 80-MB hard disc. The package uses a 9-pin dot-matrix printer. The biofeedback interface includes two channels of EMG, and one each for TEMP and ED feedback. This system improves the video display but retains limited biofeedback capabilities and will not be adequate for future software developments. The software includes 20 or more displays, video games, on-screen instructions, and statistical analyses of data. This system has limited computer and printer capabilities.

2. $8000. The same system as number 1 except the computer is an IBM clone 486 with more RAM (4 MB) and a 250-MB hard disc. It also has muscle-scanning software along with a muscle-scanning device. The package includes a 24-pin dot-matrix printer. This is a good system and would serve most biofeedback settings well. However, it lacks some modalities of feedback and channels necessary in some applications.

3. $10,000. The same system as number 2 except the biofeedback interface includes respiration, heart rate, and EEG feedback. The upgraded software allows these additional modalities. The printer is color. This is an excellent system that will meet current and future needs for many practitioners. Consider two additional EMG channels.

SOFTWARE

You are looking for *user-friendly* software. Typically, user-friendly software lessens the need for you to memorize a list of commands. It also reduces the need to refer frequently to a manual to remind you of what to do. User-friendly software has pull-down menus. I know. What are pull down menus? If you use the newer and popular word processors you know about both user-friendly and pull-down menus. For those of you who do not know, imagine a row of key words across the top of your screen such as "File" and

"Options." By selecting a particular key word, you open a menu of choices on your screen. In the case of the keyword "File," the choices might be "Load" a new file, "Save" the file you are working on, or "Exit" the software. In a biofeedback context, example keywords allow for selection of displays or setting news thresholds. You do not have to remember a lot of commands. You simply choose from the choices contained in each menu.

Another software consideration is *versatility*. Some biofeedback programs allow very few feedback displays and have very limited printing options. Others do not allow programming sequences of training. Still others do not permit making changes to the current feedback screen without leaving the feedback and going to another screen. For these reasons, make every effort to try the software before purchasing. Attend workshops or attend the Annual Meeting of the Association of Applied Psychophysiology and Biofeedback (AAPB). Nearly all vendors of biofeedback hardware and software are there. If these suggestions are not feasible for you, at least contact several users of the software and hardware you are considering.

The software you select should allow for recording and displaying several feedback modalities. Sometimes you will want or need to monitor six, eight, or more channels simultaneously. Be sure your software allows this so you have the option available to you.

Use a reliable vendor available for your questions. Ask professionals who have had experience with computer-based biofeedback about the reputation of vendors you are considering. Are phone calls returned promptly? Does the vendor have clinical skills? How long has the company been in existence? Does it sell several different systems?

CONCLUSION

I have reviewed major considerations in selecting a computer and software for biofeedback. Unlike many other products, computers have dramatically improved while their cost has dropped. They are now standard in many biofeedback offices, and this trend will undoubtedly continue with further improvements in hardware and software. I hope this chapter helps you to make a wise choice among the confusing options. However, remember that the most important element in successful biofeedback is not the computer or the software, it is the *therapist*. With a good computer-based biofeedback system, many therapists can be better therapists with the added information available. Remember that even computers are not perfect, not perfect, not perfect!

III

OFFICE ASSESSMENT AND COMPLIANCE

6

Intake Decisions and Preparations of Patients for Therapy

Mark S. Schwartz

This chapter discusses intake decisions and the preparation of patients for therapy. It begins with considerations and guidelines for making decisions about the selection of patients and the planning of appropriate interventions. It continues with discussions of both the importance of tailoring therapy goals and the cognitive preparation of patients, or patient education. Additional sections focus on interviewing, history taking, and selected self-report measures.

One basic intake decision in the therapeutic setting is whether or not to use biofeedback with a specific patient. This is particularly relevant when existing publications regarding the use of biofeedback for specific symptoms and disorders are very limited, or when research results are unclear or equivocal. Professional opinions vary about this decision due to differences among professionals, circumstances, disorders, and types of treatments available. This chapter discusses many factors in the decision-making process.

Practitioners can benefit from being aware of the information and guidelines set forth in this chapter before and during assessment interviewing. Although the selection of topics is not exhaustive, it is sufficient for many of the situations the practitioner is likely to encounter. For more intake information and considerations about specific disorders discussed in this book, the reader is referred to specific chapters (especially to Chapters 7, 14, and 15 on baselines and headache).

DISORDERS

Arriving at a list of disorders for which biofeedback and other applied psychophysiological treatments are appropriate is not an easy task. One must consider both the individual to be treated and the specific features and stage of the disorder. There are many practical considerations including the accuracy of the diagnosis. Prudent practitioners first consider the published literature and current clinical practice.

Published Literature and Current Clinical Practice

Good research is one cornerstone of clinical practice and a basis for deciding which disorders, symptoms, and patients to treat. One must therefore read many journals and books and attend professional meetings. However, research often does not capture the essence of clinical applications, and good research is lacking for many disorders. Therefore, practitioners need not rigidly require ideal research support. One need not wait for well-controlled research to support all procedures and applications before using biofeedback and associated therapies. However, practitioners need to base decisions on logical and responsible criteria. Other considerations become more important when we lack adequate research.

Prudent professionals know their limitations. They can also recognize the limits of others' experience and the limitations of published research. As practitioners, we must guard against the problem of "not knowing what we do not know." Each of us should place ourselves in the role of the patient and even a third-party payer: "Suppose I were the patient." "Suppose someone asked me to pay for the treatment of someone." "What questions would I ask?" "What compromises and accommodations would I ask for and regard as proper?" Prudent practitioners consider several sources of data.

Disorder Lists

Agreement on a list of disorders is a formidable task especially considering the diversity of health care professionals and issues and constraints among third-party payers. Complete agreement is unlikely among practitioners who endorse and use biofeedback. However, one must keep this in perspective. In this way biofeedback procedures do not differ from many diagnostic procedures and treatments that are common practice for many medical disorders. Whether or not a disorder is on an indication list depends on many factors. These include the diagnostic criteria, the individual patient, and the degree of caution exercised. Practitioners consider many sources when selecting disorders and patients for whom to recommend treatment.

I was very tempted to avoid presenting any lists of disorders. Doing so is subjective, somewhat arbitrary, subject to criticism, and the lists themselves can soon become obsolete. However, I offer the lists in Table 6.1 as examples and guidelines. The three columns and ratings convey degrees of confidence in the current literature and clinical practice. Readers will note differences from the lists in documents published by the Association for Applied Psychophysiology and Biofeedback (AAPB) (Shellenberger, Amar, Schneider, & Steward, 1989; Applications Standards Committee for AAPB, 1992). The differences result from perspective, emphasis, criteria, and opinion.

One need not consider the present lists as indisputable anymore so than one considers other lists as irrefutable. These lists reflect the perspectives of authors and committees at a given time. They are merely guidelines and are not etched in granite. Mindful practitioners never automatically accept or reject for treatment all or most patients with a disorder on any list.

Disorders on the A list are those for which there is the most confidence. Research about these is usually the best and most abundant. Agreement among practitioners and researchers is probably easier to get for these disorders. It is the "best" list by these criteria. Inclusion in the lists does not imply that biofeedback alone is always the treatment of choice or the sole or primary treatment. Exceptions are Raynaud's disease and nocturnal enuresis for which forms of biofeedback can be the primary or sole treatment.

The B list disorders enjoy research support, although the number of studies and/or the methodologies are less than for those on the A list. Forms of biofeedback are often a legitimate part of a treatment plan for these disorders. However, other treatments usually play a larger role than for those disorders in the A list.

TABLE 6.1. Selected Disorders for Which Practitioners Can Consider Using Biofeedback

A: Best	B: Good	C: Maybe
Tension-type headache	Insomnia, psychophysiological (–)	Writer's cramp (+)
Migraine headache	Anxiety disorders	Esophageal spasm
Raynaud's disease	Chronic pain (±)	Occupational cramps (musician)
Fecal incontinence	ADD/ADHD (–)	Blepharospasm
Urinary incontinence	Seizures (few)	Hyperhidrosis
Essential hypertension	Nausea/vomiting, functional	Dysmenorrhea
Nocturnal enuresis	Irritable bowel syndrome (–)	Visual disorders (–)
Dyschezia (anismus) (pelvic floor outlet obstruction syndrome)	Motion sickness (–)	Some dermatologic disorders
	Asthma (±)	Diabetes mellitus (+)
	Bruxism and TMD (+)	Fibromyalgia (+)
	Tinnitus (associated symptoms)	Posture training (+) idiopathic scoliosis
	Phantom limb pain	Menopause hot flashes
	Raynaud's, secondary	Functional voice D/Os (hyperfunctional dysphonia)

The disorders on the C list are promising and enjoy single or multiple case studies.[1] Many readers recognize that there are other disorders that could appear on this list.

One also can include disorders for which relaxation and other applied psychophysiological techniques are effective, and one uses biofeedback instruments to get a more complete assessment. Biofeedback can help some of these patients change their beliefs about themselves, including their self-confidence about making changes. For some patients, biofeedback helps improve their self-regulation. Instrumentation also allows practitioners to assess and document progress. For example, relaxation is often useful for anticipatory nausea and vomiting associated with chemotherapy and for other functional nausea and vomiting. However, I know of no studies using biofeedback. A plus (+) or minus (–) sign suggests a finer degree of grading (A–, B+, B–, or C+) or my uncertainty.

---

[1]Inclusion of vision disorders here reflects my ignorance of this application. There are several references including supportive research. I admit insufficient understanding of this application and no experience.

One could properly include several other symptoms and conditions on the three lists from the field of physical medicine and rehabilitation; omission reflects my limited knowledge and experience. Such lists are better treated separately by other professionals. For example, see Chapters 21 and 22.

Cautions and Contraindications[2]

Practitioners must consider cautions and contraindications before using biofeedback and other physiological self-regulatory therapies. One can expect serious problems to occur when providing relaxation and/or some forms of biofeedback for patients for whom such cautions and contraindications apply.

Experts generally agree about many of the cautions and contraindications. However, there is no single, agreed upon document listing or discussing all cautions and contraindications. Available and useful lists and discussions include the *Standards and Guidelines for Biofeedback Applications* (AAPB, 1992)—the official but provisional statement of the AAPB. This document replaced the listing and discussion in the original *Applications Standards and Guidelines* of the Biofeedback Society of America (now the AAPB) (Schwartz & Fehmi, 1982). Adler and Adler (1984, 1989a, 1989b) offered sage opinions regarding limitations of biofeedback. I encourage all practitioners to read their chapters.

Most practitioners consider the following disorders and conditions as outright contraindications or ones providing the need for much caution. These include severe depression, acute agitation, acute or fragile schizophrenia or a strong potential for psychotic decompensation, mania, paranoid disorders such as with delusions of influence, severe obsessive–compulsive disorder (OCD), delirium, acute medical decompensation, or a strong potential for a dissociative reaction, fugue state, or depersonalization. There is very little or no literature on patients with these disorders, as logic precluded such interventions with these patients.

When a practitioner can justify using relaxation and biofeedback with a patient with one of these diagnoses or conditions, then prudent standards of practice dictate using special assessment and treatment procedures. For example, one might treat tension or migraine headaches in a patient with OCD or the potential for psychotic decompensation.

Caution also must be employed with some forms of biofeedback and relaxation therapies for certain other patients. These are not contraindications. However, providers must be very knowledgeable and experienced with these conditions and be well versed in using special approaches. These include patients with moderate to severely impaired attention or memory, as in dementia and mental retardation, or those with some seizure disorders. One also needs to be cautious with patients with significant "secondary gain" from symptoms.

For example, in a small percentage of patients with seizure disorders, certain sensory signals used in electroencephalographic feedback could result in seizure activity. Patients with significantly impaired attention, memory, or both require special approaches and much cooperation from significant others living with them. Patients with much secondary gain from their symptoms need therapy to reduce or stop competing influences on compliance and improvement.

Practitioners should tell patients taking medications for certain medical disorders and their physicians that relaxation therapies might result in a need for adjustment (usually reductions) in medication dosage.

---

[2]In the first edition of this book, this topic was discussed in Chapter 7. It now belongs in the revised version of this chapter.

They should inform patients taking medications for certain medical disorders that relaxation therapies might result in a need for reduced dosage and discuss this possibility with the patient's physician. However, we should note that reports documenting adverse effects or altered medication requirements associated with relaxation therapies and biofeedback are very rare. These disorders are diabetes mellitis, hypothyroidism, seizure disorders, hypertension, glaucoma, and asthma.

Medical Conditions Masquerading as Psychological Symptoms

Essentially all practitioners know and understand there are many symptoms that masquerade as psychological or functional ones but actually are caused by an organic medical disorder requiring different treatments (Kaplan & Saddock, 1985, pp. 1275–1277; Othmer & Othmer, 1989, pp. 226–234; Hall, 1980).

All health care professionals must be aware of this possibility. They must be familiar with the symptoms and other manifestations of diagnosed conditions and other possible diagnoses. Nonmedical practitioners are particularly in need of extra caution and consultations from medical specialists. Prudent practice standards dictate working closely with competent and proper physicians who have already ruled out other causes and diagnoses and who will reevaluate patients as indicated.

The scope of this chapter does not permit a detailed discussion of this subject that has been well treated by others. I trust the present discussion is helpful and sufficient for the scope of this volume. The reader is referred to the Reference section for excellent and more detailed information.

Neurological, endocrine, cardiovascular, collagen, and other disorders often produce psychological or psychiatric symptoms. It is in the early stages of many of these disorders that practitioners are more likely mislead.

For older patients, we must consider that irritability and depressive symptoms often are part of the early stages of a progressive dementia such as Alzheimer's disease. These patients most often do not recognize or admit to their neurocognitive impairments including their memory problems. For some patients, expressive language or spatial problems are the earliest neurocognitive impairments rather than memory problems. We must also recognize that anxiety, depression, occasionally hyperactivity, and/or grandiose behavior occur among persons with hyperthyroidism (Graves' disease; thyrotoxicosis) long before a confirmed diagnosis. Collagen diseases such as systemic lupus erythematosus (SLE) develop over a long time, often many years. This disease produces anxiety, depression, and multiple symptoms in many body systems.

Anxiety and/or depression are often manifestations of a wide variety of neurological disorders such as Wilson's disease, multiple sclerosis, and cerebral ischemia. Panic and other anxiety symptoms are common symptoms of oat-cell lung cancer, Menière's disease, hyperparathyroidism, hypoparathyroidism, and hyperadrenalism (Cushing's disease). Panic, anxiety, and headaches are among the symptoms of pheochromocytoma. Very rapid heart rate and pounding with all or several of the classic symptoms of panic disorder can occur with supraventricular tachycardia. This includes rapid onset of a heart rate often above 140 bpm and up to about 200 bpm.

Medications not used for psychiatric disorders also produce a wide variety of symptoms. These include irritability, restlessness, insomnia, anxiety, lethargy, and/or depression. For example, note the associations of one or more of these symptoms reported by Othmer and Othmer (1989, pp. 231–233) which they abstracted from Hall (1980). They list some or many of these symptoms for some anti-infection agents, ANS drugs, stimulants, hormones, diuretics, and others including antihistamines, vitamin B complex, and nicotinic acid.

Recommendations

Readers should consider the following recommendations for helping avoid important mistakes.

- Become familiar with the special features of the medical disorders seen in your practice and the unusual symptoms for disorders specific to the practice.
- Become familiar with the features of psychiatric disorders for those patients with one or more of these disorders.
- Make sure that your patients will soon have or recently had a competent medical examination. Maintain a close relationship with your patients' physicians and/or other physicians who can help.
- Recommend to patients that they maintain regular or periodic contact with their physician.
- Encourage patients to report any new symptoms, new and unusual behaviors, and changes in existing symptoms.
- Know the drugs your patients take to understand possible symptoms and side-effects.

CONSIDERATIONS

Stepped Care

The stepped-care approach usually involves first using less complicated, less expensive, and sometimes less time-consuming treatments. There is a strong precedent for this approach in medicine and other health care fields. Practitioners should, for example, consider less potent medications or lower doses before more potent or higher doses, outpatient therapy before inpatient therapy, a neck brace before surgery, diet and exercise before medication. Following a stepped-care protocol, practitioners should also consider screening measures or a basic battery of measures before more extensive batteries of tests.

There are situations when an even more conservative approach than biofeedback is appropriate and preferable to try first. Patients and referral sources will usually be grateful and respectful when practitioners are conservative and successful with "less than more" treatment. For example, one can:

1. Consider relaxation before biofeedback.
2. Consider audiotaped relaxation before live instructions.
3. Consider dietary changes before relaxation and biofeedback. All patients need not stop caffeine before starting biofeedback and related therapies. See Chapter 10 for a detailed discussion of caffeine. However, one should try to stop excess caffeine before relaxation and biofeedback for patients with headaches, anxiety, Raynaud's disease, irritable bowel syndrome (IBS), psychophysiolgical insomnia, and hypertension. As a minimum, one should discuss with patients the rationale for eliminating caffeine to reduce interference with relaxation and biofeedback. If stopping caffeine before other treatments leads to improvement, there will be a credible demonstration of the effects of caffeine. However, even when eliminating caffeine does not result in symptom relief, it still allows for a more meaningful symptom baseline. Patients also may be more motivated to comply with later recommendations and better able to do so if they first made indicated dietary changes.

Stepped care also includes other factors that are often simple to change. For example, stopping gum chewing is sometimes proper before relaxation and biofeedback. Consider the patient who chews gum a few hours per day and has tension-type headaches in the temporalis muscles or facial pain from probable daytime bruxism. This simple change is a necessary first step and might be sufficient.

Other examples of stepped care include starting with good quality patient education, realistic positive expectations, and a symptom log for a few weeks. This assumes that the initial physiological assessment or other data did not show the need to start with biofeedback.

Practical considerations often compel me to use the stepped-care model. It is very consistent with advocating and using biofeedback and very consistent with the past and future cost-containment *Zeitgeist.* Many patients get significant and often sufficient benefit with less, rather than more treatment. Many disorders lend themselves to the stepped-care approach. Among these are headaches, essential hypertension, anxiety, IBS, psychophysiological insomnia, temporomandibular disorders, tinnitus, and Raynaud's disease.

Alternative Treatments Tried and/or Available

Among the important initial factors to consider are the prior therapies tried and their outcomes. For example, let us consider a patient who is using or did use medication that helps significantly. What are the patient's reasons for wanting to or needing to stop or reduce the medications or not return to them? Such reasons include negative side effects, medical cautions, addiction, patient's preference, inconsistent benefit, or mistaken fears about the medication. If the need to decrease or stop the medication is clear and the justification for physiological self-regulation good, then the practitioner should consider a change in treatment approach. An exception would be if there is very limited or unclear research or clinical experience with biofeedback for the patient's symptoms. Practitioner's should consult the patient's physician about any medication changes.

If relaxation or biofeedback therapies were previously unsuccessful, the practitioner should:

- Ask about these therapies to avoid providing the same or similar therapy.
- Ask patients about their understanding about the rationale and treatment procedures and their compliance.
- Ask about their comfort with the prior therapist.
- Ask about the presence or absence of the therapist during sessions.
- Ask about the instrumentation and modalities used and the placement sites of electrodes.
- Ask about the types of relaxation instructions and body positions during relaxation and biofeedback.
- Ask patients to show their understanding of desired breathing techniques.
- Ask about past generalization and transfer of training procedures.

A therapist can usually get the answers to these and related questions within a few minutes. The responses can provide justification for another trial of relaxation, with or without biofeedback. A prior unsuccessful trial need not prevent another trial. However, there need to be indications that another trial could improve upon important therapy procedures.

An adequate trial of proper medication can often offer a less expensive, yet effective option that is acceptable to the patient. This suggestion may sound like heresy from an advocate of behavior therapies and biofeedback. However, the cost of some medications that result in significant improvement can be less than a series of office visits. Some prudent practitioners avoid more effective but expensive therapies when reasonable options exist that are less expensive and have not had an adequate trial. I am not implying that one should try several medications before justifying physiological self-regulation or other nonpharmacological therapies. In fact, some medications are more expensive than relaxation and biofeedback—especially when the person takes the medication for years.

Our patients, referral sources, and third-party payers appreciate concern for treatment costs. They respect practitioners offering biofeedback who are alert to and facilitate alternative effective and less expensive treatments first. In some cases, an adequate trial of an appropriate medication is a correct option. For example, some patients did not yet use preferred medications. Some used inadequate doses of an appropriate medication. Others used the medication incorrectly such as at the wrong times. Some used the wrong medications. Some used too much medication and need to reduce or stop it. Others used incorrect combinations of medications. Some used only over-the-counter medications. It often may be better to try medication if the patient is willing to do so and there are no medical cautions or contraindications.

If an adequate trial of medication is ineffective or achieves insufficient improvement, the patient's motivation can increase for options such as relaxation and biofeedback. Biofeedback and associated therapies are often more easily justified after an unsuccessful trial of other proper and cost-efficient therapies. This assumes an adequate rationale for biofeedback, a competent provider, and the presence of other necessary criteria for such therapies.

Severity and/or Seriousness of Symptoms or Disorders

The therapist should consider the seriousness or severity of the patient's symptoms and disorder when deciding about whether to offer or continue biofeedback. He or she should consider physiological self-regulatory therapies including biofeedback for a patient with serious or severe symptoms even when there is scant, insufficient, or equivocal research and/or clinical experience to support its use. This is especially true when options are nonexistent, more risky, or far more expensive. Again, this protocol assumes an adequate rationale for biofeedback, a competent provider, and the presence of other necessary criteria for such therapies.

Consider the example of a 69-year-old woman with very labile and often very high blood pressures. She asked for biofeedback to help her control her blood pressure. She had already tried most of the proper medications and had had very negative side effects to all of them. She refused to take these medications. Dietary changes were not helping enough. Physiological self-regulatory therapies appeared justified, although the published research at the time was equivocal. With biofeedback, the patient reduced her daily blood pressures reliably to a clinically significant degree.

A patient presented with hyperemesis gravidarum, a serious disorder involving frequent unrelenting nausea and vomiting during pregnancy. Antiemetic medications were either contraindicated because of her pregnancy or were no longer available in the United States. Research studies using biofeedback and relaxation therapies with this disorder did not exist. However, the clinical rationale was sound. Practitioners and research supported the successful use of such therapies with patients with functional emesis not associated with pregnancy as in patients with anticipatory emesis associated with chemotherapy for cancer. Alternative therapies for this patient were much more expensive and far less practical. The option was continued hospitalization and intravenous nutritional therapy for the remaining 6 months of her pregnancy or until the hyperemesis stopped. A brief and intensive therapy program proved successful in substantially reducing the emesis.

Patients who fully pay for their treatment have the right to decide whether the discomfort is enough to justify their investment in therapy. However, when someone else is paying all or much of the bill, there is more responsibility to assess need for treatment. The practitioner might consider avoiding or deferring treatment if the patient's symptoms are mild or infrequent enough so he or she can live comfortably with minimal or no treatment.

In this category for example, we might consider the following: patients with vascular headaches once every 2 to 3 months that last a few hours and respond well to a safe medication; patients with very mild tension-type headaches two or three times a month for a few hours each; patients with bruxism without pain or damage to the teeth or other oral structures or tissues. Some practitioners encourage these people to live with their symptoms unless a brief and inexpensive therapy program has a good chance of success.

Geographical Distance between Patients and Treatment Facilities

Consider the patient who lives beyond a reasonable driving distance from treatment facilities. Often, a suitable referral in the patient's home area is not available. Other patients prefer treatment away from their home area. Some had bad experiences there. Some prefer or need to maintain strict confidentiality away from their home area. Some prefer the type of therapy, professional care, and credibility of a specific facility. In contrast, as is often the case in some large medical centers, the patient can only stay for a very short time.

When there is good indication for biofeedback and other related therapies and options are impractical, inappropriate, or nonexistant, the practitioner should consider a "massed-practice" therapy program. Such a program involves one or two daily office sessions for a few or several days. There are advantages to this schedule, and sometimes it is the only or the best option available. This allows more time to discuss the rationale and therapy recommendations and answer questions that arise after the initial office session. When symptoms are serious or severe, massed-practice therapy can result in enough progress. It can serve to add encouragement for the patient to continue when he or she returns home.

A limitation of massed-practice therapy away from a patient's home environment and usual routine is that the patient is usually experiencing much less stress. There also may be self-imposed or implied pressure to accomplish more than is reasonable in a short period of time. This is the advantage to a customary schedule. It allows therapy to occur during the patient's usual schedule and life circumstances.

Professional's Confidence and Competence with Biofeedback

The practitioner's confidence and competence using necessary instrumentation during evaluation and therapy are important. I direct this discussion partly toward professionals asking whether to incorporate biofeedback instrumentation into their professional practices. It may be moot whether other professionals believe they can attain the same results without instrumentation. If a professional is competent to use instrumentation and prefers to do so, then it is acceptable to do so regardless of whether noninstrumentation procedures might result in similar results.

There is considerable precedent for this philosophy of practice in medicine and psychology. For example, some psychologists and psychiatrists prefer to rely usually or solely on detailed interviews and direct observations to make diagnoses and recommendations. This is a common and acceptable approach. In contrast, many professionals prefer to add and often rely on psychological assessments and testing that add significant costs to evaluations. However, the additional assessments are common practice, and many believe they often add to the quality of the diagnostic and therapy plan.

Similarly, many neurologists and other physicians get neuropsychological assessments to help confirm a diagnosis or add information about a patient's functioning. Sometimes these merely confirm the physician's clinical impressions. This is acceptable and common clinical practice. Other neurologists and other physicians believe such assessments are unnecessary. This, too, is acceptable clinical practice.

In contrast, critics sometimes differ about this issue. Some professionals avoid certain assessments and do not have confidence in them. Some are not competent to conduct the assessments or use the results. These facts do not obviate the procedure's appropriateness and value in the hands of the right professionals and when used correctly and prudently.

Alternative therapies and procedures may be equally effective. Some studies show one treatment to be better, whereas other studies show a second treatment to be better than the first, still other studies may show them to be equal. Practitioners have the right to choose among evaluative and therapeutic approaches that are consistent with their interest and confidence, since the practitioner's interest and confidence are crucial to the therapeutic outcome. Of course, practitioners must also keep in mind risks, costs, and efficacy.

Initial Physiological Evaluation and Baseline Session(s)

The results of the psychophysiological baseline assessment session(s) are an important source of information on which to base therapy decisions. For example, let us consider the situation in which the practitioner observes consistently low levels of muscle activity from multiple muscle areas during rest and stressor segments. In this situation, he or she should consider omitting or deferring biofeedback from the treatment plan.

In such a case, the instrumentation-based monitoring serves a very useful purpose. It reveals that the patient can relax to a therapeutic range. The practitioner then clearly explains the meaning of that finding and gives instructions, encouragement, and supervision for using relaxation. This includes using relaxation frequently enough, long enough, and at the right times for it to be of therapeutic value.

It might be that selected muscular tension is occurring in the patient's daily life but not in the practitioner's office. One needs ambulatory monitoring to show this, and such monitoring is usually impractical. A careful history and an accurate diagnosis are often the primary sources of information on which one makes such judgments. Without demonstration of tension in the office, it is still proper to use noninstrumentation-based physiological self-regulatory procedures in the patient's daily activities.

Another question that arises in the present context is the criteria for being sufficiently relaxed. There are no hard and fast rules and few for which professionals can agree except at the extremes. The level and duration of physiological activity needed for a positive therapeutic effect differ among patients. Practitioners often do not agree on necessary physiological criteria for relaxation to result in positive results for the symptoms and disorders treated. Reaching clear or ideal criteria during biofeedback-assisted relaxation office sessions is probably often unnecessary. Patients often improve despite somewhat tense levels in early and later baselines.

The practitioner should consider recommending to the patient that he or she needs to avoid excess tension, especially for sustained periods. A patient might benefit from reproducing the reduced tension observed in the baselines even if not to the ideally relaxed range. Indeed, the therapist should suggest and help the patient learn to do this frequently, rapidly, for various durations, and at the right times.

Baselines need to be long enough to observe increasing or decreasing physiological activity over several minutes. Baselines that are too short or those integrated over long periods can obscure such trends. See Chapter 7 for more discussion of baselines. Also, one should consider varying the conditions under which one conducts baselines. Baselines with only the patient's eyes closed can be very misleading and inadequate because many patients show much higher tension with their eyes open. In addition, monitoring only during resting conditions without stressors provides unrealistic results. Such recordings often show little or no tension or arousal, whereas with anticipation of or during stressful stimuli, tension and arousal are often greater.

We should also note that psychophysiological measurements are often unreliable across sessions. Thus, the activity in one session does not reliably occur in other sessions. In the first session, the patient may be more tense because of the novelty of the situation. That is one reason for additional baseline segments to base decisions about the need for biofeedback.

Furthermore, some patients relax adequately at home and in their real-life situations. However, they have difficulty relaxing in our offices. No matter how we present it, there is an implied evaluation atmosphere in the office that some patients find difficult to over-come. If the practitioner suspects this, he or she should evaluate how the patient views the session and what the patient feels like during office sessions. Then the practitioner should check the patient's physiological activity during practice periods outside the office.

Other useful data include the patient's physiological responses to feedback and after feedback segments. The questions to be asked include the following:

- Does the patient lower tension and arousal significantly with the feedback?
- Are the lowered arousal and tension maintained after the feedback?
- Does the feedback increase the arousal and tension?
- Do the stressors increase the arousal or precipitate arousal?

There are several questions and types of information on which one may base the decision to provide more biofeedback. Here are a few examples:

- Is there much excess tension and arousal during resting baseline and self-regulation segments without feedback?
- Are much tension and arousal precipitated or worsened with office stressors?
- Does feedback result in significantly lowered tension and arousal?
- Does the person return to baseline tension and arousal after feedback?

It is instructive for us to remember that such logical questions and criteria have not yet been clearly shown to predict the necessity of biofeedback-assisted therapies for achieving positive therapeutic outcomes. Until research supports such evidence, practitioners will continue to be cautious and conservative in making such decisions and recommendations.

Symptom Changes in the First Weeks

Symptom changes during the first weeks of therapy are important for deciding whether to continue sessions and determining which therapy procedures to pursue. Such improvements often occur early before patients reach ideal physiological mastery. If the initial intervention results in a clinically significant reduction of symptoms, practitioners need to justify more office-based therapy.

The primary goal is to decrease or stop symptoms and not to reduce microvolts or increase hand temperatures. When there are clinically significant changes in the first few weeks, one should consider deferring more biofeedback sessions even if one assumes that some patients need specific physiological mastery for reliable therapeutic changes. In addition to cost considerations, another reason for this determination is credibility—to the patient, the referral source, and the third-party payer. Patients may accept added office therapy if they do not continue to progress on their own. If they do progress further, then one saves the cost of unnecessary office sessions. Furthermore, if biofeedback has a "placebo" component for some patients, premature extended use may "use up" that component. Note that the term "component" and not the statement of biofeedback is a placebo.

Patients need preparation for the possible need of later added office therapy. As an example, we can consider the following sample statement to a patient who showed clinically significant improvement of symptoms in the early weeks of therapy.

"I am happy for your improvement in such a short time. I am sure you too are very pleased. You significantly reduced the hours of severe headache, increased the hours without headaches, and reduced your use of medications. You also are showing improved ability to reduce muscle tension in your face and head muscles. It sounds like you are applying the therapy very well.

"Reducing excess tension is probably one reason for your improvement. You know the muscle tension in your head is still tense when we measure it in the office. In the long run, it might be better to relax these muscles deeper and faster and maintain the lower levels longer.

"I want you to continue to improve, but I do not want to overdo the biofeedback sessions. More sessions now could speed more improvement, but I cannot predict that with certainty. Consider this conservative option. Continue applying the therapy and keep records of your symptoms for another few weeks. We can review your situation at that time.

"I assure you that if your improvement does not continue, we can resume the biofeedback. However, if you want to continue office sessions now, then we can consider that as well."

Patient Characteristics

There are several studies of patient characteristics associated with more benefit from biofeedback and related therapies. It is difficult to establish predictive criteria. Even when there is significant correlation with outcome, there is usually much overlap between groups. This is obvious to most clinicians. I state this for anyone who feels tempted to conclude that practitioners should not treat some patients who have certain personality characteristics. (See the discussion about the Minnesota Multiphasic Personality Inventory [MMPI] in Chapter 14.)

The results of these studies are interesting and have academic and heuristic value. The studies identify patient characteristics that differentiate more successful versus less successful results. One implication is that the patient variable(s) provide criteria for who should not receive biofeedback or related therapies. However, there are many variables that influence the relationships between patients and therapy results. These studies need replications in a variety of clinical settings and with potential "moderator variables" before one can conclude that some patients should not receive biofeedback.

As defined by Steffek and Blanchard (1991), the theoretical variable "absorption" was the subject of several studies (Qualls & Sheehan, 1981; Tellegen, 1981; Kelso, Anchor, & McElroy, 1988). "Absorption" is the ability of a person to immerse his or her awareness and imaginative and ideational capacities into periods of total attention. People with this ability can focus their attention on imaginative activities of their choosing. They are receptive to sensory and imaginal experiences and can dwell on these.

An important question to ask is what to do with patients with different characteristics? For example, do practitioners need to add more patient education? Will more frequent or more closely spaced sessions work better for some patients? Will procedural variations help? Practitioners should consider using this type of data to decide to implement more patient education and attitude-change procedures. Such data help to determine the need for more patient education, other therapy procedures, and adjustments in therapy goals.

Patient's Motivation and Compliance: Enhancement with Biofeedback

Patients need to maintain motivation for practice and application of physiological self-regulatory therapies. Relaxation therapies alone can be successful without biofeedback for many patients. However, one can still justify providing instrumentation-based measurements and feedback. These can help reinforce a patient's progress and help increase confidence in his or her ability to self-regulate physiologically.

For some patients, feedback is confirming and encouraging. It helps some patients gain or maintain confidence in the treatment and their abilities. Some question and dispute the idea that they are physically tense or autonomically aroused. Some doubt that their thoughts affect their physiological tension and arousal. Some doubt they can control their physiology. All these patients need concrete and credible evidence. Using instrumentation with physiological self-regulation procedures is not a rejection of the value of relaxation alone. It is not an either/or choice as some portray it.

Patient's Choice and Cost of Therapy

Practitioners always need to respect each patient's needs and treatment choices. They must discuss the patient's options, time needed, desired results, prognosis, and costs realistically.

As practitioners, we obviously want to see as much improvement as practical for patients. We often measure success against research criteria such as 50+%, 70+%, or 90+% reduction of symptoms along with reduced medications when indicated. Indeed, we strive for these ideal goals and encourage our patients accordingly. However, such goals are often unrealistic and even inappropriate. They may not match the patient's goals. Some patients welcome an improvement of 20–50%, especially after years of very little change.

Financial costs and time invested are important considerations for patients. If we consider an example of about 30–40% improvement and maintenance of improvement costing a few hundred dollars, the expected cost for another possible 10–20% improvement is several hundred dollars more and several more office visits. Some patients may decide that the additional improvement is not worth the additional investment. Patients show concern with the number of office visits, time away from work, and the financial costs. There are also the costs and inconvenience of transportation and child care to consider. Practitioners need not always measure success against the criteria of that which is possible. Realism allows our patients to participate in choosing how much benefit they desire or will accept for how much investment.

AN INTRODUCTION TO PATIENT EDUCATION

Rationale

Some patients have difficulty accepting the potential benefits from relaxation, biofeedback, and other applied psychophysiological treatments. They are sometimes skeptical, critical, and resistant. That should not surprise us or lead to our defensiveness. Nor should we dismiss patients as unsuitable candidates because they question treatment or appear resistant. Many patients have already seen other health professionals who were optimistic about their therapy, yet the results were unsuccessful. Practitioners are now asking them to accept a different approach often perceived as the last one of a series.

However, patients are often unfamiliar with behavioral and self-regulatory strategies. These represent approaches that are often very different from those to which patients are more familiar. Patients often do not have adequate and understandable information about the rationale for these therapies. They need information they can understand and accept. Furthermore, some patients are skeptical or defensive about nonmedical health professionals.

If we think about it from the patient's standpoint, relaxation and biofeedback therapies can appear as rather simplistic solutions. Explanations can appear very complex. Some patients probably think to themselves something like the following:

"You mean I have these pains in my head [or other symptoms] for years, went to several good doctors, took thousands of pills, and continued to suffer. Now, you tell me that relaxing each day, listening and looking at a machine measuring my muscle tension is all that I needed all this time? I would like to believe that, but I have been down this road before. Convince me!"

We should not assume that patients understand and accept the rationale for therapy or that brief explanations are usually sufficient. Nor should we assume that patients spontaneously ask questions or directly tell us their concerns. They usually do not!

Furthermore, we should not assume that patients accept and remember explanations and recommendations. Thus, we must seriously consider well-planned and well-executed patient education to increase patients' attention, understanding, recall, confidence, satisfaction, and compliance. We must devote adequate time early in the relationship and thereafter to prepare and teach patients adequately. The values of good patient education and its varied methodology are very important yet often underestimated or neglected in professional education, clinical practice, and research.

It is safe to assume that patient education also can reduce anxiety, increase the credibility of the professional and the therapy procedures, and facilitate positive expectations. As Shaw and Blanchard (1983) concluded,

Giving participants a high initial expectation of therapeutic benefit from stress management training has significant benefit in terms of self report of change and reduced physiological reactivity[,] and . . . these improvements are mediated at least in part by increased compliance with home practice instructions. . . . the procedures, per se, are not especially powerful without the appropriate set. (p. 564)

They noted as well that "a certain degree of salesmanship and trainer enthusiasm certainly can make a difference in outcome" (p. 564).

Some practitioners rush into the therapy phase with limited patient education. This is often understandable considering the high costs for health care and demands on professionals' schedules. However, cost considerations are not sufficient justification for limited patient education. There are cost-efficient methods for providing good patient education.

Good patient education can improve patients' knowledge and attitudes about the causes of their symptoms and about therapy. It can enhance the patients' perceptions of the practitioner as an expert, and as being credible and trustworthy. Compliance and therapy effectiveness partly depend on patient knowledge, beliefs, perceptions, and a positive therapeutic alliance.

Metaphors

Tailoring patient education to a specific patient depends on that patient's intelligence, education, reading ability, sophistication, and psychological mindedness. Health professionals commonly use metaphors to communicate with and educate patients. One of the major reasons for using metaphors is to help simplify information, concepts, and procedures. Metaphors are excellent for presenting part of the rationale and the concepts that patients need to understand. Metaphors allow practitioners to present ideas at a verbal experiential and indirect level. This can make ideas easier to accept and use (Combs & Freedman, 1990, pp. 59–60).

The struggle for an agreed-upon definition of metaphor is ancient. The lack of agreement continues to the present (Ortony, Reynolds, & Arter, 1978; Muran & DiGiuseppe, 1990). One view is that "a *metaphor* is a way of writing or speaking figuratively and of describing something in terms of something else" (Morris & Morris, 1985). Synonyms include figure of speech, image, and symbol.

In contrast, the interactive view (Richards, 1936; Black, 1962) posits that metaphors are much more than simply analogies. Metaphors are valuable for learning and understanding new knowledge blueprints. Muran and DiGiuseppe (1990) summarize this view and describe it as a radical constructivist view. In this view,

> . . . metaphors are seen as "cognitive instruments" by which similarities are created that previously were not known to exist . . . (Boyd, 1979) . . . one way of breaching the epistemological chasm between old and new knowledge by affording different ways of perceiving and organizing the world (Petrie, 1979). . . . (p. 71)

> It has been used for centuries as a method of teaching and communicating in many fields. (p. 70)

> Metaphorical communication conceptualized as both a *heuristic* and *epistemic* device makes it a highly persuasive means of conveying and altering thought . . . not only a vehicle for communication but also a vehicle for change. (p. 73)

Furthermore, Siegelman (1990) starts her book by stating, "Most of us, and our patients . . . find ourselves cleaving to metaphor to communicate experience that is hard to convey in any other way" (p. 1).

Practitioners of cognitive-behavioral therapies advocate analogies and metaphors as ". . . valuable means of communicating some of the complex subtleties of life . . ." (McMullin, 1986, p. 139). McMullin (1986) describes in detail many examples of perceptual shift techniques for cognitive restructuring therapy.

These techniques ". . . make a creative use of analogies to help clients who are preoccupied with damaging beliefs to understand the nature of the perceptual transition that they must undergo" (p. 73). For example, reversible drawings or embedded figures provide stimuli to help patients perceive how they can perceive situations differently or in a perceptually shifted way with practice. Other examples for the use of analogies in cognitive therapy are found in McMullin (1986).

There are many metaphors used by professionals. They develop their own and use those of others. More discussion of metaphors and examples of them are beyond the scope of this book. (Consider other sources such as Schwartz, in press.)

Cautions in the Use of Metaphor

Many linguists and psychologists warn of the potential misuse and misleading potential of metaphors. For example, the use of metaphor can foster careless thought ". . . by acting as a substitute for the hard, analytic work of determining precisely what to say, a point previously raised by Aristotle . . . when he warned of the ambiguity and obscurity inherent in metaphor" (Muran & DiGiuseppe, 1990, p. 72).

These authors review the cautions of other writers (Petrie, 1979; Beardsley, 1972; Fraser, 1979). People interpret metaphors in many different ways, and metaphors are very context sensitive thereby increasing the chances of mistakes. Thus, practitioners need to be careful specifying *why* they are using a metaphor, *with whom*, and *in what context.*

One premise of this section is that metaphors can improve cognitive preparation and education of patients. Improved cognitive preparation improves compliance for maintaining many behaviors necessary for effective therapy results (Levy, 1987).

EVALUATION/ASSESSMENT: INTERVIEWING, HISTORY TAKING, AND SELF-REPORT MEASURES

Psychological Evaluation

Deciding where to begin history taking, and whether or not as well as how soon to include psychological inquiries all depend on the patient, circumstances, and clinical judgment. With many medical patients, mental health practitioners are often wise beginning with a history of physical symptoms. However, exceptions abound. For example, patients often clearly show their psychological-mindedness from the beginning. Often, all or most of the symptom history information is available in the recorded history.

Medical patients often do not need much time for psychological evaluation. There are often practical constraints from the patient's schedule or distance from home of the therapeutic center. Many have limited psychological-mindedness and resist such an evaluation. However, even a brief psychological evaluation is often better than none. One should at least ask something like: "What are the pressures and frustrations in your life?" The practitioner should convey to the patient that she or he can talk about such matters and that such matters might be important for understanding and treating him or her. Patient education booklets help to convey these messages (Schwartz, in press).

Asking a few psychological questions can help with rapport. It can help assess the patient's receptiveness or resistance to this type of question and treatment. Further, it determines the need for more evaluation or eliminates it.

I culled and adapted the following list of psychological factors from Adler and Adler (1987). They provide an erudite, insightful, refined, and skilled commentary on history taking. One must read their original text to appreciate their style and clinical wisdom. Although it was written as a guide for interviewing people with headaches, this list and their discussion are useful for other disorders. The Adlers (1987) suggest considering evaluation of many factors. These include:

- Patient's expectations of themselves.
- Perceived expectations by others.
- Existence of past or present family conflicts.
- Sensitivity to criticism and to emotional expressions.
- Comfort and skills at being assertive.
- Illnesses and hospitalizations.
- Past or present grief or anticipated grief.
- Medication misuse.
- Perceptions of health care professionals.
- Perceived emotional triggers or factors increasing the risk of a symptom.

Do personality features and psychopathology worsen or maintain current symptoms or are they the effects of chronic symptoms? How necessary is it for practitioners to assess and treat psychopathology to significantly reduce current physical symptoms? Also, do life stressors in the past cause or contribute to current symptoms? For example, what is the role of past sexual abuse and grief on current symptoms? How necessary is it for practitioners to assess and treat these factors to reduce current physical symptoms significantly? These are complex subjects. See the section below on sexual abuse. Also, see Chapters 14, 15, and 33 for discussion of such assessment and treatment for headaches and IBS.

History Taking and Interviews

There are many resources for history taking and interviewing. Good examples include Hersen and Turner (1985) and Othmer and Othmer (1989). See Chapters 14 and 15 for a detailed discussion of a headache history and for other references.

Practitioners often use interview outlines as guides. For example, the reader should review Lacks (1987) for insomnia. The topics and specific items covered and the time invested for each depend on many factors. These include:

- Professional setting.
- Professional specialty.
- Referral source.
- Referral information available.
- Whether there will be continuing care by another professional such as the referral source.
- Results from screening measures.
- Stepped-care considerations.
- Cost consideration for the patient.
- Time available by the patient and the practitioner.
- Purpose of the consultation or evaluation.[3]

Medical and other practitioners responsible for assessment and treatment are wise to get at least some of their own history information rather than to rely on the information from others. This is true even when the other sources are competent professionals including physicians. It is tempting and sometimes necessary and acceptable to forego this process because of time and cost-containment factors. However, practitioners needing specific information often need to get it directly from the patient. One can review the prior reports aloud

---

[3]Consultations for evaluating patients for therapy and referring them elsewhere are different from consultations for starting therapy by the practitioner.

with the patient for his or her confirmation and elaboration. Even seemingly clear information such as onset, location, frequency, and duration can differ when one carefully asks the questions and listens carefully to the answers.

Even competent and experienced professionals can overlook potentially important items. That does not mean they were careless or incompetent. Patients tell different professionals different information and give different answers to the same type of question. Practitioners also can misunderstand patients' statements. Furthermore, practitioners, including physicians, sometimes get only the information needed for the purpose of their consultation. This can be to make a diagnosis, rule out serious organic pathology, prescribe medication, and/or make referrals for psychological evaluations, biofeedback, physical therapy, or other treatments.

Physicians and other practitioners with special interests and expertise in specific symptoms and disorders often get more detailed information than do other professionals. For example, for headaches, these areas of information include dietary factors, gum-chewing habits, use of bed pillows, sleep habits, stress, work postures, and other ergonomic factors, driving habits, beliefs, and sexual and physical abuse. One sometimes observes discrepancies between the recorded history information and the information the practitioner now gets from the patient. One must be alert to such inconsistencies and address them tactfully.

Sexual and Physical Abuse[4]

There are research reports that physical and/or sexual abuse are often part of the history of patients with chronic pain (Haber & Roos, 1985; Domino & Haber, 1987; Toomey, Hernandez, Gittleman, & Hulka, 1993) and common among patients with IBS (Drossman et al., 1990; Wurtele, Kaplan, & Keairnes, 1990). Percentages vary with at least the definition of abuse, the ages selected, assessment methods and questions asked, and whether there was sexual abuse, physical abuse, or both.

One crucial question is whether sexual abuse is more prevalent for these disorders than in more heterogeneous and general population samples. See Salter (1988, pp. 16–24, especially Table 1.1, p. 18) for a review of the prevalence studies of sexual abuse wherein she lauds the studies of Russell (1984) and Badgley (1984). The Russell study reported 28% of females under age 16 began to experience sexual abuse. The Badgley report noted 15% of females began experiencing abuse before age 16. These figures are very representative of studies in the 1980s. The Badgley study also reported sexual abuse for 6% of males under the age of 15. Older studies, mostly done in the 1950s and earlier, reported much higher percentages. This discrepancy may result from differences in definitions, assessment methods, and questions.

In the original study of chronic pain patients and abuse as reviewed by Bradley, Haile, and Jaworski (1992),

> abused patients, relative to those who had not been abused, were twice as likely to have suffered pain without a specific precipitating injury or identified cause and to have a significantly greater number of previous medical problems for which they had sought treatment. (p. 198)

In the next study from that group, their review notes that,

---

[4] I extend loving appreciation for the help and insights for this section to Nancy M. Schwartz, M.A., LMHC, CBT (BCIA), CSME (BCIA) whose specialties and significant experience include evaluating and treating both victims of sexual abuse and offenders.

abused patients, relative to those who were not abused, were significantly more likely to report constant daily headaches . . . [and] significantly greater number of medical problems for which they had been hospitalized as well as previous surgical procedures. (p. 198)

Therefore, this review recommends "that assessments of all chronic pain patients should include a careful evaluation of possible sexual and physical abuse" (p. 199). The interview questions from Drossman et al. (1990) in their paper are one set of questions. Practitioners should review other sources and guidelines for self-report and interview questions and consult with specialists in this field before deciding how to assess this complex and delicate topic.

Evaluating this topic and considering proper intervention are potential value in treating many patients with chronic pain and IBS. One potential value of knowing about the abuse is its possible influence on the development and/or maintenance of chronic pain, IBS, or other medical and psychophysiological problems.

However, no data show that abuse is an etiologic or contributory factor for these or other disorders commonly referred for applied psychophysiological therapies. I found no studies of these disorders in which the treatment focused on abuse. I found no studies that examined abuse as a factor in treatment failures from relaxation and biofeedback.

Nevertheless, giving a patient a chance to discuss this openly with a proper professional is often helpful (Cahill, Llewelyn, & Pearson, 1991). However, referral to specialists in abuse is often better and necessary to "resolve issues such as poor self-image, self-blame for the abuse, sexual dysfunction, and suppressed anger and rage" (Bradley, Haile, & Jaworski, 1992, p. 199).

The history of abuse often adds to general tension and arousal in addition to other factors. In some patients this could be significant. Perhaps it influences their tolerance for symptoms? Perhaps it contributes to those factors that motivate people with these symptoms to seek medical help? Perhaps it contributes to the factors that motivate people to avoid treatment? Self-blame, poor self-image, sexual dysfunction, and suppressed anger and rage could affect all of these.

Interview Outlines

The following outline or checklist offers a guideline to consider and one from which to glean ideas for interviewing and other intake procedures. Most of these questions and items apply in general clinical practice with psychophysiological, headache, and anxiety disorders. Some items and questions do not apply to other disorders such as in specialty practices for incontinence. See Chapters 14 and 15 for a more detailed discussion of taking a headache history. For tinnitus evaluation questions and self-report measures see Chapter 34.

1. Symptom(s)
   [Patients' highest priority symptoms are not always the reason for referral.]
   a. Description of symptom(s)
      What are the symptoms like? Is it . . . ? [Offer choices from which the patient can select. Do this orally or use good questionnaire.]
   b. Location(s)
      Where does it begin?
      Show me.
      Does it move around?

c. Frequency(-ies)
   How often does it occur?
   When does it increase and decrease?
d. When occurs
   When do the symptoms occur?
   At what time of day do they occur?
   Do they always or usually occur then?
e. Duration
   How long do the symptoms last? Do they last for . . . ?
   If they vary, what are the shortest, longest, and usual durations?
f. Intensity
   How bad is it? [Consider verbal or visual rating scales.]
g. Original
   When did the symptoms originally begin?
h. Development over months/years
   Has it changed over this time?
i. Course or progression
   [Over minutes, hours, days]
   Does it change after it starts? What changes?
j. Precipitants/antecedents
   [Look for dietary, environmental, postural, hormonal, emotional, work and family
   stress, or time pressures.]
   What do you think causes or starts the symptoms?
   Do you suspect anything that might be triggering it?
   Is there anything that often seems to precede it?
   Do you suspect anything that might be triggering it?
k. Aggravated/worsened by
   Does anything increase the severity? What?
l. Alleviated/helped by
   [Look for signs that relaxation, leaving a situation, heat/cold, and medications
   relieve the symptoms.]
   Does anything decrease the severity or relieve it?
   What do you do that relieves or reduces the symptoms?
m. Medications
   How soon do you get relief after taking medication?
   Are medications taken too often as when expecting symptoms?
   Does the patient take abortive medication with minimal symptoms?
   Are medications taken when he or she expects to be in a situation where he fears
   symptoms?
n. Nonrelief
   What did you try that did not seem to help you?
   What medications (doses) did you take?
   When did you take them?
   What medications can't you tolerate?
   Tell me about the relaxation that did not work.
   What did you do? Show me (breathing). What was it like?
   How long did you use the relaxation?
o. Remissions, periods of
   Are you ever totally free of symptoms for days, weeks, or longer?

    p. Associated symptoms
       What other symptoms do you get with the main one?
       Do you get . . . ? [Ask specific questions about specific symptoms.]
    q. Reactions of others
       What does your family do when you have symptoms?
    r. Behaviors before, during, and after onset
    s. Limitations in life due to symptoms
    t. Behaviors and attitudes on days without the symptoms
    u. Family members with similar or the same symptoms

2. Prior treatments
    a. Prior psychological treatments
       [Ask when, where, who, number of office visits, duration, results, patient's reactions and perceptions.]
    b. Prior experience with relaxation
       What do you recall doing?
       What do you still do?
       When do you do it?
       What about the relaxation seems to work for you?
    c. Prior experience with biofeedback
       Who provided it?
       Where on you body did he or she put sensors?
       Were your eyes open or closed most of the time?
       Were you reclining some or most of the time?
       What did you do during the sessions?
       Were you alone often or was the therapist with you most of the time?
       [Find out about their knowledge and perceptions of this treatment.]
    d. Treatments that did not help at all
       What other therapies did you try?
       When did you do it?
       What did you do?
       How many times did you go?
       Did it help at all?
       What were your reactions? What did you think about it?
       [This is when one finds out how desperate and open-minded the patient was or is. It adds more on past use of medications, physical therapy, dietary changes, and chiropractic treatment, and it helps develop a plan.]

3. Current treatments
    a. Current psychological treatments
       [Get names and addresses of professionals. Ask about attitudes, comfort, expectancies, content, preferences, questions, and plans.]
    b. Current medical treatments [Same questions as above]

4. Attitudes about health professionals, treatments, and symptoms
    a. Symptoms
       What do you think is causing your symptoms?
       Do you think anything has been overlooked?

[This is when practitioners learn of patient's beliefs and fears about an organic cause that has not yet been found.]

What are your thoughts when the symptoms start?

[Consider asking patients to write these down or audiotape them.]

What are your thoughts and fears when you have severe symptoms?

[This opens the door to cognitive factors.]

b. Treatments

What do you expect from this treatment?

What have you heard about this treatment? What did your physician tell you?

c. Professionals

What do think and feel about coming to a psychologist? What do you think would be different in your life without these symptoms or with the symptoms much reduced?

5. Why did the patient come now for treatment?

Why have you come for treatment now?

[This is when one finds out other potentially important information. It is often the entry to more psychological portions of an evaluation.]

Did you hear about this or another treatment for your symptoms?

Are your symptoms worse? Have new features? Is there a new symptom?

Did you read or hear about another disease causing these symptoms?

Are you afraid of having another disease?

Is your depression worse?

Is your job at risk?

Is your marriage at risk?

[Are there changes in life plans? For example, is a pregnancy desired and the patient must stop medications? Is the patient returning to school, changing jobs, getting married, or anticipating other major changes calling for better treatment for their symptoms? [Does the patient have another agenda? Are the symptoms and seeking help now the socially acceptable permit to the practitioner?]

6. Stressors [Check for past and current stressors. Review the records. Ask about items tailored to patient. Consider questionnaires.]

a. Interpersonal

b. Work

c. Family

d. Financial

e. Physical and emotional health

f. Time-use behaviors and habits

Schedule overload: How many hours do you work?

Perfectionism: How neat do you like your house? Your office?

Procrastination

Being disorganized

Inefficient time use

Lack of goals and priorities

g. Legal

h. Existential

i. Sexual

j. Living conditions

k. Others

7. Emotions [Observe the patient. Consider self-report measures. Ask.]
   a. Depression
   b. Anxiety
   c. Anger

8. Neurocognitive [Observe the patient, review records, ask, and assess directly to check for long-term limitations or acquired impairments.]
   a. Memory
   b. Attention/concentration
   c. Intellectual
   d. Language
   e. Reading
   f. Head and brain injuries and surgeries with residual effects

9. Physical [Observe the patient, review records, and ask the patient to check on hearing, vision, and physical limitations.]

10. Dietary and chemical intake [Check records and ask the patient to check on past, recent, and current use of items listed below.]
    a. Caffeine
    b. Tobacco
    c. Alcohol
    d. Other vasoactive substances such as tyramine and MSG.
    e. Other stimulants and depressants
    f. Gum chewing
    g. Others such as sugar/artificial sweeteners, spices, and fried foods.

11. Medications [Check records and ask about all prescription and OTC medications, results, and side-effects.]

12. Health promoting behaviors [Check on exercise, time-use management, dietary, and vacations.]

13. Social support systems [Check on family and friends. Ask about children, church/synagogue activities, volunteer and organizational activities.]
    Where do your children (grandchildren) live?
    Tell me about your relationship with them?
    Do you see or talk to them often?
    Do you belong to organizations? How often do you attend?

14. Education and work history [Recent and current status]

15. Sleep patterns and problems
    [Check for at least basics. Consider questionnaires.]
    a. Schedule for bedtime and awake time
    b. Sleep onset latency
    c. Interruptions and durations
    d. Sleep partner observations such as breath holding and teeth grinding
    e. Feeling after morning awakening
    f. Daytime sleepiness

16. Abuse, physical and sexual [Childhood, recent, and current]
    Practitioners need to be comfortable asking questions about sexual abuse. If no infor-

mation is available in the recorded history or other sources, consider inquiry part of routine practice. The intake interview is usually not the time for detailed discussion of this topic or probing unless the patient wants and needs to talk about it then. Gaining this information is very delicate and fraught with complex subtleties. There are several factors guiding this decision. These include presenting symptoms, purposes of the interview, time available, likelihood of seeing the patient again, and practitioner's experience. Consider asking at least a single question such as,

> "Did you experience any abuse, sexual or physical, as a child or adolescent?"
> "Is it possible that you experienced anything as a child or adolescent that one might consider sexual or physical abuse?"

A patient's response such as "Not that I remember" is a cue to a history of possible abuse. A practitioner with expertise and experience can inquire further or make note of the response and wait for or create chances in later sessions to inquire further. For example,

> "Earlier, I asked you about abuse, and you said that you didn't think so as far as you could remember. Some patients who have questions about possible abuse recall more as therapy progresses. Is there anything you want to ask me about definitions of abuse, the meaning and implications of possible memories?"

If this leads to the possibility, probability, or confirmation of abuse, some therapists consult with or refer patients to specially trained and experienced professionals.

17. Recommendations and plan: Considerations and discussions
    a. Further evaluation/assessment
       Interview
       Self-report questionnaires/inventories [See list]
       Neurocognitive
    b. Referral in same setting for more evaluation or consultation
    c. Referral elsewhere for more evaluation and/or treatment
    d. Psychophysiological assessment
    e. Answer questions. Discuss misperceptions and unrealistic expectations
    f. Demonstrate/model relaxation
    g. Prudent Limited Office Treatment [PLOT] with one to three office sessions
    h. Self-report symptoms diary/log
    i. Office-based treatment(s) procedures with biofeedback
       Specific modalities and rationale
       Specify sites and rationale
       Note special procedures and rationale
       Estimate expected number of sessions
       Estimate criteria for continuing, changing, or stopping plan
    j. Note topics discussed with patient
       Getting baseline for symptoms or starting treatment now
       Rationale and procedures for symptom diary/log
       Treatment options
          Medication versus nonpharmacologic

Treatment by patient alone with no office visits versus few to several office
    sessions
Single treatment versus combinations
Dietary options
Other symptom management/treatments
Stepped-care rationale and plan
Patient self-treatment versus office-based
No treatment
Using patient education
Explained relationship between
    Stress, thoughts, and symptoms
    Muscle tension, postures and symptoms
Explained goals of treatment and daily applications
Described desirable attitudes
Explained rationale and procedures for
    Relaxation and biofeedback for relaxation
    Biofeedback for other treatments (UI, FI, rehab, ADHD)
Other therapies, rationale for and consideration of
    Cognitive behavioral therapies
    Time-use management therapies
    Dietary changes
Daily Practice
Self-report mood and personality measures
Neurocognitive assessment
Answered patient's questions and dispelled myths
Costs and billing
Other recommendations
Referral information and rationale

Self-Report Measures as Part of Intake

Rationale, Uses, and Issues

The usefulness of self-report measures in clinical practice is not news nor is it debated among most practitioners. Their use has many advantages, which are summarized in a list below. Briefly, these measures can provide information about topics not obtained during interviews and observations. They can shed light on and provide hypotheses to explain unclear behaviors. They provide quantification and documentation of many variables of interest and are often necessary for reports to other professionals and third-party payers. The usual issues are selection of measures, when and how to use them, interpretation, and costs.

Some professionals argue persuasively that there are situations in which it is prudent to administer sets of such measures routinely (Bradley, Haile, & Jaworski, 1992). They state that in their inpatient program they educate, prepare, and reassure patients before the evaluation that

> the psychological evaluation [is] part of the medical diagnostic process. In order to reduce patients' concerns that their symptoms are not viewed as legitimate . . . they are informed that the psychological assessment is mandatory for all patients . . . performed . . . prior to

completion of the medical diagnostic procedures. . . . required to identify interactions between pathophysiological and psychologic[al] processes that affect patients' physical symptoms, disabilities, and social and familial activities . . . [and] also may suggest interventions
that might help to reduce the patients' suffering. (p. 194)

However, there are clinical situations in which such measures are unncessary and not
cost-efficient. They sometimes do not add enough to clinical decision making and treatment plans to justify the time and expense. They sometimes can interfere with desired
rapport and the therapeutic alliance between practitioner and patient. Many practitioners
are skilled interviewers and highly experienced clinicians. Self-report paper-and-pencil
measures often do not provide much more information than one can gain in a good interview.

Let us consider, for example, a consultation to decide the appropriateness of biofeedback for tension-type headaches for a probable work-posture related tension myalgia. Let
us further assume this is a consultation with a patient resistant to coming to see a psychologist. Now let us consider the potential perceptions and reaction of this patient to a series of
self-report mood and personality measures.

Other examples are consultation for which the decision to proceed or not to proceed
with biofeeback and related therapies will be the same regardless of information gained from
paper-and-pencil self-report measures.

Skilled practitioners can often base such decisions on prior recorded information and
an interview. This sounds like an argument against the use of the measures. That is not
my point at all. However, I maintain that one must use them prudently and not indis-
criminately or routinely in all clinical situations. Merits of self-report measures include their
ability to:

- Document symptoms, personality, beliefs, and behaviors.
- Document changes or lack of changes.
- Direct practitioners to areas needing more time and effort.
- Increase awareness of patients about their beliefs, behaviors, and personality factors.
- Provide a basis for feedback to patients about attending to their beliefs, behaviors,
  and personality.
- Correct self-misperceptions of some patients.
- Provide cautions for practitioners.
- Confirm or disconfirm impressions from interviews.
- Correct practitioner misperceptions of some patients.
- Generate hypotheses about possible problems and treatments.
- Assist the less experienced practitioner.
- Potentially save interviewing and treatment time.
- Raise topics, beliefs, and behaviors for discussion.
- Select patients needing special attention.

The selection of measures is the perogative of individual practitioners and depends
on many factors. A detailed discussion of these factors is beyond the scope of this book. A
brief listing will suffice. This list includes:

- Availability of the measures.
- Motivation and availability of the patient for the time needed.

- Practitioner experience with the measure(s).
- Brevity of the measures and ease of administration and scoring.
- Reading level of the measure(s) and reading ability of the patient.
- Useful and/or important clinical and treatment plan questions needing information obtainable from the measures.

Selecting Measures and Selected Measures

This section gives a checklist of topics and selected measures to consider when one is assessing with self-report measures. The list gives a sense of the extent of topics and measures to consider. It serves as a reminder and guideline when one is selecting measures. The extent of the list may appear overwhelming. Considering the use of many of these is unwieldy and impractical in routine clinical practice. It could take 4 to 8 hours to finish a comprehensive array of measures. This is not acceptable for many or most patients and office practices. Think of the personnel needed and the time to score and interpret the measures. Think of the costs!

A discussion of the details of these measures is beyond the scope of this book. Turk and Melzack (1992, chapters 9, 10, 12, 13, and 14) discuss the measures for the assessment of patients with pain. Their book is required reading. The categories and selected measures listed in Table 6.2 are provisional selections.

For each group, the list gives the abbreviation, full name, and one or more references. Comments follow for selected measures. Where available, I include sources for getting some measures. The order of categories is arbitrary, and there is some duplication of measures under different groups.

TABLE 6.2. Selected List of Self-Report Measures[1]

Absorption
TAS (Tellegen Absorption Scale)
(Tellegen & Atkinson, 1974; Tellegen, 1981)

Alexithymia
TAS (Toronto Alexithymia Scale)
(Taylor & Bagby, 1988; Parker, Taylor, Bagby, & Thomas, 1991; Kirmayer & Robbins, 1993; Bagby, Parker, & Taylor, 1994; Parker, Bagby, Taylor, Endler, & Schmitz, in press)

Anger
STAXI (State–Trait Anger eXpression Inventory)
(Spielberger, 1988)
MAI (Multidimensional Anger Inventory)
(Siegel, 1986)
POMS (Profile of Mood States)
(McNair, Lorr, & Droppleman, 1981
MMPI or MMPI-2 (Minnesota Multiphasic Personality Inventory)
[Examine subscales and content scales.]
(Hathaway et al., 1989)

(continued)

TABLE 6.2. (*continued*)

Anxiety

    STAI (State–Trait Anxiety Inventory)
      (Spielberger, 1983)
    POMS
    MMPI or MMPI-2 [Examine content scales.]

Assertiveness

    RAS (Rathus Assertiveness Scale)
      (Rathus, 1973)
    AI (Assertion Inventory)
      (Gambrill & Richey, 1975)

Daily stress and hassles

    DSI (Daily Stress Inventory)
      (Brantley, Waggoner, Jones, & Rappaport, 1987; Brantley & Jones, 1989)
    HS/US (Hassles Scale/Uplifts Scale)
      (Lazarus & Folkman, 1989; Kanner, Coyne, Schaefer, & Lazarus, 1981)
    SRLE (Survey of Recent Life Experiences)
      (Kohn & Macdonald, 1992)

Depression

    BDI (Beck Depression Inventory [Look at items separately for mood versus somatic items])
      (Beck et al., 1961)
    GDS (Geriatric Depression Inventory)
      (Yesavage, Brink, Rose, & Leirer, 1983)
    POMS
    MMPI or MMPI-2 [Examine subscales and content scales.]

Efficacy, self

    HSES (Headache Self-Efficacy Scale)
      (Martin, Holroyd, & Rokicki, 1993)
    GESS (Generalized Expectancy for Success Scale)
      (Fibel & Hale, 1978)
    ASES (Arthritis Self-Efficacy Scale)
      (Lorig, Chastain, Shoor, & Holman, 1989)

Illness behaviors/disability and suffering

    SIP (Sickness Impact Profile) (136 items)
      (Bergner, Bobbitt, Carter, & Gilson, 1981)
    DQ (Disability Questionnaire) (24 items)
      (Roland & Morris, 1983)
    CIPI (Chronic Illness Problem Solving Inventory)
      (Kames, Naliboff, Heinrich, & Schag, 1984)
    IBI (Illness Behavior Inventory)
      (Turkat & Pettegrew, 1983)

TABLE 6.2. (*continued*)

Life events, major, and stress

> LES (Life Experiences Scale)
> > (Sarason, Johnson, & Siegel, 1978)
> SRE (Schedule of Recent Events)
> > (Holmes & Rahe, 1967)

Locus of control, health

> MHLC (Multidimensional Health Locus of Control)
> > (Wallston, Wallston, & DeVellis, 1978)
> HSLC (Headache-Specific Locus of Control)
> > (Martin, Holroyd, & Penzien, 1990; VandeCreek & O'Donnell, 1992)

Multidimensional measures of psychopathology

> MMPI-1 or MMPI-2
> MDI (Multiaxial Diagnostic Inventory)
> > (Doverspike, 1990)

Obsessive–compulsive

> Leyton Obsessional Inventory (LOI, M/F)
> > (Cooper, 1970; Snowdon, 1980; Stanley et al., 1993)
> CAC (Compulsive Activity Checklist)
> > (Freund, Steketee, & Foa, 1987)
> MOCI (Maudsley O–C Inventory)
> > (Hodgson & Rachman, 1977)
> YBOCS (Yale–Brown Obsessive Compulsive Scale)
> > (Goodman, Rasmussen, et al., 1989)

Pain:
  Affect

> MPQ (McGill Pain Questionnaire), Affect scale
> > (Melzack & Katz, 1992)
> PDS (Pain Discomfort Scale)
> > (Jensen, Karoly, & Harris, 1991; Jensen & Karoly, 1992)

  Beliefs

> SOPA (Survey of Pain Attitudes)
> > (Jensen, Karoly, & Huger, 1987)
> PAIRS (Pain and Impairment Relationship Scales)
> > (Riley, Ahern, & Follick, 1988)
> PBAPI (Pain Beliefs and Perceptions Inventory)
> > (Williams & Thorn, 1989)
> PIBQ (Pain Information and Beliefs Questionnaire)
> > (DeGood & Shutty, 1992)

(*continued*)

TABLE 6.2. (*continued*)

Coping

CSQ (Coping Strategies Questionnaire)
(Rosenstiel & Keefe, 1983)
VPMI (Vanderbilt Pain Management Inventory)
(Brown & Nicassio, 1987)
WOC (Ways of Coping)
(Folkman & Lazarus, 1980)

Intensity (See Jensen & Karoly, 1992, pp. 137–144)

VAS (Visual Analogue Scale) (10 centimeter line labeled at extremes)
GRS (Graphic Rating Scales) (VAS with intensity-denoting points)
BRS (Behavior Rating Scale) (often 6 points, 0–5)

Sensory and affect

MPQ (McGill Pain Questionnaire)
(Melzack, 1975; Melzack & Katz, 1992)
SF-MPQ (Short Form-McGill Pain Q)
(Melzack, 1984; Melzack & Katz, 1992)

Multidimensional measures of psychosocial context

WHYMPI (West Haven–Yale Multidimensional Pain Inventory)
(Kerns, Turk, & Ridy, 1985)
CIPA (Chronic Illness Problem Inventory)
(Kames, Naliboff, Heinrich, & Schag, 1984)
PSPI (Psychosocial Pain Inventory)
(Getto & Heaton, 1985)

Perfectionism

MPS-H (Multidimensional Perfectionism Scale—Hewitt)[2]
(Hewitt, Flett, Turnbull-Donovan, & Mikail, 1991)
MPS-F (Multidimensional Perfectionism Scale—Frost)
(Frost, Marten, Lahart, & Rosenblate, 1991)

Reality testing

BORRTI (Bell Object Relations and Reality Testing Inventory)
(Bell, 1989; Bell, Billington, & Becker, 1985)
MMPI/MMPI-2

Self-control/self-management styles

MBSS (Miller Behavioral Style Scale)
(Miller, 1987, 1990, in press a, in press b, in press c; Steptoe, 1989; Gattuso, Litt, & Fitzgerald, 1992; Ludwick-Rosenthal, & Neufeld, 1993)

TABLE 6.2. (*continued*)

RLRS (Rosenbaum Learned Resourcefulness Scale) (Self-Control)
   (Rosenbaum, 1990)
PSI (Problem Solving Inventory)
   (Heppner & Peterson, 1982)

Sexual abuse

Sexual Abuse Questionnaires (Used to assess if abuse occurred)
   (Russell, 1984; Badgley, 1984; Drossman et al. 1990)
Sexual Victim Trauma Assessment [Used to assess impact of abuse.]
   (Hindman, 1989)

Social support

ISSI (Interview Schedule for Social Interaction)
   (Henderson, Duncan-Jones, Byrne, & Scott, 1980)
ISEL (Interpersonal Support Evaluation)
   (Cohen, Mermelstein, Kamarck, & Hoberman, 1985)
SSQ (Social Support Questionnaire)
   (Sarason, Levine, Basham, & Sarason, 1983)

Tinnitus (See Chapter 34)

Note. Sources of measures:
BORRTI, Morris D. Bell, Ph.D., Psychology Service, 116B, V.A. Medical Center, West Haven, CT 06516; *DSI* and *STAXI*, Psychological Assessment Resources, Inc., P.O. Box 998, Odessa, FL 33556, (800)331–TEST; *Hassles and Uplifts Scales, STAI*, and *WOC*, Consulting Psychologists Press, 577 College Ave, Palo Alto, CA 94306; *MDI*, from Doverspike (1990); *MPS-Hewitt*, Paul L. Hewitt, Ph.D., Department of Psychology, University of Winnipeg, Manitoba, R3B 2E9, Canada, (204)786–7811; *MPS-Frost*, Randy O. Frost, Ph.D., Department of Psychology, Smith College, Northampton, MA 01063, (413)585–3911; *Pain*, Several measures, Turk and Melzack (1992); *POMS*, Educational and Industrial Testing Service, San Diego, CA 92107; *Sexual Victim Trauma Assessment*, Data Collection Form, AlexAndria Associates, 911 S. W. 3rd St., Ontario, OR 97914, (503)889–8938; *Y-BOCS*, Wayne K. Goodman, M.D., Clinical Neuroscience Research Unit, Connecticut Mental Health Center, 34 Park St., New Haven, CT 06508.

[1]In addition to the references listed by each measure, useful summary information for several are in Fisher and Corcoran (1994). The measures include the GDS, MHLC, GESS, PSI, RAS, RI, IBI, MOCI.

[2]The two MPSs are different and developed by different authors at about the same time, published in different journals, and developed presumably without awareness of the other; hence the same name. This is unusual and a little confusing. Refer to these for now with the name of the authors until they resolve the name issue.

CONCLUSION

This chapter discusses topics and guidelines for selecting whom to treat with biofeedback and other applied psychophysiological interventions including other physiological self-regulation therapies. It includes topics and guidelines for intake interviewing and self-report measures as well as guidelines for introducing patient education.

REFERENCES

Adler, C. S., & Adler, S. M. (1984). Biofeedback. In T. B. Karasu (Ed.), *The psychiatric therapies: The American Psychiatric Association Commission on Psychiatric Therapies.* Washington, DC: American Psychiatric Association.

Adler, C. S., & Adler, S. M. (1987). Evaluating the psychological factors in headache. In C. S. Adler, S. M. Adler, & R. C. Packard (Eds.), *Psychiatric aspects of headache* (pp. 70–83). Baltimore: Williams & Wilkins.

Adler, C. S., & Adler, S. M. (1989a). Biofeedback and psychosomatic disorders. In J. V. Basmajian (Ed.), *Biofeedback: Principles and practice for clinicians* (pp. 233–248). Baltimore: Williams & Wilkins.

Adler, C. S., & Adler, S. M. (1989b). Strategies in general psychiatry. In J. V. Basmajian (Ed.), *Biofeedback: Principles and practice for clinicians* (pp. 249–264). Baltimore: Williams & Wilkins.

Applications Standards Committee of the Association for Applied Psychophysiology and Biofeedback. (1992). *Standards and guidelines for biofeedback applications in psychophysiological self-regulation.* Wheatridge, CO: Association for Applied Psychophysiology and Biofeedback.

Badgley, R. (1984). *Sexual offenses against children: Report of the Committee on Sexual Offenses Against Children and Youths.* Ottawa: Government of Canada.

Bagby, R. M., Parker, J. D. A., & Taylor, G. J. (1994). The twenty-item Toronto Alexithymia Scale—I: Item selection and cross validation of the factor structure. *Journal of Psychosomatic Research,* 38(1), 23–32.

Bagby, R. M., Taylor, G. J., & Parker, J. D. A. (1994)). The twenty-item Toronto Alexithymia Scale—II: Convergent, discriminant, and concurrent validity. *Journal of Psychosomatic Research,* 38(1), 33–40.

Bass, E., & Davis, L. (1992). *The courage to heal* (rev. ed.). New York: Harper Perennial.

Beardsley, M. C. (1972). Metaphor. In P. Edwards (Ed.), *The encyclopedia of philosophy* (Vol. 5). New York: Macmillan.

Beck, A. T., Ward, C. H., Mendelson, M., et al. (1961). An inventory for measuring depression. *Archives of General Psychiatry, 4,* 561–571.

Bell, M. D. (1989). *An introduction and brief interpretive guide to the Bell Object Relations and Reality Testing Inventory* (BORRTI). Unpublished manual, V.A. Medical Center, West Haven, CT.

Bell, M. D., Billington, R. J., & Becker, B. R. (1985). Scale for the assessment of reality testing: Reliability, validity, and factorial invariance. *Journal of Consulting and Clinical Psychology, 53*(4), 506–511.

Bergner, M., Bobbitt, R. A., Carter, W. B., & Gilson, B. S. (1981). The Sickness Impact Profile: Development and final revision of a health status measure. *Medical Care, 19,* 787–805.

Black, M. (1955). Metaphor. *Aristotelian Society Proceedings, 55,* 273–274.

Black, M. (1962). *Models and metaphor.* Ithaca, NY: Cornell University Press.

Black, M. (1979). More about metaphor. In A. Ortony (Ed.), *Metaphor and thought* (pp. 19–43). New York: Cambridge University Press.

Boyd, R. (1979). Metaphor and theory change: What is metaphor for. In A. Ortony (Ed.), *Metaphor and thought* (pp. 356–408). New York: Cambridge University Press.

Bradley, L. A., McDonald-Haile, J., & Jaworski, T. M. (1992). Assessment of psychological status using interviews and self-report instruments. In D. C. Turk & R. Melzack (Eds.), *Handbook of pain assessment* (pp. 193–213). New York: Guilford Press.

Brantley, P. J., & Jones, G. N. (1989). *Daily Stress Inventory.* Odessa, Florida: Psychological Assessment Resources.

Brantley, P. J., Waggoner, C. D., Jones, G. N., & Rappaport, N. B. (1987). A daily stress inventory: Development, reliability, and validity. *Journal of Behavioral Medicine, 10*(1), 61–74.

Brown, G. K., & Nicassio, P. M. (1987). The development of a questionnaire for the assessment of active and passive coping strategies in chronic pain patients (Vanderbilt Pain Management Inventory [VPMI]). *Pain, 31,* 53–65.

Cahill, C., Llewelyn, S. P., & Pearson, C. (1991). Treatment of sexual abuse which occurred childhood: A review. *British Journal of Clinical Psychology, 30,* 1–12.

Cohen, S., Mermelstein, R., Kamarck, T., & Hoberman, H. M. (1985). Measuring the functional components of social support (Interpersonal Support Evaluation [ISEL]). In I. G. Sarason & B. R. Sarason (Eds.), *Social support: Theory, research, and applications* (pp. 73–94). The Hague: Martinus Hijhoff.

Combs, G., & Freedman, J. (1990). *Symbol, story, and ceremony: Using metaphors in individual and family therapy.* New York: Norton.

Cooper, J. (1970). The Leyton Obsessional Inventory. *Psychological Medicine, 1,* 48–64.

DeGood, D. E., & Shutty, M. S. Jr. (1992). Assessment of pain beliefs, coping, and self-efficacy. In D. C. Turk & R. Melzack (Eds.), *Handbook of pain assessment* (pp. 219–220). New York: Guilford Press. (Includes Pain Information and Beliefs Questionnaire [PIBQ] in Appendix 13A, pp. 227–228.)

Domino, J., & Haber, J. (1987). Prior physical and sexual abuse in women with chronic headache: Clinical correlates. *Headache, 27,* 310–314.

Doverspike, W. F. (1990). Multiaxial Diagnostic Inventory: Adult clinical scales and personality scales. *Innovations in clinical practice: A source book* (Vol. 9, pp. 241-260). Sarasota, FL: Professional Resource Exchange.

Drossman, D., Lagerman, J., Nachman, G., Li, Z., Gluck, H., Toomey, T., & Mitchell, C. (1990). Sexual and physical abuse among women with functional and organic gastrointestinal disorders. *Annals of Behavioral Medicine, 113,* 828–833

Fibel, B., & Hale, W. D. (1978). The Generalized Expectancy for Success Scale—A new measure. *Journal of Consulting and Clinical Psychology, 46,* 924–93. (See Fischer, J., & Corcoran, K. [1994].)

Fischer, J., & Corcoran, K. (1994). *Measures for clinical practice: A sourcebook* (2nd ed.). New York: The Free Press.

Folkman, S., & Lazarus, R. (1980). An analysis of coping in a middle-aged community sample. *Journal of Health and Social Behavior, 21,* 219–239.

Fraser, B. (1979). The interpretation of novel metaphors. In A. Ortony (Ed.), Metaphor and thought (pp. 172–185). New York: Cambridge University Press.

Freund, B., Steketee, G. S., & Foa, E. B. (1987). Compulsive Activity Checklist (CAC): Psychometric analysis with OCD. *Behavioral Assessment, 9,* 67–79.

Frost, R. O., Marten, P., Lahart, C., Rosenblate, R. (1990). The dimensions of perfectionism. *Cognitive Therapy and Research, 14*(5), 449–468.

Gambrill, E. D., & Richey, C. A. (1975). The assertion inventory for use in assessment and research. *Behavior Therapy, 6,* 550–561.

Gattuso, S. M., Litt, M. D., & Fitzgerald, T. E. (1992). Coping with gastrointestinal endoscopy: Self-efficacy enhancement and coping style. *Journal of Consulting and Clinical Psychology, 60*(1), 133–139.

Getto, C. J., & Heaton, R. K. (1985). A manual for the psychosocial pain inventory. Odessa, FL: Psychological Assessment Resources.

Getto, C. J., Heaton, R. K., & Lehman, W. E. (1983). PSPI: A standardized approach to the evaluation of psychologic factors in chronic pain. In J. J. Bonica (Ed.), *Advances in pain research and therapy* (pp. 885–890). New York: Raven Press.

Goodman, W. K., Price, L. H., Rasmussen, S. A., Mazure, C., Fleischmann, R. L., Hill, C. L., Heninger, G. R., & Charney, D. S. (1989). The Yale–Brown Obsessive Compulsive Scale (Y-BOCS). *Archives of General Psychiatry, 46,* 1006–1011.

Goodman, W. K., Rasmussen, S. A., Price, L. H., Mazure, C., Heninger, G. R., & Charney, D. S. (1989). *Yale–Brown Obsessive Compulsive Scale (Y-BOCS),* Clinical Neuroscience Research Unit, Connecticut Mental Health Center, 34 Park Street, New Haven, CT 06508.

Haber, J. D., & Roos, C. (1985). Effects of spouse abuse and/or sexual abuse in the development and maintenance of chronic pain in women. *Advances in Pain Research and Therapy, 9,* 889–895.

Hall, R. C. W. (Ed.). (1980). *Psychiatric presentations of medical illness.* New York and London: Spectrum.

Hathaway, S. R., McKinley, J. C., Butcher, J. N., Dahlstrom, W. G., Graham, J. R., Tellegen, A., & Kaemmer, B. (1989). *Minnesota Multiphasic Personality Inventory—2: Manual for administration.* Minneapolis: University of Minnesota Press.

Henderson, S., Duncan-Jones, P., Byrne, D. G., & Scott, R. (1980). Measuring social relationships. The interview schedule for social interactions [ISSI]. *Psychosomatic Medicine, 10,* 723–734.

Heppner, P. P., & Petersen, C. H. (1982). The development and implications of a personal problem-solving inventory. *Journal of Counseling Psychology, 29,* 66–75.

Heppner, P. P. (1988). *The Problem Solving Inventory.* Palo Alto: Consulting Psychologists Press.

Hersen, M., & Turner, S. M. (1985). *Diagnostic interviewing.* New York: Plenum Press.

Hewitt, P. L., Flett, G. L., Turnbull-Donovan, W., & Mikail, S. F. (1991). The Multidimensional Perfectionism Scale: Reliability, validity, and psychometric properties in psychiatric samples. *Psychological Assessment, 3*(3), 464–468.

Hindman, J. (1989). *Sexual Victim Trauma Assessment: Data Collection Form* (Used in conjunction with *Just Before Dawn*). Ontario, OR: AlexAndria.

Hodgson, R. J., & Rachman, S. (1977). Obsessive–compulsive complaints. *Behaviour Research and Therapy, 15,* 349–395.

Holmes, T. H., & Rahe, R. H. (1967). The social readjustment scale. *Journal of Psychosomatic Research, 11,* 213–218.

Jensen, M. P., & Karoly, P. (1985–1986). Control theory and multiple placebo effects. *International Journal of Psychiatry and Medicine, 15*(2), 137–147.

Jensen, M. P., & Karoly, P. (1992). Self-report scales and procedures for assessing pain in adults. In D. C. Turk & R. Melzack (Eds.), *Handbook of pain assessment* (135–151). New York: Guilford Press.

Jensen, M. P., & Karoly, P. (1991). Control beliefs, coping efforts, and adjustment to chronic pain. *Journal of Consulting and Clinical Psychology, 59,* 431–438.

Jensen, M. M., Karoly, P., & Harris, P. (1991). Assessing the affective component of chronic pain: Development of the Pain Discomfort Scale. *Journal of Psychosomatic Research, 35,* 149–154.

Jensen, M. P., Karoly, P., & Huger, R. (1987). The development and preliminary validation of an instrument to assess patients' attitudes toward pain. *Journal of Psychosomatic Research, 31*(1), 393–400.

Kames, L. D., Naliboff, B. D., Heinrich, R. L., & Schag, C. C. (1984). The chronic illness problem solving inventory [CIPI]: Problem-oriented psychosocial assessment of patients with chronic illness. *International Journal of Psychiatry in Medicine, 14,* 65–75.

Kanner, A. D., Coyne, J. C., Schaefer, C., & Lazarus, R. S. (1981). Comparison of two modes of stress management: Daily hassles and uplifts versus major life events. *Journal of Behavioral Medicine, 4,* 1–39.

Kaplan, H. I., & Sadock, B. J. (1985). *Comprehensive textbook of psychiatry.* Baltimore: Williams & Wilkins.

Kelso, H., Anchor, K., & McElroy, M. (1988). The relationship between absorption capacity and electromyographic biofeedback relaxation training with a male clinical sample. *Medical Psychotherapy, 1,* 51–63.

Kerns, R. D., Turk, D. C., & Ridy, T. E. (1985). The West Haven–Yale Multidimensional Pain Inventory (WHYMPI). *Pain, 23,* 345–356.

Kerns, R. D., & Jacob, M. C. (1992). Assessment of the psychosocial context of the experience of chronic pain. In D. C. Turk & R. Melzack (Eds.), *Handbook of pain assessment* (pp. 235–253). New York: Guilford Press.

Kirmayer, L. J., & Robbins, J. M. (1993). Cognitive and social correlates of the Toronto Alexithymia Scale. *Psychosomatics, 34*(1), 41–52.

Kohn, P., & Macdonald, J. E. (1992). The survey of recent life experiences: A decontaminated hassles scale for adults. *Journal of Behavioral Medicine, 15*(2), 221–236.

Lacks, P. (1987). Behavioral treatment for persistent insomnia. New York: Pergamon.

Lazarus, R. S., & Folkman, S. (1989). *Manual for the Hassles and Uplifts Scales.* Palo Alto, CA: Consulting Psychologists Press.

Levy, R. L. (1987). Compliance and clinical practice. In J. A. Blumenthal & D. C. McKee (Eds.), *Application in behavioral medicine and health psychology: A clinician's source book* (pp. 567–587). Sarasota, FL: Professional Resource Exchange.

Lorig, K., Chastain, R. L., Ung, E., Shoor, S., & Holman, H. R. (1989). Development and evaluation of a scale to measure perceived self-efficacy in people with arthritis. *Arthritis and Rheumatism, 32*, 37–44.

Ludwick-Rosenthal, R., & Neufeld, R. W. J. (1993). Preparation for undergoing an invasive medical procedure: Interacting effects of information and coping style. *Journal of Consulting and Clinical Psychology, 61*(1), 156–164.

McMullin, R. E. (1986). *Handbook of cognitive therapy techniques.* New York: Norton.

McNair, D. M., Lorr, M., & Droppleman, L. F. (1981). *Manual of the Profile of Mood States (POMS).* San Diego: Educational and Industrial Testing Service.

Martin, N. J., Holroyd, K. A., & Penzien, D. B. (1990). The Headache-Specific Locus of Control Scale: Adaptation to recurrent headaches. *Headache, 30*(11), 729–734.

Martin, N. J., Holroyd, K. A., & Rokicki, L. A. (1993). The Headache Self-Efficacy Scale: Adaptation to recurrent headaches. *Headache, 33*(5), 244–248.

Martin, P. R., & Soon, K. (1993). The relationship between perceived stress, social support and chronic headaches. *Headache, 33*, 307–314.

Martin, P. R., & Theunissen, C. (1993). The role of life event stress, coping and social support in chronic headaches. *Headache, 33*, 301–306.

Melzack, R. (1975). The McGill Pain Questionnaire: Major properties and scoring methods. *Pain, 1*, 277–299.

Melzack. R. (Ed.). (1983). *Pain measurement and assessment.* New York: Raven Press.

Melzack, R., & Katz, J. (1992). The McGill Pain Questionnaire: Appraisal and current status. In D. C. Turk & R. Melzack (Eds.), *Handbook of pain assessment* (pp. 152–168). New York: Guilford Press.

Miller, S. M. (1987). Monitoring and blunting: Validation of a questionnaire to assess style of information seeking under threat. *Journal of Personality and Social Psychology, 52*, 345–353.

Miller, S. M. (1990). To see or not to see: Cognitive information styles in the coping process. In M. Rosenbaum (Ed.), *Learned resourcefulness: On coping skills, self-control, and adaptive behavior.* New York: Springer.

Miller, S. M. (in press a). Monitoring and blunting in the face of threat: Implications for adaptation and health. In L. Montada, S. H. Filipp, & M. J. Lerner (Eds.), *Life crisis and experiences of loss in adulthood.* Hillsdale, NJ: Erlbaum.

Miller, S. M. (in press b). Tuning in and tuning out: Confronting the effects of confrontation. In H. W. Krohne (Ed.), *Attention and avoidance: Strategies in coping with aversiveness.* New York: Springer-Verlag.

Miller, S. M. (in press c). Individual differences in the coping process: What to know and when to know it. In B. Carpenter (Ed.), *Personal coping: Theory, research, and application.* New York: Praeger.

Morris, W., & Morris, M. (1985). *Harper dictionary of contemporary usage* (2nd ed.). New York: Harper & Row.

Muran, J. C., & DiGiuseppe, R. A. (1990). Towards a cognitive formulation of metaphor use in psychotherapy. *Clinical Psychology Reviews, 10*, 69–85.

Ortony, A. (Ed.). (1979). *Metaphor and thought.* New York: Cambridge University Press.

Ortony, A., Reynolds, R., & Arter, J. A. (1978). Metaphor: Theoretical and empirical research. *Psychological Bulletin, 85*(5), 919–943.

Othmer, E., & Othmer, S. C. (1989). *The Clinical Interview Using DSM-III-R.* Washington, DC: American Psychiatric Press.

Parker, J. D. A., Taylor, G. J., Bagby, R. M., & Thomas, S. (1991). Problems with measuring alexithymia. *Psychosomatics, 32*(2), 196–202.

Parker, J. D. A., Bagby, R. M., Taylor, G. J., Endler, N. S., & Schmitz, P. (in press). Factorial validity of the twenty-item Toronto Alexithymia Scale. *European Journal of Personality.*

Petrie, H. G. (1979). Metaphor and learning. In A. Ortony (Ed.), *Metaphor and thought* (pp. 438–461). New York: Cambridge University Press.

Qualls, P. J., & Sheehan, P. W. (1981). Imagery encouragement, absorption capacity and relaxation during EMG biofeedback. *Journal of Personality and Social Psychology, 41,* 370–379.

Rathus, S. A. (1973). A 30-item scale for assessing assertive behavior. *Behavior Therapy, 4,* 398–406.

Richards, I. A. (1936). *The philosophy of rhetoric.* London: Oxford University Press.

Riley, J. F., Ahern, D. K., & Follick, M. J. (1988). Chronic pain and functional impairment: Assessing beliefs about their relationship. *Archives of Physical Medicine and Rehabilitation, 69,* 579–582.

Roland, M., & Morris, R. (1983). A study of the natural history of back pain: Part I. Development of a reliable and sensitive measure of disability in low-back pain. *Spine, 8,* 141–144.

Rosenbaum, M. (Ed.). (1990). *Learned resourcefulness: On coping skills, self-control, and adaptive behavior.* New York: Springer.

Rosenstiel, A. K., & Keefe, F. J. (1983). The use of coping strategies in low-back pain patients: Relationship to patient characteristics and current adjustment. *Pain, 17,* 33–40.

Russell, D. (1984). *Sexual exploitation: Rape, child sexual abuse, and workplace harassment.* Beverly Hills, CA: Sage.

Salter, A. C. (1988). *Treating child sex offenders and victims: A practical guide.* London: Sage.

Sarason, I. G., Johnson, J. H., & Siegel, J. M. (1978). Assessing the impact of life changes: Development of the Life Experiences Survey. *Journal of Consulting and Clinical Psychology, 46,* 932–946.

Sarason, I., Levine, H., Basham, R., & Sarason, B. (1983). Assessing social support: The Social Support Questionnaire. *Journal of Personality and Social Psychology, 44,* 127–139.

Schwartz, M. S. (Ed.). (in press). *Patient education: A practitioner's guide.* New York: Guilford Press.

Schwartz, M. S., & Fehmi, L. (1982). *Applications standards and guidelines for providers of biofeedback services.* Wheatridge, CO: Association for Applied Psychophysiology and Biofeedback.

Shaw, E. R., & Blanchard, E. B. (1983). The effects of instructional set on the outcome of a stress management program. *Biofeedback and Self-Regulation, 8*(4), 555–565.

Shellenberger, R., Amar, P., Schneider, C., & Turner, J. (1994). *Clinical efficacy and cost effectiveness of biofeedback therapy: Guidelines for third party reimbursement.* (2nd ed.). Wheatridge, CO: Association for Applied Psychophysiology and Biofeedback.

Siegel, J. M. (1986). The multidimensional anger inventory. *Journal of Personality and Social Psychology, 51*(1), 191–200.

Siegelman, E. Y. (1990). *Metaphor and meaning in psychotherapy.* New York: Guilford Press.

Snowdon, J. (1980). A comparison of written and postbox forms of the Leyton Obsessional Inventory. *Psychological Medicine, 10,* 165–170.

Spielberger, C. D. (1983). *Manual for the State–Trait Anxiety Inventory (STAI).* Palo Alto: Consulting Psychologists Press.

Spielberger, C. D. (1988). *State–Trait Anger Expression Inventory (STAXI) Manual.* Odessa, FL: Psychological Assessment Resources.

Stanley, M. A., Prather, R. C., Beck, J. G., Brown, T. C., Wagner, A. L., & Davis, M. L. (1993). Psychometric analyses of the Leyton Obsessional Inventory in patients with obsessive–compulsive and other anxiety disorders. *Psychological Assessment, 5*(2), 187–192.

Steffek, B. D., & Blanchard, E. B. (1991). The role of absorption capacity in thermal biofeedback treatment of vascular headache. *Biofeedback and Self-Regulation, 16*(3), 267–275.

Steptoe, A. (1989). An abbreviation version of the Miller Behavioral Style Scale. *British Journal of Clinical Psychology, 28,* 183–184.

Taylor, G. J., & Bagby, R. M. (1988). Measurement of alexithymia. Recommendations for clinical practice and future research. *Psychiatric Clinics of North America, 11* (3), 351–366.

Tellegen, A. (1981). Practicing the two disciplines for relaxation and enlightenment: Comment on the role of the feedback signal in EMG biofeedback: The relevance of attention by Qualls and Sheehan. *Journal of Experimental Psychology: General, 110,* 217–226.

Tellegan, A., & Atkinson, G. (1974). Openness to absorbing and self-altering experiences (absorption): A trait related to hypnotic susceptibility. *Journal of Abnormal Psychology, 83,* 268–277.

Toomy, T. C., Hernandez, J. T., Gittleman, D. F., & Hulka, J. F. (1993). Relationship of sexual and physical abuse to pain and psychological assessment variables in chronic pelvic pain patients. *Pain, 53,* 105–109.

Turk, D. C., & Melzack, R. (Eds.). (1992). *Handbook of pain assessment.* New York: Guilford Press.

Turkat, I. D., & Pettegrew, L. S. (1983). Development and validation of the Illness Behavior Inventory. *Journal of Behavioral Assessment, 5,* 35–47.

VandeCreek, L., & O'Donnell, F. (1992). Psychometric characteristics of the headache-specific Locus of Control Scale. *Headache, 32,* 239–241.

Wallston, K. A., Wallston, B. S., & DeVellis. (1978). Development of the Multidimensional Health Locus of Control Scales. (MHLOC). *Health Education Monographs, 6*(2), 160–170.

Williams, D. A., & Thorn, B. E. (1989). An empirical assessment of pain beliefs. *Pain, 36,* 351–358.

Wurtele, S. K., Kaplan, G. M., & Keairnes, M. (1990). Childhood sexual abuse among chronic pain patients. *Clinical Journal of Pain, 6,* 110–113.

Yesavage, J. A., Brink, T. L., Rose, T. L., & Leirer, V. O. (1983). Development and validation of a geriatric depression screening scale: A preliminary report. *Journal of Psychiatric Research, 17,* 37–49.

7

Baselines

Mark S. Schwartz

The gathering of useful baselines of physiological and symptom data is usually very important and an integral part of clinical practice. There are many proper ways to gather useful baseline data. Documents of the Association for Applied Psychophysiology and Biofeedback (AAPB) provide brief discussions of baselines (Applications Standards Committee of the Association for Applied Psychophysiology and Biofeedback, 1992).

REALISTIC CONSIDERATIONS FOR SYMPTOM BASELINES

In routine clinical practice, it is not always practical and necessary to gather pretreatment symptom baselines, although the procedure is useful and often important. Good therapists often strive to obtain such pretreatment baselines whenever practical, but they often do not gather this information. Patients usually expect to start treatment when they are first seen by practitioners. In addition, referring doctors often expect that their patients will start treatment when first seen. Furthermore, some clinicians' offices are too busy to permit one or more weeks to pass while they gather baseline symptom data.

However, in research one must get pretreatment symptom baselines. For headaches, Blanchard, Hillhouse, Appelbaum, and Jaccard (1987) offer good support for a 2-week baseline in research with tension-type headaches. They support at least 3 weeks of baseline with migraine headaches and 3 weeks for patients with both types of headaches.[1] For clinical use, they suggest 1 week for tension-type headaches, 2 weeks for migraines, and 2 weeks when both types are present.

These authors based their conclusions on the statistical variance accounted for in a 4-week baseline using approximations from the data from 1, 2, or 3 weeks. Their arbitrary criteria were reasonable. They required the shorter periods to account for 90% of the variance of the 4-week baseline in research and 75% of the variance in clinical practice. I did not find similar studies of baseline guidelines for other disorders.

When a practitioner believes it is practical and in the interest of a patient, then he or she should obtain this type of recommended baseline. However, asking patients to defer therapy many days or for 2 weeks or more might result in reduced motivation, although patients might not openly express their concerns about delays. However, I admit to being unaware of any research on this subject. The practitioner should clearly explain the ratio-

[1]They use the older term "combination" headaches.

nale for the baseline, although some patients might not accept the rationale even after an adequate explanation. Reduced motivation during a baseline could detract from the similarity of some research and frequent clinical conditions.

I do not intend to diminish the value of a pretreatment baseline of symptoms. Such baselines are often ideal. However, an important question for clinicians is whether there are adequate and practical alternatives (Houtler & Rosenberg, 1985). Often, the ideal is not practical and might even be counterproductive for some patients. There is another way to get useful information with which to compare symptom changes during and after therapy. A careful interview can get reasonable estimates of baseline data (Houtler & Rosenberg, 1985). Furthermore, the first weeks of treatment can serve as a type of baseline. An example of how to achieve this is to start with a conservative intervention during those weeks within a stepped-care program. A provider who adopts this approach might say something such as the following to a patient:

"You and I both want to be confident that the therapy is working and to what degree it is working. It would be better to record your symptoms for at least a week or longer before starting therapy. That would give us a more accurate record of your present symptoms to compare with the effects of therapy. However, I know you are hurting and you want to start therapy and feel better as soon as you can. Therefore, I am not going to ask you for a pretreatment baseline of your symptoms. Instead, I am going to ask you about the details of your symptoms. You can begin keeping a record of your symptoms after today so we can measure your progress."

SAMPLE INTERVIEW QUESTIONS

Here is a portion of a sample interview, illustrating how one might ask a patient about headache-free days:

INTERVIEWER: Do you have any headache-free days—days in which you are completely free of headaches and any head discomfort all day?

PATIENT: Yes.

INTERVIEWER: You mean you do not have even slight or mild discomfort on these days from the time you awaken in the morning until bedtime?

PATIENT: Yes.

INTERVIEWER: How many such days do you have in a typical week?

PATIENT: I have one or two.

INTERVIEWER: How many such days have you had in the past week?

PATIENT: One.

Other periods such as 2 weeks, 1 month, or the like, are also appropriate to put forth. One also can say the last question this way: "How many days without any symptoms have you had since _____?" The practitioner should try to choose a specific date, such as the beginning of the month or the last major holiday. One can pick a recent event such as returning from vacation or starting a new job.

A different version of the above conversation might be as follows:

INTERVIEWER: Do you have any symptom-free days?

PATIENT: No.

INTERVIEWER: You never have a whole day with no symptoms at all?

PATIENT: Well, sometimes.

INTERVIEWER: How many symptom-free days do you have in a typical month? [Here it may be useful to lead the patient a little with examples.] Would you say you have one a week? Are there 2 or 3 days a month? Could there be one in a month?

PATIENT: I have about two or three a month.

The questions might then proceed to symptom severity:

INTERVIEWER: On the days you have headaches, how many hours do you think they are severe to very severe?

PATIENT: It varies.

INTERVIEWER: I understand. However, during a typical week would you estimate you have 1–3 hours, 4–6 hours, 7–9 hours, 10–12 hours, or all hours awake?

It can be helpful to repeat patients' responses, but in different words. This allows patients to hear what they have said. It also provides for further reflection by the interviewer and another chance for patients to change if needed. Here is an example:

INTERVIEWER: You estimated you had about 5–7 hours of severe to very severe headache in each of the past two weeks. You said this was typical of the past few months. On some days, you had 2–3 hours of severe to very severe headache. During these past 14 days, you estimated there was only 1 day during which you didn't have a headache at all. Do I understand correctly? You did not even have slight or mild tension, a rating of 1 or a 2, during all your waking hours that day?

The times of day at which symptoms occur are also important:

INTERVIEWER: Do you awaken with some headache in the morning?

PATIENT: Yes.

INTERVIEWER: What percentage of your mornings do you awaken feeling slight or more intense sensations or headache? [If the patient has difficulty giving an estimate, give some prompts or examples to choose among: "Is the percentage 10%, 25%, 50%, 75% or 90%?" Or "In the past 2 weeks, were there 1–2, 3–4, 7–8, 10–11, or 12–13 such mornings?"]

Again, the strategy of repeating patients' responses in somewhat different words can be helpful:

INTERVIEWER: Do you awaken with some headache in the morning?

PATIENT: No

INTERVIEWER: You are saying that you never awaken with a headache in the morning. All your headaches develop during the day?

PATIENT: Well, once or twice a week I do wake up with a mild headache.

The above examples provide a flavor of detailed interviews that practitioners can conduct to get reasonable estimates of pretreatment symptoms. The interview can, and should, include questions about duration, circumstances, medication usage, and anything else the interviewer thinks may be important for future comparisons. It sounds like it might require a lengthy time to get such detailed information. However, it usually need not require more than a few minutes.

FURTHER JUSTIFICATION AND ADVANTAGES OF SYMPTOM BASELINES AND CAREFUL INTERVIEWS

Many patients overestimate or underestimate their progress when asked general or global questions about whether they are better. There are many research reports documenting the discrepancy between global estimates versus symptom logs (Andrasik, Burke, Attanasio, & Rosenbaum, 1985; Andrasik & Holyrod, 1980; Cahn & Cram, 1980). This is even true when patients have also kept symptom records. Some patients perceive that they did not improve, although their self-report records do show improvement. This discrepancy may be the result of an increase in symptoms in the past few days. Some patients may be reacting to a discrepancy between their expectations for more improvement compared to their actual improvement. Often, they do not realize there has been improvement. For example, a patient could have fewer hours of severe-intensity symptoms and more symptom-free hours. However, that patient could be focusing on days with symptoms that did not change.

Some patients overestimate their improvement. They may say "I am 90% better!" However, their records or prior estimates may show a much smaller degree of improvement—perhaps 50%, or even less. There are various possible interpretations for these overestimates. The patients' expressions may be figures of speech, or they may not recall their earlier symptom estimates. They may want to stop coming in for therapy and may exaggerate their improvement to accomplish this in a "face-saving" manner.

Sometimes, self-report data do not reflect improvement when improvement actually did occur. When a discrepancy appears between patients' verbal reports and their records, then further inquiry may provide evidence of improvement. One example of such a discrepancy would be when check marks on an hourly record form reflect symptom activity, but the symptoms were shorter than an hour in duration. Some patients confidently state their symptoms are shorter now than in prior weeks of treatment or before therapy. Another example is the absence of symptoms under particular conditions under which they have previously occurred. When they *do* occur, these symptoms might do so with much less intensity, duration, or both.

Potentially contributing factors to the discrepancy are people who complete their symptoms logs inaccurately, such as at times other than those requested. Many people complete retrospective symptom logs at the end of a day instead of at the instructed and self-reported times (Hermann & Blanchard, 1993). The above problems do not cast doubt on the reliability and validity of standard self-report symptom logs for most patients. However, they do raise questions of the reliability and validity for some. This situation could be one source of the discrepancies between different estimates of pain and other symptoms.

Whatever the reasons for overestimates or underestimates, baselines or good retrospective estimates offer useful data. They aid in better evaluation of progress and serve to reassure and encourage some patients. Symptom baselines or good retrospective estimates are useful for other reasons. These include:

1. *Referral sources.* Such data are useful when we contact referral sources later about patients' progress.

2. *Referrals made to others.* Such data are helpful when we refer patients to other professionals.

3. *Peer review.* Such data can be useful in documenting patients' progress when insurance forms are submitted. This helps to justify the need for continued therapy.

4. *Communicating to patients.* As stated above, some patients are unaware of their symptom changes or the degree of change. Baseline symptom data serve as reminders and demonstrations that changes have occurred. This verification of progress can help patients' motivation if the changes are not yet large enough to be obvious to them.

5. *Therapists' confidence.* As therapists, we want to believe that our patients are improving. However, patients' perceptions of improvement are not always accurate. Most practitioners believe that accurate feedback is useful and often important for learning to take place. Therefore, we must adopt that model for the continued learning and application of our therapies. We often need accurate symptom and physiological data to evaluate therapy. Accurate information or feedback about changes in symptoms and physiology allows us to support effective strategies. This also allows us to face the limitations of therapy plans and revise them, no matter how well-conceived our investment in them. Our confidence in the therapies that are effective will increase with the availability and proper use of such data.

6. *Check patient's behavior.* Real and implied checks on patients' applications of our recommendations can be useful. Repeating selected physiological baselines adds to this check. Reviewing patients' self-report records across therapy can enhance this check. It is not proper to communicate mistrust of our patients. However, we are aware of the tendency for patients to distort or otherwise misinform themselves and us. These evaluative measures communicate to them the need for accuracy and compliance for their own benefit.

For excellent and detailed discussions of measurement scales and procedures for assessing chronic pain, see Jensen and Karoly (1992), Keefe and Williams (1992) and other chapters in Turk and Melzack (1992). For information about measures for other symptoms, see the chapters on headaches, Raynaud's Disease, hypertension, attention-deficit/hyperactivity disorder, urinary and fecal incontinence, hyperactivity, and enuresis (Chapters 14, 15, 17, 18, 20, 23, 25).

PHYSIOLOGICAL BASELINES

This section focuses on physiological baselines.[2] Physiological baselines and stress-profile evaluations with instrumentation are proper to obtain for many patients seen for one or more sessions. The individual patient and circumstances dictate the feasibility, appropriateness, and need for physiological baseline data in single-contact consultations.

Researchers and clinical practitioners commonly get physiological baselines, often with multiple modalities. They standardize procedures to attempt to get reliable comparisons

[2]After reviewing the final chapter, Fred Shaffer, Ph.D. suggested a section that ties together factors affecting baselines. I could not write this but am grateful for this suggestion and include his list.

- Clothing restrictiveness affects respiratory measures. See Chapter 11 on breathing.
- Cognitive preparation.
- Body position and posture affect cardiovascular, EMG, and respiratory measures (Shaeffer et al., 1991).
- Limb position affects blood volume pulse and skin temperature.
- Many medications and "social" drugs affect all measures. See Introduction for note about the lack of a chapter on this topic.

among patients and across sessions. They also often use conditions such as adaptation or habituation, sitting quietly, simple relaxation instructions, cognitive and physical stressors, poststress phases, and postrelaxation phases. Getting this much baseline data during multiple sessions is not usually feasible in applied practice. However, practitioners should consider such extensive baselines during at least one session and selected baseline data during parts of other sessions.

Reasons for getting physiological baselines include permitting later comparisons and educating patients about their physiological and psychophysiological activity, reactivity, and recovery. Baselines often strengthen the rationale for starting therapy and selecting a therapy plan. In addition, later comparisons of physiological self-regulation can strengthen patients' confidence in their changes in self-regulation.

There are many acceptable and useful procedures for getting physiological baselines. Common phases include adaptation or habituation, one or more phases of resting quietly and instructed relaxation, office stressors, and one or more recovery phases. Therapists sometimes ask patients to loosen clothing such as neckties and belts and to remove eyeglasses, wristwatches, and shoes. Patients sometimes remove contact lenses unless keeping their eyes closed for several minutes will not be a problem.

One can omit these phases when baselines should closely approximate real-life conditions. Thus, the practitioner should omit these to more closely approximate real-life resting baseline tension and arousal, reactivity, recovery, and relaxation.

Adaptation/Habituation/Stabilization Phase

Rationale

The adaptation, habituation, or stabilization phase allows patients to adapt or adjust to the novel conditions of the office, instrumentation, and recording. This is especially important in early sessions. Furthermore, presession activities and environment also require adjusting to office conditions and the ambient temperature of the office. Examples of such activities are presession stress, rushing to the appointment, walking up flights of stairs, and significant temperature discrepancies between the outdoors and the office. One must allow the effects of these to subside.

For useful data and interpretation of baselines and other physiological data later in a session, it is crucial to start with sufficient adaptation (Sturgis & Gramling, 1988). The duration of adaptation periods varies in the published literature. Sallis and Lichstein (1979) and Meyers and Craighead (1978) report preliminary and limited guidelines for some physiological variables and recording conditions.

Frontal electromyographic (EMG) stabilization occurred in an average of 11 minutes across a very small group of 17 undergraduate, nonclinical students (Sallis & Lichstein, 1979). However, among these subjects, there was "considerable idiosyncrasy of the EMG adaptation response" (p. 339). This suggests there would probably be much variability among clinical patients especially for those who are showing high levels of head muscle tension.

One report argued for providing subjects with the "maximum clarity and certainty about what will occur during the adaptation period" (Meyers & Craighead, 1978, p. 355).

- Physical appearance of the office may affect measures. See Chapter 9 on compliance for discussion of physical appearance of the office.
- Office temperature affects at least skin temperature and blood volume pulse.
- Therapist behaviors and appearance can affect measurements.

This can reduce the chance that they will view this period as an "arousing task." This calls for cognitive preparation about the expected length of time, events, and procedures. At least some psychophysiological variables might respond differently in an adaptation depending on the cognitive preparation information or instructional set.

For example, Meyers and Craighead (1978) reported differences between not knowing what to expect ("maximal uncertainty") compared with instructions providing much less uncertainty. I admit that the data and their interpretations are confusing to me. However, it is clear and important that these researchers found differences. This supports the need for practitioners to attend to the cognitive preparation before adaptation. This study helps us realize the potential impact of cognitive preparation and instructional set on autonomic physiological functioning. Lacey's (1967) theory of "idiosyncratic patterning of somatic responses and the multidimensional nature of arousal" also received support (Meyers & Craighead, 1978, p. 360).

Therefore, one must be aware of and consider many factors when planning for and implementing adaptation and baseline recordings. This also is true for psychophysiological feedback. After doing so, one still expects individual differences in responses and patterns among patients and subjects. "One size (or adaptation) does *not* fit all."

In clinical practice, one usually tailors the cognitive preparation and adaptation time to the individual person and situation. There is no standard and agreed-upon cognitive preparation or instructional set. Practitioners need be aware of the potential impact of instructional set on patients and should consider standardizing it or documenting the set used. Practitioners will appreciate a research report that includes this information. It can ease replication and application to clinical practice.

The total duration of the stabilization phase varies and depends on several factors including time in the waiting room. Other practical factors include the physical condition of the patient arriving at the office, the physiological activity monitored, the therapist's purpose, and the number of prior sessions. Respiration rate, finger pulse volume, heart rate, and basal skin resistance can reach stability in an average of about 6 minutes (Meyers & Craighead, 1978) although there is variability.

Definitions

The common use of the term "adaptation" refers to the beginning of the session before baselines. This precedes relaxation instructions, stressors, recovery, and feedback phases.

"Habituation" is the reduction of a physiological response with repeated or continuous presentation of a stimulus or stimuli. It refers to a "decrease in response magnitude during repeated or extended presentations of a stressor" (Haynes, Gannon, Orimoto, O'Brien, & Brandt, 1991, p. 357). Neuronal firing and physiological reactivity habituate, and different physiological systems habituate at different rates and in different times (O'Gorman, 1983). For example, cardiovascular and electrodermal activity change differently. Greater intensity, uniqueness, or complexity of stimuli all can reduce the habituation process (O'Gorman, 1983). As Sturgis and Gramling (1988) point out, the "orienting response" and the "defensive response" affect habituation. The first provides an alerting function, is reflexive, and happens instantly after slight environmental changes.

Technical Considerations

Practitioners should monitor and record moment-by-moment physiological functioning to check the potential effects of brief orienting responses and should, for example, watch for events such as noises. Brief orienting responses are of potential clinical use as well. For example, the person who is more physiologically responsive to low-level environmental stimuli may require different procedures. Habituation is rapid after orienting responses but can affect summary scores of adaptation and other periods.

Psychophysiological arousal can occur with perceived and bona fide threatening stimuli present. Habituation of this type of response is usually slow and variable (Sturgis & Grambling, 1988). Several potentially threatening factors associated with office visits can increase muscle tension and autonomic arousal. An example occurs in a person who feels threatened by doctors or mental health professionals. Sitting quietly for several minutes, reclining, and connection to the instruments are other examples for some persons. Practitioners should check these factors when planning and interpreting adaptation and other baseline periods. Repeated exposure to potentially threatening stimuli within a longer initial session or repeated sessions might be necessary to obtain adequate baselines. Further development of better guidelines for adaptation needs more research.

Reduced arousal during a longer adaptation while the patient is generally relaxing probably involves habituation to the stimuli. This is one explanation for the therapeutic effects of exposure therapies such as systematic desensitization and flooding. Repeated exposure to the instrumentation and associated stimuli may be a version of exposure therapy. The treatment effect with the office stressors may not be from relaxation or biofeedback but from prolonged and repeated exposure to the stimuli.

One commonly needs at least 5 minutes for adaptation. However, sitting quietly for up to 20 minutes may be necessary for some patients. For example, Taub and School's (1978) anecdotal report suggests that for some persons even 30 minutes is not enough for stabilization of hand temperature. Shorter times are probably enough for most people seen in clinical practice. Adaptation is often between 3 to 5 minutes with instruments attached, especially for patients who waited several minutes in a waiting room.

Neutral conversation is acceptable if the goals are adjustment of body position and adjustment to the instruments. Therapists should consider omitting conversation if the goal is allowing the physiological systems of interest to settle down. During this phase, therapists typically give no specific instructions to the patient except to sit quietly and get comfortable.

Resting Baselines

Rationale

A period of sitting quietly with eyes open and then with eyes closed can be useful. This is different from the adaptation and other phases. Many practitioners call this the baseline. It is a baseline, but not the only type of baseline. The purposes are to observe and measure resting basal physiological activity.

Methods of Measuring

Some therapists conduct this phase only or mostly with the patient's eyes closed. This is suitable for conditions such as insomnia. However, it is not realistic for assessing baseline physiology for headaches and other symptoms that occur with eyes open. For example, using only an eyes-closed baseline can lead a therapist to incorrectly conclude there is no excess muscle activity. It is common to observe more muscle activity in the head and facial muscles when eyes are open. The reverse is also sometimes present.

Therapists' should get baseline data with eyes open when patients' symptoms start with their eyes open and when biofeedback with eyes open is planned. Observing lower arousal with eyes open than with eyes closed is potentially useful. It provides cues about what it means for patients to close their eyes. It raises questions to answer about what patients are thinking about and doing when they close their eyes. When eyes are kept open, therapists should consider instructing patients to include time calmly gazing at an object such as a picture or plant. They should remind patients to avoid staring or examining the object they are looking at as well.

Intersession Stability of Psychophysiological Responses

Adequate test–retest reliability of resting baseline measurements is an essential topic. There is statistical reliability but more variability than consistency in muscle and autonomic functioning (Arena, Blanchard, Andrasik, Cotch, & Meyers, 1983; Faulstich et al., 1986; Arena, Goldberg, Saul, & Hobbs, 1989; Waters, Williamson, Bernard, Blouin, & Faulstich, 1987; Shaffer, Sponsel, Kice, & Hollensbe, 1991).

For example, in one comprehensive study (Waters et al., 1987) of 10 baseline segments of psychophysiological activity before the first stimulus, six were significant, although the reliability was modest between $r = .4$ to $.6$. Only one (respiration rate) was above that range at $.75$. About two-thirds of all the intersession correlations between the interstimulus presentations were in this range.

Waters et al. (1987) also used a more complex analysis of pattern similarity called the Profile Similarity Index (Buco & Blouin, 1983). This provided a single index of overall similarity or reliability of the two response profiles. For four of the five sets of baselines,[3] nearly all subjects (87–100%) had PSIs indicating similarity. The exception was after the quiz and before the stressful imagery with only about 50% showing similarity between the sessions.

Technical Considerations

One observation by Arena et al. (1983) with implications is the rise of basal hand temperatures across three sessions. The first two sessions were 1 day apart and the third 7 days later. The mean temperature rose from 85.6° F to 88.4° F and then to 91.2° F. After 20 more days, the basal temperature dropped to 82.4° F. The authors' interpretation was a significant basal habituation effect for hand temperature with sessions repeated within 1 week. This effect dissipated with sessions spaced more than 1 week apart. One implication noted is that increases in temperature sometimes attributed to relaxation or biofeedback often could be habituation to the clinical situation.

Clinical Implications

For resting baselines and for office-based stressors, clinical practitioners need be very cautious when interpreting autonomic data. Comparisons of resting baselines across sessions are complex for many subjects. Knowing this is important when we generalize to other situations and when we compare data across sessions. Many practitioners view each session's resting baselines as largely new situations at least for most autonomic-mediated variables.

---

[3]Before each stimulus presentation. Four of these are between the stimuli and are also recovery periods as they also follow a stimulus and precede the next stimulus.

Marked shifts in muscle and autonomic activity often occur after the patient is sitting quietly for several minutes. Muscle activity can steadily or suddenly drop. Finger temperature can gradually or suddenly increase. Heart rate can drop. Therefore, baseline periods should be considered in a very early session and in some therapy sessions that can capture these changes. This can require segments of up to 15 minutes in a very early session and in some therapy sessions. It also helps check for physiological changes that occur in the extended relaxation periods outside the therapist's office. There is no fixed or proper time for all people and all circumstances!

Realizing that these changes can occur before therapy can help to increase a patient's confidence. It also is important to document the lack of change, especially when changes begin occurring later during feedback and nonfeedback phases. This information is useful for the therapist. Such changes in an initial session do not mean that one needs therapy less. Among the important therapeutic goals are shortening the time before the therapeutic changes occur and increasing the degree and reliability of such changes.

Shorter baseline phases, such as 1 to 3 minutes, also are feasible and proper under many conditions. For example, if we consider the patient sitting quietly with eyes closed, his or her muscle activity may remain low and steady with very little variability for about 1 to 2 minutes among multiple muscles in the head and neck. The muscle activity will probably not change significantly over the next few minutes. Cost containment and other pragmatic factors argue for the shortest baseline phases that can typically answer evaluative and therapy questions.

The therapist should consider the question of whether the patient can relax selected muscle areas into a selected range. Observing that degree of relaxation for 1 to 2 minutes is often sufficient. Evaluating finger temperatures of a patient with Raynaud's disease requires the patient to sit quietly for up to about 20 minutes. Selecting the duration of baseline phases depends on the evaluative clinical or research questions and the physiological modality monitored. It also depends on the physiological changes observed during the initial parts of the baseline phase.

There are circumstances in which one wants or needs additional baseline data. Obtaining such data can entail more than one baseline session and extending some baseline phases even beyond 15 minutes. For example, when there is much variability within or between sessions, one can justify longer resting baselines. Another example occurs for disorders such as sleep-onset insomnia when the relaxation sessions at home are long.

Some patients show increasing muscle activity, cooling hands, increasing pulse, and/or restlessness during the first few minutes of a baseline. More than a few minutes of a baseline might be unnecessary and counterproductive. Even about 5 minutes may be enough. In such a case, the therapist should consider that relaxation induced anxiety (RIA) may be present. He or she should consider the therapeutic goal of gradually increasing periods of sitting quietly without increases in physiological arousal.

Pretreatment and periodic physiological baselines are less practical under some circumstances. For example, there are limitations in the schedules of some patients as in the case of the patient who lives a few hundred miles from the therapist where there is no qualified professional to refer the patient. The therapist is consulting only for one session and that session focuses on the intake interview and patient education for treatments thought to help reduce physical symptoms. There is time for a brief biofeedback session—but not enough time for a desired baseline. The therapist decides instead to get only a brief baseline of about 5 minutes and invest the remaining instrumentation time to providing feedback. The therapist instructs the patient in relaxation, and gives patient-education booklets and audiotapes. The patient then goes home and practices relaxation as instructed.

The lack of physiological baseline data does not always compromise therapy. One properly adjusts priorities, maintains the patient's best interests, and can initiate therapy. If this patient returned for further therapy, one could still get a physiological baseline. Practitioners can discuss the ideal with the patient and note in their reports the reasons for proceeding differently.

Conversely, there are conditions for which one can justify multiple physiological baseline segments or sessions. One such situation occurs when one suspects that the patient may be better or worse at different times. Examples of such times are soon after specific *eliciting* or *emitting* events such as eating, upsetting discussions, physical activity, and certain times of day. Therapists should consider scheduling office sessions to coincide with or immediately follow such events.

The absence of excess tension or arousal during a resting baseline does not mean the person has adequate control. This also is true for patients who show a lack of significant reactivity to a stressor. Therapists should always consider such factors as the possible effects of medications, the office environment, baseline conditions, and the limitations of simulated stressors. For example, some people do not react to office stressors. There are individual differences in how therapists present stressors. Presentation style can affect the stressor's effect.

Physiological tension and arousal, reactivity, and slow recoveries in one office session often do suggest similar functioning in daily life. However, office sessions do have limits. Tension, physiological reactivity, and slow recovery in one session do not mean that the person reacts the same way in other situations. At best, these are snapshots or glimpses of a person's psychophysiological activity in daily life. Office procedures are sources of hypotheses and information for productive discussions. However, they are not always reliable evidence for a patient's daily functioning.

Sitting Quietly with Eyes Open and Eyes Closed

Starting this baseline assumes that patients become as comfortable and stable as practical by the end of the adaptation stage. Patients then continue to sit quietly with minimal instructions. The baseline is sometimes the last part of the adaptation phase. Therapists should consider instructing patients to sit quietly with their eyes open and just gaze across the room. They should instruct patients to avoid talking and moving. Therapists often add a period with eyes closed.

Instructed Relaxation

A common variation, used in addition to a resting baseline, involves giving basic relaxation instructions. For example, some therapists instruct patients to employ whatever relaxation strategies they already use or think might be helpful. Instructions also may give some ideas such as relaxing specific muscle areas. This phase often results in lowered muscle activity and other lowered arousal. It checks patients' abilities to apply their current relaxation skills and the results of simple instructions. Let's consider the following instructions.

> "Now, rest quietly a little longer. Use whatever methods you think best to relax. Focus on the muscles of your face, head, and shoulders. Let yourself go and release the tension in different parts of your body. If you feel that you have to move, scratch, sneeze, or something else, go ahead and do it. This phase lasts a few minutes. Don't think of problems or upsetting events and do not worry about how well you are doing. Whatever degree of relaxation achieved is all right."

Stressor Reactivity or the Stimulation Phase

Rationale

It is sometimes useful to introduce cognitive and physical stressors to check for psychophysiological reactivity and rate of recovery. Both reactivity effects and recovery can help identify causes and correlates of biobehavioral disorders and can potentially help predict those persons at risk for these disorders (Haynes et al., 1991). These authors also note that assessing reactivity can help develop effective interventions. This section discusses reactivity, and the next section focuses on recovery.

Although many providers use stress stimuli before starting therapy, some do not always use them. However, using stress stimuli can help therapists answer some patients' questions about the ways that physiology reacts to stimuli. Some patients benefit from seeing their reactivity and recovery.

For some patients there is very little, if any, excess tension or arousal as they are sitting quietly or relaxing. The therapist may suspect that this is not typical for a specific patient. Stimulation allows one to show the increases and lack of rapid or adequate recovery.

Mechanisms and Mediators of Reactivity

There are two interdependent pathways in which physiological stress occurs (Haynes et al., 1991). One is the *autonomic nervous system* pathway (ANS), especially the *sympathetic nervous system* (SNS) division. The other is the *hypothalamic–pituitary–adrenal cortex system* pathway. The hypothalamus organizes the ANS pathway with input from cortical and subcortical brain structures. This tends to have a rapid onset and short equilibrium time that is the duration of maximum effect. The effects are mostly the results of nerve endings releasing epinephrine and norepinephrine and from the adrenal medulla. In the second pathway, the hypothalamus also regulates the release of adrenocorticotropin hormone (ACTH) from the pituitary gland. This promotes the release of cortisol from the adrenal cortex. These effects are slower and have a longer equilibrium latency or time until maximum effects. The time is longer than that resulting from epinephrine and norepinephrine.

Thus, the duration of a stressor strongly influences its impact. Many studies show that short-duration stressors elevate neurotransmitters, but longer-duration stressors suppress them. Longer-duration stressors deplete norepinephrine, lift the inhibition of ACTH, release cortisol, and suppress the immune system. Transient stressors often used in laboratory studies and clinical practice may not be sufficient for health-inhibiting effects.

The nature of the stress—physiological or psychological—is important. For measuring primarily psychological stressors, therapists should be aware that serum cortisol responds more to subjectively distressing, uncontrollable, and psychologically prominent stress (Dienstbier, 1989). In contrast, the ANS-mediated catecholamine responses, such as epinephrine and norepinephrine, respond to nearly all stimuli such as startle, cognitive, exercise, and mild electric shock (Haynes et al., 1991). See Asterita (1985) and Haynes et al., (1989) for more detailed discussions of this topic.

Stress and stimulation constitute part of evaluation and treatments for conditions other than those treated with relaxation. For example, when evaluating patients with fecal incontinence, therapists should use simulated stimulation to the lower bowel. This checks for reactivity of the internal and external anal sphincters. It also checks for ineffective tensing of the gluteal and abdominal muscles.

With patients with urinary incontinence, therapists sometimes introduce fluid into the bladder to check for sphincter control. During this procedure, practitioners also check for ineffective tensing of abdominal muscles. Other examples involve patients undergoing muscle re-education. Therapists often ask them to hold, carry, walk, push, or bend to evaluate their muscle activity.

Definitions and Methods of Measuring

Response magnitude such as peak reactivity during a stressor is a commonly used psychophysiological response parameter for assessing the effects of stress (Haynes et al., 1991). Researchers and practitioners use cognitive and physical stressors to examine ANS- or central nervous system (CNS)-mediated reactivity. A variety of stimuli are in use in clinical practice. Practitioners assume that the stimuli are stressful. However, for some individuals this may not be the case. In some cases, it is merely orienting or mild stimulation. The following are a few stimuli in clinical and research use and abbreviated sample instructions. For each, the therapist should assume an introductory phrase such as "In a few moments I will ask you to . . ." or "When I ask you to, please. . . ."

1. *Silent arithmetic.*[4] Close your eyes and. . . . count backwards from 450 by 7s. Count backwards from 450 by 8s. Count backwards from 450 by 9s. Count backward from 951 by 13s. Read silently (or aloud)[5] each math problem and write down the answer (e.g., 121 + 767 = ?; 326 − 74 = ?; 18 x 12 = ?).

2. *Tense muscles.* Make a fist. Clench your teeth. Try to open this tightly closed jar. Bend slightly at the waist. Hold this package with both hands.

3. *Personal imagery.* Imagine something very unpleasant for you.

4. *Memory tasks.* Remember this story exactly as I say it.

5. *Hyperventilation.*[6] Inhale and exhale very quickly and deeply for 2 minutes. Inhale and exhale through both your mouth and nose. Each time you inhale try to fill your lungs completely. Each time you exhale try to empty your lungs completely. Inhale every time I say "In." Exhale every time I say "Out." (One can use an audiotape to signal inhalations and exhalations.)

6. *Prerecorded loud noises or other unpleasant sounds.* Examples are a baby crying, car horns repeatedly blowing, or listening to people screaming at each other.

7. *Cold exposure and cold pressure.* Hold this glass of ice water for 2 minutes. Place your hand up to your wrist in this bucket of ice water. Then close your eyes. Please keep your hand in the ice water until it becomes too uncomfortable (hurts badly enough) to continue or until I tell you to stop.

8. *Action and challenging video games.*

9. *Slides of stressful scenes or videotaped traumas.* Look at these slides (or video).

10. *Difficult quizzes.* Complete this quiz. Most people get a score of at least _____.

11. *Holmes–Rahe Visualizations.*[7] Please close your eyes. Visualize yourself in the following situation(s). Try to see yourself in the situation. Feel just how this situation hits you. Really get into it! Try to make it as real and vivid as you can including the sights,

---

[4]One example for each stressor presentation for math and tense muscles.

[5]Sample equations and the purpose of reading aloud from Linden (1991).

[6]See Chapter 11 for discussion of hyperventilation, Hyperventilation Provocation Test, and cautions.

[7]Developed by Rosenthal et al. (1989) for research. Instructions modified very slightly.

sounds, smells, and emotions. Imagine how you would react as clearly as possible. (See discussion below.)

12. *Your Everyday Life Pressures* (*YELP*).[8] Sharpen your imagination. Put yourself in this situation. (Subject/patient reads along silently as experimenter/practitioner reads each scenario aloud.) Try to see yourself in the situation. Feel just how this situation hits you. Really get into it! Try to make it as real and vivid as you can including the sights, sounds, smells, and emotions. Imagine how you would react as clearly as possible. (Rosenthal et al., 1989; see discussion below).

Obviously, one does not use all or most of these techniques with each patient. Research and clinical practice usually include from one to three stressors. Most require at least 1 minute and usually up to 4 minutes for each presentation. There are individual differences in reactivity, hence the rationale for using multiple stimuli of different types.

Instructions probably have an arousal effect at least for some physiological responses such as heart rate (Furedy, 1987; Sharpley, 1993). This probably results from several factors such as attending to the instructions and anxiety associated with the uncertainty and challenge of the task. This additional arousal effect can confound the assessment of reactivity of the stressor. Therefore, the therapist should consider measuring the reactivity during the instructions and separating this from the stressor task data. With computer-based psychophysiological systems, one can create periods or trials designated as instructions.

Some practitioners insert another period of about 1 minute after the instructions and before instructing the patient to start the task. They assume this allows the patient to relax and allows for measuring the effects of instructions and anticipation. However, some patients may prematurely start some cognitive task during this period. Therapists can circumvent this easily by instructions such as "In a few moments I will ask you to. . . . Keep relaxing until I say to begin." For counting backwards, therapists should wait until after the interspersed postinstruction period to give the numbers.

Mental Arithmetic. This is probably the most commonly used office stressor in research and clinical practice. There are several advantages (Linden, 1991) for mental math as a stressor. It is easy to administer. It does not require equipment as do video games, reaction times, or cold pressors. At most it needs only a method to visually present equations. It should raise no ethical concerns from an Institutional Review Board (IRB), Human Subjects Research Review Committee, Ethics Committee, or Clinical Practices Committee. In addition, the technique of mental arithmetic offers a wide range of variations for adapting it for specific patients and for repeated presentations. However, a potential problem for comparing studies and procedures stems from the lack of universally accepted standardized procedures.

Linden (1991) provides a useful review and a series of studies of the effects of vocal versus written versions, noise distraction, and different types of math tasks. The most arousing, at least for cardiovascular reactivity, are those involving vocal responding, noise distraction, and solving visually presented equations (Linden, 1991). One may expect some attenuation of the reactivity with repeated presentations of the same math task (Sharpley, 1993). Thus, the therapist should consider different math tasks if he or she uses repeated stressor presentations involving math.

Your Everyday Life Pressures and Holmes–Rahe Visualizations. Rosenthal et al. (1989) developed two brief and practical stressor tasks for research that are of potential clinical use. I

---

[8]Developed by Rosenthal et al. (1989) for research. Instructions modified very slightly.

present a summary of these here. The Holmes–Rahe scenes are from the Holmes–Rahe (1967) Social Readjustment Scale. One also could use items from other life stress inventories. The patient visualizes either a short version (e.g., fired at work, divorce, or jail term) or a detailed version. Examples of detailed versions are "Going to jail for a long time," "With no real warning, you are out of job," "Going through a divorce. You don't really want it but can't stop it" (Rosenthal et al., 1989). The two versions did not differ in terms of various ratings by college students.

The subjects ranked 20 Holmes–Rahe life events items and visualized their top three choices in ascending order each for 2 minutes. The mean of these ratings consistently and significantly indicated more stress than did a videotape of dramatic scenes from a major chemical fire and a child and father nearly drowning. The Holmes–Rahe visualization ratings were also consistently and significantly more stressful than the ratings for 2 minutes of visualizing an individually selected personal worst experience in the past 6 months.

The YELP task involved eight selected vignettes "depicting frustrating, disappointing, or otherwise noxious" situations. Many doctoral-level clinicians selected these from among 48 potential items. I present two vignettes as examples. The rest are in Rosenthal et al. (1989).

> 8. You've been asked to plan a project and go to a meeting to give your ideas. You've put much time, thought, and effort into your proposal and have a lot of confidence in it. Most of the other people start off agreeing with you. But one tease keeps shooting you down in a very funny way that gets everyone laughing. You become angry but don't know what to do. Even though your ideas are very solid the tease makes them sound silly. You lose your cool. You get all tense and tongue-tied. The others keep laughing at you. You feel like a helpless fool and want to crawl into a hole. (p. 553)
> 4. You have some very personal worries on your mind. You need a sounding board and share your worries with a close friend. Your friend listens sympathetically, gives some advice, and promises never to breathe a word to anyone. Later, you learn the friend gossiped about your personal problems. That made things worse, as well as losing your trust in the friend. (p. 553)

The stress ratings for Holmes–Rahe visualizations were consistently higher than the three other stressors. The YELP procedure was about the same or slightly more stressful than one's own worst event. In studies 3 and 4, Rosenthal et al. (1989), obtained heart rate and frontal EMG from two samples of 12 (6 men and 6 women) college-aged subjects each receiving either Holmes–Rahe visualizations or YELP stressors with three presentations of 2 minutes each using different items. All 24 subjects also received three mental arithmetic tasks (i.e., counting backwards from 450 by 7s, by 8s, and from 500 by 9s) and a cold pressor stress presented three times each for 2 minutes.

The major finding from the psychophysiological reactivity and recovery data was that the two "new stressors had an impact fairly similar to mental arithmetic and very close to each other" (p. 557) "and were commensurate in impact with cold pressor and mental arithmetic" (p. 560).

Advantages of the Holmes–Rahe visualization and YELP tasks are the availability of stressors for repeated presentations and the probable acceptance of institutional review committees. Limitations are the lack of data for patients although the authors planned such research. They state the customary and proper caution to use for research. I agree. However, I see no convincing reason to avoid the Holmes–Rahe and YELP tasks in clinical psychophysiological assessments. Many practitioners will find these types of tasks useful; however, one must gain experience in clinical settings to evaluate their potential value.

Considering the wide range of stressors and procedures used in clinical settings, there can be no harm in trying these. As with all office-based stressors, one must be very cautious about interpreting the meaning and implications of psychophysiological reactivity and recovery. Prudent practitioners will use all of them cautiously.

Technical Considerations

Absolute scores are more stable than difference scores, although the correlations among repeated measures are modest, and some are unreliable across procedures (Waters et al., 1987). Single psychophysiological responses are much less useful than multiple types of responses for showing psychophysiological reactivity. Multivariate statistical analyses examine patterns of reactivity and reveal the more meaningful reliability indices than less complex comparisons. However, they are not usually practical and often not possible in routine clinical practice with currently available and most commonly used instruments and software.

Some psychophysiological functions react more to the body's needs and physiological demands than to emotional reactivity to office stressors. One example is pulse rate. Individual differences in cardiac demand among patients and between sessions are often unassessable in routine practice.

There are occasionally decreases in arousal during cognitive tasks intended to increase arousal. For example, Sharply (1993) points out "that some cognitive tasks elicit heart rate increases and other cognitive tasks elicit heart rate decreases" (p. 234). He reports "testing over 600 subjects with the same style of mental arithmetic task. Subjects from five to 63 years are almost uniform in their heart-rate reactivity (HRR) being an increase, but some instances of HRR as a decrease were observed across all ages" (p. 234). Of the 72 subjects in the research reported, "7 showed HRR which were decreases" (p. 234). This underscores the need to look at individual data rather than only group data that typically will obscure such differences.

Review of Studies

Arena et al. (1989) continued their series of studies of psychophysiological stability during office procedures, individual response stereotypy, and stimulus–response specificity. They correctly assume that "it is important to determine the response system in which individuals are most reactive and to then examine that dominant response more closely" (p. 610).

Subjects. The group used 46 female and 18 male college students and community volunteers with a mean age of 33 (SD = 13) and an age range from 17 to 75.

Modalities and Sites. Using Coulbourn instruments, they measured bifrontal EMG, finger temperature, and pulse rate. The EMG bandpass was 90–250 Hertz. Finger temperature was from the volar surface of the third phalanx of the left hand's second digit. Pulse rate was from a finger photoplethysmogragh on the volar surface of the third phalanx of the left hand, presumably the second digit. The subjects sat in an easy chair in contact with the experimenter via a window and intercom. Recordings were on four days—1, 2, 8, and 28.

Psychological Measures. Results from several measures[9] are in a separate report.

---

[9]The State–Trait Anxiety Inventory, Beck Depression Inventory, Social Readjustment Rating Scale, SUNY-Albany revision of the Cox Psychosomatic Symptom Checklist, and Hassles and Uplifts Scale.

Adaptation. The instructions for subjects were to sit quietly with their eyes closed for 20 minutes.

Resting Baseline. This was from an added 2 minutes under the same conditions. The data were the average EMG from the last second of the 12 10-second intervals. Temperature samples were from the end of the 10-second intervals. Pulse rate data were from all the data in each interval.

Stressors. With the subjects' eyes closed, the mental stress was counting backwards by 7s from a large random three-digit number for 4 minutes. After recovery from the mental stress and with their eyes closed, the patients' physical stress was up to 4 minutes of a cold pressor with their right hand immersed up to the wrist in a bucket of ice water. They could stop if it became too uncomfortable. The data were the average from the first minute of each stress.

Reactivity. Computations of standard z scores allowed determining the modality producing the largest arousal for each stressor. Each subject experienced eight stress events across the 4 days. Response stereotypy was showing the most reactivity in the same system for at least six of the eight stressor periods. Stimulus–response specificity was showing more reactivity in one response system to one stressor in at least three of the four sessions and the most frequent arousal from a different system during the other stressor. Five clinicians provided the ratings of the data. Preset criteria applied to the standard scores showed 42% ($N = 27$) with response stereotypy and 20% ($N = 13$) with stimulus–response specificity. The other 24 subjects did not fit either classification.

Research Implications and Limitations. The use of nonclinical subjects is a limitation but understandable given the stage of this type of research. The authors note the limited array of stressors and suggest others be incorporated in the future to improve clinical relevance. They also note the limitation of using only three psychophysiological responses and suggest the use of others to improve clinical relevance. There were no manipulation checks on compliance with mental stress.

Agreement among clinician ratings was only about 50%, and agreement with empirical classification based on deviation scores only 29%. The authors also note the potential use of other classification systems for response stereotypy and specificity. For example, they note that reducing the criterion from six to five of the eight trials would increase the percentage of subjects classified as showing stereotypy from 42% to 67%.

Strengths. The use of 4 days of comparisons and a large sample were strengths of this study. Investigating response stereotypy and following stimulus–response specificity were other strengths. Continuing a series of studies in the same area also is praiseworthy.

Clinical Implications. Many subjects (42% in this study), and by implication many patients, show reliable responding over time or individual response stereotypy, regardless of the nature of the stress. A substantial percentage of subjects (20% in this study) respond differently to different types of stressors. One implication of the latter is to direct treatment at all response systems affected by different stressors. To determine this, one must first include different types of stressors and different types of modalities. This would call for more therapy than for those showing response stereotypy. Each type of stressor does not show the same type of physiological response. Subject factors appear more important determinants of the response system.

Clinicians can determine the psychophysiological response patterns but appear to need specialized statistical procedures to discern these patterns. However, these are not readily available or not yet practical in routine clinical practice. Incorporating these statistical analyses into standard biofeedback software packages and making them user friendly is necessary for routine clinical use.

The correlations of baseline and reactivity data across sessions indicate there are many factors other than known procedural factors affecting the reliability of psychophysiological measures. Each of these three responses showed statistical reliability. However, the magnitudes of the 54 correlations[10] were only moderate. Two-thirds of them were between $r = .4$ to .7, and only one was above $r = .7$. This does not suggest that other procedures and subjects will produce a similar degree of reliability. However, it does caution us to be careful relying on data from one session.

Additional Research. However, a reanalysis of their data using the intraclass correlation coefficient (I-CCC; Kirk, 1982) showed large coefficients (Arena & Hobbs, 1993). This indicates substantially better temporal stability for absolute scores than previously shown. Absolute scores are most important and used most commonly in research and clinical practice. The I-CCC accounts for changes in *values* of scores and allows analysis of three or more sets of data for the same subjects. Pearson product correlation coefficients, used previously in research on temporal stability of psychophysiological responding, accounts for the *relative proportion* of scores for *two sets* of scores. Analyses of difference scores or percent change of raw scores from baseline show much lower correlations as expected for difference scores.

The I-CCCs for temperature were +.77 for baseline and mental arithmetic across the four sessions. For frontal EMG, the coefficients were +.87 and +.84 respectively and for heart rate, +.77 and +.70. The coefficients for the cold pressor also were impressive for skin temperature (+.82) and heart rate (+.99)—although less so for frontal EMG (+.63).

The more positive findings from the reanalyses do not detract from the need to study the other factors that affect the temporal stability of psychophysiological responding (Arena & Hobbs, 1993). In a subsequent study of the original 1989 sample, Arena and Hobbs (in press) studied trait anxiety in their search for factors affecting temporal stability. Their anxiety measure was the Spielberger Trait Anxiety Inventory (STAI; Spielberger, Gorsuch, & Luchene, 1970).

The low-anxiety group of 17 subjects had a an average score of about 26 which is at about the 21st percentile. The high-anxiety subjects had an average score of about 48 at the 90th to 92nd percentiles for male and female subjects. The average age of the college and community volunteer sample was about 32 (*SD* = nearly 13, range 18–75).

This factor showed significant effects on psychophysiological temporal stability but not magnitude of reactivity. Lower-anxious subjects show more stability than high-anxious subjects for hand surface temperature but not for frontal EMG or heart rate. The latter two did not show a consistent relationship. Thus, correlations for hand temperature across sessions are substantially higher for lower-anxious than higher-anxious subjects. There is extreme lability between sessions in higher trait-anxious subjects. The investigators "strongly

---

[10]Three conditions, three responses, and between 4 days (three comparisons).

recommend to both clinicians and researchers that they employ additional measures of arousal and relaxation, instead of relying solely on hand surface temperature response" (Arena & Hobbs, in press).

Aside from understandably using a nonclinical sample and "only three psychophysiological responses," the only limitation of this study was the lack of control for nicotine and caffeine. The authors note this but suggest that this "would not typically occur in practice settings." However, both caffeine and nicotine are more commonly used by high-anxious people and both affect hand temperatures through peripheral vasoconstriction. Therefore, one needs to control for these. Practitioners anxiously await research with patients and look for controls for caffeine and nicotine.

Waters et al., (1987) compared 30 college students with 5 stimuli and 10 psychophysiological measures over 2 weeks. The magnitude and range of correlations were similiar to the later study by Arena et al. (1989). About 40% of the correlations for reactivity were between $r = .4$ to .7. They also analyzed pattern similarity with the Profile Similarity Index (Buco & Blouin, 1983) providing a single index of overall similarity or reliability of the two response profiles. For reactivity, at least 87% of the subjects showed similarity indicated by the PSI.

Probably the most revealing analysis was from comparing the ranks from 10 to 1 of the subjects with a ranked hierarchy of standardized physiological scores for each subject and for the 10 psychophysiological measures. Waters et al. averaged the ranks across the stimulus procedures. Fifteen of 30 subjects ranking 10th in one session, and 14 ranking 9th were 10th or 9th in the second session. Similarly, 29 of the subjects ranked 2 or 1 in the first session were 2 or 1 in the second session. Those ranked between these extremes in the first session varied considerably in the second, and some went to the other extreme.

The researchers concluded that "it is thus clear that the most extreme responses in an individual's psychophysiological response hierarchy are the most stable (reliable) across experimental sessions" (Waters et al., 1987, p. 219). Thus, the subjects ranked highest (10 or 9) and those ranked lowest (1 or 2) were the reasons for stability of the overall analysis. This "helps account for the significant but modest Test–Retest correlations of single measures . . ." (p. 220).

Shaffer et al. (1991) studied the 1-week reliability of resting baseline psychophysiological activity for several ANS variables assessed for 5 minutes after a 15-minute stabilization period. The 21 male and female undergraduates, aged 18 to 21, reclined with their legs supported and their eyes open. There were statistically significant reliability correlations for several variables. The stability was high for skin conductance level ($r = .89$), moderate and statistically significant for heart rate ($r = .63$), abdominal amplitude ($r = .63$), finger temperature ($r = .54$), and respiration rate ($r = .49$), and low and nonsignificant for blood volume pulse ($r = .23$).

See the detailed discussion of the study by Flor, Turk, and Birbaumer (1985) later in this chapter. I present it separately because it involves more than reactivity and reliability—and because of unique and commendable features.

Clinical Considerations

We learn from the available studies such as Waters et al. (1987) that reliabilities vary across procedures, responses, and subjects. Response patterns also vary among procedures and subjects. About half of subjects[11] at one extreme in one session will also show reactivity at

---

[11]We can assume this is true for patients, but we do not yet have enough evidence.

the same extreme in a second session up to 2 weeks later. However, the other subjects will vary. Therapists must consider both individual–response stereotypy and stimulus–response specificity when designing psychophysiological evaluation and therapy procedures and when interpreting at least baselines and reactivity data.

Practitioners hope that research will address remaining questions. For example, do therapists need to evoke intense psychophysiological reactions or will milder reactivity be sufficient to accomplish evaluation and therapy goals?

Therapists should consider stressors longer than 1–2 minutes. However, reduced arousal during a longer stressor, while generally relaxing, could be habituation to the stressor. Remember, this is one explanation for the therapeutic effects of exposure therapies such as systematic desensitization and flooding. Repeated exposure to short stressors followed by relaxation or biofeedback-assisted relaxation may be a version of exposure therapy. Reduced reactivity to stressors may not be the result of relaxation or biofeedback but rather pro-longed exposure or repeated short exposures to the stressor stimuli.

Some practitioners may ask whether one can accomplish desired goals of evaluation and therapy using exposures to stressors of 1–2 minutes rather than longer ones such as 4 minutes. This depends on the goals. If one uses short stressors and gets arousal, it gives the therapist information to use in patient education. It may not matter if the arousal is less than that occuring in daily life. However, if there is very little or no arousal from a short exposure, the therapist should consider a longer exposure, a different presentation of the stressor, or another stressor.

Poststress Recovery Stage

Rationale

Psychophysiological and other biobehavioral disorders often have important physiological components. Implicated as causal factors are environmental and other stressors. However, the interactions among behavioral, cognitive, and physiological factors are complex.

The strength of the relationship between the magnitude of reactivity and other indices of psychological functioning is often modest (Haynes et al., 1991). These authors also note a modest ability for reactivity to distinguish persons with a disorder from those without it. Hence the interest in both the rate and degree of recovery to help explain etiology and plan clinical interventions.

The goal of many clinical interventions is changing the psychophysiological response to stress (Cacioppo, Berntson, & Anderson, 1991; Haynes, Falkin, & Sexton-Radek, 1989). Therefore, psychophysiological poststress recovery is of crucial importance.

Implications include etiology and treatment of psychophysiological disorders. Specifically, recovery indices can help identify causal mechanisms of many biobehavioral disorders. They can help identify persons at risk for these biobehavioral disorders and help develop effective interventions and evaluations of treatment (Haynes et al., 1991).

Within-study differences between stressor versus poststress recovery results constitute a very important index of the importance and potential use of poststress recovery. This implies that these two indices stem from different mechanisms. Eighty-one of 180 statistical analyses reported by Haynes et. al. (1991) showed nonsignificant effects of stressors. Of these 81, 74% showed significant recovery phase effects. Conversely, when stressor effects were significant in 74 analyses, recovery phases showed nonsignificant effects for 42% of the same variables. Stress effects and recovery are very often different and of differential sensitivity and potential utility.

Definitions and Methods of Measurement

Impaired recovery or *slowness of recovery* after psychophysiological reactivity to one or more stressors is the focus of using poststress recovery stages. Specific definitions of poststress recovery vary in the literature. Arena et al. (1989) defined recovery as a return to the quiescent baseline state after stress-induced reactivity. The EMG recovery was a return to 5% of the mean of initial resting baseline. Hand temperature recovery was a return to within 5% of the baseline mean. Heart-rate recovery was recovery to within 2 beats/minute of the baseline.

Other definitions of recovery are "changes in stressor-induced responses following stressor termination" and "the rate and degree to which a psychophysiological response approaches prestress levels following a stressful experience" (Haynes et al., 1991, p. 356). These definitions allow for nonlinear and bidirectional changes. It is different from a return to a prestressor quiescent baseline state. The time course of *recovery* is the magnitude of the response over time after stopping a stressor. It is sometimes nonlinear and may diverge from prestressor levels. For example, arousal sometimes increases or becomes unstable.

Recovery differs from habituation (Haynes et al., 1991; Konarska, Stewart, McCarty, 1989). "Latency to recovery" is the time required to reach the prestressor level. "Relative recovery to baseline" is the absolute degree or percentage the physiological variable approaches the prestressor baseline level after a specified time. Freeman (1939) called this the "Physiological Recovery Quotient." "Relative recovery from a stressor" is the absolute degree or percentage the physiological variable changes from the peak magnitude during a stressor after a specified time. The "recovery slope" is the units of change per unit of time and the form of that slope. Examples of the latter are linear and parabolic.

Review of Studies Assessing Recovery

A representative sample of 24 studies of recovery are in Haynes et al. (1991). Forty-one more studies from 1984 through the first half of 1990 are available from the first author. This a nonexhaustive list but probably representative. Diverse methods and questions about proper measurement methods of some studies complicate interpretation.

Time Period to Assess Recovery

There are very few studies specifically focused on the time period needed to assess poststress recovery adequately (Arena, 1984; Arena, Bruno, Brucks, & Hobbs, 1992[12]). The physiological variables in these two studies were cephalic vasomotor response, frontal and forearm flexor EMG, hand temperature (left hand), heart rate, and skin resistance.

Arena (1984) studied 15 college undergraduates. All were about age 20. He reported a 3-minute poststress period adequate to return to a basal quiescent state for most of several psychophysiological measures. Frontal EMG needed 6 minutes to recover. This study "indicated good intrasession reliability on all measures except frontal EMG, whereas there was inadequate intersession reliability" (Arena et al., 1992).

The recent study did "not completely replicate or support the major findings of" their earlier study. Most subjects (about 78%) returned to baseline with 6 minutes for heart rate. Average times were 3.7 and 2.9 minutes for the two poststress periods.

---

[12]The abstract in the Proceedings of the 23rd Annual Meeting of the AAPB included analyses of only 20 subjects. Interested readers can write to Dr. Arena for a copy of the paper based on the analyses of all 64 subjects.

However, for both EMG sites, only 48% returned to baseline in the 6 minutes. The average time was 4.6 minutes and 5.1 minutes for the two poststress periods.

For hand surface temperature, 6 minutes "was clearly inadequate" for most subjects. Only about 38% returned to baseline in this period. The average time was about 4.5 minutes and 5.6 minutes during the two poststress periods. The percentages returning to baseline appeared higher in the first poststress period. For example, hand temperatures returned to baseline in nearly 48% compared to only about 26% in the second poststress period.

Although the earlier study suggested about 3 minutes for cardiovascular and electrodermal modalities to recover back to a prestress basal level, the latter study indicates much longer times are necessary. The authors speculation about the differences focuses on the larger sample size and the wider age range of the recent study. The age range was 17–75, and the mean age was nearly 33.

These two studies used serial 7s from a large random three-digit number as the cognitive stressor and cold pressor (presumably right hand) as the physical stressor. Exposure was 4 minutes for the cognitive and up to that for the physical. This cognitive stressor is probably milder than many others in use, and the cold pressor is a more intense physical stress than most clinicians use. It also is more likely to evoke cardiovascular effects that would take longer to recover from than most other office-based physical stressors. The subjects were college students and community volunteers of various ages, hence one must use caution generalizing to patients. However, it is reasonable to assume that the implications from the more recent study are more similar to patients.

Except for the limits of these studies, the research of Arena and his colleagues is important and useful. They supported the need to allow for recovery periods. They showed the differences in the durations of these periods among modalities, and they documented the duration of the recovery periods under specified conditions. Poststress periods may need to be at least 6 minutes if one needs patients to return to a baseline. This is feasible in clinical practice using two or three stress periods during an evaluation session. However, it is typically not practical during routine therapy sessions if one uses multiple stressors or intense stressors. The cognitive stress in these studies is only serial 7s for 4 minutes. For some, that is stressful, but for many it is not.

Methods of Measuring and Technical Considerations

Common measures include simple change scores. An example of a change score is the difference between the poststimulus compared to the prestimulus and stressor. Other examples are between the resting baseline and a stressor and between pretreatment and posttreatment phases. Criticism of change scores occurs because they contain measurement error from both pre- and poststimulus phases. Thus, they tend to have poor test–retest reliability as can the use of regression procedures or residualized change scores thought by Lacey (1959) to be a solution and, thus, can be misleading (Cacioppo et al., 1991).

The direction and magnitude of autonomic responses have multiple sources of influence and restriction. One is the "law of initial values" (Wilder, 1957; Oken & Heath, 1963; Sturgis & Gramling, 1988). The law of initial values asserts that the prestimulus level of a system being measured affects the magnitude of the physiological reactivity to a specific stimulus or situation. One assumes an implicit "ceiling effect." Smaller increases in reactivity and larger decreases may occur after a higher prestimulus level. It is more applicable to cardiovascular and vasomotor responses than others such as skin resistance responses although not usually to skin conductance responses. The extent this law operates across various physiological systems needs more research. Serious implications are that change scores are less useful and statistical power is compromised unless one uses special statistical analyses such as covariance and autonomic lability score (Lacey, 1956; Benjamin, 1967; Coles, Gratton, Kramer, & Miller, 1986, p. 213). The autonomic lability score requires the same constraints and debates as ANCOVA (Coles et al., 1986, pp. 212–213), and research rarely uses it.

Implications for clinical practice are the needs to be aware of the effects of prestimulus levels on reactivity and to be very careful interpreting change scores especially without complex statistical analyses.

The law of initial values is one case of a broader law of dynamic range that includes floor and ceiling effects on autonomic functioning (Cacioppo et al., 1991; Berntson, Cacioppo, & Quigley, 1991; Cacioppo & Tassinary, 1990a, 1990b).

One should consider using the latency to recovery, the relative recovery to baseline, the relative recovery from a stressor, and/or the recovery slope. To measure nonlinear recovery, one needs time-series measurements or frequent sampling across time. Psychophysiological systems have different recovery time courses and require different sampling rates. One that shows fast changes, such as from many ANS systems, requires a frequent sampling rate.

The magnitude of stress response reactivity affects all recovery measures. The relative recovery to baseline, a proportional index, is more strongly affected by baseline values than are absolute indices. The tie to the prestress baseline is stronger for the latency to recovery and the relative recovery to baseline. The tie is weaker for the prestress baseline to the relative recovery from the stressor and the recovery slope.

Statistical Analysis Considerations

Multiple regression analysis for linear and nonlinear functions allows estimates of variance in a recovery index. Variables contributing to this are:

- The prestress baseline
- The magnitude of the response to the stressor
- The time since stopping the stressor
- The duration of the stressor
- Subject characteristics
- The specific response measured

Clinical Considerations and Uses in Stress Profiling

I offer clinical considerations that I based partly on the research of Arena and his colleagues. Recovery to a basal level is idiosyncratic and depends on many factors. These include the manner in which one presents stressors, the specific meaning of the stressor for the individual, the specific person's physiology, and individual response stereotypy and stimulus–response specificity (Arena et al., 1989).

Based on Haynes et al. (1991), I offer these inferences for the clinical use of recovery in stress profiling. Delayed poststress recovery should alert therapists to possible behaviors or thoughts increasing the persistence of the stressor-induced reactivity. It also should alert the therapist to the person's inability to regulate the physiological reactivity proficiently.

Impaired poststress recovery suggests unhealthy functioning of physiological, homeostatic control mechanisms involving the ANS, CNS, and endocrine systems. This may be the result of chronic, stressor-triggered, physiological activation. That may have direct unhealthy effects such as prolonged elevations of blood pressure, migraines, and tension-type headaches. There also may be indirect deleterious effects such as modifying negative feedback systems. For example, altered baroreceptor sensitivity interferes with normal reductions of blood pressure.

Signs of delayed poststress recovery can help guide intervention decisions. With this information, therapists can often uncover specific behavioral, cognitive, or physiological events to target during treatment. This augments interventions that focus on preventing and avoiding life stressors or only using relaxation to moderate their effects. Shorter poststress recovery time and/or sharper recovery slopes can serve as measures of therapy effectiveness.

Practitioners hope that research will address remaining questions. For example, do therapists need each physiological response to recover to a basal level to accomplish evaluation and therapy goals?

Selected Study of Stress Profiling

Flor et al. (1985) gave us an excellent study of the value of stress profiling. It was from the doctoral dissertation of the first author at the Univerisity of Tübingen. The data do not address stability of responses but do give us valuable information on logical and predicted muscle reactivity differences between groups, the importance of office stressors, and the value of recovery data. Another important asset is the inclusion of the diathesis–stress model of chronic back pain for conceptualizing the procedures and explaining the results.

Subjects

There were 17 subjects each in groups of patients with chronic back pain (CBP), chronic general pain (GP) unrelated to the back, and nonpain hospital patients with other medical problems such as diabetes. Of the 51 patients, 40 were male patients, and the age range was 23 to 73 with an average age of 47. The CBP group had seven patients with degenerative disc disease/spondylosis, four with low back pain (LBP) of unknown origin, and three with disc hernias. Nine of the CBP patients showed X-ray evidence of moderate-to-severe degenerative changes, and the other patients showed minimal or no changes.

Modalities and Sites

The EMG recordings were made with a Cyborg Biolab. Electrodes were placed on the lumbrosacral erector spinae muscles for the 14 patients with LBP and a trapezius muscle of the 3 with upper back pain. The fixed bandpass filter was 100–250 Hz.

Recording of frontal EMG, a theoretically irrelevant muscle site, was for assessing the response specificity of the stressors for patients with back pain. Heart-rate recordings from the right hand second digit and skin resistance level from the left hand helped check the stressor manipulations.

Psychological Measures

The Pain Experience Scale (PES; Turk, 1981) was used to assess emotional and cognitive reactions to pain. Combined with the Beck Depression Inventory (BDI), these two measures were the most useful measures for predicting EMG reactivity. The PES and BDI accounted for almost 76% of the variance of EMG reactivity. Readers should refer to the original article for information about the other measures.

Adaptation/Resting Baseline

The authors did not specify an adaptation period. However, they did record 10 minutes of a resting baseline with the subjects sitting still with their eyes open. The average resting EMG activity was higher for the CBP group. However, this came from only four of the CBP patients who showed extreme muscle activity very different from the other patients in this group during this phase.

Stressors

Cognitive stressors consisted of recalling and describing for 1 minute a recent personal stressful event or a recent pain episode. General stress consisted of quickly counting backwards by 7s from 758. The neutral task was reciting the alphabet. The order of the tasks varied among the patients. The ANS measures of heart-rate and skin-resistance level and self-report ratings of the stressors supported the stressor manipulation.

Reactivity

Reactivity was the average EMG of the 1-minute stressor task. The EMG reactivity of patients with CPB was significantly greater only to the personal stressors. For example, with a personal stress, the CBP group showed 4.5 microvolts (SD = 5.1) compared to the prestress 2.6 microvolts. In contrast, the other groups showed 1.8 and 1.4 microvolts reactivity compared to their 1.5 and 1.1 prestress EMG activity. The pain recall stressor showed the same result with an average increase of 2.2 microvolts compared with essentially no increase for the other groups. The other tasks showed significantly less increases of about .6 and .3 microvolts for the CBP group.

Recovery

Recovery was the average number of seconds for a patient's muscle tension to return to the level of the 1-minute pretrial baseline up to the maximum of the 5-minute recovery period. The CBP patients showed slower recoveries of bilateral back muscles after the personal stressors.

Limitations

The authors note the possible limitation of using a fixed 100- to 250-Hz bandpass filter. This does not discredit the reactivity results. It implies that a wider bandpass would capture more muscle activity. The inability to control for the potential effects of analgesic medications may be a limitation of the study. However, the CBP and GP groups did not differ in type and amount of these medications. The published account also does not specify the exact trapezius placement.

The study combined patients with widely variable causes for their CBP. Depression and reactions to pain might be related to the type of CPB diagnosis and other variables associated with the pain and diagnosis. The study did not report which aspects of depression were more predictive of reactivity. The details of the sitting position were vague in the published report; for example, we do not know if there was back support.

Strengths

The use of clinical patients is unique and applauded. Comparison of a specific clinical group with a clinical control group and a nonclinical control group raises more applause. Providing stressors with clinical practicality and relevance eases clinical application. Controlling for order and body movement effects adds to the strength of the conclusions. Excessive movement resulted in excluding only two subjects. Further adding to the clinical usefulness is the inclusion of measures of mood and self-reported emotional effects of symptoms to predict physiological changes. Finding no differences among the groups for a theoretically irrelevant muscle site, the frontal, helps support a response-specificity model.

The study controlled for the possible effects of surgery and possible effects of denervation potentials. Comparing personal stressors with a general stressor and a neutral task is another strength.

Research Implications and Needs

One can effectively and usefully study the effects of stress on physiological reactivity among clinical patients. One can derive useful data for application to clinical practice. Future research needs to assess the aspects of depression and self-reported attitudes about the symptom effects. This could help better predict psychophysiolgical reactivity and recovery. We also need assessment of more intense and longer duration stressors. This would assess whether such stressors result in more reactivity and more significant delays in recovery and could help bridge the gap from office procedures to daily life. Assessing a wider bandpass that captures more of the electrical activity of the muscles is another research need.

One needs to study these procedures with more homogeneous causes for the CBP. The authors note the need for further study of the potential effects of surgery, medication effects, and denervation of muscles.

Clinical Implications

Measuring muscle reactivity to personal stressors and measuring recovery after these stressors can be useful and may be necessary at least with some patients with CBP. Therapists should consider using and comparing the effects of multiple stressors including personal stress, general stress, and a neutral task.

Measuring logically related muscles in the target areas of the pain is appropriate. The use of frontal EMG is of limited value for assessing patients with CPB with these procedures. Although the levels of muscle reactivity were low, they are enough to justify patient education about patient reactivity and recovery in daily life.

Aspects of depression probably interact with psychophysiological reactivity. Thus, one should assess depression among patients with CPB and use this in clinical decisions. There are subgroups of patients with CPB for whom these psychophysiological measures are more useful. Patient reactions and perceptions of the effects of pain probably interact with reactivity. Depression and reactions to pain might be the result of the type of CPB diagnosis or other variables associated with the pain and diagnosis. Practitioners should consider this when they assess depression and pain reactivity rather than rely solely or primarily on self-ratings alone. For example, depression and pain reactivity ratings may change with various interventions. We do not yet know if this would alter their relationships with psychophysiological reactivity and recovery.

Psychophysiological Reactivity, Recovery,
and Treatment Efficacy: Conclusions

More of a discussion of this very complex subject is beyond the scope of this chapter and this author. However, some discussion was necessary to provide some basic and useful information, a sense of the complexity of this subject, and a direction for readers.

One must use caution about inferences about psychological and psychophysiological significance based on clinical procedures. Readers are cautioned to treat these data as preliminary hypotheses and to recognize the limits of most clinical recordings and procedures. They are urged not to use simple change or difference scores to indicate robustly reliable or clinically meaningful inferences. Readers are encouraged to use the physiological data to generate hypotheses about the patient and to use such information for patient education and to work toward applied psychophysiological changes.

A good example to consider might be a patient showing increased physiological reactivity during presentation of a stressor and a rapid recovery to the prestimulus baseline. One can point to this as an example or glimpse at how the process *could* occur in daily life. Two good uses of such data would be to help the patient change his or her self-efficacy beliefs and to provide encouragement and reinforcement for the patient's daily practice. However, it would be a mistake to suggest this as clear evidence of a patient's frequent reactivity or ability to recover adequately in daily life.

SUMMARY

Symptom and physiological baselines are very often useful aspects of evaluations and therapy. Obtaining and interpreting such data are complex activities and require much attention to details. Individual variations among patients are common. No single procedure or set of procedures is adequate or ideal for all patients. Clinical judgment and skills continue to be important.

The practitioner should: Be careful! Be wary! Do not jump to conclusions! I offer a variation of Neal Miller's famous dictum. "Be bold in what you think, but cautious in what you say and do." Also, consider this variation of the classic dictum, "Use it or lose it." For stress profiling, "use a good stressor sparingly or risk losing it."

GLOSSARY

ADAPTATION (HABITUATION). Allows patients to adapt to or adjust to novel conditions or stimuli such as an office, instrumentation, psychophysiological recordings, or auditory or visual stimuli.

ADRENAL MEDULLA. Two endocrine organs, one on top of each kidney. Each has two distinct parts, the medulla or inner core and the cortex or outer layer. Epinephrine (adrenaline) and a small amount of norepinephrine (noradrenaline) are secreted by the medulla. Release of one or both of these typically occurs during anticipation of and actual physical and emotional stress. (See *epinephrine*; Chapter 18.)

ADRENOCORTICOTROPIC HORMONE (ACTH). Hormone released from the pituitary gland.

BARORECEPTOR SENSITIVITY. The sensitivity of special sensory nerve endings stimulated by pressure changes and located in parts of the heart and blood vessel walls. A physiological negative feedback system.

BASAL SKIN RESISTANCE. An electrodermal measurement term less commonly used and less preferred now than skin conductance. It is the reciprocal of skin conductance (1 divided by conductance). Two types are response and level. The general term is skin resistance activity. (See Chapter 4.)

CATECHOLAMINES. Sympathetically mediated chemicals such as epinephrine and norepinephrine. Epinephrine is a hormone and neurotransmitter secreted by the adrenal medulla and involved in regulation of metabolism. Norepinephrine is a hormone and neurotransmitter secreted by the adrenal medulla. (See *adrenal medulla*.)

CEPHALIC VASOMOTOR RESPONSE. Vasomotor refers to nerves that control the smooth muscles of blood vessel walls. Cephalic refers to the head. Sympathetic nervous system stimulating fibers typically vasocontrict vessels.

COGNITIVE PREPARATION INFORMATION OR INSTRUCTIONAL SET. Alternative terms referring to verbal and/or printed information provided by experimenters, clinicians, and therapists to prepare patients for various assessment and therapy procedures. Can often influence expectations and affect responses and compliance.

COGNITIVE STRESSORS. Stress induced by presenting one or more of a variety of mental tasks or presumably stressful visual or auditory stimuli. (See text for several examples.)

CORTISOL. The major natural glucocorticoid hormone released from the adrenal cortex. Regulates aspects of metabolism. A type of corticosteroid pharmaceutically often called hydrocortisone. (See Chapters 18, 35, 37.)

DEFENSIVE RESPONSE. A reflexive reaction occurring immediately after threatening stimuli. Physiological changes include increased muscle tone, vasoconstriction of peripheral blood vessels and cephalic vessels, increased heart rate, respiration changes, activation of certain EEG activity, and increased sensitivity of some sense organs. Habituation of this general response is typically slow, especially compared to the orienting reflexive response, which adapts rapidly.

ELECTRODERMAL. A general term for measurements of the electrical activity or potential of the skin. Includes skin conductance, skin resistance, and skin potential. Measurements may be basal level (EDL) or response (EDR) within each of these. (See Chapter 4.)

ELICITING EVENTS OR STIMULI. Stimuli that elicit responses, presumably automatically. They may be innate, as in reflexes, or conditioned with experience or training. Contrast with emitting events or stimuli.

EMITTING EVENTS OR STIMULI. Stimuli that emit responses rather than eliciting them. In this model (operant or instrumental conditioning), the emphasis is on the stimuli that follow and reinforce behavior. Emitting events provide the occasion and conditions for operant behavior to occur. Operant behavior is emitted.

EPINEPHRINE. Adrenaline. Hormone secreted by the adrenal medulla. (See *catecholamines* and *norepinephrine*.)

EQUILIBRIUM TIME. The duration of a maximum effect.

FINGER PHOTOPLETHYSMOGRAPH. Instrument that measures the amount of blood flow passing through a finger.

FINGER PULSE VOLUME. Amount of blood flowing through blood vessels. An index of the force of the flow from the heart.

FLOODING. A type of behavioral exposure therapy in which exposure times are long until the anxiety and arousal diminish with relaxation and/or cognitive methods and/or with habituation to the stimuli.

FOREARM FLEXOR EMG. Measure of EMG activity from the flexor muscles of the forearm.

FRONTAL EMG. A general and common term referring to bilateral EMG of the forehead and adjacent areas, usually measured with one active electrode on about the middle of each frontalis muscle. By itself, it provides no information about the independent action of each frontalis nor allows one to distinguish the exact source of muscle activity. Commonly used as very indirect feedback site in general relaxation, although the reasons why it seems to work for many persons is still unknown. It is not useful for measuring electrical activity of the cervical neck muscles or occipital muscles. (See Chapters 14, 15.)

HABITUATION. See *adaptation.*

HEART RATE. Beats per minute.

HYPOTHALAMIC–PITUITARY–ADRENAL CORTEX SYSTEM PATHWAY. The hypothalamus organizes the ANS pathway with input from cortical and subcortical brain structures.

IDIOSYNCRATIC PATTERNING OF SOMATIC RESPONSES. Lacey's concept of individuals responding with their own pattern of physiological responses. For example, some people respond mostly with skeletal muscles. Others respond mostly with constriction of peripheral blood vessels. Others respond with perspiration. Others respond with bowel and/or stomach symptoms. Others respond with a combination.

LATENCY TO RECOVERY. The time required to reach prestressor level.

LAW OF INITIAL VALUES. The prestimulus level of a system being measured affects the magnitude of the physiological reactivity to a specific stimulus or situation. One case of a broader law of dynamic range that includes floor and ceiling effects on autonomic functioning.

MULTIDIMENSIONAL NATURE OF AROUSAL. Psychophysiological arousal typically has two or more dimensions or types of arousal.

NOREPINEPHRINE (ALSO, NORADRENALINE). A natural neurohormone and neurotransmitter released by sympathetic nerve endings. Also found in the brain. One type of *catecholamine,* a body compound having a sympathomimetic action. A powerful vasopressor (constrictor of capillaries and arteries). Others include epinephrine and dopamine. Norepinephrine is released by postganglionic adrenergic nerves and the adrenal medulla. Has mostly alpha-adrenergic activity and some beta-adrenergic activity. Pharmaceutical agent is norepinephrine bitartrate (also called levarterenol bitartrate). (Also see Chapters 14, 15, 17, 20, 36.)

ORIENTING RESPONSE. A reflex that alerts the person to sudden environmental stimuli (see Sturgis & Gramling, 1988).

PHALANX, THIRD. Section of a finger that includes the tip.

RECOVERY SLOPE. The units of physiological change per unit of time and the form of that slope.

RELATIVE RECOVERY TO BASELINE. The absolute degree or percentage by which a physiological variable approaches the prestressor baseline level after a specified time.

RELATIVE RECOVERY FROM A STRESSOR. The absolute degree or percentage by which a physiologic variable changes from the peak magnitude during a stressor after a specified time.

RESPIRATION RATE. Breaths per minute. (See Chapter 11.)

RIA. Relaxation-induced anxiety. (See Chapters 11 and 12.)

RESPONSE STEREOTYPY [STE'RE-O-TI"PE]. Psychophysiological responding in the same body system across different stimuli.

STIMULUS–RESPONSE SPECIFICITY. Psychophysiological responding specific to certain stimuli.

SYSTEMATIC DESENSITIZATION. A common and highly successful type of behavioral therapy for fear and phobia responses. There is gradual exposure for very limited periods from the least anxiety producing to increasingly anxiety producing. Exposures usually occur with relaxation. Exposure is imagined, with artificial stimuli (e.g., pictures, video) known as in vitro and real-life stimuli known as in vivo. (See Chapter 18.)

VOLAR SURFACE. Palm side of fingers. More accurate and precise term than palmar surface.

REFERENCES

Applications Standards Committee of the Association for Applied Psychophysiology and Biofeedback (1982). *Applications Standards and Guidelines for providers of biofeedback services.* Wheatridge, CO: Association for Applied Psychophysiology and Biofeedback.

Applications Standards Committee of the Association for Applied Psychophysiology and Biofeedback. (1992). *Standards and Guidelines for biofeedback applications in psychophysiologic self-regulation.* Wheatridge, CO: Association for Applied Psychophysiology and Biofeedback.

Andrasik, F., Burke, E. J., Attanasio, V., & Rosenblum, E. L. (1985). Child, parent, and physician reports of a child's headache pain: Relationships prior to and following treatment. *Headache, 25,* 421–425.

Andrasik, F., & Holroyd, K. A. (1980). Reliability and concurrent validity of headache questionnaire data. *Headache, 20,* 44–46.

Arena, J. G. (1984). Inter- and intra-reliability of psychophysiological post-stress adaptation periods. *Journal of Behavioral Assessment, 6,* 247–260.

Arena, J. G., Blanchard, E. B., Andrasik, F., Cotch, P. A., & Myers, P. E. (1983). Reliability of psychophysiologic assessment. *Behaviour Research and Therapy, 21*(4), 447–460.

Arena, J. G., Bruno, G. M., Brucks, A. G., & Hobbs, S. H. (1992, March 19–24). What is an adequate psychophysiologic post-stress adaptation period? From *Proceedings of the 23rd Annual Meeting of the Association for Applied Psychophysiology and Biofeedback, Colorado Springs* (pp. 90–92). Wheatridge, CO: Association for Applied Psychophysiology and Biofeedback.

Arena, J. G., Goldberg, S. J., Saul, D. L., & Hobbs, S. H. (1989). Temporal stability of psychophysiological response profiles: Analysis of individual response stereotypy and stimulus response specificity. *Behavior Therapy, 20,* 609–618.

Arena, J. G., & Hobbs, S. H. (1993, March 25–30). Temporal stability of psychophysiological stress profiles: A re-analysis. *Proceedings of the 24th Annual Meeting of the Association for Applied Psychophysiology and Biofeedback, Los Angeles.* Wheatridge, CO: Association for Applied Psychophysiology and Biofeedback.

Arena, J. G, & Hobbs, S. H. (in press). Reliability of psychophysiological responding as a function of trait anxiety. *Biofeedback and Self-Regulation.*

Asterita, M. F. (1985). *The physiology of stress.* New York: Human Sciences Press.

Benjamin, L. S. (1967). Facts and artifacts in using analysis of covariance to "undue" the law of initial values. *Psychophysiology, 4,* 187–206.

Berntson, G. G., Cacioppo, J. T., & Quigley, K. S. (1991). Autonomic determinism: The modes of autonomic control, the doctrine of anatomic space, and the laws of autonomic constraint. *Psychological Review, 98*(4), 459–487.

Blanchard, E. B., Hillhouse, J., Appelbaum, K. A., & Jaccard, J. (1987). What is an adequate length of baseline in research and clinical practice with chronic headache? *Biofeedback and Self-Regulation, 12*(4), 323–329.

Buco, S. M., & Blouin, D. C. (1983). *Use of similarity coefficients when populations parameters are unknown*. Paper presented at the Meeting of the Southeastern Psychological Association, New Orleans. (Reported in Waters et al., 1987)

Cacioppo, J. T., Berntson, G. G., & Anderson, B. L. (1991). Psychophysiological approaches to the evaluation of psychotherapeutic process and outcome: Contributions from social psychophysiology. *Psychological Assessment, 3*(3), 321–336.

Cacioppo, J. T., & Tassinary, L. G. (1990a). Inferring psychological significance from physiological signals. *American Psychologist, 45*, 16–28.

Cacioppo, J. T., & Tassinary, L. G. (1990b). *Principles of psychophysiology: Physical, social, and inferential elements*. New York: Cambridge University Press.

Cahn, T., & Cram, J. R. (1980). Changing measurement instrument at follow-up: A potential source of error. *Biofeedback and Self-Regulation, 5*, 265–273.

Coles, M. G. H., Gratton, G., Gramer, A. F., & Miller, G. A. (1986). Principles of signal acquisition and analysis. In M. G. H. Coles, E. Donchin, & S. W. Porges (Eds.) *Psychophysiology: Systems, processes, and applications*. New York: Guilford Press.

Dienstbier, R. A. (1989). Arousal and physiological toughness: Implications for mental and physical health. *Psychological Review, 96*, 84–100.

Faulstich, M. E., Williamson, D. A., McKenzie, S. J., Duchmann, E. G., Hutchinson, K. M., & Blouin, D. C. (1986). Temporal stability of psychophysiological responding: A comparative analysis of mental and physical stressors. *International Journal of Neuroscience, 30*, 65–72.

Flor, H., Turk, D. C., & Birbaumer, N. (1985). Assessment of stress-related psychophysiological reactions in chronic back pain patients. *Journal of Consulting and Clinical Psychology, 53*(3), 354–364.

Freeman, G. L. (1939). Towards a psychiatric plumsoll mark: Physiological recovery quotients in experimentally induced frustration. *The Journal of Psychology, 8*, 247–252.

Furedy, J. J. (1987). Beyond heart rate in the cardiac psychophysiological assessment of mental effort: The T-wave amplitude component in the electrocardiogram. *Human Factors, 29*, 183–194.

Haynes, S. N., Falkin, S., & Sexton-Radek, K. (1989). Psychophysiological measurement in behavior therapy. In G. Turpin (Ed.), *Handbook of clinical psychophysiology* (pp. 175–214). London: Wiley.

Haynes, S. N., Gannon, L. R., Orimoto, L., O'Brien, W. H., & Brandt, M. (1991). Psychophysiological assessment of poststress recovery. *Psychological Assessment, 3*(3), 356–365.

Hermann, C. U., & Blanchard, E. B. (1993, March 25–30). The role of the hand held computer in headache treatment and research. *Proceedings of the 24th Annual Meeting of the Association for Applied Psychophysiology and Biofeedback, Los Angeles* (pp. 29–33). Wheatridge, CO: Association for Applied Psychophysiology and Biofeedback.

Holmes, T. H., & Rahe, R. H. (1967). The social readjustment scale. *Journal of Psychosomatic Research, 11*, 213–218.

Houtler, B. D., & Rosenberg, H. (1985). The retrospective baseline in single case experiments. *Behavior Therapist, 8*, 97–98.

Jensen, M. P., & Karoly, P. (1992). Self-report scales and procedures for assessing pain in adults. In D. C. Turk & R. Melzack (Eds.), *Handbook of pain assessment* (pp. 135–151). New York: Guilford Press.

Keefe, F. J., & Williams, D. A. (1992). Assessment of pain behaviors. In D. C. Turk & R. Melzack, *Handbook of pain assessment* (pp. 277–292). New York: Guilford Press.

Kirk, R. E. (1982). *Experimental design: Procedures for the behavioral sciences* (2nd ed.). Belmont, CA: Brooks/Cole.

Konarska, M., Stewart, R. E., & McCarty, R. (1989). Habituation of sympathetic–adrenal medullary responses following exposure to chronic intermittent stress. *Physiology and Behavior, 45*, 255–261.

Lacey, J. I. (1956). The evaluation of autonomic responses: Towards a general solution. *Annals of the New York Academy of Science, 67*, 123–164.

Lacey, J. I. (1959). Psychophysiological approaches to the evaluation of psychotherapeutic process and outcome. In E. A. Rubinstein & M. B. Parloff (Eds.), *Research in psychotherapy*. Washington, DC: American Psychological Association.

Lacey, J. I. (1967). Somatic response patterning and stress: Some revisions of activation theory. In M. H. Appley & R. Trumbull (Eds.), *Psychological stress* (pp. 14–42). New York: Appleton-Century-Crofts.

Linden, W. (1991). What do arithmetic stress tests measure? Protocol variations and cardiovascular responses. *Psychophysiology, 28*(1), 91–102.

Meyers, A. W., & Craighead, W. E. (1978). Adaptation periods in clinical psychophysiological research: A recommendation. *Behavior Therapy, 9,* 335–362.

O'Gorman, J. G. (1983). Habituation and personality. In A. Gale & J. Edwards (Eds.), *Physiological correlates of human behavior: Vol. 3. Individual differences and psychopathology.* London: Academic Press.

Oken, D., & Heath, H. A. (1963). The Law of Initial Values: Some further considerations. *Psychosomatic Medicine, 25*(1), 3–12.

Rosenthal, T. L., Montgomery, L. M., Shadish, W. R., Edwards, N. B., Hutcherson, H. W., Follette, W. C., & Lichstein, K. L. (1989). Two new, brief, practical stressor tasks for research purposes. *Behavior Therapy, 20,* 545–562.

Sallis, J. F., & Lichstein, K. L. (1979). The frontal electromyographic adaptation response: A potential source of confounding. *Biofeedback and Self-Regulation, 4,* 337–339.

Shaeffer, F., Sponsel, M., Kice, J., & Hollensbe, J. (1991, March 15–20). Test–retest reliability of resting baseline measurements. *Proceedings of the 22nd Annual Meeting of the Association for Applied Psychophysiology and Biofeedback, New Orleans* (pp. 128–130). Wheatridge, CO: Association for Applied Psychophysiology and Biofeedback.

Sharpley, C. F. (1993). Effects of brief rest periods upon heart rate in multiple baseline studies of heart rate reactivity. *Biofeedback and Self-Regulation, 18*(4), 225–235.

Spielberger, C. D., Gorsuch, R. L., & Lushene, R. E. (1970). *STAI Manual for the State–Trait Anxiety Inventory.* Palo Alto, CA: Consulting Psychologists Press.

Sturgis, E. T., & Gramling, S. (1988). Psychophysiological assessment. In A. S. Bellack & M. Hersen (Eds.), *Behavioral Assessment: A Practical Handbook* (3rd ed., pp. 213–251). New York: Pergamon Press.

Taub, E., & School, P. (1978). Some methodological considerations in thermal biofeedback training. *Behavior Research Methods and Instrumentation, 10,* 617–622.

Turk, D. C. (1981). *The Pain Experience Scale.* Unpublished questionnaire, Yale University.

Turk, D. C., & Melzack, R. (Eds.). (1992). *Handbook of pain assessment.* New York: Guilford Press.

Waters, W. F., Williamson, D. A., Bernard, B. A., Blouin, D. C., & Faulstich, M. E. (1987). Test–retest reliability of psychophysiological assessment. *Behaviour Research and Therapy, 25*(3), 213–221.

Wilder, J. (1957). The law of initial value in neurology and psychiatry. *Journal of Nervous and Mental Diseases, 125,* 73–86.

8

Therapist Presence or Absence

Mark S. Schwartz
Audrey L. Gemberling

Should biofeedback therapists be present during physiological monitoring and feedback therapy phases? This is a delicate, important, and potentially controversial question. Its implications are very important, since therapists can have an impact upon a patient's developing, transferring, and generalizing physiological self-regulation, as well as upon symptom changes. Also important is the implication for treatment costs, and hence the cost–benefit ratio. Another consideration is the impact on the investment of professionals in the procedures used by many therapists.

Considerable variation exists in current practice. This ranges from therapists always being present to therapists seldom being present. A solo practitioner is more likely to be present all or most of the time. In some settings, patients are alone most of the time and often without observation even through a one-way window. Current practice will probably remain unchanged until there is convincing evidence to guide practitioners.

This chapter discusses some topics about therapist presence or absence that need consideration. We hope this will stimulate professionals into thinking about this issue more carefully. We hope it will help practitioners consider revisions of their practice. Most of the topics probably do not yet lend themselves to firm guidance. However, we offer some directions for consideration.

We hope this chapter will be of heuristic value and will stimulate research. The questions of therapeutic effectiveness are obviously important. However, we do practice in an atmosphere of cost containment and competitiveness in health care. Therefore, the costs of options may be of similar importance to providers, clinics, and hospitals. Biofeedback providers who can provide biofeedback services with less presence during some sessions could have advantages in competing for health care dollars. This assumes that they do so with effectiveness and at lower costs. The crucial questions are:

Is the effectiveness of the two approaches significantly different?
How much difference is there between the costs when therapists are present or absent?

UNANSWERED QUESTIONS

At present we have no research information, or very little, to answer the following questions:

1. For which modalities, and at which phases of sessions, are therapists' presence needed?
2. Which types of patients need therapists present? Who can or should be alone during parts or much of therapy?
3. Does the presence or absence of therapists affect the development of physiological self-regulation?
4. Are symptom changes affected by therapists' presence or absence? If this affects symptom changes, then what type or combination of presence and absence is important?

It could be better sometimes to leave patients alone when using less demanding electromyographic (EMG) feedback. Examples of such feeback would include single-site head or facial monitoring and feedback while the patient sits quietly. This would be in contrast to using multiple modalities. It would also contrast with thermal feedback alone when one therapy goal is helping a patient in reduction of general sympathetic arousal. However, this is still far from a confirmed finding. Several factors would probably influence this decision. For example, experienced therapists often prefer being with their patients until the patients begin to show self-regulation. With procedures such as autogenic relaxation with feedback in the background, the therapist's role is often only that of an observer.

Occasionally, it might be better for some patients to be alone for a while—although probably not for an entire session. The rest of a session could include discussion of procedures, effects on symptoms, and transfer to nonoffice conditions. However, therapists should avoid conveying or implying they are leaving the patient alone while they are going to attend to other patients. When this is necessary, one should be careful to do so only with patients who are likely to understand and accept the reason. It is better for a therapist to leave a patient alone for a few sessions only after having spent a few sessions with that patient. This sequence certainly could be better than the reverse for physiological effects (Borgeat, Hade, Lauouche, & Bedwani, 1980).

For some patients, a therapist's presence might result in higher muscle activity compared to when the therapist is absent. No one knows whether this helps to promote physiological self-regulation and symptom changes. Some characteristics of therapists probably will affect the development of physiological self-regulation for many patients. Both the amount and type of interactions between patients and therapists obviously influence the relevance and impact of these characteristics. Taub and School (1978) showed the importance of therapists' characteristics for learning to reduce peripheral vasoconstriction. Therapists' presence during the biofeedback sessions obviously affects these interactions. However, we do not yet know whether this is true for EMG biofeedback-assisted relaxation. We also need to know whether other aspects of therapy can override some or all these characteristics. For example, can a therapist's credibility and good cognitive preparation of patients compensate for some other characteristics?

ADVANTAGES AND DISADVANTAGES OF THERAPIST PRESENCE

The advantages of therapists being present include:

1. The therapist can observe patients for sources of artifact. Examples are swallowing, movement, eyes opening or closing, hand positions, and breathing changes. Windows

into therapy rooms or remote video cameras can accomplish this but are luxuries not usually available.

2. The therapist can make suggestions during and between segments of sessions. These include adaptation, baselines, office stressors, and feedback segments.

3. The therapist's presence provides more "real life" situations for generalization to occasions when other people are present.

4. The therapist can be more flexible in altering sessions' protocols when needed or desired.

5. The therapist can reduce a patient's frustration during long feedback segments such as longer than 20 minutes. The therapist can stop such segments or switch to different feedback signals or modalities.

6. The therapist's presence demonstrates interest in the patient.

7. The therapist can record data from the instruments in short trials, such as those of 15, 30, or 60 seconds, when computers or other automated data acquisition systems are unavailable.

8. The therapist can provide the attention that some patients expect and need.

9. The therapist can take opportunities to employ other therapy procedures when using biofeedback to facilitate relaxation or neuromuscular rehabilitation.

10. The therapist's presence may sometimes permit the use of less complex and less expensive instrumentation.

The disadvantages of the therapist being present, or, conversely, the advantages of the therapist being absent, include:

1. The therapist's presence increases costs of biofeedback sessions.

2. The therapist's presence creates an implied scrutiny or evaluation atmosphere. This could increase muscle tension and sympathetic arousal.

3. The therapist's presence interferes with patients' opportunities to explore and to relax in circumstances more similar to when they are alone elsewhere.

4. If the therapist's characteristics and behaviors are much less than ideal or are undesirable, then his or her presence could create tension in patients. This could interfere with physiological self-regulation and self-confidence.

We need definitions of physical distances between therapists and patients and barriers between them that constitute presence and absence. In addition, when and how often should therapists be present or absent? Also, what are the criteria for determining when a therapist should provide verbal statements, and what types of statements should these be?

LEAVING PATIENTS ALONE:
A CONSERVATIVE VIEWPOINT

We offer a conservative position on leaving patients alone. It is consistent with the Biofeedback Society of America's *Applications Standards and Guidelines for Providers of Biofeedback Services* (Schwartz & Fehmi, 1982) and the revised Standards by other authors (Applications Standards Committee of the Association for Applied Psychophysiology and Biofeedback, 1992). The revised document states,

> The presence of a skilled and qualified therapist throughout the treatment process is a necessary part of adequate biofeedback. . . . There may be sessions in which necessary brief

absences of the therapist occur or where a planned brief solo practice interlude is made a part of the treatment process at advanced levels. . . . However, it is not appropriate when doing general relaxation . . . for psychophysiological disorders to leave a patient to practice alone, listening to tapes with minimal or no supervision during the . . . session. (p. 40)

There are times when it is acceptable to leave patients alone even without observation from another room. One may do this to allow patients to explore and further develop physiological self-regulation. Such phases should be less often than those with direct observation or with a therapist present.

There are practitioners who schedule many of a patient's therapy sessions alone and without observation or communication with them during the session. For example, these therapists provide an intake session and one or two biofeedback sessions with themselves present. However, they then provide several sessions with the patient alone and unobserved between the time the therapist attaches the transducers and the time he or she removes them. It is inappropriate to provide most therapy sessions with patients alone, without direct and nearly continuous observation, and without the capacity to interact with them. It also may be unethical.

We strongly suspect that such practices are a major concern to third-party payers who view them as "biofeedback factories." When unsuccessful, such experiences probably create a negative impression of biofeedback in the minds of patients. They often do not seek biofeedback again and become disillusioned and skeptical the next time someone suggests it. The motivation of some practitioners to leave their patients alone during many office sessions is probably the result of ignorance and misinformation about proper procedures. However financial factors probably motivate some practitioners.

We emphasize that we are not against ever leaving patients alone. We are against overutilizing such sessions. Overly relying on patients to learn for themselves from instrumentation feedback is not in the best interests of most patients. It is also not good for the biofeedback field in general.

SUGGESTIONS FOR WHEN PATIENTS ARE LEFT ALONE

If a practitioner decides to leave patients alone we suggest consideration of the following:

1. Practitioners will want instruments that allow recording and storage of all the trials of physiological data. They should use brief trials to improve assessment of changes and variance among the trials. Recording many trials also allows observing outlying trials that suggest possible artifacts such as patients' movements.

2. Therapists should provide careful instructions beforehand about the purposes of the segment. They should consider telling patients what produces artifacts and therefore what to try to avoid or remember to note later. Practitioners might consider the following sample instructions when the recording instruments are in the same room as the patient and without automated recording or direct observation. Many practitioners still use this type of instrument. Computer-based instruments make these recordings easier.

"I am going to leave the room for 15 minutes. I will be very close by but cannot hear or see you. Are you comfortable with being alone for 15 minutes?" [If the answer is 'Yes,' then consider saying the following:] This will give you a chance to explore self-regulation. Use the feedback to help guide you to become more aware of changes.

"If you must get up, you can disconnect the cable [or sensors] like this. [Demonstrate this.] I do not think that will be necessary, but I want you to know how just in case. I will be back in exactly 15 minutes, at ___. [The therapist should give the time and be sure there is a clock within view or that the patient has a watch. The therapist must be sure to return on time. For many patients, a few minutes extra will not matter. However, for some, their confidence and comfort depend partly on the therapist's promptness.]

"Try this and see how you feel about doing it this way. If your eyes are open, please note where the meter needle is most of the time [or with digital integration most of the numbers are on the screen]. If you close your eyes during the relaxation segments, then recall what the sound was like most of the time." [Set the gain so the audio is comfortable.]

If there is direct observation, an intercom, or automated storage of physiological data, then one can substitute different statements for the script given. The therapist might consider "I will be next door and can see and hear you. If you need me, just tell me, and I will be available." One can omit statements about the need for patient recall or adjustments.

3. Therapists should leave patients alone only for short periods such as 5–20 minutes.

4. Ideally, there will be some type of observation, although it is not required.

5. There should be a way for selected patients to signal therapists in case they are uncomfortable. Practitioner judgment dictates the need for a signaling system.

6. Therapists should ask patients beforehand about their thoughts and feelings about being alone. Prudent therapists know to give patients a realistic chance to express themselves. They are able to create an atmosphere in which patients are comfortable expressing themselves about any concerns. They will avoid asking a patient, "Do you want to be left alone for a while?" or, "Is my presence bothering you?" Good therapists will say something like the following:

"Sometimes patients find it distracting or a little interfering to have someone else always in the room. How would you feel about being alone for a few minutes? How much time do you think you would be comfortable alone to explore self-regulation? Are you comfortable with being alone for 10 minutes?"

7. Conscientious therapists often adjust the fees of such sessions to reflect the different costs associated with the therapists' absence. If one leaves a patient alone for about 15 minutes or longer, some professionals consider it excessive and inappropriate to charge the same rate as when the therapist is present. One can justify the same rate if the therapist is observing from another room.

SUGGESTIONS FOR WHEN THERAPISTS ARE PRESENT

When the therapist is present in the same room with the patient, then:

1. The therapist should consider noting the physical proximity to the patient. For example, is the therapist next to, behind, or in front of the patient? How close is the therapist to the patient?

2. The therapist should consider noting what he or she says to the patient during different phases. The therapist should also note *when* he or she says it as well as any noises or other potentially interfering events that occur. If a therapist provides therapy with supervision, he or she should discuss and agree with what to say and do in different segments and contingencies.

3. Therapists should ask patients about their thoughts and feelings about the therapist's presence. They should aim to create an atmosphere in which patients feel comfortable expressing themselves about any concerns.

RESEARCH

Borgeat et al. (1980) were the first to study the topic of therapist presence and absence. Their discussion showed good insight and sensitivity about some factors that could have affected their results. They also provided some future directions for research. As a first attempt at such research, it was worthwhile. However, some information was lacking and some statements were ambiguous.

We mean no disrespect for the journal's editorial process or to the authors, but there were some serious problems with the research. For example, in specifying that "patients with frontalis EMG mean level below 2 [microvolts] at the evaluative session were excluded . . ." (p. 277), the authors did not mention whether this was with eyes open or closed. They also did not mention whether this was for the baseline or the entire session. There was no information given about the experience of the therapists as psychotherapists and as biofeedback therapists. Also, the use of a sensitivity scale of ×0.3 or ×1 and with 3 to 4 microvolts would probably result in a rather high-pitched sound. With only 30% improvement among the subjects, one wonders about how they practiced relaxation and what other variables were present. There was no analysis of the headache or medication changes in block 1. In addition, there were only three sessions over 3 weeks. Furthermore, the use of average headache intensity is not the most sensitive measure. There was also no specification about coaching or the like. Finally, what was the relationship between the reported subjective improvement and the patients' self-report records?

Borgeat, Hade, Larouche, and Gauthier (1984) continued their research with 16 patients with tension headaches. Each patient received eight sessions alternating therapist presence and absence. Experienced psychiatrists were the therapists. They found that therapist presence and absence did not significantly correlate with general physiological arousal. They suggested that patients' EMG and electroencephalographic (EEG) data reflected a trend toward greater arousal during therapist presence. However, skin conductance showed decreased activity during therapist presence. They did not find a significant effect of therapist presence and EMG activity as they had in their previous work. They suggested that more than one session was necessary to see an interaction with the therapist present or absent. They also found that the patients' anxiety and increased muscle tension vary when the therapist is present.

They found one of the four therapists' patients had significantly lower EMG levels during active presence of the therapist. Therefore, they suggest considering measurement of individual therapist variables to determine more completely the effects of therapist presence or absence and the therapist–patient relationship.

Bregman and McAllister (1983) also studied the effects of therapist presence versus absence, but with thermal biofeedback. They concluded that therapist's presence hinders biofeedback performance. They did not state the type of subjects; however, these were probably college students. They also did not report the starting temperatures of the subjects or any information about them.

The investigators noted that one might overcome the negative effects of the experimenter's presence. They cited social facilitation theory (Zajonc, 1965) to help explain the hindering effects of the presence of others upon task performance. They also noted that the same theory might also facilitate such performance "once a subject learns to control a biofeedback modality" (p. 546). With clinical insight, they noted as well the possibility "that a warm supportive experimenter/therapist [might] . . . reduce and possibly overcome the negative learning effects found in the present study" (p. 546). However, they offered no information about the personality or the behavior of the experimenter present with the subjects. Nor did they tell readers whether the experimenter was blind to the major hypothesis of the study, that, "an experimenter's 'mere' presence would hinder the acquisition of thermal control" (p. 544).

Dumochel (1985) studied the effects of therapist presence or absence and an index of "rate of learning" of physiological self-regulation during thermal and frontal EMG biofeedback. He refered to "lower EMG levels" and "increases in temperature" during sessions compared to baseline. Nearly all patients were women in treatment for various types of headache. Therapist presence or absence did not affect the patients' "rate of learning." This ambitious research is commendable. We should note that the patients had considerable cognitive preparation, good rapport, support, encouragement, and positive expectations. They had both in-office relaxation instructions and relaxation tapes to use outside the office. All or some of these factors probably affected the results.

Furthermore, even in the therapist-absence condition, the therapist was present for several minutes early in the session, periodically during the sessions, and at the end. However, he was available much less and provided much less help during the baseline and feedback portions.

One conclusion is there are conditions in which therapists may be absent from the therapy room for short periods without adversely affecting some physiological progress. The author has acknowledged the limitations of his study and the need for more research.

More recently, Borgeat, Elie, and Castonguay (1991) studied 32 patients with tension headaches using frontal EMG. Each patient had six sessions and a 2-month follow-up session. A male psychiatrist and a female psychiatric nurse were the therapists. This study attempted to determine if muscle tension levels correlate with the presence of a therapist and clinical improvement. The authors' suggest that EMG levels during a pretraining period with the therapist present can predict symptomatic improvement during therapy.

These authors also suggest that the decrease in muscle activity with the therapist present may be the result of the therapeutic relationship or process in the beginning of training. However, they did not measure interpersonal factors nor did they consider the differences between the two therapists such as one being a male psychiatrist and the other being a female psychiatric nurse.

CONCLUSION

There is still very limited research about the topic of whether therapists should be or need to be present during all, most, some, or none of biofeedback sessions. We still do not have adequate information about major factors that could affect results. There are many factors to consider. There are different definitions of presence or absence as well.

Those differences might influence or affect patient compliance and the development of physiological self-regulation at different stages of sessions and treatment.

Aside from a paragraph in the *Standards and Guidelines* (Applications Standards Committee of the Association for Applied Psychophysiology and Biofeedback, 1992) there are no guidelines. The present chapter has discussed aspects of this issue, reviewed the research, and provides some guidelines.

There are studies that do not favor therapist presence during biofeedback sessions, although there are substantial limits in methodology and completeness in these studies. These investigators correctly note the need for much more research. They suggest that presence of therapists might be better under some conditions. For example, the more recent work supports the clinical lore supporting the importance of individual therapist variables.

Professionals base their decisions on their preferences, judgments, and the circumstances. Prudent professionals think carefully about the many factors before deciding what to do. We think that prudent practitioners prefer tailoring therapy procedures to the individual patient.

We hope this chapter will serve heuristic purposes and help stimulate useful research. Until sufficient research and further guidelines exist, most biofeedback practitioners will probably not leave most patients alone without direct observation most of the time. On the other hand, the therapist's presence in the same room may be less desirable for certain patients in some situations.

REFERENCES

Applications Standards Committee of the Association for Applied Psychophysiology and Biofeedback. (1992). *Standards and guidelines for biofeedback applications in psychophysiological self-regulation.* Wheatridge, CO: Association for Applied Psychophysiology and Biofeedback.

Borgeat, F., Elie, R., & Castonguay, L. (1991). Muscular response to the therapist and symptomatic improvement during biofeedback for tension headache. *Biofeedback and Self-Regulation, 19*(2), 147–155.

Borgeat, F., Hade, B., Larouche, L. M., & Bedwani, C. N. (1980). Effect of therapist's active presence on EMG biofeedback training of headache patients. *Biofeedback and Self-Regulation, 5,* 275–282.

Borgeat, F., Hade, B., Larouche, L., & Gauthier, B. (1984). Psychophysiological effects of therapist's active presence during biofeedback as a simple psychotherapeutic situation. *The Psychiatric Journal of the University of Ottawa, 9*(3), 134–137.

Bregman, N. J., & McAllister, H. A. (1983). Voluntary control of skin temperature: Role of experimenter presence versus absence. *Biofeedback and Self-Regulation, 8,* 543–546.

Dumouchel, B. D. (1985). *Patient's perceived control, therapist's presence/absence, and the optimization of biofeedback learning.* Unpublished doctoral dissertation, New York University.

Schwartz, M. S., & Fehmi, L. (1982). *Application standards and guidelines for providers of biofeedback services.* Wheatridge, CO: Biofeedback Society of America. [now Association for Applied Psychophysiology and Biofeedback]

Taub, E., & School, P. J. (1978). Some methodological considerations in thermal biofeedback training. *Behavior Research Methods and Instrumentation, 10,* 617–622.

Zajonc, R. B. (1965). Social facilitation. *Science, 149,* 269–274.

9

Compliance

Mark S. Schwartz

Patients must understand and accept therapy in order for treatment to be effective and beneficial. They must cooperate with recommendations and maintain attitudes and behaviors compatible with successful results. Being able to educate, persuade, and motivate patients adequately influences the effectiveness of all health care professionals. This is true no matter how effective the treatments and regardless of the therapist's knowledge. It also is true irrespective of the professional's good intentions. Social psychology and the literature on compliance give us much research and guidance for enhancing practitioners' effectiveness and helping patient compliance.

This chapter discusses factors that promote compliance. Prudent professionals are aware of these factors and adjust their professional behaviors accordingly. They strive toward integrating them into their professional activities. The intent here is not to criticize those professionals who have not mastered all or most of the behaviors. None of us can attend to everything, or agree with and incorporate all that is ideal. However, we can all strive to change our behaviors and environment so as to improve our effectiveness.

This chapter summarizes many ideas and conclusions from the extensive literature on compliance with medical and psychological treatments (DiMatteo & DiNicola, 1982). Another focus of the chapter is the rationale for carefully developed patient education. It also presents considerations about conducting one's professional practice.

The term "compliance" is complex and controversial for many professionals. It suggests an approach to patient care that implies a duty by the patient to follow blindly the practitioner's orders (DiMatteo & DiNicola, 1982). Some professionals use other interchangeable terms including "adherence," "cooperation," "collaboration," and "therapeutic alliance." I use the term compliance in this chapter because it is still a commonly employed term and the one used by DiMatteo and DiNicola (1982). However, they correctly point out that compliance should not "imply varying power relationships between the practitioner and patient" (p. 8).

Each of us asks whether our patients understand and accept our recommendations. Do they feel comfortable to admit their lack of understanding and acceptance? Furthermore, do they always tell us the truth? Suggesting that patients sometimes do not tell us the truth may appear callous and critical. However, I certainly do not intend to criticize patients. I feel devoted to them and to the best delivery of services possible.

Experienced professionals probably already realize that some patients distort and slant the truth to please us and to avoid embarrassment. They also do this to avoid perceived and expected criticism and rejection and for other reasons and combinations of reasons. In addition, they often simply forget. Some patients did not understand or accept much of what we asked them to remember and do.

Solutions to compliance problems are not simple. However, practitioners can usually include improvements into their professional practices. This chapter's guidelines and considerations apply to most settings in which practitioners provide biofeedback.

For the purposes of the present discussion, the topic of compliance is divided into three major categories and 11 subcategories, outlined as follows:

1. The professional
    A. Professional setting and nontherapy and therapy personnel
    B. Referral source's attitudes and behaviors
    C. Provider's characteristics and behaviors
    D. Interaction and relationship between the provider and patients
    E. Cognitive preparation of patients
2. The patient
    A. Patient's perceptions
    B. Patient's expectations
    C. Patient's affect
    D. Other patient factors
3. Evaluation and intervention
    A. Selected methods of assessing compliance
    B. Selected methods of increasing compliance

THE PROFESSIONAL

Professional Setting and Nontherapy and Therapy Personnel

The waiting room, therapy office, and office personnel all affect patient compliance. They influence patients' impressions, confidence, and satisfaction. Office neatness and comfort, and friendly and efficient personnel can help to promote patients' comfort, confidence in the professionals, compliance, and therapy effectiveness. Prudent practitioners consider neatness, a therapy room without unnecessary display of wires, comfortable temperatures, proper friendliness, office efficiency, reasonable waiting times, and related factors. They also are aware that the office color scheme and furniture affect patients' comfort and impressions, and potentially, compliance. Consistency in which professionals provide therapy also may be an advantage for many patients.

In summary, personnel who are friendly, efficient, and professional in their appearance and behaviors affect patients' impressions, comfort, satisfaction, and compliance. Comfortable, neat, and uncluttered office rooms also probably help. Short waiting times and consistency of therapists are additional factors that promote compliance.

Referral Source's Attitudes and Behaviors

Practitioners may benefit from knowing the referral reason given to the patient. Did the referral source give up trying to treat the patient and convey this attitude to the patient? Did the referral source convey that the referral for biofeedback is a logical next step in an organized plan?

Patients should be asked about their perceptions of what the referral source conveyed to them. Therapists should consider discussing with referral sources their viewpoints about biofeedback and what they convey to patients when they make referrals. This helps a practitioner know how much attention to direct toward a patient's confidence in the therapy rationale, recommendations, and procedures.

For example, some referral sources say to patients, "I do not know what else to do for you. Maybe biofeedback will help. Why don't you try biofeedback?" Practitioners should contrast this with, "We tried several therapy approaches. The next step is to try biofeedback, an often effective approach." Diplomatic and educational communications to referral sources can encourage preferred communications to patients. Therapists should consider sending educational reading materials and including useful, informative, and sensible content in letters to referral sources.

The prudent professional should be aware of the attitudes of the referral source toward him- or herself as a practitioner using biofeedback. These attitudes influence the referral source's messages to patients about both biofeedback and the therapist as a professional. This can help guide patient education and patient management.

Well-written letters to referral sources and well-written notes in patients' records influence referral sources' attitudes and behaviors. They are educational and help create an image. Prudent therapists should consider including and discussing the rationale for biofeedback and related therapies and the procedures planned and used. They should also consider including the results expected and achieved. A well-informed referral source can be an ally and help with cognitive preparation.

One can avoid writing a long letter or repeating what the reader already knows about the patient. The following is a sample letter to a referral source. In some cases, the professional might include some data and graphs.

Dear _____,

Thank you for referring Ms. _____ for evaluation of biofeedback treatments of her tension headaches. I will not repeat most of the history, of which you are aware. I met with her on __/__/95. I agree with you that including biofeedback is a very reasonable approach for her.

Psychophysiological assessment of her muscle activity used four sites: the standard bifrontal, bilateral posterior neck, and both right and left frontal–posterior neck placements. Baseline assessment was with her eyes open and then closed, and while sitting with her back and head supported and while standing. The assessment involves doing this during rest and in response to mild office stressors. The procedures then include visual and audio feedback to check her response and begin to develop her physiological self-regulation.

The muscle activity from the neck area while at rest with her eyes open showed excess muscle activity, mostly 4 to 6 microvolts (integral average, with a 100–200 Hertz bandpass). While she was standing and trying to relax, the patient showed more excessive muscle activity in her neck, mostly 9 to 12 microvolts. These are particularly high. The muscle activity from the other sites was only slightly tense for resting muscles while the patient was sitting and only slightly higher while she was standing. Visual feedback was very helpful to her in reducing the muscle activity, especially while she was standing. When the feedback was not available to her, the muscle tension increased and remained elevated.

I discussed the rationale for therapy and the procedures in detail. Evaluation of stress and psychosocial factors did not suggest enough to warrant other forms of stress management now. Also, the patient was not receptive to other forms of stress management. I provided audiotapes and patient-education booklets to her to help prepare her for therapy.

I have seen Ms. _____ for five sessions focused on physiological self-regulation. She is working on blending this into her daily activities. She continues to show increasing ability to lower muscle activity during resting conditions and to maintain even lower muscle activity after feedback is stopped each session. In the last two sessions, her muscle activity during some phases was in a therapeutic range below 2 microvolts.

Her self-report hourly symptom log showed a 75% reduction of severe headaches, a 50% reduction of total hours of headaches, and an 80% decrease in medication use compared to her initial reports. She agreed to two more office sessions to add to her confidence and help her consolidate her gains.

Thank you for referring this pleasant lady. I am happy to be of some help to her. Contact me with any questions.

Sincerely yours,

_____

Practitioners' Characteristics and Behaviors

Patients are constantly assessing the credibility of practitioners. This credibility is a major element in patients' attitudes, and it affects compliance and therapy effectiveness. Much of what practitioners do is attitude change. We enhance or detract from our credibility by our presentation and the amount of and quality of time we spend with patients. Our appearance, behaviors, personality, offices, instruments, and procedures all affect our credibility. The recommendations and patient education we provide to patients also influence our credibility. We cannot rely solely on our reputation and the reputation of the treatment.

Patients attend closely to our behaviors and personality. This influences their satisfaction, and many patients comply better when they are very satisfied with their therapist. This can be especially important when patients have much self-doubt and limited sources of reinforcement.

Trustworthiness is another major factor in achieving attitude changes and compliance. All of us need to reflect periodically upon the trust our patients place in us. What are we doing to maintain and enhance that trust? Trustworthy practitioners increase and maintain trust by being on time, maintaining confidentiality, and being consistent in their approach. They realistically discuss therapy goals and expectations. They also discuss expected and possible changes in therapy well in advance.

A personal model of relaxation also is important. The appearance of a relaxed therapist, or one who effectively shows relaxation when needed, conveys an important teaching model. It also influences one's credibility. The therapist might consider some self-disclosure about how he or she has used physiological self-regulation to prevent and manage symptoms such as headaches, anxiety, and tachycardia.

Effective communication of information and recommendations is another important factor. Practitioners need to make presentations to patients that are logical, coherent, understood, accepted, and remembered. Patients who do not understand or accept the information will be less likely to follow recommendations. Effective communication requires that it is within the "latitude of acceptance" of the patient. Thus, is must be acceptable at the time the patient receives it. A provider with a rigid conceptual framework and a rigid approach to therapy will often not evoke compliance from patients whose attitudes are outside the limits of the information and therapy plan. Patients' attitudes must be compatible with explanations about the causes of their symptoms. Their attitudes must be compatible with the therapy rationale, procedures, and recommendations.

For example, practitioners communicate about topics that may be unfamiliar or "ego dystonic" for a patient. These topics may be outside their range of attitude acceptance. They include recommendations about both the ideal frequency of relaxation and the timing of it. We must consider how "letting go" and a "nonstriving attitude" sound to many patients.

Asking a patient to avoid perfectionism in learning physiological self-regulation is another example. Stopping caffeine and other dietary vasoactive chemicals, stopping nicotine, and changing work schedules are outside the acceptance range for some patients.

Therefore, a flexible approach is in order. It is often not advisable to push or insist for total early compliance for nearly everything. Instead, the therapist should consider explaining the role of each factor, and develop a flexible stepped-care approach. The use of metaphors can help these explanations. Consider the following sample explanation to a patient:

> "Mrs. _____, we talked about the potential advantages of stopping caffeine, changing some foods you eat, and managing your time use more effectively. Caffeine and nicotine interfere with effective relaxation. More effective use of time will help you make time for enough relaxation to help you. I know you see some of these as major changes, and you might not feel ready for them. I am not saying that all are completely necessary for you to reduce or stop your symptoms. However, some are necessary. You know I want to help you. My responsibility to you is to tell you everything that could help.
>
> "Please, seriously consider these recommendations. The decision about what to do now and later is up to you. You can start with _____ and _____ for a trial and then see how far you get. Some changes are not permanent. You probably will make better progress by making changes. What do you think, and how do you feel about this?"

The above presentation does not imply preference for starting with less than the ideal. Flexibility, laced with clear communication and empathy, is often more likely to lead to acceptance than rigid insistence.

Interaction between the Practitioner and Patients

For many professionals, their interaction with patients is a major cornerstone of therapy and very often a necessary part. The list below presents a checklist of selected considerations.

1. Attend to your personal characteristics and behaviors.
2. Provide enough time with patients.
3. Provide an active interaction.
4. Acknowledge the legitimacy of the patient's complaints.
5. Present an organized, systematic, and flexible approach.
6. Include appropriate, but limited, social conversation.
7. Provide reassurance, support, and encouragement.
8. Provide and reinforce realistic positive expectations.
9. Provide choices for patients.
10. Allow patients to question recommendations.
11. Tailor therapy whenever indicated and practical.
12. Demonstrate and model selected procedures.
13. Provide appropriate self-disclosure.
14. Show attention and interest in patients through tone of voice, facial expression, and physical posture.
15. Convey appropriate affect.
16. Maintain frequent eye contact.
17. Touch patients appropriately.
18. Observe for signs of anxiety, resistance, and confusion.

Some of the items in this list are discussed elsewhere in this chapter. Others are so obvious they need no elaboration. The following discussion elaborates on items 9, 11, 13, 14, and 17.

Providing Choices for Patients: Tailoring Therapy

First, I discuss together the closely related topics of providing patients with choices and tailoring therapy whenever possible. There is a place for predesigned therapy programs. However, they may detract from compliance. For example, for patients with headaches, there are several ways to begin. One may start with a baseline symptom log, a medication trial, dietary changes alone, relaxation therapy alone, or a few biofeedback sessions followed by a few weeks of practice. Or one could start with several office sessions combining biofeedback and relaxation therapies. Or one could start with cognitive stress management or psychotherapy.

Several factors affect the choice among these options. Tailoring therapy means basing the plan on interview information and the psychophysiological assessment. Tailoring includes consideration of the patient's attitudes, schedule, and finances. One also considers the symptoms during the first days and weeks of therapy and the first few biofeedback sessions.

One need not discuss all choices in detail with every patient. However, having choices and knowing the potential advantages and disadvantages of each help to convey that the patient is actively participating in the design of her or his program. Such an approach also conveys that the practitioner is considering the patient's situation, preferences, and needs. I assume that such tailoring helps compliance and recommend the therapist consider these factors among those influencing a therapy plan soon after it starts.

1. Improvement of symptoms sometimes occurs after a physician gives convincing reassurance to a patient about the nonserious nature of his or her symptoms.

2. Recently starting a new medication or changing dosage can improve symptoms.

3. Recent changes in life-style, work, exercises, and/or dietary intake can result in significant decrease in symptoms.
(In these three examples, compliance with a time-consuming treatment will often be less than ideal. This is especially true if the patient believes the symptom changes result from the above reasons. In such circumstances, tailoring the therapy plan can involve deferring more office-based biofeedback.)

4. Another factor that should alert the practitioner to the need for tailoring is a lack of physiological tension and arousal and/or rapid return to a "therapeutic range"[1] after intentional arousal during office sessions. This suggests that the patient can relax adequately but needs to apply his or her ability to do so.

5. Some patients show significant improvement of symptoms in the first weeks of therapy regardless of the physiological self-regulation shown in the office. It is sometimes surprising and difficult to explain this rapid improvement of symptoms. The scientist in each of us wants to know why and how this is occurring. The skeptical and cautious part of us is suspicious and may want more office sessions for confidence. However, the clinician in us, especially the cost-conscious and pragmatic part, accepts the progress and may defer more office therapy. Compliance may be better if the symptoms increase later. The patient will then realize he or she needs more therapy.

---

[1]The term "therapeutic range" may or may not be the same as a relaxed range. The criteria for relaxed range differ among practitioners. They also differ at different stages of therapy and for different therapeutic goals. I prefer the term "therapeutic range."

6. Therapists should consider deferring or stopping office-based biofeedback sessions with patients who continue noncompliance with necessary parts of therapy. For example, some patients do not practice relaxation at all or do so for much less time than suggested. Many continue life-style behaviors such as caffeine usage, work habits, and schedules that are inconsistent with making progress.

7. Assessment and feedback sites may need tailoring. Patients may perceive repeated sessions semireclined, with eyes closed, lights dimmed, and with feedback only from one area as meaningless. Tailoring both the sites and conditions provides fresh tasks and can increase patient confidence. Physiological recordings and feedback in different body positions are often proper. For example, therapists should consider including regimens sitting up in a straight-backed chair, standing, and working at a desk. Making the sessions more sensible to patients can increase confidence in the therapy, and hence compliance.

8. Physiological arousal to images of cognitive stressors and activities offers rich therapeutic data with which to tailor therapy. For example, let us suppose a patient shows good relaxation in multiple muscle areas, warm hands, and low skin conductance during resting baselines. Further, suppose this is similar during a standard cognitive stressor and in different positions. Now let us suppose that this patient has significantly decreased finger temperatures while imagining or talking about work or family stress. The therapist may consider options to provide biofeedback during resting conditions and only encourage relaxation between stressors. Another option would be to repeat the arousal scenes several times with and without feedback and explore the content further. Or, one could encourage relaxation before, during, and immediately after work situations. The choice would depend partly on the patient's preference and willingness to focus on such issues.

9. Long geographic distance between the patient and the treatment office will require tailoring of the therapy. The prudent therapist may consider office sessions twice a day for two or more consecutive days, with a few weeks between such phases. For some patients, such a schedule may be preferable to the one-session-per-week schedule. This is not practical for most patients. However, for patients who live too far away for weekly sessions, a "massed-practice" schedule is proper. It conveys that the therapist is willing to extend himself or herself to provide such a schedule. If such a schedule helps increase physiological self-regulation, it will presumably increase patient confidence and compliance.

Providing Appropriate Self-Disclosure

Limited self-disclosure by practitioners includes brief and proper descriptions of how they effectively use physiological self-regulation in their own lives. In this manner therapists can communicate that they know firsthand that this methodology works. The therapist should consider saying something like this:

> "Before I give a talk, relaxing my muscles and using diaphragmatic breathing help me feel much more comfortable. I also talk to myself differently at these times. [Explain this.] I get a warning sign that a migraine headache may be starting. I get a scintillating scotoma [explained]. Relaxation usually stops the warning and prevents the headache. Relaxed breathing stops my tachycardia [explained] nearly every time it happens."

Showing Attention and Interest in Patients through Tone of Voice, Facial Expression, and Physical Posture; Touching Patients Appropriately

I discuss these items together for convenience and because they have overlapping features. The practitioner's voice, facial expressions, body posture, and other nonverbal behaviors all convey interest, trust, sincerity, experience, and confidence. I am not suggesting that health care professionals need voice and posture lessons. However, many need awareness of or reminders of the potential impact of nonverbal behaviors on our patients.

Touch also can be important. Touching patients is part of the practice of physicians, nurses, physical therapists, occupational therapists, dentists, and other health care professionals. Psychologists and other persons providing biofeedback do not typically use physical contact in their other contacts with patients. Some are probably uncomfortable and inexperienced with touching. Even those with experience may not know how to use touch to help convey sincerity, support, and encouragement.

There are several obvious chances to use touch properly aside from the initial handshake. They include times when the therapist is attaching electrodes and other transducers to patients and when he or she is directly helping in relaxation or muscle re-education. For example, the therapist might consider how he or she moves a patient's hair and grasps the patient's arm. It can be enlightening for practitioners to ask themselves how the contact would feel if they were the patient?

There are other opportunities for the careful use of touch that support and enhance the rapport between the practitioner and his or her patients. These occur during the early interviews and periodically afterward. For a patient who needs much reassurance and hope, consider the impact of the following:

"This treatment is correct for you. You are on the right road now, and I will help you stay on that road."

The practitioner conveys even more impact if, near the end of that statement, he or she gently but firmly places a hand on the patient's forearm. He or she might give a mild squeeze or brief pat on the arm. Such contact is no longer than about 2 seconds.

The practitioner should not appear patronizing. Also, he or she must always be sensitive about contact. Some patients may not like such contact or may distrust it. However, if not overdone in intensity or frequency, the technique can have positive effects.

Other chances for reassuring with touch include occasions when patients express frustration, fear, life stress, and difficulty with physiological self-regulation. Proper use of touch helps a practitioner to convey caring about the patient's welfare. It bears repeating that touch should not be overdone.

Touch also can have a negative effect. For example, consider the possible impressions of female patients touched by male practitioners. I am not suggesting that one should avoid such contacts altogether. However, the duration and frequency of the contacts can convey the wrong message. Consider the difference between a possible undesirable message from a touch of about 5 seconds compared to a desirable one of about 2 seconds. I do not need to elaborate on this point. If the practitioner's hands are cold, moist, or both, he or she should consider touching clothed parts of the body and not bare skin. This also probably needs no elaboration.

Cognitive Preparation of Patients

Cognitive preparation includes correcting misperceptions. It includes providing needed information about many topics. These include: (1) the rationale for physiological self-regulation, (2) the therapy process, (3) therapy goals, (4) use of medications, (5) generalization, (6) therapy options, (7) stepped-care, and (8) the symptom log.

Prudent practitioners try to avoid overloading their patients during one session. Some information may need presentation during the first few sessions and then need to be repeated later for emphasis and to help patients recall. Carefully developed patient-education scripts, booklets, and audiotapes help provide information.

A checklist can help organize presentations and help the therapist avoid overlooking some information. This is useful for the neophyte and practitioner who does not see many patients for biofeedback and physiological self-regulation.

Most patients forget much of what they hear. Thus, the therapist should consider repeating some information from the booklets and tapes. Therapists should expect that most patients will have at least some compliance problems. However, compliance problems will probably be less for patients when the information is readily available to them every day.

Cognitive preparation includes promoting the attitude of self-responsibility. If that is within the patient's "latitude of acceptance," he or she will more likely accept it. Shaping acceptance of self-responsibility is one of the challenging aspects of clinical practice.

Cognitive preparation also includes expecting slow progress, plateaus, and setbacks. Practitioners want to communicate realistic positive expectations. It can be useful to show patients graphs of developing physiological self-regulation and symptom changes from prior patients. In addition, it can be helpful to tell the patient something like the following:

> "You have a good chance of making progress in reducing or stopping your symptoms. However, I do not know how long this will take. You know this type of therapy is not like taking medicine for an infection. Some patients show much improvement within days or weeks. Others progress more gradually over several weeks or a few months. Plateaus and even temporary reversals happen. If they occur, remember they are normal and a natural part of learning. You need not feel discouraged.
>
> "Remember that athletes and musicians expect unevenness in developing and keeping their skills. Even bright people often have difficulty learning some motor skills. People like me need more time learning how to fix mechanical and electrical appliances and equipment. Someone else develops those skills faster. Also, keep in mind that even accomplished athletes have *off days*. Not even a great baseball player, golfer, or tennis player always hits the ball well."

We are all acquainted with the resistance, skepticism, and pessimism that patients often display. Often, they have gone to several doctors and have tried various treatments. They had positive expectations yet felt disappointment with the results. For some patients, our treatment approach appears too simplistic, despite our professional reputation and careful explanations. If their healthy skepticism leads to our being defensive or rejecting of them, then we unnecessarily risk losing them and not starting therapy.

The prudent therapist will consider investing extra time checking and discussing the perceptions of selected patients. He or she will offer creative explanations of the rationale for a therapeutic trial and discuss options. This is especially appropriate if reasonable options do not exist. In these ways and others, the professional can gently, compassionately, and empathetically overcome patient resistance. It is too easy to give up and label such patients unsuitable for therapy. For such patients, the challenge to the therapist is greater. The challenge is to establish a therapeutic alliance and mobilize these patients realistically. In addition, the challenge is to shape their attitudes and perceptions of the therapy. Thus, the therapist shapes their self-confidence, their optimism, and their willingness to engage in a realistic therapy trial. The therapist should consider saying something like the following to show that he or she understands the patient:

> "If I put myself in your place, I would be skeptical. After all, you went to several doctors and tried several treatments, all without success. I understand that you were hopeful before and then disappointed. I suppose part of you is asking yourself why is this going to be

any different. You do not want to get your hopes up because you do not want that disappointment again. I understand that and I think it is perfectly normal.

"You know I cannot promise you will improve. I cannot promise how much improvement you will have. However, I can tell you that many patients I treated did well despite being unsuccessful with past therapies. Thousands of professionals all over the country report the same experiences with their patients. You are not being fair to yourself by being extremely skeptical and pessimistic.

"There are several approaches we can take. If the first is less than ideal, then, there are variations and other approaches. Biofeedback is not one therapy. It is many therapies. The way we start can be different from the way we finish. Do not hesitate to ask me any questions or express any concerns and doubts. I will be with you as long as I can help and as long as you are willing to keep trying.

"Some of the therapy may appear to you as too simple to work. I admit these methods can appear that way. In fact, I do not want them to appear complicated. They are not as simple as they appear, but neither are they very complicated. Even long-term symptoms often do not require complex solutions.

"For example, I treated many patients who were vomiting for months or years. I treated others with severe and frequent headaches for decades. [Practitioners will insert their own experiences and those of others.] These treatments helped most of them. Many of those patients thought these treatments were probably not enough for them. I might think that also if I had those symptoms for so long. Yet, they got better.

"Relaxation and biofeedback treatments are often enough alone. However, sometimes we also need other therapies."

Some, even much of the cognitive preparation, can be standard for many patients. However, practitioners must always consider the need for tailoring the presentation. Early sessions also can be useful in achieving the following:

1. Explaining about and showing how biological feedback can help patients develop improved physiological self-regulation.
2. Showing patients the effects of muscle tension on symptoms.
3. Assessing patients' awareness of increasing and decreasing tension.
4. Mobilizing patients' positive expectations.
5. Increasing patients' confidence.
6. Explaining about and show patients how generalization and transfer of training works.
7. Correcting misperceptions.

When discussing therapy goals, practitioners can use physiological data including the patient's current abilities for physiological self-regulation. The data are often useful when discussing the rationale for reminders for frequent daily applications of avoiding excess tension and using relaxation.

Some readers may perceive the above as suggesting too much information and too much cognitive preparation for only one session. "All of this in one, 45–60 minute session?" the reader may logically ask. "Yes," is the answer. A practitioner can do all of this in one session. However, it is often impractical to do all this in one session without overloading the patient. Thus, the therapist should consider patient-education booklets and audiotapes that contain much of the necessary and useful information. One can get booklets and tapes prepared by others or develop one's own. Therapists should also consider consultations with professional patient-education writers and editors about readability, style, and grammar (Schwartz, in press). Compliance counseling begins during or after the initial session.

THE PATIENT

The patient's perceptions, expectations, and mood are among the important aspects of therapy and compliance. This assumes that patients' cognitions affect compliance, an assumption with which few professionals would disagree. The list below provides a catalogue of many specific patient perceptions, expectations, affective factors, and other factors. All of these can affect compliance and therapy results. Their order and the space devoted to discussing each topic does not confer relative importance. The therapist should consider the entire list during evaluation, cognitive preparation, and treatment.

I.   Perceptions
   A. Biofeedback and relaxation
      1. Patients may perceive biofeedback/relaxation as psychological treatment.
      2. Patients may perceive biofeedback/relaxation as insufficient or useless therapy.
      3. Patients may perceive relaxation as a waste of time.
      4. Patients may perceive biofeedback as the last chance for help, thus increasing stress.
   B. Therapy
      1. Patients may perceive therapy as preprogrammed and resist such a program.
      2. Patients may perceive the need for alternative therapies based on prior medical consults.
      3. Patients may perceive aspects of biofeedback/relaxation as silly or embarrassing.
      4. Patients may perceive the therapy as too costly and impractical.
      5. Patients may perceive the therapy program as taking too long.
      6. Patients may perceive the explanations of the rationale and therapy procedures as too complex.
      7. Patients may perceive self-report symptom logs as impractical.
      8. Patients may perceive the time needed daily as an interference with other priorities.
   C. Therapist
      1. Patients may distrust doctors and health care professionals in general.
      2. Patients may not perceive their professional/therapist as an ally.
   D. Symptoms
      1. Patients may perceive their symptoms as organic, hence requiring alternative therapy.
      2. Patients may perceive their symptoms as out of their control.
   E. Self and others
      1. Patients may fear using passive therapies.
      2. Patients may expect loss of control with relaxation therapy.
      3. Patients may perceive a lack of cooperation from significant others.

II. Expectations
    A. Patients may have unrealistic negative expectations.
    B. Patients may have unrealistic positive expectations.
    C. Patients may have experienced inadequate biofeedback/relaxation and may expect it again.
III. Affect and symptom discomfort
    A. Anxiety may interfere with patients' attention.
    B. Symptoms may interfere with patients' attention.
    C. Depression may interfere with patients' attention and compliance.
IV. Other factors
    A. Patients may be reluctant to speak candidly about psychological, interpersonal, and other stressful matters.
    B. Symptoms may be reinforcing, and symptom relief perceived as threatening.
    C. Patients may resist stopping caffeine, nicotine, alcohol, other vasoactive dietary chemicals, chewing gum, and unnecessary, ill-advised, and risky medications.
    D. Patients may have neurocognitive functioning that is impaired enough to interfere with their attention.

Perceptions

Perceptions of Biofeedback and Relaxation

Patients May Perceive Relaxation/Biofeedback as Psychological Treatment. It is probably still more common for mental health professionals than other health care professionals to provide biofeedback-assisted relaxation. It is therefore understandable that many patients perceive biofeedback as a psychological approach. Many health care professionals also consider biofeedback as a psychological technique. However, these therapies are multidisciplinary and not uniquely or exclusively within the provence of psychology. Surely, professionals with psychology education, training, and experience have advantages for treating many patients. However, that does not mean that the therapies are psychological in orientation.

The important points here are the patients' perceptions and feelings about psychological therapies and that many patients resist psychological therapies. Even when accepting a referral to a mental health professional, the patient may still be uncomfortable with the perceptions of psychological therapies. The practitioner should consider explaining that many professionals do not view biofeedback and relaxation as psychological treatments.

Such a discussion is pertinent when one is treating patients with medical disorders. One may not need to discuss the multidisciplinary nature of biofeedback with patients who voluntarily seek mental health help. Furthermore, nurses, physical therapists, occupational therapists, and dentists providing or supervising these therapies need not have this type of discussion with patients. Whatever the individual practitioner's discipline, he or she should consider portraying physiological self-regulation and biofeedback as having many unique features in addition to any psychological aspects.

My suggestions here may sound defensive or even apologetic for providing psychological therapies. That is not at all my intent. After all, I am a clinical psychologist and provide a variety of psychological services for which I take pride. However, when faced with a patient's discomfort caused by his or her perception of a therapy, I feel it necessary to help that patient develop a different perception. This will help the patient accept and be comfortable with the therapy. Furthermore, to consider biofeedback as a psychological technique implies that other professionals should not provide these therapies. This is inconsistent with the presence of many fine practitioners in other legitimate disciplines who do have licenses to provide psychological therapies.

Patients May Perceive Biofeedback/Relaxation as Insufficient, Useless, or as a Waste of Time. Relaxation and biofeedback-assisted relaxation may appear to some patients as insufficient or useless. This can be especially true when patients think of the intensity, frequency, and the chronicity of their symptoms. For some patients, prior unsuccessful therapies can diminish the credibility of self-regulation therapies. They harbor these perceptions and yet do not openly express them. One result can be an extreme form of noncompliance—dropping out of treatment early.

A corollary of the first perception is that relaxation is simply a waste of time. Such a perception is especially common among medical patients who have chronic physical symptoms. Laypeople very often do not perceive these symptoms as caused by or worsened by psychophysiological tension and arousal. This perception is also common among patients who were unsuccessful with several therapies, such as medications, that have face validity as powerful. Practitioners should show their awareness of these perceptions. For example, one might say:

> "I imagine that you may be thinking, 'How is this therapy going to help me? I have had these symptoms so long and tried so many treatments recommended by doctors with whom I had confidence. I got my hopes up before and the treatments did not help. How is this going to be different? You are saying to me that I need to spend a lot of time each day. This is time away from activities important to me. I have a busy schedule. Relaxation appears so simplistic compared to what I already tried. I am having trouble believing this can be enough and not a waste of time.' If this or similar thoughts are in your mind then we should discuss it."

If the patient admits such thoughts, then, the therapist can explain carefully the rationale for therapy, how it can help the patient despite the chronicity of his or her symptoms and all the prior, unsuccessful treatments. The therapist should describe time spent as an investment.

Patients May Perceive Biofeedback as the Last Chance for Help. Some patients, who tried several therapies without adequate success, perceive relaxation and biofeedback as therapies of "last resort." This perception is especially common among patients seen in tertiary medical centers. Many patients there have exhausted primary and secondary sources of health care. As with other misperceptions, patients are usually hesitant to report this perception spontaneously.

I believe that such a perception is an added source of anxiety and can heighten physiological arousal and tension. It can interfere with the patient's attending to what the professional is presenting and to compliance with therapy recommendations. The increased tension and symptoms that sometimes result can lead to more frustration and discouragement. Some patients then consider giving up entirely and dropping out of therapy.

One can change and even stop this perception by conveying the conviction to the patient that there are several therapies and approaches available. There are, after all, many relaxation procedures, several biofeedback modalities, and several biofeedback procedures.

In addition, there are life-style changes, dietary changes, cognitive stress management therapies, other stress management approaches, and various combinations of these. Of course, a particular patient need not use all of these. This information can significantly alter the perception of biofeedback as a single therapy, or as the therapy of last resort.

Patients may even resist or be less than ideally cooperative with therapy recommendations if they are perceived as the last resort. Implicitly, the patient might be saying that he or she would prefer not to try very hard rather than try and fail. Rather than saying "It is better to have tried and lost," patients act according to a different belief—"It is better not to try and still have some hope that a good therapy might still exist."

Perceptions of Therapy

Patients May Perceive the Therapy Program as Preprogrammed and Resist Such a Program. Practitioners sometimes provide biofeedback and related therapies in preprogrammed packages. This sometimes includes a specified number of sessions, standard placements of transducers, standard body positions, and therapy session conditions. There are often specific physiological criteria for branching to the next stage or to a different strategy.

Such packages are acceptable and useful in some settings and for some patients. However, some patients and practitioners resist preprogrammed packages and prefer tailored therapy. We need to be aware of these potential perceptions and adjust our therapies accordingly.

Patients May Perceive that Other Therapies Are Needed, Based on Prior Medical Consultations. Physicians with whom the patient consulted probably discussed and recommended therapy options. These include new or different medications, dosage changes, surgery, or psychotherapy. Before pursuing those other therapies, the patient came to a provider using biofeedback and related therapies. However, the other options often remain in the patient's perceptions as viable and possibly effective. The therapist should uncover these perceptions and deal with them as soon as practical.

Patients May Perceive Aspects of Biofeedback/Relaxation as Silly or Embarrassing. Some patients perceive certain aspects of relaxation as silly or embarrassing. These include tensing and releasing facial muscles, diaphragmatic breathing, listening to audiotaped relaxation, and relaxing in public places. Patients will usually not spontaneously voice such perceptions and feelings even after a therapist discusses it with them. Assuming that these perceptions exist and potentially affect compliance, the next question is how to revise them.

Some practitioners and therapists model some aspects of the relaxation. Therapist self-disclosure that he or she uses these procedures in daily life also can be reassuring. Some patients also may feel more comfortable once they know that many professionals, executives, athletes, entertainers, and others also often use these procedures. Explaining the credible rationale and application of each procedure also can help to put it in better perspective.

Patients May Perceive the Therapy as Too Costly and Impractical; Patients May Perceive the Therapy Program as Taking Too Long. Some patients perceive the costs and duration of treatment as beyond their capabilities and patience. This discourages them, hence decreases compliance. Solving this problem is not easy. In many professional settings, costs sometimes are substantial. Therapy can extend over several months. The duration of a therapy program is adjustable for many patients. The stepped-care approach offers a model within which to adjust the number of office sessions.

The quality of the relationship between the practitioner and the patient can help the patient accept the costs and duration of therapy. The credibility of the professional and other factors discussed in this chapter also can help. Practitioners support reduced fees when standard fees are a hardship for the patient and when there is a clear need for therapy. This practice is often easier in public institutions, but large private institutions and some private practitioners also adjust fees. Such humanistic and generous adjustments result in appreciation and can increase compliance. Fee adjustments have become more difficult in recent years, and this may worsen because of reimbursement problems throughout the health care system.

Patients May Perceive the Explanations of the Rationale and Therapy Procedures as Too Complex. Patients need to understand clearly an explanation for the therapy rationale and procedures. Patients need to relate the procedures logically to symptom reduction. Otherwise, they may perceive treatment as being too complex or irrelevant for them. This can affect compliance.

Patients May Perceive Self-Report Symptom Logs as Impractical. Self-report symptom logs should be practical and easy for patients. If not, then patients will perceive this as too much of a chore. This perception can lead to passive rebellion and a lack of records, contrived data, or withdrawal from therapy.

Patients May Perceive the Time Needed Daily as an Interference with Other Priorities. This type of therapy often involves considerable time commitments by patients. Even when not perceived as a waste of time, therapy takes time away from other important activities. A therapist's urging for an hour or more a day of relaxation is more than some patients have available. Of course, when patients' schedules are very full, there is often a greater need for balance and relaxation. However, patients may not perceive the situation that way. Practitioners often try to persuade them of this need but may be unconvincing. Appropriate time commitment is just impractical for some patients.

Examples of people whose schedules do not permit time for ideally applying treatments are farmers, tax accountants, and other seasonable workers whose schedules change significantly. It often is better to be flexible and wait than "beat one's professional head against a stone wall." In such cases, the therapist might, for example, consider shorter daily relaxation sessions. Or, he or she might consider more instructions for blending the physiological self-regulation into daily activities.

Another strategy in this situation would be to defer some treatment and focus the therapy on altering the patient's schedule and priorities. Some call this "time use therapy" (Schwartz & Schwartz, in press). One can defer therapy until the patient's schedule changes or the patient can shift priorities and behaviors compatible with therapeutic recommendations. For example, some people need to delegate, to drop items from their daily and weekly list, learn to do some tasks with less perfection, and/or to get better organized.

Perceptions of the Therapist

Patients May Distrust Doctors and other Health Care Professionals. Some patients learned to mistrust health care professionals. Such distrust often stems from their experiences or others' opinions. I am not speaking of paranoid patients. Those patients are extremely difficult to treat regardless of who we are and what we do. I am talking mostly about patients who experienced mistreatment or were mislead. Some received treatment from insensitive providers. Some may have experienced abuse. Some know people who had such experiences. It is very disappointing but not surprising to hear about health care professionals who are incompetent, marginally competent, or who take advantage of patients. Patients who experience such health care professionals sometimes have limited positive experiences to counteract the negative perceptions.

Professionals who add to the negative perceptions of some patients include those who provided inadequate relaxation, biofeedback, and associated therapies. For example, many patients react negatively to being alone for most or all sessions. These patients report feeling abandoned, anxious, confused by what to do, and frustrated. These feelings have added to their negative perception of biofeedback and professionals offering such services. Professionals can modulate such experiences by creating the perception of being, at last, different from the others. We do this by the quality of our interactions with the patient. We need to be sensitive to this type of experience and perception. The therapist needs to inquire about the patient's prior experiences if he or she does not volunteer the information and it is otherwise unknown. Extra efforts on the therapist's part can be important when a patient presents verbal or nonverbal cues of mistrust.

Some patients will candidly describe their negative experiences with other professionals. Other patients will sit quietly with a distrustful look on their face or provide no obvious visible clues of their distrust. For some patients, even sincere and reasonable efforts result in continued mistrust and antagonism. Some people do not want to be in our office or follow our advice. This is true no matter who we are, what we say, and how pleasant we are.

Patients May Not Perceive Their Practitioner as an Ally. Even patients without negative experiences may not perceive us as their ally in the battle against their symptoms. We may be credible and even highly competent. However, they might see us as too formal, too distant, not devoted enough, or too busy to provide the time they perceive as needed. They also might view us as too interested in making money or too interested in using their data and them as case studies.

Both our behavior and the therapeutic relationship affect these perceptions. We need to get out from behind our desks and our formality and convey that we do care about them as people, not only as patients or cases. It is difficult for some professionals to adopt Will Roger's dictum—"I have never met a man [or woman] I did not like." However, it helps to keep striving to show our liking for all patients, perhaps with a few exceptions.

Perceptions of Symptoms

Patients May Perceive Their Symptoms as Organic, Hence Requiring Other Therapy. A patient's perception may be that, "If only my doctors believed me and did more tests, they would find the cause." In this case, patients continue to believe that an organic cause is the major factor explaining their symptoms. They hold this perception despite their doctors' conclusions that a referral was proper for relaxation, biofeedback, and related therapies.

Patients often limit their compliance in such a case. To comply properly, patients need to believe that stress, or tension and arousal could cause or worsen their symptoms. They need to believe that organic factors are minor or nonexistent. Superficial compliance with the mechanics of therapy might still occur. However, these patients only "go through the motions." They often wait for another chance to get more medical tests. They may even view such compliance as a chance for them to show that the symptoms indeed are organic. They do this by failing to improve.

Such a situation is typically very difficult to manage. This is especially true after exhaustive and highly expert medical examinations and laboratory tests have ruled out an organic explanation for the symptoms.

When such patients are in primary or secondary levels of the health care system, they often go to highly credible tertiary medical centers. Resulting examinations and tests sometimes do find organic disease explanations for some patients' symptoms. There are sometimes physical and emotional symptoms that appear functional but are in fact organic. Examples of organic diseases that can produce symptoms that can appear as functional include pancreatic carcinoma, pheochromocytoma, some occult brain tumors, and thyroid disorders. (See Chapter 6 for more examples.) These cases are usually the exceptions. Ruling out organic causes by the best and credible medical examinations can help patient acceptance of physiological self-regulation and related therapies. I hope government regulations and third-party payers continue to permit this vital health care practice.

It is usually wiser to defer office relaxation, biofeedback, and related therapies if the patient is not yet sufficiently convinced of the functional nature of his or her symptoms or other rationale. Otherwise, one risks souring the patient's experience with failure from a treatment that might later be successful when the patient is more accepting.

Patients May Perceive Their Symptoms as Out of Their Control. Patients can believe their symptoms are beyond their control even if they accept a functional or psychophysiological explanation and believe that psychophysiological therapies can help symptoms in many people. This sometimes involves the perception of themselves as inadequate to relieve their symptoms. They also may perceive the intensity or chronicity of the symptoms as so severe that these therapies could not possibly work for them. A caring and skilled clinician can convince patients of the potential for help despite the chronicity and severity of the symptoms. One can mobilize these patients for enough compliance to achieve successful results.

Perceptions of Self and Others

Patients May Fear Using Passive Therapies. Some patients perceive relaxation therapies as tantamount to becoming passive—a threatening perception for those patients who avoid anything passive. Practitioners should be aware of the chance that this perception is present. They should look for this if the patient is avoiding relaxation practice. Such avoidance sometimes is clear in the first psychophysiological assessment session. The therapist should reassure the patient that relaxation does not equal passivity in any broad sense. Relaxation practice is not going to increase passivity. One can gradually introduce relaxation practice and gradual acceptance of using relaxation. Briefer periods of passive relaxation are sometimes helpful. The therapist should consider suggesting that patients periodically raise themselves out of the relaxed state. This can reassure patients that they can do this anytime they need to.

Patients May Expect Loss of Control with Relaxation Therapy. Some patients fear losing control even without a history of such a loss. Such patients require extra reassurance and gradual exposure to treatment procedures. Practitioners expecting these perceptions introduce preparatory information early that physiological self-regulation therapies increase self-control rather than lessen it.

Patients May Perceive Lack of Cooperation from Significant Others. Patients often need support and cooperation from their family and others. Some patients believe these people will not be understanding, accepting, and cooperative. Such perceptions are often accurate. These people may misunderstand and even ridicule the patient, although probably in jest. However, such behaviors can decrease compliance.

In this situation, the therapist can consider four options. First, he or she should consider giving patient-education booklets and/or tapes to patients. Patients should be encouraged to share these with the other people to help convey the rationale and procedures.

A second approach is to encourage patients to explain the rationale and procedures directly to the others. Increasing the patient's assertiveness to gain the understanding, acceptance, and cooperation of others is ideal. Patients must clearly understand and remember the essential details. This underscores the importance of patient education to provide the resources for patients to rely upon in learning what they need to communicate. One problem is persuading some of these patients to assert themselves enough to discuss these matters with the people who need to know.

Practitioners sometimes consider directly contacting the other people, with the patient's permission. Therapists may consider this third option when cooperation from the other people is necessary, but the patient is not getting it. A fourth approach suggests the patient use relaxation procedures only when other people are not around. This is the least desirable option.

For some patients, practitioners should consider enlisting others to give direct cooperation and help. For example, others can take care of some household or work responsibilities, reduce noise, and answer phone calls for a few minutes. Others can remind the patient about body postures and relaxation. However, cooperation and help could threaten some patients' perceptions of self-sufficiency. Many patients want to conduct their therapy without help from other people. This is desirable and commendable. However, one should not foster this attitude because then patients may perceive themselves as unable to get such help and cooperation.

There are legitimate reasons for patients not to seek help and cooperation from others. Some patients get along poorly with people in their life. There may be a history of poor cooperation from those people after similar requests. Some patients have a strong preference and capability for independence and a good history of self-discipline. Others have ample chances to apply the treatment procedures without the cooperation and help from others.

Expectations

Patients May Have Unrealistic Positive or Negative Expectations

Patients' expectations are often unrealistic in either positive or negative directions. Most practitioners know that unrealistic negative expectations interfere with compliance. However, unrealistic positive expectations are also common and involve expecting greater or faster benefit than usual. Patients base such expectations on what they have heard, read, or want or need to believe. Unrealistic positive expectations can result in disappointment and later noncompliance when the expectations do not match reality.

In the first session, practitioners usually get a sense of patient expectations. Discerning practitioners assume that unrealistic expectations may be present and that cognitive preparation should include promoting realistic positive expectations.

Patients May Have Experienced Inadequate
Biofeedback/Relaxation and May Expect It Again

Patients may perceive these therapies as inadequate when they did not get successful results with it in the past. However, the prior practitioner may have provided less than ideal biofeedback and related therapies. Reversing such negative expectations requires extra care, especially if one wants to avoid disparaging the prior practitioner. One may consider saying something like the following:

> "The treatment you received in the past sounds like what many professionals provide. You know there are differences in opinion and practice among professionals. Education and training of professionals vary. Some professionals did not have much formal education and training in biofeedback because it was not easily available then. It still is not easily available for many professionals. Some professionals cannot travel as much as others to get the training.
>
> "Furthermore, some professionals specialize in biofeedback. They devote more time to developing specialized knowledge, skills, and procedures. Others are less specialized. Some professionals are not in places that allow them to get preferred instruments. Most practitioners mean well, but often they do not know what they do not know. There is much we can add to the therapy you had in the past. This can be important and helpful for you."

Affect and Symptom Discomfort

Practitioners usually know that patients' affect and symptoms have an impact on what they remember from spoken patient education. Affect and symptom discomfort interfere with the attention and experience during feedback. This probably does not need more discussion.

Other Factors

Patients May Be Reluctant to Speak Candidly About Psychological, Interpersonal, and Other Stress Matters

Some patients view a referral for relaxation and biofeedback therapies as "face-saving" in contrast with a psychological evaluation. These patients sometimes expect that psychological topics will not be a focus of the evaluation and treatment. They often are reluctant to speak candidly about psychological matters that are of potential importance in the formulation of an effective treatment program.

For some of these patients, practitioners can skirt such topics at least in the early sessions. It often is sufficient to focus on physiological self-regulation therapies, reduction of or stopping chemical stressors, and making related changes. However, there are many other patients who need psychological therapies to reduce or stop symptoms. Many practitioners wisely develop and convey an understandable and acceptable rationale for discussing psychosocial and related topics.

Symptoms May be Reinforcing, and Symptom Relief May Be Perceived as Threatening

Most practitioners know that symptoms can serve reinforcing value despite the discomfort and impairment. Some patients expect that significant symptom relief will result in threatening effects. However, some practitioners forget or are less aware of this. Practitioners often struggle with ways to discuss this delicate topic with patients. Without ample caution and tact, the result can be loss of a patient's confidence and trust.

Discreet practitioners consider using examples when discussing this topic and checking for the possible role of this factor in maintaining patients' symptoms and in compliance problems. One example occurs with persons who are chronically very obese, often from their adolescence. These people often face very different heterosexual situations when they lose considerable weight and approach a normal figure. They may not believe that they have the interpersonal skills and stress management strategies to adjust to such conditions. They may or may not be aware of the approach–avoidance conflict. In either case, they will probably be reluctant to discuss them spontaneously. A common result is lack of compliance with a weight-loss program.

Another example might be a married couple with a very poor relationship. When one moves toward divorce, one faces expectations about other negative conditions. Loneliness and financial hardships are two examples of these. One common result of such realization is retreat back into the marriage, often without constructive steps to improve the marriage. Such behavior can occur several times, resulting in a "revolving door" type of behavior.

Some practitioners experienced severe physical symptoms themselves and have thereby gained an awareness for and increased empathy with patients' expectations and behavior. Some practitioners even experienced the temptation for others to take care of them. They gained temporary relief from onerous responsibilities and escaped distasteful situations. They know firsthand the temptation to maintain this state. If such practitioners are comfortable with limited self-disclosure, then, sharing these experiences may be helpful. They give legitimacy for the patients to admit to these thoughts.

Patients May Resist Stopping Caffeine, Nicotine, Alcohol,
Other Vasoactive Dietary Chemicals, Chewing Gum,
and Unnecessary, Ill-Advised, and Risky Medications

Typically, most patients accept stopping caffeine, chewing gum, and some foods with vasoactive chemicals. However, they do commonly resist stopping nicotine, alcohol, and medications. What do we do when patients plan to continue ingesting chemicals that we know detract from the effectiveness of physiological self-regulation therapies? There is no general agreement about this decision.

Practitioners advise patients of the potential negative effects on treatment. They explain the physiological effects of caffeine, nicotine, and other chemicals. They try to persuade patients to avoid such chemicals during the hour or so before relaxation and biofeedback sessions. The effects of gum chewing on temporalis muscles are not clear to most patients: They require patient education and a demonstration. Ideally, practitioners will persuade patients to stop these. I sometimes say to patients something like the following:

> "I know your symptoms are very distressing to you, and you want to reduce or stop them. I've explained how _____ interferes with relaxation and self-regulation of your body. I know you want to make progress as fast as practical. You probably want to limit the number of office sessions needed. Continuing to consume these chemicals can detract from your progress and prolong therapy. The decision is yours whether you stop them or not. I am willing to help you as long as there is a chance to reach your goals. However, I do not want you to waste your time and money. I will do everything I can to help you withdraw from and stop these chemicals. Please give this some thought, and we can discuss this further."

Patients' Neurocognitive Functioning May Be Impaired
Enough to Interfere with Their Attention

Impaired neurocognitive functioning in patients often results in their inability to remember the instructions and therapy recommendations and to attend to therapy tasks. These present special problems and challenges. Practitioners can sometimes successfully treat such patients with enough involvement and help from cooperative persons living with the patient.

EVALUATION AND INTERVENTION

There are several methods for assessing compliance:

1. Patients can self-monitor frequency and durations of relaxation, and the times they use it.
2. Patients can keep a self-report log of symptoms.
3. Patients can self-monitor subjective physiological sensations associated with relaxation.
4. Patients can self-monitor cognitions associated with relaxation.
5. Patients can self-monitor chemical intake including caffeine, nicotine, and other vasoactive chemicals.
6. Patients can self-monitor physiological parameters, such as skin temperatures, pulse rates, and blood pressures. They can do this before, during, and after relaxation sessions.
7. Practitioner interviews are often revealing.
8. Periodic psychophysiological assessments are often revealing.
9. Observation of a patient's breathing and body postures is often revealing.
10. Reports from other people in a patient's daily life are helpful.
11. Patients' motor functioning often provides a useful index.
12. Patients' daily activities often provide a useful index.

The practitioner should encourage patients to maintain a self-report log. This conveys the importance of the information requested. It conveys the intent of the therapist to review such information. However, requesting too much or too complicated record keeping can be counterproductive if it creates too much bookkeeping. There are a variety of record-keeping systems used.

Patients do not need to be 100% accurate or complete for practitioners to obtain useful information and assess compliance. The log is often enough to allow practitioners to check on compliance and to stimulate discussion.

Therapists should devote some portion of office sessions to reviewing the log. When logs are not available or incomplete, they should use the interview to get information about patients' experiences and compliance. Experienced and competent clinicians know that simple questions are often not enough to elicit needed and useful information. Patients often provide incorrect and misleading responses in interviews. For example, let us consider the value of the response "yes" to the following questions.

- Are you practicing your relaxation?
- Are you practicing your relaxation as instructed?
- Are you feeling relaxed when you use the relaxation?
- Are you practicing your relaxation daily?

- Are you practicing your relaxation at various times each day?
- Are you feeling much better?

These and similar questions are inadequate alone to elicit useful information. Patients can answer such questions with a "yes" or "no," interpreting the questions in ways they prefer. These are not always the ways the practitioner intends. When patients say "yes" to practicing daily, does that mean "daily," or does it mean "most days" or just "some days"?

Limited time to question patients in detail or limited interviewing skills results in not enough information for assessing compliance and progress. If there is no self-report log or it is incomplete, the therapist might consider the following examples of interview questions. One might start in this manner:

"Let us review your relaxation practice. As accurately as you can recall, please tell me how you have been progressing toward your goals. How often and when are you ____?"

Depending on the completeness of the patient's response to such an initial question, the clinician should consider the specific questions:

"How many times each day, during the past week, did you relax for 15–20 minutes each? How many brief relaxations of 2–10 minutes each?
"Are there days on which you were not been able to relax? How many days?"
"Let's talk about those days. What are the problems?"
"How do you feel during your relaxation sessions? What sensations are you experiencing during relaxation? What do you experience after your relaxation sessions? How long do those sensations and feelings last?"
"In what situations did you use relaxation during the past week?"
"When could you benefit from relaxation but are not using it?"

Physiological measures during office sessions also can help assess compliance. However, one must be careful to avoid misusing or misinterpreting such data. For example, it is reasonable to assume that warmer baseline skin temperatures, faster increases in skin temperature, lower baseline muscle activity, and/or faster drops of muscle activity all reflect good relaxation experiences between office sessions. However, one cannot assume these are clear signs of compliance.

Improved baseline psychophysiological functioning can reflect increasing comfort or habituation to the office, instrumentation, and the therapist. Such psychophysiological data are often consistent with verbal reports of compliance with relaxation, reduction of undesired chemicals, and/or other life-style changes. In such cases, one can use the data as a valuable basis for positive verbal reinforcement from the therapist. Conversely, we cannot assume a lack of compliance from the lack of psychophysiological progress during baselines.

Observations of patients by persons living or working with the patients may help assess compliance. These include observation of patients' restlessness, posture, breathing, facial muscles, and other visible cues of tension and relaxation.

INCREASING COMPLIANCE AND SUMMARY

The purpose of this chapter is to help answer the question asked by all practitioners: "What can I do to help assure or increase the likelihood that my patients will do what I recommend?" Some of the answers appear throughout the chapter. Three arbitrary divisions for dividing and summarizing the methods and considerations for increasing compliance are summarized below.

Persons and factors that prevent or decrease noncompliance include:

- Professional setting and office personnel.
- Professional's characteristics and behaviors.
- Interaction between professional and patient.
- Cognitive preparation of patients.
- Patients' perceptions, expectations, and affect.
- Patients' family and others in their daily lives.

Specific interventions include the following:

- Use readily accessible, easy to use self-report record systems.
- Ask patients to record readily observable and meaningful behaviors.
- Instruct patients why and how to self-monitor.
- Reinforce patients' accuracy and completeness.
- Convey that one will review the patient's records.
- Encourage patients to record behaviors, experiences, and symptoms when they occur.
- Establish subgoals, and review and revise them as needed.

General considerations include:

- Be willing to accept less than ideal compliance and therapeutic progress.
- Successively approximate and shape compliance.
- Allow patients to set their own goals and discuss cost–benefit considerations.

The items for preventing or decreasing noncompliance do not need elaboration here. This chapter has already discussed in detail the factors under each of these six rubrics. Self-report logs relate to the seven items listed as specific interventions for increasing compliance. Therapists should give positive verbal reinforcement to those parts of self-report logs that are present and appear accurate. One can encourage or shape more accuracy and completeness. For example, one might say:

"These records are a good beginning. You have the idea. Allow me, please, to suggest [or ask] that you add and develop your records a little more by doing the following. . . ."

Patients ideally record their symptoms and behaviors when they occur, and not hours later. Exceptions are when the symptoms are very severe for hours or when there are no symptoms for hours. Preaddressed and prestamped envelopes also ease communications for those patients not seen often in the office.

Practitioners should review the records with the patients and share the tabulations and graphs derived from the data. This conveys that the practitioner is using the records to make therapy changes and recommendations. It reinforces the usefulness and importance of the records *and* the professional's interest in the patients.

Practitioners need to be patient with their patients. We need to be willing to accept less than ideal compliance and therapy progress without conveying negative criticism, displeasure, or disappointment. Implied scolding or expressions of disappointment may signal reappraisal of the question "Who is treating whom?"

It is useful to remind ourselves that we are here to serve our patients—and not the reverse. We fulfill many of our responsibilities when we provide a good rationale for our recommendations and present practical and achievable methods to reach therapy goals. We fulfill other responsibilities by maintaining our credibility in the views of our patients and preserving positive rapport with them.

Patients usually know better than practitioners the degree of symptom improvement that is enough for them. They know the limits of their time, money, and the inconvenience they are willing and able to invest for the desired benefits. Determining and reviewing of subgoals can help compliance. For example, the goal of eliminating symptoms is too distant and too unrealistic for many patients. Subgoals include tailoring the number of minutes of relaxation and separate relaxation periods per day. Another subgoal is to achieve percentage reductions of caffeine or nicotine use. One also can aim for specific reductions of symptom frequency or intensity, and increases in symptom-free hours. There are many other behavioral and physiological signs of improvement that can be partial goals (Schwartz & Fehmi, 1982).

It is abundantly clear that compliance is a very complex and many-sided concept. Patient compliance requires great care, preparation, ingenuity, persistence, and patience on the part of practitioners. It requires reviews of one's own professional behaviors, setting, and procedures. It requires tailoring to the individual. Professional and humane characteristics and skills impact on patient compliance. Practitioners need adequate time to develop their program, and patients need enough time to apply recommendations. Practitioners also need to tolerate and function with ambiguity and within the less than ideal world of clinical practice. We need to continue to strive toward further cultivation and growth of our skills to help our patients cultivate compliance, healthy attitudes, and behaviors.

REFERENCES

DiMatteo, M. R., & DiNicola, D. D. (1982). *Achieving patient compliance.* New York: Pergamon Press.

Schwartz, M. S. (Ed.). (in press). *Patient education: A practitioner's guide.* New York: Guilford Press.

Schwartz, M. S., & Fehmi, L. (1982). *Applications standards and guidelines for providers of biofeedback services.* Wheatridge, CO: Biofeedback Society of America.

Schwartz, M. S., & Schwartz, N. M. (in press). Time use management: A patient education manual. In M. S. Schwartz (Ed.), *Patient education: A practitioner's guide.* New York: Guilford Press.

IV
CULTIVATING LOWER AROUSAL

10

Dietary Considerations:
Rationale, Issues, Substances,
Evaluation, and Patient Education

Keith I. Block
Mark S. Schwartz

Many professionals believe and many patients report that certain dietary elements and patterns aggravate or trigger some physical symptoms. Health professionals advise their patients to alter those elements that they believe cause or aggravate those symptoms. Many conditions treated with physiological self-regulation overlap with the symptoms treated by changing food and beverage intake. Among them are migraine headaches, anxiety, and irritable bowel syndrome (IBS). Among the dietary changes suggested for these conditions are: elimination of certain foods, beverages, and medications; avoiding eating under stress; increasing fiber intake; and altering eating patterns that result in hypoglycemia.

Links between caffeine and anxiety or insomnia, and between fiber and bowel problems, are well established clinically. Links between diet and migraine headache have been controversial. In the last 10 years, however, this connection was extensively explored and has received substantial validation. Because of the work in this field—which has been difficult for both patients and professionals to accept in the past—the present chapter emphasizes the relationship between diet and migraines, although it does not exclude the other conditions listed above.

There is anecdotal, clinical, and research support for including dietary recommendations in clinical practice with migraine patients as well as for those with some nonmigraine headaches. The relationship between these substances and the onset or aggravation of symptoms is neither completely clear nor agreed upon by experts. However, a growing body of work now confirms early observations of dietary triggers for migraine and establishes possible mechanisms of action.

Practitioners should remember that the association between dietary factors and migraine headaches is variable. Headache sufferers are sensitive to widely different foods or food classes; they typically react to more than one food. Even for the individual, a particular food may not trigger headaches every time one ingests it, possibly because of differences in stress levels and recent consumption of other migraine-aggravating foods. Changes in the status of the detoxification pathways of the liver and gut may lead to variation in the body's ability to excrete foreign substances that aggravate migraines. Variation in permeability of the gut wall to food-borne migraine trigger compounds may also account for this response variability. Health professionals should be aware of these sources of variable response. They should also keep abreast of the controversies in research in this field in order to allow realistic discussion with patients and with other health professionals who may regard the diet–migraine link with skepticism.

This chapter helps readers to assess dietary factors in clinical practice. Our specific goals are as follows:

1. We discuss general issues of methodology involved in the hypothesized relationships between dietary factors and physical symptoms.
2. We discuss the allergy–migraine hypothesis.
3. We discuss the vasoactive contents found in several foods, beverages, and medications, and the possible role of these substances in migraine.
4. We discuss problems with the use of caffeine.
5. We provide alternative strategies for when and how to introduce dietary advice into clinical programs and to discuss the implications of each strategy.

We begin with a brief account of the current state of research on the pathophysiology of migraine as a framework for discussion of the actions of migraine trigger foods.

MECHANISMS OF MIGRAINE

People susceptible to migraines appear to be unusually reactive to events and substances that trigger vasoconstriction or vasodilatation. Two theories of migraine mechanisms are now under investigation. One theory views migraines as a result of dilatation of cranial blood vessels triggering head pain; the other theory views the pain as resulting from plasma leaking out of cranial vessels, causing inflammation of surrounding tissues. In both of these theories, serotonin plays a major role—although it is not certain just what that role is. Serotonin (5-hydroxytryptamine or 5-HT) is an important neurotransmitter with vasoconstrictor activity. It seems to be released in large quantities from blood platelets in migraine: Its metabolites appear in the urine following migraine, and platelet serotonin level has been shown to decrease by 40% during migraines (Humphrey, 1991).

Many migraine triggers and inhibitors have activities related to serotonin. Reserpine, a drug that causes the release of serotonin from platelets, causes migraine-like headaches in migraine sufferers. Red wine, a common migraine trigger, has been shown to cause release of serotonin from platelets in vitro (Jarman, 1991). Many antimigraine drugs react with serotonin receptors, including sumatriptan, ergot derivatives, and methysergide. However, these drugs also show other relevant activities, such as vasoconstriction (Saxena & DenBoer, 1991). Giving serotonin intravenously abolishes migraine symptoms. Feverfew (*Chrysanthemum parthenium* Bernh.), a herb in the daisy family found useful in migraine prophylaxis, blocks release of serotonin from platelets in experiments. It also reduces platelet aggregation induced by serotonin in migraine patients who use it regularly. Feverfew also, however, blocks prostaglandin synthesis, another possible migraine-inhibiting mechanism (der Marderosian & Liberti, 1988). Ginger (*Zingiber officinale* Roscoe) is another botanical reported useful in aborting migraine headaches in a case study: It also inhibits prostaglandin synthesis as well as thromboxane generation (Mustafa & Srivastava, 1990).

Exactly what serotonin does in the brain neurovascular system to cause migraines is not clear. Some theorize that migraine is a manifestation of serotonin deficiency in the brain, caused, possibly, by factors that trigger serotonin release from storage sites in platelets and other tissues, and consequent depletion. The depletion might cause vasodilatation and the pain of migraine. The situation may, however, be more complex. Serotonin receptors also help to modulate release of plasma from brain blood vessels, which could cause inflammation in surrounding brain tissue (Moskowitz & Buzzi, 1991). The trigeminal nerve and blood vessels associated with it may also be implicated in migraine. Both the nerve and vessels can send and receive pain signals (Edmeads, 1991). Other substances, including prostaglandins, histamine, and hormones also play a role in migraine symptoms, although their activities are even less well worked out than that of serotonin. How migraine trigger foods fit into the picture is not well understood, except that most of them have some vasoactive components.

METHODOLOGICAL ISSUES

There are important factors to consider when discussing the relationships between what people consume and their symptoms. For example, Kohlenberg (1980) presented interesting and valuable arguments supporting an interaction or combination theory rather than targeting one substance alone. His idea was that multiple dietary substances and other risk factors such as stress can result in symptoms in some persons. Stress includes a wide variety of environmental, psychological, and somatic factors. Olesen (1991), for instance, lists emotional upset, hormonal changes, fatigue, smoke, strong light, weather, and high altitudes as some of the nondietary physical stresses that may trigger migraines. Missed meals or erratic blood sugar may trigger migraines (Egger, 1991). The combinations and interactions of these factors, as well as those of diet, vary significantly both within and between individuals. This makes it more difficult to determine what relationships are active in each case.

Furthermore, for some persons, the circumstances surrounding the consumption of suspected substances could be as important, or even more important than the substances themselves. For example, people commonly consume many of the suspected foods and beverages in the evenings, on weekends, at parties, or at sports events. Examples of such foods are red wine, aged cheeses, sausages, chocolate, and hot dogs. Social activities and sporting events often involve additional sources of tension, arousal, and fatigue. These could lead to symptom onset caused by sympathetic arousal, general muscle tension, or both.

In addition, people are more likely to recall times when symptoms followed soon after ingestion of specific foods and beverages. They are less likely to recall the times symptoms did not occur or times they occurred several hours later. Once a person experiences symptoms soon after ingestion of specific foods or beverages, he or she may expect the symptoms the next time the substances are consumed—regardless of whether the food or beverage physiologically caused symptom onset. This expectancy itself can increase the chance that symptoms will occur. Alternatively, an inconsistent or variable association can lead patients to believe mistakenly that there is no relationship between the dietary element and their symptoms.

The complex interactions among potential migraine triggers can manifest themselves in puzzling research results. Salfield et al. (1987), for instance, randomized a group of children with migraines to either a diet low in vasoactive amines or a high-fiber diet, which served as a placebo. Both groups had significant reductions in headache, and headaches were reduced in the placebo and low-amine groups by the same amount. This could be a result of placebo or nonspecific effects. It could also have resulted from a reduction in hypoglycemia by the high fiber content of the placebo diet, since fiber frequently stabilizes blood sugar levels. The higher fiber content may have assisted in natural detoxification mechanisms. The children on the high-fiber diet may also have previously eaten "junk food" high in other potentially vasoactive substances such as monosodium glutamate (MSG) and sodium nitrate, which were displaced by the high-fiber foods (Radnitz, 1990).

A further complication of migraine headaches is the time lag that often follows intake of migraine trigger foods. Gettis (1987a) describes an excellent example of this in his case report of a male in his late 30s, a vegetarian who suffered from common migraines. He kept a daily diary of headache incidence and the number of 325-milligram aspirin tablets taken. Eventually the constant aspirin ingestion led to gastrointestinal bleeding. The subject was then put on a bland diet of white bread, macaroni, oatmeal, cottage cheese, milk, baked potato, applesauce, scrambled eggs, cooked spinach, and peas. Within days of undertaking this "ulcer diet" his migraines disappeared. The subject then began adding new foods to his diet, recording in a food diary whether headaches occurred after the reintroduction of a new food. He would eat a new food for 3 consecutive days and then wait 4 days before introducing a new food. If he reacted to a food, he would test it a second time using the same procedure.

Eventually the subject isolated three foods that triggered his headaches: bananas, citrus, and cheese, (all of which contain vasoactive compounds including serotonin, dopamine, and tyramine) (Riggin, McCarthy, & Kissinger, 1976). His detailed records and careful plan of food introduction also revealed that he had a delayed reaction to his trigger foods: His headaches occurred 48–72 hours following ingestion of the offending foods. This observation is of distinct clinical importance, since migraine sufferers may fail to observe the relationship between specific foods and migraines because of such time lags and may therefore assume there is no connection between foods and their headaches.

Gettis (1987b) discusses the importance of this meticulously documented time lag in research on food-related migraines. In the light of this phenomenon, many studies did not leave adequate time for the development of migraines after intake of the foods or compounds under study. Many appear to have assumed that migraines triggered by food or chemicals would appear within 24–48 hours. This assumption led investigators to administer test substances and placebos within 48 hours of each other. If some subjects are reacting to test substances after 48 hours, this would lead to headaches following placebo administration that were actually caused by the test substance—explaining in part the high rate of reaction to placebo seen in many migraine studies (Radnitz, 1990).

Gettis (1987b) also points out that some studies do not control the intake of other potentially migraine-causing foods by their subjects and suggests that control of diet during the testing period could lead to more consistent results. Finally, subjects must eliminate all migraine-causing foods from their diets to give accurate results (Gettis, 1987a). If the subject described above had eliminated bananas, citrus, and cheese one at a time and reintroduced them before eliminating the other foods, he never would have been able to determine the causes of his headaches, since his diet would never have been free from his migraine trigger foods.

THE ISSUE OF ALLERGY AND MIGRAINE

Some professionals refer to the relationship between certain dietary factors and migraines as an allergic one. Speer (1977), a pediatric allergist, argues for an allergic etiology for many migraines. He discusses in detail many dietary and nondietary factors. Unfortunately, the literature he refers to is mostly from the 19th and early 20th centuries and anecdotal in nature. However, Speer's book is interesting. It contains some potentially useful information about dietary and nondietary factors that have been anecdotally reported to contribute to migrane and are therefore worth keeping in mind.

There were no well-controlled studies that showed that vascular headaches represented an allergic reaction until the ambitious study by Egger, Wilson, Carter, Turner, and Soothill, (1983a). This study supported an allergic pathogenesis for migraines among many children of ages 3–16. Children were put on a diet low in foods known to be commonly allergenic for 2 weeks. Of the 88 children who completed the diet, 78% reported full recovery from migraines. Forty of the children then underwent double-blind challenges at weekly intervals with allergenic foods. Thirty-nine percent of children reported migraines from cow's milk, 31% from wheat, 36% from eggs, and 17% from corn—all foods commonly found to be highly allergenic. Adverse reactions, however, were idiosyncratic for each child. Other commonly allergenic foods found to trigger migraines were orange, tomato, rye, fish, and soy. Some foods suspected to contain vasoactive substances also caused migraines, including chocolate, cheese, coffee, and malt (Egger, 1991). Podell (1984) provided an excellent summary of the study.

Identifying food sensitivities is not easy in clinical situations. Comprehensive dietary elimination-and-challenge procedures are often not practical, especially as one of the first evaluative and treatment approaches. Many professionals described the Egger, Wilson, Carter, Turner, and Soothill (1983a) study as a landmark. We need, however, to be careful not to overgeneralize or overinterpret the findings from even such a well-done study. We need replications and extensions of these findings with other samples of children and adults.

Letters to *Lancet* in response to this study noted questions and caveats (Cook & Joseph, 1983; Stephenson, 1983; Gerrard, 1983; Hearn & Finn, 1983; Peatfield, 1983; Feldman, 1983). Egger, Wilson, Carter, Turner, and Soothill (1983b) responded to some of the questions. There are several reasons for not easily extrapolating these findings to adults. The percentage of adults who are prone to atopic diseases is less than for children. There is no compelling theoretical basis explaining how the immune system mediates migraines. The children in this study (Egger et al., 1983a) had many other behavioral and somatic symptoms, creating some doubt about the representativeness of their sample. Egger (1991) has argued that the effect of allergenic foods may be to increase gut permeability, allowing increased vasoactive substances in other foods to enter the circulation in greater quantities. Radnitz (1990) points out that the response to the diet could have been the result of placebo effect, especially since the trial period was only 2 weeks. Food allergies were not confirmed with more sophisticated tests such as IgE or skin tests. Finally, childhood migraine responds well to a number of manipulations, including biofeedback, so that the response rate could represent a nonspecific effect.

Other workers, however, have argued for the validity of the food allergy hypothesis. Mansfield, Vaughn, Waller, Haverly, and Ting (1985) eliminated wheat, milk, corn, eggs and other foods to which individuals had positive skin tests from the diets of selected adults. Of 16 subjects with positive skin tests, 11 experienced relief of migraines; of 27 who had negative skin tests, only 2 experienced relief. In a later paper, Mansfield (1990) argued for histamine-mediated causes of allergic migraines. Specialized immune cells in the gut, termed mast cells, release histamine in the presence of allergenic foods. Histamine inhibits uptake of serotonin by brain cells, possibly leading to depletion of serotonin and consequent migraine. Intravenous infusions of histamine lead to throbbing headaches in normals and migraine sufferers; the latter usually develop pain first on the side that is clinically affected in migraine, and respond to lower doses of histamine than normals.

Giacovazzo and Martelletti (1989) tested 24 patients with food-triggered migraine who had positive skin tests or radio-allergo-sorbent test (RAST; a sophisticated method of detecting allergies) to relevant foods. The foods identified as migraine triggers were eliminated from the diet, and dosing with sodium cromolyn begun (sodium cromolyn is a drug given prophylactically to block allergic responses). At the start of the trial, before drug dosing or diet, the trigger foods were tested to develop baseline headache index values for each food. After 1 and 2 months on the diet-drug trial, and 1 month after the trial was ended, foods were tested again. Headache index values fell during the first and second months, and rose again after the trial, although not to the baseline values.

Immune complexes are commonly formed in the blood after sensitive persons ingest allergenic foods. Sodium cromolyn inhibits histamine release from gut mast cells, which is triggered by the presence of immune complexes. The authors suggest that such inhibition blocks a sequence of events leading to release of serotonin from circulating platelets.

Weber and Vaughan (1991) review several studies that correlated the release of allergic mediators, such as histamine, with migraine headaches and then attempted to relate these reactions to skin-test data. Migraines, they report, have been reported to be associated with increases in histamine following exposure to known allergenic foods. For instance, in a patient with beef-induced migraine, a migraine headache was observed to be preceded by a tripling of histamine levels following beef ingestion. Skin tests and RAST for beef were both negative. A study of five patients with food-induced migraines showed major increases in histamine levels following challenges with allergenic foods. The increased histamine levels were followed by migraine headaches. Skin tests for the allergenic foods, however, were negative.

Other workers reporting evidence of headache relief after elimination of foods shown to be allergenic include Monro, Carini, Brostoff, and Zilkha (1980), Grant (1979), Radnitz and Blanchard (1991), Weber and Vaughan (1991), Lucarelli et al. (1990), and Hughes, Gott, Weinstein, and Bingelli (1985). Egger, Carter, Soothill, and Wilson (1989) found that elimination of allergenic foods brought relief in epilepsy–migraine syndrome. Pradalier, Weinman, Launay, Baron, and Dry (1983) and Wilson, Kirker, Warnes, and O'Malley (1980), however, found no relationship between food allergy and migraine. Some of the variability in results may arise because allergy-triggered migraines probably affect only a small—and unknown—percentage of migraine sufferers. There does, however, appear to be enough data to regard the food allergy–migraine hypothesis as one worth clinical consideration. Skin tests and RAST, however, may be of less value than food elimination and challenge in detecting allergy-related migraine trigger foods, as the studies reviewed by Weber and Vaughan (1991) suggest.

VASOACTIVE CONTENTS (NOT INCLUDING CAFFEINE) OF FOODS AND BEVERAGES

Aside from caffeine (discussed separately later), other vasoactive chemicals may trigger or increase the likelihood of migraine headaches. Commonly mentioned substances are tyramine, sodium nitrate, phenylethylamine, monosodium glutamate, levodopa, alcohol, and the noncaloric sweetener aspartame. These substances are in many foods and beverages and may lead to migraine headaches in a variety of ways. The effectiveness of foods containing vasoactive substances in triggering migraine is shown in a study by Lai, Dean, Ziegler, and Hassanein (1988), who fed red wine, chocolate, and sharp cheddar cheese to subjects who reported migraines associated with these foods, in order to cause migraines for electrophysiological study. Of the 38 subjects tested, 42% reported migraines after eating the offending foods in a clinical situation.

Tyramine

Tyramine is the most commonly discussed vasoactive substance. Chemically, it is an amine, or a breakdown product of an amino acid. Amines result when proteins are chemically altered by decarboxylation by enzymes during metabolism, or by bacterial contamination after death. The pressor amines are a group of amines that can stimulate the sympathetic nervous system. This group includes serotonin, tryptophan, histidine, and tyramine, the amine derivative of the amino acid tyrosine (interestingly, the Greek word "tyros," from which tyrosine and tyramine are derived, means cheese).

Health professionals became aware of tyramine's vasoactive properties when investigators discovered its interaction with monoamine oxidase inhibitors (MAOI), drugs used in the treatment of depression and hypertension. Serious adverse biochemical interactions (even death) have occurred when patients consume tyramine while taking these medications. Tyramine and other pressor amines are usually harmless, as they are detoxified in the liver and intestines. Monoamine oxidase mediates this oxidative mechanism. The MAOI drugs significantly interfere with detoxification, allowing large amounts of amines to reach the bloodstream, triggering hypertensive crises and migraine-like headaches.

The mechanism by which tyramine might trigger migraine headaches may be analogus to the activity of MAOI drugs. Some workers have hypothesized that 5–10% of migraine sufferers have a genetic deficiency of monoamine oxidase activity, allowing excessive amounts of tyramine to reach the bloodstream. The vasoactive effect of this pressor amine may then cause a migraine headache (Gettis, 1987b).

Hanington (1980; Hanington, Horn, & Wilkinson, 1969) and colleagues were the first to investigate the relationship of tyramine to migraine headaches. They gave a group of migraine sufferers capsules containing tyramine or placebo. Over the series of trials they conducted, headaches resulted after tyramine 80% of the time and after placebo only 8% of the time (Radnitz, 1990). Several other workers were unable to replicate these studies, possibly because tyramine sensitivity may affect only 5% of migraine sufferers. Relationships between tyramine-containing foods and headache can, however, be documented, as shown, for example, in the case report by Gettis (1987a). Tyramine sensitivity must therefore be considered clinically when one is treating migraines that appear to be food related. Tyramine, however, is not the only vasoactive amine that may cause migraine headaches, although it receives the most attention because of its interaction with MAOI drugs. Other agents, such as the octopamine in citrus fruits, must also be considered.

Tyramine content varies significantly not only among foods, but even between samples of the same food. For example, in yogurt and sour cream, the manufacturing process and contamination may or may not result in vasopressor amines (see *Nutrition Reviews*, 1965, cited in McCabe & Tsuang, 1982). For instance, Horowitz, Lovenberg, Engelman, and Sjoerdsma (1964) found no detectable tyramine in the yogurt they analyzed. One should instruct persons with tyramine-related migraines that if they eat dairy foods, they should consume only fresh products manufactured by a reputable source and stored appropriately. Some may then tolerate moderate servings of yogurt and sour cream, even though they commonly contain small amounts of tyramine.

Tyramine usually increases with the aging process in cheeses. However, the appearance of looking aged and mature does not always correlate with greater tyramine content than in the appearance of pale, mild-flavored cheese (McCabe & Tsuang, 1982). Although increasing times of maturation usually increase tyramine level, other factors also affect it. Such factors include types of microorganisms or decarboxylating enzyme levels. Thus, a short-maturation cheese, such as Camembert, can contain high levels of tyramine. Likewise, a long-maturation cheese can contain low amounts of tyramine if there is lower decarboxylation or if other enzymes transform the tyramine. Moreover, the bacteriological quality of the milk is a major factor affecting the final concentration of tyramine (Antila, Antila, Mattila, & Hakkaraineu, 1984, cited in Vidaud, Chaviano, Gonzales, & Garcia Roche, 1987).

Furthermore, cheese closer to the rind of a block can contain much more tyramine than samples from the center of the block (Price & Smith, 1971). They reported a difference in tyramine concentration from 11 to 1184 micrograms per gram with distances of 7 down to 0 centimeters from the rind of several pieces of Gruyère cheese. Most tyramine was close to the rind—less than about 3 centimeters. Concentrations near the rind varied widely nearer the rind (e.g., from 250–1184 micrograms per gram) among the samples, but the gradients of distance were similar.

Sen (1969) suggested that tyramine content of fish may be the result of bacterial contamination. Meat also can undergo such contamination. There are reports, for example, of hypertensive crises among persons taking MAOI who had consumed ground beef 3 days after cooking it. Problems have resulted from eating tuna fish 2 days after opening the can or eating beef liver stored for 1 week before preparation (Boulton, Cookson, & Paulton, 1970; Lovenberg, 1973). Any food with much protein has the potential of undergoing degradation from tyrosine to tyramine if contaminated and consumed after storage of a few to several days. The implication is that one should instruct patients to avoid leftover foods and potentially spoiled foods.

Bananas are often in lists of food for patients with migraines to avoid or reduce. Although there are several amines in banana peels that could produce pressor activity, the banana pulp contains smaller concentrations of the amines. Dopamine levels of 22–48 micrograms per gram for fruit pulp and 210–720 micrograms per gram for fruit peel, for instance, have been reported (Riggin et al., 1976). Banana peels also contain much more tyramine than banana pulp (see Table 10.1). One published report of a hypertensive crisis associated with bananas was a patient who had consumed whole green bananas stewed in their skins (Blackwell & Taylor, 1969). This is presumably not a common dish, at least in the United States. The case report by Gettis (1987a) shows that some migraine sufferers do react to bananas. Perhaps the cumulative effect of the several amines in combination with other amine-containing foods was the problem in this subject, who ate 2–3 servings of bananas, citrus, and cheese daily. Some lists discourage eating significant quantities of other fruits such as oranges, which have small tyramine concentrations but may contain other potentially problematic amines.

Yeast extracts are also commonly on the lists in question. Published reports from the British literature referred to brands that do contain very large concentrations of tyramine. Brewer's yeast in pill or liquid form does contain significant concentrations of tyramine. This is found in health food and drug stores as a vitamin supplement. Reports about plain yeast-leavened bakery products show negligible tyramine concentrations, yet some headache clinics recommend that food-related migraine patients avoid hot, fresh homemade bread.

Levodopa or dopamine, another pressor amine, is in fava beans in significant amounts (Hodge, Nye, & Emerson, 1964). Fava green beans or broad beans, often marketed as "Italian" green beans, are much wider, more than ½ inch, compared to common green beans.

Many foods and beverages contain tyramine and other vasoactive amines, and these frequently appear on lists of foods for dietary migraine sufferers to avoid. One finds differ-

TABLE 10.1. Tyramine-Containing Foods, Beverages, and Condiments, and Concentrations[a,b]

Food or beverage	Tyramine concentration (micrograms/gram or micrograms/milliliter)
Cheeses	
Cheddar	
English	0–953
New Zealand	471–580
Australian	226
New York State	1416
Canadian	251–535
Old, center cut	1530
Aged in ale	1000
Center cut	192
Fresh	120
Aged in beer	136
Processed, pasteurized	26
Gruyere	
American	516
British	11–1184
Finland	102
Stilton	
American	466
English	2170
Stilton blue	2170
Emmenthal	225
Emmentaler	225–1000
Brie	
American	180
Danish	Nil
Camembert[a]	
American	86
Danish	23–1340
Mycella (Camembert type)	1340
Cuban (average = 208)	34–425
American	*Low*
Processed	
American	50
Canadian	26
Cuban salami (average = 16)	2–27
Hungary	9
Roquefort (French)	27–520
Blue	
Danish	31–256
French	203
Bourmandise (Blue type)	216
Boursault (French)	1116
Parmesan	
Italy	65
United States	4–290

(continued)

TABLE 10.1. (*continued*)

Food or beverage	Tyramine concentration (micrograms/gram or micrograms/milliliter)
Cheeses	
Romano (Italian)	238
Provolone (Italian)	38
Cracker Barrel (Kraft)	214
Brick, natural (Canadian)	524
Mozarella (Canadian)	410
Gouda	
Canadian	20
Cuban (averages = 137 and 155)	40–280 mg/kg
Cream cheese	Nil
Cottage cheese	Nil
South African	6.6
Fontina (Cuban) (average = 88)	54–167
Broodkaase (Cuban) (average = 41)	0–163
Dambom (Cuban) (average = 90)	26–150
Carré (Cuban) (average = 126)	52–200
Mahon (old) (Spanish)	369
Cáceres (cured) (Spanish)	225
Cáceres (Spanish)	102
Malaga (fresh) (Spanish)	22
Dry/fermented sausage	
Hard salami (average = 210)	to 392
Pepperoni (average = 39)	to 195
Summer sausage (average = 184)	to 184
Farmer salami (average = 314)	to 314
Genoa salami (average = 534)	to 1237
Smoked landjaeger (average = 396)	to 396
Dry sausage (average = 244)	to 244
Semi-dry sausage (average = 85.5)	to 85.5
Dry fermented, Belgian	102–1506
Others (Tyramine in micrograms/gram or per milliliter)	
Marinated (pickled) herring (? spoiled)	3030
Herring (Canadian)	470
Fish	
Unrefrigerated, fermented	*Moderate*
Dried	*Moderate*
Meat Unrefrigerated, fermented	*Moderate*
Caviar (estimated high, but no published analysis)	High
Pods of broad beans (e.g., Fava)	? Concentration
Shelled beans and other legumes permitted	
Sour cream	Variable but often nil
Yogurt	Variable but often nil, especially from reputable brands

TABLE 10.1. (*continued*)

Food or beverage	Tyramine concentration (micrograms/gram or micrograms/milliliter)
Others (Tyramine in micrograms/gram or per milliliter)	
Chicken liver	
Cooked, not kept refrigerated	94–113
Fresh cooked	Nil
Beef liver	
Fresh/frozen	5.4/4.8
Unrefrigerated, fermented	*Moderate*
Canned figs	? Concentrations could be negligible
Pork, ham, bacon	? Concentrations; also nitrates
Ham, country cured	Nil
Red wine	Highly variable, some nil
White wine	*Little or none*
Bourbon, gin, vodka	? Concentrations probably negligible
Red vinegar	
Barley, germinating (used to make malt)	26
Nuts	Insignificant amounts
Peanut butter	? Tyramine
Avocado	23
Orange pulp	10
Raspberries, fresh	12.8–92.5
Raspberry jam	up to 38.4
Raisins	? Concentrations; grapes = none
Beer	
Canadian	0.6–11.2
American	1.8–4.4
Ale	Mean = 8.8
Chianti wine	1.76–24.5
Japanese wines[c] (red)	Mean = 1.8; 0.13–9.51
Japanese wines (white)	Mean = 0.98; ND–7.8
Banana (peel/pulp)	63–65/7
Yeast products	
Plain	Nil
Canadian brand (unspecified)	66–84
Yeastrel	101
Barmene	152
Befit	419
Yex	506
Marmite	1087–1639
English brand (unspecified)	2100

(*continued*)

TABLE 10.1. (*continued*)

Food or beverage	Tyramine concentration (micrograms/gram or micrograms/milliliter)
Far Eastern foods, beverages, and condiments in Zurich, Switzerland[a,d,e]	
Preserved foods	
Vegetarian curd, cooked, Taiwan	32.4
Vegetarian curd, cooked, Taiwan	48.0
Seasoning for sauces and cooking	
Soya beans, fermented, Singapore	713 (50 g)[f]
Soya beans, Taiwan	878 (10 ml)[f]
Soya sauce, Swiss, Dr. Dunners	293 (10 ml)[f]
Dried soya bean products	
Bean flour, to thicken sauces, etc., Thailand	0.10
Dried bean curd, China, P.R.	0.29
Dried duck, China	
Breast	35.3
Shank	19.9
Rib	2.3
Sausages	30.6
Soya bean drinks	
Singapore; Swiss	Nil[g]
Dehydrated, China, P.R.	0.23
Soya bean curd (Tofu)	
Japan	Nil
Dehydrated mix, Japan	0.09
Baked, Japan	0.01
Fried, Hong Kong	0.66
Soya bean, condiment, Formosa	939 (20 g)[f]
Soya bean soups	
Soya bean fermented, miso soup, Japan	1.82
Soya bean paste, fermented, Korea	206.00 (50 g)
Soya bean soup, prepared, Korea	0.22
Soya bean soup, concentrate, Japan	2.22
Sample foods from Zurich restaurants[a,b,c]	
Large Chinese restaurant	
Beef, dry roasted	1.3
Bean curd with pork	1.2
Bean curd with vegetables	4.8
Sea cucumbers	4.5
Fried rice	0.8
Fried noodles	2.9
Indian/Indonesian midsize restaurant	
Indonesian salad	0.3
Spring roll	0.2
Malaysian curry	12.7
Dry curry (Indian)	0.5
Rice (Indian)	0.4
Beer	1.0
Campari	0.2
Mineral water	Nil

TABLE 10.1. (*continued*)

Food or beverage	Tyramine concentration (micrograms/gram or micrograms/milliliter)
Sample foods from Zurich restaurants[a,b,c]	
Small Chinese restaurant	
Duck, roasted	0.1
Soya bean salad	0.1
Fried noodles	10.6
Squid in soya bean sauce	31.4
Canned fruit from Far East	Nil
Very small Thai restaurant	
Papaya salad	3.6
Fried rice with beef	1.7
Grilled squid	7.1
Fried noodles	2.9
Chicken with coconut sauce	63.1
Fried chicken with ginger	10.8
Thai sausages, grilled	101.5
Chicken in bamboo curry	22.5
Beer, Thai Singha	1.0
Beer, Heineken	1.0
Large Korean restaurant	
Bean curd base soup	4.4
Glass noodles with mushrooms	33.6
Fried fish	0.3
Fried seaweed	0.5
Zucchini/soya beans	0.1
Hot vegetable pickles, radish	31.4
Rice, white	0.2
Sweet and sour beef	21.8
Beer, Korean	39.9

Note. All tyramine < 1 mg/portion unless specified. Portions: most meat/vegetables, 50–75 g (1.8–2.6 oz.); salads, 50–100 g (1.8–3.5 oz.); most rice, 150–200 g (5.3–7.0 oz.); most soups, 100–150 ml (3.4–5.1 oz.); most drinks, 250–350 ml (8.5–11.8 oz.).

[a]Normal portions are variable. However, as a guide, Vidaud et al. (1987) note a normal portion of Camembert cheese is about 23 g (0.8 oz., avoirdupois) and of Gouda about 30 g (1.06 oz.).

The concentrations are from: Maxwell (1980), reporting the concentrations as reported by Horowitz et al. (1964), McCabe (1986), Sen (1969), Boulton et al. (1970), Coffin (1970), Hedberg et al. (1966), Marley and Blackwell (1970), Orlosky (1982), Udenfriend et al. (1959); Cuban and Spanish data from Vidaud et al. (1987); Zurich data from Da Prada and Zurcher (1992), Bruyn (1980), Johansson and Schubert (1990), Rice, Eitenmiller, and Kohler (1975, 1976; cited by McCabe, 1986), Rice and Kohhler (1976), Rivas-Gonzalo, Santos-Hernandez, and Marine-Font (1983; cited by McCabe, 1986). Data from Orlosky are inserted in italic (no specific concentrations given).

[b]Vidaud, Chaviano, Gonzales, and Garcia Roche (1987) reviewed eight studies with ranges of 13–2000 milligrams per kilogram. All but one study (Asatoor, Levi, & Milne, 1963) reported average tyramine content of less than 211.

[c]From Ibe, Saito, Nakazato, Kikuchhi, Fujinuma, and Nishhima (1991). Samples of 32 samples of red and 43 samples of white wine. No specification of country of origin for wines. Many other amines analyzed. Only tyramine and phenethylamine presented here as only two with particular psychoactivity and vasoactivity and considered risks for migraine. Only other amines with significant concentrations were PU (putrescine), a polyamine, and HI (histamine). PU in red wine up to 28.6 (mean = 4.84) and HI up to 10.0 (mean = 1.9). In white wine, PU up to 10.4 (mean = 1.2) and HI up to 9.9 (mean = 1.1).

ences among lists by different sources, although most lists contain similarities. The concentrations of vasoactive substances vary significantly among listed foods and beverages. However, most lists treat items as about equal and do not refer to the wide variations in concentrations. A major reason for the absence of such information in most lists is that it is difficult to obtain. There are many factors that result in differences, even for the same food or beverage. The information available about concentrations is important. This is especially true if we assume the importance of the interaction or additive effects among factors. Selected tyramine concentrations for many foods are in Table 10.1. We added information about the published tyramine concentrations of many items. This provides readers with a sense of the wide variations among items even within the same food group. The implication is that the items are not necessarily of equivalent potential in causing or increasing the likelihood of migraines or contributing to other problems (e.g., negative interactions such as hypertensive crisis with MAOI antidepressants).

Phenylethylamine

Phenylethylamine is a compound found in chocolate and in red and white wines (Ibe et al., 1991) that may be a cause of diet-related migraines. It is similar in chemical structure to epinephrine, norepinephrine, dopamine, ephedrine, amphetamine, tyramine, and numerous other sympathomimetic drugs with vasoconstrictor and pressor activities. It is, in fact, the basic chemical structure that all these compounds share (Gilman, Rall, Nies, & Taylor, 1990).

Chocolate has been reported clinically to trigger migraines. Sandler, Youdim, and Hanington (1974) gave phenylethylamine capsules to 36 patients who reported migraines from chocolate and found that phenylethylamine triggered three times as many headaches as placebo capsules. Other workers attempted to trigger migraines using chocolate in placebo-controlled studies but did not duplicate these results, perhaps because of insufficiently high dosages of phenylethylamine (Dalessio, 1980; Moffet, Swash, & Scott, 1974). Gibb et al. (1991), however, challenged 12 patients with chocolate and a closely matched placebo in a double-blind, parallel group study. Chocolate was followed by migraine in 5 of 12 patients who received chocolate and none of 8 patients who received placebo. It should be noted that octopamine, another potentially bioactive amine, has been isolated from chocolate (cacao) beans (Kenyhercz & Kissinger, 1978).

Monosodium Glutamate

The reality of the "Chinese restaurant syndrome," although it has been reliably grounded in a number of research studies, is still not without challenge (Radnitz, 1990). Some of the difficulty certain researchers have found in documenting the syndrome may result from

---

[d]Based on analyses of "typical Far Eastern foods purchased from specialised food stores [and] served in . . . restaurants in Zurich [Switzerland]." Adapted from Da Prada and Zurcher (1992) with permission. See original for seven sample menus from Zurich Chinese, Indian/Indonesian, Thai, Korean restaurants. Full meals range from 1.61 mg to 20.94 with 5 ≤ 5 mg. A milligram is a much larger amount (1000 times) than a microgram.

[e]The rationale for including the international items is for patients traveling to foreign countries, the potential similarity to imported products, and the use of this book in countries other than the United States.

[f]Amount consumed in a normal serving.

[g]Nil = n.d. (not detected) = under detection limit.

different dosages employed. Variability may also arise from the amounts of background dietary intake of monosodium glutamate (MSG), which is almost ubiquitous in processed foods.

This syndrome is characterized by facial tightness, sweating, and a throbbing headache. Most of the work validating it was done in healthy subjects. It is not certain that MSG is a specific trigger for migraine headaches. Neverthless, Scopp (1991) presents a case study of a patient who was able to nearly eliminate her migraine headaches, plus a constant muscle contraction headache, by removing MSG from her diet. Merritt and Williams (1990) have investigated the effect of MSG on rabbit aorta and have indicated a possible mechanism by which MSG may trigger migraines in sensitive subjects. Solutions of MSG were applied to strips of rabbit aorta. When applied at high concentrations, MSG or glutamine was observed to cause contraction of the blood vessels. It also relaxed contractions induced by serotonin, norepinephrine, prostaglandin, and histamine, and it subsequently contracted the vessels. Tyramine potentiated the effects of glutamine by over 200%. Although the concentrations used were high, the authors stated these can occur in humans. These experiments show a clear vasoactive potential for this substance.

Eliminating MSG from the diet is not an easy task within the context of contemporary American eating habits. The substance appears in nearly all processed foods under a variety of names. From 3–5 grams of MSG may now be present in a typical American meal, taking MSG effects out of the Chinese restaurant and into the culture at large.

MSG, the sodium salt of glutamine, a naturally occurring amino acid, is typically made from hydrolyzed plant proteins. It is used to impart a fresh flavor to processed foods. It typically comprises 10–30% of such hydrolyzed plant proteins. After 1986, the FDA permitted the food industry to drop the name "MSG" from flavor enhancers containing glutamine. MSG is thus now known under a variety of names, including hydrolyzed vegetable protein, natural flavor, flavoring, and *kombu* extract. Table 10.2 shows a variety of foods and food components containing MSG. Amounts of MSG are not listed specifically in most cases, as this information is industrially sensitive and varies widely with the processor.

Other Substances

"Hot dog headache" may be a reaction to sodium nitrate and ingestion of nitrite by persons sensitive to these substances that can result in headaches. Henderson and Rashin (1972) gave 10 milligrams of sodium nitrate or placebo to one migraine sufferer. Headaches occurred in 8 of 13 trials of sodium nitrate, and no headaches occurred after placebo. Ten healthy volunteers had no headaches after nitrate or placebo. Amyl nitrite, formerly used in treatment of angina, often caused vascular headaches, possibly because of vasodilator action. Nitrites used in the munitions industry cause headaches in some individuals (Diamond, Prager, & Freitag, 1986).

Headaches followed ice cream ingestion in 31% of 49 nonmigraine subjects, and 93% of 59 migraine sufferers in one experiment. This phenomenon may result from the sudden cooling of the oral pharynx. It represents an excessive vasomotor reaction to cold and could be a manifestation of the erratic vasomotor regulation common in migraine patients (Diamond et al., 1986).

Alcohol is a known vasodilator and may trigger headaches or worsen existing ones. Certain types of alcoholic drinks contain other vasoactive substances as well: Red wine is a well-known migraine trigger with serotonin-releasing properties (Jarman, 1991). Littlewood (1988), for instance, compared red wine and vodka and found that red wine triggered headaches in 11 dietary migraine patients, whereas vodka did not. The migraine triggering ac-

TABLE 10.2. Possible Migraine-Inducing Dietary Factors: Monosodium Glutamate

Food ingredients containing MSG
  Autolyzed yeast
  Calcium caseinate
  Hydrolyzed oat flour
  Hydrolyzed protein
  Hydrolyzed vegetable protein (HVP)
  Hydrolyzed plant protein
  Kombu extract
  Sodium caseinate
  Textured protein
  Yeast extract
  Yeast food

Food ingredients usually containing MSG
  Barley malt
  Bouillon
  Malt extract
  Malt flavoring
  Natural flavoring
  Natural beef flavoring
  Natural chicken flavoring

Food products usually containing MSG or HVP	
Beef bouillon cubes	40–46% HVP
Poultry bouillon cubes	30–50% HVP
Canned cream soups	0.25–0.6% HVP
Canned beef broths	0.5–2.0% HVP
Canned gravies	0.5–2.0% HVP
Dehydrated soups	
Meat type (oxtail, kidney)	15–25% HVP in dry product
Poultry type	5–10% HVP in dry product
Vegetable (mixed vegetable, pea)	3–10% HVP in dry product
English sausage	0.15–0.35% HVP
Frozen dinner entrees	
Gravy powders	20–40% HVP in dry product
International foods	
Liver sausage	0.25–0.5% HVP
Luncheon meats	0.25–0.5% HVP
Most diet foods and weight loss powders	
Most sauces in jars and cans (e.g., tomato and barbecue)	
Most salad dressings and mayonnaises	
Potato chips and prepared snacks	
Prepared beef products (e.g., beef stews, beefburgers, hot pot, hashes etc.)	0.5–1.0% HVP

Note. Material in this table is taken from Scopp (1991) and NOMSG (1992).

tivity of red wine has sometimes been attributed to phenolic flavonoids, which may result in increased catecholamine concentrations by inhibiting catechol-o-methyltransferase. This hypothesis has not been thoroughly examined (Radnitz, 1990).

The artificial sweetener aspartame may cause headaches in some people. Lipton, Newan, Cohen, & Solomon (1989) queried 171 headache patients about whether aspartame, alcohol (a positive control), and carbohydrates (a negative control) caused headaches.

Nearly 50% reported headaches caused by alcohol, 8% by aspartame, and 2% by carbohydrates. Migraine patients were significantly more likely to report alcohol, and three times more likely to report aspartame as headache triggers than nonmigraine patients. Koehler and Glaros (1988) studied 25 subjects who suffered migraines in a double-blind, placebo-controlled trial in which 300 milligrams per day aspartame or placebo were given for 4 weeks separated by a week-long washout period. Significantly more headaches occurred during the aspartame period than in the baseline or placebo periods.

Harrison (1986) suggests that copper may be a unifying factor in several migraine-related foods. These foods either contain large amounts of copper or increase its absorption into the body. Chocolate, glutamate, nuts, shellfish, whiskey, wheat germ, and citrate are examples of copper-containing or copper-transporting foods. Histamine, produced in allergic reactions, may also transport copper ions into the bloodstream. The mechanism by which copper might trigger migraines could be through a defect in a copper-containing enzyme, ceruloplasmin. The enzyme defect may reduce inactivation of vasoactive amines such as serotonin and tyramine. Table 10.3 summarizes the other possible migraine-inducing foods discussed here.

CAFFEINE

Status of Effects on Health and Disease

Caffeine continues to be the focus of considerable attention by health professionals and the public. One major concern is that caffeine might play a role in a variety of serious diseases such as heart disease. The experimental evidence, however, does not support a clear or consistent relationship (Curatolo & Robertson, 1983).

The other concern is that caffeine, as a psychotropic stimulant, elicits or aggravates physiological symptoms associated with several other disorders. These disorders include migraine headaches, anxiety, Raynaud's disease, IBS, hypertension, premenstrual syndrome, and sleep-onset insomnia. These are among the disorders treated by health professionals using physiological self-regulatory and other applied psychophysiological treatments. Caffeine use is clearly inconsistent with the goals of reducing sympathetic arousal and general muscle tension.

Action, Metabolism, and Toxicity

Caffeine is a bitter-tasting crystalline substance and probably the world's most popular drug. In North America, 80–90% of adults consume caffeine-containing beverages (Hughes et al., 1991; Fennelly, Galletly, & Purdie, 1991), and consumption estimates are above 200 milligrams a day (Griffiths et al., 1990). In usual doses, caffeine stimulates the central nervous system and hence raises mood. The effects vary from pleasant stimulation and alertness to unpleasant stimulation and tension. It can reduce fatigue by increasing skeletal muscle

TABLE 10.3. Possible Migraine-Inducing Dietary Factors: Other Items

Item	Substance contained or action in the body
Alcohol	Nonspecific vasodilator
Chocolate	Phenylethylamine
Hot dogs	Nitrate
Ice cream	Cooling of oropharynx

contractions. Caffeine can ease performance of simple tasks. However, it may disrupt more complex tasks involving motor reaction time and fine motor coordination. Higher doses can stimulate breathing. There are both central and peripheral effects on heart rate. These partly offset each other except at high doses. Increased heart rate results from high doses.

Caffeine causes vasoconstriction in cerebral circulation. This effect helps explain its presumed efficacy in relieving some headaches (i.e., reducing cerebral vasodilatation from other sources). Presumably, the timing of the ingestion of caffeine can be important for the latter. At other times, one would not seek to constrict cerebral blood vessels.

Caffeine spreads rapidly through the body where body tissues and fluids quickly absorb it. About 90% metabolizes in the liver, and people excrete the rest unchanged in the urine. Individuals differ in sensitivity and tolerance to caffeine. It reaches all tissues of the body within about 5 minutes. Peak plasma levels vary widely and range from 15 minutes to as long as 2 hours.

Half-life estimates also vary, from about 1.5 hours to as long as 7.5 hours. The average is about 3–4 hours (Curatolo & Robertson, 1983; Gilbert, 1981). The effects of caffeine continue in the body for lengthy periods. This is so whichever reports one accepts, or whichever turn out to be more accurate for all or specific persons. Some variation results from individual differences, tolerance, smoking, and the person's usual consumption of caffeine. For example, smokers metabolize caffeine more rapidly than nonsmokers (Gilbert, 1981). There is no day-to-day accumulation of caffeine in the body.

Caffeine metabolism appears to be related to dosage, as shown in a chronic dosing situation controlled for 16 days in inpatient research subjects (Denaro, Brown, Wilson, Jacob, & Benowitz, 1990). The authors observed disproportionate increases in blood levels with increasing daily doses, which may be a factor adding to the observed adverse effects seen among persons consuming higher levels. The dosage-dependent relationship occurred even in low-dose conditions with doses only moderately higher than the average consumption of adults.

Toxicity occurs at about 1 gram. A lethal dose in adults requires 5 to 10 grams orally. For drip coffee, which has the highest caffeine content, such a dose could require as few as 34 5-ounce cups. More likely, it would require closer to 68 cups.

Toxicity, however, could occur with 7–14 cups drunk in a very short period. For highly caffeinated carbonated beverages, a lethal dose requires 77–150 12-ounce cans. It is unlikely and uncommon for toxicity to occur. It is also unlikely and uncommon for a lethal dose to occur. Caffeine is, nevertheless, a potent chemical that can have harmful effects.

Caffeine Effects

Migraine

The role of caffeine in migraine headaches is not precisely defined. A survey of migraine sufferers in the 1940s found that 19% reported headaches triggered by caffeine; in 20% of these cases, however, the headaches were not migraine headaches (Radnitz, 1990). Caffeine might cause migraines because of its actions on cerebral veins. Consuming caffeine causes vasoconstriction: It can thus be useful in stopping headaches. This vasoconstriction, however, is later followed by a rebound vasodilatation, which may cause headache. Matthew and Wilson (1985) studied cerebral blood flow changes induced by caffeine. Increased cerebral blood flow is correlated with migraine headaches. They found that caffeine intake in a group of caffeine users with high daily intake was immediately followed by a decrease in cerebral blood flow. In 24 hours, however, cerebral blood flow increased, providing a possible migraine-triggering mechanism.

Anxiety and Other Conditions

One of the effects of caffeine with many implications for practitioners is its effect on anxiety. Several recent reports support the effect of caffeine on anxiety (Bruce & Lader, 1989; Bruce, 1990; Bruce, Scott, Shine, & Lader, 1992). Most patients with anxiety disorders are probably not consuming large quantities of caffeine. In an uncontrolled series, however, 24 patients diagnosed with generalized anxiety disorder or panic disorder withdrew from caffeine for 1 week prior to a planned start of anxiolytic medication. Six of these patients showed significant reductions of anxiety symptoms with only caffeine abstention and remained improved for at least 6 months.

Not all reports support the relationship between caffeine and anxiety among anxiety patients (Matthew & Wilson, 1990), although those reports were based on dosages of only 250 milligrams. There is another report of anxiety induced by similarly low doses of caffeine (Griffiths et al., 1990).

Caffeine's impact on other conditions commonly treated with physiological self-regulation may be substantial. A syndrome termed "caffeinism," which is difficult to differentiate from anxiety attacks, is brought on by excess caffeine consumption. Some evidence has been adduced that people with panic disorders have unusual sensitivity to caffeine. Because of increased heart rate and force of contraction, caffeine may potentiate cardiovascular responses to stress. Caffeine stimulates gastric secretion and may cause chronic stomach pain. It may also aggravate IBS and ulcers (Sargent & Solbach, 1988).

Some reports (Rossignol, 1985; Rossignol & Bonnlander, 1990) support the relationship between several premenstrual symptoms and caffeine consumption with a dose–response relationship not explained by total fluid intake. This relationship was clearer for those women with more severe symptoms. However, methodological factors still limit definitive conclusions. The clinical implication for women with these symptoms is to stop consuming caffeine for at least several months before or with other treatments.

Caffeine Contents of Beverages and Foods

Estimates of the caffeine content in coffees vary significantly. This depends upon the strain of coffee bean and the condition of the beans—whether they are green or roasted. It also depends on the type of coffee (i.e., drip, percolated, or instant). Brewing time also affects caffeine content. There are several studies of the caffeine content of coffees and other beverages, such as cocoa, tea, and carbonated drinks (Bunker & McWilliams, 1979; "Caffeine: What It Does," 1981; Gilbert, Marchman, Schwieder, & Berg, 1976). The results vary, depending, in part, on the analyses. Table 10.4 provides the ranges and averages given by Pennington and Church (1985) and Anonymous (1991).

Longer (e.g., 10 minutes vs. 5 minutes) percolation of coffee usually increases caffeine by about 4–15 milligrams per 150 milliliters. In general, the ratio of ground coffee to water is about 71–78 grams to 48 ounces of water.

A small chocolate bar contains about 25 milligrams of caffeine. Soft drinks contain between 33 and 65 milligrams of caffeine. Consider the example of a child of about 27 kilograms (59–60 pounds) who ingests three caffeinated soft drinks and three small chocolate bars. This is about 7.2 milligrams per kilogram and is the equivalent of about 8 cups of instant coffee for a 174-pound (79-kilogram) adult.

We need not know the exact amount of caffeine in a specific patient's coffee. It does not pay to invest expensive professional time exploring the strain of coffee bean and brewing time used by the patient. One can estimate the caffeine intake from coffee from the general type (i.e., instant, drip, or percolated) and the number of ounces drunk. Profes-

TABLE 10.4. Ranges and Average Caffeine Content of Coffee and Other Beverages

Beverage	Range	Estimated averages per 5 ounces (150 milliliters)	Estimated per 1 ounce
Coffee			
Percolated	93–134		23
Automatic	99–134	117	
Nonautomatic	93–130	108	
Drip	106–164		27
Automatic	110–164		
Nonautomatic	106–145		
Instant	47–68	60	12
Flavored from mixes (6 fl. oz.)	27–74		8+
Orange cappuccino		74	12+
Cafe Amaretto		60	10
Irish mocha mint		27	4+
Tea			
American black, bagged (5 minutes)	39–50	46	9+
American black, bagged (3 minutes)	35–46	42	8+
American black, bagged (1 minute)	21–33	28	5+
Imported black (5 minutes)	63–67	65 (6 oz.)	11
Instant	32–35	33 (6 oz.)	5+
Green (5 minutes)	26–36	31	6+
Green (1 minute)	9–19	14	3
Mint (5 minutes)	36–63	50 (6 oz.)	8+
Chocolate and foods with it			
Candy (mostly about 1+ oz.)	4–8		
Sweet (dark) (1 oz.)	5–35	20	
Special dark (Hershey) (1 oz.)		23	
Semisweet chips (Nestle) (1 oz.)		17	
Cocoa, dry, Hershey (1 oz.)		70	
Cocoa, dry, Hershey (1 oz.)		5	
Chocolate milk	2–7	5 (8 oz.)	
Most other powders, puddings, cocoa	4–8/serving		
Carbonated beverages (12 oz.)	21–57		
Mountain Dew		54	4.5
Mr. Pibb, Diet		57	
Mello Yello		53	
Most others[a]	36–45	40	3.3

Note. Data from Pennington and Church (1985).

[a]Consumer Reports (Anonymous, 1991) reports most colas 36–48 mg per 12 oz.

sionals should also inquire about the size of the cup used as most people use the term cup when they are actually drinking from larger-sized mugs. A cup can vary from about 5–12 ounces or even more.

    The value of using questionnaires to estimate patterns of caffeine consumption received qualified support (p. 507) from James, Bruce, Lader, and Scott (1989). Self-report and saliva assays are significantly but modestly correlated. There are some methodological limitations in this study. Their subjects, for instance, were volunteer medical students who might be more accurate than the average patient. We must be cautious in relying entirely on questionnaire sources. Careful clinical interviewing and attempts at precise daily record keeping may be necessary if one needs accuracy.

Caffeine Withdrawal

Regular use of as little as 100 milligrams of caffeine per day can induce a form of physical dependence, interruption of which elicits characteristic withdrawal symptoms in some people (Griffiths et al., 1990). This is a much lower critical dosage, and there are more symptoms reported than in earlier studies. Until recently, the focus was on the regular use of more than about 350 milligrams of caffeine per day, interruption of which elicits a characteristic withdrawal syndrome (Gilbert, 1981). Until recently the most conspicuous feature of caffeine withdrawal was noted to be a severe headache relieved by consuming more caffeine. Greden, Victor, Fontaine, and Lubetsky (1980) reported that 42 patients had caffeine withdrawal headaches after using as little as 500 milligrams per day. Fennelly et al. (1991) report that "headache after general anesthesia is related to preoperative caffeine withdrawal consequent upon moderate daily levels of caffeine intake" (p. 453). Among 287 patients they found "a highly significant difference in caffeine consumption" between patients with and without headache (p. 449). The more caffeine, the greater the probability of headache developing both preoperatively and postoperatively. One-hundred-milligram increases resulted in 12% and 16% increases, respectively. Other articles support this relationship between caffeine withdrawal and postoperative headache (Weber, Ereth, Danielson, & Ilstrup, 1993; Harper, 1993).

The importance and implications of the studies by Griffiths and his colleagues (Griffiths et al., 1990; Silverman & Griffiths, 1992; Mumford et al., 1994) are clear. They provide strong support for the presence of more types of withdrawal symptoms and a higher incidence of symptoms. Withdrawal symptoms occur from much lower daily doses than previously recognized and with different dosing schedules. People discriminate low doses of caffeine below 20 milligrams. Their data support "an orderly, time-limited caffeine withdrawal syndrome after abstinence from low dietary doses of caffeine" (Griffiths et al., 1990, p. 1129). The important point is that it requires very little daily use of caffeine to create physical dependence and withdrawal symptoms.

The authors also report their findings as "the first evidence that caffeine withdrawal produces craving for caffeine-containing foods" (p. 1130). Readers should examine these reports, especially that of Griffiths et al. (1990) which is the most convincing study in the series until that time. Although it was based only on seven subjects, the methodology and results are impressive. The authors, of course, call for replication. The subjects were the "scientist-colleagues who worked together doing behavioral pharmacological research at The Johns Hopkins University School of Medicine. They participated both as subjects and co-investigators . . ." (p. 1124). One phase was a simple ABA (baseline-treatment-baseline), double-blind design with ". . . exposure to 100 mg/day of caffeine for 9 to 14 days, substitution of placebo for 12 days and . . . re-exposure to 100 mg/day of caffeine for 7 to 12 days" (p. 1125).

The subjects knew there would be one or more times when caffeine would start and restart but did not know the number or durations. They ingested 10 capsules of 10 milligrams each at hourly intervals from about 8:00 A.M. to 5:00 P.M. and rated 33 dimensions of mood and behavior four times each day. Four of the seven showed strong evidence of withdrawal peaking on either the first or second day and decreasing progressively over about 1 week.

Before the next phase, the investigators reviewed the data from all the subjects. Then they repeatedly substituted placebo for a series of 5 ". . . 1-day periods separated by an average of 9 days" and 15–19 days with caffeine. The subjects again did not know when they ingested placebo. All subjects showed withdrawal effects.

In the first phase, the subjects reported:

> a significant decrease in ratings of alert/attentive/observant, well being, social disposition, motivation for work, able to concentrate, energy/active, self-confidence, urge to do task/work-related activities and content/satisfied, and a significant increase in ratings of headache, irritable/cross/grumpy, depressed, muscle pain or stiffness, lethargy/fatigue/tired/sluggish, cerebral fullness, craving for caffeine-containing foods . . . and flu-like feelings. (Griffiths et al., 1990, p. 1127)

The strong withdrawal effects might be the result of the relatively long abstinence, 39 hours in Phase II; the repeated withdrawal testing of each subject, multiple symptoms, and "subjects who were conscientious about avoiding all dietary sources of caffeine and in whom caffeine abstinence was verified biologically" (p. 1131). Note that some withdrawal effects did not peak until 27 hours after stopping caffeine. The important points are that it requires very little daily use of caffeine to create physical dependence and withdrawal symptoms and that there are probably many more withdrawal symptoms than headaches.

Another study (van Dusseldorp & Katan, 1990) supported the high frequency of caffeine withdrawal headaches in 19 of their 45 recruited subjects in their double-blind study of other effects of caffeine withdrawal. Six weeks of drinking coffee with an average of 435 milligrams of caffeine per day were counterbalanced with 6 weeks with decaffeinated coffee with a total of 30 milligrams of caffeine per day. It is instructive to note also that five of their patients recorded fewer headache complaints during withdrawal. Important methodological fine points were that they accomplished the withdrawal by having an independent source switch the caffeinated and decaffeinated coffee. Only seven of the subjects reported awareness of the switch. Unfortunately, the analyses reported did not eliminate these.

In another study (Caraco, Zylber-Katz, Granit, & Levy, 1990) intending to look at metabolism of caffeine, 10 of 11 subjects reported caffeine withdrawal symptoms, with the most frequent and most troublesome being headache. The symptoms started soon after caffeine restriction and lasted up to 48 hours.

A patient's medication alone can contain enough caffeine to create or add to the problem. Even some migraine medications, notably certain ergotamine tartrate preparations, contain caffeine (Sargent & Solbach, 1988). Table 10.5 presents the caffeine content in several prescription (Rx) and over-the-counter (OTC) preparations. Considerable searching for a comprehensive list of all or even most preparations with caffeine did not result in finding such a source. The Physician's Desk References (1982a, 1982b) for prescription and nonprescription drugs and the Food and Drug Administration provide only a small percentage of such preparations. Pharmacists contacted did not have a comprehensive list.

The American Drug Index (ADI) is the most comprehensive source located, but there is no index for caffeine. The only way to get such a list is a page-by-page review of the ADI. This review revealed more than 200 such preparations with many more being OTC than Rx preparations. Most contain about 32–40 milligrams (range 6.5–250). If a person took a few doses each day, then one could consume a considerable amount of caffeine. Such usage is common for analgesic purposes, weight control, use of cold and allergy preparations, and for alertness.

Practitioners should inquire of patients about all OTC and Rx preparations used to determine caffeine intake. Inclusion of a comprehensive list here is beyond the scope of this chapter.

TABLE 10.5. Caffeine Content of Selected Prescription and Nonprescription Preparations

Trade Name	Manufacturer	Caffeine content (milligrams)
Prescription		
ABC compound with codeine	Zenith	40
Amaphen	Trimen	40
Anaquan	Mallard	40
A.P.C.	Burroughs-Wellcome	32
B-A-C	Mayrand	40
Beta-Phed	MetroMed	32
Cafemine TD Capsules	Legere	75
Cafergot	Sandoz	100
Damason-P	Mason	32
Di-Gesic	Central	30
Dihydrocodeine compound	Schein	30
Ergocaf	Robinson	100
Ergo Caffein	CMC	100
Ergothein	Wolins	100
Esgic	Forest	40
Ezol	Stewart Jackson	40
Fioricet	Sandoz	40
Fiorinal	Sandoz	40
Florital	Cenci	40
Hyco-Pap	LaSalle	30
Korigesic	Trimen	30
Medigesic	U.S.Pharm	40
Migralam	A.J. Bart	100
Norgesic	Riker	30
Norgesic Forte	Riker	60
Orphengesic	Various	30
Orphengesic Forte	Various	60
Pacaps	LaSalle	40
Propoxyphene compound 65	Schein	32.4
Repan tablets	Everett	40
Soma compound	Wallace	32
Synalgos-DC	Wyeth	30
Tencet	Hauck	40
Two-Dyne	Hyrex	40
Triad	UAD	40
Wigraine	Organon	100
Nonprescription		
Anacin	Whitehall	32
Appedrine Maximum Strength	Thompson Medical	100
Arthritis Strength BC powder	Block	36
Aqua Ban	Thompson Medical	100
Aqua Ban Plus	Thompson Medical	200
Caffedrine	Thompson Medical	200
Caffin T-D	Kenyon	250
CP	Western Research	140
CCP Cough and Cold tablets	Medique	64.8

(continued)

TABLE 10.5. (*continued*)

Trade Name	Manufacturer	Caffeine content (milligrams)
	Nonprescription	
Codexin Extra Strength	Arco	200
Cope	Mentholatum	32
Coryban-D	Pfipharmecs	30
DeWitt's Pills	DeWitt	6.5
Dietac	Menley & James	200
Dristan Advanced Formula	Whitehall	16.2
Efed II (black)	Alto	200
Enerjets	Chilton	65
Excedrin Extra Strength	Bristol-Myers	65
Goody's Headache Powders	Goody's	32.5
Keep-A-Wake	Stayner	162
Lerton Ovules	Vita Elixir	250
Midol	Glenbrook	32.4
No Doz	Bristol-Myers	100
Periodic	Towne	60
Prolamine	Thompson Medical	140
Quick-Pep	Thompson Medical	150
Revs Caffeine T.D.	Vitarine	250
Sinapils	Pheiffer	32.5
Sta-Wake Dextabs	Approved	97.2
Stay-Alert	Edward J. Moore	250
Stay Awake	Towne	200
Slim Plan Plus	Whiteworth	200
Summit	Pheiffer	100
Tirend	Smith, Kline, Beecham	100
Triaminicin	Dorsey	30
Vanquish	Glenbrook	33
Verv Alertness	APC	200
Vivarin	Smith, Kline, Beecham	200
Wakoz	Jeffrey Martin	200

Note. Appreciation is extended to Judith Lukach, R.Ph., Brian Lukach, M.S., and Scott Apelgren, M.S., R.Ph., for their important assistance with preparation of the original 1987 table. For the current revision, I thank Deborah Crumb, R.Ph., for helping to update this table. She found five new Rx and seven new OTC preparations, deleted five Rx, and revised information on five others from the two groups.

In attempting to assist patients in cessation of caffeine use, professionals should inform them of the potential for caffeine withdrawal headaches and other withdrawal symptoms. Some patients may have to be advised to reduce their caffeine consumption gradually in order to diminish severe withdrawal symptoms that could disrupt compliance.

THERAPEUTIC STRATEGIES

The proportion of migraine sufferers whose headaches are triggered by diet or caffeine-containing medications is not known. Some estimate that 5% of migraine sufferers are sensitive to tyramine (Radnitz, 1990). Owen, Turkewitz, Dawson, Casaly, and Wirth

(1992) report that 60% of head pain patients seen at their clinic have food-related headaches, but they do not distinguish migraines from other headache types. Thus, the health professional cannot assume that a migraine sufferer's symptoms are related to diet. It may also be unwise, however, to assume that diet plays no role. Some patients, if they have been informed of the diet–migraine connection, may be able to correlate their symptoms with particular foods on their own. Only 75% of headache patients appear to know about possible food–headache links (and only half of these have been informed of these links by medical professionals) (Guarnieri, 1990). Treatment principles applicable to migraine can also, of course, be applied to other potentially diet-related conditions commonly treated with self-regulation.

Different practitioners have offered suggestions for treating headaches that are possibly diet-related. Owen et al. (1992) conduct a comprehensive nutritional assessment to assess intake of possible trigger foods. These foods are systematically eliminated from the diet for 4 weeks and reintroduced one by one. Food intakes and headache are monitored to determine which foods trigger headaches. When the trigger foods have been identified, instruction is given in recognizing them on product ingredient labels and in restaurants. Low blood sugar and eating under stress are discussed, as well as overuse of vitamin supplements, as headaches are symptoms of vitamin A and vitamin D toxicity (Gilman et al., 1990).

Diamond et al. (1986) provide a comprehensive list of foods to avoid and foods to eat as a migraine headache treatment diet. They also make certain practical suggestions for dietary migraine diagnosis and treatment. Patients are told to eat and sleep at regular times, to keep headache diaries to help discover links between diet (or other factors) and headache. In reintroducing prohibited foods, patients should be cautioned that the absence of headache in one trial should not be considered evidence that the food is definitely harmless. Medication that patients are taking may have protected them from headache, and even foods known to provoke migraines do not do so on all occasions for some patients.

Radnitz and Blanchard (1991) used a two-step dietary treatment program with 10 patients with vascular headaches who were unsuccessful with biofeedback. In the first phase, patients got a list of foods to avoid. These included both allergenic foods, such as wheat, corn, dairy, and foods with caffeine or other vasoactive compounds, such as citrus, cheese, MSG, and coffee. For patients who did not report a 50% decrease in headaches with this diet, they employed a comprehensive elimination diet followed by challenges with suspected trigger foods. They assessed compliance with diets with food diaries. Six of the subjects noted substantial reductions in headaches with this program, whereas four did not. Those who did not achieve reduction in headaches were younger than the successes, reported more suspected food sensitivities, and complied with the dietary restrictions less faithfully. Thus, even though they claimed more food sensitivity, they were less methodical in avoiding the foods to which they claimed sensitivity.

There are, as this study shows, many problems in introducing dietary advice into the comprehensive treatment of migraine. The fact that for a possibly large percentage of patients food will have no relation to migraines is only the first of these. Diet changes are difficult to accomplish, even for what should be highly motivated patients. Other problems revolve around conflicts that patients might feel between dietary advice and treatment modes such as physiological self-regulation or stress management.

Much of the dietary counseling in migraine treatment is based on lists of prohibited foods. Some health professionals advise patients to stop consuming all foods and beverages on a list at the start of a treatment program, without efforts to either use the list as a preliminary elimination diet or to take into account the relative concentrations of offending chemicals in foods on the list. For many patients this tactic would be inconvenient, could be unnecessary, and might result in compliance problems. Professionals making such blanket recommendations could compromise their credibility and the therapist–patient relationship unless they make clear to patients the strong effect that diet appears to have on migraines in many people. The therapist must give a thorough explanation of the place of an elimination diet in therapy and must be prepared to deal with compliance issues.

For instance, making such recommendations at the beginning of a treatment that also involves other interventions might cloud or at least delay understanding the relationships of dietary factors and symptoms. Such combinations of treatments when started simultaneously can lead a patient to perceive the treatment program as a shotgun approach. This can diminish the focus and relative importance and usefulness of the other applied psychophysiological treatments including biofeedback.

Insisting that patients stop consuming everything that conceivably might result in symptoms on a permanent basis early in treatment also creates a demand that patients may not be ready to accept. Diet is, after all, fraught with psychological, familial and sociocultural complications and implications. Patients may not accurately report problems in following the diet, or lack of compliance, to the health professional who is not sensitive to the emotional dynamics of dietary change.

However, these concerns must be weighed against the increased possibility of success if diet is indeed an important factor in the symptoms of any particular patient. Success and rapid relief of symptoms are, after all, paramount in the patient's point of view and should be equally prominent in that of the therapist. If a patient's migraines are related to diet, symptoms will disappear much more quickly with proper dietary change—possibly within days (Gettis, 1987a) or within 2 or 3 weeks. If the symptoms are not related to diet, a few weeks of avoiding certain foods will not hinder relief of migraines. Indeed, since many of the foods that seem to trigger migraines are not healthful (chocolate, MSG-laden processed foods, sausages, cheese, alcohol, hot dogs), such patients may note improvements in general health or learn valuable lessons about the possibility of productive diet changes.

From this point of view, integrating self-regulation training with diet gives patients both short-term benefits and long-term prophylactic effects whether their symptoms are diet-related or not. This can be considered a highly positive and appropriate therapeutic strategy for migraines, IBS, and the other multifactorial conditions treatable with self-regulation.

Integrating the dietary and self-regulation components of a comprehensive migraine treatment program can be done in several different ways. One option in evaluating dietary connections to migraine symptoms is to query patients about their own observations on diet, medications, and symptoms (at the risk of delaying symptom relief). If they have not considered the question, they could perhaps be allowed a few weeks to make such observations, bearing in mind suggestions about foods that migraine sufferers commonly find troublesome. More typically, however, the therapist should consider the following strategies of implementing the comprehensive approach. The order in which they are presented does not imply preference.

1. *Self-regulation only.* Do not stop foods or beverages before or while carrying out applied psychophysiological treatments. This approach assumes that the professional does not accept the potential validity of dietary or allergy factors.

2. *Diet first.* Stop all or most of the suspected substances. The patient alters the diet and medication use of at least the items with higher concentrations of suspected elements and those with more suspected potential of adding to symptoms. True evaluation of the potential of the dietary approach requires, of course, a thorough, if temporary, elimination

diet. The practitioner and patient can then proceed with as many challenges as possible. No other treatment occurs until one adequately checks the results of this approach alone. This requires several weeks, or possibly longer.

3. *Stepped care.* The patient starts a physiological self-regulation treatment program for at least several weeks. Depending on the results, one adds dietary treatment later if still of potential additional benefit. This is proper, for example, if there is not enough improvement in symptoms.

4. *Self-regulation plus trigger avoidance.* The professional may start the patient on an applied psychophysiological treatment program and a few, patient-acceptable, dietary restrictions. Although this leaves the relative contribution of each approach unclear, it nevertheless is not likely to interfere with compliance. The focus of the intervention is still nondietary.

5. *Self-regulation plus elimination diet.* The therapist stops all or most of the suspected substances and proceeds with other applied psychophysiological treatments at the same time. The therapist should clearly explain to the patient the rationale and need for such an approach, along with the strategy for gradual reintroduction of initially prohibited foods. This approach is common, but it confounds the relative contributions of the two treatments. The possibility of such confusion could be discussed with the patient in light of the potentially more rapid symptom relief (a consideration, perhaps, especially in severe and frequent headaches). Later, when there are clinically significant symptom reductions, patients may change the dietary regimens and test themselves by reintroducing suspected trigger foods at weekly intervals (e.g., Gettis, 1987a).

Professionals may, of course, combine cognitive and other stress management treatments with other applied psychophysiological treatments. One also may defer these in the stepped-care model of intervention to more adequately assess their relative contribution.

There are advantages and disadvantages for each of the alternative strategies we have presented for integrating list-based dietary counseling with physiological self-regulation treatment. All are justifiable and reasonable under specific circumstances. We do not favor omitting dietary considerations entirely from presentations to patients. By understanding the advantages and disadvantages of each strategy, professionals and patients can make adequately informed decisions. Table 10.6 describes selected advantages and disadvantages of each strategy.

Certain migraine cases have proven refractory to list-based dietary counseling. Some of these have been helped by comprehensive diet revision based on a positive program emphasizing whole, natural foods (preferably locally grown) and vegetarian protein sources, and radically excluding processed foods, dairy products, and refined sugar. The first author of this paper uses this program as a comprehensive health regimen in his practice. It certainly does not exclude the appropriate use of medications, but it does emphasize the need for self-care and self-reliance and discourages the overreliance on medications seen in some migraine patients. The diet is low in fats and allergenic foods and high in fiber. It avoids many sources of vasoactive compounds, such as tropical fruits (bananas, citrus), cheese, chocolate, caffeine sources, and processed foods that may contain MSG or artificial sweeteners. It is also low in many allergenic foods, including cow's milk and eggs. Wheat and corn, common grain allergens, are present in the diet but are deemphasized in favor of whole-grain rice, a staple of the program. The high fiber content of the diet, the emphasis on vegetable proteins, and the absence of refined sugars may assist those whose headaches are related to low blood sugar. In addition, the diet is fully compatible with emerging recommendations for general health and prevention of cancer and heart disease.

TABLE 10.6. Advantages and Disadvantages of Five Strategies for Including Dietary Changes in Therapy Programs of Selected Patients

Strategy	Advantages	Disadvantages
Self-regulation only	No need to do without selected foods and beverages; no inconvenience from checking the ingredients of foods and beverages.	May decrease chances of ameliorating symptoms sooner; may eventually cost more for other therapies, such as medications.
Diet first	May be sufficient for clinically significant symptom reduction in some patients; may save the expenses of other therapies.	May take longer to reduce or eliminate symptoms; may be inconvenient to check dietary factors; requires patient's compliance with dietary regimen; may defer symptom reduction if dietary factors are unimportant or only part of the problem.
Stepped care	No initial need to do without desired foods and beverages; no initial inconvenience from checking ingredients; opportunity to evaluate the relative effects of physiological self-regulation and dietary therapy at separate times; may increase later compliance with either or both types of therapy when their relative contributions are better identified.	May cost more because of longer physiological self-regulation therapy; may defer symptom reduction if dietary factors are important.
Self-regulation plus trigger avoidance	No initial need to do without all or most of the foods and beverages; may result in faster reduction of symptoms if both therapies are relevant and needed; may be more acceptable to some patients, hence increasing compliance with dietary changes.	May be impossible to determine the relative contributions of each type of therapy; may decrease compliance with one approach if patient relies on the other; may cost more if more dietary changes are needed; may defer symptom reduction if more dietary changes are needed.
Self-regulation plus elimination diet	May decrease or eliminate symptoms faster.	May be impossible to determine the relative contributions of each type of therapy; may decrease compliance with either or both if the patient relies on one or does not take either seriously.

The positive diet program revolves around five food groups: grains, vegetables, fruits, proteins, and fats. Carbohydrates are the main source of calories, so grains are the centerpiece of the diet. Recommended grains for daily use are brown rice, barley, oats, millet, and kasha. Grains are to be eaten as whole cooked grains, with less emphasis on flours and other processed forms.

Vegetables recommended for daily use are leafy vegetables (kale, collards, mustard greens, but not spinach), squashes, carrots, onions, turnips, and cruciferous vegetables (broccoli, cauliflower, cabbage, brussels sprouts). Tomatoes (often allergenic and high in sugar) are deemphasized.

Fruits recommended for daily use are apples, apricots, melons, pears, cherries, peaches, and other temperate-zone fruits. Citrus fruits, bananas, figs, papaya, mango, avocado, and other tropical fruits are to be reduced and if necessary eliminated (many of these are on lists of migraine trigger foods).

Proteins include aduki beans, garbanzos, soy foods (e.g., tofu and soy milk, both good calcium sources), lentils, and other small beans; larger beans may be eaten less frequently. Fish may be eaten 2–3 times weekly if desired (chicken may be used when patients are making the transition to the full program). If patients feel they must eat dairy products, and are found not to be sensitive to them after elimination and reintroduction, skim milk products and low-fat yogurt are preferable to other forms. Modifications in this part of the regimen might be necessary in the case of allergies to fish, to soy, or to other beans.

Fats include nuts, seeds, and oils: canola and olive oil are emphasized. Sweeteners used include brown rice syrup, maple syrup, and natural fruits. Recommended drinks include water (preferably spring water), teas such as bancha or herbal tea, or grain coffee substitutes. Caffeine-containing beverages, sodas, and wines are to be avoided. Practical suggestions for meal plans are found in a few cookbooks (e.g., Colbin, 1979). Formalized nutritional need assessment and exchange lists are available for the diet.

People using the diet must be certain to obtain enough calcium from such sources as leafy green vegetables, calcium-fortified soy milk, garbanzo beans, tofu, broccoli, and other natural calcium sources. Calcium supplements are allowable if patients are not able to structure their diets adequately; vitamin B_{12} supplements may be needed for those who may choose strict vegetarian diets; high-quality multivitamin supplements are also allowable.

This diet has also proven successful with many patients presenting with IBS and other bowel diseases. Some patients with IBS have been found to respond well to increases in dietary fiber, which is greatly increased in this diet. Some authors have noted that high-fiber diets tend to normalize bowel function, diminishing both constipation and diarrhea, both of which are features of IBS (Harvey, Pomare, & Heaton, 1973; Payler, Pomare, Heaton, & Harvey, 1975). It should be noted that some patients who present with symptoms resembling IBS are actually lactase-deficient or lactose-intolerant individuals, making either a hydrogen breath test for lactase deficiency or a trial elimination of dairy products a good strategy. Not all patients with IBS respond to diet, however, and there remains some controversy concerning the impact of fiber on bowel disease (Ritchie, Wadsworth, Leonard-Jones, & Rodgers, 1987; Heaton, Thornton, & Emmet, 1979; Hillman, Stace, Fisher, & Pomare, 1982). Nevertheless, a trial of increasing dietary fiber, preferably through overall diet changes that include elimination of dairy products, rather than simply fiber supplements (Soltoft, Gudmand-Hoyer, Krog, Kristensen, & Wulff, 1986), is justified in patients with IBS who have not previously attempted it.

Some patients may be interested in the botanical migraine remedies mentioned above. Feverfew is taken as a migraine preventive. It has been studied in dosages of 50 milligrams per day, or two fresh leaves chewed daily (der Marderosian & Liberti, 1988). Some patients experience mouth ulcerations while taking fresh leaves and may need a capsule form. Dried ginger, available in supermarkets, was taken by one patient to abort migraine headaches. At the onset of aura, 500–600 milligrams of powdered ginger was mixed with water and consumed. An abortive effect was noticeable in 30 minutes. Following this, the same dose was taken twice every 4 hours until the attack was over, and for 3 to 4 days after. The subject experienced no ill effects, and eventually began including fresh ginger in her daily diet, which proved to be an effective migraine preventive (Mustafa & Srivastava, 1990).

Regardless of which alternative you select, there are additional considerations to incorporate into treatment plans. First, most patients can easily avoid heavy caffeine consumption even if they have been heavy consumers. Second, patients should avoid dietary items they strongly suspect cause symptoms. This will be acceptable to most patients. Third, patients should avoid dietary substances known from the literature or strongly suspected to cause headaches (e.g., alcohol, MSG). Finally, if list-based dietary counseling is used, professionals should be very specific about the foods to avoid. Therapists should periodically assess how well patients are adhering to their dietary restrictions, and be prepared to offer practical suggestions for making dietary changes. As in any therapeutic situation, therapists must equip themselves to handle compliance problems.

CONCLUSION

In the last decade, studies of diet and migraine have progressed considerably. We still need, however, much more information about the concentrations of tyramine and other substances in the foods and beverages listed in Tables 10.1 through 10.4. The relative lack of such information probably results from the complexity of such analyses. The variations within a given item depend on factors such as how one prepares the particular food and where it comes from. We also suspect that there may be other reasons for the limited research about the concentrations of these substances. One such reason is the presumed equivocal nature of the research about the relationships between these substances and migraines. There are professional disagreements about the importance of this area. We hope eventually to better identify and adjust concentrations of vasoactive substances for persons who are or might be susceptible to the effects of such substances. Further research on the nature and physiology of diet-related migraine is also warranted: Such research might take advantage of certain new technical methods such as ELISA-ACT (enzyme-linked immunosorbent assay—activated cell test) testing for food allergies.

Discussion of migraine headache prevention may seem beside the point at this date, since the autoinjectable migraine-abortive drug sumatriptan has recently entered the U.S. pharmaceutical market. This drug is a highly effective migraine abortive used for debilitating headaches that is effective with minimal side effects in approximately 80% of patients. Obviously, the remaining 20% of patients still need to concern themselves with prevention of migraines.

Is the elimination of migraine-triggering foods or the control of migraines through physiological self-regulation still a reasonable goal for the 80%? We feel that it is. A number of patients avoid sumatriptan because it is injectable, rather than oral. Many practitioners still prefer to treat migraines with the older medications, in part because sumatriptan is a fairly expensive drug: Its current cost is approximately $30 per dose. For the patient who has only a few migraines per year, this is not an unreasonable expense, whether paid through reimbursement schemes or out-of-pocket funds. For patients who suffer from frequent migraines, however, the yearly cost becomes quite high. Even if paid from a reimbursement scheme, governmental or private, costs associated with sumatriptan treatment of the many patients who have frequent migraines become a substantial drain on the overall health care costs of the nation. We feel it is of more importance than ever that patients learn to control the incidence of migraines now that a costly drug has become one of the first-line treatments for debilitating headaches. Otherwise, our health care system faces the specter of yet another high-tech medication adding billions of dollars to our total health care budget. Practitioners involved in dietary or physiological self-regulation treatment of migraine headaches should feel no embarrassment in continuing to advocate their treatment strategies.

In conclusion, there are many factors to consider when checking the possible contribution of dietary factors in patients' symptoms and when advising dietary changes. However, the data available to date suggest that unifocal care of migraines and other diet-related conditions is never complete care. This evidence warrants serious consideration of dietary changes for at least some patients. How one conveys this information and carries out the changes should involve careful thought and planning. It is not as simple as telling patients to abstain from certain foods. Dietary change is difficult emotionally and socially. Changing ingrained eating patterns requires both practical help and technical knowledge. Clinicians and researchers can be most effective if they are thoroughly familiar with dietary considerations when providing biofeedback and other applied psychophysiological treatments.

GLOSSARY

ABA DESIGN. An experimental design in which a baseline period (A) precedes an intervention or treatment (B), followed by another baseline (A). Often used in single-case research.

AMINE. Result when proteins are chemically altered by decarboxylation by enzymes during metabolism or by bacterial contamination after death. The "pressor amines" are a group of amines that can stimulate the sympathetic nervous system (SNS). This group includes serotonin, tryptophan, histidine, and tyramine. (See Chapter 18.)

ANXIOLYTIC MEDICATION. Medications for reducing anxiety.

CATECHOL-O-METHYLTRANSFERASE. Methyltransferase is any enzyme of a subgroup of enzymes of the transferase class. Transferase enzymes transfer a chemical group from one compound (donor) to another compound (acceptor). Methyltransferase (or transmethylase) catalyzes the transfer of a methyl group from one compound to another. Methyl is the radical CH_3 in organic chemistry. For example, it is part of methyl alcohol (CH_3OH). Catechol is catechin, catechuic acid, or pyrocatechol; it is part of the catecholamine structure.

ERGOT DERIVATIVES. Type of medication for migraine. (See Chapters 14 and 15.)

HISTAMINE. A histidine product found in all body tissues, especially mast cells. Highest concentrations in lungs. Also present in ergot. Has several functions, including dilatation of capillaries, contraction of most smooth muscle tissue, increased gastric secretion, and increased heart rate.

IMMUNE COMPLEXES. Antigen–antibody compounds commonly formed in the blood after sensitive persons ingest allergenic foods.

IMMUNOGLOBULIN E (IgE). One of the five classes of immunoglobulins. Has the unique function of mediating immediate hypersensitivity reactions.

LEVODOPA (L-DOPA). A form of the amino acid dopa used to treat parkinsonism and other conditions. Dopamine forms from dopa, an intermediate product in norepinephrine synthesis. Acts as a CNS neurotransmitter. (See *norepinephrine*; Chapters 7, 17, 18.)

MAST CELLS. In most connective tissue, especially on paths of blood vessels. Contain heparin (anticoagulant) and histamine (vasoconstrictor). Also called tissue mast cells or histogenous mast cells to distinguish from mast cells in blood.

METHYSERGIDE. Potent serotonin antagonist having vasoconstrictor effects. Inhibits or blocks serotonin. Used as analgesic for treating some patients with migraines (m. maleate is Sansert). Several contraindications including peripheral vascular disease, severe hypertension, pulmonary disease, collagen diseases, and others.

MONOAMINE OXIDASE INHIBITORS (MAOI). Drugs used in the treatment of depression. Significantly interfere with detoxification of amines from foods and drinks and allow large amounts of amines to reach the bloodstream.

MONOSODIUM GLUTAMATE (MSG). A preservative and flavor enhancer used in many foods and spices. The sodium salt of glutamine, a naturally occurring amino acid. It is typically made from hydrolyzed plant proteins. It is used to impart a fresh flavor to processed foods.

PHENOLIC FLAVONOIDS. Flavonoid is a generic term for aromatic oxygen heterocyclic compounds that are widely distributed in higher plants. They are grouped in order of increasing oxidation state. Aromatic, in organic chemistry, denotes a compound having a ring system stabilized by a closed circle of conjugated double bonds or nonbonding electron pairs (e.g., benzene). Phenolic refers to phenol, a generic term for any organic compound having one or more hydroxyl groups attached to an aromatic or carbon ring.

PHENYLETHYLAMINE. A compound found in chocolate and in red and white wines. It may be a cause of diet-related migraines. It is similar in chemical structure to epinephrine, norepinephrine, dopamine, ephedrine, amphetamine, tyramine, and numerous other sympathomimetic drugs with vasoconstrictor and pressor activities. It is the basic chemical structure that all these compounds share. (See *epinephrine, norepinephrine, catecholamines, adrenal medulla*; Chapters 7, 17, 18.)

PROSTAGLANDIN SYNTHESIS. Prostaglandins (PGs) are a group of 20-carbon unsaturated fatty acids that have many potent biological effects and affect many organs. They are not classified as hormones because they act as local inter- and intracellular modulators of the tissue's biochemical activity and are not mediated by plasma. They are derived mostly from arachidonic acid. They all bind to specific cell-surface receptors and cause increased intracellular second messenger cyclic AMP and sometimes cylic GMP. The increased cyclic AMP increases PG synthesis, resulting in more increases in cyclic AMP. Prostaglandin D_2 is the major PG made by mast cells in the immune system. The PGs have many physiological influences in varied parts of the body.

RADIO-ALLERGO-SORBENT TEST (RAST). A sophisticated skin test method of detecting allergies to relevant foods.

SEROTONIN. Important neurotransmitter and vasocontrictor synthesized in humans in certain intestinal cells or in central or peripheral neurons. Found in high concentrations in many blood tissues as well as intestinal mucosa, pineal body, and CNS. Synthesis starts with uptake of tryptophan into serotonergic neurons. Tryptophan is changed (hydroxylated) by an enzyme to become 5-hydroxytryptophan and then changed (decarboxylated) by another enzyme to serotonin (5-HT). There are three types of receptors: $5-HT_1$, $5-HT_2$, and $5-HT_3$, and four subtypes of $5-HT_1$. It has many physiological properties including inhibiting gastric secretions, stimulating smooth muscle, and serving as a central neurotransmitter. Also often called "5-hydroxytryptamine (5-HT)." A major factor in medical/neurological and psychiatric conditions such as migraines and depression. About 90% occurs in the gastrointestinal tract, about 8% in blood platelets, and the rest in the brain. About 8% of 5-HT (serotonin) is found in blood platelets. It falls at the onset of a migraine attack and is normal between attacks (Saper et al., 1993). (See Chapters 14, 15.)

SODIUM CROMOLYN. A drug given prophylactically to block allergic responses. Inhibits histamine release from gut mast cells triggered by the presence of immune complexes.

SUMATRIPTAN. Recently introduced antimigraine medication. Trade name is Imitrex.

SYMPATHOMIMETIC. Producing or mimicking effects of adrenergic stimulation of postganglionic fibers of sympathetic nervous system. Also called adrenergic.

THROMBOXANE GENERATION. Thromboxane is one of two compounds, A_2 and B_2. The word derives from *thrombocyte* (a blood platelet) plus an oxane ring. It is extremely potent as an inducer of platelet aggregation and platelet release reactions. It also is a vasoconstrictor. It is synthesized by platelets and is very unstable.

TYRAMINE. An amine resulting from the breakdown of an amino acid. The most commonly discussed vasoactive substance.

ACKNOWLEDGMENT

We sincerely thank Charlotte Gyllenhaal, Ph.D., University of Illinois at Chicago College of Pharmacy, who contributed to the research and writing of this chapter.

REFERENCES

Anonymous. (1991). The cola wars. *Consumer Reports Magazine, 56,* 518–525.

Antila, P., Antila, V., Mattila, J., & Hakkarainen, H. (1984). Biogenic amines in cheese. 1. Determination of biogenic amines in Finnish cheese using high performance liquid chromatography. *Milchwissenschaft, 39,* 81–85.

Asatoor, A. M., Levi, A. J., & Milne, M. P. (1963). Trancylpromine and cheese. *Lancet, ii,* 733–734.

Blackwell, B. (1963). Tranylcypromine. *Lancet, ii,* 414.

Blackwell, B., & Taylor, D. C. (1969). "Cold cures" and monoamine-oxidase inhibitors. *British Medical Journal, 2,* 381–382.

Boulton, A. A., Cookson, B., & Paulten, R. (1970). Hypertensive crisis in a patient on MAOI antidepressants follow a meal of beef liver. *Canadian Medical Association Journal, 102,* 1394–1395.

Bruce, M. S., & Lader, M. (1989). Caffeine abstention in the management of anxiety disorders. *Psychological Medicine, 19,* 211–214.

Bruce, M. S. (1990). The anxiogenic of caffeine. *Postgraduate Medical Journal, 66*(Suppl. 2), 18–24.

Bruce, M., Scott, N., Shine, P., & Lader, M. (1992). Anxiogenic effects of caffeine in patients with anxiety disorders. *Archives of General Psychiatry, 49,* 867–869.

Bruyn, G. W. (1980). The biochemistry of migraine. *Headache, 20,* 235–246.

Bunker, M. L., & McWilliams, M. (1979). Caffeine content of common beverages. *Journal of the American Dietetic Association, 74,* 28–32.

Caffeine: What it does. (1981, October). *Consumer Reports,* 595–599.

Caraco, Y., Zylber-Katz, E., Granit, L., & Levy, M. (1990). Does restriction of caffeine intake affect mixed function oxidase activity and caffeine metabolism? *Biopharmaceutics and Drug Disposition, 11,* 639–643.

Coffin, D. C. (1970). Tyramine content of raspberries and other fruit. *Journal of the Association of Official Analytic Chemists, 53,* 1071–1073.

Colbin, A. (1979). *The book of whole meals.* Brookline, MA: Autumn Press.

Cook, G. E., & Joseph, R. (1988). Letter. *Lancet, ii,* 1256–1257.

Curatolo, P. W., & Robertson, D. (1983). The health consequences of caffeine. *Annals of Internal Medicine, 98,* 641–653.

Dalessio, D. J. (1980). Migraine therapy. In D. J. Dalessio (Ed.), *Wolff's headache and other head pain* (pp. 131–162). New York: Oxford University Press.

Da Prada, M., & Zürcher, G. (1992). Tyramine content of preserved and fermented foods or condiments of Far Eastern cuisine. *Psychopharmacology, 106*(Suppl.), S32–S34.

Denaro, C. P., Brown, C. R., Wilson, M., Jacob, P. III, & Benowitz, N. L. (1990). Dose-dependency of caffeine metabolism with repeated dosing. *Clinical Pharmacologic Therapy, 48,* 277–285.

der Marderosian, A., & Liberti, L. (1988). *Natural product medicine.* Philadelphia: George F. Stickley.

Diamond, S., Prager, J., & Freitag, F. G. (1986). Diet and headache. Is there a link? *Postgraduate Medicine, 79*(4), 279–287.

Edmeads, J. (1991). What is migraine? Controversy and stalemate in migraine pathophysiology. *Journal of Neurology, 238,* S2–S5.

Egger, J. (1991). Psychoneurological aspects of food allergy. *European Journal of Clinical Nutrition, 45*(Suppl. 1), 35–45.

Egger, J., Carter, C. M., Soothill, J. F., & Wilson, J. (1989). Oligoantigenic diet treatment in children with epilepsy and migraine. *Journal of Pediatrics, 114,* 51–58.

Egger, J., Wilson, J., Carter, C. M., Turner, M. W., & Soothill, J. F. (1983a). Is migraine food allergy? A double-blind controlled trial of oligoantigenic diet treatment. *Lancet, ii,* 865–869.

Egger, J., Wilson, J., Carter, C. M., Turner, M. W., & Soothill, J. F. (1983b). Letter. *Lancet, ii,* 1424.

Feldman, W. (1983). Letter. *Lancet, ii,* 1424.

Fennelly, M., Galletly, D. C., & Purdie, G. I. (1991). Is caffeine withdrawal the mechanism of postoperative headache? *Anesthesia and Analgesia, 72,* 449–453.

Galletly, D. C., Fennelly, M., & Whitwam, J. G. (1989). Does caffeine withdrawal contribute to postanesthetic morbidity? *Lancet, i,* 1335.

Gerrard, J. W. (1983). Letter. *Lancet, ii,* 1257.

Gettis, A. (1987a). Serendipity and food sensitivity: A case study. *Headache, 27,* 73–75.

Gettis, A. (1987b). Viewpoint: Food induced "delayed reaction" headaches in relation to tyramine studies. *Headache, 27,* 444–445.

Giacovazzo, M., & Martelletti, P. (1989). Letter. *Annals of Allergy, 63,* 255.

Gibb, C. M., Davies, P. T., Glover, V., Steiner, T. J., Clifford Rose, F., & Sandler, M. (1991). Chocolate is a migraine-provoking agent. *Cephalalgia, 11,* 93–95.

Gilbert, R. M. (1981). Caffeine: Overview and anthology. In S. A. Miller (Ed.), *Nutrition and behavior: The proceedings of the Franklin Research Center's 1980 working conference on nutrition and behavior; New research directions* (pp. 145–166). Philadelphia: Franklin Institute Press.

Gilbert, R. M., Marchman, J. A., Schwieder, M., & Berg, R. (1976). Caffeine content of beverages as consumed. *Canadian Medical Association Journal, 114,* 205–208.

Gilman, A. G., Rall, T. W., Nies, A. S., & Taylor, P. (Eds.). (1990). *Goodman and Gilman's the pharmaceutical basis of therapeutics* (8th ed.). New York: Pergamon Press.

Grant, E. C. G. (1979). Food allergies and migraine. *Lancet, i,* 966–968.

Greden, J. F., Victor, B. S., Fontaine, P., & Lubetsky, M. (1980). Caffeine-withdrawal headache: A clinical profile. *Psychosomatics, 21*(5), 411–413, 417–418.

Griffiths, R. R., Evans, S. M., Heishman, S. J., Preston, K. L., Wannerud, C. A., Wolf, B., & Woodson, P. P. (1990). Low-dose caffeine physical dependence in humans. *Journal of Pharmacology and Experimental Therapeutics, 255*(3), 1123–1132.

Guarnieri, P., Radnitz, C. L., & Blanchard, E. B. (1990). Assessment of dietary risk factors in chronic headache. *Biofeedback and Self-Regulation, 15,* 15–25.

Hanington, E., Horn, M., & Wilkinson, M. (1969). Further observations on the effects of tyramine. In *Background to migraine, 3rd symposium* (pp. 113–126). New York: Springer.

Hanington, E. (1980). Diet and migraine. *Journal of Human Nutrition, 34,* 175–180.

Harper, J. V. (1993). For want of a cup of coffee (Editorial). *Mayo Clinic Proceedings, 68,* 928–929.

Harrison, D. P. (1986). Copper as a factor in the dietary precipitation of migraine. *Headache, 26,* 248–250.

Harvey, R. F., Pomare, E. W., & Heaton, K. W. (1973). Effects of increased dietary fibre on intestinal transit. *Lancet, i,* 1278–1280.

Hearn, G., & Finn, R. (1983). Letter. *Lancet, ii,* 1081–1082.

Heaton, K. W., Thornton, J. R., & Emmett, P. M. (1979). Treatment of Crohn's disease with an unrefined-carbohydrate, fibre-rich diet. *British Medical Journal, 2,* 764–766.

Hedberg, D. L., Gordon, M. W., & Glueck, B. C. (1966). Six cases of hypertensive crisis in patients on tranylcypromine after eating chicken livers. *American Journal of Psychiatry, 122,* 933–937.

Henderson, W. R., & Raskin, N. (1972). Hot dog headache: Individual susceptibility to nitrite. *Lancet, ii,* 1162–1163.

Hillmann, L. C., Stace, N. H., Fisher, A., & Pomare, E. W. (1982). Dietary intakes and stool characteristics of patients with the irritable bowel syndrome. *American Journal of Clinical Nutrition, 36,* 626–629.

Hodge, J. V., Nye, E. R., & Emerson, G. W. (1964). Monoamine-oxidase inhibitors, broad beans, and hypertension. *Lancet, i,* 1108.

Horowitz, D., Lovenberg, W., Engelman, K., & Sjoerdsma, A. (1964). Monoamine-oxidase inhibitors, tyramine and cheese. *Journal of the American Medical Association, 188*(13), 1108–1110.

Hughes, E. C., Gott, P. S., Weinstein, R. C., & Binggeli, R. (1985). Migraine: A diagnostic test for etiology of food sensitivity by a nutritionally supported fast and confirmed by long-term report. *Annals of Allergy, 55,* 28–32.

Hughes, J. R., Higgins, S. T., Bickel, W. K., Hunt, W. K., Fenwick, J. W., Gulliver, S. B., & Mireault, G. C. (1991). Caffeine self-administration, withdrawal, and adverse effects among coffee drinkers. *Archives of General Psychiatry, 48,* 611–617.

Humphrey, P. P. A. (1991). 5–Hydroxytryptamine and the pathophysiology of migraine. *Journal of Neurology, 238,* S38–S44.

Ibe, A., Saito, K., Nakazato, M., Kikuchi, Y., Fujinuma, K., & Nishima, T. (1991). Quantitative determination of amines in wine by liquid chromatography. *Journal of the Association of Official Analytical Chemists, 74,* 695–698.

James, J. E., Bruce, M. S., Lader, M. H., & Scott, N. R. (1989). Self-report reliability and symptomatology of habitual caffeine consumptoms. *British Journal of Clinical Pharmacology, 27,* 507–514.

Jarman, J., Glover, V., & Sandler, M. (1991). Release of (^{14}C)5-hydroxytryptamine from human platelets by red wine. *Life Sciences, 49,* 2297–2300.

Johansson, I. M., & Schubert, B. (1990). Separation of hordenine and N-methyl derivatives from germinating barley by liquid chromatography with dual-electrode coulometric detection. *Journal of Chromatography, 498*(1), 241–247.

Kenyhercz, T. M., & Kissinger, P. T. (1978). Determination of selected acidic, neutral and basic natural products in cacao beans and processed cocoa. Liquid chromatography with electrochemical detection. *Lloydia, 412,* 130–139.

Koehler, S. M., & Glaros, A. (1988). The effect of aspartame on migraine headache. *Headache, 28,* 10–14.

Kohlenberg, R. J. (1980). *Migraine relief: A personal treatment program.* Seattle: Biofeedback and Stress Management Clinic.

Lai, C. W., Dean, P., Ziegler, D. K., & Hassanein, R. S. (1989). Clinical and electrophysiological responses to dietary challenge in migaineurs. *Headache, 29,* 180–186.

Lipton, R. B., Newman, L. C., Cohen, J. S., & Solomon, S. (1989). Aspartame as a dietary trigger of headache. *Headache, 29,* 90–92.

Littlewood, J., Gibb, D., Glover, V., Sandler, M., Davies, P. T., & Rose, F. C. (1988). Red wine as a cause of migraine. *Lancet, i,* 558–559.

Lovenberg, W. (1973). Some vaso- and psychoactive substances in food: Amines, stimulants, depressants, and hallucinogens. In National Research Council (U.S.) Food Protection Committee (Ed.), *Toxicants occurring naturally in foods* (2nd ed., rev.). Washington, DC: National Academy of Sciences.

Lucarelli, S., Lendvai, D., Frediani, T., Finamore, G., Grossi, R., Barbato, M., Zingdoni, A. M., & Cardi, E. (1990). Hemicrania and food allergy in children. *Minerva Pediatrica, 42,* 215–218.

Mansfield, L. E. (1990). The role of antihistamine therapy in vascular headaches. *Journal of Allergy and Clinical Immunology, 86,* 673–676.

Mansfield, L. E., Vaughn, T. R., Waller, S. F., Haverly, R. W., & Ting, S. (1985). Food allergy and adult migraine: Double blind and mediator confirmation of an allergic etiology. *Annals of Allergy, 55,* 126–129.

Marley, E. (1977). Monoamine oxidase inhibitors and drug interactions. In D. G. Grahame-Smith (Ed.), *Drug interactions.* Baltimore: University Park Press.

Matthew, J., & Wilson, W. H. (1985). Caffeine consumption, withdrawal and cerebral blood flow. *Headache, 25,* 305–309.

Maxwell, M. B. (1980). Reexamining the dietary restrictions with procarbazine (an MAOI). *Cancer Nursing, 3*, 451–457.

McCabe, B. J. (1986). Dietary tyramine and other pressor amines in MAOI regimens: A review. *Journal of the American Dietetic Association, 86*(8), 1059–1064.

McCabe, B., & Tsuang, M. T. (1982). Dietary considerations in MAO inhibitor regimens. *Journal of Clinical Psychiatry, 43*, 178–181.

Merritt, J. E., & Williams, P. B. (1990). Vasospasm contributes to monosodium glutamate-induced headache. *Headache, 30*, 575–580.

Moffet, A. M., Swash, M., & Scott, D. F. (1974). Effect of chocolate in migraine: A double-blind study. *Journal of Neurology, Neurosurgery and Psychiatry, 37*, 131–162.

Monro, J. A., Carini, C., Brostoff, J., & Zilkha, K. (1980). Food allergy in migraine. *Lancet, ii*, 1–4.

Moskowitz, M. A., & Buzzi, M. G. (1991). Neuroeffector functions of sensory fibres: Implications for headache mechanisms and drug actions. *Journal of Neurology, 238*, S18–S22.

Mumford, G. K., Evans, S. M., Kaminski, B. J., Preston, K. L., Sannerud, C. A., Silverman, K., & Griffiths, R. R. (1994). Discriminative stimulus and subjective effects of theobromine and caffeine in humans. *Psychopharmacology, 115*(1–2), 1–8.

Mustafa, T., & Srivastava, K. C. (1990). Ginger (*Zingiber officinale*) in migraine headache. *Journal of Ethnopharmacology, 29*, 267–273.

NOMSG. (1992). *Hidden sources of MSG*. Santa Fe, NM 87504: Author.

Olesen, J. (1991). A review of current drugs for migraine. *Journal of Neurology, 238*, S23–S27.

Orlosky, M. (1982). MAO inhibitors in sickness and in health. *Massachusetts General Hospital Newsletter. Biological Therapies in Psychiatry, 5*, 25–28.

Owen, M. L., Turkewitz, J., Dawson, G. A., Casaly, J. S., & Wirth, O. (1992). Nutritional education as a part of a multidisciplinary behavior modification approach to the treatment of head pain (abstract). *Headache, 32*, 265–266.

Payler, D. K., Pomare, E. W., Heaton, K. W., & Harvey, R. F. (1975). The effect of wheat bran on intestinal transit. *Gut, 32*, 209–213.

Peatfield, R. C. (1983). Letter. *Lancet, ii*, 1082.

Physicians' Desk Reference for Nonprescription Drugs 3rd ed. (1982). Oradell, NJ: Medical Economics Co.

Physicians' Desk Reference, 47th ed. (1992). Oradell, NJ: Medical Economics Co.

Podell, R. N. (1984). Is migraine a manifestation of food allergy? *Postgraduate Medicine, 75*(4), 221–225.

Pradalier, A., Weinman, S., Launay, J. M., Baron, J. F., & Dry, J. (1983). Total IgE, specific IgE and prick tests against foods in common migraine—a prospective study. *Cephalalgia, 3*, 231–234.

Price, K., & Smith, S. E. (1971). Cheese reaction and tyramine. *Lancet, i*, 130–131.

Radnitz, C. L. (1990). Food-triggered migraine: A critical review. *Annals of Behavioral Medicine, 12*(2), 51–71.

Radnitz, C. L., & Blanchard, E. B. (1991). Assessment and treatment of dietary factors in refractory vascular headache. *Headache Quarterly, Current Treatment and Research, 2*(3), 214–220.

Rice, S. L., Eitenmiller, B. R., & Kohler, P. E. (1975). Histamine and tyramine content of meat products. *Journal of Milk Food Technology, 38*, 256–258.

Rice, S. L., Eitenmiller, B. R., & Kohler, P. E. (1976). Biologically active amines in food: A review. *Journal of Milk Food Technology, 39*, 353–358.

Rice, S. L., & Kohhler, P. E. (1976). Tyrosine and histidine decarboxylase activities of *Pediococcus cerevisiae* and *Lactobacillus* species and the production of tyramine in fermented sausages. *Journal of Milk Food Technology, 39*, 166–169.

Riggin, R. M., McCarthy, M. J., & Kissinger, P. O. (1976). Identification of salsolinol as a major dopamine metabolite in the banana. *Journal of Agricultural and Food Chemistry, 24*, 189.

Ritchie, J. K., Wadsworth, J., Leonard-Jones, J. E., & Rogers, E. (1987). Controlled multicentre trial of a unrefined carbohydrate, fiber-rich diet in Crohn's disease. *British Medical Journal, 295*, 517–520.

Rivas-Gonzalo, J. C., Santos-Hernandez, J. G., & Marine-Font, A. (1983). Study of the evolution of tyramine content during the vinification process. *Journal of Food Science, 48*, 417–418.

Rossignol, A. M. (1985). Caffeine-containing beverages and premenstrual syndrome in young women. *American Journal of Public Health, 75,* 1335–1337.

Rossignol, A. M., & Bonnlander, H. (1990). Caffeine-containing beverages, total fluid consumption, and premenstrual syndrome. *American Journal of Public Health, 80*(9), 1106–1110.

Salfield, S. A. W., Wardley, B. L., Houlsby, W. T., Turner, S. L., Spalton, A. P., Beckles-Wilson, N. R., & Herber, S. M. (1987). Controlled study of exclusion of dietary vasoactive amines in migraine. *Archives of Diseases of Childhood, 62,* 458–460.

Sandler, M., Youdim, M. B. H., & Hanington, E. (1974). A phenylethylamine oxidising defect in migraine. *Nature, 250,* 335–337.

Sargent, J., & Solbach, P. (1988). Stress and headache in the workplace: The role of caffeine. *Medical Psychotherapy, 1,* 83–86.

Saxena, P. R., & DenBoer, M. O. (1991). Pharmacology of antimigraine drugs. *Journal of Neurology, 238,* S28–S35.

Scopp, A. L. (1991). MSG and hydrolyzed vegetable protein induced headache: Review and case studies. *Headache, 31,* 107–110.

Sen, N. P. (1969). Analysis and significance of tyramine in foods. *Journal of Food Science, 34,* 22–26.

Soltoft, J., Gudmand-Hoyer, E., Krag, B., Kristensen, E., & Wulff, H. R. (1986). A double-blind trial of the effect of wheat bran on symptoms of irritable bowel syndrome. *Lancet, i,* 270–272.

Speer, F. (1977). *Migraine.* Chicago: Nelson-Hall.

Stephenson, J. B. P. (1983). Letter. *Lancet, ii,* 1257.

Stewert, M. M. (1976a). MAO inhibitors and foods: Reality and mythology. *Neuropharmacology, 16,* 527.

Stewert, M. M. (1976b). MAOIs and foods: Fact and fiction. *Adverse Drug Bulletin, 58,* 200.

Stewert, M. M. (1977). MAO inhibitors and food: Reality and mythology. *Neuropharmacology, 16,* 527.

Udenfriend, S., Lovenberg, W., & Sjoerdsma, A. (1959). Physiologically active amines in common fruits and vegetables. *Archives of Biochemistry and Biophysics, 85,* 487–490.

van Dusseldorp, M., & Katan, M. B. (1990). Headache caused by caffeine withdrawal among moderate coffee drinkers switched from ordinary to decaffeinated coffee: A 12 week double blind trial. *British Medical Journal, 300,* 1558–1559.

Vidaud, Z. E., Chaviano, J., Gonzales, E., & Garcia Roche, M. O. (1987). Tyramine content of some Cuban cheeses. *Die Nahrung 31*(3), 221–224.

Weber, J. G., Ereth, M. H., Danielson, D. R., & Ilstrup, D. K. (1993). Prophylactic oral caffeine and postoperative headache. *Mayo Clinic Proceedings, 68,* 842–845.

Weber, R. W., & Vaughan, T. R. (1991). Food and migraine headache. *Immunology and Allergy Clinics of North America, 11*(4), 831–841.

Wilson, C. W., Kirker, J. G., Warnes, H., & O'Malley, M. (1980). The clinical features of migraine as a manifestation of allergic disease. *Postgraduate Medical Journal, 56,* 617–621.

11

Breathing Therapies

Mark S. Schwartz

Practitioners very commonly use relaxed breathing therapies[1] for reducing physiological tension and arousal and for treating a wide variety of specific symptoms and disorders. Some researchers and practitioners consider many symptoms as breathing-related ones (Janis, Defares, & Grossman, 1983; Lichstein, 1988; Fried, 1987, 1993a, 1993b; Ley, 1988a, 1988b, 1992, 1993; Timmons & Ley, 1994).[2] This view asserts that breathing incorrectly frequently increases the risk for developing or triggering many symptoms. Some believe that most symptoms are caused by organic dysfunction and that breathing irregularities exacerbate the symptoms (R. Fried, personal communication, March 13, 1994). Therefore, breathing therapies are essential in the treatment of patients with many different symptoms and disorders.

Those symptoms directly implicated for breathing therapies include panic, functional chest pain, and asthma. Breathing therapy is also part of the treatment of many other symptoms and disorders. These include irritable bowel syndrome (IBS), migraine headaches, and hypertension. Practitioners sometimes use breathing therapies alone. They also use them in combination with other relaxation therapies, behavioral therapies, and other forms of stress management. Some authors (Janis et al., 1983) speculate that it is possible that altered breathing patterns mediate some of the positive effects of relaxation therapies and biofeedback-assisted relaxation through autonomic nervous system changes.

This chapter is an overview and summary of selected topics related to breathing and breathing therapies. It is especially designed for nonmedical readers and others not well versed in breathing therapies. Respiration and hyperventilation are extremely complex topics. A detailed discussion of these is far beyond the scope of this chapter and book. As Aronson (1990) reminds us about respiration, "To understand it even at an elementary level requires some preparation in physics, biochemistry, and physiology" (p. 349). Practitioners using biofeedback often do not have this background. See Naifeh (1994) and Fried (1993) for basic anatomy and physiology of the respiratory system and autonomic nervous system.

---

[1]This chapter uses the terms "breathing therapy" and "relaxed breathing therapy" instead of "breathing retraining" used in other references. This is for consistency throughout the book. I prefer "therapy" instead of "training." The term "training" has an educational and instructional denotation. I agree with many practitioners that it also is acceptable in many settings. We do educate and instruct patients, but therapy is more consistent with activities of therapists. Third-party reimbursement also may prefer therapy rather than training.

[2]I know good professionals with far more knowledge than I who could write more scholarly and more authoritatively on this subject. However, I sought to learn more, and writing this has been a wonderful learning experience. I also thought I could be more objective than many others. I intend no disrepect to these fine professionals and hope that they keep this in perspective. This chapter does not compete with the extensive treatments of this subject by others.

Many articles and chapters include a bewildering amount of technical information. Only some specialists understand most of this information. However, most practitioners using breathing therapies should know some of it. Thus, this chapter provides selected information that will be useful to many readers. There is no way to avoid technical information. However, I try to present this in ways that I trust most readers will understand. The chapter provides a unique array of information not found in any single source.

The chapter focuses on hyperventilation and breathing therapies for selected disorders. It discusses proposed mechanisms, selected issues, and provides a review of breathing therapies and biofeedback techniques used for breathing therapy. More discussion of relaxation-induced anxiety may be found in Chapter 12. Chapter 37 includes more discussion of asthma. Limits of the chapter are due to space and my own limitations. I trust that curtailing the scope and details in the chapter does not diminish its value.[3] For more information, one must read other sources. I especially encourage reading Fried (1993) and Timmons and Ley (1994) as they are very recent.

ANATOMY AND PHYSIOLOGY

The lungs themselves have no intrinsic muscles for breathing. The diaphragm is a major muscle of breathing. It is a sheet-like muscle stretching from the backbone to the front of the rib cage that separates the chest cavity from the abdominal cavity (see Figure 11.1A and 11.1B). It forms a flexible, moving floor for the lungs. When at rest, the shape of the diaphragm is a double dome, and it extends upward into the chest under the lungs.

To start inhalation, the diaphragm contracts, flattens downward, and descends. This allows expansion of the chest cavity and allows the lungs to fill more completely. It displaces the abdominal contents, expanding the belly. The natural return of the diaphragm to its resting state occurs with exhalation. Other muscles involved in breathing include the intercostal muscles acting on the rib cage and the scalene muscles that raise the chest by lifting the first and second ribs. In some cases, the muscles of the abdominal area contract to push the abdominal contents upward and push upward on the diaphragm. See Naifeh (1994) and Fried (1993) for detailed presentations on the anatomy and physiology of breathing.

HYPERVENTILATION AND
HYPERVENTILATION SYNDROME

Some definitions of *hyperventilation* (HV) focus on rapid cycles of inhaling and exhaling (*tachypnea*) and/or breathing voluminous amounts of air in each breath (*hyperpnea*). Ley (1993) asserts that one also must consider the amount of air breathed per unit of time (*minute volume*) and compare this to the person's metabolic demand for oxygen at the time. Thus, HV is breathing beyond what the body needs to meet the immediate needs for oxygen and removal of carbon dioxide (CO_2), that is, HV is low CO_2 for any reason. Thus, the physiological definition of HV is low CO_2—pCO_2 less than an average of 38 torr at sea level. There is a range of values dependent on individual fitness.

---

[3]For example, the discussion of anatomy and physiology is intentionally very brief. Many other references cover this topic (Aronson, 1993; Naifeh, 1994; Fried, 1993; Macklem & Mead, 1986). There is no inclusion of special populations such as children and adolescents.

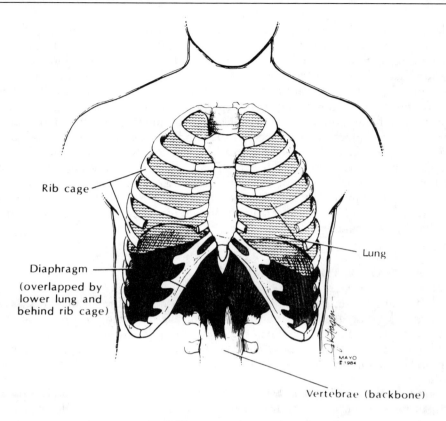

Rib cage

Lung

Diaphragm
(overlapped by
lower lung and
behind rib cage)

Vertebrae (backbone)

FIGURE 11.1A. Front view.

The implications of this for hyperventilation syndrome (HVS), panic, relaxation induced anxiety (RIA), and other symptoms will become more clear later in the chapter. For now, the implication is that one may not be breathing rapidly or deeply to create a state of HV. If HV lasts long enough, it can lead to "constriction of arteries of the brain and hand, increased neural excitability, increased production of lactic acid, and lowering of [the] phosphate level in arterial blood" (Garssen, deRuiter, & van Dyck, 1992, p. 142).

HVS is a variety of somatic symptoms associated with hypocapnia and induced by hyperventilation (Dorland, 1988; Lewis & Howell, 1986; see Table 11.1). Many people with HVS are unaware of their HV. They often attribute their symptoms to other causes and worry unnecessarily. Voluntary HV usually reproduces some or all of the symptoms.

A useful distinction is between "chronic" versus "acute" or "periodic" hyperventilation (Ley, 1988a, 1988b). Periodic hyperventilation is often normal as a part of reactivity to stress and physical demands. However, chronic hyperventilation is abnormal and troublesome. In addition to the variety of symptoms, it produces physiological conditions that can explain the paradoxical reactions of RIA and panic during sleep (Ley, 1988a, 1988b). Briefly, people who chronically hyperventilate are frequently in a continuous state of reduced plasma bicarbonate with a low level of pCO_2. Reduced plasma bicarbonate is a necessary compensatory homeostatic mechanism. This results in being near the threshold of severe hypocapnia or low alveolar CO_2. Low blood CO_2 is "hypocarbia." These are definitions

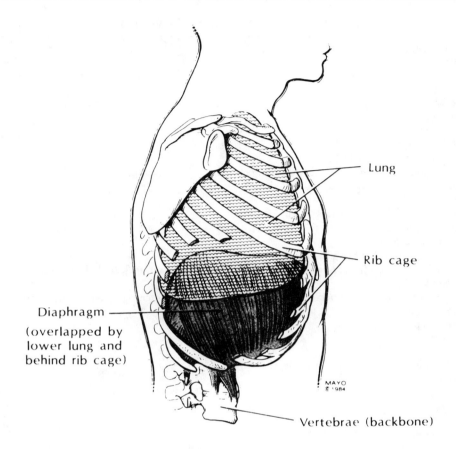

FIGURE 11.1B. Side view.

and not disease states, although they may contribute to diseases. According to one view (Ley, 1988a, 1988b), when people in a chronic state of HV and low pCO_2 reduce their metabolism further during relaxation or sleep, they increase their risk of symptoms. (See the section on Mechanisms for more details.)

Assessing Hyperventilation

Methods for assessing HV include observations, interviews, self-report questionnaires, HV provocation, blood assays, a transcutaneous instrument that roughly estimates CO_2, and a noninvasive instrument that measures the percentage of exhaled CO_2. The last instrument is an infrared gas analyzer called a capnometer that can produce a capnograph. Physiological monitoring can be during rest and during office stress challenges. It can be performed while the patient is supine, seated, or standing.

During HV provocation, one compares the similarity of the symptoms during the provocation with the presenting complaints. Voluntary hyperventilation during provocation re-

TABLE 11.1. Symptoms of Hyperventilation[a]

Central neurological
    Unreality
    Dizziness
    Faintness
    Unsteady feelings
    Lightheadedness
    Disturbance of consciouisness
    Feeling far away
    Confused or dream-like feeling
    Concentration impairment/trouble thinking clearly
    Disturbance of vision (blurred, double vision)

Peripheral neurological
    Numbness (tongue, face, hands, feet)
    Coldness (general, hands or feet)
    Shivering/cold shudders
    Heat/warmth, feeling of (e.g., head, general)
    Paresthesia (tingling) (fingers, arms, face, circumoral [around mouth], body legs, feet), pins and
        needles
    Tetany (hyperexcitability of nerves and muscles, with spasms, twitching, and cramps—rare)

Muscular skeletal
    Tremor (e.g., hands)
    Shakiness
    Tight muscles
    Muscle pain (and cramps, e.g., toes, legs)
    Stiffness (finger, arms, legs)
    Hands tight and hard to open

Cardiovascular
    Heart racing—tachycardia
    Heart pounding—palpitations
    Irregular heart beat
    Precordial pain (chest, over heart, lower thorax)
    Raynaud's phenomenon

Gastrointestinal
    Nausea
    Vomiting
    Diarrhea
    Globus/pressure, lump, or knot in throat
    Epigastric pain
    Stomach feels blown up
    Stomach cramps
    Aerophagia

Other somatic
    Dry mouth and throat
    Headache
    Sweating
    Weakness (general)
    Fatigue (general, low stamina, tires easily)

Respiratory/thoracic
    Shortness of breath (while awake or from sleep)
    Suffocating feeling/need for air
    Unable to breathe deeply enough
    Chest pain, atypical (around heart region)

TABLE 11.1. (*continued*)

Chest tightness
Yawning
Faster or deeper breathing than normal
Sighing
Affective
  Apprehension
  Fear of inability to breathe
  Anxiousness/nervousness
  Unrest or panic feelings
  Tension
  Nightmares
  Giddiness/feeling excited without reason
  Crying fits without obvious reason
Response bias
  Catarrh[b]
  Drowsiness
  Stinging
  Choking
  Earache
  Ringing in ears/tinnitus
Others
  Talking difficulty

[a]Sources are primarily Missri and Alexander (1978), Clark and Hemsley (1982), Lewis and Howell (1986), and Fried (1987, 1993b).

[b]Inflamed mucous membranes and discharges in air passages of head and throat.

sults in considerable individual variability of symptoms and patterns (Clark & Hemsley, 1982; see Fried, 1993, for adverse effects, dangers, and contraindications for HV provocation).

Relying on patients to report all the symptoms is insufficient. They often do not recall or report many of the symptoms unless these are provoked in the office. Observing unprovoked breathing patterns in the office also is insufficient.

Criteria for Diagnosing HV

Criteria for diagnosing HV vary but typically involve measures of CO_2. Physiology textbooks do not disagree according to Fried (personal communication, March 14, 1994) It is low CO_2. It is less than 38 torr (less than 5% $PetCO_2$). This criterion is independent of symptoms. However, symptoms can emerge with higher and lower levels of $PetCO_2$ (Fried, 1993b). Practitioners typically focus on symptoms rather than CO_2 level. One view (Fensterheim, 1994) is that clinicians want and need to avoid failing to diagnose HV when it is present. He also agrees with the belief of Bass and Gardner (1985) and Gardner (1994) that no symptom or clinical definition of HVS is widely accepted. Thus, they can be less precise than the researcher who tries to avoid including a nonhyperventilator in a hyperventilator group and hence must use a strict physiological critierion.

Some practitioners and researchers use a criterion of a respiration rate at rest equal to or more than a specified number of breaths per minute (b/min) such as 16. There is no universally accepted normal breathing rate. A resting breathing rate of 8–14 b/min reported by Holloway (1994) is a commonly accepted criterion. However, there are reports of 16–17 b/min (± nearly 3 b/min) (Tobin et al., Sackner, 1983) for younger and older persons monitored without their awareness. Other reports suggest that men and people in their early 20s show slightly lower rates than women or older people (Jammes, Auran, Gouvernet, Delpierre, & Gimaud, 1979, as reported in Fried, 1993b). Fried (1993b) suggests a goal of "no more than 9 to 12 b/min" (p. 246) for a person at rest. He assumes normal tidal volume and pCO_2.

People with organic diseases that affect respiration typically show faster respiration rates from about 18–28 b/min (± 8) (Fried, 1993b).

Therefore, using a breathing rate above 16 is a crude and insuffient criterion for HV, and one cannot rely on this. Ley (1993), Fried (1993b), and Timmons and Ley (1994) provide a good discussion of this topic. For example, Ley states that even sound operational definitions are often insufficient unless they include information about the person's conditions at the time.

Hyperventilation Provocation Test
or Forced Hyperventilation Provocation Test

The hyperventilation provocation test (HVPT) or the forced hyperventilation provocation test (FHVPT) involves directed, intentional, and very rapid and usually deep breathing. Instructions often include something like filling the lungs with each inhalation and exhaling as completely as possible. The purpose is to reproduce the patient's symptoms and complaints as a diagnostic aid. There are cautions and critics, but this technique remains in common clinical practice.

Methods reported usually involve a specified rate (b/min) of at least 20 sometimes as many as 60 b/min.[4] Patients do this for a specified time of at least 60 seconds and usually 2–3 minutes. There are guidelines but no standard protocol exists (Timmons, 1994). Howell (1990) suggests the 20 Deep Breaths Test. Folgering and Colla (1978) use "one minute of deep breathing" (Timmons, 1994). Bonn, Readhead, and Timmons (1984) added breathing with the upper chest and 60 b/min.

Some research and many practitioners rely only on the rate and time method. This can be very unpleasant for some patients. Therefore, practitioners sometimes stop when many of the symptoms appear. Some use a pacing device such as a fast metronome or audiotape (Salkovskis & Clark, 1990). Others also specify a percentage (e.g., 50%) drop in pCO_2 as an alternative criterion (Craske & Barlow, 1990).

One can specify a specific level of alveolar pCO_2. Criteria vary, for example, less than 19 millimeters Hg (19 torr) (Nixon & Freeman, 1988) to below 38 torr (Fried, 1993b). Gardner (1994) uses the criterion of "below about . . . 30 mm Hg at rest or during or after exercise, or remains low 5 minutes after voluntary overbreathing" (p. 109). (A torr is 1 millimeter Hg. It is a measurement unit for gas pressure, for example CO_2.) Opinions of normal pCO_2 include 38 and 40 millimeters Hg.

There are individual differences in the level below which symptoms appear. This also *always* depends on other factors such as whether the office is at sea level or at much higher altitudes. Measures of $PetCO_2$ are usually sea level measures. The measurement drops as altitude increases because of decreased air pressure at higher altitudes; $PetCO_2$ is a percentage of CO_2 relative to air pressure in the surrounding environment. $PetCO_2$ is less at higher altitudes and in cities such as Denver.

---

[4]Some readers may question whether one can breathe at 60 b/min. I just did 20 in 15 seconds, and I am dizzy. Okay, dizzier. It can be done. Whether a practitioner wants or needs patients to breathe that fast in a HVPT is another question.

Some consider a patient's awareness of the similarity of naturally occurring symptoms to HVPT-induced symptoms as "the most important element in the diagnosis of HVS" (Garssen et al., 1992, pp. 149–150; Lewis & Howell, 1986). However, studies of this criterion are rare. In the few studies available, "the response to the HVPT does not predict the occurrence of HV during panic attacks" (Garssen, de Ruiter, & van Dyck, 1992, p. 150). This review summarized studies that concluded there was no difference in the recognized symptoms typical for HV during the HVPT compared to those occuring during a stressful time-pressured task without decreased $PetCO_2$. The task was the Stroop Color Word test. One must read Ley's (1993) comments about these studies and the Garssen et al. (1992) review. Ley is more favorable about the HVPT. He points out that the absence of a HVPT effect does not mean a patient does not have a HV-related problem.

Garssen et al. (1992) note that although some patients recognize symptoms during a HVPT, carbon dioxide does not always drop during ambulatory monitoring of panic. He is referring to the study by Hibbert and Pilsbury (1989) who used a transcutaneous estimate of the partial pressure of the CO_2 ($p_{tc}CO_2$). Furthermore, this study concluded that some patients do not recognize the provoked symptoms. These include patients who show large drops in $p_{tc}CO_2$ during panic. One interpretation is that panic can cause HV rather than HV always causing panic. The transcutaneous method is slow in showing changes that usually occur for each breath. Thus some practitioners and researchers who have tried it have not found it useful, especially for office assessments.

In a study with nonclinical subjects, Huey and West (1983) avoided raising expectations of anxiety and avoided using the term hyperventilation in the instructions to overbreathe. Nevertheless, HV led to more symptoms than during a modified overbreathing technique that avoided hypocapnia. They called the technique the "isocapnic overventilation technique" (IOT). It artificially prevents lowered end-tidal CO_2 ($PetCO_2$) during HV by using a mixture of air enriched with CO_2. Under these conditions, the patients did not differ from subjects not overbreathing. This supports the HVS explanation.

One view is that HV is a necessary factor for most of the somatic symptoms associated with HVS but not sufficient for panic symptoms. For example, cognitive factors also are necessary according to Garssen et al. (1992). Thus, cognitive therapy is necessary for treatment. Ley (1992) agrees with this for a subset of patients.

A problem is that HVPT does not always evoke the symptoms in question for a specific person. For example, chest pain is not easy to reproduce.

Other views are critical about the role of HV for panic and the value of HVPT as the only or best criterion. For example, stressful mental tasks with only small decreases in alveolar CO_2 also can evoke HVS symptoms (Garssen et al., 1992). However, the decreases in $PetCO_2$ were 1.2 milligrams Hg. Furthermore, a mental task of thinking about various stressful topics led to HV and decreased pCO_2[5] among more subjects (33/54, or 61%) than did the HVPT (7/54, or 13%) (Nixon & Freeman, 1988).

Some practitioners (Fried, 1993) are far more cautious about HVPT. Fried considers it hazardous and recommends against this procedure. However, he provides no exceptions and guidelines about when it may be acceptable. He is cautious partly because he is a nonphysician. He is very concerned about inducing changes in blood acid–base balance and coronary and cerebral vasoconstriction and ischemic hypoxia. This is worrisome to him, as it should be to everyone, because a patient could have an undiscovered and undiagnosed organic disease that places the patient at risk. For example, the patient with diag-

---

[5]pCO_2 is the partial pressure of CO_2 in alveolar (or atmospheric) air. It is not a partial pressure measure of arterial blood CO_2 which is p_aCO_2.

nosed "functional chest symptoms" might turn out to have an organic cardiac disease for which induced biochemical and cardiovascular changes increase the risks. However, he adds that "in fairness to my colleagues . . . a number of them use the procedure and have reported no consequent ill effects in their clients"(p. 42).

Compernolle, Hoogduin, and Joele (1979) caution against using voluntary HV with patients with chronic anemia or vascular diseases. They refer to loss of consciousness and fatal accidents with HV followed by breath-holding during underwater swimming and diving competition (Hill, 1973; Craig, 1976). Neurological impairment and fatal accidents also have occurred following HV in children with sickle cell anemia (Allen, Imbus, Powars, & Haywood, 1976). However, aside from the examples cited, they noted:

> nothing in the literature to substantiate the fear that provoking hyperventilation may be dangerous. There are no reports of accidents resulting from two to five minutes of hyperventilation followed by breathing into a bag. (p. 616)

Prudent practitioners are extra cautious with people at risk for syncope for which there are many causes. Causes include certain cardiovascular, metabolic, or neurological disorders such as seizures. The clinician must remember that hypocapnia-induced vasoconstriction from hyperventilation reduces cerebral blood flow (Berkow & Fletcher, 1992). Thus, caution is necessary for many elderly patients and those with compromised cerebral blood flow. The clinician should also be aware that there are many organic medical conditions that can cause HV (Gardner, 1994). Thus, practitioners must be very careful lest they provoke unintended and potentially risky symptoms. For example, even psychologically distressed patients who hyperventilate as a result of functional habit and anxiety also can have diabetes. Induced HV may affect or at least interact with blood glucose (Guthrie, Moeller, & Guthrie, 1983; Lum, 1994). If blood glucose is very low because of poorly controlled diabetes, induced HV can add to the acidosis and intensify symptoms.

Practitioners and researchers who believe they need to use the HVPT or intend to do so for other clinical or research reasons must get medical clearance. This is crucial particularly in patients with a history of respiratory, cardiovascular, or some neurological diseases. For example, a history of or evidence for coronary artery disease or unexplained chest pain raises clear caution.

A related caution stems from the potential for some patients to self-initiate breathing procedures. Some patients may self-initiate breath-holding or the Valsalva maneuver to abort symptoms including those from HVS and panic. Quiet breath-holding, or apneas, combined with irregular breathing is a pattern associated with just as many problems as the obvious hyperventilation pattern (Holloway, 1994). There is one report (Sartory & Olajide 1988) of the use of the Valsalva[6] maneuver as a potential treatment for panic symptoms. Physicians suggest using the Valsalva to abort paroxysmal atrial tachycardia for selected patients. Such information may encourage patients to try these without proper consultation. For example, the case reported by Rapee (1985) began aborting her panic symptoms by holding her breath without instructions to do so. In most people, these attempts are not dangerous, but one must be cautious and complete in patient-education instructions.

In some weight lifters "hyperventilation before lifting causes hypocapnia, cerebral vasoconstriction, and peripheral vasodilation" (Berkow & Fletcher, 1992, p. 432). The lifting involves the Valsalva maneuver, which affects blood return to the heart reducing cardiac out-

---

[6]The Valsalva maneuver is forced exhalation effort with the glottis closed. It substantially increases intrathoracic pressure and disrupts venous blood returning to the heart. *Eastern* breathing advocates avoid it because of its risks (Chandra, 1994).

put and altering CO_2 levels. Potentially, systemic vasodilation and decreased blood pressure may occur increasing the risk of syncope for some people engaged in similar activities.

Although for most people the risks do not exist, there are enough reasons to be very cautious and obtain approval from a qualified physician. Prudent practitioners may decide to avoid the procedure unless it is absolutely necessary to make a diagnosis or to convince a patient of the diagnosis.

Exclusion Diagnoses and Organic Causes of Hyperventilation

Prudent practitioners consider medical disorders for which one expects altered breathing and symptoms not caused by incorrect breathing. This underscores the importance of appropriate medical examination and tests before one concludes that symptoms are the result of HV. Even a partial list of such tests is beyond the scope of this chapter.

Many organic medical disorders also cause HV (Gardner, 1994). This does not eliminate the role of breathing therapies totally, but it does raise cautions about diagnosis and therapy procedures. Although providing a complete list is beyond the scope of this chapter, some readers may find a partial list of such conditions useful. Examples of drugs are salycilate (e.g., aspirin) intoxication and stimulants such as caffeine, nicotine, and amphetamines. Examples of diseases are hepatic (liver) and renal failure, even mild asthma, interstitial lung diseases, and various pulmonary and vascular diseases. Focal lesions of the respiratory centers of the brain stem constitute another example. See Gardner (1994) and medical texts for further discussion of this topic.

SYMPTOMS OF HYPERVENTILATION

Consulting different references results in some differences in the lists of hyperventilation symptoms. The list in Table 11.1 (Symptoms) contains most symptoms reported by patients and sometimes thought to be assocated with HVS. One finds nearly all these symptoms reported by at least some patients diagnosed with HVS. Obviously, patients do not present most of these symptoms and many of them do not differentiate between people with HVS and those without HVS.

Nevertheless, this list alerts or reminds practitioners about the scope of symptoms associated with HV. It reflects the complexity of making the HVS diagnosis. It also may serve as a source for patient education and is an aid for developing checklists. It is useful to divide the list into areas, although there is overlap. Several of the specific symptoms could be under different headings.

These lists presumably imply that the symptoms stem from hyperventilation. However, that is not clear. Many symptoms often accompany hyperventilation. Therefore, they could result from other physiological and cognitive events that often coexist with hyperventilation (Clark, 1986; Garssen et al., 1992).

According to this view, cognitive factors can increase the risk of developing HV and HV-related symptoms. This can occur after other causes for physiological arousal and the onset of other symptoms. For example, anticipation of symptoms, perceptions of lack of control over symptoms or feelings of helplessness, and a lack of understanding of symptom origin can increase the risk of developing various symptoms and HV.

All practitioners should remember that many of these symptoms also accompany medical and neurological disorders as well as other stress disorders. Diagnosis is by exclusion as well as inclusion.

SYMPTOMS, DISORDERS, MECHANISMS, AND BREATHING THERAPY

Symptoms and disorders for which relaxed breathing therapy is part of the treatment plan include HVS, panic, and functional chest pain. I also include relaxation-induced anxiety in this section.

Hyperventilation Syndrome

There is a surprising paucity of studies using breathing therapies alone for HVS. Reports and studies of breathing therapy alone for HVS do show clinically significant reductions of HVS symptoms (Grossman, De Swart, & DeFares, 1985; Fried, 1993b; Timmons & Ley, 1994). However, methodological problems and equivocal results from studies detract from firm conclusions. Studies of cognitive restructuring, relaxation, breathing, feedback for respiration rate, and patient education also lead to significant improvements (Bass, 1994; Ley, 1994). However, using breathing therapies alone for HVS remains a logical and sound approach. Practitioners probably will continue to combine breathing therapy with good patient education, other relaxation procedures, and cognitive approaches. The specific need for biofeedback-assisted breathing therapy (e.g., respiration rate, diaphragmatic breathing, CO_2 feedback, and volumetric feedback) also remains logical although unsubstantiated. The value for feedback is at least for therapist information, documentation, and to obtain information for patient motivation and confirmation.

Functional Chest Pain and Functional "Cardiac" Symptoms

There are many patients with noncardiac chest pain. Often, there is no objective or probable organic cardiac pathology explaining these symptoms. One correctly assumes that psychophysiological factors play a role in these symptoms for many patients (Clouse, 1992; Hegel, Abel, Etscheidt, Cohen-Cole, & Wilmer, 1989). However, chest pain associated with symptomatic HV is not "psychogenic" in the sense of being purely cognitive in origin. There are physical reasons, albeit, often psychophysiological ones. Muscle tension, spasm, and fatigue in the intercostal muscles constitute one such mechanism (Bass, Gardner, & Jackson, 1994). Many physicians refer to this musculoskeletal explanation as chest-wall pain.

Some physicians suggest that a distended stomach caused by aerophagia places excess pressure on the diaphragm and can cause chest pain (Bass et al., 1994). Diaphragm spasms may create chest symptoms. For some, esophageal involvement contributes to these symptoms (Clouse, 1992). Here too, psychophysiological factors often play a role in some of these patients (Drossman et al., 1990). This international panel of clinical investigators provided a preliminary consensus report of functional gastrointestinal disorders. Included among these disorders was "functional chest pain of presumed oesophageal origin" (p. 163). This is "midline chest pain with or without dysphagia for at least three months; *and* no evidence for oesophagitis, cardiac or other disease to explain symptoms" (p. 163). Although esophageal disorders are common in these "chest" symptoms, the authors recognize the etiological potential for psychological factors.

One also must consider reduced blood flow to the heart (Fried, 1993b); HV can trigger paroxysmal vasospasms in the heart (and the brain). The effects of HV on cardiac functioning are not in question. They are real and accepted by all experts. In fact, HV and high arousal contribute to many of the occurrences of cardiac symptoms of organic origin such as angina pectoris and infarction (Nixon, 1989; Fried, 1993b).

However, a question of clinical significance for practitioners is whether the cardiac changes with HV indicate an organic cardiac diagnosis. They often do not. Saying that breathing changes and thoughts affect various parts of the brain does not mean the patient has an organic brain disorder.

Another question of clinical significance is whether there are noncardiac reasons to explain functional chest pain that may appear to patients (and practitioners) as having a cardiac origin. The answer is yes. There are musculoskeletal, diaphragm-related, and esophageal-related causes often stimulated and provoked by psychophysiological factors. Many people are hypervigilant and focus on their bodily sensations more keenly than is needed or desired. These people attribute dire causes to sensations and symptoms that are within the range of normal physiological sensations and events or at least not at all dangerous. This can result in cognitive anxiety and worry, and physical musculoskeletal tension and ANS arousal. These in turn can lead to or accompany the physical changes that produce the chest symptoms.

Treatments of potential value include psychopharmacological therapy such as low-dose antidepressants (Clouse, 1992), cognitive therapy (Salkovskis, 1992), behavioral therapies similar to those for chronic pain (Bradley, Richter, Scarinci, Haile, & Schan, 1992), and breathing therapies (DeGuire, Gevirtz, Kawahara, & Maguire, 1992; also see the review by Garssen et al., 1992). There are no studies of the combination of these therapies and no comparisons among the therapies.

This chapter focuses on the study using breathing therapies (DeGuire et al., 1992). Breathing therapies and patient education led to significantly reduced symptoms among patients with functional cardiac symptoms who showed signs of hyperventilation.

Patients received one of three breathing therapies: (1) without physiological feedback, (2) visual biofeedback from thoracic and abdominal strain gauges, or (3) end-tidal CO_2 feedback. Therapy common to all patients consisted of:

1. Verbal patient education about respiratory physiology and the hypothesized effect of hyperventilation on functional cardiac symptoms.
2. Instructions for diaphragmatic breathing.
3. Demonstration of diaphragmatic breathing by the therapist.
4. Office practice and correction of errors.
5. Encouragement to endure and reassurance about the expected decline of the discomfort of slow diaphragmatic breathing often reported by patients.
6. Encouragement to avoid increasing tidal volume or amount of air inhaled to compensate for changes in rate of respiration.
7. Encouraged slow-paced rate of respiration less than 14 b/min.[7]
8. Encouragement to practice this during conversations and while visualizing situations in which patients were having problems maintaining the new breathing.
9. Physiological monitoring and feedback typically occurred in later sessions.

---

[7]This rate of 4–5 seconds per inhalation/exhalation cycle is faster than often recommended and instructed in relaxed breathing therapy. Note that nearly all patients reduced their breathing to 8–9 b/min (SD = 2 to 3)—much less than 14 b/min. This is slightly faster than the goal of 6 cycles per minute or 10 seconds per cycle that many practitioners recommend. This finding supports the robust nature of the treatment.

The patients met several criteria for success. Improvement included the number of days with symptoms and the frequency of cardiac symptoms. Patients completed self-reported ratings of symptom frequency and severity. There were six treatment sessions over 3 weeks. The study partly based improvement on symptom changes between a 2-week baseline and the 2 weeks after treatment. The three breathing therapy groups reduced the days on which symptoms occurred from 8–10 of 14 days down to 4–5 of 14 days. The control group showed no drop from 10 of 14 days with symptoms.

The treated groups reduced their frequency of cardiac symptoms from an average of 21 symptoms (range 15–25) down to about 9 (range 4–15). All three groups showed reduced symptoms compared to the control group that did not change. The three treatment groups dropped from 23 to 4 symptoms after treatment, from 15 to 9, and from 25 to 15 compared to the control group with 27 to 26 symptoms. The authors note that they did not measure duration of symptoms and that this resulted in underestimating the effect. For example, some patients recorded one episode of chest pain all day and then episodic mild pain. They appeared to show increased symptoms rather than improvement that would be a more accurate interpretation.

Reduced respiratory rate and increased end-tidal CO_2 also occurred. Respiratory rate dropped from 15–18 to 8–9 breaths per minute compared to the control group who showed no change from 15 breaths per minute.

The breathing therapies led to end-tidal CO_2 increases. They started with 34–38 torr and increased to 39–41 torr showing a more normal level of CO_2. Some experts report 38 torr and higher as normal (Fried, 1993b).

Reduction of cardiac symptoms and increased end-tidal CO_2 occurred more so among those with reduced breathing rate. The reduced respiration rate correlated with reduced frequency of symptoms ($r = .53$, $p < .001$), number of days with symptoms ($r = .59$, $p < .001$), and increased end-tidal CO_2 ($r = .38$, $p = .018$). Deguire et al. (1992) note that, "the use of end-tidal CO_2, abdominal and thoracic strain gauge monitors did not add significantly to either reducing the frequency of cardiac symptoms or facilitating changes in physiology (p. 676)."

However, there was a trend for patients using strain-gauge monitors with computer-based visual biofeedback to produce the largest effect. The authors caution that the extent to which physiological feedback information added to the new attributions about symptoms is unclear. The presence of mitral valve prolapse did not detract at all from the success of these subjects.

Practitioners should consider including breathing therapies for patients diagnosed with functional chest pain and functional cardiac symptoms. However, it should be noted that functional chest symptoms and HVS are not synonymous (Bass, 1994). These authors also remind us that HV only provokes chest pain in less than half the patients assessed. Using breathing therapy for these patients is logical considering the successful use of this therapy for many patients with panic symptoms and the frequency of panic symptoms among these patients (see below). See Chapter 33 for a discussion of the potential of breathing therapies for menopausal hot flushes.

We can also note the potential benefit of relaxation therapies with breathing therapy during cardiac rehabilitation for patients after myocardial infarctions (van Dixhoorn, Duivenvoorden, Staal, Pool, & Verhage, 1987; van Dixhoorn & Duivenvoorden, 1989; van Dixhoorn, 1990). They report fewer second coronary events, rehospitalizations, and less unstable angina episodes and other serious cardiac events. Van Dixhoorn (1992, 1993, 1994) presents variations of breathing therapy that emphasize attentional states and total body involvement.

Relaxation-Induced Anxiety

RIA is the paradoxical arousal response that a small percentage of people experience during various relaxation procedures. Hyperventilation as a cause of RIA seems contradictory, but there is logic and support for this. The assumption and hypothesis of excess hypocapnia occurring during relaxation together constitute one possible explanation for RIA. This phenomenon appears to occur mostly in people who often hyperventilate. However, this explanation cannot and does not account for all RIA as one realizes from the detailed discussion of RIA in Chapter 12 and in Ley (1988b). However, HV may be a factor for some or many such people. Thus, practitioners should consider this during evaluation and treatment with relaxation therapies.

Panic

Breathing therapy constitutes a basic part of current treatments for many patients with panic symptoms and panic disorder. The debate continues as to whether HV causes panic or merely accompanies it in some patients with panic symptoms. Ley (1993) is a prolific, tenacious, and persuasive advocate of the role of HV for panic and the necessity of breathing therapy for these patients (see Ley, 1985, 1987a, 1987b, 1988a, 1988b, 1991, 1992). Contrary views by Garssen et al. (1992), Clark and his colleagues (Salkovskis & Clark, 1990), and Barlow and his colleagues (Barlow, 1988) provide balance and perspective. Ley's (1992, 1993) proposal helps resolve some differences in opinion.

Some studies report more benefit from respiratory control with exposure to situations in which symptoms occur compared with only exposure without breathing therapy. However, breathing therapy often leads to mixed results whether or not one includes cognitive components. This contrary view is that "recent studies do not support the idea that HV is an important *causal* mechanism in producing panic attacks" (Garssen et al., 1992, p. 149). Rather, HV accompanies panic in some patients with panic according to this view. Garssen et al. (1992) conclude that methodology problems make for impossible interpretations and conclusions for the specific role of breathing therapy. Examples of problems include combining therapies, very small samples, and lack of controls. The specificity and mechanism of breathing therapy are unclear and elusive.

> The majority of the studies point to a therapeutic effect of breathing retraining and cognitive reattribution of physical symptoms to hyperventilation for patients suffering HVS and the closely related panic disorder with or without agoraphobia. . . . The conclusion seems warranted that both . . . [treatments] help alleviate anxiety in patients with HVS or related disorders. (Garssen et al., 1992, pp. 148–149)

However, Ley (1992, 1993) provides a studious resolution to the disagreement about the relationship of HV and panic. He has proposed three types of panic attack (Ley, 1992). He calls the classic panic attack Type I or Classic PA. He distinguishes this from Anticipatory PA (Type II) and Cognitive PA (Type III). There are distinctive and objective physiological features of Type I especially compared to Type III. These features are: (1) sharp drops in $pCO_2 > 10$ millimeters Hg, (2) sharp increases in respiration rate and/or tidal volume, (3) sharp increases in heartrate >10 b/min, (4) sharp increases in electrodermal activity, and (5) low finger temperature < 80°F. He suggests that practitioners should expect the most benefit from breathing therapy for patients with Type I symptoms and expect the most benefit from cognitive therapies for Type III. One should read at least these two references to appreciate his position. A discussion of the proposed relationship between HV and panic is considered in a later section of this chapter.

Panic and Functional Chest Pain

Panic symptoms occur in many patients with unexplained or functional chest pain (Beitman, 1992) and among patients with unexplained cardiac symptoms in some cardiac care units (Carter et al., 1992). Another study reported that patients with panic disorder report more panic symptoms than patients with chest pain but no coronary artery disease (Beck, Berisford, Taegtmeyer, & Bennitt, 1990). However, both groups report similar severity of "chest pain, dyspnea, paresthesias, and fear of having a heart attack" (p. 249).

Mechanisms

The logic for this chapter wanes rapidly if HV is not a cause of the symptoms and disorders discussed above. Therefore, the emphasis here is on the Ley and related views. Whether entirely valid or not, this view has both good logic and support. HV probably is an important factor and therefore is a cornerstone in the rationale for this chapter.

To understand the proposed role of HV and to understand breathing therapy for these symptoms and disorders require a comprehension of the technical aspects of hypocapnia. The text is as nontechnical as I could make it. (See the Glossary for technical information.)

Hypoxia and/or Hypocapnia

"Hypoxia" is a bodily state of insufficient or low oxygen (O_2). "Hypocapnia" is a bodily state of insufficient or low CO_2. There are many causes of hypoxia and hypocapnia. The focus here is on people without organic diseases that cause impaired oxygenation or metabolic changes in blood pH closely linked to CO_2. For example, the chapter does not discuss environmental conditions such as high altitudes that cause impaired oxygenation.

One must consider both O_2 and CO_2 in a discussion and understanding of breathing and HV. However, the relative focus may be different. One contemporary view (Fried, 1987, 1993a, 1993b) focuses more on insufficient O_2. The author focuses on the end-product of HV. Ley (1988a, 1988b, 1992, 1993) focuses more on insufficient CO_2. Each view acknowledges the importance of the other gas (CO_2 and O_2) in its formulations. Although the relative focus may be different, I think that Ley and Fried agree on the importance of both. These are not fundamentally different viewpoints or points of focus. Hypoxia results from reduced CO_2 because, as pH rises (alkalosis), it leads to decreases in the dissociation of O_2 from hemoglobin thus producing hypoxia (R. Ley, personal communication, March 23, 1994). However, inspection of the references of several of the publications of each author reveals a curious omission of references by the other. I do not speculate about this avoidance and only point to it for the reader's notation. The contributions of each view are useful and important for practitioners. The reader should also note that despite the focus on O_2, Fried (1993b) measures and feeds back end-tidal carbon dioxide ($ETCO_2$). Changes in $PetCO_2$ indicate changes in O_2. That is, increased $PetCO_2$ indicates less hypoxia—increased cellular uptake of O_2.

Both Fried and Ley are researchers and clinicians. Both are theorists, prolific writers, and considered authorities in this field. They write for sophisticated readers who are familiar with and understand much of the technical content. Their style of writing is often complex. I try here to present this in a style and with terms that more readers can understand as well as to steer a tactful course within a diplomatic channel. If any readers believe I ran aground, I request their indulgence and understanding. I trust that the rising tide and favorable winds of this chapter will carry me back to smooth navigating.

First, let us follow Ley's line of thinking. Assuming constant metabolism, significantly increased volumes[8] of air inhaled (and exhaled) can lead to an excess loss of CO_2. This results in the sensations that typify many panic attacks. Ley (1988a) states that even a person's metabolism attempting to compensate, by increasing the CO_2 level, does not keep up with the effects from the increased volumes of air (Ley, 1987, 1988a, 1988b). Thus, hypocapnia can occur despite the body's attempt to regain balance and a desired level of CO_2.

People with chronic and severe HV maintain low levels of CO_2 in their blood and normal blood pH. The low level of CO_2 is only slightly above the threshold of nonspecific sensations produced by hypocapnia. The lowered CO_2 from HV *increases* the pH. It moves the pH toward alkalinity and away from a normal pH of 7.4.[9] The kidneys compensate for this by excreting bicarbonate to *lower* the pH and thus produce normal pH despite the low CO_2.

However, there is a problem for people who chronically hyperventilate. That is, there is a physiological lag between metabolic regulation of CO_2 and the breathing regulation of it. As Ley (1988a) reminds us, "breathing is a slave to metabolism" (p. 255). Thus, decreases in metabolism lag behind the decreases in respiration. The reverse is true as well.

Relaxation reduces metabolic demands. However, the temporal lag in the respiratory adjustment produces a temporary drop in CO_2 and a *rise* in pH (respiratory alkalosis). This depends on the degree and rate of decreased metabolism. These people cannot easily adjust to the sudden difference. They do not adjust well to the lag between respiratory changes and the metabolic production of CO_2. Thus, it takes less overbreathing to reach a low level of CO_2 in these people compared to asymptomatic people who maintain a normal CO_2 level at rest. When symptomatic people overbreath, CO_2 drops further and depleted bicarbonate buffers cannot compensate fast enough. The kidneys control a small part of the acid–base balance but most is mediated by the lungs.

When a person sits or reclines to relax, the metabolic production of CO_2 can suddenly drop. If the volumes of air remain steady, there is an increase in the intensity of sensations of hypocapnia and symptoms of panic or HV.

---

[8]A problem develops when we consider the use of the term "minute volume" (MV) (see the Glossary). Ley (1988a) refers to MV as the sum of tidal volumes breathed per minute. A tidal volume (V_t) is the amount of air inspired and expired during one normal respiratory cycle. Ley's definition of MV suggests the *total volume* of air. However, readers familiar with other definitions of MV may view MV as something slightly different. For example, two medical dictionaries define MV as the volume or quantity of air *expelled* from the lungs per minute (*Dorland's Illustrated Medical Dictionary*, 1988; *Melloni's Illustrated Medical Dictionary* [Dox, Melloni, & Eisner, 1979]). A third wording of the definition, "volume of air *inspired* per minute" in the classic book *Psychophysiology* (Kaufman & Schneiderman 1986, p. 112), could lead some readers to slightly different conclusions. I was bewildered and initially frustrated with these seemingly different definitions.

I offer the following resolution that I trust is satisfactory. Despite the different wording and potential implications, they all mean the same thing. The dictionary definitions refer to expelled air. Another definition refers to inspired air. Since what comes in typically goes out, they include the volume of air inhaled. Thus, they all imply that MV refers to the *total volume of inhaled or exhaled air in a minute*. Also, the term "expelled" eliminates breath holding during measurements. Holding one's breath for 1 minute means an MV of zero. Naifeh (1994) said it clearly. "*Minute ventilation* refers to the total volume of air inspired (or expired) in a minute and is expressed in liters per minute. The normal value at rest is 6 liters per minute" (p. 26).

[9]Normal pH is 7.4. A pH lower than 7.4 is acid, and a pH above 7.4 is alkaline (base). The terms acidosis and alkalinity are relative terms in human tissue.

Exercise

Ley (1988a) also states there are other situations when metabolism drops and volumes of air inhaled per minute are steady or increase. He cites the common example of abruptly stopping somewhat vigorous exercise. This assumes the person does not also voluntarily and rapidly reduce the volume of air per minute.

Exercise leads to a rise of CO_2 and *decreased* pH into the acid range (respiratory acidosis). Thus, CO_2 is higher and pH is lower during exercise. The degree of these shifts depends on the degree and rate the metabolism increases. When the person who chronically hyperventilates stops the exercise, the problem develops. The metabolic production of CO_2 drops. The lag in respiratory adjustment also adds to the fall in CO_2 and creates a temporary state of elevated pH (respiratory alkalosis). The degree of this depends on the degree and rate of metabolic decrease. Part of the problem occurs because people who chronically hyperventilate typically overbreathe longer than others after stopping the required overbreathing during exercise. Combining the overbreathing from exercise and that from their chronic breathing habit causes larger drops in CO_2. This leads to hypocapnia and potentially to panic. The problems develop after the stimulation rather than during it. This reasoning could account for patients with panic symptoms often avoiding exercise and excitement (Ley, 1988a).

Habituation and/or Homeostatic Changes
in Electrolytes and Blood Gases

Some investigators observe that panic symptoms often become less pronounced during persisting and clinically significant hypocapnia—at least with the nonpatients studied by van den Hout, de Jong, Zandbergen, and Merckelbach (1990). They speculate that this may be the result of a "special case of habituation" (p. 447) as the symptoms lose their novelty over time. However, this explanation may have less application to clinical patients who continue to worry about their symptoms.

Another view involves a physiological explanation for the gradual reduction and cessation of some sensations that often accompany HV and panic. These sensations include paresthesia, dizziness, and depersonalization. This view has more relevance for clinical practice.

Briefly, van den Hout et al. (1990) suggest that internal and natural biological changes occur and cause changes in internal feedback. These changes alter the sensations that often lead to anxiety and more HV. This explanation focuses on natural and homeostatic changes in calcium and potassium (K^+) affecting changes in paresthesia, and bicarbonate and pH that result in dizziness and a sense of depersonalization. This view states that despite continued very low CO_2, there are compensatory mechanisms that change the body's electrolytes (calcium and potassium). These changes can result in decreased symptoms or cessation of some symptoms in less than an hour in some people.

This view does not negate the hypocapnic explanation for the onset of symptoms. However, it suggests that physiological stabilization and homeostasis often occur in about 30–90 minutes, and this reduces symptoms. Interventions may need to work in less time to show their specific therapeutic value.

Chronic versus Acute or Periodic Hyperventilation

It is crucial to distinguish between "chronic hyperventilation" and "acute or periodic hyperventilation" to understand the mechanisms underlying many of the symptoms discussed in this chapter. "Chronic hyperventilation" is hypothesized to produce a "steady state of diminished plasma bicarbonate" (Ley, 1988a). One expects all patients who chronically exhibit HV to show many classic symptoms. These include "breathlessness, other respiratory complaints, low pCO_2 but normal pH, dizziness, low finger temperature, nausea, fatigue, malaise, dry mouth, and frequent micturation" (Ley, 1988a, p. 258). Relaxation during periods of HV results in reduced metabolism. However, without reduced ventilation, the increased intensity in hypocapnia produces the unpleasant, anxiogenic effects of respiratory alkalosis. The implication is that one does not expect the effects during relaxation and related conditions for people who periodically hyperventilate.

PROPOSED MECHANISMS OF ACTION FOR BREATHING THERAPY

Historical Interest Views

Air from Nasal Inhalations Has a Calming Effect

An old idea of historical interest is that warming and humidifying inhaled air exerts a soothing function (Ballentine, 1976; reviewed by Lichstein, 1988, p. 35). Typical instructions in breathing therapies are to inhale through the nose. This view suggests that the shifting patterns of airflow through the nasal passages stimulate nerve endings, and this has a calming effect on the nervous system.

Yoga masters instruct trainees to alternate nostrils. One belief is this results in shifts in cerebral lateral dominance (Chandra, 1994; Backon, 1989). The reader is also directed to reviews by Fried (1993b) and Barelli (1994) for a summary of nasopulmonary physiology.

At least nasal inhalations help the therapist assess whether the patient can breathe through the nose. Another interpretation of the calming effect is that breathing through the nose (or pursed lips discussed below) slows ventilation. The airways are smaller and offer more resistance (R. Ley, personal communication, March 23, 1994; Barelli, 1994). Fried (1993b) agrees and points out "one cannot easily hyperventilate when breathing through the nose" (p. 238).

Vagal Stimulation and Parasympathetic Dominance via Nasal Breathing and Diaphragm Movements Have a Calming Effect

This explanation suggests that in breathing therapy the regularity of the diaphragm's motion and/or the lungs' actions cause the abdominal contents to stimulate the vagus nerve gently. This promotes increased parasympathetic functioning (Hirai, 1975; Ajaya, 1976; Rama, 1979). The reader is directed to the review by Lichstein (1988) who notes that this is "plausable but unvalidated" (Lichstein, 1988, p. 35).

Contemporary Views

Contemporary views involve CO_2 changes or cognitive changes. The CO_2 view is the dominant one.

Carbon Dioxide

Briefly, the CO_2 level in the body is a vital psychophysiological gas. Part of it passes out in each exhalation. However, the blood must maintain a certain level of CO_2. It is necessary for regulating bodily processes such as blood pH and for stimulating automatic or involuntary respiration.

When the level of CO_2 is too high, the resulting condition is *hypercapnia*. This has important implications for relaxation. Insufficient breathing increases the CO_2 level. Hypoventilation leads to elevated arterial CO_2, that is, hypercapnia. Breath-holding for several seconds (e.g., 5–10) and shallow, slow breathing producing *hypoventilation* are two common examples of how people create mild hypercapnia. The first increases the CO_2 much faster.

Mild hypercapnia occurs from an increase of only about 10%. It starts a complex central and peripheral body process with several effects. These include slowing heart rate, dilation of peripheral vasculature, stimulation of gastric secretions, depressed cortical activity, and global sensation of mild somnolence (Lichstein, 1988, pp. 36–37; Ley, 1988a). This normally occurs in the transitions from wakefulness to drowsiness to sound sleep (Lichstein, 1988; Naifeh, Kamiya, & Sweet, 1982).

Too much breathing is too much of a good thing. Hypocapnia means not enough CO_2 in the blood. This brings us to HV, or too much breathing. Ley (1988a, 1988b, 1993) asserts that hypocapnia occurs when the total amount of air breathed exceeds the metabolic needs of the body. Breathing with more than the number of breaths needed at a particular time (respiration rate) and/or taking in larger volumes of air than needed (tidal volume) per minute (minute volume) reduces the CO_2 in the blood.

Hypocapnia also involves increased pH or the alkalinity level of the blood. The kidneys automatically compensate by excreting bicarbonate (base) which, in turn, helps maintains the pH balance. In essence, this model suggests that when a person breathes too much air and does so too often, it creates a chronically altered level of pCO_2. This gives rise to increased risk for hyperventilation symptoms when CO_2 drops further during rapid, deep breathing or during relaxation and sleep.

Cognitive Views

There are two models of how cognitive activity could be the active process explaining how breathing therapy reduces symptoms. I refer to these as "cognitive diversion" and "cognitive restructuring."

Cognitive Diversion. This view proposes that shifting attention away from worrisome, annoying, irritating, and similar thoughts results in a temporary, although incomplete, reduction of anxiety. This process is inherent in all relaxation therapies (Lichstein, 1988; Rosenthal, 1980).

One explanation of how relaxation procedures are successful for helping people with sleep-onset insomnia is that they divert attention from cognitive activity that contributes to the patient's staying awake. That does not mean that relaxation procedures have no physiological relaxation properties that are necessary for some patients. The cognitive explanation for how relaxation procedures help facilitate sleep onset means that for some patients cognitive activity is probably more important than physiological tension and arousal for maintaining wakefulness. Furthermore, cognitive activity often has arousal properties. For these people, relaxation procedures that divert attention away from this cognitive activity successfully help reduce the latency to sleep onset.

As Lichstein (1988) states, "breath manipulations fill our mind with unprovocative content . . . like any other emotionally neutral act capable of consuming attention" (p. 38). If this is true, then "more difficult or complex breathing patterns that naturally command more careful attention should prove to be more powerful relaxation techniques (Hirai, 1975, cited in Lichstein, 1988, p. 38). There is some indirect support, albeit incomplete, for this hypothesis (Worthington & Martin, 1980, cited in Lichstein, 1988, p. 38). Many Eastern and Western relaxation procedures (e.g., breath meditation, breath mindfulness, yoga, Zen, Benson's relaxation response, autogenic training, and Jacobson's progressive muscle relaxation [PMR]) focus on or include breathing. The reader is referred to Lichstein (1988) for an extensive discussion of this topic.

Cognitive Restructuring. Another cognitive model focuses on the anticipation of symptoms and cognitive beliefs or attributions about the symptoms. These cognitions can increase the risk of developing HV after physiological activation (see Garssen et al., 1992). For example, many people feel helpless and believe they have no control over the symptoms. They often lack understanding of the origin of the symptoms and attribute them to a serious disease. They often anticipate symptoms and engage in this type of cognitive activity that results in physiological arousal and some symptoms. Therefore, according to this model, these cognitions can increase the risk of developing HV after physiological activation.

Cognitive therapies include cognitive reattribution of the symptoms to HV rather than to a serious disease. Therapy also involves developing beliefs of self-efficacy and control over the symptoms. The implication is that patient education and cognitive-behavior therapies can be useful and sometimes essential parts of therapy. Breathing therapies often provide immediate relief, and relief can lead to cognitive restructuring that helps prevent future arousal and symptoms.

For the practitioner, it may not matter whether the patient's improvement is the result of practicing corrected breathing regularly, the diversion properties of relaxed breathing, altered cognitions, or a combination of these. For that matter, it may not matter to many patients. Prudent practitioners include both the physiological and cognitive components.

BREATHING THERAPY TECHNIQUES: NONINSTRUMENTATION-BASED/NONFEEDBACK AND PROPOSED MECHANISMS

There are several types of breathing therapy techniques that are used without psychophysiological monitoring and biofeedback. These include slow diaphragmatic breathing, paced respiration, breath meditation/breath mindfulness, rebreathing, and pursed-lip breathing (Berkow & Fletcher, 1992, p. 632).

Diaphragmatic Breathing, Slow

Slow diaphragmatic breathing is a very common technique used by practitioners. It probably is *the* most common. Using it, one teaches the patient to breathe with the diaphragm and minimize or stop the use of mid- to high-chest and accessory breathing muscles (e.g., shoulder raising). One standard goal is slowing respiration to about 6–8 b/min. This is much less than the 12–15 b/min typical for most people. Some practitioners strongly recommend 3–5 b/min. This often includes widening of the lower ribs. There is often a short pause after each exhalation.

Proposed mechanisms include increases in pCO_2. Cognitive elements of distraction and restructuring also may be important. Practitioners often use various types of biofeedback instruments with this technique. These include stretch gauges for chest and abdominal movements, EMG from accessory breathing muscles, volume devices, and capnographic measures of pCO_2 and O_2.

Paced Respiration

Inhaling and exhaling at a predetermined rate is called *paced respiration* (Clark & Hirschman, 1990; Lichstein, 1988). Therapists who use this technique suggest that patients coordinate the rate with a device such as a metronome that allows a preset rhythm. A summary of the rationale, value, and research with paced respiration (Clark & Hirschman, 1990) emphasizes the justification of paced respiration. For example, reduced electrodermal responsiveness and lowered ratings of subjective discomfort in response to threat both occur with paced respiration below the baseline rate of nonclinical and clinical subjects (Clark & Hirschman, 1990).

Clark and Hirschman (1990) point to the potential advantage of using respiratory cues over other somatic and autonomic nervous system (ANS) cues. They note the evidence supporting the generalized ANS effects accompanying respiratory changes because of the coupling of the somatic and ANS systems. They also note the association of anxiety and tension with respiratory changes and the fact that various stress reduction techniques include variations of paced respiration. They understandably focus on the reduction of symptoms such as panic attacks and HV that can accompany use of paced respiration.

This rationale for paced respiration is the same for most or all relaxed breathing therapies. They involve slowing the respiratory rate to below the usual or baseline rate and involve a regular breathing rhythm. The advantage of so-called "paced respiration" is the use of an external pacing device. This may be especially useful for some people in the early stages of breathing therapy and when the clinician is providing abbreviated office therapy in a stepped-care protocol.

In a sample of alcohol-dependent male inpatients with high trait anxiety, Clark and Hirschman (1990) used a 10-minute pacing procedure. This resulted in significantly more reduction of self-reported tension and state anxiety than an attention-control procedure. The use of an external cue with tones helped them pace themselves better than without it. The external cue was an audiotaped alternation of two tones (800 and 900 Hz) changing every 3 seconds providing a rate of 10 respiration cycles per minute. The investigators have suggested longer training periods especially to consolidate the learned pacing rate that drifted back to baseline without the external pacing signal.

One may wonder about the 10-cycles-per-minute pacing procedure. It was slower than the typical baseline of about 16+ b/min in the subjects of Clark and Hirschman (1990), a rate often associated with anxiety. However, it was not as slow as the more common goal of 6–8 b/min used in other breathing therapies. Clark and Hirschman (1990) report the average rate for these subjects as 11, but their table shows a rate of 13–14. Both figures are slower than the control group average of 18, but not the 10 b/min specified. One wonders how relaxing it is to breath at a rate of 11 or 13 b/min while listening to alternating tones at a rate of 10 per minute. Last, this study examined only intrasession relaxation.

Caution

Some authorities (R. Fried, personal communication, March 13, 1994; E. Peper, personal communication, March 20, 1994) express concern about the potential for harm from fixed-paced breathing. Part of their concern is that this technique alone ignores the vital role of increased tidal volume with normal pCO_2. When tidal volume rises, breathing rate drops proportionately assuming constant metabolism. Slowing breathing without raising tidal volume can result in hypoventilation. In a patient with emphysema, O_2 drops abruptly.

Breath Meditation and Breath Mindfulness

Methods of breath meditation noted by Lichstein (1988) include *passive breath mindfulness* and *breath holding*. The origins of these methods include yoga and Zen Buddhism. Western-derived relaxation procedures such as PMR also include being mindful of breathing. Lichstein (1988) provides a review of the theories, methods, and research for breath meditation and mindfulness, and other meditative methods. Practitioners should have access to that book.

In most methods, patients focus their attention on breathing. This allows the emergence of natural breathing and thus facilitates altered breathing. In meditative techniques, one often combines the breathing focus with "a mantra, counting, fixed gaze on an external object, or a relaxation cue word" (Lichstein, p. 163). Other schools of meditation also include breathing but with less focus upon it.

The methods of slow diaphragmatic breathing and paced respiration are more contemporary and secularized versions. Unlike the meditation methods, these allow open eyes and do not require imagery. These changes probably make the methods more practical and acceptable to more people.

Various theories attribute the positive therapeutic effects of these breathing techniques to cultivating right-hemisphere functioning, nasal air flow, diaphragm movement and gentle stimulation of the vagus nerve, CO_2 changes, and cognitive distraction. Most research supports the CO_2 hypothesis. The research for the other theories and methods is less supportive and equivocal at best. However, this should not detract from consideration of the use of breath-meditative procedure and breath-mindfulness procedures with selected patients. One matches procedures with patients and symptoms.

Rebreathing

Rebreathing is obviously not a relaxation technique. However, it is a noninstrumentation technique for stopping HV and physiological panic symptoms. It is an old and very common technique recommended by many physicians (Compernolle, Hoogduin, & Joele, 1979) and some respiratory and physiotherapists (Holloway, 1994). Interestingly, there were no controlled studies of rebreathing found before the analog study by van den Hout, Boek, van der Molen, Jansen, and Griez (1988). They studied medical students and supported the value for rapidly raising pCO_2.

However, restoring pCO_2 faster in a closed system did not reduce physical symptoms faster than when subjects were rebreathing in an open system that they thought was closed. Thus, rebreathing expired air into a bag that was in a semiclosed system yielded similar results in symptom changes compared to the closed system. This study did not reliably support the physiological rationale for the effectiveness of the technique among healthy young medical students. The interpretation was that distraction and/or instructions, and patient's expectations, may be important factors in its success. The authors acknowledge the limits of generalizing this to clinical patients. This study should not discourage practitioners from using the paper-bag technique for some patients. It does support the role of expectation and other cognitive factors for at least some patients. It casts some doubt on the necessary relationship of restoring CO_2 and the subsiding of symptoms.

Holloway (1994, pp. 170–171) suggests using the paper-bag rebreathing method in emergencies when other methods are not successful. She recommends 6–12 easy and natural breaths in the bag covering the nose and mouth. The patient should continue abdominal breathing after removing the bag. The technique may be repeated as necessary.

van den Hout et al. (1988) suggested that some people may "show marked post-rebreathing hypocapnia overshoots" (p. 308). This occurs after using the rebreathing technique with a fully closed system. The study used normal subjects. However, this is consistent with their earlier work (van den Hout & Griez, 1985) on posthypercapnic overshoot leading to hypocapnia in some panic patients. The authors speculated that the mechanism is a hypersensitive chemoreceptory system, at least in panic patients. They argued for caution using rebreathing, at least with panic patients. Readers should note that the Compernolle et al. (1979) technique involves placing a few fingers "inside the bag to provide some air and prevent hypoxemia which can cause hyperventilation" (p. 621).

The rebreathing technique with a paper bag has value for some patients. The value of the research from the Netherlands group is in providing some cautions and supporting the role of cognitive factors. As long as the CO_2 levels theory remains prominent as an explanation for the cause of symptoms of many patients, then a rebreathing technique is logical. The role of cognitive factors at least for some people is not surprising. It does not negate the role of CO_2. Both physiological and cognitive factors are operative with many applied psychophysiological and behavioral therapies for physical symptoms among many patients.

Holloway (1994) cautions against using this method "as an easy way out" (p. 171). Also, she cautions, avoid plastic bags!

Pursed-Lip Breathing

Pursed-lip breathing (PLB) is a commonly used respiratory therapy indicated for patients with "advanced [chronic obstructive pulmonary disease] COPD who hyperinflate their lungs during attacks of bronchospasm, panic, or exercise; and as an adjunctive measure in patients undergoing exercise rehabilitation or respiratory muscle training" (Berkow & Fletcher, 1992, p. 632). The patient exhales very slowly with lips partially closed "as if ready to whistle" (p. 632). Patients with advanced COPD take small inhaled breaths to avoid and decrease hyperinflation. Tiep et al. (1986, 1992) used this technique successfully with O_2 feedback for patients with COPD. The mechanisms by which they felt this could help patients included increased oxygen saturation, breathing at higher lung volumes, slower breathing rate, and increased expiratory volumes.

Patients without COPD can use pursed-lip breathing with deeper breaths. It makes good sense to consider this technique with non-COPD patients. Ideally, one would use O_2 monitoring/feedback instruments, although they are probably not needed for all patients. I could find no research on the use of PLB with patients other than those with COPD.

INSTRUMENTATION-BASED BREATHING FEEDBACK

There are several instrumentation-based breathing feedback systems used to enhance relaxed breathing. All are logical and in use by practitioners. There is no research showing any differential outcomes among them. Practitioners use those systems that are available and for which they feel most comfortable.

Nasal-Air-Flow Temperatures[10]

A thermistor (an electrical resistor that measures temperature) taped below a nostril detects the changes in temperature of air inhaled and exhaled. Inhaled air is cooler, and exhaled air is warmer. With a computer-based visual display set sensitively, a therapist and patient can clearly see the rapid changes in temperature. During inhalation, the temperature falls, and then rises during exhalation. One sees hills and valleys in the curve on the screen. One goal is to make the hills and valleys about the same size and duration. The patient watches the curve and with this feedback regulates the size and timing of breaths to create a regular rhythm of hills and valleys in the curve.

The clinician should set the display screen width to a time reflecting a few inhalations and exhalations. The temperature should be centered in the middle of the screen, and the range of temperature (sensitivity) set to create hills and valleys that are easy to see. The temperatures should not extend beyond the limits of the screen. The range depends partly on the patient. Therapists starting to use this technique will often try it with themselves first. They should consider starting with a display in which the range is at or less than about 5° Fahrenheit and tailor it for the individual.

This is a simple technique requiring only one temperature feedback unit and a simple computer-based software display. However, it does not give any other information such as that about muscles used and CO_2. Therefore, practitioners often use it in conjunction with other feedback instruments.

One caution is that to avoid transmission of infections from the nose, therapists must be very careful to disinfect the thermistor between sessions for all patients.

Strain Gauges

Many practitioners use stretchable devices wrapped around the abdomen, chest, or both. These allow monitoring and feedback about abnormal breathing patterns such as irregularity, breath-holding, and apneas. Therapists also use this to help teach new breathing patterns. It is better than observation alone (Timmons, 1994). The device has sensors that convey the degree of expansion. These connect to a computer-based feedback system that allows viewing the signals on a computer monitor. The purpose of this type of system is to see the expansions in each body area. One sees the difference between the abdominal area and the chest area during each breath. The specific numbers are unimportant and may be different for each person. The numbers depend on the tightness of the bands and the sensitivity setting. The feedback signal provides hills and valleys that depend on the size of the breath and body area used. This is similar to the nasal-air measure. However, the advantage over the nasal-air measure is that it gives information about abdominal versus chest breathing. The reader should note the use of a strain gauge in the DeGuire et al. (1992) study of breathing retraining for hyperventilation for patients with functional chest or cardiac symptoms. Like the nasal-air-temperature measure, this method provides no information about other muscles or CO_2. There are technical limitations to this type of measurement. Movement artifact is one problem. Recalibration after movements and position

---

[10]Dr. Fried reminded me (personal communication, March 13, 1994) that he believes he was the first to use a thermistor to monitor nasal air flow. However, he expressed some embarassment as it was *only* a demonstration! His concern related to the potential for transmitting infections (e.g., staphillococcus). I thank him for this and have added the caution for careful disinfecting of the thermistor between all sessions.

changes may be necessary (Timmons, 1994). The reader is directed to Fried (1993b, p. 40), Timmons (1994, pp. 281–282), and Timmons and Meldrum (1993) for more discussion and references for using strain gauges.

Electromyography from Accessory Breathing Muscles

Practitioners also use electromyography (EMG) from accessory breathing muscles. They should consider using the sternomastoids, upper-back muscles including the rhomboids and levator scapulae, upper-chest muscles including the pectoralis and/or scalene muscles. The selection of muscles depends on therapist preference and practical considerations. The purpose is to show whether there are EMG increases from these muscles during each inhalation, the degree of the increases, and to give feedback to help the patient reduce these increases.

Incentive Inspirometer

This instrument is the one of choice by Erik Peper and his colleagues (Peper, Smith, & Waddell, 1987; Roland & Peper, 1987; Peper & Tibbetts, 1992; MacHose & Peper, 1991). They recommend the Voldyne "incentive inspirometer" (Sherwood Medical Corporation[11]) and the 4000-ml Coach inspirometer (DHD Medical Products[12]) to provide calibrated information about inhalation volume. An inspirometer is a device with a calibrated cylinder into which there is a movable piston that moves as one inhales. The position of the piston shows the amount inhaled. The capacity is 4,000 milliliters of air. Peper and Tibbetts (1994, in press) emphasize the need for an inspirometer that permits slow inhalations.

Advantages of this method include its very low cost and face validity. Each person has his or her own device costing less than $20. Each is reusable many times by the same person. Therapists can use this alone at least for part of therapy but often use other physiological measures as well. See Table 11.2 for a summary of the procedures adapted from Peper and his colleagues (Peper, Smith, & Waddell, 1987; Roland & Peper, 1987).

Peper and Tibbetts (in press) now combine EMG feedback from the scalene and trapezius muscles with the use of incentive inspirometer feedback for patients with asthma. They also use this combination with other patients. The rationale is to combine the teaching of slower breathing and with larger volumes while also reducing upper-thoracic EMG activity. The goal is to allow slow effortless inhalation after complete exhalation.

The authors used this combination with a protocol for desensitizing asthmatic-provoking triggers. They suggest that the combination of feedback modalities and an adaptation of their desensitization protocol could be useful for patients with HVS and panic.

Noncontact Respiration Feedback[13]

A noncontact infrared sensor suspends above the abdomen in this technique. The instrument detects the breathing rhythm, amplifies the signal, and converts this into visual and audio signals. The audio signals are a triad organ sound or white noise. Hooded goggles over the eyes and earphones provide synchronized feedback signals with inhaling and exhaling. During inhalation, lightness and volume increase; they grow dimmer and softer with exhalation. Available accessories provide for fading of music or voice. One also can

[11]11802 West Line Industrial Drive, St. Louis, MO 63146.

[12]125 Rasbach Street, Canastota, NY 13032.

[13]Human Dynamics, 6000 Park of Commerce Blvd, Boca Raton, FL 33487. Models 5000S and 1600.

TABLE 11.2. Procedures for Using Incentive Inspirometer and Other Physiological Modalities

Introduction and practice
1. Loosen tight/restrictive clothing (e.g., belt, buttons, upper part of pant zipper).
2. Sit upright.
3. Place inspirometer on table/desk at mouth level.
   (Use a second one if needed for inhalations larger than 4000 milliliters).
4. Explain general outline of session to patient.
5. Instruct in use of incentive inspirometer.
6. Practice one or two breaths to show understanding of the instruction to "breath in through the mouth and out through the nose."
7. Consider including EMG from trapezius and scalene muscles and strain gauges around the chest and abdomen. Using EMG feedback may help the patient avoid gasping. Also consider finger temperature, electrodermal, and/or pulse rate and/or blood volume pulse, nasal-air-flow temperatures, and/or CO_2.

Baseline recordings
1. Close your eyes.
2. Take five normal breaths.
   a. Tell patient when piston returns to zero line before next breath.
   b. Record maximum volume inhaled for each breath.
3. Instruct patient to take five maximum volume breaths.
   a. Record maximum volumes for each.
   b. The maximum volume may reach or exceed 4000 milliliters. Instruct patient to hold his or her breath for a moment and continue inhaling with the other inspirometer.
4. Instruct patient to perform tasks such as talking, writing, and cognitive stressors and observe breathing pattern, and record EMG, strain gauge information, and consider other modalities.

Diaphragmatic breathing instructions: No inspirometer/more baseline
1. Tell the patient to open his or her eyes.
2. Explain the rationale for diaphragmatic breathing.
3. Allow very slow inhalations. Allow the abdominal area and sides of rib cage to expand before filling the chest cavity.
4. Relax the shoulders and chest until the end of inhalation.
5. Practice exhaling by slightly pulling in the abdomen at end of each exhalation. Wait for inhalation to occur.
6. Repeat instructions and demonstrate diaphragmatic breathing two to three times.
7. Ask the patient to close his or her eyes.
8. Added baseline: Instruct the patient to take five maximum inhalations. Record the maximum volume for each.

Therapy procedures
(This is inhalation volume feedback and guidance.[a] One may do this over multiple sessions. The goal is effortless breathing.}
1. Help patient's exhalation by applying gentle pressure to abdomen and/or sides of the abdomen with therapist's hand.
2. Help patient's inhalation by placing therapist hands on his or her abdomen and/or sides and encouraging the patient to *expand* slightly.
3. Help the patient to relax his or her shoulders:
   a. Apply slight pressure on top of the shoulders.
   b. Gently shake or rock the shoulders.
   c. Instruct some patients to tense slightly and relax.
4. Discuss patient's feelings and sensitivity about the abdomen expanding.
5. Practice relaxation of shoulders and upper chest during inhalations.
   a. Give verbal and/or EMG biofeedback from either trapizius or scalene muscles about relaxation of shoulders. At the volume peak, record the EMG.

(*continued*)

TABLE 11.2. (*continued*)

Therapy procedures

6. Practice increasing volumes while reducing scalene and trapius EMG. Exhaling slowly and completely are the main goals. Patient should inhale increased volume (e.g., 500, 1000, . . . 4000 milliliters) for at least two trials.
7. Compare chest versus diaphramatic breaths.
   a. Take large chest breath and observe volume.
   b. Take slow diaphragmatic breath and observe volume.
8. Patient observes pattern with inspirometer, EMG, and strain gauge feedback.
9. Patient shows any problems with breathing. Repeat diaphramatic breathing.
10. Instruct patient in various strategies for exhalations.
    a. Whispering "Haaaa" sound.
    b. Using pursed lips.
    c. Therapist modeling and exhaling audibly slightly longer than patient during practice.
    d. Patient imagining air flowing in and out through body or balloon expanding and contracting.
    e. Using gentle contact with patient's shoulders and abdomen.
11. Reduce upper-thoracic breathing during inhalations. Increase abdominal displacement. Increase exhalation time.
12. In addition to volume, EMG, and strain gauge information, consider using electrodermal, pulse, and temperature information as guides. Generally, temperature should increase or remain warm, SCL should decrease or remain low, pulse rate should decrease or remain low. Respiratory sinus arrhythmia (RSA) should increase. Patient should breathe effortlessly to maximize RSA.

Postinstruction

1. Sustain relaxed breathing for at least 10 minutes with eyes closed and open.
2. Sustain relaxed breathing during selected tasks graduated in arousal potential: cognitive stress, writing, using a computer keyboard, standing, walking, talking.
3. Continue to observe feasible psychophysiological modalities as guides.
4. Review instructions for daily practice and applications.
   a. Self-observations of breathing.
   b. Resume relaxed breathing for various periods (few minutes to 15+ minutes) as indicated (i.e., regardless of arousal or symptoms, when anticipating stress, during all resting and relaxation periods, and with first signs of arousal or symptoms).
   c. Repeat several times a day.

Notes. Each modality and physiological variable may be different for each patient. Peper and Tibbitts (1994) properly warn against forcing breathing to match standards such as volume and rate. They also wisely warn practitioners to discourage patients from premature discontinuing of prescribed medications. They also allude to potential negative side effects associated with exhaling too rapidly, hyperventilation, and a variety of RIA symptoms (see Chapter 12) and encourage practitioners to be aware and prepared for these.

*a*Not all needed with every patient. Typically used are: 1, 2, 3, 5, 7.

provide visual feedback away from the patient's head instead of in the goggles. Recorded summary data are for comparisons across sessions and patients.

The Capnometer and Oximeter Method

This method allows measurement and feedback of end-tidal CO_2 and good estimates of arterial blood O_2 saturation (PaO_2). One inserts a narrow plastic tube about .25 inches into either nostril (Fried, 1987, 1993b, personal communication, March 13, 1994).[14]

[14]Fried (1993) specified the right nostril but did not specify why. He tells me that either nostril is acceptable. He used the right nostril for convenience because he sits to the right of the patient.

The tube's outer width is about 4 millimeters. One tapes the tube to the skin near the upper lip.

This method allows continuous sampling of end-tidal breath conducted to an infra-red gas analyzer. The signal then goes to a computer that feeds back the wave of rising and falling $PetCO_2$ on a video monitor. It provides hard copy output of the pattern and gives statistics for specified periods. The therapist can place a goal wave for size and rate of the breaths. Fried (1993b) uses a capnograph and a J & J physiological monitoring and feedback system. One needs a system that recognizes and displays analyzed blood gas data.

Spirometry

For therapists without access to a capnometer, L. C. Lum (cited in Timmons, 1994) recommends "spirometry." This is a measure of the amount of air moved. Nonphysicians and nonphysiologists should consider the smaller, less expensive, and relatively accurate Wright spirometer (Timmons, 1994). This allows an estimate of overbreathing by providing an estimate of minute volume. Normal resting minute volume is about 6 liters (Naifeh, 1994). An example of a criterion for overbreathing is 30 liters per minute (L. C. Lum, 1991, personal communication to Timmons).

Arterial Blood Oxyhemoglobin Saturation: Oximetry

Fried (1993b) uses and recommends this measure. One uses a device called an oximeter attached to the index finger. One also could use an ear lobe, a practice commonly employed by sleep laboratories for overnight oximetry for assessing decreased O_2 saturations in patients with obstructive sleep apnea. The output from the oximeter connects to a physiological monitoring system (e.g., J & J I-430 System I-801 module). The oximeter shows percentage of saturated hemoglobin (OHb), and the biofeedback display shows the saturation of arterial blood oxygen over each breath cycle.

This display shows variations of O_2. It gives an index of the O_2 delivery to tissues during monitoring $PetCO_2$. For example, normal pCO_2 and elevated O_2 perfusion in the blood (SaO_2) reflects O_2 perfusion expected with deep diaphragmatic breathing. Some experts wonder about the accuracy of this index. Contrast this to reduced O_2 in the tissues associated with hypocapnia.

Skin Temperatures: Hand and Head-Apex

This is an indirect measure of breathing according to Fried (1993b). He attaches the temperature sensor to the fifth digit of the nondominant hand. Other practitioners may use other digits. By itself, skin temperature is not a good index. However, it is a common index of relaxation and often monitored during breathing therapy procedures.

Fried's (1993b) unique contribution is the temperature sensor attached to the scalp apex. Normal levels of CO_2 increase cerebral blood flow. Fried asserts that this placement gives an index of blood flow in the brain. This procedure and its value as an indirect index of normalized and relaxed breathing await research.

Plethysmography: Pulse Rate and Sinus Rhythm

Another indirect measure is pulse information (Fried, 1993b). A common placement is the second digit of the right hand. A biofeedback interface allows for measurement of variations of beat-to-beat pulse. This is an index of vagal tone and respiratory sinus arrhythmia (RSA) during the breath cycles and provides an indirect index of cardiopulmonary status.

Invasive Instruments

All the above instruments are totally or essentially noninvasive. The capnographic method requires a small nasal cathether inserted only ¼ inch into a nostril. This is not invasive. Invasive instruments include *blood gas analyzers*. These *directly* measure acid–base balances (pH), partial pressures of arterial oxygen (pO_2) and carbon dioxide (pCO_2), bicarbonate level (HCO_3), and arterial oxygen saturation (SaO_2). This chapter does not discuss them as they are used in psychophysiological research and not in clinical practice.

SELECTED ISSUES, QUESTIONS, AND METHODOLOGY PROBLEMS

There remain many issues and questions about breathing therapies in clinical practice. The following represent only a sample of those that impress me as important and pertinent.

- When can practitioners use breathing therapies alone and when do they need to combine these with other therapies such as other relaxation and cognitive therapies? For example, will breathing therapy alone be sufficient for a patient whose symptoms appear primarily or only to result from HV?
- What are the proper or fundamental qualifications for practitioners and therapists providing breathing therapies? Several authorities caution that therapists must be properly trained and competent (Timmons, 1994, pp. 269, 278; Holloway, 1994, pp. 173– 174). Knowledge of anatomy, the mechanics of breathing, and respiratory diseases is essential. Furthermore, these authors recommend that therapists be models of relaxed abdominal breathing. Clinical or counseling psychology education, training, and competence are often useful and sometimes necessary (Fried, 1993b). Emotional and clinically important content often arises during relaxation sessions including those with breathing retraining. This is consistent with the teachings of L. C. Lum, a chest physician and pioneer in this field (cited in Timmons, 1994) who "often emphasized in his teaching, the single most important characteristic of therapists in this field is *empathy*" (p. 269).
- When should practitioners use biofeedback as part of breathing therapies? The answer is probably similar to that for other applications. Most practitioners do not have capnographic feedback. They must rely on other measures of breathing. When does the advantage of direct measures of the gases affect clinical results? Does it matter what information the therapist feeds back to the patient? There is no research comparing techniques, instruments, and procedures. Individual practitioner preferences and experience are still the main determinants.
- What should practitioners communicate to patients about the role of breathing and symptoms and the effects of breathing therapies? This is a very complicated and challenging subject for many professionals to understand. Thus, it is more complex for most patients to understand. However, patients need some rationale. There are no patient-education booklets on this subject.
- It is also possible that larger than normal *increases* in pCO_2 occur during sleep for some people (see Craske & Barlow, 1990, and the critical commentary by Ley, 1991, of

Craske & Barlow). One would need monitoring during sleep in a sleep laboratory to show this. This is not practical in routine clinical practice except perhaps in extreme cases. An example of such an extreme case would be when the symptoms are very severe and disabling, and other less expensive and more conservative assessments and interventions were not enough to give relief. Also, it should be noted that some patients hyperventilate during sleep (R. Fried, personal communication, March 13, 1994).

• Which specific breathing rates and pCO_2 levels are necessary to achieve desired effects for specific patients? The literature contains various recommendations.

• A serious methodological problem is that patients usually are unavailable during their panic symptoms in the natural environment. Thus, practitioners must make inferences based on history, office monitoring, and attempts to provoke symptoms. Monitoring baseline breathing and symptoms in the office is of limited value. For example, patients with presumed muscle tension-related symptoms can have normal resting muscles in the practitioner's office. So too, people with presumed HV-related symptoms can have normal breathing and blood chemistries.

The "chicken and egg" problem also is crucial.[15] Hyperventilation and symptoms occurring simultaneously do *not* mean that HV caused the symptoms. Similarly, a drop in arterial pCO_2 during HV and presence of symptoms do *not* mean that the drop in pCO_2 caused all the symptoms. Ambulatory transcutaneous monitoring of pCO_2 offers a partial remedy for this problem and might help answer many vexing questions. A recently developed method for transcutaneous (tc) monitoring referred to as $p_{tc}CO_2$ attempts to accomplish this. It has potential value in research and perhaps in clinical practice. However, there are questions and concerns about its reliability. Timmons (1994) notes the "slow response time and insensitivity to small changes in pCO_2" (p. 283). This instrument typically requires a multidisciplinary and collaborative approach.

• People with chronic frequent HV are easier to study. They often, but not reliably, show blood chemistry changes reflecting renal compensation for respiratory alkalosis. However, one study showed this in only 14% of HVS patients (Folgering, 1986, cited in Garssen et al., 1992).

CONCLUSIONS AND TREATMENT IMPLICATIONS

This chapter assumes that abnormal breathing styles such as HV are major factors resulting in or aggravating an array of symptoms. These include HVS, panic episodes of many patients while awake and during sleep, RIA, and noncardiac chest pain and related chest symptoms. Another assumption is that respiration therapies are logical and proper for these symptoms. Relaxed breathing methods often rapidly result in physiological relaxation. These methods can reduce or stop emotional distress even for patients not treated with other relaxation methods.

There are multiple explanations for how relaxation therapies work in general. Similarly, there are multiple explanations for how breathing therapies work. There is no universal agreement among practitioners and researchers about how these therapies work. Possible explanations include altered CO_2 and altered O_2 levels, cognitive changes, and cortical and subcortical changes.

---

[15]I include Fried's playful commentary (personal communication, March 13, 1994). He informed me that when someone asked Darwin "Which came first, the chicken or the egg?" Darwin replied, "It was an almost chick that laid the egg from which the chicken emerged." From this, Fried concludes that "the egg came first!"

This chapter assumes that these therapies often alter biochemical mechanisms crucial to causing symptoms and crucial for stopping them. A very common assumption and particularly promising explanation is that altered carbon dioxide (pCO_2) is often crucial.

Slow, diaphragmatic (abdominal) breathing is the most common breathing method. Deeper than usual breathing is a common part of this method. However, slow and abdominal breathing also characterize other relaxation techniques. Furthermore, breathing therapy procedures require voluntary actions and thus a diversion from other cognitive activity such as anxious and angry thoughts.

Another assumption is that many people who often experience HV are more prone to RIA and panic symptoms. A vulnerable situation arises when one abruptly stops vigorous exercise without voluntarily reducing the volume of air breathed each minute. For people who chronically experience HV, there may be more risk of symptoms during sedentary activities after hyperpneic breathing (increased depth and rate of respiration; panting) (Ley 1988a). Such occasions might include while driving or watching television or movies. Minute volume remains constant and greater than normal or may increase in heavy traffic or when the patient is watching violence. One expects low metabolic production of CO_2 because of low physical energy needs during these activities. Panic attacks may occur, however, from this combination of events.

Therapy Implications

Respiration therapy should be included in the treatment of a variety of symptoms and disorders. These include the symptoms of many patients with anxiety disorders such as panic, functional chest and cardiac symptoms, some tachycardia conditions, RIA, HVS, and asthma.

1. *Practitioners and cautions.* There are signs on the ski lift poles of a Colorado ski resort that read "Know your limit, ski within it." That saying applies to many aspects of life. In this context, know your limit, *practice* within it. Understanding breathing physiology and measurement and using this knowledge in treatment are complex. Employing this method requires both considerable knowledge and proper training. Several authorities emphasize the importance of practitioners having proper understanding of anatomy, physiology, disorders, and breathing techniques and cautions. For example, Timmons (1994) emphasizes that "faulty technique or inexperience may lead to complications in treatment" (p. 276). Discussing the importance of proper qualifications for practitioners and therapists, she refers to Bass (1994) and states that "it is possible to make some hyperventilators worse with breathing exercises, at least in the early stages of training" (p. 278).

Close collaboration with properly trained and credentialed professionals is prudent. Practitioners should collaborate with physicians who treat patients with chronic lung diseases. This is important for nonphysician practitioners. They should consider learning and using techniques used by properly credentialed respiratory and physical therapists experienced with chronic lung diseases. They should consider collaboration with these therapists, as well. Referral of selected patients is sometimes more prudent.

2. *Matters concerning intake, patient education, and starting therapy.* Credible patient education is an important component in treating breathing-related symptoms and disorders. Holloway (1994) emphasizes and discusses patient education and demonstrations for patients. The therapist should consider using a printed patient-education booklet. Holloway (1994) suggests the patient-education book on HVS by Bradley (1991). I am not yet familiar with this volume and reserve judgment about it.

Some patients should consider having a spouse or close friend present to help reinforce the procedures at home and remind the patient of the procedures. This may be especially useful for patients with impaired concentration and memory (Holloway, 1994, p. 164).

Therapists should consider using the HVPT and stressful tasks to provoke symptoms in the office. Stressful tasks include time-pressured difficult tasks and thinking about personal events associated with naturally occurring symptoms. Proper safeguards must be employed when one is using HVPT.

Some clinicians suggest that some patients become "obsessed" with their breathing (Timmons, 1994). Timmons agrees but adds that this is rare. It is not a contraindication to using breathing retraining for most patients. Experienced and prudent practitioners can assess this tendency and manage it early. For example, Timmons (1994) suggests helping these patients focus on general relaxation.

Many patients are using tranquilizers and/or sleeping medications when they present for relaxation and breathing therapy. Timmons (1994) states that "many psychotherapists consider it unethical to accept clients who are on tranquilizers or sleeping medications" (p. 279). The reason given is they are "unlikely to learn while their feelings are blunted [*and*] the ability to learn new breathing patterns may be diminished as well" (p. 279).

However, many patients need to continue these medications, at least for a while. Examples are patients with severe anxiety. They may need the medications to lower their arousal level enough to cooperate with other treatments. Furthermore, I know of no research that shows that these patients cannot or do not benefit from breathing therapies. However, some patients probably should withdraw from the medications before breathing therapy. For example, reduction or cessation of some medications may allow HV symptoms to emerge that were suppressed by the drug.

3. *Therapy without instrumentation.* Practitioners can provide successful breathing therapy without physiological instrumentation-based feedback. For example, many therapists use a light sandbag (a few pounds) or an open, large city telephone directory or other large book placed on the abdomen. This provides sensory feedback from the pressure of the weight. It helps maintain the patient's awareness of the body area and thus provides continuous feedback. Also, therapists can place one hand over the sternum or chest and the other hand over the abdominal wall. At first, some therapists may place their hands over or under the patient's hands.

4. *Therapy with instrumentation.* Feedback instrumentation is often useful for many patients. This chapter describes such instruments. The usefulness of such instruments is increasingly recognized in research and clinical practice (see Chapter 3B for part of the rationale for instrumentation-based feedback).

Physiological measures, such as CO_2, can be useful in therapy and are often necessary in research. Furthermore, physiological monitoring of breathing probably has value for the practitioner even when it has less value for the patient. It provides much information and more accurate information for both the therapist–practitioner and the patient. It quantifies breathing parameters so the therapist can sometimes treat the patient more efficiently. For example, instrumentation provides information about respiration rate, the magnitude and volume of breaths, the areas of the body used in the breaths, the pattern and regularity of breaths, blood chemistries, and changes within and between sessions.

However, the absence of physiological measures does not mean that one cannot treat successfully. Physiological changes are probably only part of the reason explaining improved symptoms from HV. Distraction and other cognitive techniques affecting attributions and expectations probably are important for many patients.

5. *Techniques.* A common relaxed breathing method consists of slow, deep, abdominal

inhalations for a few to several seconds and slow exhalations. The respiration cycles are typically at least 50% less than typical breathing rates. Holloway (1994) encourages patients "to count slowly and silently while practicing breathing exercises, aiming for a rate of 6–8 breaths per minute" (p. 166). Inhalations are from 4–8 seconds.

Some techniques include brief pauses for a few to several seconds after the inhalation. This increases blood CO_2. However, contrary to some other methods of breathing therapy, some therapists caution against pausing after the inhalation and recommend pausing after the exhalation (Holloway, 1994).

> There must be no holding of inspired air. . . . [It] exacerbates some symptoms, particularly cardiac arhythmias and chest pains. . . . The inspiratory phases should flow naturally into the relaxed expiratory phase. . . . A pause is encouraged after the expiration. [Also], contrary to many methods of breathing exercise, *inspiration* is the active phase. Expiration is passive and relaxed, and a pause should occur at the end of expiration. (p. 165)

However, I found no data supporting either of these cautions and recommendations.

Patients should be instructed to feel themselves becoming more relaxed as they slowly exhale. Therapists should consider saying cue words with the exhalation. The therapist repeats this cycle a few times for about 1 minute and usually longer. Practice periods are often at least once per day for 5–20 minutes each. Application is often for briefer periods many times per day to reduce the frequency of HV throughout waking hours. Patients do this with eyes open or closed. The use of a pacing method or device comparable to a metronome (sometimes called paced respiration) may help some patients.

Therapists should use structured tasks that distract patients from their anxiety and other symptoms. The goal is to increase the perception of control and increase thoughts of self-efficacy. Techniques including general relaxation, breathing therapies, cognitive distraction, and cognitive reattribution can serve this purpose.

Practitioners might also consider brief periods of breath-holding up to 5–10 seconds or pursed-lip breathing to increase the CO_2 level. They should consider suggesting these methods to avoid hypocapnia for selected patients.

A mirror may be used to help the patient "observe areas of movement while breathing. Attention may be drawn to sternomastoid tensing and movement of the sternum and clavicles" (Holloway, 1994, p. 166).

After the patient has demonstrated ability to maintain a desired breathing pattern in a relaxed posture, the therapist might suggest changing to other positions to help transfer of training. For example, he or she can switch the patient to sitting upright, standing and leaning against a wall, standing, slow walking, and fast walking (Holloway, 1994). There is less abdominal excursion while standing. The therapist should discourge tightening of the abdominal muscles and carefully note breathing rhythms and correct patients when he or she observes abdominal tensing and noisy breathing. The toning of abdominal muscles should be encouraged and abdominal exercises tailored to the patient. Age, general condition, and back problems must all be considered.

6. *Daily practice and application.* Therapists should correct faulty breathing patterns during daily activities. They should discourage patients from "talking continuously in a steady stream, using long sentences, and then gasping and taking a sudden inhalation before setting off again! . . . [and, instead,] encourage short, concise sentences in a low register most of the time" (Holloway, 1994, p. 169).

Patients should also avoid "tight trousers or jeans, corsets, panty girdles, and belts" (Holloway, 1994, p. 170; also, see MacHose & Peper, 1991). These encourage upper-chest movements and inhibit abdominal movement. Weaning patients away from tight clothing can be difficult for many patients.

Patients should be encouraged to reduce breathing rate and volume when starting relaxation. They should reduce inhalation volume very soon after stopping exercise or gradually slow down near the end of exercising. For example, patients can walk and cool off until breathing is slower. They can get up often while watching television or otherwise move around, which might reduce the frequency of the symptoms. They can also do isometric exercises.

Therapists can encourage patients to suppress coughs, sighs, sniffs, and yawns. Patients can control sighs and yawns by either "swallowing or hold[ing] the breath to a count of five, breathing out slowly, holding to five again, and then resuming easy abdominal breathing" (Holloway, 1994, p. 166).

Therapists should consider instructions for the paper bag technique as an emergency technique, and patients should practice this first with supervision.

Closing Remark

"It is better not to change a patient's breathing unless you know what you're doing" (L. C. Lum, 1991, cited in Timmons, 1994, p. 276).

GLOSSARY

ACIDOSIS. Acidosis stems from a buildup of acid or depletion of the alkaline reserve (bicarbonate content) in blood and body tissues. There is an increased concentration of hydrogen ions. This is *decreased* pH. *Hypercapnic acidosis*, also called *respiratory acidosis*, results from excessive *retention* of CO_2. *Compensated respiratory acidosis* occurs when the kidneys compensate and raise the low pH toward normal. There also are other causes. Compare with alkalosis.

ALKALOSIS. Alkalosis stems from a buildup of base or alkali or from a loss of acid without comparable loss of base in body fluids. There is decreased hydrogen ion concentration. This *increases* pH. *Respiratory alkalosis* results from excess loss of CO_2 from the body. *Compensated respiratory alkalosis* occurs when the blood pH returns toward normal by acid retention or kidney mechanisms that excrete base (bicarbonate). There also are other causes. Compare with acidosis.

BASE. In chemistry, a base is the nonacid part of a salt. It produces hydroxide ions in liquids such as blood.

BICARBONATE. A type of salt (HCO_3^-). *Blood bicarbonate* is an index of the alkaline reserve level.

BREATHS PER MINUTE (B/MIN). Normal b/min usually ranges from 8–15, sometimes slighty higher. An abnormally high rate usually is above 15.

BUFFER AND BICARBONATE BUFFERING SYSTEM. In biochemistry, a buffer is any chemical system preventing change in concentration of another chemical substance such as hydrogen ion concentration (pH). The kidneys release bicarbonate as part of the *bicarbonate buffering system* of the body.

CAPNIA. A suffix referring to carbon dioxide. *Hypocapnia* is low or below-normal CO_2. *Hypercapnia* is high or above-normal CO_2.

CATARRH. Inflamation of mucous membranes with free discharge, especially of air passages of head and throat.

CIRCUMORAL. Around or near the mouth.

DYSPNEA. Labored or difficult breathing. *Functional dyspnea* is dyspnea not related to exercise and without an organic cause. *Sighing intermittent dyspnea* is very deep sighing respirations without a significant change in rate, without wheezing. It has functional or emotional causes rather than organic causes.

END-TIDAL pCO$_2$. A valid estimate of arterial pCO$_2$ in normal lungs.

HYPOCAPNIA. A deficiency of carbon dioxide in the blood resulting in alkalosis. Hyperventilation is one cause.

HYPOVENTILATION. Hypoventilation occurs when there is too little air entering the pulmonary alveoli.

HYPERPNEA. Breathing large volumes of air in each breath (cf. *tachypnea*).

HYPOXIA. Reduced oxygen to tissues below required levels. This can occur despite sufficient blood in the tissues. It can occur if not enough oxygen enters the blood, as with decreased barometric pressures at high altitudes. It can occur from decreased oxyhemoglobin (OHb) in the blood, which is partly a function of the pH of the blood and is affected by fluctuations of carbon dioxide and other gases. There are other causes.

ISOCAPNIC OVERVENTILATION TEST (IOT). A technique that artificially prevents lowered end-tidal CO$_2$ (PetCO$_2$) during hyperventilation by using a mixture of air enriched with CO$_2$.

PARESTHESIA. An abnormal sensation such as burning or prickling.

pH. pH represents the concentration level and ratio of alkalinity to acidity. A pH of 7.35 to 7.45 is neutral for blood. Above 7.45 means more alkalinity, and below that means more acidity. The symbol pH refers to the hydrogen ion (H$^+$) concentration or activity of a solution such as blood.

PRECORDIAL PAIN. Chest pain specifically over the heart and lower thorax. The thorax is between the neck and respiratory diaphragm.

PULMONARY ALVEOLI OR VESICLES. Tiny sacs at the ends of the bronchial tree through which gas exchanges with the pulmonary capillaries.

TACHYPNEA. Rapid cycles of inhaling and exhaling (cf. *hyperpnea*).

TORR. The unit of pressure equal to 1 millimeter Hg. It is used in the measurement of end-tidal CO$_2$.

Capacities

FUNCTIONAL RESIDUAL CAPACITY (FRC). The amount of air remaining at the end of normal quiet respiration.

INSPIRATORY CAPACITY (IC). The volume of gas that one can take into the lungs on a full inspiration. It starts from the resting inspiratory position and equals the tidal volume plus the inspiratory reserve volume.

TOTAL LUNG CAPACITY (TLC). Volume of gas contained in the lungs at the end of a maximal inspiration.

VITAL CAPACITY (VC). Volume of gas that one can clear from the lungs from a full inspiration, with no limit to the duration of expiration. It equals the inspiratory capacity plus the expiratory reserve volume.

Volumes

EXPIRATORY RESERVE VOLUME (ERV). Maximal amount of air expired from the resting end-expiratory level. Amount between tidal volume (V_T) and residual volume (RV). Vital capacity (VC) equals inspiratory capacity (IC) plus ERV.

INSPIRATORY RESERVE VOLUME (IRV). Maximum or limit of air one can inhale from the end-inspiratory position.

MINUTE VOLUME (MV). (1) "Quantity of gas (air) expelled from the lungs per minute" (*Dorland's Medical Dictionary*, p. 1847); (2) "volume of air expelled from the lungs per minute" (Dox et al., p. 521); (3) "sum of tidal volumes breathed per minute" (Ley, 1988a, p. 253); (4) "volume of air inspired per minute" (Kaufman & Schneiderman, 1986, p. 112).

RESIDUAL VOLUME (RV). Amount of gas remaining in the lungs at the end of a maximal expiration.

TETANY. Hyperexcitability of nerves and muscles. Muscular twitching, cramps, and exaggerated reflexes (hyperreflexia) are among the characteristics.

TIDAL VOLUME (V_T). Amount of gas inspired and expired (i.e., ventilation) during one respiratory cycle of a normal breath.

Abbreviations Involving Oxygen

P_AO_2. Partial pressure of alveolar oxygen.

P_AO_2. Arterial partial pressure of oxygen.

SaO_2. Arterial blood saturation.

Abbreviations Involving Carbon Dioxide

$ETCO_2$. Partial pressure of CO_2 in end-tidal breath. Values usually in torr but can be in percent.

pCO_2. Partial pressure of CO_2 in alveolar (lung) air. Values in torr or percent. High positive correlation between $ETCO_2$ and pCO_2 often makes them interchangeable. When $ETCO_2$ is in percent, it is percent of end-tidal CO_2 or $PetCO_2$ (e.g., 38 torr = 5% $PetCO_2$).

$PaCO_2$, PCO_2, pCO_2. All three abbreviations, found in the literature, mean partial pressure of carbon dioxide. The first is arterial CO_2, and the others are options for the generic version.

$PetCO_2$. Percentage end-tidal CO_2.

$P_{TC}CO_2$. Transcutaneous estimate of pCO_2. It is closely related to arterial pCO_2, but with some delay from blood changes to transcutaneous values (Pilsbury & Hibbert, 1987).

ACKNOWLEDGMENTS

I am very thankful to Ronald Ley, Ph.D., Robert Fried, Ph.D., Eric Peper, Ph.D., and my colleague Charles D. Burger, M.D., for their reviews of an earlier draft of this chapter. Their many comments, suggestions, and corrections helped considerably. This appreciation in no way implies their endorsement of any of the content of this chapter.

I also pay respect to our Japanese colleagues (Umezawa, 1992, 1994) now adding to the knowledge in this area.

REFERENCES

Allen, J. P., Imbus, C. E., Powars, D. R., & Haywood, L. J. (1976). Neurologic impairment induced by hyperventilation in children with sickle cell anemia. *Pediatrics, 58,* 124-126.

Aronson, A. (1990). *Clinical voice disorders* (pp.349–369). New York: Thieme.

Backon, J. (1989). Nasal breathing as a treatment for hyperventilation: Relevance of hemispheric activation. *British Journal of Clinical Practice, 43,* 161–162.

Bacon, M., & Poppen, R. (1985). A behavioral analysis of diaphragmatic breathing and its effects on peripheral temperature. *Journal of Behavior Therapy and Experimental Psychiatry, 16,* 15–21.

Barlow, D. H. (1988). *Anxiety and its disorders: The nature and treatment of anxiety and panic.* New York: Guilford Press.

Bass, C. (1994). Management of patients with hyperventilation-related disorders. In B. H. Timmons & R. Ley (Eds.), *Behavioral and psychological approaches to breathing disorders* (pp. 149–155). New York: Plenum Press.

Beck, J. G., Berisford, M. A., Taegtmeyer, H., & Bennitt, A. (1990). Panic symptoms in chest pain without coronary artery disease: A comparison with panic disorder. *Behavior Therapy, 21,* 241–252.

Beitman, B. D. (1992). Panic disorder in patients with angiographically normal coronary arteries. *American Journal of Medicine, 92*(Suppl. 5A), 33–40.

Berkow, R., & Fletcher, A. J. (Eds.). (1992). *The Merck manual of diagnosis and therapy* (16th ed.). Rahway, NJ: Merck.

Bonn, J. A., Readhead, C. P. A., & Timmons, B. H. (1984). Enhanced adaptive behavioural response in agoraphobic patients pretreated with breathing retraining. *Lancet, ii,* 665–669.

Bradley, L. A., Richter, J. E., Scarinci, I. C., Haile, J. M., & Schan, C. A. (1992). Psychosocial and psychophysiological assessments of patients with unexplained chest pain. *American Journal of Medicine, 92*(Suppl. 5A), 65–73.

Brandly, D. (1991). *Hyperventilation syndrome.* Auckland, New Zealand: Tandem.

Carter, C., Maddock, R., Amsterdam, E., McCormick, S., Waters, C., & Billett, J. (1992). Panic disorder and chest pain in the coronary care unit. *Psychosomatics, 33*(3), 302–309.

Clark, D. M., & Hemsley, D. R. (1982). The effects of hyperventilation: Individual variability and its relation to personality. *Journal of Behavior Therapy and Experimental Psychiatry, 13*(1), 41–47.

Clark, M. E., & Hirschman, R. (1990). Effects of paced respiration on anxiety reduction in a clinical population. *Biofeedback and Self-Regulation, 15*(3), 273–284.

Clark, D. M., Salkovskis, P. M., & Chalkley, A. J. (1985). Respiratory control as a treatment for panic attacks. *Journal of Behavior Therapy and Experimental Psychiatry, 16*(1), 23–30.

Clouse, R. E. (1992). Psychopharmacologic approaches to therapy for chest pain of presumed esophageal origin. *American Journal of Medicine, 92*(Suppl. 5A), 106–113.

Compernolle, T., Hoogduin, K., & Joele, L. (1979). Diagnosis and treatment of the hyperventilation syndrome. *Psychomatics, 19,* 612–625.

Craig, A. B. (1976). 58 cases of loss of consciousness during underwater swimming and diving. *Medical Science and Sports, 8*(3), 171–175.

Craske, M. G., & Barlow, D. H. (1990) Nocturnal panic: Response to hyperventilation and carbon dioxide challenges. *Journal of Abnormal Psychology, 99*(3), 302–307.

DeGuire, S., Gevirtz, R., Kawahara, Y., & Maguire, W. (1992). Hyperventilation syndrome and the assessment of treatment for functional cardiac symptoms. *American Journal of Cardiology, 70,* 673–677.

De Ruitter, C., Garssen, B., Rijken, H., & Kraaimaat, F. (1992). The role of hyperventilation in panic disorder: A response to Ley (1991). *Behaviour Research and Therapy, 30*(6), 643–646.

Dorland's illustrated medical dictionary (27th ed.) Philadelphia, PA: W. B Saunders.

Dox, I., Melloni, B. J., & Eisner, G. M. (1979). *Melloni's illustrated medical dictionary.* Baltimore, MD: Williams & Wilkins.

Drossman, D. A., Thompson, W. G., Talley, N. J., Funch-Jensen, P., Janssens, J., & Whitehead, W. E. (1990). Identification of subgroups of functional gastrointestinal disorders. *Gastroenterology International, 3*(4), 159–172.

Fensterheim, H., & Wiegand, B. (1991). Group treatment of the hyperventilation syndrome. *International Journal of Group Psychotherapy, 41*(3), 399–403.

Folgering, H., & Colla, P. (1978). Some anomalies in the control of paCO$_2$ in patients with a hyperventilation syndrome. *Bulletin Européen de Physiopathologie Respiratoire, 14,* 503–512.

Fried, R. (1987a). Relaxation with biofeedback-assisted guided imagery: The importance of breathing rate as an index of hypoarousal. *Biofeedback and Self-Regulation, 12*(4), 273–279.

Fried, R. (1987b). *The hyperventilation syndrome.* Baltimore: The Johns Hopkins University Press.

Fried, R. (1993a). Respiration in stress and stress control. In P. Lehrer & R. L. Woolfolk (Eds.), *Principles and practice of stress management* (2nd ed., pp. 301–331). New York: Guilford Press.

Fried, R. (1993b). *The psychology and physiology of breathing: In behavioral medicine, clinical psychology, and psychiatry.* New York: Plenum Press.

Gardner, W. N. (1994). Diagnosis and organic causes of symptomatic hyperventilation. In B. Timmons & R. Ley (Eds.), *Behavioral and psychological approaches to breathing disorders* (pp. 99–112). New York: Plenum Press.

Garssen, B., de Ruiter, C., & van Dyck, R. (1992). Breathing retraining: A rationale placebo? *Clinical Psychology Review, 12,* 141–153.

Grossman, P., De Swart, J. C. G., & Defares, P. B. (1985). A controlled study of a breathing therapy for treatment of hyperventilation syndrome. *Journal of Psychosomatic Research, 29*(1), 49–58.

Guthrie, D., Moeller, T., & Guthrie, R. (1983). Biofeedback and its application to the stabilization and control of diabetes mellitus. *American Journal of Clinical Biofeedback, 6,* 82–87.

Hegel, M. T., Abel, G. G., Etscheidt, M., Cohen-Cole, S., & Wilmer, C. I. (1989). Behavioral treatment of angina-like chest pain in patients with hyperventilation syndrome. *Journal of Behavior Therapy and Experimental Psychiatry, 20*(1), 31–39.

Hibbert, G. A., & Chan, M. (1989). Respiratory control: Its contribution to the treatment of panic attacks. *British Journal of Psychiatry, 154,* 232–236.

Hibbert, G. A., & Pilsbury, D. (1988). Hyperventilation in panic attacks: Ambulant monitoring of transcutaneous carbon dioxide. *British Journal of Psychiatry, 152,* 76–80.

Hibbert, G. A., & Pilsbury, D. (1989). Hyperventilation: Is it a cause of panic attacks? *British Journal of Psychiatry, 155,* 805–809.

Hill, P. McN. (1973). Hyperventilation, breath holding and alveolar oxygen tensions at the breaking point. *Respiratory Physiology, 19,* 201–203.

Holloway, E. A. (1994). The role of the physiotherapist in the treatment of hyperventilation. In B. H. Timmons & R. Ley (Eds.), *Behavioral and psychological approaches to breathing disorders* (pp. 157–175). New York: Plenum Press.

Holmes, D. S., McCaul, K. D., & Solomon, S. (1978). Control of respiration as a means of controlling responses to threat. *Journal of Personality and Social Psychology, 36*(2), 198–204.

Howell, J. B. L. (1990). Behavioral breathlessness. *Thorax, 45,* 287–292.

Huey, S. R., & West, S. G. (1983). Hyperventilation: Its relation to symptom experience and to anxiety. *Journal of Abnormal Psychology, 92,* 422–432.

Janus, I., Defares, P., & Grossman, P. (1983). Hypervigilant reactions to threat. In H. Selye (Ed.), *Selye guide to stress research* (Vol. 3). New York: Scientific and Academic Editions.

Kaufman, M. P., & Schneiderman, N. (1986). Physiological bases of respiratory psychophysiology. In M. G. H. Coles, E. Donchin, & S. W. Porges (Eds.), *Psychophysiology: Systems, processes, and applications* (pp. 107–121). New York: Guilford Press.

Lehrer, P. M., Sargunaraj, D., & Hochron, S. (1992). Psychological approaches to the treatment of asthma. *Journal of Consulting and Clinical Psychology, 60*(4), 639–643.

Lewis, R. A., & Howell, J. B. L. (1986). Definition of the hyperventilation syndrome. *Clinical Respiratory Physiology (Bulletin of European Physiopathologic Respiration), 22,* 201–205.

Ley, R. (1987). Panic disorder and agoraphobia: Fear of fear or fear of the symptoms produced by hyperventilation? *Journal of Behavior Therapy and Experimental Psychiatry, 18*(4), 305–316.

Ley, R. (1988a). Panic attacks during relaxation and relaxation-induced anxiety: A hyperventilation interpretation. *Journal of Behavior Therapy and Experimental Psychiatry, 19*(4), 253–259.

Ley, R. (1988b). Panic attacks during sleep: A hyperventilation-probability model. *Journal of Behavior Therapy and Experimental Psychiatry, 19*(3), 181–192.

Ley, R. (1991). *Hyperventilation and panic attacks during sleep: A critical commentary on a study by Craske and Barlow.* Unpublished manuscript.

Ley, R. (1992). The many faces of pan: Psychological and physiological differences among three types of panic attacks. *Behavior Research and Therapy, 30*(4), 347–357.

Ley, R. (1993). Breathing retraining in the treatment of hyperventilatory complaints and panic disorder: A reply to Garssen, DeRuiter, and Van Dyck. *Clinical Psychology Review, 13,* 393–408.

Ley, R. (1994). Breathing and the psychology of emotion, cognition, and behavior. In B. H. Timmons & R. Ley (Eds.), *Behavioral and psychological approaches to breathing disorders* (pp. 81–95). New York: Plenum Press.

Lichstein, K. L. (1988). *Clinical relaxation strategies* (pp. 34–39, 43, 57–60, 162–165, 209). New York: Wiley-Interscience.

Lum, L. C. (1975). Hyperventilation: The tip and the iceberg. *Journal of Psychosomatic Research, 19,* 375–383.

MacHose, M., & Peper, E. (1991). The effects of clothing on inhalation volume. *Biofeedback and Self-Regulation, 16*(3), 261–265.

Missri, J. C., & Alexander, S. (1978). Hyperventilation syndrome: A brief review. *Journal of the American Medical Association, 240*(19), 2093–2096.

Naifeh, K. H. (1994). Basic anatomy and physiology of the respiratory system and the autonomic nervous system. In B. H. Timmons & R. Ley (Eds.), *Behavioral and psychological approaches to breathing disorders.* New York: Plenum Press.

Naifeh, K. H., Kamiya, J., & Sweet, D. M. (1982). Biofeedback of alveolar carbon dioxide tension and levels of arousal. *Biofeedback and Self-Regulation, 7*(3), 283–299.

Peper, E., & MacHose, M. (1993). Symptom prescription: Inducing anxiety by 70% exhalation. *Biofeedback and Self-Regulation, 18*(3), 133–139.

Peper, E., Smith, K., & Waddell, D. (1987). Voluntary wheezing versus diaphragmatic breathing with inhalation (Voldyne) feedback: A clinical intervention in the treatment of asthma. *Clinical Biofeedback and Health, 10*(2), 83–88.

Peper, E., & Tibbetts, V. (1992). Fifteen-month follow-up with asthmatics utilizing EMG/incentive inspirometer feedback. *Biofeedback and Self-Regulation, 17*(2), 143–151.

Peper, E., & Tibbetts, V. (1994). *Refresh and renew with effortless diaphragmatic breathing.* Unpublished paper.

Peper, E., & Tibbetts, V. (in press). Incentive inspirometry feedback for desensitization with asthmatic provoking triggers: A clinical protocol. *Medical Psychotherapy.*

Pilsbury, D., & Hibbert, G. (1987). An ambulatory system for long-term continuous monitoring of transcutaneous pCO_2. *Clinical Respiratory Physiology, 23,* 9–13.

Rapee, R. M. (1985). A case of panic disorder treated with breathing retraining. *Journal of Behavior Therapy and Experimental Psychiatry, 16*(1), 63–65.

Roland, M., & Peper, E. (1987). Inhalation volume changes with inspirometer feedback and diaphragmatic breathing coaching. *Clinical Biofeedback and Health, 10*(2), 89–97.

Rosenthal, T. L. (1980). Social cueing processes. In M. Hersen, R. M. Eisler, & P. M. Miller (Eds.), *Progress in behavior modification* (Vol. 10, pp. 111–146). New York: Academic Press.

Salkovskis, P. M. (1992). Psychological treatment of noncardiac chest pain: The cognitive approach. *The American Journal of Medicine, 92*(Suppl. 5A), 114–121.

Salkovskis, P. M., & Clark, D. M. (1990). Affective responses to hyperventilation: A test of the cognitive model of panic. *Behaviour Research and Therapy, 28*(1), 51–61.

Salkovskis, P. M., & Clark, D. M. (1991). Cognitive therapy for panic attacks. *Journal of Cognitive Psychotherapy, 5,* 215–226.

Sanderson, W. C., Rapee, R. M., & Barlow, D. H. (1988). Panic induction via inhalation of 5.5% CO_2 enriched air: A single subject analysis of psychological and physiological effects. *Behaviour Research and Therapy, 26,* 333–335.

Sartory, G., & Olajide, D. (1988). Vagal innervation techniques in the treatment of panic disorder. *Behaviour Research and Therapy, 26*(5), 431–434.

Stout, C., Kotses, H., & Creer, T. L. (1993). Improving recognition of respiratory sensations in healthy adults. *Biofeedback and Self-Regulation, 18*(2), 79–92.

Suess, W. M., Alexander, A. B., Smith, D. D., Sweeney, H. W., & Marion, R. J. (1980). The effects of psychological stress on respiration: A preliminary study of anxiety and hyperventilation. *Psychophysiology, 17*(6), 535–540.

Tiep, B., Branum, N., & Burns, M. (1992, March 19–24). Biofeedback breathing retraining reduces dyspnea and improves gas exchange. In *Proceedings of the 23rd Annual Meeting of the Association for Applied Psychophysiology and Biofeedback, Colorado Springs* (p. 55). Wheatridge, CO: Association for Applied Psychophysiology and Biofeedback.

Tiep, B., Burns, M., Kao, D., Madison, R., & Herrera, J. (1986). Pursed lips breathing training using ear oximetry. *Chest, 90,* 218–221.

Timmons, B. H., & Ley, R. (Eds.). (1994). *Behavioral and psychological approaches to breathing disorders.* New York: Plenum Press.

Timmons, B. H., & Meldrum, S. J. (1993). *Behavioral applications of respiratory measurements.* Unpublished manuscript.

Umezawa, A. (1992). Effects of stress on post expiration pause time and minute ventilating volume. *Current Biofeedback Research in Japan 1992.* Tokyo: Shinkoh Igaku Shuppan.

Umezawa, A. (1994, March 3–8). *Stress, relaxation, and respiratory function: Changes of minute ventilating volume and post expiration pause time under stress and relaxation.* Paper presented at the 25th annual meeting of the Association for Applied Psychophysiology and Biofeedback, Atlanta, GA.

van den Hout, M. A., Boek, C., van der Molen, G. M., & Griez, E. (1988). Rebreathing to cope with hyperventilation: Experimental tests of the paper bag method. *Journal of Behavioral Medicine, 11*(3), 303–310.

van den Hout, M. A., De Jong, P., Zandbergen, J., & Merckelbach, H. (1990). Waning of panic sensations during prolonged hyperventilation. *Behavior Research and Therapy, 28*(5), 445–448.

van den Hout, M. A., Griez, E., van der Molen, G. M., & Lousberg, H. (1987). Pulmonary carbon dioxide and panic-arousing sensations after 35% carbon dioxide inhalation: Hypercapnia/hyperoxia versus hypercapnia/normoxia. *Journal of Behavior Therapy and Experimental Psychiatry, 18*(1), 19–23.

van der Molen, G. M., van den Hout, M. A., Merckelbach, H., van Dieren, A. C., & Griez, E. (1989). The effect of hypocapnia on extinction of conditioned fear responses. *Behaviour Research and Therapy, 27*(1), 71–77.

van Dixhoorn, J. (1992). *Cardiac events after myocardial infarction: Four year follow-up of exercise training and relaxation.* Paper presented at Fifth World Congress of Cardiac Rehabilitation, Bordeaux, France.

van Dixhoorn, J. (1993, Sept.). *Breath relaxation—stress management in East and West.* Paper presented at 3rd International Conference on Biobehavioral Self-Regulation and Health, Tokyo.

van Dixhoorn, J. (1994, March). *Breath relaxation.* Workshop presented at the 25th Annual Meeting of the Association for Applied Psychophysiology and Biofeedback, Atlanta, GA.

van Dixhoorn, J., & Duivenvoorden, H. J. (1989). Breathing awareness as a relaxation method in cardiac rehabilitation. In F. J. McGuigan, W. E. Sime, & J. M. Wallace (Eds.), *Stress and tension control 3* (pp. 19–36). New York: Plenum Press.

van Dixhoorn, J., Duivenvoorden, H. J. Staal, J. A., Pool, J., & Verhage, F. (1987). Cardiac events after myocardial infarction: Possible effect of relaxation therapy. *European Heart Journal, 8,* 1210–1214.

van Doorn, P., Folgering, H., & Colla, P. (1982). Control of the end-tidal PCO_2 in the hyperventilation syndrome: Effects of biofeedback and breathing instructions compared. *Bulletin Européen de Physiopathologie Respiratoire, 18*(6), 829–836.

Waites, T. F. (1978). Hyperventilation—chronic and acute. *Archives of Internal Medicine, 138,* 1700–1701.

12

Problems with Relaxation and Biofeedback-Assisted Relaxation and Guidelines for Management

Mark S. Schwartz
Nancy M. Schwartz

Relaxation therapies and biofeedback-assisted relaxation procedures commonly lead to positive therapeutic results. Most people using these therapies do so without problems. Nevertheless, a few people do experience uncomfortable reactions and other problems with these therapies. These negative reactions can disrupt therapy, alarm patients and therapists unnecessarily, and result in stopping potentially useful therapy. The experience of negative reactions can reduce compliance with recommended relaxation. This in turn can reduce the chances for improvement (Borkovec et al., 1987).

Fortunately, significant negative reactions are uncommon, and serious negative reactions are rare. One can usually avoid negative reactions. Practitioners who are aware of the potential negative reactions to relaxation and possible causes can prevent or lessen the effects of many of them.

Bernstein and Borkovec (1973) identified several possible problems and negative side effects of progressive muscle relaxation. Schultz and Luthe (1969) discussed potential problems and negative side effects associated with autogenic therapy. The reader is referred to these excellent discussions and their suggested solutions.

NEGATIVE REACTIONS, RELAXATION-INDUCED ANXIETY, AND OTHER PROBLEMS

Negative Reactions

A partial list of the potential negative reactions reported includes the following:

1. *Musculoskeletal activity.* Examples of such activities are tics, cramps, myoclonic jerks, spasms, and restlessness.
2. *Disturbing sensory experiences.* These experiences include sensations of heaviness, warmth, cooling, depersonalization, misperceived body size, floating, and a variety of visual, auditory, gustatory, and olfactory experiences.

3. *Sympathetic nervous system activity.* These reactions include increased heart rate and increased electrodermal activity.
4. *Cognitive-affective, emotional, and intrusive thoughts.* Examples include feelings of sadness, anger, depression, disturbing thoughts, intrusive thoughts or mind wandering, tearfulness, increased anxiety, and fears such as fear of losing control.
5. *Other* possible negative side effects. These include hypotensive reactions, headache, sexual arousal, and psychotic symptoms.

Relaxation-Induced Anxiety

"Relaxation-induced anxiety" (RIA) is the term used to denote a variety of negative reactions associated with relaxation procedures. Heide and Borkovec (1983) defined RIA as "paradoxical increases in cognitive, physiological, or behavioral components of anxiety as a consequence of engaging in systematic relaxation training" (p. 171). Carrington (1977) described intense restlessness, profuse perspiration, shivering, trembling, pounding heart, and rapid breathing associated with a type of meditation. In essence, RIA is increased anxiety associated with attempts at relaxation.

Most negative reactions are with relaxation rather than biofeedback. Furthermore, we found no reports specifically with only biofeedback. Thus, one cannot separate the reports of negative reactions with biofeedback from those from relaxation. We cannot determine the incidence or prevalence of negative reactions with biofeedback from any of the published reports.

Incidence of Relaxation-Induced Negative Reactions

Until recent years, there was little attention in the clinical and research literature given to these problems. There is very limited information about the incidence of negative reactions and problems. There are very few studies and almost none with medical patients. What studies do exist involve very few subjects. Most research rarely mentions or ignores them as if they did not exist. Available reports are mostly anecdotal, surveys of mental health professionals, observations of subjects or patients in studies, and small samples of patients with anxiety disorders. Survey studies are helpful but fraught with methodology problems.

Jacobson and Edinger (1982) and Edinger and Jacobson (1982) were among the early reports about some negative side effects associated with relaxation therapies. They conducted a brief mail survey of behavior therapists who used relaxation therapies. The 116 clinicians who responded reported a total of 17,542 patients and clients. An estimated 3.5% of patients had experienced negative reactions that interfered with relaxation therapy. They partially defined interference as "noncompliance or client-initiated termination of treatment" (Edinger & Jacobson, 1982, p. 137). The professionals surveyed reported "discontinuing relaxation" because negative side effects confounded treatment in another 3.8% of their patients and clients.

The data from Edinger and Jacobson (1982, p. 138) indicated the more commonly reported negative reactions were "intrusive thoughts" in 15% and "fears of 'losing control'" in 9.3%. The less commonly reported reactions were "disturbing sensory experience" in 3.6%, "sexual arousal" when the client and the therapist were of different sexes in 2.3%, "muscle cramps" in 2.1%, "spasms/tics" in 1.7%, "sexual arousal" when the client and the therapist were of the same sex in 0.85%, "emergence of psychotic symptoms" in 0.4%, and "other" or "miscellaneous" such as "sleep, increased anxiety, and depersonalization" reported by no more than two clinicians or 2.5%.

The investigators acknowledged that there are problems with survey research and that "no attempt was made to examine client population(s) being treated and exact relaxation procedure(s) . . . being used by respondents" (Edinger & Jacobson, 1982, p. 138). They concluded, however, that "side-effects are generally infrequent and inconsequential" and that "very few . . . appear sufficient to stop therapy by an experienced and knowledgeable therapist except perhaps the sexual arousal and emergence of psychotic symptoms," the latter of which occurred in only about "1 out of every 263 cases treated" (p. 138).

In the one study of medical patients (Blanchard, Cornish, Wittrock, & Fahrion, 1990), 73 hypertension patients received temperature biofeedback and relaxation. Of these, 4–9% reported negative sensations or experiences in any one session, but all were minor and none were RIA. Among a group of 30 undergraduates reporting chronic anxiety, 5 (17%) "reported increased anxiety" during a taped session of progressive relaxation (Braith, McCullough, & Bush, 1988, p. 193).

We believe that very few people have undesirable or negative reactions to biofeedback instruments and feedback signals alone. The few who do are probably anxious about biomedical instruments and the process of recording internal body activity. They are probably anxious about various types of evaluations and seeing doctors.

Heide and Borkovec (1983, 1984) provided a very thoughtful review of RIA. They conceded that, although the evidence for RIA was mostly anecdotal, it was present often enough to be of concern. They reviewed the suggested mechanisms presumed to underlie the phenomenon and suggested procedures for relieving some problems.

Also, they found physiological correlates of anxiety in some subjects who did not report anxiety. In some subjects reporting anxiety, physiological measures were lower—although not as low as those reporting reduced tension. Thus, RIA is a difficult phenomenon to understand in general terms. It is often a subjective experience possibly more clearly understood through in-depth study of individual cases.

Proposed Causes of Relaxation-Induced Anxiety and Risk Factors

There are several hypothesized causes of RIA. Any one or combination could apply to an individual. The first five are from Heide and Borkovec (1984).

1. *Cognitive fear of unfamilair sensations.* Some people may have a cognitive fear of sensations associated with relaxation. Sensations include tingling, heaviness, warmth, and muscle jerks. Patients may view these physiological-behavioral reactions and the cognitive-affective reactions as uncomfortable or unfamiliar rather than as positive signs that relaxation is automatically occurring. This may be more common in people who rarely or never attend to body sensations or among those who interpret body sensations as negative.

A related hypothesis (Denny, 1976) suggests that stimuli produced by relaxation may become conditioned to fear when paired with a history of punishment during relaxation or safety times. Another idea is that some chronically anxious people might become frightened with the unfamiliar sensations of deep relaxation. These thoughts could then trigger body chemical changes.

2. *Fear of losing control.* Some people are preoccupied with maintaining control over their physical and psychological processes (Braith et al., 1988; Lehrer, 1982). Furthermore, some people fear losing control and may use active, effortful relaxation strategies. Our culture assumes that exercising control requires active effort. Seligman (1975) defined control as being able to change outcomes by voluntary actions. Patients may display a pattern of trying too hard. They need to maintain a high degree of activity out of fear that without it they will waste time and accomplish nothing.

Fearing inactivity may give rise to anxiety. This may be more common among people who avoid rest and reflection and those intent on maintaining control with active and effortful activity. For people with generalized anxiety, "daily maintenance of higher-then-normal tension may be a learned avoidance response to relaxation" (Borkovec et al., 1987, p. 887). This fear of anxiety also fits in the next explanation.

Associated with the loss of control is the perception that relaxation "signifies vulnerability, lack of control over anger and sexual desire, overpassivity, etc." (Lehrer, 1982, p. 424). This may be the cause of the angry feelings evoked by five patients when asked to relax by Abromowitz and Wieselberg (1978).

3. *Fear of experiencing anxiety.* Relaxation-induced anxiety is more common in persons who are chronically anxious. Relaxation methods often direct people to focus away from external stimuli and to focus on body sensations or thoughts. This may increase their awareness of current internal cues often associated with higher levels of anxiety. In the past, these cues were distressing as the person viewed them as meaning "out of my control" or they associated the cues with heightened anxiety including panic. For example, specific thoughts about anxiety may result in cognitive anxiety (Norton, Rhodes, & Hauch, 1985).

4. *Fear of encountering oneself.* This is the hypothesized fear of attending to the heightened awareness of internal experience, in general. Some professionals view this phenomenon as one resulting from dissatisfaction with oneself or from fearing the increased awareness of inner conflicts.

5. *Situation-produced worry or intrusive thoughts and worries.* Patients may find, as they reduce their focus from external stimuli, that their own thoughts and worries arise and become more dominant. This situation is the same as with the cognitive intrusions that interfere with sleep onset. Note these thoughts do not relate to relaxation but become associated with the relaxation experience (see also Lichstein, 1988, p. 138).

6. *Breathing.* Another interesting and logical hypothesis with support is that of Ley (1988). Physical changes from breathing occur during relaxation and could cause or increase the chance of having RIA. Chronic hyperventilation alters the amount of carbon dioxide and other body chemicals in the blood. This could lead to RIA as the person shifts from activity to inactivity without changing breathing pattern to match the inactive state. The reader is referred to Chapter 11 for a more detailed discussion of breathing.

7. *Parasympathetic or trophotropic response.* An old hypothesis is the parasympathetic or trophotropic response hypothesis. According to this view, some people tend to have more parasympathetic responses. RIA is a compensatory ergotropic sympathetic nervous system (SNS) response. This is similar to theories such as the one proposed by Stampler (1982) suggesting that relaxation might directly stimulate the "complex interplay of psychological and physiological factors" (Cohen, Barlow, & Blanchard, 1985, p. 99) that could lead to RIA in susceptible people.

For example, DeGood and Williams (1982) reported a case of a 40-year-old female patient treated with autogenic training and electromyographic (EMG) biofeedback for low-back and leg pain. They monitored her finger temperature and skin conductance. She developed acute headaches with nausea soon after each of the first two sessions. Revising the training procedure to having the patient sit upright with her eyes open helped to stop the postsession symptoms. The authors speculated that the negative symptoms were caused by "vagal rebound" or "parasympathetic overcompensation" (p. 464) after physiological deactivation during the relaxation.

This explanation focuses on the possible role of the anterior hypothalamus (Gellhorn, 1965, 1967; Mefford, 1979, cited in Cohen et al., 1985, p. 99). According to this view, "lowered somatic activity . . . tends to be accompanied by increased activation of the trophotropically dominant anterior hypothalmus and related structures (DeGood & Williams, 1982, p. 464).

8. *Switching from passive to active coping.* Another possibility involves switching from a passive, immobilized, nonpreparatory, and relaxed state to the anticipation of or preparation for action (Elliott, 1974; Obrist, 1976, 1981; Cohen, et al., 1985). Heart rate is slower during passive coping. The person switching from a passive to an active coping method could experience large accelerations of heart rate according to this explanation (Cohen et al., 1985). Such accelerated heart rate is presumably not because of increased anxiety but because of cardiac–somatic coupling. This is the close relationship between heart rate and striate muscle activity. Thus, preparation for action may produce increased somatic arousal and increased heart rate.

9. *Other explanations.* Other examples of those who experience RIA are people who are competitive with themselves and who fear failure. In other individuals, relaxation may arouse thoughts and feelings of sexual arousal. Still other people take certain medications and confuse the side effects or interactions with RIA.

Guidelines for Avoiding, Minimizing, and Managing RIA

People who experience RIA are among those who often most need psychophysiological self-regulation. The implication for practitioners is not to avoid relaxation and biofeedback but to be aware of and anticipate reactions. Practitioners should provide understandable and realistic patient education and select types of relaxation and biofeedback that are less likely to have these reactions. A positive therapy alliance can help practitioners manage these reactions.

Patient preparation for relaxation should include an explanation that the patient may experience sensations and thoughts during relaxation that are normal signs that relaxation is taking place. This is especially important for patients with chronic anxiety. One should expect intrusive thoughts in early sessions of relaxation. This will diminish as the patient's skills and confidence increase. The clinician should explain relaxation as increased control rather than as diminished control. He or she can explain that people often achieve relaxation proficiency and increased autonomic nervous system (ANS) control through less effort rather than through more effort.

The therapist can consider a switch to a different type of relaxation. People rarely experience RIA with two different types of relaxation. If one is using a bodily focus type, a switch to a more cognitive approach might achieve desired results. If one is using a cognitive method, a switch to an active, external attentional focus or to a bodily focus type might be tried. An example of this would be focusing on external sounds in or outside the office rather than a mental focus on body awareness (Wells, 1990; see the discussion under Distraction and Intrusive Thoughts).

Other Problems

In addition to the above more intense and distressing negative reactions, other problems can arise with relaxation. These include:

1. Embarrassment and self-consciousness about relaxation.
2. Problems with concentration and distracting thoughts.
3. Subjective and physical discomfort associated with sitting or lying "still."
4. Difficulty following instructions for relaxation or biofeedback, or ignoring some instructions.

5. Listening to the audiotaped relaxation procedures or being exposed to biofeed-back-assisted relaxation but not following or participating in the procedures.
6. Fear of failure.
7. Selected body areas remaining tense.
8. Poor cooperation from family members or other significant persons.
9. Increased awareness of symptoms.
10. Falling asleep during relaxation and biofeedback.
11. Movements: laughing, talking, coughing, sneezing, body movements.

Guidelines for Avoiding, Reducing, and Managing Other Problems

Some practitioners do not ask their patients about whether they are experiencing negative reactions or other problems with relaxation. Some researchers do not ask their subjects these questions. Both practitioners and researchers should consider the following guidelines.

1. *Embarrassment problem.* Some patients feel embarrassed or self-conscious about tensing certain muscles, such as those of the face. Others feel embarrassed about other relaxation procedures.

Solutions: Modeling the procedures and offering reassurance and supportive statements sometimes can help. In earlier trials, one can look away from the patient and look at the visual display while the patient tenses muscles.

2. *Gender or sexual problems.* Some patients may feel sexually aroused, self-conscious, or threatened. Some patients may feel this when there are cross-gender therapist–patient combinations. Others will feel this with same-gender combinations and homosexual fantasies. Reclining in a darkened room and using suggestive or other relaxation terms with double meanings can add to subjective discomfort. Self-consciousness and similar discomfort also can occur with patients unaccustomed to the passive role in any situation. Now, they find themselves asked to recline passively. This can be psychologically uncomfortable.

We suspect that very few patients will explain these reasons for their discomfort, and many are not aware of the reasons. Constrictive clothing, that a patient is wearing also may influence comfort or discomfort.

Solutions: Practitioners should consider starting such patients in a sitting-upright posture, to which patients are more accustomed and with which they may be more comfortable. Professionals should be sensitive to this factor and should adjust the procedures accordingly. One can adjust the position of a recliner and foot rest to reduce this potential problem. Professionals should be certain to maintain boundaries and be careful about touching these patients.

3. *Script problem.* The contents of relaxation scripts are comfortable for many patients but uncomfortable for others. This depends on the patients' perceptions, attitudes, and fantasies. For example, the therapist might consider the potential effect of "feelings of heaviness" with patients with actual or perceived overweight problems.

Solutions: Professionals should provide sufficient patient education and tailor the scripts.

4. *Distraction and intrusive thoughts problem.* There are many sources of distraction from the concentration needed during relaxation and body-awareness procedures in the therapist's office and elsewhere. Distractions include associations from the content of the relaxation script. Some people think about their life and responsibilities at these times.

Solutions: The therapist should discuss this problem with patients and reassure them that these distracting thoughts and images are normal. Then, he or she can assist patients in ways to lessen them. To achieve such a goal, the therapist might consider shorter sessions; he or she might include more breaks, or start with eyes open or partly open. Practitioners should also consider using active sensory awareness exercises such as the example by Wells (1990) of external attentional focusing on sounds in the environment.

One can expand this to training patients to mentally focus on sensory awareness of the environment rather than internal awareness and a self-attentive focus. For example, the therapist can guide or direct a patient to attend to the texture of the armchair, sounds in the office, and the color of a wall. He or she can then guide the patient through switching from one to another to increase the patient's ability to choose and control his or her mental focus. The therapist should do these slowly but for only a few seconds each. For example:

> "Right now, think about the color of the wall. Right now, think about the texture of the chair. Right now, think about the sound of. . . . Now, switch your attention from one to another."

Another suggestion is for patients to think of the distracting thoughts as words or pictures on a movie or television screen. The therapist can encourage the patient to imagine the screen becoming smaller and smaller until it becomes tiny and distant or disappears entirely. Patients can imagine they are moving farther away or the screen is moving farther away. Sitting close to a big, color screen is more distressing than seeing the same words and image on a 1–3-inch black and white screen several feet away.

5. *Silence, motionless, and restlessness problem.* Being silent and being motionless are paradoxically uncomfortable for some people. These people become restless with longer sessions. Some may have features of the syndrome sometimes known as adult attention-deficit/hyperactivity disorder.

Solutions: Practitioners should assess and prepare for this early for all patients. They should ask whether the patient has any concern about sitting quietly for the planned amount of time. If the practitioner anticipates patient discomfort, he or she should discuss this early, reassure patients, and suggest adjusted body positions and durations as indicated. The therapist can assure patients they can easily make adjustments. Patients should be given choices about physical positions, lighting, and time to make adjustments. Sessions can be shortened or interspersed with breaks. Patients may keep eyes open or partly open. Therapists' should also avoid long silences without verbal instructions, discussion, changes in feedback displays and tasks, or physiological changes obvious to the patient.

6. *Low self-efficacy and fear of failure.* Patients often do not have the needed self-confidence in their abilities to develop effective relaxation skills. The theme in their self-statements is "I cannot do it." They also may not have realistic goals. They may expect the goal of therapy to be *mastery*. Similarly, fear of failure is a common problem. Patients say and ask themselves: "Am I doing this right?" "Am I doing this better than the last time?" "I will never get the feelings and benefits I need!"

Solutions: The therapist should explain and remind patients that learning new physical and mental skills has peaks, valleys, and plateaus. He or she should also explain to patients that developing or cultivating low or lower tension and arousal is often a gradual process. Using examples from the acquisition of athletic, musical, or other skills is often helpful. Therapists should encourage and remind patients to avoid hurrying, and of the "three Ps" of patience, practice, and persistence.

Prudent therapists should expect and discuss fear of failure early and periodically. They help patients replace the negative thoughts with positive ones. They suggest that patients remind themselves often that most people can make progress and guide patients away from viewing physiological self-regulation as something that one passes or fails.

Patients should be encouraged to allow the relaxation to happen or to let go rather than try to make it happen. They should focus on increasing their awareness of feelings associated with physiological self-regulation. Therapists should change the goals away from specific numbers: Patients need not become olympic competitors.

7. *Awareness of tension problem.* A few patients report increased symptoms during early stages of relaxation therapies. General relaxation permits more awareness of tension of selected body areas. Patients may perceive themselves as more tense than they were before. This is an example of the Gestalt psychology phenomenon of "figure–ground." As some stimuli fade, others appear more salient. This does not mean that patients are more tense. The background has changed. This can also result from increased focus on symptoms with the use of self-report symptom logs. Furthermore, some relaxation procedures, such as tensing muscles, can increase some symptoms.

Solutions: Therapists should discuss this phenomenon and reassure patients that such perceptions are common and normal. By noticing tension earlier, one can reduce the tension and prevent symptoms. Prudent practitioners help patients reframe this belief as increased awareness.

8. *Significant-others problem.* Family and other significant people in a patient's life who are around him or her during relaxation therapy may not be understanding and cooperative.

Solutions: If such people are not present during office sessions, therapists should provide the patient with patient-education materials explaining the rationale, procedures, and need for cooperation from others. Practitioners may need to counsel some patients on how to discuss this with others and how to increase cooperation from family members.

9. *Other factors not related to starting therapy.* Factors other than starting relaxation therapy can increase symptoms. If a patient is not cognitively prepared for the therapy, he or she can experience increased concern, emotional arousal, and tension, and therefore increased symptoms. Another factor is the presence of sufficient stress occurring and even increasing in the patient's life, thereby adding to the symptoms.

Solutions: Discussion of current life events and counseling, adjustments, and reassurance are appropriate. One must obviously rule out other causes, such as an incorrect diagnosis and treatment strategy.

10. *Viewing treatment as stressful problem.* Some patients view some aspects of treatment as stressful, and this can add to symptoms. Therapists should consider the time and arrangements required for patients to attend office sessions. This includes time away from other duties and responsibilities and explanations to employers and supervisors. It often means extra work when patients get back from appointments. Patients also invest time and effort following homework assignments, maintaining self-report records, and completing questionnaires. These time pressures are stressful. Added to these pressures are the expenses for therapy. Thoughts about any or all of these added sources of stress can intrude.

Solutions: Sensitivity and flexibility on the practitioner's part about scheduling and assignments can help decrease the effects of this stress.

11. *Disregarding instructions.* Patients sometimes disregard instructions during biofeedback and other relaxation procedures in the practitioner's office and elsewhere. For example, they may not imagine the stress stimuli the practitioner presents. They also may imagine the stress stimuli for only part of the time. In addition, some patients intentionally think of topics other than the biofeedback signal or verbal relaxation instructions. Patients

are unlikely to admit such diversions without careful questioning. The therapist must be careful discussing this to avoid giving the impression of being critical.

Solutions: Sensitivity and flexibility on the practitioner's part about assignments and instructions can help. Therapists should provide adequate patient education. They can change the content of the relaxation script and procedures. Or, they may consider saying something like the following:

> "Sometimes, you might be thinking about other topics during relaxation and biofeedback. It is normal for that to occur at times, and I understand. However, I need to know if you shift away from the instructions here or in your practice at home. Please understand when I ask you about that. Please share it with me when it is happening so we can discuss it."

12. *Not focusing on physiology.* Some people only listen to audio relaxation tapes but do not focus on their physiology. Some patients just listen to or watch feedback signals but with minimal or no focusing on their physiology. It is as if they are expecting or hoping that the relaxation instructions and biofeedback signals will induce the desired outcome by itself.

Solutions: The therapist can anticipate this potential problem and discuss it. He or she can guide patients away from a scenario of passively expecting the audiotape or feedback signal to be therapeutic by itself. Biofeedback gives patients information, suggestions, guidelines, and samples to use, but the patients themselves are responsible for the changes.

13. *Falling asleep.* Some patients fall asleep during relaxation procedures.

Solutions: Therapists should be aware of potential sleepers. Patients can keep their eyes open. Patients can schedule sessions earlier in the day. They should avoid relaxation after meals unless it is needed for postprandial symptoms. Therapists can conduct a sleep-disorder evaluation and treat the causes of the hypersomnia. For example, they can check for sleep apnea, psychophysiological insomnia, sleep–wake schedule disorders, and narcolepsy.

14. *Misuse of audio relaxation tapes.* Some patients are dependent on tapes and use them too often and too long. They rely on them and do not learn to relax without them.

Solutions: Patient education includes the proper role of tapes to avoid potential dependence on them. Therapists should taper patients from tapes using fading and related behavioral techniques and should consider using tapes with progressively briefer scripts. Patients should consider turning the tape player off progressively earlier in the script and continuing the relaxation. They can progressively lower the volume.

15. *Not having or taking enough time to practice and apply relaxation.* This is a very common problem. Many patients who particularly need to develop and apply relaxation therapies also have substantial time-use problems. They do not know how to or have not applied effective time-use management in their lives.

Solutions: The therapist should conduct or refer such patients for an evaluation and for education about time-use management. For example, practitioners can help such patients learn to set goals and priorities. Other valuable lessons for patients include learning to delegate, avoiding or reducing time wasters, reducing perfectionism, and managing procrastination (Schwartz & Schwartz, in press). The therapist should encourage patients to schedule relaxation and make practice and application a priority.

Problems with Biofeedback Procedures and Their Management

In addition to the problems with relaxation, there are specific problems that occur during biofeedback-assisted relaxation sessions that are specific to the biofeedback (Gaarder &

Montgomery, 1981, p. 94). These remain relevant, although with the technological advantages of microcomputer-based biofeedback, there is a broader array of solutions. We include some of these and suggest a few solutions for consideration. Experienced and very competent therapists develop their own repertoire.

1. *Often, there are very small changes in a physiological parameter or the patient does not think the feedback signal is changing. Solutions:* Therapists can use the threshold or change it to ease the task. The gain can be increased so the visual display feedback or audio feedback changes are more obvious with less physiological changes. Therapists can encourage shifting attention to other sites or cognitions as well as switching to a different task or feedback site. They can use varied verbal relaxation instructions and change the visual display as well.

The therapist can ask the patient to close his or her eyes for a few moments and then freeze the visual display if it changes in the desired direction. Then, the therapist can ask the patient to open his or her eyes gently to see the change. This should be repeated as needed.

2. *Often, the feedback signal moves in the undesired direction. Solutions:* The therapist should stop instrumentation-based feedback to the patient. He or she can discuss "trying too hard" and provide quiet, brief, and clear verbal feedback when the therapist sees the signal moving in the desired direction. The therapist should observe the patient's posture, breathing, and movements and suggest adjustments as needed. He or she should shift focus to other sites, tasks, or techniques. The therapist should use varied verbal relaxation instructions and ask about patients' cognitions. He or she should discuss and suggest changes as needed. Increased control is the ability to move the signal in either direction. The experienced practitioner will notice what makes it go in the wrong direction as this can give clues for moving it the desired direction.

3. *Some patients become bored with the feedback signal or task. Solutions:* The therapist should change feedback displays. With computer-based systems, there are a wide variety of feedback options. The therapist can also consider shorter sessions. He or she should adjust goals of a session to increase the chance of obvious successes and reinforce changes.

RESEARCH ON NEGATIVE REACTIONS AND PROBLEMS

Practitioners need much more research about the incidence and mechanisms of negative reactions associated with relaxation therapies including biofeedback-assisted relaxation (Poppen, 1984; Edinger, 1984). Practitioners also need much more research on patient variables associated with negative reactions and on preventive and management procedures. We trust that those conducting such research will consider and incorporate most or all of the following.

Retrospective survey research is fraught with enough methodology problems to preclude its value for estimating the incidence. Imagine receiving a survey with questions about how often each of several negative reactions and other problems occurred in your practice. Such recall is of doubtful accuracy. Some of the more common problems are:

1. One has to recall such events among hundreds of patients.
2. One has to recall such events over years of practice.
3. Practitioners do not systematically inquire about such events among their patients.
4. Practitioners often supervise others who provide the relaxation and biofeedback therapies.

5. Retrospective surveys lack control over varied relaxation and biofeedback proce-
    dures, audiotapes, types of patients, therapist characteristics, patient education,
    durations of sessions, and environments.

One recommendation is that a major professional organization develop comprehensive and carefully constructed questionnaires and make these available for clinicians and
researchers to use prospectively. Cooperative efforts between the organization gathering the
prospective data and a national data bank would provide useful data.

Such a clinical research questionnaire would probably include questions and controls
for many variables. Examples are varied relaxation procedures, presence or absence of therapist, patient education, duration of sessions, locations of negative reactions, eyes open or
closed, and postural and lighting information, therapist characteristics, types of symptoms
and disorders, patient's experience with these and other therapies, and names, doses, and
side effects of medications.

CAUTIONS AND CONTRAINDICATIONS

There are other, more serious factors to consider when providing physiological
self-regulatory therapies. These constitute the cautions and contraindications (see Chapter 6
for a discussion of these). One expects potentially serious problems to occur if one provides
such therapies for patients for whom such cautions and contraindications apply. However,
one can use special approaches for carefully selected patients with some of these disorders and
conditions if the practitioner is knowledgeable about and experienced with these disorders.

CONCLUSION

Problems can and do occur when using relaxation therapies and biofeedback-
assisted relaxation. The experience of negative reactions such as RIA can reduce compliance with recommended relaxation. However, very few patients are at risk, and very few
experience negative reactions. Prudent practitioners use available information, wisdom from
experience, skills, precautions, and good judgment in patient selection and implementing
treatments. It is proper here to remind readers that

> Every patient should be treated with biofeedback by a professional with the appropriate
> credentials who is qualified to understand and treat both the illness and the patient without
> biofeedback, or by someone under the direct and personal supervision of a professional so
> qualified. (Adler & Adler, 1984, p. 612)

REFERENCES

Abromowitz, S. I., & Wieselberg, N. (1978). Reaction to relaxation and desensitization outcome: Five
angry treatment failures. *American Journal of Psychiatry, 135,* 1418–1419.
Adler, C. S., & Adler, S. M. (1984). Biofeedback. In T. B. Karasu (Ed.). *The psychiatric therapies: The
American Psychiatric Association Commission on Psychiatric Therapies.* Washington, DC: Ameri-
can Psychiatric Association.
Bernstein, D. A., & Borkovec, T. D. (1973). *Progressive relaxation training.* Champaign, IL: Research
Press.

Blanchard, E. B., Cornish, P. J., Wittrock, D. A., & Fahrion, S. (1990). Subjective experiences associated with thermal biofeedback treatment of hypertension. *Biofeedback and Self-Regulation, 15*(2), 145–159.

Borkovec, T. D., Mathews, A. M., Chambers, A., Ebrahimi, S., Lytle, R., & Nelson, R. (1987). The effects of relaxation training with cognitive or nondirective therapy and the role of relaxation-induced anxiety in the treatment of generalized anxiety. *Journal of Consulting and Clinical Psychology, 55*(6), 883–888.

Braith, J. A., McCullough, J. P., & Bush, J. P. (1988). Relaxation-induced anxiety in a subclinical sample of chronically anxious subjects. *Journal of Behavior Therapy and Experimental Psychiatry, 19*(3), 193–198.

Carrington, P. (1977). *Freedom in meditation.* New York: Doubleday-Anchor.

Cohen, A. S., Barlow, D. H., & Blanchard, E. B. (1985). Psychophysiology of relaxation-associated panic attacks. *Journal of Abnormal Psychology, 94*(1), 96–101.

DeGood, D. E., & Williams, E. M. (1982). Parasympathetic rebound following EMG biofeedback training: A case study. *Biofeedback and Self-Regulation, 7*(4), 461–465.

Denny, M. R. (1976). Post-aversive relief and relaxation and their implications for behavior therapy. *Journal of Behavior Therapy and Experimental Psychiatry, 7,* 315–322.

Edinger, J. D. (1984). Re: Adverse reactions to relaxation training [Response to Poppen, 1984]. *The Behavior Therapist, 7*(7), 138.

Edinger, J. D., & Jacobson, R. (1982). Incidence and significance of relaxation treatment side-effects. *The Behavior Therapist, 5,* 137–138.

Elliott, R. (1974). The motivational significance of heart rate. In P. A. Obrist, A. H. Black, J. Brener, & L. V. DiCara (Eds.), *Cardiovascular psychophysiology: Current issues in response mechanisms, biofeedback, and methodology* (pp. 505–537). Chicago: Aldine.

Gaarder, K. R., & Montgomery, P. S. (1981). *Clinical biofeedback: A procedural manual for behavioral medicine* (2nd ed.). Baltimore: Williams & Wilkins.

Gellhorn, E. (1964). Motion and emotion: The role of proprioception in the physiology and pathology of the emotions. *Psychological Review, 71,* 457–472.

Gellhorn, E. (1965). The neurophysiological basis of anxiety: A hypothesis. *Perspectives in Biology and Medicine, 8,* 488–515.

Gellhorn, E. (1967). *Principles of autonomic–somatic integrations: Physiological basis and psychological and clinical implications.* Minneapolis: University of Minnesota Press.

Heide, F. J., & Borkovec, T. D. (1983). Relaxation-induced anxiety: Paradoxical anxiety enhancement due to relaxation training. *Journal of Consulting and Clinical Psychology, 51,* 171–182.

Heide, F. J., & Borkovec, T. D. (1984). Relaxation-induced anxiety: Mechanisms and theoretical implications. *Behaviour Research and Therapy, 22,* 1–12.

Jacobson, R., & Edinger, J. D. (1982). Side effects of relaxation treatment. *American Journal of Psychiatry, 139*(7), 952–953.

Lehrer, P. M. (1979). Anxiety and cultivated relaxation: Reflections on clinical experiences and psychophysiological research. In F. J. McGuigan (Ed.), *Tension control: Proceedings of the fifth annual meeting of the American Association for the Advancement of Tension Control.* Chicago: American Association for the Advancement of Tension Control.

Lehrer, P. M. (1982). How to relax and how not to relax: A reevaluation of the work of Edmund Jacobson—I. *Behaviour Research and Therapy, 20,* 417–428.

Ley, R. (1988). Panic attacks during relaxation and relaxation-induced anxiety: A hyperventilation interpretation. *Journal of Behavior Therapy and Experimental Psychiatry, 19*(4), 253–259.

Lichstein, K. L. (1988). *Clinical relaxation strategies.* Wiley: New York.

Mefford, R. B. (1979). The developing biological concept of anxiety. In W. E. Fann, I. Karacan, A. D. Pokorny, & R. L. Williams (Eds.), *Phenomenology and treatment of anxiety* (pp. 111–124). New York: Spectrum Publications.

Norton, G. R., Rhodes, L., Hauch, J., & Kaprowy, E. A. (1985). Characteristics of subjects experiencing relaxation and relaxation-induced anxiety. *Journal of Behavior Therapy and Experimental Psychiatry, 16*(3), 211–216.

Obrist, P. A. (1976). The cardiovascular–behavioral interaction as it appears today. *Psychophysiology*, *13*, 95–107.

Obrist, P. A. (1981). *Cardiovascular psychophysiology: A perspective*. New York: Plenum Press.

Poppen, R. (1984). Adverse reaction to relaxation training [Letter to the Editor]. *The Behavior Therapist*, *7*(1), 18.

Schultz, J. H., & Luthe, W. (1969). *Autogenic therapy: Vol. 1. Autogenic methods*. New York: Grune & Stratton.

Seligman, M. E. P. (1975). *Helplessness: On depression, development and death*. Freeman: San Francisco.

Schwartz, M. S., & Schwartz, N. M. (in press). Time use management. In M. S. Schwartz (Ed.), *Patient education: A practitioner's guide*. New York: Guilford Press.

Wells, A. (1990). Panic disorder in association with relaxation induced anxiety: An attentional training approach to treatment. *Behavior Therapy*, *21*, 273–280.

13

The Use of Audiotapes for Patient Education and Relaxation

Mark S. Schwartz

Audiotapes are in common use for patient education and relaxation therapies. They have a legitimate place in the clinical practice of applied psychophysiology, biofeedback, behavior therapy, and behavioral medicine. There are distinct advantages for providers, patients and their families, institutions, and third-party payers. This chapter focuses on the advantages of using audiotapes and provides considerations in their use.

Practitioners disagree about whether or not to use relaxation tapes and how to use them. Practitioners often lack education both about how to make good tapes and how to make good use of them. There also is limited research on these topics, and the use of tapes for patient education has a very limited literature.

I discuss in this chapter the advantages of using audiotapes for patient education and relaxation. I then focus on the actual use of relaxation tapes, including the dimensions of such tapes. Making one's own tapes versus getting commercially available ones and the issue of taped versus live relaxation therapy are other topics explored here.

ADVANTAGES OF USING AUDIOTAPES

Some advantages of audiotapes for patient education are part of the extensive discussions of audiotapes and patient education by Doak, Doak, and Root (1985). This chapter includes aspects of their cogent discussions, which conclude that tapes can be very useful for patient education.

Professional Advantages

Conservation of Time

Of foremost importance is that using tapes can conserve a practitioner's time, freeing it for other activities. Prudent practitioners consider carefully prepared tapes combined with face-to-face presentations and printed materials.

Increased Flexibility

In busy professional settings, there is often not enough time or energy to fully discuss the rationale for therapy and to answer many of the patients' questions. Patients often want to know enough for them to decide whether to invest in a program that involves biofeedback and other forms of applied psychophysiology. They often have limited time and money themselves to learn about these therapies. Printed patient-education booklets have a place in helping to inform and prepare patients. However, these are impractical for some patients and not enough for others. Audiotaped patient education increases flexibility both for patient education and relaxation.

Reduced "Burnout" from Repetition

Providers who see many new patients each week repeat the same or similar information to many or all patients. Although practitioners usually often prefer face-to-face presentations of patient-education and relaxation procedures, these presentations often become tedious. Frequent repetition of the same information, even with new patients, often results in practitioners losing interest. The use of well-developed audiotapes ease routine instructions (Doak et al., 1985) as well as help to maintain quality control over the information provided.

Language

Audiotapes often have language advantages (Doak et al., 1985). For example, they can be informal, use colloquial and natural language, and allow more variability. Futhermore, accents can enhance comprehension for some patients. However, these authors note that accents also can detract from other patients' comprehension.

Practical Considerations

Lower Costs

The costs of providing face-to-face patient-education and relaxation therapies have increased substantially over the years. The cost of providing about 1 hour of such therapy is now approaching $200. Compare this to the small fee for audiotapes and printed booklets. Costs partly depend on whether practitioners make their own tapes or buy them and on the quantities purchased. Nevertheless, providing all relaxation therapy with office-based interactions costs much more than supplementing office relaxation therapy with tapes.

Everyone in health care is very concerned about cost containment. The proper use of effective audiotapes is very important for achieving cost containment. Third-party payers should welcome these cost-saving measures and should consider reimbursing for them.

Increased Number Of Patients

Practitioners can see more patients and provide more services when they properly use audiotapes. Everyone should value providing more services to a greater number of patients while using less professional time as long as they can maintain quality of treatment.

Increased Credibility and Enthusiasm

A well-prepared audiotape is often better organized, more complete, and more professional than presentations made in face-to-face situations. Some patients can also benefit from the increased credibility of patient-education and relaxation procedures prepared by credible sources on commercially available tapes. Credibility and enthusiasm conveyed on a tape can increase both the confidence and positive expectations of many patients.

Learning Time

Reduced learning time is a potential advantage of audiotapes for some patient education (Doak et al., 1985). As an example, we can assume that for most patients faster learning can result from increased patient satisfaction, comprehension and knowledge, and increased interest and motivation.

Patient Considerations

Increased Comprehension and Retention

A large percentage of patients display poor comprehension of printed instructions (Doak et al., 1985). Many patients do not understand or remember live, spoken instructions. Tapes can be a very useful patient-education modality for many patients. Tapes can improve comprehension, hence knowledge, for many patients. Doak et al. (1985) particularly recommend considering tapes for patients who learn better by listening, those visually impaired, and those with low literacy. Other patients who can benefit are those who need variety to overcome attention span problems and those who prefer repetition of taped learning. There also are patients whose language differs from the providers. For example, some patients do not speak or understand English, or English is a second language for them. Tapes in the patient's language have obvious advantages.

In addition, there often is not enough time in face-to-face sessions for practitioners to present all or even most of the information needed. Some information presented to patients will not reach family members. Practitioners probably present the same topics differently to different patients. Some of these presentations may be less clear and less complete at certain times. Well-constructed scripts can help solve that problem, but then one still has the problems associated with repetition.

Furthermore, most patients forget most new information in a few minutes or hours after face-to-face communications. Tape-recorded information that permits patients to listen to the material more than once probably increases retention.

Patient Satisfaction

Many patients prefer face-to-face presentations, but this depends partly on the practitioner's verbal skills and personality. Properly developed audiotaped presentations can be as satisfactory or more satisfactory than face-to-face presentations. I know of no data comparing taped patient-education presentations with face-to-face presentations. In a pilot study of 50 consecutive patients, I found that nearly all were very satisfied with a taped patient-education presentation supplementing a face-to-face presentation.

Motivation and Compliance

Well-developed and well-presented audiotaped patient-education and relaxation procedures could help to enhance patient understanding and interest in the recommendations and therapy procedures. This, in turn, could increase patient motivation and compliance. There is no research for this assumption. However, the alternative assumption—that face-to-face presentations are better for increasing patient motivation and compliance—also has no data. Until there are adequate studies, the less costly approach is justified.

Consistency of Information and Therapy Procedures

Well-developed audiotapes increase the consistency of the information and standardize the information and procedures. Patients who receive such tapes at least receive the same information and procedures.

Provision of Information to Family Members

Family members of patients often need education about the therapy rationale and procedures. When patients bring family members with them, it is easier to educate them if the practitioner's schedule permits. However, patients usually come alone. Involvement of family members can help increase compliance with relaxation procedures for some patients. It is very often difficult for patients to communicate adequately to family members. Audiotapes allow patients added ways to share information with their families. Some spouses and children participate with the patient and reportedly benefit from the experience.

Reduction of Distractions

Distractions occur often when patients are learning relaxation, especially in early phases. This can occur when tapes are used, but it is probably less likely. Clinical experience suggests that the taped voice helps to keep patients focused on the procedures. This assumption deserves formal study.

Assistance in Pacing and Timing of Relaxation

Some patients rush through relaxation. Some lose track of a good pace. Tapes can help to reduce this problem because they provide instructions over fixed times and use standard pacing.

In tertiary professional practices, audiotapes are useful for all the reasons given above. Practitioners in tertiary practices see many patients who live long distances away and see some patients only once. The responsibilities in that first and often only session include patient education and the answering of questions. One needs to give the patients much useful and necessary information and explain many therapy procedures in the short time available. One must conserve time, be flexible, contain costs, and see some patients with very little notice.

When practical, tertiary practitioners usually try to refer patients to a practitioner much closer to the patient's home. The referral will probably result in more evaluative and explanatory interview time. Thus, one should strive to reduce unnecessary duplication. Audiotapes allow presentations of useful information and procedures in a cost-efficient manner. Since one also has face-to-face discussions with all patients, the use of tapes allows one to review and select patient-education topics specifically indicated by the situation.

There are some potential *disadvantages* of using tapes. There are the risks of relying too much on them, or of using tapes with poorly developed scripts, inadequate recording style, and technically inadequate recordings. These factors can reduce both the efficiency and value of the tapes. There are many useful ideas for making patient-education tapes in

Doak et al. (1985). The use of too many tapes for a given patient may overburden that patient. Practitioners need to be flexible and use good clinical judgment for when, how, and with whom to use tapes. The following section addresses several considerations in using and making audio relaxation tapes.

CONSIDERATIONS IN THE USE OF AUDIOTAPED RELAXATION

Awareness of considerations in selecting, recording, and using audiotaped relaxation is useful. Again, for emphasis, it is not my intention to promote substitution of tapes for all live relaxation therapies. Instead, my intent is recommending careful, prudent, cost-efficient, and effective use.

Dimensions of Relaxation Tapes

Several dimensions of relaxation tapes are important for patients' preference, comfort, compliance, and effectiveness. Gaarder and Montgomery (1981) published the best listing and discussion of these dimensions. The interested reader should refer to their discussion of each dimension (pp. 149–154).

- Length
- Source of voice
- Tonal quality of voice
- Hypnotic quality of voice
- Pace
- Voice quality
- Authoritarian suggestion
- Authoritativeness
- Suggestiveness
- Gender
- Dialect and vocabulary
- Background sound

- Focus on:
  Breathing
  Muscle relaxation
  Muscle tensing
  Body parts
  Sensations
  Body imagery
  Mental imagery
  Subjective cues

Patients differ in their preference at least for some of these dimensions. These preferences probably will influence their use of the tapes and their psychological and physiological responses. In turn, these responses affect the results from the use of tapes. The practitioner should consider these dimensions when purchasing commercially available tapes, recording tapes, and when recommending tapes to patients and colleagues.

There are no official guidelines or research to help us decide about which tapes to use and when we should record scripts ourselves. There are no guidelines or research to help us match patients with dimensions of tapes. Practitioner preferences may not match patient preferences. Relying on one tape or one set of tapes may not be satisfactory for all patients no matter how good the tape. A library of alternatives may be preferable. This allows patients to try different tapes and to choose the one or those tapes with which they are most comfortable.

A later section discusses research comparing taped versus live relaxation therapies. Those studies usually provide no information about any of the dimensions of the tapes. The studies also do not include evaluations or ratings by practitioners or by the patients or subjects.

These studies often assume that a single tape is satisfactory for all or most subjects. This is usually a tape developed by the investigator. The implicit assumption is that a tape is a tape is a tape. This is as erroneous as assuming that biofeedback is biofeedback is biofeedback. Assessing the physiological and psychological responses of patients to different tapes is an important area that at present has not been adequately researched.

In conclusion, many practitioners use a variety of relaxation tapes. Careful practitioners listen to and try to relax with each tape they plan to give to their patients. This includes those tapes made by the practitioner. The therapist should recognize and respect the fact that some patients may want choices and benefit from selecting their own tape.

Making One's Own Tapes

This section focuses on making both patient-education and relaxation tapes. Some information on patient-education tapes also applies to relaxation tapes. Doak et al. (1985) provide many useful ideas for making patient-education tapes. Advantages for practitioners making their own tapes include the patient's hearing his or her own doctor's or therapist's voice. However, this is not always an advantage. Many providers do not have the voice quality for such recordings. Their voices may be distracting or disturbing to some patients. I doubt that most patients expect personalized, taped instructions.

Tapes permit the use of informal, natural, and colloquial language. Tapes also permit local or regional language and allow the use of dialects and accents that can enhance comprehension and acceptance.

Practitioners should consider the many similarities between reading printed information and listening that are noted by Doak et al. (1985). Both use the same language decoding process by patients and provide cues via their structure, grammar, sequence, and tempo. Both demand attention and memory to increase comprehension and rely on prior knowledge to integrate new information.

Therapists should also consider the differences noted by Doak et al. (1985). The rate of flow of information is usually not controllable by the listener listening to tapes. There are no visual stimuli or graphics unless in an accompanying book or with slides.

As with printed materials, in devising scripts for audiotapes, practitioners should define the purpose and scope of the message explicitly. What new behaviors does the therapist want patients to do? What are the main points? The following guidelines for patient-education scripts are presented by Doak et al. (1985) who suggest the practitioner

- Use conversational language.
- Use short, common-usage words.
- Vary sentence lengths.
- Use a predictable, repetitive format such as instructions followed by examples.
- Maintain consistency in terms.
- Draw attention to key points.
    Change tone of voice.
    Use repetition.
    Give emphasis in the summary and ask questions.
- Use a normal rate of speech between 100–150 words per minute (Sticht, 1975).
- Consider combining tapes with worksheets or workbook.

The duration of tapes can be as brief as 5–10 minutes. This duration is better for those with low literacy skills and patients with very short attention spans. When making longer tapes for all patients, the clinician should consider breaks about every 5 minutes. These intervals permit reviews, questions, and interactions with printed materials. The breaks also help to maintain patient attention.

Practitioners who consider writing their own scripts and making their own patient-education tapes and relaxation tapes should consider asking their colleagues and patients to listen to sample recordings. They should request comments and criticisms. They should also assess patients' physiological responses and subjective reactions and attitudes. The prudent clinician will plan to revise these tapes a few times.

Providers who prefer to tape-record relaxation procedures individually for each patient, as some do, may benefit from the same guidelines. That is, they should have colleagues and patients listen to and critique different versions. Practitioners should not assume that some factors do not matter unless shown not to matter. Finally, clinicians should remember that buying commercially available tapes in quantity substantially reduces the cost per tape.

Making Relaxation Tapes

Practitioners can review Gaarder and Montgomery (1981), Gevirtz (1987), Smith (1989) for further ideas about relaxation tapes. They should consider the following suggestions gleaned and adapted from these sources as well as my own experience.

- Consider 10–20 minutes duration for longer periods and briefer times for some applications.
- Read several sample scripts aloud.
- Listen to several samples of published relaxation tapes for script and other ideas and for your own impressions.
- Specify all details in your script.
- Use a colloquial style as if you were talking to someone.
- Before starting, decide to use one relaxation method or to combine methods. Consider stretch–release, tense–release, passive, breathing, relaxing thoughts, or images.
- If you decide to do separate scripts for each method and put them all on the same tape, then select a sequence.
- Decide between directive instructions versus permissive instructions. For example, "my arms are feeling heavier" is more directive, and "feelings of heaviness are developing in my arms" is more permissive.
- Consider including words, phrases, and mental pictures to help deepen the relaxation and relaxed feelings. See Smith (1989) for ideas.
- Consider including statements or suggestions to permit acceptance of relaxing beliefs and commitment. Consider "I trust the relaxing powers within myself" or "I am becoming more accepting of the relaxing powers within me."
- Consider writing brief pauses and quiet periods into the script. These can be as brief as 2–5 seconds or longer if the patient will be repeating phrases.
- Type out the script with a word processor.
- Read it aloud several times. Jot down emphasis places.
- Assess the script with the help of others. Check the length. Be sure the instructions are specific and avoid instructions that are vague or uncertain. Avoid statements that patients will view as unrealistic and will not believe even with repetition (Smith, 1989, p. 214).
- Revise, revise, revise.
- Ask someone else to read it to you in the manner intended.

- Read the final script several times for familiarity.
- Record your script and listen to yourself a few times while trying to relax with it. Remember that your voice sounds different to you than it does to others. Change the script and rerecord as needed. Arrange for someone else in your office to record it if your voice is not relaxing.

Taped versus Live Relaxation

A basic and very important question is whether live relaxation therapy is more effective than taped relaxation procedures. Some professionals in this field are very critical of the use of any relaxation tapes. Others are critical of commercially available relaxation tapes compared to those made by the practitioner for his or her own patients.

One of the arguments against commercially available tapes (and, by implication, many provider-made standard tapes) is that they provide noncontingent reinforcement and poor pacing of the procedures. One contention is that contingent reinforcement and optimal pacing require looking at patients and carefully examining their musculature, facial expressions, and emotional responses. The research supporting the superiority of live over taped relaxation typically focuses on the tensing and releasing portion of this progressive muscle relaxation. Face-to-face therapy may be more useful for this early stage of progressive muscle relaxation during which one uses tensing and releasing of muscle groups. Lichstein (1988) noted that "there is no data on the question of live versus taped presentations of other relaxation methods" (p. 98).

There is no disagreement here with the value of office-based live relaxation therapies provided by practitioners competent in their use. Nor is there disagreement with the assumption that such therapy can provide better learning of relaxation than some taped procedures for many patients. The disagreement is with blanket assumptions that one approach is superior to the other in all or even most respects for all or even most patients. There are simply too many factors and circumstances for adopting such an assumption. For example, we can consider the many characteristics of taped procedures, the many procedures other than tensing–releasing, the cost–benefit ratio, and the feasibility of office-based sessions for many patients. We may also consider the advantages of audiotapes for other reasons discussed earlier in the chapter.

Reviews of studies comparing the physiological differences between taped relaxation therapy versus live relaxation therapy in the office report statistically significant differences in favor of live relaxation therapy (Borkovec & Sides, 1979; Lehrer, 1982; Lichstein, 1988).

However, there is a lack of assessment and specifications of the tapes used in those studies. Published studies also typically do not provide much or any description of the many dimensions of tapes that can influence patient or subject acceptance and comfort. Studies concluding that live therapy is better have typically used the tape only in the office and only for a few sessions. There is also no indication of the researcher's bias. Research results are incomplete and inconclusive.

We may consider the recent study by Craw, Newton, and Newman (1993) who concluded that "taped and live procedures are equivalent when differences in cognitive preparation and expectancy inherent in these procedures are controlled for between groups" (p. 62). Cognitive preparation was live for all 40 treated male Veterans Administration inpatients in a substance abuse program. Treated patients reduced heart rate and galvanic skin reaction (GSR), increased finger temperature, and decreased state anxiety over four sessions. Live presentation of relaxation or taped presentation with the therapist present did not affect the results. Audio–video format was not better than audio alone. This study needs replication and extension, but it does illustrate one way in which audiotaped relaxation can be as effective as live presentation.

To dismiss the use of taped relaxation on the basis of the other available research is unwise. One cannot conclude that live relaxation is always or usually better than taped relaxation. Limiting relaxation therapies to live and office-based procedures limits the flexibility of a clinical practice. It creates unnecessary constraints on researchers of relaxation therapies. It increases costs to the professional, the patient, the health care institution, and third-party payers. It ignores the cost differential between these two methods and other advantages of tapes discussed elsewhere in this chapter. For example, are the clinical differences always or usually worth the greater costs associated with live presentations? Can taped relaxation therapy result in clinically meaningful and patient acceptable therapeutic gains for some patients? Within a stepped-care model of treatment, can practitioners reserve live relaxation therapy for those patients having trouble or insufficient results with taped procedures?

Another concern is that practitioners should not use relaxation tapes to provide instructions to patients during office-based sessions with the therapist absent. Some professionals go even so far as to consider this bordering on unethical professional behavior. The issue of therapist presence or absence during biofeedback sessions is the topic of Chapter 8. Many of the same professional concerns and considerations about leaving patients alone without professional observation apply here.

There may be some circumstances in which leaving a patient alone for a few minutes while he or she is listening to a relaxation tape is appropriate. However most professionals frown on doing so for several sessions and with good cause. Admittedly however, it is still an empirical question whether such a practice is less efficacious with selected patients than other office procedures.

Until adequate data are available, it is prudent and sensible to avoid or at least limit such practices. Practitioners should adjust fees for such sessions. When they are used at all, practitioners would be wise to provide clear and defensible justifications to the patient, referral source, and third-party payers. I am unaware of justifications.

CONCLUSIONS

The criticism of audiotaped relaxation is an unresolved empirical issue. The issue is far more complex than choosing either one approach or another. All tapes should receive critical evaluation and be used prudently. This chapter has discussed considerations for selecting tapes and guidelines for their use. In fact, it is partly because of my agreement with many of the concerns with the indiscriminate use of commercially available and other tapes that I wrote this chapter.

Live patient education and relaxation can be more expensive compared to the proper use of well-prepared tapes for many patients. Unanswered is the question of whether the repetitive use of taped relaxation therapy outside the practitioner's office yields similar results as office-based live relaxation therapy. Other unanswered questions include whether good patient education can increase the usefulness of taped relaxation therapies.

Finally, the practitioner is urged to consider audiotapes for patient education for biofeedback and relaxation therapies and other applied psychophysiological therapies. The prudent therapist will consider them for providing *some* relaxation therapies for *many* patients. There are many considerations in making, selecting, and using audiotapes. Therapists should consider using a variety of relaxation tapes for patients because patients have different preferences and needs. Cost–benefit considerations have become increasingly important in the changing health care financial environment. Well-developed and prudently used audiotapes probably often help to provide more effective and cost-efficient patient education and relaxation therapies than avoiding their use would incur. However, research needs in this area remain substantial.

REFERENCES

Borkovec, T. D., & Sides, J. K. (1979). Critical procedural variables to the physiological effects of progressive relaxation: A review. *Behaviour Research and Therapy, 17,* 119–125.

Craw, M. J., Newton, F. A., & Newman, R. G. (1993, March 25–30). Biofeedback assisted relaxation training within a substance abuse program: A comparison of taped versus live instructions. In *Proceedings of the 24th Annual Meeting of the Association for Applied Psychophysiology and Biofeedback, Los Angeles.* Wheatridge, CO: Association for Applied Psychophysiology and Biofeedback.

Doak, C. C., Doak, L. G., Root, J. H. (1985) *Teaching patients with low literacy skills* (pp. 77–101). New York: J. B. Lippincott.

Gaarder, K. R., & Montgomery, P. S. (1981). *Clinical biofeedback: A procedural manual for behavioral medicine* (2nd ed.). Baltimore: Williams & Wilkins.

Gevirtz, R. (1987). Appendix: How to make a personalized relaxation tape. In E. M. Catalano (Ed.), *The chronic pain control workbook* (pp. 203–207). Oakland, CA: New Harbinger Publications.

Lehrer, P. M. (1982). How to relax and not to relax: A re-evaluation of the work of Edmund Jacobson—I. *Behaviour Research and Therapy, 20,* 417–428.

Lichstein, K. L. (1988). *Clinical relaxation strategies.* New York: Wiley-Interscience.

Smith, J. C. (1989). *Relaxation dynamics: A cognitive-behavioral approach to relaxation.* Champaign, IL: Research Press.

Sticht, T. G. (Ed.). (1975). *Reading for working: A functional literacy anthology* (pp. 98–104). Alexandria, VA: Human Research Resources Organization.

V
DISORDERS NEEDING LOWER TENSION AND AROUSAL

14

Headache: Selected Issues and Considerations in Evaluation and Treatment
Part A: Evaluation

Mark S. Schwartz

Applied psychophysiological treatments, including relaxation and biofeedback therapies are commonly accepted as standard treatment for tension-type and migraine headaches. There is widespread clinical application of many biofeedback procedures for treating people with these types of headaches. Indeed, patients with headaches comprise the largest group of patients seen by many practitioners.

I confidently estimate that relaxation and biofeedback therapies in clinical settings have resulted in the successful treatment of at least hundreds of thousands of people. This is not surprising. One need only consider the prevalence of these headaches and the costs associated with chronic and frequent headaches. Included are the costs of visits to physicians, the costs of medications, and the cost from time lost from work and other activities.

Many studies over the past 20 years have used relaxation and biofeedback[1] for treating people with headaches termed "muscle tension," "vascular," "migraine," and "combination" or "mixed" headache. There probably are more publications about relaxation and biofeedback treatments for people with headaches than there are for other disorders. Blanchard and Andrasik (1987) and Andrasik and Blanchard (1987) reviewed the out-come research. More recent research has continued to support the value of these therapies. Furthermore, the heuristic value of biofeedback stimulated considerable research. This includes research about the causes of headaches, treatment effectiveness, and mechanisms of treatment.

Biofeedback and associated therapies for the treatment of patients with headaches are here to stay and will continue to grow. However, the ways that practitioners apply these treatments will probably undergo changes.

This chapter discusses many of the conceptual and practical topics for applied psychophysiological treatments of headaches. Compared to the first edition, this chapter reflects extensive editing, updating, and several new topics. The reader is referred to other chapters for more discussions of related topics.[2]

---

[1]For convenience, this chapter uses the term "biofeedback" instead of specifying EMG or temperature biofeedback and instead of cumbersome terms such as biofeedback-assisted physiological self-regulatory therapies, augmented proprioception, and applied clinical biofeedback.

[2]These include intake and cognitive preparation of patients (Chapter 6), compliance (Chapter 9), definitions (Chapter3B), audiotapes (Chapter 13), and dietary considerations (Chapter 10).

Some providers rely primarily on biofeedback and relaxation therapies. Others include these therapies with selected patients and incorporate these approaches in the context of broader behavioral and stress management therapy programs.

Research in the past few years has helped to provide useful information and answers to many questions and issues such as those below. Nevertheless, prudent practitioners are mindful of these questions and issues. This chapter discusses in some depth several of these questions and concerns.

- When should one use biofeedback versus other nonpharmacological therapies?
- Which biofeedback procedures are more effective than others?
- What placements of electromyographic (EMG) electrodes should one consider and use?
- Is treating to specified physiological criteria needed? Thus, how much skill do patients need?
- To what degree does patient education affect results?
- Who should provide biofeedback therapies?
- What are the mechanisms of therapeutic success?
- What are the most cost-effective ways to provide biofeedback and related therapies for patients with headaches.
- How much assessment and what types of assessment does one need before and during treatment?
- What are the effects of medications on headaches and biofeedback?
- What other therapies should one consider?
- Can biofeedback and related therapies be useful with special populations such as elderly and pediatric patients, and how does one provide the therapies?
- Can biofeedback and related therapies be useful with menstrual-related headaches and migraines during pregnancy?
- What is the role of dietary changes in treating headaches?
- What is the role of sleep assessment and treating sleep disorders in treating headaches?
- Do clinical practitioners achieve higher or lower rates of success than in controlled studies?
- How close do clinical applications need to be to research procedures for similar or better efficacy?

These questions require credible responses. However, their existence alone is not enough to place a moratorium on the clinical applications and reimbursement of biofeedback for headaches. Third-party reimbursement for biofeedback treatments of headaches has increased over the past several years. Yet, some health insurance companies still show reservation about reimbursing for biofeedback treatments for headaches. Assuredly, a major concern for them is financial. They realize the scope of the headache problem and probably fear the potential for substantial costs. These companies apparently do not know there are ways to reduce their costs by increasing reimbursement for biofeedback and related clinical services.

Clinical biofeedback is justifiable and cost efficient for treating many patients with headaches. Published research and clinical experience are sufficient to support reimbursement. However, practitioners also are aware of and sensitive to the questions and concerns raised by very cautious and sometimes critical professional peers. Practitioners need to remain aware of the questions and concerns of the critics and those providing payments.

Practitioners must adequately respond to the questions, concerns, and reservations of the critical professionals. It is not sufficient simply to point to the widespread clinical use of biofeedback and to those studies that support its use.

In addition, we need to be careful about who provides the services, how, for whom, and when one uses biofeedback. We also need to be willing to tailor our procedures and to provide clinical services in cost-effective and efficient ways. My intention for this chapter is to add to the understanding, acceptance, and improved uses of biofeedback and related therapies. There are good responses and counterarguments to the critics. Before discussing these and other questions and issues, I present a selected review of diagnosis.

DIAGNOSIS

The proposed revision of classification and diagnostic criteria for headache disorders, cranial neuralgias, and facial pain (Olesen, 1988) offers some advances over the prior 1962 system. The focus here is on the proposed new groups of "tension-type headaches" and "migraines with and without aura" (Andrasik, 1992; Olesen, 1988; Saper, Silberstein, Gordon, & Hamel, 1993). A listing of the diagnostic criteria is beyond the scope of this chapter.

With the proposed system, practitioners make a diagnosis for each distinct headache form. Criteria are more precise than in the prior system. The new system acknowledges a possible continuum between pure migraines and pure tension-type headaches. The proponents dropped the diagnoses of "mixed," "combination," or "tension-vascular" headache. If a patient has both types of symptoms, one now uses both a migraine without aura and a tension-type diagnosis. The system also states the order of diagnosis when diagnoses are listed. Migraine comes before tension-type when one makes both diagnoses. We should note this is not consistent with the common observation that muscle tension and muscle symptoms often appear to precede other symptoms.

The acknowledgment of a possible continuum may appear curious and unexpected considering the criteria implying distinct types of headache. One can resolve this apparent inconsistency by interpreting it to mean that patients can have combinations of headache types rather than have a headache that is a combination headache.

Some professionals propose combining separate diagnoses into a unitary diagnosis such as "recurrent benign headache." Part of the rationale for this proposed merge is the considerable overlap in the symptoms and treatments for headaches within the existing diagnoses. There also is potential benefit from using medications for headaches other than the original intended use for any one type of headache. If the practitioner adopts the view of an amalgam diagnosis, then he or she should consider specifying the predominant features.

In clinical practice, systems with separate diagnoses remain in use. Physicians and other practitioners often are not familiar with the proposed new system or the merged concept or do not see the relevance and importance of these in daily practice. After all, relaxation and biofeedback often are part of the treatment plan regardless of the specific diagnostic name. Yet there are indeed advantages for the proposed new system, especially for research, which is consistent with one of its major goals. I expect it will take several more years to fully replace the older system practice.[3]

---

[3]For practitioners using biofeedback therapies, there is no difference in treatment tied to the second- and third-digit-level subdiagnoses.

One problem with the new system lies in differentiating headaches associated with versus those not associated with a disorder of pericranial muscles. However, there are no criteria for muscle tenderness and EMG microvolts. The system acknowledges both this and the difficulty with this distinction. The purpose for this subdivision is to "stimulate research." The proposed system notes the subdivision is optional "in view of the poor scientific basis for the subdivision." Specifically, the document states that:

> There is not yet sufficient evidence available regarding the limits of normality of pericranial muscle tenderness. Neither has sufficient attention been given to the methodology of pericranial palpation. Evidence concerning normal EMG levels of pericranial muscles is similarly deficient. Until evidence accumulates concerning tenderness on palpation and pericranial EMG, each investigator must judge as best he (*she*) can on the basis of experience with non-headache sufferers and by comparing symmetrical sites. . . . (Olesen, p. 30)

The new system specifies that one assumes or suspects a "psychogenic" etiology if one cannot find evidence of muscle involvement based on tenderness or EMG. However, this assumption fails to consider the problem of lack of criteria. It also ignores patients whose headaches suggest a muscle and postural contribution but for whom muscle involvement does not show in the office. For example, we can consider patients whose daily activities involve probable or clear excess muscle tension but who relax well in the practitioner's office.

The new system acknowledges many of its limitations. My comments intend to bring attention to or remind readers of selected issues and to offer some comments and suggestions on some of these diagnostic issues.

Selected implications of this diagnostic scheme include the following:

1. Consider using tension-type headaches and migraine with or without aura. Consider using multiple diagnoses instead of mixed or combination headache.

2. Consider using multiple criteria for assessing muscle tension. Use multiple muscle sites. Use multiple postures including sitting and standing. Use multiple conditions of recording including resting, stressors, eyes open, eyes closed, sitting and standing.

3. Use multiple methods for assessing stress and other potential causes or aggravating factors. Include a careful history and consider self-report measures.

4. If there are no signs of excess muscle tension in the office during resting baselines, apply relaxation treatments to daily life.

5. Within a stepped-care model, start with less evaluation of muscle activity and tenderness and add more later.

MECHANISMS OF HEADACHE CAUSES AND TREATMENT EFFICACY

Different models and explanations exist for explaining the etiology and progression of tension-type and migraine headaches. There also are different views about the mechanisms of successful therapies. Challenges even continue for the assumption that muscle contraction causes all tension-type headaches. Challenges also exist for the view that vascular changes triggered by biochemical agents are the primary or sole causative factors for migraine headaches. Questions about the role of stress and emotion also remain. The following section summarizes several of the major models of etiology and treatment mechanisms. I offer selected comments, conclusions, and implications.

Resting EMG of People with and without Headache Diagnoses

Most earlier studies do not show a consistent difference between resting EMG levels in the frontal and/or neck regions of subjects with tension-type headache versus subjects without tension-type headaches (Andrasik, Blanchard, Arena, Saunders, & Barron, 1982; Marcus, 1992; Flor & Turk, 1989). One implication is that muscle activity during rest is not a good differential factor. Another implication is that there is more than muscle activity involved in the etiology of tension headaches. Third, resting muscle activity may not be the best source of data upon which to base the decision for providing biofeedback.

Most prior comparisons involve only the frontal area, reclining or partially reclining postures, and eyes closed. More recent studies support a difference (Ahles et al., 1988; Schoenen, Gerard, DePasqua, & Juprelle, 1991; Hatch et al., 1992). In Ahles et al. (1988), the difference compared to a small group of nonheadache subjects ($N = 21$) was for tension, migraine, and mixed headaches. There were no meaningful differences among the headache types. The difference from the nonheadache control group was for three different body positions. The positions were reclining, sitting without back supported, and standing with hands at sides. All conditions were with subjects' eyes closed. The sitting and standing positions had higher bilateral trapezius tension than the reclining. We must also note that 40–50% of their sample did not show abnormal EMG activity in any positions. The authors logically speculate that their patients may represent a group with more severe and refractory headaches. The clinical setting in which this study took place is a tertiary headache clinic.

The more recent study by Schoenen et al. (1991) compared patients with tension-type headaches and healthy controls in reclining and standing postures and with a math stressor. They recorded the left frontalis, temporalis, and trapezius muscles. The EMG activity was higher in the patients than the controls. This occurred for both postures, with the math stress, and for all sites. Most patients (62.5%) showed EMG levels exceeding the control groups by two standard deviations considering all three muscles and recording conditions. Only 2 of the 32 patients showed EMG activity outside the defined normal range during all recordings.

Hatch et al. (1992) reported that "headache subjects showed significantly greater EMG activity than controls during baseline and stressful task performance" (p. 89). The Lichstein et al. (1991) study also showed statistically higher frontal EMG activity during sitting resting baselines than in normal controls. This occurred during a headache-free session and with an even greater difference during the active headache period.

There were methodological limits in these studies. However, the conclusions are that differences can and do exist for patients compared to nonheadache controls, and placements and postures can be important. It is speculative yet logical to also conclude that the differences may be more likely in clinical settings in which practitioners see patients with more severe and refractory headaches.

Nevertheless, EMG recordings are still not of clear diagnostic use. Using multiple recording sites and multiple conditions might eventually be a more useful procedure, but this too is speculative. Furthermore, these studies are not contrary to the possibility that there is more than muscle activity involved in the etiology of tension-type and migraine headaches. Most data indicate that resting muscle activity in reclined postures does not differentiate between patients and nonheadache controls.

The EMG during Headache-Active and Headache-Free States

People with tension-type headaches often do not show a difference between their EMG activity during headaches and when no headache is present. The Hatch et al. (1992) review noted "conflicting results" (p. 90). Some studies showed

> greater EMG activity during a headache and another larger group showing no difference . . . [and] one study . . . [reported] frontal EMG levels . . . significantly lower during the headache state than when they were headache free. (Hatch et al., 1992, p. 90)

This topic has not been the focus of much research, especially in recent years. An example of recent research is the study of Lichstein et al. (1991) of 13 people with migraines with prodrome and 8 with both episodic and chronic tension-type headache. They found no reliable difference in frontal muscle tension between headache-active and headache-free sessions with subjects sitting quietly in a recliner chair. Again, one can assert that limited body positions (Ruff, Sturgis, & St. Lawrence, 1986) and recording sites obscured the difference. Furthermore, there might be more than muscle activity involved in tension-type headaches, and the muscle sites monitored may not be the ones involved. For some subjects, the muscle activity might be greater before and after the monitoring. Nevertheless, the fact remains that again there was no difference shown.

It is reasonable to study headache-active versus headache-free time. However, the lack of a difference in EMG activity is not enough to conclude that muscle tension does not cause these headaches, since the absence of a difference does not prove the absence of its effect. We have only to consider a person carrying something heavy long enough to produce pain in the arms and shoulders. We may observe no excess tension during recordings after the individual puts the burden down even if the pain continues. This is so obvious that it does not need further explanation.

Relationship between EMG Changes and Pain across Sessions

Some patients treated for tension-type headaches show a relationship between changes in office-recorded EMG activity across sessions and reduced headaches. Other patients do not show this relationship. This seldom and inadequately researched question "remains an area of controversy" (Blanchard, 1992, p. 539).

Most published reports do not show a consistent relationship. This suggests that there may be something other than muscle tension involved with decreased tension-type headaches. There is some support for the idea that cognitive factors may play an important role in these changes (Holroyd et al., 1984; Blanchard, 1992). I believe this is true for some patients. However, one also must consider that limitations in recording muscle activity during office procedures are less likely to reflect clinically relevant changes. Changes in patients' daily activities are probably more related to symptom changes than office-recorded muscle activity. Furthermore, recording other muscle sites may be more appropriate than the ones commonly chosen in research.

Relationship between EMG Activity and Pain in Tension-Type Headaches

Practitioners often observe patients starting a relaxation session with a headache. Many of these patients clearly lower their cephalic or neck muscle tension and report decreased intensity or elimination of the headache during the session. It is not surprising that many practitioners still assume there is a significant relationship between muscle tension and headache intensity for some patients.

However, research shows no clear or consistent relationship between EMG activity and pain intensity or pain frequency in patients experiencing tension-type headaches (Lichstein et al., 1991; Hatch et al., 1992). Showing that variations of EMG activity result in changes in pain intensity and frequency has been elusive. The logic is good, but there is scant research on this topic.

A more recent study, however, did support the relationship (Hatch et al., 1992). The latter noted that "pain ratings and EMG activity increased during task performance and then showed a parallel decline during recovery periods" (p. 110). All their subjects denied a headache when they arrived at the laboratory but some reported head or neck pain during the procedures.

Other factors besides decreased muscle tension could account for the clinical observations. These include reduced SNS arousal and various cognitive factors. Most patients want to feel better. These sessions allow distraction from their stressful daily activities. Nevertheless, reduced and resting muscle tension also are likely factors for many of these patients. Practitioners should consider other monitoring sites and consider that muscle activity may be higher before the office monitoring starts.

Relationship between EMG and Site of Headache

There is not enough research about EMG activity and pain sites. During rest or stress, there is sometimes more EMG activity from nonpain sites and sometimes more activity from pain sites. We may consider three possible explanations. Referred pain from one site to another could produce this effect. The muscle activity at the pain site may have been greater before the recordings. Some or most of the muscle activity was outside the range of the EMG bandpass.[4]

The EMG of People with Tension-Type versus Migraine Headaches

Patients with tension-type headaches do not show more resting EMG activity than patients with migraines. Older and more recent studies find similarities between the muscle tension in patients diagnosed with tension-type or migraine headaches. Lichstein at al. (1991) showed this with small groups of headache-free and headache-present patients diagnosed with tension-type or with migraines. Thus, muscle tension might play a role in the etiology of migraines. Furthermore, muscle tension is probably not the differentiating factor between the two diagnoses. This type of finding has led some to assert that the difference between headaches with these diagnoses is more a degree on a continuum than two distinct and separate diagnoses (Marcus, 1992).

Involvement of Head and Neck Muscles in Tension-Type Headaches

Excess tension in the frontal, temporal, occipital, upper trapezii, and posterior neck muscles contributes to tension-type headaches. However, most research and some clinical practice

---

[4]Many practitioners and some research customarily record EMG activity within a 100–200 Hertz bandpass. However, much muscle activity occurs below and some above this range. Advances in instrumentation allow power spectrum displays of muscle activity. This will allow research to answer this question and permit practitioners to tailor bandpass filters to each patient.

still often focus on the frontal area. Some studies have looked beyond the frontal area. Hudzinski and Lawrence (1988, 1990) and Hatch et al. (1992) are among those who looked at more than the frontal area. Hudzinski and Lawrence (1988, 1990) studied the *frontal–posterior neck* (FpN) placement. Hatch et al. (1992) studied the left and right temporalis and cervical neck sites.

Hudzinski and Lawrence (1990) noted that "conventional frontal surface EMG does not appear to reliably discriminate between muscle contraction headache sufferers or to be a means by which to distinguish the headache from nonheadache subject" (p. 24). The FpN placement encompasses multiple cephalic and neck muscles. Referring to their research on this placement, the authors reported that it is "the most discriminating" between headache and nonheadache activity" (p. 24). (See Chapter 15 for more discussion of this electrode placement.) Hatch et al. (1992) reported the temporalis muscles, the frontal area, and the posterior neck muscles reacted significantly to laboratory stress for both patients and controls.

Continued Excess Muscle Activity versus Level of Activity

Continued excess muscle tension could be more important for causing pain than the specific intensity or level of muscle tension. However, no research yet exists that supports this theory (Hovanitz, Chin, & Warm, 1989; Hatch et al., 1992). As Hatch et al. (1992) state, "at the present time, it is not known how much muscle activity over what time interval is necessary or sufficient to elicit the pain experience" (p. 108). Nevertheless, practitioners often assume that sustained excess muscle activity is a causative or aggravating factor. An implication for practitioners who adopt this concept is to recommend that patients need to release excess muscle activity often. Thus, one recommends reducing the intensity, frequency, and durations of excess tension to patients rather than only improving the depth of the relaxation.

The EMG Reactivity of People with Headaches Prone to Stress Reactions

The relationship between EMG reactivity to stress for patients with tension-type headaches compared to those without headaches appears inconsistent in the available research. This inconsistency implies that not all patients with tension-type headaches respond to stress with increased muscle tension. However, the stressors used in some research may be too weak in content and/or duration. Again, the muscle sites monitored may not be the most reactive. It also is possible that some people with tension-type and migraine headaches show changes in autonomic nervous system (ANS) reactivity, biochemical changes, and cephalic blood flow (CBF). That idea is congruent with the CBF studies of Gannon, Haynes, Cuevas, and Chavez (1987) and Haynes, Gannon, Bank, Shelton, and Goodwin (1990) discussed next. The reader should also see Hatch et al. (1992).

Cephalic Blood Flow and ANS Reactivity in People with Headaches

According to Haynes et al., 1990:

> Changes in extracranial cephalic blood flow in response to stressors has long been suggested as a possible mechanism to account for migraine pain and associated symptoms . . . [*and*] . . . suggested as a possible causal factor for muscle-contraction headache. . . . (p. 468)

The studies of Haynes et al. (1990) and Gannon et al. (1987) are very important. These researchers demonstrated experimentally rather than only with correlations that environmental psychological stress can *induce* headaches. They also showed the involvement of CBF in both types of headaches. The first relates to the proposed mechanism of stress and headaches. The second relates to the present topic.

These well-known and respected researchers demonstrated that CBF patterns occurred in an analogue situation with recruited volunteers. Their studies with somewhat limited sample sizes improved on cross-sectional and correlational studies of stress and headaches. They helped clarify the uncertainty of whether observed psychophysiological changes follow or precede headaches.

Their method used a 1-hour cognitive stressor with subjects without headaches at the start of the procedure. The subjects reported histories of frequent headaches diagnosed as muscle-contraction, migraine, or mixed. Their earlier study showed that this stressor leads to "significant increases in multiple psychophysiological indices, subjective reports of stress, and headache reports by about 80% of subjects" (Haynes et al., 1990, p. 471). I include their description of their stressor.

> Subjects were informed that "in this phase we are attempting to see how accurately and quickly you can think." They were exposed to a cognitive stressor consisting of arithmetic problems (e.g., 237–349) every 15 sec. for 1 hr. In addition, they were informed that if their performance fell below the average for college sophomores, they would hear a buzzer. Buzzes (approximately 50 dB) were presented 22 times throughout the hour on a set variable-interval schedule. (Haynes et al., 1990, p. 471)

This stressor is impressive. Sixteen of 17 subjects diagnosed with tension headache diagnosis reported headaches. Two of 5 subjects with migraines reported headaches as did 13 of 14 with mixed headaches. Average headache severity increased over the hour.

The study continuously measured blood volume pulse amplitude (BVPA) from six sites. The sites were two supratrochlear sites, two superficial temporal sites at the bifurcation of the temporal artery, and two cervical vertebrae sites at the spinalis–semispinalis site. The analyses indicated BVPA changes over the hour. Most of the subjects showed a significant relationship between CBF patterns and the induced headaches. The authors admitted they did not know whether the changes represented a primary cause of headache or a correlate of other processes in the central autonomic or neurotransmitter systems. Furthermore, individual differences in BVPA pattern occured. The pathophysiological mechanism might be different for headache types, as there was vasoconstriction in those subjects with migraines and vasodilation in those subjects with tension-type features.

The authors conservatively noted that BVPA patterns might vary with different stressors. They also noted that other blood vessels might play a role and noted no confirmation of the factors regulating the vasomotor responses. The relationship between the vasomotor responses in the analogue situation and natural situations is also unknown.

One mechanism that may explain the relationship of CBF and headache is the sustained contraction of cephalic and neck muscles such as from sustained psychosocial stress. This may restrict blood flow or create ischemia resulting in anoxia and increased concentration of lactic acid. Ischemia at other local sites also might result in compensatory distention of the cephalic arteries and other changes. Examples are increased circulatory neurokinins, catecholamines, vasopressin, and platelet serotonin. These two explanations are not mutually exclusive. Another idea is that the cessation of stress might result in a rebound distention of some cephalic blood vessels.

The proposed role of CBF is consistent with the vascular and neurogenic theories of migraines. Either the CBF leads to headaches or a central neurogenic dysfunction leads to CBF and headache. A CBF link is also consistent with the theory that sustained muscle contraction results in vascular and CBF changes among persons with tension-type headaches.

There are several implications from this research area. It helps support the justification for treating psychosocial stress and reactivity. The CBF research helps explain the inconsistent findings of research using weaker office stressors. It suggests the use of both stronger stressors and longer durations of stressors than are now typical in clinical practice. It supports the potential use of the CBF modality for monitoring and feedback. It supports the evidence that different types of treatment can result in decreased headaches. It also implies that the use of each type or treatment does not preclude the role of the others. Thus, one can intervene with the psychosocial stressor, the muscle tension, and/or the biochemical and blood-vessel stage. The next topic also supports the role of psychosocial and emotional factors contributing to headaches and supports interventions based on the role of these factors.

Influence of Psychological, Stress, and Other Factors

The commonly hypothesized and usually accepted relationship between psychological, emotional, and stress factors as causing and/or worsening headaches is an "age-old" assumption and another complex topic. There is considerable support for the relationship although it is very difficult methodologically for research to demonstrate a clear, unequivocal, and strong causal relationship. More complex is the clear demonstration of and full elucidation of the mechanisms, although many researchers and practitioners believe there is an accumulation and cascade of events needed and/or sufficient.

Practitioners, many researchers, and many or most patients continue to assume that many factors can affect the likelihood of developing or worsening a headache. Examples include:

- Major stressors and high-density minor daily stressors.
- Negative cognitive perceptions and apprisal of stress events.
- Excess or prolonged emotional reactions to stress.
- Inadequate stress management skills and behaviors.
- Certain personality features (e.g., obsessive–compulsiveness, avoidance of expressing anger).
- Lack of stress moderating factors (e.g., social support).

See Adler, Adler, and Packard (1987) for more examples and discussions of the literature about these factors. This belief and assumption does not preclude other "risk factors" or "triggers." The research below does not suggest or support migraine or tension headache personalities.

Many practitioners (and researchers) may wonder why this hypothesized and long held assumption even needs research support. "Everyone already knows it" may be "on the lips" or "out of the lips" of many professionals. However, consider that at least for many people with migraines, and perhaps for many people with tension-type headaches, and the other diagnoses related to these "distinct" types, there are many other and very different types of factors thought to act as "triggers" and contributing factors to these headaches when present alone or in combination. Consider, for example, the list below for migraines[5] and some tension-type headaches, the assumed and patient reported roles of:

[5]Adapted from Blau and Thavapalan (1988).

- Lack of food as in fasting, delayed or missed meals.
- Specific foods and drinks.
- Sleep abnormalities (i.e., excess and insufficient sleep).
- Hormones associated with menstruation, menopause, and pregnancy.
- Posture, head and neck positions, other ergonomic factors, sleeping positions, and incorrect pillows.
- Temporomandibulor behaviors.
- Visual factors (e.g., eye strain, glare, flicker, and staring at a video display terminal screen).
- Environmental factors (e.g., barometric pressure, heat, and cold).
- Environmental irritants (e.g., noise, odors, smoke, and allergens).
- Activities such as exercise and automobile travel.
- "Let down" phenomenon called "weekend headache," "Sunday headache," or "relaxation headache."

Further complicating the understanding of and demonstration of a relationship is the probability that many people with these types of headaches and a few or several of the assumed "psychological–affective–behavioral–physiological" risk factors, also have other probable major, exclusive, or sufficient causes for their headaches (e.g., postures, muscle tension habits, sleep problems, dietary; see below for more of these). Even assuming the relationship in question exists, and I do make that assumption, and assuming the presence of these "risk factors" in a given person, does not mean that the risk factors are causing the headaches for that person. Furthermore, it does not necessarily mean that one must treat these cognitive and psychophysiological factors in order to obtain therapeutic effectiveness.

Although some research addresses either migraines or tension-type headaches, this discussion combines both because,

1. Many studies addressed both headache types.
2. There is disagreement about the distinction between the types.
3. Some studies refer to chronic primary headache and do not make a distinction between migraines and tension-type headaches.
4. The headache classification system is changing.
5. Different investigators use different diagnostic terms.
6. Frequently both types exist in the same person.
7. Even with distinct types, they often interact with each other.
8. Psychological and emotional factors influence both types.

Evidence from studies on psychological, emotional, and stress factors support their role for contributing directly or indirectly to headaches (Hovanitz et al., 1989; Blanchard, Kirsch, Appelbaum, & Jaccard, 1989; Nattero, DeLorenzo, Biale, Torrie, & Ancona, l986; Holm, Holroyd, Hursey, & Penzien, 1986; Levor, Cohen, Naliboff, McArthur, & Heuser, 1986; Nattero et al., 1989; Kohler & Haimerl, 1990; Rugh et al., 1990; Leijdekkers & Passchier, 1990; deBenedittis, Lorenzetti, & Pieri, 1990; Hatch, Schoefeld, et al., 1991; Passchier, Schouten, van der Donk, & van Romunde, 1991; Hatch et al., 1992; deBenedittis & Loranzetti, 1992; Martin & Theunissen, 1993).

A summary of all, or even many, of these studies is beyond the space and time constraints of this author. Interested readers are directed to the references for their own reviews. I assume that my scholarly colleagues at universities will continue to analyze these and forthcoming studies and write detailed summaries and commentaries.

Nevertheless, I offer a brief review of a few of the studies as illustrations. This in no way implies preference for or an impression of superiority of these studies compared to the others.

To start, we know laboratory stress can induce headaches (Gannon et al., 1987; Haynes et al., 1990). Additionally, we know there is support for ratings of stress being higher during periods before and on the day of migraine headaches (Levor et al., 1986). Support for the effect of stress on migraines also comes from a careful, prospective 6-month study showing that stress increased the day before the clear-cut migraine occurred for six of seven subjects and during the headache day for 3 more of 13 German postal employees (Kohler & Haimerl, 1990). Eleven of these had "common migraine," two had "classic migraine," and some also had so-called "mixed" headaches. On the day before 109 of 192 migraines, patients scored in the upper third of the distributions on a 10-item ipsative stress questionnaire. This led the researchers to conclude that "the effects of stress on the occurrence of migraine attacks are considerable" (Kohler & Haimerl, 1990, p. 871). There was no significant relationship between low air pressure on the day of the migraines for any of the individuals. However, that factor was significant for the group and occurred on the days of 81 of 192 migraines. Compared with stress the day before, low air pressure had a weaker effect.

An interesting and clinically useful discussion of "weekend headaches" in Nattero et al. (1989) provides the following insights into the potential psychological explanations for this phenomenon. People with "weekend headaches" tend to have headaches, usually diagnosed as migraines, during a "let-down" period rather than in the midst of stress. These investigators compared patients with only weekend headaches to those with common migraines without reference to day. For the present topic, I include their clinical speculations about the characteristics of the weekend headache patient. The investigators try to explain,

> The ... headache with "a loss in his structure of the week" ... might be generated by that feeling of emptiness experienced ... in view of drab weekend days, where the patient has no real interests outside of work. ... Some upsetting situations in patients' private lives, such as marital conflicts, can also be considered as precipitants especially during weekends. (Nattero et al., 1989, p. 97)

The Minnesota Multiphasic Personality Inventory (MMPI), Beck Depression Inventory, and the State–Trait Anxiety Inventory (see Chapter 6) suggest, that compared to the common migraine patients, the weekend headache patient, reports more of a "lack of a real interest in sexual life, poor family and social life, dissatisfaction with what they have accomplished and low self esteem" (Nattero et al., 1989, p. 98) and has higher elevations of scales 1, 2, 3, 7, and 8 for females and scales 1, 2, 3, 4, and 7 for males. My inspection of the profiles suggest that the differences for scales 1, 2, and 3 for both sexes, and for scales 7 and 8 for females, is also clinically significant. The authors acknowledge that:

> Whether the stress burden is greater in these weekend headache patients than in the others, or whether these patients have a lesser capacity to cope with stress, is still an open field of research. (p. 98)

The physiological disregulation model of Gary Schwartz (1977, 1978) provides useful concepts to explain factors affecting the risk of developing a headache. Briefly,

> Physiological disregulation may occur when an individual does not or cannot attend to his/her physiological state and does not take corrective action to return to normal functioning. Failure to attend to or act upon physiological status may result from any of a number of

causes, including (1) environmental demands that preempt attention or action, (2) CNS information processing (genetic or learned, such as life-style or personality) that results in inappropriate attention or response to external stimuli, (3) physiology that responds in a hyper- or hypoactive manner to CNS stimulation, and (4) absent or inappropriate sensory feedback to the CNS from a peripheral organ. (Hovanitz et al., 1989, p. 56)

For detailed discussions of the role of psychological and cognitive factors in the genesis of and worsening of headaches, and a discussion of the role of cognitive and psychotherapy treatments for headaches, see Martin (1993) and Adler et al. (1987).

Inclusion in the preceding list does not imply a demonstration of a clear and direct relationship or a lack of methodological limitations with the studies. However, the sheer number of supportive studies and the aggregate conclusions are consistent with aspects of these traditional views. At least for people prone to developing headaches, in some people not so prone, and those already with headaches, there are psychophysiological, in the broadest sense of that term, "triggers" and "risk factors" that can increase the risk of developing and/or worsening a headache. This presumably occurs through increased muscle activity, biochemical changes associated with ANS changes, or both (Gannon et al., 1987; Haynes et al., 1990). Therapy often needs to address both these contributions. Marcus (1993) proposes a "combined biochemical–vascular–muscular" or "neurovascular" model (p. 165). For an excellent review and graphic illustrations of the role of triggers and risk factors resulting in changes in serotonin and other neurotransmitters and resulting in headaches see Marcus (1993).

The present assumed relationship and research support is fundamental and essential for those practitioners engaged in providing cognitive-behavioral and other forms of psychotherapy for patients with these headaches. Despite this long held belief among practitioners, research support is needed to support these types of interventions and to support improvements in selection of patients for these types of therapies.

This assumption is also useful for practitioners using stressors in psychophysiological assessments ("stress profiling") (see Chapter 7). For example, if one can induce "sufficient" psychophysiological reactivity and assess this and the recovery from the stimulations, and if these psychophysiological measures are useful for patient education, fostering cognitive changes, and treatment planning including biofeedback procedures, then supporting and demonstrating the hypothesized relationships achieves practical importance.

Furthermore, research support in this area helps identify factors that are precursors of the muscle tension and/or biochemical changes that are the presumed physiological correlates and assumed necessary contributing factors to causing or worsening headaches. See Chapter 6 for measures of relevant variables such as alexithymia, anger, perfectionism, obsessive–compulsiveness, depression, and anxiety.

Conclusions and Implications for Clinical Practice

It is reasonable to assume that many risk factors and triggers exist for headaches. These include excess and/or sustained muscle tension, and habits that increase and result in this tension; major and daily stress; anger, anxiety, depression, and other personality and mood factors; psychological/cognitive and psychophysiological effects of exposure to stressors; and social supports. In addition to these, properly putting psychological and stress factors in perspective requires that practitioners be aware of and assess other potential risk factors and triggers including eating habits, dietary chemicals, drugs, hormonal status, postures and related factors, sleep schedules and abnormalities, visual factors, and other potentially relevant factors including the days on which and conditions in which the headaches occur.

Individual differences abound for both people prone to headaches and those that are not so prone. For the headache prone person, one or a few risk factors or triggers may be enough to cause a headache. For other people, several more risk factors and triggers within a relatively short time may be needed to result in a headache. Furthermore, headaches are often "timelagged," occurring several hours or days after the obvious exposure to the risk factors and triggers. Prudent and knowledgeable practitioners realize that the risk factors and triggers of the moment are often not just those that immediately precede a headache.

Assessment of patients with headaches usually requires multidimensional assessment and multicomponent treatment options and planning tailored to the individual. If one assumes the importance of the roles of serotonin and other neurotransmitters in at least many patients with headaches (e.g., the neurovascular model), then treatment options include avoidance of triggers and/or providing therapies that affect these neurotransmitters in desired directions. The latter are often medications, but the explanation for the mechanism of relaxation therapies, biofeedback, and cognitive therapies probably involves alterations of serotonin and other neurotransmitters. After all, beliefs do have biological correlates and effects. Our treatments are rather on a molar level but there must be molecular changes that occur.

Type of Stress Events versus Cognitive Appraisals

Is it that stressful events often lead to headaches or is it the perceptions of stressful events that result in headaches? Implicated in the answer to this question is the role of cognitions in the development of headaches. Other implications are the roles of cognitive-behavioral therapy and patient education in the treatment of headaches. "Recurrent tension headaches are not typically triggered by major life changes but rather occur in conjunction with the chronic everyday stresses experienced by most people" who tend "to perceive stressful events as more distressing and disturbing occurrences than do controls" (Holm et al., 1986, p. 165).

One might propose that people with chronic benign headaches are not necessarily exposed to more stress but, rather, prone to a "tendency to interpret any life event, within his cognitive and emotional framework, as being more arousing or impactful than those people who remain healthy or develop less serious illness" (De Benedittis et al., 1990, p. 66). This is the "cognitive appraisal" hypothesis. This study was a cross-sectional and retrospective study of people with chronic headaches compared to a matched headache-free sample. The headache diagnoses included 29 diagnosed as chronic tension-type, 21 with migraines, and 6 with mixed headaches. Personal negative ratings of stressful life events in the year before onset of headaches were *predictive* of headaches. There were many more such events in the headache groups than in the control group.

Another retrospective study (Nattero et al., 1986) reported more prolonged stress in the 10 years before onset of tension-type and mixed headaches but not before the onset of vascular headaches. However, the differences were not in the year before onset of the headaches.

Another unique study used ambulatory EMG recordings of the posterior neck (Hovanitz et al., 1989). The study showed more EMG activity on days with stress than on days without stress. They found this for both patients with tension-type headaches and for nonheadache control subjects. Elevated muscle activity was not more associated with pain. However, even with the very small sample, headache subjects reported more subjective negative affect compared to nonheadache subjects. This is one of the more interesting and important studies in recent years. It provides good data, offers good interpretations, raises good methodological questions, and is of much heuristic value. Among the conclusions is the "strong support for the role of disregulation in the etiology of tension headaches" (p. 68).

Psychopathology

Another basic question is whether people with headaches develop more psychopathology. There was not much support for headaches resulting in psychopathology in the cross-sectional and retrospective study of tension-type headaches and migraines by Blanchard, Kirsch et al. (1989). However, headache patients did show more psychological distress on several self-report measures than did nonheadache control patients. Those with tension headaches showed more distress than those with migraines. Those with mixed headaches were between the other two groups but closer to the migraine group. The study controlled for life-stress differences in the prior year.

There was more psychopathology, as operationally defined in this study, associated with headache severity for persons with tension-type headaches than for those with migraines. Furthermore, partial correlations showed that duration did not moderate this relationship. However, the type of headache did moderate the association. Furthermore, there was no association between longer durations of headaches and psychopathology. In fact, there was less psychopathology for patients with 2 years of headaches compared to those with 1 year. Those with 1–3 years of headaches reported the most distress on measures of somatic concern but not much depression. However, distress was less for groups with 4–13 years and for those with 14–22 years of headaches. There was only slightly more distress among those with 23 or more years of headaches.

For patients aged 19–30 and headaches for 3 years or less, there was a higher correlation with somatization on the MMPI. We should note that several of the MMPI items involve headache-related content. For persons aged 31–41 years, this same relationship existed with more recent onset of headaches associated with more depression on the BDI. For the group aged 42 and older, more recent onset of headaches is associated with more depression.

Thus, this study argues against chronic headaches increasing long-term psychopathology. One finds, as expected, more distress with very recent onset but not increasing with more years of headaches.

Methodological Notes

This section notes a few observations about the methodologies of the above studies. I include it for students and those planning research on these topics.

Conclusions based on studies with college subjects and recruited subjects may be different from studies with patients in primary-care and tertiary-care institutions. The conclusions based on patients with less refractory headaches may be different from conclusions based on patients with more refractory headaches.

Retrospective and cross-sectional studies may have different conclusions than prospective, longitudinal studies. We should consider that the accuracy and completeness of recall of life events and perceptions diminish with time.

The selection of self-report measures can affect results. For example, there are items reflecting headache symptoms and direct effects of headaches in measures such as BDI, Spielberger Trait Anxiety Inventory (STAI), Psychosomatic Checklist (PSC), and in MMPI scales 1, 2, 3, and 7. One must be careful to avoid drawing conclusions about depression, anxiety, psychosomatic tendencies, and somatization unless one controls for these items in analyses. We should consider looking at MMPI subscales and analyzing these and other scales for nonheadache-related items. We should also look at BDI items separately for those with mood content versus those with somatic content.

Specifically, we can use multiple measures to measure daily stress, and we should consider including both normative measures comparing subjects to others and ipsative measures within each person. For example, Kohler and Haimerl (1990) defined a stress day as the top 33% or the top 20% of an individual's (ipsative) distribution based on selected items. One such item was "time urgency, strain, or overburdening during the past day." Subjects responded with ratings from 1 or "very much less than usual" to 5 signifying "very much more than usual." Ipsative measures are legitimate in that each person defines his or her subjective stress.

Physiological monitoring in the office and laboratory permits more control and fewer sources of signal variability and confounding factors. It is less expensive than ambulatory monitoring. However, ambulatory monitoring (Arena, Bruno, & Brucks, 1993; Arena, Hannah, Bruno, Smith, & Meador, 1991; Arena, Sherman, Bruno, & Young, 1989, 1991; Sherman & Arena, 1992; Sherman, Evans, & Arena, 1993; Hatch et al., 1991; Schlote, 1989; Arena, Bruno, Brucks, et al., 1994a, 1994b; Arena, Bruno, Bruck, Meador, & Sherman, 1993; Sherman, Arena, Searle, & Ginther, 1991) will probably advance our knowledge more than relying solely on studies with office and laboratory measures. Of course, we must control for other factors that could affect headaches.

ASSESSMENT

Assessment of headaches involves many topics. It includes a description and history of the headaches and other potentially related symptoms and conditions. Assessment includes a medical and neurological physical examination, laboratory tests, and diagnosis. Often, it includes psychological consultation, self-report measures, and sometimes psychiatric and sleep-disorder consultations. Self-report measures include those of stress, emotions, and personality. Measurement of headaches involves a daily self-report log. Assessment requires that practitioners understand the myriad of etiological factors that can cause, emit, maintain, and aggravate headaches. It requires knowing the myths and facts about headaches.

This chapter discusses selected topics. Excellent sources of information and guidelines for assessing patients with headaches include Andrasik (1992), Andrasik and Baskin (1987), Adler et al. (1987), Blau (1990a), and Saper et al. (1993). Also, see Chapter 6 for more discussion of intake considerations.

Nonphysician practitioners using biofeedback wisely prefer referrals from and collaboration with physicians, especially those with much expertise with headaches. Differential diagnosis is basic (e.g., Saper et al., 1993). Nonphysician practitioners need to know the *danger signs* that suggest immediate referral to a physician (Andrasik & Baskin, 1987; Andrasik, 1992, p. 345). If the practitioner does not know the diagnostic and danger signs, he or she should consult these sources or others.

Interview and/or Questionnaire

Practitioners should resist the temptation to rely on a self-report questionnaire for diagnosing headaches. The careful clinical interview remains the gold standard. Rasmussen, Jensen, and Olesen (1991) made a good effort to develop a self-administered questionnaire for studying large populations but concluded that "a questionnaire is not a satisfactory tool in diagnosing headache disorders" (p. 290). Other writers complimented them on their efforts and encouraged the continued development of improved measures (Lipton, Stewart, & Solomon, 1992). As an aid in office practice, some questionnaires might be useful as adjuncts to the interview but not as the primary method of data gathering. The following quote by Andrasik (1992) explains the complexity of assessing and treating patients with headaches. It implies the need for a careful clinical interview and continuing assessment.

> The biopsychosocial model of headache states that the likelihood of any individual experiencing headache depends upon the specific pathophysiological mechanisms that are "triggered" by the interplay of the individual's physiological status (e.g., level of autonomic arousal), environmental factors (e.g., stressful circumstances, certain foods, alcohol, toxins, hormonal fluctuations), the individual's ability to cope with these factors (both cognitively and behaviorally), and consequential factors that may serve to reinforce, and thus increase, the individual's chance of reporting head pain. (Andrasik, 1992, p. 350)

Symptom Records: The Headache Diary

Self-report measures of headaches are necessary for properly checking clinical results. There are primarily two types of self-report measures. The most common measure is daily rating of headaches, typically hourly or four to six times a day. These measures use a 6-point rating scale from 0 to 5 or a 10-point scale. Other information usually recorded includes frequency of relaxation, the use of medications, caffeine, alcohol, and comments about the day.

The second type of measure is the global rating by the patient. Patients do this periodically or at the end of therapy. Global ratings can be verbal or on a printed rating scale. Global ratings are common in clinical practice but rarely acceptable for evaluating outcome in research. Daily ratings are the norm in research and in clinical practice.

Andrasik and Holroyd (1980) compared the use of a headache questionnaire at the beginning of treatment to the use of continuous daily hourly ratings over the next 2 weeks. The similarity between the two methods with 99 subjects was very poor with very small and nonsignificant correlations. The questionnaire reports underestimated the frequency of headaches, overestimated intensity, and both overestimated and underestimated headache durations. The questionnaire test–retest reliability was high and significant. However, it did not correspond well to the data obtained with the daily ratings using a 10-point scale. The authors suggested "that questionnaire methods of assessing headache symptoms should be supplemented by daily headache recordings whenever possible" (p. 46).

The relationship between patients' ratings and those by "significant others" was the focus of the interesting and useful study by Blanchard, Andrasik, Neff, Jurish, and O'Keefe (1981). The relationship between patients' four-times-daily ratings and the ratings obtained from the "significant others" at the end of therapy was significant, although with only a modest correlation ($r = .44$, $p <. 002$). The authors point out that the correlation " . . . is comparable to correlations between other concurrent measures of change used in behavior therapy research and does indicate a significant degree of social validation for improvement detected from the diary" (p. 714).

The correlation between the patients' daily ratings and global rating on a 200-millimeter visual analogue scale was even more modest ($r = .36$, $p < .002$). The linear regression analyses between the two global ratings and the patients' daily ratings suggested that the global ratings may "produce overestimates of patient improvement" (p. 714).

It is easier to ask a patient for a subjective global estimate of change. For example, professionals ask whether patients' headaches are any different than before therapy. Are they any different compared with the prior week or month? These estimates are verbal or with standard measures such as a visual analogue scale. The problem is that patients often overestimate the changes. In my experience, many patients provide subjective global over-estimates of their improvement compared to their hourly and daily records. This is consistent with the results of Blanchard, Andrasik, et al. (1981).

However, self-report daily records are not fully accurate either. They too are subject to limitations (Collins & Thompson, 1979; Hermann & Blanchard, 1993). They are the most commonly used because they are practical and the best available. The alternatives are less accurate and more likely to lead to erroneous conclusions. For example, if a patient says that he or she is 50%, 75%, or 90% better, a therapist might stop therapy. Perhaps, the patient is indeed better. The question is the accuracy of how much better.

The accuracy of the time the patient made the rating is often another problem. There are data indicating a lack of accuracy of patient's reported times. At least during a baseline of 2 weeks, many subjects often record their ratings restrospectively (Hermann & Blanchard, 1993). However, we do not know whether this is crucial for accuracy. It is of concern if one assumes that retrospective ratings depart from accurate ratings. This question begs for research.

It is necessary to consider the reasons patients overestimate their improvement. Perhaps, the patient is responding only to the improvement of the last few days? Perhaps, he or she desperately wants to be better and deceives himself or herself into believing the degree of improvement. The reason for such self-deception also may be a desire to end therapy. A patient may be uncomfortable telling the therapist he or she wants to end therapy. The patient also may want to please the therapist. Thus, that patient may tell the therapist what he or she thinks the therapist wants or *needs* to hear. The use of adequate daily records reduces these global overestimates.

Less frequent in my experience are those patients who underestimate the degree of improvement indicated by their daily ratings. Ratings may show reduced hours of severe headache, increased hours with no headache, and reduced use of medications compared to a patient global estimate.

There are several methods for analyzing patient symptom data. No one method is completely satisfactory by itself. Therapists should consider using multiple measures of change. A common method is the average headache intensity. One calculates this by multiplying the hours each day for each intensity. Then, one sums the total and divides this sum by the number of recorded hours.

Practitioners should also, consider tracking the number of hours of severe and very severe intensities and headache-free hours. The number of days that are completely or almost completely headache-free is another useful index. Medication use is still another obvious index.

The "self-report headache diary" or "log" is the standard method (Andrasik, 1992). Many practitioners consider hourly ratings ideal. Regular review, praise, and mailing in the log during gaps between office visits are ways to help promote compliance. (See compliance section in this chapter and Chapter 9.)

However, compliance issues demand flexibility and options for some patients. Practitioners should consider ratings at regular preset times. For example, ratings can be done soon after morning awake time, at noon, at the end of the workday, and again in the late evening. An option is every 3–4 hours, such as 7 A.M., 11 A.M., 3 P.M., 7 P.M., and 11 P.M. These two options are useful for patients with pain during nearly all waking hours. However, these options have limitations. For example, using them, one does not see patterns. One cannot get a complete measure of the hours with headache, the exact durations, and the frequency of discrete headaches.

Patients also record their medication usage in the log. This is very important. It helps to document medication changes and assesses if symptom improvement is the result of medication or of nonpharmacological therapies. It also helps to assess possible analgesic-induced and rebound headaches. Some practitioners choose to rate the potency of each medication and derive a medication index (Andrasik, 1992). One multiplies the potency of each medication by the number taken and sums the total weekly.

There are alternative and supplementary headache-measurement approaches used in some research and clinical practices (Andrasik, 1992). These include separately measuring multiple features of pain such as the McGill Pain Questionnaire (Melzack & Katz, 1992) and methods for separating sensory and affective features of pain (Jensen & Karoly, 1992). Some patients report improvements in their affective reactions to their pain even without pain reduction. The practitioner should also consider a checklist of behaviors such as avoidance, activities, complaints, and help-seeking behaviors (Philips & Jahanshahi, 1986; Andrasik, 1992; also see Andrasik, 1992, for more ideas and discussion).

Getting a Headache History

Getting a headache history is well described in many references (Kunkel, 1987; Andrasik, 1992; Blau, 1990a; Swanson, 1987; Dalessio, 1986). Chapters in Adler et al. (1987) are among the best sources describing the psychological assessment of people with headaches. I could not do justice to this complex topic in the space available or present it better than the Adlers.

All practitioners with the responsibility for assessment and treatment are wise to avoid relying entirely on the history information from other health professionals. This is true even when the prior history has been from competent physicians. It is tempting, and sometimes necessary and acceptable, to forego this added history-taking because of time- and cost-containment factors.

Physicians with a special interest and expertise in headaches will usually get detailed information. However, if a practitioner needs to know specific information, he or she should get it directly from the patient. The practitioner should consider reviewing the prior written reports aloud with the patient for confirmation. Patients sometimes give different professionals different answers to the same type of question. Some practitioners misunderstand patients' statements. Other practitioners often get only that information needed for a diagnosis, to rule out serious pathology, and to prescribe medication. Patient reports of information such as onset, location, frequency, and duration are sometimes different when another practitioner asks the questions and listens carefully to the answers.

Discrepancies from Prior History

• *Lower-grade headache versus the bad headaches.* One sometimes reads a history of a specified number of headaches per month such as six headaches each for 1–2 days. Then one finds out there are nearly daily lower-grade headaches. Yet the patient told the prior doctor only about the *bad headaches.* "I have about five to six headaches a month" can mean that the patient does not want to complain about the others of lesser intensity. "I didn't think the doctor wanted to know about those other headaches," is a comment often heard.

• *Long history of less-frequent and less-intense headaches versus recent onset of headaches.* Patients sometimes report the onset of their headaches as when they became more intense or more frequent. The recorded history might say 1 or 2 years, but the onset could have been many years earlier.

• *Less frequent headaches, but other sites of pain.* Some patients report the location of their headaches as the areas in which the pain is the worst or most frequent. Practitioners must ask about other areas that may be important for diagnosis and therapy.

• *Items overlooked in interviews.* Even experienced and competent professionals sometimes miss or overlook potentially important information. These items include dietary factors, gum chewing, sleep problems, work postures, and driving habits. Many practitioners do not ask about the patient's bed pillow, the using of too many pillows, or using no pillow. Incorrect pillows or sleep positions often can contribute to or cause headaches, especially those starting in the neck.

Headache Interview and History Questions

The following is a summary of topics and questions to use when taking a headache history. Each item often requires more than one question. Many of the items and questions are mainly for diagnosis. However, most also have implications for assessment and therapy by providers of applied psychophysiological methods. The focus here is less on diagnosis and more on the other uses and implications. Diagnosis is not less important, but other published sources cover the diagnostic implications. I adapted the items and questions from multiple sources including Blau (1990a), Swanson (1987), and Dalessio (1986). I encourage reading Blau (1990a). It is an erudite, insightful, refined, and skilled commentary on history taking.

Number of Headaches and Types. Find out the number of different types of headache occuring recently and in past years. This is for diagnosis, treatment plan, and the self-report symptom diary.

Onset. This is Blau's first "time" question. The duration and age of the patient are important mostly for diagnosis. Consider these questions: How long have you had this type of headache? How old were you when this type of headache started? When did the headaches begin? How did they begin? Did you have headaches in grade school, in high school, or in college?

One is more concerned with a headache beginning in an elderly patient especially if it starts suddenly and is severe. The crucial decisions involve determining if the diagnosis is temporal arteritis or an expanding intracranial lesion such as from a hemorrhage or brain tumor. A headache that changes very little over many years is probably benign.

For practitioners planning biofeedback for the headaches, the value of knowing onset information is to help understand the patient's experience with headaches and the patient's expectations. A very long history of headaches suggests many treatments, many disappointments, and a life-style focused on headaches. Consider these when making a treatment plan.

Frequency, Regularity, and Periodicity. If episodic, what is the frequency and regularity of the headaches? This information is necessary for diagnosis and baseline information. It is Blau's second "time" question. Consider questions such as: When do you get headaches? How often are the headaches? How many days a week or month do you have no headache at all? Do your headaches increase at certain times of the month or year? Have you ever thought that your headaches increased before or during certain times of the year or events? (see Chapter 7 for discussion of baselines).

In searching for potential triggers, one is looking for possible hormonal and other calender events. These can be as simple as regular work events. They can be more complex such as holidays, birthdays, or the anniversaries of deaths, divorces, and marriages. This is another chance to gauge the patient's receptivity and readiness to possible psychological explanations and treatments.

Time of Headaches. This variable refers to whether the headache starts while the patient is awake or during sleep and at the same time each day or at different times. Consider such questions as: "When or at what time of day do they occur?" "Do they always or usually occur then?" In addition to diagnostic purposes, this information is for understanding precipitating events and timing of relaxation. For example, some tension-type headaches typically start on the way to work. Some start or worsen at about the same time at work or near the end of the work day. This information has implications for timing relaxation.

Characteristics of the Pain.

- *Location.* To determine location of pain, it is helpful to ask: "Where does the pain begin?" "What is the location at onset of pain and how does it evolve?" For example, it can be useful to know whether the headache starts in the posterior neck, the temples, or the occipital area. "Does the pain move around?" (Blau's "site" questions 4 and 5 [1990a, p. 132].)
- *Description of pain and intensity.* (Blau's questions 10 for "quality" and 11 for "quantity" [p. 133].] Ask about *quality.* What is the pain like? Is it aching, burning, throbbing, or stabbing? Practitioners often offer choices from which the patient can select. One usually does this orally, but this is a good use of questionnaires such as the McGill Pain Questionnaire.

  "Is the pain deep as in a stomach ache?" "Is it near the surface like something digging into your skin?" (Blau's "site" question 6 [p. 132].) These questions are more for diagnosis than for treatment. For example, a short and stabbing pain occurring up to several times per minute and sometimes occurring in waves suggests trigeminal neuralgia. Sensations that are band-like, feel like a tight cap, or general tightness suggest a tension-type headache.

  Ask about *quantity* of pain—the intensity. "How bad is the pain?" This is the severity-type question and subjective. Rating scales are often helpful. One can verbally or visually present the scale. An important part of a rating scale of intensity and severity is the effect on the patient's activities. A related question is, "How do the headaches affect your life?" This often unveils signs and discussion of depression and anxiety that may require separate evaluation.
- *Duration of pain.* "How long does it take for the headache to reach the maximum intensity?" (Blau's "time" question 3 [p. 132].) Sample questions are: "How long do most of your headaches last?" "Do they last for minutes, an hour or so, a few hours, a half-day, a whole day, or more than a day?" "If the lengths vary, what are the shortest, longest, and usual lengths?"

  The value of this information is mostly for diagnosis. However, it is also useful for understanding the impact of the headaches on the person, for treatment, and for assessing progress. For example, are the headaches disabling enough to justify treatment beyond the earliest steps of stepped care? Are the headaches shorter as treatment progresses?

Prodromal Symptoms. These are the signs before "migraines with aura." One use of knowing about these is for timing of relaxation and other treatments. Prodromes last for several minutes up to 30 or more minutes. Some are visual, neurological, or psychological. Examples include visual scotomata, vertigo, paresthesias, intense feelings of unusual well-being, restlessness, depression, or fatigue. The prodrome often gives the person a chance to use relaxation to abort or prevent a severe headache.

Practitioners should ask: "What else happens when you have this headache?" In this way they can look for diagnostic and warning signs. This involves specific questions about symptoms such as nausea, sweating, visual changes, nasal discharge, muscle tension in specific areas, and colder hands or feet. A patient with migraines without aura may report that his or her spouse remarks that the patient's hands are much colder before the migraine starts. Another patient diagnosed with cluster headaches and with all the classic signs also may note muscle tension in the neck before the headache. Both have obvious implications for using relaxation and biofeedback.

Precipitation. "What will bring on a headache?" "What do you think causes or starts the pain?" "Is there anything that often seems to precede the pain?" "Do you suspect anything that might be triggering the headache?" (Blau's question 7 [p. 132].) In asking these questions, the practitioner is looking for dietary, environmental, hormonal, postural, and psychosocial factors such as anger, anxiety, or depression. These are for diagnosis and for treatment. The practitioner should, for example, look for signs that bright light, weather changes, carbon monoxide, certain smells, or cigarette smoke bring on a headache. Do the headaches occur before or with menses? What foods or drinks does the patient suspect is triggering headaches? (see Chapter 10 on dietary factors). If bending, lifting, or other physical exertion precipitates a headache, the practitioner should consider an intracranial lesion. However, some benign headaches start with this type of activity.

Associated Symptoms. "What else happens when you have this headache?" Ask specific questions about specific symptoms (Blau's question 12 [p. 133] for other features.) This involves systemic and neurological questions and implications. Discussion of these is beyond the intent and scope of this chapter.

Aggravation. Do coughing, exercise, or other activities increase the headache? Does anything increase your pain? (Blau's question 8 [p. 132].) Here the practitioner is looking for signs of organic factors (e.g., intracranial, musculoskeletal). Discussion of this topic also is beyond the intent and scope of this chapter.

Relief and Nonrelief Factors. What factors often reduce a headache? "What do you do that relieves or reduces your pain?" "What does not help?" "What medication doses do or did you take and when?" "How soon do you get relief after taking the medication?" (Blau's question 9 [p. 132].) Other questions include: "Tell me about the relaxation?" "What do or did you do with relaxation?" "How long would you relax?" "Where do or did you apply the heat or cold?"

The practitioner is looking to see if relaxation, heat, cold, and medications relieve the pain. This is often a good chance to check misuse of medications. Does the patient take medications too often and when expecting a headache? Does the patient take abortive medication when the signs of a headache are minimal or when the headache is only slight? Does the patient take medications when he or she anticipates being in a situation where the person fears getting a headache?

Practitioners can ask questions such as: "Some people sometimes take medicine when they think they might get a headache." "Some take medicine when they feel very slight signs of a headache starting." "Have you ever done that?" "Do you do that sometimes?" "How often do you do that?"

Since nonrelief factors can also be illuminating, practitioners can ask: "What have you tried that did not seem to help?" "What medication doses did you take?" "When did you take them?" "What medications can't you tolerate?" "Where did you apply the heat or cold?" "Tell me about the relaxation that did not work?" "What did you do?" "What was it like?" "How long would you use the relaxation?"

Patients sometimes take abortive medications too late. Analgesic doses are sometimes too small or only taken once. Some patients take insufficient doses of prophylactic medications and some incorrectly use prophylactic medications to abort headaches.

Consider using Blau's (1990a) metaphor for communicating to patients about relying on medication to treat headaches and insufficient dosage by reminding patients that "spectacles do not cure my eyesight and . . . half-strength lenses do not result in normal visual acuity" (p. 133).

Many patients use relaxation often with no more than tensing and releasing muscles or the first phase of Jacobson's progressive relaxation. Patients forget or have never been instructed to progress beyond that phase. Tensing might worsen or not relieve the pain. If patients thought of tensing and releasing muscle tension as relaxation therapy, then correcting that myth becomes important.

Family History. "Do other family members have a history of headache?" This provides clues to the patient's perceptions and expectations. For example, does she believe that because her mother had headaches she, too, is destined to have them?

Previous Therapies. These questions add more focus on the past use of medications, physical therapy, relaxation and biofeedback, dietary changes, psychotherapy, and chiropractic treatment. "What other treatments did you try?" "When did you do it?" "What did you do?" "How many times did you go for treatment?" "Did it help at all?" "What were your reactions?" "What did you think about it?"

These questions help practitioners learn how desperate and how open-minded the patient is to find relief, and the answers they elicit help develop the treatment plan. For example, if the patient never used physical therapies or used them long ago with some benefit, or used them incorrectly, then the practitioner should consider physical therapy in the plan. However, if the patient used extensive physical therapy without benefit, then the therapist should consider deferring more.

These questions help practitioners find out more about the patient's prior use of relaxation and biofeedback. "Who provided it? Where on your body did the therapist put sensors?" "Were your eyes open or closed?" "Were you sitting quietly most of the time?" "Were you reclining some or most of the time?" "What were you doing during the sessions?" "Were you alone often or was the therapist with you most of the time?"

Patient's Ideas. What ideas does the patient have about his or her headaches? "What do you think is the cause of your pain?" "What thoughts and fears do you have during bad headaches?" (Blau's question 14 [p. 133].) This is when a practitioner learns of the patient's beliefs and fears about an organic cause not yet found.

Practitioners can also open the door to the cognitive and stress factors that patients also suspect, whether accurate or inaccurate. Consider asking more questions about patients' cognitions before and during the first signs of a headache. "What are your thoughts when you get the first signs of a headache?" Cognitive-behavioral practitioners often ask patients to write down or tape-record these thoughts.

Why Is the Patient Seeking Help Now? "Why have you come for treatment now?" (Blau's question 15 [p. 133].) This is when practitioners learn other potentially important information. It is often the entry port to the more psychological portion of an evaluation. "Are the headaches worse?" "Is the depression worse?" "Is your job at risk?" "Is your marriage at risk?" "Are there upcoming major changes in your life?" "For example, are you returning to school, changing jobs, getting married, or planning other major changes that require better treatment for your headaches?" "Is a pregnancy planned, and do you need to stop prophylactic and other medications?" Other questions may include: "Do the headaches have new features?" "Is there a new type of headache?" "Did you hear about a new treatment for headaches?" "Did you read or hear about a disease causing headaches?" "Are you afraid of having another disease?"

Be alert for other motivations. For example, are the headaches and biofeedback a socially acceptable "permit to the practitioner" and psychotherapy? "What would be different in your life if and when you have many fewer headaches or if they are much shorter or much less intense?" "Is the company you work for in financial trouble?"

Description of a Typical Headache from Onset. This description is an added and optional question that sometimes reveals information missed by other questions.

Medical History. Such histories are mostly for diagnoses and typically part of medical and neurological evaluations. Practitioners ask about past illnesses, concurrent diseases, traumas, surgeries, and allergies to medications, foods, and beverages.

Other Factors. Some *sleep* disorders can cause or worsen headaches. At least ask a few questions about the patient's sleep. "How are you sleeping?" "How long does it take for you to start sleep?" "How often do you wake in the night and for how long?" "Is your sleep restless?" "Do you snore?" Consider a more detailed sleep history or a referral to a sleep-disorder specialist if you suspect a problem. For example, there is no sense trying to use relaxation and biofeedback if there are signs of excess daytime somnolence.

Pursue inquiry into potential *emotional* and other *psychological* factors that could be worsening the headaches or interfere with treatment. Consider referring the patient to a clinical psychologist or psychiatrist for further evaluation.

Psychological Evaluation

Whether to evaluate psychological factors, where to begin, and how soon to introduce questions all depend on the patient, circumstances, and the practitioner's judgment. In many professional settings, such as medical clinics, even mental health practitioners are often wise to begin with a headache history or a review of the available recorded history. However, exceptions abound. For example, there are psychologically minded patients who show this clearly from the beginning. All or most of the headache history information is already available in the recorded history for many patients.

Not all or even most patients need a psychological evaluation. There are often practical constraints that result from a patient's schedule and distance from home. Many patients show a limited or total lack of psychological-mindedness or display resistance to such inquiries and evaluation. However, a brief psychological evaluation is often better than none. Asking even a few psychosocial questions can help with rapport. It helps check a patient's receptiveness or the resistance to this type of question and treatment. The practitioner assays the potential need for a more detailed evaluation then or whether one can defer or eliminate it. At the very least, the practitioner should infer the patient's mental status from the interview unless there is an obvious need for a more direct examination.

As a minimum, ask about the pressures and frustrations in the patient's life. In some way convey to the patient that she or he can talk about such matters. Convey that this might be important for understanding and treating him or her. Tell the patient that even if these matters are not evaluated fully now, they might become more important later. Patient-education booklets can help convey this message (Schwartz, in press).

I adapted and culled the following list of psychological factors from Adler and Adler (1987, pp. 70–83). This represents another erudite, insightful, refined, and skilled commentary on history taking. One must read the original to appreciate fully the authors' clinical wisdom and style. They suggest considering evaluation of many factors including:

- Patients' expectations of themselves
- Perceived expectations by others
- Existence of past or present family conflicts
- Sensitivity to criticism and to emotional expressions
- Comfort and skills at assertiveness
- Illnesses and hospitalizations
- Past or present grief or anticipated grief
- Medication misuse
- Experience, perception, and misperception of health care professionals
- Perceived emotional triggers or factors that increase risk of a headache

Personality and Psychopathology as Cause or Effect of Headaches

This topic includes evaluation of psychopathology, including depression, as a cause or an effect of headaches. The prior section on mechanisms of headache discusses the causes for headaches and some implications for treatment. This section focuses on the evaluation of psychopathology and personality. The implications of this topic for assessment and treatment include:

- Should the practitioner assess psychopathology?
- Should the practitioner treat the psychopathology?
- What can one expect during and after nondrug treatment?
- What could account for changes or lack of changes in headaches?

The older view is that psychopathology predisposes people to, contributes to, or causes tension and vascular headaches. A different view is that personality changes, depression, anxiety, and other psychopathology result from living with headaches. Both views have proponents, and both have support. Practitioners and researchers know that the two views represent the extremes, and both have practical and heuristic value. Both are probably true for some persons.

A third view is probably also true for many people. The anxiety, depression, and personality features of many people probably enhance the chance of developing headaches. For many of those with frequent headaches, there are effects on their moods, life-style, personality, behaviors, and reactions to stress.

Measures of anxiety and depression may show slight positive changes during and after relaxation and biofeedback treatments for headaches without changes in headaches. Practitioners and investigators speculate on the explanations. Analyses of the measures need to look closely at the aspects of depression and anxiety that change. For example, some measures like the BDI and STAI deal with varied elements of each emotional construct. Reduction of a total score does not tell us what specific aspects changed. One also must note the changes of specific items and sets of items.

For example, the BDI pretreatment scores of 6 to 11 reported in Blanchard, Steffek, Jaccard, and Nicholson (1991) are not higher than scores of nondepressed or mildly depressed patients. Among nondepressed medical patients, such scores and even slightly higher scores do not reliably mean a depression diagnosis. One can respond to these items and get slightly to mildly elevated scores for a variety of reasons. Practitioners who use the BDI know this and inspect individual items. However, I agree that some patients, who do not show clinically significant improvements in their headaches, do report improvements in mood.

A notable example of mood and anxiety improvement without changes in the target physical symptom is found among patients with tinnitus (ear ringing; see Chapter 34). These patients often report improved mood, reduced anxiety, and better adjustment despite no objective improvements in the tinnitus. "The ringing is the same, but I am sleeping much better and feel much better," some patients say. Such reports could be a response to implied demands of the clinical interview. They could be a way for a patient to reduce "cognitive dissonance" and justify his or her investment in treatment. Nevertheless, I believe that many patients do sleep better and experience less anxiety and depression.

One reasonable speculation about implicated reduction of depression and anxiety without changes in physical symptoms comes from Blanchard, Steffek, et al. (1991). They propose that depression reduction occurs because "most patients 'learn' a greater sense of being in control of their headaches as a function of receiving treatment . . . [and] . . . for many patients who achieve little actual reduction in headache activity, there is nevertheless a consistent inclination to perceive positive change" (p. 253). These investigators further speculate that anxiety reduction may occur because of reduced *unpredictability* rather than *controllability*. Anxiety decreases "may . . . be attributed to increased awareness of, knowledge about, and sensitivity to biopsychosocial factors mediating headache activity" (p. 253). Both speculations are credible and deserve more research attention.

Practitioners know that depression and other psychological factors can play a role in headache development and maintenance. Antidepressant medications are a major part of treatment programs for headaches. However, it is not the antidepressant effects of the medications that account for the improvements. The dose often used for headaches is much less than that used for depression. Changes in sleep and changes in brain biochemistry are two other explanations. Packard and Andrasik (1989a) note that "the exact mechanism by which depression causes headache has not been determined (p. 17)."

For discussions of the role of depression and other psychological factors in headache, and treatments, readers should see Chapters 8, 12, 13, 24, 30, and 31 in Adler et al. (1987). Practitioners should not underestimate the potential value of pharmacotherapy and nonbehavioral psychotherapy in the treatment of many persons with headaches. Assessment of psychosocial behaviors and emotions becomes increasingly important as one accepts the potential role of these factors in causing and maintaining headaches and in interfering with successful treatments.

Measures: The Minnesota Multiphasic Personality Inventory

The focus here on the MMPI reflects its prominence in the headache literature. In a discussion of the assessment of headaches, it is hard to exclude this topic. However, it is a complex topic requiring more space and time than practical here. There are multiple ways the MMPI is woven into the headache literature. It is a measure of various types of psycho-pathology, personality characteristics, and psychological well-being. Practitioners often use it to classify persons, predict treatment outcome, and monitor treatment progress.

The gist of this discussion is that the MMPI has value for assessing some patients with headaches but less value than some professionals assert. The MMPI can help alert practitioners to special problems and needs of selected patients. However, the MMPI or other self-report inventories should not be the criteria for avoiding relaxation and biofeedback for a specific patient or groups of patients.

Classifying Patients with Headaches

One origin for the attention to the MMPI and headaches is the MMPI subgroups found with chronic low back pain patients reported in the mid-1980s (Costello, Hulsey, Schoenfeld, & Ramamurthy, 1987; Kinder, Curtis, & Kalichman, 1991). Several attempts to find MMPI types associated with different headache types have usually met with meager results. Dieter and Swerdlow (1988) reviewed much of the research including the review of Williams, Thompson, Haber, and Raczynski, (1986). The original Kudrow and Sutkus (1979) classification system did not get much support from Andrasik, Blanchard, Arena, Teders, and Rodichok (1982), nor from Dieter and Swerdlow (1988).

Patients with different types of headaches show elevations on scales 1[6] and 3. These elevations, as expected, decrease with relaxation and biofeedback treatment. Whether or not this is a reduction of psychopathology or a reduction of the headache-related complaints among several items is not clear. Clearly, some of the reduction probably comes from headache-specific items.

Another classification approach looks at the MMPIs of people with different types of headaches. Patient groups with headache diagnoses often produce higher elevations on MMPI scales than those with other diagnoses.

Most MMPI differences among the headache diagnostic groups in these studies are subclinical. They are below the elevations and differences that professionals usually consider clinically important. Nevertheless, note that the MMPIs of those people with migraines and cluster headache are often closest or indistinguishable from nonheadache, normal control subjects. In contrast, those with tension-type headaches show higher elevations than most other headache groups, and those with posttraumatic headaches sometimes show the highest elevations.

A recent paper[7] on this topic by Williams, Raczynski, Domino, and Davig (1993) briefly reviewed other reports. Their data also show that patients with tension headaches have higher elevations on several scales than those with migraines. Furthermore, the migraine patients had higher scores on scales 1, 2, 3, and 7 than control subjects who were nonpatients.

---

[6]I encourage practitioners and authors to shift from using the MMPI scale letters and names to using only the MMPI scale numbers. This practice has been common for many years among many professionals. The rationale is to stop using outmoded and ill-advised concepts and names for these scales. Also, remember that each scale measures multiple concepts and that elevations often do not imply the designated entity embodied in the name. The use of the old names is confusing and misleading in interprofessional communications. They also can be very troublesome and misleading with patients. One exception is scale 2 or depression.

[7]Note that the authors refer to "occipital EMG" recorded from "just below the hairline of the neck adjacent to the spinal column" (p. 150). I suspect they meant "neck EMG." This is not important for the MMPI part of their study which is the major thrust of their paper. I mention it only to help readers avoid using this placement to assess occipital activity. See section "Placement of Electrodes" in Chapter 15 for a detailed discussion of occipital EMG.

The only study using the MMPI-2 also showed significant elevations on scales 3, 1, and 2 for patients with posttraumatic headaches and no differences from those patients with the diagnoses of status migraine with or without analgesic rebound (Kurman, Hursey, & Mathew, 1992).

Note that after removing headache-related items, a mixed headache group became the lowest on scales 1 and 3 in the Dieter and Swerdlow (1988) data. The order of the other groups differed from that reported by other studies. The posttraumatic group remained with the highest elevations at T score 70 and 71 for scales 1 and 3. This probably reflects the damage and symptoms resulting from trauma.

The "pain density" concept of Sternbach, Dalessio, Kunzel, and Bowman (1980) refers to the overall time with pain. It might explain some of the headache group differences. Thus, patients with the diagnoses of posttraumatic headaches often experience the most time with pain each year. Patients with tension-type headaches and "mixed headaches" often experience less time with pain than those with posttraumatic headaches. Patients with posttraumatic headache experience more time with headache than most patients with migraines. This hypothesis awaits more research.

Williams et al. (1993) offered some support for the potential role of the MMPI with patients with headaches. However, there are significant limits using the MMPI with these patients and problems using it to classify patients. There is much variability in MMPI responses among persons with headaches, and their responses vary to items on scales 1 and 3 including the headache-related items. Dieter and Swerdlow (1988) refer to this as the "disconnection" between the MMPI and headaches in that some patients with chronic headaches do not endorse the obvious headache items.

The MMPI as a Measure and Correlate of Psychopathology and Stress

Another way to use the MMPI is to identify subgroups[8] of patients with headaches based on their MMPI profiles and elevations of scales. Studies support the potential value of using the MMPI this way to identify subgroups of patients regardless of their diagnosis. The MMPI helps assess patients' pain coping as a probable "interaction between a person's resources (general psychological status, pain coping style, social support, etc.) and the nature of the headache or pain complaint . . ." (Robinson, Geisser, Dieter, & Swerdlow, 1991, p. 114). However, no one knows whether the MMPI responses predate the headaches. The MMPI could be unrelated to the headaches or be a reaction to the headaches. The reaction hypothesis has more support. Robinson et al. (1991) replicated the MMPI clusters of the Robinson, Swimmer, and Rallof (1989) and Costello et al. (1987) studies with nonheadache pain groups. These studies support the use of the MMPI in this way. The five MMPI clusters are with:

1. No significant elevations on any scales.[9]
2. High elevations of only scales 1, 3, and 2.

---

[8]Another consideration is the similarity of scales 1, 2, and 3 among some of the groups in these studies. There are only a few points difference for scale 2. It seems tenuous to differentiate groups with such similar scores.

[9]Another observation and comment pertains to considering a profile with the T scores on scales 1 and 3 at 62 and 65, and on scale 2 at 55 as "relatively normal" and not the "Conversion V." The elevations are higher than those in Rappaport, McAnulty, Waggoner, and Brantley (1987), and the configuration is the same. Clinical lore and research (Schwartz, Osborne, & Krupp, 1972) support the configuration as being more important than the elevation for this profile.

3. No significant elevations but some elevations between T scores 60 and 70 mostly on scales 1, 3, and 2 and higher than those in cluster number one.
4. Significant elevation on scale 2 and on scales 1 and 3.
5. Significant elevations on several scales (K, 1, 2, 3, 4, 6, 7, and 8).

The more recent study had a larger sample than prior studies and added the fourth cluster with an elevation on scale 2. As expected "none of the clusters characterized a particular diagnostic group" (p. 114). They did not find a relationship between the MMPI clusters and headache frequency, whereas Rappaport et al. (1987) did find such a relationship.

At about the same time as the Robinson et al. (1991) study, Kinder et al. (1991) independently published their review and study of 508 patients. They reported it as "the largest headache sample that had been cluster analyzed to date" (p. 226). They advocated the need for a very large sample and suggested separating male and female patients. They also recommended separate criteria from the low back pain studies for determining the number of clusters and special cluster-analysis statistics.

They agreed with prior research showing no reliable or useful relationship between the MMPI and headache diagnosis for male patients. Female patients with normal MMPIs more often had migraine headaches than female patients in other MMPI groups. However, about two-thirds of the patients with normal MMPIs had tension-type headaches and "migraine headache cannot be said to characterize this group of females patients" (p. 231). This study found four MMPI clusters for male and female patients but not exactly the same four reported by Rappaport et al. (1987). Furthermore, the clusters were different for male patients and female patients.

These studies find a normal group, which is usually the largest group. Furthermore, the studies usually find a group with several elevations. They refer to this as the "psycho-pathological profile." Another group found is the so-called "distressed" group after Sternbach (1974). This group has elevations on scales 1, 2, 3, and sometimes other scales. The Kinder et al. (1991) study found this for male and female patients. The pattern with scale 2 several T-score points higher than other scales and no other high elevations also appears in this study. The pattern with scales 1 and 3 predominant and a lower scale 2 did not show up in this study. Prior studies, including Rappaport et al. (1987), reported this group.

The Kurman et al. (1992) study also showed three types of MMPI-2 clusters. Their 86 patients had more severe headache diagnoses of posttraumatic, and status migrainous with and without analgesic rebound. There were 13 cases with considerable psychopathology indicated by several MMPI high elevations mostly above T score 70. Another 29 patients showed less psychopathology indicated by several lower elevations but showed very high elevations on scales 3, 1, and 2 above T score 70. Thirty-nine other patients had only mild elevations on scales 1 and 3 and no other elevations. Anxiety, depression, health concerns, low self-esteem, and work interference characterize the most elevated group.

Issues and Considerations. I raise a few questions and issues to consider when one is using the MMPI with patients with headaches, when interpreting research, and when developing research ideas.

1. Should a practitioner treat patients with MMPI elevations and MMPI-indicated psychopathology differently from other patients? For example, does one need to add psychotherapy from the beginning of treatment with all or most such patients? Does one need more relaxation and biofeedback sessions? Does one need different self-regulatory proce-

dures with these patients? Does one need to add more encouragement and patient education?

2. How much elevation of specific MMPI scales and what combinations of elevations might exclude a patient from relaxation and/or biofeedback? I know of no data that shows that most or nearly all patients with specific MMPI elevations or many elevations do not do well with this type of therapy regardless of how it is applied.

3. Remember the past cautions and contraindications about using these therapies with patients with a diagnosis of schizophrenia, elderly patients with a variety of diagnoses including headaches, and those with moderate to severe developmental disabilities. See Chapter 36 for a discussion of how relaxation therapies and biofeedback work very well for these groups.

4. Here are technical points to consider. First, some elevations on MMPI clinical scales often result from the addition of the scale "K correction" rather than items from clinical scales. Some MMPI experts interpret such elevations differently. A second issue not addressed in most of these MMPI studies is partialing out the MMPI items directly addressing headache-related symptoms and other symptoms associated with co-existing medical conditions. This is especially important for interpreting MMPIs of other medical and neurological groups such as those with chronic back pain and seizure disorders. Third, using subscales helps with interpreting the parent scales and the clusters of items contributing to an elevated scale. For example, an elevation of scale 3 does not always mean endorsement of excess somatic items: *An elevation is not an elevation is not an elevation.*

The existing MMPI research with patients with headaches is of academic interest, has at least heuristic value, and some clinical use. The MMPI alerts practitioners to:

- Avoid overlooking a patient's problems.
- Become more aware of patient's cognitions needing attention.
- The potential need for added evaluation.
- The potential need for modified therapy procedures.
- The potential need for adding other forms of therapy.
- Show increased patience with some patients.
- Other interpretations of psychophysiological data.
- Other interpretations for lack of progress.

Thoughtful and skilled practitioners can continue to use these therapies regardless of the MMPI until and unless research and/or widespread clinical experience shows otherwise.

Other Measures of Personality and Psychopathology. There are self-report measures assessing the beliefs of patients with pain. See Chapter 6 for a more detailed discussion of intake measures. Others measure patients' self-efficacy expectations and still others measure patients' strategies for coping with pain. For a recent review of these measures see DeGood and Shutty (1992). Many practitioners find some of these of potential use for assessing patients with headaches. The Bakal Headache Assessment Questionnaire (Bakal, 1982; Penzien, Holroyd, Holm, & Hursey, 1985), and the West Haven–Yale Multidimensional Pain Inventory (Kerns, Turk, & Rudy, 1985; Kerns & Jacob, 1992) are among those to consider.

The Headache-Specific Locus of Control Scale (Martin, Holroyd, & Penzien, 1990; VandeCreek & O'Donnell, 1992) is a recently developed and promising 33-item self-report measure. It can help practitioners better understand the beliefs of patients about their perceived control of their headaches. Another scale to consider is the 51-item Headache Self-Efficacy Scale (HSES; Martin, Holroyd, & Rokicki, 1993). "It assesses [an] individual's belief that they are able to do the things necessary to prevent a moderately painful headache when confronted with personally relevant headache precipitants" (p. 244). It appears to have incremental use in addition to the locus of control scale.

Self-report measures for assessing stress are also sometimes helpful. To appreciate this, use the Daily Stress Inventory (Brantley, Waggoner, Jones, & Rappaport, 1987; Brantley & Jones, 1989) or the Hassles Scale (Kanner, Coyne, Schaefer, & Lazarus, 1981; Lazarus & Folkman, 1989) with a few patients.

The Millon scales, Millon Behavioral Health Inventory (MBHI) and Millon Clinical Multiaxial Inventory (MCMI), receive very little attention in the published literature on headaches. Two studies suggest potential use of these measures for assessing treatment-related factors, predicting response to treatment, and differentiating headache patients from other pain groups. I do not discuss these because of the limited literature, small samples, and my limited personal experience with them.

Implications of Using Self-Report Measures. When considering the MMPI and other self-report measures, consider these implications:

1. Do not use the MMPI to classify people with different headache types.
2. People with headaches differ substantially in personality and psychopathology.
3. Most people with headaches probably will not produce clinically significant elevations beyond the expected scales 1 and 3, and some on scale 2. These elevations may reflect headache-related symptoms and reactions to their headaches.
4. Consider the MMPI clusters, other MMPI indices, and/or other measures to assess the strengths and limits of each patient.
5. Do not assume that reductions in MMPI scores reflect clinical improvements beyond headache-related symptoms.
6. Consider checking and inquiring about headache-related items for those patients with headaches—especially if they did not endorse these items.
7. The relationship between headache frequency and MMPI cluster type is uncertain.
8. Consider measures other than the MMPI clinical scales. For example, consider measures of daily stress. Consider the Headache-Specific Locus of Control Scale (Martin et al., 1990; VandeCreek & O'Donnell, 1992) and the HSES (Martin et al., 1993). Also, consider the Daily Stress Inventory (Brantley et al., 1987).
9. If the MMPI is used before treatment, consider using it to check on the need for further assessment. Consider using it if clinically relevant questions or indications arise in clinical interviews. Consider it to increase confidence in clinical impressions and decisions.
10. Some practitioners defer the MMPI and related measures until later in treatment unless clearly indicated earlier. If treatment will be the same, they ask, why invest the time and expense? There are no data to indicate that practitioners cannot successfully treat patients with headaches using relaxation, biofeedback, and cognitive-behavioral therapies without using the MMPI.

I do not advocate avoiding the MMPI. I use the MMPI-1[10] and MMPI-2 often in clinical practice. However, it is misleading to assume that the MMPI is necessary for many patients. For example, note that in one study (Kinder et al., 1991) of 145 male patients,

---

[10]The designation for the original MMPI does not contain the -1. I use it here only for convenience to distinguish it from the MMPI-2. Practitioners still commonly use both in clinical practice. Essentially all research with headaches used the MMPI-1. I expect future research will address the present issues with the MMPI-2. A discussion of the MMPI-2 is beyond the scope of this chapter.

only 6 had *psychopathological* profiles. Of 363 female patients, only 20 had such profiles. Furthermore, research does not show that the same treatments have different results for patients with different MMPI patterns. If future research shows otherwise, then a pattern assessment will be more valuable.

In evaluating and treating people with headaches, consider the following:

1. Assess at least depression, anxiety, and somatization variables.
2. Provide patient education to help patients understand the relationship between their behaviors, life events, and the impact on headaches.
3. Provide patient education for realistic expectations about the potential for positive changes in depression and anxiety.
4. Consider using relaxation and biofeedback with selected patients with headaches and consider deferring treatment for depression and anxiety. If depression and anxiety improve significantly, the practitioner and patient could avoid more treatment.
5. Consider that some reported improvements in areas other than target physical symptoms are probably real. However, some probably result from patients' self-deception or their perceived need to convey improvements. Awareness of these potential explanations, early patient education, and skilled clinical interviewing all help practitioners discern innocent deception. This does not mean that practitioners should defer psychotherapy or pharmacological treatments for anxiety and depression until after relaxation and biofeedback. When depression is clear and significant, then treating this first is common, appropriate, and sometimes necessary before relaxation and biofeedback can be initiated. This decision is a clinical one tailored to each patient by each practitioner. However, research and clinical experience support deferring psychotherapy and pharmacological treatment for many patients with headaches.
6. Factors other than psychological ones can interfere with successful use of relaxation and biofeedback. For example, smoking and caffeine can contribute to symptoms and/or interfere with treatment.
7. If depression, anxiety, or other psychological distress persist after adequate treatment with relaxation and biofeedback therapies for headache, plan other treatments.

Volunteers for Research: Methodological Notes

Therapists should consider the potential differences between volunteers and patients seen in clinical practice when recruiting or soliciting volunteers with headaches for research. Investigators sometimes note and discuss this potential difference (Philips, 1976) but rarely study it.

Practitioners should also note the potential difference between volunteers with headaches who present themselves almost immediately or within about 1 month compared to others who defer volunteering especially beyond 6 months. These groups may differ in important factors such as psychopathology. One study (McAnulty et al., 1986) reported differences measured with the MMPI. Early volunteers showed higher scores on scales 2, 7, and 8. Some early volunteers may show more signs of depression, anxiety, and other features that could affect treatment, correlates, and outcome. Thus, researchers should consider the order of self-referral if recruitment takes place over several months and control for self-referral order when assigning research subjects to experimental groups. Early versus later self-referred groups should be analyzed separately when possible.

General Implications for Assessment

1. Patients self-referred to nonphysicians or referred by physicians for relaxation and biofeedback may differ from patients self-referred to physicians with headaches. The probability of a neurological abnormality causing the headaches is extremely low for the group referred by physicians.

2. Neurological tests are for diagnosis, reassurance, and sometimes for medical–legal reasons. Reassurance of patients sometimes requires neurological tests despite their often limited diagnostic value for most patients.

3. Some abnormalities on neurological tests are of no clinical relevance for headaches. Relaxation and biofeedback can result in significant reduction of headaches even among patients with some of these abnormalities (Morrill, Blanchard, Barron, & Dentinger, 1990).

4. Self-referred patients presenting to nonphysicians need competant medical and/or neurological examination.

5. "Patients complaining of abrupt or radical changes in headache should be referred to a competent neurologist before proceeding . . ." (Morrill et al., 1990, p. 35).

Medical and Neurological Consultation and Laboratory Tests

All nonphysicians should know that nearly all patients with headaches need competent medical and/or neurological consultation. There are exceptions, but the prudent nonphysician practitioner errs on the careful side.

One example of a patient who might *not* need another medical or neurological examination is a patient in the 30s with a history of many years of clearly unchanging headaches diagnosed as tension-type headache. In this example, the patient has had multiple medical and/or neurological examinations over the past few years. He or she has had appropriate and thorough laboratory studies over these years. In this scenario, the person goes to an independently licensed psychologist who is highly experienced in assessing and treating headaches. Perhaps a phone call or other brief contact with the patient's physician might be sufficient without the necessity to repeat more medical or neurological examinations. There is a potential risk here, but it is tiny.

The reason for discussing this scenario is not to encourage this practice. However, in reality, it occurs. Sometimes, patients ask for nonpharmacological treatments and want or need to avoid the added expense and time for medical or neurological examination. Such situations might increase the ability to contain the costs and financial hardships for many people obtaining medical and neurological services.

Practitioners wanting to treat such a patient yet uncomfortable with even the low risk and perceived ethical problems can sometimes do the following:

1. Discuss the issue candidly with the patient.
2. Suggest and offer to arrange for the medical and/or neurological services.
3. Allow the patient to refuse those services for a specified period while starting treatment. Prudent practitioners will clearly document this interchange in the official session notes; more cautious practitioners will ask the patient to sign a document.

Morrill et al. (1990) found, among 278 highly select patients with headaches, that "the majority of clients with abnormal laboratory tests (most of which were mildly abnormal) still saw substantial headache reduction with self-regulatory treatment for chronic headache" (p. 27). Only 1 or 2 of the 278 patients had a serious structural abnormality. Of 112 patients getting a routine electroencephalograph (EEG), 14 (12.5%) had some abnormality, with most only being mildly abnormal. Of these, 12 completed treatment with 3 improving 64–100%, and 1 improving 30%. The others showed slight or no improvement.

Of 166 patients not getting routine tests, 57 had one or more tests with 13 abnormal. The only abnormalities were for 1 of 29 with skull films, 6 of 45 with EEGs, 5 of 14 with CT scans, and the one with a sinus X-ray. The overall abnormal rate was 22.8% among those selected for tests. Ten of the 13 patients completed treatment, with 6 showing clinically meaningful improvement of 48–81% and 2 others of 37%. "For those . . . with abnormal test findings who completed treatment, 29 percent of tension headache . . . and 40 percent of vascular headache . . . showed clinically significant . . . reduction in headache activity" (p. 34).

The selection of tests for each patient depends on the individual case and the physician's experience and opinion. This chapter is not the place to discuss the decision-making process and criteria for selecting laboratory tests. A brief discussion serves as a review for some readers and a basic knowledge for others when reviewing medical and neurological assessments. Practitioners should look for such items as a *complete blood count, biochemical profile, electrolytes, sedimentation rate,* and *total thyroxine.* These are often routine and easy to get tests for screening for possible systemic diseases. The sedimentation rate is a test for *temporal arteritis* and especially important for elderly patients with a recent onset of headaches in the distribution of these blood vessels.

Some headache specialists argue for skull X-rays, a computed tomography (CT) or magnetic resonance imaging (MRI) scan, and an EEG for selected symptoms. Other specialists recommend the CT scan as the best clinical neurological test for detecting structural brain lesions. These specialists deemphasize the value of skull films and an EEG. "The yield for plane skull films and EEGs [is] very low and infrequently of value" (Swanson, 1987, p. 20). The appropriateness of the CT or MRI is especially important in ascertaining the etiology of a headache different from a patient's prior headaches or one that is getting progressively worse.

The value of routine CT or MRI scans for patients presenting with headaches is the subject of disagreement. Mitchell, Osborn, and Grosskreutz (1993) reviewed several studies and added their own data. They emphasize the strong preference for a careful history and neurological examination. From a statistical view, they argue persuasively against the value and cost–benefit ratio of routine brain CTs for patients with headaches who have normal neurological exams and physical exams without focal findings or unusual clinical symptoms. However, they note that the value of the CT could vary in different patient populations.

Another logical and necessary view is that of Campbell (1993). His contrasting view departs from the "cold statistics" and takes into account the realities of the individual patient and the physician in clinical practice. In summary, he asks "what if it [were] your head?" and "Now tell the jury, doctor . . ." (p. 52). The current *Zeitgeist* is heavy with the need for cost containment, government and other third-party payer involvement in medical practice, and no restrictions on our litigious society. Somewhere between the extremes of expensive routine tests and very few of these tests exists the choice that constitutes the correct compromise.

Nonphysicians treating patients with headaches need to be aware that the yield from routine CTs is low for many populations of patients with headaches, and therefore their patients may not have a CT or MRI. Part of the rationale for discussing this topic is that it heightens the importance of being sure the patient does have a very competent neurological history, examination, and that there are no unusual clinical symptoms. Being alert to changing symptoms and danger signs of nonbenign headaches will become more important for some practitioners. Working very closely with competent physicians including neurologists will become increasingly important.

If there were a trauma involved, then cervical spine X-rays are appropriate. This is especially valid if the pain is mainly occipital or if the pain comes with bracing of neck muscles. See Swanson (1987), Saper et al. (1993), and other references for more discussions of this topic.

TREATMENT OF SPECIAL POPULATIONS

The populations discussed in this section are the elderly, pregnancy-related headaches, menstrual-related headaches, and high-medication users. (See Chapter 15 for a discussion of pediatric headaches.) Obviously, each of these categories could involve a separate section or an entire chapter. The purposes here are to call the reader's attention to special considerations for each group, summarize selected conclusions, and provide selected references.

Elderly Patients with Benign Headaches

Tension-type and migraine headaches are very common among the elderly. Further development of nonpharmacological treatments for these benign headaches in the elderly is important. The percentage of our population that is elderly is steadily growing (Williams, 1991). In one medical center outpatient sample (Solomon, Kunkel, & Frame, 1990), 4.3% (359/8289) of those with a diagnosis of headache (excluding temporal arteritis) were aged 65 or older. Of these, 31.7% were tension, 17.8% migraine, and 15.9% were mixed headaches. Hence, two-thirds had diagnoses for which practitioners consider treatment with relaxation, biofeedback, and other applied psychophysiological methods.

Very little data exist on the prevalence of these diagnoses among the elderly. People of various ages with headaches very often do not seek treatment. During a routine office visit in a well-studied elderly population in Dunedin, Florida, 9.1% (117/1284) reported frequent headaches. Female patients reported headaches more than twice as often as male patients (11.2% of 819 versus 5.4% of 465). However, we do not know the specific diagnosis of each group. I note this to give a sense of the prevalence of headache among the elderly. The average age was 78 for those reporting headaches.

In a Japanese sample of 288 elderly patients with various types and degrees of dementia, 75 reported headaches. Of these, 43 (58.9%) had tension-type headaches, 15 (20.5%) had migraines without aura, and 2 had both types (Takeshima, Taniguchi, Kitagawa, & Takahashi, 1990). Of those with tension-type, 12 were chronic and 31 episodic. Among the 59 patients with dementia of the Alzheimer type (DAT), 15 (25.4%) had headaches, including 11 with tension-type headaches. Among the 160 with cerebrovascular disease (CVD), 135 had vascular dementia, and 34 (21.3%) of the 160 had headaches without a direct relationship to their old CVD episodes. Among 160 with cerebrovascular disease, 135 had vascular dementia. Of the 160, 34 (21.3%) had headaches without a direct relation to their old CVD episodes. Twenty of these had tension-type headaches, and seven had migraines without aura. Others had combinations or uncertain diagnoses.

One conclusion is that tension-type and migraine headaches are common among the elderly—including those with various degrees of dementia. Age and neurocognitive impairments compromise the quality of life among many of these people. They often are unlikely to complain about their headaches for many reasons. These include impaired memory, impaired verbal expressive abilities, depression, and lack of opportunity. We should note that the Takeshima et al. (1990) study excluded those patients "who did not have the ability to complain of headaches" (p. 735).

Practitioners expect more coexisting symptoms, diseases, and use of medications among the elderly. This potentially affects and complicates diagnosis and treatment. Notable examples include hypertension and depression. It is worth noting that the Dunedin program (Hale, May, Marks, Moore, & Stewart, 1987) reported an association of headaches among male patients with "paroxysmal nocturnal dyspnea, feeling lonely, and feeling depressed" (p. 274). Female patients reported many symptoms with their headaches including brief losses of speech and temporary losses of vision. These could be caused by transient ischemic attacks (TIAs) or microinfarctions and/or the migraines (Hale et al., 1987). Other symptoms included feeling depressed and perceptions that other people did not care about them.

The diagnoses significantly ($p < .0001$) related to frequent headaches included arthritis, peptic ulcers, angina, cataracts, and diverticulosis among female patients. Among men, the diagnoses were temporal arteritis and kidney stones. It makes sense to think of osteoarthritis linked to tension headaches among the elderly. However, most with this diagnosis did not have an association with headache. The authors suggest that the headaches for those with angina and ulcers were likely caused by drug-induced complications. Examples are those from nonsteroidal anti-inflammatory agents used by persons with headaches and from nitroglycerin taken for angina. Unexpectedly, there was no significant association between hypertension and headache in this study. The only medications associated with frequent headaches were nitroglycerin and aspirin among women but none for men.

For many of these people, medications are not sufficient or contraindicated because of medical conditions. This supports the role of nonpharmacological treatments if efficacious.

Biofeedback and Self-Regulatory Treatment for Headaches

The limited literature until about 1988 was pessimistic about the effectiveness of relaxation and biofeedback for treating headaches in the elderly. This literature was retrospective and based on single cases or anecdotal reports. The general belief was that these treatments were not successful for older patients especially those with very long-term symptoms. However, that was not the experience from some clinical practitioners who observed success with elderly patients. There was limited support for this treatment without a published literature.

Fortunately, some determined investigators prospectively studied series of older patients and found successful use of these treatments for headaches in the elderly (Arena, Hightower, & Chang, 1988; Kabela, Blanchard, Appelbaum, & Nicholson, 1989; Arena, Hannah, Bruno, & Meador, 1991). Pessimism and poor expectations by investigators may have resulted in poor results before these studies. Now, optimism and positive expectations exist.

The ages of the patients in the Kabela et al. (1989) study were 60–77 (mean = 65) for the 16 treated patients. The ages were 62–71 (mean = 65) for the 8 patients reported by Arena et al. (1991). Some practitioners, especially this author, who is 53, do not consider patients in their early and mid-60s as elderly (see Chapter 36).

One can only commend Arena, his colleagues, and others for their sensitivity and efforts to tailor the instructions and treatment for older subjects. The therapists simplified instructions, spoke more slowly, and summarized information. They made extra efforts to be patient and spend more time listening. I question whether asking subjects to "repeat verbally each session's instructions" (p. 384) is necessary for most patients, especially those without signs of neurocognitive impairments. However, as an advocate for more efforts for patient education, I agree with the intent.

The outcome of these series, totalling 34 patients, showed 21 or 62% (21/34) with improvements of 50% or greater. Others showed improvements of lesser degrees. The number of treatment sessions varied from 3 to 19 sessions. Most had between 8 and 12 sessions. This included patients treated only with limited portions of treatment such as using only frontal EMG, only relaxation instructions, or only three office visits. The authors encouraged daily practice. These series are encouraging, and the results open the door to improvements. Tailoring treatment to the individual and good professional judgment are still acceptable practice for treating the elderly.

The authors correctly point out the limits of their studies. For example, we do not yet know the efficacy of these treatments for elderly non-Caucasians. We do not know the efficacy with patients with major psychological problems and those with concomitant medical and neurological problems. Nevertheless, the results are encouraging and help to justify these treatments for this population.

Conclusions

1. Consider treating older and elderly patients with relaxation and biofeedback, including some patients with dementia.
2. Interview patients carefully about their headaches, and encourage caretakers to do the same.
3. Arrange for medical, neurological, and/or psychiatric evaluation. Monitor those symptoms that could affect accurate diagnosis and/or affect relaxation and biofeedback treatments.
4. Note and monitor all medications that could affect treatment.
5. Develop special patient education and cognitive preparation for treatment of elderly patients to reassure them and to increase their understanding and compliance.
6. Assess and treat depression and sleep disorders, as needed, at least before and/or during applied psychophysiological treatments. Note that treating depression and/or sleep problems could help decrease headaches in some patients.
7. Include elderly patients' spouses, other family members, or caretakers, in evaluation and treatment, as needed.
8. Treatment might require 10–19 office sessions with some elderly patients. However, fewer office sessions also can be successful with some patients.

Pregnant Women

Among pregnant women, many medications for headaches are often ill-advised or contraindicated, especially for migraines. During pregnancy, some women report relief from headaches, others report more headaches, and others note no change. Some women without a history of headaches report an onset of migraines during preganacy, especially in the third trimester. Medications such as propranolol and ergotamine are risk factors for fetal damage, as is caffeine (Hickling, Silverman, & Loos, 1990; Hughes & Goldstein, 1988).

I found only one report for applied psychophysiological treatment of vascular headaches during pregnancy (Hickling et al., 1990). The authors reported on an uncontrolled series of five women treated with a combination of treatments. Treatment included muscle and autogenic-type relaxation, EMG and thermal biofeedback, and cognitive psychotherapy. The presentation and description of the data are less than ideal, but the overall result is encouraging. There was significant improvement in all five women at the end of between 4 and 12 sessions. Improvement usually started in the second trimester. Clear interpretation of results is impossible. However, the improvements at the end of treatment and at follow-up of 4–17 months support this type of treatment for at least some of these women. There are no contrary reports.

High-Consumption Headache Medication Users

Practitioners often encounter patients with tension-type and/or migraine headaches who regularly consume large amounts of headache medications. Several investigators report the observation of drug-induced headaches including those from chronic use of analgesics or ergotomine.

Practitioners often begin applied psychophysiological treatments while patients continue their medication. Therapists monitor the medications and look for reductions of both headaches and medication. Many patients resist or fear stopping medications before another treatment. However, the drugs themselves are part of the problem for many of these people. The drugs can confound treatment and interpretation of results.

Within a stepped-care framework, practitioners can consider starting with conservative relaxation and limited office visits during the medication withdrawal stage. They can then consider adding more office visits if still needed after withdrawal is complete. An excellent report with 10 such patients (Blanchard, Taylor, & Dentinger, 1992) supports this approach.

Features of "analgesic rebound" are "almost continuous low- to moderate-intensity headache" with typically daily use of "high levels of analgesic medication" (Blanchard et al. 1992, p. 180). These authors further report "exacerbation of head pain" when patients try to reduce or stop the medications. The regular use of ergotomines and prophylactic medications also appears to cause or worsen headaches in susceptible persons.

Treatment of these patients is more difficult than others with headaches. Hospital-based detoxification is proper for many patients—but very costly. However, it is impractical for many and unavailable for others. Blanchard et al. (1992) present three common clinical options here:

1. Ask patients to withdraw on their own or with a physician-prescribed tapering schedule.
2. Add self-regulatory treatment to choice 1. Consider a few sessions of relaxation and psychological support during the withdrawal. Add more self-regulatory treatment after withdrawal.
3. Start a multicomponent self-regulation treatment and withdrawal of medication.

In their report, Blanchard et al. (1992) added more progressive relaxation or combined this with cognitive therapy for tension-type headaches. For vascular headaches, they combined thermal biofeedback, progressive relaxation, and/or cognitive therapy. They used the second approach with eight patients in a clinical replication series. They switched to the third approach with two other patients. There was "a meaningful reduction in medication level in 6 . . . [of] the 8 patients who made a serious attempt at medication withdrawal" (p. 200). Interested practitioners should review the individual data for these patients in the original article.

Two of the 10 patients significantly reduced their headaches after only withdrawal (patients 1 and 3). Two more did so with combined withdrawal and treatment (patients 9 and 10). The headaches of two others did not improve after drug withdrawal but *did* improve after treatment (patients 2 and 4). Three others significantly reduced their medications, but this did not reduce their headaches, and they did not enter treatment. The two patients reached in follow-up did not significantly improve. The headaches worsened during a marked reduction or total withdrawal of medication in a few but not most patients. Thus, rebound is not inevitable among these patients. Tailoring the approach to the patient and good professional judgment are crucial.

Implications and Recommendations

1. Some patients should stop medications before starting treatment.
2. Patient education and support are very important before and during withdrawal.
3. For some patients, combine withdrawal, support, and relaxation or with other treatments.

Patient education should deemphasize dependency on medications. Explain how medications can lead to less effectiveness. Focus on the medications as the culprit rather than the patient as the problem. However, support and emphasize the patient's responsibility for changing.

Do not focus on or encourage negative attitudes toward the physicians who prescribed the medications. Consider telling patients that medications are standard treatments and often successful despite the undesirable result in some people. This is a delicate line to walk. I do not see benefits from arousing or reinforcing patients' ire against other doctors. There may be exceptions when the patients' prior doctors misused medications, and mismanagement raises ethical and malpractice questions.

Women with Menstrual-Related Migraines

For many women, migraine headaches worsen before, during, and/or at the end of menstruation. There are few studies of the efficacy of thermal biofeedback for menstrual-related migraines, and conclusions are not yet clear. Reports include those by Solbach, Sargent, and Coyne (1984a), Szekely et al. (1986), Gauthier, Fournier, and Roberge (1991), and Kim and Blanchard (1992). The most recent of these summarizes the methodological shortcomings of these studies. A discussion of biochemical and methodological factors related to this topic is beyond the scope of this chapter. However, a summary of selected information is relevent here.

The use of thermal biofeedback may or may not be effective. This depends on the definition of menstrual-related migraine, the treatment components, the data one selects, and the interpretation one adopts. It is obvious why confusion surrounds the topic. As Kim and Blanchard (1992) point out,

> There is a clear conflict in the literature: Solbach et al. (1984a) interpret their study as showing no effect of nonpharmacological treatment on menstrual migraine (as do Szekely et al., 1986), whereas Gauthier et al. (1991) interpret their data as showing that biofeedback treatments work equally well with menstrual and nonmenstrual migraine. (p. 198)

There is some support, although weak, for the use of thermal biofeedback and relaxation procedures for menstrual-related migraine headaches. It is reasonable to introduce this type of treatment if medications are not enough and if the headaches are interfering with the person's life. Practitioners should ask patients to keep clear symptom records and clearly define the criteria for menstrual-related versus other migraine headaches. Patients should try to note midcycle ovulation headaches and consider them to be another type of menstrual-related migraine.

Definitions of Menstrual Migraine

There is no consensus on the definition of menstrual-related headaches. Do we use a patient's subjective definition? Do we use specific time limits such as 3 days before or after menses or 7 days before and after onset of menses? For Szekely et al. (1986), the definition is headache occurring regularly during the menstrual phase. They define this phase as a constant 15 days, plus and minus 7 days around the onset of menses. Solbach et al. (1984a) did not distinguish menstrual-related headaches from other migraines. She defined the menstrual phase as the 3 days before the onset of menses, during menses, and the 3 days following menses. Gauthier et al. (1991) defined the menstrual phase the same way.

Kim and Blanchard (1992) classified these migraines and nonmenstrual migraines from the subjects' subjective report confirmed by their headache log. Some women with menstrual migraines reported worsening during 1 week before onset of menses, during menses, during ovulation, or at both menses-related and other times. Subjects defined the time when they thought their menstrual migraines were most likely to occur. These were either during the week before the menses or during the menses. See Silberstein (1992) for a discussion of biochemical factors and definitions. He proposes a differentiation of menstrual migraine from premenstrual migraine.

Results and Conclusions

I focus on the Kim and Blanchard (1992) study as the most recent and one that controls for factors not previously controlled for. They reported on various combinations of relaxation, temperature biofeedback, and cognitive therapy with extended or limited office-based programs. As a group, these treatments were similarly effective for both menstrual and nonmenstrual migraine groups. They were significantly more effective than nontreated subjects. Among the group of 38 women reporting menstrual migraines, 16 (42%) reported at least 50% improvement compared with a similar 33/60 (55%) of those with nonmenstrual migraines. Other percentages of improvement were also similar. Those with menstrual migraines showed slightly less improvement in headaches and medication reduction. However, they did improve compared to pretreatment.

Because of possible limitations of the first study, the researchers studied another 15 subjects reporting both menstrual-related and nonmenstrual-related migraines. They used only temperature feedback presumably with relaxation home practice. This group did not do as well as a group. However, four patients reduced their nonmenstrual migraines by at least 50% (average = 74%). Three of these also reduced their menstrual migraines by at least 50% (average = 88%). Another subject improved her menstrual migraines by nearly 81%. Note that four subjects worsened when comparing the 4 weeks after treatment to the pretreatment baseline.

These treatments can result in significant improvements for many women with menstrual-related migraines. One can certainly justify this treatment approach. Practitioners should consider using a subjective definition of menstrual-related migraine and verify these with headache logs.

SUMMARY

A major application of relaxation therapies, biofeedback therapies, and other applied psychophysiological therapies is in the treatment of tension-type and migraine headaches. An extensive research and clinical literature exists with good support for these treatments. There are still many unanswered questions about causes, evaluation and assessment, mechanisms of cause, and the treating of special populations.

The focus throughout Part A has been on diagnosis, proposed mechanisms of cause, evaluation and assessment, and treatment of selected special populations. The focus of Part B is treatment. The topics are considerations for cost containment, pediatric headaches, selected factors affecting headaches and interfering with treatments, patient education, compliance, placement of electrodes, and selected treatment-process variables.

Note. References and Glossary for this chapter are located at the end of Chapter 15.

15

Headache: Selected Issues and Considerations in Evaluation and Treatment
Part B: Treatment

Mark S. Schwartz

COST-CONTAINMENT CONSIDERATIONS

Many health care professionals using biofeedback are making significant efforts to contain costs for evaluations and treatments of headaches while preserving quality of care. This challenge is essential, complex, and has achievable goals. This section focuses on the rationale for and factors involved in the stepped-care model for providing health care. This model involves starting with less complicated and less expensive, effective therapies and continues as an integral part of health care. An example of the stepped-care approach is the treatment of essential hypertension. Dietary and exercise recommendations typically precede diuretics, which, in turn, usually precede other medications.

The major treatments for tension-type and migraine headaches often proceed with medications, selected dietary changes, relaxation and biofeedback therapies, physical therapies, stress management, and psychotherapy. One starts with a prudent number of office visits. The order does not imply a preference or standard of practice. It is one logical order. The order also logically starts with relaxation with limited biofeedback and limited office visits and then proceeds to extensive biofeedback. One often then adds physical therapy, dietary changes, stress management, psychotherapy, and then medication. Different medications and different dietary changes could appear at both ends.

The terms "home-based," "minimal-therapist," and "limited-contact" in the published literature fit well within a stepped-care model and are equivalent terms. For convenience, I refer to these as "prudent limited office treatment" (PLOT) and discuss this later.

This chapter does not review the literature on the cost-effectiveness of biofeedback for treating people with headaches. That topic requires more time and space than available here. Practitioners, policy makers, and third-party payers should review Shellenberger, Amar, Schneider, and Stewart (1989).

O'Grady's (1987) study is impressive and definitely worth noting. It illustrates how biofeedback can reduce medical utilization and medication usage among patients with chronic headaches. In a large health management organization (HMO) setting, 63 patients with chronic headaches completed biofeedback treatment with from 6 to 20 sessions. O'Grady compared these patients with 17 others completing 5 sessions or less. At 1 year follow-up, those with more sessions had 75% fewer physician office visits for headache!

They also used 56% less medication and had 19% fewer emergency room visits! They also made 16% fewer phone calls to their physicians at 1 year. Office visits for headache remained consistently low over 5 years after treatment! In the year before treatment, patients had made an average of more than six visits per year for headaches. Over the next 5 years, the average was less than two visits per year.

Medication

Most people with headaches go to physicians first, and physicians usually prescribe medications. That practice is logical and often effective. One may disagree with this approach, but it remains a standard of practice. For that reason, I start with considerations for cost containment for pharmacological therapies and focus on the migraines. I do this because of the potential for high costs for treating migraines with prophylactic and abortive medications. However, cost-containment considerations for tension-type headache are also pertinent.

Pharmacological Treatment of Migraines: Prophylaxis

Many practitioners still consider propranolol as the "most widely used pharmacological treatment [for migraine prophylaxis] and the 'gold standard' against which new pharmacological agents are evaluated" (Holroyd & Penzien, 1990, p. 1). These authors conducted a meta-analysis of 25 clinical studies of propranolol and 35 clinical studies of relaxation and thermal biofeedback with a combined total of 2445 patients. The studies reveal no consistent advantage for either approach. In the studies using daily symptom ratings, the reduction of headaches is about 45% for short-term periods. With less conservative outcome measures, such as physician ratings or patient global reports, the improvement is about 20% better. Both treatments are much better than studies with placebo or untreated subjects, both of which typically produce little or no improvement. Other prophylactic medications such as beta blockers, calcium channel blockers, and antidepressants are also useful for individual patients. However, none are consistently better than propranolol (Holroyd, Penzien, & Cordingley, 1991).

Therefore, one makes the choice between propranolol or other medications versus using relaxation and biofeedback on grounds other than effectiveness. Such factors include patient convenience, contraindications, professional preferences and habit, and, finally, cost. At one pharmacy in Jacksonville, Florida, the cost of a generic brand, nonsustained release propranolol is about $600 a year for a 160-milligram/day dose. The trade-name product and the sustained release version are more expensive, up to about $750/year. Over a 3-year period, the medication could cost from about $1800 to about $2250.

Unanswered questions involving pharmacological treatment include the following:

- What is the comparative effectiveness over longer periods?
- What is the effect of combinations of treatment?
- Are there differential effects on specific subgroups of patients?
- Are there differential effects on quality of life and disability?
- What are the differential iatrogenic effects of these treatments?

Until we know the answers to these questions, the decision to start with a prophylactic medication such as propranolol or a nonpharmacological treatment such as relaxation and biofeedback, depends on:

- Patient preference
- Physician preference

- Patient experience with medication
- Negative side effects
- Medical contraindications
- Practical considerations, such as:
  Availability of relaxation and biofeedback
  Treatment costs
  Reimbursement

Pharmacological Treatment: Abortive

I found one study comparing long-term effects of abortive pharmacological therapy compared with relaxation and thermal biofeedback (Holroyd, Holm, et al., 1989). Both treatments resulted in clinically significant improvements. The patients maintained most of their gains at the 3-year follow-up. However, six were still using this treatment among the eight patients treated with relaxation and biofeedback. Only two had added other treatment. Furthermore, none were using prophylactic or narcotic medications at follow-up. In contrast, only 2 of 11 patients who started with ergotamine were still using it, and 5 were using prophylactic medications or narcotics. Two of the seven who changed treatments did so because of side effects of the ergotamine.

Compliance with ergotamine and other medications for headache has been troublesome. A brief patient-education manual and one brief session helped to teach patients with chronic migraines to use their abortive medications effectively. Social learning theory was the basis of both. Presumably, this helped patients transform their knowledge into behaviors compared to a standard therapy group without the patient-education experience.

Therefore, practitioners should be sure patients are taking abortive medication when comparing this treatment with nonpharmacological treatments. This is important when comparing clinical experience and research. One often needs good patient education to help assure compliance.

Thus, abortive medications have a place in the treatment of migraines. However, compliance can be a problem. Long-term reliance on abortive medications might not be as good as relaxation and biofeedback. We need more studies of long-term comparisons.

Dietary

Practitioners should consider stopping selected dietary substances before any other treatments if a patient or practitioner strongly suspects this could reduce the patient's migraines. This is often easy to do, especially if the patient agrees, and it does not involve an extensive change in dietary habits. However, extensive dietary changes and challenges are occasionally proper before or after other treatments. Such a regimen should be tailored to this individual patient, and the probability of success, time involved, feasibility, and costs—especially doing this before other treatments—considered. See Chapter 10 for a detailed discussion of dietary factors and migraines.

Cognitive and Other Psychotherapies

Rationale

Cognitive therapies have a long history in the treatment of migraine and tension headaches. One can logically justify the use of cognitive therapies for many patients with headaches and research to show their specific value. However, research results vary in support of cognitive therapies with less-than-desired demonstration of their added value. The reasons for continued research and clinical use of cognitive-behavioral therapies include the following:

1. Many clinical practitioners and researchers believe that cognitive factors and therapies are more important than shown thus far by research.
2. Practitioners and researchers desire to improve treatment for those patients who do not get ideal results from relaxation and biofeedback therapies.
3. Documenting the value of the added investment of time and expense for cognitive therapies is more important now.

Each of these is independently worthwhile. The rationale for cognitive therapies for headaches is well summarized by Appelbaum et al. (1990). They propose that patients' perceptions and experience of stressful situations account for the worsening and/or maintenance of headaches. Automatic thoughts that accompany a patient's perceptions probably mediate stress reactivity and headache onset for many patients. In turn, one or both of two factors may mediate tension-type headaches. One is the individual's perception of a lack of control when facing these stressful situations. Another is the chronic muscular tension and sympathetic arousal that occurs in response to these situations.

Review of Studies

Tension-Type Headaches. This section summarizes several studies of cognitive therapies for tension-type headaches. Pure cognitive therapy was more successful than a self-regulatory approach with relaxation and bifrontal electromyographic (EMG) auditory biofeedback for recruited subjects (Holroyd, Andrasik, & Westbrook, 1977).

Adding cognitive therapy to muscle relaxation therapy improves the percentage of patients showing clinically significant improvement within a regular office-contact model (Blanchard, Appelbaum, Radnitz, Michultka, et al., 1990). The Headache Index data did not support the advantage for adding cognitive therapy. However, 10 (62.5%) of 16 patients showed at least 50% reduction of headaches compared to 6 (31.6%) of 19 in the relaxation only group.

We should note that this study used progressive muscle relaxation without biofeedback. We can also note that the relaxation only group did not fare as well as expected based on other studies and fared *no better* than a "pseudomeditation" group. The data support the addition of cognitive therapy. However, it is not clear that it always yields results better than the results from relaxation alone or with biofeedback.

Combining a tailored cognitive therapy and a relaxation procedure was more effective than relaxation alone in a limited-contact, self-administered format (Tobin, Holroyd, Baker, Reynolds, & Holm, 1988). Tailoring involved problem solving and cognitive restructuring for each patient. The relaxation therapy was progressive muscle relaxation. One limitation was the lack of a control group.

Another study showed cognitive therapy better than a combination of muscle and autogenic relaxation procedures without biofeedback (Murphy, Lehrer, & Jurish, 1990). The authors speculate that the reason might result from the patients' improved ability to manage stressors. Cognitive therapy can result in improvement. A valuable finding is that criteria other than the Headache Index sometimes provide more useful information. In this case, improvement was reduced frequency of days with headaches and reduced severity of the worst headache each week.

One must note that the improvement for both groups was below that of other studies. For example, the Headache Index improvement showed only about 30% for relaxation and 47% for the cognitive therapy. These were both lower than rates found elsewhere using similar therapies. The authors admit doubting whether their subjects in both groups actually used the specific techniques. Thus, this was a study of *exposure* to therapy rather than of the *use* of therapy. The authors asked if the difference from other studies could have resulted from the slightly older ages of their subjects. The ages of their subjects were from the mid-20s to the early 50s. The mean age was about 40. However, other studies (Appelbaum et al., 1990) do not suggest that this age should do worse than younger patients.

A limited-contact study showed no advantage for combining a fixed set of cognitive procedures and relaxation therapies compared with relaxation alone (Appelbaum et al., 1990). In contrast to the Tobin et al. (1988) study, the patients were 9 years older (37 vs. 28) and had suffered headaches 6 years longer. Furthermore, the cognitive therapy protocol was fixed instead of tailored. These factors could result in reducing the advantage of cognitive therapy. The authors consider whether more time and more cognitive therapy would help. It might take longer than 1 month for the effects of cognitive therapy to show. The authors also consider a possible "ceiling effect." Adding more strategies to an already valid therapy might prove contraproductive. In summary, there are conditions in which adding cognitive therapy to relaxation does not help. However, the reasons for this are not clear.

In conclusion, the potential advantage of adding cognitive therapy to relaxation alone or to a combination of relaxation and biofeedback is not clear. We also do not know whether brief and tailored cognitive therapy for each patient would be sufficient. Nevertheless, many practitioners continue to believe that cognitive factors and therapies are valuable—at least for selected patients. The logic is too strong to ignore this in clinical practice. The vital questions include what types of cognitive therapy are useful, what specific procedures are most useful, for whom are they useful, and when should one introduce cognitive therapy? Prudent clinical judgment, the use of a stepped-care model, and cost containment remain in the forefront of clinical practice until research answers these questions, and support for them arrive. It will arrive for selected patients, procedures, and therapy conditions.

Migraines and Mixed Headaches. The focus here is selected research with cognitive therapies for migraines and patients with both migraine and tension-type headaches (mixed headaches). One study combined cognitive therapy with temperature biofeedback (TBF) and compared this combination to TBF and relaxation without the cognitive therapy component (Blanchard, Appelbaum, Nicholson, et al., 1990). The patients had vascular or mixed headaches. Treatment was within a limited-office model. All treatment was better than a symptom-monitoring, waiting-list control group. However, cognitive therapy did not result in better results than without it.

Another study showed that in a regular office-contact model, combining cognitive therapy with TBF had about the same results as TBF alone for patients with vascular (migraines and mixed) headaches (Blanchard, Appelbaum, Radnitz, Morrill, et al., 1990). Treatment was better than no treatment.

There was no advantage for providing a combination of relaxation and cognitive therapy for patients with migraines treated in a clinic-based model with eight sessions versus a limited-contact model with two sessions (Richardson & McGrath, 1989). Both treatment groups fared better than a waiting-list control.

Conclusions and Recommendations for Cognitive Therapies

1. Practitioners can justify combining cognitive therapies with relaxation and biofeedback for selected patients. However, the added value is not consistent for all patients.

Do not routinely start with the combination when using a stepped-care model and seeking cost containment.

2. Use multiple measures of improvement. Any one measure might not be sufficient. Consider using the Headache Index, a medication index, and the number of days with a headache.

3. Consider a questionnaire such as that of Murphy et al. (1988). This allows assessments of patients' ability to prevent headaches and function with headaches. It also allows assessment of patients' perceived personal control over their headaches.

4. Patient education is probably very important to explain the rationale for cognitive and other therapies and to provide therapy instructions.

5. Consider tailoring cognitive therapies.

6. Results and the "ceiling effect" from relaxation and biofeedback may depend on several factors. Consider asking these questions:

A. Is biofeedback used to change patients' cognitions about their sense of control?
B. Is the feedback information adequate?
C. Is the relaxation with biofeedback tailored to patients? For example, was it from different muscle areas such as the cervical neck, trapezii, and occipital muscles. Is the feedback with varied postures and activities?
D. Are there other therapy changes during and after therapy?
E. Is there sufficient patient education to teach the rationale, procedures, and expectations for relaxation and biofeedback?
F. What is the frequency and timing of relaxation practice?

One can speculate that these factors can result in approaching or reaching maximum effectiveness. If so, then cognitive therapy might not add much. Each practitioner decides the role of cognitive therapies and tailors treatment for patients while continuing to review research and gain more clinical experience.

Prudent Limited Office Treatment

Using fewer office sessions is a treatment model different from the traditional model for relaxation and biofeedback treatments. This model has much validity in the atmosphere emphasizing cost containment. Various terms denote this model. The terms "minimal therapist," "home-based," and "limited-contact" are interchangeable in the literature. None of these terms is ideal, and patients and professionals may misunderstand them. Of these, I prefer "limited-contact" (Guarnieri & Blanchard, 1990). Minimal implies least or insignificant, and that is certainly not the intent. The term home implies a specific place for treatment rather than everywhere other than in the professional's office.

I propose the term "prudent limited office treatment" with the acronym PLOT for convenience. I use the term "prudent" in the sense of discerning, judicious and logical, careful, conscientious, and economical. It is a conservative approach but not an extreme one. The term prudent does not imply that using more office sessions is imprudent or excessive. There are many cases in which it is proper to start with more sessions rather than fewer sessions. The acronym PLOT intends to communicate that it is prudent to consider the least number of office sessions to accomplish therapeutic goals. It implies that this approach is often appropriate, sufficient, and cost containing.

There are patients whose headaches respond to uncomplicated therapies. They do not need extensive office-based relaxation and biofeedback. Research supports the strategy of preceding biofeedback with relaxation therapy for some patients to determine which patients benefit from relaxation alone (Blanchard, Andrasik, Neff, et al., 1982). In that study, the therapists used office-based relaxation sessions. However, that is probably as expensive as biofeedback sessions.

Relaxation therapies and/or biofeedback-assisted relaxation need not involve a lengthy series of office sessions to be effective. There are now several studies supporting PLOT to be as effective as longer, office-based programs. Preliminary reports were by Jurish et al. (1983), Teders et al. (1984), and Blanchard, Andrasik, et al., (1985). The last group noted that their

> treatments are not entirely self-help or do-it-yourself treatments. There is the need for training by a professional at crucial points in the total regimen as well as the availability of telephone consultation between the monthly office visits. (Blanchard, Andrasik, et al., 1985, p. 219)

A summary of their regimen is:

> three office visits, approximately once per 4 weeks, and two scheduled telephone consultations of 10–15 minutes between office visits. Total therapist time was scheduled to be 2 hours, 30 minutes. In addition to the office visits, the patient received 5 audiotapes and a set of 8 manuals to guide him through the training. (p. 215)

These studies reported that PLOT programs were far more cost-effective for reducing vascular, mixed, or tension headaches than traditional office-based treatment. They divided the percentage of improvement by the total therapist contact time and compared the two approaches. They concluded that home-based treatment was "more than twice as cost-effective" for treating patients with tension headaches. For patients with migraines, it was four times more cost-effective. For mixed headache, it was six times more cost-effective. Clinical practice is more variable, and these figures will probably differ in other settings. Thus, PLOT could be more cost-effective depending on the costs of delivering care, the specific treatment components, and the professional time needed in each approach.

The PLOT cost-containment approach extends to treating pediatric patients with migraines (Burke & Andrasik, 1989; Guarnieri & Blanchard, 1990; Allen & McKeen, 1991). Based on a sample of nine children in a limited-contact and eight children in a clinic-based approach, Guarnieri and Blanchard (1990) found "no significant difference in efficacy between the two conditions" (p. 179). The average age was 11 and ranged from 8–16. All the children had migraines for at least 1 year, and the average was 3.7 years.

Five children in the clinic-based protocol and three in the limited-contact protocol showed at least 50% reduction of headaches at the 4-week follow-up. Although this difference ($p < .15$) did not reach a customary significance level, the authors sensed from anecdotal evidence that the home environment was more important in the limited-contact condition than in the clinic-based approach. They speculated that

> when the home environment is supportive and generally stable, the home-based treatment leads to good results: However, when the home environment is somewhat chaotic or nonsupportive, then the home-based treatment does not give as good results. (Guarnieri & Blanchard, 1990, p. 183)

This makes sense for a pediatric population but requires further study.

One implication is that a PLOT approach can work for pediatric patients. This approach increases the need for family involvement and support. Cautious practitioners will check the home environment before deciding upon this approach in clinical practice. Practitioners need to foster "a home environment supportive of adaptive coping behaviors" (Allen & McKeen, 1991, p. 467).

With a "multiple-baseline" or "time-lagged control" design, Allen and McKeen (1991) studied 21 children with migraines without aura. The children were aged 7 through 12 and had had headaches for an average of 3.4 years with the range from 6 months to 6 years. There were two treatment visits over 2 weeks in addition to the initial interview. A fourth visit was for assessing psychophysiological changes after treatment. Of the 15 children who showed compliance and whose parents showed compliance, 13 (87%) showed a reduction of headaches of at least 70%. Six of these reported no headaches at the end of treatment.

The children showed similar success at 3 and 8 months follow-up. Headaches also improved for another three children who complied with relaxation but whose parents did not follow the guidelines for behavior management. However, they then gradually worsened over treatment and did not do as well as the others. These three children had a lower headache index during the baseline. Only the children with noncompliant parents did not significantly reduce their medication use during treatment. There was a significant association of more practice, better hand warming, and decreased headache frequency. The data "suggest that both biofeedback and environmental support were important to the success of the program" (Allen & McKeen, 1991, p. 471). This study supports the cost-containment value of treating children within a PLOT protocol. See Allen and McKeen (1991) for details and discussion of the treatment.

Implications

The implication from the PLOT studies is not that one should treat all or most patients within a PLOT model. The point is there are alternatives for many patients, and cost containment is possible. The practitioner should consider starting a treatment trial within a PLOT model and include a suitable instructional or patient-education package. If clinically significant and patient-acceptable symptom improvement does not occur, then more office-based therapy can always be added.

The following example contains steps to consider in the treatment of many headache patients.

1. In the first sessions, include some or all of the following:

   - Make necessary dietary changes.
   - Stop gum chewing, especially with temporalis headaches.
   - Change easy-to-modify life stressors.
   - Assess multiple muscle sites and finger temperature during baseline resting and responses to stress.
   - Provide limited biofeedback for one to three sessions.
   - Use audiotaped relaxation and printed instructions.
   - Use verbal, printed, and taped patient education.
   - Provide brief live relaxation instructions.
   - Use a self-report log to assess headaches, medication usage, relaxation practice, caffeine, and so forth.
   - Arrange for follow-up in a few weeks.

2. Consider adding more office-based therapy if headaches do not decrease a clinically significant degree in a few weeks.

   - Consider face-to-face relaxation therapy.
   - Consider a few more biofeedback-assisted relaxation sessions if indicated.
   - Consider further evaluation and other treatments.

3. If headaches still do not decrease to an acceptable degree, consider different office-based therapy, as indicated.

- Consider more biofeedback-assisted relaxation, as indicated.
- Consider cognitive and other stress management therapies, as indicated.

The stepped-care example can have other elements and sequences. For example, one can defer treatment if the patient expects a major life change in a few weeks, and the change will probably result in a reduction of stress and symptoms. For example, one can defer treatment for a teacher seen in May who reports that symptoms typically improve substantially in the summer.

A stepped-care approach is not the model of choice for all patients. Many patients show considerable excess physiological tension and/or considerable stress in their lives. At the outset of therapy, they often need intervention strategies such as those in steps 2 and 3.

PEDIATRIC HEADACHES[1]

A chapter about headaches and biofeedback should include a discussion of the application of relaxation therapies and biofeedback for pediatric patients. The rationale for this application to pediatric patients includes the facts that headaches in children are common, the relaxation therapies with biofeedback are very effective, and we know that a large percentage of children with headaches will continue to have them as adults. This section summarizes the major conclusions from the published literature.

Prevalence and Prognosis

Headaches are common in children of all ages and increase over childhood and adolescence (Bille, 1962, 1981, 1989, 1990; Blanchard & Andrasik, 1985; Linet, Stewart, Celentano, Ziegler, & Sprecher, 1989). The classic and ongoing Swedish questionnaire studies of 9,059 children by the pediatrician, Bo Bille, showed 39% of 6-year-old children and 70% of 15-year-old children with headaches. A U.S. study included 3,158 children ages 12–17 whose families were contacted by telephone (Linet et al., 1989). Among their many findings were that 56% of the males and 74% of the females reported a headache in the past 4 weeks, 27% of the males and 41.4% of the females reported two or more headaches, and 4.5% of the males and 9.4% of the females reported four or more headaches in the past month. The average intensity was moderate on a 1–10 scale (4.5 males; 4.7 females) and the mean duration was 5–6 hours.

The specific diagnosis is difficult to make in many cases and, as discussed elsewhere in Chapter 14, there is disagreement among experts for diagnosis in adults. Furthermore, the categories and labels change over time. Some practitioners and researchers suggest that it is even more difficult to make specific diagnoses for children (Silberstein, 1990). Confounding factors include the role of regular use of analgesics or ergot derivatives that often can transform migraines and episodic tension-headaches into chronic daily headache.

Some professionals believe that in teenagers "masked depression" is often associated with chronic tension-type headache (Silberstein, 1990, p. 721). This author notes that

---

[1]A discussion of this application could also have been put in Chapter 33 on Special Populations. In addition to headaches, there are many successful biofeedback applications for pediatric patients (e.g., see Chapters 21, 24, and 25). Some practitioners and researchers support the contention that biofeedback applications for adults are appropriate for pediatric patients.

depressed teenagers are very unlikely to admit to being depressed on the more obvious self-report depression measures. Thus, the clinical interview may be a better assessment method. Silberstein (1990) looks for "evidence of sleep disturbance, loss of energy, loss of interest, and diminished ability to concentrate. The child frequently looks and behaves depressed but denies depressed affect" (p. 721).

I admit to having no useful clinical experience with depression in teenagers and accept the premise that many of the teenagers with chronic tension headaches also are depressed. However, it may be worth noting that all or most of the symptoms included by Silberstein (1990) are also those symptoms that result from sleep deprivation—a common self-imposed behavior pattern.

The prognosis of benign headaches is far from desirable. In the 30-year follow-up (Bille, 1989) of a large Swedish sample with migraine headaches as children, only 62% were migraine-free for 2 or more years as young adults (Silberstein, 1990). However, after 30 years there were only 40% who continued to be migraine free. Bille (1990) reported that "53 percent of the migraine children had migraine as adults, and one-third had recurrent attacks since childhood" (p. 39).

The prognosis of treatments other than relaxation and biofeedback show a progressive reduction of up to 50% of headaches in treated and control groups (Silberstein, 1990). Research on treatment of headaches in pediatric patients must have control groups, and success must be better than about 50% to be taken seriously.

Effectiveness of Relaxation and/or Biofeedback Treatments

Published research strongly supports the effectiveness of biofeedback-assisted relaxation as a nonpharmacological treatment of headaches in children and adolescents. The review by Duckro and Cantwell-Simmons (1989) concluded that relaxation training with and without biofeedback is effective for managing chronic headache among children and adolescents. They concluded that nearly all (88%) of the children treated in seven studies met the criterion of a reduction in the headache composite index of at least 50%. Silberstein's (1990) impression is that relaxation and biofeedback are "perhaps more effective in children than in adults" and "are useful alone and as an adjunct to pharmacotherapy" (p. 722). Blanchard's (1992) more recent review was even more emphatic and more favorable toward biofeedback. He focused on temperature biofeedback (TBF) and stated that,

> TBF, usually with adjunctive autogenic training, has consistently led to significant improvement and to 67% or better of the samples being clinically improved. . . . For the most part . . . the headache reductions noted at the end of treatment have been maintained at follow-up of up to 1 year. Relaxation training has also been shown to be effective in the treatment of pediatric migraine . . . but perhaps not as effective as TBF. . . . TBF may be the treatment of choice for pediatric migraine. (pp. 546–547).

I arrived at the same conclusion favoring biofeedback from my review of the literature of relaxation without biofeedback and using various methods for teaching and administering relaxation procedures. One exception is the study by Fentress, Masek, Mehegan, and Benson (1986) which compared relaxation and biofeedback and found both groups to be equally very successful in their small sample.

This conclusion is based on reviewing the studies of the use of relaxation without biofeedback for treating pediatric headaches (Richter et al., 1986; Larsson, Melin, Lamminen, & Ullstedt, 1987; Larsson & Melin, 1988; McGrath et al., 1988; Wisniewski, Genshaft,

Mulick, Coury, & Hammer, 1988; Larsson, Melin, & Döberl, 1990; Passchier et al., 1990; Engel, Rapoff, & Pressman, 1992).

I reviewed several investigations using biofeedback as part of treatment (Labbe & Williams, 1984; Andrasik et al., 1984; Werder & Sargent, 1984; Mehegan, Masek, Harrison, Russo, & Leviton, 1984; Blanchard & Andrasik, 1985; Burke & Andrasik, 1989; Grazzi, Lelone, Frediani, & Bussone, 1990; Guarnieri & Blanchard, 1990). There is insufficient data to evaluate any age differences in response to these treatments.

Some of the biofeedback studies report that all or nearly all of the subjects did extremely well usually with at least 80% improvement in headaches. Those using only relaxation often show some improvement but with much lower percentages of the groups showing improvement and far less improvement, typically less than 50%.

It is instructive to add here that some children, as with some adults, "prefer the feedback and do less well without it. Other patients seem to be bothered by the feedback" (Duckrow & Cantwell-Simmons, 1989, p. 432). "In either case, the information is still useful for the therapist" (p. 432).

One must also point out that, as with adults, the relationship between symptom changes and physiological changes during and across office treatment sessions is not clear and not established. At least one study did provide some support for a relationship between muscle tension and tension headache improvement (Grazzi et al., 1990). The complexity of this relationship is discussed in Chapter 14.

The effectiveness of "home-based, minimal-therapist" relaxation and biofeedback for children and adolescents may be affected by the family environment (Blanchard, 1992; Burke & Andrasik, 1989; Guarnieri & Blanchard, 1990; also see discussion of PLOT in this chapter).

Preventive Prophylactic Medications

Prudent practitioners will consider prophylactic medications based partly on the frequency of the headaches, the severity and durations of the headaches, and the effectiveness of simple analgesics for the child. Prophylactic medications are useful for some children with chronic headaches, especially those who have "severe, frequent attacks" and those "complicated by neurological symptoms" (Silberstein, 1990, p. 721). The use of medications does not preclude the use of biofeedback and relaxation.

Other Nonpharmacological Treatments for Children

There are other useful considerations and treatment recommendations for children. In tailoring treatment to the individual, some of these may be tried first within a stepped-care model. Many of these also are relevant for adults as well. Silberstein (1990) reminds us of these:

- Reassure the family about benign condition.
- Adjust the life-style of the child including "regular bedtime, a reasonable meal schedule, and the avoidance of overload in activities" (p. 722).
- Identify and eliminate headache triggers ("physical exertion, hunger, noise, traveling, light glare, certain foods, and head trauma") (p. 722).
- "In children with a disturbed home life, significant depression, or abuse, family and individual psychotherapy is indicated" (p. 722).

For a brief discussion of dietary factors for headaches in children, see Silberstein (1990) who concludes that this is still a "very controversial" area (also, see Chapter 10).

Conclusion

Relaxation therapy, often with biofeedback, is appropriate and may be the best treatment for many pediatric-aged patients with chronic headaches. A stepped-care approach is appropriate for many of these patients although the treatment must be tailored to the individual patient.

OTHER SELECTED FACTORS AFFECTING HEADACHES AND INTERFERING WITH TREATMENTS

Medications

Negative Effects on Headaches

There are at least two broad aspects to this topic. One is the effect on headaches of taking large amounts of analgesics or other medications. This subdivides into the effects of the medications on maintaining headaches and the initial increase of headaches when the medication is stopped ("rebound headache"). Stopping such medications can have an efficacious result.

The other aspect is the effect of trying to use relaxation and biofeedback with patients who are still taking large amounts of analgesic and other headache medications. This section focuses on both aspects. The summary of this topic is that:

- The chronic use of some analgesics and some other headache medications worsens headaches. They can interfere with improvement in some patients.
- There is also evidence arguing against the role of analgesics causing headaches, especially for migraines, in that some patients do well on chronic analgesics.
- Withdrawal from medications can reduce headaches in some patients.
- As both a cause and treatment for headaches, the evidence is stronger for ergotamine tartrate than for other analgesics.
- For patients taking large amounts of these medications, the efficacy of treating them with relaxation and biofeedback is still unclear. The prognosis is probably poor.
- The value in combining a withdrawal program with relaxation and biofeedback treatments is promising.

Analgesic Rebound Headache: The Concept and the Data

The first paper describing "analgesic rebound headache" was by Kudrow (1982). It became a focus of clinical and research attention by Rapoport and his colleagues (Rapoport, Sheftell, Weeks, & Baskin, 1983; Rapoport, Weeks, Sheftell, Baskin, & Verdi, 1985; Rapoport, 1988). Practitioners now often encourage withdrawal as a treatment. The implications for stepped care are obvious.

The proposed syndrome is "almost daily use of relatively high levels of analgesic medication combined with chronic low-to-moderate levels of headache" (Blanchard, 1992, p. 543). Severe headaches for several days follow stopping or markedly reducing chronic use of analgesics. However, continued abstinence often results in substantial reductions of headaches. Starting other medications for headaches during and after withdrawal of analgesics confounded interpretation of results in early and many later studies.

All the patients in the Mathew, Kurman, and Perez (1990) study had EMG and temperature biofeedback and a low-caffeine and low-tyramine diet. For those stopping symptomatic medications, 14 of 28 dropped out despite the relaxation, biofeedback, and dietary counseling. That group had the highest drop-out percentages. Those stopping these medications but continuing prophylactic medication had the second highest drop out rate of 27.5% (16 of 58). Among those who stopped all medications, headaches initially rose during about the first 2 weeks and then dropped steadily over several weeks. Those patients who did not stop medications showed no change in headaches.

The improvement of patients without any medications was about the same as among those patients in other medication groups. The latter included patients continuing prophylactic medications without symptomatic medications. This led Mathew et al. (1990) to conclude that "concomitant use of symptomatic medications nullifies the effects of prophylactic medications" and "discontinuing daily symptomatic drugs enhances the beneficial effects of prophylactic medications" (p. 637). Details of the relaxation and biofeedback procedures are scant. One has a sense that this was a very basic version of relaxation and biofeedback.

One question is whether or not relaxation and biofeedback can play a role in withdrawal from analgesics and in what ways would this help? Based on available data, the results from relaxation and biofeedback treatments are much less satisfactory for high users of analgesics (Michultka, Blanchard, Appelbaum, Jaccard, & Dentinger, 1989). These patients are among the more refractory to behavioral treatments such as relaxation and biofeedback. This result does not appear related to personality differences among patients.

The 10 high-medication-user female patients reported by Blanchard, Taylor, and Dentinger (1992) illustrate the complexity of this problem. This report further shows the difficulty some patients have stopping medications even with help. However, applied psychophysiological treatment appeared to help some patients withdraw from medications. Treatment included relaxation, biofeedback, cognitive therapy, support, or combinations. For these patients, practitioners may properly care less about the element of the treatment package that is working. Withdrawal and significant clinical improvement are far more important.

Inpatient withdrawal may sometimes be necessary but is often impractical because of financial and other factors. Of interest is the study of 10 patients with tension-type headaches and 44 with migraines in Vienna (Baumgartner, Wessely, Bingol, Maly, & Holzner, 1989). That study reported that 60% of the patients "experienced a long lasting relief of headaches" and 76% "a significant reduction of analgesic abuse" (p. 513). Like most other studies in this area, this one had many confounding factors. The treatment package was multicomponent, and the types of patients and variables were complex.

Comprehensive inpatient treatment (Lake, Saper, Madden, & Kreeger, 1993) is a consideration for patients with "severe, intractable, persistent migraine (chronic daily headache)" (p. 55). One of seven criteria for admission is "sufficient analgesic drug useage to render likely a significant withdrawal response or so-called 'rebound' headache" (p. 56). The other criteria involved pain. Relaxation and biofeedback are components in the treatment program. Despite the nearly $5000 average cost per patient for an average of 8.5 days, the authors' logic and justification are persuasive. The more conservative data indicate a reduction of days with severe headache by at least 50% in about two-thirds of 91 patients. There was long-term maintenance of the substantial reduction of pain medications. Interested readers should read the details of that study.

Description of Analgesic Abuse Headaches. Some describe these headaches as "rather uniform and independent of the initial headache type and of the pharmacological substance abused" (Baumgartner et al. 1989, p. 510). "Drug-induced headache features" can include a constant, dull, and daily occipital pressure that spreads along both parietal areas (Baumgartner et al., 1989). The headache can also feel like a helmet that fits too tightly. There may be other headache attacks superimposed on these. Accompanying symptoms include: asthenia, nausea, irritability, memory problems, and sleep disturbances.

Among the Mathew et al. (1990) patients, most of these headaches were bilateral and diffuse with scalp tenderness, including suboccipital tenderness. Severity and location of headaches varied. Nearly everyone had some daily headaches consistent with migraine "even though they rarely show the typical and distinct pattern of migraine attacks" (p. 637). Furthermore, "Most of the time it is difficult to distinguish [the drug-induced headache] from the primary headache disorders" (p. 637).

Accompanying features were asthenia, nausea, restlessness, irritability, memory problems, difficulty in intellectual concentration, and depression. Seventy-nine percent showed combinations of these. "One of the most striking features of drug-induced headache is the early morning awakening (2 A.M. to 6 A.M.)" (p. 638). This could be an effect from withdrawal.

Withdrawal features described by Baumgartner et al. (1989) included "increased headache intensity (rebound headache), sleep disturbances, vegetative symptoms (nausea, vomiting, hypotension), mood disturbance, and non-specific heart sensations" (p. 511). One patient had an epileptic seizure. Withdrawal symptoms were most severe on days 3 and 4 after stopping the drug, and symptoms lessened substantially after that.

The criteria of Baumgartner et al. (1989, p. 511) for the diagnosis of analgesic abuse were proposed by Diener (1988a):

• More than 20 days a month with headachess.
• More than 10 hours of headache each day.
• More than 20 days a month ingesting analgesics.
• Regularly using analgesics and/or ergotamines combined with barbiturates, codeine, caffeine, antihistamines, or minor tranquilizers.
• Increased headache intensity and frequency after stopping analgesics.
• Initial headache types irrelevant for developing this syndrome.

See Baumgartner et al. (1989), Mathew et al. (1990), Rapoport (1988), Askmark, Lundberg, and Olsson (1989), Blanchard et al. (1992), and Michultka et al. (1989) for information about analgesics and details of their studies.

Arguments against Analgesic Rebound Headaches. One proposed mechanism for rebound headache is that analgesics produce more brain serotonin that paradoxically increases pain in patients with headaches. If this is true, the question is how does this mechanism account for the lack of increased headaches among patients with arthritis who take larger doses of aspirin than do patients with headaches. The same question applies to people taking aspirin daily to help prevent arterial thrombosis (Fisher, 1988). Optional answers are that: (1) this mechanism is incorrect; (2) patients with headaches are biologically different from other persons with chronic pain; or (3) there is some other factor beyond the "biochemical rebound effects" of chronic analgesic use that results in persistent headaches and improvement after withdrawal.

Could it be because analgesics mask some pain and some of the body's internal or natural biofeedback? Could this add to the physiological disregulation and/or the discrepancy between tension and awareness of tension? This analgesic masking of pain could add to increased tension without awareness and therefore to worse and maintained headaches.

Another concern by Fisher (1988) is whether "rebound" is the proper term. It implies that "as the medication wears off headache comes back even worse" (p. 666). However, there are suggestions of habituation to analgesics. This leads to the need for more medication that can interfere with the effects of other medications such as amitriptyline. This suggests that pain gets worse with the use of the medication.

Another question is how tension-type headaches, presumably often caused and worsened by muscle contraction, can worsen by a central origin without muscle contraction? A further question is how tension-type headaches can worsen by a "central origin" without muscle contraction? This relates to the issue of whether or not these headaches are distinct or on a continuum with other headaches.

Lance, Parkes, and Wilkinson (1988) reported that among 89 rheumatology clinic patients, 50 were taking more than 14 analgesic pills per week, typically for several years. This report preceded Rapoport (1988). Based on interview data, these patients did not have more headaches than those taking less than 14 pills. This "Letter to the Editor" discussed the issue for migraine headaches.

Lance et al. (1988) take issue with the assertion that the mechanism of analgesic abuse is a "suppression or down-regulation of a central anti-nociceptive system" (p. 61). If this were true, then patients with chronic pain but without migraines should experience increased headaches with the use of "high numbers of analgesics." For this proposed mechanism to be accurate, "the anti-nociceptive system of a migrainous population must be already partly suppressed, or set at a different level to the rest of the population, so that analgesics in the quantities described tip the migraineur over the threshold into daily headache" (p. 61). However, their data did not support this assumption.

There is another problem with some studies thought to support the effect of regular use of analgesics causing headaches and improvement after withdrawal. Other medications used could account for the improvements. However, some reports did not substitute other medications. Those data offer stronger support for the negative effects of chronic analgesics.

In conclusion, there is research support for the view that chronic use of analgesics daily or almost daily can worsen and maintain headaches. However, the mechanisms remain unclear. Nevertheless, strong advice to selected patients to withdraw from these medications is now common practice. This fits well within a stepped-care model.

Nonheadache Medications Causing Headaches

Practitioners treating headaches need to know about nonheadache medications that can provoke headaches. It is beyond the scope of this chapter to discuss this topic in detail. A short list and brief discussion will suffice. Askmark et al. (1989) summarize the "drugs most frequently associated with headache according to 10,506 reports to [World Health Organization] WHO from five countries." The countries are Australia, New Zealand, Sweden, United Kingdom, and the United States. "The ten drugs most frequently reported . . . were *indomethacin, nifedipine, cimetidine, atenolol, trimethoprim–sulfamethoxazole, zimeldine, glyceryl trinitrate, isosorbide dinitrate, zomepirac,* and *ranitidine*" (p. 441; emphasis added). Oral contraceptives also were among the most reported drugs. The most common mechanism proposed for drug-related headaches from some drugs is "vasodilatation and salt and water retention with subsequent redistribution of intracranial fluid" (p. 441). The mechanism is unknown for other drugs.

Implications for the Effects of Medications on Headaches

Assessment. Get information about all medications and include in daily symptom and medication log. Consider self-report measures of self-efficacy to assess patient's beliefs and perceptions.

Stepped Care. The issues to be considered include: Should one use outpatient or inpatient treatment? How much patient education and cognitive preparation is necessary before withdrawal? Should one use physiological self-regulation treatments before and/or during withdrawal? Does one continue or start prophylactic medications to cover the withdrawal?

For some patients, one could proceed with a protocol similar to this:

1. Provide comprehensive patient education and cognitive preparation. Include information about aspects of addiction and preparation for withdrawal. Discuss the potential role of medications causing headaches, a withdrawal plan, and options. Provide considerable encouragement and reassure the patient about the practitioner's support.
2. Start limited relaxation and cognitive therapies, as indicated.
3. Consider prophylactic medications in selected patients.
4. Start with outpatient withdrawal.
5. Instruct patients in the use of a symptom and medication log.
6. Add more relaxation, biofeedback, and cognitive therapies, as indicated.
7. Follow closely with office visits and/or telephone follow-up for at least several weeks.
8. Consider inpatient withdrawal, as indicated.

The above sequence is only one acceptable sequence. For selected patients, one could start with an inpatient protocol. Include most or all of the other elements, as indicated.

Medication Effects on Biofeedback

The Jay, Renelli, and Mead (1984) report noted an "extreme paucity of information describing the physiological effects on biofeedback training of medication used concurrently to treat a specific headache or pain problem" (p. 59). Unfortunately, there remains a paucity of research on this topic. I did not locate another study specifically focused on this topic and do not have a clear explanation for the lack of research. This type of research is very complex, and there is very little funding for it. Thus, we must infer the potential effects of medications on biofeedback from what we know about the medications.

The study (Jay et al., 1984) examined one beta blocker, propranolol (Inderal), and amitriptyline (Elavil) during biofeedback for developing vascular and neuromuscular control. Patients started medication at least 4 days before starting a sequence of eight relaxation, EMG, and thermal biofeedback sessions. The results suggested that the beta blocker led to a "markedly increased variability in the ability of patients to control" their hand temperature. This also occurred for patients taking amitriptyline alone and trying to master muscle control. The use of either or both "may make concurrent biofeedback . . . more difficult by increasing physiological variability" (p. 67). Baseline physiological functioning varied markedly early in the sessions and after several sessions. However, this did "not prevent biofeedback-enhanced relaxation . . . from occurring" (p. 67). However, for some patients it was particularly difficult.

The physiological variability when using each medication alone was less than for patients using both medications. All patients reached the criteria of 92°F and less than 1 microvolt. The authors did not specify either the conditions in which this occurred or the duration of these. We also do not know whether these patients decreased their headaches. We are grateful to these authors for their pioneering work; however, practitioners need improved studies and understandable data presentations.

These two medications probably result in physiological variability that could make treatment more frustrating for some patients. This could result in patients ending treatment prematurely, but there are no data indicating this will happen. There are no data showing that these patients do not do as well as those treated without the medications. The authors ask "Does the combination of both medications make biofeedback training easier by decreasing the physiological variance on the measures . . . ?" (Jay et al., 1984, p. 69). We do not know about other medications. Practitioners will continue to use relaxation and biofeedback with patients taking medications known or thought to affect physiological activity including muscle tension and autonomic nervous system (ANS) reactivity and recovery.

Dietary Vasoactive Chemicals

Despite our best efforts and those of our patients, some patients with migraines do not benefit from relaxation, biofeedback, cognitive therapies, and other forms of stress management. Thus, some practitioners suggest dietary treatments after unsuccessful trials with these other treatments.

Published studies report inconsistent outcomes thought to result from methodological problems (Radnitz, 1990; Radnitz & Blanchard, 1991). The two proposed mechanisms for food-triggered migraines are allergic and vasoactive mechanisms. There exist enough data supporting one or both mechanisms to justify a trial of dietary changes (see Chapter 10 for a detailed discussion of dietary factors). Prudent practitioners are very careful in selecting the foods and substances for patients to avoid on a long-term basis.

Sleep

In addition to headaches often occuring during sleep, sleep problems can cause or worsen headaches. Many practitioners may not be aware of the latter and can benefit from this knowledge. Otherwise, they may overlook sleep variables as one of the causes of headache. A detailed discussion of this topic is beyond the scope of this chapter. However, a brief summary of selected information and references will help some readers. Association with an accredited sleep disorders center is ideal but not practical for most practitioners. A very brief but good review of sleep and headaches is by Sahota and Dexter (1990).

Headaches occur during and after nocturnal sleep and after brief periods of *diurnal* sleep. Migraines occur during *Stages III, IV,* and *rapid eye movement (REM)*. Cluster headaches and *chronic paroxysmal hemicrania* occur with REM. Sleep deprivation, excessive sleep, and sleep disruptions can all lead to headaches. *Sleep apnea* is commonly associated with headaches that are often bilateral or diffuse. Some *parasomnias*, especially sleep walking (*somnambulism*), correlate with headaches, especially migraines. Sleep and headaches may have common substrates involving anatomy, electrophysiology, and biochemistry. For example, serotonin and other amines are often important for both headaches and sleep.

Disturbed sleep in patients with headaches could also result from anxiety, depression, or other causes besides the headaches themselves. The effects of headaches on sleep are highly variable, and not all patients with headaches report sleep disturbance. Migraines, cluster, and chronic paroxysmal hemicrania probably receive the most study as probable causes of sleep disturbance.

Implications

Assessment of patients with headaches should include information about their sleep patterns. If there is a suggestion of a possible sleep disorder, especially one associated with headaches, then further evaluation should be considered. Sometimes an evaluation and treatment of a headache-related sleep disorder occurs about the time of a relaxation and biofeedback consultation for treating the headaches. Prudent practitioners will consider deferring treatments such as relaxation and biofeedback until after the sleep disorders evaluation and treatment.

Aerobic Exercise

There is very little research about aerobic exercise and headaches. The available literature often suggests that exercise can cause migraines. There are reports of headaches caused by or aggravated by varying degrees of exercise. See the references in Darling (1991). However, there are other reports that suggest that exercise is not uniformly a risk factor for migraines. In some persons, exercise might even help reduce migraines.

One interesting case reported by Darling (1991) suggests that it is possible for aerobic exercise to abort classic migraines. However, the subject of that report presented an unusual combination of features. She was a professional dancer and had exercised with aerobics and running several times a week for many years. At age 43, she reported that the exercise aborted the migraines either during a visual aura or if she exercised during the headache phase. Thus, this case could be atypical.

In a group of volunteers with classic migraines, Lockett and Campbell (1992) reported no increase in migraines for 11 women undergoing low-impact aerobic dancing and calisthenics. The sessions were three times a week for 6 weeks. Each session was 45 minutes including a 10-minute warm-up, and a 10-minute cool-down period. In this small sample, there was a nonsignificant tendency toward improvement on multiple variables. For this discussion, the important point is that the headaches did not worsen.

Caution in interpreting the role of exercise in causing migraines is wise. Some of the reports involve very strenuous exercises such as running and strenuous exercise without a warm-up period. Another factor is the wearing of tight swimming goggles. It would be misleading to consider aerobic exercise a treatment for most persons with migraines. However, practitioners will keep their clinical antennae up for that possibility.

A related topic of potential relevance to the management of headaches is exercise-induced analgesia (EIA) (Padawer & Levine, 1992). Anecdotal reports by dancers and athletes that they felt no pain during strenuous exercise links to the idea of exercise releasing endorphins resulting in pain reduction. The proposal and acceptance by some of EIA stem from this linkage. However, research support for the proposed EIA confounds the effects of exercise with pain test-reactivity. Thus, it provides only weak support according to Padawer and Levine (1992), whose study does not support EIA. The purpose here is only to introduce the EIA concept and suggest that it remains controversial. Practitioners can use this information when discussing exercise with those patients who ask about it. Practitioners should consider recommending that many patients with headaches avoid strenuous exercise.

COGNITIVE PREPARATION OF PATIENTS: PATIENT EDUCATION

Many professionals consider that cognitive preparation of patients and patient education are extremely important for relaxation and biofeedback therapies. Nevertheless, professionals often ignore or give inadequate attention to this topic. Variation in cognitive

preparation of patients is considerable, and research is scant on the topic of patient education and cognitive preparation for relaxation and biofeedback treatments.

There is a sizable literature on expectations for success and their importance to outcome. This literature does not specifically address relaxation and biofeedback treatments
of headaches. Patient education and cognitive preparation can influence expectations, and
expectations can influence outcome. There is an extensive literature on patient education
and medical practice and on its effect on patient satisfaction, compliance, and outcomes.
(See Schwartz, in press, for a detailed discussion of patient education.)

The practitioner should consider the following questions when reviewing cognitive
preparations of headache patients for biofeedback and associated therapies:

1. Did I adequately cover the patient's concerns, questions, misperceptions, and
   anxiety about therapy?
2. Does the patient understand the rationale for therapy, the procedures, the goals,
   and his or her responsibilities?
3. Does the patient remember enough information for therapy to proceed effectively?
4. Is the content of printed and audiotaped presentations clear enough and within
   the reading and intellectual range of the patient?
5. Are the methods for patient education acceptable to the patient?
6. Are the methods for patient education cost-effective?
7. Is the content of the presentations complete enough to anticipate the questions
   and concerns that are likely to arise after therapy starts?

These questions take on more importance when we consider that some professionals
rely on the use of self-help manuals and a PLOT protocol (Jurish et al., 1983; Teders et al.,
1984).

The growth in use of self-help manuals is well known. Content and readability remain
important even if we limit our focus to the printed materials professionals give to their
patients as part of office-based treatment (Andrasik & Murphy, 1977; O'Farrell & Keuthen,
1983). The importance of content, readability, and understanding increases with limited
therapist contact. Increased needs for cost containment will motivate many professionals
to rely more on printed and audiotaped patient-education material and preparation for
treatments. Research topics needing attention include necessary minimal content, matching of content to patient, and readability of printed patient-education materials.

The practitioner should consider reviewing examples of existing cognitive preparations for biofeedback and associated therapies for headache. Schwartz (in press) provides
discussions of patient education. The discussions of cognitive preparation, compliance, and
audiotapes in Chapters 4, 6, and 8 of this book provide added ideas.

COMPLIANCE

Compliance is extremely important in the treatment of headaches. Therapists
make many requests and recommendations that require considerable cooperation from patients. For example, a self-report log involves frequent ratings of headache intensity and
other information. It often includes information about medications and caffeine usage. The
log sometimes includes finger temperatures before and after relaxation. A log for many weeks
places considerable demands on patients.

Practitioners need to consider the office visits, cognitive stress management assignments, and dietary changes as well. Patients need to practice and apply relaxation often,

and at those times when it will be of benefit. In addition, there are often suggestions for life-style changes involving work, social, and family activities. Reminding oneself to think and act differently before and during stressful events requires much cooperation. Patients often need to change their sitting, standing, and working postures. They need to change their sleeping positions and the type of pillow and placement of their pillow(s) during sleep. These all require understanding, acceptance, and cooperation by patients.

It is not surprising that many patients do not follow some or many recommendations. Pain helps motivate many patients to cooperate with recommendations. However, it is often painfully inadequate (pun intended) as a sole motivator. Never assume that pain is sufficient to provide all or even most of the incentive needed for adherence to the therapy recommendations.

Many therapists believe that some patients need comprehensive programs that involve many recommendations. This gives the term "therapeutic alliance" a new dimension. Professionals have much responsibility insuring that a patient's involvement in the alliance is sufficient to follow recommendations. Otherwise, patients waste time, effort, and money, and their needs often remain unmet.

It is not enough only to make recommendations to patients. It is not enough to expect them to take responsibility for complying with recommendations. They are trying to apply these recommendations while they also are trying to develop confidence in their abilities and also carrying out their daily lives.

Patient responsibility is very important, but we often must cultivate it. One cannot assume that it adequately exists from the onset of therapy. This is especially important for patients for whom we make many recommendations. It is especially important as well for patients for whom compliance is difficult even for a few recommendations. We can emphasize patient responsibility but must be patient and persistent as we ask our patients to do the same. We also need to examine our professional behaviors and practices (see Chapter 6 for more discussion of compliance).

PLACEMENT OF ELECTRODES

Rationale

Bilateral frontal ("bifrontal") EMG feedback for patients with tension-type headaches is still a common placement. Practitioners know that other muscles contribute to these headaches. They know that the bifrontal site does not adequately measure or reflect the activity of the other muscles. Other muscle areas include the cervical neck, upper trapezii, and occipital muscles. Nevertheless, therapy using bifrontal EMG feedback often leads to successful results in a large percentage of patients with tension-type headaches (Blanchard & Andrasik, 1985). The reasons for the association between this EMG site and successful results are still unclear. Some practitioners and researchers adopt a cognitive model for explaining the association of biofeedback and decreased tension-type headaches. For these professionals, the placement of electrodes may make little or no difference. This chapter assumes that decreasing muscle tension is important for many or even most patients with tension-type headaches.

The purpose here is to discuss other recording placements in addition to the bifrontal placement. One intent is to show that occipital activity is undetected or inadequately detected by bifrontal or posterior neck placements. I will discuss ways to record more of the head and neck muscles and review existing research. I include cases and illustrations of recordings, and discuss advantages, limitations, and implications of alternative placements.

Some practitioners and researchers assume that reduced frontal activity reflects reductions in other head and neck muscles. The frontal placement is useful when the headaches involve the frontal area. However, when one suspects or knows there are other muscles involved, it is logical to record and provide feedback from those areas. These other muscle areas include the posterior neck muscles, upper trapezii, occipital, and suboccipital muscles. Research supports the value of recording from head and neck area sites other than the bifrontal (Hart & Cichanski, 1981; Hudzinski, 1983; Hudzinski & Lawrence, 1988; Pritchard & Wood, 1983; Sanders & Collins, 1981).

Blanchard and Andrasik (1985) reminded us that "some controversy has arisen as to the most appropriate electrode placement. . . ." They reviewed four studies (Martin & Mathews, 1978; Hart & Cichanski, 1981; Philips, 1977; Hudzinski, 1983). The studies reviewed compared bifrontal versus posterior neck sites. The authors concluded from those results that "we are left without a clear answer" (Blanchard & Andrasik, 1985, p. 91). They based their suggestions on their own data and other research. Their conclusion was that practitioners should "start with frontal EMG biofeedback in all cases" (p. 91). For those "patients who complain that the typical headache starts in the back of the neck . . ." (p. 91) they suggested neck feedback if frontal feedback did not lead to headache relief. They also noted that neck EMG feedback was more useful for six of six patients in one study (Hudzinski, 1983) reporting headaches starting and spreading from the neck.

I do not argue with the results reported in the literature by Blanchard and Andrasik (1985) and others. Bifrontal feedback and relaxation may generalize to other muscle areas including the occipital area for some patients. Some patients who attend to their head muscles and relax them often also will relax the occipital muscles. However, my experience suggests that some patients do not relax the occipital area even with excellent relaxation of the frontal and cervical neck areas.

The Frontal–Posterior Neck Placement

History

The occipitalis area is a site of headaches for some patients. Many years ago, I wanted to see if I could indirectly measure occipitalis tension without directly recording from those muscles, as direct measurement is inconvenient. I used different electrode placements and multiple simultaneous recording sites. The placements were bifrontal, bilateral posterior neck, and a new placement I called the frontal–posterior neck (FpN) placement. The last involves one electrode on a frontalis muscle and another electrode on one side of the posterior neck. The EMG recorded also includes activity from other cephalic and neck muscles. This includes occipital area activity (Nevins & Schwartz, 1985).

Hudzinski and Lawrence (1988, 1990) thoughtfully referred to the FpN placement as the "Schwartz–Mayo Method." I was aware of their research when it started. However, I was unaware of the first article and their name choice for this placement until publication.[2]

To test whether this placement was actually recording the occipital area, I first recorded myself. The bifrontal site showed about 1 microvolt. The bilateral posterior neck site showed between 1–2 microvolts. I then selectively tensed the occipitalis muscles. The FpN recordings rose to 20 microvolts and much higher while the other two sites continued to show very low activity.

---

[2]I am very grateful to those investigators for providing the first published studies of this electrode placement and for their thoughtfulness. However, I admit embarrassment about their name for the placement. I am more comfortable calling it the FpN placement.

Brad Nevins, then a biofeedback therapist,[3] worked with me and was of great help and support in developing this placement. We directly recorded the occipitalis muscles on a few patients and nonpatients. The data quickly convinced us that frontal and cervical neck placements did not show occipitalis tension. However, it was clear that occipitalis tension did show on the FpN channel, albeit much less so than on the direct occipital channel (Nevins & Schwartz, 1985). Although one can feel occipital tension via proprioceptive feedback and/or palpation, it is very difficult.

Independently and at about the same time, others had related ideas. Pritchard and Wood (1983) reported that patients with tension or migraine headaches showed significantly higher occipital activity than frontal activity during an experimental stress.

Hudzinski (1983) published his paper on the importance of recording and feedback from the posterior neck muscles. He reported that his patients thought that the "neck, rather than the frontalis musculature, was the more useful electrode placement site for reducing their muscle activity" and that "14 of the 16 patients . . . reported that using both electrode placement sites was more effective for understanding the muscle activity involved in their headaches" (p. 88).

Hudzinski (1983) concluded that "both clinician and patient can gain significant information about head pain by using the neck electrode site, in addition to frontalis musculature, in the diagnostic assessment and treatment of chronic muscle contraction headache" (pp. 88–89). Another of Hudzinski's important conclusions was that "one cannot assume . . . that a decrement in EMG activity in the frontalis or the neck musculature is representative of the activity from other muscle sites" (p. 89). This was consistent with earlier studies supporting the independence of the frontal and posterior neck muscles (Shedivy & Kleinman, 1977; Whatmore, Whatmore, & Fisher, 1981).

These studies suggested and were consistent with the search for recording and feedback placements other than the frontal area. They were consistent with including the neck, frontal, and occipital areas. One practical problem was how to get information about occipital tension in routine clinical practice.

Occipitalis Muscles and EMG Placement

The occipitalis muscles pull the scalp back. They are under less voluntary control than the frontalis muscles. Their function is more limited than that of the frontalis, and hence they have less internal or proprioceptive biofeedback. When patients are asked to tense only the occipitalis muscles, most have much more difficulty than when asked to tense the frontalis muscles. In fact, very few people can tense only the occipitalis muscles *on command*. One can use the term "occipital" to describe the direct bilateral placement in a similar way one uses the term "frontal."

It is preferable to record directly from the occipitalis. However, such recordings are less practical in routine clinical practice because hair usually covers the recording area. Shaving of hair, done by Pritchard and Wood (1983), is undesirable in clinical practice. Furthermore, many practitioners use electrodes that do not easily remain in good skin contact in the hair.

One can record a bilateral occipital site with standard cup electrodes without shaving any hair. It requires extra care and a few more minutes to properly attach the electrodes with extra conductive gel, extra tape, and the use of other procedures such as bobby pins to keep the hair away from the site. However, this is not practical for routine sessions. Fig-

[3]Now Brad Nevins, Ph.D.

ure 15.1 shows a single channel bilateral occipital placement and the posterior neck placement portion of the montage described in the Appendix at the end of the chapter.

Research

Nevins and Schwartz (1985) have shown that:

1. The frontalis, posterior neck, and occipitalis muscles can contract independently. One can substantially tense the occipitalis muscles independently from the frontal muscles and the posterior neck muscles (see Figure 15.2).
2. There is a relationship between muscle activity recorded from the FpN placement and that recorded directly from an occipital placement (see Figure 15.2).
3. There is a greater relationship between occipital activity and the FpN placement than between occipital activity and frontal activity.

Hudzinski and Lawrence (1988, 1990) published their rationale and normative data on the FpN placement. Hudzinski and Lawrence (1988) were interested in two major clinical and research issues. One was the inconsistent relationship between resting EMG activity in the frontal and neck areas for people with chronic tension headaches compared to people without headaches. The second issue was the inconsistent relationship among people with chronic tension headaches during their headaches compared to their headache-free periods.

These authors used both right- and left-sided FpN sites with 25 patients during and without tension headaches. They compared these with 25 age-matched nonheadache, non-ill, control subjects. They compared the EMG activity for five different head and neck sites. Frontal measurement was with the muscle scanning method. Measurement from each

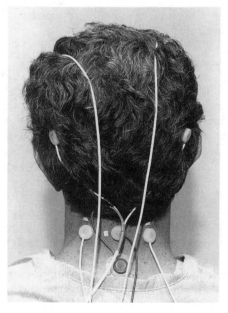

FIGURE 15.1. Photograph of a single channel bilateral occipital placement and the posterior neck placement for electrodes number 3 and number 4 of the 5 electrode/4 channel FpN montage. The two frontal electrodes are on the forehead in the standard sites.

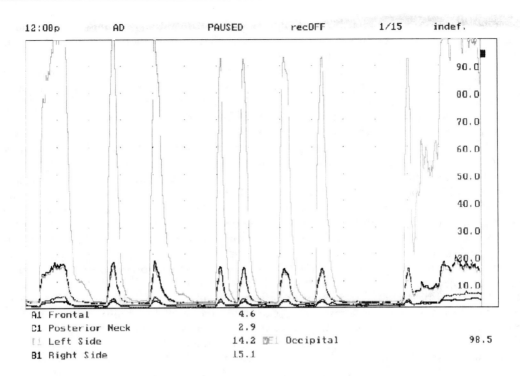

A1 Frontal   4.6
C1 Posterior Neck   2.9
[1 Left Side   14.2 ▓▓ Occipital   98.5
B1 Right Side   15.1

FIGURE 15.2. This figure demonstrates, in a normal subject, the very high intensity of muscle tension that can be produced from the occipitalis muscles and the minimal reflection of this muscle activity in the bifrontal and bilateral posterior neck channels.

The occipitalis channel is the one with the highest peaks up to and exceeding 100 microvolts. The bifrontal and bilateral posterior neck channels are the lowest two, and the two FpN channels are above those. Note the rises and falls of the two FpN channels occurring simultaneously with the changes in occipital tension.

Note that the scale is 0–100 root mean square microvolts (100–200 Hertz bandpass). This scale is used here for demonstration purposes only and necessary because of the amount of occipital tension used in the demonstration. All channels are on the same 0–100 scale.

frontalis muscle is a better measure of specific frontalis activity than a bilateral frontal site. However, it does not provide the same microvolt activity as from the more common bilateral frontal site.

The Hudzinski and Lawrence (1988) study showed that the FpN placement "was able to significantly discriminate headache from nonheadache activity" (p. 32). It also discriminated between patients with chronic headaches when they had a headache compared to sessions when the same patients did not report a headache. There was increased microvolt activity with the headaches. These authors helped pave the way for studies to resolve many clinical and research dilemmas.

Their placement involves, on each side, an active electrode "on the forehead over the pupil . . . approximately one inch above the eyebrow . . . [and] . . . the other active electrode . . . on the ipsilateral cervical paraspinals at the C_4 site one-half inch lateral from the spine (Hudzinski & Lawrence, 1990, p. 24). This is the placement to use if one uses their norms. For assessing possible occipital activity in clinical practice, one can put the posterior neck electrode at the hairline and slightly lateral from the paraspinals. The frontalis muscle site also can be slightly higher. There are no data comparing these slightly different placements for reflecting occipital activity.

Hudzinski's normative subjects sat on a stool 20 inches high. Their hands were in their laps and feet were flat on the floor. Their eyes were open, and they sat quietly and motionless in an upright position. In their earlier study, they had used a reclining chair. The posterior neck electrode site was less specifically described in the earlier report but presumably was the same as that later described.

Hudzinski and Lawrence (1990) present normative data for 100 normal subjects. They recorded left and right sides, in sitting and standing positions and with two bandpaths of from 100 to 200 Hertz and from 25 to 1000 Hertz. They present data for three age groups, ages 14–29 ($N = 51$), 30–49 ($N = 39$), and 50–74 ($N = 10$). They also present nine percentile points (1, 5, 10, 25, 50 . . . 95, and 99) for the eight conditions. The eight are two-band paths, sitting and standing, and left and right sides. They checked the test–retest reliability for 32 subjects measured about 2 weeks apart. There was a drop in EMG between the 2 weeks. However, significant correlations ranged from $r = .54$ to .81. The narrow-band correlations were higher ($r = .74$ to .81) than the wide-band correlations in both sitting and standing postures.

Another finding of interest was an age effect. The subjects of Hudzinski and Lawrence, aged 50–74, showed about 1 microvolt more EMG activity than their younger groups. Although a small sample, this finding is consistent with other studies with other recording sites (Arena, Blanchard, Andrasik, & Myers, 1983). The authors also noted the importance of subtle postural deviations and/or "laterality differences in facial expression" (Hudzinski & Lawrence, 1990, p. 27) as possible explanations for a consistently higher left side.

Uses of the FpN Placement

There are advantages for using an FpN placement. First, it is an indirect measure of possible occipital activity when used in combination with frontal and posterior neck sites. Second, it is a more sensitive indirect measure of temporalis activity than the bifrontal placement. Third, the FpN is a more comprehensive measure of muscle activity in the head and neck than other single EMG channels. Fourth, it is a more useful indicator of resting muscle tension of patients with tension-type headaches (Hudzinski, 1983). Fifth, the availability of four channels of muscle activity provides assessment of the right and left sides of the head and neck.

Higher than expected FpN recordings raise the question of occipital tension. One must rule out other causes of the elevated FpN signal. Thus, to interpret FpN activity, one needs to know from where the muscle tension emanates. One needs at least simultaneous recordings from the frontal area and from the posterior neck area. This helps determine how much tension in those areas contributes to the microvolts shown on the FpN channel. For example, some people swallow without touching their upper and lower teeth together. They tense other muscles including the sternomastoids. This muscle activity shows on the FpN channels. Muscle activity often remains low or unchanged in the frontal channel during these swallows.

I use the electrode assembly described in the Appendix at the end of the chapter. I consider an FpN elevation indicating possible excess tension in muscles other than frontal and posterior neck areas when FpN microvolts exceed the sum of the bifrontal and bilateral posterior neck. This is an estimate based on clinical experience. Sometimes one observes elevated occipital activity from a fifth channel, and the FpN is not more than the sum of the frontal and posterior neck channels. The patient's headache description and reported location and clinical judgment indicate when to directly record the occipital area rather than rely on the FpN placement.

The two temporalis muscles contribute to FpN microvolts. However, temporalis tension is usually unlikely given the resting posture of the head and jaw during recording sessions. This is because of the action of the temporalis muscles. Travell and Simons (1983) remind us that "all fibers of the temporalis muscle contribute to its primary function of elevation (closure) of the mandible. The posterior fibers, in addition, are important for retrusion and lateral deviation of the mandible to the same side" (p. 239).

Thus, there is no activity in the temporalis muscles unless the patient closes his or her jaw with contact of the upper and lower teeth, moves the jaw from side to side, or retracts or thrusts it forward. Furthermore, activity in the anterior fibers with clenching or grinding shows in the channel recording frontal activity. These jaw and teeth positions sometimes occur but are uncommon during recording sessions. They are easily observed and modifiable. Careful observation and instructions to patients minimize this potential source of muscle activity.

When Is the FpN Needed or Not Needed?

Some readers might say: "I get good results with bifrontal recordings." Some say, "the literature supporting the use of EMG biofeedback with headaches usually uses the bifrontal site." I agree with both. A single bifrontal site might be sufficient for some patients. One can justify this if the frontal site shows elevated activity and/or the headaches are mostly in the frontal area. However, suppose the symptoms include the back of the head. Suppose the bifrontal area is consistently or mostly relaxed even with office stressors. Furthermore, suppose symptom reduction is inadequate using only the frontal placement. Then, the practitioner should consider recording elsewhere and adding unilateral or bilateral FpN placements.

Case Example

A clinical vignette helps to illustrate the potential diagnostic value of the FpN placement. A patient told me her headaches were in her forehead. The referring physician's notes stated the same, and my initial clinical interview did not reveal other headache sites. The psychophysiological assessment proceeded with recording from the left and right FpN placements, and the bifrontal and bilateral posterior neck placements. There was an elevation of FpN beyond that expected from observing the muscle tension from the frontal and neck sites.

I then asked the patient again about the location of her headaches, and she pointed to her forehead. Undaunted and still inquisitive, I asked if she ever had headaches in the back of her head. I pointed to the occipital area on my head. She said, "Sometimes." I asked how often that meant, and she responded "about 20% of the time." She paused and added with emphasis, "but, they are the worst ones." We then recorded directly from the occipital area and noted excess tension far beyond resting levels.

What are the lessons learned from such an experience? A patient's interpretation of interview questions is sometimes different from our intention and understanding of the interview questions. For this patient, the question of "Where are your headaches," meant, "Where are *most* of them?" She had focused on frequency. Perhaps she temporarily forgot the other headaches. The FpN elevation and the pattern suggested additional clinical inquiry and what I believe was important clinical information. Sometimes one sees brief elevations in the FpN channel without obvious origins other than the occipital area. This alerts the practitioner to further inquiry and assessment. I see several patients each year with occipital headaches and with excess occipital EMG.

Conclusions and Implications

- Some patients with headaches have symptoms in the occipital area for which the occipital muscles contribute. Inclusion of monitoring that reflects this tension can be useful.
- Some patients with headaches have symptoms in the posterior neck that contribute to their condition. Inclusion of EMG monitoring of that site can be useful.
- In patients with low frontal and/or posterior neck muscle activity, professionals might conclude there is insufficient head and neck muscle activity to justify biofeedback. One also might conclude that there is sufficient relaxation of other cephalic muscles during the recording conditions. Both assumptions are sometimes incorrect.
- Frontal and/or posterior neck placements inadequately measure occipital tension. The FpN placement is the best *indirect* measure of occipital activity when used with bifrontal and posterior neck placements. Ideally, one uses both left and right FpN placements.
- Using four EMG channels with two from the FpN indirectly measures temporalis and sternomastoid tension better than do bifrontal or posterior neck placements.
- Ideally, one uses multiple body positions including sitting up without neck and/or back support, and standing (Sturgis & Arena, 1984; Ruff, Sturgis, & St. Lawrence, 1986). Psychophysiological assessment includes various office stressors (see Chapter 7).
- If one suspects occipital tension, then consider occipital recording and feedback. One can do this either directly or with multisite recordings including the FpN placement in addition to frontal and posterior neck sites. One may suspect an occipital tension origin for headaches from a patient's report of symptoms. Headaches from the back of the head and/or vertex raise this possibility. Headaches in the back of the head also can emanate from other sources such as the suboccipital and posterior neck.
- If there is clear excess tension in the occipital area, especially without involvement from other muscle sites, then one must consider a direct occipital placement. It can ease physiological self-regulation of that area.
- If symptom reduction is inadequate using other placements, then one considers recording elsewhere and considers the FpN.
- When only one EMG placement on the head or neck is used, the FpN is a more comprehensive index of muscle activity than other single placements.
- Providing feedback from muscle sites for which there is more muscle activity can help patient acceptance and increase therapy credibility.
- However, sometimes patients with excess occipital tension generalize their relaxation from frontal feedback and/or with instructions to relax all the head muscles. In such cases, occipital or FpN feedback may not be necessary.
- Practitioners and researchers who adopt an exclusive or primarily cognitive model of explaining relaxation and biofeedback effects might not agree with needing multiple placements. They might attribute improved outcome to the cognitive changes from recording and feeding back from any credible EMG site.
- Practitioners should always use EMG recordings in conjunction with careful clinical interviews and observations during interviews and psychophysiological monitoring. They should watch a patient's face, ears, temples, neck, and scalp while talking to them. Practitioners should watch patients while they are talking, listening, and during stressors.
- As with headaches in other areas of the head and neck, practitioners must assess and rule out other sources of the headaches such as the cervicogenic described by Pfaffen-

rath and his colleagues (Pfaffenrath, Dandekar, & Pollman, 1987; Sjaastad, Fredricksen, & Pfaffenrath, 1990; Sjaastad & Stovner, 1993).

Research Needs

We need research to answer the following questions among others about the FpN and other electrode placements.

1. Does feedback from the FpN and direct occipital placements yield larger or faster reductions of muscle activity and headache activity than using other feedback placements?
2. What is the relative value of FpN and/or occipital feedback for patients whose headaches are primarily occipital compared to patients whose headaches are primarily frontal?
3. What proportion of patients with tension-type headaches with occipital and vertex symptoms show excess occipital-area muscle tension?
4. What activities, stressors, and positions of the head, neck, and jaw show excess muscle tension in the occipital muscles?
5. What muscles significantly contribute to the FpN placement EMG other than frontalis, posterior neck, occipitalis, temporalis, and sternomastoid?
6. Does direct occipital feedback result in better reductions of muscle activity and headaches than the FpN?

SELECTED TREATMENT PROCESS VARIABLES

Baseline Length

There are multiple factors affecting a practitioner's decision to obtain a headache baseline and over what span of time (see Chapter 7 for a more detailed discussion of baselines). Proposed criteria and data from Blanchard, Hillhouse, Appelbaum, and Jaccard (1987) offer useful guidelines. They examined headache diaries of 212 subjects over 4 weeks of a pretreatment baseline. There were 81 patients with tension headaches, 60 with migraines, and 71 with mixed diagnoses. They also examined 54 patients for 4 weeks after treatment. They compared the correlations between the total of the 4 weeks with different numbers of weeks. These were the first week, the first 2 weeks, and the first 3 weeks. They proposed that correlations must account for 75% of the variance for clinical purposes and 90% for research purposes. A correlation of between $r = .864$ and $.866$ yields a variance of 75% with rounding. This is a reasonable, although an arbitrary criterion.

For clinical purposes, Blanchard et al. (1987) recommend an adequate baseline is 1 week for tension headaches and 2 weeks for migraine and mixed headaches. For research purposes, the baselines should be 2 weeks for tension headaches and 3 weeks for migraine and mixed headaches. Practical considerations suggest that a 1-week baseline would probably be acceptable in at least some clinical situations without doing an injustice to the 75% criteria.

For follow-up, they suggest 1 week for migraine and tension headaches and 2 weeks for mixed headaches. Practitioners may use these guidelines and recommendations for individual cases and studies. The data and recommendations have clear practical use for clinical practitioners and researchers. They support the acceptability of a shorter baseline than was often thought needed prior to their study. Practitioners know that these data are group data. Thus, individual factors dictate the need for baselines of different lengths.

Composition of Sessions and Conditions within Sessions

There are many session protocols in use in clinical practice and in research studies. The type of clinical protocol selected for use depends upon several factors. These include available time, presence or absence of the therapist, type of instrumentation, and number and type of modalities. They also include patient motivation, patient's learning ability, therapy stage, and practitioner preferences. No single protocol meets all needs and circumstances. However, there are some basic stages and variations in many protocols. The reader should see Chapter 7 for detailed discussion of this topic. The following are examples of segments of psychophysiological assessment protocols.

1. Adaptation: This is a quiet period of a few to several minutes. There are no specific instructions. The patient settles in and becomes adjusted to the instrumentation, attachments, and body positions.
2. Baselines: These periods last a few minutes each, often 3–5 or more minutes. They often include one and usually more conditions such as eyes open, eyes closed, sitting, and standing. These are for assessing a patient's physiological activity without specific therapy instructions. One can compare the results of these segments with the same conditions after feedback and with baselines in later sessions. Some baselines such as for skin temperature are longer such as 15–20 minutes.
3. Self-regulation: These are a few minutes each, often 3–5 or more minutes. The therapist provides brief instructions to *relax* or *let go* of tension in the head, face, neck, and shoulders. This permits assessment of the patient's ability to relax without biofeedback.
4. Stimulation: In this stage, the professional presents office stressors to assess physiological reactivity and the rate and degree of recovery. Such stimulation takes the forms of cognitive stress, clenching fists, tensing shoulders, head, face muscles, or all these. The duration of each stimulation is often 1–3 minutes. A therapist might repeat the stimulation in the same session and later sessions.
5. Biofeedback: These periods are about 3–5 or more minutes in one or more conditions and positions. These include with eyes open, eyes closed, sitting, and/or standing. The patient observes and/or listens to visual and/or audio external biofeedback.
6. Reassessment of self-regulation:[4] This stage repeats the initial baseline and/or the self-regulation stage. The patient attempts relaxation again after the stimulation. The purpose is to assess recovery rate, degree, and duration of relaxation within the practical time limits of a session. Consider 3–5 minutes for each. Practitioners usually end sessions with a discussion of the session and recommendations.

Factors Potentially Affecting/Enhancing Treatment and Outcome

Determining Changes in Skin Temperature

There is no single or generally agreed upon criterion for determining whether peripheral skin warming occurred because of a person's own volitional efforts or is sufficient for a therapeutic effect. There are several possible criteria and comparisons (Morrill & Blanchard, 1989). One can compare baseline samples with a self-regulation and/or feedback sample. Therapists often start with a stable temperature near the end of a baseline of several min-

---

[4]After this, one can repeat stages with feedback, self-regulation, stimulation, and self-regulation again.

utes (see Chapter 7 on baselines). They compare this with a stable temperature at or near the end of the self-regulation or a feedback phase.

One can use the highest skin temperature in the session as a criterion for change, especially if it is maintained for a few minutes. Reaching and maintaining a target temperature is another criterion favored by some practitioners. (The reader should consult the discussion later in this chapter on dose–response.)

The number of sessions that the patient increased temperatures above a stable baseline is yet another criterion. The absolute temperature may not always be as important as the fact that the patient is making the changes. Smaller reductions in temperature during office-stressors and/or faster recovery to or near baseline temperatures are other criteria used clinically.

Two problems are adaptation and baseline periods that are too short (see Chapter 7). In either case, one can mistakenly assume that the relaxation and/or biofeedback procedures are useful in the warming process. Natural warming often takes place with the stopping of activities and especially with rest. Natural warming takes place after longer periods following ingestion of caffeine, nicotine, and other chemicals. Body positions affect reduced sympathetic nervous system (SNS) arousal and peripheral blood flow. Warming caused by these factors may be desirable to show patients how they affect physiology in a desired direction. Such demonstrations also can increase patient confidence and self-efficacy especially early in treatment. However, this is not the same as volitional psychophysiological self-regulation. Stopping activity, resting, and avoiding certain chemicals are important. However, this type of therapy also seeks to help people learn to use postures, breathing, images, and various cognitive changes to effect physiological changes. To show this credibly means adequate adaptation and stable baselines for comparison. It means stable temperature changes within and across sessions and stress conditions.

A related problem is using integration periods that are too long. There is no generally agreed upon duration. However, several trials of a few to several seconds each will show trends and stability better than trials integrated over longer periods such as a minute or longer.

One issue is that the relationship of these and other criteria to improvement remains within the realm of research questions. This relates to the questions of mechanism of treatment and to dose–response relationships. Thus, practitioners should consider multiple criteria and use caution when interpreting any single criterion.

Temperature feedback sensitivity is a separate topic. Feedback should often reflect the smallest temperature changes the instrument can produce accurately. For example, watching or listening to feedback that changes .25°F or more is probably too large for many patients' and therapy goals. Consider much smaller changes. Some practitioners and researchers recommend changes such as .01° and even smaller. One exception may occur when the temperature lability and variability are large enough to be distracting, confusing, and upsetting for the patient. Gradually increasing the sensitivity is an option in such situations.

Possible Effects of EMG Filter Bandpass on Results

The commonly used bandpass of 100–200 Hertz is above that for most muscle activity. There is a paucity of research on selecting the ideal bandpass for individual patients and recording conditions. Many practitioners also use a wide bandpass such as from 20–1000 Hertz. That includes all muscle activity.

Recent advances in instrumentation allow inspection of the "power spectrum" of EMG activity. This should help answer many research and clinical questions about the frequencies where the muscle activity is occurring for individual patients and recording conditions. Eventually, this should improve clinical practice. However, most practitioners and researchers will probably defer investing in such instrumentation.

Possible Role of Cognitive Factors in Symptom Changes

A "cognitive-attributional" model is another explanation for interpreting symptom changes occurring during and after EMG biofeedback therapies (Holroyd et al., 1984). The essence of this model is that reductions in headache symptoms are "mediated more by cognitive changes induced by performance feedback than by reductions in EMG activity" (p. 1049). The authors gave false verbal feedback indicating high success after the session. These subjects reported significantly more symptom reduction than did false postsession feedback suggesting moderate success. However, we should note that the study used undergraduate volunteers aged 18–19 with recurrent headaches but who were not seeking treatment. Generalization to more common clinical populations requires more research. Blanchard (1992) reminds us that the Holroyd study "needs to be replicated with the more prototypical tension headache patient, someone in his or her late 30s who has had headaches for 15–20 years" (p. 539).

One should not take false feedback seriously as a therapeutic approach. It raises serious ethical questions. However, that caution does not detract from the value of the study. The study supports the idea that cognitive factors could be important in explaining some individual differences in outcomes among patients and differences among studies.

Other related theories and research support the importance of patients' perceptions of their own progress and of their self-efficacy (Bandura, 1977, 1982; Bandura, Taylor, Williams, Mefford, & Barchas, 1985). Beliefs, in large part cultivated in the cognitive preparation phase and during therapy, probably do affect outcome.

It is not surprising that a patient's belief that he or she is doing well is sometimes more related to reduction of headaches than is EMG activity. This should not be disappointing to anyone. The lack of EMG changes during some sessions and across sessions for some patients does not dismiss muscle tension reductions in daily life as important for successful results. However, support for cognitive factors does suggest the limitation of relying solely on EMG data and feedback as the only method on which to base a therapeutic strategy. For this, we are grateful to Holroyd and his colleagues.

Consider this common clinical scenario. The patient feels helpless, has low self-efficacy about improvement, and has insufficient understanding of the causative role of muscle tension in his or her headaches. Furthermore, there are discrepancies between the patient's excess muscle tension versus his or her awareness of the tension. The practitioner presents the patient with the rationale for relaxation, the need to relax often, and uses biofeedback to show the patient his or her own capacity to do so. The patient's self-efficacy and confidence changes. The patient will often then change his or her daily behaviors for reducing excess tonic muscle tension and frequency of phasic excess tension. The symptoms decrease. What was the role of biofeedback? It was not to teach relaxation! The therapist used it to show and convince the patient that he or she could do it. That therapeutic involvement could be enough to motivate the patient to comply in daily life.

In this model, one may observe symptom changes even if EMG activity in the office remains unchanged. One assumes the practitioner is persuasive. One further assumes that the patient understands the explanations and accepts them. This changes the patient's self-efficacy beliefs about therapy and reduces his or her sense of helplessness. A single biofeedback session might be sufficient in this model. One also assumes that the patient makes behavioral changes in his or her daily life. As a practitioner, I have no problems with such a model.

However, there are conditions in which more biofeedback is probably more useful and probably necessary. These include conditions when the practitioner is less persuasive and/or the patient needs more convincing. Additional biofeedback is useful and probably necessary when muscle tension levels are high in the office and, by inference, also in daily life. One can make similar statements about SNS arousal and other feedback modalities for migraines.

The Peripheral Warming, the Dose–Response Model, and the Generalized ANS Model as Mechanisms for Thermal Biofeedback Treatment of Migraine Headaches

It is more than 20 years since the incidental finding of an association between hand warming and reduced migraines. After many reports and reviews (Blanchard & Andrasik, 1987; Hatch, Fisher, & Rugh, 1987) about this association, we still are unsure of the mechanism. Thermal biofeedback, practiced in various ways, results in a reduction of headaches of about 50–60%.

Is Warming Necessary? Some doubt the specific role or necessity of hand warming. Some researchers and practitioners point to data suggesting that temperature biofeedback warming (TBF-W) is sometimes not better than general relaxation. Some report that TBF-cooling also might be as effective as warming. However, these studies of the early 1980s had very small samples, did not control for practice, and had other methodological problems. For example, Blanchard's (1992) review included analysis of the work of Kewman and Roberts (1980). He noted that "analysis of those who actually warmed their hands compared with those who cooled them, found a trend for hand warmers to experience more headache relief" (Blanchard, 1992, p. 539).

How Warm is Enough? Is There an Ideal Temperature Criterion? Is This a Dose–Response Relationship? The dose–response relationship received no strong or clear support in the Blanchard, Andrasik, Neff, et al. (1983) study. However, the more often there was hand warming, the more headache relief occurred overall. Some support for a temperature criterion relationship comes from Morrill and Blanchard (1989). This is the temperature threshold theory suggested years earlier by Fahrion (1977) and by Libo and Arnold (1983). Those patients who reached at least 96°F more often reported clinically significant headache relief than those reaching slightly lower temperatures (Blanchard, Andrasik, Neff, et al., 1983). In their data, 63% (17/30) of subjects above this level were successes in reducing migraines. Comparisons were with those below 96°F and with treatment failures. However, this is not the same as a dose–response relationship. A dose–response relationship implies the degree of temperature change. This is the specific criterion or the threshold criterion.

Many practitioners were very skeptical about needing such a high temperature before the data of Morrill and Blanchard (1989). These data helped open the door or kept the door open to the temperature criterion or threshold model.

Do General ANS Changes Occur with Reduced Migraines?

A related model is the generalized ANS conditioning or conditioned-adaptation–relaxation reflex theory of Dalessio and Sovak and their colleagues in the late 1970s. They reported (Sovak,

Kunzel, Sternbach, & Dalessio, 1978) that in those migraineurs who clinically improve, TBF results in decreases of sympathetic tonic outflow. They measured this by multiple cardiovascular measures including heart rate and vasomotor response of the supraorbital and temporal arteries. Morrill and Blanchard's (1989) data on heart rate also are consistent with this model. Only "successful migraineurs had a strong and consistent reduction in heart rate after completing treatment" (p. 174). Unfortunately, there is a paucity of direct research on this model of TBF. Support for it would suggest and be consistent with using some types of relaxation and other biofeedback modalities and procedures with migraines.

Is Relaxation Practice Necessary? If So, What Amount is Necessary?

The assumption for the need for practice is integral to the treatment of many symptoms and conditions. Research addresses the role of practice in the treatment of tension, migraine, and mixed headaches. Recommendations to practice daily and repeated encouragement to do so are a basic part of relaxation and biofeedback-assisted therapy by essentially all practitioners. However, there are only a few reports specifically examining this assumption even for headaches for which there are more reports than for other disorders (Hillenberg & Collins, 1983; Libo & Arnold, 1983; Solbach, Sargent, & Coyne, 1984b; Lake & Pingel, 1988; Blanchard, Nicholson, Radnitz, et al., 1991; Blanchard, Nicholson, Taylor, et al., 1991).

These reports find both support and lack of support for the necessity of practice or a dose–response relationship involving the amount of practice. Most reports support the value of practice. However, there are methodological limitations in these reports, and questions remain.

Nevertheless, applying relaxation in daily life is logical and prudent. Most practitioners continue to encourage applications of relaxation in daily life. It is ludicrous to think otherwise at this time. This section examines selected issues, research, and methodological limitations. I speculate on factors that could resolve some disagreements and draw some conclusions.

Issues Regarding Relaxation Practice. Therapists should at least consider these issues when evaluating and planning research on practice and in clinical practice. There are several items for which definitions or criteria for practice differ or are unclear. Some specify "practice frequency" as regular or frequent and define this as six or more times per week or one or more times per week. Others refer to using relaxation as needed, when stressed, or occasionally. Some report practice versus no practice (Hillenberg & Collins, 1983), and others report more versus less practice (Lake & Pingel, 1988).

A common definition of "improvement" is at least a 50% reduction of the Headache Index (HI) or a 25% or greater reduction of three of four factors comprising the HI. Some report global ratings, and others use symptom logs. "Confirmation of practice" varies from self-report to more objective measurement (Hoelscher et al., 1984, 1986). Reports usually do not specify the "quality of practice," although some do (Solbach, Sargent, & Coyne, 1989). Research usually does not use rating scales for assessing "relaxation proficiency." It is no wonder we still have questions.

Research on Relaxation Practice. Conventional wisdom for the usefulness and importance of practice frequency in treating headaches has research support (Libo & Arnold, 1983; Lake & Pingel, 1988; Solbach et al., 1989; Blanchard, Nicholson, Taylor, et al., 1991; Allen & McKeen, 1991; Blanchard, Nicholson, Radnitz, et al., 1991; Gauthier, Côte, & French, 1994).

For patients with tension-type headaches, Blanchard, Nicholson, Radnitz, et al. (1991) supported the advantage of home practice. They relied on PMR without biofeedback as the primary treatment. There were 10 sessions over 8 weeks, and they used audiotapes to help with home practice. Instructions for the no-home-practice group gently discouraged home practice. The home-practice group showed greater improvement in their headaches than those without home practice. Their proficiency at relaxing in the office sessions also was better than the no-practice group. There was no symptom improvement among those monitoring their symptoms. The data indicated that expectation of improvement probably did not account for the effects, and medications did not change for any of the groups.

For vascular headaches, home practice combined with TBF and a brief introduction to autogenic phrases did not clearly result in more symptom improvement than no practice. However, the authors admit to limitations in the study. A crucial limitation is that 30% of the subjects in the no-practice group did practice despite instructions to avoid practice. Inspection of their data suggests that home practice had some advantage for some subjects.

Lake and Pingel (1988) relied on a retrospective questionnaire from a large sample of patients with a diagnosis of mixed headaches. The frequency of daily brief relaxations as short as a few seconds and extended relaxations correlated with improvement of headaches defined in several ways. The 102 fee-paying and mostly female (82%) patients reported brief relaxation as more useful than extended relaxation. Improvements include intensity, duration, aborting headaches, and medication usage. The authors concluded that "the analyses show a consistent and strong relationship between . . . frequency of brief relaxation—and headache control . . . most of whom [with] chronic daily pain" (p. 126). Treatment was multicomponent with patient education, several types of relaxation including tapes, thermal and EMG biofeedback, and some cognitive aspects.

Related to the quality of relaxation and cognitive aspects was the report from most patients that the most helpful aspect of treatment was the "awareness of thoughts and feelings related to headache" (p. 127). The correlation between a patient's age and improvement was nonsignificant. There was a wide enough range of age (13–73 with a mean and median of 33) to show the difference if one were present. The number of biofeedback sessions ranged from less than 5 to more than 16. This also did not correlate significantly with the results.

The *age* of patients related to the effects of practice receives very little attention. Patients under age 36 were more compliant than older patients in the study of Solbach et al. (1989). For children, aged 7–12, being treated for migraines, frequency of home practice was one significant factor related to treatment results (Allen & McKeen, 1991). The correlation between headache frequency and the average number of practices per day was significant ($r = .61$, $p < .01$). More frequent practice more often resulted in better patient ability to warm hands without biofeedback ($r = .50$, $p < .01$).

Toward Understanding the Mixed Support for Practice. One variable that could affect the relationship of practice to headache changes is reducing high levels of tension rather than the practice of relaxation. Consider the logic and potential for reducing high-intensity tension. This includes intensity, frequency, and/or durations of high tension. Periods of high-intensity tension such as from teeth clenching, raised shoulders, shifting or tilting the head forward, and occipital tension probably contribute significantly to onset and maintenance of symptoms.

One would not expect deep relaxation once or twice a day or several brief relaxations each day could counteract such tension. Reducing high-intensity tension could be as important or more important for many patients as increasing the frequency, duration, depth, and quality of their deeper relaxation. This could help explain why relaxation practice sometimes does not show a relationship to decreased headaches.

Many practitioners often seek to increase patients' awareness of excess tension. Some specifically instruct patients to attend to these episodes of high tension and stop or reduce them. However, research studies do not mention this latter type of instruction. We do not know if research studies include this instruction. Studies of practice and most other studies also do not report changes in other behaviors that can affect headaches. These include sleep efficiency, sleep and daytime postures, type of pillow used, and dietary changes. Were they mentioned in any sessions? Did patients become aware of them from other sources and make these changes? In addition to including or controlling for these other factors, we need measures of muscle activity with ambulatory multichannel EMG recordings.

These other factors may be about equal in groups who practice more and those who practice less or do not practice. However, in small samples, it might not be true even with random assignment. Future research will address these other changes.

For tension-type headaches, a measure of the "quality of relaxation" was more important than the quantity of relaxation in Solbach et al. (1989). Quality included awareness of muscle relaxation in the head and neck during practice, experiencing warmth sensations, and throbbing or fullness sensations in the hands. Thus, aside from quantity of practice, assessing quality may be useful.

Conclusions about Relaxation Practice.

- There is research support for practice, and there is more logic and support for it than for no practice—at least for people with tension-type headaches.
- There is both logic and support for using many brief and extended relaxations daily for patients with tension-type headaches.
- Practitioners and researchers need to continue evaluating and focusing on measuring the quality of relaxation in addition to quantity.
- It probably is not necessary for some patients to relax as often as others need to in order to achieve good results.
- For patients with migraines, practice may not be necessary for all patients. Limited research raises some questions about conventional wisdom, but it is not enough to justify abandoning practice for these patients. One interpretation of the available data suggests that some patients might benefit from office-based relaxation and TBF without practice. It is consistent with research with Raynaud's disease (see Chapter 17). That is encouraging even if it is counterintuitive.
- Consider focusing on and recording the reduction of the frequency, intensity, and duration of high-tension episodes. Some practitioners already do this, but research usually focuses on relaxation practice.

SUMMARY

Relaxation and biofeedback therapies in the treatment of tension-type and migraine headaches are major application areas and often the treatment of choice. Part B has focused on treatment. Topics discussed include cost containment, factors affecting headaches and interfering with treatments, patient education, compliance, placement of electrodes, and selected treatment-process variables.

GLOSSARY

AAPB. Association for Applied Psychophysiology and Biofeedback.

AMITRIPTYLINE. (Trade names Elavil and Endep) A tricyclic antidepressant (TCA) drug used in smaller doses for headaches (especially chronic daily headache), episodic tension-type headache, atypical face pain, neck pain, and pain syndromes with sleep disturbance or anxiety. Also used for intermittent migraine and related headaches. Also can help sleep-onset insomnia. Proposed mechanisms include increased synaptic norepinephrine or serotonin, inhibition of 5-HT and norepinephrine reuptake, effects on 5-HT_2 receptors, and decreased beta-receptor density.

ANALGESIC REBOUND HEADACHE. Almost continuous headache associated with regular daily use of high levels of analgesic medications (see text).

ANOXIA. Literally, total lack of oxygen. Often used interchangeably with hypoxia to mean a reduced supply of oxygen to the tissues.

ASTHENIA. Loss or lack of strength. Especially weakness from cerebellar or muscular disease.

ATENOLOL (Trade name Tenormin). An antiadrenergic $beta_1$-selective adrenoreceptor-blocking agent. Used as an antihypertensive and heart drug.

BIFURCATION OF THE TEMPORAL ARTERY. Site where the temporal artery divides into two branches, one to the frontal region and the other to the parietal region.

BANDPATHS (Also bandwidth or bandshape). Range of an amplifier's frequency (hertz) sensitivity (see Chapter 4).

BIOCHEMICAL PROFILE (blood chemistry group). ". . . May include an analysis of electrolytes (see *electrolytes*) and glucose (blood sugar), a series of liver function tests . . . , and tests for uric acid, creatinine (a kidney function test), and albumin (a major protein in the blood). Sometimes different combinations of tests are used" (Larson, 1990, pp. 1282–1283). It is another screen for possible systemic diseases.

BLOOD VOLUME PULSE AMPLITUDE (BVPA). Amount of blood in a pulse beat. Compare finger pulse amplitude (FPA), finger pulse volume (FPV), and cephalic pulse amplitude (CPA).

C_4. Fourth cervical spine.

CATECHOLAMINES. Body compounds having a sympathomimetic action. Include epinephrine, norepinephrine, and dopamine. Epinephrine (also adrenaline) is a hormone and neurotransmitter secreted by adrenal medulla. It is involved in regulation of metabolism. *Norepinephrine* (also, noradrenaline) is a neurohormone and neurotransmitter released at sympathetic nerve endings. Also found in the brain. (See these terms in Chapters 7, 18.)

CEILING EFFECT. The highest value a parameter, such as a physiological activity, can reach, thereby limiting changes depending on the starting point of the measurement.

CENTRAL ORIGIN. Starting in the central nervous system.

CEPHALIC. Referring to the head. Another term for headache is *cephalalgia*.

CEPHALIC BLOOD FLOW (CBF). In the present chapter, extracranial cephalic blood flow. Also, cerebral blood flow.

CERVICAL PARASPINALS. Muscles next to and on either side of the cervical spine and parallel to it.

CHRONIC PAROXYSMAL HEMICRANIA (CPH). A type of headache classified with cluster headaches. May be a variant form of cluster headache and often confused with it. Mostly in women and young girls. May be provoked by flexion and sometimes neck rotation. This latter finding distinguishes it from cluster headaches. Features include unilateral pain in the temple, forehead, ear, eye, or occipital areas. Attacks average 10 to 15 minutes and last 5 to 30 minutes, in contrast to cluster headaches, which last longer, an average of 45 minutes. Sufferers average 10 to 15 attacks per day but may have up to 30. Attacks may awaken some from sleep. Autonomic symptoms are similar to cluster headaches. One must rule out intracranial diseases that can mimic CPH. These include ophthalmic artery aneurysm and pituitary tumor. Treatment includes indomethacin and sometimes corticosteroids.

CIMETIDINE (Trade name Tagamet). A histamine H_2-receptor antagonist (blocker). Used in the treatment of duodenal and gastric ulcers and other gastrointestinal disorders.

COGNITIVE DISSONANCE. An unpleasant feeling arising when there is a lack of agreement (dissonance, discord, or disagreement) among one's ideas, beliefs, and/or behaviors.

COMPLETE BLOOD COUNT (CBC). Most common and basic blood test. "Involves counting the number of each type of blood cell in a given volume of . . . blood and examining the cells under a microscope to check for any abnormalities in their size or shape" (Larson, 1990, p. 476). Part of the CBC determines the hematocrit value (HCT or Hct), the percentage of total blood volume occupied by red blood cells. Another part is hemoglobin status (Hb), "the iron-rich molecule in the red blood cell that binds oxygen and delivers it to the cells of . . . [the] body" (Larson, 1990, p. 477). Other parts of the CBC include the WBC count (the number and kinds of white blood cells) and platelet count. Indications include a screen for possible systemic diseases including suspected hematologic (e.g., anemia, leukemia) and infectious diseases.

CRANIAL NEURALGIA. Neuralgia along the course of a cranial nerve.

DISCONNECTION BETWEEN THE MMPI AND HEADACHES. Some patients with chronic headaches do not endorse obvious headache items on the MMPI.

DISTENTION. Being distended or enlarged, such as of cephalic arteries.

DIURNAL. Occurring during the day.

DIVERTICULOSIS. Multiple pouches projecting out from the colon wall, usually the lower (sigmoid) portion. Usually not painful or productive of other symptoms. Unknown cause. Risk increases with age. Incidence in Western countries is 20–50% over age 50. With inflammation, pain occurs, probably from undigested food and bacteria lodged in it; condition is then called diverticulitis. Pain may be severe and cramping, usually on the left side. Pain may be mild for several days before getting worse. Fever and nausea are often present. This can result in a small abscess to a massive infection or perforation. If this occurs, the inflamed diverticulum spills intestinal contents into the abdominal cavity, causing peritonitis, a medical emergency. Often symptoms of irritable bowel syndrome (IBS) are incorrectly blamed on diverticulosis.

EIA. Exercise-induced analgesia (see text).

ELECTROLYTES. Substances that dissociate into ions when fused or in solution and thus become capable of conducting electricity. Examples are potassium, sodium, chloride, and phosphate. Blood chemistry group laboratory tests include electrolytes as a screen for possible systemic diseases.

ERGOTAMINE. Ergot alkaloid used in treating moderate to severe migraine and related headaches such as cluster headaches, status migrainosis (dihydroergotamine, DHE), chronic daily headache (DHE), and menstrual migraine. Ergot is derived from rye plant fungus. Available as ergotamine tartrate (Cafergot, Wigraine, Ergomar, Ergostat, Bellergal-S, Migrogot) and dihydroergotamine (DHE-45) injections (intravenous, intramuscular, or subcutaneous). The DHE differs from ergotamine tartrate: It is a weaker arterial vasoconstrictor, has selective venoconstricting properties, substantially less emetic (nauseating) features, and fewer uterine effects. Both have agonist action on serotonin (5-HT$_{1a}$ and 5-HT$_{1d}$) and alpha-adrenergic receptors. Both create vasoconstriction by stimulating arterial smooth muscle through 5-HT receptors. Both constrict venous capacitance. Both inhibit reuptake of norepinephrine at sympathetic nerve endings. Both reduce vasogenic/neurogenic inflammation (Saper et al., 1993). (See *sympathetic*, Chapter 18 and others.)

FRONTAL POSTERIOR NECK (FpN). One EMG electrode on one frontalis muscle and another electrode on the ipsilateral side of cervical neck near the hairline. Proposed as a broader and better measure of cephalic muscle tension. Also provides an indirect indication of occipitalis tension when frontalis, posterior neck, and sternomastoid tension are ruled out as contributing to the EMG signal. Usually used with bilateral frontal and bilateral neck electrodes. Ideally also used with matched set of FpN electrodes on the contralateral side. Thus, an ideal EMG montage is four EMG channels.

GLYCERYL TRINITRATE. Nitroglycerin.

HERTZ (Hz). Unit of frequency equal to 1 cycle per second (cps) (see Chapter 4).

HOME-BASED TREATMENT. See text and *prudent limited office treatment.*

INDOMETHACIN. An analgesic and anti-inflammatory drug. A nonsteroidal anti-inflammatory.

IPSATIVE. Criterion-referenced as opposed to norm-referenced. Thus, comparison is with a criterion rather than a normative group.

IPSILATERAL. Situated on, pertaining to, or affecting the same side, as opposed to contralateral (*Dorland's Illustrated Medical Dictionary*, 1988).

ISCHEMIA. Deficiency of blood flow in a body part as a result of functional constriction or actual obstruction of a blood vessel.

ISOSORBIDE DINITRATE (Trade names Isordil and Sorbitrate). An antianginal heart drug. An organic nitrate. Vasodilator with effects on veins and arteries.

LACTIC ACID. Formed in muscle cells during intense muscular tension, as in heavy exercise or tense muscles, by the breakdown of glucose (glycolysis), the hydrolysis of sugar by enzymes in the body. This provides energy anaerobically, without inspired oxygen.

LIMITED-CONTACT TREATMENT. See *prudent limited office treatment.*

MEASURES AND SELF-REPORT TESTS.
Millon Behavioral Health Inventory (*MBHI*): A T–F self-descriptive measure of coping styles, attitudes about illness and treatment, and personality factors that may affect reactions to illness and treatment.
Millon Clinical Multiaxial Inventory (*MCMI*): A T–F self-descriptive measure of personality patterns, personality disorders, and other clinical syndromes.
MMPI subscales: Each of the original MMPI scales has subgroups of items focused on different aspects of the longer ("parent") scale. For example, scale 2 (Depression) has five subscales. Others with subscales are scales 3, 4, 6, 8, 9, and 0.

MINIMAL-THERAPIST TREATMENT. See *prudent limited office treatment.*

MULTIPLE-BASELINE DESIGN. A special type of single-case design with multiple baseline lengths for subjects and/or symptoms.

NEURALGIA. Paroxysmal pain extending along the course of one or more nerves.

NEUROKININS, CIRCULATORY. A peptide is one of many compounds that yield two or more amino acids on hydrolysis. A kinin is one of a group of peptides that cause contraction of smooth muscle and have other physiological effects.

NIFEDIPINE (Trade name Procardia). One type of calcium channel antagonist in the dihydro-properadine group. Also called calcium ion influx inhibitor or slow channel blocker. These are drugs used to lower blood pressure by decreasing vascular resistance. Antianginal drug. May worsen headache in up to 30% of patients. Less commonly used for migraines than the more widely used verapamil (Trade names Calan, Isoptin, Verelan, Verapamil HCl) of the phenylal-kylamine group of calcium channel blockers.

OCCIPITAL. Pertaining to or situated near the occiput or occipital bone (back part of the head or skull). *Occipital muscles* are above the posterior neck hairline, connected to the frontalis muscles by tendonous tissue. Their function is to pull the scalp back. They are under voluntary control but very difficult for nearly all people to control.

OPERATIONALLY DEFINED. The meaning of the term or concept consists of the operations (method) performed to demonstrate it. For example, anxiety or any emotion may be operationally defined as the score on specific self-report questionnaires. Pain intensity, such as headache intensity, may be operationally defined by specified ratings.

OSTEOARTHRITIS. (Also called degenerative joint disease and wear-and-tear arthritis; osteoarthrosis.) Wear and tear is the main cause. Athletes with joint injuries and laborers who challenge joints daily are at greater risk. One of the most common disorders affecting tens of millions of people and more common in elderly people. Usually strikes only one joint if knee or hip is involved. If fingers are affected, often multiple joints become arthritic. Appropriate exercise, such as range-of-motion and muscle strengthening, can be valuable treatments. Other therapies include heating pads, hot water bottles, hot baths, and a cervical collar during acute episodes affecting the neck. Weight control and good posture are invaluable adjuncts. Aspirin or other anti-inflammatory drugs are effective for pain and discomfort. Corticosteroid injections are for severe inflammation such as in a weight-bearing joint. Hip or knee replacement or hand surgery is sometimes indicated after long-term deterioration.

PAIN DENSITY. Concept of Sternbach et al. (1980). Refers to the overall time with pain. For example, people with tension-type headaches usually have a greater pain density than those with migraines, that is, more time with pain.

PARASOMNIAS. Normal and abnormal movements and behaviors during sleep. Examples of normal parasomnias are hypnic jerks and brief myoclonic jerks at sleep onset. Examples of abnormal parasomnias are sleepwalking, sleeptalking, sleep terror, periodic leg movements, head banging, bruxism, nocturnal enuresis, and sleep-related cluster headaches and chronic paroxysmal hemicrania.

PARESTHESIAS. Abnormal sensations, for example, prickling.

PAROXYSMAL. Spasm, sudden recurrence or intensification.

PAROXYSMAL NOCTURNAL DYSPNEA. Respiratory distress ususally thought to result from congestive heart failure with pulmonary edema. Sudden attacks of air hunger and difficult breathing during sleep and related to reclining. Patients awaken gasping and must sit or stand to catch their breath. Similar to the causes of orthopnea. Precipitated by increased venous return of blood to a damaged left ventricle that cannot manage the overload. May occur in patients with aortic insufficiency, mitral stenosis, hypertension, and other left ventricle conditions.

POWER SPECTRUM. Advanced method of analyzing electrical signals, especially the complex waveforms of the EEG. Provides all frequency and amplitude components, including dominant and subdominant, of a waveform.

PRODROMAL SYMPTOMS OF MIGRAINES. Visual (most common), motor, sensory, brainstem, or psychological signs indicating the onset of a *migraine with aura*. Less often, it occurs with or after onset of headache phase. A common visual aura is the *fortification spectra* or *scotomata*—zig-zag or *scintillating* (sparkling) image. Motor aura (much less common) includes hemiparesis or aphasia. Sensory aura includes hypersensitivity to feel and touch or reduced sensation. Other disturbances include ataxia (e.g., irregular muscle control/unsteadiness), vertigo (illusion of movement; sensation of the external world revolving around patient or patient revolving in space; not the same as dizziness), tinnitus (ear ringing; see Chapter 34), hearing loss, diplopia (double vision), loss or change in level of consciousness, paresthesia (e.g., prickling sensation), dysarthria (imperfect speech articulation from disturbed muscular control). Psychological prodromal symptoms can include depression, anger, euphoria, or hypomania. Other prodromal features associated with migraines include stiff neck (distinguish from tension type), chilled feeling and peripheral vasoconstriction, fatigue, increased urination frequency, anorexia, fluid retention, and food cravings.

PROPRANOLOL (Trade name Inderal). An antiarrhythmia heart drug also used for migraines. It is a nonselective beta-adrenergic blocking agent that competes with beta-adrenergic receptor stimulant agents for available receptor sites.

PRUDENT LIMITED OFFICE TREATMENT (PLOT). Term proposed to replace home-based, minimal-therapist, and limited-contact treatment.

RANITIDINE. A histamine-blocker ulcer drug.

SCHWARTZ–MAYO METHOD. Name given by Dr. L. Hudzinski for the FpN placement of EMG electrodes (see *FpN*).

SEDIMENTATION RATE (SED RATE). (Also erythrocyte sedimentation rate or ESR) "Blood test . . . determines the rate at which red blood cells settle to the bottom of a container. If the cells settle faster than normal, this can suggest an infection, anemia, inflammation, rheumatoid arthritis, rheumatic fever, or one of several types of cancer" (Larson, 1990, p. 1283).

SEMISPINALIS CERVICUS. Muscle that rotates vertebral column.

SEROTONIN. (Also called 5-hydroxytryptamine, 5-HT.) Vasoconstrictor. Synthesized in humans in certain intestinal cells or in central or peripheral neurons. Found in high concentrations in many tissues, including intestinal mucosa, pineal body, and CNS. Synthesis starts with uptake of tryptophan into serotonergic neurons. Tryptophan is hydroxylated by an enzyme to become 5-hydroxytryptophan, then decarboxylated by another enzyme to serotonin 5-HT. There are three types of receptors (5-HT_1, 5-HT_2, 5-HT_3) and four subtypes of 5-HT_1. It has many physiological properties including inhibiting gastric secretions, stimulating smooth muscle, and serving as a central neurotransmitter. A major factor in medical/neurological, and psychiatric conditions such as migraines and depression. About 90% occurs in the gastrointestinal tract, about 8% in blood platelets, and the rest in the brain.

Platelet serotonin. About 8% of 5-HT is found in blood platelets. It falls at the onset of a migraine attack and is normal between attacks (Saper et al., 1993).

SLEEP APNEA. An obstructive sleep disorder. Recurrent episodes of stopping breathing during sleep caused by obstruction of air in the upper respiratory passages. The throat muscles (pharynx) relax, so the walls collapse as the person approaches deeper sleep. The person moves rapidly to a lighter level of sleep after several seconds (up to 20 to 30 seconds). It prevents reaching restorative sleep.

The muscles regain normal tone, relieving the obstruction, and the person gasps for air. Signs and symptoms include excessive daytime sleepiness despite suitable sleeping time, loud snoring, and episodes of breath stopping during sleep observed by another person. Morning headaches can occur. Diagnosis needs confirmation in a sleep laboratory. Sleep apnea is a major factor in many people's daytime drowsiness. Treatment includes substantial weight loss in those who are obese. Many people successfully use a special machine that delivers air through a mask at a pressure above ambient air. This is called continuous positive air pressure (CPAP).

SOMNAMBULISM. Sleepwalking. A parasomnia.

SPINALIS. Muscle that extends vertebral column.

STAGES III, IV, REM. Three of the five sleep stages (others are I and II.) Stages III and IV are deeper levels of sleep than I and II. Stage IV is sometimes called "restorative" sleep. It occurs in the early period of a sleep cycle. REM stands for rapid eye movement and is typically associated with dreaming.

STATUS MIGRAINE (STATUS MIGRAINOSUS; INTRACTABLE MIGRAINE). Severe, debilitating migraine attacks that last for weeks.

SUBJECTIVE GLOBAL ESTIMATE. A patient's estimate of his or her pain without using a specific rating scale or procedure. Often refers to retrospective estimates. For example, "I feel 50% better," "The headaches are 50% improved."

SUPRATROCHLEAR. In this context, above the trochlear nerve (fourth cranial nerve), the motor nerve for the superior oblique muscles of the eyeball that rotate the eyeball downward and outward.

SYMPATHOMIMETIC. "Mimicking the effects of impulses conveyed by adrenergic postganglionic fibers of the sympathetic nervous system" (*Dorland's Illustrated Medical Dictionary*, 1988). Also called *adrenergic*. (See *sympathetic* in Chapter 18 and others.)

T SCORE. Common statistical transformation of raw scores to allow comparison among different scales and psychological tests. T scores have a mean of 50 and a standard deviation of 10. Thus, about 68% of a population have T scores between 40 and 59, and about 95.4% between 30 and 69.

TBF. Thermal biofeedback.

TEMPORAL ARTERITIS. Also known as cranial arteritis and giant cell arteritis. Inflammation of an artery in the head, often near the temple. Probably a form of disordered immune reaction. Can thicken the lining of the affected artery, blocking blood flow, most commonly to the eyes. Can cause partial or total blindness if untreated. Condition of older people, usually between ages 60 and 75 and almost exclusively older than 50, in women slightly more than in men. Diagnosis sometimes is a problem because it mimics other ailments, and symptoms may be vague (e.g., feeling "run down"). Usual symptoms include throbbing headaches, loss of vision, temple area pain, jaw pain when chewing, and sore scalp. Only sure diagnostic test is biopsy of a piece of the artery, an outpatient procedure done with a local anesthetic. Treatment is usually with oral corticosteroid drugs, usually daily, often for one or more years. Initial large doses are usually prescribed and lowered after several weeks (Larson, 1990).

TERTIARY. Third in order. Often used to refer to very large medical centers that provide a variety of health care services including resolution of medical and/or psychological diagnoses and treatment questions unresolved by primary and second opinions. Could be large specialty medical centers.

TOTAL THYROXINE (TOTAL SERUM THYROXINE OR T_4). A rapid, simple, direct, and inexpensive blood test of the thyroid hormone thyroxine.

TRANSIENT ISCHEMIC ATTACK (TIA). Temporary deficiency in blood supply to part(s) of the brain, usually lasting a few minutes. Most often caused by atherosclerosis when plaque deposits form inside arteries. Major risk factors are hypertension, some types of heart disease, smoking, diabetes, and older age. Usually rapid onset, brief duration, and return to normal functioning. Signs and symptoms include sudden weakness, tingling, or numbness, typically on one side. Vision loss, speech difficulty, vertigo, double vision, imbalance, or incoordination of limbs are other signs and symptoms. These are similar to an ischemic stroke but disappear completely within 24 hours with TIAs. May occur repeatedly in the same day or later. Regard as a warning of possible stroke later, which occurs in about one-third of people. Another third have more TIAs, and the others have no more cardiovascular symptoms. Treatments include medications for blood pressure, reducing blood clots, and/or reducing or eliminating plaque. Carotid endarterectomy surgery for carefully selected patients removes arterial plaque (Larson, 1990).

TRIMETHOPRIM–SULFAMETHOXAZOLE. An antibiotic combination drug.

VASOPRESSIN. One of two hormones formed by neuronal cells of the hypothalmic nuclei. Stored in the posterior lobe of the pituitary gland. Stimulates contraction of muscular tissue of capillaries and arterioles. Raises blood pressure. Also, promotes contraction of intestinal muscles, increases peristalsis, and has some contractile effect on uterus. The pharmaceutical preparation is prepared synthetically or from pituitary of healthy domestic animals used for food by man. Used mainly as antidiuretic, especially for treating diabetes insipidus. Also called *antidiuretic hormone (ADH)*.

VERTIGO. Illusion of movement. Sensation of the external world revolving around patient or the patient revolving in space. Not the same as dizziness.

VISUAL ANALOGUE SCALE (VAS). A straight line, usually 10 cm long, with ends labeled as the extremes of pain intensity (e.g, *no pain* to *pain as bad as it could be*) or pain affect (e.g., *not bad at all* to *the most unpleasant feeling possible for me*). May have specific points along the line labeled with intensity-denoting adjectives or numbers, called graphic rating scales (GRSs). Patients indicate which point along the line best represents their pain intensity (and/or pain affect). The distance from the *no pain* (or *not bad at all*) end to the mark made by the patient is the pain intensity (or pain affect) score (Jensen & Karoly, 1992).

VISUAL SCOTOMATA. See *prodromal symptoms of migraine*.

WHO. World Health Organization.

ZIMELDINE. An antidepressant withdrawn from the market by the FDA.

ZOMEPIREC. An analgesic and anti-inflammatory withdrawn from the market by the FDA.

ACKNOWLEDGMENT

I am very thankful to neurologist and headache subspecialist, William P. Cheshire, M.D., of Mayo Clinic Jacksonville, for his review of sections of this chapter. His comments and suggestions were very helpful. This appreciation does not imply his endorsement of the content of this chapter.

REFERENCES

Adler, C. S., & Adler, S. M. (1985). An analysis of therapeutic factors seen in a ten-year study of psychophysiologically and psychodynamically oriented treatment for migraine In F. C. Rose (Ed.), *Migraine* [Proceedings of the 5th International Migraine Symposium. London, 1984] (pp. 186–196). Karger: Basel.

Adler, C. S., & Adler, S. M. (1987). Evaluating the psychological factors in headache. In C. S. Adler, S. M. Adler, & R. C. Packard (Eds.), *Psychiatric aspects of headache* (pp. 70–83). Baltimore: Williams & Wilkins.

Adler, C. S., Adler, S. M., & Packard, R. C. (1987). *Psychiatric aspects of headache*. Baltimore: Williams & Wilkins.

Ahles, T. A., & Martin, J. B. (1989). The relationship of electromyographic and vasomotor activity to MMPI subgroups in chronic headache patients: The use of the original and contemporary MMPI norms. *Headache, 29*, 584–587.

Ahles, T. A., Martin, J. B., Gaulier, B., Cassens, H. L., Andres, M. L., & Shariff, M. (1988). Electromyographic and vasomotor activity in tension, migraine, and combined headache patients: The influence of postural variation. *Behaviour Research and Therapy, 26*(6), 519–525.

Allen, K. D., & McKeen, L. R. (1991). Home-based multicomponent treatment of pediatric migraine. *Headache, 31*, 467–472.

Anderson, C. D., & Franks, R. D. (1980). Migraine and tension headache: Is there a physiological difference? *Headache, 21*(2), 63–71.

Andrasik, F. (1992). Assessment of patients with headache. In D. C. Turk & R. Melzack (Eds.), *Handbook of pain assessment* (pp. 344–361). New York: Guilford Press.

Andrasik, F., Attanasio, V., Blanchard, E. B., Burke, E., Kabela, E., McCarran, M., Blake, D. D., & Rosenblum, E. L. (1984, November). Behavioral treatment of pediatric migrain headache. In F. Andrasik (Chair), *Recent developments in the assessment and treatment of headache*. Symposium conducted at the annual meeting of the Association for Advancement of Behavior Therapy, Philadelphia, PA. [Summarized in Blanchard & Andrasik, 1985.]

Andrasik, F., & Baskin, S. (1987). Headache. In R. L. Morrison & A. A. Bellack (Eds.), *Medical factors and psychological disorders: A handbook for psychologists* (pp. 325–349). New York: Plenum Press.

Andrasik, F., & Blanchard, E. B. (1987). The biofeedback treatment of tension headache. In J. P. Hatch, J. G. Fisher, & J. D. Rugh (Eds.), *Biofeedback: Studies in clinical efficacy* (pp. 281–321). New York: Plenum Press.

Andrasik, F., Blanchard, E. B., Arena, J. G., Saunders, N. L., & Barron, K. D. (1982). Psychophysiology of recurrent headache: Methodological issues and new empirical findings. *Behavior Therapy, 13*(4), 407–429.

Andrasik, F. A., Blanchard, E. B., Arena, J. G., Teders, S. J., & Rodichok, L. D. (1982). Cross-validation of the Kudrow–Sutkus MMPI classification system for diagnosing headache type. *Headache, 22*, 2–5.

Andrasik, F., & Holroyd, K. A. (1980). Reliability and concurrent validity of headache questionnaire data. *Headache, 20*, 44–46.

Andrasik, F., & Murphy, W. D. (1977). Assessing the readability of thirty-nine behavior modification training manuals and primers. *Journal of Applied Behavior Analysis, 10*, 341–344.

Appelbaum, K. A., Blanchard, E. B., Nicholson, N. L., Radnitz, C., Michultka, D., Attanasio, V., Andrasik, F., & Dentinger, M. P. (1990). Controlled evaluation of the addition of cognitive strategies to a home-based relaxation protocol for tension headache. *Behavior Therapy, 21*, 293–303.

Arena, J. G., Blanchard, E. B., Andrasik, F., & Appelbaum, K. (1986). Obsessions and compulsions in three kinds of headache sufferers: Analysis of the Maudsley questionnaire. *Behaviour Research and Therapy, 24*(2), 127–132.

Arena, J. G., Blanchard, E. B., Andrasik, F., Appelbaum, K., & Myers, P. E. (1985). Psychophysiological comparisons of three kinds of headache subjects during and between headache states: Analysis of post-stress adaptation periods. *Journal of Psychosomatic Research, 29*(4), 427–441.

Arena, J. G., Blanchard, E. B., Andrasik, F., Catch, P. A., & Myers, P. E. (1983). Reliability of psychophysiological assessment. *Behaviour Research and Therapy, 21*(4), 447–460.

Arena, J. G., Blanchard, E. B., Andrasik, F., & Myers, P. E. (1983). Psychophysiological responding as a function of age: The importance of matching. *Journal of Behavioral Assessment, 5*, 131–142.

Arena, J. G., Bruno, G. M., & Brucks, A. (1993). *Biofeedback treatment of the chronic headache sufferer*. Toronto: Thought Technologies Press.

Arena, J. G., Bruno, G. M., Brucks, A. G., Meador, K., & Sherman, R. A. (1993, March 25–30). Ambulatory monitoring of bilaterial upper trapezius surface EMG in tension and vascular headache sufferers. *Proceedings of the 24th Annual Meeting of the Association for Applied Psychophysiology and Biofeedback, Los Angeles*. Wheatridge, CO: Association for Applied Psychophysiology and Biofeedback.

Arena, J. G., Bruno, G. M., Brucks, A. G., Searle, J. R., Meador, K., & Sherman, R. A. (1994, March 3–8). Preliminary results in tension headache sufferers of pre- to post-treatment ambulatory neck EMG monitoring: Generalization of EMG biofeedback training and EMG changes as a function of treatment outcome. *Proceedings of the 25th Annual Meeting of the Association for Applied Psychophysiology and Biofeedback, Atlanta* (pp. 4–7). Wheatridge, CO: Association for Applied Psychophysiology and Biofeedback.

Arena, J. G., Bruno, G. M., Brucks, A. G., Searle, J. R., Sherman, R. A., & Meador, K. J. (1994). Reliability of an ambulatory electromyographic activity device for musculoskeletal pain disorders. *International Journal of Psychophysiology, 17*, 153–157.

Arena, J. G., Hannah, S. L., Bruno, G. M., & Meador, K. J. (1991). Electromyographic biofeedback training for tension headache in the elderly: A prospective study. *Biofeedback and Self-Regulation, 16*(4), 379–390.

Arena, J. G., Hannah, S. L., Bruno, G. M., Smith, J. D., & Meador, K. J. (1991). Effect of movement and position on muscle activity in tension headache sufferers during and between headaches. *Journal of Psychosomatic Research, 35*, 187–195.

Arena, J. G., Hightower, N. E., & Chang, G. C. (1988). Relaxation therapy for tension headache in the elderly: A prospective study. *Psychology and Aging, 3*(1), 96–98.

Arena, J. G., Sherman, R. A., Bruno, G. M., & Young, T. R. (1989). Electromyographic recordings of five types of low back pain subjects and non-pain controls in different positions. *Pain, 37*, 57–65.

Arena, J. G., Sherman, R. A., Bruno, G. M., & Young, T. R. (1991). Electromyographic recordings of five types of low back pain subjects and non-pain controls in different positions: Effect of pain state. *Pain, 45*, 23–28.

Askmark, H., Lundberg, P. O., & Olsson, S. (1989). Drug-related headache. *Headache, 29*, 441–444.

Bakal, D. A. (1982). *The psychobiology of chronic headache*. New York: Springer.

Bakal, D. A., Demjen, S., & Kaganov, J. A. (1981). Cognitive behavioral treatment of chronic headache. *Headache, 21*(3), 81–86.

Bandura, A. (1977). Self-efficacy: Toward a unifying theory of behavioral change. *Psychological Review, 84*, 191–215.

Bandura, A. (1982). Self-efficacy mechanism in human agency. *American Psychologist, 37*, 122–147.

Bandura, A., Taylor, C. B., Williams, S. L., Mefford, I. N., & Barchas, J. D. (1985). Catecholamine secretion as a function of perceived coping self-efficacy. *Journal of Consulting and Clinical Psychology, 53*(3), 406–414.

Baumgartner, C., Wessely, P., Bingol, C., Maly, J., & Holzner, F. (1989). Long term prognosis of analgesic withdrawal in patients with drug-induced headaches. *Headache, 29*, 510–514.

Bell, N. W., Abramowitz, S. I., Folkins, C. H., Spensley, J., & Hutchinson, G. L. (1983). Biofeedback, brief psychotherapy and tension headache. *Headache, 23*(4), 162–173.

Bille, B. (1962). Migraine in schoolchildren. *Acta Paediatrica Scandinavia, 51*(Suppl. 136), 1–151.

Bille, B. (1981). Migraine in childhood and its prognosis. *Cephalalgia, 1*, 71–75.

Bille, B. (1989). Migraine in children: A 30 year follow-up. In G. Lanzi, U. Balotin, & A. Cernibori (Eds.), *Headache in children and adolescents* [Excerpta Medica, International Congress Series 833] (pp. 19–26). Amsterdam: Elsevier.

Bille, B. (1990). The development of pediatric headache research. *Headache Quarterly, Current Treatment and Research, 1*(1), 39–42.

Blanchard, E. B. (1992). Psychological treatment of benign headache disorders. *Journal of Consulting and Clinical Psychology, 60*(4), 537–551.

Blanchard, E. B., & Andrasik, F. (1985). *Management of chronic headaches: A psychological approach*. New York: Pergamon Press.

Blanchard, E. B., & Andrasik, F. (1987). Biofeedback treatment of vascular headache. In J. P. Hatch, J. G. Fisher, & J. D. Rugh (Eds.), *Biofeedback: Studies in clinical efficacy* (pp. 1–79). New York: Plenum Press.

Blanchard, E. B., Andrasik, F. A., Ahles, T. A., Teders, S. J., & O'Keefe, D. M. (1980). Migraine and tension headache: A meta-analytic review. *Behavior Therapy, 11,* 613–631.

Blanchard, E. B., Andrasik, F., Appelbaum, K. A., Evans, D. D., Jurish, S. E., Teders, S. J., Rodichok, L. D., & Barron, K. D. (1985). The efficacy and cost-effectiveness of minimal-therapist-contact, nondrug treatment of chronic migraine and tension headache. *Headache, 25,* 214–220.

Blanchard, E. B., Andrasik, F., Arena, J. G., Neff, D. F., Saunders, N. L., Jurish, S. E., Teders, S. J., & Rodichok, L. D. (1983). Psychophysiological responses as predictors of response to behavioral treatment of chronic headache. *Behavior Therapy, 14*(3), 357–374.

Blanchard, E. B., Andrasik, F., Arena, J. G., & Teders, S. J. (1982). Variation in meaning of pain descriptors for different headache types as revealed by psychophysical scaling. *Headache, 22*(3), 137–139.

Blanchard, E. B. Andrasik, F., Neff, D. F., Arena, J. G., Ahles, T. A., Jurish, S. E., Pallmeyer, T. P., Saunders, N. L., Teders, S. J., Barron, K. D., & Rodichok, L. D. (1982). Biofeedback and relaxation training with three kinds of headache: Treatment effects and their prediction. *Journal of Consulting and Clinical Psychology, 50,* 562–575.

Blanchard, E. B., Andrasik, F., Neff, D. F., Jurish, S. E., & O'Keefe, D. M. (1981). Social validation of the headache diary. *Behavior Therapy, 12,* 711–715.

Blanchard, E. B., Andrasik, F., Neff, D. R., Saunders, N. L., Arena, J. G., Pallmeyer, T. P., Teders, S. J., Jerish, S. E., & Rodichok, L. D. (1983). Four process studies in the behavioral treatment of chronic headache. *Behaviour Research and Therapy, 21*(3), 209–220.

Blanchard, E. B., Appelbaum, K. A., Guarnieri, P., Neff, D. F., Andrasik, F., Jaccard, J., & Barron, K. D. (1988). Two studies of the long-term follow-up of minimal therapist contact treatments of vascular and tension headache. *Journal of Consulting and Clinical Psychology, 56*(3), 427–432.

Blanchard, E. B., Appelbaum, K. A., Nicholson, N. L., Radnitz, C. L., Morrill, B., Michultka, D., Kirsch, C., Hillhouse, J., & Dentinger, M. P. (1990). A controlled evaluation of the addition of cognitive therapy to a home-based biofeedback and relaxation treatment of vascular headache. *Headache, 30,* 371–376.

Blanchard, E. B., Appelbaum, K. A., Radnitz, C. L., Jaccard, J., & Dentinger, M. P. (1989). The refractory headache patient—I. Chronic daily, high intensity headache. *Behaviour Research and Therapy, 27*(4), 403–410.

Blanchard, E. B., Appelbaum, K. A., Radnitz, C. L., Michultka, D., Morrill, B., Kirsch, C. L., Hillhouse, J., Evans, D. D., Guarnieri, P., Attanasio, V., Andrasik, F., Jaccard, J., & Dentinger, M. P. (1990). Placebo-controlled evaluation of abbreviated progressive muscle relaxation and of relaxation combined with cognitive therapy in the treatment of tension headache. *Journal of Consulting and Clinical Psychology, 58*(2), 210–215.

Blanchard, E. B., Appelbaum, K. A., Radnitz, C. L., Morrill, B., Michultka, D., Kirsch, C. L., Guarnieri, P., Hillhouse, J., Evans, D. D., Jaccard, J., & Barron, K. D. (1990). A controlled evaluation of thermal biofeedback and thermal biofeedback with cognitive therapy in the treatment of vascular headache. *Journal of Consulting and Clinical Psychology, 58*(2), 216–224.

Blanchard, E. B., Hillhouse, J., Appelbaum, K. A., & Jaccard, J. (1987). What is an adequate length of baseline in research and clinical practice with chronic headache? *Biofeedback and Self-Regulation, 12*(4), 323–329.

Blanchard, E. B., Jaccard, J., Andrasik, F. Guarnieri, P., & Jurish, S. E. (1985). Reduction in headache patients' medical expenses associated with biofeedback and relaxation treatments. *Biofeedback and Self-Regulation, 10*(1), 63–68.

Blanchard, E. B., Jurish, S. E., Andrasik, F., & Epstein, L. H. (1981). The relationship between muscle discrimination ability and response to relaxation training. *Biofeedback and Self-Regulation, 6,* 537–546.

Blanchard, E. B., Kirsch, C. A., Appelbaum, K. A., & Jaccard, J. (1989). The role of psychopathology in chronic headache: Cause or effect? *Headache, 29*(5), 295–301.

Blanchard, E. B., Nicholson, N. L., Radnitz, C. L., Steffek, B. D., Appelbaum, K. A., & Dentinger, M. P. (1991). The role of home practice in thermal biofeedback. *Journal of Consulting and Clinical Psychology, 59*(4), 507–512.

Blanchard, E. B., Nicholson, N. L., Taylor, A. E., Steffek, B. D., Radnitz, C. L., & Appelbaum, K. A. (1991). The role of regular home practice in the relaxation treatment of tension headache. *Journal of Consulting and Clinical Psychology, 59*(3), 467–470.

Blanchard, E. B., Steffek, B. D., Jaccard, J., & Nicholson, N. L. (1991). Psychological changes accompanying non-pharmacological treatment of chronic headache: The effects of outcome. *Headache, 31*, 249–253.

Blanchard, E. B., Taylor, A. E., & Dentinger, M. P. (1992). Preliminary results from the self-regulatory treatment of high-medication-consumption headache. *Biofeedback and Self-Regulation, 17*(3), 179–202.

Blau, J. N. (1990a). Headache history: Its importance and idiosyncrasies. *Headache Quarterly, Current Treatment and Research, 1*(2), 129–135.

Blau, J. N. (1990b). Migraine theory and therapy: Their relationship. *Headache Quarterly, Current Treatment and Research, 1*(1), 15–22.

Blau, J. N., & Thavapalan, M. (1988). Preventing migraine: A study of precipitating factors. *Headache, 28*, 481–483.

Bowdler, I. (1988). The association between analgesic abuse and headache—coincidental or causal? *Headache, 28*(7), 494.

Brantley, P. J., & Jones, G. N. (1989). *Daily Stress Inventory*. Odessa, FL: Psychological Assessment Resources.

Brantley, P. J., Waggoner, C. D., Jones, G. N., & Rapoport, N. B. (1987). A daily stress inventory: Development, reliability, and validity. *Journal of Behavioral Medicine, 10*(1), 61–74.

Bruyn, G. W. (1980). The biochemistry of migraine. *Headache, 20*, 235–246.

Burke, E. J., & Andrasik, F. (1989). Home versus clinic-based treatments of pediatric migraine headache: Results of treatment through one year follow-up. *Headache, 29*, 434–440.

Campbell, J. K. (1993). CT or not CT—That is the question [Editorial]. *Headache, 33*, 52.

Collins, F. L., & Thompson, J. K. (1979). Reliability and standardization in the assessment of self-reported headache pain. *Journal of Behavioral Assessment, 1*(1), 73–86.

Costello, R. M., Hulsey, T. L., Schoenfeld, L. S., & Ramamurthy, S. (1987). P-A-I-N: A four-cluster MMPI typology for chronic pain. *Pain, 30*, 199–209.

Cram, J. R. (1980). EMG biofeedback and the treatment of tension headaches: A systematic analysis of treatment components. *Behavior Therapy, 11*, 699–710.

Dalessio, D. J. (1986, January 30–February 1). Headache, history, physical examination and laboratory tests. In *Headache: Theory, diagnosis, psychological aspects and therapy* (pp. 11–26). Proceedings of the Annual Meeting of the American Association for the Study of Headache, Scottsdale, AZ.

Dalessio, D. J., Kunzel, M., Sternbach, R., & Sovak, M. (1979). Conditioned adaptation-relaxation reflex in migraine therapy. *Journal of the American Medical Association, 242*(2), 102–104.

Darling, M. (1991). The use of exercise as a method of aborting migraine. *Headache, 31*, 616–618.

deBenedittis, G., & Lorenzetti, A. (1992). Minor stressful life events (daily hassles) in chronic primary headache: Relationship with MMPI personality patterns. *Headache, 32*, 330–332.

deBenedittis, G., Lorenzetti, A., & Pieri, A. (1990). The role of stressful life events in the onset of chronic primary headache. *Pain, 40*, 65–75.

DeGood, D. E., & Shutty, M. S. Jr. (1992). Assessment of pain beliefs, coping, and self-efficacy. In D. C. Turk & R. Melzack (Eds.), *Handbook of pain assessment* (pp. 214–234). New York: Guilford Press.

Dexter, J. D. (1988). Headache and sleep. *Headache, 28*, 671–672.

Diener, H. C. (1988a). Clinical features of analgesic-induced chronic headache [Review; German]. *Deutsche Medizinische Wochenschrift, 113*(12), 472–474.

Diener, H. C. (1988b). Therapy of analgesic-induced chronic headache [German]. *Deutsche Medizinische Wochenschrift, 113*(12), 475–476.

Diener, H. C., Dichgans, J., Scholz, E., Geiselhart, S., Gerber, W. D., & Bille, A. (1989). Analgesic-induced chronic headache: Long-term results of withdrawal therapy. *Journal of Neurology, 236*(1), 9–14.

Dieter, J. N., & Swerdlow, B. (1988). A replicative investigation of the reliability of the MMPI in the classification of chronic headaches. *Headache, 28,* 212–222.

Dorland's illustrated medical dictionary (27th ed.). (1988). Philadelphia: W. B. Saunders.

Duckro, P. N., & Cantwell-Simmons, E. (1989). A review of studies evaluating biofeedback and relaxation training in the management of pediatric headache. *Headache, 29,* 428–433.

Edmeads, J. (1989). Four steps in managing migraine. *Postgraduate Medicine, 85*(6), 121–124, 127–128, 131–132, 134.

Elkind, A. H. (1991). Drug abuse and headache. *Medical Clinics of North America, 75*(3), 717–732.

El-Mallakh, R. S., Kranzler, H. R., & Kamaniz, J. R. (1991). Headaches and psychoactive substance use. *Headache, 31,* 584–587.

Elmore, A. M., & Tursky, B. (1981). A comparison of two psychophysiological approaches to the treatment of migraine. *Headache, 21*(3), 93–101.

Engel, J. M., Rapoff, M. A., & Pressman, A. R. (1992). Long-term follow-up of relaxation training for pediatric headache disorders. *Headache, 32,* 152–156.

Evans, D. D., & Blanchard, E. B. (1988). Prediction of early termination from the self-regulatory treatment of chronic headache. *Biofeedback and Self-Regulation, 13*(3), 245–256.

Fahrion, S. L. (1977). Autogenic biofeedback treatment for migraine. *Mayo Clinic Proceedings, 52,* 776–784.

Fentress, D. W., Masek, B. J., Mehegan, J. E., & Benson, H. (1986). Biofeedback and relaxation-response training in the treatment of pediatric migraine. *Developmental Medicine and Child Neurology, 28,* 139–146.

Fisher, C. N. (1988). Analgesic rebound headache refuted. *Headache, 28,* 666.

Flor, H., & Turk, D. C. (1989). Psychophysiology of chronic pain: Do chronic pain patients exhibit symptom-specific psychophysiological responses? *Psychological Bulletin, 105,* 215–259.

Gannon, L. R., Haynes, S. N., Cuevas, J., & Chavez, R. (1987). Psychophysiological correlates of induced headaches. *Journal of Behavioral Medicine, 4,* 411–423.

Gauthier, J., Côté, G., & French, D. (1994). The role of home practice in the thermal biofeedback treatment of migraine headache. *Journal of Consulting and Clinical Psychology, 62*(1), 180–184.

Gauthier, J. G., Fournier, A.-L., & Roberge, C. (1991). The differential effects of biofeedback in the treatment of menstrual and nonmenstrual migraine. *Headache, 31,* 82–90.

Grazzi, L., Leone, M., Frediani, F., & Bussone, G. (1990). A therapeutic alternative for tension headache in children and 1-year follow-up results. *Biofeedback and Self-Regulation, 15*(1), 1–6.

Guarnieri, P., & Blanchard, E. B. (1990). Evaluation of home-based thermal biofeedback treatment of pediatric migraine headache. *Biofeedback and Self-Regulation, 15*(2), 179–184.

Haber, J. D., Thompson, J. K., Raczynski, J. M., & Sikora, T. L. (1983). Physiological self-control and the biofeedback treatment of headache. *Headache, 23*(4), 174–178.

Hale, W. E., May, F. E., Marks, R. G., Moore, M. T., & Stewart, R. B. (1987). Headache in the elderly: An evaluation of risk factors. *Headache, 27,* 272–276.

Hart, J. D., & Cichanski, K. A. (1981). Comparison of frontal EMG biofeedback and neck EMG biofeedback in the treatment of muscle-contraction headache. *Biofeedback and Self-Regulation, 6,* 63–74.

Hatch, J. P., Fisher, J. G., & Rugh, J. D. (Eds.). (1987). *Biofeedback: Studies in clinical efficacy.* New York: Plenum Press.

Hatch, J. P., Moore, P. J., Borcherding, S., Cyr-Provost, M., Boutros, N. N., & Seleshi, E. (1992). Electromyographic and affective responses of episodic tension-type headache patients and headache-free controls during stress task performance. *Journal of Behavioral Medicine, 15*(1), 89–112.

Hatch, J. P., Prihoda, T. J., Moore, P. J., Cyr-Porvost, M., Borcherding, S., Boutros, N. N., & Seleshi, E. (1991). A naturalistic study of the relationship among electromyographic activity, psychological stress and pain in ambulatory tension-type headache patients and headache-free controls. *Psychosomatic Medicine, 53,* 576–584.

Hatch, J. P., Schoefeld, L. S., Boutros, N. N., Seleshi, E., Moore, P. J., & Cyr-Provost, M. (1991). Anger and hostility in tension-type headache. *Headache, 31*, 302–304.

Haynes, S. N., Cueves, J., & Gannon, L. R. (1982). The psychophysiological etiology of muscle contraction headache. *Headache, 22*(3), 122–132.

Haynes, S. N., Gannon, L. R., Bank, J., Shelton, D., & Goodwin, J. (1990). Cephalic blood flow correlates of induced headaches. *Journal of Behavioral Medicine, 13*(5), 467–480.

Hering, R., & Steiner, T. J. (1991). Abrupt outpatient withdrawal of medication in analgesic-abusing migraineurs. *Lancet, 337*, 1442–1443.

Hermann, C. U., & Blanchard, E. B. (1993, March 25–30). *The role of the hand held computer in headache treatment and research.* Paper presented at the 24th Annual Meeting of the Association for Applied Psychophysiology and Biofeedback, Los Angeles, CA.

Hickling, E. J., Blanchard, E. B., Schwarz, S. P., & Silverman, D. J. (1992). Headaches and motor vehicle accidents: Results of psychological treatment of post-traumatic headache. *Headache Quarterly, 3*, 285–289.

Hickling, E. J., Blanchard, E. B., Silverman, D. J., Schwarz, S. P. (1992). Motor vehicle accidents, headaches and post-traumatic stress disorder: Assessment findings in a consecutive series. *Headache, 32*, 147–151.

Hickling, E. J., Silverman, D. J., & Loos, W. (1990). A nonpharmacological treatment of vascular headache during pregnancy. *Headache, 30*, 407–410.

Hillenberg, J. B., & Collins, F. L. Jr. (1983). The importance of home practice for progressive relaxation training. *Behaviour Research and Therapy, 21*(6), 633–642.

Hoelscher, T. J., Lichstein, K. L., & Rosenthal, T. L. (1984). Objective vs. subjective assessment of relaxation compliance among anxious individuals. *Behaviour Research and Therapy, 22*, 187–193.

Hoelscher, T. J., Lichstein, K. L., & Rosenthal, T. L. (1986). Home relaxation practice in hypertension treatment: Objective assessment and compliance induction. *Journal of Consulting and Clinical Psychology, 54*, 217–221.

Holm, J. E., Holroyd, K. A., Hursey, K. G., & Penzien, D. B. (1986). The role of stress in recurrent tension headache. *Headache, 26*, 160–167.

Holroyd, K. A., Andrasik, F., & Westbrook, T. (1977). Cognitive control of tension headache. *Cognitive Therapy and Research, 1*(2), 121–133.

Holroyd, K. A., Cordingley, G. E., Pingel, J. D., Jerome, A., Theoganous, A. G., Jackson, D. K., & Leard, L. (1989). Enhancing the effectiveness of abortive therapy: A controlled evaluation of self-management training. *Headache, 29*, 148–153.

Holroyd, K. A., Holm, J. F., Penzien, D. B., Cordingley, G. E., Hursey, K. G., Martin, N. J., & Theofanous, A. (1989). Long-term maintenance of improvements achieved with (abortive) pharmacological and nonpharmacological treatments for migraine: Preliminary findings. *Biofeedback and Self-Regulation, 14*(4), 301–308.

Holroyd, K. A., Nash, J. M., Pingel, J. D., Cordingley, G. E., & Jerome, A. (1991). A comparison of pharmacological (amitriptyline HCl) and nonpharmacological (cognitive-behavioral) therapies for chronic tension headaches. *Journal of Consulting and Clinical Psychology, 59*(3), 387–393.

Holroyd, K. A., & Penzien, D. B. (1990). Pharmacological versus nonpharmacological prophylaxis of recurrent migraine headache: A meta-analytic review of clinical trials. *Pain, 42*, 1–13.

Holroyd, K. A., Penzien, D. B., & Cordingley, G. E. (1991). Propranolol in the management of recurrent migraine: A meta-analytic review. *Headache, 31*, 333–340.

Holroyd, K. A., Penzien, D. B., Hursey, K. G., Tobin, D. L., Rogers, L., Holm, J. E., Marcille, P. J., Hall, J. R., & Chila, A. G. (1984). Change mechanisms in EMG biofeedback training: Cognitive changes underlying improvements in tension headache. *Journal of Consulting and Clinical Psychology, 52*(6), 1039–1053.

Hovanitz, C. A., Chin, K., & Warm, J. S. (1989). Complexities in life-stress-dysfunction relationships: A case in point—tension headache. *Journal of Behavioral Medicine, 12*(1), 55–75.

Hudzinski, L. G. (1983). Neck musculature and EMG biofeedback in treatment of muscle contraction headache. *Headache, 23*, 86–90.

Hudzinski, L. G., & Lawrence, G. S. (1988). Significance of EMG surface electrode placement models and headache findings. *Headache, 28*, 30–35.

Hudzinski, L. G., & Lawrence, G. S. (1990). EMG surface electrode normative data for muscle contraction headache and biofeedback therapy. *Headache Quarterly, Current Treatment and Research, 1*(3), 23–28.

Hughes, H. E., & Goldstein, D. A. (1988). Birth following exposure to ergotamine, beta blockers, and caffeine. *Journal of Medical Genetics, 25*, 396–399.

Jay, G. W., Renelli, D., & Mead, T. (1984). The effects of propranolol and amitriptyline on vascular and EMG biofeedback training. *Headache, 24*, 59–69.

Jensen, M. P., & Karoly, P. (1992). Self-report scales and procedures for assessing pain in adults. In D. C. Turk & R. Melzack (Eds.), *Handbook of pain assessment* (pp. 135–151). New York: Guilford Press.

Jurish, S. E., Blanchard, E. B. Andrasik, F., Teders, S. J., Neff, D. F., & Arena, J. G. (1983). Home-versus clinic-based treatment of vascular headache. *Journal of Consulting and Clinical Psychology, 51*(5), 743–751.

Kabela, E., Blanchard, E. B., Appelbaum, K. A., & Nicholson, N. (1989). Self-regulatory treatment of headache in the elderly. *Biofeedback and Self-Regulation, 14*(3), 219–228.

Kaganov, J. A., Bakal, D. A., & Dunn, B. E. (1981). The differential contribution of muscle contraction and migraine symptoms to problem headache in the general population. *Headache, 21*(4), 157–163.

Kanner, A. D., Coyne, J. C., Schaefer, C., & Lazarus, R. S. (1981). Comparison of two modes of stress management: Daily hassles and uplifts versus major life events. *Journal of Behavioral Medicine, 4*, 1–39.

Kerns, R. D., & Jacob, M. C. (1992). Assessment of the psychosocial context of the experience of chronic pain. In D. C. Turk & R. Melzack (Eds.), *Handbook of pain assessment* (pp. 235–253). New York: Guilford Press.

Kerns, R. D., Turk, D. C., & Rudy, T. E. (1985). The West Haven–Yale Multidimensional Pain Inventory (WHYMPI). *Pain, 23*, 345–356.

Kewman, D., & Roberts, A. H. (1980). Skin temperature biofeedback and migraine headache: A double-bind study. *Biofeedback and Self-Regulation, 5*, 327–345.

Kim, M., & Blanchard, E. B. (1992). Two studies of the nonpharmacological treatment of menstrually-related migraine headaches. *Headache, 32*, 197–202.

Kinder, B. N., Curtiss, G., & Kalichman, S. (1991). Cluster analysis of headache-patient MMPI scores: A cross-validation. *Journal of Consulting and Clinical Psychology, 3*(2), 226–231.

Kohler, T., & Haimerl, C. (1990). Daily stress as a trigger of migraine attacks: Results of thirteen single-subject studies. *Journal of Consulting and Clinical Psychology, 58*(6), 870–872.

Kudrow, L. (1982). Parodoxical effects of frequent analgesic use. *Advances in Neurology, 33*, 335–341.

Kudrow, L., & Sutkus, B. J. (1979). MMPI pattern specificity in primary headache disorders. *Headache, 19*, 18–24.

Kunkel, R. S. (1987). First things first: The physical workup. In C. S. Adler, S. M. Adler, & R. C. Packard (Eds.), *Psychiatric aspects of headache* (pp. 59–63). Baltimore: Williams & Wilkins.

Kurman, R. G., Hursey, K. G., & Mathew, N. T. (1992). Assessment of chronic refractory headache: The role of the MMPI-2. *Headache, 32*(9), 432–435.

Labbé, E. L., & Williamson, D. A. (1984). Treatment of childhood migraine using autogenic feedback training. *Journal of Consulting and Clinical Psychology, 52*(6), 968–976.

Lake, A. E. III. (1981). Behavioral assessment considerations in the management of headache. *Headache, 21*(4), 170–178.

Lake, A. E. III, & Pingel, J. D. (1988). Brief versus extended relaxation: Relationship to improvement at follow-up in mixed headache patients. *Medical Psychotherapy, 1*, 119–129.

Lake, A. E. III, Saper, J. R., Madden, S. F., & Kreeger, C. (1993). Comprehensive inpatient treatment for intractable migraine: A prospective long-term outcome study. *Headache, 33*, 55–62.

Lance, F., Parkes, C., & Wilkinson, M. (1988). Does analgesic abuse cause headache *de novo*? *Headache, 28*, 61–62.

Langemark, M., Olesen, J., Poulsen, D. L., & Bech, P. (1988). Clinical characterization of patients with chronic tension headache. *Headache, 28,* 590–596.

Largen, J. W., Mathew, R. J., Dobbins, K., & Claghorn, J. L. (1981). Specific and non-specific effects of skin temperature control in migraine management. *Headache, 21*(2), 36–44.

Larson, D. E. (1990). *Mayo Clinic family health book.* New York: William Morrow.

Larsson, B., & Melin, L. (1988). The psychological treatment of recurrent headache in adolescents—short-term outcome and its prediction. *Headache, 28,* 187–195.

Larsson, B., & Melin, L. (1989). Follow-up on behavioral treatment of recurrent headache in adolescents. *Headache, 29,* 249–253.

Larsson, B., Melin, L., & Doberl, A. (1990). Recurrent tension headache in adolescents treated with self-help relaxation training and a muscle relaxant drug. *Headache, 30,* 665–671.

Larsson, B., Melin, L., Lamminen, M., & Ullstedt, F. (1987). A school-based treatment of chronic headaches in adolescents. *Journal of Pediatric Psychology, 12*(4), 553–566.

Lazarus, R. S., & Folkman, S. (1989). *Hassles and Uplifts Scales.* Palo Alto, CA: Consulting Psychologists Press.

Leijdekkers, M. L. A., & Passchier, J. (1990). Prediction of migraine using psychophysiological and personality measures. *Headache, 30,* 445–453.

Levor, R. M., Cohen, M. J., Naliboff, B. D., McArthur, D., & Heuser, G. (1986). Psychosocial precursors and correlates of migraine headache. *Journal of Consulting and Clinical Psychology, 54,* 347–353.

Libo, L. M., & Arnold, G. E. (1983). Relaxation practice after biofeedback therapy: A long-term follow-up study of utilization and effectiveness. *Biofeedback and Self-Regulation, 8*(2), 217–227.

Lichstein, K. L., Fischer, S. M., Eakin, T. L., Amberson, J. I., Bertorini, T., & Hoon, P. W. (1991). Psychophysiological parameters of migraine and muscle-contraction headaches. *Headache, 31,* 27–34.

Linet, M. S., Stewart, W. F., Celentano, D. D., Ziegler, D., & Sprecher, M. (1989). An epidemiologic study of headache among adolescents and young adults. *Journal of the American Medical Association, 261,* 2211–2216.

Lipton, R. B., Stewart, W. C., & Solomon, S. (1992). Questionnaire versus clinical interview in the diagnosis of headache [Letter to Editor]. *Headache, 32*(1), 55–56.

Lockett, D. M., & Campbell, J. F. (1992). The effects of aerobic exercise on migraine. *Headache, 32,* 50–54.

Marcus, D. A. (1992). Migraine and tension-type headaches: The questionable validity of current classification systems. *The Clinical Journal of Pain, 8,* 28–36.

Marcus, D. A. (1993). Serotonin and its role in headache pathogenesis and treatment [Review article]. *Clinical Journal of Pain, 9,* 159–167.

Martin, N. J., Holroyd, K. A., & Penzien, D. B. (1990). The Headache-Specific Locus of Control Scale: Adaptation to recurrent headaches. *Headache, 30,* 729–734.

Martin, N. J., Holroyd, K. A., & Rokicki, L. A. (1993). The Headache Self-Efficacy Scale: Adaptation to recurrent headaches. *Headache, 33,* 244–248.

Martin, P. R. (1993). *Psychological management of chronic headaches.* New York: Guilford Press.

Martin, P. R., & Mathews, A. M. (1978). Tension headaches: Psychophysiological investigation and treatment. *Journal of Psychosomatic Research, 22,* 389–399.

Martin, P. R., Nathan, P. R., Milech, D., & van Keppel, M. (1989). Cognitive therapy versus self-management training in the treatment of chronic headaches. *British Journal of Clinical Psychology, 28*(4), 347–361.

Martin, P. R., & Theunissen, C. (1993). The role of life event stress, coping and social support in chronic headaches. *Headache, 33,* 301–306.

Mathew, N. T., Kurman, R., & Perez, F. (1990). Drug induced refractory headache—clinical features and management. *Headache, 30,* 634–638.

McAnulty, D. P., Rappaport, N. B., Waggoner, C. D., Brantley, P. J., Barkemeyer, C., & McKenzie, S. J. (1986). Psychopathology in volunteers for headache research: Initial versus later respondents. *Headache, 26,* 37–38.

McGrath, P. J., Humphreys, P., Goodman, J. T., Keene, D., Firestone, P., Jacob, P., & Cunningham,

S. J. (1988). Relaxation prophylaxis for childhood migraine: A randomized placebo-controlled trial. *Developmental Medicine and Child Neurology, 30*, 626–631.

Mehegan, J. E., Masek, B. J., Harrison, R. H., Russo, D. C., & Leviton, A. (1984). *Behavioral treatment of pediatric headache.* Unpublished manuscript, Boston Children's Hospital, Boston, MA.

Melzack, R., & Katz, J. (1992). The McGill Pain Questionnaire: Appraisal and current status. In D. C. Turk & R. Melzack (Eds.), *Handbook of pain assessment* (pp. 152–168). New York: Guilford Press.

Michultka, D. M., Blanchard, E. B., Appelbaum, K. A., Jaccard, J., & Dentinger, M. P. (1989). The refractory headache patient—II. High medication consumption (analgesic rebound) headache. *Behaviour Research and Therapy, 27*(4), 411–420.

Mitchell, C. S., Osborn, R. E., & Grosskreutz, S. R. (1993). Computed tomography in the headache patient: Is routine evaluation really necessary? *Headache, 33*, 82–86.

Mizener, D., Thomas, M., & Billings, R. (1988). Cognitive changes of migraineurs receiving biofeedback training. *Headache, 28*, 339–343.

Morrill, B., & Blanchard, E. B. (1989). Two studies of the potential mechanisms of action in the thermal biofeedback treatment of vascular headache. *Headache, 29*, 169–176.

Morrill, B., Blanchard, E. B., Barron, K. D., & Dentinger, M. P. (1990). Neurological evaluation of chronic headache patients: Is laboratory testing always necessary? *Biofeedback and Self-Regulation, 15*(1), 27–35.

Moss, R. A., Ruff, M. H., & Sturgis, E. T. (1984). Oral behavioral patterns in facial pain, headache and non-headache populations. *Behaviour Research and Therapy, 22*(6), 683–687.

Murphy, A. I., Lehrer, P. M., & Jurish, S. (1990). Cognitive coping skills training and relaxation training as treatments for tension headaches. *Behavior Therapy, 21*, 89–98.

Nattero, G., De Lorenzo, C., Biale, L., Allais, G., Torre, E., & Ancona, M. (1989). Psychological aspects of weekend headache sufferers in comparison with migraine patients. *Headache, 29*, 93–99.

Nattero, G., De Lorenzo, C., Biale, L., Torrie, E., & Ancona, M. (1986). Idiopathic headaches: Relationship to life events. *Headache, 26*, 503–508.

Nevins, B. G., & Schwartz, M. S. (1985, April 12–17). An alternative placement for EMG electrodes in the study and biofeedback treatment of tension headaches. *Proceedings of the 16th Annual Meeting of the Biofeedback Society of America, New Orleans* (pp. 100–104). Wheatridge, CO: Association for Applied Psychophysiology and Biofeedback.

O'Farrell, T. J., & Keuthen, N. J. (1983). Readability of behavior therapy self-help manuals. *Behavior Therapy, 14*(3), 449–454.

O'Grady, S. J. (1987). Changes in medical utilization after biofeedback treatment for headache: Long-term follow-up (Doctoral dissertation, Pacific Graduate School of Psychology, Menlo Park, CA). *Dissertation Abstracts International, 49*, 49-01B (University Microfilms, No. 88-03939).

Olesen, J. (1988). Classification and diagnostic criteria for headache disorders, cranial neuralgias, and facial pain (1st ed.). *Cephalalgia, 8*(Suppl. 7), 1–96.

Packard, R., & Andrasik, F. (1989a). *Psychological aspects of headache in adults and children.* Manual for workshop presented at the 20th Annual Meeting of the Association for Applied Psychophysiology and Biofeedback, San Diego, March 17–22.

Packard, R., & Andrasik, F. (1989b). *Posttraumatic headache.* Short course presented at the 20th Annual Meeting of the Association of Applied Psychophysiology and Biofeedback, San Diego, March 17–22.

Padawer, W. J., & Levine, F. M. (1992). Exercise-induced analgesia: Fact or artifact? *Pain, 48*, 131–135.

Passchier, J., Schouten, J., van der Donk, J., & van Romunde, L. K. J. (1991). The association of frequent headaches with personality and life events. *Headache, 31*, 116–121.

Passchier, J., van den Bree, M. B. M., Emmen, H. H., Osterhaus, S. O. L., Orlebeke, J. F., & Verhage, F. (1990). Relaxation training in school classes does not reduce headache complaints. *Headache, 30*, 660–664.

Penzien, D. B., Holroyd, K. A., Holm, J. E., & Hursey, K. G. (1985). Psychometric characteristics of the Bakal Headache Assessment Questionnaire. *Headache, 25*, 55–58.

Pfaffenrath, V., Dandekar, R., & Pollman, W. (1987). Cervicogenic headache—the clinical picture, radiological findings and hypotheses on its pathophysiology. *Headache, 27*(9), 495–499.

Philips, C. (1976). Headache and personality. *Journal of Psychosomatic Research, 20*, 535–542.

Philips, C. (1977). The modification of tension headache pain using EMG biofeedback. *Behaviour Research and Therapy, 15*, 119–129.

Philips, H. C., & Hunter, M. S. (1982). A psychophysiological investigation of tension headache. *Headache, 22*, 173–179.

Philips, H. C., & Jahanshahi, M. (1986). The components of pain behavior report. *Behaviour Research and Therapy, 24*, 117–125.

Pritchard, D. W. (1989). EMG cranial muscle levels in headache sufferers before and during headache. *Headache, 29*, 103–108.

Pritchard, D. W., & Wood, M. M. (1983). [MG levels in the occipitofrontalis muscles under an experimental stress condition. *Biofeedback and Self-Regulation, 8*(1), 165–175.

Radnitz, C. L. (1990). Food-triggered migraine: A critical review. *Annals of Behavioral Medicine, 12*(2), 51–71.

Radnitz, C. L., & Blanchard, E. B. (1991). Assessment and treatment of dietary factors in refractory vascular headache. *Headache Quarterly, Current Treatment and Research, 2*(3), 214–220.

Rapoport, A. M. (1988). Analgesic rebound headache. *Headache, 28*, 662–665.

Rapoport, A. M., Sheftell, F. D., Weeks, R. E., & Baskin, S. M. (1983). Analgesic rebound headache. In *Proceedings of the 12th meeting of the Scandanavian Migraine Society*, 37–88.

Rapoport, A. M., Weeks, R. E., Sheftell, F. D., Baskin, S. M., & Verdi, J. (1985). Analgesic rebound headache: Theoretical and practical implications. *Cephalalgia, 5*(Suppl. 3), 448–449.

Rappaport, N. B., McAnulty, D. P., Waggoner, C. D., & Brantley, P. J. (1987). Cluster analysis of Minnesota Multiphasic Personality Inventory (MMPI) profiles in a chronic headache population. *Journal of Behavioral Medicine, 10*(1), 49–60.

Rasmussen, B. K., Jensen, R., & Olesen, J. (1991). Questionnaire versus clinical interview in the diagnosis of headache. *Headache, 31*, 290–295.

Reik, L. Jr., & Hale, M. (1981). The temporomandibular joint pain–dysfunction syndrome: A frequent cause of headache. *Headache, 21*(4), 151–156.

Reinking, R. H., & Hutching, D. (1981). Follow-up to: "Tension headaches: What form of therapy is most effective?" *Biofeedback and Self-Regulation, 6*(1), 57–62.

Richardson, G. M., & McGrath, P. J. (1989). Cognitive-behavioral therapy for migraine headaches: A minimal-therapist-contact approach versus a clinic-based approach. *Headache, 29*, 352–357.

Richter, I. L., McGrath, P. J., Humphreys, P. J., Goodman, J. T., Firestone, P., & Keene, D. (1986). Cognitive and relaxation treatment of paediatric migraine. *Pain, 25*, 195–203.

Robinson, M. E., Geisser, M. E., Dieter, J. N., & Swerdlow, B. (1991). The relationship between MMPI cluster membership and diagnostic category in headache patients. *Headache, 31*, 111–115.

Robinson, M. E., Swimmer, G. I., & Rallof, D. (1989). The P-A-I-N MMPI classification system: A critical review. *Pain, 37*, 211–214.

Ruff, M., Sturgis, E. T., & St. Lawrence, J. S. (1986, November). *EMG levels in tension headache sufferers: Does position make a difference?* Paper presented at the 1986 Annual Meeting of the Association for Advancement of Behavior Therapy, Chicago.

Rugh, J. D., Hatch, J. P., Moore, P. J., Cyr-Provost, M., Boutros, N. N., & Pellegrino, C. S. (1990). The effect of psychological stress on electromyographic activity and negative affect in ambulatory tension-type headache patients. *Headache, 30*, 216–219.

Sahota, P. K., & Dexter, J. D. (1990). Sleep and headache syndromes: A clinical review. *Headache, 30*, 80–84.

Sanders, S. H., & Collins, F. (1981). The effect of electrode placement on frontalis EMG measurement in headache patients. *Biofeedback and Self-Regulation, 6*, 473–482.

Saper, J. R., Silberstein, S., Gordon, C. D., & Hamel, R. L. (1993). *Handbook of headache management*. Baltimore: Williams & Wilkins.

Schoenen, J., Gerard, P., De Pasqua, V., & Juprelle, M. (1991). EMG activity in pericranial muscles during postural variation and mental activity in healthy volunteers and patients with chronic tension-type headache. *Headache, 31*, 321–324.

Shellenberger, R., Amar, P., Schneider, C., & Stewart, R. (1989). *Clinical efficacy and cost effectiveness of biofeedback therapy: Guidelines for third party reimbursement.* Wheatridge, CO: Association for Applied Psychophysiology and Biofeedback.

Schlote, B. (1989). Long term registration of muscle tension among office workers suffering from tension headache. In C. Bischoff, H. Traue, & H. Zenz (Eds.), *Clinical perspectives on headache and low back pain.* New York: Hogrefe.

Schwartz, G. E. (1977). Psychosomatic disorders and biofeedback: A psychobiological model of disregulation. In J. D. Maser & M. E. P. Seligman (Eds.), *Psychopathology: Experimental models.* San Francisco: W. H. Freeman.

Schwartz, G. E. (1978). Psychobiological foundations of psychotherapy and behavior change. In S. L. Garfield & A. E. Bergin (Eds.), *Handbook of psychotherapy and behavior change: An empirical analysis* (2nd ed.). New York: Wiley.

Schwartz, M. S. (Ed.). (in press). *Patient education: A practitioner's guide.* New York: Guilford Press.

Schwartz, M. S., Osborne, D., & Krupp, N. E. (1972). Moderating effects of age and sex on the association of medical diagnoses and 1–3/3–1 MMPI profiles. *Journal of Clinical Psychology, 28*(4), 502–505.

Shading, D. I., & Kleinman, K. M. (1977). Lack of correlation between frontalis EMG and either neck EMG or verbal ratings of tension. *Psychophysiology, 14,* 182–186.

Sherman, R. A., & Arena, J. G. (1992). Biofeedback in the assessment and treatment of low back pain. In J. Basmajian & R. Nyberg (Eds.), *Spinal manipulative therapies* (pp. 177–197). Baltimore: Williams & Wilkins.

Sherman, R. A., Arena, J. G., Searle, J. R., & Ginther, J. R. (1991). Development of an ambulatory recorder for evaluation of muscle-tension related low back pain and fatigue in soldier's normal environments. *Military Medicine, 156*(5), 245–248.

Sherman, R. A., Evans, C., & Arena, J. G. (1993). Environmental–temporal relationships between pain and muscle tension: Ramifications for the future of biofeedback treatment. In M. Shtark & T. Sokhadze (Eds.), *Biofeedback—2: Theory and practice* (pp. 108–114). Moscow, Russia: Nauka. (Russian with English abstract)

Silberstein, S. D. (1990). Twenty questions about headaches in children and adolescents. *Headache, 30,* 716–724.

Silberstein, S. D. (1992). Menstrual migraine (Guest Editorial). *Headache, 30*(6), 312–313.

Sjaastad, O., Fredriksen, T. A., & Pfaffenrath, V. (1990). Cervicogenic headache: Diagnostic criteria. *Headache, 30*(11), 725–726.

Sjaastad, O., & Stovner, L. J. (1993). The IHS classification for common migraine. Is it ideal? *Headache, 33*(7), 372–375.

Solbach, P., Sargent, J., & Coyne, L. (1984a). Menstrual migraine headache: Results of a controlled, experimental outcome study of nondrug treatments. *Headache, 24,* 75–78.

Solbach, P., Sargent, J., & Coyne, L. (1984b). An analysis of home practice patterns for non-drug headache treatments. *Headache, 29,* 528–531.

Solbach, P., Sargent, J., & Coyne, L. (1989). An analysis of home practice patterns for non-drug headache treatments. *Headache, 29,* 528–531.

Solomon, G. D., Kunkel, R. S., & Frame, J. (1990). Demographics of headache in elderly patients. *Headache, 30,* 273–276.

Sovak, M., Kunzel, M., Sternbach, R. A., & Dalessio, D. J. (1978). Is volitional manipulation of hemodynamics a valid rationale for biofeedback therapy of migraine? *Headache, 18,* 197–202.

Sovak, M., Kunzel, M., Sternbach, R. A., & Dalessio, D. J. (1981). Mechanism of the biofeedback therapy of migraine: Volitional manipulation of the psychophysiological background. *Headache, 21,* 89–92.

Sternbach, R. A. (1974). *Pain patients: Traits and treatments.* New York: Academic Press.

Sternbach, R. A., Dalessio, D. J., Kunzel, M., & Bowman, G. E. (1980). MMPI patterns in common headache disorders. *Headache, 20,* 311–315.

Sturgis, E. T., & Arena, J. G. (1984). Psychophysiological assessment. In M. Hersen, P. Miller, & R. M. Eisler (Eds.), *Progress in behavior modification* (Vol. 17, pp. 1–30). New York: Academic Press.

Sturgis, E. T., Schaefer, C. A., Ahles, T. A., & Sikora, T. L. (1984). Effects of movement and position in the evaluation of tension headache and nonheadache control subjects. *Headache, 24*(2), 88–93.

Sutton, E. P., & Belar, C. D. (1982). Tension headache patients versus controls: A study of EMG parameters. *Headache, 22*(3), 133–136.

Swanson, J. W. (1987). History, examination, and laboratory tests for headache. *Journal of Craniomandibular Disorders Facial and Oral Pain, 1*, 17–20.

Szekely, B., Botwin, D., Eidelman, B. H., Becker, M., Elman, N., & Schemm, R. (1986). Nonpharmacological treatment of menstrual headache: Relaxation-biofeedback behavior therapy and person-centered insight therapy. *Headache, 26*, 86–92.

Takeshima, T., Taniguchi, R., Kitagawa, R., & Takahashi, K. (1990). *Headache, 30*, 735–738.

Teders, S. J., Blanchard, E. B., Andrasik, F., Jurish, S. E., Neff, D. F., & Arena, J. G. (1984). Relaxation training for tension headache: Comparative efficacy and cost-effectiveness of a minimal therapist contact versus a therapist-delivered procedure. *Behavior Therapy, 15*, 59–70.

Thompson, J. K., & Figueroa, J. L. (1980). Dichotomous vs. interval rating of headache symptomatology: An investigation in the reliability of headache assessment. *Headache, 20*, 261–265.

Tobin, D. L., Holroyd, K. A., Baker, A., Reynolds, R. V. C., & Holm, J. E. (1988). Development and clinical trial of a minimal contact, cognitive–behavioral treatment for tension headaches. *Cognitive Therapy and Research, 12*, 325–339.

Travell, J. G., & Simons, D. G. (1983). *Myofacial pain and dysfunction: The trigger point manual.* Baltimore: Williams & Wilkins.

Vandecreek, L., & O'Donnell, F. (1992). Psychometric characteristics of the headache-specific Locus of Control Scale. *Headache, 32*, 239–241.

Werder, D. S., & Sargent, J. D. (1984). A study of childhood headache using biofeedback as a treatment alternative. *Headache, 24*, 122–126.

Werder, D. S., Sargent, J. D., & Coyne, L. (1981). MMPI profiles of headache patients using self-regulation to control headache activity. *Headache, 21*, 164–169.

Whatmore, G. B., Whatmore, N. J., & Fisher, L. D. (1981). Is frontalis activity a reliable indicator of the activity in other skeletel muscles? *Biofeedback and Self-Regulation, 6*(3), 305–314.

Williams, D. E., Raczynski, J. M., Domino, J., & Davig, J. P. (1993). Psychophysiological and MMPI personality assessment of headaches: An integrative approach. *Headache, 33*, 149–154.

Williams, D. E., Thompson, J. K., Haber, J. D., & Raczynski, J. M. (1986). MMPI and headache: A special focus on differential diagnosis, prediction of treatment outcome, and patient–treatment matching. *Pain, 24*, 143–158.

Williams, T. F. (1991). Health care trends for older people. *Biofeedback and Self-Regulation, 16*(4), 337–347.

Wisniewski, J. J., Genshaft, J. L., Mulick, J. A., Coury, D. L., & Hammer, D. (1988). Relaxation therapy and compliance in the treatment of adolescent headache. *Headache, 28*, 612–617.

TECHNICAL APPENDIX:
FOUR-CHANNEL ELECTRODE ASSEMBLY
FROM FIVE ELECTRODES
Michael J. Burke[5]
Mark S. Schwartz

This technical appendix describes an electrode assembly developed at the Mayo Clinic, Rochester. When monitoring four EMG channels, it decreases the number of electrodes from 12 to 5. This includes the one common ground electrode. This substantially reduces the time needed to attach the electrodes. We provide this technical information for interested readers.

Construction of the Five-Electrode Assembly

Figure 15A.1 depicts the wiring diagram. From each of the four electrodes, paired wires create four comparison recordings. These are A (1–2), B (2–3), C (3–4), and D (4–1). All comparisons use the one common ground electrode.

A photograph of the electrode cable, leads, and connection container is in Figure 15A.2. One should periodically test the integrity of the wiring with a standard test load board as shown in Figure 15A.3.

Construction of this electrode assembly is not practical for most practitioners. A practitioner should enlist the help of someone skilled in such technical electrical work or get help from a biofeedback instrument manufacturer or distributor.

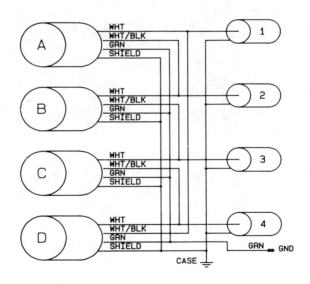

FIGURE 15A.1. EMG wiring diagram.

[5]Section of Engineering Development, Mayo Clinic Rochester.

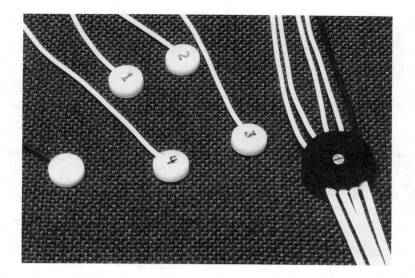

FIGURE 15A.2. Photograph of EMG cable, leads, and connection container.

FIGURE 15A.3. Four-point EMG test load (and ground).

16

Temporomandibular Disorders

Richard N. Gevirtz
Alan G. Glaros
Deborah Hopper
Mark S. Schwartz

Temporomandibular disorders (TMD), sometimes called TMJ disorders, are important disorders for dentistry, medicine, and psychology. TMD refers to disorders of the jaw muscles and the temporomandibular joint (TMJ), including associated facial, head, and neck pain. Dental professionals and other health professionals recognize psychological and emotional factors as playing key roles in the etiology, maintenance, and treatment of TMD disorders (Dworkin & LeResche, 1992). This creates an increasing role for clinicians using biofeedback in the treatment team for TMD. See Rugh (1983) for an overview of the subject and Taddey (1990) for a lay explanation. Excellent patient education is available from Aetna Health Plans and the National Institute of Dental Research.

Many fine reviews of the literature on psychological and psychophysiological aspects of TMD are available (Glaros & Glass, 1993; Flor & Turk, 1989). This chapter presents data on TMD that can help practitioners using biofeedback understand the relationship between psychological, behavioral, or emotional factors and TMD symptoms. This understanding should then serve as a basis for treatment appropriate to the underlying pathogenesis.

ANATOMY AND PHYSIOLOGY OF THE TMJ AND ASSOCIATED MUSCULATURE

We begin with a brief description of the anatomy and physiology of the TMJ and its associated musculature. Practitioners need to have this knowledge for understanding diagnosis and for treating people with TMD (Okeson, 1989). Readers should see Glaros and Glass (1993) and Taddey (1990) for drawings of the anatomy involved.

The major structures of the TMJ include the *condyle*, the *articular disc*, the *articular fossa*, and the associated membranes, fluids, and ligaments. The condyles arise from the U-shaped mandible and are within the *glenoid fossa* located directly in front of the ears. Assisting condylar movement is the articular disc. The disc is made up of dense fibrous connective tissue and lacks nerves and blood supply. These structures and the associated muscles provide for normal functions of the teeth and jaw.

Normal functioning of the TMJ is unusual for a joint in that it involves two components to its movement. When the jaw initially opens, the joint works on a ball and socket principle in which the condyle rotates within the fossa. As the jaw continues to open, the condyle translates over a bony, articular eminence, or dislocates over a protruding process in the upper jaw. One can conveniently think of the articular disc as biological Teflon that makes the smooth, pain-free translation of the condyle past the eminence possible.

Many conditions can adversely affect the condyle. Degenerative disorders can lead to erosion and flattening of the condyle or form undesirable growths called bone spurs. Both conditions may result in decreased function, pain, or both. Alterations of normal disc function also may be present in TMD. These can include the temporary or permanent displacement (derangement) of the disc from its normal position, resulting in clicking, popping, or grinding noises upon opening or closing, or difficulty opening or closing the jaw (Bell, 1986; Taddey, 1990). Abnormal loads placed on the joint by clenching or grinding may cause these derangements (Laskin, 1992). A large proportion of the population experience TMJ noises. Although often very bothersome to individuals, they are generally not cause for concern in the absence of pain, limited range of motion, or changes in opening pattern (Glaros & Glass, 1993).

The most important muscles for jaw function are the masseter muscles, temporalis muscles, and lateral and medial pterygoids. The *masseter muscles* elevate the mandible during mastication. One can palpate the masseters by placing fingers slightly above the angle of the mandible—the point of the jaw—while the person clenches. The *temporalis muscles* also close the jaw and retract the mandible. One can palpate this muscle by placing fingers on one or both temples while the person clenches.

The *lateral (external) pterygoid muscle* protrudes and depresses the mandible and aids lateral movement to the opposite side. One normally palpates this muscle from within the mouth. The *medial (internal) pterygoids* close the jaw, produce lateral movement to the opposite side, and aid in protrusion. Like the external pterygoid, one normally palpates this muscle from inside the mouth. Other muscles that may be important in patients with TMD include the *sternomastoids, hyoids*, and *digastrics*. A wonderful sourcebook is the landmark work of Travell and Simons (1983) that details the basic anatomy and physiology of the masticatory, head, and cervical muscles.

Most cases of TMD involve myalgia (muscle pain) not involving any disturbance to the TMJ. This pain can arise for a variety of reasons. The most important reason is probably parafunctional clenching and grinding. Psychological stress can trigger these behaviors that often occur without awareness. They can occur during normal activities such as reading, watching television, or driving a car and can become a habit independent of circumstances.

Another pathway implicated in TMD involves parafunctional oral activity such as chewing gum, pencils and erasers, ice, and cheeks and lips (Moss, Sult, & Garrett, 1984). Work-related behaviors and ergonomic variables also can be involved in TMD. For example, raising a shoulder to hold a telephone receiver to an ear puts pressure against the TMJ and increases muscle tension primarily in the neck and shoulder. This can aggravate the problem and increase pain. Poor positioning of a computer keyboard or monitor can increase or maintain pain in TMD patients.

Travell and Simons (1983) propose that some or most chronic muscle pain is a result of trigger points. These are palpable taut bands of muscle tissue that are tender to palpation. There is a characteristic pattern of pain associated with active trigger points. Research shows that careful needle electrode techniques can detect high levels of EMG activity in the trigger point itself, where the adjacent nontender muscle is silent (Hubbard & Berkoff, 1993). Additionally, data recorded from the trigger point needle EMG electrode now show responses to psychological stress, while the adjacent nontender muscle is silent during this stress (McNulty, Gevirtz, Hubbard, & Berkoff, 1994).

Work by several investigators such as Passatore, Grassi, and Filippi (1985) shows that sympathetic pathways innervate the muscle spindle which is a proprioceptive component of muscle. However, little evidence exists for autonomic control of "extrafusal" or ordinary muscle fibers. These findings suggest that trigger points may be an important link between muscle pain of TMD and psychological stressors (Carlson, Okeson, Falace, Nitz, & Lindroth, 1993b). Sympathetically mediated trigger points associated with the muscle spindles might develop because of stress. Prolonged emotional factors, particularly anger, might maintain this.

This may help us to explain the link between behavioral or emotional factors and mechanisms of muscle pain. Research is under way to determine the exact process in the musculature responsible for muscle pain related to trigger points. However, it now appears that the sympathetic nervous system is involved in the innervation of trigger points and that emotions play a role through this pathway.

SYMPTOMS AND ETIOLOGY OF TMD

A patient with TMD may report a wide variety of oral conditions and painful disorders, including:

1. Accelerated wear on the dentition without other known causes.
2. Myofascial pain of the face, head, and neck without other known organic etiology.
3. Fractured or mobile teeth or defective restorations ("fillings") without other known causes.
4. Broken restorations.
5. Teeth-grinding noise disturbing to patient's spouse, other family members, or other sleeping partners or roommates.
6. Headaches, ear pain, tinnitus ("ringing" or "buzzing" in the ears), or dizziness without other known causes.
7. Derangements of the articular disc or other structures of the TMJ without other known etiology.
8. Hypertrophy and/or tenderness of the masticatory muscles.
9. TMJ pain without other known etiology.

In addition to dentists, it is not surprising that physicians and psychologists also often participate in evaluating and treating people who present with TMD symptoms. Psychologists' involvement in evaluating and treating patients with TMD stems from research support for stress being a major etiological and contributing factor to many TMD symptoms. Research also supports the benefits of psychological and biofeedback therapies in managing and treating these symptoms (e.g., Dalen, Ellertsen, Espelid, & Gronningsaeter, 1986).

The complicated nature of TMD requires that practitioners maintain a good working relationship with a dentist competent in TMD, and with other properly trained health professionals including neurologists, otorhinolaryngologists (ENTs), and rheumatologists. The symptoms of TMD can mimic a variety of physical conditions. Thus, proper assessment and early intervention for TMD may reduce individual and societal costs associated with the care of these patients. Furthermore, psychologists and other practitioners using biofeedback can assist other providers by pointing out the importance of myalgia in patients with TMD and the role that psychological and biofeedback-assisted therapies have for this disorder. Myalgia implies muscle problems, stress factors, and parafunctions. These are amenable to biofeedback and psychological interventions. Furthermore, psychologists and other practitioners can help other providers by showing the value of relaxation therapies, biofeedback, and other applied psychophysiological therapies for patients with TMD.

Our coverage of the etiologies of TMD addresses the roles of parafunctional activity, occlusion, psychological variables, psychophysiological variables, trauma, and abuse.

Parafunctional Activity

Clenching and grinding are parafunctional behaviors and both important causes and aggravating factors for TMD symptoms. Clenching occurs both during the day and at night, whereas grinding typically occurs at night (Glaros & Melamed, 1992). Several studies investigated the sleeping EEGs of patients who engage in nocturnal parafunctional activities. Wruble, Lumley, and McGlynn (1989) present a thorough review of the subject. This nocturnal activity primarily occurs during Stage II sleep, REM sleep, and with sleep transitions to lighter stages, especially to Stages I and II. Rugh and Ware (1986) and Ware and Rugh (1988) suggested that this parafunction during REM sleep is very intense, more associated with facial pain, and also may be more destructive to the teeth. We can note that the relationship between EEG activity and nocturnal grinding and clenching is characterized by a great deal of individual variation. For this reason, group data are misleading. A thorough review can be found in McGlynn, Cassisi, and Diamond (1985) or Rugh and Harlan (1988).

Occlusion

Malocclusion is the relative failure of the upper and lower teeth to fit together properly. Occlusal theories of the cause of TMD remain popular among many dentists. The dental literature contains a variety of clinical reports indicating the importance of malocclusion. For example, one author states that "it has been shown experimentally and observed innumerable times clinically that occlusal interferences may precipitate" clenching and grinding and that these behaviors "can be alleviated or eliminated by correction of occlusal disharmony" (Mohl, 1979, p. 190).

However, more recent reviews strongly suggest that occlusion plays a minor role at best (Glaros & Glass, 1993; Seligman & Pullinger, 1991). Epidemiological studies suggest that deviations from ideal occlusion are statistically normal in both child and adult populations (Kirveskari, Alanen, & Jämsä, 1992; Ramfjord & Ash, 1983). For example, over 95% of 5- and 10-year-old children showed occlusal interferences in one study (Kirveskari et al., 1992). Furthermore, there is no compelling experimental evidence to support the hypothesis that occlusal disharmony causes teeth clenching and grinding behaviors (Bell, 1986).

Psychological Variables

Some researchers and practitioners theorize a significant relationship between TMD and particular personality variables and posit that these variables must therefore play an etiological role. Glaros and Rao (1977) reviewed much of the early literature and concluded that the evidence does not support the existence of a personality type that is more prone to clenching and grinding. Further discussion of the topic may be found in Moss, Garrett, and Chiodo (1982) and Carlson et al. (1993a).

Glaros and Rao (1977) also noted that the directionality of effect can work both ways. Behaviors can lead to pain symptoms that in turn may promote changes in other behaviors, moods, and personality variables. Many studies show that patients with TMD have significantly more depressive symptoms than normal controls. Although there is more depression compared to normal controls, most of these patients do not show clinically significant depression. One study reported 30% of patients with TMDs showing evidence of major depression based on a structured clinical interview (Kinney, Gatchel, Ellis, & Holt, 1992). Wright, Deary, and Geissler (1991) reported only 13.5% of their patients with TMDs had clinically elevated depression scores on the Beck Depression Inventory (BDI).

Psychophysiological Variables

The psychophysiological approach to TMD muscle pain symptoms suggests that people react to stress with different bodily systems. Some react via the head and neck muscles, and some of these become TMD patients (Kapel, Glaros, & McGlynn, 1989; Laskin, 1969; Rugh & Solberg, 1976; Zarb & Carlsson, 1979).

Many studies report that patients with TMD show more intense facial muscle activity responses to experimental stressors (Clarke & Gevirtz, 1991; Flor, Birbaumer, Schulte, & Roos, 1991; Flor, Birbaumer, Schugens, & Lutzenberger, 1992; Kapel et al., 1989; Mercuri, Olson, & Laskin, 1979; Moss & Adams, 1984; Rao & Glaros, 1979). Other research suggests that these patients may have deficits in muscle discrimination abilities (Flor, Schugens, & Birbaumer, 1992). However, the evidence in favor of chronically elevated postural tone or unconscious bracing of muscles in TMD is sparse (Carlson et al., 1993b; Flor & Turk, 1989).

Many studies have also documented a relationship between stress and nocturnal clenching and grinding (Rugh, 1975; Rugh & Solberg, 1975; Clark, Rugh, Handelman, & Beemsterboer, 1977; Clark, Rugh, & Handelman, 1980; Funch & Gale, 1980; Hopper, Gevirtz, Nigl, & Taddey, 1992). Funch and Gale (1980) were among the first researchers to point out the importance of anticipatory anxiety rather than stressful life events in clenching and grinding. In our work (Hopper et al., 1992), we found that the degree to which subjects worried or were anxious about tomorrow's stressors predicted the amount of masticatory muscle activity each night. This has implications for clinical intervention, as we shall discuss later.

Trauma and Abuse

Physical trauma to the TMJ, whether by accident or deliberate abuse, is an important etiological factor in TMD. An emerging area of research also suggests that a considerable proportion of these patients suffered from emotional or sexual abuse during childhood (Harness & Donlon, 1988; Harness, Donlon, & Eversole, 1990). Studies suggest that patients with histories of abuse are likely to present with a variety of physical and psychological problems (Browne & Finkelhor, 1986; Cunningham, Pearce, & Pearce, 1988; Finkelhor et al., 1986). The nature of the complaints from the patient who repeatedly seeks medical care, despite lack of clear pathophysiology, appears to represent a disguised form of help-seeking (Drossman et al., 1990).

The important point for our discussion is that practitioners must be alert to the possibility that the patient is not going to respond to a dental/behavioral treatment in the ways outlined below. Instead, biofeedback may serve as a "Trojan horse" (Wicramsekera, 1988). Many patients view biofeedback as a medical treatment and not strictly a psychological treatment. Therefore, it may attract those patients who would otherwise reject psychological interpretations for their symptoms. However, once the patient is in the office, the rapport established between provider and patient might allow the patient an opportunity to discuss his or her traumatic past. Prudent clinicians need training to evaluate and treat such problems or need to refer such patients to someone who can.

ASSESSMENT

Assessing the effectiveness of treatment for nocturnal clenching or grinding involves both self-report and EMG data. We (R.G. & D.H.) use small, EMG devices we (D.H.) built that store cumulative data over several hours based on the design reported by Burgar and Rugh (1983). This device, while slightly cumbersome, adds objectivity to the assessment of treatment outcomes. Most patients are unwilling to wear a portable EMG monitoring device during daytime hours. Thus, checking the effects of treatment for daytime clenching typically involves only self-report measures.

Self-report measures for pain are useful (Karoly & Jensen, 1987). Self-report measures of symptoms specific to TMD also may be useful. Examples are clenching, grinding, joint mobility, and noise. These measures should be used cautiously because patients are often initially unaware of their parafunctional behaviors (Glaros & Glass, 1993). As patients become more aware of their parafunctional behaviors, they may report more of these behaviors. This increase may reflect greater awareness of the behaviors but not reflect treatment failure. The practitioner should consider using visual analogue scales daily to assess muscle pain symptoms. This includes scales dealing with chronic aching pain, pain with function, and morning pain.

TREATMENT

Based on the above, it is important to target treatment toward the mechanisms thought to underlie the symptoms. For example, if the practitioner thinks grinding or clenching of teeth is the primary cause of symptoms, he or she should target treatment at that particular problem. However, if the practitioner thinks the symptoms are primarily myogenic in origin and unrelated to grinding or clenching, then he or she should aim treatment at muscular relaxation. Sometimes, reported symptoms seem to arise more from an overreaction to normal physiological events. In these cases, the therapist might consider a cognitive-behavioral approach.

Dental

The most common dental treatment for TMD is a hard "interocclusal" appliance or mouthguard called an intraoral splint that covers the maxillary or mandibular teeth. The device prevents grinding behavior from causing additional damage to the teeth but does not always reduce the amount of grinding. For clenching, the device reduces masticatory muscle activity (Clark, Beemsterboer, Solberg, & Rugh, 1979) and spreads the forces associated with the remaining activity over a larger area of the teeth, typically resulting in reduced pain (Holmgren, Sheikholeslam, & Riise, 1993).

Occlusal adjustment treatment involves "equilibration" or adjustment of the fit between the upper and lower teeth. Dentists accomplish this by selectively grinding the teeth to fit better. However, research indicates that occlusal factors do not typically contribute to the etiology of TMD and occlusal adjustments are seldom needed (Glass, Glaros, & McGlynn,

1993). Since the effects of equilibration are not reversible, current recommendations strongly discourage its use (American Academy of Orofacial Pain, 1993).

Behavioral

Behavioral treatments include cultivated low arousal and stress management, massed practice, alarm systems, and habit reversal.

Cultivated Low Arousal

Cultivated low arousal techniques such as biofeedback-assisted relaxation and stress management are widely used treatments for TMD. Many studies (Mealiea & McGlynn, 1987) indicate that using EMG biofeedback is an effective treatment for TMD. The most common sites for biofeedback involve the masseter, temporalis, or frontal areas, combined with other relaxation procedures or stress management (Glass et al., 1993). Treatment typically ranges from 6 to 12 sessions. Many patients need to learn to position the jaw and teeth properly. They also need to learn how mild, sustained tooth contact increases EMG activity in the temporalis and masseter muscles. Learning these skills helps patients progress quickly.

Verifying physiological data can be instructive to patients. For example, a multimodal psychophysiological stress profile can illustrate both the existence and extent of patients' psychophysiological responses to stressors. Showing patients their psychophysiological baseline, reactivity, and recovery data can be instructive to them. A multimodal psychophysiological assessment can illustrate patients' psychophysiological responses to stressors and recovery after stressors. This may involve multiple EMG sites such as frontal, temporalis, or masseter muscles. The more general frontal–posterior neck EMG placement may also be considered. This includes frontalis, cervical neck, temporalis, occipitalis, and sternomastoid muscles. (See Chapter 15 for a detailed discussion of this placement.)

Psychophysiological assessments also often include finger temperature, skin conductance, heart rate, and/or respiration rate and pattern. After a stabilization or adaptation period of several minutes, the practitioner should obtain a baseline of at least 5 minutes. Then one introduces stressors such as counting backwards by 7s from a large three-digit number and/or imagining a personal stressor for at least 3 minutes. Recovery periods of at least 3 minutes typically follow each stressor. Later, one may show the patterns of reactivity, lability, and recoveries to the patient. However, the EMG data from masticatory muscles should be excluded while patients are speaking. (See Chapter 7 for a detailed discussion of adaptation, baselines, reactivity, and recovery in psychophysiological assessments.)

For patients who engage in daytime clenching, a log of clenching events may suggest that certain persons, events, or situations are triggers for clenching.

A functional analysis of these stimuli suggests the need for assertiveness or anger-management therapy or other psychotherapy. For patients who clench or grind during sleep, relaxation procedures and cognitive-behavioral therapy procedures can reduce or stop ruminative thinking prior to sleep. Patients should continue evaluation of their complaints of pain and other jaw problems throughout treatment and periodically supplement this by proper assessments by the dentist.

Interventions include relaxed breathing, audiotaped relaxation, biofeedback-assisted muscle and temperature relaxation as indicated, and cognitive stress inoculation as indicated. Relaxation procedures include muscle relaxation, autogenic procedures, imagery, or combinations (Gevirtz, 1987). Cognitive interventions should focus on anticipated stressors (Hopper et al., 1992).

After patients show low arousal in the therapist's office, the therapist can use procedures to generalize the low arousal to the daily environments and activities. Patients use stress management methods to maintain awareness, manage stress, and maintain lowered arousal in daily life. These methods include relaxation reminders such as colored, adhesive dots and cognitive techniques.

Specific Muscle Training

The masseters are the common targets for relaxation. Practitioners often use EMG biofeedback to enhance masseter relaxation or to enhance general relaxation. Mealiea and McGlynn (1987) reviewed the scientific evidence for masseter biofeedback. Several studies since then also support the use of EMG feedback from masseter muscles for the treatment of TMD-related pain (Flor & Birbaumer, 1993; Crocket, Foreman, Alden, & Blasberg, 1986). However, the role and value of masseter feedback need more research (McGlynn et al., 1990).

Another view focuses on the lateral pterygoids as the muscle of interest. Scott and Lundeen (1980) show that overuse of this muscle through excessive protrusion can reproduce pain patterns identical to those often reported by TMD patients. Furthermore, during physical examination with these patients, this muscle is often highly sensitive to palpation. Gevirtz (1990) described an intraoral EMG device for recording from this hard-to-reach muscle.

Studies suggest that biofeedback-based treatments for TMD offer a competitive alternative to regular dental or pharmacological approaches (Crockett et al., 1986; Hijzen, Slangen, & VanHouweligen, 1986; McGlynn et al., 1990). For example, Dahlström, Carlsson and Carlsson (1982) compared EMG biofeedback to splints. Both groups improved with treatment, with maximal mouth opening improving only in the biofeedback group. Furthermore, a 1-year follow-up (Dahlström & Carlsson, 1984) showed that both groups maintained their gains. Turk, Zaki, and Rudy (1993) reported that stress management techniques provided less short-term reduction of TMD pain than using dental splints. However, longer-term follow-up suggested that patients receiving combined dental and stress management techniques fared better.

The mechanism by which biofeedback works is not clearly understood. Studies show that TMD patients receiving biofeedback typically show decreases in facial muscle activity and decreases in self-reported pain (e.g., Burdette & Gale, 1988). One hypothesis suggests that biofeedback works directly by promoting decreased EMG activity that, in turn, is responsible for the reduction in self-reported pain. However, an indirect challenge to this hypothesis comes from experimental studies showing that jaw pain markedly subsides seconds after subjects cease sustained maximum clenching (Christensen, 1979).

In none of the studies reported to date were TMD patients specifically selected for high baseline levels of EMG, nor did any reach a criterion level of EMG activity considered normal (cf., Shellenberger & Green, 1986, 1987). If biofeedback works because of reductions in EMG activity, then patients with elevated baseline levels of EMG activity would most likely benefit from biofeedback, especially if they reached and maintained this criterion level of EMG activity.

An alternative hypothesis for the efficacy of biofeedback suggests that using biofeedback helps patients develop general relaxation skills and better coping strategies. Many of the biofeedback studies incorporate relaxation training (Funch & Gale, 1984; Gale, 1979) or some type of cognitive awareness or stress management techniques into the treatment program (e.g., Burdette & Gale, 1988; Crockett et al., 1986). Biofeedback also may increase the patient's awareness of tension (Dalen et al., 1986). For example, becoming aware of daytime clenching might be sufficient to produce desirable changes.

Massed Negative Practice

"Massed negative practice" is the term for scheduling deliberate and repeated jaw clenching. A few studies show that this can reduce subsequent nocturnal, EMG-measured jaw activity (Rugh & Solberg, 1974). Unfortunately, the procedure also exposes patients to the risk of broken teeth, increased pain, and more severe TMD. We cannot recommend this procedure considering the limited evidence for it and its aversive nature.

Alarm Systems

A sleep-interruption alarm called a nocturnal alarm may help patients who clench and/or grind during sleep. A nocturnal alarm monitors EMG activity from a masseter or temporalis muscle as the patient sleeps. An alarm sounds when EMG activity exceeds a threshold for a specified time or when a certain number of suprathreshold EMG events occur within a brief period. During treatment with nocturnal alarms, patients typically show reductions in nocturnal EMG events, particularly when sounding of the alarm is associated with a task that requires wakefulness (Cassisi, McGlynn, & Belles, 1987). Follow-up data suggest that the efficacy of nocturnal alarms may be limited to the active treatment period (see also Hudzinski & Walters, 1986; Cassisi & McGlynn, 1988; Hudzinski & Lawrence, 1992).

The use of alarm systems may result in sleep disturbance at least until the procedures significantly suppress the nocturnal bruxing activity. Some patients may experience rebound effects. Thus, after stopping the use of the alarm system, patients may experience higher levels of clenching or grinding (Cassisi et al., 1987). Practitioners need to be aware that most commercially available devices for nocturnal monitoring of TMD-relevant EMG activity cannot discriminate parafunctional clenching and grinding from normal swallowing or gross motor activities that may occur during sleep (e.g., turning over in bed). Current limitations in battery life make it difficult to monitor all night for multiple nights. Clinicians and researchers can select between devices that sample EMG activity at fixed intervals, that "wake up" when EMG activity exceeds a preset threshold, or that record continuously for limited periods of time—usually no more than a few hours. One can usually monitor from only one EMG site with a single device, and it is difficult to assess the meaningfulness of the data obtained by such devices (Biedermann, 1984; Burdette & Gale, 1990; Hatch, Prihoda, & Moore, 1992).

These limitations curtailed the widespread clinical use of alarm systems. Some practitioners use a small portable EMG device with a threshold for auditory feedback (alarm) set to sound above a preset level such as 20 microvolts. They instruct patients to complete a task requiring wakefulness and to relax their jaw muscles each time the alarm sounds. An intermittent schedule of feedback may produce more enduring results (Hudzinski & Walters, 1986).

Clark and his colleagues recently reported on the use of mild electrical shock to the upper lip as the contingent feedback (Clark, Koyano, & Browne, 1993). When this system was used during sleep, heart rate and respiration did not change, but there was considerable reduction of activity of masticatory muscles. Data on the endurance of the effect are not yet available. However, if favorable, they would represent a promising feedback approach to nocturnal clenching and grinding.

Habit Reversal

Habit reversal (Azrin & Nunn, 1973, 1977) may be a useful technique for managing daytime clenching. This technique involves detecting the preclench state, substituting an incompatible behavior in the place of clenching, and having subjects overlearn this response in every stimulus situation where clenching might occur (Rosenbaum & Ayllon, 1981). This usually involves office monitoring, coaching, and lots of practice between sessions. Therapists should encourage patients to keep their lips together and their teeth apart. Also, they should place the tip of the tongue gently between the front teeth.

A STRATEGY FOR TREATING THE TMD PATIENT

Our approach to treating the TMD patient involves stepped care, beginning with assessment and moving to various treatment modalities. The following serves as a guide for each segment of assessment and treatment.

I. General assessment
   A. Rule out other medical factors (Glaros & Glass, 1993; Glaros & Rao, 1977).
   B. Obtain dental consultation to assess the condition of the TMJ and masticatory musculature. If information from the dentist does not include information about the patient's response to muscle palpation, and if you have proper credentials and training, consider performing palpation. Consider asking the dentist to perform this. See Dworkin and LeResche (1992) for specific directions for performing such palpations.
   C. Obtain a detailed history of the condition, including prior treatments.
   D. Assess psychological, psychophysiological, and behavioral patterns that might be salient.
   E. Obtain relevant self-monitoring data, including daytime logs of clenching or presleep cognitive logs that target worrying, rumination, and dysfunctional cognitions.

II. Psychosocial and behavioral assessment. Assess and determine the amount of:
   A. Depression.
   B. Sleep disturbance, including sleep-onset and sleep-maintenance insomnia.
   C. Obsessive or ruminative worrying.
   D. Anxiety.
   E. Daily/weekly life stressors.
   F. Parafunctional clenching and grinding.
   G. Other parafunctional oral habits such as chewing ice, biting fingernails, and chewing gum.
   H. Adequacy of skills to cope with situational stressors.
   I. Reinforcers for pain.
   J. Other relevant factors.

III. Psychophysiological assessment
    Use psychophysiological assessment to detect salient modalities for cultivating low arousal, reducing reactivity, and improving recoveries after stress. Assess patients' attributions about their symptoms. This is important to shape their beliefs about TMJ

dysfunction versus occlusion versus psychophysiological muscle habits and reactivity to stress.

A. Recording from at least two muscle placement sites:
1. Masseters, bilateral, or one or both individually.
2. Temporalis, bilateral, or one or both individually.
3. Frontalis, bilateral.
4. Combination, including masseters.
5. Frontal–posterior neck.
B. Resting baseline assessment of facial and head muscles while reclining, sitting up, during manual tasks, etc.
C. Assessment of reactivity of facial and head muscles during office stress stimulation.
D. Assessment of recovery of facial and head muscles after stress stimulation.
E. If appropriate, sleep-time assessment, including nocturnal activity frequency, amplitudes, durations, and time of night.

IV. Patient education: Setting the stage for treatment

Confirm that the patient understands the basics of the explanation for the pain syndrome. Assure that the patient has an accurate understanding based on a version of the hyperactivity and/or trigger-point models. The patient must *think muscle*! Assess understanding by asking the patient to repeat the rationale for treatment. There will be limited or no treatment success if the patient continues to believe inaccurately that the pain is caused by a deteriorating jaw joint rather than stress-induced muscle tension. This is especially true for patients who continue to hear clicks, pops, and grinding sounds from their TMJ.

A. Describe the normal anatomy and physiology of the TMJ and associated muscles.
B. Describe the patient's data about the physical state of the TMJ and muscles.
C. Describe the effects of stress and parafunctional activities on the TMJ and muscles.
D. Describe the relationship between the assessment data and the proposed treatment.
E. Describe proposed treatment, and provide take-home pamphlets and other informational sources.
F. Assess patient's understanding of the disorder at the start of treatment and periodically during treatment. The patient should have a working model in mind for each treatment phase.

V. Initial treatment

A. Have dentist fabricate intraoral splint by dentist, if appropriate.
B. Use analgesics and/or tricyclic antidepressants for management of pain, if appropriate.
C. Demonstrate effects of parafunctional activities on masticatory muscles.
D. Begin office-based EMG feedback from masseters, temporalis, and/or frontal–posterior neck placements. Include resting, stressor, and activity reactivity and recovery. Include relaxation procedures for daily use. Consider relaxation tape.

Start with either temporalis or masseter muscles. Use the "rule of thirds" to place the electrodes over a masseter muscle. Use the anterior portion of a temporalis muscle. If using one channel, consider placing an active electrode on opposite sides of the face and the reference electrode under the chin (Rugh & Lemke, 1984). This placement may be satisfactory, but it cannot distinguish right from left. If one suspects asymmetry, consider two channels with one set of electrodes on each side. Teach the patient to find jaw positions that maximize relaxation of the masticatory muscles. Instruct the patient to slowly open his or her mouth as if to eat a small piece of food. This usually produces the lowest EMG readings. Then use other maneuvers until the patient can easily relax the jaw.

Use feedback thresholds to help the patient achieve very low levels of muscle activity in this region. Consider this early in treatment. It may take only one session or much longer.

Consider EMG feedback from unilateral or bilateral frontal–posterior neck placement.[1] Consider bilateral if one has multiple EMG channels. This wide placement requires general relaxation of several muscles in the head and neck including frontalis, temporalis, masseters, and several neck muscles.

Consider using bilateral, dual-channel, "dynamic EMG feedback." Some practitioners use this to help patients develop symmetrical muscle activity. This assumes that significantly more tension exists on one side than the other and is contributing to dysfunctional muscle tension patterns. Consider doing this in different body positions and during simulated tasks. We know of no research with this procedure, but it is a logical and currently accepted clinical practice.

VI. Second-step treatment if the first stage is not adequate
    A. Cognitive therapies focusing usually on anger management.
    B. More EMG feedback sessions, incorporating additional facial and cervical muscles.

Cognitive therapies are often used for selected patients for whom the preceeding treatments were not satisfactory. Focusing on issues of anger management, assertion, and avoiding confrontation is often critical when treating people with muscle tension disorders. Help patients become aware of and change dysfunctional beliefs about not being assertive or angry. This can allow for gradual changes in behavior and reduce chronic self-depreciating rumination. The use of these procedures requires proper professional credentials and training.

Patients often are seeing other treating professionals at the same time you are treating them. For example, patients are often in treatment with chiropractors or physical therapists when they come for biofeedback. Taddey (1990) offers a lay description of the various modalities used by physical therapists and others.

Treatment in conjunction with biofeedback is most effective when the health care provider concentrates on muscles or trigger points as described by Travell and Simons (1983). Be careful that different concurrent therapies are not confounding your therapies and evaluations. Discussion with the other treating professionals and coordination of treatment are often prudent.

VII. Third-step treatment if above is not adequate
    A. More extensive cognitive therapy.
    B. Alarm system, if appropriate.
    C. Re-evaluation of presenting complaints.

When the above treatments are insufficient, seriously reconsider the initial diagnosis of TMD or reconsider the treatments. For example, examine more closely

---

[1]See Chapter 15 for discussion of this placement.

the possible roles of dysfunctional family or marital relationships, prior sexual and physical abuse, and "secondary gain."

CONCLUSION

Biofeedback and other applied psychophysiological therapies have a place in the treatment of temporomandibular disorders. Working closely with dentists and other health professionals is critical to increase treatment effectiveness. This chapter emphasizes the importance of identifying proposed mechanisms that play an important role in the etiology of TMD symptoms and matching treatments to these mechanisms. Research suggests that the behavioral and psychological interventions presented in this chapter can be effective in treating these patients. Most patients will experience considerable relief from their symptoms if they conscientiously use these techniques.

GLOSSARY

ALARM SYSTEMS. Sleep interruption biofeedback from a masseter and/or temporalis muscle with a loud auditory stimulus contingent on clenching and grinding of teeth when it exceeds a preset threshold of intensity, duration, and/or frequency. Potentially useful but with limitations. (See Chapter 25 for an example of a highly useful form of sleep-interruption biofeedback for nocturnal enuresis.)

ARTICULAR DISC. Articular refers to a joint. The TMJ articular disc assists movement of the condyle and pads or absorbs shock. It is a dense fibrous connective tissue lacking nerves and blood supply. In the TM joint, it is between the ball and socket.

ARTICULAR FOSSA. The TMJ socket part of the temporal bone.

COGNITIVE THERAPIES. Behavioral therapies involving becoming aware of and changing dysfunctional beliefs and self-statements.

CONDYLES. Bony structures arising from the U-shaped mandible and within the *glenoid fossa*. The ball in a ball-and-socket-type joint. Located directly in front of the ears and on top of the jawbone.

CULTIVATED LOW AROUSAL. Various psychophysiological methods, usually various relaxation methods, to move toward and achieve a state of low psychophysiological arousal.

DIGASTRIC MUSCLE. Raises hyoid bone and base of tongue and lowers mandible.

DYNAMIC EMG FEEDBACK. Multichannel EMG feedback during different body postures and simulated tasks.

EQUILIBRATION. Adjustment of the fit between the upper and lower teeth. Dentist accomplish this by selectively grinding the teeth to fit better.

EXTRAFUSAL MUSCLE FIBERS. Ordinary muscle fibers.

FRONTAL–POSTERIOR NECK PLACEMENT. Electrode placement for EMG recording. (See Chapters 14 and 15.)

HABIT REVERSAL. A behavioral therapy in which the person detects the preclench state, substitutes an incompatibe behavior in place of clenching, and overlearns this response in every situation where clenching might occur. It may be a useful technique for managing daytime clenching.

HYOID MUSCLES. Muscles that control the hyoid bone—the horseshoe-shaped bone at the base of the tongue. Muscles include the stylohyoid, thryrohyoid, and geniohyoid. These muscles draw the hyoid bone upward and backward, depress the hyoid bone and elevate the larynx, and elevate the hyoid bone, respectively.

HYPERTROPHY. Enlargement or overgrowth of an organ or part as a result of an increase in size of its constituent cells. Can be caused by increased activity.

INTEROCCLUSAL APPLIANCE. An orthotic device or mouthguard called an intraoral splint covering the *maxillary* or *mandibular* teeth. Intended to protect the teeth from wear from grinding (bruxism) and/or to modify the position of the ball in the socket.

MANDIBULAR TEETH. Teeth of the lower jaw (mandible).

MASSED PRACTICE (massed negative practice). A behavioral therapy involving intentionally engaging in the undesired behavior under voluntary control (e.g., clenching) to increase awareness and help eliminate it. An aversive and risky procedure not recommended here.

MAXILLARY TEETH. Teeth of the upper jaw (maxilla).

MYOGENIC. Originating in muscle.

OCCLUSION. Dental bite or alignment of maxillary and mandibular teeth when one closes the jaw or makes functional contact. Occlusal disharmony or malocclusion means improper or bad dental bite.

PARAFUNCTIONAL MUSCLE ACTIVITY. Clenching and grinding independent of chewing food. Nonfunctional.

PSYCHOPHYSIOLOGICAL ASSESSMENT. The use of various physiological modalities (e.g., EMG, EDR, skin temperature, pulse, breathing, and/or EEG) to assess psychophysiological resting levels, reactivity, and recoveries in response to various conditions such as relaxation, cognitive and physical stimuli, and postural changes (see Chapter 7).

PTERYGOID MUSCLES. Two pairs of muscles (medial or internal pterygoid and lateral or external pterygoid) controlling jaw movements. Located deep and inside the mouth and hence not easily available for direct palpation. The lateral pterygoid assists in opening the mandible (jaw) by pulling the head of the mandible forwards. It also protrudes the mandible and moves it to either side. The medial pterygoid closes the jaw and assists in lateral movements.

RAPID EYE MOVEMENT (REM) SLEEP. The stage of sleep when most dreaming occurs. Alternates with NREM sleep about every 90 minutes. Occurs about 20–25% of the total sleep time and becomes longer as the sleep phases progress.

RESPIRATION RATE. Breaths per minute (see Chapter 11).

RUMINATIVE THINKING. Cognitive preoccupation with one or more ideas or thoughts, and difficulty dismissing or stopping them.

SECONDARY GAIN. Advantages that a person gets from being ill. Examples are attention from others, being cared for, and avoiding responsibilities. People are often unaware of this as a potential contributing factor in maintaining their symptoms and disorder. It is not the same as malingering.

SKIN CONDUCTANCE. A common type of electrodermal activity (see Chapter 4).

STABILIZATION OR ADAPTATION (HABITUATION). Allows patients to adapt to or adjust to novel conditions or stimuli such as an office, instrumentation, psychophysiological recordings, or auditory or visual stimuli. Allows the physiological parameter to become stable. (See Chapter 7.)

STAGE I SLEEP. The lightest level of NREM sleep. A transition from being awake to sleep. About 5% of a normal adult's sleep time.

STAGE II SLEEP. The second level of NREM sleep with specific EEG waveforms. Occurs about half of the time one sleeps. *Stage III and IV NREM* sleep, known together as slow-wave sleep, are the deepest levels. They occur about 10% to 20% of the sleep time.

STERNOMASTOID. Sometimes still called the sternocleidomastoid muscle. Muscles connecting the sternum (breastbone) and the clavicle (collar bone) to the mastoid process of the temporal bone at the nuchal line of the occipital bone (back of the lower part of the ear). Rotates and extends head. Flexes vertebral column.

REFERENCES

American Academy of Orofacial Pain. (1993). *Temporomandibular disorders: Guidelines for classification, assessment, and management.* Chicago: Quintessence.

Azrin, N. H., & Nunn, R. G. (1973). Habit reversal: A method of eliminating nervous habits and tic. *Behaviour Research and Therapy, 11,* 619–628.

Azrin, N., & Nunn, R. G. (1977). *Habit control: Stuttering, nail biting, and other nervous habits.* New York: Simon and Schuster.

Bell, W. (1986). *Temporomandibular disorders: Classification, diagnosis management.* Chicago: Yearbook Medical Publishers.

Biedermann, H.-J. (1984). Comments on the reliability of muscle activity comparisons in EMG biofeedback research with back pain patients. *Biofeedback and Self-Regulation, 9,* 451–458.

Browne, A., & Finkelhor, D. (1986). Impact of child sexual abuse: A review of the research. *Psychological Bulletin, 99,* 66–77.

Burdette, B. H., & Gale, E. N. (1988). The effects of treatment on masticatory muscle activity and mandibular posture in myofascial pain-dysfunction patients. *Journal of Dental Research, 67,* 1126–1130.

Burdette, B. H., & Gale, E. N. (1990). Reliability of surface electromyography of the masseteric and anterior temporal areas. *Archives of Oral Biology, 35,* 747–751.

Burgar, C. G., & Rugh, J. D. (1983). An EMG integrator of muscle activity studies in ambulatory subjects. *IEEE Transactions on Biomedical Engineering, BME-30*(1), 66–69.

Carlson, C., Okeson, J., Falace, D., Nitz, A., Curran, S., & Anderson, D. (1993a). Comparison of psychologic and physiologic functioning between patients with masticatory muscle pain and matched controls. *Journal of Orofacial Pain, 7,* 15–22.

Carlson, C., Okeson, J., Falace, D., Nitz, A., & Lindroth, J. (1993b). Reduction of Pain and EMG activity in the masseter region by trapezius trigger point injection. *Pain, 55,* 397–400.

Cassisi, J. E., & McGlynn, F. D. (1988). Effects of EMG-activated nocturnal alarms on nocturnal bruxing. *Behavior Therapy, 19,* 133–142.

Cassisi, J. E., McGlynn, F. D., Belles, D. R. (1987). EMG-activated feedback alarms for the treatment of nocturnal bruxism: Current status and future directions. *Biofeedback and Self-Regulation, 12,* 13–30.

Christensen, L. V. (1979). Some subjective–experiential parameters in experimental tooth clenching in man. *Journal of Oral Rehabilitation, 6,* 119–136.

Clark, G. T., Beemsterboer, P. L., Solberg, W. K., & Rugh, J. D. (1979). Nocturnal electromyofascial evaluation of myofascial pain dysfunction in patients undergoing occlusal therapy. *Journal of the American Dental Association, 99,* 607–611.

Clark, G., Koyano, K., & Browne, P. (1993). Oral motor disorder in humans. *California Dentistry Association, 21*(1), 19-30.

Clark, G. T., Rugh, J. D., & Handelman, S. L. (1980). Nocturnal masseter muscle activity and urinary catecholamine levels in bruxers. *Journal of Dental Research, 59,* 1571–1576.

Clark, G. T., Rugh, J. D., Handelman, S. L., & Beemsterboer, P. L. (1977). Stress perception and nocturnal muscle activity. *Journal of Dental Research, 56* (Special Issue B), B161.

Clarke, R., & Gevirtz, R. (1991). Physiological responses to interpersonal stress in temporomandibular disorder. *Biofeedback and Self-Regulation, 16,* 294–295.

Crockett, D. J., Foreman, M. E., Alden, L., & Blasberg, B. (1986). A comparison of treatment modes in the management of myofascial pain dysfunction syndrome. *Biofeedback and Self-Regulation, 11,* 279–291.

Cunningham, J., Pearce, T., & Pearce, P. (1988). Childhood sexual abuse and medical complaints in adult women. *Journal of Interpersonal Violence, 3*(2), 131–134.

Dahlström, L., Carlsson, G. E., & Carlsson, S. G. (1982). Comparison of effects of electromyographic biofeedback and occlusal splint therapy on mandibular dysfunction. *Scandinavian Journal of Dental Research, 90,* 151–156.

Dahlström, L., & Carlsson, S. G. (1984). Treatment of mandibular dysfunction: The clinical usefulness of biofeedback in relation to splint therapy. *Journal of Oral Rehabilitation, 11,* 277–284.

Dalen, K., Ellertsen, B., Espelid, I., & Gronningsaeter, A. G. (1986). EMG feedback in the treatment of myofascial pain dysfunction syndrome. *Acta Odontologica Scandinavica, 44,* 279–284.

Drossman, D., Leserman, J., Nachman, G., Li, Z., Gluck, H., Toomey, T., & Mitchell, C. (1990). Sexual and physical abuse among women with functional and organic gastrointestinal disorders. *Annals of Behavioral Medicine, 113,* 828–833.

Dworkin, S. F., & LeResche, L. (Eds.). (1992). Research diagnostic criteria for temporomandibular disorders: Review, criteria, examinations and specifications, critique. *Journal of Craniomandibular Disorders: Facial and Oral Pain, 6,* 301–355.

Finkelhor, D., Araji, S., Baron, L., Browne, A., Peters, S. D., & Wyatt, G. E. (1986). *A sourcebook on child sexual abuse.* London: Sage.

Flor, H., & Birbaumer, N. (1993). Comparison of efficacy of electromyographic biofeedback, cognitive-behavioral therapy, and conservative medical interventions in the treatment of chronic musculo-skelatal pain. *Journal of Consulting and Clinical Psychology, 61,* 653–658.

Flor, H. Birbaumer, N., Schugens, M., & Lutzenberger, W. (1992). Symptom-specific psychophysiological responses in chronic pain patients. *Psychophysiology, 29,* 452–460.

Flor, H., Birbaumer, N., Schulte, W., & Roos, R. (1991). Stress-related electromyographic responses in patients with chronic temporomandibular pain. *Pain, 46,* 145–152.

Flor, H., Schugens, M. M., & Birbaumer, N. (1992). Discrimination of muscle tension in chronic pain patients and healthy controls. *Biofeedback and Self-Regulation, 17,* 165–177.

Flor, H., & Turk, D. (1989). Psychophysiology of chronic pain: Do chronic pain patients exhibit symptom-specific psychophysiological responses? *Psychological Bulletin, 105,* 215–259.

Funch, D. P., & Gale, E. N. (1980). Factors associated with nocturnal bruxism and its treatment. *Journal of Behavioral Medicine, 3,* 385–397.

Funch, D. P., & Gale, E. N. (1984). Biofeedback and relaxation therapy for chronic temporomandibular joint pain: Predicting successful outcomes. *Journal of Consulting and Clinical Psychology, 52,* 928–935.

Gale, E. N. (1979). Biofeedback for TMJ pain. In B. Ingersoll & W. McCutcheon (Eds.), *Clinical research in behavioral dentistry* (pp. 83–89). Morgantown, WV: West Virginia University.

Gevirtz, R. (1987). Temporomandibular disorders; and how to make a relaxation tape. In E. Catalano (Ed.), *The chronic pain control workbook.* Oakland: New Harbinger Press.

Gevirtz, R. (1990). Recording the lateral pterygoid in MPD patients. *Biofeedback, 18*(1), 45–47.

Glaros, A. G., & Glass, E. G. (1993). Temporomandibular disorders. In R. Gatchel & E. Blanchard (Eds.), *Psychophysiological disorders* (pp. 293–355). Washington, DC: American Psychological Association.

Glaros, A. G., & Melamed, B. G. (1992). Bruxism in children: Etiology and treatment. *Applied and Preventive Psychology, 1,* 191–199.

Glaros, A. G., & Rao, S. (1977). Bruxism: A critical review. *Psychological Bulletin, 84,* 767–781.

Glass, E. G., Glaros, A. G., & McGlynn, F. D. (1993). Myofascial pain dysfunction: Treatments used by ADA members. *Journal of Craniomandibular Practice, 11,* 25–29.

Harness, D., & Donlon, W. (1988). Cryptotrauma: The hidden wound. *Clinical Journal of Pain, 4,* 257–260.

Harness, D., Donlon, W., & Eversole, L. (1990). Comparison of clinical characteristics in myogenic, TMJ internal derangement, and atypical facial pain patients. *Clinical Journal of Pain, 6,* 4–17.

Hatch, J. P., Prihoda, T. J., & Moore, P. J. (1992). The application of generalizability theory to surface electromyographic measurements during psychophysiological stress testing: How many measurements are needed? *Biofeedback and Self-Regulation, 17,* 17–39.

Hijzen, T. H., Slangen, J. L., & VanHouweligen, H. C. (1986). Subjective, clinical and EMG effects of biofeedback and splint treatment. *Journal of Oral Rehabilitation, 13,* 529–539.

Holmgren, K., Sheikholeslam, A., & Riise, C. (1993). Effect of a full-arch maxillary occlusal splint on parafunctional activity during sleep in patients with nocturnal bruxism and signs and symptoms of craniomandibular disorders. *Journal of Prosthetic Dentistry, 69,* 293–297.

Hopper, D., Gevirtz, R., Nigl, A., & Taddey, J. (1992). Relationship between daily stress and nocturnal bruxism. *Biofeedback and Self-Regulation, 17,* 309.

Hubbard, D., & Berkoff, G. (1993). Myofascial trigger points show spontaneous needle EMG activity. *Spine, 18,* 1803–1807.

Hudzinski, L., & Lawrence, G. (1992). Effectiveness of EMG biofeedback in the treatment of nocturnal bruxism: A three-year retrospective follow-up. *Biofeedback and Self-Regulation, 17,* 312.

Hudzinski, L., & Walters, P. (1986). Use of portable electromyograms in determining and treating chronic nocturnal bruxism. *Psychophysiology, 23,* 442–443.

Kapel, L., Glaros, A. G., & McGlynn, F. D. (1989). Psychophysiological responses to stress in patients with myofascial pain dysfunction syndrome. *Journal of Behavioral Medicine, 12,* 397–406.

Karoly, P., & Jensen, M. P. (1987). *Multimethod assessment of chronic pain.* Oxford: Pergamon Press.

Kinney, R. K., Gatchel, R. J., Ellis, E., & Holt, C. (1992). Major psychological disorders in chronic TMD patients: Implications for successful management. *Journal of the American Dental Association, 123*(10), 49–54.

Kirveskari, P., Alanen, P., & Jämsä, T. (1992). Association between craniomandibular disorders and occlusal interferences in children. *Journal of Prosthetic Dentistry, 67,* 692–696.

Laskin, D. M., (1969). Etiology of the pain-dysfunction syndrome. *Journal of the American Dental Association, 79,* 147–153.

Laskin, D. M. (1992). Temporomandibular disorders: Diagnosis and etiology. In B. G. Sarnat & D M. Laskin (Eds.), *The temporomandibular joint: A biological basis for clinical practice* (4th ed., pp. 316–328). Philadelphia: W. B. Saunders.

McGlynn, F. D., Cassisi, J. E., & Diamond, E. L. (1985). Bruxism: A behavioral dentistry perspective. In R. J. Daitzman (Ed.), *Diagnosis and intervention in behavior therapy and behavioral medicine* (Vol. II, pp. 2, 28–87). New York: Springer.

McGlynn, F., Gale, E., Glaros, A., LeResche, L., Massoth, D., & Weiffenbach, J. (1990). Biobehavioral research in dentistry: Some directions for the 1990's. *Annals of Behavioral Medicine, 12,* 133–149.

McNulty, W., Gevirtz, R., Hubbard, D., & Berkoff, G. (1994). Needle electromyographic evaluation of trigger point response to a psychological stressor. *Psychophysiology, 31,* 313–316.

Mealiea, W. L., & McGlynn, F. D. (1987). Temporomandibular disorders and bruxism. In J. P. Hatch, J. G. Fisher, & J. D. Rugh (Eds.), *Biofeedback: Studies in clinical efficacy* (pp. 123–151). New York: Plenum Press.

Mercuri, L. G., Olson, R. E., & Laskin, D. M. (1979). The specificity of response to experimental stress in patients with myofascial pain dysfunction syndrome. *Journal of Dental Research, 58,* 1866–1871.

Mohl, N. D. (1979, May). Behavioral management of functional oral disorders: Comments and critique. In P. S. Bryant & E. N. Gale (Eds.), *Oral motor behavior: Impact on oral conditions and dental treatment* (Workshop proceedings, NIH Publication No. 79-1845). Washington, DC: Government Printing Office.

Moss, R. A., & Adams, H. E. (1984). Physiological reactions to stress in subjects with and without myofascial pain dysfunction symptoms. *Journal of Oral Rehabilitation, 11,* 219–232.

Moss, R. A., Garrett, J., & Chiodo, J. F. (1982). Temporomandibular joint dysfunction and myofascial pain dysfunction syndromes: Parameters, etiology, and treatment. *Psychological Bulletin, 92,* 331–346.

Moss, R. A., Sult, S., & Garrett, J. C. (1984). Questionnaire evaluation of craniomandibular pain factors among college students. *Journal of Craniomandibular Practice, 2,* 364–368.

Okeson, J. P. (1989). *Management of temporomandibular disorders and occlusion.* St. Louis: C. V. Mosby.

Passatore, M., Grassi, C., & Filippi, G. (1985). Sympathetically-induced development of tension in jaw muscles; the possible contraction of intrafusal muscle fibers. *Pfluegers Archiv, 405,* 297–304.

Ramfjord, S. P., & Ash, M. M. (Eds.). (1983). *Occlusion* (3rd ed.). Philadelphia: Saunders.

Rao, S. M., & Glaros, A. G. (1979). Electromyographic correlates of experimentally induced stress in diurnal bruxists and normals. *Journal of Dental Research, 58,* 1872–1878.

Rosenbaum, M. S., & Ayllon, T. (1981). Treating bruxism with the habit-reversal technique. *Behaviour Research and Therapy, 19,* 87–96.

Rugh, J. D. (1975). *Variables involved in extinction through repeated practice therapy.* Unpublished doctoral dissertation, University of California, Santa Barbara.

Rugh, J. (1983). Psychological factors in the etiology of masticating pain and dysfunction. In O. Laskin, W. Greenfield, E. Gale, J. Rugh, P. Niff, C. Alling, & W. Ayer (Eds.), *The president's conference on the examination, diagnosis and management of temporomandibular disorders.* Chicago: American Dental Association.

Rugh, J. D., & Harlan, J. (1988). Nocturnal bruxism and temporomandibular disorders. In J. Jankovich & E. Tolosa (Eds.), *Advances in neurology: Facial dyskinesias* (Vol. 49, pp. 329–341). New York: Raven Press.

Rugh, J. D., & Lemke, R. R. (1984). Significance of oral habits. In J. D. Matarazzo, S. M. Weiss, J. A. Herd, N. E. Miller, & S. M. Weiss (Eds.), *Behavioral health: A handbook of health enhancement and disease prevention* (pp. 947–966). New York: Wiley.

Rugh, J. D., & Solberg, W. K. (1974). Identification of stressful stimuli in the natural environments using a portable biofeedback unit. *Proceedings of the 5th annual meeting of the Biofeedback Research Society, Colorado Springs.* Wheatridge, CO: Association for Applied Psychophysiology and Biofeedback.

Rugh, J. D., & Solberg, W. K. (1975). Electromyographic studies of bruxist behavior before and during treatment. *Journal of the California Dental Association, 3*(9), 56–59.

Rugh, J. D., & Solberg, W. K. (1976). Psychological implications of temporomandibular pain and dysfunction. *Oral Science Review, 7,* 3–30.

Rugh, J. D., & Ware, J. C. (1986). Polysonigraphic comparison of nocturnal bruxists with and without facial pain. *Journal of Dental Research, 65* (special issue abstract #97), 181.

Scott, D. S., & Lundeen, T. F. (1980). Myofascial pain involving the masticatory muscles: An experimental model. *Pain, 8,* 207.

Seligman, D., & Pullinger, A. (1991). The role of functional occlusal relationships in temporomandibular disorders: A review. *Journal of Craniomandibular Disorders: Facial and Oral Pain, 5,* 265–276.

Shellenberger, R., & Green, J. (1986). *From the ghost in the box to successful biofeedback training.* Greeley, CO: Health Psychology Publications.

Shellenberger, R., & Green, J. (1987). Specific effects and biofeedback versus biofeedback-assisted self-regulation training. *Biofeedback and Self-Regulation, 12,* 185–209.

Taddey, J. (1990). *TMJ: The self-help programs.* Surrey: Book Press.

Travell, J. G., & Simons, D. G. (1983). *Myofascial pain and dysfunction: The trigger point manual.* Baltimore: Williams & Wilkins.

Turk, D., Zaki, H., & Rudy, T. (1993). Effects of intraoral appliance and biofeedback/stress management alone and in combination in treating pain and depression in patients with temporomandibular disorders. *Journal of Prosthetic Dentistry, 70,* 158–164.

Ware, J., & Rugh, J. (1988). Destructive bruxism: Sleep stage relationship. *Sleep, 11,* 172–181.

Wickramsekera, I. (1988). *Clinical behavioral medicine.* New York: Plenum Press.

Wright, J., Deary, I. J., & Geissler, P. R. (1991). Depression, hassles and somatic symptoms in mandibular dysfunction syndrome patients. *Journal of Dentistry, 19,* 352–356.

Wrumle, M. K., Lumley, M. A., & McGlynn, F. D. (1989). Sleep-related bruxism and sleep variables: A critical review. *Journal of Craniomandibular Disorders and Oral Facial Pain, 3,* 152–158.

Zarb, G. A., & Carlsson, G. E. (1979). *Temporomandibular joint function and dysfunction.* Copenhagen: Munksgaard.

17

Raynaud's Disease: Selected Issues and Considerations in Using Biofeedback Therapies

Mark S. Schwartz
Mark F. Kelly

This chapter provides information about Raynaud's disease and guidelines for evaluating patients with Raynaud's disease and using thermal biofeedback in the treatment of this disorder.

DEFINITIONS, SYMPTOMS, DIAGNOSIS, AND CAUSES

Raynaud's symptoms involve spasm of arterioles and small arteries in the digits of the hands and feet. Triphasic skin-color changes are classic. They involve whiteness (blanching or pallor), blueness (cyanosis), and redness (rubor, cynosis, or reactive hyperemia). Some people show biphasic skin-color changes involving the cyanosis and then reactive hyperemia. Occasionally, symptoms include the nose and tongue. They rarely involve the thumb. The duration of spasms ranges from minutes to hours. Cold exposure is the usual stimulus for the spasms. However, emotional and other psychological events also can provoke an attack in many patients. Estimates vary widely for the incidence of this type of stimulus.

An important distinction is between "primary" or "idiopathic Raynaud's" (Raynaud's disease) that has no known cause and Raynaud's symptoms secondary to another condition sometimes called "secondary Raynaud's." Examples of such conditions are connective tissue disorders such as rheumatoid arthritis (RA), systemic lupus erythematosus (SLE), and most commonly, scleroderma (progressive systemic sclerosis, or PSS). Nearly all patients with PSS experience these vasospastic episodes. Others include mixed connective tissue disease, Sjögren's syndrome, polymyositis, and dermatomyositis (Coffman, 1991).

Other conditions that cause these symptoms include obstructive arterial diseases such as thromboangiitis obliterans and arteriosclerosis obliterans (Coffman, 1991). Trauma as from traumatic vasospastic disease (vibration-induced) is another secondary cause. Carpal tunnel syndrome and thoracic outlet obstruction syndromes are common causes (Coffman, 1991). Reflex sympathetic dystrophy, dysproteinemias, polycythemia, myxedema or adult hypothyroidism, primary pulmonary hypertension, and renal disease add to the list. The list of uncommon causes extends even further (Coffman, 1991).

Drugs also can result in the spasms and are secondary causes. Notable examples are ergot preparations, methysergide, beta-adrenegic blocking agents, and imipramine (Coffman, 1991). Prudent nonmedical practitioners understand the necessity of proper medical examination and testing. Useful testing includes differentiating occlusive versus vasospastic disease.

Raynaud's disease usually affects females from preadolescence to early middle age. The estimated ratio of females to males is about 4:1. It has bilateral involvement and the presence of symptoms for at least 2 years without progression and without evidence of another cause. Occasionally, it takes longer for the underlying disease to become manifest. Some patients initially diagnosed as having idiopathic Raynaud's disease later learn that their symptoms are secondary to another disorder unrecognized earlier in the history of the symptoms. Trophic changes in the skin and gangrene, if present at all, are minimal in persons with the primary type.

In 1862 Maurice Raynaud first defined this clinical syndrome as episodic digital ischemia provoked by cold, cyanosis, and emotion. In 1888 Raynaud suggested that hyperactivity of the sympathetic nervous system caused the increased vasoconstrictive response to cold. Lewis (1929) proposed a "local fault" theory in which there was excess sensitivity to local cooling of precapillary resistance vessels. Current theories still include increased activity of the sympathetic nervous system (SNS) and local fault in the digital arteries, and there is supportive evidence for each position or the combination (Coffman, 1991). Other theories of pathophysiology include serotonin, platelets, and blood viscosity. The significant correlation of Raynaud's disease, migraine headaches, and variant angina pectoris suggests a possible common systemic mechanism involving vasospasms in digital, cerebral, and coronary circulatory beds (Berkow & Fletcher, 1992; Coffman, 1991). Some speculate about a blood-borne, neurological, or general abnormality of vascular smooth muscles. The vasospasm of pulmonary hypertension correlates with Raynaud's, but there is no systemic disease implicated. The theories of a general vascular abnormality cannot account for the differences in drug responses and neurogenic controls among the different circulatory beds. In conclusion, many factors may contribute to the vasospasms in digits.

TREATMENTS

There are no universally accepted medical treatments for Raynaud's disease. Stepped-care treatment and sensible first treatments involve protecting the body and extremities from cold, stopping smoking, and stopping caffeine. There is surprisingly no mention of other vasoactive dietary substances in the references I have reviewed (see Chapter 10 for these dietary substances).

Advances in pharmacotherapy show promise and are part of current medical practice (Berkow & Fletcher, 1992). However, the drugs are nonspecific, and negative side effects are a problem. This is a limitation of medication treatments. A discussion of pharmacotherapy is beyond the scope of this chapter. However, we include a brief mention of several medications for interested readers. One notable example is nifedipine, a calcium entry blocker (Coffman, 1991). Others include other calcium entry blockers, sympatholetic agents such as reserpine and guanethidine, and prazosin and thymoxamine. These drugs often have bothersome side effects. Others in this class have mixed results, poor results, and/or intolerable side effects. See Coffman (1991) for a discussion of all these drugs and others.

We note certain types of medications because they are contraindicated for their use with Raynaud's. They induce digital vasoconstriction and may actually worsen the condition. Notable examples are beta blockers or beta-adrenergic receptor antagonists, clonidine, and ergot preparations (Berkow & Fletcher, 1992; Coffman, 1991).

Regional sympathectomy often has major drawbacks and complications. There is limited long-term success especially for the hands. When considered at all, regional sympathectomy is usually a last resort for patients with Raynaud's disease who are suffering from progressive disability. It is contraindicated for secondary Raynaud's (Coffman, 1991) and of "doubtful value in the primary disease" (Coffman, 1991). However, relief may last from 1 to 2 years for the upper extremities, and there are reports of considerable and lasting benefit for lumbar sympathectomy to relieve the spasms in the toes (Coffman, 1991).

Well-controlled research supports the use of thermal biofeedback-assisted treatment of idiopathic Raynaud's disease. Combining thermal biofeedback with cold stress challenges can improve initial and long-term results. See the studies by Freedman and his colleagues (Freedman, 1987; Freedman, Ianni, & Wenig, 1985) for thermal biofeedback without and with cold stress challenges. However, including cold stress challenges is not yet a standard or common clinical practice because of very limited access to such equipment to create the cold challenges.

Surprising are the omissions of the biofeedback and cold stress challenge studies in the otherwise excellent and useful review by Coffman (1991). There is only one sentence referring to biofeedback, and there are no references. Coffman very briefly alludes to the "Pavlovian conditioning" method involving immersing the hands in warm water while the body is in cold ambient air (Jobe et al., 1985; see discussion of this later in this chapter).

To a much smaller degree than for Raynaud's disease, a few case studies and limited research support biofeedback as part of the clinical management for Raynaud's secondary to connective tissue disorders (Stambrook, Hamel, & Carter, 1988).

THE USEFULNESS OF THERMAL BIOFEEDBACK
IN TREATING RAYNAUD'S DISEASE

The reduction of peripheral vasoconstriction and vasospastic attacks often lessens significantly with various forms of physiological self-regulation. Some practitioners and researchers still believe that autogenic therapy and similar relaxation techniques can be effective without biofeedback. In this view, biofeedback procedures are superfluous. This may be true for some patients with Raynaud's disease as it is for headaches. However, based on the experimental literature, the "jury is still out" on this issue.

There are several publications describing the use of thermal biofeedback and other biobehavioral therapies for Raynaud's disease (Grove & Belanger, 1983; Sedlacek, 1984, 1989; Rose & Carlson, 1987). The most convincing and best controlled between-groups experimental study is by Freedman, Ianni, and Wenig (1983). This study and the follow-up reports (Freedman, 1987) over 3 years strongly support the advantage of thermal biofeedback over autogenic relaxation for treating Raynaud's disease. The ambitious treatment study employed a focal cold stimulus as part of the therapy with biofeedback. The authors reported a 32.6% reduction of vasospastic episodes in the autogenic therapy group. However, there was a 66.8% reduction in the thermal biofeedback group and a 92.5% reduction in the thermal biofeedback plus cold stress challenge group. Major methodological advantages of this study included ambulatory monitoring and a 1-year initial follow-up during the same cold months in which therapy began. The results lasted at least 3 years following treatment (Freedman, Ianni, & Wenig, 1985, 1987). Currently, there is a federally funded, multi-institution study of these procedures that is in the first of 5 years.

If other practitioners do not get the same results with these treatment approaches, this would not lessen the value of thermal biofeedback. Relevant issues and questions include:

1. What are the biological mechanisms causing Raynaud's episodes?
2. What are the mechanisms involved in successful therapy with thermal biofeedback and other physiological self-regulatory therapies?
3. What are the mechanisms involved in focal cold stimulus challenges?
4. What are the mechanisms involved with the counterconditioning technique of immersing hands in very warm water while the body is in cold ambient air?
5. When should a practitioner consider the counterconditioning approach?
6. Are there common mechanisms between the focal cold challenge with thermal biofeedback and the counterconditioning warm water/cold air approach?
7. For which patients are thermal biofeedback therapies and other procedures needed to achieve the best therapeutic results?
8. When should a practitioner include thermal biofeedback and focal cold challenge stimuli for patients with Raynaud's disease?
9. What therapeutic procedures in thermal biofeedback are more appropriate and useful than others?
10. Are there preferred therapist characteristics and skills needed to provide effective thermal biofeedback for Raynaud's disease?
11. Would combinations of selected medications and biobehavioral therapies attain better results than either does alone.

GUIDELINES FOR TREATING RAYNAUD'S DISEASE

1. Practitioners should be sure that a very careful clinical interview, medical examination, and tests establish the diagnosis as either Raynaud's disease or Raynaud's phenomenon. Review the patient's medical history. Look for environmental, physiological, and psychological factors that contribute to the vasospastic episodes. Be sure the patient avoids vasospastic-inducing medications and other vasospastic chemicals. Contact with cold stimuli, environmental cold, emotional, and other stressors are the common triggers of vasospastic episodes. See Table 17.1 for an outline gleaned and adapted from Freedman, Lynn, and Ianni (1982).

2. Secondary gains are possible. Investigate this, and, if they are present, discuss and try to make changes.

3. Assess peripheral vascular activity and reactivity in response to temperature, cognitive, and other stressors. Paper-and-pencil stress measures can provide useful information for stressors. Standard stressful cognitive tasks such as mental arithmetic are not stressful for all patients. See Chapter 7 for information and guidelines.

4. To evaluate results faster, start treatment in the late summer or early fall if cold is the main precipitating factor. This is especially important if symptoms are infrequent, easily managed in warm weather, and respond to nonphysiological, self-regulatory procedures. What if patients request treatment in the late winter or early spring? Should a practitioner defer treatment for several months? The answer is "not always." Other choices are acceptable.

    a. Consider telling the patient that treatment can begin now, but it will probably require several office visits over 1 to 3 months and considerable practice. Explain that the motivation to practice may be less because his or her symptoms

TABLE 17.1. Interview Protocol for Raynaud's Disease

1. When did your symptoms begin?
2. Please describe your symptoms.
   A. Where do they occur?
      Do they occur in your hands? Do they occur in one or both hands?
      Do they occur in your feet? Do they occur in one or both feet?
      Do the symptoms occur in your face?
   B. What sequence of color changes occurs? Do they get white, blue, and red?
   C. Are these changes always the same?
   D. What do your hands, feet, or face feel like during each color change?
      Do they feel cold, numb, burning, tingling, and/or painful?
3. How long does a typical attack last? How long does a mild attack last?
   How long does your worst attack last?
4. How frequent are your attacks?
   A. In what month do you usually get most attacks?
      How many do you get in that month?
   B. In what month do you tend to get the least attacks?
      How many attacks occur in that month?
   C. When your problem was the worst, how often did you get attacks?
   D. When your problem was the least troublesome, how often did you get attacks?
   E. What is the longest period you recall without an attack?
   F. What is the longest period in cold weather you recall without an attack?
5. Do you wear special clothing to prevent attacks?
6. Do you regulate the room temperature to decrease attacks?
   At what room temperature do you feel most comfortable?
7. Assuming you are not wearing protective clothing, what outside temperature would begin to create problems for you?
8. When you are wearing protective clothing, at what temperature do you begin to have problems?
9. In what circumstances are you likely to get attacks?
10. What do you do when you get an attack? Do you do anything to reduce it?
11. What kinds of events, thoughts, or feelings seem to cause an attack?
    Try to be specific.
12. How do you feel when you get an attack?
    What do you think about when you get an attack? Try to be specific.
13. Does Raynaud's disease prevent you from doing anything?
14. If you did not have Raynaud's, how would your life change?
15. Are you taking any medication? Are you in any treatment? Tell me about it.
16. How helpful is your treatment?
17. How helpful do you think this treatment will be?

Note. Adapted from Freedman, Lynn, and Ianni (1982). Copyright 1982 Grune & Stratton. Reprinted by permission.

are much less frequent. The patient and therapist may choose to delay office visits until such time that motivation to practice is stronger. However, this is a good time to get a self-report log for a few weeks. Such a log includes the frequency and intensity of the vasospastic episodes and precipitating factors. For example, the patient can provide to the practitioner information about cold exposure, emotional stress, nicotine, caffeine, and other dietary contributions to vasoconstriction. One can then plan for thermal biofeedback in late summer or early fall.

    b. A reasonable second alternative is to begin a self-report log for a few weeks and then to introduce nonbiofeedback, physiological self-regulation procedures and cognitive stress management, if indicated. Emphasize the need for practice, self-regulation, and a self-report log during these warmer months. Explain that the expected reduction of vasospastic episodes is probably no more than about one-third with this approach. Realistically explain the difficulty in evaluating progress during this period. Discuss the possibility or probability of needing to add thermal biofeedback in the upcoming fall or winter. This compromise allows the professional to start therapy in a realistic context.

    c. Third, one can begin with a self-report baseline, thermal biofeedback with or without a cold stress challenge, and other indicated therapies such as stress management. Include realistic explanations and expectations as described in paragraphs a and b above.

        One must be realistic with patients and with oneself as the professional that the season will probably influence motivation and symptoms. Effective treatment is more than learning to warm one's extremities in the office and elsewhere. It also must be effective in response to precipitating stimuli. If emotional and stressful events precipitate many attacks, the season will be a less important factor. In this case, the third option with emotional stimuli incorporated into the therapy program would be more realistic at any time of year.

5. Practitioners should gather adequate self-report data of vasospastic attacks outside the office in comparable ambient temperatures. The self-report symptom log is the major method for getting symptom data. Some experts believe that the most useful datum is the frequency of vasospastic attacks (Freedman et al., 1982). Carefully educate patients as to what constitutes a vasospastic episode. Many patients are surprisingly unaware of the criteria for such episodes.

6. The therapist should be someone who has the personal characteristics and skills to foster comfort in the therapy procedures.

7. Practitioners should provide advice and recommendations to reduce or stop caffeine, nicotine, and other vasoconstrictive substances whenever applicable (see Chapter 10).

8. Ambient room temperature and humidity need to be proper and constant. Ideally, from 72–74°F should be suitable. Significant fluctuations in temperature and moisture are likely to cause artifacts and other problems.

9. Prevent drafts of all kinds. Avoid any varying air flow from vents, air conditioning, fans, and heaters that selectively warms or cools the patient.

10. Use adequate adaptation and baseline periods to assess the thermal biofeedback properly. Remember, warming occurs while sitting quietly in a warmer environment after coming in from cooler outside temperatures especially with eyes closed. Also, warming occurs after hurrying to make the appointment while sitting quietly in a calmer environment. If the adaptation and baseline periods are too short, one may observe warming during feedback that is unrelated to the feedback.

It is common for patients to show little or no warming in the first several minutes of sitting quietly. Then, many patients show rapid warming without physiological feedback or any specific relaxation procedures taught by the therapist. Without adequate adaptation and baseline periods, therapists may mistakenly think that the biofeedback experience is important for this warming. Sometimes, therapists want their patients to know that such sitting and relaxing often results in warming. In such cases, providing physiological feedback after a shorter-than-ideal baseline is reasonable once or even a few times. However, one still needs an adequate adaptation period (Taub, 1977). Furthermore, this is separate from the physiological feedback that occurs after clear plateaus of skin temperature.

The duration of the adaptation and baseline periods is partly a matter of professional choice and practicality. Where was the patient before the session, and what was he or she doing? For example, a period of sitting quietly in the waiting room for 15 minutes and a 10-minute baseline after being attached to the instruments are often sufficient (see Chapter 7 for discussion of adaptation and baseline periods).

11. A thermal biofeedback training phase of about 15 minutes or slightly longer is probably sufficient. Much longer phases, such as 20 minutes or longer, may result in frustration and impatience. Tailor the duration to the patient, therapist, and situation.

12. The therapist should remember that even minute amounts of perspiration on or near the thermistor site(s) will probably affect the temperature. One must control or account for this in some way. If this occurs, the baseline period becomes even more important. Consider simultaneous electrodermal measurement to assess the contribution of perspiration to skin temperature changes. Also, consider physiological measurement of blood flow to control for perspiration and "thermal lag" (Freedman et al., 1982).

"Plethysmography" is a common skin-surface measure of blood flow. It measures blood volume pulse (BVP), also called finger pulse volume (FPV). The infrared emitter and detector in the sensor measure these small variations in blood volume that occur with every heartbeat. Specifically, BVP is a measure of the amplitude of each pulse, thus representing an index of blood flow.

Another approach sometimes used to monitor blood flow and vessel occlusion is Doppler ultrasound. This procedure employs high-frequency sound waves directed and reflected by red blood cells moving through a vessel. The red cells shift the frequency by an amount proportional to their velocity (the Doppler effect). This frequency shift produces an audible signal and visual pulse waves (Strandness & Sumner, 1975).

13. Practitioners should plan for many office sessions with some or most employing thermal biofeedback. This can require 8–16 sessions or even more.

14. Practitioners should consider bidirectional thermal biofeedback.

15. If one uses guided imagery to enhance relaxation and warming, it should be tailored to the patient.

16. Practitioners should assess the transfer of training and generalization of reduced vasoconstriction to daily-life situations.

17. Therapists should do as much as necessary and possible to increase both short-term and long-term compliance. Patients need ample motivation to comply with the many therapeutic recommendations and the duration of therapy and follow-up. Skeptical patients require more cognitive preparation to maintain compliance. Patients who are too enthusiastic and have unrealistic expectations also require special attention to give them a realistic context for treatment.

18. Therapists should remind patients that despite the potential success of treatment, they need to continue using reasonable protective measures to minimize or avoid cold exposure. For example, they need adequate clothing, hand protection, and must avoid unnecessary direct cold exposure.

19. Therapists should get adequate self-reports of vasospastic episodes during the next cold season comparable to the symptom baseline.

20. During the redness phase (the reactive or hyperemic phase), patients can experience much pain and burning. The prudent practitioner must be aware that many patients are very hesitant about learning hand-warming skills because of the fear of exacerbating the

hyperemic phase. This is a difficult problem. Until more research is done in this area, clinical sensitivity and careful observations are recommended.

RECENTLY PROPOSED PHYSIOLOGICAL MECHANISMS IN RAYNAUD'S DISEASE AND THERMAL BIOFEEDBACK

Research in recent years by Robert Freedman and his colleagues sheds new light on the physiological mechanisms involved in digital temperature changes (Freedman, 1991, 1994; Freedman, Sabharwal, et al., 1988; Freedman, Morris, et al., 1988; Freedman, Mayes, & Sabharwal, 1989; Freedman et al., 1991; Freedman, Keegan, Rodriguez, & Galloway, 1993). There are important implications for treatment including with biofeedback.

The palmar surface and tips of the fingers are replete with arteriovenous shunts that function with the capillaries. These shunts can rapidly change their size and blood flow rate in response to external temperature, mainly as a result of activity in the sympathetic adrenergic vasoconstrictor nerves. Circulating vasoactive substances interact with biochemical alpha- and beta-adrenergic receptors and affect finger blood flow circulation. Sympathetic vasoconstricting nerves also affect circulation in fingers.

Freedman and his colleagues showed that feedback-assisted vasodilation operates at least partly via a nonneural, beta-adrenergic mechanism. It does not require activity of efferent digital nerves. One can block these nerves and still get vasospastic attacks. This research challenges the previously assumed sole and primary role of general decreased sympathetic activity for feedback-assisted vasodilation. Finger temperature increases can and do occur with thermal biofeedback but without other signs of decreased sympathetic activation. Those researchers showed this with normal subjects (Freedman et al., 1993) and with patients with Raynaud's disease (Freedman et al., 1991). Measures of SNS activation included heart rate, blood pressure, and the circulating catecholamines epinephrine and norepinephrine. This research supports a local or focal role of blood flow and finger temperature biofeedback for Raynaud's disease.

Furthermore, these investigators supported the idea that different mechanisms mediate feedback-assisted vasoconstriction and vasodilation (Freedman, Sabharwal, et al., 1988; Freedman, Morris, et al., 1988). Thus, the mechanism is probably different when patients engage in bidirectional temperature feedback.

What are the implications for practitioners? One implication is that thermal biofeedback is preferable to other physiological self-regulation therapies that focus only on general reductions of sympathetic arousal.

Other research with clinical implications focuses on possible differences in ease of hand warming between the sexes and races. These studies compared beta-adrenergic activity in blacks and whites (McGrady & Roberts, 1991), and female and male patients (Freedman, Sabharwal, & Desai, 1987). Whites and male patients could warm their hands with thermal biofeedback more easily than blacks and female patients. Comparisons between black female patients and white female patients were similar to comparisons between male and female patients. Research suggests that blacks and female patients have decreased alpha- and beta-adrenergic receptor density in the peripheral vasculature. Therapists will have to consider this when treating such individuals for Raynaud's disease with biofeedback and tailor expectations, procedures, and physiological goals accordingly.

CONDITIONING PROCEDURES
AND THE USE OF BIOFEEDBACK THERAPY

Hand warming under conditions of induced cold directly to the finger resulted in the best short-term and long-term effects with thermal biofeedback using the paradigm employed by Freedman and his colleagues. Jobe et al. (1985) used a different paradigm to create vasodilation and hand warming during a cold challenge. They formulated their rationale and procedures within a classical or Pavlovian counterconditioning model. The cold stressor was cold ambient air viewed as the conditioned stimulus (CS). The conditioned response was rapid hand warming via immersing the hands (or feet) in hot tap water. Their subjects with Raynaud's disease showed significantly higher digital temperatures when exposed to cold after this treatment. The results also suggested that this procedure has an enduring effect at the 1-year follow-up survey data.

One can speculate that the Freedman paradigm and the Jobe paradigm may have something in common. Both involve hand warming during induced cold challenges. However, there are not enough data yet with the Jobe procedures. We look forward to research that replicates the Jobe procedures, compares these techniques, and studies possible common biochemical, physiological, and conditioning mechanisms. Both are practical for clinical application.

CONCLUSIONS

Raynaud's disease is not uncommon. However, its symptoms rarely occur naturally or fully in the research laboratory or practitioner's office. This holds true for spontaneous symptoms or those induced with cold challenges. Causes of and mechanisms of Raynaud's disease probably involve multiple factors and combinations. These include physiological, biochemical, environmental, and local cold stimuli, as well as emotional and psychological factors.

Biofeedback-assisted therapy has a place in the treatment of Raynaud's disease. There are many factors to consider when using biofeedback for Raynaud's. The interfaces between and among biofeedback, psychology, psychophysiology, biochemistry, and pharmacology will help to further our understanding of this disease and its treatment.

GLOSSARY

ALPHA-ADRENERGIC RECEPTORS. Receptors that respond to epinephrine and specific blocking agents. Includes sites that produce vasoconstriction.

ARTERIORSCLEROSIS OBLITERANS. Peripheral atherosclerotic disease. Occlusion of blood to the extremities by atherosclerotic plaques (atheromas).

ARTERIOVENOUS SHUNTS. Can rapidly change their size and blood flow rate in response to external temperature, mainly as a result of activity in the sympathetic adrenergic vasoconstrictor nerves.

ATHEROSCLEROSIS. The major arteriosclerotic disease. One of several diseases in which arterial walls become thickened and lose elasticity. Major risk factors are hypertension, elevated low-density lipoproteins (LDL) and reduced levels of high-density lipoproteins (HDL), cigarette smoking, diabetes mellitus, obesity, being male, and family history of premature atherosclerosis. Other risk factors may include physical inactivity and older age.

BETA-ADRENEGIC BLOCKING AGENTS (BETA BLOCKERS). Drugs that block adrenergic transmission at either beta$_1$- or beta$_2$-adrenergic receptors or at both. For example, drugs used to lower blood pressure by decreasing cardiac output by adrenergic blockade. Also used for cardiac arrhythmias, migraines, and other conditions. Examples are propranolol (Inderal), atenolol (Tenormin), metoprolol tartrate (Lopressor).

BETA-ADRENERGIC RECEPTORS. Adrenergic receptors that respond to norepinephrine and certain blocking agents. May be beta$_1$- or beta$_2$-adrenergic receptors.

BIDIRECTIONAL THERMAL BIOFEEDBACK. Thermal biofeedback procedures to assist patients to alternately warm and cool fingers in order to increase physiological self-regulation.

BLANCHING OR PALLOR. Whiteness of skin that results from decreased blood supply.

BLOOD VISCOSITY. "Resistance offered by a fluid to change of form or relative position of its particles due to attraction of molecules to each other" or "state of being sticky or gummy." (Thomas, 1989) Compared to standard liquid such as water.

CALCIUM ENTRY BLOCKERS (CALCIUM CHANNEL BLOCKERS). Drugs used to lower blood pressure by decreasing vascular resistance. Example: Verapamil (Calan).

CARPAL TUNNEL SYNDROME. Swelling or inflamed tissues in the passageway through the wrist (carpal or wrist tunnel) that compresses the median nerve. Involves numbness and tingling sensations in fingers and hand, wrist pain shooting into the forearm or into palm or surfaces of fingers. Pain and numbness are usually worse at night. Common to typists, carpenters, grocery clerks, factory workers, meat cutters, violinists, mechanics, and some others, all of whom are subject to repeated stress and strain of the wrist and who often pinch or grip instruments with a flexed wrist. Numbness does not involve the little finger. Conservative treatments are resting the joint and wearing a splint that immobilizes the wrist. Steroid drugs such as cortisone are the next treatment. Surgery is usually successful if the other treatments are insufficient.

CATECHOLAMINES. Autonomic nervous system chemicals such as epinephrine and norepinephrine. *Epinephrine* is a hormone and neurotransmitter secreted by the adrenal medulla and involved in regulation of metabolism. *Norepinephrine* is a hormone and neurotransmitter secreted by the adrenal medulla. (See *norepinephrine*.)

CIRCULATING VASOACTIVE SUBSTANCES. Interact with biochemical alpha- and beta-adrenergic receptors and affect finger blood flow.

CLONIDINE. An antihypertensive drug taken orally or applied to and entering the skin in a patch form or ointment (*transdermal clonidine*). (See Chapter 37.)

COLLAGEN. An essential fibrous insoluble protein in connective tissue, as skin, bone, ligaments, and cartilege. About 30% of the protein in the body. Functions as a frame or network for many tissues. *Collagen vascular diseases* are *diffuse connective tissue* diseases. These include rheumatoid arthritis, systemic lupus erythematosus, scleroderma (progressive systemic sclerosis), polymyositis and dermatomyositis, vasculitis, Sjögren's syndrome.

CONNECTIVE TISSUE DISORDERS. Group of diseases of connective tissue with similar anatomic and pathological features. Many believe these are autoimmune diseases in which the immune system malfunctions and attacks itself, resulting in damaged skin, muscles, and other parts of the body. The common clinical sign is inflammation, of unknown cause, of the connective tissue and often blood vessels. (See *collagen vascular diseases*, Chapter 23.)

CYANOSIS. Blueness of skin caused by slow blood flow (reduced oxyhemoglobin, usually less than S$_{aO2}$) in blood vessels. Can result from pulmonary or cardiac disease. For Raynaud's, the second stage when there are three stages. Can be the first stage.

DERMATOMYOSITIS. See *connective tissue disease, polymyositis.*

DOPPLER ULTRASOUND. Uses high-frequency sound waves directed and reflected by red blood cells moving through a vessel. Red cells shift the frequency by an amount proportional to their velocity (the Doppler effect). This frequency shift produces an audible signal and visual pulse waves. One use is measuring blood flow in fingers in patients with Raynaud's.

DYSPROTEINEMIAS. "Derangement of protein content of the blood" (*Dorland's Illustrated Medical Dictionary,* 1988). Proteinemia is excess protein in the blood.

EFFERENT DIGITAL NERVES. A nerve, such as a motor nerve, carrying impulses from the CNS to the digits (fingers or toes). Contrast with *afferent* nerves.

EPINEPHRINE. Adrenaline. Hormone secreted by the adrenal medulla. (See *catecholamines* and *norepinephrine.*)

ERGOT PREPARATIONS. Ergot alkaloids are used in treating moderate to severe migraine and related headaches such as cluster headaches, status migrainosis, chronic daily headache, and menstrual migraine. Ergot is derived from rye plant fungus. Available as *ergotamine* tartrate (Cafergot, Wigraine, Ergomar, Ergostat, Bellergal-S, Migrogot) and dihydroergotamine (DHE-45) injections (intravenous, intramuscular, or subcutaneous). The DHE differs from the tartrate. For example, it is a weaker arterial vasoconstrictor, has selective venoconstricting properties, substantially less emetic (nauseating) features, and less uterine effects. Both have agonist action on serotonin (5-HT_{1a} and 5-HT_{1d}) and alpha-adrenergic receptors. Both create vasoconstriction by stimulating arterial smooth muscle through 5-HT receptors. Both constrict venous capacitance. Both inhibit reuptake of norepinephrine at sympathetic nerve endings. Both reduce vasogenic/neurogenic inflammation. (See *sympathetic,* Chapter 18, and others.)

GUANETHIDINE. A drug that depresses postganglionic adrenergic nerves, inhibiting sympathetic activity. Has been used in treating hypertension. (Guanethidine monosulfate is an ingredient in Esimil.)

HYPEREMIA. Excess of blood in a part. Two causes are local or general relaxation of arterioles or blocked outflow from the area. Reactive hyperemia involves temporary arrested flow and restoration such as in Raynaud's.

HYPOTHYROIDISM, ADULT. (See *myxedema.*) Caused by an underactive thyroid gland. A shortage of thyroid hormone slows the basal metabolic rate. It usually develops slowly over months or years. It is not common but not unusual. It afflicts men and women of any age, but most commonly middle-aged women. The person feels physically and mentally sluggish. Usually, an abnormal antibody destroys the thyroid gland. Sometimes, the pituitary does not produce thyroid-stimulating hormone (TSH). Sometimes, the treatment for hyperthyroidism produces hypothyroidism because it works too well. Hashimoto's disease (lymphocytic thyroiditis) may cause it. The cause is unknown in some cases. Symptoms include constant tiredness, muscle aches, slowed heart rate, constipation, dry and lusterless skin, thickened skin, hoarse voice, hearing loss, puffy face, dry hair, goiter in some people, heavy and prolonged menstrual periods, decreased interest in sex, and/or an inability to stay warm in cool or cold ambient temperatures. Increased weight, if present, is slight. Treatment is usually successful. *Hyperthyroidism* is the excessive secretion of hormone by the thyroid gland. (See Chapter 18 for more on hyperthyroidism.)

IMIPRAMINE HYDROCHLORIDE (TOFRANIL). The first tricyclic antidepressant, also used for other purposes such as nocturnal enuresis. Action is not primarily by stimulating the CNS. Blocks uptake of norepinephrine at nerve endings and thus potentiates adrenergic synapses. (See Chapter 25.)

LUMBAR SYMPATHECTOMY. (See *sympathectomy.*) Cutting of the sympathetic nerves from the lumbar spine.

METHYSERGIDE. Potent serotonin antagonist having vasoconstrictor effects. Inhibits or blocks serotonin. Used as analgesic for treating some patients with migraines (methysergide maleate is Sansert). Several contraindications including peripheral vascular disease, severe hypertension, pulmonary disease, collagen diseases, and others.

MIXED CONNECTIVE TISSUE DISEASE (MCTD). A rheumatic disease with overlapping features similar to three connective tissue diseases: SLE, scleroderma, and polymyositis/dermatomyositis. Immune factors are implicated. May be a distinct clinical disease. Women comprise about 80% of patients with MCTD. Very serious disease with average mortality of about 13% in an average of 6 to 12 years. Most patients respond to corticosteroids if treated early, and long-term remissions do occur. (See *connective tissue disease.*)

MYXEDEMA. (See *hypothyroidism, adult.*) Untreated hypothyroidism for several years. Myxedema coma involves drowsiness and a sensation of intense intolerance for cold. Profound lethargy and unconsciousness follow this. Sedatives may precipitate this. Requires emergency medical treatment usually with hormone injections.

NIFEDIPINE (Trade name Procardia). One type of calcium channel antagonist in the dihydro-properadine group. Also called calcium ion influx inhibitor or slow channel blocker. These are drugs used to lower blood pressure by decreasing vascular resistance. Antianginal drug. May worsen headache in up to 30% of patients. Less commonly used for migraines than most widely used verapamil (other trade names Calan, Isoptin, Verelan, Verapamil HCl) of the phenylalkylamine group of calcium antagonists. (Also, Chapters 14 and 15.)

NOREPINEPHRINE (NORADRENALINE). A natural neurohormone. One type of *catecholamine*, a body compound having a sympathomimetic action. A powerful vasopressor (constrictor of capillaries and arteries). Others include epinephrine and dopamine. Norepinephrine is released by postganglionic adrenergic nerves and the adrenal medulla (see Chapters 7, 18). Has mostly alpha-adrenergic activity and some beta-adrenergic activity. Pharmaceutical is norepinephrine bitartrate (Also called levarterenol, bitartrate). (Also see Chapters 7, 14, 15, 20, 36.)

OBSTRUCTIVE ARTERIAL DISEASES. Examples include thromboangiitis obliterans and arteriosclerosis obliterans.

PLATELETS (THROMBOCYTES). Round or oval discs in blood. Do not contain hemoglobin. Important role in coagulation, hemostasis, and thrombus formation. Adhere to each other and the edges of an injured small vessel and thus clot or plug it.

PLETHYSMOGRAPHY. A common skin surface index of blood flow. Measures blood volume pulse (BVP), also called finger pulse volume (FPV). An infrared emitter and detector in the sensor measures small variations in blood volume occurring with every heartbeat. The BVP is a measure of the amplitude of each pulse and is an index of blood flow.

POLYCYTHEMIA VERA (TRUE). Caused by bone marrow producing too many red blood cells. There also are increased white blood cells and platelets. Usually develops gradually and appears in late middle age and slightly more often in men. Differentiate from secondary polycythemia caused by heavy smoking of cigarettes, severe lung disease, abnormal hemoglobin, or living at high altitudes. The secondary form is the body overcompensating for low concentration of oxygen and making too many red blood cells. Treatment is necessary to avoid thicker (more viscous) blood, increasing the risk of stroke or a heart attack. The first treatment is often withdrawing blood to achieve normal or low hemoglobin. Medication, such as radioactive phosphorus, can reduce production of blood cells by the bone marrow.

POLYMYOSITIS: A rare disorder of inflamed muscles. The presence of skin and muscle inflammation is *dermatomyositis*. Women are twice as likely to have these, and these disorders occur at any age. Both disorders can disappear within a few months. However, when they affect the throat muscles and swallowing, death can occur. Prednisone is the main drug therapy, or immunosuppressive drugs such as methotrexate, if prednisone does not work.

PRAZOSIN (HYDROCHLORIDE). (Trade names Minipress, Minzide). Causes vasodilation. Used as antihypertensive drug.

PRIMARY PULMONARY HYPERTENSION. Very uncommon obliterative disease involving small and medium pulmonary arteries. Narrowing of the vessels lumen always occurs. This results in failure of the right ventricle or fatal syncope in 2 to 5 years. Females have this 5 times more often than males. Raynaud's phenomenon and arthralgias often present and often precede, by years, the apparent onset of PPH.

RECEPTOR DENSITY. Alpha- and beta-adrenergic receptor density in the peripheral vasculature.

REFLEX SYMPATHETIC DYSTROPHY (RSD). Burning sensation or pain and tenderness caused by water retention, usually in a hand or foot. Other symptoms are thin or shiny skin along with increased sweating and hair growth. It can develop weeks or months after an injury, heart attack, or stroke. Can affect a kneecap or hip. In the second phase, which usually develops over months, the skin becomes cool and shiny. Contracture may occur. Usually occurs after age 50, in men and women about equally. Loss of minerals in bones is typical and revealed by X-rays. If not treated promptly, irreversible damage can occur. Analgesics, heat and cold, and exercise are common treatments. Corticosteroid drugs are useful for some people.

REGIONAL SYMPATHECTOMY. Sympathectomy is an interruption of some portion of the sympathetic nervous pathway by transection, resection, or other means.

RENAL. Kidney.

RESERPINE. Older drug previously used as an antihypertensive. Also has sedative effects. Side effects can include depression.

RHEUMATOID ARTHRITIS (RA). An autoimmune, systemic disease presumably stimulated by an unknown virus. The immune system attacks itself. Contrast with osteoarthritis, caused by wear and tear in normal use, and affects only the musculoskeletal system.

RUBOR. Redness of skin caused by excess blood. Often accompanied by painful, throbbing, or burning sensations. Reactive hyperemia. In Raynaud's, the third stage when there are three color changes (triphasic).

SCLERODERMA (PROGRESSIVE SYSTEMIC SCLEROSIS, OR PSS). Means hard skin. This connective tissue disorder leads to a permanent tightness and shiny skin in affected areas. Common areas are arms, face, or hands. Other symptoms are puffy hands and feet, especially in the morning, and joint pain and stiffness. Women are about four times as likely to get it. Management depends on the severity and body systems affected. One treats the hypertension with medication, the joint pain with analgesics, and intestinal problems such as atrophy of the intestinal walls with antibiotics. When skin is affected, exercise is essential to limit stiffening and maintain blood flow. One needs to stop smoking. Antireflux therapy and avoiding eating 3 to 4 hours before bedtime are for heartburn. Antacids protect the esophagus muscular lining.

SECONDARY CAUSE OF REYNAUD'S. Raynaud's caused by another disease such as scleroderma. Contrast with the more common primary idiopathic Raynaud's.

SEROTONIN. Vasoconstrictor. Synthesized in humans in certain intestinal cells or in central or peripheral neurons. Found in high concentrations in many blood tissues including intestinal mucosa, pineal body, and CNS. Synthesis starts with uptake of tryptophan into serotonergic neurons. Tryptophan is changed (hydroxylated) by an enzyme to become 5-hydroxytryptophan, then changed (decarboxylated) by another enzyme to serotonin (5-HT). There are three types of receptors, 5-HT$_1$, 5-HT$_2$, and 5-HT$_3$, and four subtypes of 5-HT$_1$. It has many physiological properties, including inhibiting gastric secretions, stimulating smooth muscle, and serving as a central neurotransmitter. Also often called *5-HT, 5-hydroxytryptamine.* A major factor in medical/neurological and psychiatric conditions such as migraines and depression. About 90% occurs in the gastrointestinal tract, about 8% in blood platelets, and the rest in the brain.

PLATELET SEROTONIN. About 8% of 5-HT (serotonin) is found in blood platelets. It falls at the onset of a migraine attack and is normal between attacks.

SJÖGREN'S SYNDROME. A connective tissue disease. Symptoms are dryness of the eyes, with a sandy or gritty feeling, and dry mouth. Often occurs with rheumatoid arthritis or other disorders such as lupus, scleroderma, or polymyositis. Mostly found in middle-aged women. Eye drops and stimulating saliva are the main treatments to relieve symptoms. Severe cases may require corticosteroids.

SYMPATHOLYTIC AGENTS. Agents that oppose the effects of adrenergic postganglionic fibers of the SNS (hence, *antiadrenergic*). Contrast with *sympathomimetic.* (See Chapters 14, 15, and others.)

SYSTEMIC LUPUS ERYTHEMATOSUS (SLE). A life-long and usually episodic disease affecting 10 times more women than men and usually starting between 15 and 35. Frequently affects the synovial membrane in joints and produces inflammation, swelling, and pain, usually in the fingers and wrists. Other symptoms include rashes, especially on the nose and cheeks; localized chest pain and coughing; sunlight sensitivity causing rash and fever; and baffling fatigue. Diagnosis is by a blood test, an antinuclear antibody test that detects a specific protein usually found in persons with SLE. Other tests, such as creatinine to assess kidney function, also are used. It is a serious disease that can affect all organ systems. For some people it can cause internal bleeding, reduced resistance to infection, depression, kidney disease, and serious damage to joints. However, for many people, SLE is not major. Treatments include corticosteroids and anti-inflamatory drugs. Other drugs also are common.

THERMAL LAG. Lag between change in the amount of peripheral blood flow regulated by the diameter of peripheral blood vessel and the change in skin surface temperature, as detected by the thermistor.

THORACIC OUTLET OBSTRUCTION SYNDROMES. Group of ill-defined syndromes with symptoms of arm pain and paresthesias in the hand, neck, shoulder, or arms; vasomotor symptoms including Raynaud's phenomenon. Several causes are proposed.

THROMBOANGIITIS OBLITERANS (BUERGER'S DISEASE). A rare disorder. An obliterative or occlusive disease with ischemia and superficial phlebitis and inflammation in small and medium-sized veins and arteries of the hands and feet. Early symptoms include coldness, numbness, tingling, or burning (Raynaud's phenomenon). Pain from severe ischemia then develops, and ulcers or gangrene appear later. Usually (about 95%) occurs in young and middle-aged men who smoke cigarettes. Unless one stops smoking early and avoids other factors (e.g., trauma from tight shoes, thermal injury), amputation is typical.

TRAUMATIC VASOSPASTIC DISEASE (VIBRATION DISEASE). The continuous use of vibratory tools can cause diminished flexion of the fingers, loss of cold, heat, and pain perception, blanching, and osteoarthritic changes in the arm joints.

THYMOXAMINE. A sympatholytic agent that is mainly an alpha$_1$-adrenergic receptor antagonist also with some alpha$_2$-adrenergic receptor blocking effects. May have fewer side effects than prazosin. Not available in the United States.

TROPHIC CHANGES. Changes (e.g., in skin) caused by nutritional changes.

VASOACTIVE SUBSTANCES. Interact with biochemical alpha and beta adrenergic receptors, affect finger blood flow circulation.

REFERENCES

Belch, J. J. F. (1990). The phenomenon, syndrome and disease of Maurice Raynaud. *British Journal of Rheumatology, 29*(3), 162–165.

Berkow, R., & Fletcher, A. J. (1992). *The Merck manual of diagnosis and therapy* (16th ed.). Rahway, NJ: Merck.

Blanchard, E. B., Andrasik, F., Neff, D. F., Arena, J. G., Ahles, T. A., Jurish, S. E., Pallmeyer, T. P., Saunders, N. L., Teders, S. J., Barron, K. D., & Rodichok, L. D. (1982). Biofeedback and relaxation training with three kinds of headache: Treatment effects and their prediction. *Journal of Consulting and Clinical Psychology, 50*, 562–575.

Coffman, J. D. (1991). Raynaud's phenomenon: An update. *Hypertension, 17*, 593–602.

Dorland's illustrated medical dictionary (27th ed.). (1988). Philadelphia, PA: W. B. Saunders.

Freedman, R. R. (1987). Long-term effectiveness of behavioral treatments for Raynaud's disease. *Behavior Therapy, 18*, 387–399.

Freedman, R. R. (1989). Quantitative measurements of finger blood flow during behavioral treatments for Raynaud's disease. *The Society for Psychophysiological Research, 26*(4), 437–441.

Freedman, R. R. (1991). Physiological mechanisms of temperature biofeedback. *Biofeedback and Self-Regulation, 16*(2), 95–115.

Freedman, R. R. (1994, March 3–8). Mechanisms of temperature biofeedback. *Invited Citation Lecture Presented at the 25th Annual Meeting of the Association for Applied Psychophysiology and Biofeedback, Atlanta, GA.* Aurora, CO: Sound Images, Inc.

Freedman, R. R., & Ianni, P. (1983). Self control of digital temperature: Physiological factors and transfer effects. *Psychophysiology, 20*, 682–689.

Freedman, R. R., Ianni, P., & Wenig, P. (1983). Behavioral treatment of Raynaud's disease. *Journal of Consulting and Clinical Psychology, 51*, 539–549.

Freedman, R. R., Keegan, D., Migály, P., Vining, S., Mayes, M., & Galloway, M. P. (1991, March 15–20). Plasma catecholamines during behavioral treatments for Raynaud's disease. In *Proceedings of the 22th Annual Meeting of the Association for Applied Psychophysiology and Biofeedback, Dallas* (pp. 8–11). Wheatridge, CO: Association for Applied Psychophysiology and Biofeedback.

Freedman, R. R., Keegan, D., Rodriguez, J., & Galloway, M. P. (1993, March 25–30). Plasma catecholamine levels during temperature biofeedback training in normal subjects. In *Proceedings of the 24th Annual Meeting of the Association for Applied Psychophysiology and Biofeedback, Los Angeles, CA* (pp. 92–95). Wheatridge, CO: Association for Applied Psychophysiology and Biofeedback.

Freedman, R. R., Lynn, S. J., & Ianni, P. (1982). Behavioral assessment of Raynand's disease. In F. J. Keefe & J. A. Blumenthal (Eds.), *Assessment strategies in behvioral medicine.* New York: Grune & Stratton.

Freedman, R. R., Mayes, M. D., & Sabharwal, S. C. (1989). Induction of vasospastic attacks despite digital nerve block in Raynaud's disease and phenomenon. *Circulation, 80*(4), 859–862.

Freedman, R. R., Morris, M., Norton, D. A., Masselink, D., Sabharwal, S. C., & Mayes, M. D. (1988). Physiological mechanism of digital vasoconstriction training. *Biofeedback and Self-Regulation, 13*(4), 299–305.

Freedman, R. R., Sabharwal, S. C., Ianni, P., Nagaraj, D., Wenig, P., & Mayes, M. D. (1988). Nonneural beta-adrenergic vasodilating mechanism in temperature biofeedback. *Psychosomatic Medicine, 50*, 394–401.

Freedman, R. R., Sabharwal, S. C., & Nagaraj, D. (1987). Sex differences in peripheral vascular adrenergic receptors. *Circulation Research, 61*(4), 581–585.

Grove, R. N., & Belanger, M. T. (1983). Biofeedback and Raynaud's diathesis. In W. H. Rickles, J. H. Sandweiss, D. W. Jacobs, R. N. Grove, & E. Criswell (Eds.), *Biofeedback and family practice medicine* (pp. 193–232). New York: Plenum Press.

Jobe, J. B., Beetham, W. P., Roberts, D. E., Silver, G. R., Larsen, R. F., Hamlet, M. P., & Sampson, J. B. (1985). Induced vasodilation as a home treatment for Raynaud's disease. *Journal of Rheumatology, 12*(5), 953–956.

Keefe, F., Surwit, R. & Pilon, R. (1980). Biofeedback, autogenic training, and progressive relaxation in the treatment of Raynaud's disease: A comparative study. *Journal of Applied Behavior Analysis, 13,* 3–11.

Lewis, T. (1929). Experiments relating to the peripheral mechanism involved in spasmodic arrest of circulation in the fingers, a variety of Raynaud's disease. *Heart, 15,* 7–101.

McGrady, A., & Roberts, G. (1991). Racial differences in the relaxation response of hypertensives. *Psychosomatic Medicine, 54,* 71–78.

Raynaud, A. G. (1862). *De l'asphyxie locale et de la gangrène symétique des extrémités.* Paris: Rigoux.

Raynaud, M. (1988). *New research on the nature and treatment of local asphyxia of the extremities* (T. Barlow, Trans.). London: New Sydenham Society.

Rose, G. D., & Carlson, J. G. (1987). The behavioral treatment of Raynaud's disease: A review. *Biofeedback and Self-Regulation, 12*(4), 257–272.

Schwartz, M. S., & Fehmi, L. (1982). *Applications standards and guidelines for providers of biofeedback services.* Wheatridge, CO: Biofeedback Society of America.

Sedlacek, K. (1984). Biofeedback treatment of primary Raynaud's. In F. J. McGuigan, W. E. Sime, & J. M. Wallace (Eds.), *Stress and tension control.* New York: Plenum Press.

Sedlacek, K., (1989). Biofeedback treatment of primary Raynaud's disease. In J. V. Basmajian (Ed.), *Biofeedback: Principles and practice for clinicians* (3rd ed., pp. 317–321). Baltimore: Williams & Wilkins.

Simpson, D. D. & Nelson, A. E. (1976). Specificity of finger pulse volume feedback during relaxation. *Biofeedback and Self-Regulation, 1*(4), 433–443.

Strandness, D. E. Jr., & Sumner, D. S. (1975). Applications of ultrasound to the study of arteriosclerosis obliterans [Review]. *Angiology, 26*(2), 187–198.

Stambrook, M., Hamel, E. R., & Carter, S. A. (1988). Training to vasodilate in a cooling environment: A valid treatment for Raynaud's phenomenon. *Biofeedback and Self-Regulation, 13*(1), 9–23.

Taub, E. (1977). Self-Regulation of human tissue temperature. In G. E. Schwartz & J. Beatty (Eds.), *Biofeedback: Theory and research.* New York: Academic Press.

Thomas, C. L. (1989). *Tabor's cyclopedic medical dictionary* (16th ed.). Philadelphia: F. A. Davis.

18

Biobehavioral Treatment of Essential Hypertension

Angele McGrady
R. Paul Olson
J. Suzanne Kroon

This chapter begins with a summary of the basic physiology of blood pressure (BP) regulation. It proceeds to the classification of BP, the definition of hypertension, and finally describes the characteristics of hypertensive disease. The chapter reviews traditional pharmacotherapy for hypertension according to the revised stepped-care approach and discusses briefly nonpharmacological treatments other than biofeedback and relaxation. For the most part, the chapter consists of a detailed description of a composite treatment plan for essential hypertension. This plan utilizes and references key research from several biofeedback treatment centers and psychophysiological laboratories. We develop characteristics of baseline, treatment, and follow-up, discuss patient education, and list evaluation criteria for outcome. The next section of the chapter deals with how to preselect patients to enhance their chances for success in lowering BP. The chapter ends with suggestions for further research.

Also germane to the treatment of patients with essential hypertension are (1) the general principles of biofeedback measurement, (2) considerations in developing low physiological arousal, (3) the intake process, (4) cognitive preparation of patients, (5) compliance, and (6) generalization. In this chapter, however, we discuss only selected topics that are specific to treatment of essential hypertension.

NORMAL REGULATION OF BLOOD PRESSURE

A basic understanding of the physiology of blood pressure (Vander, Sherman, & Luciano, 1994; Ganong, 1991) is necessary before the biofeedback practitioner can implement a treatment plan to reduce high BP. Appreciation of the complexities of neural and endocrine influences is not essential. However, the practitioner must (1) understand the variables that determine BP and the elements of BP regulation, and (2) explain to patients in layman's terms the potential effects of biofeedback and relaxation on BP.

Blood pressure is expressed as systolic/diastolic in millimeters of mercury. Systolic BP (SBP) is the maximum pressure during ejection of blood from the heart, and diastolic BP (DBP) is the minimum pressure during cardiac relaxation. Mean arterial pressure (MAP) is the average blood pressure driving blood through tissues.

445

Cardiac output and total peripheral resistance determine blood pressure (see Figure 18.1). One calculates cardiac output by multiplying heart rate (beats per minute) by stroke volume output. The latter is the amount of blood ejected with each beat of the heart. Factors controlling heart rate and stroke volume include sympathetic and parasympathetic nerve activity. Total peripheral resistance (TPR) is the resistance or impediment to the flow of blood in the arteries, arterioles, and to a minor extent, the veins. Sympathetic activity, circulating substances in the blood, and local conditions in the tissues all influence TPR. For example, if sympathetic activity increases, arterioles constrict and present a larger resistance to the flow of blood, raising BP.

Neural, kidney, and hormonal factors all control BP. The nervous system is very important in the rapid control of arterial pressure. Baroreceptors located in the walls of the heart and blood vessels are stretch receptors that monitor BP. The baroreceptors respond to distention caused by increased pressure by sending an electrical signal through nerves to the vasomotor center in the medulla of the brain. Here, groups of neurons exert control of blood pressure. Nerve responses begin within a few seconds and can decrease pressure significantly within 5–10 seconds. The baroreceptor system is most important for short-term regulation of arterial pressure, whereas long-term regulation requires mechanisms based in the kidney (renal) and in the endocrine systems.

Blood volume is a critical determinant of long-term BP level. For example, when the circulatory system contains too much fluid, arterial pressure rises. Increased BP in turn signals the kidneys to excrete the excess fluid (pressure diuresis). Loss of fluid through the urine then returns fluid balance to normal and decreases blood pressure. The hormone aldosterone, released from the adrenal cortex and the renin–angiotensin system, is also important in BP regulation. Reabsorption of sodium by the kidney is controlled by aldosterone. In turn, aldosterone secretion is stimulated by the renin–angiotensin hormonal complex. For example, decreased plasma volume instigates a neural and endocrine reflex re-

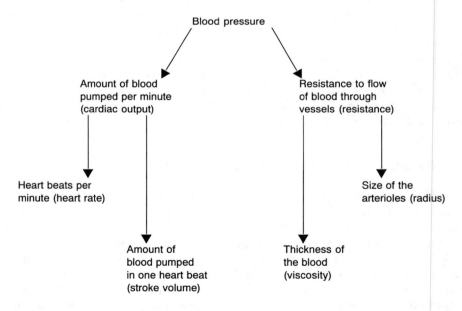

FIGURE 18.1. Determinants of blood pressure. Data from Vander, Sherman, and Luciano (pp. 452–453).

sponse that consists of increased renin–angiotensin and aldosterone, resulting in increased sodium reabsorption. Fluid loss decreases, and fluid balance is restored.

Maintenance of blood flow to the vascular beds, such as those in skin and muscle, requires a certain level of blood pressure. If BP is too low, the tissues will not receive enough blood. The variation in the proportion of blood flow to different tissues depends on the metabolic needs of those tissues. The end products of metabolism build up in active tissues, then dilation of blood vessels occurs to ensure delivery of more oxygenated blood. This is local regulation. On the other hand, some substances circulate within the bloodstream and affect tissues distant from where the substance was originally produced and secreted. For example, the adrenal medulla releases epinephrine that dilates the vessels in skeletal muscles. The atrial natriuretic peptide, secreted by the heart, antagonizes the actions of various vasoconstrictor chemicals. Other vasoactive compounds are released by the walls of blood vessels (e.g., endothelium-derived relaxing factor), affect tone and diameter, and, therefore, affect resistance and BP.

In summary, receptors (monitoring structures) keep track of BP. Change in BP alerts the nerve cells in the vasomotor center. Response to the change in BP involves modulation of the two basic determinants of BP: cardiac output and total peripheral resistance by nervous, renal, or hormonal action.

Assessment of Blood Pressure

Practitioners must recognize the many possible errors in routine BP measurements by patients and professionals inadequately trained to measure blood pressures. The most accurate BP instruments are the standard mercury sphygmomanometers. The second choice is a properly calibrated aneroid sphygmomanometer. Practitioners should recalibrate the aneroid sphygmomanometer against a mercury sphygmomanometer every 3–12 months depending on the frequency of its use. For office professional use, automatic BP monitors can be purchased. They provide reliable measures of SBP, DBP, and heart rate. If a practice contains a significant number of hypertensive patients, an investment in a 24-hour ambulatory device may be worthwhile.

Practitioners should help patients select good quality, easy-to-use instruments and train them in their use. To do this, practitioners need to be familiar with several brands and models of sphygmomanometers. Electronic BP instruments that provide a digital readout are also available and may be useful to individuals with poor hearing for home use. All BP instruments need to be recalibrated at regular intervals. Medical supply stores frequently stock several types of monitors and help patients with assembly and calibration of their instruments.

Both standardized and repeated BP measurement are critical to establishing the patient's actual pretreatment BP and evaluating therapy effects. Blood pressures measured under very similar conditions are more nearly standard than such measurements obtained under different conditions. Many factors, including those listed below, either artificially increase or decrease the values obtained. The four categories that subsume these factors are patient, practitioner, setting, and equipment (adapted from Kaplan, 1986, and Joint National Committee, 1993).

Patient
1. The arm that is used. One should initially measure BP in both arms.
2. The position and level of the patient's arm. The arm and back should be supported; position the arm at heart level.

3. The position of the patient: sitting, standing, supine. Measurements should begin after the patient has been sitting for 5 minutes.
4. Whether or not the patient is talking or quiet. The patient should be quiet during measurements.
5. The breathing rate of the patient.
6. The emotional state of the patient shortly before or at the time one obtains the BP. Consider his or her attitudes toward both BP measurement and the professional doing the measuring.
7. The length of time since the patient ate or exercised.
8. Recent use of nicotine, caffeine, or other chemicals. Patients should not have had caffeine or smoked within 30 minutes of BP measurement.
9. Current diet and recent dietary changes (e.g., sodium intake).
10. The interval between BP measurements in the same session. Average at least two measurements separated by 2 minutes.
11. Body weight and fluid retention.
12. Changes in types or dosages of antihypertensive medications, other prescription, and over-the-counter medications.

Practitioner
13. The person measuring the BP (e.g., patient, nurse, physician, biofeedback practitioner).
14. The manner (attitude) of the person measuring the BP.

Setting
15. The time of day, day of the week, season of the year.
16. The site and setting of BP measurement (e.g., work, home, professional's office).
17. The patient's familiarity with or habituation to the environment in which one measures the BP.

Equipment
18. The instrument used, whether it be a manual sphygmomanometer, or an electronic model. The same instrument should be used each time.
19. The calibration of the instrument.
20. The placement of the cuff on the arm and the rate of deflation of the cuff.
21. A cuff size appropriate to arm circumference.

An incorrect cuff size may significantly alter BP readings. A cuff that is too small produces a falsely high BP reading. As a result, one could incorrectly classify obese patients as having hypertension. For arm circumferences of less than 33 centimeters, we recommend a regular size adult cuff (12 × 23 centimeters). The recommendation for arm circumferences between 33 and 41 centimeters is a large size (15 × 33 centimeters). Use a thigh size cuff of 18 × 36 centimeters for those arms larger than 41 centimeters. Practitioners often purchase cuffs of different sizes for the clinical setting so a properly sized cuff will be available when needed.

Classification of Blood Pressure

The Joint National Committee (JNC) is a group of professionals expert in the diagnosis and treatment of hypertension. They meet approximately every 4 years to study and discuss results of epidemiological studies and therapeutic trials. Their published reports guide practitioners who care for patients with hypertension. The fifth and latest report presents the classification of BP shown in Table 18.1 (Joint National Committee, 1993). The terminology for levels of BP above normal was revised. "Mild," "moderate," "severe," and "very severe" are now stages 1–4. The term "nonpharmacological therapy" is now "life-style modifications." The report discusses recommendations for treatment using life-style modification and antihypertensive medications. Target BPs are < than 90 millimeters Hg DBP and < 140 millimeters Hg SBP.

HYPERTENSION

Definitions and Characteristics

"Hypertension" is a complex disease characterized by sustained elevations of SBP, DBP, or both. "Essential" or "primary" hypertension is elevated BP of unknown etiology and is the diagnosis for more than 90% of people with chronically elevated BP (Kaplan, 1986). Professionals agree that environmental, endocrine, neurological, hemodynamic, and psychosocial factors interact to hasten the appearance of hypertension in individuals predisposed to elevated BP by heredity, personality, or both.

"Secondary" hypertension results from a specific disease or pathological abnormality in the body. Some examples are diseases of the kidney, tumors of the adrenal gland, Cushing's disease, primary aldosteronism, and diseases of the thyroid gland (hyperthyroidism) (Kaplan, 1986). Medical and surgical management of secondary hypertensive disorders usually supersede psychophysiological therapy. Thus it is unlikely that physicians would refer these individuals for biofeedback for their hypertension.

The detrimental effects of hypertension are well documented. Sustained elevations of BP can damage the brain, kidneys, heart, and blood vessels. Untreated hypertension contributes to premature death through stroke, heart attack, or kidney failure. The presence of laboratory values outside the normal range in addition to elevated BP increases the incidence of complications of hypertensive disease. The presence or absence and the type of organ damage are also part of classifying hypertension and determining its severity.

The incidence of essential hypertension increases with age. The prevalence is higher for young adult men and middle-aged men than same-aged women; elderly women have a higher incidence than men. About 25% of children with one hypertensive parent will have sustained elevated BP. If both parents have hypertension, then about 50% of their children will develop the disease. Hypertension develops about 10 times more often in persons over-

TABLE 18.1. Classification of Blood Pressure in Adults Aged 18 Years or Older

Category	Systolic (mm Hg)	Diastolic (mm Hg)
Normal	<130	<85
High normal	130–139	85–89
Hypertension		
Stage 1 (mild)	140–159	90–99
Stage 2 (moderate)	160–179	100–109
Stage 3 (severe)	180–209	110–119
Stage 4 (very severe)	≥ 210	≥ 120

Note. Based on data from Joint National Committee (1993). *Archives of Internal Medicine, 153,* 154–183. Adapted by permission.

weight by 20% over normal body weight compared to those maintaining normal body weight (Joint National Committee, 1993). African Americans are much more likely to have elevated BP and more severe hypertension than whites (Dressler, 1991).

There are risk factors associated with the development of essential hypertension. These are: age, sex, heredity, race, obesity, dietary factors (alcohol, high sodium diet), lack of physical activity, psychological stress, sociocultural variables, and personality (Kaplan, 1986). Anxiety, anger, and depression are the primary personality factors that have been investigated (Byrne, 1992). Scientists cannot reliably identify a single characteristic or risk factor as the causal factor in the development or maintenance of elevated BP. For example, only about 30% of hypertensive individuals are sensitive to sodium and to volume. Their BP decreases by greater than 10 millimeters Hg MAP with sodium and fluid depletion (Weinberger, 1993).

Attempts have been made to describe the pathophysiology of hypertension in terms of disordered cardiac output or total peripheral resistance or both. The hypersympathetic state of initial BP elevation depends on high cardiac output. As hypertension progresses, high resistance predominates (Julius, 1991). It is clear that the diagnosis of essential hypertension alone tells us very little about causes and psychophysiological characteristics of this heterogenous condition. Rather, a mosaic of behavioral, psychological, and physiological factors leads to the development of chronically elevated BP.

Life-Style Modifications

The JNC (1993) placed "life-style modifications" (formerly called nonpharmacological therapies) as Step 1 in the algorithm for treatment of hypertension. Life-style modifications include sodium and alcohol restriction, physical exercise, weight control, and smoking cessation. The Joint National Committee recommends the following life-style modifications:

Lose weight if overweight

Limit alcohol intake to ≤ 1 ounce per day of ethanol (24 ounces of beer, 8 ounces of wine, or 2 ounces of 100-proof whiskey)

Exercise (aerobic) regularly

Reduce sodium intake to less than 100 millimole per day (< 2.3 grams of sodium or approximately < 6 grams of sodium chloride)

Maintain adequate dietary potassium, calcium, and magnesium intake

Stop smoking

Reduce dietary saturated fat and cholesterol intake for overall cardiovascular health; reducing fat intake also helps reduce caloric intake—important for control of weight and Type II diabetes

Health professionals who offer psychophysiological therapies, including biofeedback, should question patients about their life-style during the initial interview and then consider recommending changes in behavior. Providers of biofeedback and associated therapies, however, would do well to enlist the services of dietitians, smoking cessation experts, and established exercise programs to complement the biofeedback and relaxation therapies. If one combines other therapies with relaxation and biofeedback, it becomes difficult to determine the relative contributions of each to lowered BP. In the clinical setting, the analysis of separate efficacy of each treatment is often less important, since the overall objective is to lower BP to normotensive levels and decrease medication requirements. However, knowing the relative contribution of each therapy can sometimes be useful information, could help compliance, and makes it easier to justify each therapy.

The introduction of life-style changes should include an explanation to those patients being asked to change their behaviors and habits. Explain to patients that since sodium causes retention of fluid, the increased blood volume increases BP. Caffeine and nicotine are stimulants that acutely increase heart rate, therefore, cardiac output and BP. Encourage an exercise program, especially aerobic exercise. Discuss the conditioning effect of exercise on the muscles. For example, explain that active muscles need more blood; dilation of blood vessels decreases the resistance to blood flow and thereby lowers BP. The sedentary patient should get proper medical screening and approval before beginning a program of moderate or strenuous aerobic exercise. Set a contract with the patient—"Let's try life-style changes first. We'll recheck monthly for 4–6 months, then discuss alternatives."

Pharmacological Therapies

Pharmacotherapy is the core of treatment for persons with Stages 3 and 4 hypertension. With regard to the high-normal, mild, or moderate hypertensive groups, one may delay medication while the person attempts to implement life-style changes (Joint National Committee, 1988, 1993). Actually, compliance with taking medication may be poor in individuals who do not have noticeable symptoms. Medication can also have disturbing psychological and somatic side effects.

Research does not consistently support the notion that once individuals start medications, they require them for life. Tapering off and cessation of medication ("step-down therapy") do not automatically lead to resumption of elevated BP (Veterans Administration, 1975). Blood pressure may remain within normal limits for as long as 1 year. Thus, consider step-down therapy and drug withdrawal after BP remains stable for 1 year on medication. Regular follow-ups should be continued.

Formerly, many physicians used a standardized pharmacological stepped-care approach to treating hypertension. A revision of the stepped-care approach was prompted by the following factors:

1. Concern for patients' quality of life (Croog et al., 1986).
2. Development of new and effective pharmacological agents with fewer side effects.
3. Increased involvement of patients in their own self-care.
4. Research that supports matching one class of drug with a subset of the hypertensive population.

Major classes of antihypertensive drugs include diuretics, beta blockers, angiotensin converting enzyme (ACE) inhibitors, and calcium channel blockers. Diuretics increase sodium and water excretion by the kidney and, therefore, decrease TPR. Beta blockers decrease cardiac output and indirectly decrease blood volume. The ACE inhibitors lower vascular resistance. The calcium channel blockers inhibit blood vessel wall contraction, thus decreasing TPR (Mycek, Gertner, & Perper, 1992). The Joint National Committee (1993) recommends beginning pharmacological therapy with diuretics or beta blockers because of demonstrated reduction in morbidity or mortality. If BP response is inadequate, further therapy includes an increase in drug dose, substitution of a drug from another class (ACE inhibitors, calcium channel blocker, alpha blockers, alpha and beta blockers), or the addition of a second agent (Joint National Committee, 1993).

PSYCHOPHYSIOLOGICAL THERAPY: A MULTICOMPONENT APPROACH INCORPORATING BIOFEEDBACK

The biobehavioral therapies including biofeedback are useful in treating essential hypertension. They are adjuncts to standard pharmacological treatments in the moderate hypertensive patient or as an alternative to medication in the mild or borderline (Stage 1 or 2) hypertensive patient. Early reports (Patel, 1973, 1977; Benson, Shapiro, Tursky, & Schwartz, 1971; Kristt & Engel, 1975) demonstrated the effectiveness of biofeedback alone or combined with relaxation in lowering BP in individuals with essential hypertension. The 1988 report by the JNC stated that "relaxation and biofeedback therapies produce modest long term reductions in BP in selected groups." However, the more recent report (1993) states that ". . . The role of stress management techniques . . . is uncertain."

In our view, there are valid criticisms of many of the published biofeedback studies because of deficiencies in design and methodology. These critiques include the absence or inadequacy of pretreatment BP monitoring, medication changes during treatment, lack of clearly defined outcome measures, questionable generalization of the decreased BP to the home or work setting, and poorly designed or absent long-term follow-up (Jacob, Chesney, Williams, Ding, & Shapiro, 1991).

However, close inspection of the results of even the criticized studies reveals that a percentage of participants do lower BP and/or medication significantly. The benefits of maintaining normotensive BP with reduced or no medication are noteworthy. Therefore, we conclude that one can justify the psychophysiological therapies in the treatment of high BP. The practitioner should *implement the psychophysiological therapies in all essential hypertensive patients before medication in Stage 1, before medication with close medical supervision in Stage 2, and concurrently with medication in Stages 3 and 4.*

Therapy Rationale and Justification

The psychophysiological therapies are indicated when:

1. The medication side effects are severe.
2. The patient is young or has early, high normal, or Stage 1 hypertension.
3. Life-style changes alone were not enough to lower the BPs to the normotensive range.
4. The patient's physician opposes prescribing medication for the patient.
5. The patient has a specific interest in the self-regulation of physiological function and has realistic expectations.
6. The patient has a family history of hypertension and cardiovascular disease and wishes a preventive measure.
7. The patient has a stressful life-style and notices a slow increase in BP over time.
8. The patient can participate as a research subject in clinical trials of biofeedback and relaxation.

Consider the cost effectiveness of psychophysiological therapy and the possible use of alternative, less expensive methods such as losing weight, stopping smoking, reducing sodium intake, moderating alcohol intake, increasing physical activity, or combinations of these. Obviously, altering these risk factors is a less costly alternative for both patients and third-party payers.

Combined Pharmacotherapy and Psychophysiological Therapy

Biofeedback has been studied as an adjunct to diuretic therapy (Jurek, Higgins, & McGrady, 1992), beta-blockers, and other medications (Hatch et al., 1985; Glasgow, Engel, & D'Lugoff, 1989; Blanchard et al., 1986). Patients provided with adjunctive biofeedback and/or relaxation therapy are often able to decrease BP more than patients on medication alone. These two treatment modalities can be advantageously combined in the care of patients with essential hypertension. In fact, Brody suggested that the extent of a patient's psychological distress is directly proportional to the amount of medication required to control his or her BP (Brody, 1981).

If BP decreases to below 140/90 millimeters Hg and remains at that level, then reduction in medication is a possibility. Consult the patient's physician and ask for a withdrawal schedule for reducing medication. Whereas one can abruptly stop some antihypertensive drugs, one must taper others. If reduction of medication before treatment is not approved by the physician or if patients enter treatment medicated but with still elevated pressures, then at the end of biofeedback treatment, medication withdrawal should again be considered. Other possibilities are to reduce the dosage of medication or, if the patient is medicated with more than one type of antihypertensive medication, to withdraw one type while maintaining the other one. Similar to the life-style modifications, one can implement biofeedback before antihypertensive medication, concurrently with medication, or in a patient already stabilized on medication.

Stages of Treatment

Patient Education

Health care professionals provide various types of patient education throughout all the stages of treatment. During baseline, one may give the essential facts about hypertension, instruct the patient in the accurate measurement of BP, and give a simple explanation of the major factors affecting BP. During treatment one can provide the rationale for psychophysiological therapies as each procedure is introduced. One should also provide detailed information about each intervention, in layman's terms. Most patients can comprehend the basic biology of BP and how specific biological, chemical, and psychological factors affect their BP. Written materials and videos are helpful adjuncts to oral explanations, particularly in teaching groups of patients.

Baseline

The first treatment stage consists of a baseline period during which the therapist repeatedly monitors and records BPs. Multiple measurements of BP can, in a portion of the hypertensive population, result in decreases in BP that are statistically and clinically significant (Engel, Gaarder, & Glasgow, 1981; McGrady & Higgins, 1990). Decreases in office BP to normal levels with only monitoring do not always coincide with equal declines in home BP, so both office and home BPs should be available to the practitioner. Although the mechanism underlying the reduction in BP with monitoring is unknown, decreased anxiety or desensitization to BP measurements may be relevant factors.

Give patients careful instructions in how to take their own BPs. Lend them a BP device or encourage them to purchase one. Calibrate instruments and recheck them against the clinic instruments. Training patients to take their own BP is quite important. Demonstrate positioning of the arm and rest of the body, and step-by-step procedures. Give patients a written set of instructions with their log sheets. If you can, train them with a teaching stethoscope where both you and the patient hear the sounds simultaneously. Model correct techniques in your setting. Establish a standard rest period before measuring the BP. Usually, 3–5 minutes of sitting quietly is sufficient. Allow 1–2 minutes between two or three measurements. Discourage dialogue between measurements.

The BP log sheets should have space for recording date, time of day, caffeine/alcohol consumption, smoking, exercise, and all medications taken. In this way, patient and practitioner can identify variations in BP coincident with time of day and activities. During the baseline period, patients also have weekly professionally obtained BP in the health care provider's office. Both office and home BP values are necessary because discrepancies are common between BPs measured in the office and those measured elsewhere by the patients.

Baselines are necessarily flexible and variable in length. In a research setting, 3–4 weeks of BP monitoring allows the BP to stabilize. In clinical practice, however, a lengthy pretreatment period is impractical. The practitioner must reach the best compromise. If the patient already owns a BP monitoring device, ask him or her to log BPs and bring them to the first appointment. Otherwise begin monitoring at the first appointment. Assuming appointments are 1 week apart, the interview, initial psychophysiological measurements, and beginning therapy will still give the practitioner 10–14 days (20–40 values) of patient BP readings.

Biofeedback

Researchers and practitioners use several different types of biofeedback in treating essential hypertension. These include thermal, direct BP, electromyographic, and electrodermal feedback.

"Direct BP feedback" was described by Glasgow, Gaarder, and Engel (1982) as a BP-lowering technique utilizing direct blood pressure feedback. The procedure was introduced by Tursky, Shapiro, and Schwartz (1972) and revised by Kristt and Engel (1975).

> In this procedure the patient is trained to inflate the BP cuff to about the systolic pressure and to try to inhibit brachial artery sounds. Patients . . . attempt to control brachial artery sounds for about 25–30 seconds, after which they . . . deflate the cuff for about 15 seconds. If successful in inhibiting 25% of sounds on the previous trial, the patient . . . inflates the cuff to a pressure level 2 mm Hg less than that of the previous trial. The procedure was repeated until the patient could no longer lower SBP on two consecutive trials. . . . Patients were urged to practice . . . several times daily, but were especially encouraged to practice at the time of day when their pressures were likely to be highest as indicated by the findings during baseline. For most patients this was the afternoon. (p. 158)

Patients learn the procedure over a 3-month period. They develop the ability to identify the sensations that accompany reduction in SBPs and devise personalized techniques to lower BP. Generalization is also explained to patients so they may continue to apply the techniques without the sphygmomanometer many times each day and in many places and situations.

"Thermal biofeedback" has been studied extensively in two laboratories (Fahrion, Norris, Green, Green, & Snaar, 1986; Blanchard et al., 1986, 1988; reviewed in Blanchard, 1990). With thermal biofeedback, the practitioner instructs the individual to pay attention to the information indicating the temperature of his or her finger or toe. Patients attempt to warm their hands or feet using this feedback.

In an uncontrolled study (Fahrion et al., 1986), 77 patients monitored BP and received thermal biofeedback, muscle feedback, instructions in diaphragmatic breathing, and relaxation techniques. Criterion was 95°F for the hands and 93°F for the feet. Criteria were also set for breaths per minute and for muscle tension. Fifty-eight percent of the medicated patients eliminated medication; an additional 35% of the medicated patients reduced medications by half. The decreases in BP and medications were stable at 33 months.

The results of Blanchard's controlled studies favored monotherapy with thermal biofeedback over progressive relaxation in a group of medicated patients. Specific temperature criteria were not set. Patients trained with thermal biofeedback reduced BP more than patients trained with progressive relaxation. Supine and standing norepinephrine levels decreased concomitant with thermal biofeedback-mediated reduction in BP (McCoy et al., 1988).

McGrady (1994) utilized thermal biofeedback and relaxation therapy in a group format. Forty-nine percent of the sample met the criterion for success, a decrease in mean arterial pressure of 5 millimeters Hg. Significant decreases in measures of anxiety and plasma aldosterone also occurred in the treated patients and not in the untreated controls.

The physiological rationale for the use of thermal biofeedback is that increased sympathetic activity commonly observed during stress constricts the blood vessels in the skin. The decreased blood flow results in cooler temperature. In contrast, decreased sympathetic activation results in less vasoconstriction. So, as individuals warm their hands, the practitioners are actually training decreased neurally mediated vasoconstriction and subsequently decreased TPR. A criticism of this explanation is that the skin vasculature actually contributes only a small percentage to the overall total peripheral resistance. Furthermore, Freedman (1991) showed in his laboratory that the small but statistically significant increases in temperature mediated by thermal feedback in normotensives depend on nonneural factors whose identities are presently unknown. Others have argued that a generalized reduction in arousal occurs with thermal biofeedback particularly when it is combined with relaxation therapies (Fahrion et al., 1986).

"Electromyographic feedback" was the modality used in early studies by McGrady, Yonker, Tan, Fine, and Woerner (1981) and recent studies by Goebel, Viol, and Orebaugh (1993), Jurek et al. (1992), and McGrady and Higgins (1989). The theoretical framework underlying the use of EMG feedback in hypertension is that EMG feedback mediates general relaxation and, therefore, decreases in autonomic arousal. Changes in blood flow to skeletal muscle occur during contraction and relaxation of muscles. Control of circulation to skeletal muscles, the largest vasculature, is brought about both by neural and local factors. Strong contractions of skeletal muscles impede blood flow within those muscles. Early fatigue and pain can occur during prolonged skeletal muscle activity and ischemia (reduced blood supply) can result from a chronic contracted state. Thus, sustained contraction is associated with increased BP. On the other hand, one can maintain weaker or intermittent contractions for prolonged periods. With weak muscular contractions, the muscle receives more blood flow than the blood flow sent to that muscle during a strong contraction. Vasodilation in muscle can decrease TPR and BP (Vander et al., 1994).

McGrady et al. (1981) and McGrady and Higgins (1989) showed that decreases in SBP and DBP occurred in medicated and unmedicated patients trained with EMG biofeedback and relaxation therapy. In the earlier study of medicated patients, significant SBP and DBP decreases were observed only in the treated patients and not in the controls. Concomitant decreases were also demonstrated in cortisol and aldosterone in the treated patients. In the later study, 39 unmedicated hypertensive patients monitored BP for 6 weeks. This was followed by 16 sessions of EMG and temperature biofeedback combined with autogenic or progressive relaxation. Patients practiced relaxation at home twice daily for 15 minutes. For 6 weeks after therapy, BPs were measured weekly in the laboratory and at home by patients. Twenty-three patients reduced their BPs by at least 5 millimeters Hg MAP; seven reduced their MAP by less than 5 millimeters Hg, whereas nine showed no change or an increase (McGrady & Higgins, 1989).

Goebel et al. (1993) reported on 12 years of research in 117 hypertensive patients. Simple relaxation, relaxation plus EMG feedback, relaxation plus direct BP feedback, and BP feedback alone each produced small, consistent decreases in BPs and in medication use. Patients in the active and believable control condition did not show similar BP decreases.

"Electrodermal feedback" depends on sweating, a sympathetically mediated response to change in ambient temperature. Sweat also is secreted under stressful conditions. Electrodermal activity is directly proportional to the amount of sweat (see Chapter 4). Galvanic skin response (GSR) is a form of electrodermal feedback. Therefore, treatment with the latter should accomplish the same results as those reported for GSR. Patel (1973) and Patel and Marmot (1988) used GSR combined with EMG feedback in groups of hypertensive patients as part of their multimodal treatment program. Patients received information about the electrical conductance of their skin. In the recent report (Patel & Marmot, 1988), groups of patients participated in 1-hour weekly sessions provided by general practitioners for 10 weeks. Education took place in the first half-hour, and the second half-hour included relaxation training, breathing exercises, and GSR feedback. Patients practiced at home daily. The net drop in SBP was 7.3 millimeters Hg (significant); DBP decreased 2.2 millimeters Hg (not significant). This cost-effective way of providing treatment to hypertensive patients should be explored further.

Relaxation

Practitioners use relaxation therapies as unimodal treatments or in combination with biofeedback modalities in stepped psychophysiological approaches for treatment of essential hypertension. Although the relaxation therapies differ in instructions and processes, each shares a common goal of enhanced calmness and reduced sympathetic arousal. The types of relaxation include:

- Progressive relaxation (Jacobson, 1977; Bernstein & Borkovec, 1973; McGuigan, 1993)
- Autogenic therapy (Luthe, 1969); modified autogenic therapy (Green, Green, & Norris, 1980; Linden, 1990)
- Hypnotic relaxation (Deabler, Fidel, Dillenkoffer, & Elder, 1973)
- Transcendental meditation (Wallace, 1970; Schneider, Alexander, & Wallace, 1992)
- Benson's "relaxation response" (Benson, Beary, & Carol, 1974)
- Yogic meditation including deep breathing (Patel, 1973; Patel & North, 1975)

No one type of relaxation has been shown conclusively to be more efficacious than other types in treatment of hypertension. However, the incorrect use of progressive relaxation may be problematical for patients with hypertension for the following reasons. The first is that the muscle contraction component of progressive relaxation may produce breath-holding and a Valsalva response (Herman, 1989). The Valsalva response results in an increase in cardiac output and, thereby, increased SBP and DBP. Second, breath-holding initiates an increase in sympathetic neural activity that will increase blood pressure. Third, the type of tensing done during progressive relaxation is of the isometric variety in contrast with the isotonic or aerobic type. Isometric exercises produce an increase in both SBP and DBP. Tensing muscles very tightly or for too long impedes blood flow to the muscles, as described earlier.

Yet progressive relaxation is too valuable a therapeutic modality to eliminate it completely from the treatment of hypertension. The practitioner can use progressive relaxation to help patients discriminate tension and relaxation. However, it is important to:

1. Attend to the breathing pattern of patients who are using this technique.
2. Encourage patients to monitor their breathing and to make sure that they do not hold their breath during the muscle tension phase.
3. Instruct patients to use the minimal amount of tension that allows them to learn to discriminate between the tension and the relaxation state.
4. Shorten the time for tensing compared to the time for the relaxation phase.
5. Remember to include passive relaxation procedures after ending progressive relaxation practice.

"Sequencing" relaxation and biofeedback was described by Glasgow, Engel, and D'Lugoff (1989) as follows:

1. After a 1-month BP monitoring phase, if the BP levels are still elevated, one starts the SBP feedback procedure. If BPs fall to acceptable levels, patients may not need further treatment; check BP at 6 months or yearly.
2. If SBP feedback does not lower BP to normotensive levels, the relaxation procedures should be implemented. Progressive relaxation is used to assist patients in differentiating tense and relaxed muscles. Passive relaxation therapy facilitates lowered arousal. If BP is sufficiently low, then start the follow-up protocol.
3. If BP still is too high, recommend appropriate pharmacological intervention.

The number of office sessions varies depending on the severity of the hypertension and patient compliance. Patients use the relaxation procedures multiple times each day, especially if they find their BPs elevated. Patients who received biofeedback first and relaxation second did slightly better than those who received the therapies in reverse order. Furthermore, patients who received *both* treatments were better at long-term follow-up than patients who received only one of the treatments (Engel, Glasgow, & Gaarder, 1983).

It is likely that biofeedback and relaxation operate through different physiological mechanisms. Relaxation may have a generalized effect in reducing sympathetic nerve activity that affects heart rate and thereby decreases stroke volume. On the other hand, biofeedback may work primarily through vasomotor control, since BP increased and decreased (with biofeedback) without a concomitant change in heart rate. Thus, biofeedback and relaxation are complementary rather than alternative methods in BP control (Engel & Baile, 1989).

Cognitive strategies are also included in psychophysiological therapies. Development of coping skills assists patients in managing their anxiety and their reactions to stress (Davis, Eshelman, & McKay, 1988). Sometimes significant anxiety occurs when a patient hears the diagnosis of essential hypertension. Practitioners should consider evaluation of anxiety and cognitive strategies before the biofeedback component begins. Then, one can integrate the training of new coping skills into the biofeedback and relaxation therapies.

Since essential hypertension is a complex, multidimensional illness, it is logical to expect that people with it will respond with varying degrees of success to relaxation and biofeedback. As with pharmacological agents, each modality helps some individuals. Tailoring the treatment program to the person is critical to success.

Home Practice

Steptoe, Patel, Marmot, and Hunt (1987) demonstrated a significant association between relaxation practice and reduced BP. However, in the study by Wittrock, Blanchard, and McCoy (1988), patients succeeding and failing to reduce their BPs reported a similar frequency of practice and sensations of relaxation. Nonetheless, researchers and clinicians usually agree that relaxation practice is essential if a patient is to transfer or generalize what he or she has learned in the clinical setting to home or work.

A common recommendation for home practice is at least twice a day for 15–20 minutes. Practice encompasses relaxation with or without simple biofeedback devices. Consider a daily record of practice and a more detailed diary of thoughts and feelings during practice. Instruct the patient in the procedures, and then provide written scripts and relaxation tapes. Emphasize the importance of learning the relaxation procedures well enough so that lowering of BP occurs without scripts or tapes. Home practice using the direct SBP feedback techniques was explained above. Patients can incorporate thermal biofeedback into home relaxation practice using small, inexpensive temperature devices. Alternatively, patients can borrow or rent digital thermal biofeedback devices from the practitioner.

Instruct patients to measure the temperature of their hands, feet, or both before and after relaxation practice. They also may use continuous visual feedback during relaxation practice. Patients should keep their bodies warm by covering themselves (excluding the hands and feet) if necessary. It is more difficult to elicit a hand- or foot-warming response in a room that is cold. This may be particularly significant for the elderly and for economically challenged persons who may be keeping their thermostats set at lower levels. The elderly often have some difficulty maintaining adequate blood supply to the extremities. Their hands, therefore, may start out colder.

Follow-Up

Long-term follow-up is very important for patients who complete a clinical program for reducing their BP. Hypertension is a progressive disease, thus one expects BP increases over time as part of the aging process. Long-term maintenance of reductions in BP resulting from relaxation and/or biofeedback therapies were reported early by Taylor, Farquhar, Nelson, and Agras (1977), Agras, Southam, and Taylor (1983), Engel et al. (1983), Blanchard et al. (1986, 1988), Fahrion et al. (1986), more recently by Leserman et al. (1989), McGrady, Nadsady, and Schumann-Brzezinski (1991), and Goebel et al. (1993). Although the percentage of patients retaining the treatment effects varies, some patients maintain criterion BPs for 1–3 years.

The necessity of continued home practice of either relaxation, biofeedback, or diaphragmatic breathing for long-term BP effects lacks consensus. Some research supports the use of practice of relaxation as an essential component of maintaining lowered BP. However, other studies have not been able to demonstrate conclusively the necessity for continued relaxation practice. It seems logical for practitioners to suggest, nonetheless, continued practice of relaxation. The improved cognitive processing of stressful stimuli initiated during treatment should be emphasized. If research confirms the necessity of consistent practice, then the psychophysiological therapies can be viewed in the same context as aerobic exercise. Although exercise may lower BP during a short-term 4–6 month program, it too requires continued adherence to maintain the gains achieved during conditioning. If one stops exercising, the cardiovascular and skeletomotor systems decondition faster than the training period necessary to build them up. It is wise, therefore, in a clinical practice, to make clear and organized arrangements for follow-up with patients before they end treatment.

The design of an efficacious follow-up program for patients is challenging. Several options are:

1. Mail blood pressure log sheets to patients, and ask them to return the log in a preaddressed stamped envelope.
2. Contact patients by phone at regular intervals, and ask for their blood pressures.
3. Schedule periodic follow-up booster or refresher sessions with relaxation and biofeedback. For example, patients may receive one refresher therapy session every other week for 6 weeks, followed by monthly sessions for 6 months, and then yearly follow-up sessions.
4. In a physician-based or collaborative setting, obtain the BPs from the physician's office after the patient's regular check-ups.

SPECIAL POPULATIONS

Pregnant Women

The efficacy of biofeedback-based and relaxation-based interventions in pregnancy-induced hypertension (PIH) was investigated. PIH is a serious condition where pregnant women develop high blood pressure, protein in their urine, and edema late in gestation. Traditional treatment for PIH is bed rest and obstetrical monitoring. Frequently, women find compliance difficult particularly if they have other family obligations.

In a study by Somers, Gevirtz, Jasin, and Chin (1989), women with PIH were divided into three groups. One group received standard medical care. The second group was provided with an additional 4 hours of education to increase compliance to bed rest. The active-intervention group received treatment consisting of self-monitoring of blood pressure, thermal biofeedback-assisted relaxation, hand and foot warming, and diaphragmatic breathing. Total therapy time was also 4 hours. Instructions to subjects were to practice the techniques twice daily at home in bed. Subjects in the biobehavioral group maintained their BP at a significantly lower level compared to the group on bed rest alone or the group with enhanced compliance to bed rest. Thus, biobehavioral intervention may be used as a low-risk adjunct to standard treatment in mild PIH (Somers et al., 1989).

Elderly Persons

Isolated systolic hypertension is a relatively common problem in the elderly. These individuals have an abnormal SBP, but their diastolic pressure is below 90 millimeters Hg. Pearce, Engel, and Burton (1989) trained 15 individuals over the age of 60 with SBP feedback to lower SBP using their own sphygmomanometers. Relaxation training followed the biofeedback period. Significant decreases averaging 13 millimeters Hg SBP were recorded in the 15 hypertensive patients.

The positive results from preliminary studies of these special populations are promising and certainly indicate a need for larger clinical trials.

TREATMENT OUTCOME: OUTCOME MEASURES
AND ASSESSMENT OF SUCCESS

An evaluation of the effects of biobehavioral interventions for essential hypertension in *individual* patients includes the following specific questions:

1. Did the patient succeed in reducing BP into the normotensive range?
2. Is the reduction of BP clinically significant and statistically significant?
3. Has the patient reduced his or her medication? Has the BP remained normotensive with less or no medication? Has the patient added any other medications that may have a BP-lowering effect?
4. If the BP is normal, did the patient alter his or her life-style or dietary habits (e.g., sodium intake, weight loss, exercise) after treatment? If so, could these changes account for the reductions of BP?
5. Has the patient shown positive transfer of physiological self-regulation? That is, can he or she lower BPs and maintain lower BPs at work, home, in the physician's office, as well as in the biofeedback practitioner's office?
6. For how long after completion of therapy is the BP in the normal range?
7. Has the patient achieved specified and credible criteria for physiological self-regulation? For example, if peripheral skin temperature of 95°F is the established criterion, is the patient consistently able to raise the temperature to that level for specified durations?

Evaluation of clinical applications of biofeedback in "group outcome studies" should include the following considerations:

1. The clinical significance of the decreases in SBP and DBP.
2. The statistical significance of the decreases in SBP and DBP.
3. The stability of BP decreases.
4. The fraction of the treated patients that improved significantly.
5. The degree of transfer of BP changes obtained in the laboratory to the patients' environments.
6. Sufficient length of baseline and posttreatment period to separate treatment effects from monitoring or habituation effects.
7. Documentation of learning of the relaxation or biofeedback therapy.
8. Adequate controls for medication changes.
9. Adequate controls for weight, dietary sodium, and physical exercise.

PREDICTION OF RESPONSE

It is cost effective and efficient to attempt to describe characteristics of patients that enhance their ability to lower their BP. Before a practitioner accepts a hypertensive patient for biobehavioral treatment, he or she should insure that a physician ruled out secondary hypertension. Determination of the pretreatment BP and medication history is also important. Furthermore, if an individual's diagnosis is essential hypertension and the BP is already well controlled, then psychophysiological therapies may not produce any further lowering of BP. Under these circumstances, the clinical goal can be reduction in medication.

Compliance with therapists' recommendations is also part of the patient-selection process. If a person resists the BP monitoring recommendations and misses appointments during the baseline period, then that person's compliance with biofeedback and relaxation instructions is in doubt. If a patient shows poor compliance (missed appointments, sporadic monitoring, unwillingness to learn the measurement technique), then compliance with relaxation instructions is also apt to be problematical. However, poor compliance with antihypertensive medication does not automatically translate into poor compliance with relaxation instructions. Some people oppose beginning antihypertensive medication in the early stages of treatment. A better test of a patient's willingness to comply with psychophysiological therapy is the baseline period. At that time practitioners should discuss potential compliance problems with the patient. In all professional biobehavioral therapy settings, patients need a high level of involvement and motivation. Patients must understand clearly their own responsibilities and the need to self-manage medication regimes, to obtain BPs according to instructions, to attend office sessions, and to apply therapy procedures.

There have been several attempts at characterizing patients to assess their chances of success in biofeedback programs. Early work pointed to successful patients having higher neurogenic tone (Cottier, Shapiro, & Julius, 1984), higher anxiety, forehead muscle tension, and cortisol (McGrady, Utz, Woerner, Bernal, & Higgins, 1986). Later, McGrady and Higgins (1989) and Weaver and McGrady (1995) suggested a predictor profile potentially useful in recommending treatment to patients. The factors tested in this profile include indicators of the classical stress response and substances related to the pathophysiology of hypertension. Patients with the best chances for success in lowering BP had higher pretreatment anxiety scores, heart rate, cortisol, plasma renin activity, and lower hand temperatures. Confirmation of this profile requires testing in large enough samples of individuals to assess its true impact on patient selection.

Other work on medicated patients did not isolate similar biochemical or physiological factors but instead identified factors related to process and outcome. In a controlled comparison between thermal biofeedback and progressive relaxation, the three variables investigated were: expectancies, skill acquisition, and home practice. There were no significant differences in practice between treatment groups or between succeeders and failures; for thermal biofeedback, skill acquisition and expectancies were related to outcome; for the progressive relaxation group, perceptions of relaxation correlated with success (Wittrock et al., 1988).

THE WELL-EQUIPPED OFFICE

The well-equipped office for treating patients with essential hypertension includes:

- A mercury sphygmomanometer
- Several different sized BP monitoring cuffs
- A teaching stethoscope so that both the patient and the practitioner can listen to the BP sounds at the same time
- A *Physicians' Desk Reference*
- A manual of drug interactions
- Self-monitoring BP devices to lend to patients
- Written instructions for the measurement and recording of BP by the patients
- A variety of written and visual aids for patient education
- Log sheets for recording BP and home practice

DIRECTIONS FOR FUTURE RESEARCH
AND UNANSWERED QUESTIONS

We encourage professionals to use appropriate clinical research designs to test patients' response to biofeedback and related therapies and to help advance the basis for using these therapy procedures. A useful resource for designing experimental protocols for single cases or clinical series is the book by Barlow and Hersen (1984). The most effective biobehavioral therapy programs are treatment *packages* that include education, BP monitoring, positive expectancies, one or more relaxation therapies, and direct or indirect biofeedback modalities. Each of the individual components may contribute a unique or overlapping modulation of cardiac output or total peripheral resistance.

Some of the unresolved questions in this field include:

1. What is the role of home practice of relaxation in short-term and long-term outcome?
2. Can one predict BP responses to biofeedback and relaxation?
3. Can the efficacy of biofeedback and relaxation be demonstrated in special populations?
4. Can one improve cost-effectiveness using a group format instead of individual therapy sessions?
5. What are the physiological and biochemical effects of each therapeutic modality?
6. Are the patients who respond to biofeedback and relaxation the same patients who respond to salt restriction and exercise?
7. Subject, therapist, and procedural variables all need investigation. We need to learn more about which therapies work better for different patients, provided by whom, how often, for how long, and under what conditions.
8. Are these therapies as effective or more or less effective in minority populations?

CONCLUSIONS

The final goal of health care practitioners is for their patients to have BPs adequately controlled with a treatment regimen that the patient can maintain for a long time with the least amount of medication. There is considerable evidence that individuals can develop and retain effective self-regulation of their BP. Combined pharmacological and nonpharmacological therapies including life-style changes hold great promise in management of hypertension. Further research will clarify which persons can benefit most from biofeedback and relaxation therapy as well as which therapies are preferentially efficacious.

GLOSSARY

ADRENAL CORTEX. Outer region of each adrenal gland, which secretes aldosterone, cortisol, and androgens.

ADRENAL GLANDS. A pair of endocrine glands located above each kidney. The outer portion of the gland is the *adrenal cortex*. The inner portion is the *adrenal medulla*.

ADRENAL MEDULLA. The medulla or inner core of the *adrenal glands*. Epinephrine (adrenaline) and a small amount of norepinephrine (noradrenaline) are secreted by the medulla.

ALDOSTERONE. Hormone secreted by the adrenal cortex that regulates balance of electrolytes.

ALDOSTERONISM. An abnormality of electrolyte metabolism caused by excessive secretion of aldosterone.

ANGIOTENSIN II. Hormone that stimulates secretion of aldosterone from adrenal cortex. Promotes smooth muscle contraction.

ANGIOTENSIN-CONVERTING ENZYME INHIBITORS (ACE INHIBITORS). Drugs used to lower BP by decreasing vascular resistance. Example: enalapril (Vasotec).

ARTERIAL BARORECEPTORS. Stretch receptors in the carotid sinus or aortic arch. Sensitive to stretch induced by changes in arterial blood pressure.

ATRIAL NATRIURETIC FACTOR (ANF). Hormone secreted by atrial cells that causes a decrease in reabsorption of sodium by the kidney. More sodium is excreted.

AUTONOMIC NERVOUS SYSTEM (ANS). Part of the peripheral nervous system that consists of sympathetic and parasympathetic subdivisions. Innervates cardiac muscle, smooth muscle, and glands. (See Chapter 1 for more on ANS.)

BETA BLOCKERS. Drugs used to lower BP by decreasing cardiac output by adrenergic blockade at either beta$_1$- or beta$_2$-adrenergic receptors or at both. Example: propranolol (Inderal).

CALCIUM CHANNEL BLOCKERS. Drugs used to lower BP by decreasing vascular resistance. Example: verapamil (Calan).

CARDIAC CYCLE. One contraction–relaxation cycle of the heart.

CARDIAC OUTPUT. Blood volume pumped by each ventricle per minute.

CORTISOL. The major natural glucocorticoid hormone released from the adrenal cortex. Regulates aspects of metabolism. (See Chapters 7, 18, 35, 37.)

CUSHING'S DISEASE. Syndrome in which the pituitary secretes excessive adrenocorticotropic hormone. The adrenal cortex secretes too much cortisol.

DESENSITIZATION (SYSTEMATIC DESENSITIZATION). A common type of behavior therapy to assist patients to decrease fear, phobias, and arousal responses associated with certain stimuli. There is gradual exposure for very limited periods from the least anxiety-producing to increasingly anxiety-producing. Exposure is imagined, with artificial stimuli (e.g., pictures, video), known as in vitro, and/or with real-life stimuli, known as in vivo. For example, gradually exposing a person to blood pressure instruments and procedures so the person can become accustomed to them.

DIASTOLIC BLOOD PRESSURE (DBP). Minimum blood pressure during relaxation of heart or during cardiac cycle.

DIURETICS. Drugs that increase the excretion of urine thus decreasing plasma volume. Example: hydrochlorothiazide (Dyazide).

EPINEPHRINE. Hormone secreted by adrenal medulla; involved in regulation of metabolism. Also a neurotransmitter.

HEMODYNAMIC. Pertaining to the movements involved in the circulation of the blood.

HG. Mercury; millimeters Hg are units of pressure.

HYPERTHYROIDISM. Excessive secretion of hormone by the thyroid gland; characterized by increased metabolic rate, goiter, and disturbances in the autonomic nervous system.

ISCHEMIA. Reduced blood supply.

MEAN ARTERIAL PRESSURE (MAP). The average pressure during the cardiac cycle. It is calculated by adding diastolic pressure to one-third pulse pressure.

METABOLISM. Total chemical reactions that occur in a living organism.

NEURAL. Having to do with nerve cells or nervous system.

NONNEURAL. Not related to nerve cells or nervous system.

NOREPINEPHRINE. (Also noradrenaline.) A natural neurohormone and neurotransmitter released by postganglionic adrenergic nerves and the adrenal medulla (see Chapters 7, 18). Also found in the brain. One type of *catecholamine*, a body compound having a sympathomimetic action. Others include epinephrine and dopamine. Has mostly alpha-adrenergic activity and some beta-adrenergic activity. Pharmaceutical is norepinephrine bitartrate (also called levarterenol bitartrate). (See Chapters 7, 14, 15, 17, 20.)

PARASYMPATHETIC. A subdivision of the autonomic nervous system whose fibers originate from brainstem and sacral region of spinal cord.

PLASMA. Liquid portion of the blood.

RENIN. Enzyme secreted by the kidney that catalyzes formation of angiotensin I; important in BP regulation.

SPHYGMOMANOMETER. Device that consists of a cuff, which can be inflated, and a pressure gauge used for measuring blood pressure. In the *aneroid* type, the pressure gauge does not contain liquid. In the *mercury* type, the pressure gauge contains mercury.

STROKE VOLUME. Amount of blood ejected by a ventricle during one heartbeat.

SYMPATHETIC. Subdivision of the autonomic nervous system whose fibers originate in the thoracic and lumbar regions of the spinal cord.

SYSTOLIC BLOOD PRESSURE (SBP). Maximum arterial blood pressure during cardiac cycle.

TOTAL PERIPHERAL RESISTANCE (TPR). The sum of all resistances to blood flow in all the systemic blood vessels.

VALSALVA MANEUVER. Forcible exhalation effort against a closed glottis. Increases intrathoracic pressure and interferes with venous return to the heart. Forced exhalation effort against occluded (pinched) nostrils and closed mouth. (Also see Chapters 23, 37.)

VASCULAR. Pertaining to blood vessels or indicative of a copious blood supply.

ACKNOWLEDGMENTS

We thank hypertension subspecialists Sheldon G. Sheps, M.D., and Gary L. Schwartz, M.D. of Mayo Clinic Rochester, for their reviews of drafts of this chapter. Their comments and suggestions were very helpful. This does not imply their endorsement of the content of this chapter.

REFERENCES

Agras, W. S., Southam, M. A., & Taylor, C. B. (1983). Long-term persistence of relaxation induced blood pressure lowering during the working day. *Journal of Consulting and Clinical Psychology, 51,* 792–794.

Barlow, D. H., & Hersen, M. (1984). *Single case experimental designs: Strategies for studying behavior change* (2nd ed.). New York: Pergamon Press.

Benson, H., Beary, J. F., & Carol, M. P. (1974). The relaxation response. *Psychiatry, 37,* 37–46.

Benson, H., Shapiro, D., Tursky, B., & Schwartz, G. E. (1971). Decreased systolic blood pressure through operant conditioning techniques in patients with essential hypertension. *Science, 173,* 740–741.

Bernstein, D. A., & Borkovec, T. D. (1973). *Progressive relaxation training: A manual for helping professions.* Champaign, IL: Research Press.

Blanchard, E. B. (1990). Biofeedback treatments of essential hypertension. *Biofeedback and Self-Regulation, 15*(3), 209–228.

Blanchard, E. B., Khramelashvili, V. V., McCoy, G. C., Aivazyan, T. A., McCaffrey, R. J., Salenko, B. B., Musso, A., Wittrock, D. A., Bereger, M., Gerardi, M. A., & Pangburn, L. (1988). The USA–USSR collaborative cross-cultural comparison of autogenic training and thermal biofeedback in the treatment of mild hypertension. *Health Psychology, 7,* 175–192.

Blanchard, E. B., McCoy, G. C., Musso, A., Gerardi, M. A., Pallmeyer, T. P., Gerardi, R. J., Cotch, P. A., Siracusa, K., & Andrasik, F. (1986). A controlled comparison of thermal biofeedback and relaxation training in the treatment of essential hypertension: I. Short-term and long-term outcome. *Behavior Therapy, 17,* 563–579.

Brody, D. S. (1981). Psychological distress and hypertension control. *Journal of Human Stress, 6*(1), 2–6.

Byrne, D. G. (1992). Anxiety, neuroticism, depression, and hypertension. In E. H. Johnson, W. D. Gentry & S. Julius (Eds.), *Personality, elevated blood pressure, and essential hypertension* (pp. 67–85). Washington: Hemisphere Publishing Corporation.

Cottier, C., Shapiro, K., & Julius, S. (1984). Treatment of mild hypertension with progressive muscle relaxation. *Archives of Internal Medicine, 144,* 1954–1958.

Croog, S. H., Levine, S., Tessta, M. A., Brown, B., Bulpitt, C. J., Jenskin, C. D., Klerman, G., & Williams, G. H. (1986). The effects of antihypertensive therapy on the quality of life. *New England Journal of Medicine, 314,* 1657–1664.

Davis, M., Eshelman, E. R., & McKay, M. (1988). Coping skills training. In M. Davis, E. R. Eshelman, & M. McKay (Eds.), *The relaxation and stress reduction workbook* (3rd ed., pp. 118–129). Oakland: New Harbinger.

Deabler, H. L., Fidel, E., Dillenkoffer, R. L., & Elder, S. T. (1973). The use of relaxation and hypnosis in lowering high blood pressure. *American Journal of Clinical Hypnosis, 16,* 75–83.

Dressler, W. W. (1991). Social class, skin color, and arterial blood pressure in two societies. *Ethnicity and Disease, 1*(1), 60–77.

Engel, B. T., & Baile, W. S. (1989). Behavioral applications in the treatment of patients with cardiovascular disorders. In J. B. Basmajian (Ed.), *Biofeedback: Principles and practice for clinicians,* (3rd ed., pp. 223–231). Baltimore: Williams & Wilkins.

Engel, B. T., Gaarder, K. R., & Glasgow, M. S. (1981). Behavioral treatment of high blood pressure: I. Analyses of intra- and interdaily variations of blood pressure during a one-month, baseline period. *Psychosomatic Medicine, 43,* 255–270.

Engel, B. T., Glasgow, M. S., & Gaarder, K. R. (1983). Behavioral treatment of high blood pressure: II. Follow-up results and treatment recommendations. *Psychosomatic Medicine, 45*(1), 23–29.

Fahrion, S., Norris, P., Green, A., Green, E., & Snaar, C. (1986). Behavioral treatment of essential hypertension. A group outcome study. *Biofeedback and Self-Regulation, 11*(4), 257–259.

Freedman, R. R. (1991). Physiological mechanisms of temperature biofeedback. *Biofeedback and Self-Regulation, 16,* 95–115.

Ganong, W. F. (1991). *Review of medical physiology* (15th ed.). Los Altos, CA: Lange Medical Publications.

Glasgow, M. S., Engel, B. T., & D'Lugoff, B. C. (1989). A controlled study of a standardized behavioral stepped treatment for hypertension. *Psychosomatic Medicine, 51,* 10–26.

Glasgow, M. S., Gaarder, K. R., & Engel, B. T. (1982). Behavioral treatment of high blood pressure: II. Acute and sustained effects of relaxation and systolic blood pressure biofeedback. *Psychosomatic Medicine, 44*(2), 155–170.

Goebel, M., Viol, G. W., & Orebaugh, C. (1993). An incremental model to isolate specific effects of behavioral treatments in essential hypertension. *Biofeedback and Self-Regulation, 18*(4), 255–280.

Green, E. E., Green, A., & Norris, P. A. (1980). Self-regulation training for control of hypertension. *Primary Cardiology, 6,* 126–137.

Hatch, J. P., Klatt, K. D., Supik, J. D., Rios, N., Fisher, J. G., Bauer, R. L., & Shimotsu, G. W. (1985). Combined behavioral and pharmacological treatment of essential hypertension. *Biofeedback and Self-Regulation, 10*(2), 119–138.

Herman, J. (1989). Valsalva response during progressive relaxation: An extension study. *Scholarly Inquiry for Nursing Practice: An International Journal, 3*, 217–225.

Jacob, R. G., Chesney, M. A., Williams, D. M., Ding, Y., & Shapiro, A. P. (1991). Relaxation therapy for hypertension: Design effects and treatment effects. *Annals of Behavioral Medicine, 13*(1), 5–17.

Jacobson, E. (1977). The origins and development of progressive relaxation. *Journal of Behavior Therapy and Experimental Psychiatry, 8*, 119–123.

Joint National Committee. (1988). The 1988 report of the Joint National Committee on Detection, Evaluation and Treatment of High Blood Pressure. *Archives of Internal Medicine, 148*, 1023–1038.

Joint National Committee. (1993). The fifth report of the Joint National Committee on Detection, Evaluation and Treatment of High Blood Pressure. *Archives of Internal Medicine, 153*, 154–183.

Julius, S. (1991). Autonomic nervous dysfunction in essential hypertension. *Diabetes Care, 14*(3), 249–259.

Jurek, I. E., Higgins, J. T. Jr., & McGrady, A. (1992). Interaction of biofeedback-assisted relaxation and diuretic in treatment of essential hypertension. *Biofeedback and Self-Regulation, 17*(2), 125–141.

Kaplan, N. M. (1986). *Clinical hypertension* (4th ed.). Baltimore: Williams & Wilkins.

Krist, D. A., & Engel, B. T. (1975). Learned control of blood pressure in patients with high blood pressure. *Circulation, 51*, 370–378.

Leserman, J., Stuart, E. M., Mamish, M. E., Deckro, J. P., Beckman, R. J., Friedman, R., Benson, H. (1989). Nonpharmacologic intervention for hypertension: Long-term follow-up. *Journal of Cardiopulmonary Rehabilitation, 9*, 316–324.

Linden, W. (1990). *Autogenic training: A clinical guide.* New York: Guilford Press.

Luthe, W. (1969). *Autogenic therapy.* New York: Grune & Stratton.

McCoy, G. C., Blanchard, E. B., Wittrock, D. A., Morrison, S., Pangburn, L., Siracusa, K., & Pallmeyer, T. P. (1988). Biochemical changes associated with thermal biofeedback treatment of hypertension. *Biofeedback and Self-Regulation, 13*(2), 139–150.

McGrady, A.V. (1994). Effects of group relaxation training and thermal biofeedback on blood pressure and related psychophysiological variables in essential hypertension. *Biofeedback and Self-Regulation, 19*(1), 51–66.

McGrady, A. V., & Higgins, J. T. Jr. (1989). Prediction of response to biofeedback-assisted relaxation in hypertensives: Development of a hypertensive predictor profile (HYPP). *Psychosomatic Medicine, 51*, 277–284.

McGrady, A. V., & Higgins, J. T. Jr. (1990). Effect of repeated measurements of blood pressure on blood pressure in essential hypertension: Role of anxiety. *Journal of Behavioral Medicine, 13*(1), 93–101.

McGrady, A. V., Nadsady, P. A., & Schumann-Brzezinski, C. (1991). Sustained effects of biofeedback-assisted relaxation therapy in essential hypertension. *Biofeedback and Self-Regulation, 16*(4), 399–413.

McGrady, A. V., Utz, S. W., Woerner, M., Bernal, G. A. A., & Higgins, J. T. (1986). Predictors of success in hypertensives treated with biofeedback-assisted relaxation. *Biofeedback and Self-Regulation, 11*(2), 95–103.

McGrady, A. V., Yonker, R., Tan, S. Y., Fine, T. H., & Woerner, M. (1981). The effect of biofeedback-assisted relaxation training on blood pressure and selected biochemical parameters in patients with essential hypertension. *Biofeedback and Self-Regulation, 6*(3), 343–353.

McGuigan, F. J. (1993). In P. Lehrer & R. Woolfolk (Eds.), *Principles and practice of stress management* (2nd ed., pp. 17–51). New York: Guilford Press.

Mycek, M. J., Gertner, S. B., & Perper, M. M. (1992). *Pharmacology* (Chapter 19). Philadelphia: J. B. Lippincott.

Patel, C. H. (1973). Yoga and biofeedback in the management of hypertension. *Lancet, ii*, 1053–1055.

Patel, C. H. (1977). Biofeedback-aided relaxation and meditation in the management of hypertension. *Biofeedback and Self-Regulation, 2*(1), 1–41.

Patel, C., & Marmot, M. (1988). Can general practitioners use training in relaxation and management of stress to reduce mild hypertension? *British Medical Journal, 296*, 21–24.

Patel, C. H., & North, S. (1975). Randomized controlled trial of yoga and biofeedback in management of hypertension. *Lancet, ii*, 93–99.

Pearce, K. L., Engel, B. T., & Burton, J. R. (1989). Behavioral treatment of isolated systolic hypertension in the elderly. *Biofeedback and Self-Regulation, 14*(3), 207–219.

Schneider, R. H., Alexander, C. N., & Wallace, R. K. (1992). In search of an optimal behavioral treatment for hypertension: A review and focus on transcendental meditation. In E. H. Johnson, W. D. Gentry, & S. Julius (Eds.), *Personality, elevated blood pressure, and essential hypertension* (pp. 291–316). Washington: Hemisphere Publishing Corporation.

Somers, P. J., Gevirtz, R. N., Jasin, S. E., & Chin, H. G. (1989). The efficacy of biobehavioral and compliance interventions in the adjunctive treatment of mild pregnancy-induced hypertension. *Biofeedback and Self-Regulation, 14*(4), 309–318.

Steptoe, A., Patel, C., Marmot, M., & Hunt, B. (1987). Frequency of relaxation practice, blood pressure reduction and the general effects of relaxation following a controlled trial of behaviour modification for reducing coronary risk. *Stress Medicine, 3*, 101–107.

Taylor, C. B., Farquhar, J. W., Nelson, E., & Agras, W. S. (1977). Relaxation therapy and high blood pressure. *Archives of General Psychiatry, 34*, 339–343.

Tursky, B., Shapiro, D., & Schwartz, G. E. (1972). Automated constant cuff pressure system to measure average systolic and diastolic blood pressures in man. *IEEE Transactions on Biomedical Engineering, 19*, 271–276.

Veterans Administration Cooperative Study Group on Antihypertensive Agents. (1975). Return of elevated blood pressure after withdrawal of antihypertensive drugs. *Circulation, 51*, 1107–1113.

Vander, A. J., Sherman, J. H., & Luciano, D. S. (1994). *Human physiology* (6th ed.). New York: McGraw-Hill.

Wallace, R. K. (1970). Physiological effects of transcendental meditation. *Science, 167*, 1751–1754.

Weaver, M. T., & McGrady, A. (1995). A provsional model to predict blood pressure response to biofeedback-assisted relaxation. *Biofeedback and Self Regulation, 20*.

Weinberger, M. H. (1993) *Hypertension primer*, Dallas, TX: American Heart Association.

Wittrock, D. A., Blanchard, E. B., & McCoy, G. C. (1988). Three studies on the relation of process to outcome in the treatment of essential hypertension with relaxation and thermal biofeedback. *Behaviour Research and Therapy, 26*(1), 53–66.

VI
NONTRADITIONAL
APPLICATIONS

19

Biofeedback-Assisted Relaxation and Diabetes Mellitus

Angele McGrady
Barbara Bailey

This chapter first describes the characteristics of diabetes mellitus and discusses the traditional management of the disease. It then explores the impact of psychological factors and life-style adjustments on the control of diabetes. The chapter mainly addresses general clinical procedures for treatment with biofeedback and relaxation combined with traditional medical therapy. We discuss recommendations for types of and number of treatment sessions, home practice, and communication with the patient's physician. Next, we summarize considerations important when using biofeedback with persons with diabetes, and we discuss possible contraindications to treatment. A brief summary of eight studies is given at the end of the chapter.

More research is necessary to further establish and improve this treatment approach. However, the results are encouraging overall, and practitioners using relaxation and biofeedback are receiving referrals of patients with diabetes. The treatment of diabetes involves special risks and requires specialized knowledge. Thus, practitioners using relaxation and biofeedback must have this knowledge and work as part of a treatment team.

DEFINITIONS AND TYPES OF DIABETES MELLITUS

Definition of Diabetes Mellitus

Diabetes mellitus is a chronic disorder of metabolism affecting about 14 million people or about 6% of the United States population. High blood glucose (sugar), known as hyperglycemia, characterizes diabetes. Hyperglycemia results from either relative or absolute insulin deficiency. Glucose is one of the products that results from metabolism, the breakdown of ingested food, principally carbohydrates. Glucose is the body's main fuel source and typically the brain's only energy source. Blood glucose numbers are recorded as milligrams per deciliter or in millimoles per liter (Krall & Beaser, 1989).

The glucose level in the blood normally rises after a meal. This increase prompts the pancreas, an organ that lies behind the stomach, to secrete the regulatory hormone insulin. By combining with cell surface receptors, insulin allows glucose to enter cells and increases storage of fatty acids, amino acids, as well as glucose. The counterregulatory hormone, glucagon, is also secreted by the pancreas. Glucagon mobilizes glucose, fatty acids, and amino acids from storage sites into the blood when needed. Other counterregulatory hormones, namely epinephrine, growth hormone, and cortisol, are also important to maintain normal blood glucose between meals (Goodman, 1988). The normal ranges of venous blood glucose levels are: 70–105 milligrams per deciliter before breakfast, less than 160 milligrams per deciliter 1 hour after meals, and less than 120 milligrams per deciliter 2 hours after eating. In people with diabetes, either the pancreas is not able to produce enough insulin or the cells are unable to use insulin efficiently. Without insulin, the cells are not able to use glucose for fuel, and hyperglycemia ensues (Krall & Beaser, 1989).

An important laboratory test commonly performed on the blood of individuals with diabetes is for glycosylated hemoglobin (hemoglobin A_{1C}). This test, used to check glycemic control, reflects the average blood glucose level for the preceding 2–3 months. The range of values depends to some extent on the laboratory method of analysis. In our laboratory normal is 3.3–5.6. Excellent control is below 7. Some authorities consider < 8–8.59 as good control. Fructosamine, another laboratory test done on blood plasma, represents the average blood glucose for the preceding 2–3 weeks. Although hemoglobin A_{1C} is the gold standard in diabetes management, fructosamine more accurately reflects recent interventions to control blood glucose. In our laboratory, the ranges are 200–272 for normal, and up to 381 millimoles per liter for controlled diabetics (Armbruster, 1987; Springer, 1989). Physicians order these tests because they are useful for assessing glycemic control and treatment efficacy for up to 3 months. However, many authorities do not commonly use the test for fructosamine.

Types of Diabetes

There are two main types of diabetes mellitus: (1) IDDM or Type I and (2) NIDDM or Type II (Guthrie, DeShelter, & Hinnen, 1988; Krall & Beaser, 1989) (see Figure 19.1). With IDDM, the pancreas makes minimal or no insulin. Therefore, the person needs to take one or more injections of insulin daily to keep the blood glucose level under control. People usually develop this type of diabetes before age 30, and the signs and symptoms of the disease may appear abruptly. The major symptoms are hyperglycemia, weight loss, polydipsia, polyphagia, and polyuria. About 10–20% of the population with diabetes have IDDM.

Most people with diabetes (80–90%) have NIDDM. The pancreas produces reduced, normal, or even above-normal amounts of insulin, but blood glucose levels remain higher than normal. Insulin resistance plays a key role in this type of diabetes. The tissues do not use insulin efficiently. People with this type of diabetes usually develop it after age 40. They are often obese and have a family history of the disorder. The signs and symptoms of their hyperglycemia appear gradually. Physicians make the diagnosis of diabetes based on plasma glucose values and symptoms.

TRADITIONAL MANAGEMENT
OF DIABETES MELLITUS

There is no cure yet for either type of diabetes. However, one can manage the disease with diet, physical exercise, and hypoglycemic medication. Educating patients to carry out the prescribed treatment regimen is an integral component in effective diabetes self-care (Cox & Gonder-Frederick, 1992). Management requires lifelong daily attention. Self-management is "a set of skilled behaviors engaged to manage one's own illness" (Goodall & Halford, 1991). It is the cornerstone of treatment for people with diabetes.

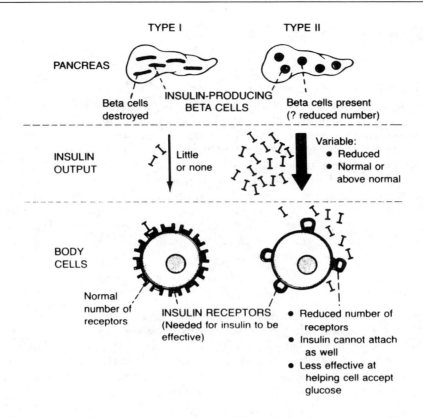

FIGURE 19.1. Diabetes: Type I refers to insulin dependent diabetes. Type II indicates noninsulin dependent diabetes. From Krall and Beaser (1989). Copyright 1989 Lea & Febiger. Reprinted by permission.

Education

People with diabetes can learn from diabetes educators specific behaviors to keep their blood glucose level within an acceptable range. Adhering to a treatment regimen requires that people with diabetes learn certain skills to attain glycemic control. Primarily, they need to take an oral hypoglycemic agent or learn how to administer insulin to lower their blood glucose level. Diabetics must understand specific dietary principles and alter previous patterns of eating. Learning how to use a blood glucose meter to check the blood glucose level and interpret results is vital in both IDDM and NIDDM. Practitioners and diabetes educators also encourage regular physical activity to assist in lowering the blood glucose level and to achieve and maintain desired weight.

In summary, to compensate for the effects of the disease, each person with diabetes faces adjustments from former living habits. The integration of these new skills and activities into an established daily routine may be difficult and stressful. Practitioners and diabetes educators also direct education toward management of the acute and chronic complications of long-standing diabetes.

Hypoglycemic Agents

Insulin

The types of insulin differ in their onset of action, peak, and duration. The type of insulin used determines the time for an insulin dose to begin to lower the blood glucose, the time to reach its peak effect, and the duration of the effect (see Table 19.1). One cannot take insulin orally because it is destroyed by the stomach's digestive juices. Therefore, one injects insulin into the subcutaneous fat tissue using a needle and syringe. Suitable injection sites include the abdomen, upper arms, anterior thighs, and buttocks. The abdomen is the preferred site, but sites should be rotated. Physicians prescribe the type(s), amount(s), and frequency of insulin injections. They base this on the patient's weight, degree of glycemic control desired, the patient's response to insulin, and the patient's projected level of physical activity over the next few hours. Alternatives to the traditional insulin injections with a syringe are: (1) continuous insulin infusion pumps, (2) insulin delivery pens, and (3) jet injectors.

Oral Hypoglycemic Agents

Oral hypoglycemic agents (Guthrie et al., 1988; Krall & Beaser, 1989) are tablets often prescribed for individuals with NIDDM. These agents are not insulin. Thus, they are not effective for individuals who have Type I diabetes. The oral agents' effectiveness depends on the ability of the patient's pancreas to make insulin. Oral agents promote increased insulin release from the pancreas, decrease the production of glucose by the liver, and enhance formation of cellular receptors to combine with insulin.

The first generation of oral agents produced included tolbutamide (Orinase), acetohexamide (Dymelor), tolazamide (Tolinase), and chlorpropamide (Diabinese). The second generation of oral agents proved more effective at lower dosages, produced fewer side effects, and displayed different duration of action. These agents are glyburide (DiaBeta, Glynase PresTabs, Micronase) and glipizide (Glucotrol). Physicians may prescribe one-half tablet, or one or more tablets daily to maintain glycemic control.

Self-Monitoring of Blood Glucose

Self-monitoring of blood glucose (SMBG) methods have markedly improved over the last decade as a result of advances in technology and the relative ease of performing the procedure (American Diabetes Association, 1992). People with diabetes monitor their blood glucose with their own blood glucose meter or with test strips alone (visual method). The blood glucose meter gives a precise number showing the actual blood glucose level. In con-

TABLE 19.1. Types and Action of Insulin

Types	Onset	Peak	Duration
Rapid-acting	½–1 hour	2–4 hours	5–12 hours
Intermediate acting	1–4 hours	8 ± 2 hours	16–24 hours
Long-acting	4–6 hours	18 hours	36+ hours

Note. Data from Guthrie et al. (1988, p. 70).

trast, the visual method gives only an approximate range. The visual method also requires the person to discriminate a color change in the test strip and compare it to a color bar. The blood glucose meters are small, lightweight, portable, and battery operated. People with diabetes purchase a meter for home use to check their blood glucose level multiple times a day. This helps to determine the effectiveness of the prescribed treatment regimen. The results of SMBG provide valuable information about the person's management of diabetes and glycemic control. With this data, the diabetes care team can better determine how well therapy is controlling blood glucose and whether the physician needs to make changes in the person's diabetes management plan.

Health professionals must competently provide patients with the education and training needed to monitor their blood glucose. For example, an improperly done blood test that does not follow the manufacturer's directions may be inaccurate. Blood glucose meters need to be calibrated and cleaned on a regular basis and checked for quality control. The diabetic patient should be evaluated on how well he or she performs a blood test and the accuracy of his or her log book.

COMPLICATIONS OF DIABETES

Both acute and chronic complications can occur in persons with IDDM and NIDDM. The acute complications discussed below are hypoglycemia, diabetic ketoacidosis (DKA), and hyperglycemic hyperosmolar nonketotic syndrome. The chronic complications discussed later may appear after an individual has had diabetes for years and can seriously affect many organ systems of the body.

Acute Complications

Hypoglycemia

Hypoglycemia refers to a low blood glucose (below 50 milligrams per deciliter) caused by too high a dose of insulin or oral hypoglycemic tablets, a delayed or skipped snack/meal, more physical activity than usual, or a combination of these (Guthrie et al., 1988). The initial warning signs and symptoms (adrenal stage) are those associated with increased sympathetic nervous system activity: sweating, hunger, tachycardia, anxiety, weakness, occasional nausea and vomiting, increased blood pressure, cold hands, and hyperalertness. The cerebral stage of hypoglycemia occurs when there is a severe lack of glucose supplied to the brain. It results in neuroglycopenic symptoms and confusion. Hypoglycemia can progress to the point of unresponsiveness, seizures, and coma (Havlin & Cryer, 1988).

Diabetics need to check their blood glucose level when they experience mild signs and symptoms of hypoglycemia. If blood glucose monitoring equipment is unavailable or it is impractical to test, patients must assume that the symptoms are the result of hypoglycemia and require proper self-treatment.

Treatment of hypoglycemia consists of eating or drinking something containing sugar to raise the blood glucose level. The person takes about 10–15 grams of quick-acting carbohydrate (Guthrie et al., 1988). Examples of foods that can provide this amount of carbohydrate are: 4 ounces of fruit juice, 6 ounces of regular (not sugar-free) soft drink, 8 ounces of milk, a tablespoon of honey, 6–8 Lifesavers, or 2–3 glucose tablets. After self-treatment, it may take 10–15 minutes before the person feels better. Some people are frightened by hypoglycemia and overtreat themselves causing a rebound hyperglycemia. Blood glucose monitoring is recommended after self-treatment to verify that the blood glucose level has increased. If the next scheduled snack or meal is more than 30 minutes away, the person should ingest starch and protein (e.g., cheese and crackers) to prevent the blood glucose level from going down again. For episodes of severe hypoglycemia where the person is unresponsive and unable to swallow, someone should give the person an injection of glucagon to raise the blood glucose level. If glucagon is not available, enlist emergency medical assistance.

Some individuals who have diabetes for many years may experience "hypoglycemia unawareness." They lose the capacity to recognize early warning signs and symptoms of low blood sugar. This happens because of an absent or diminished counterregulatory hormone (epinephrine) response. As a result, these people may experience episodes of severe hypoglycemia. They require a glucagon injection by another person and/or emergency medical assistance. Encourage patients who experience hypoglycemic unawareness to monitor their blood glucose levels regularly. Instruct them to treat themselves with glucose promptly if their blood glucose level is < 50 milligrams per deciliter or if they recognize signs and symptoms of hypoglycemia. Educate family members about hypoglycemia. A prescription for a glucagon emergency kit for home use should be obtained from the physician.

Diabetic Ketoacidosis

DKA results from a profound insulin deficiency and is a more common complication of IDDM than NIDDM. Key features of DKA usually include a blood glucose level remaining above 240 milligrams per deciliter, and a positive test for ketones, dehydration, and electrolyte depletion. Precipitating factors that can lead to DKA are acute illness, infection, or inadequate insulin dose (Guthrie et al., 1988).

Hyperglycemic Hyperosmolar Nonketotic Syndrome

This syndrome, or HNKS, occurs from a relative lack of insulin and is more common in persons with NIDDM, especially in elderly people. This complication is also characterized by a high blood glucose level, severe dehydration, and neurological deficits. Unlike DKA, there is usually an absence of acidosis (Guthrie et al., 1988). Both DKA and HNKS are serious conditions that require intervention by a physician and urgent therapy.

Chronic Complications

Persons with either IDDM or NIDDM are at risk for developing chronic complications such as "microvascular," "macrovascular," and "neuropathic" complications. These serious health problems can develop in individuals after they have had diabetes for years. However, it remains unclear why some people with diabetes develop them, whereas others do not. Nonetheless, recent research emphasizes the importance of good glycemic control and use of hypoglycemic agents to prevent or delay the occurrence of complications.

The Diabetes Control and Complication Trial (DCCT) was a large-scale clinical trial of more than 1400 patients with IDDM. The purpose of the study was to determine the effect of intensive therapy of diabetes on incidence of long-term complications. Half of the patients continued their usual care, and the other half received intensive treatment (3–4 injections per day and multiple monitoring of blood glucose). Results were striking. The intensive therapy group decreased average blood glucose and glycosylated hemoglobin. Long-term complications of the eye, kidney, and nervous system were reduced by more than one-half (DCCT, 1993).

Microvascular Complications

Microvascular complications involve the small blood vessels in the eye (retinopathy) and kidney (nephropathy). Damage occurs to the small blood vessels in the retina causing leakage or bleeding in the eye. Damage to and hemorrhage of the fragile blood vessels of the eye may result in loss of vision if not treated. Patients should schedule annual or more frequent visual examinations with an ophthalmologist.

About one-third of the people with IDDM develop "proteinuria," and 5–10% of these develop kidney failure after about 20 years. Damaged filtering units of the kidneys called glomeruli can no longer adequately filter waste products resulting in increased accumulation of these waste products in the blood. Other problems are infections in the kidneys, the tubes leading to the bladder, and the bladder. If the kidneys fail, individuals will require hemodialysis or peritoneal dialysis to remove the waste products of metabolism. Kidney transplantation is an alternative to dialysis (Krall & Beaser, 1989).

Macrovascular Complications

Macrovascular complications refer to damage to larger blood vessels of the body. There are three major types of macrovascular disease: (1) coronary artery disease, (2) cerebral artery disease (cerebrovascular), and (3) peripheral vascular disease. Therefore, myocardial infarctions, cerebral vascular accidents, and lower extremity amputations occur more frequently among people with diabetes than in the general population (Guthrie et al., 1988).

Neuropathy

Diabetes and its metabolic abnormalities also can affect the nerves of the body (neuropathy). There are four major categories of neuropathy (Guthrie et al., 1988).

1. *Mononeuropathies* involve nerve damage to a single nerve or groups of nerves. Examples are carpal tunnel syndrome, footdrop, or third cranial nerve palsy (ptosis).
2. *Proximal motor neuropathies* affect the muscles of the legs.
3. *Peripheral neuropathy* (distal symmetrical polyneuropathy) is the most common type of neuropathy and affects the legs, feet, arms, and hands. The symptoms of neuropathy in the feet are numbness, cold, and pain. Because of impaired sensation, patients with neuropathy must pay special attention to care of the feet to avoid tissue damage.
4. *Autonomic neuropathy* affects the nerves to the sweat glands, gastrointestinal, genitourinary, and cardiovascular systems. Problems that can occur as a result of autonomic neuropathy are diminished sweating, digestive difficulties, diarrhea, neurogenic bladder, and sexual dysfunction, particularly impotence.

THE ROLE OF PSYCHOLOGICAL STRESS IN DIABETES

The Effects of Stress on Metabolism

A proposed model describes the impact of stress on metabolism and on the acute and chronic complications of diabetes (Evans, 1985; Surwit & Feinglos, 1988). Emotional distress activates several physiological pathways. Stimulation of the sympathetic nervous system releases glucagon from the pancreas and decreases secretion of insulin.[1] Decreased parasympathetic (vagal) nerve activity also results in less insulin. These autonomic imbalances result in lower blood levels of insulin, decreased entry of glucose to cells, and hyperglycemia. In addition, sympathetic stimulation causes the release of catecholamines (epinephrine and norepinephrine) from the adrenal medulla. These hormones also have an anti-insulin effect contributing to the hyperglycemia.

The other pathway activated during stress is via the anterior pituitary gland. It causes the adrenal cortex to release cortisol, and the pituitary to release growth hormone. It also causes the thyroid gland to release thyroxine, although this has little to do with acute glycemic regulation. These hormones stimulate biochemical processes (glycogenolysis and gluconeogenesis) in the liver resulting in increased blood glucose. Lack of insulin makes glucose unusable. This increases hepatic and adipose tissue lipolysis resulting in increased blood levels of fatty acids and ketones in the urine. Hyperlipidemia and DKA may occur as a result.

Thus, this controversial model proposes that stress increases blood glucose through sympathetic and adrenal medullary pathways. But single stressors can decrease blood glucose in some persons under laboratory conditions. Individuals react to stress with either hypo- or hyperglycemia (Gonder-Frederick, Carter, Cox, & Clarke, 1990). Nonetheless, chronic severe stress may have a continuing disruptive effect on blood glucose, elevating average blood glucose levels, and increasing variability. Whether stress contributes to the onset of IDDM or NIDDM remains unclear.

The Effects of Stress on the Person with Diabetes

Psychological factors can impact on the individual's ability to adjust to diabetes, whether the disease starts in adolescence or adulthood (Cox & Gonder-Frederick, 1989). Receiving the diagnosis itself may be a traumatic event. Initially there may be a sense of relief, since before the diagnosis the person was feeling very sick, weak, and tired without knowing why. However, most individuals go through a grief process after being told the diagnosis. Components of this process consist of anxiety, fear, denial, anger, bargaining, depression, and finally acceptance.

Immediately after diagnosis many patients feel overwhelmed by the amount of information they must absorb and what they need to do to implement and maintain glycemic control. Sometimes, many educational sessions are necessary before the person feels competent to manage his or her disease. However, knowledge gained does not mean that the person has accepted the disease, will adhere to the treatment regimen, or will achieve glycemic control. Adjustment to diabetes is a lifelong process. Worsening of the disease or developing complications present further challenges to control and acceptance.

Acute and chronic stress may affect management of diabetes in several ways. Acute and severe distress distract some patients from attending to their usual self-care regimen. For example, they may miss an insulin dose, overeat, skip a meal, and decrease the frequency of blood glucose monitoring. During periods with frequent daily stress, some people with diabetes sacrifice their usual self-care activities and, instead, concentrate on managing the stress. This can lead to poor glycemic control. Forgetting or deliberately omitting insulin is a common cause of ketoacidosis requiring hospitalization (Wilkinson, 1987). A person's perception of stress and its effects can strongly influence the neural and endocrine impact on blood glucose. Individuals competent in stress management may show only minor short-lasting blood glucose instability under stressful conditions.

---

[1]This mechanism does *not* cause hyperglycemia in IDDM. Capacity to manufacture insulin naturally is already lost.

TEAM APPROACH IN USING BIOFEEDBACK-ASSISTED RELAXATION WITH DIABETIC PATIENTS

Members of the Team

The team approach is optimal for working with patients with diabetes. Assessing the psychological and physiological effects of stress, stress management, and biofeedback on blood glucose control are necessary. In addition to a physician with special expertise in diabetes, the team[2] consists of at least a certified biofeedback practitioner, a certified diabetes educator, and the patient. The team works together in evaluating the effects of treatment on the physiological and psychological aspects of glycemic control. Most biofeedback practitioners do not have expertise in diabetes education and management. However, when they treat patients with diabetes, they need to know the basic physiology of diabetes and the fundamentals of diabetes management.

Role of the Psychologist Practitioner Who Uses Biofeedback

The psychologist practitioner carries out an initial interview with the diabetic patient to determine stress-related physical and emotional symptoms. One assesses the patient's perception of the effects of stress on his or her blood glucose and his or her perceived capabilities and management strategies (see Chapter 6). Psychological testing also may be used to assess the person's levels of depression, anxiety, anger, and current stress.

This practitioner also conducts a psychophysiological assessment. Practitioners differ on the specifics of this assessment but often monitor multiple modalities. These often include muscle tension, skin conductance, and blood flow in the hands (via skin temperature), heart rate, and breathing during the resting baseline, and during and after various standard office stressors (see Chapter 7). Our laboratory measures frontal electromyography (EMG), heart rate, blood pressure, and finger temperature while patients sit quietly with their eyes closed.

The practitioner provides biofeedback, relaxation therapies, and stress management. Relaxation and biofeedback can help patients feel more in control of their physiology, psychological state, and their illness. Furthermore, decreased plasma levels of stress hormones and sympathetic activity mediate lowered arousal (Benson, Beary, & Carol, 1974), and diminished hyperglycemia.

Role of the Diabetes Educator

The diabetes educator (and/or physician) can interpret blood glucose values because he or she understands the effects of hypoglycemic medications, diet, and exercise on blood glucose. This person also obtains information about the person's diabetes care regimen using the following outline.

---

[2]Biofeedback practitioner is a general term that includes a variety of professionals with varied qualifications and competencies in addition to biofeedback. For the present discussion, we assume this is a properly qualified and credentialed professional. Whoever is in this role must be state licensed to conduct the specified parts of the evaluation and treatment. If not, then the team also needs another properly credentialed professional such as a psychologist. In some medical settings, a registered dietician is a useful part of the team. Therefore, the team could involve a physician, biofeedback therapist, diabetes educator, dietician, psychologist, and the patient.

History

1. Year of diagnosis and symptoms that led to the diagnosis.
2. Family history of diabetes.
3. Other medical problems.
4. Use of prescription and nonprescription medication.
5. Self-concept/self-image relative to diabetes.
6. Previous diabetes education.

Medical Treatment Regimen for Diabetes, Knowledge,
and Management

1. *Medications*
   a. *Insulin*: type(s), source, frequency of injections, prescribed doses, injection site(s), problems with preparing or giving injections, knowledge of onset, peak, and duration of action.
   b. *Oral hypoglycemic agents*: types, dosage, and knowledge of effects.
2. *Diet*: usual caloric intake, restrictions, times of meals, types and amounts of food eaten, meal-planning skills, compliance problems.
3. *Activity/exercise*: types, frequency, duration, problems with activity.
4. *SMBG*: type of blood glucose meter, frequency and time(s) of testing, record keeping, and monitoring problems.
5. *Weight, height*.

Acute/Chronic Complications of Diabetes, Knowledge,
and Management

1. *Hypoglycemia*: frequency of episodes, signs and symptoms, and usual causes.
   a. *Treatment(s)*: use of a glucagon emergency kit, and availability of a quick-acting carbohydrate source.
   b. *Precautions*: wearing of a Medic-Alert or similar bracelet or necklace, and carrying a wallet card.
2. *Ketoacidosis and HNKS*: number of episodes since diagnosis, cause(s) for episode(s), testing of urine for ketones when ill.

Education and Instruction

With the above information, one identifies the patient's knowledge, current self-management, self-care deficits and problems, and capabilities to make appropriate decisions and manage his or her disease. This information provides the basis for instructing the patient about diabetes care and addressing problems with daily management during later sessions.

USING BIOFEEDBACK WITH PATIENTS
WITH DIABETES MELLITUS

Choice of Patients

Type of Diabetes

See the research summary for details of controlled studies of the successful use of biofeedback-assisted relaxation with persons with NIDDM (Surwit & Feinglos, 1983) and IDDM (McGrady et al., 1991).

Time Since Diagnosis and When to Start Biofeedback

Starting at the time of diagnosis, patients with diabetes need to adjust their life-style and behavior significantly. They must incorporate diabetes management behaviors into their daily routine. Psychosocial adjustment to IDDM and NIDDM often is problematic. Therefore, counseling and supportive psychotherapy can be useful during the early weeks and months after diagnosis.

However, beginning a biofeedback-assisted relaxation program may not be appropriate. Adding the clinic appointments for biofeedback and home practice requirements necessary to learn relaxation techniques might overload the resources of the patient. Furthermore, it would be difficult to attribute improvement in glycemic control to the biofeedback and relaxation because the patient is starting multiple new behaviors concurrently.

Another reason for deferring biofeedback during the first year after diagnosis is the so-called diabetic "honeymoon period." This phenomenon is the partial or complete remission of the signs and symptoms of diabetes soon after the onset of IDDM when the pancreas temporarily produces insulin. The blood glucose level may stabilize at close to normal, and the need for exogenous insulin may decrease significantly or completely. This period may last one, several, or, rarely, 12 months (Krall & Beaser, 1989). One could mistakenly attribute a decreased need for exogenous insulin to the biofeedback and stress management treatment instead of to temporary pancreatic insulin production. When the honeymoon period ends and the patient's beta cells are no longer capable of producing insulin, the patient could misattribute the renewed need for exogenous insulin as a total failure of the self-regulation process.

Within a stepped-care model, consider starting more conservative relaxation therapy or office-based biofeedback-assisted relaxation sooner than 12 months after diagnosis for selected patients. For example, one could start with audio cassette relaxation instructions and printed patient education about relaxation. The material should include information to avoid misattributions about the honeymoon period.

Acknowledged Impact of Stress

Patients must at least partially accept the idea that stress can negatively impact on glycemic control. Increased average blood glucose, a wider range of values, an increase in fasting blood glucose, and sometimes more frequent hypoglycemia are common stress effects reported by patients. If a patient is unaware of or rejects the correlation between stress and blood glucose, then perhaps stress is not affecting that person's blood glucose. However, if he or she does not understand stress and is unaware of the potential for its effects, the person may misunderstand its impact. In this case, educate the patient about stress and its relationship to blood glucose. This can improve the chance for treatment to help normalize blood glucose levels.

Cooperation from the Patient's Physician

The physician must approve the referral for biofeedback and should agree to be available for consultation as needed. Practitioners should document the patient's glucose data before, during, and after a biofeedback-assisted relaxation treatment program. They should share this with the patient's physician during and after treatment.

The physician should give the patient guidelines to adjust his or her daily insulin dosages. Patients can adjust the dosages when the blood glucose level exceeds an acceptable level and the patient cannot explain the hyperglycemia by diet, exercise, or insulin. One can use algorithms to make insulin adjustments. For example, some individuals use a "split-and-mixed" insulin regimen such as using intermediate-acting and short-acting insulin twice a day. Physicians may instruct them to increase one type of insulin by a predetermined number of units to compensate for unexplained hyperglycemia. For circumstances such as illness that immediately increase the body's insulin requirement, physicians may prescribe supplementary doses of short-acting regular insulin to prevent progressive loss of glycemic control (Skyler, Skyler, Seigler, & O'Sullivan, 1981).

Reduction of insulin doses may become necessary as a patient progresses with biofeedback therapy. Equally important, patients with severe and unresolved glycemic control problems should be instructed to contact their physician for guidance and possible changes in their medical treatment regimen.

Compliance with the Prescribed Medical Regimen

Patients who consistently do not comply with recommendations for diet, hypoglycemic medication, and/or blood glucose monitoring are not good candidates. They probably will not comply with relaxation practice assignments. Furthermore, improved compliance with the medical regimen may result in better glucose control, but it will confound interpretation of the effects of biofeedback treatment on blood glucose.

Physical Setting

An office for treating diabetic patients needs to maintain sources of quick-acting carbohydrates. Examples are fruit juice, glucose tablets, and regular (not sugar-free) soft drinks. A meter to test for blood glucose, including test strips and lancets, should be available. The equipment to download and calculate values is helpful but not necessary. A diabetes patient manual such as the *Joslin Diabetes Manual* (Krall & Beaser, 1989) is useful. Contact the American Diabetes Association or your local chapter for patient-education materials.

Evaluation of Outcome

The primary treatment outcome measure is blood glucose. We use four indicators[3] of blood glucose to evaluate end-of-treatment outcome. One calculates these from about 50 measurements made before and the same number after completion of therapy. The indicators we use are:

1. Average blood glucose
2. Percentage of the values above 200 milligrams per deciliter
3. Percentage of morning, (fasting) values between 80 and 120 milligrams per deciliter
4. Number of hypoglycemic episodes (or values equal to or below 50 milligrams per deciliter)

A secondary outcome variable is dosage of hypoglycemic agent. Compare the number of tablets of oral hypoglycemic medication or number of units of rapid, intermediate and long-acting insulin used before and after therapy.

---

[3]These indicators and the specific values may differ in other medical clinics.

GENERAL CLINICAL PROCEDURES

Goals

The goals of biofeedback-assisted relaxation are to:

1. Increase the person's ability to perceive and effectively manage stress.
2. Decrease the neural and endocrine systems' effects on blood glucose and insulin.
3. Reduce average blood glucose and increase the percentage of fasting blood glucose values at target range.
4. Reduce dosage of hypoglycemic medication if blood glucose levels are well controlled at entry.

Baseline: Blood Glucose Monitoring

Practitioners must have sufficient data about glycemic control before starting biofeedback for patients with IDDM or NIDDM. We suggest at least 2 weeks of blood glucose data. Try to assess the accuracy of the patient's blood glucose values reported during the initial interview and reassess after treatment. Patients can make gross errors in self-reports of blood glucose values (Mazze, Shamoon, Pasmantier, Lucido, & Murphy, 1984). In these cases, recommend a meter with a memory. Some meters permit downloading the data to a device that prints blood glucose results with the date and time of each test. One can compare these data to the patient's log book results. Occasionally, individuals feel under great pressure to produce "good data" for the practitioner. One must review the patient's blood glucose data carefully and with sensitivity and consideration of his or her efforts in maintaining good glycemic control. Regular blood glucose monitoring must continue during treatment.

Request patients to bring their meter and blood glucose log book to all treatment sessions. Review blood glucose values with them, discuss trends in glycemic control, and address problems with glycemic control such as hypoglycemia. If necessary, contact the physician to adjust the medical treatment regimen.

It also may be helpful for patients to record daily anxiety or stressful events and time. This helps identify work and family stressors to be discussed later in the stress management intervention. Physiological assessment and psychological testing occur during baseline.

One must check body weight, particularly in NIDDM and with persons overweight when treatment starts. Weight loss and accompanying decreases in blood glucose level may require adjustment of the medication dose. Furthermore, when significant weight loss occurs during treatment, one cannot attribute decreases in blood glucose solely to relaxation or biofeedback therapies. We recommend weekly weights for NIDDM patients, and pretreatment and end-of-treatment weights for IDDM patients.

Relaxation Therapy

Relaxation therapies involve slow, diaphragmatic breathing (see Chapter 11), meditation, autogenic phrases, and/or progressive muscle relaxation. One also may use "positive imagery" with other relaxation therapies (Davis, Eshelman, & McKay, 1988). Measure the person's blood glucose before and after at least the first relaxation session. In our program, most sessions include instruction and practice of autogenic phrases. About one-fourth of the sessions involve progressive relaxation.

Biofeedback

Avoid these office sessions at times of low blood glucose or within an hour after strenuous exercise. Do not proceed with a relaxation or biofeedback session if the patient is experiencing hypoglycemic symptoms. Wait until symptoms have resolved and it has been confirmed (by monitoring) that the blood glucose levels have increased to more normal levels.

We offer therapy encompassing 12 60-minute sessions. These consist of counseling for 15 minutes, a 5-minute EMG and thermal baseline, 15 minutes of biofeedback, 5 minutes of debriefing, and 15–20 minutes of reviewing blood glucose logs. The relaxation therapies can be coupled with EMG or thermal biofeedback. One may use one or multiple sites for EMG. Selection depends on suspected or known tension areas for individual patients.

Thermal biofeedback can be used with most patients, since loss of thermal sensation in the hands is uncommon and occurs late in the progression of peripheral neuropathy. A single case study (Bailey, Good, & McGrady, 1990) reported that a patient with IDDM learned to increase finger temperature despite sensory deficits. The patient had little sensation of changes in hand temperature, yet she could warm her hands. Thermal biofeedback may be useful in maintaining circulation to the hands and feet (Hartje et al., 1992). The data on this potential benefit of biofeedback are incomplete and require further study.

Home Practice of Relaxation

We recommend starting with once- or twice-daily practice of relaxation for 15–20 minutes. The biofeedback practitioner, the diabetes educator, and the patient determine the optimal time(s) for practice. This is important so relaxation practice does not coincide with peak insulin times and thus increase the risk for hypoglycemia. Avoid relaxation practice after 9 P.M. to prevent potential exacerbation of nighttime hypoglycemia (Bendtson, Gade, Thomsen, Rosenfalck, & Wildschiodtz, 1992).

At about the midtreatment point, we recommend starting mini-relaxation periods many times per day for 30–60 seconds each. The diabetic person may use the mini-relaxation periods when monitoring his or her blood glucose. Between the application of the blood on the test strip in the glucometer and the display of the result, there is usually a brief waiting period of 60 or 120 seconds. The suggestion to use this time for a mini-relaxation is usually very well accepted by patients. Patients can use mini-relaxations after 9 P.M.

Review of Blood Glucose and Insulin Data

In our setting, patients are with the diabetes educator for 15–20 minutes each session. This is for review of their blood glucose documentation and to identify trends of hypoglycemia or hyperglycemia. The educator discusses possible reasons for the identified trend(s) and suggests strategies to avoid recurrences. He or she notes the relaxation practice times and scrutinizes its effects on the next blood glucose value.

Long-Term Follow-Up

There are no long-term follow-up studies with diabetic populations treated with biofeedback or relaxation. However, we suggest periodic refresher sessions as is common practice when treating other chronic disorders. The practitioner and the patient determine the timing of the follow-up office sessions. One periodically evaluates glycemic control as described earlier.

FINDING PATIENTS WITH DIABETES

Many practitioners and researchers work in large hospitals or medical clinics that treat many patients with diabetes mellitus. Professionals in other settings can locate patients who may benefit from biofeedback-assisted relaxation treatments through various sources. Local hospitals may have diabetes care centers. Patient support groups are common. The local office of the American Diabetes Association may print a monthly newsletter and may hold regular meetings for people with IDDM or NIDDM. For information about basic and clinical research in diabetes, several professional journals are good sources of information. Examples are *Diabetes Care, The Diabetes Educator, Diabetic Medicine*. Subscriptions to *Diabetes in the News* and *The Diabetes Forecast* are useful for patients.

POSSIBLE CONTRAINDICATIONS TO TREATMENT

The following concerns were brought to our attention and require comment.

1. *Deep relaxation has a tendency to lower blood glucose to hypoglycemic levels. This is very unlikely.* Early reports, such as Fowler, Budzynski, and Vandenbergh (1976), expressed concerns about the effects of EMG biofeedback on blood glucose in patients with diabetes. This report identified hypoglycemia as a potential serious problem and advised practitioners to be very cautious in treating patients with IDDM. However, at the time of that case study, SMBG was uncommon, and meters were expensive and difficult to use. That case study patient did not monitor blood glucose daily. We suggest that the risks of using biofeedback-assisted relaxation in NIDDM as well as in IDDM are low if SMBG is in place and if a trained professional is available to interpret those glucose records. The practitioner should be aware of the possibility of hypoglycemia if patients are not maintaining proper nutrition, or are exercising excessively and not eating additional food to compensate for the synergistic effect of exercise and insulin. Furthermore, a patient who is not monitoring and logging blood glucose data is not a good candidate for biofeedback or relaxation treatment.

2. *Patients can misinterpret hypoglycemia as anxiety. This can happen.* Many of the symptoms associated with hypoglycemia are also characteristic of an anxiety reaction. These include sweating, cold hands, hyperalertness, tachycardia, increased blood pressure. Indeed, the symptoms of hypoglycemia and the symptoms of the stress response are both caused by excess sympathetic, adrenal medullary, and adrenal cortical activity. In fact, epinephrine, cortisol, and glucagon are critical to compensate for hypoglycemia (Ganong, 1991). If the person is experiencing hypoglycemia but interprets it as anxiety, his or her blood glucose could continue to decrease to dangerous levels while the patient attempts to "relax away" the symptoms. Therefore, instruct patients in the appropriate responses to symptoms of hypoglycemia. First, test blood glucose to check for low blood sugar. Then treat appropriately with a quick-acting source of carbohydrate followed by retesting. Relaxation will *not* stop the symptoms of hypoglycemia.

It may be possible to use biofeedback to help patients differentiate the stress response from hypoglycemia. For example, increased facial muscle tension, commonly experienced during a stress response, is not a common sign of hypoglycemia. Learning to discriminate facial muscle tension using EMG biofeedback may help some patients to distinguish the two states. This suggestion is anecdotal and not documented in research studies and thus requires testing. The only accurate way of identifying hypoglycemia is testing the blood.

3. *People with diabetes use hyperventilation to counteract acidosis; therefore, do not teach them deep breathing. This not true. Acidosis stimulates hyperventilation.* In persons without

and with diabetes, the respiratory system attempts to compensate for shifts in blood acidity (see Chapter 11; Fried, 1993; Timmons & Ley, 1994). People with diabetes may hyperventilate in their attempt to reregulate blood acidity through respiratory compensation. However, instructions or training to breathe slowly and deeply with the diaphragm do not and cannot override the strong signals from the brain's respiratory center. If the patient is acidotic, attempts at voluntary control of breathing are overridden quickly. Patients should also test their urine for ketones to distinguish DKA from hyperventilation secondary to anxiety.

What are the implications for using slow, deep, diaphragmatic breathing with patients with diabetes? Question the patient about any history of ketoacidosis and assess hyperventilation (see Chapter 11). Observe and measure breathing during initial interviews and when patients practice breathing therapy procedures. SMBG must continue throughout treatment, and the data used to monitor any changes in average blood glucose levels.

RESEARCH SUMMARY

The following are brief summaries of research that considered the effects of biofeedback or relaxation for patients with IDDM or NIDDM. We present them in chronological order and have excluded single case studies. A detailed description and a critique of the studies are beyond the scope of this chapter.

Rosenbaum (1983) treated four patients with IDDM diabetes and two with NIDDM with biofeedback, relaxation, and family therapy. She presented the results in a case-study type format and followed the patients for up to 4 years. Five of the six patients showed improvement in at least one of three outcome measures: average plasma glucose, insulin dosage, and/or range of blood glucose. There were no complications related to biofeedback treatment.

Surwit and Feinglos (1983) used biofeedback and relaxation in a hospital setting to treat six patients with NIDDM and compared these with another six without treatment. The treated patients had five daily sessions of progressive relaxation and EMG biofeedback, and they significantly improved their glucose tolerance. There were no changes in insulin sensitivity or glucose-stimulated insulin secretory activity.

Seven patients with IDDM were treated with biofeedback-assisted relaxation (EMG and thermal). Four of the seven achieved a decrease in units of insulin required to maintain control of blood glucose (Guthrie et al., 1983).

In a combined clinic and home-practice format, four patients with IDDM received 6 weekly sessions of progressive muscle relaxation (Lammers et al., 1984). Two of the four patients significantly decreased blood glucose during the 6 weeks of treatment.

Five diabetic patients who monitored blood glucose daily and were well controlled on insulin participated in a study by Landis et al. (1985). Treatment consisted of 15 weekly 1-hour sessions of biofeedback-assisted relaxation and three subsequent monthly sessions. Therapists used EMG, thermal, and skin conductance feedback. Average glucose levels and insulin remained stable during treatment. However, in four of the five patients, the median and the range of values for blood glucose decreased.

One study focused on 20 patients with poorly controlled IDDM (Feinglos et al., 1987). The study used glycohemoglobin to assess outcome. Ten patients received EMG biofeedback-assisted progressive muscle relaxation, and 10 patients received no treatment. Treatment consisted of 1 week of in-hospital training followed by 6 weeks of practicing relaxation at home. There was no improvement in glycohemoglobin or total insulin dose reported in the trained group compared to the untrained group.

McGrady et al. (1991) divided 18 patients with IDDM into a treatment and a no-treatment group. Patients received 10 treatment sessions. These included eight sessions of autogenic relaxation and two with progressive relaxation. Five sessions contained electromyograph biofeedback, and five included thermal feedback. All patients monitored blood glucose at least three times a day. Patients met weekly or every other week with a clinical nurse specialist to review blood glucose and insulin dosages. The study reported significant improvements in blood glucose. The experimental and control groups differed significantly on three criteria of improvement: the average level of blood glucose, the percentage of blood glucose values above 200 milligrams per deciliter, and the percentage of fasting blood glucose values at target. There were no significant changes in the insulin dosages in either group. A more recent controlled study of 16 patients confirmed the positive effects of biofeedback-assisted relaxation on blood glucose (McGrady, Graham, Bailey, & Nelsen).

CONCLUSION

Research using biofeedback and relaxation as adjunctive treatment for persons with diabetes mellitus is encouraging. Recent advances in knowledge of the immune aspects of diabetes may further the understanding of psychoneuroimmunological factors in the regulation of blood glucose. Rapid improvements in technology allow diabetic patients and their health care providers to anticipate fewer invasive procedures, better control, and a more normal life.

Learning relaxation techniques with biofeedback may be a valuable adjunct to the usual medical care. Certainly, the adjunctive techniques cannot substitute for diet, activity, hypoglycemic medication, or blood glucose monitoring. However, patients with diabetes can achieve better self-care by learning psychophysiological self-regulation including various types of stress management. Since self-care is indeed the cornerstone of glycemic control, the self-regulatory therapies such as relaxation with biofeedback are logical components of overall management of diabetes. More research is necessary to determine ideal selection of patients and the most efficacious relaxation and biofeedback procedures.

GLOSSARY

BACKGROUND DIABETIC RETINOPATHY. Microaneurysms in the retina.

DIABETIC KETOACIDOSIS. An acute complication of diabetes caused by a deficiency of insulin resulting in hyperglycemia, ketosis, acidosis, dehydration, and electrolyte imbalance.

FRUCTOSAMINE. A laboratory serum test that measures the amount of glycated protein and indicates the level of glycemic control for the preceding 2–3 weeks.

HEMOGLOBIN A_{1C}. A laboratory blood test that measures the percent or fraction of hemoglobin that has glucose attached. The test is used to evaluate glycemic control for the preceding 2–3 months.

HONEYMOON PERIOD. Phenomenon that may occur shortly after the onset of type I diabetes in which there is partial or complete remission of signs and symptoms of the disease. It may last up to 12 months.

HYPERGLYCEMIA. Increased blood glucose.

HYPOGLYCEMIA. An acute complication of diabetes in which the blood glucose level is low (<50 mg/dl) as a result of an imbalance of activity, food intake, and/or hypoglycemic medication.

HYPOGLYCEMIA UNAWARENESS. An inability to recognize the early warning signs and symptoms of low blood sugar because of an absent and/or diminished counterregulatory hormone response. As a result, the person may experience episodes of severe hypoglycemia requiring the use of glucagon and/or emergency medical treatment.

INSULIN RESISTANCE. Glucose is unable to enter cells because there are fewer insulin receptors on the cell surface. Combination between insulin and these receptors is necessary for glucose entry.

KETONE BODIES. Chemicals formed during the metabolism of fat. Normal blood and urine concentration is low. Excessive ketones may accompany insulin deficiency in IDDM.

LIPOLYSIS. Metabolism of fat for energy.

MACROVASCULAR COMPLICATIONS. Damage to larger blood vessels of the body involving the coronary arteries, cerebral arteries, and peripheral blood vessels.

MICROVASCULAR COMPLICATIONS. Changes in the small blood vessels of the eye (retinopathy) and kidney (nephropathy) that may lead to blindness and kidney failure, respectively.

NEUROPATHY. Damage to nerve cells of the body that results from diabetes.

POLYDIPSIA. Excessive thirst.

POLYPHAGIA. Excessive hunger.

POLYURIA. Excessive urination.

PROTEINURIA. Protein (albumin) in the urine due to damage to the filtering units of the kidney.

ACKNOWLEDGMENTS

We thank endocrinologists, Thomas P. Fox, M.D., and Geoffrey S. Gates, M.D., of Mayo Clinic Jacksonville; Robert A. Rizza, M.D., of Mayo Clinic Rochester; and James Horner, M.D., of the Medical College of Ohio, for their reviews of drafts of this chapter. Their comments and suggestions were very helpful. This does not imply their endorsement of the content of this chapter.

REFERENCES

American Diabetes Association. (1992). Consensus statement: Self-monitoring of blood glucose. *Diabetes Care, 15*(2), 56–61.

Armbruster, D. A. (1987). Fructosamine: Structure, analysis and clinical usefulness. *Clinical Chemistry, 33*, 2153–2163.

Bailey, B. K., Good, M. P., & McGrady, A. V. (1990). Clinical observations on behavioral treatment of a patient with insulin-dependent diabetes mellitus. *Biofeedback and Self-Regulation, 15*(1), 7–13.

Bendtson, I., Gade, J., Thomsen, C. E., Rosenfalck, A., & Wildschiodtz, G. (1992). Sleep disturbances in IDDM patients with nocturnal hypoglycemia. *Sleep, 15*(1), 74–81.

Benson, H., Beary, J. F., & Carol, M. P. (1974). The relaxation response. *Psychiatry, 37*, 37–46.

Cox, D. J., & Gonder-Frederick, L. A. (1989). The role of stress in diabetes mellitus. In D. J. Cox & L. A. Gonder-Frederick (Eds.), *Behavioral medicine handbook of diabetes mellitus* (pp. 1–27). Champaign, IL: Raven.

Cox, D. J., & Gonder-Frederick, L. A. (1992). Major developments in behavioral diabetes research. *Journal of Consulting and Clinical Psychology, 60*(4), 628–638.

Davis, M., Eshelman, E. R., & McKay, M. (1988). *The relaxation and stress reduction workbook* (pp. 21–36, 55–64, 81–90). Oakland, CA: New Harbinger.

DCCT Research Group. (1993). The effect of intensive treatment of diabetes on the development and progression of long-term complications in insulin-dependent diabetes mellitus. *New England Journal of Medicine, 329,* 977–986.

Evans, M. (1985). Emotional stress and diabetic control: A postulated model for the effect of emotional distress upon intermediary metabolism in the diabetic. *Biofeedback and Self-Regulation, 10,* 241–255.

Feinglos, M. N., Hastedt, P., & Surwit, R. S. (1987). Effects of relaxation therapy on patients with type I diabetes mellitus. *Diabetes Care, 10,* 72–75.

Fowler, J. E., Budzynski, T. H., & Vandenbergh, R. L. (1976). The effects of an EMG biofeedback relaxation program on the control of diabetes. *Biofeedback and Self-Regulation, 1,* 105–112.

Fried, R. (1993). Respiration in stress and stress control. In P. Lehrer & R. L. Woolfolk (Eds.), *Principles and practice of stress management* (2nd ed., pp. 301–331). New York: Guilford Press.

Ganong, W. F. (1991). *Review of medical physiology* (15th ed.). Greenwich, CT: Lange Medical Publications.

Gonder-Frederick, L. A., Carter, W. R., Cox, D. J., & Clarke, W. L. (1990). Environmental stress and blood glucose change in insulin-dependent diabetes mellitus. *Health Psychology, 9*(5), 503–515.

Goodall, T., & Halford, N. K. (1991). Self management of diabetes mellitus: A critical review. *Health Psychology, 10*(1), 1–8.

Goodman, M. A. (1988). *Basic medical endocrinology.* New York: Raven.

Guthrie, D., DeShelter, E., & Hinnen, D. (Eds.). (1988). *Diabetes education: A core curriculum for health care professionals.* Chicago: American Association of Diabetes Educators.

Guthrie, D., Moeller, T., & Guthrie, R. (1983). Biofeedback and its application to the stabilization and control of diabetes mellitus. *American Journal of Clinical Biofeedback, 6*(2), 82–87.

Hartje, J. C., Roura, M. F., Morrisey, P. J., Montgomery, C. T., Wilson, W. J., & Rust, M. J. (1992, March 19–24). Biofeedback therapy as treatment for the autonomic deficiencies found in the neuropathy of diabetes mellitus. In *Proceedings of the 23rd Annual Meeting of The Association for Applied Psychophysiology and Biofeedback, Colorado Springs* (pp. 154–155). Wheatridge, CO: Association of Applied Psychophysiology and Biofeedback.

Havlin, C. E., & Cryer, P. E. (1988). Hypoglycemia: The limiting factor in the management of insulin-dependent disbetes mellitus. *Diabetes Educator, 14,* 407–411.

Krall, L. P., & Beaser, R. S. (1989). *Joslin diabetes manual* (12th ed.). Philadelphia: Lea & Febiger.

Lammers, C. A., Naliboff, B. D., & Straatmeyer, A. J. (1984). The effects of progressive relaxation on stress and diabetic control. *Behaviour Research and Therapy, 22*(6), 641–650.

Landis, B., Jovanovic, L., Landis, E., Peterson, C. M., Groshen, S., Johnson, K., & Miller, N. E. (1985). Effects of stress reduction on daily glucose range in previously stabilized insulin-dependent diabetic patients. *Diabetes Care, 8,* 624–626.

McGrady, A. V., Bailey, B. K., & Good, M. P. (1991). Controlled study of biofeedback-assisted relaxation in type I diabetes. *Diabetes Care, 14*(5), 360–365.

Rosenbaum, L. (1983). Biofeedback-assisted stress management for insulin-treated diabetes mellitus. *Biofeedback and Self-Regulation, 8*(4), 519–532.

Skyler, J. S., Skyler, D. L., Seigler, D. E., O'Sullivan, M. J. (1981). Algorithms for adjustment of insulin dosages by patients who monitor blood glucose. *Diabetes Care, 4*(2), 311–318.

Springer, R. (1989). Glycated protein tests. *Diabetes Self Management,* January/February, 44–46.

Surwit, R. S., & Feinglos, M. N. (1988). Stress and autonomic nervous system in type II diabetes. *Diabetes Care, 11,* 83–85.

Surwit, R. S., & Feinglos, M. N. (1983). The effects of relaxation on glucose tolerance in noninsulin dependent diabetes mellitus. *Diabetes Care, 6,* 176–179.

Timmons, B. H., & Ley, R. (Eds.). (1994). *Behavioral and psychological approaches to breathing disorders.* New York: Plenum Press.

Wilkinson, G. (1987). The influence of psychiatric, psychological and social factors on the control of insulin-dependent diabetes mellitus. *Journal of Psychosomatic Research, 31*(3), 277–286.

VII
NEUROFEEDBACK APPLICATIONS

20

Neurofeedback for the Management of Attention-Deficit/ Hyperactivity Disorders

Joel F. Lubar

Attention-deficit/hyperactivity disorder (ADHD) exists in all countries and in all cultures. Its recognition and characteristics became considerably clearer in the last decade. It is a very significant disorder affecting a large number of children and many adults. Certainly, ADHD can be debilitating in terms of achieving educational objectives, maintaining employment, and developing careers. It is a disorder that can be extremely disruptive within family systems and affects most aspects of one's ability to function effectively in a complex society and to set and achieve important life goals.

In this chapter, I describe a relatively new, very promising, and powerful adjunctive procedure called electroencephalographic (EEG) neurofeedback training (neurofeedback) for treatment and long-term management of this disorder. My work in this area began in the mid-1970s. A recent paper (Lubar, 1991) has described the details of the development of the neurofeedback treatment approach for ADHD. During the early development of this technique, the treatment involved what was commonly called EEG biofeedback training. However, in the last few years, a new term emerged—neurofeedback. This specifically refers to feedback designed to alter a condition which displays evidence that it is neurologically based.

However, neurofeedback in a broader sense is defined as biofeedback linked to a specific aspect of the electrical activity of the brain such as the frequency, amplitude, or duration of activity such as theta (4–8 Hertz), alpha (8–13 Hertz), or beta (13 Hertz or greater) from certain scalp or brain locations. Neurofeedback can also be linked to components of auditory, visual, or somatosensory event-related potentials or slow DC shifts in cortical excitability as recently shown by Schneider et al. (1992) for schizophrenic patients.

Currently, there are over 300 organizations using EEG neurofeedback in the treatment of ADHD. These include private clinics, university-based groups, and individuals working within school systems. Neurofeedback is employed by a wide range of practitioners including pediatricians, psychiatrists, clinical and counseling psychologists, clinical psychophysiologists, social workers, educational specialists, nurses, and other health care providers.

This chapter covers the description of ADHD, its characteristics, a brief historical review, and a description of some of the existing therapies for this disorder. Next, I present a detailed description of the EEG characteristics of ADHD, along with the rationale for developing a data base from EEG measures including both age-related and intelligence-related considerations. I then discuss the rationale for neurofeedback including the criteria for an effective intervention with specific individuals. I also describe the details of instrumentation and treatment protocols that should be used for this type of training and how they vary as a function of age, intelligence, and severity of the disorder. Pre- and posttreatment measurement used to determine the effectiveness of neurofeedback is the next topic. I then describe the results from our clinic, our research, and those of others. The next section of this chapter focuses on the integration of neurofeedback with other therapies, including the use of medications, family therapy, individual therapy, and parent support groups. Finally, I outline future directions that need to be considered for the further development of neurofeedback training for ADHD.

It is important to emphasize that treatment of ADHD is not simple. In fact, it is very challenging. Fortunately, the treatment risks are low in that we are not treating a life-threatening disorder such as seizures and some cardiovascular disorders in which considerations regarding mortality must be taken into account. However, considerations of which amplitude and frequency characteristics of the EEG need to be enhanced and which need to be decreased, and what electrical parameters need to be incorporated into the instrumentation are important. Careful management of these specific training parameters will greatly determine whether the outcome of the treatment is a success in terms of decreased behaviors associated with ADHD or whether nothing significant occurs. In our early studies in the late 1970s that employed blinded crossover designs where we purposely trained children to increase slow activity in the EEG, there was a deterioration of behaviors observed in the classroom, that is, more ADHD behaviors emerged. When the children were trained to decrease the slow activity and increase faster activity, their behaviors improved. These data will be described in more detail later on, but they show that careful attention to what is being trained in the EEG is important if we are to obtain improvements in ADHD-related behaviors. No single treatment, no matter how powerful, can totally bring ADHD under control with long-term maintenance. This is because ADHD affects so many aspects of one's life. The integration of neurofeedback with other modalities is crucial to obtain the potential for maximum results. It is imperative that individuals planning to use neurofeedback have proper training. New practitioners should receive intensive training and that includes observing and supervised working with patients with ADHD. It is my experience that regardless of a therapist's background, to become a seasoned neurofeedback practitioner often requires the equivalent of an internship of 1–2 years. One needs to understand the complexity of ADHD, its many components, and how they interact and affect the lifestyle and family systems of individuals with this disorder.

DESCRIPTION OF ATTENTION-DEFICIT/ HYPERACTIVITY DISORDER

The description of ADHD in this chapter is not exhaustive. There are many excellent published reviews of this disorder. In 1991, a special supplement of the *Journal of Child Neurology* was devoted entirely to ADHD. In the introduction to that special edition, it is stated that even 10 years ago there were more than 2000 papers published about this disorder and that the number of papers and books has grown exponentially since then (Voeller, 1991). There is still considerable disagreement as to the best diagnostic and treatment approach. It is becoming clearer that attention-deficit disorder (ADD) occurs in two main forms—with or without hyperactivity. The form with hyperactivity is sometimes referred to as ADHD or ADD+; the form without hyperactivity is referred to as ADD or ADD– (Barkley, 1989).

In the 1950s and 1960s, this disorder was referred to as minimal brain dysfunction syndrome (MBD). At that time many believed that there was something structurally wrong within the central nervous system with some type of brain injury or inadequate integration of perceptual mechanisms (Anderson, 1963). G. F. Still, a British physician, published a very early description of this disorder in *The Lancet* in 1902. He referred to the complex of behaviors we now call ADHD as "Abnormal Deficits in Moral Control . . . and Wanton Mischievousness and Destructiveness." We recognize this today as a combination of ADHD, conduct disorder (CD), and oppositional defiant disorder (ODD). Even at present, Barkley (1990) describes one aspect of ADHD as a deficit in rule-governed behavior. In some ways, this refers to some of the same problems that Still recognized almost 100 years ago.

Currently, in *The Diagnostic and Statistical Manual of Mental Disorders* for the American Psychiatric Association (DSM-IV), the term attention deficit/hyperactivity disorder is the most common description. Lahey, Schaughency, Hynd, Carlson, and Nieves (1987) working with the DSM-IV committee strongly suggested that ADD without hyperactivity be considered a separate entity from ADHD even though they can overlap. This is partly because ADD has some characteristics that are different from ADHD.

Figure 20.1 shows some relationships between ADHD and other disorders. Regardless of the nosology, one underlying emerging fact seems very clear: ADD+ and ADD- have a strong biological basis. In many families, these may be familial and most likely, neurologically based. Their neurological basis may be structural in some instances where there is overlap with severe specific learning disabilities such as developmental dyslexia. Furthermore, there is likely an abnormality in neurometabolism as shown by recent PET scan studies. This provides the basis for the use of stimulant medication therapy for dealing with certain aspects of this disorder (Zametkin & Rapoport, 1987; Zametkin et al., 1990).

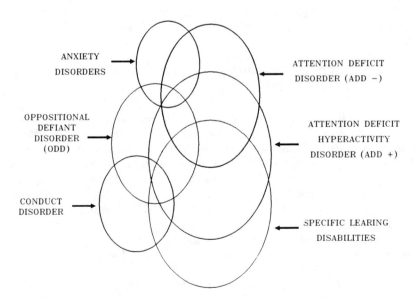

FIGURE 20.1. Schematic diagram illustrating relationship between ADD with and without hyperactivity and other comorbid conditions. The circles are meant to be representations and are not drawn to a scale that represents the amount of overlap of the different disorders but to show that there is a relationship between them.

Many children with pure ADD without hyperactivity experience considerable lethargy, lack of motivation, daydreaminess. In children where there is a hyperkinetic or hyperactive component (ADHD), the latter may be associated with impulsive behavior or oppositional defiant disorder. In severe cases, oppositional defiant disorder may evolve into a true conduct disorder and, if untreated, may further evolve into an antisocial personality disorder in adulthood. However, it must be emphasized that the latter represents a very small fraction of the ADHD population and also represents the extreme end of a continuum (Lahey, 1991).

Children and adults with ADD without significant hyperactivity may often experience anxiety disorders. Both ADD and ADHD individuals may also experience depression. Occasionally this disorder is associated with ticks and in rare cases, seizures. As far as the genetics of ADHD are concerned, Noble, Blum, Ritchie, Montgomery, and Sheridan (1991) provided evidence that there may be a cluster of alleles on chromosome eleven associated with a familial form of this disorder. In this case, many family members who are blood relatives might experience some of the manifestations of ADHD. Interestingly, the authors described the location of these alleles close to other alleles on the same chromosome that may be associated with certain tic disorders, alcoholism, and bipolar depression. Furthermore the incidence of these comorbid conditions is higher in the ADHD population than it is in control populations.

When alcoholism is present in the family structure, the use of neurofeedback for individuals with ADD or ADHD might be quite problematic according to Peniston and Kulkosky (1989). The reason for this according to these investigators is that alcoholics tend to have increased beta activity and decreased theta and alpha activity. As we shall see later, training for ADD and ADHD involves increasing beta and decreasing theta and sometimes alpha activity. Theoretically, this might be counterindicated if the individual experiences ADD or ADHD and alcoholism simultaneously. At the present time, there is not enough research available to indicate exactly how to proceed in this particular situation.

CHARACTERISTICS OF ATTENTION-DEFICIT/ HYPERACTIVITY DISORDER

Since ADHD has a strong biological–neurological basis, its manifestations are often apparent from very early childhood. Some children are extremely hyperactive (hyperkinetic) almost from birth. They have great difficulty falling asleep, often whine a great deal, and parents describe them as difficult children. Some of the children who eventually develop ADD without hyperactivity are very lethargic and may have a lower activity level than siblings or other children without this disorder.

Usually by age 4, the characteristics of this disorder are apparent. Children lose interest in toys very readily. They have difficulty interacting with children who do not have ADHD in regard to playing games with them and sustaining attention to tasks. Sometimes children with ADHD are characterized by peers, educators, and even parents as mentally retarded although they may in fact be normal, superior, or even gifted. This disorder occurs at all levels of the intelligence scale. In contrast, there are many individuals with IQs of less than 80 who have very good attentional capability and can often focus on a particular task for long periods of time without distraction. They will sometimes work very well with a tutor even though their learning capability is significantly limited. The ADD children, on the other hand, display inattentiveness, impulsivity, and hyperactivity as described by Barkley

(1990), particularly if they are ADHD. If they are ADD−, they display inattentiveness as their main characteristic.

One view of ADHD is as a motivational disorder. In addition to rapidly losing interest in their toys, these children also lose interest in friendship relationships and have difficulty developing good peer relationships. They have a decreased response to punishment that is related to their problems with rule-governed behaviors. They experience rapid extinction to new stimuli or satiate more rapidly to new situations (Barkley, 1990). This is particularly relevant in any kind of behavioral intervention and has direct implications for how neuro-feedback sessions have to be carried out in order to maintain motivation and interest.

Both ADD and ADHD are more common in the male population than in the female population, ranging anywhere from 3:1 to 6:1, depending on which review one reads (Whalen & Henckler, 1991). Whereas ADD without hyperactivity does not go away as one matures, ADD with hyperactivity often changes in that the hyperkinetic component may decrease with age. Many professionals now believe that a significant proportion of both ADHD and ADD individuals continue to experience this disorder throughout their life history. As far as inattentiveness and difficulty with rule-governed behavior is concerned, especially with adolescents, there is difficulty maintaining or sustaining activity leading to completion of tasks. This is the case with homework in high school, meeting deadlines imposed in work situations, and maintaining commitments in social or marital relation-ships later in life.

The differential diagnosis of ADHD from other disorders is often difficult and re-quires considerable skill. In order to develop a comprehensive treatment program, it is necessary to determine the extent the individual is experiencing other comorbid conditions. This is especially the case if the program involves neurofeedback combined with medica-tion, family intervention, individual psychotherapy, and behavior therapy. These comorbid conditions include ODD, CD, learning disabilities (LD), anxiety and affective disorders, and various thought disorders.

Common tools for determining diagnoses and comorbidities involve extensive inter-viewing and family history, medical history, and, in some cases, detailed medical workups involving EEG, neurological scanning (MRI or PET) techniques, blood work, and even genetic studies. The use of psychodiagnostic tools such as the Minnesota Multiphasic Per-sonality Inventory (MMPI) and metrics designed specifically for children can be useful as part of the assessment of possible thought and affective disorders.

Neuropsychological measures are particularly useful for assessing possible organic brain dysfunction and specific learning disabilities. These techniques include but are not limited to the Halstead–Reitan battery, Luria Neuropsychological battery, Wechsler Intelligence Scale for Children (WISC-R) or (WISC-III) or the Wechsler Adult Intelligence Scale—Revised (WAIS-R), Woodcock–Johnson Psychoeducational Evaluation—Revised (WJ-R), and other neuropsychological and achievement measures.

For the behavioral–observational assessment of ADD and ADHD, there are excellent rating scales available. These include Barkley (1987), Conners' Parent and Teacher Ques-tionnaire (Conners, 1969), Hawthorne, Achenbach Child Behavior Checklist, the Child Activity/Attention Profile of Edelbrock, Home and School Situation Questionnaire, and others in development. Many of these are checklists filled out by parents or teachers and often include items based on the DSM-IV categorization of ADHD. The same checklist should be employed before and after an intervention to determine the extent that the treat-ment affected the behaviors described. This is particularly important for neurofeedback as a treatment method still being established.

CURRENT THERAPIES

Most prevalent approaches for the treatment of ADHD currently involve the use of antihyperactive medications, primarily stimulants occasionally supplemented by (1) tricyclic antidepressants, (2) alpha blockers, and in rare cases, (3) antipsychotic medications. Other nonmedical therapies involve (1) the extensive use of behavior therapy involving complex schedules of rewards and punishments (Barkley, 1990; Wolraich et al., 1990), (2) cognitive-behavioral therapy, (3) traditional individual psychotherapy, and (4) the family systems approach. Other techniques such as visual–motor integration and dietary management have proved effective only in rare cases and are not at the present time part of the treatment mainstream.

The use of stimulant medications for the treatment of the hyperactive component of ADHD, and in many cases, the treatment of ADD without hyperactivity is represented by literature dating back at least to the 1940s. As early as 1937, Bradley reported that amphetamine sulfate significantly decreased the hyperkinetic behavior of children and allowed them to function better socially and in academic settings. At that time, the explanation for the positive results from using stimulants with hyperactivity was not understood. Very briefly, the two main hypotheses that have been developed to explain how stimulants may be useful for these children are (1) the low arousal hypothesis, developed by Satterfield and Dawson in 1971 and further elaborated by Satterfield, Lesser, Saul, and Cantwell (1973), and (2) the noradrenergic hypothesis developed over years and elegantly elaborated by Zametkin et al. (1990).

Essentially, these two hypotheses propose that children with ADHD experience low arousal. This low arousal comes about as the result of decreased impact of sensory stimuli, in all modalities, acting on the central nervous system mechanisms for sensory integration and resulting in the child engaging in stimulus-seeking behavior. Self-stimulation and object play are primary features of the hyperactive (hyperkinetic) syndrome (Lubar & Shouse, 1976, 1977; Shouse & Lubar, 1978). Children with hyperactivity often exhibit intense but brief interest in new stimuli. For example, they rub objects against their bodies, smell them, taste them if they can, and often engage in other stimulus-seeking behaviors such as excessive movement, spinning around, running from place to place within a room, picking up one object after another and examining it. If they are in a room where there is very little stimulation, they will very often fall asleep after a brief flurry of activity.

The basis for this stimulus-seeking behavior might lie in decreased noradrenergic activity particularly in the brainstem reticular formation and perhaps in the basal ganglia as well. Heilman, Voeller, and Nadeau (1991) proposed that in many of these children, as well as adults with this disorder, there is a defect in response inhibition and particularly in the nigrostriatal frontal system, more on the right side of the brain than the left side. Motor restlessness may reflect not only frontal lobe dysfunction but possible impairment of the dopaminergic system as well. Basically, we think of arousal being mediated by (1) connections from the brainstem reticular formation, which receives inputs from all of the sensory modalities except olfaction, (2) the transmission of this information to the diffuse thalamic (reticular) projection system, and (3) the basal forebrain, which does receive olfactory projections. These input systems, in conjunction with the basal ganglia and the cerebellum, which is involved in programming the output of the motor cortex, are all affected by decreased noradrenergic activity. Norepinephrine, a key transmitter in this system, is produced by a very important brainstem nucleus located in the midbrain, the locus coeruleus. This nucleus has extensive projections with these mesolimbic–striatal and forebrain systems. Not only is the neuroanatomy of these systems complex, but the resulting neurochemical dysfunctions and/or neuropathology associated with them are also complex. The latter include movement disorders and affective disorders. As we discuss below, these abnormalities in neurochemistry and neurophysiology are reflected in EEG measures, event-related potential measures, and in regional brain metabolism.

At the current time, three primary stimulants are used in trying to restore noradrenergic balance. In younger children, the use of dextroamphetamine is common. In children from age 6 through adolescence and even adulthood, two other medications are in common use: methylphenidate (Ritalin) and pemoline (Cylert). Children and adults who experience either impulsive behavior or have extreme difficulty with organizational and planning skills might respond positively to small amounts of a tricyclic antidepressant, such as norpramine or imipramine. The latter has more anticholinergic side effects than the former. In some children when the impulsive behavior also becomes very aggressive, the use of clonidine, an alpha-adrenergic blocker, is sometimes helpful. There is little doubt that between 60–80% of children with ADHD show varying degrees of positive response to these medications when properly administered. In some cases, the response is ideal in that the child no longer exhibits all components of the hyperactive syndrome or any great attentional difficulties. Individuals who have this ideal response can remain on these medication regimens for a long time without any significant negative side effects. Other individuals show partial responses to the medications and may exhibit a variety of side effects. In some cases, these include anorexia, varying degrees of sleep disturbance, and mood changes. Some children respond to Ritalin with an almost totally flat affect. They are sometimes described as "zombie-like" by parents or others familiar with the child. Such a response would warrant the use of either a different medication or a nonmedication alternative.

Of the 20–25% of children who do not respond well to medications, there may be a combination of reasons: (1) either more serious side effects including gastrointestinal disturbances, (2) increased tic disorders when tics are present (a possible problem with Ritalin), (3) seizure disorders, (4) headaches, (5) urinary problems, or (6) changes in affect unacceptable to the person or family. One of the main problems with medication is that its effects can be short-lived or state-dependent. Ritalin clears the system rapidly within 3–4 hours. Cylert and amphetamine clear less rapidly, often within 8 hours of administration. The effects of the medication are then gone. For this reason, it is often necessary to give two or three doses of the medication a day, particularly for Ritalin. One solution to this is to use a time-release form, but this is not always as effective as individual dosages. Ritalin is very commonly administered with a larger dose in the morning, a second dose at noon, and a very small dose after school to help the child to complete homework assignments.

The administration of these medications is rarely based on body weight, and more appropriately based on response. An adult or a large child may respond very effectively to 5 milligrams of Ritalin, whereas a small child may require 40 milligrams or more to obtain an adequate response. The important factor is not how much Ritalin is administered per unit of body weight but how much of it enters the central nervous system. As far as basic mechanisms are concerned, there is a significant literature indicating that Ritalin does improve certain characteristics of the evoked response such as the latency and amplitude of the P3 component associated with sensory discrimination (Klorman, 1991).

There is little present evidence that Ritalin has any effect on cortical EEG. This may explain one of the reasons why there is a very limited carryover effect with the use of these medications. One of the major complaints of parents is that the child performs well with the medication, but the effect is medication-dependent. As soon as the medication is gone or often during holiday periods or weekends, many of the undesirable behaviors return, and the child is still not able to get work done, especially in academic settings. Sometimes when Ritalin is given for long periods of time, that is, several years, there is a carryover effect for several months after administration is stopped, but many of the undesirable behaviors eventually may return.

It is my experience working with children with ADHD that as they mature, if there is a hyperkinetic component, this motor component will very often decrease with age. It may even disappear or be replaced by fidgetiness and inability to sit still for long periods of time. Nevertheless, the attention deficit associated with the ADHD may actually become worse as one becomes older. The reason for the latter is because the demands of society, particularly academic demands become greater. Many children who do well in grade school begin to experience decreased performance in junior high or middle school. They then begin to get failing grades in many courses by the seventh or eighth grade because they cannot keep up with the work and do not hand in long and tedious assignments.

In summary, although the view of this chapter that neurofeedback is a powerful adjunctive technique, treatment is usually integrated with medications where medications are necessary or desirable. Medication is a powerful adjunct to other therapy. Medication is often combined with the use of behavior-modification techniques based on Skinnerian principles of reinforcement, including withdrawal of rewards or punishment where appropriate. The use of "time out" as a primary technique, or cognitive-behavioral therapy techniques that try to change the child's perception of why certain behaviors are inappropriate are often part of a behavioral regimen.

Cognitive-behavioral therapy often involves the use of self-induced messages to try to maintain behavioral control. This technique has not been used extensively, and the results are variable. The main criticism of the behavioral therapies is that they are effective in only 40–60% of cases. When they are effective, the techniques have to be used extensively on a moment-by-moment basis, every day for many months and years. The administration of these schedules of reinforcement is tedious and often resented by the parents because it dominates their life circumstances and requires extensive parent training to maintain the various schedules of reinforcement.

One of the biggest problems in ADHD is that there is often underlying prefrontal lobe dysfunction. The prefrontal lobes of the brain are the "executive" portions of the brain involved in planning and judgment. Inappropriate behaviors occurring today can lead to very significant future consequences. Children with ADHD often live for the present. It has very little meaning for them when they are told that they may get a bad grade at the end of a grading period if their assignments are not completed. This is especially true if the end of the grading period is several weeks or months away. Behavior therapy, on the other hand, would reward the child for getting a particular assignment done and perhaps punish the child by withdrawal of rewards or "time outs" for not getting the assignment done. This technique might work fine for a particular circumstance but may not generalize well and would have to be repeated on a day-to-day basis. Non-ADHD children have the cognitive abilities to understand why not getting the assignment done will be important for them. They more readily stop engaging in nonproductive behaviors that lead to punishment or withdrawal of rewards because they can plan for the future and understand the consequences of behaviors.

Individual psychotherapy for children experiencing depression or severe adjustment problems is very importantly integrated with family systems approaches. Many children with ADD are adopted. These are children who, with the genetic basis for ADD/ADHD, are often adopted by families that do not have this disorder, do not understand it, and do not know how to deal with it. Another unfortunate fact is that in many families where there is ADHD or ADD, the family system is destroyed by the child's behaviors, and as a result, separation or divorce are more prevalent. In situations where there are custody issues, severe conflicts between parents and between the child and his or her biological and/or stepparents, family systems approaches are often much more important than the use of behavior therapy or medication alone.

The main hypothesis underlying the use of neurofeedback is simply stated: If ADHD and ADD are associated with neurological dysfunction, particularly at the cortical level and primarily involving prefrontal lobe function, and if the underlying neurological deficit can be corrected, the ADHD child may be able to develop strategies and insights (paradigms) that non-ADHD children already have. With the use of these paradigms, the abilities to organize, plan, and understand the consequences of inappropriate behavior are facilitated. As a result, there is a much stronger carryover of the effectiveness of rewards, time outs, and other behavioral approaches. The need for medication may actually diminish if we can show that, by changing cortical functioning, there is also a change in brainstem function such as brainstem or cortical event-related potentials or measures of sensory integration. The long-term effects of neurofeedback have already been documented (Tansey, 1990; Lubar, 1991, 1992). Therefore, this technique, which leads to normalization of behavior, can lead to normalization of neurological dysfunction in the ADHD child and can have long-term consequences for academic achievement, social integration, and overall life adjustment.

ELECTROENCEPHALOGRAPHIC CHARACTERISTICS OF ADHD

Abnormalities in EEG were reported in children now classified as ADD and ADHD as early as 1938 (Jasper, Solomon, & Bradley, 1938). There is an extensive literature, much of it reviewed in the supplement to the *Journal of Child Neurology* published in 1991. Basically, EEG studies show excessive slow activity in central and frontal regions of the brain. These studies are supported by recent PET scan and SPECT scan studies that also indicate abnormalities in cerebral metabolism in these particular brain areas. Current research in progress by Daniel Amen and J. H. Paldi (1993) have uncovered several patterns of EEG abnormalities in children with ADD. One pattern involves frontal lobe deactivation. These children experience decreased metabolism in prefrontal regions of the brain, and according to these investigators, are good candidates for the use of stimulant medications as well as neurofeedback. Other children show deficits in limbic system activity and are characterized as having oppositional behavior, emotional outbursts, and impulsiveness. These children also show significant decreased metabolism in their prefrontal lobes. They are good candidates for the use of tricyclic antidepressants such as imipramine or norpramine. The third subgroup comprises individuals who have increased activity in the medial superior frontal gyrus. These individuals experience the opposite of ADD and are often characterized as having an attention deficit with obsessive–compulsive disorder. They have a very short attention span and are often impulsive and oppositional. They take a long time to get required work done because they become obsessed with sometimes irrelevant material and cannot seem to discriminate between what is essential and what is nonessential in completing a homework assignment. These patients sometimes respond to Anafranil. By far the most common group of ADD children are those with excessive slow activity in frontal and central brain regions.

In a recent study (Mann, Lubar, Zimmerman, Miller, & Muenchen, 1991), we examined the difference between a group of 25 children with ADD without hyperactivity or learning disability and 27 carefully matched controls. The subjects were matched for IQ and socioeconomic status. They were all right-handed male children. In that study, we published a multicolored topographic brain map showing differences between the groups for baseline studies and during reading and drawing challenges. The data clearly showed that during the academic challenges, there were significant increases in slow (4–8 Hertz) theta activity along the midline and in the frontal regions and decreased beta activity, especially along the midline and posteriorly. This was the first quantitative, multichannel neurological study to show that children with *pure* ADD as opposed to ADHD are statistically different in terms of their EEG characteristics.

During the past 2 years, we collected data on the Lexicor NRS24 system (Boulder, Colorado) to develop a data base examining one particular measure of EEG activity. This measure is the percentage power ratio of 4–8 Hertz theta activity divided by 13–21 Hertz beta activity. This baseline study involved the following protocol: a cap (Electro Cap, Inc.) containing all 19 of the electrodes according to the international 10–20 system of electroencephalography is fitted to the child, adolescent, or adult's head. There are different size caps depending on head size (see Figure 20.2). The cap is connected to a harness that holds it tightly in place and to a band that is placed around the chest. Electrode gel is placed into each of the electrode cups embedded in the cap, and impedances of less than 7 kilohms are

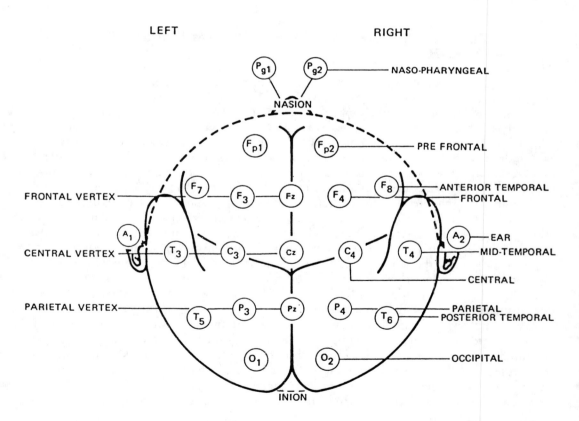

FIGURE 20.2. Locations of the standard 19 electrode placements according to the International 10–20 system of electroencephalography.

obtained before recording can be started. Linked ears are used as references for the 19 cortical channels. The subject is placed in front of an easel, which is used to present materials at different times during the test protocol. The test consists of six parts: first an eyes-open baseline during which approximately 3 minutes of EEG activity is recorded followed by an eyes-closed baseline for 3 minutes. The subject is then requested to read material silently that is grade- or age-level appropriate. This is tested by reading out loud for fluency before the material is presented silently. The child next reproduces figures from the Beery–Bender Visual Motor Gestalt Test and then completes the Raven's Progressive Color Matrices Test. The next task involves reading to the subject content that continues the material that the child has read silently before. Each portion of this examination lasts for about 3 minutes. Additional tasks sometimes follow the formal data-base testing. These may involve the coding task from the WISC-R or other measures from the Halstead–Reitan Battery to see whether there are unusual patterns of cognitive activity associated with these neuropsychological tasks. This portion of the evaluation is still experimental.

The data from the 19 recording channels are analyzed by compressed power spectral analysis and displayed as a multicolored topographic brain map showing the absolute activity in microvolts for each of the different band passes of interest. A second set of maps compares all of the band passes on the same numerical scale so that it is possible to evaluate where the primary activity is occurring, that is, theta, beta, or some other band pass.

Figure 20.3 shows the current status of our data base for three groups of individuals with ADD. These data consist of children, adolescents, and adults not taking any medication. A small group of matched control subjects is compared to the 15-year and older group

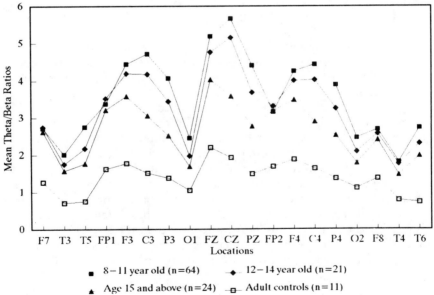

FIGURE 20.3. Current status of data base for three groups of individuals with ADD and matched controls for the adult group. The measure illustrated is the ratio of 4–8 Hertz theta activity to 13–21 Hertz beta activity, measured in terms of percentage total power. Note that the highest ratios are obtained in location CZ for children and at FZ for older adolescents and adults.

of ADDs. There is a large difference between the theta–beta ratios of these two adult groups. Age-matched control groups for the other subjects are currently being developed.

The data base that originally developed in the Mann et al. (1991) study, was based on 16 channels of information recorded with electrodes placed on the International 10–20 sites using Nihon Kohden Elefix paste for electrode attachment. The data from the Nihon Kohden EEG was analyzed by an off-line analysis system called Stellate (1990). Some of those data were presented in my review paper (Lubar, 1991). The two groups in that study were very carefully matched (8- to 11-year-olds). Significant difference ($p < .5$ and $< .001$) levels were obtained for many central and frontal locations. The current data base replicates those findings and extends it for the older groups.

An important point in the development of an EEG data base is that EEG is age dependent. For example, there are many published studies (Gasser, Verleger, Bacher, & Sroka, 1988), that illustrate age-related differences in the distribution of EEG activity in different bands from low delta to high beta. The current figure illustrates that, for ADD children, the differences between 8- to 11-year-olds and 12- to 14-year olds are relatively small. The difference between groups is probably somewhat larger for normal controls. Our current data base includes both male and female subjects with all being right-handed. The current data base is heterogeneous for IQ and includes individuals with full-scale IQs ranging from 85 to 140. In contrast, in our previous study (Mann et al., 1991), the IQ range was very restricted in the normal range (101–107). Both age and IQ differences may be important.

We are currently evaluating differences in theta–beta ratios and alpha–beta ratios as a function of IQ for children in the 8- to 11-year-old group. Differences between theta–beta ratios are quite small, but larger differences appear to be developing in alpha–beta ratios and may ultimately be important in further refining our data base for differentiating ADHD and ADD individuals with controls based on theta–beta ratios, alpha–beta ratios, and IQ considerations.

Figure 20.4 shows a raw EEG sample gathered from an adolescent male with ADD during a reading task. Normally we associate active processing tasks with blocking alpha and theta and increased beta activity. However, it is clear from the figure that there is considerable slow activity in many of the frontal central and posterior channels. This consists primarily of theta and some alpha activity and characterizes the ADD/ADHD EEG. In many children as well as adolescents and even adults, the degree of slowing is very apparent without any numerical analysis. Another interesting point is that alpha activity often occurs in ADD and ADHD adults even more than theta and shows lack of blocking to complex stimuli. This may result from the normal evolution of the EEG in that for children, there is primarily slower activity than for adults. At approximately age 12–14, alpha finally reaches its adult frequency and stabilizes, whereas in children below the age of 6, alpha activity actually occurs in the below-8-Hertz range, although it has different physical characteristics and is generated by different subcortical regions than theta activity. Alpha also has a pathognomonic waxing and waning characteristic. It is very sinusoidal in its appearance, whereas theta is more irregular and sporadic in its appearance and rate of occurrence.

RATIONALE FOR NEUROFEEDBACK

This section discusses the rationale for neurofeedback and examines criteria for effective intervention in terms of patient characteristics, instrumentation specifications, training, and background of therapists. It then discusses treatment protocols for neuro-

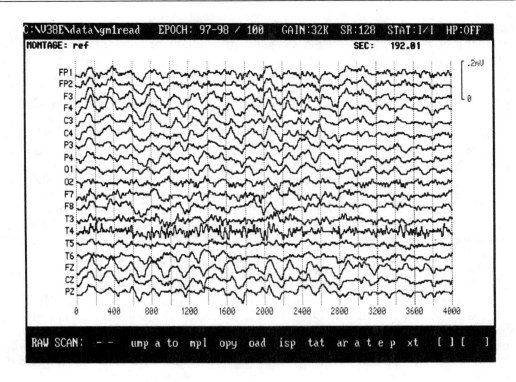

FIGURE 20.4. Example of EEG recorded from an adolescent, age 14, with ADHD on Ritalin. The main features of this EEG recording are the large slow waves between 4 and 6 Hertz in the theta range seen in almost all channels except for temporal locations. Excessive theta activity and lack of beta activity are the primary neurological landmarks of ADHD.

feedback sessions, pre- and posttreatment measures, and describes some results from the author's clinic and other clinics currently using neurofeedback training.

Part of the rationale for neurofeedback treatment for ADD with or without hyperactivity relates directly to some of the characteristics of the children described earlier. A primary problem that the ADD/ADHD individual experiences is difficulty in completing tasks that are long, repetitive, and perceived as boring. This relates to much of the activity that occurs in the school setting, including homework. Another characteristic of the ADD/ADHD individual mentioned previously is difficulty in accepting the reality that socially appropriate behavior is governed by rules, and rule-following behavior is essential in order to progress through the various developmental milestones necessary to achieve a functional adulthood. Individuals who are not able to follow these rules may ultimately experience ODD, CD, or in the worst cases, antisocial personality disorders. This does not mean that all ADD children have this pathway as an inevitable consequence of their behaviors, but there *is* a higher incidence of such problems in the ADD/ADHD population.

Two other general characteristics of the ADD/ADHD population are poor motivation and rapid habituation to the reward properties of stimuli. Thus, play activities and toys do not remain interesting very long for these children. There is also the thrill-seeking behavior sometimes seen in ADD/ADHD adolescents. The use of stimulant medication, whether it be Ritalin (methylphenidate), Cylert (pemoline), or Dexadrine (amphetamine sulfate), is primarily directed toward increasing arousal or impact of stimulation. There is very little clear evidence that these medications, particularly methylphenidate, change cortical function.

A common complaint of many parents of ADD/ADHD children is that with the medication, the child does better in school, concentrates better, and is less hyperactive, but the same child still has difficulty getting required work done, still has difficulty following the rules, and still has difficulty understanding why, when he or she acts inappropriately, these behaviors need to be corrected. These latter problems arise from altered cognitive functioning and in large part, with frontal lobe functioning. The frontal lobes are the executive portions of the brain, particularly the frontal pole, orbital frontal cortex, and dorsal surface of the frontal lobe extending back centrally along the midline to the premotor cortex. These are the cortical areas that have decreased metabolism in ADD adults and probably in ADD children and decreased fast EEG activity and excessive slow EEG activity.

Neurofeedback works best with medication in ADHD children if one can change cortical functioning as well as arousal functions. By changing cortical functioning, we are attempting to establish a "cortical template" that responds, in terms of its EEG signatures, similarly to that of non-ADD/ADHD individuals in those circumstances and situations that cause problems for the ADD/ADHD child, adolescent, or adult. Many groups working with these children report that once they learn the neurofeedback techniques, when they behave inappropriately and this behavior is pointed out to them, they can move readily to correct it. They do not repeat the inappropriate behavior as much once they understand why the behavior was inappropriate. In essence, ADD/ADHD children provided neurofeedback training often experience long-term transfer of the training to school and home settings because they begin to function cortically more like non-ADD individuals. Hence, rule-following behavior increases, impulsiveness decreases, inappropriate social behaviors decrease, and motivation levels improve.

During the past 3 years, work carried out by the author and colleagues and other groups working with ADD and ADHD children has helped to clarify a number of matters that have led to the development of a position statement for the treatment of ADD/ADHD with neurofeedback. The position statement is as follows:

Previous and current results of the treatment of ADD/ADHD with neurofeedback are promising for those individuals demonstrating certain quantitative EEG and behavioral characteristics. Practitioners utilizing this treatment modality recognize that the disorders of ADD or ADHD are complex and have a wide range of symptoms, etiologies, and therapeutic interventions. Neurofeedback offers patients a psychophysiological treatment that, when combined with other traditional therapies, produces significant improvement for many patients. More research, currently being conducted, is needed to extend these results. To date, this treatment has been successfully applied for over 3000 children treated by approximately 300 health care organizations. Neurofeedback is neither a panacea nor a cure but a powerful adjunctive technique.

1. *Who is a candidate for neurofeedback therapy?* Anyone with a *primary diagnosis* of ADD or ADHD, between the ages of 7 and 45, with low-average, average, or above-average intelligence is a candidate. Neurofeedback treatment should not be offered with comorbidity of:

- Mental retardation
- Childhood psychosis
- Severe depressive or bipolar illness
- Significant seizure disorder where medications interfere with learning (i.e., sedating medications)
- Hyperkinesis, where multiple medications or high dosages with monotherapy have been ineffective
- Learning disabilities *without* ADD or ADHD as a primary problem
- Dysfunctional families who refuse to participate in indicated therapy

2. *What symptoms can be improved with neurofeedback?*

- Attention, focus, and concentration
- Task completion and organizational skills
- Impulsiveness
- Mild hyperactivity

3. *What are the results of treatment?*

- Improved behavior and learning
- Improvement in school grades
- Increased self-esteem
- Better job performance
- Greater realization of innate potential
- Higher intelligence test scores
- Improved scores on parent–teacher rating scales

4. *How effective is this treatment approach?* When the above criteria are used to select candidates for therapy and treatment, the majority of patients completing treatment show marked improvement. The improvement is measured and validated by improvement in the results listed above as well as measured by independent observers and testing and by reports by teachers, parents, and other involved health care professionals. This position statement is an evolving document. As more data are gathered on more patients, modifications will probably occur. Those using neurofeedback in their practice or in research can help refine this position statement through an interactive dialogue that will continue to develop among practitioners using neurofeedback.

SPECIFICATION CRITERIA
FOR NEUROFEEDBACK INSTRUMENTATION

At the present time, there are about a half-dozen instruments designed and developed for the use of neurofeedback for ADD/ADHD. The main requirements for appropriate instrumentation include very accurate signal processing with the ability to discriminate changes as small as 0.1 microvolt for purposes of setting thresholds. Ideal instrumentation should always allow the researcher–clinician to observe the raw signal and to see either how it is processed in order to produce reward or inhibition of reward and to observe the relationship between changes in events in the raw EEG and the feedback. Excellent systems employ both analog and digital processing. Such systems have been described in detail previously (Lubar & Culver, 1978; Lubar, 1991).

Those persons engaged in neurofeedback treatment have to fulfill several well-defined physiological criteria simultaneously. They have to increase either (1) sensorimotor rhythm (SMR) (between 12 and 15 Hertz) especially if they are hyperactive, or (2) beta activity (often defined as 16–20 Hertz), and they must do so at the same time they are not producing excessive theta, movement, or EMG activity. The task is to isolate the SMR or beta activity and to increase its duration, prevalence, and, if possible, its amplitude, while simultaneously decreasing the amplitude and percentage of theta, EMG activity, or gross movement. To do this, the subject or patient has to be very alert, but also relaxed and quiet. One of the main problems that children with ADD/ADHD have is staying on task as often measured by poor performance in continuous performance tasks such as the Gordon Diagnostic System or the Test of Variables of Attention (TOVA). The essence of neurofeedback treatment involves engagement in a continuous performance type task under an *altered EEG state* for significant periods. For this specific reason, ADD/ADHD children are able to play Nintendo or other computer and arcade games for long periods of time with no significant transfer to homework situations or other situations that are long, boring, and repetitive such as school-related tasks. Similarly, it is unlikely that training children to perform continuous performance tasks by themselves would have any significant carryover, but being able to perform these types of tasks in the altered but more normal EEG state *does* appear to work.

There are different explanations regarding the mechanism of how neurofeedback works. If one believes that the individual becomes aware of the different EEG states and can discriminate when they are producing alpha, theta, or beta, then the argument is quite simple. Individuals simply learn to produce the desired EEG pattern in the appropriate setting. They learn to produce beta when they need to concentrate, theta when they want to relax and experience a considerable amount of visual imagery, and alpha when they want to relax in a more blank-mind, "open focus" state. However, many individuals undergoing neurofeedback tell us that they do not know exactly how they produce the different EEG patterns, but they are often able to do it on request.

At one level, this is evidence that there are unconscious processes operating in this type of learning phenomenon and that one can learn without direct awareness. Evidence to support learning without awareness has been discussed and debated (Kamiya, 1979) for more than a quarter of a century as the field of biofeedback evolved. Non-ADD individuals are very aware of changes in their levels of alertness. If one is reading a very exciting passage or engaged in listening to a particularly powerful audio presentation or speech, one usually becomes very alert, fixated on the speaker or on the material being presented, and actively processes the content. If, after a while, the individual experiences fatigue, wandering of attention, or forgetting the content, the EEG shows a shift toward lower frequencies. We can sometimes force ourselves into an attentive state, and this is associated with higher frequency EEG activity. Individuals with ADD and ADHD probably have greater difficulty making these discriminations. Therefore, they need the augmented information, in the form of feedback, presented for many sessions before they begin to develop in demand settings an almost reflexive normal response to shifts in attention. This allows them to increase their level of concentration and focusing.

Instrumentation appropriately designed for this type of treatment must provide very clear feedback stimuli indicating when different conditions have been met. Some of the instruments use game displays such as color wheels that light up sequentially with different colors every time a burst of beta activity occurs with a specific duration and specific amplitude. Another display is an airplane flying above a specified threshold level line and a tone that changes in frequency or intensity. Both signals correspond to the amplitude and duration of beta activity. These instruments also provide warning lights, usually red circles or light displays, that activate when the person produces theta or, in some cases, alpha above a set threshold or EMG activity above threshold. Gross body movement will usually activate the theta filter. In some cases, filters with lower band passes in the 0–2 Hertz or 0–4 Hertz region also are used to respond to gross body movements.

High-quality instrumentation should also record and score data for each session including parameters as (1) average microvolt levels of reward or inhibit activities, (2) percentage of reward or inhibit activities above or below their appropriate thresholds, (3) threshold settings, and perhaps, (4) ratios of fast to slow activity measured either in power units, percentage units, or amplitude units. They should record information about (5) the duration of the entire session, (6) number of points achieved if using a point system, and (7) the activities taking place during the training session. These data should be maintained on a day-to-day or session-to-session basis and be either transportable into database or graphing programs such as Lotus, Excel, or Quattro, or have the capability to display graphically the data either within and/or over sessions.

Ideally designed instruments will allow the therapist or researcher to access this graphical material and print it out either in black and white or multicolors for purposes of reports to patients, schools, insurance companies, referral sources, or for publication. The data should be stored in a form that can be transported into statistical programs for regression analysis, that is, changes over sessions, and individual data should be gathered in such a way as to be combined into group data to look at group differences in controlled studies.

Instruments that have all of these capabilities including computer systems containing 386 or 486 chips capable of running at 20–50 megahertz and, with printers, range in price from about $5,000 to over $20,000. The more expensive instruments often have multichannel capacity where additional channels are primarily used for assessment purposes. Feedback is based on either a bipolar electrode montage with ear reference, or in some cases, a referential montage with a forehead ground and ear reference. At present, not enough data are available to determine which is the best montage. Each has its advantages and disadvantages.

Bipolar Montage

The bipolar montage has the advantage that there is common-mode rejection of signals that occur simultaneously in phase at both of the electrode inputs. This will include 60-Hertz activity, perhaps certain types of movement activities, and other physiological artifacts including cardiac artifacts. However, the signal that is processed represents the algebraic subtraction of the EEG activity at two different points. It does not tell us about the absolute activity at each individual electrode site. Referential recording uses a single electrode. Training with a single electrode involves training over a smaller area than bipolar training. However, the EEG that is being trained represents the actual electrical activity at that point as compared with a reference, either a ground and/or ear references that are supposedly electrically more neutral. Larger signals are obtained from monopolar recordings; however, these are much more prone to artifact because of lack of common mode rejection, hence there may be more inhibit circuit activity, and training may be somewhat more difficult.

It would be instructive to compare a controlled study with matched groups in which one group receives monopolar recording and the other receives bipolar training to see if there is any significant difference between the two.

One manufacturer has an instrument that has the capability of recording from up to five channels simultaneously and processing the average activity from all of these channels together in order to provide feedback. This type of training provides coverage over a larger area of the scalp but, at the present time, no data are available using this multichannel montage, so that it is not known whether this approach is more or less beneficial than the referential or bipolar recordings currently in use. If one is using a bipolar montage, it is essential that one very carefully measures the distance between the electrodes every session. For example, if the distance between the electrodes for a person is 4.5 centimeters, it should remain at that distance, plus or minus 1 millimeter, for all sessions. Otherwise, data relating to microvolt levels will be inaccurate for bipolar recordings. The magnitude (amplitude) of the signal depends on the interelectrode distance. Accurate electrode placement is necessary if we are to obtain meaningful data from which we can draw conclusions relating to whether learning is actually taking place.

Electrode Materials

Electrode materials employed usually are gold plated or silver-cup 22 electrodes with a hole in the middle for the extrusion of excess electrode paste. Impedances between the electrode and skin should be 5 kilohms or less, and, for some instruments, it is extremely important that there be no significant offset voltage between the electrodes and the skin. Offset voltages occur when electrodes act as batteries and impose a voltage upon that which is already imposed by the EEG. This can cause a baseline shift of the entire signal sent to the amplifier and sometimes results in distortion of the wave forms. In some cases, it is impossible for the signal to be processed, and only noise appears on the screen. Many manufacturers offer an impedance meter that measures both impedance between the electrodes and voltages offset. We have found that, with offsets of less than plus or minus 30 millivolts and an impedance of less than 5000 ohms, outstanding recordings occur consistently with reliable repeatable data over sessions.

Electrode Locations

Electrode preparation is very simple. Electrode sites are shown in Figure 20.2. Measurements are taken as follows: For training the sensorimotor rhythm, we place electrodes at international 10–20 locations C_3 and C_4. In order to locate these two points, it is necessary to locate CZ, the vertex. To do this, a tape measure is applied from the nasion at the top of the bridge of the nose where the forehead is indented to the inion, just underneath the occipital condyle, the bump at the back of the head. Half this total distance is marked with a dry marker, the same type of marker that is often used on white boards. The tape is then placed from the preauricular notch of the left ear through this marked spot to the preauricular notch on the right ear. Half the distance again is measured. Where the two cross locates CZ. When CZ is obtained, then 20% of that total distance from ear to ear is calculated. That distance is then marked from the vertex toward the left ear and the right ear along the line between the two ears. This is the location of C3 and C4. If one is working with beta training, we have found that the best location is a point 10% of the total distance from nasion to inion, in front of CZ and behind CZ. These two points are halfway between CZ and FZ and halfway between CZ and PZ. Once the appropriate locations are marked, the marking dot is removed with Omniprep, a gel that contains a small amount of pumice.[1] Next, a small mound of electrode paste is placed over the cleansed spot. Either 10–20 conductive paste or Nihon Kohden or Grass Instrument Co. paste can be used. The electrode

[1]Omniprep can be obtained from D. O. Weaver Company, Aurora, CO 80033.

is then pushed down on the mound until the paste extrudes through the small hole in the middle of the electrode. Our preference has been to use grass E5SH electrodes and in some cases, the smaller E6SH electrode works equally well. A cotton ball is finally pushed down on top of the electrode in the mound of paste, and this completes the electrode application for the head. For the ear, a Grass Instrument Co. ear-clip electrode is used. This involves two cup electrodes placed in a small plastic holder. The ear is simply cleaned by rubbing it with Omniprep, wiping the Omniprep off, and then placing some electrode paste in the cups of the electrode and placing the ear clip on the ear.

Some neurofeedback systems require only three electrodes, two active electrodes for the scalp and one ear clip. Others require the active electrodes on the head, an ear clip, and a forehead ground. These requirements are outlined by the specific manufacturers. Once the electrodes are placed, the subject experiences no discomfort. There may be some discomfort on the scalp during the application of electrodes. It is usually not significant and might occur from rubbing the Omniprep, which is mildly abrasive, on the scalp before placing the electrode in its appropriate location. Since this procedure has been tolerated very well in children as young as age 6, it is not a major problem. In adolescents and adults, there is hardly any response at all to this preparation procedure. Typically, a well-trained therapist can perform the entire electrode connection in 2 minutes or less. At the end of the session, one simply removes the electrodes by lifting them from the head. The paste is cleansed either with a mild soap solution, with warm water, or isopropyl alcohol. Patients tolerate the removal of electrodes without difficulty. The term "sensors," rather than electrodes, is better to use, especially with children.

TREATMENT PROTOCOLS

If our goal is providing comprehensive treatment for persons with ADD/ADHD, it is important to do this in the context of the activities where they are having difficulty. Many children with this disorder score poorly on measures of reading, handwriting, auditory skills, spelling, or mathematical computational skills. This is one of the reasons why pretesting information is important before beginning neurofeedback. Once the therapist knows in which areas the child is experiencing the most difficulty, the neurofeedback session can be designed to help the child overcome some of these problems.

The typical session, for example, might consist of a 2-minute baseline in which there is neither auditory nor visual feedback. The computer screen can be turned off, and the data gathered in order to determine the baseline measures. These measures include (1) microvolts of theta, (2) microvolts of beta, (3) percentage of theta below the theta threshold, (4) percentage of beta above the beta threshold, (5) perhaps ratios of theta to beta activity, and (6) threshold settings.

After a complete baseline, the child might engage in a feedback component for about 5 minutes. During this portion of the session, the child sits in front of the screen in an upright chair with eyes open and tries to obtain as high a score as possible using the various feedback displays. The child should be introduced to each display in the first session and given the chance to choose those displays that he or she prefers. Next, the child can receive auditory feedback with a reading task. The goal of this portion of the session is to read and, at the same time, produce the desired EEG activity.

If the person starts producing too much theta, one can cue him or her to stop reading, try to restart the feedback again, and then continue reading. The idea is to be able to perform the academic tasks while producing the feedback. Since the task is a reading task, auditory feedback is appropriate as visual feedback would interfere with the task. Next, one can present a 5-minute period in which the person uses both auditory and visual feedback without additional tasks. One can then present another academic component such as a listening task in which the child experiences the visual feedback while listening to a story. An option is a listening task with very low amplitude auditory feedback in the background.

Other conditions can involve an initial baseline, several feedback components, and several academic components. These academic components might involve math problems plus feedback, spelling plus feedback, and handwriting plus feedback. The type of feedback should be appropriate for the task so as not to interfere with the task but to give the person cues in the background linked to changing the EEG while that person performs the task. It is very important for the therapist to be involved in the feedback process. With young children, the therapist should always be in the room.

Sometimes children become bored during a session. If this happens, tell the child that if he or she obtains a specified number of points, you will stop and play a game. The game can be a board game such as checkers, a thinking game such as 20 questions, a short card game, or something else familiar to the therapist and the child. Games are used as rewards for good performance.

However, if the child does not meet feedback goals, the therapist should be understanding and make the criteria for the game rewards easier. Realize that, often, this treatment is taking place after school—the time of day when children are most fatigued. If the child is able to perform well under these conditions, the transfer into school settings is even better than if they do all of their training in the early morning—the time of day when they are most alert.

I do not use recliner chairs in reclined positions for this type of treatment because in classrooms, children sit at desks and maintain upright postures. In this way, EEG neurofeedback for ADD/ADHD is very different from relaxation training for anxiety disorders or stress reduction.

From time to time, therapists should question the child or adult to determine whether the patient is aware of EEG changes and what is making the displays work and what makes the displays stop. In other words, what is producing beta, SMR, and what is producing theta and EMG. This awareness is important because the information gathered can be used in the classroom setting for teachers to cue the child when they see the child is not attending.

In research settings, one is interested in determining the most important factors in neurofeedback training. One asks questions such as: Are the therapist variables important? Is the nature of the display important? To what extent does the neurofeedback have a positive effect compared with neurofeedback integrated with academic skills, therapy, or other techniques? Answers to these questions are best learned by research designs with carefully matched groups. Such a design should include a control group that receives no training, but all pre- and postmeasures are taken over the same time interval as other groups receiving treatment. There should be (1) a group receiving only neurofeedback with a relatively neutral therapist in terms of therapist–patient interaction; (2) a group that might receive some other type of biofeedback such as EMG or thermal feedback; (3) a group receiving some other treatment such as behavior therapy or psychotherapy; and perhaps (4) groups receiving neurofeedback combined with some of these other approaches. The last would help determine whether the effects are additive or more than additive.

There is a very critical need for controlled studies of this kind if neurofeedback for ADD/ADHD is to be accepted by those professionals who believe that only double-blind studies or studies with matched control groups are valid. Consider this important point about double-blind studies: They are excellent for determining whether short-acting drugs are effective, particularly in the context of methylphenidate. In this situation, one administers a drug that clears body systems within 6 hours. It is relatively easy to do double-blind studies when one group receives methylphenidate, another group receives a placebo, and then a crossover is employed. It is also easy in an A-B-A design, when one group first receives methylphenidate alone, then a placebo, and then methylphenidate alone.

In our early laboratory-based work, we carried out blinded studies of this type. However, one of the drawbacks is that children require treatment over many weeks and months, and part of that time, they receive feedback that may exacerbate their symptoms. For ethical reasons, one cannot do this in a fee-for-service setting. There also is the question of whether it is appropriate to expose children for a significant period, that is, 15 or more sessions, where they receive a type of feedback that could make them worse or lead them to become disappointed in the treatment resulting in stopping the treatment in worse condition than when they started. For this reason, I personally do not advocate double-blind studies with this population. These children are very fragile, and their families are very sensitive to negative outcome. However, studies with accurately matched groups could be more convincing.

Clinical case outcome studies that are being carried out at the present time, some of which are being published, are extremely important. They help to define the groups that are appropriate for neurofeedback training. It is through clinical work that we have been able to develop the position statement. Based on this statement, it is easier to design and carry out controlled outcome studies than it was before knowing the types of children, adolescents, or adults appropriate for this type of treatment. As in many other treatments for other disorders, the results with controlled outcome studies may not be as strong as those done in clinical settings where feedback is integrated into a multicomponent treatment program.

PRE- AND POSTTREATMENT MEASURES

I strongly recommend pre- and posttreatment measures on all patients whenever possible. This is for purposes of validating treatment as well as extending the validity of neurofeedback training for ADD/ADHD. These measures can include measurements from intelligence tests, psychoeducational assessments, continuous performance tasks, and single or multichanneled EEG assessments. Behavior rating scales also are excellent but are less reliable than other behavioral measures because of their subjectivity, especially when completed by parents. It is particularly important to obtain follow-up data from patients for as long as possible and provide periodic "booster" sessions, as indicated.

OVERVIEW OF RESULTS OF RECENT RESEARCH

Figures 20.5 and 20.6 show the results of a retrospective study recently completed. This study is an independent telephone survey of 52 patients seen over a 10-year period. The surveyor had no contact with any of the patients during their treatment or evaluation and did not meet any of the patients. The criteria for inclusion in this study were that these patients completed treatment and were available. Many more patients completed treatment over the 10 years. However, one of the problems was that some of the older persons reached adulthood, left the area, and were not available. Other families also moved from the area and were not available. The survey used 16 items from Conners'

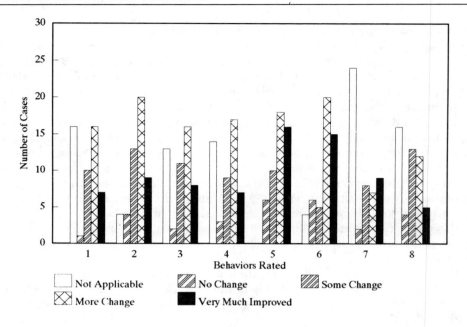

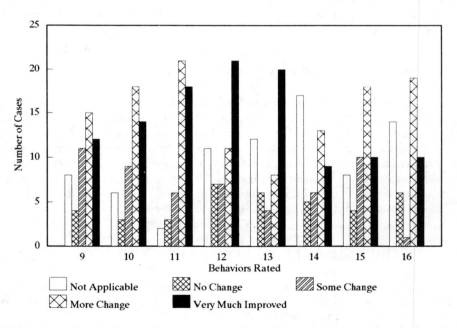

FIGURES 20.5 and 20.6. Results from a retrospective study employing Conners' Questionnaire for 51 patients extending from less than 1 year to 10 years posttreatment. See text for detailed explanation.

Parent Teacher Questionnaire. The results are shown in Figures 20.5 and 20.6: The first graph shows changes in 8 behaviors, and the second shows behaviors 9 through 16.

Note that the highest ratings are in the two categories "Very Much Improved" and "More Change." This was particularly the case for reductions in constant fidgeting, demanding or easily frustrated, restless or overactive, excitable, inattentive, fails to finish things, and temper outbursts or moody behavior. Note the improvements in overall behavior, attitude, homework, grades, family interactions, and general relationships. The *greatest* changes were for completing homework and improved grades. In some cases, there were many "Not Applicable" (N/A) responses. This was particularly the case for fidgeting, easily frustrated, cries often, disturbs others, relationship with friends, and general relationships. The reason for these N/A responses was at least 50% of the subjects had finished treatment between 1 and 10 years ago. For those subjects who moved into adolescence or adulthood, these categories no longer apply.

Perhaps the most important finding in our retrospective study was that the greatest improvements occurred in the areas in which parents and schools are most concerned, that is, behavior, attitude, homework, and grades. In each case, the parent doing the rating was asked specifically to what extent that individual felt the neurofeedback had played a significant role in the change and to what extent this change was the result of maturation. Although this is a subjective question, virtually all parents felt that the changes were the result of the neurofeedback experience. In many cases, parents said that they believed that these changes would not have taken place without the neurofeedback. Again, it must be emphasized that retrospective data are highly subjective. Parents will often report positive results more readily than negative results because they do not like to feel that their child had failed at a particular task or treatment. It is very likely that some of the positive results obtained over long periods of time will be shown to have come about as the result of other factors such as maturation or possibly other treatments that may have been employed during the period over which the study was done. To answer these criticisms would require essentially a series of controls followed for an equally long period of time where either no treatments were employed or other treatments were employed and compared with groups where neurofeedback was the primary or only treatment.

It is important that all practitioners using neurofeedback for ADD/ADHD collect the type of data described above. Other behavioral rating scales may be as good and perhaps more appropriate than the one used in this example. The important point is that patients are not successful if they just complete treatment and only do better at that point. Success is best judged by long-term changes and in individuals for whom a significant life change occurs.

Another study being carried out by Michael Linden in California is finishing its second replication. It includes a waiting control group given the WISC-R and behavior rating scales before and after the waiting period and an active neurofeedback group that used the theta–beta paradigm. The active neurofeedback group showed an increase of 10 WISC-R Full Scale points and a significant decrease in inattentiveness. The waiting control group showed no changes in either of these measures.

Daniel Chartier and Ned Kelly in North Carolina followed their patients for more than 6 months posttreatment and used Conners' Scale. They followed 16 patients and obtained identical results to our results. Ziegfried Othmer and his associates in California measured WISC-R subscales changes after and before neurofeedback treatment. There are four subscales that are most closely associated with attentional deficits. These are arithmetic, coding, information, and digit span, often referred to as the "acid" test. Statistically significant increases were observed for these subtests of the WISC-R as well as others. The largest changes were obtained in picture completion, comprehension, arithmetic, similarities, picture arrangement, digit span, and coding. The smallest change was obtained in block design. Since there is a practice effect following test and retest on the WISC-R, this was taken into account by doing all of the posttesting more than 6 months after the initial pretest. Othmer found significant improvements in TOVA scores after treatment as well as changes of more than 10 points in verbal and performance IQ. Some individuals showed more than a 20-point change. Tansey (1990, 1991) reported increases of more than 15 points in the Full Scale WISC-R score following neurofeedback. However, Tansey's population included primarily reading-disabled children rather than children with primarily ADD/ADHD.

At present, a number of insurance carriers consider this treatment as promising but still experimental and are awaiting more published results before allowing more coverage for this type of treatment.

INTEGRATION OF NEUROFEEDBACK WITH OTHER THERAPEUTIC APPROACHES

Many children, adolescents, and some adults are treated with stimulant medications, especially if the diagnosis is ADHD. The main stimulant medications are amphetamine sulfate (Dexadrine), pemoline (Cylert), and methylphenidate (Ritalin). At present, it appears that at least for methylphenidate and perhaps Cylert, there is very little effect on cortical EEG activity.

I plan to carry out studies to determine if, in fact, these medications affect cortical functioning, evoked potentials, and specific behavioral measures related to ADD/ADHD. There is no evidence that these medications interfere with neurofeedback. Still, many parents and children prefer to avoid them. My personal view is *not* to promise medication reduction or elimination as part of a neurofeedback-based treatment program. However, if a person responds very well to neurofeedback and the child (and parents, if the subject is a minor) feels that he or she would like to try medication-reduction trials, this should be undertaken in conjunction with an appropriate physician specialist.

I find that the best regimen for Ritalin is to reduce it gradually even though it clears the system very quickly. For example, if a child is on 20 milligrams of Ritalin in the morning, 10 milligrams at noon, and 5 milligrams in the late afternoon, the medication reduction might be as follows: 20, 10, 0; then 20, 5; then 10, 5; then 5, 5; 5, 0; then 0. One should carry out the stepwise reduction about one step every 4–7 days. If, in the process of medication reduction, the child or adolescent appears to be losing control over hyperkinesis or impulsiveness, stop the medication reduction at that point, or perhaps increase the medication.

Cylert is usually administered in a dosage of 37.5 milligrams sometimes once a day or occasionally twice. Medication reduction might be simply stopping the afternoon dose and then, if possible, stopping the morning dose 2 weeks later. One can reduce amphetamine very much in the same manner as Ritalin. Sometimes medication reduction appears to work very well for a period of 1–2 months, and then the child begins to show signs of needing medication again. If this is the case, one can reintroduce the medication if requested by a physician, the parent, or the school. Many children with ADHD are able to completely eliminate medications with follow-up periods of up to 5 years or longer without reintroducing medication at any time. These are the most fortunate outcomes and probably represent one end of a continuum. If a child is on high doses of stimulant medication and still has poor control, that child is probably a poor candidate for neurofeedback, does not meet the requirements in our position statement, and therefore should not be treated with neurofeedback.

There are other medications commonly used in treating ADD comorbidity problems. These problems include impulsiveness, depression, seizure disorders, and tic disorders. Such medications as desipramine (Norpramin) and imipramine (Tofranil) are often prescribed especially for depression and occasionally for impulsiveness. Clonidine (Catapres), an alpha-blocking agent, is also in use. These drugs, especially the tricyclics, take several weeks to reach maximum blood levels and a similar time period to clear the body. Medication reduction must be carried out much more slowly and under careful medical supervision.

Many patients, particularly children and adolescents, in neurofeedback treatment and/or on medications, also may need to participate in individual or family therapy. Many families with children with ADD/ADHD experience degrees of dysfunctionality. Adolescents with ADD/ADHD often have children and are not emotionally and financially capable of raising a child and place these children for adoption. These children are often adopted by families with no history or current evidence of ADD/ADHD, and the parents are unprepared to manage the child. Occasionally these children are physically or emotionally abused. These families need considerable counseling and parent education to understand the biological nature of ADD and to accept that it is not their fault that the child has this disorder. Sometimes the children and adolescents have issues, such as abuse and neglect, needing attention. There are many parents who do not know how to manage children with ADD, especially ADD with hyperactivity. These parents benefit significantly from parenting groups.

I recommend that practitioners using neurofeedback for ADD/ADHD offer services to help parents develop skills for helping their children who (1) refuse to do their homework, (2) claim that the homework does not exist, (3) lose their school materials, (4) are continuously teased, (5) are separated from other children by teachers, and/or (6) are left out of peer activities.

The majority of children with ADD, with or without hyperactivity, know they have problems. They know that they are different from other children. They have enormous problems feeling good about themselves. Some of them seek drugs and/or alcohol because their self-esteem is low. The incidence of suicide also is higher among ADD and ADHD adolescents than most other adolescents. The incidence of incarceration for crimes is higher among adolescents and adults with ADD/ADHD.

The progression from ODD to CD to antisocial personality disorder is tragic and sometimes can be circumvented by appropriate family interventions. It is very important that practitioners and others not view neurofeedback as a cure-all or a single stand-alone approach for the treatment of these children. The best neurofeedback instrument does not replace a poor therapist who is not empathetic to the needs of the person and does not understand the complexity of the disorder. Similarly, an outstanding health professional can only go so far in helping a person manage this disorder unless that therapist can intervene either pharmacologically and/or neurologically to change the underlying neurophysiology of the system.

CONCLUSION AND FUTURE DIRECTIONS

The development of neurofeedback in the treatment of ADD/ADHD progressed slowly and steadily since the late 1970s. During the past 3 years, the development of this area rapidly accelerated. Many more health care professionals now are being trained and are providing this type of treatment. There are some traditionalists who challenge neurofeedback. Their position usually focuses on the absence of controlled studies and that most work that does exist is primarily clinical in nature. There is a need for multiple-group, controlled-outcome studies as well as more and improved clinical studies. The position statement needs modification as more is learned. The limits of neurofeedback and the integration of the technique with other traditional approaches need more thorough investigation. There are many parent support groups formed to promote understanding and treatment for ADD/ADHD.

The evolution of this treatment will be a slow process. Third-party reimbursement for neurofeedback as a treatment modality is necessary to treat most children appropriate for this treatment modality. The majority of children with ADD/ADHD live in family situations of modest income.

We can now anticipate future directions of instrumentation development. We need development of EEG pattern recognition programs that more accurately analyze the EEG and provide feedback that is more contingent and more precisely paired with specific EEG characteristics. The detection of activity in the EEG is presently either through active band pass filters with the analog and/or digital processing imposed upon filter outputs or through Fourier-Spectral analyses of EEGs. This is not the approach taken by professional electro-encephalographers when making a determination regarding abnormal or normal EEG activity. The human brain does a pattern analysis. A trained expert can very clearly see complex patterns in the EEG consisting of the interweaving of slow, fast, normal, and abnormal activity. Development of such programs could help increase the rate of learning and make it possible to successfully treat more difficult cases and perhaps show more clearly the power and the specificity of neurofeedback as a treatment modality.

Long-term follow-up of patients is very important, not just for 1 year, but for 5–15 years. Only through longitudinal studies can we learn if neurofeedback fulfills the promise of being able to offer a technique that changes cognitive functioning and produces long-term shifts in cerebral function.

Neurofeedback offers other possibilities now being seen on the horizon. One is the increase in human cognitive functioning. If we identify electrophysiological activity associated with special abilities and higher intellectual functioning, then perhaps we can raise neurocognitive functioning. In a sense, neurofeedback holds a promise for everyone if it can be shown to enhance human potential, creativity, and a better quality of life.

GLOSSARY

A-B-A DESIGN. An experimental design in which a baseline period (A) precedes an intervention or treatment (B), followed by another baseline (A). Often used in single-case research.

ALLELES. One of two or more different genes that occupy corresponding positions (loci) on paired chromosomes. They are usually indicated by a capital letter for the dominant and a lowercase letter for the recessive gene.

BASAL FOREBRAIN (FOREBRAIN; PROSENCEPHALON). One of three major subdivisions of the brain (also midbrain and hindbrain)—the most forward part. It includes the telencephalon (front or end brain) containing the basal ganglia, limbic system, olfactory bulb and tract, and lateral ventricles. Also includes the thalamus of the diencephalon (posterior portion of the forebrain).

BASAL GANGLIA. Collection of four masses of gray matter located deep in the cerebral hemisphere and mainly under the anterior region of the neocortex and to the side of the thalamus. Involves extrapyramidal regulation of motor activity and probably other functions including sequencing complex movements into a smoothly executed response. Often referred to as the *extrapyramidal system.*

BIPOLAR ELECTRODE MONTAGE. Refers to an electrode configuration where activity between two electrodes is subtracted and compared to a reference or neutral ground electrode.

BLINDED STUDIES. Research design in which the experimenter(s) do not know which subjects are in which treatment condition(s).

BRAINSTEM RETICULAR FORMATION. The brainstem connects the cerebral hemispheres with the spinal cord. Reticular means in the form of a network. The reticular formation is a diffuse network of groups of cells and fibers throughout the brainstem. They connect the ascending and descending tracts. They are important (essential) in their influence on and control of alertness, waking, sleeping, and several reflexes. The reticular formation includes the *reticular activating system* (RAS), which initiates and maintains wakefulness and directs attention, and which extends to the entire cerebral cortex.

CEREBELLUM. The cerebellum plays an important role in coordination of and regulating voluntary movements of skeletal muscles. It is a large structure behind the pons and medulla oblongata of the brainstem. It does not initiate movements but interrelates with brainstem structures in execution of many movements, including posture, balance, walking, running, writing, dressing, eating, playing musical instruments, and eye movement tracking. It controls speed, acceleration, and trajectory of movements.

COMMON MODE REJECTION. Refers to the ability of a bipolar recording to reject signals that are identical in both electrode leads simultaneously and are also in phase, for example, in-phase eye blinks, gross body movements, EKG, and other artifacts that might contaminate the EEG signal. (Also see Chapter 4.)

COMORBIDITY. Referring to other disorders that occur at the same time as the target disorders. Examples would be depression, CD, or ODD associated with the target disorder, ADHD.

CZ, THE VERTEX. EEG electrode placement on the top of the head.

DOPAMINERGIC SYSTEM. The system of tissues influenced by dopamine, a catecholamine neurotransmitter that is the immediate precursor in norepinephrine synthesis. (See *norepinephrine, catecholamine* in Chapter 17.)

EAR REFERENCE. Reference electrode placed on an ear. The point of reference against which the voltage from other active electrodes is gauged.

EVENT-RELATED POTENTIAL MEASURES. A scalp surface measure of evoked cortical potential. These are changes in electrical activity in response to physical stimuli, associated with psychophysiological processes, and/or in preparation for motor responses. Special computer analysis of the EEG allows measurement of the latency, duration, and amplitude of selected cortical wave forms. (See *somatosensory evoked potential,* Chapter 37.)

INION. The most prominent point or center of the external protuberance of the occipital bone.

INTERNATIONAL 10–20 SITES. Standard sites for surface EEG electrodes.

LOCATIONS C_3 AND C_4. Specific sites for two of the EEG surface electrodes near and lateral to C_z. C stands for central.

LOCUS COERULEUS. Structure in the midbrain which produces most of the norepinephrine in the CNS.

NASION. Skull location or landmark immediately above the nose, roughly at the depression at the nose root, and just lower than the position of the eyebrows.

NEUROFEEDBACK. The term that typically refers to EEG feedback designed to alter a condition for which there is evidence that it is neurological. A form of EEG biofeedback training.

NIGROSTRIATAL FRONTAL SYSTEM. Projects from the substantia nigra to the corpus striatum (one of the parts of the basal ganglia). Substantia nigra ("black" or deep gray substance) is involved with extrapyramidal motor control. It is located from the upper edge of the pons into the subthalamic region. The neurotransmitter is dopamine. (See *basal ganglia*.)

NIHON KOHDEN ELEFIX PASTE. EEG electrode paste made by this manufacturer.

NORADRENERGIC ACTIVITY. Activated by or secreting norepinephrine. (See *norepinephrine*.) The source in the CNS is the locus coerulus.

NOREPINEPHRINE. Also called noradrenaline. A natural neurohormone and neurotransmitter released by sympathetic nerve endings and in the brain. One type of *catecholamine*, a body compound having a sympathomimetic action. Norepinephrine is released by postganglionic adrenergic nerves and the adrenal medulla. Has mostly alpha-adrenergic activity and some beta-adrenergic activity. (See Chapters 7, 14, 15, 17, 20, 36.)

OCCIPITAL CONDYLE. The bump at the back of the head.

OFFSET VOLTAGE. Voltage produced when electrodes act as batteries and impose a voltage.

PREAURICULAR NOTCH OF THE LEFT EAR. In front of the auricle of the ear. The auricle is the part of the external ear not within the head. Also called the flap or pinna. The notch (incisura anterior auris) is the depression between the crus of the helix (upper end of outer hook-like structure) and the tragus (small knob-like protuberance lower and to the side of the opening to the ear canal (external acoustic meatus). The preauricular notch is just anterior to this ear location and posterior to the hair as at the top of a sideburn.

REFERENTIAL MONTAGE. A combination of EEG electrodes that obtain information about the electrical activity of specific areas of the brain compared with a relatively neutral ground or reference.

RESPONSE INHIBITION. The ability to inhibit responding to inappropriate stimuli. Measured by computer-based continuous performance tests. Used in the assessment of ADHD.

SPECT SCAN. Single proton emission computerized tomography, similar to PET scan (positron emission tomography), a technique that allows for the evaluation of blood flow and metabolism in the living brain.

TEST OF VARIABLES OF ATTENTION (TOVA). A computer-based continuous performance test for assessing very detailed information about sustained attention. Used in the assessment of ADHD.

REFERENCES

Amen, D. G., & Paldi, J. H. (1993, May). Evaluating ADHD with brain SPECT imaging. (Abstracts of the American Psychiatric Association, San Francisco)

American Psychiatric Association. (1994). *Diagnostic and statistical manual of mental disorders* (4th ed.). Washington, DC: Author.

Anderson, W. W. (1963). The hyperkinetic child: A neurological appraisal. *Neurology, 13,* 968–973.

Barkley, R. (1987). *Defiant children: A clinician's manual for parent training.* New York: Guilford Press.

Barkley, R. (1989). Attention-deficit hyperactivity disorder. In E. J. Mash & R. A. Barkley (Eds.), *Treatment of childhood disorders* (pp. 39–72). New York: Guilford Press.

Barkley, R. A. (1990). *Attention deficit hyperactivity disorder: A handbook for diagnosis and treatment.* New York: Guilford Press.

Bradley, C. (1937). The behavior of children receiving benzedrine. *American Journal of Psychiatry, 94,* 577–585.

Conners, C. K. (1969). A teacher rating scale for use with drug studies with children. *American Journal of Psychiatry, 127,* 884–888.

Gasser, T., Verleger, R., Bacher, P., & Sroka, L. (1988). Development of the EEG of school-age children and adolescents. I. Analysis of band power. *Electroencephalography and Clinical Neurophysiology, 69,* 91–99.

Heilman, M., Voeller, K. S., & Nadeau, S. (1991). A possible pathophysiologic substrate of attention deficit hyperactivity disorder. *Journal of Child Neurology, 6,* S76–S81.

Jasper, H. H., Solomon, P., & Bradley, C. (1938). Electroencephalographic analysis of behavior problems in children. *American Journal of Psychiatry, 95,* 641–658.

Kamiya, J. (1979). Autoregulation of the EEG alpha rhythm: A program for the study of consciousness. In E. Peper, S. Ancoli, & M. Quinn (Eds.), *Mind/body integration: Essential readings in biofeedback* (pp. 289–297). New York: Plenum Press.

Klorman, R. (1991). Cognitive event-related potentials in attention deficit disorder. *Journal of Learning Disabilities, 24*(3), 130–140.

Lahey, B. B. (1991, October). Presentation at the 4th Annual Meeting of CH.A.D.D. Conference, Washington, DC.

Lahey, B. B., Schaughency, E., Hynd, G., Carlson, C., & Nieves, N. (1987). Attention deficit disorder with and without hyperactivity: Comparison of behavioral characteristics of clinic-referred children. *Journal of the American Academy of Child Psychiatry, 26,* 718–723.

Lubar, J. F. (1989). Electroencephalographic biofeedback and neurological applications. In J. V. Basmajian (Ed.), *Biofeedback: Principles and practice for clinicians* (3rd ed., pp. 67–90). Baltimore: Williams & Wilkins.

Lubar, J. F. (1991). Discourse on the development of EEG diagnostics and biofeedback treatment for attention-deficit/hyperactivity disorders. *Biofeedback and Self-Regulation, 16,* 201–225.

Lubar, J. F. (1992, October). *Point/counterpoint: Is EEG neurofeedback an effective treatment for ADHD?* Presented at the 5th Annual Meeting of CH.A.D.D., Chicago.

Lubar, J. F., & Culver, R. M. (1978). Automated signal-detection methodologies for biofeedback conditioning. *Behavior Methods and Instrumentation, 10,* 607–617.

Lubar, J. F., & Shouse, M. N. (1976). EEG and behavioral changes in a hyperkinetic child concurrent with training of the sensorimotor rhythm (SMR): A preliminary report. *Biofeedback and Self-Regulation, 3,* 293–306.

Lubar, J. F., & Shouse, M. N. (1977). Use of biofeedback in the treatment of seizure disorders and hyperactivity. In B. B. Lahey & A. E. Kazdin (Eds.), *Advances in Clinical Child Psychology* (pp. 203–265). New York: Plenum Press.

Mann, C., Lubar, J., Zimmerman, A., Miller, C., & Muenchen, R. (1991). Quantitative analysis of EEG in boys with attention-deficit-hyperactivity disorder: Controlled study with clinical implications. *Pediatric Neurology, 8,* 30–36.

Noble, E., Blum, K., Ritchie, T., Montgomery, A., & Sheridan, P. (1991). Allelic association of the D_2 dopamine receptor gene with receptor-binding characteristics in alcoholism. *Archives of General Psychiatry, 48,* 648–654.

Peniston, E. G., & Kulkosky, P. J. (1989). Alpha-theta brainwave training and beta-endorphin levels in alcoholics. *Alcoholism: Clinical and Experimental Research, 13,* 271–279.

Satterfield, J. H., & Dawson, M. E. (1971). Electrodermal correlates of hyperactivity in children. *Psychophysiology, 8,* 191–197.

Satterfield, J. H., Lesser, R. I., Saul, R. E., & Cantwell, D. P. (1973). EEG aspects in the diagnosis and treatment of minimal brain dysfunction. *Annals of the New York Academy of Science, 205,* 274–282.

Schneider, F., Rockstroh, B., Heimann, H., Lutzenberger, W., Mattes, R., Elbert, T., Birnbaumer, N., & Bartels, M. (1992). Self-regulation of slow cortical potentials in psychiatric patients: Schizophrenia. *Biofeedback and Self-Regulation, 17*(4), 277–292.

Shouse, M. N., & Lubar, J. F. (1978). Physiological bases of hyperkinesis treated with methylphenidate. *Pediatrics, 62,* 343–351.

Still, G. F. (1902). The Coulstonian lectures on some abnormal psychiacal conditions in children. *Lancet, i,* 1008–1012,1163–1168.

Tansey, M. A. (1990). Righting the rhythms of reason, EEG biofeedback training as a therapeutic modality in a clinical office setting. *Medical Psychotherapy, 3,* 57–68.

Tansey, M. A. (1991). Wechsler's (WISC-R) changes following treatment of learning disabilities via EEG biofeedback training in a private setting. *Australian Journal of Psychology, 43,* 147–153.

Whalen, C. K., & Henckler, B. (1991). Therapies for hyperactive children: Comparisons, combinations, and compromises. *Journal of Consulting and Clinical Psychology, 59,* 126–137.

Wolraich, M. L., Lindgren, S., Stromquist, A., Milich, R., Davis, C., & Watson, D. (1990). Stimulant medication use by primary care physicians in the treatment of attention-deficit hyperactivity disorder. *Pediatrics, 86,* 95–101.

Zametkin, A. J., Nordahl, T. E., Gross, M., et al. (1990). Cerebral glucose metabolism in adults with hyperactivity of childhood onset. *New England Journal of Medicine, 323,* 1361–1366.

Zametkin, A. J., & Rapoport, J. L. (1987). Noradrenergic hypothesis of attention deficit disorder with hyperactivity: A critical review. In H. V. Metsler, (Ed.), *Psychopharmacology: The third generation of progress* (pp. 837–842). New York: Raven.

VIII
NEUROMUSCULAR APPLICATIONS

21

Biofeedback in Neuromuscular Re-Education and Gait Training

David E. Krebs

"I can't! It just won't move that way!" Too often therapists hear similar retorts from motor-impaired patients, such as those with postsurgical disorders, lower-motor neuron lesions, or amputations. Current therapeutic exercise incorporates facilitation, positioning, resistance, repetition, and other manual techniques to provide patients with increased access to the information and skills necessary to move their limbs or walk in a normal fashion. Distressingly, we must often acknowledge that our efforts are insufficient—that patients' protestations are accurate.

THE USE OF FEEDBACK IN PSYCHOLOGICAL INFORMATION SYSTEMS

At the outset, we must address our current crude state of understanding of human information processing and motor control. Historically, we have studied mechanical models and applied the knowledge thus obtained to humans. Although many machines require input–output and servomechanical feedback from their actions in order to successively approximate desired outcomes, little evidence exists that humans primarily depend upon such feedback (Mulder & Hulstyn, 1984). In fact, recent work on enhancing normal human performance emphatically denies the utility of massed practice and immediate feedback (whether bio- or otherwise), suggesting that distributed practice with summary knowledge of results on a scheduled (time-delayed) basis generates more permanent learning (Druckman & Bjork, 1991; Winstein, Christensen, & Fitch, 1993).

Normal motor control has been reviewed elsewhere at length and in great detail (Brooks, 1981; Herman, Grillner, Stein, & Stuart, 1967). Motor control, however, has few unifying theories, and the limited work that has been done on abnormal populations often contradicts areas of agreement in work on normal subjects. Physical therapists merely need to recall having learned to put their hands "just so" for proprioceptive neuromuscular facilitation patterning and then to reflect on the current view that such careful manual placements may be a waste of time! Yet, every day, motor-impaired patients improve despite our "ignorance."

Clearly human movement control requires visual, vestibular, and proprioceptive information. What is profoundly unclear is how that information is processed. Attempts to dogmatically view biofeedback, or any other artificial information system, as a substitute for lost proprioceptive pathways can therefore only be a crude approximation, at best, to the extremely sophisticated control systems that have evolved in humans. The fact that biofeedback, in conjunction with therapeutic exercise regimens, helps patients regain motor function has been repeatedly demonstrated. How the feedback aids the process, however, remains enigmatic.

Biofeedback-assisted neuromuscular re-education, as practiced today, must always be viewed as an adjunctive agent; therapists who depend upon the instruments to restore motor behavior are very likely to be unsuccessful. The skills of therapists remain of paramount importance. However, an understanding of biofeedback and some of the physiological events monitored with biofeedback instruments may certainly improve patients' (and therapists'!) skills.

Some Motor Learning Considerations

Feedback must be relevant in order to enhance learning. Therapists are well aware that providing verbal cues can improve motor performance. This feedback may, for example, be in the form of verbal cues to focus attention on agonist muscles, praise the patient who has just mastered straight-leg raising after knee arthroscopy, or congratulation to the child who has for the first time gained control of a prosthetic myoelectric hand.

Studies of specificity of information, in which, for example, subjects are asked to pitch a ball at a target, demonstrate that performance decrements can occur with each piece of lost information. However, the converse may not be true; that is, more feedback is not necessarily better. As noted in the examples above, the timing and type of feedback, whether exogenous or endogenous, may be as important as the amount of feedback. General verbal encouragement is often a relatively nonspecific and inefficient means of aiding motor performance. In addition, there are the frequent long delays (i.e., latency) between completion of tasks by patients and the provision of verbal feedback by therapists. In some cases these delays may be more effective in motor performance enhancement than immediate biofeedback (Gable, Shea, & Wright, 1991).

Although therapists may describe the location of agonist and antagonist muscles, and even make attempts to describe the "feelings" patients should experience if the proper muscles are used appropriately, there is still no way to communicate which motor units to activate. How should the motor units be recruited? Should they be activated synchronously or asynchronously? Electromyographic (EMG) biofeedback can provide some useful information regarding motor unit activity that patients do not otherwise have available.

Disagreement exists regarding the utility of providing EMG feedback, because most forms of feedback are tantamount to merely communicating "more" or "less" EMG activity. The information provided to patients via current technology is decidedly unsophisticated and incomplete compared to that which intact nervous systems can provide during muscle contractions. Therefore, many therapists prefer to work with devices that directly measure and feed back force or joint range of motion (ROM). This preference is based on the assumption that EMG signals are not sufficiently informative or sophisticated to be true "process" feedback, and that EMG does not adequately reflect actual outcome (e.g., limb displacement or torque) to provide accurate knowledge of results. This is discussed further, below.

In summary, feedback must be accurate and relevant in order to qualify as assistance in neuromuscular re-education.

Speed of Information

Feedback must be timely with regard to the therapy tasks. Several studies have demonstrated that the utility of feedback from the environment is greatest in unfamiliar tasks and that feedback is nearly worthless or even counterproductive in well-learned, rapid movements (e.g., typing or playing the piano) (Mulder & Hulstyn, 1984). The fastest cortical feedback loops (i.e., those loops that could reflect changes in environmental conditions) have latencies of at least 100–200 milliseconds. For example, a pianist performing a fast "run" cannot possibly rely on visual or auditory feedback during the "run." If a mistake has occurred, several more notes will be played (i.e., about 0.2 second of music) before any adjustments to the motor plan can be made. At that point, the performer must make a decision to ignore the mistake or to back up and correct it. Either way, timely auditory feedback is critical.

Ambulation also requires a series of preplanned motor events. If a disruption occurs, feedback of the "mistake" must be acted upon and built into the plan for ensuing steps. Normal walking speed is about 1 cycle per second. Ankle dorsiflexors, for example, must resist foot slap from heel strike to foot flat for about 60 milliseconds. Therapists attempting to encourage normal gait in hemiplegic patients using feedback from dorsiflexor EMG cannot possibly hope for correction of inadequate dorsiflexor motor unit activity during that gait cycle. The information is that EMG activity was inadequate during the past gait cycle, and patients must therefore figure out how to increase that activity before ensuing heel strikes.

In addition to endogenous latencies within patients, most EMG biofeedback instruments have built-in integrators or averages, which may slow the signal within the instruments. Furthermore, all EMG processors delay electrical events during amplification. A further latency results at the audio speaker and visual meter because of inherent mechanical delays from inertia. In short, most commercial EMG feedback instruments introduce delays of 50–100 milliseconds before the signal can even reach the ears and eyes of patients.

Summary of Requirements
for Information Feedback

Information to be fed back to patients must be relevant and timely to be of therapeutic use. Therapists must choose, from a variety of modalities, the instrument or device that provides the most meaningful information to patients. Commercially available EMG instruments can provide timely feedback if the events being monitored are at least 0.5 seconds in duration. Thus, for feedback during 5-second isometric contractions, adequate time may be available for patients to adjust the motor program and change the number of motor units being activated during contractions. During most functional activities, however, the "feedback" acts as an error signal or knowledge of results, to be used in planning future skeletal movements. For amputees, prosthetic feedback during training may help compensate for severed sensory systems. The following sections examine some application of biofeedback in the rehabilitation of patients with neuromotor dysfunction and amputation.

NEUROMUSCULAR RE-EDUCATION
USING EMG FEEDBACK

In this section, the origins of the EMG signal are briefly reviewed, and its progress is traced on a hypothetical round trip from a patient's central nervous system (CNS) (starting with the intention to move) through monitoring instrumentation, and back to the CNS for the patient to reprocess (i.e., proprioception and exteroception). The astute reader will note that, as in any other journey, a potential problem lurks at every junction and intermediate step. This section should help therapists avoid those hazards, or at least to recognize them.

Muscle Physiology: Where Does the EMG Signal Arise?

After the CNS causes the anterior horn cell to discharge, the motor nerve depolarizes, conducting its electrical current about 40–60 meters per second. Because a motor unit is, by definition, the anterior horn cell, its nerve, and all the muscle fibers it innervates, the amount of muscle to be excited depends upon the size of the motor field (i.e., the number of muscle fibers innervated by each anterior horn cell and its axon). In EMG feedback, we most often use surface electrodes that sum all potentials beneath their surfaces.

The size of a motor unit varies among muscles. Skeletal muscles that require very fine control, such as the extraoccular or intrinsic hand muscles, have very few muscle fibers in one motor unit—often as few as four to five fibers per anterior horn cell. Conversely, large postural muscles need less fine control and may have as many as 1,000 muscle fibers supplied by a single anterior horn cell.

Variations also exist within muscles. By differentially recruiting large and small motor units within a muscle, the CNS has the ability to activate the same motor units over and over again, to do so more quickly or slowly, and to apportion the amount of muscle firing to the tension generation requirements. That is, at least two recruitment methods can increase tension within a given muscle: activating *more* motor units, increasing the motor unit firing *rate*, or both.

Controversy exists regarding the preferred recruitment training method for use with patients having very low levels of muscle activation. Therefore, the paretic patient being trained to increase EMG signals may be learning to recruit more motor units or to activate the same motor units more quickly; most EMG biofeedback instruments cannot discriminate between these two methods, and in any case, it is unknown which recruitment method is more therapeutic. The rectified and smoothed EMG signal will increase whether patients are developing increased activation of small motor units more rapidly and synchronously, or a greater number of units are being recruited.

After the terminal branches of a motor nerve have discharged, the action potential hits the neuromuscular junction. The distal end of the nerve releases acetylcholine, which diffuses across the synaptic cleft to begin the muscle action potential (see Figure 21.1). The acetylcholine receptors cause the muscle action potential to occur, in the "sarcolemma," or jacket, surrounding the muscle (Greek, sarcos = "flesh," lemma = "sheath"). The sarcolemmal depolarization (action potential) is much slower than the nerve action potential propagation. It is this sarcolemmal electrical event that the EMG instrument records. After the electrical excitation travels through the muscle, the action potential reaches a storage area for calcium ions, the sarcoplasmic reticulum. Only after the electrical depolarization reaches this storage area and causes calcium to be released does the mechanical event—muscle contraction—occur. That is, the nerve action potential travels about 60 meters per second, reaches the muscle, and causes a chemical reaction that causes another electrical event, the muscle action potential, traveling at about 5 meters per second. The muscle electrical action potential normally results in calcium ion release, which in turn causes tension (force) production by the muscle.

The preceding paragraph indicates clearly that measuring a muscle's electrical production with EMG, is *not* equivalent to measuring the muscle's tension production. A common example may help clarify the difference between a muscle's electrical and mechanical events. Most people have experienced a "charley-horse." These painful muscle contractions are apparently the result of the spontaneous calcium liberation from the sarcoplasmic reticulum. They have no EMG activity associated with them, because no sarcolemmal discharge precedes the mechanical event. That probably explains why one cannot stop

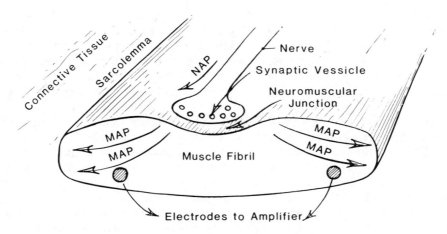

FIGURE 21.1. Schematic representation of neuromuscular electrical events. Following nerve depolarization, the nerve action potential (NAP) travels distally to the synaptic vesicles, which release acetylcholine across the synaptic cleft at the neuromuscular junction. The resulting muscle action potential (MAP) is the event recorded by the EMG, whether via intramuscular electrodes (shown) or surface electrodes.

a charley-horse by voluntarily contracting the muscle. Mechanically stretching the muscle, which dissociates the actomyosin and allows the calcium to return to the sarcoplasmic reticulum, however, promptly relieves the pain.

In short, measuring muscles' electrical activity with EMG, is not synonymous with specifically measuring muscle activity. Some discussion of this is found in Chapter 5. A more detailed discussion of the biochemical and electrical activity is beyond the scope of this chapter. The important point for biofeedback is that the EMG signal arises *before*, and occasionally independent of, muscle mechanical activity, so the EMG device can indeed be misleading.

Relationship between the EMG Device's Signals and Normal Muscle Activity

The EMG biofeedback device is simply a very sensitive voltmeter. Like any voltmeter, EMG instruments can only measure electrical signals if one pole of an instrument is negative with respect to the other pole. After the electrical signal is measured, most biofeedback instruments "condition" EMG signals so that positive and negative impulses are "rectified" (the machine finds the signal's absolute amplitude); then the device "smooths" (filters) the signal prior to display, to decrease the normal, minor fluctuations present in the muscle's electrical output. Thus, although the electrical event within the patient occurs prior to the mechanical contraction, the mechanical event may be over by the time the EMG machine "conditions" the signal for feedback to patients. Of course, these delays are on the order of milliseconds, but nonetheless, the type of signal processing affects the feedback delivered to the patient.

Input Impedance

At the time of contraction, each muscle fiber produces a signal of several thousandths of a volt. The summated current from all the firing fibers must pass through the resistive skin and subcutaneous tissues, thus further reducing its voltage, sometimes by 100-fold. Thus, tissues intervening between the electrodes and muscles tend to attenuate the signals. Therefore, EMG signals from obese patients or from limb sites with above-average amounts of adipose tissue appear less than normal, even if the signals from the muscle are equivalent to these from other muscles with less intervening tissue. Indeed, any intervening tissue will increase the effective resistance to muscles' electrical signals. Atrophic, necrotic, or very oily skin will also attenuate signals.

Ohm's Law states that resistance (impedance) is inversely related to voltage. If a large resistance is found at the skin, the measured muscle signals will be reduced. If, on the other hand, the EMG machine's impedance is *much* greater than skin impedance, a more valid measure of the muscle's electrical activity will be obtained. The clinical relevance of Ohm's Law is that EMG instruments should have at least 1,000 times as much input impedance as that measured between the two active electrodes. One can easily measure skin electrode impedance by attaching an ohmmeter to the surface electrodes after they are attached to the skin. Generally, a standard, careful skin preparation to remove dead surface skin and excess oil will decrease resistance to 1,000 ohms or less, as much as necessary with older instruments having about 100-megohm input impedance. Newer instruments, with input impedances in the gigohm and higher range, seem to require little skin preparation beyond a quick alcohol wipe on the skin.

Common-Mode Rejection Ratio

Modern EMG instruments use differential amplifiers. Their chief characteristic is that the voltage of one active electrode is compared to the voltage at the other active electrode. The ground electrode may be placed almost anywhere on the patient. When muscle action potentials occur, the signals produced are compared between the two active electrodes. If the voltage travels down the muscle and arrives at both electrodes simultaneously, no difference between the electrodes is registered, and the instrument reflects no change of activity. Therefore, therapists must choose electrode placements that maximize the likelihood that EMG signals will first reach one active electrode and later reach the other active electrode.

In practice, therapists should generally place one electrode on the muscle belly as far away from other muscles as possible (more on this "cross talk" potential later), and the other 1 centimeter or less distal to it and parallel to the direction of the fibers. Thus, when the action potential's signal propagates down the muscle, the EMG instrument will record a temporal difference in voltage between the two sites.

The advantage of the differential recording system is its "rejection" of extraneous voltages. Although we may not be aware of it, patients' skin receives a great many voltages, such as from lights, motors, and other hospital appliances; these produce currents that travel through the air and can affect surface EMG recordings. Muscles other than the ones of interest (e.g., myocardium) also produce voltages within patients' bodies. If the electricity from these other sources reaches the two active electrodes simultaneously, the differential amplifier will "reject" those artifactual signals.

The voltage from lights and other exogenous generators nearly always reaches the two skin electrodes simultaneously, so room current (60 Hertz) interference is often minimal if common-mode rejection ratio (CMRR) is high enough. Myocardial activity, however, is often a problem when recording near the heart, such as on the chest or upper back. Since the anatomical progression of the cardiac "R" wave is well known, therapists who perceive a regularly alternating signal unrelated to the skeletal muscle(s) of interest should refer to a vector cardiography map and place the electrodes perpendicular to the progression of the R wave, so that the electrocardiographic (EKG) signal arrives at both electrodes concurrently. In practice, it is usually sufficient simply to experiment with different electrode placements until the EKG artifact is minimized.

CMRR is not perfect. If a signal of 60 Hertz interferes with a therapy session, the therapist should turn off the room lights or look for a nearby whirlpool or diathermy machine as the culprit. An ungrounded appliance operating from the same electrical circuit as the EMG feedback instrument will occasionally interfere with EMG recordings. If the EMG instrument cannot operate by batteries, then the therapist should disconnect the ungrounded appliance. Many therapists require that electricians install an outlet isolated from other appliances, thus eliminating feedback interference from power lines.

As with input impedance, higher is better. CMRRs should be at least 200,000:1. If the muscles being monitored are especially paretic and generate only a few microvolts, then large amplifier gains are required; large gains, unfortunately, also amplify the artifacts. Therefore, high CMRR are especially important when recording the low myoelectric signals common in neuromuscular re-education.

Frequency Response (Bandwidth)

"Bandwidth" is the range between the lowest- and highest-frequency response of an EMG instrument. Most of the power at surface kinesiological EMG recordings is between 20 and 200 Hertz. Thus manufacturers often dictate that their EMG instruments need no more than 200 Hertz as the highest cutoff frequencies. However, responsiveness of instruments relates not only to the frequency of the monitored signal, but also to how quickly the signal changes. Fourier theory tells us that any EMG wave can be decomposed into a number of sine waves; the highest frequency of a powerful sine wave will correspond to the highest-frequency component of the EMG wave. So even if an EMG signal occurs at a frequency of only once a minute, it will contain some high-frequency component if it rises or falls quickly; this will require a rapid (high-frequency) response from the EMG instrument for accurate recording. Therefore, the high end of the machine's bandwidth should exceed 200 Hertz to enable the machine to respond faithfully to all components of the signal.

For the EMG instrument to reproduce faithfully the input signal, it must react as quickly or slowly as the signal itself. It must also recover, ready to record the next signal. In stereo equipment, this extreme faithfulness, or "high fidelity," was a technological breakthrough in the late 1950s. It enabled listeners to hear music signals approximately as they were recorded. A wide bandwidth in EMG allows high fidelity with regard to muscle action potentials. In general, a bandwidth of 20–1000 Hertz is adequate for surface kinesiological EMG feedback.

Why shouldn't the bandwidth be wider? In an ideal world, a bandwidth of 0–20,000 Hertz would provide coverage for any situation likely to be encountered. Alas, life and EMG instrumentation require tradeoffs. Artifact and noise become prominent features outside the bandwidth of 100–200 Hertz. Hence many manufacturers provide machines with only 100–200 Hertz bandwidth, promising low noise or "artifact-free" EMG signals—but conveniently ignoring true EMG signals mixed in with the frequencies of < 100 or > 200 Hertz. Such machines can be made more cheaply because their frequency range is attenuated—but *caveat emptor*!

Movement artifact signals have their greatest power below 5 Hertz, so whenever patients move limbs monitored at low frequencies, movement artifact signals will be fed back to patients, even if the muscle(s) are not generating muscle electrical activity. Of course, a high CMRR will help solve the problem, but most commercial portable EMG instruments simply are not technically up to that challenge, so some manufacturers opt instead for a less expensive solution—low-frequency cutoffs of 100 or even 200 Hertz. As a result, the surface EMG signal's power beyond 100–200 Hertz may be lost.

High-frequency response capabilities greater than 250 Hertz are rare in commercially available EMG feedback instruments. Again the reason is cost. To make the high-frequency cutoff as high as, for example, 10,000 Hertz would require noise-suppression circuits or high-quality (low inherent noise) components, which would increase manufacturer, and hence purchaser, costs. All circuits have natural noise in them resulting from electron vibration, temperature, and other interference. Less expensive components often carry with them more "leakage" and noise. Thus, cutting off the signal amplification at 200 Hertz allows a less expensive, although less useful, biofeedback instrument.

Noise Level of EMG Instruments

In information theory, "noise" is anything that interferes with the information being sampled. Noise intrinsic to the recorder is most problematic when amplifying signals from paretic muscles. The high gains necessary to amplify the electrical signal from a weak muscle contraction also amplify the noise of the instrument. In instruments with, for example, a noise level of 2 microvolts, trying to feed back a 0.8-microvolt contraction is impossible, because the signal-to-noise ratio is too low.

In general, the lower the noise, the better. Fortunately, most commercially available instruments have noise levels of less than 2 microvolts.

False Signals (Artifacts) from EMG Instruments

The characteristics described above pertain to instrumentation specifications, which are provided by the manufacturer. Even a perfect EMG instrument, however, could not ensure that therapists and patients will obtain clean signals. The following section describes other kinesiological EMG feedback artifacts and their possible clinical remedies.

Movement artifact is perhaps the most common signal error seen when monitoring patients while they are exercising. The movements of limbs and/or cables attached to the electrodes induce voltages that instruments cannot distinguish from "real" EMG voltages. Because most limb movements are under 5 Hertz, the low-frequency cutoff of most biofeedback instruments automatically eliminates them. However, sudden or very rapid movements also have high-frequency components in them and may still result in distortions of EMG signals. Cable movements can have high-frequency components and relatively high voltage compared to EMG signals, and hence they are a frequent cause of artifact.

Several solutions to movement artifact are available. The most common way to decrease cable movement artifact is to eliminate the source of it by fastening the electrode wires and cables to patients' limbs. It may be helpful to shorten the cables, thus keeping the amplifier as close as possible to the electrodes.

Electronic solutions are also available. Movement artifact results from muscle voltages being on the order of millionths of a volt (i.e., microvolts), whereas movement artifact is on the order of thousandths of a volt (i.e., millivolts) or even more. Both signals are greatly amplified, perhaps 1,000- to 100,000-fold by the device. If preamplification can be performed at the recording site (i.e., the skin), movements resulting in artifacts as great as several hundred millivolts are then trivial in comparison to the preamplified signal voltage (i.e., volts) coming to the main amplifier, and thence to the meter, oscilloscope, or speaker. In addition, both the amplifier and the limb move simultaneously.

There are several commercially available biofeedback instruments with preamplifiers at the electrode site. Most gait laboratories and kinesiological EMG researchers have adopted skin-site preamplification for use when EMG recordings might be contaminated with movement artifact. Biofeedback clinicians will surely adapt these instruments for neuromuscular re-education as well.

Currently, a few biofeedback companies offer radio-telemetered systems, which obviate the need for cables between the preamplifier and the main instrument. No doubt the subminiature electronics and 3-D display monitors and headsets developed for modern personal computers will contribute further to suppression of artifact in future biofeedback instruments.

Volume-conducted artifact results when signals from nearby muscles are inadvertently picked up by the surface electrodes. Because differential amplifiers merely compare the voltage at one active electrode to the voltage at the other, contraction of any muscle in the vicinity of the surface electrodes may result in "feedback" to patients. Because volume-conducted signals pass through more tissues than does the signal from the muscle directly underlying the electrodes, directly displayed volume-conducted potentials appear less sharp on an oscilloscope and sound like low-pitched rumblings on the speaker. Unfortunately, most biofeedback instruments have neither an oscilloscope nor a direct speaker connection for examining the myopotentials.

Using an amplitude meter and clicks or a pitch for feedback, therapists are unable to determine whether the increase in amplitude of EMG (i.e., higher meter readings or greater frequency of clicks or tones) is the result of an increase in the motor-unit activity in the muscle underlying the electrodes or of an increase in motor-unit activity of distant muscles.

Without an oscilloscope or direct speaker output, therapists may palpate the suspected muscle to determine whether the antagonist or some other nearby muscle is contracting. However, this method is not foolproof. Tendons and muscle bellies become palpably tense from being passively stretched, thereby misleading a therapist to believe that an antagonist is actively contracting during nonisometric contractions of the agonist. The most reliable method now available, short of using indwelling needle electrodes, is to put a second set of electrodes over the antagonist muscle and to monitor it on another channel.

For example, a therapist may ask a hemiplegic patient to actively dorsiflex and increase the EMG amplitude in the anterior tibialis. Spastic patients may have difficulty in achieving changes in range of motion, so the therapist may be satisfied with increased EMG amplitude measured by the electrodes over the anterior tibialis. However, if the triceps surae is contracting and preventing dorsiflexion, a volume-conducted impulse from the spastic calf muscles could be the reason for the ostensible increase in "anterior tibialis" EMG amplitude. Dr. Carlo DeLuca and colleagues at Boston University have shown that volume conduction from 1-centimeter interelectrode placements and properly conditioned signals is usually 17% or less.

The volume conduction problem is similar in patients with paretic muscles. Because paretic muscles (e.g., from peroneal palsy) have few active motor units, these low signals must be amplified greatly (e.g., a meter scale of 0–10 microvolts) in order to discern any motor-unit activity. Patients try to please therapists and to show themselves that "there is life in my muscle," so they clench their teeth and co-contract throughout the limb. Often, they are successful in increasing the response of the biofeedback instrument, but in this case, the patients may be rewarded for functionally useless motor behavior.

I have seen several patients with neuropathy referred by therapists who noted, "The patient can increase the muscle's EMG but can't achieve any functional gains." With such patients, I use multichannel biofeedback. Therapy concentrates on inhibition of the antagonists and muscles surrounding the agonists, while attempting to increase the response of the agonist's channel. Many patients require three or more sessions to "undo" the effects of previous "biofeedback" (which was in fact artifact feedback); hence biofeedback must have had a powerful effect!

EKG and *60-Hertz* (i.e., power-line) *artifacts* are discussed above in connection with CMRR. Occasionally, it is impossible to eliminate the EKG or 60-Hertz artifact. In such cases, therapy to increase the EMG signal above the amplitude of the regularly occurring EKG artifact (e.g., 72 beats per minute) or power-line artifact (i.e., 60 Hertz) is the only alternative to abandoning feedback therapy for that muscle.

EMG as a Kinesiological Monitor during Movement

Even if artifacts are eliminated, a "clean" EMG signal must be interpreted with caution. Many researchers have shown that EMG amplitude is linearly related to force production only under isometric conditions. Since the 1950s, it has been known that once joint movement occurs, the EMG-force relationship depends upon the speed of contraction and the length of the associated muscle (Lenman, 1959; Lippold, 1952). It is well known that muscles exert greater or lesser force in a given joint at different points in the ROM because of biomechanical factors such as changes in the joint's lever arm and the degree of sarcomere (i.e., actomyosin) overlap. Much less is known about neurophysiological influences governing muscle activity over different arcs of motion within the same joint (Basmajian, 1974).

To investigate the neurophysiological mechanisms of muscle control, my colleagues and I studied the effects of knee and hip joint positions on EMG amplitude of normal, maximally contracting quadriceps muscles and those of patients with joint mechanoreceptor deficits (Krebs, Staples, Cuttita, & Zickel, 1983). In normal subjects, maximum EMG activity occurred with the knees and hips at 0° flexion; less EMG amplitude was observed with knees and hips flexed, although all subjects were requested to give maximal effort in all positions.

Patients who had recent anterior joint capsule incisions following meniscectomy responded quite differently from normal subjects. Maximum EMG activity was found in the affected limb with the knee at 30° knee flexion and the hip at 15° flexion. We concluded that motor-unit activity depends not only on joint angle, but also upon the integrity of the joint structures. Therefore, the neurophysiological control and activation of muscles with disruption of their peripheral joint receptors may be very different from those of normal limbs, even during maximal effort and at equivalent joint angles.

Activation aside, what information does EMG amplitude contain regarding force output? Under isometric conditions and equivalent joint angles, force and EMG are at least approximately linearly related for an individual subject: an increase in EMG amplitude is accompanied by a proportional increase in force production. This relationship also appears to hold if only length is changed: Nelson (1976) at New York University (NYU) has demonstrated that subjects performing constant-speed (isokinetic) exercise show a proportional increase in force output and in EMG amplitude.

Functional activities, however, rarely occur at either constant speed or constant muscle length, the only known conditions under which EMG amplitude is a valid predictor of force output. Nearly all biofeedback sessions include procedures with active, functional movements. During functional movement, force, muscle length, joint position, and movement velocity freely change (Keefe & Surwit, 1978). Under such conditions, therapists must not equate increases in EMG amplitude with functional gains or muscle force improvement. Some studies show a weak relationship between EMG amplitude increases and functional gains, but large numbers of subjects are required to show a statistically significant effect (Krebs, 1989). Even in laboratory settings with sophisticated equipment, the EMG output for a given activity in a given subject can be significantly variable (Shiavi, Champion, Freeman, & Griffin, 1981).

The comments above are not intended to suggest that no relationship exists between EMG and limb force output from muscles contracting at various speeds. Rather, the relationship is simply unknown. My colleagues and I recently reported that maximum EMG amplitude, Manual Muscle Test (MMT) scores, and isokinetic scores are significantly correlated, at least in severely paretic quadriceps muscles following knee arthrotomy (Krebs, Staples, Cuttita, Chui, & Zickel, 1982). The relationship, however, is a moderate one ($r = .70$). That is, as patients recover following surgery, functional and muscle power improvements may in part result from improvements in recruitment of motor units.

Recruitment of motor units may be aided by EMG biofeedback. Much more research is needed before EMG biofeedback can provide valid information to patients under movement conditions. In the meantime, most of us will simply view the EMG amplitude "with a grain of salt," and will depend upon other objective means for validating the efficacy of biofeedback in motor learning.

Summary

Instruments used for neuromuscular re-education biofeedback must be of the same quality as those used in kinesiological EMG measurement to obtain "clean" and useful signals. Surface electrodes summate the electrical muscle action potentials, which are filtered and attenuated as they pass through body tissues. Most biofeedback instruments then rectify and smooth the signal to provide an indication of the absolute amplitude of muscle activity. Skin resistance should be minimal (e.g., less than 1,000 ohms), whereas the input impedance should be as large as feasible (i.e., at least millions of ohms), so the muscle voltage will be accurately conveyed to the amplifier and then to the patient. High CMRRs (e.g., 200,000:1 or more) should also be sought from EMG instruments to minimize artifacts present at both electrodes.

Therapists must be especially careful to eliminate EKG, power-line, movement, and volume-conducted artifacts. Some artifacts can be controlled electronically. Filters, such as for 60-Hertz artifact, may be used to selectively suppress frequencies that commonly contain more noise than signal. However, surface EMG has most of its power in the 20–200 Hertz bandwidth, so instruments with restricted bandwidth (e.g., "60-Hertz notch filters") generally should be avoided. A frequency response or bandwidth of 20–1,000 Hertz is adequate for kinesiological EMG feedback. Machine noise levels of less than 2 microvolts are necessary for use with paretic muscles.

Use of EMG Feedback in Clinical Settings

Having considered some limitations of the EMG signal, we can now turn to clinical applications. Bear in mind the sources of contamination of EMG signals, because the unlearning of bad habits formed by inadvertently feeding back artifact or "unclean" EMG signals is not only of no benefit, it may actually make the condition worse. The following discussion assumes that the therapist has obtained a clean signal and now wants to proceed with treatment.

General Considerations

A behavioral paradigm of positive reinforcement is preferred and often employed with biofeedback therapies (Barton & Wolf, 1992). When patients generate appropriate motor behaviors, they are positively reinforced. Rewarding or positively reinforcing motor activity is frequently done verbally, with therapists commenting on the patients' progress in an effort to shape the motor responses toward normality. The audio and visual feedback, however, are usually much faster and more accurate than a therapist's comments.

Even if a patient does not fully understand the feedback signals, the therapist's knowledge of that patient's kinesiology should be enhanced by the biofeedback signals. The therapist's increased access to the patient's physiological functions probably underlies much of the reported successes of biofeedback as a treatment (Krebs, 1989).

I most often use a "two-thirds success" criterion. That is, the "magnitude threshold" for hearing the audio feedback or turning on the visual feedback is set so that, on the average, patients achieve success on two-thirds of their attempts that are in the correct *direction*. I make no claim that this two-thirds ratio has been scientifically validated, but I find it a useful starting point for most neuromuscular re-education applications. If the "success" criterion is achieved too often, the patients are not challenged; if "success" is achieved on fewer than 50% of the trials, the patients tend to become frustrated, hence diminishing their motivation.

Biofeedback is slower and less complete than natural proprioception. The therapist should relate patients' kinesthetic feelings during functional tasks to the EMG feedback during successful movements. After patients regularly attain the target criteria, they are requested to perform the activities without feedback. Then, it becomes clear whether patients have learned the tasks and whether they can generalize the internal sensations achieved during activities performed with feedback to those performed without feedback (e.g., during home exercises). Thus, merely learning to control the audio or visual feedback signals is functionally useless. The ability to call upon the internal correlates of useful movement—without biofeedback—is the hallmark of successful training.

Treatment Overview

In general, the therapist should start with easy tasks and progressively make the activities more difficult (i.e., more functional). One method is the following. First, the therapist explains the task to the patient, perhaps demonstrating with the therapist's own limbs. At this point, electrodes may be attached to the patient's contralateral limb, if it is uninjured, so the task may be understood and "normal" EMG levels established. If both limbs are affected, I often attach the electrodes to one of my muscles and demonstrate exactly what the patient is expected to do. The therapist's familiarity with the instrument and a simple explanation of what the EMG is measuring can accelerate the patient's understanding and achievement of the motor task.

When feedback is obtained from a paretic muscle, the thresholds must initially be set very low (or the gains set very high), so any muscle activity results in audio or visual feedback. Establishing and recording a baseline are important, so that progress within the first session, and during subsequent sessions, can be compared (see Figure 21.2). To enhance the validity of the initial assessment, a maximum isometric contraction of the monitored muscle is requested, and the criterion thresholds and gains are adjusted accordingly.

After maximum activity is recorded, the therapist should set the instrument so that achievement of the criterion occurs on about two-thirds of the trials, as noted above. A period of 5–10 minutes of working with any one muscle group is usually the maximum desirable time, since longer periods seem to lead to fatigue, boredom, and thus less than optimal learning.

After amplitude improvement occurs, the patient should be trained for temporal muscle activity control (ability to rapidly activate motor units) (see Figure 21.3, last two lines). One way of accomplishing this with EMG biofeedback instruments is to set a time limit

Patient
Name: _____

Hosp.
#: _____

Date of
Exam: _____

Birthdate: _____   Sex: _____   Duration/Onset Date: _____

See attached appendices for problem-specific evaluation forms, if any.

PROM:

MMT:

DTR's: <u>BJ</u> <u>TJ</u> <u>KJ</u> <u>AJ</u> <u>Clonus</u> <u>Babinski</u> <u>Hoffman</u>

Right:
Left:

Sensory and Proprioception:

ADL & Gait:

Other Therapies/Information:

Skin Condition: Atrophic?   Obesity?   Skin Preparation:

BF Device Used: Electrode Size: Separation Distance:

Electrode Placement:

Pretreatment: Resting Level: Maximum Isometric (2 sec.):

Treatment: Threshold Settings:

Posttreatment: Reseting: Max. Isometric:

Electrode Placement, Size, & Preparation of Other Muscles:

Pretreatment: Resting Level: Max. Isometric:

Posttreatment: Resting Level: Max Isometric:

Electrode Placement, Size, & Preparation of Other Muscles:

Pretreatment: Resting Level: Max. Isometric:

Posttreatment: Resting Level: Max Isometric:

FIGURE 21.2. Initial evaluation form for neuromuscular re-education via biofeedback, PROM, passive range of motion; DTR's, deep tendon reflexes; BJ, biceps jerk; TJ, triceps jerk; KJ, knee jerk, AJ, ankle jerk. Developed by David E. Krebs for use at St. Luke's Hospital Center Biofeedback Clinic, New York, NY; used by permission of St. Luke's Hospital.

and amplitude threshold, asking the patient to reach the threshold as many times as possible within the time limit. I use a microvolt level of about 60–80% maximum isometric activity and count the number of times the threshold light comes on during a 10-second trial. To score a valid trial, the muscle must relax completely between each repetition (i.e., the meter must return to the relaxation level before the next attempt is made to exceed the threshold). The relaxation requirement is especially difficult for patients with spasticity, so care should be taken not to frustrate a patient by performing this test too early in the course of treatment.

Sophisticated EMG instruments can calculate the rate of increase in EMG for each contraction. Higher rates of isometric EMG development mean faster tension development. This task may be made more functional, and more difficult, by making it contingent upon simultaneous relaxation of the antagonist and/or other muscles.

There is now good evidence that EMG biofeedback is an effective adjunct in restoring motor function to patients with hemiplegia (Schleenbaker & Mainous, 1993). In my experience, normalization of hemiplegic gait may require development of rapid dorsiflexor tension with concomitant relaxation of spastic plantar flexors. For example, requesting rapid alternating 0- to 60-microvolt relaxation and activation of the anterior tibialis muscle for 10 seconds, while maintaining electrical silence in the triceps surae, is a difficult task, but patients who improve their performance on this test seem to walk better. It seems especially helpful to have patients perform this test while standing, although this functional position makes the rapid EMG activity alternations more difficult.

At minimum, therapy must be functionally relevant. Attention to mobility and muscle power must not be neglected in favor of biofeedback therapy. Biofeedback is only a tool to aid therapeutic exercise. If the exercises are inappropriate, they will remain so even after feedback is added. If biofeedback-assisted skills cannot be generalized to functional situations, patients and therapists have wasted their time. Therefore, patients must always be asked to perform activities of daily living (ADL) without feedback as tests of the efficacy of the treatment regimen by timing or rating the task in some way (e.g., see Figure 21.3, third line).

However, the clinical situation is rarely a sufficient test. The clinical environment may differ radically from a patient's normal surroundings (see Cataldo, Bird, & Cunningham, 1978). In my city office, the closed, quiet, clean surroundings are quite different from the situation on the street just outside, or on the subway or bus. Only after a patient can perform the activities without feedback in his or her normal, open environment should a therapist feel treatment has been successful.

Summary

In summary, patients with neuromuscular impairments often need movement re-education. Biofeedback does not re-educate; therapists and practice do. Used properly, biofeedback may be a useful adjunct to therapeutic exercise (Inglis, Campbell, & Donald, 1976; Schleenbaker & Mainous, 1993).

The critical elements of success with biofeedback-enhanced therapeutic exercise are:

1. The task should be explained clearly, with a demonstration on the unimpaired side if possible.
2. As biofeedback success occurs, the tasks should be incremented toward function and nonfeedback conditions.

Name: _____ Hosp. #: _____ Date: _____

Home Practice Regimen:

Functional Status:

Treatment Strategy:

   Muscle(s):   Skin Preparation: Device:

   Electrode Size: Separation Distance:

Pretreatment:

Threshold Settings (Best):

Posttreatment:

Rapid Alternating Activity Increase & Decrease:

Goals: Time:

FIGURE 21.3. Treatment record form for neuromuscular re-education via biofeedback. Used by permission of St. Luke's Hospital, New York, NY.

3. The therapist must be sure to test the patient's progress on functional tasks. Therapy that teaches control of audio signals, meters, and lights may be seductive to the therapist, but it does not help the patient!

Clinical Example: EMG Feedback of Quadriceps Activity for Postmeniscectomy Patients

Patients with paretic muscles from lower-motor neuropathy or postsurgical disorders appear to benefit greatly, at least in muscle power, from biofeedback-assisted therapeutic exercises. It should be borne in mind that ROM, ambulation, and ADL instructions may be higher priorities than muscle power enhancement for some paretic patients. The message here, as throughout this chapter, is that therapists should not suspend their clinical judgment for this "magic" therapy; patients should be treated according to their functional needs, not according to what equipment is available.

I find EMG feedback helpful for muscles with MMT scores of "fair-plus" (F+) or below. Stronger muscles can and should be given resistive exercises rather than EMG feedback. Consider the typical patient referred following knee arthrotomy. The patient is unable to straight-leg raise, and ipsilateral quadriceps activity is barely palpable—certainly less than F+. The usual treatment regimen might include 20 minutes of "quad setting" (i.e., isometric contraction of quadriceps with the knee and hip at 0°), straight-leg raising, and gait training, if possible. Biofeedback can be very useful in such cases.

Several years ago, I randomly assigned patients to two groups, and found that the "conventional" treatment group achieved only one-tenth as much improvement in EMG activity as, and significantly less improvement in Manual Muscle Test (MMT) Scores than the group receiving the identical regimen using EMG feedback (Krebs, 1981). A more recent paper, however, showed that the usual "quad set" position (hip and knee at 0° is not optimal for developing maximum EMG activity in postmeniscectomy quadriceps (Krebs et al., 1983). Flexion of 0° apparently inhibits the quadriceps in postmeniscectomy limbs, whereas slight flexion enhances motor-unit activity. A logical synthesis of currently available information is needed to optimize treatment regimens, since a definitive empirical study of postarthrotomy recovery has yet to be reported. The following treatment description incorporates elements from basic physical therapy procedures, from my research, and from general biofeedback considerations.

Before treatment, a thorough history and a physical examination are conducted. The latter includes an assessment of upper-extremity muscle power and sitting–standing balance, to determine whether gait training can be accomplished with crutches or other assistive devices. The patient's motivation, psychological status, and discharge plans are also reviewed. Discharge planning should determine whether unusual barriers (such as carpets or stairs) that would impede independent function with assisting devices are present in patients' homes. Outpatient follow-up care may then be more adequately planned.

Because improvement of one muscle, the quadriceps femoris, is the primary goal of strengthening exercises, a one-channel (one-muscle) EMG feedback instrument may be used. The affected limb is placed on a "short arc quad board" (see Figure 21.4), which positions the knee at 30° and the hip in enough flexion to accommodate the knee flexion.

The electrode sites are then chosen. Because the quadriceps muscles are multipennate (i.e., its fibers run in many directions), nearly any electrode placement on the skin is acceptable as long as the placement is as remote as possible from other superficial muscles, such as adductors and hamstrings. The location of the electrodes must be marked on the skin and noted in the patient's record for replication during ensuing therapy sessions (see Figure 21.5). It is most convenient simply to develop a consistent placement for each muscle, which is used for all treatment sessions. Such a standardized placement speeds application of electrodes and enhances comparability of between-session recordings of EMG activity without confounding the measures by variability of electrode placements.

The skin may be prepared by abrading the chosen electrode site and then wiping the

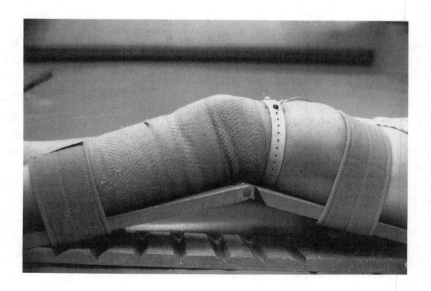

FIGURE 21.4. Short-arc quad board.

site with alcohol. If unusually thick epithelium, skin atrophy, excessive oil, or dirt is present, a more extensive skin preparation is performed. Often merely wiping the skin vigorously with alcohol "prep" pads or cotton soaked with alcohol will result in the pinkish hue indicative of hyperemia, and hence minimal skin resistance. If skin resistance is not yet sufficiently reduced, then conductive gel, cream, or paste may be introduced into the skin with a cotton-tipped swab. However, one must be especially careful to rub the conductive medium only onto a very small area, because if the skin between the EMG electrodes is permeated with conductive medium, the electrical signal conducts from one active electrode to the other, creating a "short circuit." The "short circuit" eliminates the differential amplitude between the recording sites, resulting in artifact.

The patient is then asked to "straighten your leg as hard as you can; make a muscle with your thigh." After several such efforts without feedback to the patient have been recorded for baseline assessment, the biofeedback training can begin. The patient is instructed in the use of EMG biofeedback during isometric exercise. The therapist may say,

> "Use the instrument to help you know when the muscle is active. The higher the meter reading, the stronger your muscle contraction. Experiment with different speeds of tightening the muscle and other methods. Try to make the reading as high as possible, by straightening your knee."

Patient: Date:

Meniscectomy type & location:

Age: Sex:

Tourniquet time:

Location of electrodes:

Spacing:

Date of Operation:

		Day 1	Day 2	Day 3	Day 4
Resting microvolts	Pre				
	Post				
Maximum microvolts	Pre				
	Post				
Muscle grade or straight-leg raise	Pre				
	Post				
Crutch walking: Weight bearing?					

FIGURE 21.5. Treatment record form for biofeedback therapy for postmeniscectomy patients. Used by permission of St. Luke's Hospital, New York, NY.

After 10 minutes or a little longer, the patient may be reassessed, the results recorded on a form such as that shown in Figure 21.5, and the EMG instrument disconnected. Instructions in active knee extension and straight-leg raising then begin. Once the patient can straight-leg raise, gait instructions with weight bearing to tolerance usually follow.

After the patient can easily generate maximum motor unit activity, and the MMT score is G– or greater, active resistive exercises replace EMG feedback.

Consider the perceived disadvantages of EMG biofeedback. Therapists have complained that it is time consuming to apply electrodes and teach the patient how to use the instrument. Although the initial time investment is greater than that for nonfeedback therapy, patients usually can be left alone to exercise, hence freeing the therapist for other activities (Krebs, 1981). Indeed, portable instruments can be lent to very motivated and intelligent patients to use between therapist contacts; these permit practice to occur at other times and on other days.

Given an informational tool like biofeedback, many patients can improve upon the exercises provided to them by therapists. In fact, the idea to flex the knee during postmeniscectomy exercises came directly from watching patients struggle at 0° knee flexion, but masterfully control their quadriceps at 30°.

EMG Feedback Training for Myoelectric Prosthesis Control

Biofeedback as a therapeutic tool has grown out of several fields. One such field is prosthetics. More than four decades ago, Berger and Huppert (1952) at NYU reported that EMG might be used to control motors to open and close prosthetic hands and to control other prosthetic functions. Battye, Nightingale, and Whillis (1955), from England, reported the first successful application of myoelectric signals in the control of a prosthetic hand.

The concept was simple. As Berger and Huppert explained, "Since the electric motor supplies the power for the artificial arm movements, the amputee's only responsibility is the control of the motor" (1952, p. 110). Despite the early work in this area, clinical application of EMG-controlled prostheses remains of controversial efficacy. Until recently, poor energy sources for the motors and mechanical systems made electrically powered prostheses rather inefficient and subject to frequent repair (Wirta, Taylor, & Finley, 1978). A number of electric prosthetic control systems now exist, including switches and harnesses. This section focuses on training for myoelectrically controlled systems without attempting to address the issue of which control system is more nearly optimal.

Two types of myoelectric control are currently available. "Dichotomous control" is similar to threshold control of biofeedback (i.e., turning an audio or visual signal on and off). For example, the EMG signal from the flexors of the below-elbow amputee's forearm can control prosthetic hand closing. If their EMG exceeds a threshold value, the prosthetic hand "flexes." Similarly, EMG activity in the forearm extensors that exceeds a threshold value opens the hand.

"Proportional control" is featured on the newer myoelectric prostheses, although it is an old concept. Analogous to biofeedback's continuous EMG amplitude feedback from a meter, or proportional audio tone or clicks, a large signal results in proportionally faster or more forceful prosthetic movement. Low-amplitude EMG signals result in slow movement for fine control. My colleagues and I have recently added another control variable: prosthetic joint stiffness. This "impedance controller" prosthesis appears to be a more natural use of the EMG signal in prosthetics (Popat et al., 1993).

General Considerations

Because EMG signal control is prerequisite to myoelectric prosthesis control, EMG bio-feedback occurs prior to functional training with the prosthesis. Indeed, this is one of the few cases in which the acquisition of biofeedback skill is a prerequisite to other therapy. Until the amputee can control the EMG signal from the control-site muscles, the myoelectric prosthesis is merely an expensive passive appliance.

Availability of a strong EMG signal from the proposed control site (see Figure 21.6) is the first factor to examine in the potential candidate. Most amputees, congenital or surgical, are capable of generating currents from the amputation limb, whether or not surgical myodesis has been performed. Congenital amputees, having never had the opportunity to functionally use their severed muscles, often meet with difficulty in the early stages of EMG biofeedback; after they learn to generate some signal, no matter how small, training usually proceeds apace.

Control sites are carefully chosen to meet three criteria: (1) The muscles must be superficial, so that surface electrodes may be employed; (2) EMG activity from the muscle must exceed the noise and movement artifacts, so that prosthetic activation does not inadvertently occur (the same EMG artifacts may be present in EMG amplifiers and electrode systems for prostheses as described for biofeedback systems); and (3) the patient must become capable, with training, of rapid, reliable, and repeated voluntary activation and relaxation of the EMG signal.

Frequently, the control muscle is chosen for its ontological function. For example, hand opening is usually controlled by forearm extensors in the below-elbow amputee. However, no empirical evidence exists supporting the validity of such reasoning. Indeed, above-elbow amputees must control prehension with muscles that ontologically function at the elbow or shoulder. These amputees apparently fare none the worse in their control of prehension. In most cases, the control-site electrode placements are generally the same as those used in other upper-limb EMG feedback situations.

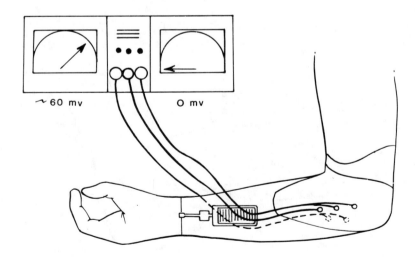

FIGURE 21.6. Myotestor biofeedback unit monitoring below-elbow residuum's flexor EMG. Note that extensors (dial on right) are quiescent.

No matter what control muscles are selected, biofeedback therapy goals are as follows:

1. Facilitation of EMG output from the control muscle.
2. Rapid EMG generation to the threshold necessary for prosthetic activation.
3. Inhibition of EMG during antagonist activation.

Most often, therapy starts with conventional EMG biofeedback instruments. Several prosthetic manufacturers even supply their own EMG instruments for preprosthetic biofeedback therapy; although the amplifier specifications (e.g., input impedance, CMRR, bandwidth, and noise level) are frequently suboptimal, the obvious advantage of such machines is their compatibility with the EMG signal conditioning used in the prosthesis.

Many myoelectric prostheses are fitted to children. To maintain children's attention, various "myotoys" have been developed. For example, the truck shown in Figure 21.7 moves forward and backward contingent upon flexor or extensor muscle activation, respectively. Children often attend to toys more readily than to lights, clicks, or meters. Proportional speed control can be introduced so greater EMG activity moves the toy faster than less EMG activity.

For all patients, therapy with a bench-mounted or hand-held prosthesis, such as that shown in Figures 21.8 and 21.9, proceeds after initial EMG and control skills have been acquired. The unilateral amputee should learn such manual skills as holding jars while screwing the top on or off with the unimpaired hand. Holding the prosthesis in his or her unimpaired hand, the amputee may then learn crude prehension activities (see Figure 21.9).

It is important to pause and digress somewhat at this point. A prosthetic hand is a poor substitute for the natural member. Most of the unilateral amputee's ADL will be

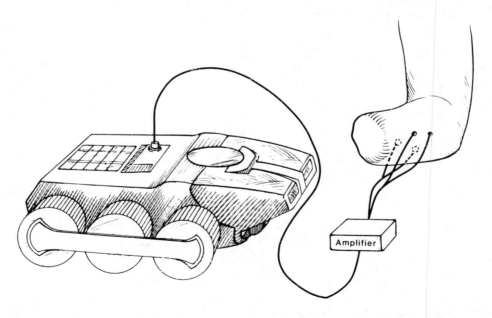

FIGURE 21.7. Myotoy (made by Milton-Bradley, Springfield, MA). EMG activity controls the toy's movement, such that agonist–antagonist EMG causes movement in opposite directions.

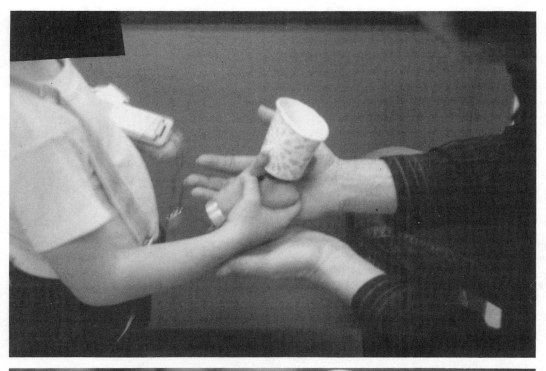

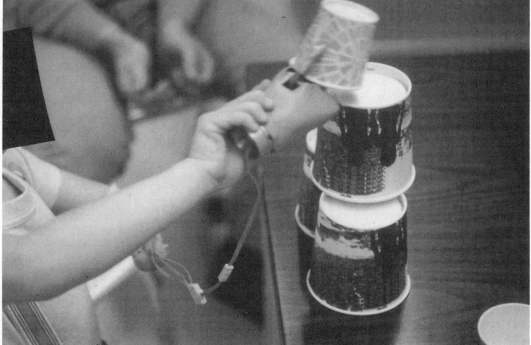

FIGURE 21.8. Two illustrations of therapy with a young amputee, using a hand-held prosthesis.

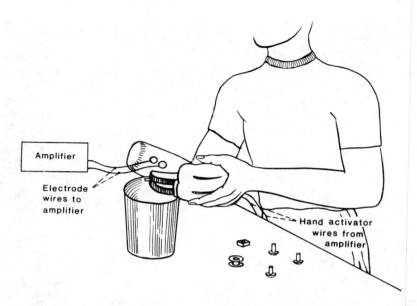

FIGURE 21.9. The patient in Figure 21.8 progresses to crude prehension activities with the hand-held prosthesis.

performed with the unimpaired limb (Krebs, 1987). The prosthetic device is most often used for assistance, and then only when unilateral prehension is insufficient. Therefore, training in complex prosthetic prehension tasks (e.g., picking up jelly beans or holding an egg), although impressive to some clinicians, is largely irrelevant to functional prosthetic use. Just as frustration may result from training with the prosthetic hand prior to acquiring sufficient EMG control, so may ennui ensue from training for unrealistic prosthetic goals.

Prosthetic hands are said to be less functional than hooks; their bulk and mechanical complexity limit visual feedback and fine prehension. Myoelectric hands, in addition, are much more costly, heavier, and probably break down more frequently than do body-powered ("conventional") hooks.

Only two myoelectric hooks are currently available commercially. The Synergistic Hook invented by Childress uses EMG control, but an elegant mechanical design provides the force–velocity priority for this terminal device (Childress, 1973). Current prosthetic options are suboptimal: It is critical to train the amputee in functional, realistic activities, accommodating current prosthetic limitations.

Summary

In summary, as electronic and prosthetic technologies improve, amputees will be afforded more kinesiological control of their prosthetic devices. Therapists must design biofeedback programs that mimic the control system of the prosthesis. The design limitations of any artificial limb, however, define the maximum functional capacity of the user.

LOCOMOTOR TRAINING

The Gait Cycle

Human locomotion is normally a regular, rhythmical, and repeatable series of oscillating stance and swing phases. When the foot touches the floor, the limb is in stance phase. Stance phase constitutes about 60% of a normal gait cycle. Advancing the limb through the air is called the swing phase. The joint motions (i.e., kinematics) and the forces that produce the motions (i.e., kinetics) have been studied extensively in normal populations. Much less is known regarding abnormal gait, the subject of most therapists' attention. A gait deviation such as a unilateral limp (i.e., decreased stance time) may result from a variety of kinematic or kinetic abnormalities including loss of motor power, pain, fear, and/or poor neuromuscular coordination. Sherman and Arena (1992) provide a superb literature review on back pain biofeedback and its relationship to motor function.

Colborne, Olney, and Griffin (1993) recently reported significant advances in the gait of patients with hemiplegia treated with *both* soleus EMG and ankle-joint electrogoniometric biofeedback; EMG is often used to estimate muscle contribution to locomotion. However, muscle force is just one of many biomechanical determinants of locomotion. Gravity, inertia, and the floor reactions are at least as important as the forces generated by superficial lower-extremity muscles that are accessible to surface EMG feedback (Krebs, 1992). Joint motion electrogoniometry captures the limb motions resulting from all these force sources.

Although EMG feedback attempts to provide information and answers to patients, we practitioners do not fully understand the question. We encourage subjects to activate their muscles in a prescribed sequence, but we do not yet know the correct sequence for normal muscle activity, let alone the complex compensations required by pathomechanics or pathophysiology (e.g., lower-limb amputation or CNS disorders).

Several authors have reported that EMG activity for a given muscle varies widely even within the same subject under identical walking conditions. Indeed, even Basmajian (1974) has suggested that EMG amplitude should only be classified as "none," "minimal," "moderate," or "marked," and not given numerical values. Of course, I do not mean to imply that EMG feedback for gait training is de facto useless; rather, therapists should be cautious in attaching too much importance to the EMG signal. Winter (1984) and Yang and Winter (1984) have recently provided insight into the reliability of various EMG-averaging methods; as such work progresses, therapists will have a more meaningful scientific basis for EMG-feedback-assisted gait training.

Neurophysiological control mechanisms aside, force resultants in gait have been fairly well documented. It is known, for example, that weight-bearing forces and stance times must be shared approximately equivalently by the lower extremities; otherwise, asymmetry and increased energy consumption result. Achievement of symmetric timing occurs by moving right and left extremity and spinal joints through approximately equivalent arcs at similar speeds. Thus, although the impetus for the motions may derive from complex interactions of exogenous (e.g., gravity and inertia) and endogenous (i.e., muscle) locomotor forces, the resultant kinematics and kinetics are mechanically somewhat easier to measure and therefore may be more amenable to error detection and biofeedback therapy.

Several forms of kinematic and kinetic biofeedback are clinically available. Unlike EMG feedback, electronic processing of gait motions and forces is rather direct. The primary equipment consideration is linearity of output (i.e., feedback) to input (i.e., joint motion or force reaction). That is, the signal reaching the patient should closely track kinematic or kinetic activity. Although 100% linearity is never achieved, technical specifications should be scrutinized before purchasing any such instrument to ensure that the feedback to patients is valid.

Most biofeedback gait therapy uses an audio signal, thus allowing the patient's visual system to attend to the walking environment. The most widely used devices are those providing electrogoniometric and floor-reaction force feedback (i.e., limb load monitors). These therapy aids are designed to provide patients and therapists with indications of limb positions or applied loads (Binder, 1981; Gapsis, Grabois, Borrell, Menken, & Kelly, 1982). After a few sessions, most patients can use the devices without constant supervision.

Kinematic Feedback

An electrogoniometer (see Figure 21.10) is simply a potentiometer (i.e., variable-resistor rheostat). Potentiometers are common: They control the volume of stereos and dim the room lights. Turning the potentiometer causes its resistance to electric currents to increase or decrease. Since voltage is inversely proportional to resistance, turning the potentiometer causes the stereo volume to change or the light's brightness to vary.

In gait measurement, two "arms" are attached to the potentiometer as in Figure 21.10—one to its base and the other to the movable rheostat. The arms are strapped to the limb segments, so joint rotation changes the potentiometer's resistance to current. Just as a 20° turn of the volume control knob on a stereo should always result in the same change of audio volume, so should a 20° knee flexion always result in the same change of voltage in an electrogoniometer. The voltage through the electrogoniometer is provided by a battery. Joint movement causes a pitch or buzz of known frequency from the audio feedback system (Gilbert, Maxwell, George, & McElhaney, 1982).

For example, a high pitch may indicate knee flexion, whereas a low pitch or no pitch tells the patient that the knee is extended and that it is therefore safe to accept weight for the ensuing stance phase. Frequently, the signal is dichotomized, so that knee flexion of more than 10° results in a warning signal, and silence indicates knee extension (Wooldridge, Leiper, & Ogston, 1976). Applications of the electrogoniometer to the therapist's knee will demonstrate "normal" knee motions and feedback tones. The patient attempts to simulate the normal pitch with the involved knee (Koheil & Mandel, 1980).

An electrogoniometer is especially useful in training an above-knee amputee how to control the prosthetic knee (Fernie, Holden, & Soto, 1978). Patients are instructed to load the prosthesis only when its knee is extended (i.e., only when the warning buzzer is not heard). After stance-phase weight bearing is safely achieved during prosthetic knee extension, joint-angle feedback may be employed to teach knee flexion during the swing phase.

Joint-position biofeedback, whether for patients with amputation, hemiplegia, or osteoarthritis, should proceed using the same general guidelines as any biofeedback therapy to attain relative normality. Positive reinforcement is emphasized, and the "two-thirds" success rule may be applied. Thus, patients must be given the opportunity to achieve successive approximations to normality, by setting the "error" warning range quite broadly during initial training and incrementing the tasks toward replication of normal (or safe!) kinematics as skill improves. Dichotomous feedback is often provided during initial training. I find that the introduction of continuous feedback is simply too much information for patients to act upon until a fairly normal gait is established.

It is critical that therapists be fully familiar with normal gait kinematics (see Figure 21.11). I have seen patients valiantly struggling to comply with the admonishments of therapists to dorsiflex beyond neutral during the swing phase, despite the fact that the ankle

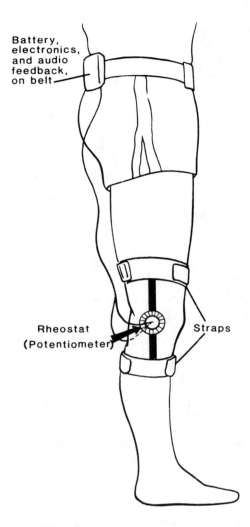

FIGURE 21.10. An electrogoniometer.

reaches only 0° or so during the swing. If the therapists had only applied the electro-goniometer to their own ankles, the futility of the task would have been obvious.

Therapists must appreciate the differences between normal persons' and amputees' gaits, because prostheses move quite differently from normal limbs. The normal knee flexes just after heel strike, at the beginning of the stance phase (see Figure 21.11). The knee then extends to about 7° and begins to flex again in anticipation of the swing phase. No commercially available prosthetic knees (except the BRADU "bouncy" knee from Nuffield Labs, England) allow this "double-flexion wave" in stance. Most prosthetic knees must remain fully extended, or the prosthesis will buckle during weight bearing.

It is important to be cognizant of the major compensations for neuromotor abnormality. For example, patients with paretic quadriceps will often compensate by strongly plantar flexing the shank during midstance, thus extending the knee. Ankle–foot orthoses

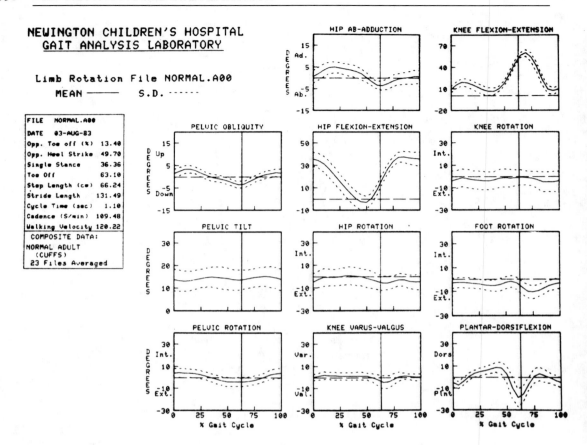

FIGURE 21.11. Gait kinematics of 14 healthy adults walking at their preferred rate on a smooth, level surface. *Solid line* indicated mean; *dashed line*, ± 1 standard deviation. Reprinted permission of Newington Children's Hospital, Newington, CT.

are frequently prescribed with the ankle set at 5° plantar flexion in order to help provide this extension moment to the knee. Training such patients to mimic normal knee kinematics will obviously result in a poor gait.

West Park Hospital, in Toronto, has devised a device for training knee control that may be useful for patients who persist in knee flexion while that limb is loaded. A buzzer is silent only if knee extension occurs while the foot switch, indicating stance phase, is closed. Although the system was designed for above-knee prosthesis training, it should be useful in training wearers of above-knee orthoses. For example, arthritic patients could be trained to bear weight on an involved limb more normally while simulating normal stance kinematics.

The components of an electrogoniometer are quite inexpensive and may be fabricated by anyone with a rudimentary knowledge of electricity (Gilbert et al., 1982). The engineering or electrical maintenance shops of most hospitals can provide a usable feedback device, using components costing less than $10. As long as the potentiometer is of high quality (i.e., > 90% linearity), it should be perfectly adequate for clinical purposes. Additional contingency or logic features, such as heel switches to indicate stance or swing phases, may be added, but are obviously "luxury" items.

Kinetic Feedback

A limb load monitor may be employed to provide patients with information regarding the amount or rate of loading on the lower limbs. Generally, an audio signal, linearly proportional to vertical load, warns patients of excessive or insufficient weight bearing.

The simplest type of limb load monitor is a foot switch (see Figure 21.12.) This biofeedback device is readily fabricated by any clinician. A tone generator (e.g., a buzzer) and speaker are connected in series with a battery to metal strips. When the strips are approximated during the stance phase, the circuit is completed, and audible feedback results. Although no indication of the amount of weight bearing can be discerned from foot-switch biofeedback, information regarding stance duration may help achieve symmetrical lower-limb timing.

One foot switch for each limb may be placed under the patient's heel, providing incentive to achieve heel strike at the beginning of each stance phase. Hemiplegic patients are asked to equalize duration of the audible tones from both foot strikes. This simple device can be used in the physical therapy department, or virtually anywhere. Switches attached to the heels of children with cerebral palsy (CP) have successfully decreased the frequency of "toe-walking" by reinforcing heel contact. Heel switches can also be used to document the efficacy of EMG relaxation therapy for spastic calf muscles in improving CP patients' gait.

Most limb load monitors in clinical use have provision for feedback of the amount of weight borne on a limb. In essence, a strain gauge is inserted between the floor and the patient's limb, usually into the sole of a sandal attached to the patient's shoe (see Figure 21.13). The two plates shown are really a type of transducer, so that as more weight is applied, resistance through the transducer decreases (Wolf & Binder-Macleod, 1982).

Limb load feedback is most often used to help patients attain partial weight bearing on a lower limb with a fracture or recent hip or knee endoprosthesis. A threshold level is set

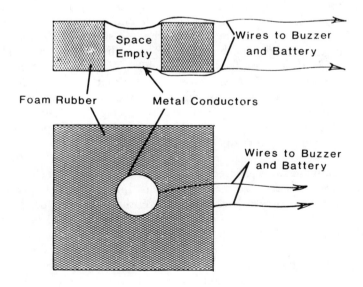

FIGURE 21.12. A simple foot switch. Contact of metal conductors during stance causes auditory or visual feedback.

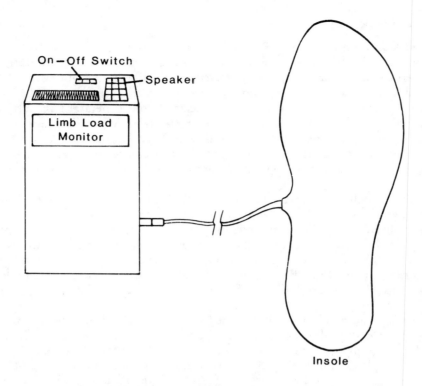

FIGURE 21.13. A more sophisticated limb load monitor.

to indicate the maximum allowable weight to be applied on the limb. When weight bearing exceeds the threshold, an audible tone is emitted. Thus, non- or partial-weight-bearing ambulation can be achieved by training, to keep the unit silent. In biofeedback with post-fracture gait training, elimination of the guesswork regarding weight on the limb is a most attractive feature of limb load biofeedback (Craik & Wannstedt, 1985; Wannstedt & Herman, 1978). Winstein et al. (1993), however, report that delayed, or summary, knowledge of results rather than concurrent biofeedback enhances both acquisition and retention of the skills needed for successful partial weight-bearing gait. Winstein et al. used only normal, healthy subjects, so more research on impaired populations precedes firm conclusions on biofeedback versus knowledge of results.

Encouraging patients to increase the load on their limbs, by progressively increasing the threshold as therapy sessions proceed, is somewhat more complex (Warren & Lehman, 1975). Successive approximation to the "normal" loading and time sequence, positive reinforcement, and the "two-thirds" success ratio incentive all remain operative.

Increasing limb stress can be accomplished by loading the limb horizontally as well as vertically. Limb load feedback is intended only to monitor the vertical component of the floor reaction force. Although fore–aft, torsional, and horizontal shear forces are well known from force-plate gait studies, limb load biofeedback essentially ignores these components, because of complex problems of measurement and patient-information processing. Clinically, this means that, especially during early and late stance when shear stresses are great, limb load monitors may provide invalid information regarding the forces the limb is experiencing. The practical result of the kinetic limitations of limb load monitors is often an artifactually high feedback at heel strike and toe off, especially during fast walking.

Krusen Research Center of Moss Rehabilitation Hospital in Philadelphia has reported (Wannstedt & Herman, 1978) that output from the device it has developed and markets, perhaps the most widely used limb load monitor, corresponds closely to the vertical component output from force plates during static standing and loading activities. However, I am not aware of research that reports the relationship between output from the biofeedback device and force plates from abnormal (e.g., hemiplegic or amputee) gait.

For the amputee, the ability to bear full weight on the prosthetic limb is critical, and vertical force kinetic feedback can be profitably employed for such patients (Kegel & Moore, 1977). Reports of technicians attempting to train above-knee amputees with force-plate readouts during gait have appeared. These were apparently designed to include the non-vertical components of kinetic biofeedback. Although laudable in theory, training of patients to simulate all components of normal gait kinetics is practically impossible. Practicing therapists must again recall that complex adaptations are used by amputees to attain energy-efficient gaits. No prosthetic knee (nor, indeed, a severely arthritic knee) can perform exactly like a normal knee, simply because it is physically quite unlike a normal knee. Thus, therapists are again cautioned against expecting biofeedback to cure all gait ills. The "errors" fed back to amputees may, in fact, be normal compensations of patients seeking to walk as efficiently as possible, given their mechanical limitations.

More recently, standing posture and kinetic biofeedback to reduce falls in the elderly have gained favor (Krebs, 1990; Hu & Woollacott, 1992). For example, Jobst (1989) randomly assigned 72 subjects with postural ataxia, primarily from encephalitis and cerebellar disease, to center-of-pressure biofeedback or physical training alone. Following treatment, the biofeedback group performed significantly better than the controls in locomotion and other ADL tasks.

Moore and Woollacott (1992) provide an excellent literature review describing the usefulness of biofeedback in patient treatment. Patients are encouraged to increase, reduce, or simply become aware of the normal postural sway experienced during quiet standing. There is at present no evidence that such feedback is helpful; there are several reports that such feedback is detrimental (Sheldon, 1963) or at best not helpful (Winstein et al., 1989). My colleagues and I suggest part of the problem may be that the wrong variable is fed back to the patients (Benda, Riley, & Krebs, 1994). Although most commercially available "posture and balance" feedback devices claim to monitor the subject's center of gravity, instead, all monitor the center of pressure beneath the feet. In normal quiet standing, the center of pressure and center of gravity do move together, but in subjects with poor balance or during locomotion, the center of pressure *must* be decoupled from the center of gravity (Zachazewski, Riley, & Krebs, 1993; Benda et al., 1994).

In summary, it would appear that clinical application of limb load feedback should be limited at present to informing patients of gross errors in timing and weight bearing.

Kinematic and Kinetic Biofeedback in a Clinical Setting

Therapists using both joint-position and force feedback should begin sessions by familiarizing patients with the equipment and the desired outcomes of therapy. Because biofeedback is essentially a learning process, I generally begin therapy sessions with gait training. Therapeutic exercise is tiring, and fatigue seems to interfere with skill acquisition. Most frequently, following an overview of the goals of therapy (including a gait demonstration from a normal subject, usually the therapist), the first session is devoted to static standing activities.

Biofeedback sessions should be brief, to avoid fatigue. With the patient in the parallel bars, training begins by practicing walking in place. Frequent rests should be interspersed with therapeutic trials of 30–60 seconds. If the idea of weight-bearing feedback is not quickly comprehended by a patient, I often use two bathroom scales (Peper & Robertson, 1976). For static biofeedback, these cheap and familiar devices are often overlooked in biofeedback's preoccupation with high technology!

After a patient can successfully perform the activity statically, weight shifting begins. The patient should be asked to advance the more involved limb while eliciting the appropriate biofeedback signal. By the second session, patients can usually shift their weight from limb to limb, and can practice stance- and swing-phase biofeedback. Once performance is error-free on over half (e.g., two-thirds or more) of the trials, ambulation for short distances can be attempted.

At this point, each patient should be reassessed. Questions that should be asked include: (1) Are the therapy goals appropriate for this patient? (2) Is biofeedback enhancing or interfering with progress in other areas of therapy?

Most sessions beyond the first two or three should include static weight shifting and dynamic gait activities, so the basic skills learned in the first sessions are not lost.

After the patient acquires ambulatory skills, it is imperative to check his or her performance without biofeedback. Gait should be a smooth, automatic, subconsciously controlled activity. In contrast, biofeedback requires voluntary attention to the tasks to be developed. Hesitation may develop if the patient attends excessively to the biofeedback instruments, thereby inhibiting normal gait.

While locomotor skills are developing, it is critical that normal walking speed be incorporated into the regimen. I have seen patients who could walk with fairly "normal" kinematics while using biofeedback, but when they were asked to walk at a normal pace (about 1 cycle per second), their control disappeared. I had neglected to train for the correct timing and speed of movement.

In summary, effective kinematic and kinetic biofeedback must start with appropriate goals. Hemiplegic patients should generally be encouraged to flex the affected knee during stance, but above-knee amputees should not. Application of lower-limb orthoses and prostheses will interact with gait, and they may require modification of treatment goals. Biofeedback therapy should always be targeted to achieve the most energy-efficient gait possible, consistent with safety and stability.

NEW CONCEPTS AND AREAS FOR FURTHER RESEARCH

Throughout this chapter, the role of biofeedback as an adjunctive modality in rehabilitation has been emphasized. Electronic monitoring devices can only be useful in informational feedback if they provide valid and timely data for patients and therapists. Movement brings measurement problems to any electrokinesiological feedback device, but without movement, neuromuscular re-education is pointless. Biofeedback during therapeutic exercise can be a helpful tool in increasing patient awareness, but it must not be allowed to act as a proxy for therapeutic exercise. Biofeedback is merely a powerful learning aid; by itself, it cannot hypertrophy muscles or increase limb mobility. Whether the feedback should be scheduled at infrequent intervals to provide "knowledge of results" or concurrent as in classic biofeedback remains unknown at this time, and this is one clear area for further research.

The addition of microcomputer interfaces to biofeedback-assisted therapy adds another dimension to information processing. Storing normal movement records in the microcomputer and subsequently requesting patients to approximate those movement patterns have been widely advertised to be effective in teaching neuromuscular skills. However, microcomputers, with their enormous memories, can easily overwhelm patients and therapists with information. Although new graphics and software programs are providing a means to simplify kinesiological biofeedback, it still remains the responsibility of therapists to provide valid therapy paradigms. With the increasing three-dimensional imaging capacity of modern medicine, I believe that one concept soon to make its way into biofeedback practice will be three-dimensional limb motion feedback. Already "virtual reality" environment devices are used for entertainment; some of my colleagues are using these computer assisted three-dimensional images for biofeedback to patients. How long it will be before fully three-dimensional motion images (see, e.g., Krebs, 1992) are available for therapeutic biofeedback is anyone's guess.

Much research is required before the enormous potential of biofeedback can be fully exploited. Studies of information feedback and human information processing are far from complete. Current knowledge of electromyographic, kinematic, and kinetic parameters and their relationship to functional activities is, at this time, quite crude. For example, one of the greatest practical impediments now facing clinicians is ignorance of the muscle force–EMG relationship during nonisometric contractions. How weight bearing and timing control are reflected by kinematic and kinetic gait measurements of persons with lower-limb disability is also unclear. Worse, little information exists on the gait patterns of slow-walking normal persons; current data are primarily from young normal subjects.

Electronic advances should be exploited clinically to the advantage of disabled populations. Biofeedback is a very promising adjunctive modality for neuromuscular re-education.

GLOSSARY

ACETYLCHOLINE. Transmitter released by motor neuron that diffuses across the synaptic cleft to begin a muscle action potential.

AGONIST. A muscle directly involved in contraction and opposed by the action of an antagonist muscle that needs to relax for proper function of the agonist muscle. For example, to bend the elbow, the biceps brachii muscle, as the agonist, contracts, and the triceps muscle is the antagonist. Contrast with *antagonist.*

ANKLE DORSIFLEXOR. A dorsiflexor muscle flexes or turns upward, as the foot or toes. Bending or inverting the foot toward the extensor (anterior) aspect of the leg using the tibialis anterior muscle. (See *anterior tibialis* muscle.)

ANTAGONIST. A muscle that opposes or resists the action of an agonist muscle or prime mover. Can impede the action of another muscle. Also, balances opposite forces, thus helping produce smooth movement. (See *agonist.*)

ANTERIOR TIBIALIS (TIBIALIS ANTERIOR). Arises from the tibia to and across the ankle. Dorsiflexes the foot. (See *ankle dorsiflexor.*)

COMMON-MODE REJECTION RATIO (CMRR). See text and Chapter 4.

DICHOTOMOUS. Two exclusive conditions, such as on or off.

ELECTROGONIOMETER. A potentiometer. A variable-resistor rheostat. Example of use in physical therapy is training knee flexion and, for above-knee amputees, to control prosthetic knee. (See text.)

ENDOPROSTHESIS, HIP OR KNEE. Endo- is a prefix designating *within*. An endoprosthesis of the hip or knee is within the hip or knee.

EXTEROCEPTION. An exteroceptor is a sensory nerve terminal stimulated by the immediate external environment such as the skin and mucous membranes. Contrast with proprioception.

F+. Physical therapy MMT rating of fair-plus.

G–. Physical therapy MMT rating of good or less.

INPUT IMPEDANCE. See Chapter 4.

KNEE ARTHROTOMY. Large surgical incision into a joint, in this case a knee.

KR. Knowledge of results. Contrast with biofeedback.

LOCOMOTOR. Relating to locomotion (walking) and body apparatus for locomotion.

MEGOHM. One million ohms.

MENISCECTOMY. Surgical removal of meniscus cartilage from a knee. This is the cartilage between the ends of the bones of the thigh and lower leg.

MMT SCORES. Physical therapy technique to scale muscle performance.

MUSCLE ACTION POTENTIAL. Change in electrical potential of stimulated nerve or muscle fibers. Responsible for EMG signal.

OHM'S LAW. Resistance or impedance is inversely related to voltage. (See Chapter 4.)

PARETIC MUSCLES. Slight or incomplete paralysis of a muscle.

PERONEAL PALSY. Paralysis related to the fibula or lateral (outer) portion of the leg.

QUADRICEPS MUSCLES. Great leg extensor muscles forming main muscle on the front of the thigh and covering the front and side of the femur. Actually four muscles—rectus femoris, vastus intermedius, vastus lateralis, vastus medialis. Control movement and stability of the knee.

ROM. Range of motion.

SARCOPLASMIC RETICULUM. "Network of fine tubules, similar to endoplasmic reticulum, present in muscle tissues. . . . Composed of or containing sarcoplasm—semifluid interfibrillary substance of striated muscle cells. The cytoplasm of muscle cells" (Thomas, 1989).

SERVOMECHANICAL FEEDBACK. "A servomechanism is a control system in which feedback is used to control errors in another system" (*Dorland's Illustrated Medical Dictionary*, 1985, p. 1194).

SYNAPTIC CLEFT. Synapse is the junction between nerve cells. This is the narrow extracellular gap of millionth of an inch between the pre- and postsynaptic cell membranes at the synapse. Nerve impulses pass through this gap from one nerve to another by release of a transmitter substance and reception on the next one.

TRICEPS SURAE. Triceps muscle, muscle on the back of the upper arm.

VOLUME-CONDUCTED ARTIFACT. Signals from nearby muscles inadvertently picked up by surface electrodes on other muscles (see text).

REFERENCES

Barton, L. A. & Wolf, S. L. (1992). Is EMG feedback a successful adjunct to neuromuscular rehabilitation? *Physical Therapy Practice* 2(2),41–49.
Basmajian, J. V. (1974). *Muscles alive* (3rd ed.). Baltimore: Williams & Wilkins.

Battye, C. K., Nightingale, A., & Whillis, J. (1955). The use of myoelectric currents in the operation of prostheses. *Journal of Bone and Joint Surgery, 37B*, 506.

Benda, B. J., Riley, P. O., Krebs, D. E. (1994). Biomechanical relationship between center of gravity and center of pressure during standing. *IEEE Transactions on Rehabilitation Engineering, 2*, 3–10.

Berger, N., & Huppert, C. R. (1952). The use of electrical and mechanical muscular forces for the control of an electrical prosthesis. *American Journal of Occupational Therapy, 6*, 110–114.

Binder, S. A. (1981). Assessing the effectiveness of positional Feedback to treat an ataxic patient: Application of a single-subject design. *Physical Therapy, 61*, 735–736.

Brooks, V. B. (Ed.). (1981). *Handbook of physiology* (Sec. 1: *The nervous system*, Vol. 2: *Motor control* [Part I]). Bethesda, MD: American Physiological Society.

Cataldo, M. E., Bird, B. L., & Cunningham, C. E. (1978). Experimental analysis of EMG feedback in treating cerebral palsy. *Journal of Behavioral Medicine, 1*, 311–322.

Childress, D. S. (1973). An approach to powered grasp. In M. M. Gavrilovic & A. B. Wilson Jr. (Eds.), *Advances in external control of human extremities*. Belgrade: Yugoslav Committee for Electronics and Automation.

Colborne, G. R., Olney, S. J., & Griffin, M. P. (1993). Feedback of ankle joint angle and soleus electromyography in the rehabilitation of hemiplegic gait. *Archives of Physical Medicine and Rehabilitation, 74*, 1100–1106.

Craik, R. L., & Wannstedt, G. T. (1975). The limb load monitor: An augmented sensory feedback device. In *Proceedings of a conference on Devices and Systems for the Disabled* (pp. 19–24). Philadelphia, PA: Krusen Research Center.

Dorland's illustrated medical dictionary (26th ed.). Philadelphia, PA: W. B. Saunders.

Druckman, D., & Bjork, R. A. (Eds.) (1991). *In the mind's eye: Enhancing human performance*. Washington, DC: National Academy Press.

Fernie, G., Holden, J., & Soto, M. (1978). Biofeedback training of knee control in the above-knee amputee. *American Journal of Physical Medicine, 57*, 161–166.

Gable, C. D., Shea, C. H., & Wright, D. L. (1991). Summary knowledge of results. *Research Quarterly for Exercise and Sport, 62*, 285–292.

Gapsis, J. J., Grabois, M., Borrell, R. M., Menken, S. A., & Kelly, M. (1982). Limb load monitor: Evaluation of a sensory feedback device for controlled weight bearing. *Archives of Physical Medicine and Rehabilitation, 63*, 38–41.

Gilbert, J. A., Maxwell, G. M., George, R. T. Jr., & McElhaney, J. H. (1982). Technical note—Auditory feedback of knee angle for amputees. *Prosthetics and Orthotics International, 6*, 103–104.

Herman, R. M., Grillner, S., Stein, P. S. G., & Stuart, D. G. (Eds.). (1967). *Neural control of locomotion*. New York: Plenum Press.

Hu, M. H., & Woollacott, M. H. (1992). A training program to improve standing balance under different sensory conditions. In M. H. Woollacott & F. Horak (Eds.), *Posture and gait: Control mechanisms*. Portland, OR: University of Portland Books.

Inglis, J., Campbell, D., & Donald, M. W. (1976). Electromyographic biofeedback and neuromuscular rehabilitation. *Canadian Journal of Behavioral Science, 8*, 299–323.

Jobst, U. (1989). Posturographic-biofeedback-training (bei gleichgewichtsstorungen). *Fortschrift Neurology und Psychiatry, 57*, 74–80.

Keefe, F. J., & Surwit, R. S. (1978). Electromyographic feedback: Behavioral treatment of neuromuscular disorders. *Journal of Behavioral Medicine, 1*, 13–25.

Kegel, B., & Moore, A. J. (1977). Load cell: A device to monitor weight bearing for lower extremity amputees. *Physical Therapy, 57*, 652–654.

Koheil, R., & Mandel, A. R. (1980). Joint position biofeedback facilitation of physical therapy in gait training. *American Journal of Physical Medicine, 59*, 288–297.

Krebs, D. E. (1981). Clinical electromyographic feedback following meniscectomy: A multiple regression experimental analysis. *Physical Therapy, 61*, 1017–1021.

Krebs, D. E. (1987). *Prehension assessment: Prosthetic therapy for the upper-limb child amputee*. Philadelphia: Charles B. Slack.

Krebs, D. E. (1989). Isokinetic, electrophysiologic and clinical function relationships following tourniquet-aided arthrotomy. *Physical Therapy, 69,* 803–815.

Krebs, D. E. (1990). Biofeedback in therapeutic exercise. In J. V. Basmajian & S. L. Wolf (Eds.), *Therapeutic exercise* (5th ed., pp. 109–124). Baltimore, MD: Williams & Wilkins.

Krebs, D. E. (1992). Seize the moment: Dynamics and estimated moments of force in locomotion analysis. In *12th Annual Eugene Michels Researchers' Forum* (pp. 109–119). Alexandria, VA: American Physical Therapy Association.

Krebs, D. E., Stables, W. H., Cuttita, D., Chui, C. T., & Zickel, R. E. (1982). Relationship of tourniquet time to post-operative quadriceps function (Abstr). *Physical Therapy, 62,* 670.

Krebs, D. E., Stables, W. H., Cuttita, D., & Zickel, R. E. (1983). Knee joint angle: Its relationship to quadriceps femoris activity in normal and postarthrotomy limbs. *Archives of Physical Medicine and Rehabilitation, 64,* 441–447.

Lenman, J. A. E. (1959). Quantitative electromyographic changes associated with muscular weakness. *Journal of Neurology, Neurosurgery and Psychiatry, 22,* 306–310.

Lippold, O. C. J. (1952). Relation between integrated action potentials in human muscle and its isometric tension. *Journal of Physiology, 117,* 492–499.

Moore, S. & Woollacott, M. H. (1992). The use of biofeedback devices to improve postural stability. *Physical Therapy Practice 2*(2), 1–19.

Mulder, T., & Hulstyn, W. (1984). Sensory feedback therapy and theoretical knowledge of motor control and learning. *American Journal of Physical Medicine, 63,* 226–244.

Nelson, A. J. (1976). Fusimotor influence on performance of ankle dorsiflexors in young adults. *Physiotherapy, 62,* 117–122.

Peper, E., & Robertson, J. (1976). Biofeedback use of common objects: The bathroom scale in physical therapy. *Biofeedback and Self-Regulation, 1,* 237–240.

Popat, R. A., Krebs, D. E., Mansfield, J., Russell, D., Clancy, E., Gill, K. M., & Hogan, N. (1993). Quantitative assessment of four men using above-elbow prosthetic control. *Archives of Physical Medicine and Rehabilitation, 74,* 720–729.

Schleenbaker, R. E., & Mainous A. G. (1993). Electromyographic biofeedback for neuromuscular re-education in the hemiplegic stroke patient: A meta-analysis. *Archives of Physical Medicine and Rehabilitation, 74,* 1301–1304.

Sheldon, J. H. (1963). The effect of age on the control of sway. *Gerontologia Clinicica, 5,* 129.

Sherman, R. A., & Arena, J. G. (1992). Biofeedback in the assessment and treatment of low back pain. In J. V. Basmajian & R. Nyberg (Eds.), *Spinal manipulation therapies* (pp. 177–197). Baltimore, MD: Williams & Wilkins.

Shiavi, R., Champion, S., Freeman, F., & Griffin, P. (1981). Variability of electromyographic patterns for level-surface walking through a range of self-selected speeds. *Bulletin of Prosthetic Research, 10*(35), 5–14.

Thomas, C. L. (Ed.). (1989). *Taber's cyclopedic medical dictionary.* Philadelphia, PA: Davis.

Wannstedt, G. T., & Herman, R. M. (1978). Use of augmented sensory feedback to achieve symmetrical standing. *Physical Therapy, 58,* 553–559.

Warren, C. G., & Lehmann, J. F. (1975). Training procedures and biofeedback methods to achieve controlled partial weightbearing: An assessment. *Archives of Physical Medicine and Rehabilitation, 56,* 449–455.

Winstein, C. J., Gardner, E. R., McNeal, D. R., et al. (1989). Standing balance training: Effect on balance and locomotion in hemiparetic adults. *Archives of Physical Medicine and Rehabilitation, 70,* 755.

Winstein, C. J., Christensen, S., & Fitch N. (1993). Effects of summary knowledge of results on the acquisition and retention of partial weight bearing during gait. *Physical Therapy Practice, 2*(4), 40–51.

Winter, D. A. (1984). Pathologic gait diagnosis with computer-averaged electromyographic profiles. *Archives of Physical Medicine and Rehabilitation, 65,* 393–398.

Wirta, R. W., Taylor, D. R., & Finley, F. R. (1978). Pattern-recognition arm prosthesis: A historical perspective—A final report. *Bulletin of Prosthetic Research, 10*(30), 8–35.

Wolf, S. L., & Binder-Macleod, S. A. (1982). Use of the Krusen limb load monitor to quantify temporal and loading measurements of gait. *Physical Therapy, 62,* 976–982.

Wooldridge, C. P., Leiper, C., & Ogston, D. G. (1976). Biofeedback training of knee joint position of the cerebral palsied child. *Physiotherapy Canada, 28,* 138–143.

Yang, J. F., & Winter, D. A. (1984). Electromyographic amplitude normalization methods: Improving their sensitivity as diagnostic tools in gait analysis. *Archives of Physical Medicine and Rehabilitation, 65,* 517–521.

Zachazewski J. E., Riley P. O., & Krebs, D. E. (1993). Biomechanical analysis of body mass transfer during stair ascent and descent in normal subjects. *Journal of Rehabilitation Research and Development, 30,* 412–422.

22

Biofeedback-Assisted Musculoskeletal Therapy and Neuromuscular Re-Education

Eric R. Fogel

This chapter focuses on selected biofeedback techniques for specific applications in physical therapy and muscle re-education. I discuss the rationale and limitations of specific clinical biofeedback techniques that can help patients be more aware of how to use their bodies and aid their learning.

The therapy techniques of physical rehabilitation differ in many ways from other biofeedback interventions. The differences include the patient's neurological status, structural deformities, and levels of awareness. The feedback process is "assistive" because the feedback information acts as an adjunct to the therapist's knowledge and skills in assisting the therapy.

Using biofeedback instrumentation expands the patient's natural and internal biofeedback and allows the patient to be aware of self-induced changes. Physical and occupational therapies always try to help patients increase their physiological self-regulation within their natural environments. External biofeedback offers unique chances for such help to be more direct and effective. The major advantages are the increased speed of the information and the therapist's more accurate observation of the physiological activity and changes. Therapists help patients change their awareness and reactions and help them incorporate new physical activities into new routines and habits.

To work more effectively with biofeedback, all therapists from all disciplines, should understand learning theories including operant conditioning. Therapists set up goals and help patients develop new skills, feelings, routines, and functions that improve patients' lives. There is a constant need for reassessment and changing of therapy programs. Therapy is an interaction between the therapist and the patient, with the biofeedback instrument functioning as an observer and partner. There are conditions when patients need feedback time alone to practice newly developed skills and further advance these skills toward becoming habits. I do not advise leaving rehabilitation patients alone with augmented biofeedback when they are first trying to change physiological activity.

During therapy, many events often take place that are beyond therapists' understanding of patients' needs. A therapist in one discipline often lacks training and experience in other disciplines. Such a therapist could incorrectly miss a deteriorating situation or one that is inconsistent with positive change. Ethical clinicians practice within the scope of their professional education, training, and license. Therefore, interdisciplinary referral and cooperation are essentials to successful therapy.

To set up biofeedback within musculoskeletal and neuromuscular re-education, one must follow sound therapy practices of rehabilitation programs. External biofeedback instruments cannot substitute for a good evaluation, realistic therapy, and proper consideration of the patient's physiological and environmental limitations. Although augmented biofeedback can speed up therapy, one must still work toward realistic goals. In clinical applications, one must measure a patient's rate of progress in terms of "functional improvement."

Wolf and his colleagues (Wolf, Regenos, & Basmajian, 1977) developed a measurement scale for grading patients as they make functional progress. This scale is particularly applicable to patients who have had cerebral vascular accidents (CVAs). One must not make the mistake of only measuring a patient's improvement in muscle activity measured by the instruments. I discuss this further in the instrument section of this chapter.

Research criteria often differ from clinical criteria. The goal of clinical therapy is patient improvement. In addition to providing information for learning, biofeedback can provide a valuable source of added documentation for the "functional" clinical improvements approaching therapy goals. Statistically significant changes are insufficient justification for protocols using biofeedback.

It is important to again stress the importance of therapists' having skills to help patients become aware of that which the therapists are trying to convey. It is essential to know the instrumentation capabilities and how to focus and reinforce patients' attention to information shown by the instruments. Later in this chapter, I discuss various procedures that help accomplish this in clinical applications.

Before discussing criteria for starting biofeedback, I remind therapists that their attitudes and interests in the therapy and patient are strong positive reinforcers. A therapist's absence from the room and/or a rigid therapy regime can often be interpreted by a patient negatively and can contribute to a lack of success.

CONSIDERATION IN IMPLEMENTING AND USING BIOFEEDBACK THERAPY

The field of biofeedback still does not have as many precise physiological criteria for its use and for therapy progress as are desired. However, there are criteria that are clear through clinical observation and cataloging of information such as criteria for when to use biofeedback. For example, research by Wolf (1982) showed that decreased proprioceptive awareness may be one of the crucial factors in muscle re-education. A patient compensates somewhat for the lack of position perception with muscle or positional feedback. However, the transference of skills to activities of daily living (ADL) depends upon the patient's ability to derive other forms of "self-feedback." The patient must incorporate new skills into new movement patterns.

One clear advantage of electromyographic (EMG) biofeedback, as in the treatment of peripheral nerve injury, is its ability to help the patient to exercise an affected muscle before he or she has perceptible muscle movement. Thus, with an incomplete lesion, biofeedback allows for developing activation and functional use via feedback from the remaining intact motor units.

Basmajian's (1977) research showed that humans could control single motor units. Therapists hope to get muscle "hypertrophy" or "budding" to occur through actively exercising the remaining motor units. It is not clear that feedback can increase the chance of "sprouting" or "budding." However, active exercises with strength development and motor unit recruitment or muscle activation may increase the chance of "functional improvement." This leads to a second criterion.

One must establish whether the final goal of therapy is mostly strength or refined control. An example of a strength goal is strengthening the quadriceps to support the knee. If refined control is the goal sought, then the chances of improvement lessen if the patient's diagnosis involves loss of motor units such as with anterior poliomyelitis. Improvements in facial expression or hand control are other typical goals involving refined control.

Proper diagnosis, appropriate and complete evaluation, and careful planning are needed for successful results. For emphasis, I again mention the importance of using feedback to develop useful skills that will be used by the patient to maintain functional control. Learning may be accelerated by developing progressive exercise homework that is directly connected to actual events learned by the patient at the clinic. Studies by Wolf (1982) indicate that the retention of skills and the transference of them to daily living are much more successful if the strength is coupled with the functional activity during the therapy process.

A third factor affecting implementing biofeedback therapy is the presence of both normal and pathological reflex activity. Historically, clinical and research reports first indicated the possibility of reducing spasticity with the use of biofeedback. I observed that some patients improve their ability to control the secondary effects caused by spasticity and can reduce the number of reflex spasms. I believe it is a secondary effect resulting from the maintained reduction of muscle tone, which also may reduce the stress on the protective reflex system. During exercise programs, I found it helpful to stretch the involved muscle, teach maintenance of this lengthened state, and strengthen the antagonist muscle to maintain the integrity of the corrected position. When working with patients who have spasticity, I believe that this process may allow for a possible reseting of the muscle tone protection system (as in ankle clonus). The clonus activity may change from stretch-induced, passive dorsiflexion at 25° plantar flexion to a delay at 5° dorsiflexion. The arc of clonus is thus brought within functional levels. I discuss the use of reflex activity positioning to facilitate activities later in this chapter.

Many patients come for therapy following traumatization of a body part (physical or psychological) and "splinting" or "bracing" muscle activity developed to protect that body segment. Such muscle activity initially may have had functional value, by preventing movement, providing security, and, in broad terms, shielding an area from further trauma. The duration and frequency of the "protective spasm" may determine the level of structural change that occurred in the muscle. A realistic and functional goal for corrective change is to bring the patient to the point of maximum pain-free use of the affected body part rather than a goal based on an instrument's numerical readouts.

Chronically increased muscle tone distorts the sensory perception of a body part. After therapeutic correction, a therapist may often hear the patient say, "That doesn't feel right to me." The patient must then learn to become comfortable with the corrected position and incorporate it into his or her daily activities.

The process of becoming aware of one's body is often contingent on many physical and emotional factors. Teaching someone to change his or her "body image" may require an interdisciplinary approach with careful operant conditioning. Classic examples of diagnoses with distorted sensory perception are CVA, reflex dystrophy, amputation, and severe trauma. Some clinicians may show surprise at how much more easily instrumentation-based feedback can communicate information to patients than methods without the instruments. A therapist's more complicated and uncertain verbal attempts may be very confusing to a patient with sensory distortion. The instrument can become a patient's only contact with his or her internal environment. An old but still useful article by Marinacci and Horande

(1960) discusses the use of EMG feedback for muscle re-education, the causes of loss of body use, return of muscle function, and progression of return.

In summary, I remind clinicians to be aware of the patient's presenting diagnosis, all physical and psychological factors, realistic goals based on stages of graduated progression, and the need to periodically change the patient's therapy program.

POSITIVE AND AVERSIVE REINFORCEMENT

Positive reinforcement is usually more effective than aversive reinforcement. However, sometimes adding aversive consequences for a competing behavior is more effective for strengthening a specific alternative behavior. Therapists must tailor reinforcers for each patient.

When using biofeedback in the treatment of spasmodic torticollis, one can use the combination of positive and aversive consequences (Brudny, Grynbaum, & Korein, 1974). That study compared EMG feedback to reduce the unwanted muscle spasm in one sterno-mastoid muscle with mild electric shock to the other side. The study also discussed the importance of strengthening the muscle on the opposing side[1]—the antagonist.

TREATMENT DEVELOPMENT

It is desirable to use biofeedback within a conceptual approach. Awareness training is a concept running through all of the therapies I use, although not the only conceptual approach for using biofeedback. In the discussion that follows I assume that the suggestions are only selected possible methods for managing difficult therapy situations.

When treating a patient with an upper motor neuron disorder, such as from a CVA, the practitioner must first assess dominant reflex patterns and functional capabilities. One directs progressive goals for learning toward EMG-assisted control over parts of neurological reflex patterns. The patient strengthens "static controlled behavior" and then progresses to actively disrupting these patterns during activity. The newly learned skills are directed toward more functional patterns. This treatment approach is founded on Brunnstrom's approach to therapy (Brunnstrom, 1970).

One may use other forms of therapy while monitoring with EMG biofeedback. The EMG feedback continuously informs the patient of muscle status regarding activity or inactivity. By repeatedly attending to the signal, the patient remains aware of "what is going on." Two additional approaches toward muscle training are proprioceptive neuromuscular facilitation (Knott & Voss, 1969) and the use of facilitation and inhibition vibratory techniques as suggested by Hagbarth and Eklund (1969) and Hagbarth (1973). During vibratory facilitation techniques, the EMG feedback signals the patient to be attentive to changing muscle status.

One may evoke muscle reactions by using other facilitory or inhibitory techniques. Rapid stretching of a muscle or reducing the stretch placed on a muscle will each cause a change in muscle tone. One then directs therapy efforts toward making the patient recognize and be able to reproduce the target response. The patient must work to maximize the control of this activity and to incorporate this activity into functional patterns.

---

[1]A postural muscle that is in spasm for a long time is stronger than the opposing muscle, thus requiring strengthening of the side not in spasm.

Failure to control environmental factors during therapy sessions may lead to false or misleading feedback signals. For this reason, proper structuring of therapy sessions is critical. Important questions to ask oneself while designing the therapy session are: (1) Is the monitor site "gravity dependent" or supported; (2) Is a monitored muscle being stretched quickly or over a prolonged period of time; and (3) Does the patient's body position facilitate or inhibit muscle influencing sensory input patterns? Case descriptions presented later in this chapter suggest some positional and environmental controls. Therapists familiar with manual muscle testing positions can use this knowledge to isolate target muscles in an attempt to create greater specificity of signal.

There are many other neuromuscular re-education techniques that benefit the learning process. A therapy goal is to create an environment in which a patient can learn new tasks without being distracted by dominant patterns and pain. Many patients have secondary factors associated with their condition. Thus, it is often necessary to attend to these needs first. The therapist must create a learning environment by eliminating any overriding dominant symptoms. Later in this chapter, I discuss a progression of techniques that I found helpful for controlling the secondary symptoms and promoting the desired goal.

At this point I must mention the importance of developing patients' responsibility for their own health care. There are various available assessment methods to determine how patients relate to their condition. The therapist must not allow patients to isolate their learning to the clinic environment. Each patient should understand the instrumentation and how it provides a means to increase physiological control elsewhere. Homework assignments and training sessions should be structured around functional activities. The more closely a learned activity resembles daily living, the greater the chance the patient will learn it as part of his or her normal routine.

A GENERAL TREATMENT STRATEGY

Patients often are in pain or have some debilitating aspect to their posture when they first present themselves. Many patients have various means of achieving instant relief, but these are usually of short duration. One goal of therapy is to provide a means for correction of long duration and for prevention of a return of symptoms. A corrective therapy process may be long in duration when compared to the patient's own quick relief methods. Therapists often need to provide temporary relief before trying to help a patient achieve self-regulation. Compliance can increase when the patient no longer worries about the pain.

In attempts to create a positive progression with each patient, the following are the steps used in my professional practice:

1. Pain suppression. Use the most effective method. This varies among patients.
2. Awareness therapy.

   a. *Postural.*
   b. *Functional.* The goal is for patients to prevent symptoms from occurring by becoming aware of early warning signs (subclinical) that produce symptoms.

3. Self-control and preventative measures (reduction of clinical intervention).

   a. *Postural awareness* (during functional activities).
   b. *Therapeutic exercise* (to strengthen newly learned positions and posture).
   c. *Pain reduction techniques* (self-initiated methods).
   d. *Homework* (designed to strengthen newly learned skills during activities of daily living).

4. *Progressive therapeutic exercise* (with realistic goals).
   a. *Homework* (self-regulation away from the clinic).
   b. *Reassessment* (evaluate functional value of new skills).
   c. *Progressing of program* (attempt to maximize training results).
   d. *Review.* At later date, determine if learned skills have been habituated and if further beneficial learning can be achieved.

During this process, the therapist's job is re-evaluating and adjusting the goals for each patient. The therapist must frequently assess functional improvement and potential structural changes. One sometimes enhances additional learning with ambulatory instruments or "home trainers." I discuss these later in this chapter.

There is also a need to quantify results and measure changes in therapy programs. Beyond statistical purposes, such quantification can help justify the existence and continued use of therapies and thereby provide the therapist with important feedback.

INSTRUMENTATION CAPABILITIES AND MEASUREMENT

Most of the therapeutic procedures described in this chapter use EMG feedback. Feedback does not have to involve elaborate or complicated instrumentation. One can use inexpensive instrumentation and devices with effective therapeutic procedures.

Neophytes in this field may consider conventional surface-electrode-based EMG biofeedback to be the answer to all of their quantification needs. If everyone used needle electrodes and adhered to strict research methodology and techniques, then EMG might well meet everyone's quantification needs. To measure muscles located more than one layer below the skin surface, however, needle electrodes or indwelling wires for accurate assessment must be used. Surface measurement technology has consistently improved over the last 10 years, but there are still limitations in the use of some equipment when one is trying to monitor activity during movement.

There has been considerable development in the specificity of surface EMG technology, and this has expanded the use of surface electromyography. Although this new technology has produced a desirable preciseness of signal, the technology of feedback to the patient has progressed more slowly. Evaluation of surface muscles during movement depends on the specificity of signal, the selection of target muscles, the interpretation of statistical recordings, the reproducibility of results, and the development of templates for movement patterns. Biomechanical evaluation of movement patterns is not merely a measurement of surface electromyographic activity. When a person moves, the muscle system works in an elaborate coordination of synergists, antagonists, agonists, stabilizers, and prime movers. The elaborate relationship of muscle synergy, antagonist, agonist, stabilizer, and prime movers has not been clearly established. Multisite recordings of one system of the body may be deceptively simple when compared to self-regulation during movement of all those sites. "Functional activity" again becomes the focus of concentration for therapy.

Readers might ask, why use biofeedback at all? If you can obtain and maintain a useable signal and transform it to a functional task, feedback can speed the learning process and increase the amount of information that a patient can learn.[2]

[2]See Chapter 3B for other discussion of the biofeedback signal within the definition of biofeedback and understanding how it probably helps behavior change.

To create a learning environment for your patient, you must first understand certain characteristics of both your patient and the biofeedback instrument. Evaluate the patient for sensory awareness. The choice of primary feedback should communicate with the patient's dominant and controllable sensory system (e.g., visual, auditory, tactile, proprioceptive).

Electromyography remains the leading source of feedback, but there are many other forms of feedback information. Force-plate feedback for proprioceptive feedback and goniometry for angular change feedback are examples. Instrument displays are now more sophisticated and often more complicated than a few years ago. The teaching system that you use should remain clear to the patient.

The EMG feedback instrumentation should have certain capabilities to facilitate therapy. First, the placement of electrodes should isolate the muscle's signal as much as possible. The therapeutic task is to facilitate an event, rather than simply to make a recording. The therapist should be more careful about the consistency of electrode placement across sessions and what activity is being positively reinforced than about the specificity of a signal.

A suggested method of controlling the feedback sampling is offered by Basmajian (1979). You can reduce or increase the area of muscle that you monitor by spreading the distance between electrodes or placing them more closely aligned.

Two types of feedback are essential for enhancing the therapy process: continuous and threshold. The type used can affect the results. The next step is deciding whether to use continuous feedback or to set up a threshold criterion.

When using continuous feedback, one provides a patient with a signal that reflects the entire range of muscle activity. The patient can investigate different feelings and see the response these cause on the continuous feedback. This may be more helpful in the initial learning of a new skill. Continuous feedback gives information about the total distance of the patient from the desired behavior.

Threshold feedback restricts feedback to the presence or absence of desired physiological activity. I find threshold settings helpful to refine general responses. Threshold feedback also refines the reinforcement contingencies for specific behaviors within general response patterns. This helps speed the transference to functional activity. Your choice of whether to use continuous or threshold feedback depends on the therapy goal.

Biofeedback instruments also should contain a wide range for the audio feedback and different times for the signal to cross the computer screen. This differentiates very small changes in physiological activity and helps show precise control. The audio feedback is particularly effective for ambulatory activities and those activities where visual displays are impractical. Use the volume control for accentuating or reducing the sound.

More than one channel allows one to switch target sites without repetitious preparation. Feedback instruments also should include scales (gains) such as fractions of a microvolt. This permits measurement and monitoring within a very small range of physiological activity. It helps differentiate very small changes in physiological activity and shows precise control. Ease of operation and mobility also are important.

GENERAL CLINICAL PROCEDURES

Intake Processes

Designing a biofeedback program for the specific needs of one's patients obviously requires planning and careful thought. First, one needs general intake procedures. Not every patient is suitable for biofeedback. One must be selective and identify good candidates.

Evaluations include physical and psychological status. The medical diagnosis provides criteria for establishing some expectations. This does not mean that patients with the same condition will have similar results. One must be aware of each patient's neurological progression and clinical signs of improvement versus regression, and one must constantly rate progress. When there is no progress, re-evaluation may lead to work with another body part, to focus on separate functions, to the use of other techniques, or perhaps to the use of other feedback or instruments. Being aware of the patient's interest can help one modify the program.

Evaluation includes identification of any central nervous system (CNS) disorders or upper-motor-neuron lesions. Predominant reflex patterns, tonic reflexes, hyperreflexia, strength, range of motion, and the patient's attention span must all be part of the assessment. Peripheral nerve injuries and lower-motor-neuron lesions require several different assessments, including severity of nerve injury (complete or incomplete), the degree of sensory loss, muscle flaccidity, and whatever mental association the patient has with the body part. The degree to which the patient has phantom pain and negative emotional associations with his or her condition should be analyzed.

Included in the physical analysis is a posture component. The therapist checks the patient's structural and functional posture during both rest and activity. One must analyze how an adverse posture developed and whether it is correctable without any further detriment to the patient. There are some basic procedures that can make these tasks easier. One should first direct efforts toward reducing antagonist muscle spasm before trying to facilitate agonist strength. This applies to reducing splinting activity that protects or supports a joint and its associated body part. A helpful guide to targeting a muscle is to locate the pain or "trigger" points (Travell & Simons, 1983) to reduce the discomfort, and then to stretch and teach spasm reduction in the involved muscles.

It is helpful to determine the speed at which a patient can release the involved muscle. My experience agrees with that of Wolf (1982) and suggests that the release of the involved muscle must be done during activities related to the functional goal. It is therefore important to use feedback while "putting the patients through their paces" in routine activities.

Frequency of Office Sessions

The frequency of office sessions is another important consideration. A therapist should tailor the frequency of sessions to each patient's needs. Normally, I see my patients three times a week until they appear to have some control of the tasks; then, I reduce the frequency to create independence both from the therapist and the biofeedback instruments. Sessions often last from 45 minutes to 1 hour but may be shorter if a patient becomes too fatigued or frustrated. When the patient achieves independence from the instruments, the therapist can reduce the office sessions to once every other week for about another 6 weeks. One may then decide to discharge the patient to a home-care program and again review the patient in either 3 or 6 months. The review time depends upon the severity of the condition being treated, the learned goals, and the patient's retention. Patients receiving relaxation therapy are obviously different from neuromuscular rehabilitation patients and may require less frequent sessions.

Three to five feedback sessions addressing poor kinesiological or functional behavior are often appropriate for most patients. These sessions, often interspersed among other sessions, involve focusing on relief of symptoms by changing the patient's posture when it is affecting the patient's symptoms.

Home Trainer Devices and Homework

Another consideration in planning a biofeedback program is the decision whether to use "home trainer" devices. If the therapist is confident that the patient will correctly and accurately practice the intended activities, then consider a home unit. One must avoid home reinforcement of incorrect muscle strength or incorrect patterns. Remember that patients often practice what they do best—and often that is what the clinician is trying to avoid. Thus, if home use of an EMG instrument is encouraging the wrong goals, then avoid it.

Homework assignments, however, are very appropriate. Every patient has tasks to do at home. These tasks range from corrective exercises to relaxation under stressful conditions. In my practice, I often use relaxation audiotapes given with instructions and a schedule for use.

Reassessment and Evaluation

Frequent reassessment is important, and evaluation at the end of a therapy program is helpful to rate its success and determine future goals. Re-evaluation involves: (1) instrumentation-based data and statistical analysis, (2) functional improvement, and (3) clinical observation of the patient's attitudes, postures, and other developed behaviors.

Although statistical analyses of physiological data have limitations, the data can provide good indications of progress when carefully obtained. However, the data must agree with functional and observed changes to constitute true measure of change in the patient.

General Instructions

There is a need to use general relaxation therapy procedures in physical therapy and rehabilitation. Many practitioners continue to use the frontal area for judging muscle tension from a wide upper body area and as a feedback source for general relaxation. The following discussion focuses on other recording sites and methods that I find useful.

Patients' presenting symptoms are the first source of information about the location of muscle tension. They are the best basis for selecting the placement site(s) of electrodes to teach general relaxation as well as control of specific muscles. Commonly presenting symptoms and diagnoses include: low back pain, cervical tension, bruxism, temporomandibular joint syndrome (TMJ), myofascial pain dysfunction (MPD), shoulder bursitis, reflex sympathetic dystrophy (RSD), and many more areas involving tension components. The initial evaluation should involve physiological recordings tailored for each patient.

Therapists should consider the following technique when providing general relaxation. One active electrode is placed on the anterior surface of each forearm, and the ground electrode on either forearm (Johnson & Hockersmith, 1989) (see Figure 22.1). Some professionals believe that this placement allows for monitoring of the entire upper thorax, neck, jaw, arms, and breathing mechanism. Although the heart rate may appear as an artifact, it still provides useful information for relaxation therapy. The heart rate base can be used as a goal or eliminated with instrument filters.

The following is one suggested procedure: The patient initially is fully reclined in a recliner chair. With the lights dimmed, the EMG audio feedback is turned to a very low volume. The clinician monitors the muscle activity; pillows may be used to support and comfort the patient. One important goal is to help the patient recognize a state of general relaxation.

The session begins with instructions on relaxation and the instrumentation. The specific relaxation instructions used vary according to therapist preferences. For example, one

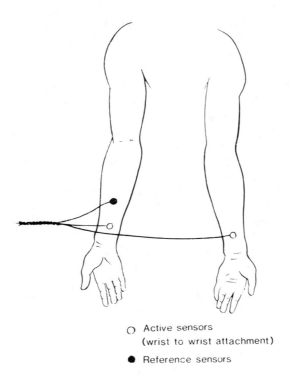

○ Active sensors
(wrist to wrist attachment)

● Reference sensors

FIGURE 22.1. Electrode placement for general relaxation, suggested by H. Johnson (1972).

may use progressive muscle relaxation, autogenic relaxation, guided imagery, or others. When the patient reaches a relaxed state, slightly turning up the audio allows the patient to monitor his or her own physiological state, receive positive reinforcement, verification, and increases confidence in being able to reach the relaxed state.

The patient may then be asked to think about tension in his or her forearms, a process that will often produce a small rise in the EMG signal. If such an increase occurs, one may explain that even thoughts of tension may produce an increase in body tension. It may also be explained that constant awareness of pain or tension may cause the patient to "splint" or tense that area. Patients may accommodate or habituate to chronic muscle tension and lose awareness of it.

The next step, while the patient is relaxed, is to request that the patient tighten and release selected muscle groups (e.g., making fists, shrugging shoulders, clenching teeth, and taking a very deep breath). One assesses the degree to which the patient has control of his or her muscles in both contraction and release and the time required to accomplish the full release and return to baseline or lower. "Splinting" activity may produce an increase in general tension recordings with greater loss of muscle control. Patients often have difficulty rapidly releasing one of the target areas. The inability to let go both rapidly and completely suggests limited muscle control.

Failure to return to baseline or a relaxed state shows residual tension that may inhibit normal muscle pattern movements. If the patient's presenting symptoms coincide with the disruption in movement pattern, one may have evidence for establishing the target muscles for relaxation training. One especially tailors relaxation for tense muscles that disrupt the proper function of the muscles involved with the presenting symptoms. In addition to looking for muscles remaining tense, the therapist should be aware of the patient's ability to control each muscle group. Prolonged muscle contraction can cause myofibrotic adhesions that may reduce a person's ability to contract that muscle.

This general technique for monitoring muscle tension is admittedly not specific. It can serve as an option until the therapist locates the specific muscles. Presently there are attempts to use surface electromyography to analyze and locate target muscles. Some professionals are using muscle scanning instruments and procedures to help locate tense or dysfunctional target muscles. This relationship between co-contracting muscles remains elusive and requires more research. Speed of feedback to the patient is more critical for learning than recording capabilities. I believe any increased specificity improves treatment; but, it is difficult to isolate one muscle as the prime cause of pattern disruption during movement.

While the patient is in a state of relaxation, the clinician should notice if there is an increase in EMG activity during each inspiration of air. Such increased EMG activity suggests use of accessory breathing muscles in the neck and shoulders, and the therapist should consider instruction in diaphragmatic breathing.

Patients can practice with feedback for a few minutes (e.g., 10–15 minutes) during an early session. They may gently contract and release muscle to learn of problem areas and recognize how relaxation feels. Patients may perform better while alone or with a therapist assisting them. The therapist must recognize when to reduce his or her presence in the room. (See Chapter 8 for a discussion of therapist presence or absence.)

During successive office sessions, patients attempt to reach a set baseline level while experiencing more simulated common postures and activities, and some stressors. Therapists may increase the room lights, increase the audio feedback volume, make the chair position more upright, have the patient stand, or change chairs. The therapist may speak to the patient or distract him or her. The goal is to develop maintenance of relaxation under simulated daily life conditions. Another goal is for the patient to achieve relaxation rapidly within seconds or a few minutes. Although one encourages longer relaxation sessions, brief relaxation periods are more practical for integration into daily life. The patient should not only relax, but should become aware of developing muscle tension that leads to symptoms.

Another excellent general relaxation technique for most patients is diaphragmatic breathing. Two separate EMG channels are often useful. One set of electrodes should be placed on a sternomastoid or upper trapezius muscle and a second set on the rectus abdominus muscle (Johnson & Lee, 1976) (see Figure 22.2). This electrode placement helps facilitate minimum activity from the neck musculature while it allows the abdomen to rise. Patients are next instructed to exhale while increasing the activity from the abdominal muscles. Practice may need to be for short periods initially, with gradual increases in time.

CASE DESCRIPTIONS

The following case descriptions illustrate therapy procedures and the rationale for change of both general and specific muscle tension. I discuss the use of biofeedback and how to incorporate it into each therapy program. Many of the following procedures require specific and adequate knowledge of anatomy and physiology. I remind and caution readers to avoid such therapy programs without appropriate education and training.

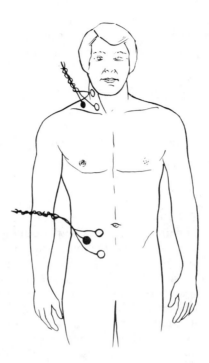

FIGURE 22.2. Technique for monitoring diaphragmatic breathing via two EMG channels, suggested by R. Johnson and Lee (1976).

Each clinician bases his or her progressive therapy goals on his or her knowledge of anatomy and dynamic motion. There is a tendency to create a "cookbook" approach to learning progressions; but, each patient's program must be developed according to the patient's characteristics and needs.

There are factors that influence the selection of target muscle sites. For example, if one is working with body extremities, it is necessary to establish joint stability before trying to teach motion. This may require working with muscles that stabilize a joint rather than move it. Peripheral joints are dependent on the stability of the proximal joints. Furthermore, one first trains proximally and then moves to distal functions. In some cases, one may find that a muscle will appear strong but actually may lack strength through normal range of motion. Fatigued muscles may lose elasticity and compensate by fibrosing in a shortened position. The patient may appear to have a shortened muscle in spasm, whereas he or she may have actually lost the ability to use that muscle during its normal function. Recent literature on surface electromyography discusses possible muscle dysfunction.

Muscles must be trained during functional tasks. Each muscle may have different functions during different tasks. A muscle can work as a "prime mover," a "synergist," an "agonist," an "antagonist," or it may perform a stabilizing function. During "ballistic motion," a muscle may serve to accelerate or decelerate a body part. One must train the muscle during "eccentric" or "concentric" function dependent on its specific task. One must evaluate the target muscles within their "kinetic chain." The feedback program should not concern itself with specific cookbook protocols. The design of a program should deal with functional muscle relationships and how to adapt them to a higher level of dynamic control. Progress through a protocol comes from the evaluator's ability to recognize patient substitutions of maladaptive behavior and chronic dysfunctional patterns.

Case 1: "Splinting" of Muscle Activity Associated with Pain

Presenting Diagnosis

Cervical paraspinal muscle spasm tension with radicular symptoms peripheral to the left fourth and fifth digits.

History and Medical Information

This 30-year-old female secretary had been in three rear-end automobile accidents over 2½ years. She had cervical-area pain and spasm with periodic symptoms of radiculitis after each accident. After the first two accidents, her symptoms had disappeared with conventional physical therapy treatment consisting of hydrocollator packs, ultrasound, and neck-stretching exercises. She had spasms of her neck muscles and headaches averaging two per week since the third accident, and she could not control the radicular symptoms. She felt her posture was worsening, and she had become very irritable. Her cervical spine X-rays were negative for pathology, but did show signs of paraspinal muscular spasm and decreased joint spaces. A diagnostic EMG showed no abnormalities. The neurologist thought there was partial anesthesia of the fourth and fifth digits and also the ulnar nerve distribution proximal to the wrist.

    The patient complained of soreness in the cervical paraspinal muscles and numbness in digits four and five of her left hand. The numbness was present for 1½ weeks, and the patient reported feeling periodic weakness in her left arm. The tension headaches were a "band"-like feeling around her head and earaches increased to three to four times per week despite her report that her accident had been "mild." She reported that her symptoms were more severe than before, and she was "unable to get any relief." However, she had learned to "live with" neck discomfort. Her prior therapies had addressed her symptoms, but it became clear during the evaluation that the prior therapies had not recognized or treated her deteriorating posture and bruxism. Prior dental records showed no apparent dental problems before the first accident.

Evaluation

Tightness in the upper trapezius musculature was present, with more tightness on the left side. Soreness was present in the upper and lower trapezius, posterior cervical, scaleni, and pectoral "trigger points." Tenderness was present in the left TMJ. The joint "cracked" when the patient opened her mouth, which she could do beyond normal limits. The jaw opening deviated with an S curve to the right, and the cervical anterior compartment musculature was also sore on the left. Shoulder depression did not show peripheral signs. Evaluation of spinal range of motion showed hyperextension of the cervical spine and hypoextension of the thoracic spine. She had limitation of 50% in motions of right lateral flexion and rotation to the left. She had a 33% decrease in lateral flexion to the right, and a 25% decrease in forward flexion. At the end points in ranges of motion in all directions, the patient described soreness at the left neck "trigger points" and a shooting-type sensation into her left shoulder. Muscle testing showed strength within normal limits.

Goals of Therapy

1. To limit pain and allow for increased range of motion.
2. To increase active pain-free range of motion.
3. To provide prevention techniques for home care through use of muscle-awareness training and relaxation techniques.
4. To strengthen thoracic extensors, neck flexors, and other support musculature.

Treatment

Treatment began with ice massage to the cervical paraspinal musculature, and continued with active stretching followed by ultrasound. These were all attempts to reduce muscle spasm and temporarily "release" the muscles. Transcutaneous nerve stimulation was then used to further suppress the pain.

During the initial period of pain control, other modalities reduced the myofascial pain. This allowed the patient to become free of pain so she could relax her muscles without increased pain. Additional techniques to help her become more amenable to corrective posture therapy included electric acutherapy, iontophoresis with lidocaine and dexamethasone sodium phosphate, and spinal joint mobilization (for a temporarily corrected spinal position).

Muscle control techniques started after three pain-blocking sessions in 1 week. The pain-blocking modalities continued, but now generalized relaxation techniques followed the pain-blocking sessions. Relaxation included diaphragmatic breathing to reduce the patient's "neck breathing." Further assessment of muscle tension suggested increased tightness and inability to release tension quickly in the left upper trapezius and neck accessory breathing muscles.

After the patient could significantly relax her muscle activity to a low level unassisted by the therapist, she was started on a neck awareness exercise with five sessions of EMG feedback over 2 weeks. With those exercises, she learned to release her neck muscles while in different positions (see Figure 22.3). She learned to release the involved muscles and demonstrated consistent control as shown by the EMG. She then progressed to practicing the control during functional activity exercises in six sessions, twice per week. The activity involved reciprocal upper trapezius contraction and relaxation, and then strengthening of thoracic extension while relaxing the upper trapezius muscles (see Figure 22.4).

The patient was by now asymptomatic in her left hand, and the frequency of her headaches decreased to once every 2 weeks. The location of her headaches suggested left masseter involvement. These symptoms and their frequency were at about the levels that

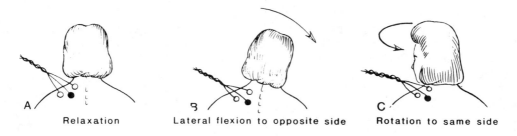

A   Relaxation   B   Lateral flexion to opposite side   C   Rotation to same side

FIGURE 22.3. Technique for releasing the muscles of the neck while in different positions (A–C).

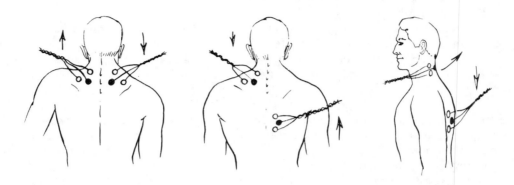

A EMG activity: Up on one side
    and kept down on opposite side

B Thoracic extension while shoulders are kept down

FIGURE 22.4. (A) Reciprocal upper trapezius contraction and relaxation. (B) Strengthening of thoracic extension while relaxing the upper trapezius.

she recalled having before the third accident. Biofeedback therapy then focused on reducing masseter muscle tension. The patient showed more difficulty releasing the left masseter than the right, suggesting an imbalance in the use of her jaw muscles (Carlsson, 1975; Rugh, 1977). Therapy then proceeded with more relaxation and instructions for equalizing right and left jaw functions (see Figure 22.5). Progressive resistive exercises continued at home to help thoracic extension and to decrease the patient's cervical lordosis. In addition, she practiced facial exercises designed to equalize the activity of right and left facial muscles. After sessions once a week for 3 weeks, the patient was able to control the tightness of her jaw muscles and had not experienced a headache for 3 weeks.

The therapist reviewed general and specific relaxation with EMG biofeedback 2 and 4 weeks later, and again at 6 and 12 months. Follow-up at 4 years continued to show no radicular symptoms, two or three headaches per year, 95% full range of motion of the cervical spine, and increased thoracic range of motion. The patient continued to be aware of and attentive to her posture and aware when she was irritating her neck. However, she reported being able to correct herself before developing symptoms.

Biofeedback therapy appeared to have helped this patient's awareness of (1) a maladaptive posture; (2) corrective positioning by use of her muscles; and (3) when increasing muscle tension could lead to symptoms. She could prevent impending symptoms, thus requiring reduced medical care. This case illustrates the need of checking many possible factors adding to symptoms.

Case 2: Low Back Pain

Presenting Diagnosis

Low back strain/sprain with stiffness.

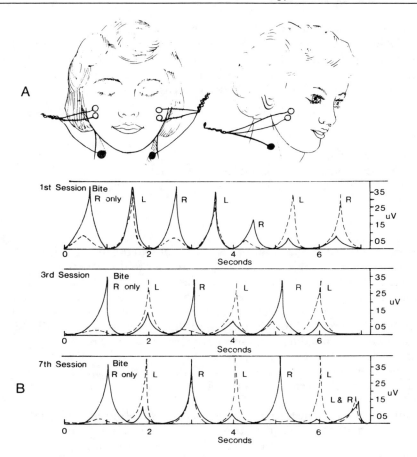

FIGURE 22.5. (A) Electrode placement for therapy to equalize right and left jaw functions. (B) Printout derived from Hyperion "Bioconditioner" EMG, demonstrating the patient's progressive ability to control right and left bite tension.

History and Medical Information

This 61-year-old man worked on a loading dock lifting packages weighing up to 50 pounds. On one occasion, when bending to lift a crate off the dock, he experienced back pain immediately. One day later he felt stiffness and pain from the right lumbar 3 (L$_3$) area to the sacroiliac and right buttock. For 3 weeks following the incident, he used home baths, showers, and hot packs; but these treatments did not decrease his symptoms. X-rays of the thoracic and lumbosacral spine were negative for pathology. He showed no neurological abnormalities.

Evaluation

The patient entered the clinic with his body held in a forward flexed position. When asked to step down on his right leg, he maintained the limb in slight flexion at the knee. There appeared to be no lateral shift of the spinal column posture. There was a decrease in spinal range of motion as follows: a decrease of 33% in forward flexion and a decrease of 25% in the motions of extension, extension with rotation, and lateral flexion. These motions caused pain on both right and left movement. Straight-leg raising showed tight hamstring muscles, both right and left, with the limit of elevation at 65° on the right. Muscle strength was within normal limits, and sensations appeared intact.

Goals of Therapy

1. To decrease pain.
2. To increase range of motion in the lower back.
3. To teach self-regulation for prevention of future injury.

Treatment

Therapy started with ice application, ultrasound, transcutaneous electrical nerve stimulation (TENS), and spinal mobilization, all in an attempt to decrease the patient's pain and to allow for release of involved muscle groups. There was a 50% reduction in pain after six sessions spread over 2 weeks. The patient was then taught a general relaxation program. The electrode placements of wrist to wrist and diaphragmatic breathing were both used for 10 sessions with 2 per week. During this period there were also three EMG feedback sessions focusing directly on reducing spasms of the patient's lower back. These sessions were to create more freedom during rotation of the lower back. He was also instructed in conventional "Williams flexion exercises" with EMG electrodes on the lumbar paraspinal muscles. This electrode placement was to help call attention to lower back relaxation (see Figure 22.6A).

In addition, the patient learned to contract one side (hip hiking) while relaxing the opposite side. He performed this in a sitting position (see Figure 22.6B). This procedure is a generalized approach to allow increased freedom of movement for vertebral rotation. One cannot isolate specific back muscles with this electrode placement. The goal is general movement. Research at Emory Regional Rehabilitation Center (S. L. Wolf, personal communication) suggests that spasm occurs in the deep rotator muscles that lie parallel to the spinal column.

Therapy proceeded with EMG monitoring/feedback and the development of relaxation of the hamstring muscles. The patient accomplished this by passive straight-leg raising and self-controlled hamstring stretching (see Figure 22.7). The hamstring control portion lasted three sessions, two of which were provided after general relaxation training. General relaxation taught the patient how to relax many muscles. Functional therapy training with feedback also included forward bending and maintaining a pelvic tilt position.

The patient returned to work asymptomatic. Follow-up review 1 year after the injury revealed maintenance of his asymptomatic state and full employment. Biofeedback provided an additional source of information for learning standard exercises and probably accelerated the learning process.

Case 3: Medial Meniscectomy

Presenting Diagnosis

Inability to control the left quadriceps muscle after a left knee medial meniscectomy.

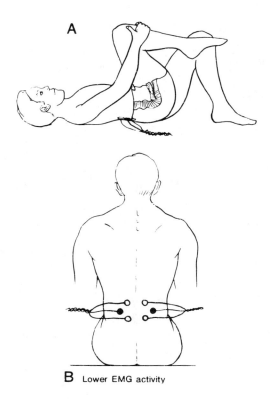

FIGURE 22.6. (A) "Williams flexion exercises." (B) Hip hiking while relaxing the opposite side in a sitting position.

History and Medical Information

This patient was a 26-year-old woman who suffered immediate pain with twisting and popping of her left knee joint after falling down stairs. . For 2 weeks she used ice applications, elevation, and immobilization to lessen the swelling and pain. The symptoms were partially controlled over the next month, but she continued to experience daily pain and began to develop a "favoring" stance; 2½ months following the accident, she began to develop locking at the knee.

An arthroscopic medial meniscectomy was performed with good healing. The left quadriceps muscle remained inactive after surgery. Despite 3 months of physical therapy to limit pain, increase range of motion, and increase strength, the patient made little to no progress. Her quadriceps muscles would not function properly, and her left knee remained sore. There was minimal muscle activity, and range of motion was 0–25° flexion without pain. Because of weakness and lack of knee stability, the patient was walking with a three-point crutch gait with minimal weight bearing on the left leg.

Evaluation

The patient had trace to poor-minus quadriceps activity of the left leg and was hypersensitive to touch around the knee joint. Range of motion did not improve and caused pain.

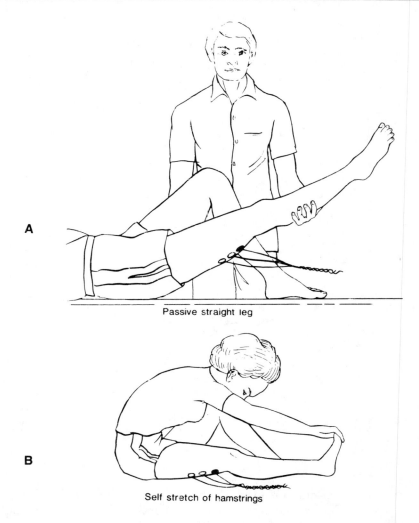

A

Passive straight leg

B

Self stretch of hamstrings

FIGURE 22.7. Hamstring exercises: (A) passive straight-leg raising; (B) self-stretching.

The patella was fixed and nonsliding. Her skin tone was pale on the left thigh, and the left thigh was 3 inches smaller in girth compared to the right. Ambulation required a three-point crutch gait, and the patient exercised extreme caution before placing any weight on the left leg.

In summary, she became extremely protective of the knee joint after experiencing pain for more than 6 months. The quadriceps functioning appeared similar to a reflex dystrophy, but the circulation remained intact. She had disuse atrophy with decreased range of motion due to pain.

Goals of Therapy

1. To decrease knee pain.
2. To mobilize the patella.

3. To promote activity of the quadriceps.
4. To strengthen knee musculature.
5. To increase joint range of motion.
6. To improve and re-educate gait pattern.
7. To develop functional activities without feedback.

Treatment

The first step was to control pain. The next step was to desensitize the left knee with xylocaine and iontophoresis across the kneecap and allow the patient to experience comfort during motion. When the knee was numb, the therapist mobilized the kneecap proximal–distal and medial–lateral. She held the knee fully supported in an extension position. The therapist placed EMG electrodes on the vastus medialus obliqus (VMO) portion of the quadriceps muscle. With EMG feedback, she tried to tighten the quadriceps without creating pain.

During the next session, the increased EMG activity showed the patient could maintain longer and stronger contractions with more repetition. Pain control and mobilization continued in the third session. The next task was for the patient to try holding her knee in a straight position while support for the lower leg decreased. This slow release of muscle under tension is known as "eccentric contraction" (see figure 22.8A).

During the next four sessions, the patient could maintain the increased quadriceps contraction. Therapy progressed to active terminal extension of the knee the last 15°. The patient still used ice packs prior to exercise. The EMG biofeedback came from the vastus medialis (see Figure 22.8B and 22.8C). She successfully straightened her leg, but she lacked strength. She also had protective spasm of the antagonistic muscle group, the hamstrings. In two sessions, she learned to control these spasms with self-stretching (see Figure 22.7B). The patient then began a home progressive resistive exercise program to strengthen the quadriceps.

The focus of the therapy program then switched to range of motion. The patient used EMG from the quadriceps while passively flexing the knee. Her task was to control quadriceps activity during stretch. Pain-free flexion improved over the next several sessions. She then proceeded to practice knee strengthening, knee range of motion, and increased weight bearing (see figure 22.9).

Gait training started when the quadriceps reached a fair muscle grade status (50%). While progressing from partial weight-bearing crutch gait to full weight-bearing cane gait, the patient received threshold biofeedback. Each time she extended her knee to full extension and contracted the muscle sufficiently, she received audio EMG feedback from the vastus medialis muscle (see Figure 22.10). This instruction included walking, sidestepping, backward walking, and pivoting. She progressed to a nonassisted gait without biofeedback in 15 sessions (see Figure 22.11). The sessions were twice a week until the last two sessions every 2 weeks.

At a 1½ year review, the patient maintained pain-free range of motion 0–125°. She could do 3 sets of 10 straight-leg raises with 22 pounds and normal-grade quadriceps activity and terminal extension with 25 pounds. Thigh girth was equal on both legs, and her gait required no assistance with unlimited endurance.

In summary, this patient learned to use her left quadriceps muscle without pain. Pain blocking was the first priority to elicit cooperation. Once the contractions were replicable, it was necessary to teach relaxation of the antagonist muscles. When she could maintain muscle integrity and support, she progressed to a gait without assistive devices. She increased her knee range of motion by actively releasing the quadriceps muscle. All activities pro-

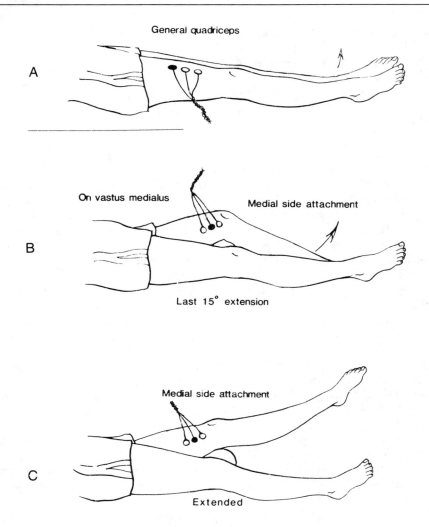

FIGURE 22.8. (A) "Eccentric contraction" of the quadriceps. (B–C) Extension of the knee the last 15°, with EMG feedback from the vastus medialus.

gressed to functional patterns. Biofeedback provided her with immediate information and reinforcement of the correct activities. Use of multiple modalities and careful progression of the therapy program were both of primary importance. She learned to use her left leg without pain.

Case 4: Tendon Repair

Presenting Diagnosis

Postsurgical repair for traumatic tearing of the flexor digitorum sublimus tendons of the second, third, and fourth right-hand digits.

With passive support

FIGURE 22.9. Relaxation of quadriceps with passive support, to aid in controlled knee flexion.

History and Medical Information

The patient was a 29-year-old, right-handed man who injured his right hand when a drinking glass broke and lacerated his palm. The laceration was deep and severed the flexor digitorum sublimus tendons of the second, third, and fourth digits. Three weeks after surgical repair of the tendons, the surgical scars were healed, and therapy began. The only remaining pathology was severe limitation in finger range of motion.

Evaluation

The patient had considerable edema of the right hand. He had active motion of his entire hand and all finger movements. Because of edema, pain, stiffness, and muscle weakness, the patient had restriction in digital flexion. There was 75% decreased flexion at the metacarpal–phalangeal and interphalangeal joints of the right second, third, and fourth digits.

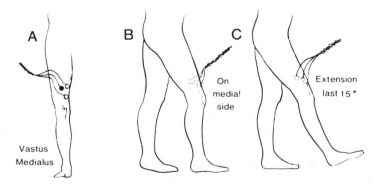

FIGURE 22.10. Extension of the knee in weight bearing, with EMG feedback from the vastus medialus.

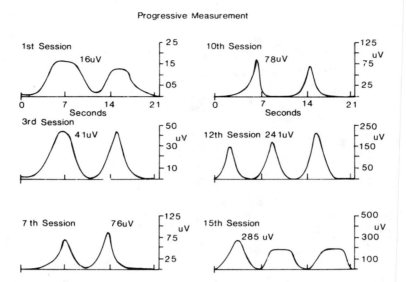

FIGURE 22.11. Printout derived from Hyperion "Bioconditioner" EMG, demonstrating the progressive strengthening of the patient's quadriceps.

The patient showed an increase in forearm flexor and extensor muscle groups, with decreased wrist "joint play" (McMennell, 1951). He was "splinting" his forearm muscles. Passive range of motion of the joint showed limitation at endpoint because of the above-noted factors. End range of motion was "forced." Circulation and sensation were intact, except for "slight tingling" at the ends of the involved fingers. His elbow and shoulder joints were within normal limits.

In summary, this man experienced a traumatic tearing of the tendons of three fingers. Prompt surgical repair maintained tendon integrity. The forearm musculature was tight and splinting. The tightness and pain caused a decrease in range of motion. The patient was limited to gentle motion until full healing occurred.

Goals of Therapy

1. To produce full range of motion, without pain of involved fingers.
2. To provide maximum strengthening.

Treatment

Therapy began with whirlpool baths and electric acutherapy for the right hand, wrist, and forearm. The patient then received separate EMG biofeedback from the forearm extensors and flexors. First, he learned to decrease all forearm activity and allow the area to relax. Gentle passive range of motion proceeded while the patient received EMG feedback from the forearm flexor muscle group. Feedback continued during passive flexor stretching and active flexor exercise. The patient also received skin temperature biofeedback from the right index finger. This program continued three times per week for 3 weeks with home exercises for range of motion without feedback.

Full exercise then started when the patient reached medical stability. The first part of the program was continued. I told him to increase the audio and visual EMG feedback as he began practicing stronger muscle contraction with EMG feedback from the forearm flexor muscle group. Initially, to create more muscle activity, the patient received electrical stimulation to specific muscle points. The EMG feedback came between each electrical stimulation. The patient's commands were to "hold the contraction" and keep the EMG activity as high as possible.

The patient regained 50% of the full active range of motion at the end of three sessions per week for 2 weeks. He was then seen twice per week for 4 weeks, with gradual reduction of the feedback and electrical stimulation. He regained 90% of full motion and strength after that stage. His home program was reviewed and increased to resistive exercise for the next 3 weeks. Formal treatment ended when the patient regained full strength and 95% of full range of motion. On review, 6 months later, the patient had 100% active range of motion.

In summary, this man began active exercises soon after his accident. He reduced secondary problems by limiting the swelling and decreasing splinting activity. Finally, EMG biofeedback enhanced the exercises by reinforcing his efforts.

Case 5: Peripheral Nerve Injury

Presenting Diagnosis

Left peroneal palsy.

History and Medical Information

This patient was a 32-year-old man who had fallen asleep in an "awkward position" and awoke with an inability to fully lift (dorsiflex) his left foot. He had tingling sensations in the foot and toes, and was developing progressively increased "foot slap" upon heel strike during gait. Two weeks after onset of his symptoms, his muscle activity deteriorated considerably. A neurologist found no active neurological disease. X-rays were all normal, with no fractures or joint injuries evident. Circulation was intact. He was then referred for physical therapy 4 weeks after the onset of symptoms.

Evaluation

The patient presented with "trace" muscle strength of the dorsiflexors of the ankle and no pain. He walked with a "foot slap." His knee and hip were normal. He had full range of motion of the ankle; his foot temperature was normal, and the skin color appeared normal. However, he remarked that he "couldn't feel what to move."

Goals of Therapy

1. To increase active muscle contractions.
2. To maintain ankle range of motion.

Treatment

Treatment began with galvanic electrical stimulation to the dorsiflexors of the left ankle. After stimulation, the patient received EMG feedback from the tibialis anterior muscle.

With visual feedback, he had increased his muscle activity (see Figure 22.12). Sessions were three times a week for 2 weeks. At the end of the second week, muscle activity had increased slightly. The biofeedback helped provide awareness to aid in exercising the muscle; its use was not an attempt to change neurological growth or reinervation.

At the end of the third week, the patient still had poor muscle strength (25%). He was then seen twice a week for 4 weeks, after which he regained 80% of his muscle strength and active joint motion. Home exercises continued throughout the therapy program. The patient refused to use an ankle dorsiflexion brace. Six months later, he had regained 100% normal muscle strength.

In summary, I assume that this man would have experienced progressive return of muscle strength without therapy. However, biofeedback and therapeutic exercise which began immediately helped to limit the secondary effects of paralysis and to facilitate the "feel" of proper muscle contraction. Biofeedback enhanced home exercises by helping the patient know "what to do."

Case 6: Spinal Cord Lesion

Presenting Diagnosis

Incomplete lesion of the spinal cord at C_5.

History and Medical Information

This patient was a 61-year-old man in excellent physical condition before suffering a spinal cord lesion. The patient had fallen and sustained an anterior dislocation lesion of the fifth cervical vertebra. At the onset, the patient was immobilized, and the cervical spine was con-

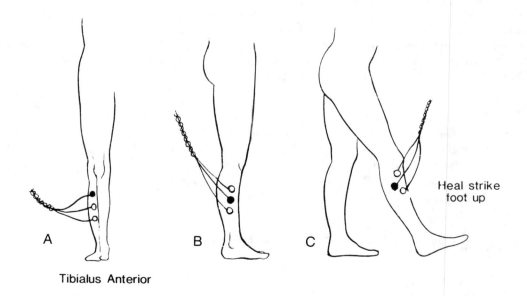

Tibialus Anterior

FIGURE 22.12. Treatment for increasing muscle activity of the ankle, with EMG feedback from the tibialis anterior muscle area.

sidered stable. He received 1 year of standard physical, occupational, and recreational therapy at a spinal cord treatment center. He had more muscle control and power than expected for his condition, and could walk unassisted with a four-legged pickup walker. He had excellent muscle activity below the lesion site, but his spasticity limited his functional use of the musculature. Hyperreflexia dominated all motions, and he had little sensory awareness below the lesion. He also was experiencing loss of bowel and bladder control.

Evaluation

The primary complaint was muscle spasticity and lack of control due to hyperreflexia causing resistance to fast movements. A general measurement of patient strength showed a fair-plus grade (60%) in the right upper extremity and a fair-minus grade (40%) for the left upper extremity. The only poor-minus motions in the upper extremity were finger abduction and adduction and thumb opposition. The strength of the left side was basically one full muscle grade below the right side in all motions. The patient could not control flexion at his elbow. Each time he would reach toward his mouth, he would have to overcome the resistance of his contracting triceps. Hand–finger flexor tightness restricted finger extension. He could not feel his finger positions.

In the lower extremities, the patient's hamstrings were extremely tight. The strength of the right hip extensors was graded good, the left graded fair-minus (40%). Bilaterally he had strong quadriceps. He showed weakness in his foot dorsiflexors, calf plantar flexors, and the hip flexors. General muscle tone on the right was fair-minus (40%), and on the left poor-minus (15%). He could not control himself when rising from a sitting position or when sitting down into a chair. Lateral stability was poor without a walker. Both of these problems were caused by his lack of position awareness. He desired training to correct these functional deficiencies.

In summary, this man presented an example of muscle strength that was uncontrolled because of a lack of natural physiological feedback on power of his muscle contractions and joint positions. Fast, overzealous movements became restricted by an overactive stretch response. Together, these problems prevented functional movements.

Goals of Therapy

1. To decrease general muscle spasms.
2. To develop position awareness with EMG biofeedback.
3. To develop functional movements.

Treatment

Therapy started with general relaxation twice per week for 12 sessions. The first specific muscle feedback therapy used continuous EMG monitoring and feedback from the triceps and biceps muscles. I instructed the patient to relax the triceps, touch his hand to his mouth, relax the biceps, and then straighten his elbow. He learned this four-count procedure. He then learned to start his contraction more slowly and to accelerate subtly. This created less resistance to movement than quick movement. His attempts were very successful, and the four-count cycle was increased in speed to two counts—touching the mouth and straightening the elbow.

The therapy then switched to EMG monitoring of the forearm, wrist, and finger flexor muscle groups. The patient learned to relax the flexor groups and then to extend his fingers while still relaxing the flexors. Continuous EMG feedback came from the flexor muscle group. The next step was to develop grip and release. He learned these behaviors well over 2½ months, and then he was able to feed himself independently. The strengthening and control programs progressed simultaneously, and both programs provided EMG feedback.

Therapy for the lower extremities started with facilitation feedback from the weakened dorsiflexors and plantar flexors and relaxation of the hamstring musculature. Relaxation of the hamstrings was accomplished by progressively higher assisted straight-leg raising, performed in a supine position on a mat table. In addition, a progressive strengthening program was started for the patient's weakened muscles. The hip flexors and abdominals were specific targets. He then learned to eccentrically lower himself to a chair while receiving EMG feedback from his quadriceps. He could associate lowering into a chair with a correct amount of EMG activity fed back during the process. This process, in reverse, helped teach rising from a chair. With his head held in front of his knees, he rocked his center of gravity forward and tightened the quadriceps muscles producing more EMG feedback. This placed him in a standing position.

I then used this procedure for developing squatting and rising from the floor. The patient also learned sidestepping and used his quadriceps as balance controllers during movement. The balance instruction taught him to maintain specific levels of EMG activity from his quadriceps during side movements. He was then transferred to a home program, with an occupational therapist and physical therapist each visiting his home one time per week. Office review sessions occurred monthly for a few months.

After 9 months of office therapy twice per week, plus the monthly review sessions, he could rise from any chair and sit down in any chair without assistance. He could rise from a floor and could crawl, both clear improvements for his functional safety. He walked unassisted with two canes, using a four-point gait. He could go up and down stairs with canes and minimal assistance. Sidestepping and lateral stability improved considerably. Upper-extremity control reached the point of unassisted feeding, and he was driving his handicapped-adapted car. He was also able to write with his dominant hand. Biofeedback helped him to identify the amount of muscle power needed to perform functional movements. The feedback also helped him create an awareness of the amount of muscle tension present during the various rehabilitative activities.

Case 7: Cerebral Vascular Accident and Femoral Fracture

Presenting Diagnoses

Right CVA with resultant left hemiplegia. Fracture of the left femoral neck, with an Austin–Moore prosthesis repair in the left hip. Reflex dystrophy of the muscles distal to the fracture. Hypertension.

History and Medical Information

This patient was a 65-year-old woman who had suffered a right CVA from a ruptured aneurysm 1 year before seeing me. She had a left hemiplegia and was able to ambulate independently with a dorsiflexion-assist leg brace and the use of a four-point cane. Her upper extremity had not responded to therapy. The left arm was spastic and carried in an elbow-flexed, internally rotated shoulder position. Nine months following the stroke, she fell and suffered a fracture of the head and neck of her left femur. An Austin–Moore prosthesis was placed in her left femur. She lost all control of her left leg and was confined to a wheelchair. She had been walking before her fracture.

Evaluation

The patient came to me in a wheelchair and wearing a short leg brace, 1 year and 3 months after the femur fracture. She showed only trace muscle activity from the left quadriceps as assessed by manual muscle testing. She had a predominant flexor withdrawal pattern in the lower extremity, a positive Marie–Foix reflex, and a hyperactive knee-jerk response. Joint range of motion remained full at all lower-extremity joints. When synergy patterns were used, the upper extremity showed some ability to flex at the shoulder. Her humeral head was well seated in the glenoid fossa. Upper-extremity motion was full at all joints. She appeared highly motivated for additional therapy. She wanted to increase her muscle awareness for walking and regain any function of her arm.

Goals of Therapy

1. To promote independent ambulation.
2. To increase function of her left arm.

Treatment

Therapy started with a program for the lower extremity. To stimulate quadriceps contraction, I tapped the patient's patellar tendon with a reflex hammer using EMG feedback from the quadriceps muscle during this procedure. She tried to maintain the audio feedback signal and keep her leg straight during each induced contraction. After 3 weeks of twice-per-week sessions, she could initiate and maintain some muscle contraction without tapping the tendon. Muscle strength was still a poor-plus (30%) muscle grade.

Therapy then shifted to using biofeedback with a progressive resistance exercise for the quadriceps. After two additional sessions over 6 weeks, she achieved and was maintaining a good muscle grade (75%). She then progressed to gait training with threshold feedback during the swing-through and heel-strike phases. She also received feedback from the tibialis anterior muscle during dorsiflexion of the foot promoted by a flexion withdrawal reflex. Training started in a 90° hip-flexed and 90° knee-flexed sitting position. As the sessions progressed, the patient performed dorsiflexion with less and less hip flexion and a straighter knee position with biofeedback provided throughout the entire progression. These procedures were to help her perform the target skill with less and less synergy pattern facilitation. She required 20 sessions of therapy to reach a point of partially controlled dorsiflexion sufficient to clear the floor. In addition, she required review of this skill once per month. She still wears a short leg brace, but without a dorsiflexion assist, and has remained on a progressive strengthening program.

Therapy for the upper extremity started first with attempts to increase external rotation of the humerus. The target muscles for EMG monitoring were the rotator cuff muscles of the scapula. The patient retracted the humerus in the glenoid while increasing the EMG signal. The next target muscles were the rhomboids and scapular stabilizers. A flexion synergy pattern helped promote arm flexion. She then worked to strengthen external rotation retraction and shoulder girdle stability. The next arm exercise was eccentric flexion 150° through 100° motion. She then learned to use the anterior deltoid for concentric arm flexion (Wolf, 1982, advocates starting proximally and proceeding distally in training).

The patient next, learned to hold her arm at 90° flexion. The next progression was holding at 90° flexion while flexing and extending the elbow. A four-count progression then followed—touching her hand to her mouth, relaxing the biceps, straightening the elbow, and relaxing the triceps and arm again. The triceps and biceps each had one separate EMG monitor. The progression helped to disrupt the synergy pattern.

Feedback also proceeded from the wrist flexors and extensors. The patient first learned to relax the wrist flexors and then learned to extend her fingers while maintaining decreased flexor muscle tone (see Figure 22.13A). When she had control of the flexors, she learned to extend the thumb. This created a useable open hand. The wrist–finger training was combined with the elbow and shoulder sessions. Total upper-extremity control was then practiced in varying positions of arm flexion and abduction–adduction. She then learned grip and release with increasingly weighted objects and in varying positions. The entire process proceeded toward functional control without feedback (see Figure 22.13B).

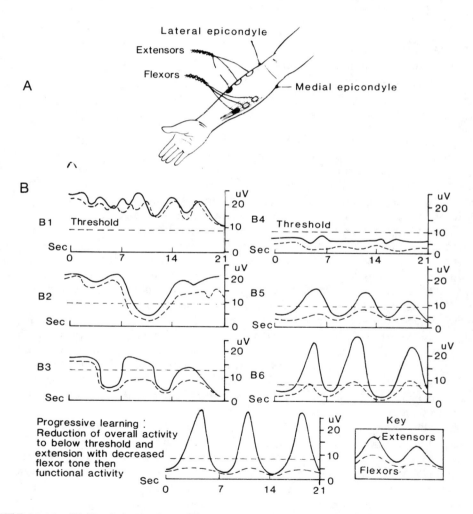

FIGURE 22.13. (A) Dual monitoring of flexor and extensor activity on two separate EMG channels. (B) Printouts derived from Hyperion "Bioconditioner" EMG, demonstrating reduction of overall activity to below threshold and extension with decreased flexor tone, and progress toward functional activity.

The upper-extremity process took 4 months, at a frequency of twice per week. The goal was to teach the patient awareness and control in functional positions. To evoke initial activity, I used synergy patterns and reflex activity. The patient then progressed toward control with less reliance on therapist facilitation. In summary, this patient developed functional control of her hand and arm. She could use it in preparing meals and in other daily activities. The patient became fully independent with a regular cane, and she could climb stairs and ambulate with minimal limitations. The biofeedback helped develop better control of the muscles and dominant patterns.

Case 8: Rotator Cuff Tear Caused by Motor Vehicle Accident

Presenting Diagnosis

Tear of the supraspinatus portion of the rotator cuff caused by rapid stretch during motor vehicle accident.

History and Medical Information

This patient was a 58-year-old man who had sustained a tear of the supraspinatus muscle at its transition from muscle into tendinous sheath. He had pain at the posterior portion of the left shoulder joint. Four days after the accident, he developed "severe weakness." For 2 days following the accident, he had periodic numbing along the posterior portion of the left forearm.

Evaluation

The patient presented with moderate soreness at the posterior left shoulder and considerable tenderness to palpation at the lateral portion of the supraspinatus muscle. He held his left shoulder in an anterior rotated position and the humerus was tight in the joint anteriorly and internally rotated. Posterior glide of the humerus in the glenoid showed tightness and resistance. The vertebral border of the scapula on the left was slightly winged, and the patient had a tender subscapularis "trigger point." He showed myofascial tightness over the left scapula and a trigger point at the infraspinatus location. Strength during external rotation of the shoulder and abduction were both reduced by 50% and painful. Shoulder range of motion was within normal limits but showed an impingement sign at 125° forward flexion and 80° of lateral abduction.

Goals of Therapy

1. Release protective spasm of the subscapularis musculature.
2. Teach patient proper use of the supraspinatus muscle (increase muscle tone).
3. Strengthen arm in all affected motions.
4. Teach home progressive resistive exercise program.

Treatment

The patient had developed a protective spasm of the subscapularis portion of the rotator cuff and, as a result, had decreased muscle tone of the supraspinatus portion of the rotator cuff. The supraspinatus was too tender to promote increased muscle strain and needed pain-controlling therapy before muscle re-education. For three times per week in the first 2 weeks, he received various modalities consisting of electric acutherapy, ice massage, and phonophoresis with corticosteroid. Next, he received myofascial stretching of the left scapular area followed by scapular mobilization promoting scapular glide and rotation. Posterior glide mobilization of the left humerus helped release the restricted joint. Next, muscle re-education started with an EMG monitor on the left supraspinatus muscle. The patient pulled his arm in shoulder retraction while the therapist gave mild resistance, and the arm was at a 45° forward flexed position. When he consistently used his supraspinatus to stabilize the joint properly, exercise progressed to strengthening. He retracted the shoulder and produced EMG activity from the supraspinatus and then performed each assigned strengthening exercise. Exercise consisted of isometric holds, isotonic movement, and isokinetic activity. During all exercises, he attended to the EMG signal.

Because of pain and tearing, the patient had lost active function of the supraspinatus muscle. He learned to use the affected muscle during all natural functioning movements. The feedback provided "muscle awareness" after controlling the pain. Feedback also reminded the patient to stabilize his joint properly during all exercise sessions. He had exercise assignments for homework. Treatment was twice a week for 6 weeks.

Case 9: Multiple Sclerosis

Presenting Diagnosis

Multiple sclerosis with complaints of knee instability and back pain.

History and Medical Information

This patient was a 54-year-old woman with a diagnosis of multiple sclerosis and lumbosacral back pain. She came to our clinic complaining of instability in both knees. She stated that she felt particularly insecure when pivoting on her legs. She felt she was "losing awareness" of her lower extremities. She had received 6 months of muscle strengthening at a major hospital's rehabilitation department.

Evaluation

The patient came to the clinic walking with a four-point pickup walker and showed considerable hyperlordosis of the lumbosacral spine while maintaining herself in a forward flexed position. When each leg began stance phase and weight bearing, she pulled back hard with the hamstring musculature to create a locked-knee position. She hyperextended her knees and had little to no push-off at the end of stance phase, on both sides. Muscle strength in the lower extremities tested as strong (90–100%), but it was used in a shortened arc of motion.

The patient had lost awareness of muscle contraction and release. She used her muscles in an all-or-none fashion. She needed feedback on when and how much to use her muscles.

Goals of Therapy

1. To increase muscle awareness for functional control of muscles during gait.
2. To teach muscle control during functional patterns.

Treatment

The patient had excellent muscle strength and a well-developed home strengthening program. Thus, therapy proceeded with specific muscle-pattern training. She received both EMG and force-dependent biofeedback. The first EMG monitor site was from the quadriceps muscles. First, she learned to control the feedback signal and use her muscles in a sitting, non-gravity-dependent position. She progressed to standing weight transfer, while required to increase the EMG signal from each leg as she bore weight on each limb. Force feedback, dependent on body weight, came from pressure-sensitive pads placed in her shoes. When 50% of body weight transferred to the support limb, an auditory feedback signaled her. She then increased the quadriceps contraction from that limb. The EMG monitor on the active quadriceps gave a threshold dependent, auditory signal showing proper levels. She progressed through various body transfers such as side-stepping, pivoting, forward and backward walking.

The next step in feedback focused on push-off at the end of the stance phase; EMG feedback came from both the hamstring muscles and the calf musculature. The patient first learned control of these muscle groups in a non-gravity-dependent sitting position. Then, she learned to flex the knee with the hamstrings rather than pulling back on the joint into knee extension. Exercise in a standing position started at this time. Electromyographic feedback from the calf musculature signaled her when she was pushing with the feet. She learned to increase push-off from midstance until the end-stance phase. Calf control helped to reduce knee hyperextension. Next, she learned ascending and descending stairs with increased control of the calf during both motions. Her task was to control the calf tension during eccentric release of the muscle. This occurred during lowering onto the foot and controlling heel impact while going down stairs. Then, she learned to push off with the foot and calf muscles while ascending stairs. Electromyographic feedback from the calf musculature was continuous.

The patient learned to control her movements during stair climbing and descending, pivoting, gait, and all weight transfers. Proper push-off decreased her forward flexion position at the back and eliminated her back pain. Her greater control allowed her to perform all standing movements independently with two forearm crutches.

Treatment sessions were twice per week for 6 weeks and one exercise review 1 month after the completion of formal therapy. Both pressure force and EMG feedback provided awareness to her, and she gained meaningful information to correct her gait. This information transferred to functional learning.

FINAL CONSIDERATIONS

There are three more general concepts important in the feedback process but not mentioned in this chapter. First, muscles that have been in spasm will often "overpower" the relaxed muscles; one must strengthen the weakened muscle to perform its normal function. Second, as in therapy for head control for cerebral palsy (Russell & Woolbridge, 1975), muscle or position feedback also must promote optimum joint position and the most functional posture for a particular patient. Third, one cannot train an isolated muscle without attending to its kinesiological partners.

SUMMARY

In this chapter, I described some techniques I believe are helpful when using biofeedback with physical therapy procedures. One must remember that feedback is simply a means for a therapist to facilitate the learning of functional awareness and control. Feedback is not the actual treatment in the present model but, rather, a cluster of electronic and electromechanical instrumentation-based techniques that convey additional useful information into a common language that facilitates the use of other therapy techniques.

GLOSSARY

AGONIST. A muscle directly involved in contraction and opposed by the action of an antagonist muscle that needs to relax for proper function of the agonist muscle. For example, to bend the elbow, the biceps brachii muscle, as the agonist, contracts, and the triceps muscle is the antagonist.

ANTAGONIST. A muscle that opposes or resists the action of an agonist muscle or prime mover. Can impede the action of another muscle. Also, balances opposite forces, thus helping to produce smooth movement. (See *agonist*.)

ASSOCIATED ANTAGONIST. "One of two muscles or groups of muscles which pull in nearly opposite directions, but which, when acting together, move the part in a path between their diverging lines of action" (*Stedman's Medical Dictionary*, 1966).

BALLISTICS. Science of motion and trajectory of guided objects or projectiles.

CONTRACTION, CONCENTRIC. A muscle developing enough tension to overcome resistance and move a body part.

CONTRACTION, ECCENTRIC. Resistance overcoming a muscle action and lengthening it.

CONTRACTION, STATIC. A muscle developing insufficient tension to move a body part against resistance.

FIXATOR (OR STABILIZER). Accessory muscle that steadies or stabilizes a part, thus allowing more precise movements in an associated structure.

KINETIC CHAIN. All the muscles involved in controlling and completing a functional movement. "Kinetic" relates to motion.

NEUTRALIZER. A muscle contracting and counteracting or neutralizing an undesired action of another muscle.

PRIME MOVER. A muscle mainly responsible for directly causing an intended action or movement.

SYNERGIST MUSCLES. Muscles that act together to have a mutually helpful (cooperative) action, such as flexor muscles.

REFERENCES

Basmajian, J. V. (1977). Learned control of single motor units. In G. E. Schwartz & J. Beatty (Eds.), *Biofeedback: Theory and research*. New York: Academic Press.

Basmajian, J. V. (Ed.). (1979, 1989). *Biofeedback: Principles and practice for clinicians* (1st & 3rd eds.). Baltimore: Williams & Wilkins.

Brudny, J., Grynbaum, B. L., & Korein, J. (1974). Spasmodic torticollis: Treatment by feedback display of EMG. *Archives of Physical Medicine and Rehabilitation, 55*, 403–408.

Brunnstrom, S. (1970). *Movement therapy in hemiplegia: A neurophysiological approach*. New York: Harper & Row.

Carlsson, S. G. (1975). Treatment of temporo-mandibular joint syndrome with biofeedback training. *Journal of the American Dental Association, 91,* 602–605.

Hagbarth, K. E. (1973). The effect of muscle vibration in normal man and in patients with motor disorders. In J. E. Desmedt (Ed.), *New developments in electromyography and clinical neurophysiology* (Vol. 3). Basel, Switzerland: S. Karger.

Hagbarth, K. E., & Eklund, G. (1969). The muscle vibrator: A useful tool in neurological therapeutic work. *Scandinavian Journal of Rehabilitation Medicine, 1,* 26–34.

Johnson, H. E., & Hockersmith, V. (1989). Therapeutic electromyography in chronic back pain. In J. V. Basmajian (Ed.), *Biofeedback: Principles and practice for clinicians* (3rd ed.). Baltimore: Williams & Wilkins.

Johnson, R., & Lee, K. (1976). Myofeedback: A new method of teaching breathing exercise to emphysematous patients. *Journal of the American Physical Therapy Association, 56,* 826–829.

Knott, M., & Voss, D. (1969). *Proprioceptive neuromuscular facilitation* (2nd ed.). New York: Harper & Row.

Marinacci, A. A., & Horande, M. (1960). Electromyogram in neuromuscular reeducation. *Bulletin of the Los Angeles Neurological Society, 25,* 57–67.

McMennell, J. B. (1951). *Manual therapy* (No. 85). Springfield, IL: Charles C. Thomas.

Rugh, J. (1977). *Learning differential control of balanced orofacial muscles.* Paper presented at the 8th Annual Meeting of Biofeedback Society of America, Orlando.

Russell, G., & Woolbridge, C. P. (1975). Correction of a habitual head tilt using biofeedback techniques—a case study. *Physiotherapy Canada, 27,* 181–184.

Stedman's medical dictionary (21st ed.). Baltimore: Williams & Wilkins.

Travell, J. G., & Simons, D. G. (1983). *Myofascial pain and dysfunction: The trigger point manual.* Baltimore: Williams & Wilkins.

Wolf, S. L. (1982). Treatment of neuromuscular problems; Treatment of musculoskeletal problems. In J. Sandweiss (Ed.), *Biofeedback reviews seminars.* Los Angeles: University of California, Los Angeles. (Two audio cassettes).

Wolf, S. L. (1983, March). *Fallacies of clinical EMG measures from patients with musculoskeletal and neuromuscular disorders.* Paper presented at the 14th Annual Meeting of the Biofeedback Society of America, Denver.

Wolf, S. L., Regenos, E., & Basmajian, J. V. (1977). Developing strategies for biofeedback applications in neurologically handicapped patients. *Physical Therapy, 57,* 402–408.

IX
ELIMINATION DISORDERS

23

Urinary Incontinence:
Evaluation and Biofeedback Treatment

Jeannette Tries
Eugene Eisman

Conservative estimates indicate that at least 11 million adults living in the community suffer from urinary incontinence [UI] (Agency for Health Care Policy and Research, 1992). Furthermore, more than 50% of all residents in nursing facilities are incontinent. Direct medical costs of caring for incontinent people in the community are more than $7 billion annually plus $3.3 billion for nursing home residents. It is difficult to estimate other, indirect costs. These include costs for protective garments, loss of income resulting from an inability to work with incontinence, or costs for caring for an incontinent person in the house. In addition to monetary costs, the psychosocial impact of UI ranges from embarrassment to depression and social isolation. It can also negatively impact health by leading to the abandonment of various activities such as exercise that promote a healthy life style (Nygrard, De Lancy, Arnsdorf, & Murphy, 1990).

Despite its prevalence and implications, individuals often do not report UI. When people do report it, health care providers often do not treat the problem comprehensively (Agency for Health Care Policy and Research, 1992). This is unfortunate, given recent estimates that we can cure or significantly improve most forms of incontinence with appropriate treatment. There is now consensus that behavioral methods, including biofeedback, are effective treatments for this troubling problem. Accordingly, for many forms of urinary incontinence, many practitioners recommend considering behavioral treatments, including biofeedback, before more invasive treatments such as surgery. This chapter reviews essential issues and procedures related to using biofeedback for urinary incontinence.

ANATOMY AND PHYSIOLOGY
OF MICTURITION AND STORAGE

Incontinence is a symptom associated with various disorders affecting bladder control. Behavioral treatments for incontinence aim to alter complex bladder-control mechanisms coordinating smooth and striated muscle activity. Considering this, biofeedback therapists must have a thorough understanding of bladder anatomy and physiology. They need this to assess bladder function and design a treatment plan tailored to the individual. Without this knowledge, the provider is merely a technician, and patients will derive minimal benefit from this potentially effective treatment.

The next sections contain a condensed summary and not a comprehensive review of anatomic and physiological concepts applicable to the behavioral treatment of urinary incontinence. By its nature, this material is complex to those unfamiliar with the anatomy of the bladder. We refer readers to the references and texts for further study of bladder anatomy and physiology before applying biofeedback techniques for UI (Mundy, Stephenson, & Wein, 1984; Hald & Bradley, 1982; Krane & Siroky, 1991; Torrens & Morrison, 1987; Ostergard & Bent, 1991; Wein & Barrett, 1988).

Those readers not intending to apply the biofeedback techniques directly may choose to skim the next sections to obtain a general knowledge of the lower urinary tract. This will help in understanding the biofeedback techniques discussed in the chapter. Within the topic of anatomy and physiology of micturition and storage, one needs to know how the following structures contribute to these processes.

- Bladder
- Bladder neck
- Levator
- Smooth muscle
- Striated muscle
- Connective tissue
- Vascular supply and epithelium
- Central nervous system (CNS)

The lower urinary tract includes the distal sections of the ureters and their uretero-vesical junction at the detrusor muscle. This is smooth muscle and forms the bladder wall. It provides the propulsive force that expels urine through the urethra. The prostate in the male and the smooth and striated muscle of the urethra are also part of the lower urinary system. Furthermore, the pelvic floor muscles connect to and support the bladder neck, the vagina, and the anal canal. The pelvic floor muscles have a significant influence on bladder control. A complex set of learned and reflexive control mechanisms govern the functions of urine storage and micturition.

Children begin to control micturition from age 2–4. More precise regulation continues for several more years. Before that time, detrusor contraction is organized neurologically at brain-stem and peripheral levels. With social conditioning, however, the detrusor reflex becomes inhibited by higher, cortical control. This process develops bladder compliance to larger volumes with bladder capacity doubling between the ages of 2 and 4 years (Hald & Bradley, 1982). However, the mechanism by which this process occurs is not well understood.

At maturity, controlled micturition is coordinated at several levels of the nervous system extending from the frontal lobe and sensorimotor cortex, to the peripheral nervous system (Hald & Bradley, 1982). Thus, normal bladder function depends upon the integrative functions of the frontal lobes, the sensorimotor cortex, the thalamus, the hypothalamus, the basal ganglia, the cerebellum, specific centers in the brain stem, the spinal cord, nerve roots, and the peripheral nerves. Damage at any of these levels may lead to bladder dysfunction that is characteristic of the level of the lesion (Torrens & Morrison, 1987).

The processes of storage and micturition also involve intact efferent and afferent activity from the sympathetic and parasympathetic branches of the autonomic nervous system (ANS). Parasympathetic nerves coming from sacral roots 2 to 4 innervate the detrusor muscle. Somatic nerves from sacral levels 2, 3, and 4 innervate the striated periurethral and levator ani muscles, primarily through the pudendal nerve. The smooth muscle of the detrusor and the proximal portion of the urethra also receive innervation from T10–L1 segments of the sympathetic nervous system.

The Process of Micturition and Storage

Afferent, or sensory signals from the somatic and autonomic nerves carry information on bladder volume to the spinal cord. This sensory feedback modulates the motor, or efferent output to the bladder and urethra. As bladder filling continues, increased sympathetic activity closes the bladder neck and suppresses detrusor contraction at the dome of the bladder and at the parasympathetic ganglia to the detrusor. Also, somatic innervation maintains static muscle tone in the striated pelvic floor and periurethral muscles producing a positive urethral closure pressure. Pudendal nerve activity at the striated sphincter also inhibits bladder contraction through sacral reflexes and suprasacral control loops (Wein & Barrett, 1988; Bhathia, 1991; McGuire, 1983).

When a person needs to urinate, sympathetic and somatic activity diminish and parasympathetic activity increases. This combination causes detrusor contraction. The brain stem and cortical centers mediate these peripheral processes. With learning, the cerebral and cerebellar influences become the predominant inhibitory control over bladder contraction.

As a dynamic process, storage and micturition depend upon the coordination of several neurophysiological mechanisms. Normally, as the bladder fills, the resting pressure in the bladder remains stable, and the compliant detrusor accommodates to the increased volume. In a normal adult, the first urge to void occurs between 250–350 milliliters. However, bladder capacity can increase easily to 400–600 milliliters. As micturition begins, bladder pressure increases because the detrusor contracts as a result of uninhibited parasympathetic activity (Hald & Bradley, 1982). Thus, an indicator of dysfunction is decreased bladder compliance to larger filling volumes. For example, one abnormal pattern occurs when one feels the first urge to void at a low volume, quickly followed by an uninhibited bladder contraction causing incontinence.

Voluntary control of micturition requires intact signals of greater bladder volumes to the spinal cord and then to the cortex. From the cortex, voiding can be inhibited through efferent excitation of the striated periurethral muscle and the sympathetically controlled smooth muscle of the proximal urethra that increases urethral resistance. Also, pudendal afferent activity inhibits the bladder through sacral and suprasacral reflexes. The cortex also inhibits the bladder contraction. This occurs at the brain stem and pelvic ganglia of the parasympathetic fibers to the detrusor. Because one can control the "involuntary" bladder muscle through the voluntary nervous system, there is in place a distinct mechanism for the "re-education" of disordered bladder function using operant learning procedures.

Once there are appropriate conditions for voiding, the voluntary muscles of the urethra relax abruptly and completely. This signals the detrusor to contract and empty without urethral resistance. During voiding, bladder pressure increases until it exceeds urethral resistance, at which point urine is expelled. As the detrusor develops a sustained contraction, the most proximal portion of the sphincter "funnels," and the external urethral sphincter relaxes. Incoordination of any of the above components or their absence can contribute to bladder disorders. These include voiding dysfunction, urinary retention, and incontinence. Unwanted urine loss occurs when bladder pressure exceeds maximum urethral pressure. A negative urethral closure pressure can occur from either of two physiological events or a combination. One is increased bladder pressure. The other is decreased urethral pressure after relaxation of either smooth and/or striated urethral muscles (Hald & Bradley, 1982). Increased bladder pressure can result from uninhibited detrusor contractions or from increased intra-abdominal pressure from contractions of abdominal muscles. Pressure from contracted abdominal muscles or descent of the diaphragm transmits pressure to the bladder.

Hald and Bradely (1982) outlined the components that interact to maintain normal bladder function. A review of these factors should help readers understand the pathophysiology of the various forms of incontinence.

The Bladder Factor

To maintain continence during filling, *intravesical pressure* must remain low compared to intraurethral pressure. During the storage phase, normal bladder compliance assures a positive pressure gradient at the urethra. Disturbance of the low intravesical pressure maintenance occurs:

- When the bladder becomes stiff and noncompliant due to *fibrosis*.
- When the bladder wall becomes *edematous*.
- With cancerous infiltration of bladder tissue.
- With overactivity of the detrusor muscle.
- When detrusor contractility diminishes and allows overdistention of the bladder.

With chronic overdistention, the person may lose the sense of urge. The bladder then fills to its physiological limit. Then, conditions such as continual *diuresis* or increased intra-abdominal pressure would increase bladder pressure to a level exceeding urethral pressure. The result is overflow leakage.

The Bladder Neck Factor

The base of the bladder is the trigone. This area takes the shape of a flat plate during the storage phase. It forms a funnel during the voiding phase. The bladder neck maintains its plate shape by two factors. First, its location is just posterior to the lower third of the pubic bone in its normal anatomic position (Tanagho, 1991). Second, there is sufficient sympathetic input to the smooth muscle of the proximal urethra. The integrity of the base plate during storage provides a barrier to urine loss when pressure is transmitted to the bladder and the bladder neck. Such pressure transmission occurs with activities that increase intra-abdominal pressure such as coughing, sneezing, or lifting.

Furthermore, DeLancey (1988, 1989b, 1990) suggests that the levator ani muscle lateral to the bladder neck is essential in supporting the bladder neck. It increases urethral pressure to maintain continence with elevations in intra-abdominal pressure. Under ideal circumstances, a rise in intra-abdominal pressure should transfer directly to the bladder neck. This mechanically helps it close. When this mechanism is intact, it maintains continence because it increases urethral pressure. That offsets the rise in bladder pressure associated with greater intra-abdominal pressure.

In summary, the bladder neck depends on three factors to remain closed. It depends on the pliancy of the urethra, which provides a sealant-like closure. It also depends on the proper anatomic placement of the bladder neck, and sufficient support and contraction of the levator ani muscle.

The "suspension factor" also contributes to normal anatomical placement of the bladder and the bladder neck. The pubourethral ligaments suspend the bladder neck. These ligaments arise from the vagina and periurethral tissue lateral to the pelvic wall (DeLancy, 1989a). They support the bladder neck within the abdominal high-pressure zone. This is the position where increases in intra-abdominal pressure are sent to the bladder neck to close the urethra. However, contraction and resting tone of the pelvic floor muscles provide the first level of support at the bladder neck. This is the levator factor discussed next.

Because the suspension factor influences the bladder neck's position and angulation (DeLancy,1989a), weakening of the muscle and ligamentous support can displace the bladder neck. This allows the base plate to funnel during the storage phase. When funneling occurs, a rise in intra-abdominal pressure would cause a decrease rather than an increase in urethral resistance. This increases the likelihood of unwanted urine loss.

The Levator Factor

The "levator factor" refers to *slow twitch*, striated muscle fibers that maintain static muscle tone and support to the pelvic structures. In contrast, *fast twitch* fibers comprise about 20% of the pelvic floor muscle. They provide an additional, active continence mechanism during situations of elevated intra-abdominal pressure. Muscle fiber type is important when considering specific training procedures used for different bladder symptoms. For example, some women develop pelvic floor muscle laxity after childbirth due to partial denervation and need to restore levator support. In such cases, therapists direct therapy with biofeedback toward improving muscle tone, endurance, and stability. Conversely, when there is a perception of impending urine loss, the voluntary muscles must respond immediately, calling upon phasic, or fast twitch muscle function. Biofeedback reinforcement for phasic muscle activity then seeks to decrease the latency of muscle recruitment.

The Smooth Muscle Factor

Smooth muscle, innervated by adrenergic sympathetic neurons, comprises the innermost layer of the proximal urethra. The location of the estrogen receptors that also supply this area is in the muscle and the epithelium of the urethra. Thus, appropriate functioning of the urethra depends on the integrity of this smooth muscle factor. An important clinical example of how this factor can be disturbed is a recent finding implicating the onset of stress incontinence in women who started taking hypertensive medications such as adrenergic antagonists (Wall & Addison, 1990; Dwyer & Teele, 1992).

The Striated Muscle Factor

The "striated muscle factor" refers to voluntary muscle fibers in the distal one-third of the urethra and periurethral area and includes the striated levator ani complex (DeLancy, 1989b). The fibers of the urethral sphincter are predominantly slow twitch fibers which maintain constant tone but still have the ability to contract with greater force when needed (DeLancy, 1991). It is known that muscle activity as measured by electromyography normally increases in the distal urethra in proportion to increased bladder volumes.

The Connective Tissue Factor and Vascular and Epithelial Factor

Collagen and elastin within urethral tissue provide a "connective tissue factor" that assists with the urethral closure function. The "vascular and epithelial factor" implies that the urethra is a contractile tube that must be soft and compliant to close off the lumen. The importance of this factor is obvious in some postmenopausal women. With the loss of estrogen, there often develops atrophy of the epithelium. This can contribute to vaginitis and irritability of the vaginal and urethral tissue. This increases the probability of incontinence. Moreover, all of the discussed peripheral factors are interdependent with the "CNS factor" that coordinates their function.

TYPES OF URINARY INCONTINENCE

The names of different types of incontinence describe the presenting symptoms associated with each group. However, the categories are not discrete. Presenting symptoms and etiologies often overlap within the same individual. Knowledge of the anatomy and physiology of bladder control is useful in understanding the distinctions between the various types of incontinence.

Stress Incontinence

Genuine stress incontinence occurs when intra-abdominal pressure exceeds urethral pressure, as with coughing or sneezing. The striated pelvic floor muscles normally support the bladder neck and exert a closing force on the urethra during conditions of heightened intra-abdominal pressure. Weakness, or laxity of these muscles usually results in stress incontinence. Stress incontinence is more prevalent in women. This is often the result of frequent pelvic floor denervation that occurs during childbirth (Allen, Hosker, Smith, & Warrell, 1990). However, it is also seen after prostatectomy following damage to the urethral sphincter or its nerve supply.

Urge Incontinence

Urge incontinence occurs with a sudden, intense, and urgent need to urinate that the person cannot inhibit. Associated symptoms include urinary frequency and low-volume urination. Urge incontinence can stem from *detrusor hyperreflexia,* a neurogenic condition marked by uninhibited bladder contractions occurring at subnormal volumes. In contrast, the term "unstable bladder" denotes a condition where uninhibited bladder contractions occur without a neurogenic etiology.

One also sees urge incontinence without uninhibited bladder contractions. This condition is *sensory urge incontinence.* The causes of both unstable bladder and sensory urge incontinence are not well understood. One predisposing factor for unstable bladder is the pattern of voiding against urethral obstruction. This occurs with an enlarged prostate or a contracted sphincter. Voiding against urethral resistance advances the development of detrusor muscle thickening, or bladder *trabeculation.* In turn, that decreases the bladder's compliance and lowers its threshold for contraction. The habit of frequent, low-volume voiding may lower the sensory threshold for the need to void. This contributes to the development of sensory urgency.

Stress incontinence often coexists with urge incontinence. This is "mixed" incontinence. Normally, activity of the pelvic floor muscles inhibits the bladder. When there is a decrease in this muscle activity, the bladder becomes disinhibited from its normal control. Urge symptoms then develop. Stress incontinence contributes to sensory urge when people develop a frequent voiding habit to avoid incontinence. Over time, bladder volumes remain at low levels. This strategy can lower sensory thresholds for the need to void.

Overflow Incontinence

Overflow incontinence occurs when the bladder cannot empty efficiently. The bladder becomes overly distended and incontinence occurs as bladder pressure overcomes urethral pressure. Overflow incontinence can develop in any condition that limits bladder emptying. This includes urethral obstruction caused by prostatic hyperplasia. It also occurs in conditions that impair sensations that cue the need to void and when there is compromised bladder contractility (e.g., bladder denervation resulting from diabetic neuropathy).

A variant of both urge and overflow incontinence is detrusor hyperactivity combined with impaired bladder contractility. Patients with this condition have urgency and frequency but have elevated postvoid residual volumes characteristic of overflow incontinence (Agency for Health Care Policy and Research, 1992).

Pharmacological and surgical treatments are traditionally and still the most often used interventions for incontinence (Agency for Health Care Policy and Research, 1992). However, these treatments have risks and side effects. They often do little to alter the basic underlying problem. In recent years, research shows that behavior techniques including biofeedback reduce UI significantly. In addition to their overall effectiveness, behavioral techniques have the advantage of being virtually risk-free. In many cases, they correct the pathophysiology contributing to the dysfunction.

BIOFEEDBACK AS A TREATMENT FOR INCONTINENCE

Biofeedback treatment for incontinence aims to alter pathophysiological responses of both smooth and striated muscles related to bladder control. Historically, protocols using biofeedback varied in the degree to which they measured, reinforced, and generalized the distinct components of bladder control.

The use of biofeedback as a treatment for urinary incontinence started with Kegel (1948). He reported on the use of a structured exercise regimen for lax pelvic floor muscles. Kegel (1948, 1951) observed that incontinence often returned after bladder suspension surgery for stress incontinence. This resulted from the hypotonic condition of the perineal muscles. Kegel (1948) posited that strengthening exercises designed to improve pelvic floor muscle tone would, in turn, enhance support to the pelvic structures and thereby reduce incontinence.

The pubococcygeus portion of the levator ani muscle provides essential support to the proximal bladder neck and urethra. To enhance greater awareness of pubococcygeus contraction, Kegel (1948) invented the pressure perineometer. From within the vagina, that device measured the contractile force of the muscle and displayed the associated pressure changes on a pressure gauge. Kegel (1951) reported significant improvements in continence among uncontrolled clinical observations of many women. Unfortunately, clinicians taught Kegel exercises without the use of his biofeedback device.

There are several disadvantages from teaching Kegel exercises without specific feedback for muscle contraction. First, weak muscles give off limited proprioceptive sensations used to gauge the effectiveness of the contraction. Second, when the pelvic floor muscles are weak, there is a strong tendency to substitute abdominal and gluteal contraction. This gives faulty feedback for the desired contraction and, in effect, makes the Kegel exercise useless or even harmful. Under conditions of urinary urgency, abdominal contraction raises intra-abdominal pressure, thus increasing the probability of urine loss. Third, when one inaccurately performs Kegel exercises, there is no change in muscle function. This reduces motivation to continue because a functional benefit is not achieved.

RESEARCH ON BIOFEEDBACK FOR URINARY INCONTINENCE

Three different biofeedback methods for UI have been researched over the past 20 years. These include procedures that:

1. Reinforce bladder inhibition.
2. Reinforce pelvic muscle recruitment to improve contractile force and muscle tone.
3. Concurrently measure and reinforce stable intra-abdominal and bladder pressures during recruitment of pelvic floor muscles.

An early study (Cardozo, Abrams, Stanton, & Feneley, 1978; Cardozo, Stanton, Hafner, & Allan, 1978) used cystometric biofeedback with 32 female subjects (mean age = 41 years) with detrusor instability and urge incontinence. Twenty-seven subjects completed the training over 4–8 sessions. The subjects watched a polygraph tracing of their detrusor contractions with instructions to inhibit them. There was no reinforcement for changes in skeletal muscle contractions. Instructions to subjects were to use the same strategies developed in the office sessions with biofeedback to control urgency and extend intervoiding intervals between sessions. The authors reported 40% cured based on patients' subjective report, with 44% of these cured measured by the objective criteria of posttreatment cystometrograms. Another 40% of the subjects reported subjective improvement confirmed in 14% with the objective criteria.

Unfortunately, only 4 of 11 subjects (36%) maintained the subjective improvement rate at 5-year follow-up (Cardozo & Stanton, 1985). This study showed that, with feedback, people could inhibit the detrusor muscle at least during and shortly after treatment. The relapse of symptoms may have resulted from the treatment's inattention to pelvic muscle recruitment that normally inhibits the bladder. It is possible that the initial improvement observed in these patients occured because pelvic floor muscle control was inadvertently reinforced, which indirectly caused bladder inhibition. However, because pelvic muscle control had not been well established with direct reinforcement, it extinguished over time.

In contrast to detrusor biofeedback, several studies used EMG biofeedback or pressure measures to reinforce pelvic muscle contractions (Baigis-Smith, Smith, Rose, & Newman, 1989; Burns, Marecki, Dittmar, & Bullough, 1985; Burns, Pranikoff, Nochajski, DeSotelle, & Harwood, 1990; Castleden & Duffin, 1981; Fisher, 1983; Henderson & Taylor, 1987; Susset, Galea, & Read, 1990; Rose, Baigis-Smith, Smith, & Newman, 1990). These research studies varied in number and duration of treatment sessions. The protocol made little effort to isolate the effect of the biofeedback from bladder exercises and home exercises. These are behavioral manipulations commonly used with biofeedback. Furthermore, many reported treatment results in terms of reduced incontinent episodes. However, they did not report correlated physiological changes.

Also, an interpretive problem arises when one measures only perivaginal muscle contractions and does not control for changes in intra-abdominal pressure. One can observe both intra-abdominal pressure and abdominal EMG artifacts in recordings of pelvic floor activity. Such artifactual recordings can inadvertently reinforce maladaptive abdominal contractions (Tries, 1990a). Unless one measures abdominal contraction separately, the transmission of abdominal artifact to perineal measures invalidates pelvic floor measures as indices of change.

Susset et al. (1990) used intravaginal pressure biofeedback to improve perivaginal contractions in 15 female patients (mean age = 28) with stress and urge incontinence. The treatment protocol included weekly clinic visits and biofeedback practice twice a day using a home-training instrument. Twelve (80%) of the subjects reported 100% improvement, and the other three reported 25–75% subjective improvement. This study reported objective improvement in 87% of the subjects. The objective criterion was a negative pad test. This test estimates urine leakage by weighing a protective pad of known weight after performing maneuvers known to cause urine leakage.

At 5–10-month follow-up, 9 of the 12 patients who reported 100% improvement and who continued the home exercises reported no recurrence of incontinence. Two reported a slight relapse. One patient was not available in the follow-up. Of the two who reported relapse, one reported stopping the exercises. The other had cystitis and required six more biofeedback sessions to regain control. These researchers emphasized the importance of a supportive and knowledgeable therapist helping patients establish and maintain muscle strength to improve bladder control.

Burns et al. (1990) compared biofeedback treatment to pelvic floor exercise without biofeedback in 135 women, aged 55 to 71. One group had instructions in pelvic floor exercises. The other group received EMG biofeedback from perivaginal muscle contractions only. All subjects were seen in the clinic for 20 minutes per week. There was no control for abdominal substitution. They compared both treatments to a control group receiving no treatment. Both treatment groups demonstrated a 54–61% reduction in incontinence compared to a 9% reduction in the control group. There was no difference between the treatment groups. They reported no follow-up data. This study showed that pelvic muscle exercises could reduce incontinence. However, the biofeedback protocol lacked specificity in that abdominal contraction was not controlled and was of limited duration. Thus, it offered little benefit beyond pelvic muscle exercises alone.

A series of studies used manometric measures of rectal and external anal sphincter pressure, and cystometric measures of bladder pressure to reinforce stability in detrusor and intra-abdominal pressures simultaneous with contraction of the pelvic muscles (Burgio, Whitehead, & Engel, 1985; Burgio, Robinson, & Engel, 1986; Burgio, Stutzman, & Engel, 1989; Middaugh, Whitehead, Burgio, & Engel, 1989; Burton, Pearce, Burgio, Engel, & Whitehead, 1988). This protocol has the advantage of providing reinforcement of pelvic floor muscle contraction isolated from abdominal contraction. It demonstrates to the patient the direct relationship of pelvic floor muscle contraction on bladder inhibition. An alternative procedure to achieve the same end uses surface abdominal EMG as a correlate measure of changes in intra-abdominal pressure while perivaginal, or external anal sphincter EMG electrodes record pelvic muscle activity (Tries, 1990a).

Using manometric biofeedback, Burgio et al. (1985) reported a reduction in incontinent episodes of 81.7% in 1 male subject and 18 female subjects with stress incontinence; a reduction in incontinent episodes of 85% in 7 male subjects and 5 female subjects with detrusor instability; and a reduction of incontinent episodes of 95% in 7 male subjects and 5 female subjects with sensory urge incontinence.

Subjects had an average of 3.6 treatment sessions over 6–12 weeks. A follow-up evaluation at 6 months indicated that patients not only maintained the level of continence obtained in treatment, but many showed more improvement.

In 23 women with stress and urge incontinence, Burgio et al. (1986) compared bladder and pelvic floor muscle exercises with multimodal manometric biofeedback to a group without the biofeedback. In the nonbiofeedback condition, pelvic muscle exercises were comprehensively taught. The examiner placed one finger in the subject's vagina and the other hand on the subject's abdomen. This procedure helped teach the subject to limit abdominal substitution during pelvic muscle contraction. The therapist then provided verbal feedback to the subject about the accuracy and intensity of the pelvic muscle contractions. The biofeedback group attained a reduction in incontinent episodes of 75.9% compared to 51% in the verbal feedback group. At 6-month follow-up, both groups showed a slight, but nonsignificant relapse in symptoms. Burgio et al. (1986) concluded that the biofeedback group showed a superior result because of the immediacy and accuracy of the instrument feedback compared to the verbal feedback.

However, Burton et al. (1988) did not find a significant difference between multimodal manometric biofeedback and behavioral therapy alone in 23 women with urge incontinence. Both groups showed a cure rate of 30% and a reduction in incontinent episodes of 79–82%. Improvements remained at 1- and 6-month follow-up. The conclusion as to why both groups responded equally well to the different treatments was because most of the subjects had urge incontinence. This condition is probably modifiable with behavioral therapy and is less reliant on precise physiological changes. Nevertheless, the authors suggested that the superior skill and knowledge of the therapist influenced the results. The authors recommended similar training for therapists applying these techniques.

Using three groups of postprostatectomy patients, Burgio et al. (1989) compared the effects of timed voiding to multimodal biofeedback combined with pelvic muscle exercise. Each treatment group had patients with distinct symptom characteristics. Eight patients with stress incontinence reduced their incontinence by 28.8% with timed voiding alone. After using biofeedback, the stress incontinence decreased by 78.3% from the pretreatment baseline. A group of eight patients with urge incontinence reported increased incontinence with timed voiding alone. However, they reduced their urge incontinence by 80.7% after biofeedback. A third group had continual urinary leakage. This group reported no change with timed voiding and only a 17% reduction in incontinence after biofeedback treatment. There was follow-up at 6–12 months posttreatment for 14 of the 25 patients. Twelve (85%) of them maintained or improved their continence from posttreatment levels. The study concluded that incontinent postprostatectomy patients without continual leaking are good candidates for biofeedback training. However, they reached this conclusion by using a training protocol that did not specifically reinforce deep levator muscle activity. Remember, this muscle normally supports the bladder neck and provides passive and unconscious resistance to urine loss.

Indeed, Burgio et al. (1989) noted that patients with continual leakage developed excellent control of the external anal sphincter given biofeedback. They learned to consciously stop the flow of urine. However, they were unable to maintain control when they did not focus their attention directly on sphincter contraction. Unpublished clinical observations by these writers indicate that men with constant leakage after prostatectomies can reduce urine loss by at least 50%. They do this when provided with specific reinforcement for deeper pelvic floor muscle contractions.

O'Donnell and Doyle (1991) observed significant reductions in incontinence in 20 elderly, inpatient men over age 65 receiving biofeedback compared to a no-treatment control group of 28 men. The treatment protocol used sterile water infusion until reaching a level of the subject's first sensation to void. Using skin surface electrodes placed at the external anal sphincter and abdominal muscles, they isolated and reinforced pelvic muscle contractions. Treatment totaled 20 sessions over 5 weeks.

There have been at least two reports describing the use of biofeedback for UI in neurologic patients (Middaugh, Whitehead, Burgio, & Engel, 1989; Tries, 1990a, 1990b). These reports lack controls. However, they indicate that treatments with biofeedback may be useful for this population. Rather than simply building pelvic floor muscle strength, these reports emphasized the training of pelvic floor muscle coordination. They achieved this by reinforcing a short latency to contract in response to the sensation of urgency. Neurological injury disrupts the normal coordination between the smooth bladder muscle and the striated sphincter during voiding, or micturition. When this occurs in a condition called *bladder-sphincter dyssynergia*, the striated sphincter does not relax during voiding. Bladder-sphincter dyssynergia prevents complete bladder emptying. The result is elevated postvoid residual volume. Sometimes, this causes urinary tract infection and damage to the bladder, ureters, and kidneys. To limit the dyssynergic voiding pattern, Middaugh et al. (1989) and Tries (1990a, 1990b) emphasized pelvic floor relaxation both at rest and during micturition.

We can consider several conclusions from the research on biofeedback for urinary incontinence. Overall, a treatment package that incorporates patient education, daily pelvic floor exercises, behavioral techniques designed to inhibit urgency, and biofeedback is very useful for reducing UI. However, as with many other rehabilitation techniques, researchers do not know the precise mechanisms for improvement.

Multiple anatomic and neurological processes mediate bladder control. Therefore, single-channel measurement techniques are typically not sufficient for increasing the strength of pelvic floor muscles in patients with bladder dysfunction. One exception may be genuine stress incontinence. However, even for stress incontinence, Burgio et al. (1986) showed the added benefit of multichannel biofeedback with Kegel exercises which allows the simultaneous reinforcement of contractions of the pelvic floor muscles and inhibition of intra-abdominal pressure.

The next section outlines the essential components of a biofeedback treatment package for UI. One must remember there is little research identifying the mechanism of action and benefits of individual components. Thus, the present recommendations evolved from personal observations of what works well. Further empirical work will determine the degree to which each part of treatment is necessary for optimal results for each type of bladder dysfunction.

INSTRUMENTATION

Before discussing the treatment components, a discussion of instrumentation is necessary. To address the various components of bladder dysfunction, the biofeedback instrumentation for UI should include several recording channels which measure and display changes in pelvic floor and abdominal muscle contractions simultaneously. Measurement is with EMG or pressure. Furthermore, *cystometric feedback*, which displays changes in bladder pressure during sterile water infusion, is useful in the assessment and treatment of urge incontinence.

Figure 23.1 shows a display of cystometrogram measurements of bladder pressure. The measurements used surface abdominal EMG, pelvic floor EMG, and rectal pressure. Figure 23.2 displays the anatomic placements of the recording devices. The multichannel display allows for the reinforcement of appropriate perineal muscle contraction and inhibition of bladder pressure and abdominal contraction. Abdominal contraction increases intra-abdominal pressure that mechanically elevates bladder pressure. One can readily measure rectal pressure with a small finger cot tied to the end of polyvinyl tubing connected to a pressure transducer (see Figure 23.2). However, when pressure measures with a rectal balloon are not available, abdominal EMG measures are an easy-to-use substitute. There are disadvantages using abdominal EMG instead of rectal pressures. First, one may not be able to distinguish a Valsalva maneuver from an actual bladder contraction because intra-abdominal pressure transmits directly to the bladder. A rectal pressure measure verifies the presence of the Valsalva. Second, abdominal EMG measures become very attenuated on obese individuals. For this problem, one should make three adjustments. First, use a very high-gain setting to amplify the abdominal response. Second, increase the interelectrode distance. Third, move the EMG electrodes more laterally on the external abdominal oblique where there may be less adipose tissue. However, these departures from standard placements limit the reliability of measures over sessions.

Figure 23.3 shows various types of recording probes typically used to measure perineal muscle activity. Generally, the design of these probes calls for placement in either the vagina or anal canal. They provide a single measure of pelvic floor muscle activity.

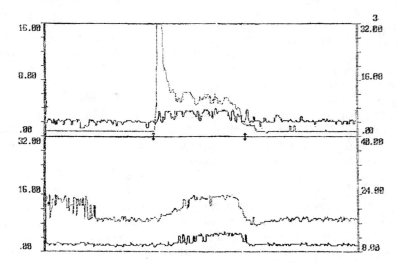

FIGURE 23.1. Cystometrogram recordings over 36 seconds showing changes in measurements during a voluntary pelvic floor muscle contraction indicated by the area between the event markers. The four tracings represent (1) abdominal EMG (upper dark), (2) paravaginal EMG (upper light), (3) rectal pressure (lower dark), and (4) bladder pressure (lower light). This measure shows a rapid fatiguing pelvic floor contraction concurrent with abdominal contraction which increases both rectal and bladder pressure. This response would be associated with urine loss rather than retention.

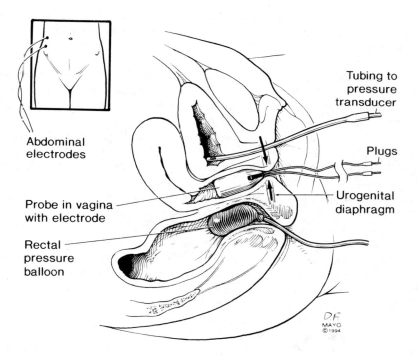

FIGURE 23.2. Schematic of probe placement during a cystometrogram biofeedback procedure.

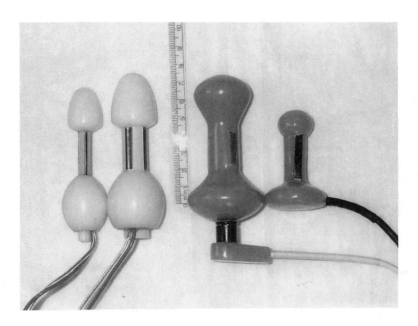

FIGURE 23.3. Various vaginal and anal EMG probes from left to right to include: the McGowan anal, the McGowan vaginal, the Perry vaginal, and the Perry anal. (These examples are for illustrative purposes only. More recent versions of these probes may be available.)

Figure 23.4 displays a recently developed vaginal EMG probe (Eisman & Tries, 1991). This design permits recording EMG from above the urogenital diaphragm that maintains the vagina in an undilated state. This probe measures perivaginal muscle activity in the sitting and standing positions and during voiding (Eisman & Tries, 1991). As a result, the therapist can reinforce pelvic floor muscle contraction specifically in positions and during movement often associated with urine loss. An example is moving from sitting to standing. This probe is completely internal to the vagina. Thus, one can use it to assess pelvic floor dyssynergia during voiding. It then allows for the reinforcement of relaxation of pelvic floor muscles in various positions during treatment for voiding dysfunction.

An EMG multiple electrode probe (MEP) for the anal canal is shown in Figure 23.4. This measures EMG activity at the subcutaneous, or distal portion of the external anal sphincter and at the level of the deep external anal sphincter and levator ani muscles (Eisman & Tries, 1993). Clinical observations indicate that the MEP can be especially useful in the treatment of UI after prostatectomy because it enables the practitioner to differentially reinforce contraction of the deeper levator ani muscle, which normally provides tonic support to the bladder neck to maintain passive continence. Observations indicate that the MEP's deeper, proximal measures mirror EMG activity taken intravaginally above the urogenital diaphragm. This observation is consistent with the anatomy. Recall that the levator ani muscle is proximal to the urogenital diaphragm and continuous from the pubis back to the coccyx. It functions as a support to the bladder neck, vagina, and anal canal. As such, the MEP may be useful in the treatment of stress incontinence in women who cannot use or prefer to avoid using a vaginal recording probe (e.g., women who are elderly and frail, women with vaginitis, and children).

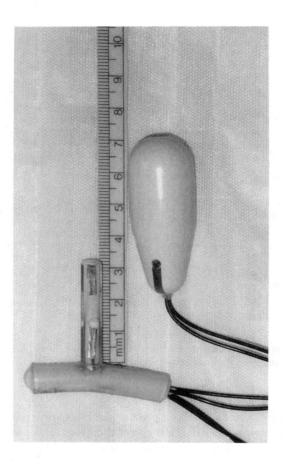

FIGURE 23.4. A vaginal EMG probe (upper right) with electrodes placed on the conical end which measure muscle activity just above the urogential diaphragm and the multiple electrode probe (MEP) which measures suface EMG activity from two sites within the anal canal. On the MEP two bipolar electrodes adjacent to the T-handle measure subcutaneous EAS activity while the proximal pair record activity from the deeper EAS and puborectalis muscles. The T-handle remains external to the anal verge when probe is positioned.

Components of Biofeedback for Urinary Incontinence

Medical Assessment

Before a biofeedback evaluation and treatment begins, there needs to be medical assessment. This includes a physical evaluation, often by the referring physician. The purposes are to rule out occult or neurological disorders, abdominal masses, or other possible causes. A rectal exam tests for rectal sensation, sphincter tone, and the bulbocavernosus reflex. It checks for fecal impaction and assesses the prostate. In women, one assesses the condition of perianal skin and rules out genital atrophy, pelvic prolapse, and urethral diverticula. In men, one assesses perineal skin condition, the foreskin, and the glans penis for abnormalities. One also checks for lower extremity edema. This is because the prone position may lead to fluid reabsorption in persons with increased excretion of urine (diuresis) and excessive urination at night (nocturia). The physical exam helps determine whether one needs further laboratory tests. A urinalysis is a basic test when there is urinary incontinence. One also must determine whether there are postvoid residuals (Agency for Health Care Policy and Research, 1992).

Verbal Interview

In the verbal interview, one gets a complete history of the onset and development of incontinence and associated symptoms. The interviewer seeks to uncover the functional relationships of symptoms and to obtain estimates of baseline data from which to judge the effectiveness of treatment. The following is a list of areas to cover in the interview.

1. *Situations in which urine is lost.* Is urine lost when there is an increase in intra-abdominal pressure? What are the specific activities that lead to urine loss (e.g., walking, bending, going up stairs, coughing, sneezing)? Specify the volume of urine loss with each activity. Note if the patient has any control of the loss of urine once it begins. Do sudden increases in intra-abdominal pressure give rise to sensations of urgency? Does the patient experience continuous or intermittent leakage? Is there urine loss without awareness?

2. *Description of sensations of urgency.* What are the antecedents and consequences of urgency? For example, does the patient experience urgency in response to certain stimuli such as running water, cold weather, changing positions, coughing, or as he or she approaches the toilet? Can he or she inhibit the urgency and for how long? Does urgency occur with a full or empty bladder? To what degree is urgency associated with incontinence, and what is the volume of urine lost with each urge-incontinent episode?

3. *Nighttime voiding pattern.* How many times does the patient usually void at night? What are nighttime voiding volumes? Does the patient wet the bed? Does the patient leak urine on the way to the toilet?

4. *Daytime voiding pattern.* What is the daytime voiding frequency, and what are typical voiding volumes? Do the patient's behaviors show a vigilance to his or her toileting needs (e.g., does the patient void before going out of the home "just in case")?

5. *Fluid intake and urine output.* Does the patient note that drinking certain beverages increases symptoms (e.g., caffeinated and NutraSweet products)? A record of 24-hour output is useful to determine adequate hydration (see Appendix 23.1). If a patient reports output to be less than 1 liter, then increase input. If a patient's output is more than 2 liters, then decrease input.

6. *Effect of emotional arousal on symptoms.* Does the patient note an increase in symptoms when emotionally aroused?

7. *Symptoms associated with voiding dysfunction.* Does the patient report any voiding hesitancy, interrupted stream, a poor flow rate, postmicturition dribble, incomplete bladder emptying, or an inability to void with perceived bladder fullness?

8. *Reflexive control.* Can the patient quickly start and stop the flow of urine? The absence of this ability does not always indicate pathology. This is because it is unphysiological to stop the flow of urine after it voluntarily starts. However, the ability to stop the urine flow in the presence of other symptoms may indicate dysfunction. For example, the ability to stop the flow without a concomitant ability to reinitiate it may be symptomatic of nonrelaxing pelvic floor muscles. Similarly, consider a patient who can readily stop and start urine flow but who has complaints of postmicturition dribble ("small volume urine loss") without elevated intra-abdominal pressure ("urge"). This suggests the presence of an uncoordinated or unstable urethral mechanism. However, these associations are based on clinical observations. As such, they are speculative and require empirical support.

9. *Use of protective garments and devices.* What type of pads does the patient use, and what is the frequency of pad change? Are other supportive devices used such as pessaries, tampons, catheters, or penile clamps?

10. *Bowel habits.* Does the patient have regular bowel movements without a need to strain? What is the normal stool consistency? Is there any complaint of fecal incontinence or staining?

11. *Symptom effects on life-style.* Has the patient restricted activities as a result of bladder dysfunction? What are the direct and indirect costs to the patient (e.g., increased laundry and cost of protective padding)?

12. *Other associated symptoms.* What is the frequency of bladder infection, perineal pain, and perineal skin irritation?

13. *Medical history.* A thorough medical, neurological, obstetric, and genitourinary history includes all prior treatments for bladder and bowel dysfunction.

14. *Current medications.* The practitioner must note if there was an onset or exacerbation of bladder symptoms associated with taking certain medications. For example, women with already weakened pelvic floor musculature may develop severe stress incontinence when they take an alpha-antagonist for hypertension (Wall & Addison, 1990; Dwyer & Teele, 1992). Conversely, any medication with anticholinergic properties may worsen urinary retention resulting in overflow incontinence. These medications include over-the-counter agents for colds or insomnia.

15. *The symptom diary or log.* For at least 1 day before the first biofeedback session, patients record all bladder symptoms and 24-hour urine output. One can send this log (see Appendix 23.1) to the patient before the interview. The patient also maintains a log throughout treatment (see Appendix 23.2). However, the patient may not need to measure volumes after the initial evaluation depending upon the evaluation outcome.

Accurate recording of symptoms is essential for the initial and ongoing assessment. In fact, therapists must assertively address noncompliance to keeping the diary. If a patient is capable but unwilling to keep it, treatment may not be practical. The diary should include several types of information. It should include the following: the time of each normal voiding, the time and estimated volume of each incontinent episode, the number of pad changes, any noteworthy antecedents to and results of incontinent episodes, and associated symptoms such as the frequency of voiding dysfunction.

Assessment with Instrumentation

Properly licensed or certified therapists whose state practice acts encompass assessment of pelvic floor muscles may conduct the physical assessment. This starts with an exam of the vagina if one uses a vaginal probe for the biofeedback. If one uses a rectal probe, then one examines the anal canal and rectum. This should be done to assure appropriate placement of the recording electrode and to assess whether the instrument measures represent the function of the perineal muscles.

For the vaginal exam, the patient's position is supine with the hips and knees flexed, thighs slightly abducted, and feet flat on the exam table. For the rectal exam, the patient is in the standard sidelying, left-lateral position, with knees and hips flexed slightly. The left-lateral position is the standard position for rectal exams because the ascending colon is on the left. Also, the abdominal electrodes are on the superiorly positioned right abdominal muscles to decrease cardiac artifact. A pillow between the patient's knees provides a comfortable resting position that the patient can maintain over a session.

During the digital exam, note the resting tone of the perivaginal or anal canal muscles. With perivaginal palpation, one can assess the pubbococcygeus muscle of the levator ani group. In the rectum, one feels the distal external sphincter just inside the anal canal. One palpates the puborectalis portion of the levator about 2.5–4.0 centimeters from the anal verge. One does this by gently moving the examination finger posteriorly toward the coccyx.

Then, the practitioner asks the patient to contract the pelvic floor muscles as if trying to stop the flow of urine or passage of stool. The instruction is to hold the contraction for 10 seconds. With the therapist's other hand on the abdomen, the patient is cued to reduce abdominal activity as much as possible while contracting the pelvic floor. After the contraction, there is a 10-second rest period. Then, the patient is asked to contract for another 10 seconds. The therapist grades the palpated contraction on a scale of 0–5 after Laycock (in press) with grading as follows:

Grade	Muscle response
0	Nil
1	Flicker
2	Weak
3	Moderate
4	Good
5	Strong

The therapist records the grade with the time in seconds that the highest grade was maintained. For example, a grade of 3/6 indicates that the patient could maintain a moderate contraction for 6 seconds. One also can extend grading to include the number of repetitions of 10-second sequences and the number of fast contractions the patient can repeat (Laycock, in press). After the manual evaluation, the therapist places the recording probe. Following manufacturer instructions, one places abdominal sensors on the right external abdominal oblique muscle. The position of one electrode is about 4–6 inches lateral to the umbilicus. The second electrode is inferior to the first, just medial to the anterior superior iliac spine.

The practitioner should obtain resting baseline measures over 1–3 minutes. Next, the therapist should ask the patient to contract the perineal muscles *for 10 seconds* as if trying to stop the flow of urine. This is followed by a period of relaxation. For reliability, one repeats the sequence of relaxation, contraction, and again relaxation. Then, one analyzes the obtained measures for the following features:

1. The amplitude and stability of the measures during the resting baseline.
2. The latency from the time the patient was cued to contract to the time of the maximum amplitude of contraction.
3. The latency from the time the patient was told to relax to the time EMG measures return to baseline.
4. The maximum amplitude recorded on each channel during the contraction.
5. The stability of the perineal contraction over 10 seconds (assessed by observation or using the standard deviation).
6. The degree to which the abdominal muscles contract during a perineal contraction.

Figure 23.5 shows EMG measures from an asymptomatic individual. One sees:

- A relatively low and stable baseline.
- A short response latency from the time of the cue to contract to the time of the maximum contraction.
- A short response latency from the time of the cue to relax to the time of return to baseline.

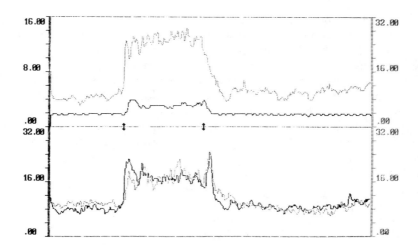

FIGURE 23.5. EMG records over 36 seconds from an asymptomatic nullipara during a voluntary contraction during the time marked by the event markers. The four tracings represent EMG from (1) abdominal muscles (upper dark), (2) paravaginal muscles (upper light), (3) inner anal canal (lower dark), and (4) outer anal canal (lower light).

- Stability over the contraction.
- A perineal contraction performed with minimal abdominal contraction.

Thus, one can compare the patient's functioning with ideal functioning. Treatment then proceeds to shape the patient's responses toward a normal model. "Shaping" refers to the gradual modification of the patient's responses through positive reinforcement of successive approximations to the ideal response.

Normally, the pelvic floor muscles relax simultaneously with the onset of both voiding and defecation. One can assess the coordinated inhibition of the pelvic floor muscles to some degree. This is done by having the patient perform a Valsalva maneuver while trying to expel the recording probe. A drop in EMG values from baseline indicates the integrity of the coordination pattern.

However, the best way to assess a voiding dysfunction is to observe the patient void with the recording electrodes in place. In this way, one observes abdominal straining, sphincter dyssynergia, and associated voiding dysfunction such as voiding hesitancy or an interrupted stream. The therapist estimates flow rate by timing the void and then dividing volume voided by the time.

Biofeedback Treatment Goals

After identifying functional problems and EMG abnormalities, the therapist should write a treatment plan with specific short-term and long-term goals. Long-term goals refer to expected functional outcomes. Short-term goals describe the training components by which the patient will achieve the functional changes. The treatment goals listed below are typically used to document progress in quantifiable terms. However, the list is inclusive because goals may vary for each patient depending upon the presenting complaints.

Long-term goals could include the following:

1. Decrease frequency of urinary incontinent episodes.
2. Decrease urinary urgency.
3. Decrease abnormal voiding frequency to four to eight voids per day and one void per night.
4. Decrease number and size of protective garments.
5. Decrease voiding dysfunction and associated risk for bladder infection and instability.

Short-term goals might be to:

1. Reinforce perineal muscle contractions toward greater amplitude and duration to improve pelvic floor muscle strength and tone.
2. Reinforce pelvic floor muscle contractions isolated from abdominal and gluteal contractions. This lessens competing responses that increase intra-abdominal pressure which results in urine loss rather than retention.
3. Improve the coordination of pelvic floor muscle by shaping perineal muscle contractions with short response latency and immediate recovery to baseline after voluntary contraction ceases.
4. Reduce chronically elevated perineal muscle activity if implicated in perineal muscle pain, voiding dysfunction, or associated bowel disorders.
5. Reduce strain voiding pattern by reinforcing perineal and abdominal muscle relaxation during micturition.
6. Provide a home program to generalize skills learned in the office to the home situation.

If one uses a cystometrogram (CMG) with the perineal measures, one should incorporate the following goals into the treatment plan. (See below for CMG procedures.)

1. Increase functional bladder capacity where abnormal.
2. Improve the coordination of perineal muscle activity to the challenge of a full bladder. During CMG, reinforce pelvic floor contraction as the patient feels urge. This mediates detrusor inhibition by activating the sphincter–detrusor inhibitory reflex that normally controls urgency.
3. Reinforce inhibition of the maladaptive abdominal contraction with urgency.
4. Improve discrimination of sensory cues that antedate uninhibited bladder contraction. Do this so that the patient learns to activate sphincter activity in a timely manner to inhibit urge.

In summary, the primary treatment goal is to optimize the striated pelvic floor muscle responses that normally mediate bladder control. The patient's diary helps the therapist to quantify the degree of dysfunction by the number of incontinent episodes, pads used, voiding frequency, and voided volumes. The diary also documents, for third-party reimbursement, objective changes with treatment. Physiological measures document bladder capacity, endurance of stable pelvic floor muscle contractions, percentage improvement in amplitude of pelvic floor muscle contraction over baseline, and percentage reduction in abdominal contraction. Some practitioners report actual changes in contractile pelvic floor strength as measured by pressure measures or surface EMG. However, we do not yet know the degree to which these physiological measures correlate with functional improvement. So, documentation of functional changes is the most meaningful way to represent the overall effect of the treatment.

Training Isolated Perineal Contractions

When there is perineal weakness or uncoordinated pelvic floor muscle activity with urgency, patients must learn to activate perineal muscles in isolation of abdominal muscles. With urge, the maladaptive habit of abdominal contraction only increases intra-abdominal pressures and encourages evacuation rather than retention. Secondly, proprioceptive feedback for muscle contraction is a function of the amplitude of the contraction. Thus, when pelvic muscles are weak, proprioceptive feedback diminishes. Consequently, afferent activity from substituting abdominal or gluteal muscle contractions can easily mask the weaker afferent signals from the pelvic floor muscles. This, in turn, limits bona fide perineal activation and later attempts at strengthening. Moreover, the afferent stimuli from the substituting muscles become associated with attempts to stop urine loss. In this way, the ineffective muscle substitution becomes conditioned to sensations of urgency. This perpetuates behaviors that increase the chances for urine loss.

Thus, the rehabilitation of bladder control requires that the person inhibit the competing, maladaptive stimulus–response patterns (urgency-substitution). Furthermore, the patient must replace them by effective pudendal nerve efferent activity that suppresses bladder contraction until one desires micturition. Toward this end, one systematically shapes isolated recruitment of the pelvic floor muscles. To do so, one uses various features of biofeedback protocol to facilitate the relearning of these skills.

Therapists instruct patients to contract their pelvic floor muscles without contracting abdominal or gluteal muscles, using the instrumentation display of the simultaneous activity of abdominal and perineal muscles for feedback. The therapist advises the patient that the initial aim of treatment is not to produce a contraction of maximum amplitude. Rather, the aim is to contract the pelvic floor muscles in isolation from other muscles and without undue effort.

Adjusting the sensitivity settings of the feedback display permits the therapist to tailor the shaping procedure to match the patient's strength and motor control. For example, one may display abdominal EMG on a scale of 0–16 microvolts, whereas one expands the display of the perineal signal on a scale of 0–8 microvolts. This can help to reinforce submaximal contractions of the latter to help disassociate them from abdominal contractions. As skill develops, therapists can use the feedback to reinforce further refinement. One does this by amplifying the abdominal signal on a scale of 0–8 microvolts and by displaying the amplitude of the pelvic floor contraction with a smaller gain.

To build muscle endurance, training proceeds with gradual increases in the duration of each contraction. As the patient improves, one may extend the contraction up to 30 seconds. Instruct the patient in diaphragmatic breathing and encourage steady, rhythmic breathing patterns as the contractions are held for more extended periods. A threshold line is useful to guide a stable contraction rather than a sawtooth display. However, use caution to avoid promoting contractions of greater duration or amplitude at the expense of allowing abdominal/gluteal substitution.

At each stage of treatment, it is useful for the patient to practice the newly acquired motor skills without instrumentation feedback. This is a rehearsal for the home exercise program. When reinforcing longer contractions, have the patient place his or her primary focus on a rhythmic breathing pattern. Gradually have the patient recruit the pelvic floor muscles as if "ramping" up to a stable contraction (see Figure 23.6). This technique seems to establish the ability to sustain an extended pelvic floor muscle contraction without effort.

Figure 23.7 displays the use of a threshold line over repeated trials for shaping deeper levator activity toward stable and sustained contractions in a postprostatectomy patient. In

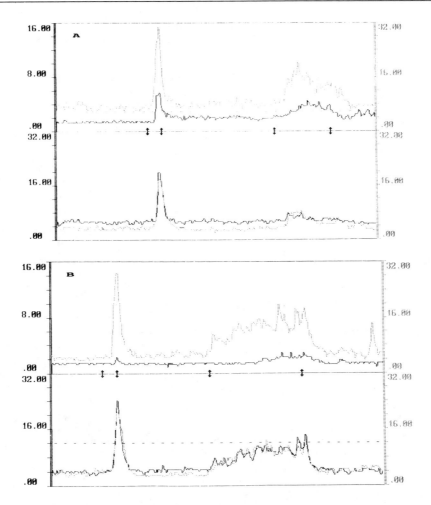

FIGURE 23.6. EMG records over 36 seconds from a 48-year-old woman with stress and urge incontinence. The four tracings represent EMG from: abdominal muscles (upper dark); paravaginal muscles (upper light); inner anal canal (lower dark); and outer anal canal (lower light). Tracing A shows early attempts to perform a quick contraction (left) followed by a sustained "ramping" contraction (right). Note inappropriate abdominal contraction, unstable vaginal recruitment, minimal anal sphincter recruitment, and muscle fatigue after only 5 seconds. In contrast, tracing B shows pelvic floor muscle contraction in the same patient after 4 months of training. It shows minimal abdominal substitution and the ability to systematically increase the recruitment pattern over 10 seconds with the greatest amplitude at the end of the contraction, signifying improvement in muscle endurance.

the first tracing, both pelvic floor measures show an unstable contraction over 12 seconds. The reader should note the relationship between abdominal EMG and pelvic floor EMG. That is, as the pelvic floor muscles fatigue, abdominal substitution increases. However, the patient learns to decrease abdominal substitution and increase the stability, amplitude, and length of the contraction to 16 seconds *over the course of the session.* In addition to the visual feedback, the patient improved with instructions in rhythmic diaphragmatic breathing and

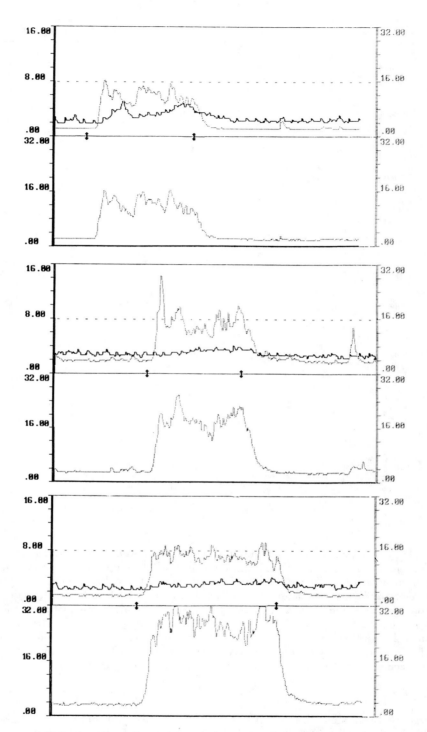

FIGURE 23.7 Abdominal and pelvic floor EMG measures using the MEP. The patient is a 62-year-old man with urinary incontinence subsequent to prostatectomy. The upper dark line indicates abdominal EMG, the upper light line displays proximal anal canal measures, and the lower light line display outer anal canal measures. A threshold line is set at 16 microvolts for the proximal anal canal and the patient is reinforced to keep abdominal muscles relaxed and maintain a stable contraction. The top tracing shows a "sawtooth" recruitment pattern and the tendency to use the abdominal muscles when pelvic floor muscles tire. The middle tracing shows greater ability to keep abdominal muscles relaxed, and the bottom tracing shows the ability to sustain a contraction for 16 seconds.

verbal cues to contract deep within the perineum. This occurred after detailed explanation to the patient about the anatomy and function of the levator ani muscle.

If the patient loses urine when going from sitting to standing, the therapist should first provide instrument feedback for perineal contraction while sitting and then continue the feedback as the patient moves to the standing position. It is often difficult for patients to recruit perineal muscles while standing. However, standing is the position in which patients are most often incontinent. With urge incontinence, for example, the intensity of the urge often increases as the person approaches the toilet. Patients respond by rushing to the toilet, thereby contracting the abdominal muscles. Thus, reinforcement for pelvic floor contraction, specifically in the standing position, fosters the generalization of behavioral strategies taught to inhibit the bladder. (See section on home program below.)

Dyssynergia and Relaxation Training

Excessive pelvic muscle activity associated with voiding dysfunction often occurs secondary to a neurological disorder. However, it also can develop as a learned response with or without a known precipitant. Furthermore, excessive striated sphincter activity occurs with a clinical condition some call "urethral syndrome." This is an exclusionary and wastebasket category. It refers to many symptoms but without any identifiable anatomic deficit or urinary tract infection. Symptoms include urgency, urinary frequency, suprapubic discomfort (aching and cramping), dysuria, ineffective and painful straining to urinate (urinary tenesmus), and low back pain. A number of these patients show excessive sphincteric activity during micturition (Raz & Smith, 1976).

Pharmacological intervention for this subcategory includes the use of muscle relaxants and benzodiazapines (Raz & Smith, 1976; Kaplan, Firlit, & Schoenberg, 1980). A procedure typically used to treat this disorder is urethral dilation despite the lack of evidence supporting its use (Agency for Health Care Policy and Research, 1992). Although there has been no research to date examining the effectiveness of biofeedback specifically for this syndrome, anecdotal observations made by these authors indicate that biofeedback training may be very effective in its treatment.

The training for pelvic floor dyssynergia starts with the systematic shaping of isolated pelvic muscle contractions described above. However, one places greater emphasis upon improving the patient's discrimination for very low levels of pelvic muscle activity. Accordingly, one can use a threshold line to reinforce the lowest possible resting baseline and an immediate return to baseline after a voluntary contraction. A strategy borrowed from progressive muscle relaxation techniques is useful here as well. The patient first contracts to a maximum amplitude and then systematically contracts at lower and lower levels. The patient does this until he or she produces only the smallest perceivable contraction followed by a period of quiescence. Then, the patient increases the duration of the contraction and always follows this by a return to the lowest possible baseline. The therapist should instruct the patient to inhibit pelvic floor activity while talking, or after gross bodily movements.

The next step is to reinforce relaxation of the pelvic floor during a gentle Valsalva maneuver. If possible, this should advance to the functional, sitting and/or standing positions. The final challenge is to have the patient void while watching the recordings to help generalize pelvic floor inhibition with micturition.

The Cystometrogram Biofeedback Procedure

A cystometrogram (CMG) is a urodynamic procedure by which one infuses either carbon dioxide or sterile water into the bladder while measuring bladder pressure and perineal muscle activity. The CMG helps assess sensations from bladder fullness, assess bladder capacity, bladder compliance, and the presence of uninhibited bladder contractions. It also provides an opportunity to observe pelvic floor and abdominal muscle responses or elevation in rectal pressure, with increasing levels of bladder fullness. The CMG requires catheterization. Thus, one gets a postvoiding residual measure. This gives important information about the patient's ability to empty his or her bladder. Interested readers will refer to texts on urodynamics for more complete descriptions of CMG diagnostic procedures. The CMG is very useful as a biofeedback technique. One must understand the procedure thoroughly before using it. This requires comprehensive training in the procedure. There are several protocols for CMG biofeedback (Burgio, Whitehead, & Engel, 1985; Burgio et al., 1986; O'Donnell & Doyle, 1991). The protocol discussed here uses an intravaginal and/or anal canal EMG probe(s), abdominal surface EMG electrodes, and a measure of bladder pressure.

Sterile water is infused through the catheter at a rate of 50 cubic centimeters per minute to a total of 400 cubic centimeters. With each incremental infusion of 50 cubic centimeters, the therapist should ask the patient to subjectively scale the sensation of bladder fullness by the following criteria (International Continence Society, 1990)

0—no urge
1—slight urge
2—moderate urge when I would normally go the bathroom
3—stronger urge
4—overwhelming urge when *I must* go to the bathroom

Notation is made of any rise in bladder pressure, whether it is sudden or gradual. Less than 15 millimeters of mercury is normal during a 400-cubic centimeter infusion. Infusion is stopped if an involuntary bladder contraction occurs. When the patient states he or she perceives an urge to void, or when the therapist observes bladder instability, the therapist coaches the patient to remain relaxed, breathe with the diaphragm, and contract the perineal muscles. This inhibits the bladder contraction and urge. To assure success, it is useful to have patients practice perineal contractions before the infusion. This optimizes their ability to recruit the sphincter when urgency occurs.

Sometimes, a patient displays bladder contractions that he or she cannot inhibit. When this occurs, the therapist should drain the bladder to a lower volume that still provides some sensation of urge and against which the patient can still practice perineal contractions. The therpist should coach the patient to maintain a rhythmic breathing pattern while staying relaxed. This limits any increase in intra-abdominal pressure. When the patient can inhibit the urge at the lower volume, the therapist can introduce a little more fluid into the bladder and then continue reinforcement of inhibitory perineal contractions. In this way, the patient slowly increases bladder capacity.

After the biofeedback procedure, the catheter should be removed and the patient allowed to void. While preparing patients to stand, the therapist should remind them to keep the abdomen relaxed while contracting the pelvic floor muscles. This allows patients to maintain control until they reach the toilet. In this way, the CMG biofeedback promotes generalization because when patients complete the voiding without incontinence, the experience of controlling the bladder strongly reinforces the inhibitory techniques. Success using this technique depends upon choosing a practicing bladder volume that the patient can inhibit but which also provides a challenge with sensations of urgency.

HOME PROGRAM

Pelvic Floor Exercise

The home program typically consists of two separate components. The first is the pelvic floor exercise. Early in the treatment program, therapists often tell patients to perform at least 60 pelvic floor contractions throughout the day. They are to divide the total so they perform 20 contractions lying down, 20 sitting up, and 20 while standing. When patients become more adept at contracting the pelvic floor muscles for extended periods, they are ready for the next step: alternating quick maximum contractions (1–2 seconds) with submaximal, extended contractions (5–30 seconds). In this way, the phasic or fast twitch muscle fibers, as well as the slow twitch fibers are stimulated. The patient's abilities displayed during the recording procedures determine the number and duration of the contractions for the home program.

For example, consider a patient who shows perineal contractions that decay with abdominal substitution or instability after 5 seconds. The therapist should instruct the patient to use 5-second contractions in the home program. Consider the patient whose contractions show a fatigue effect shown by reduced EMG amplitudes over several trials in the office. For that patient, the therapist should recommend reducing the number of contractions performed at one time in the home program. For example, instead of having the patient practice three times a day, the same number of contractions should be spread out over more frequent practice sessions. After the patient's pelvic floor muscle strength improves, the home program can be adjusted. The number and duration of the contractions should be increased to 120 per day. The patient should alternate quick and sustained contractions that range from 10–30 seconds.

The patient must be reminded that the abdominal muscles should remain relaxed during the pelvic floor contractions. Having the patient place a hand on the lower abdomen while performing the exercises provides a gross monitor of excessive abdominal contraction. The patient should be advised to relax the perineum completely between each contraction for at least 10 seconds. This amplifies the discriminative stimuli associated with the relaxed state in contrast to the contract state. This is especially important for patients with any voiding dysfunction associated with pelvic floor dyssynergia. With these patients, the relaxation period between contraction should be extended from 15 to 60 seconds.

Some practitioners and others in the field (Perry & Talcott, 1990) promote the use of pelvic floor home trainers. There is no specific research on the usefulness of these devices. However, any device or method that improves patient compliance to the exercises would be useful in strengthening the pelvic floor muscles. The disadvantage of these devices is that they monitor only pelvic muscle activity. Consequently, thoroughly train patients to inhibit abdominal contraction in the clinic before using the home devices for practice. Another disadvantage of home trainers is that the EMG trainers typically use a 100–200 Hertz bandpass filter, which filters out much of the muscle activity. The inability to measure low-frequency activity is especially detrimental when one is trying to reinforce sustained pelvic floor muscle contractions because, as the muscle fatigues, much of the muscle's electrical power shifts to frequencies below 100 Hertz.

In addition to the pelvic muscle exercises, many practitioners tell patients to stop and start the flow of urine several times per day. The purpose is to strengthen their voluntary bladder control. This exercise has good face validity for effectiveness because many patients initially report an inability to stop the urine flow when it begins. However, there is some controversy over this practice because the exercise is nonphysiological. Consequently, caution should be used when employing this technique. Caution is especially important with patients with voiding dysfunction who should not perform this maneuver until resolving their voiding dysfunction (e.g., patients with sphincter dyssynergia or those with detrusor hyperactivity with impaired contractility). Instead, those patients should focus on relaxing the pelvic floor musculature completely throughout the void.

Behavioral Strategies

The patient also gets instructions in the use of bladder-control strategies. The selection depends upon the symptoms reported in the bladder diary. Tell patients with genuine stress incontinence to contract the pelvic floor muscles before, during and after situations in which they are likely to lose urine (e.g., coughing, lifting, and moving from sitting to standing). This is to condition pelvic floor muscle contractions at times when intra-abdominal pressure increases.

The therapist should instruct patients with urge incontinence as follows. When they perceive a strong urge to urinate, they are to remain quiet, relax the abdominal muscles, and breathe rhythmically with the diaphragm. In this state, the patient then contracts the pelvic floor muscles 4–6 times to activate the sphincter–detrusor inhibitory reflex. If needed, the patient may sit if this helps regain control. The avoidance of rushing is of utmost importance. After suppressing the urge, the patient decides whether voiding is still necessary and responds accordingly. If the urge returns as the patient approaches the toilet, he or she should repeat the relax–contract cycle. There are several bladder-training protocols that encourage the gradual increase of intervoiding intervals and habit training (Agency for Health Care Policy and Research, 1992; Fantl et al., 1991; Engel et al., 1990). Habit training is a simple, timed voiding schedule without the emphasis of extending intervoiding intervals. Therapists should also read *Staying Dry* by Burgio, Pearce and Lucco (1989), which clearly outlines behavioral strategies. It is for the lay person and is an excellent resource for the appropriate patient.

Other, potentially effective methods for strengthening the pelvic floor muscles include the use of pelvic floor training weights (Peattie, Plevnik, & Stanton, 1988) and electrical stimulation (Fall et al., 1986; Sand & Wheeler, 1990). Unfortunately, controlled outcome research on the use of these devices and techniques is limited. Nonetheless, used as adjuncts to biofeedback and other behavioral strategies, these methods might afford some benefits beyond biofeedback and behavioral methods alone. Accordingly, a comprehensive treatment program could make these available, tailored to the needs of individual patients.

FREQUENCY AND DURATION OF TREATMENT SESSIONS

Practitioners often schedule the physical assessment and first biofeedback session about 1 week after the initial verbal interview. This allows one to get a baseline of bladder symptoms. It is useful to schedule the next biofeedback session 1–2 weeks after the first session, allowing time for the patient to gain the necessary neuromotor skills required to perform isolated pelvic muscle contractions for strengthening and to inhibit urgency. After that, one determines the frequency and duration of the treatment sessions by the following criteria: the severity of the problem; the motor, perceptual, and cognitive skills of the patient; and his or her ability to carry out the home program independently.

For many nonneurological patients, 6–8 sessions, which should be scheduled over a 3-month period, are usually sufficient to attain maximum benefit from biofeedback procedures. Many patients show significant improvement in fewer sessions, and more severe cases require more frequent, direct instrument reinforcement and support from the therapist. However, atrophied muscles may require 6 months of exercise to produce optimal changes in muscle function. One may need to adjust treatment accordingly to provide support and maintain the patient's motivation.

Practitioners also tailor the duration of each session for each patient. The first biofeedback session often extends to 90 minutes, especially if one performs a cystometrogram. Later treatment sessions are typically 45–60 minutes, depending upon the attention and endurance of the patient. Remember that in addition to the actual instrument feedback and reinforcement, treatment time includes other topics. The therapist reviews the previous week's bladder records and discusses with the patient what seems to be working and what is not working. There is continuing patient education and an update and review of the home exercises and behavioral strategies.

SUMMARY AND CONCLUSION

UI is a costly and embarrassing problem that affects millions of people. Until recently, the primary treatments for UI have been surgical and pharmocological, each associated with known and sometimes serious risks. Because striated muscle activity mediates bladder control, one can use operant procedures with biofeedback for increasing or regaining control disrupted by trauma, disease, or faulty learning.

However, to be effective, the practitioner must have a thorough understanding of bladder anatomy and physiology, behavioral principles underlying treatment, and the instrumentation. There is a clear need for more research to determine the benefit of certain biofeedback procedures for specific symptom clusters (e.g., the conditions best suited for using CMG biofeedback or home trainers). Furthermore, biofeedback protocols must be tailored to individual patients to adjust for idiosyncratic factors such as muscle strength, coordination, endurance, and bladder characteristics. Examples of bladder characteristics are compliance, stability, and sensation. These and other issues contributing to continence must be considered with each patient.

This chapter provides a primer for practitioners as they begin to prepare for using this effective biofeedback application.

GLOSSARY

ABDUCTED. Drawn away from the median plane.

ADRENERGIC SYMPATHETIC NEURONS. Neurons that carry impulses of adrenergic postganglionic fibers of the SNS. (See Chapters 7, 14, 15, 17, 18.)

AFFERENT. Sensory signals from the somatic and autonomic nerves that carry information to the spinal cord.

ANAL VERGE. The external (distal) boundary of the anal canal. This is the line where the walls of the anus contact during the normal state of apposition (juxtaposition).

ANTERIOR SUPERIOR ILIAC SPINE. Blunt, bony projection on anterior portion of ilium, the large portion of the hip bone.

BLADDER-SPHINCTER DYSSYNERGIA. A discoordinated voiding pattern in which there is concurrent sphincter contraction during bladder contraction in contrast to the normal pattern of sphincter relaxation during bladder contraction. The bladder sphincter does not relax during voiding, and this prevents complete bladder emptying. This is normally a neurogenic condition, but the pattern can occur from abnormal learning as well.

BLADDER SUSPENSION SURGERY. A term used to describe various types of anti-incontinence surgeries used to treat urethral hypermobility by elevating the bladder neck to its appropriate anatomic position.

BLADDER TRAINING. A behavioral strategy used primarily for urge incontinence whereby patients systematically increase the intervoiding interval to normalize voiding frequency and increase functional bladder capacity. Patients are instructed to prolong voiding to the scheduled time using relaxation techniques, distraction, or contraction of the pelvic floor muscles.

BULBOCAVERNOSUS REFLEX. (Also, bulbospongiosus reflex) Reflex associated with the bulbospongiosus muscle, one of three bilateral superficial perineal muscles. In females, the vagina separates it from the opposite side (contralateral) muscle. It constricts (compresses) the bulbous urethra or vaginal orifice in females. Innervation of the muscle is by the pudendal nerve. The bulbospongiosus stems from the central tendon of the perineum (pelvic floor and structures of the pelvic outlet), passes around the vagina, and inserts into the dorsum of the clitoris. In men, tapping the dorsum of the penis causes the bulbocavernous portion to retract by decompressing veins and allowing blood to flow out. The corpus spongiosum includes the urethra and ends in the glans. The dorsum of the penis is the anterior, more extenisve surface of the penis continuous with the anterior abdominal wall, opposite the urethral surface, which is continuous with the scrotum. In males, it starts in the median raphe over the bulb and inserts in the root of the penis. It also compresses the urethra.

COCCYX. Three to five small, fused, rudimentary vertebrae forming the caudal extremity of vertebral column (lower back, sacrum). End of spinal column.

COLLAGEN. Fibrous insoluble protein in connective tissue, such as skin, bone, ligaments, and cartilage. About 30% of the protein in the body. *Collagen vascular diseases* are diffuse connective tissue diseases. These include rheumatoid arthritis, systemic lupus erythematosus, scleroderma (progressive systemic sclerosis), polymyositis, dermatomyositis, vasculitis, and Sjögren's syndrome. (See Chapter 17.)

CYSTITIS. Inflammation of the urinary bladder, usually from an infection. It is uncommon in men. Signs and symptoms include painful urination (burning or itching feeling) and increased urinary frequency or urgent need to urinate. Others sometimes present are cloudy, malodorous, bloody urine; lower abdominal pain; and slight fever. It is not serious if treated promptly, usually with antibiotics.

CYSTOMETRY AND CYSTOMETROGRAM (CMG). A urodynamic test to assess bladder function by measuring the bladder pressure/volume relationship. One infuses either carbon dioxide or sterile water into the bladder while measuring bladder pressure and perineal muscle activity. *Cystometry* can determine the degree of detrusor overactivity, sensation, capacity, and compliance. It always involves the insertion of a catheter into the bladder.

DECREASED BLADDER COMPLIANCE. A failure to store urine in the bladder because of a loss of bladder wall elasticity and bladder accommodation. Bladder compliance can be reduced as a result of radiation cystitis, neurological bladder disorders, or inflammatory bladder conditions such as chemical cystitis or interstitial cystitis.

DENERVATION. Resection or removal of nerves to an organ or part, as can happen during childbirth.

DETRUSOR HYPERCTIVITY WITH IMPAIRED BLADDER CONTRACTILITY. A neurogenic disorder in which involuntary or uninhibited detrusor contractions coexist with bladder contractions that are inefficient in emptying the bladder without abnormal abdominal straining.

DETRUSOR INSTABILITY. The presence of involuntary detrusor contraction in the absence of a neurological disorder.

DETRUSOR MUSCLE. Detrusor means "to push down"; it is a general term for any body part that pushes down. In the lower urinry system the term refers to the smooth muscle that composes the wall of the bladder, which contracts to expel ruine.

DIURESIS. Increased excretion of urine.

EDEMATOUS. Pertaining to or affected by edema—the presence of abnormally large amounts of fluid in intercellular tissue spaces of the body, ususally referring to subcutaneous tissue.

ELASTIN. Yellow protein, sclero. The essential part of yellow elastic connective tissue.

EXTERNAL ABDOMINAL OBLIQUE MUSCLE. Flexes and rotates vertebral column and tenses abdominal wall, compressing abdominal viscera.

FAST TWITCH MUSCLE FIBERS. Striated muscle fiber type with histological characteristics that provide relatively strong and phasic (quick) contractions compared to slow twitch fibers. Some fast twitch fibers can be conditioned to resist fatigue, but other fast twitch fibers remain highly fatigable.

FIBROSIS. Formation of fibrous tissue, especially denoting an abnormal degenerative process.

FUNCTIONAL BLADDER CAPACITY. The maximum voided volume recorded on a voiding diary, which indicates the amount of diuresis that must occur before the patient feels the need to urinate.

HABIT TRAINING. A behavioral technique whereby toileting is scheduled at regular intervals that coincide with the patient's normal voiding frequency. Unlike bladder training, there is no effort to extend the intervoiding interval.

HYPERREFLEXIA. The presence of involuntary bladder contractions resulting from a neurological disorder.

HYPOGASTRIC NERVE. The nerve that carries visceral afferent and pre- and postganglionic sympathetic efferent and some parasympathetic efferent innervation to the lower urinary tract and pelvic viscera. (See *sympathetic* and *parasympathetic* in Chapter 18 and others.)

HYPOTONIC. Diminished tone of skeletal muscles. In this chapter, diminished resistance of muscle to passive stretching.

INTRAURETHRAL PRESSURE. Pressure within the urethra, the canal conducting urine from the bladder to outside the body.

INTRAVESICAL PRESSURE. Pressure within the bladder.

LEFT-LATERAL POSITION (LEFT LATERAL RECUMBENT POSITION). The person lies on the left side with right thigh and knee drawn upward. Also called an obstetric or English position (presumably based on a similarity to the manner in which women ride side-saddle).

LEVATOR ANI MUSCLE. A levator is muscle that raises a part. The levator ani muscle is a large muscle which forms the pelvic floor and supports the pelvic viscera. It has three components called the pubococcygeus, puborectalis, and iliococcygeus muscles. The levator ani is a heterogeneous mixture of slow and fast twitch muscle fibers that both supports the pelvic viscera and provides an additional occlusive force to the external urethral sphincter, especially when there is a sudden increase in intra-abdominal pressure (e.g., cough).

LEVATOR FACTOR. *Slow twitch* striated muscle fibers that maintain static muscle tone and support the pelvic structures.

LUMEN. Cavity or channel within a tube or tubular organ.

MEDIAL. Closer to the middle, median, or midline of a body or structure, or the middle layer of a structure.

MEP. EMG multiple electrode probe (see text).

MICTURITION. The voiding of urine.

MIXED INCONTINENCE. Stress incontinence coexisting with urge incontinence (see text).

NEGATIVE URETHRAL PRESSURE. The condition in which bladder pressure is greater than urethral pressure, at which point there is a loss of urine. To initiate micturition, a drop in urethral pressure precedes an increase in bladder pressure that is produced by a bladder contraction.

NOCTURIA. Excessive urination at night.

OVERFLOW INCONTINENCE. Overly distended bladder resulting in inefficient emptying of the bladder and incontinence. Bladder pressure overcomes urethral pressure (see text).

PELVIC NERVE. The nerve that contains visceral afferents and parasympathetic and sympathetic efferent innervation to the bladder and pelvic floor. (See *parasympathetic* and *sympathetic*, Chapter 18.)

PELVIC PLEXUS. A plexus formed by the hypogastric and pelvic nerves and incorporates various ganglia. Branches of the pelvic plexus convey afferent and efferent parasympathetic and sympathetic innervation to and from the internal genital organs and the lower urinary tract. (See *parasympathetic* and *sympathetic*, Chapter 18.)

PELVIC PROLAPSE. Some organs of the lower abdomen sinking (prolapsing) lower. This results from stretching or slackness of the sheet of muscles and ligaments that form the pelvic floor. This sheet supports the organs of the lower abdomen such as the bladder, uterus, and small intestines. These muscles also affect the flow of urine in the urethra as it leaves the bladder. Prolapse can result from childbirth, aging, or hereditary weakness. More common in elderly women and those who gave birth to several children. (e.g., uterus drooping into the vagina).

PERIURETHRAL MUSCLE. Muscle around the urethra.

PERIVAGINAL. Around the vagina.

PESSARY. An intravaginal device for supporting the uterus or rectum. It is also used for contraception.

POSITIVE URETHRAL PRESSURE. The situation in which urethral pressure is greater than bladder pressure and, as a result, storage is maintained.

PROSTATECTOMY. Surgical removal of part or all of the prostate gland.

PROSTATIC HYPERPLASIA. Abnormal multiplication or increase in the number of normal cells. Hypertrophy.

PROXIMAL URETHRAL RESISTANCE. Proximal means nearest or closer to any point of reference, as opposed to distal. Therefore this term refers to resistance to urine flow that is provided at the uppermost part of the urethra.

PUBOCOCCYGEUS MUSCLE. Pertaining to the pubis and coccyx or musculus pubococcygeus. Anterior portion of the levator ani muscle. From the front of the obturator canal to the anococcygeal ligament and side of coccyx. Innervated by third and fourth sacral nerves. Helps support pelvic viscera and counters intra-abdominal pressure increases.

PUBORECTALIS MUSCLE. Pertaining to the pubis (os pubis) and rectum. The pubis is the anterior inferior part of the hip bone (os coxae) on either side. Helps support pelvic large organs and counters intra-abdominal pressure increases.

PUBOURETHRAL LIGAMENTS. The pair of fibromuscular ligaments which anchor the anterior urethra to the posterior–inferior surface of the symphysis pubis in the female. Together the pubovesical and pubourethral ligaments provide support to the female bladder neck and anterior portion of the urethral wall.

PUBOVESICAL LIGAMENTS. Ligaments which extend laterally from neck of the bladder to the tendinous arch of the pelvis and assist to in bladder neck opening.

PUDENDAL NERVE. A nerve supplying the structures of the perineum including the genitalia, the urethral sphincter, and the external anal sphincter. The pudendum comprises the external genitalia of humans, especially females. The nerve arises from the sacral plexus by separate branches of the ventral rami of S2, S3, and S4.

SENSORY URGE INCONTINENCE. Urge incontinence without uninhibited bladder contractions (see text).

SLOW TWITCH MUSCLE FIBERS. Striated muscle fiber type with histological characteristics that allow for the maintenance of sustained contraction over relatively long periods and contribute to the tone that closes the urethra to maintain continence.

SUSPENSION FACTOR. Pubourethral ligaments supporting the bladder neck.

TRABECULATION, BLADDER. Detrusor muscle thickening (see text).

TRIGONE. Base of the bladder.

UMBILICUS. Navel.

UNSTABLE BLADDER. A condition in which uninhibited bladder contractions occur without a neurogenic etiology.

URETEROVESICAL. Pertaining to a ureter and the bladder.

URETHRAL DIVERTICULA. Pouch or sac defect in the lining of the urethra. Diverticulum is a pouch or sac, either natural or from herniation, of the lining mucous membrane.

URETHRAL SYNDROME. An exclusionary wastebasket category referring to many symptoms without any identifiable anatomic deficit or urinary tract infection (see text).

UROGENITAL DIAPHRAGM. A thin sheet of striated muscle stretching between the two sides of the pubic arch.

VALSALVA MANEUVER. Forcible exhalation effort against a closed glottis. Increases introthoracic pressure and interferes with venous return to the heart. Forced exhalation effort against occluded (pinched) nostrils and closed mouth. (See Chapters 18, 37.)

VISCERA (Plural of viscus). Any large interior organs in any of the three large cavities of the body, especially the abdomen.

REFERENCES

Agency for Health Care Policy and Research, Public Health Service, U.S. Department of Health and Human Services. (1992, March). *Urinary Incontinence Guidline Panel. Urinary Incontinence in Adults: Clinical Practice Guidelines.* AHCPR Pub. no. 92-0038. Rockville, MD: Author.

Allen, R. E., Hosker, G. L., Smith, A. R. B., & Warrell, D. W. (1990). Pelvic floor damage and childbirth: A neurophysiological study. *British Journal of Obstetrics and Gynaecology, 97,* 770–779.

Baigis-Smith, J., Smith, D. A. J., Rose, M., & Newman, D. K. (1989). Managing urinary incontinence in community-residing elderly persons. *The Gerontologist, 29,* 229–233.

Bhatia, N. N. (1991). Neurophysiology of micturition. In D. R. Ostergard & A. E. Bent (Eds.), *Urogynecology and urodynamics: Theory and practice* (3rd ed., pp. 31–54). Baltimore: Williams & Wilkins.

Burgio, K. L., Pearce, L., & Lucco, A. J. (1989). *Staying dry.* Baltimore: The Johns Hopkins University Press.

Burgio, K. L., Robinson, J. C., & Engel, B. T. (1986). The role of biofeedback in Kegel exercise training for stress urinary incontinence. *American Journal of Obstetrical Gynecology, 154,* 58–64.

Burgio K. L., Stutzman R. E., & Engel B. T. (1989). Behavioral training for post-prostatectomy urinary incontinence. *Journal of Urology, 141,* 303–306.

Burgio, K. L., Whitehead, W. E., & Engel, B. T. (1985). Urinary incontinence in the elderly. *Annals of Internal Medicine, 103,* 507–515.

Burns, P. A., Marecki, M. A., Dittmar, S. S., & Bullough, B. (1985). Kegel's Exercises with biofeedback therapy for treatment of stress incontinence. *Nurse Practitioner, 10*(2), 28, 33–34, 46.

Burns, P. A., Pranikoff, K., Nochajski, T., Desotelle, P., & Harwood, M. K. (1990). Treatment of stress incontinence with pelvic floor exercises and biofeedback. *Journal of the American Geriatric Society, 38,* 341–344.

Burton, J. R., Pearce, K. L., Burgio, K. L., Engel, B. T., & Whitehead, W. E. (1988). Behavioral training for urinary incontinence in elderly ambulatory patients. *Journal of American Geriatric Society, 36,* 693–698.

Cardozo, L. D., Abrams, P. D., Stanton, S. L., & Feneley, R. C. (1978). Idiopathic bladder instability treated by biofeedback. *British Journal of Urology, 50*(7), 521–523.

Cardozo, L. D., & Stanton, S. L. (1985). Biofeedback: A five year follow-up. *British Journal of Urology, 56*(2), 220.

Cardozo, L. D., Stanton, S. L., Hafner, J., & Allan, V. (1978). Biofeedback in the treatment of detrusor instability. *British Journal of Urology, 50,* 250–254.

Castleden, C. M., & Duffin, H. M. (1981). Guidelines for controlling urinary incontinence without drugs or catheters. *Age and Aging, 10,* 186–192.

DeLancy, J. O. L. (1988). Structural aspects of the extrinsic continence mechanism. *Obstetrics and Gynecology, 72,* 296–301.

DeLancy, J. O. L. (1989a). Pubovesical ligament: A seperate structure from the urethral supports ("pubourethral ligaments"). *Neurourology and Urodynamics, 8,* 53–61.

DeLancy, J. O. L. (1989b). Anatomy and embryology of the lower urinary tract. *Obstetrics and Gynecology Clinics of North America, 16,* 717–731.

DeLancy, J. O. L. (1990). Histology of the connection between the vagina and levator ani muscles: Implication for urinary tract function. *Journal of Reproductive Medicine, 35,* 765–771.

Delancy, J. O. L. (1991). Anatomy of the bladder and urethra. In D. R. Ostergard & A. E. Bent (Eds.), *Urogynecology and urodynamics: Theory and practice* (3rd ed.). Baltimore, MD: Williams & Wilkins.

Dwyer, P. L., & Teele, J. S. (1992). Prazasin: A neglected cause of stress incontinence. *Obstetrics and Gynecology, 79,* 117–121.

Eisman, E., & Tries, J. (1991). A vaginal cone for measuring EMG from the superior surface of the urogenital diaphragm. *Neurourology and Urodynamics, 10,* 409–410.

Eisman, E., & Tries, J. (1993). A new probe for measuring EMG from multiple sites in the anal canal. *Diseases of the Colon and Rectum, 36,* 946–952.

Engel, B. T., Burgio, L. D., McCormick, K. A., Hankins, A. M., Schewe, A. A., & Leahy, E. (1990). Behavioral treatment of incontinence in the long-term setting. *Journal of the American Geriatric Society, 38,* 361–363.

Fall, M., Ahlstrom, K., Carlsson, C. A., Ek, A., Erlandson, B. E., Frandenberg, S., & Mattiasson, A. (1986). Contelle: Pelvic floor stimulator for female stress-urge incontinence. *Urology, 26,* 282–287.

Fantl, J. A., Wyman, J. F., McClish, D. K., Harkins, S. W., Elswick, R. K., Taylor, J. R., & Hadley, E. C. (1991). Efficacy of bladder training in older women with urinary incontinence. *Journal of the American Medical Association, 265,* 609–613.

Fisher, W. (1983). Physiotherapeutic aspects of urine incontinence. *Acta Obstetrica Gynecologia Scandinavia, 62,* 579–583.

Hald, T., & Bradley, W. E. (1982). *The urinary bladder: Neurology and dynamics.* Baltimore: Williams & Wilkins.

Henderson, J. S., & Taylor, K. H. (1987). Age as a variable in an exercise program for the treatment of simple urinary stress incontinence. *Journal of Obstetric, Gynecologic, and Neonatal Nursing, 16*(4), 266–272.

International Continence Society for the Standardization of Terminology of the Lower Urinary Tract Function. (1990). *British Journal of Obstetrics and Gynaecology* (Suppl. 6), 1–16.

Kaplan, W. Firlit, C. F., & Schoenberg, H. W. (1980). The female urethral syndrome: External sphincter spasm as etiology. *Journal of Urology, 124*(1), 48–49.

Kegel, A. H. (1948). Progressive resistance exercise in the functional restoration of the perineal muscles. *American Journal of Obstetrics and Gynecology, 56,* 238–248.

Kegel, A. H. (1951). Physiologic therapy for urinary stress incontinence. *Journal of the American Medical Society, 146,* 915–917.

Krane, R. L., & Siroky, M. B. (1991). *Clinical neuro-urology.* Boston: Little, Brown.

Laycock, J. (in press). Pelvic floor assessment. In B. Schussler, J. Laycock, P. Norton, & S. Stanton (Eds.), *Pelvic floor re-education: Principles and practice.* London: Springer-Verlag.

McGuire, E. J. (1983). Physiology of the lower urinary tract. *American Journal of Kidney Disease, 2,* 402–408.

Middaugh, S. J., Whitehead, W. E., Burgio, K. L., & Engel, B. T. (1989). Biofeedback in treatment of urinary incontinence in stroke patients. *Biofeedback and Self-Regulation, 14,* 3–19.

Mundy, A. R., Stephenson, T. P., & Wein, A. J. (Eds.). (1984). *Urodynamics: Principles, practice, and application.* Edinburgh: Churchill Livingstone.

Nygaard, I., DeLancey, J. O. L., Arnsdorf, L., & Murphy E. (1990). Exercise and incontinence. *Obstetrics and Gynecology, 75,* 848–851.

O'Donnell, P. D., & Doyle, R. (1991). Biofeedback therapy technique for treatment of urinary incontinence. *Urology, 37*(5), 432–436.

Ostergard, D. R., & Bent, A. E. (1991). *Urogynecology and urodynamics: Theory and practice* (3rd ed.). Baltimore: Williams & Wilkins.

Peattie, A. B., Plevnik, S., & Stanton, S.L. (1988). Vaginal cones: A conservative method of treating genuine stress incontinence. *British Journal of Obstetrics and Gynaecology, 95,* 1049–1053.

Perry, J. D., & Talcott, L. B. (1990). *The Perry protocol for the treatment of incontinence using EMG biofeedback.* Strafford, PA: Perineometer Research Institute.

Raz, S., & Smith, R. B. (1976). External sphincter spasticity syndrome in female patients. *Journal of Urology, 115,* 443.

Rose, M. A., Baigis-Smith, J., Smith, D., & Newman, D. (1990). Behavioral management of urinary incontinence in homebound older adults. *Home Healthcare Nurse, 8,* 5, 10–15.

Sand, P. K., & Wheeler, J. S. (1990). *Transvaginal electrical stimulation for incontinence.* Unpublished manuscript, Rush–Presbyterian–St. Lukes Medical Center, Chicago.

Susset, J. G., Galea, G., & Read, L. (1990). Biofeedback therapy for female incontinence due to low urethral resistance. *Journal of Urology, 143,* 1205–1208.

Tanagho, E. A. (1991). Retropubic surgical approach for correction of urinary stress incontinence. In D. R. Ostergard & A. E. Bent (Eds.), *Urogynecology and urodynamics: Theory and practice* (3rd ed.). Baltimore, MD: Williams & Wilkins.

Torrens, M., & Morrison, J. F. B. (1987). *The physiology of the lower urinary tract.* London: Springer-Verlag.

Tries, J. (1990a). Kegel exercises enhanced by biofeedback. *Journal of Enterosomal Therapy, 17,* 67–76.

Tries, J. (1990b). The use of biofeedback in the treatment of incontinence due to head injury. *Journal of Head Trauma Rehabilitation, 5,* 91–100.

Wall, L. L., & Addison, W. A. (1990). Prazosin-induced stress incontinence. *Obstetrics and Gynecology, 75,* 558–560.

Wein, A. J., & Barrett, D. M. (1988). *Voiding function and dysfunction: A logical and practical approach.* Chicago: Year Book Medical Publishers.

APPENDIX 23.1. BLADDER RECORD

Name: _____ Date: _____

(Please keep the following record for a 24-hour period—before your scheduled appointment.)

1. In the 1st column mark the time (day and night) you urinate.
2. In the 2nd column mark the volume (amount) of urine—please measure this using a plastic measuring cup or jar. Do not bring with you.
3. In the 3rd column mark the time (day and/or night) accidents occur.
4. In the 4th column describe the amount of the accident—small is a few drops—large is enough to soak through outer garments if a pad is not being worn.
5. In the 5th column describe what you were doing at the time of the accident, or what caused the accident.

URINATION RECORD		ACCIDENT RECORD		
1. Time of urination	2. Amount of urine	3. Time of accident	4. Amount large/small	5. Reason for accident

Number and type of pads used today _____.

NOTE. Do not urinate right before your scheduled appointment in the clinic—we will need you to empty your bladder as part of our evaluation.

APPENDIX 23.2. SYMPTOM LOG

Date: **9-19-94, Monday**

Time	Urinated in toilet	Small accident	Large accident	Reason for accident
6:09 AM	X			
8:47 AM	X			
10:55 AM	X		X	I think I lose urine after getting dressed.
–1:40 PM	X			
2:15 PM			X	Doing paperwork
2:45 PM		X		going down basement steps.
–4:30 PM	X		X	almost 3 hrs. since urinating in toilet.
Before 8:10 I was unable to get to toilet.			X	?
–8:10 PM	X			
–11:10 PM	X			

Number of pads used today: **4**   Number of accidents: **4**

✳ Number of exercises: Lying _____ Sitting _____ Standing _____ Duration _____

Comments: _I should have changed my Depends more often, but I was taking care of my mother._

✳ _I did all of my exercises today._

24

Fecal Incontinence

Jeannette Tries
Eugene Eisman
Susan P. Lowery

Biofeedback evolved from two fields of academic psychology: psychophysiology and learning theory. Psychophysiology provided instrumentation, methods, and knowledge of the anatomy and physiology required for understanding the variety of disorders considered appropriate for this form of therapy. At first, the focus was primarily on autonomic innervated response systems. In time, this broadened to include responses innervated by both branches of the peripheral nervous system.

A major question emerging in the 1960s was whether one could use operant procedures to directly change autonomic-mediated responses. Miller and DiCara (1967) addressed this question using curarized animals. Their research indicated that operant procedures could produce bidirectional changes in heart rate, blood pressure, and glandular activity. These findings challenged the view that smooth muscle learning was possible only through classical conditioning. It gave rise to the notion that one could use operant procedures to treat disorders such as elevated blood pressure and cardiac arrhythmias. However, satisfactory replication of this research has yet to occur. Thus although numerous studies have shown that operant procedures can produce autonomic changes in noncurarized animals and humans (Bower & Hilgard, 1981), none have really employed adequate controls for skeletal muscle and central nervous system (CNS) mediation.

Although specification of the mechanisms of visceral learning is of theoretical importance, it seems less so in clinical applications because skeletal and visceral responses are inextricably linked as part of the centrally integrated response patterns (Miller, 1978). The colorectal system provides an example in which the autonomic nervous system (ANS) and the somatic branch interact to maintain bowel function. This integration provides the opportunity for use of operant procedures to alter disordered function.

Enck's (1993) critical review of the literature through 1990 found 13 adequately designed clinical studies of biofeedback treatment of fecal incontinence in adults. Only one of these studies found that biofeedback therapy did not add to the effectiveness of conventional medical treatment (Loening-Baucke, 1990). Conversely, 12 of 13 studies (Buser & Miner, 1986; Cerulli, Nikoomanesh, & Schuster, 1979; Enck et al., 1988; Engel, Nikoomanesh, & Schuster, 1974; Goldenberg, Hodges, Hersh, & Jinich, 1980; Latimer, Campbell, & Kasperski, 1984; MacLeod, 1987; Miner, Donnelly, & Read, 1990; Riboli, Frascio, Pitto, Reboa, & Zanolla, 1988; Wald, 1981a, 1981b; Wald & Tunuguntla, 1984; Whitehead, Burgio, & Engel, 1985) found that biofeedback was superior to conventional therapy. Although the investigators used diverse outcome criteria, reported improvement ranged from 50–90%, with a mean overall success rate of 79.8% among 322 subjects.

The following discussion focuses on some critical issues probably associated with improvement with biofeedback treatment of fecal incontinence. We raise questions that suggest areas in need of further research.

The use of operant procedures to improve the anorectal physiology to control incontinence was first reported by Kohlenberg (1973). He connected a water-filled balloon to a tube and to a clear cylinder. He positioned the balloon in the anal canal of a 13-year-old boy who exhibited continual fecal seepage and low sphincter pressure. When the child contracted his external anal sphincter, the height of the water column in the cylinder showed the magnitude of the squeeze pressure. Money was the reinforcement to increase his squeeze pressure. This treatment reduced his soiling but he did not become continent. The protocol improved sphincter strength but did not address other factors related to continence. For example, it did not address the sensation to rectal distention or anorectal coordination.

The seminal study of Engel et al. (1974) used a manometric three-balloon probe (described below) for a biofeedback treatment of incontinence. The elegance of this procedure is in its ability to measure and reinforce simultaneously three of the different anorectal responses that can determine continence. The training procedure simulated stool entering the rectum by causing distention of the balloon placed within the rectum. The instructions to subjects were to attend to the sensation of rectal distention and contract the external anal sphincter (EAS) in response to the distention. An important feature of the training protocol was the reinforcement of a timely EAS contraction while maintaining stable intra-abdominal pressure. The protocol used by Engel et al. (1974) addressed several factors that contribute to continence:

1. Wariness of sensory cues that normally signal impending loss of stool.
2. Timely EAS contraction to the perception of distention.
3. Reduction of a maladaptive rise in intra-abdominal pressure that frequently accompanies EAS contraction and that is counter to storage.

Thus, the sensory discrimination task provided by the balloon distention procedure reinforced a training response to specific cues that the patient could generalize to daily life. After one to four treatment sessions, four of the seven patients achieved continence. Two attained significant improvement, and one patient did not complete therapy. Other clinical reports used similar training methods and obtained comparable results (Cerulli et al., 1979; Wald, 1981a, 1981b; Goldenberg et al., 1980; Riboli et al., 1988). However, these studies did not include control groups.

Whitehead et al. (1985) used the protocol of Engel et al. (1974) with geriatric patients and obtained a reduction in incontinence of 77%. This research controlled for the effects of habit training and sphincter exercises without biofeedback. Other controlled studies, using somewhat different procedures, obtained equivalent symptom reduction (Latimer et al., 1984; Wald & Tunuguntla, 1984; Enck et al., 1988; Miner et al., 1990).

One observation made by several researchers is that a short latency response to rectal distention is essential for continence. Also, training for improved sensory discrimination is an important therapeutic goal. For example, to demonstrate the importance of rectal sensation, Buser and Miner (1986) studied a group of patients with delayed perception for rectal distention. They reported a reduction of incontinence of 92% with a protocol designed to provide reinforcement for immediate perception of, and EAS contraction to, rectal distention.

Two studies attempted to determine which components of the biofeedback training were most effective (Latimer et al., 1984; Miner et al., 1990). Latimer et al. (1984) systematically introduced reinforcement for sensory discrimination, sphincter strengthening, and sphincter coordination in a single-case experimental design. They found an association between improved rectal sensation and clinical improvement. However, EAS deficits identified by manometry did not predict an individual's response to a specific biofeedback intervention. In addition to improved rectal sensation, patients showed greater endurance for voluntary contractions of the EAS. They also showed increased magnitude of the EAS response to rectal distention. However, maximum voluntary squeeze pressure did not change significantly.

It may be that EAS strength did not increase appreciably because reinforcement for sphincter contractions was only verbal. The therapist used the feedback display only to help guide the patient. The degree to which one can shape a physiological variable with operant procedures depends upon the accuracy and immediacy of the feedback. It is unlikely that a therapist's verbal reinforcement alone can provide the kind of precise sensory information required to direct and update motor activity for improving the quality of sphincter contractions. This is especially true when trauma or disease compromises sphincter afferent and efferent activity. Furthermore, Latimer et al. (1984) did not attempt to control for increased intra-abdominal pressure that typically occurs. When it occurs, it restricts the effectiveness of sphincter training.

In the most elaborately controlled study to date, Miner et al. (1990) used a two-phase crossover design comparing sham sensory training, active sensory training, sphincter coordination training, and sphincter strength training. These workers concluded that improvement in rectal sensitivity with biofeedback contributes most to symptom reduction. They found that improved sensory discrimination always precedes reduced incontinence. However, not all patients with improved sensation developed continence.

Given these findings, it appears that adequate sensation for rectal distention is necessary but not sufficient for continence. Here again, the researchers did not employ direct visual feedback for sphincter recruitment nor did they control for abdominal substitution. Also, this study limited strength training to only three 20-minute sessions, a time rarely sufficient to strengthen muscles that are weak. Given these limitations, a comparison between strengthening procedures and sensory discrimination training is not valid in this study.

Other investigators have focused exclusively on improving EAS control (MacLeod, 1987; Schiller, Santa Ana, Davis, & Fordtran, 1979). Schiller et al. (1979) treated a woman who had daily incontinence for liquid stool. They infused increasing amounts of saline into her rectum and provided visual and verbal feedback of the retained amounts of the solution. Rectal capacity improved six-fold following this treatment. The patient became continent after 1 week of therapy although the diarrhea persisted.

In a clinical series, Macleod (1987) reported using an intra-anal EMG probe to treat 113 patients with incontinence from varied etiologies. The overall reduction of incontinence was 63%. The training procedure called for the reinforcement of EAS contractions of greater amplitude and duration up to 30 seconds. A limitation was the lack of control for unintentional abdominal contractions. During the follow-up of from 6 months to 5 years, there were no reports of relapse. MacLeod (1987) concluded that EMG biofeedback is useful for postobstetric injury and least effective for patients with anterior resection of the rectum and those with "keyhole" anal deformities.

Surprisingly, a number of reports conclude that improved continence is not necessarily associated with changes in manometric measures of sphincter strength from before to after training nor with any improvement in a saline retention test (Wald, 1981; Miner et al., 1990; Latimer et al., 1984; Loening-Baucke, 1990; Macleod, 1987; Riboli et al., 1988). It may be that the conditioning methods used and the number of treatment sessions provided by these workers were insufficient to produce measurable changes in EAS response patterns. Thus, there was limited generalization to a home exercise program that could potentially change muscle strength over time.

In contrast, other researchers showed that patients increased sphincter contractile ability (Whitehead et al., 1985; Chiarioni, Scattolini, Bonfante, & Vantini, 1993). These training protocols included direct feedback for the amplitude, quality, and duration of sphincter contractions, and the patients learned to inhibit increases in intra-abdominal pressures.

Chiarioni et al. (1993) obtained an overall 85% reduction in incontinence in 14 subjects with chronic diarrhea who had failed prior medical treatment. There was an associated improvement in the ability to sustain an EAS contraction from 19.2 seconds to 38.3 seconds. All nine patients reporting complete resolution of incontinence could sustain a 30-second EAS contraction after treatment.

The latter findings differ from an earlier study drawn from a similar patient population (Loening-Baucke, 1990). The treatment for one group was biofeedback plus conventional medical treatment. The other group received only conventional therapy. The reduction of incontinence was about 50% in both groups. Furthermore, there was no difference between the groups in the maximum voluntary contraction after therapy (Loening-Baucke, 1990). The overall percentage improvement was lower than in other studies using a comparable biofeedback protocol. The authors attributed the reduced efficacy to restricting their sample to patients with diarrhea. However, the Chiarioni et al. (1993) sample also contained only patients with diarrhea. The disparate results obtained between these two studies was more likely the result of differences in the training procedures employed. Although Loening-Baucke (1990) trained coordinated EAS contraction to rectal distention, there was no attempt to reinforce EAS contraction of sufficient duration to exceed the time required for recovery of internal anal sphincter (IAS) inhibition following rectal distention. Nor is it possible to check the adequacy of the home training program because data for the number of Kegel exercises per day were not reported. In contrast, in response to distention and without abdominal contractions, Chiarioni et al. (1993) reinforced EAS contractions of greater amplitudes and durations up to 30 seconds. In addition, there was an assigned, vigorous home exercise program including 20 30-second EAS contractions, 3 times per day.

Recently, Iwata, Nagashima, and Shimotake (1993) found that neither improved sensation nor increased sphincter strength resulted in improved continence. In this research, patients with anorectal malformations after surgical repair learned to improve sensations and voluntary sphincter contractions using visual feedback. However, continence improved for only three of the eight patients, and only anal resting pressure before treatment correlated with continence after treatment.

Like many biofeedback applications, those for fecal incontinence employ various adjunctive manipulations in conjunction with the operant conditioning of targeted physiological responses. These adjunctive procedures include bowel or habit training, dietary manipulations, and the use of medications. Usually, experimental studies do not control for these procedures. Also, biofeedback therapy is likely to be associated with nonspecific effects as from:

- The attention shown by a concerned health professional to a problem which patients generally do not discuss with others.
- The keeping of a symptom diary by the patient over the course of treatment.
- The elaborateness of the feedback procedure itself.
- The actual instrumenting of the anal canal which may improve sensory awareness of the area in, and of, itself.

Most studies have not considered these confounding factors, and only two have tried to control for them to some degree (Whitehead et al., 1985; Loening-Baucke, 1990). As a result, the degree to which these factors and adjunctive procedures contribute to clinical outcome is unknown. Moreover, there are varied treatment protocols used across studies and varied etiologies of incontinence within studies. Wald and Tunuguntala (1984), who restricted their sample to diabetes mellitus, were the exception.

Overall, the research literature indicates that some level of sensitivity to rectal distention is essential to achieve continence. Furthermore, research suggests that biofeedback therapy can be effective in improving rectal sensation. However, the association between measures of EAS strength and clinical outcome has not been consistent across studies. As a result, the degree to which improved strength contributes to continence, and to sensation itself, is unknown. The disparity between obtained changes in sensation compared to sphincter strength probably correlates with the underlying physiological mechanism(s) altered by specific biofeedback procedures. On the one hand, sensations consistently improve with biofeedback. In fact, some studies report improvement with as little as one treatment session (Buser & Miner, 1986; Cerulli et al., 1979; Goldenberg etal., 1980). As this improvement occurs rapidly, it is likely associated with relearning of neurophysiological patterns that are essentially intact but not used because of faulty sensations.

On the other hand, it is unlikely that short-term sensory discrimination training and EAS coordination training will alter muscle tone or strength sufficiently to modify a condition where EAS weakness is the primary contributor to the incontinence. Thus, when the muscles are weak but sensation is intact, symptom reduction would depend on changing muscle strength through an extended and well-designed exercise protocol. This approach was clearly shown by Chiarioni et al. (1993) in patients with diarrhea and incontinence. They attempted to improve not only the coordination of the EAS response to distention but to increase the strength of the EAS as well. Thus, it is not only possible, but desirable, to include a well-designed protocol for EAS strengthening in any program for biofeedback treatment of fecal incontinence.

STRUCTURE AND FUNCTION OF THE RECTUM AND ANUS

The biofeedback therapist must have a comprehensive understanding of the:

- Structure and dynamic functioning of the rectum and the anal canal.
- Pharmacological effects of the various drugs on bowel activity.
- Influence of diet on bowel control.
- Degree to which the measurement methods characterize the pathophysiology.

The following discussion should be viewed only as a brief outline, and the reader is referred to the sources cited for a more complete treatment of the anatomic and physiological factors that influence continence.

Anatomy and Physiology

The rectum is the most distal portion of the colon. It extends from the sigmoid segment to the anal canal. It is 12–15 centimeters long in adults and consists of circular and longitudinal smooth muscle layers like the rest of the colon. When gas or feces move into the rectum, it expands to accommodate the larger mass. Sensory nerves within the rectal walls and nearby striated muscle provide a subjective sensation of fullness and cause the urge to defecate. Contraction of the large colon and rectum provides the propulsive force to move stool toward and through the anal canal.

The *anal canal* pierces the pelvic floor muscles posteriorly. These muscles as a group are the *levator ani muscles*. They enclose the entire base of the bony pelvis and give off components that surround the urethra, vagina, and anal canal. The levator ani provides the primary support for all the organs of the lower abdomen, forming the *levator plate*. This muscle plate positions and stabilizes the various structures of the lower abdomen and pelvis. It gives off muscle fibers that funnel down to, and interdigitate with, the fibers of the EAS that surround the anal canal. The levator ani has three parts: the puborectalis, the pubococcygeus, and the illiococcygeus muscles.

The puborectalis muscle has considerable importance in the maintenance of bowel continence. The puborectalis forms a sling that extends from the pubis back and around the junction between the rectum and the anal canal. This muscle is normally in a state of contraction during the storage phase and maintains an acute angle between the rectum and the anal canal. According to some authorities, this anorectal angle is the most critical factor in the maintenance of continence (Henry & Swash, 1985). For example, if trauma or birth defect compromise the puborectalis, incontinence is almost inevitable. On the other hand, a strong puborectalis can compensate even for a disordered IAS or EAS. For a more complete discussion of the pelvic floor muscles see any comprehensive anatomy text, for example, Netter (1989) or Moore (1992).

As shown in Figure 24.1, the terminal portion of the rectum narrows into the anal canal. The anal canal length is 2.5–3.0 centimeters. It has a thickening of the circular smooth muscle layer that extends down from the rectum. This thickened portion is the IAS and normally is in a state of near maximal contraction (Henry & Swash, 1985) during the storage phase. According to the classic view, the EAS is composed of three separate bundles of striated muscle fibers. Two EAS bundles (the deep and superficial) surround the IAS at the proximal portion of the anal canal. The third, the subcutaneous, is caudal to the IAS and encircles the terminal portion of the anal canal. The EAS and pelvic floor muscles always maintain slight muscle tension during the storage phase.

The IAS relaxes several times per hour, and this allows small amounts of rectal material to enter the anal canal. This material reaches the receptor-rich anoderm, which allows for the discrimination of air, liquid, or solid. When the IAS is tonically contracted, its resting pressure provides a passive barrier to the small amounts of gas or feces that might otherwise seep out. However, when the IAS relaxes to sample the rectal contents, the EAS must contract momentarily to prevent fecal seepage. When defecation is desired, the puborectalis and the external and internal anal sphincters relax simultaneously and completely. This allows for the unresisted passage of stool through the anal canal.

Because rectal distention is the stimulus for IAS relaxation, the EAS must contract immediately with distension to prevent the accidental loss of stool. Contraction of the EAS is brief. However, it is of sufficient duration to allow the rectum to accommodate to the new volume of rectal contents and for the IAS to regain its contracted state. The urge to defecate ends with rectal accommodation until more material moves into the rectum and produces distension again.

The EAS contraction to rectal distension is so well-learned that it occurs without conscious attention and is frequently labeled an unconditioned reflex. However, research shows that the response does not occur if a person fails to sense rectal distension even when the distension is of sufficient magnitude to produce IAS relaxation. In addition, patients can inhibit the EAS response to distension when instructed to do so indicating

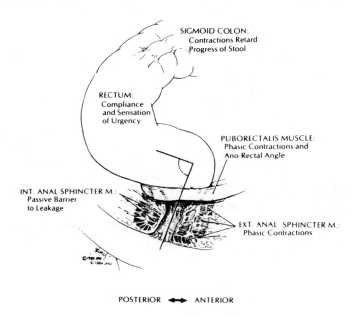

SIGMOID COLON:
Contractions Retard
Progress of Stool

RECTUM:
Compliance
and Sensation
of Urgency

PUBORECTALIS MUSCLE:
Phasic Contractions and
Ano-Rectal Angle

INT. ANAL SPHINCTER M.:
Passive Barrier
to Leakage

EXT. ANAL SPHINCTER M.:
Phasic Contractions

POSTERIOR ◄—► ANTERIOR

FIGURE 24.1. Anatomy of the anal canal, rectum, and distal colon showing some of the physiological mechanisms for preserving continence. From Whitehead (1986, p. 28). Reprinted by permission.

that the response is, in fact, under learned control (Whitehead, Orr, Engel, & Schuster, 1981).

Manometrics

Much of our understanding of normal anal sphincter function comes from anorectal manometry. This same instrumentation was used in many studies researching the effectiveness of biofeedback. This section will describe one form of pneumatic manometry that uses the Schuster anorectal probe. The Schuster probe measures simultaneously the responses of the IAS and EAS to rectal distension by simulating feces entering the rectum (Schuster, Hookman, Hendrix, & Mendeloff, 1965).

The manometry system has three major components: (1) the three-balloon rectal probe; (2) pressure transducers; and (3) a polygraph, chart recorder, or computer that records three or more channels. Figure 24.2 shows the rectal probe placed within the rectum and anal canal.

Briefly, the rectal probe consists of a double balloon tied around a hollow metal cylinder. The balloons are inserted into the anal canal so that the proximal balloon is positioned at the level of the IAS and the distal balloon is at the EAS. A third, the rectal balloon is connected to a length of tubing that is threaded through the metal cylinder that holds the IAS and EAS balloons. The rectal balloon is inserted into the patient's rectum about 10 centimeters from the anal opening. Each balloon connects to a separate pressure transducer by polyethylene tubing. The transducers produce three measurements displayed on a polygraph or computer screen.

To record baseline pressures, one places the balloons within the anal canal and rectum and inflates each of them with 10 cubic centimeters of air. (See the section on manomet-

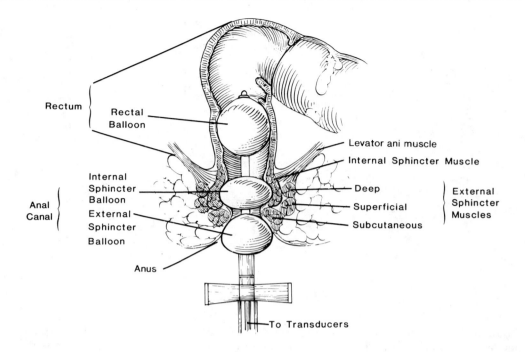

FIGURE 24.2. The rectum and anus with balloons in place.

ric assessment for a description of the insertion.) Typically, the EAS tracing will be fairly stable. The IAS and rectal tracings may exhibit a slow waveform associated with respiration. There is a sharp pressure rise in the rectal tracing as air enters the rectal balloon. Withdrawal of the air results in a quick return to baseline. When the volume of rectal distension is above the patient's sensory threshold (15 cubic centimeters is normal), the IAS tracing will show an initial pressure increase and then will drop to below baseline levels. The initial increase represents the puborectalis stretch response, and the pressure drop indicates the IAS relaxation or "inhibitory" reflex. The IAS inhibitory response may occur even if the patient does not experience the subjective sensation of distension. The magnitude and duration of the IAS relaxation have a positive correlation with the magnitude of rectal distension. Relaxation of the IAS occurs even when one does not immediately withdraw the distending volume. If the distention is maintained, the relaxation may be prolonged, but after a while, the IAS will return to baseline as the rectum accommodates to the distending volume.

The EAS tracing will show a sharp increase of pressure with an acute distension of the rectal balloon. The pressure will gradually return to baseline over the next 5–10 seconds. (see Figure 24.3A). Prolonged rectal distension results in an EAS response of longer duration. Like the IAS, the greater the rectal distension the larger the response (see Figure 24.3B).

When a voluntary EAS contraction (VS) is produced without rectal distension, a pressure increase is seen in both the IAS and EAS tracings (see Figure 24.3C). The IAS balloon records the increase in pressure because the puborectalis and EAS surround the IAS. With-

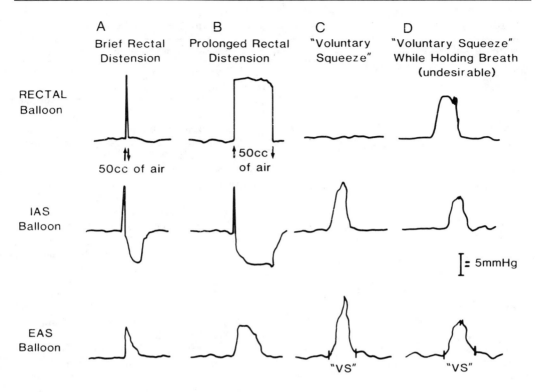

FIGURE 24.3. Sample polygraph records showing normal anal sphincter function. (A) Normal EAS response (≥5 mm Hg) and normal IAS response (initial pressure rise followed by relaxation) to rectal distension by 50 cc of air. (B) Normal EAS and IAS responses to prolonged rectal distension. (C) Normal EAS contraction in response to verbal instructions to "squeeze" without rectal distension. IAS pressure increases, since there is no rectal distension to stimulate the relaxation reflex, and the EAS muscle may indirectly produce pressure on the IAS balloon. (D) Same responses as in C, but holding of the breath results in a weaker EAS contraction.

out rectal distension and the associated IAS relaxation reflex, the IAS balloon provides an accurate measure of squeeze pressure in the proximal anal canal.

Some individuals show a rise in pressure in the rectal balloon tracing during an EAS voluntary contraction (see Figure 24.3D). This response reflects an increase in intra-abdominal pressure from abdominal muscle contraction and breath-holding. Although a slight increase in rectal pressure is normal with EAS contraction, a large increase is maladaptive. This is because the pressure pushes stool from the rectum and is the pattern of defecation rather than retention.

PATHOPHYSIOLOGY OF FECAL INCONTINENCE AND IMPLICATION FOR THERAPY

Medical and postsurgical conditions that can lead to fecal incontinence are listed in Table 24.1. One can group them into five categories based on the pathophysiology directly responsible for the incontinence. An individual patient may exhibit more than one of these deficits:

TABLE 24.1. Medical Disorders and Postsurgical Conditions That May Cause Incontinence

Disorders/conditions	Associated deficits and symptoms
Anal tumor removal	Weak EAS contraction.
Cerebrovascular accident	Impaired rectal sensation; weak EAS contraction.
Crohn's disease	Diarrhea; diminished rectal compliance; normal rectal sensation.
Diabetes	Often nocturnal incontinence; diminished rectal sensation; poor IAS resting tone; weak EAS contraction. Biofeedback is likely to decrease gross incontinence, but leakage may continue.
Encopresis, childhood	Constipation. IAS sphincter may be dilated due to large amounts of stool in rectum; may have normal EAS contraction; may have some impairment of rectal sensation due to dilation of rectum. Probably will require bowel training program and possible bulk agents or stool softeners.
Fistulectomy	Weak EAS contraction.
Hemorrhoidectomy	Weak EAS contraction.
Hirschsprung's disease	Overflow incontinence secondary to constipation (lifelong); no IAS relaxation reflex. Requires surgical correction.
Ileoanal anastomosis following colectomy and proctectomy	Liquid to soft stool; staining to gross incontinence; diminished rectal capacity; no IAS relaxation reflex; possible impairment of the EAS contraction. Requires additional dietary and/or pharmacological management of stool consistency.
Imperforate anus repair	Likely to have staining/leakage as opposed to incontinence of solid stool; diminished rectal capacity; no IAS relaxation reflex or IAS resting tone. May benefit from dietary or pharmacological therapy to solidify stool.
Irritable bowel syndrome	May have constipation or diarrhea (incontinence most common with diarrhea). Probably normal sphincter strength and function; normal rectal sensation. May have excessive rectal pressure.
Laminectomy	Weak EAS contraction or diminished rectal sensation. May be chronically constipated.
Meningomyelocele	Constipation; normal IAS reflex; very weak or nonexistent EAS contraction; generally normal rectal sensation. Probably will require bowel training program and possibly bulk agent or stool softeners. Requires more biofeedback sessions and time to achieve continence than most patients with other disorders.
Multiple sclerosis	Impaired rectal sensation; weak EAS contraction. May be chronically constipated.
Polypectomy	Weak EAS contraction.
Proctectomy	Weak EAS contraction.

TABLE 24.1. (*continued*)

Disorders/conditions	Associated deficits and symptoms
Radiation proctitis	Diminished rectal compliance. May have weak EAS contraction.
Rectal prolapse	Typically, staining after bowel movement; diminished IAS resting tone. Surgery may be best alternative.
Rectal prolapse, repaired	Weak EAS contraction.
Scleroderma	Diminished rectal compliance; no IAS relaxation reflex. May have weak EAS contraction.
Sphincter repair	Weak EAS contraction.

1. Impaired rectal sensation.
2. Inadequate contraction of the EAS.
3. Poor resting tone of the IAS.
4. Diminished rectal capacity.
5. Incomplete relaxation or paradoxical contraction with defecation.

Impaired sensation to rectal distension can result from damage to afferent nerve fibers or to sensory areas in the brain. A sensory deficit also may result from a chronically dilated rectum secondary to severe constipation. Regardless of the etiology, failure to perceive rectal distention has deleterious effects on continence. Normally IAS relaxation occurs frequently through the day. This intermittent IAS relaxation allows some rectal contents to contact the anoderm which is rich in sensory receptors. This "sampling" enables the individual to determine whether the contents of the rectum are gas, liquid, or stool. The person can then plan a course of action. That is, they can pass gas, find a toilet, or contract the EAS to inhibit the bowel movement. If rectal sensation is impaired, however, an EAS contraction does not occur concurrently with the IAS relaxation, and there is no closure of the distal anal canal as the proximal canal expands. Fecal matter sampled in the anal canal seeps outward without increased pressure at the outer anal canal.

Manometry, described in the next section, tests rectal sensation. Normally, the EAS automatically contracts at all levels of rectal distention that are perceptible. This contraction is the rectosphincteric response to distention. The amplitude of the rectosphincteric response is an index of the integrity of the sensory–motor system. It should match the patient's perception of distention.

A weakened rectosphincteric (stretch) response to distention could still result in urgency or incontinence even with normal sensation and squeeze pressures. Diminished stretch responses often occur in a muscle with low resting tone. This indicates impairment in the sensory-motor response loops of that muscle. Sensations for rectal distension occur not only in the walls of the rectum but also within the muscles of the pelvic floor (Henry & Swash, 1985). Hypotonic pelvic floor muscles reduce the response to distention by limiting the proprioceptive signal typically produced by that distention. Without an adequate proprioceptive signal, the patient has little warning for the movement of stool into the rectum. Thus, he or she cannot respond with a timely EAS contraction to close the anal canal and push the fecal material back into the rectum. Patients with this problem often perceive and report the need to have a bowel movement "too late." Improving sphincter tone with exercise may enhance the efficiency of the stretch receptor response, thus providing the patient with a more timely warning for loss of stool.

Impaired EAS contractions or muscle tone may result from partial denervation injury to the pelvic floor muscles and anal sphincter. A frequent cause for partial denervation is stretch injury during childbirth, especially where there is a prolonged second-stage labor (Allen, Hosker, Smith, & Warrell, 1990). A weak EAS contraction also may result from damage to the sphincter muscle itself such as from anal surgery, radiation, or a vaginal–rectal tear during childbirth. In these cases, incontinence occurs because the pressure from descending stool and contracting colon overcomes a low EAS squeeze pressure.

Surrounding and supporting the IAS smooth muscle at the inner anal canal is the puborectalis muscle, a striated muscle. Because of this arrangement, both smooth and striated muscle contribute to the IAS pressure recorded with manometry.

Poor IAS resting tone is often caused by damage to the IAS during anal or rectal surgery. Examples are imperforate anus repair, ileal–anal anastomosis, or hemorrhoidectomy. Poor IAS tone also may result from chronic dilation of the sphincter with constipation. In this case, normal resting tone may be restored after the patient has been disimpacted and the rectum remains empty with regular toileting. One can palpate diminished IAS resting tone during digital examination. If the involuntary IAS has a low resting baseline, the IAS relaxation reflex will show only a small amplitude change during manometric rectal distention. This is because the basal muscle activity is so low there is a limited range for muscle inhibition. If, however, the IAS smooth muscle is intact but the surrounding puborectalis muscle has low supporting tone, the IAS inhibitory response will be extreme because IAS inhibition is unopposed by any surrounding striated muscle support.

If rectal sensation and EAS contraction are adequate, individuals with poor IAS resting tone are likely to escape gross incontinence. However, they may experience leakage of liquid stool and gas in amounts too small to produce a perceived distension stimulus. The EAS will then fail to contract. Alternatively, they may complain of an urgent call to stool where there is a limited ability to inhibit a bowel movement after perceiving the sensation. This urgency may occur because the IAS inhibition and surrounding puborectalis tone contribute significantly to the sensation for impending fecal loss. These provide the first place of resistance to loss of stool or gas. When the inner anal canal has low tone, the functional length of the canal shortens. This means that the compromised anal canal has a limited area in which to elevate pressure effectively to provide resistance to fecal loss.

Rectal compliance is the ability of the rectum to adapt to a fecal mass without a sustained elevation in rectal pressure. One determines compliance by the elasticity of the rectal tissue and the degree to which the smooth muscle of the colon and rectum inhibits passage. Rectal capacity decreases when the rectal walls become noncompliant as a result of inflammation or from a reduction of the size of the rectum or colon. Noncompliance may accompany active ulcerative proctitis, scarring from rectal surgery or chronic inflammatory disease. If the rectum does not stretch and remains noncontractile to accommodate increasing amounts of stool, there is a resultant increase in pressure. This may overwhelm even the strongest EAS contraction. Also, when the colon is irritable, strong colonic contractions may inhibit a weak sphincter through neural feedback loops. The spontaneous EAS contraction that normally occurs with rectal distension not only increases pressure in the anal canal but also inhibits colonic contraction. This reduces rectal pressure until a desired evacuation time. Thus, this inhibitory effect usually reduces the need for a sustained EAS contraction to maintain continence. However, when sensory or motor deficits diminish the intensity of the EAS response, there is disinhibition of the colon from this source of control. With the loss of inhibition, incontinence is more likely to occur because rectal pressure overwhelms the anal canal squeeze pressure.

Signs of limited rectal capacity include frequent and unformed bowel movements, urgent calls to stool, and explosive bowel movements. One can assess rectal compliance manometrically by first distending the rectal balloon with 20 cubic centimeters of air, then, maintaining the distension for 2 minutes, and increasing the distending volume by 20 cubic centimeters of air in a stepwise fashion up to 200 cubic centimeters. If the rectum is compliant, the rectal channel will show a drop in pressure following the initial pressure increase. However, there will not be a return to baseline until withdrawal of the air from the rectal balloon. If the rectum is noncompliant, rectal pressure will remain high or there will be extreme variations in pressure that indicate rectal spasm.

"Paradoxical pelvic floor contraction" refers to an abnormal pattern of sphincter contraction with defecation, rather than relaxation. This coordination deficit causes an outlet obstruction constipation and straining with stool. Failure to relax the sphincter during defecation should be considered when treating incontinence because many patients become incontinent as a result of procedures done to correct the very complications that result from long-term constipation and inappropriate defecation patterns, for example, repair of rectocele, prolapse, and hemorrhoidectomy. Furthermore, chronic straining with stool is another source of pelvic floor muscle denervation that contributes to pelvic floor muscle weakness and incontinence. Therefore, patients presenting with incontinence can have both sphincter weakness and a disordered defecation pattern, which prevent complete evacuation of stool with toileting. The result of incomplete evacuation in these patients is postdefecation seepage.

The degree to which biofeedback will be successful often depends upon the complexity of the underlying pathophysiology. When EAS impairment is present but rectal sensation is adequate, biofeedback therapy is usually very effective. If the sensory deficit is slight to moderate, rectal sensation often improves with therapy. People with less notable outcomes are those who, after a bowel-training program to keep the rectum empty, do not come to sense very large volumes of rectal distension such as 50 cubic centimeters.

Some individuals with inadequate IAS resting tone and an absent IAS inhibitory reflex derive benefit from biofeedback therapy, but the results with these patients are variable. These patients may develop greater control over gross incontinence, but they may continue to have leakage. The mechanism for improvement in patients with inadequate IAS resting tone is unclear because biofeedback procedures do not directly influence the IAS, which is an involuntary muscle. The striated puborectalis muscle surrounds the IAS and contributes to the functional length of the anal canal. It may be that the mechanism for improvement in patients with poor IAS function is that with biofeedback, the puborectalis becomes more efficient at compensating for poor IAS tone.

It may be impossible to change rectal compliance where there is scar tissue or after surgical reduction of the size of the rectum. However, biofeedback may improve continence by improving the strength of the EAS to offset elevations in rectal pressure. If the noncompliance is physiological, for example, rectal spasm, biofeedback may improve compliance by enhancing the inhibitory control mechanism provided by a more effective sphincter contraction.

The medical and surgical conditions that can cause incontinence appear in Table 24.1. Biofeedback tends to be more effective when incontinence is the result of surgery as opposed to disease or functional disorders.

In addition to the physiological deficits discussed above, incontinence may result from the following:

1. There may be a lack of motivation to emit the EAS response. (This may occur, e.g., among senile, psychotic, or mentally retarded patients.)
2. Overflow incontinence may result from chronic functional constipation in children and adults.
3. Incontinence may occur with functional diarrhea.

In any of these cases, if manometric evaluation reveals normal anal function, behavioral therapy, other than biofeedback, is the preferred intervention.

TREATMENT

Treatment Providers

The biofeedback procedures for treating fecal incontinence involve minimal risk to the patient, but they are invasive. The therapist must be well trained to perform digital rectal examination done as part of the assessment and before insertion of the rectal probes. Improper insertion of the probe into a badly damaged rectum can perforate the rectal wall. Although this is unlikely, peritoneal infection can have severe consequences including death. Also, fecal incontinence and associated bowel disorders exist concurrently with other medical disorders. Patients are often taking various medications that influence bowel function. Thus, the practitioner using biofeedback must work closely with a physician.

The successful application of biofeedback for fecal incontinence is highly dependent upon the knowledge and skill of the health professional applying this therapy. This knowledge encompasses evaluation techniques, anatomic and physiological correlates of the types and symptoms of bowel dysfunction, instrumentation, and behavioral principles that guide the procedures.

Moreover, the biofeedback therapist must be sensitive to the patient's emotional needs. Many patients show initial embarrassment and/or fear the procedures. Thus, one must explain the procedures and their rationale in a clear and reassuring manner and respect the patient's modesty by keeping the individual covered as much as possible. Also, a bathroom adjoining the examination/treatment room provides privacy for patients to clean themselves and dress.

An essential feature of biofeedback is the visual information display used by the patient and the therapist to guide responses in desired directions. Thus, specific characteristics of the biofeedback instrument can optimize its clinical application. These features include speed, accuracy, availability, and reliability of the feedback signals that can be graded on a continuum. The flexibility of the biofeedback display, such as the gain and threshold settings, allow tailoring of feedback to the patient's abilities. For example, a patient cannot readily distinguish a 2-microvolt contraction on a 0- to 50-microvolt scale display when trying to recruit his or her partially innervated EAS. A 0- to 10-microvolt scale display allows magnification of a small contraction. This allows the patient to precisely discriminate response patterns resulting in optimal motor responses. Other useful features of the instrument include provisions for making permanent records of graphs and tabular data.

Moreover, the causes of incontinence are often multifactorial. These include pelvic floor muscle laxity or limited sensation to rectal distension. Thus, the more inclusive and specific the biofeedback measures and displays, the more comprehensive the treatment for the variety of symptom patterns. We recommend at least two EMG channels and manometric equipment.

Whom to Treat?

It makes sense to provide biofeedback therapy to many patients with fecal incontinence even when the potential benefit is uncertain. There may be significant functional improvement in a few sessions. This is especially true if lack of sensation is the predominant reason for the incontinence *and* the patient responds to the sensory training described below. Unfortunately, many patients coming for biofeedback have exhausted all other medical treatments. However, biobehavioral treatment can often provide functional improvement. This treatment is, in essence, a problem-solving process that can help the patient generalize physiological changes into daily life.

Some physicians also use biofeedback procedures before corrective surgery. Biofeedback treatment can improve anorectal function and helps improve surgical outcome. With biofeedback assessment, one also can detect maladaptive habits such as inappropriate sphincter contractions with defecation. Thus, one can alter the maladaptive patterns before surgery to avoid undoing its beneficial effects.

There are some patients, however, whom one should exclude from biofeedback treatment because they are almost certain to be unsuccessful. These include patients with little or no motivation to achieve continence or who cannot follow directions, for example, those with advanced dementia, psychosis, severe retardation, and children under age 5. Other patients who may have more limited improvement are those who, after a bowel-habit program to empty the rectum of stool, have a sensory deficit of greater than 50 cubic centimeters. However, this degree of sensory deficit is rare in our clinic.

BIOFEEDBACK PROCEDURES FOR BOWEL DYSFUNCTION

Functional Evaluation

After the patient's thorough medical exam, the practitioner or therapist undertakes a functional evaluation of the patient's bowel patterns and symptoms. A complete medical history of the patient should be obtained, including a detailed history of the incontinence problem (e.g., the onset of symptoms, a description of bowel patterns prior to the appearance of symptoms). Include the following questions.

1. How did the problem start, and what were the changes in bowel habits over the years?
2. What has been the duration of the fecal incontinence?
3. Were there any precipitating events such as illness, surgery, or social/psychological symptoms or disorder associated with the onset of symptoms?
4. What is the frequency of bowel movements?
5. What is the size and consistency of bowel movements?
6. Is it necessary to strain with a bowel movement? Is there any discomfort with the passage of stool?
7. Is there any feeling of incomplete evacuation? Is incomplete evacuation followed by incontinence?
8. What are the effects of various foods and other factors on bowel function?
9. Is there an "urgent call to stool" where one fears incontinence will occur if toileting is not immediate?
10. What is the approximate time from "urge" (if any) to accidental loss of stool?

11. What is the frequency of incontinent events?
12. When incontinent, what is the amount and consistency of stool? Ask the patient to distinguish stains from small amounts of stool, small amounts from large amounts, and liquid stool from solid stool.
13. Can the patient control flatus?
14. When do incontinent events occur? For example, do they occur after meals or following an incomplete evacuation? Are they nocturnal and/or diurnal?
15. What is the relationship of symptoms to diet or activity?
16. Is sensation for stool in the rectum blunted? Can they distinguish gas from stool?
17. What is the percentage of bowel movements controlled?
18. Are there factors that increase or decrease the likelihood of incontinence (e.g., type of activity, availability of rest room, and anxiety)?
19. What is the type and number of protective pads used?
20. What are the present medications?
21. Is assistance required to have bowel movements (i.e., laxatives, enemas, suppositories, or manual removal of stool)?
22. Is there pelvic floor or anal pain?
23. Is there abdominal cramping? Is it associated with meals?
24. Does the patient have any bladder symptoms such as incontinence, urgency, frequency, voiding hesitancy, or incomplete voiding?

In addition, ask the patient to give specific examples of how the problem interferes with everyday life. Some patients respond unemotionally to this question, whereas others may show considerable emotion. In addition to limiting many facets of one's life, incontinence usually affects self-concept and interpersonal relationships. Also, try to determine the degree to which emotional arousal affects symptoms, without diminishing the physical etiology of the problem even when that etiology is unclear.

Patients must feel free to discuss feelings of frustration and despair that are common among people with incontinence. Patients are very appreciative of a knowledgeable and empathetic therapist inquiring about the specific nature of the problem and their feelings. Other health care providers may have ignored the emotional side of the problem.

Instruct the patient to complete a daily symptom diary. It should include bowel frequency, incontinence episodes, feelings of incomplete evacuation, stool consistency, strain or discomfort with passage of stool, and use of enemas or laxatives. It should also include other significant information related to the patient's complaints. Ideally, the patient completes the diary for about 1 week before the initial physical evaluation and during the entire treatment. The diary documents subtle changes that guide the treatment and helps maintain the patient's motivation. Analyzing the diary with the patient during each office session impresses the patient with the importance of keeping the diary.

Physical Evaluation

The physical evaluation includes a digital exam and electromyography (EMG) of the anal canal and abdominal muscles. It also includes manometric measures of the rectum using the Schuster balloons to assess the IAS and EAS.

Digital Exam

Before inserting the Schuster probe, a digital rectal exam is necessary to assess the following:

1. The EAS and IAS resting tone felt as resistance to the finger during insertion.
2. The EAS contraction strength around the finger when instructing the patient to squeeze.
3. The strength of the contraction of the puborectalis sling muscle when instructing the patient to squeeze.
4. The presence of any discomfort when stretching the puborectalis muscle posteriorly toward the coccyx. Discomfort with this stretch may indicate excessive muscle tone and spasm.
5. The size of the rectal ampulla. Excess dilation of the rectum beyond the normal dilated state suggests chronic constipation.
6. The presence of stool in the rectum. In a normally functioning bowel, the rectum is empty. The presence of stool suggests constipation or incomplete evacuation.
7. The presence of strictures or scarring that may inhibit the passage of stool or limit rectal compliance.

EMG Assessment

In addition to EMG measurement of the pelvic floor muscles, the EMG examination should include measurement of the abdominal muscles at rest and during voluntary contraction of the pelvic floor muscles. One can view the abdominal EMG measure as a measure correlated with changes in intra-abdominal pressure. Place bipolar surface electrodes on the right abdominous oblique muscle, about 4 centimeters apart and 4 centimeters from the midline, with the rostral electrode placed laterally to the umbilicus and the caudal electrode placed perpendicular to the rostral electrode. The abdominal EMG channel uses a 100–200-Hertz bandpass filter to minimize cardiac artifact.

Use an anal plug EMG electrode to record muscle activity from the anal canal. Here, use a bandpass filter that can maximize the amount of the muscle signal, for example 15–80 Hertz. The newly designed multiple electrode probe (MEP) can differentiate muscle activity at the distal anal canal from the proximal portion of the anal canal (see Chapter 23). This function is useful when training incontinent patients to recruit the muscles specifically from the distal anal canal and when reinforcing relaxation in the deeper levator muscles as in patients with disordered defecation or levator ani syndrome. Probes with only a single pair of longitudinally placed electrodes summate activity across the entire length of the anal canal.

Position the patient in the left-lateral position with knees and hips flexed for plug insertion and recording. Before inserting the EMG probe, dilate the anal canal with a lubricated index finger as the probe is introduced into the canal with the other hand. After insertion, allow a few minutes for the surrounding muscles to adapt before taking a resting baseline measure. Examine the EMG baseline recording for elevated resting levels of either the abdominal and/or sphincter muscles. This indicates possible spasm or chronic muscle tension.

Next, ask the patient to contract the sphincter "as if trying to prevent an accident." Avoid suggesting that the patient "Contract as hard as you can" because this exhortation often results in maladaptive abdominal contraction. Examine the EMG record for the response latency, the signal's amplitude, the stability and endurance of the contraction, and the time it takes for the EMG signal to decay and recover to baseline after telling the patient to relax. Also, note the degree to which the abdominal muscles contract with the sphincter contraction. Then, ask the patient to "defecate" or push out the probe while measuring perianal muscle relaxation and abdominal contraction.

An EMG record of a normal contraction would show a:

- Relatively low baseline.
- Rapid rise to a maximum contraction.
- Stable contraction for 10 seconds.
- Short latency to return to baseline after stopping the voluntary contraction.

During the contraction, the abdominal measures should remain relatively low and stable. This indicates the patient's ability to isolate pelvic floor muscle contraction from abdominal contraction. With the "defecation" maneuver of the recording probe, the EMG from the pelvic floor muscles should drop below the baseline and to a very low microvolt level while the abdominal EMG increases as the patient elevates intra-abdominal pressure.

THE MANOMETRIC ASSESSMENT

The manometric assessment documents rectal sensitivity and the functional integrity of the anal canal. One cannot assess this only with measures of strength. Accordingly, this is an important part of the assessment and treatment of fecal incontinence. This chapter only discusses the use of the pneumatic Schuster probe as the manometric method. However, one can perform a manometric assessment and treatment with a perfusion catheter system.

Insertion of the Schuster Probe

A condom placed over the Schuster Balloon probe eases its cleaning. The condom covers the balloon with considerable slack over the balloon system, and the base of the condom just covers the T-handle. This allows advancing the rectal balloon to about 10 centimeters above the base of the EAS balloon. It is helpful to mark the rectal tube where it should line up with the base of the cylinder. This helps assure sufficient insertion into the rectum.

Deflate the balloons before insertion. Lubricate the probe well. First, dilate the opening of the anal canal with a lubricated index finger. This is a good time to conduct the full digital exam and helps the therapist visualize the anorectal angle during the balloon insertion. With the other hand, begin to insert the rectal balloon. With the tip of the rectal balloon, place some pressure against the dilating finger. In this way, one eases the rectal portion of the probe into the anal canal while it is dilated.

Once the rectal portion of the balloon is inserted, remove the dilating finger and grasp the T-handle with the same hand. Then guide the passage of the cylinder into the canal. The anorectal angle bends posteriorly. Thus, the direction of the insertion pressure may change from rostral to slightly posterior as the rectal balloon passes above the puborectalis muscle. Only one-third to one-fourth of the EAS balloon is visible with a properly placed Schuster probe. Figure 24.1 shows proper placement.

With the apparatus held to prevent it from slipping, inject 10 cubic centimeters of air into the IAS balloon. Inflation should produce a slight inward tug on the cylinder. Place 10 cubic centimeters of air in the rectal balloon and then inflate the EAS balloon with 10 cubic centimeters of air. Potential difficulties include the following:

1. If the rectum is full of firm stool, it may be difficult or impossible to advance the rectal balloon.

2. If the rectal balloon does not inflate or does so only with difficulty, check for a bent tube or to see whether the tube moved back into the cylinder.

3. If the patient has a wide anal opening, the balloon apparatus may repeatedly slip out despite proper placement and inflation. Hold the device in place by taping the crossbar of the cylinder to the patient's buttocks. However, this will probably amplify the size of the EAS responses because contractions of the gluteal muscles exert more pressure on a taped EAS balloon.

4. When the puborectalis is in spasm, passage of the probe into the canal may be uncomfortable. If discomfort persists, it may not be possible to continue with the examination. In this event, one must use an EMG probe without a retaining bulb (the MEP, or a pediatric probe) initially until the patient learns to relax the spasm.

5. Where there is considerable scar tissue or irritability of the rectal wall, there also may be discomfort. This leads to false measurements. If this occurs, use less than the 10-cubic-centimeter inflation bolus to set the balloons. Obviously, note the alteration in the standard preparation.

The Assessment

Manometric examination provides the following information:

1. The threshold of rectal sensation. This is 10–15 cubic centimeters for normal subjects.

2. The presence or absence of the IAS inhibitory reflex.

3. The integrity of the rectosphincteric response to rectal distension. The rectosphincteric response is an automatic EAS contraction that occurs to a distended rectum. Subjects show some EAS contraction in response to rectal distension even without instructions to squeeze. They also exhibit larger responses to larger distending volumes.

4. The threshold for the IAS reflex and the EAS response. In normal subjects, both should occur with distension of 10–15 cubic centimeters.

5. The timing of the IAS reflex and the EAS response. Both responses should occur immediately after rectal distension, although the IAS takes several seconds to reach its maximum inhibition. The normal inhibitory response lasts for 5–20 seconds after the rectal stimulus. The time depends upon the size of the stimulus. The greater the stimulus, the longer the inhibition reflex. In contrast, the EAS response reaches its maximum contraction within a second of the rectal stimulus.

6. The maximum voluntary squeeze pressure recorded from the EAS when instructing the patient to squeeze without rectal distension. This is greater than 20 millimeters Hg for normal subjects.

7. The degree to which the abdominal pressure maladaptively increases with voluntary contraction of the sphincter.

Examples of abnormal sphincter responses are shown in Figure 24.4. Compare these with the normal responses in Figure 24.3.

The manometric assessment is conducted as follows. Tell the patient that during the evaluation small amounts of air will be put into the rectal balloon and immediately withdrawn. During the assessment, the patient's eyes are closed or the recording display is blocked from the patient's view. Also, inflate the rectal balloon out of the patient's sight.

To demonstrate the procedure, inflate the rectal balloon with a bolus of air. Usually start with 30–50 milliliters of air and progress up to 150 milliliters of air if the patient is

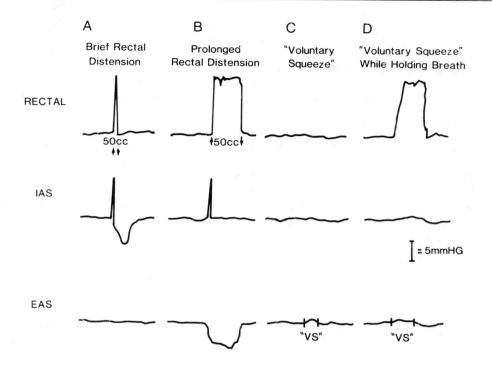

FIGURE 24.4. Sample polygraph records showing abnormal and sphincter responses. (A) No EAS response, due to either inability to sense rectal distension or impairment of the sphincter muscle. Normal IAS relaxation response. (B) Decreased EAS pressure, due to patient "bearing down" instead of contracting the sphincter. No IAS relaxation. (Both may also occur with brief rectal distension and need not occur together.) (C) Very weak EAS contraction, due to impaired sphincter strength (may occur with or without rectal distension). (D) Very weak EAS contraction, due to either impaired sphincter strength, excessive abdominal pressure, or both.

not sensitive to the initial inflation. Tell the patient that each time air is put into the rectal balloon, the examiner will ask "Did you feel that?" However, also tell the patient there will be times when the therapist will not inflate the rectal balloon and will still ask, "Did you feel that?" These "catch" trials control for the tendency to respond to the demand characteristics of the test rather than to the actual stimulus.

After asking the patient to close his or her eyes while the examiner administers rectal distension trials in a descending order of 50, 40, 30, 20, 15, 10, and 5 milliliters. After each distension, withdraw the air immediately. However, do not remove the initial 10 milliliters used to position the balloon. Wait until the pressures return to baseline before giving the next distension (about 30 seconds). The absolute sensory threshold is the lowest volume of air the patient perceives in three consecutive trials. Examine pressure changes in response to each inflation. This determines the presence and amplitude of EAS contractions and the amplitude and recovery of the inhibitory IAS reflex. Note and record both verbal and recorded response delays.

Next, observe the voluntary motor response to rectal distension. Here, one injects an air into the rectal balloon without visual or verbal feedback to the patient. Instruct the patient to squeeze the anal sphincter when feeling this stimulus, as if "trying to prevent loss of stool or flatus." Note the response time, amplitude and endurance of the sphincter contraction, increases in intra-abdominal pressure, and recovery time of the internal anal sphincter inhibitory response.

Measure the maximum squeeze pressures over an extended contraction. Ask the patient to contract the sphincter as if trying to stop a bowel movement or the loss of flatus. As with EMG, avoid the direction "contract as hard as you can." Ask for a 10-second contraction. Then, have the patient rest for about 30 seconds, and repeat the contraction for one to two more trials.

In a normal manometric record, a rectal distension of 10 milliliters results in an immediate contraction of the EAS and inhibition of the IAS. The amplitude of these responses is proportionate to the volume of air inflated into the rectal balloon. The normal sensory threshold to rectal distension above an initial 10-milliliter baseline volume is in the range of 5–15 milliliters.

Guidelines to Interpret Manometric Recordings

1. The therapist should examine the tracing and compare the size, timing, and threshold of the responses to normal responses.

2. If the IAS relaxation reflex is absent and the IAS resting tone is normal, it may signify Hirschsprung's disease. However, an absent or attenuated IAS inhibitory response may result from a rigidly contracting puborectalis muscle which surrounds the IAS. A contracting puborectalis can mask an IAS inhibitory response because it can maintain the anal canal in a rigid, tube-like state that keeps anal pressure stable. If one suspects this problem, help the patient relax and repeat the assessment. However, the nonrelaxing puborectalis muscle may be a significant contributor to the patient's symptoms. If so, the therapist will need to address this with specific behavioral strategies.

3. Compare the automatic EAS response to the maximum voluntary squeeze. They should be similar in amplitude. An attenuated automatic response may be a function of impaired sensation. It also may result from a very low resting tone that may limit stretch-receptor afferent activity normally activated with distention.

4. If there is a pressure decrease in the EAS when the patient is instructed to squeeze, the patient is probably "bearing down" as is often done in defecation. Children often confuse this response with sphincter contraction.

5. If the rectal channel shows pressure increases while the patient is squeezing, he or she is probably increasing intra-abdominal pressure by breath holding or abdominal contraction. This is the pattern of defecation and is maladaptive to sphincter contraction and fecal storage.

Patients with bowel dysfunction frequently show the following irregularities in their EMG and manometric records. Patients with incontinence frequently display EAS EMG contraction measures that are of low amplitude and limited endurance over 10 seconds. Moreover, incontinent patients usually contract the abdominal and/or gluteal muscles when asked to contract the EAS. With urgency, this abdominal contraction increases intra-abdominal and rectal pressure. In the case of incontinence, the increase in intra-abdominal pressure is difficult to offset with a weak sphincter. The patient will be more likely, therefore, to be incontinent as intra-abdominal pressure increases with urge.

In patients with an urgent call to stool and incontinence associated with little warning, one often sees an elevated sensory threshold for rectal distension or a delayed response to rectal distension. Improving rectal sensitivity where it is limited is a primary goal when using biofeedback to reduce incontinence.

Frequently, patients that report feelings of incomplete evacuation show an elevated resting EMG baseline. With the defecation maneuver, one often sees in the EAS measure either a paradoxical contraction or a failure to relax. The term for an inappropriate increase in muscle activity during defecation is "paradoxical pelvic floor muscle contraction." The term "failure to relax" is operative when muscle activity does not drop below baseline during defecation. One sees these abnormal coordination patterns in patients with outlet obstruction associated with constipation. An in-depth discussion of the biofeedback treatment for constipation is beyond the scope of this chapter (see Chapter 37). However, many patients with fecal incontinence also have symptoms of outlet obstruction (incomplete evacuation followed by fecal seepage). Consequently, if there is paradoxical contraction, it should be altered to assure optimal treatment outcome. Some patients also have difficulty appropriately raising intra-abdominal pressure with the defecation pattern. This dysfunction may be seen in patients who, through maturational delays, congenital deformity, or maladaptive learning never learned appropriate defecation patterns. Excessive EMG activity at rest also occurs in levator ani syndrome. This is a condition caused by spasm in the levator ani muscle which produces pain and discomfort in the anal canal and pelvic floor.

Biofeedback Treatment Goals

After identifying the abnormalities, specific biofeedback goals for bowel dysfunction usually include shaping the following responses:

1. Sphincteric contractions of greater amplitude and improved duration in isolation from abdominal and/or gluteal contraction and associated elevations in intra-abdominal pressure.
2. Sphincteric contractions with short response latencies and immediate recovery to baseline after voluntary contraction ceases.
3. Heightened perception to lower levels of rectal distension paired with immediate EAS contraction and IAS inhibition.
4. Sphincteric relaxation below resting baseline concurrent with appropriate elevation in intra-abdominal pressure during the defecation maneuver.
5. Reduction of chronically elevated striated sphincter muscle activity when present.

Shaping Specific Responses

Before training begins, carefully explain to the patient the anatomy and physiology of continence and the significance of the EMG and manometric findings in relation to the patient's bowel function. During treatment, the patient should learn the various roles of the striated pelvic floor muscles in bowel control and how they interact with the smooth muscle of the colon and rectum. A patient-education training manual helps. It should include lesson plans for specific training goals. One such manual is available from the Clinic for Neurophysiological Learning (Tries & Eisman, 1995).

Training Isolated Sphincteric Contractions

When there is sphincter weakness or diminished motor response with rectal distension, one must improve EAS recruitment in isolation from other muscles. With urgency, the incontinent person must learn to limit the maladaptive abdominal contraction that only increases the probability of fecal loss. Moreover, where EAS contraction is weak, there is little proprioceptive feedback for its recruitment and, therefore, the patient unknowingly substitutes ineffective muscles. This results in the weak EAS muscle being poorly activated and hence poorly strengthened.

Thus, one must systematically shape isolated pelvic floor muscle recruitment. The therapist uses various features of the biofeedback instrument to increase learning. See the section on training isolated perineal contractions in Chapter 23 for a discussion of specific pelvic floor muscle-shaping procedures using abdominal and pelvic floor EMG feedback. Therapists also can use the Schuster balloon for pelvic floor muscle re-education. One uses the EAS pressure as feedback for isolated pelvic muscle recruitment while keeping intra-abdominal pressure stable.

Improving Sensory Discrimination and Motor Coordination with Rectal Distension

Use of the Schuster balloon helps patients improve their sensation for, and the coordinated motor responses to, rectal distension. However, one usually provides sensory training using the Schuster balloon after isolated pelvic floor training. At the beginning of manometric training, inject a bolus of air into the rectal balloon. The initial training inflation volume is one that the patient perceived as rectal distention during the evaluation. Then, immediately withdraw the air and explain the automatic responses to the patient while looking at the display. Next, repeat the inflation, but tell the patient to contract the EAS immediately following the stimulus. If the patient increases abdominal pressure with the EAS contraction, remind the patient to keep the abdominal muscles relaxed.

During this procedure, tell the patient to try to identify the distention sensation and associate this with the visual feedback and the motor response (EAS contraction). Also, tell the patient to limit any delay in the EAS response to the rectal stimulus.

After the patient demonstrates immediate sphincter contractions to the perceived distention, give the air stimulus over several blind trials. The patient's eyes are closed during the distention, but the patient looks at the display immediately after the contraction to observe the accuracy of the response. If the blind trial performance is equivalent to the biofeedback trial, the therapist decreases the volume of rectal distension. The sequence is repeated with incremental reductions to 5- to 10-milliliter inflations. However, if the motor responses decay at any time in the stepwise reduction of the inflation volume, repeat the biofeedback trials at the same volume.

Relaxation Training

Patients with fecal incontinence often become anxious and panic with an urge to stool. This increases the likelihood of incontinence. General relaxation training is useful to prepare patients to cope with this anxiety. Instruct patients that when they experience an urge, they should stop their activity, relax, and breathe in a slow, deep, rhythmic manner using their diaphragm (see Chapter 11). They should stand still or sit if they can. Instruct patients to maintain overall body relaxation and then contract the EAS. This increases resistance to fecal loss and also inhibits colonic contraction.

Relaxation specific to the pelvic floor muscles aims to diminish excessive activity in the perianal, levator ani and, possibly, the abdominal muscles. Reducing excessive muscle activity is important because elevated muscle activity may cause anorectal pain, disordered or incomplete evacuation, and inefficient responses to urge.

Shaping muscle relaxation takes place with muscle-isolation training. This is because the skill required to isolate specific muscle contraction heightens discrimination for various levels of muscle activity. This discrimination then provides the basis for identifying excessive muscle activity that occurs in the life situation. It also allows for generalization of relaxation techniques outside the treatment setting.

A useful protocol for training perineal relaxation is as follows. First, establish isolated pelvic floor muscle recruitment. Then, the patient learns to recruit the perineal muscles to distinctly different amplitudes such as 15, 10, and 5 microvolts. This helps the patient discern varying levels of muscle activity. After each recruitment, reinforce the patient to immediately relax the perineal muscles. To incrementally shape greater muscle relaxation following each recruitment trial, make stepwise adjustments in the auditory and/or visual threshold. This reinforces small changes toward a lower baseline.

Additionally, instruction in diaphragmatic breathing facilitates overall relaxation of skeletal muscles, including muscles of the lower abdomen and pelvic floor. One effective technique is for the therapist to place a hand on the patient's lower abdomen and instruct the patient to inhale. The therapist's hand should elevate as the abdomen expands with the inhalation. Tell the patient to allow the abdominal muscles to relax and "become soft" so the desired expansion can occur. One of the patient's hands can then replace the therapist's hand on the lower abdomen. Position the patient's other hand on the upper thorax. In this way, the patient learns to self monitor the degree to which breathing is thoracic or diaphragmatic. Advise patients to practice breathing and relaxation skills daily, integrate the breathing technique with sphincter exercises, and when trying to control the urge to defecate.

Training Synchronous Sphincter Relaxation with Defecation

Paradoxical contraction or a failure to relax with defecation maneuvers occurs with constipation and incomplete evacuation. Many patients with incontinence also display these patterns with defecation maneuvers. They have associated complaints of incomplete evacuation followed by fecal seepage. To assure the best possible treatment outcome, therefore, correction of these abnormalities is essential.

The following procedure is useful in altering paradoxical contraction with defecation. First, initiate sphincter recruitment and relaxation training as outlined above to help the patient distinguish muscle activity from relaxation. However, one can proceed with training sphincter relaxation with defecation before the patient has fully acquired the ability to contract the sphincter at higher EMG amplitudes or over longer durations.

The patient's position is side-lying with hips and knees flexed to about 90°. The therapist instructs the patient to gently defecate or "push out" the anal probe while watching the biofeedback display. During this procedure, abdominal EMG should increase while EAS EMG signals remain stable or decrease. One gauges improvement by the ratio of abdominal EMG over EAS EMG and the degree to which the EAS EMG drops below the resting baseline.

Often, patients with congenital abnormalities, such as imperforate anus, have difficulty increasing intra-abdominal pressure with defecation. This is possibly because they did not learn coordination when younger. In this case, the therapist teaches the patient to gently use the Valsalva technique before training EAS relaxation with the defecation pattern. A useful strategy is to instruct the patient to gently blow through pursed lips while expanding the abdominal cavity. When integrating the Valsalva with pelvic floor relaxation, the patient attempts to establish the feeling of gentle dissent of the pelvic floor while keeping the sphincter EMG signal quiet. Then, one can alternate a squeeze or holding contraction of the sphincter with defecation practice. This rehearses the functional skill of sphincter recruitment followed by inhibition.

When the patient shows some reduction in sphincter EMG in the side-lying position, then rehearse defecation on the toilet or commode chair. Use the biofeedback display to reinforce sphincter relaxation. Use either the anal plug electrode or perianal electrodes. However, if the anal plug becomes easily dislodged when the patient is upright, perianal electrodes may be the better choice.

Adjunctive Behavioral Procedures

Alterations in diet and daily bowel habits can reduce many symptoms of bowel dysfunction. Ideally, one starts these modifications before the biofeedback interventions. For example, research suggests that the bowel-training program may contribute as much as, or more, than biofeedback therapy to the successful outcome achieved with meningomyelocele children (Whitehead et al., 1982).

During the initial therapy session, review the importance of dietary fiber. Give to the patient written guidelines about the recommended intake and sources of dietary fiber. For chronic constipation, Wexner and Daily (1988) recommend the gradual addition of Miller's bran to the daily diet up to ½ cup per day. The advantages of bran are that it is inexpensive and patients can systematically control its intake. Patients should be advised to limit foods high in fat. The therapist should explore the possibility of lactose intolerance if not previously determined. If one suspects or determines lactose intolerance, instruct the patient appropriately. A patient who is incontinent of frequent and liquid stool may benefit from an antidiarrheal medication. However, these medicines typically slow colon transit time. Thus, one must determine whether the incontinence is caused by fast transit time or overflow from impaction or incomplete evacuation. In the latter case, antidiarrheal medication is contraindicated.

A bowel-training program may be necessary for encopretic children or other patients with constipation when the constipation contributes to overflow incontinence and seepage. Instruct the patient to try to evacuate at the same time every day. The patient should attempt evacuation about 10–20 minutes after a meal. This takes advantage of the gastrocolic reflex stimulated with the ingestion of food. After breakfast is the ideal time for many people to attempt evacuation. This is because the colon seems to be more active shortly after awakening. However, analysis of the symptom diary may suggest a different pattern of colonic excitability. If a bowel movement does not occur for 2 consecutive days, the patient should use an enema at the time of attempted evacuation. The patient may need stronger stimulants such as suppositories or laxatives to establish regular bowel patterns. However, the therapist should wean the patient from these as soon as possible. Most stool normalizers, bulk agents, and some antidiarrheal medications are nonprescription items. Nevertheless, it is a good idea to consult the patient's physician about altering their use. A detailed description of a bowel training program is in Lowery, Srour, Whitehead, and Schuster (1985). Related assessment and therapy procedures are in Doleys, Schwartz, and Ciminero (1981).

There is little consensus about the effect of regular exercise on bowel function. However, the therapist should consider incorporating aerobic-type exercise into the home program if exercise is lacking and when there is no medical reason that prohibits it. The emotional and psychological benefits of exercise warrant its inclusion in treatment. For those patients who have not been on a regular exercise program, a walking program is advantageous. It requires no specific equipment, and one can easily modify and upgrade it to the patient's tolerance. Also, one can objectively measure performance by time and distance walked.

THE HOME PROGRAM

The home program is essential to the successful outcome of the biofeedback–behavioral treatment program. In describing a biofeedback and behavioral program for urinary incontinence, Millard and Oldenburg (1983) reported that patient compliance was the best predictor of success for reducing urinary incontinence. This appears to hold true for the treatment of bowel dysfunction as well.

Instruct patients to maintain a written log of the time of day for all appropriate bowel movements and incontinent episodes. The patients must come to realize that the diary is an integral part of the home program. Patients also should record the use of laxatives, suppositories, enemas, and sphincter exercises. A sample home record form is in the Appendix. It includes columns to record scheduled toileting and enemas if a bowel training program is part of the therapy program.

Assign daily sphincter exercises for nearly all patients seen for bowel dysfunction. For those patients showing sphincter weakness or limited endurance of EAS contraction, the obvious goal of the exercises is to improve the ability to contract the EAS for longer durations. There is a second goal for patients with elevated resting EAS muscle activity and/or paradoxical contraction of the EAS with defecation. This goal is to improve discrimination of elevated muscle activity and to reduce sphincter activity to the normal range. To date there has been no empirical determination about the optimal number of sphincter contractions needed to achieve these goals.

One must assure conditioning of both phasic and tonic muscle activity. To do this, instruct patients to alternate between quick, maximum contractions and sustained, submaximal contractions. The primary goal is to build muscle endurance without abdominal substitution. The recommended number of contractions ranges from 60–120 per day divided among three daily sessions. Patients should perform one-third lying down, one-third standing, and one-third sitting. The duration of the sustained contraction depends on how well the patient can contract the sphincter without abdominal substitution during the biofeedback phase. Instruct patients to relax the sphincter and use the breathing technique for at least 10 seconds between each contraction. Extend the relaxation period up to 30 seconds between each contraction for patients who have sphincter relaxation as a treatment goal. With improvement shown over sessions, increase each sustained contraction to between 10–20 seconds.

Also, instruct patients with delayed or weakened EAS responses to rectal distention to contract the EAS when they feel any stimulus in the rectum. This conditions the automatic EAS response to rectal distention.

CLOSING REMARKS

Fecal incontinence is a troubling problem which affects many individuals and causes serious disruption in work and social activities. Furthermore, there are a considerable number of patients who complain of both fecal and urinary incontinence. One reason this occurs is that these conditions share the common etiology of partial denervation injury at childbirth. Also, many patients complain of concurrent symptoms of disordered defecation patterns, constipation, and pelvic pain. Therefore, the clinician working this area should be prepared to deal with the multifactorial nature of fecal incontinence and understand, in a comprehensive way, the various functions of the pelvic floor and other factors which influence bowel function. It is hoped that this chapter has contributed, to some degree, to the development that understanding.

GLOSSARY

ANAL SPHINCTERS. The anal canal is surrounded by a voluntary or external (EAS) and an involuntary or internal (IAS) anal sphincter. The IAS is continuous with the circular muscle layer of the colon and surrounds the superior two-thirds of the canal. The EAS blends with the puborectalis component of the levator ani muscle and surrounds the inferior two-thirds of the canal, external to the IAS. Nonsynchronous function of these muscles contributes to the gamut of gastrointestinal disorders including constipation, incontinence, hemorrhoids, fistula, prolapse, and the like.

ANORECTAL MANOMETRY. The integrity of the anorectal muscles can be evaluated electromyographically (EMG), functionally (how much fluid can be instilled into the rectum before leakage occurs), or manometrically (how much pressure can be generated within the anal canal and rectum). Pressure may be measured by using a three-balloon system, commonly referred to as the Schuster balloons, or through use of a water perfusion catheter. Changes in balloon pressure can be displayed on a computer screen and used, for example, in a biofeedback program for strengthening the external anal sphincter, to promote relaxation in the treatment of levator ani syndrome, or to improve rectal sensitivity.

GASTROCOLIC REFLEX. Colonic activity increases approximately 30 minutes after a meal. Constipated patients may be advised to develop a pattern of toileting to coincide with this increased activity.

IAS INHIBITORY REFLEX. Distention of the rectum with a balloon causes relaxation (inhibition) of the IAS and contraction of the EAS. Inhibition of the IAS is an unconditioned reflex mediated by afferent impulses from stretch receptors in the walls of the rectum and, probably, in the levator plate; this reflex can occur without awareness, as following spinal transection. The EAS contraction, although seemingly automatic, is a learned response that is mediated through the spinal cord and, as a consequence, disappears when the sensory component is compromised.

LEVATOR ANI MUSCLES. A thin sheet of muscle that forms the pelvic floor, having three components called the pubococcygeus, puborectalis, and iliococcygeus muscles. The levator ani is a heterogeneous mixture of slow and fast twitch muscle fibers that both supports the pelvic viscera and provides an additional occlusive force to the external urethral and anal sphincters, especially when there is a sudden increase in intra-abdominal pressure, as during coughing, lifting, laughing, etc.

LEVATOR SYNDROME. A number of conditions, including proctalgia fugax, levator spasm, levator ani syndrome, and coccygodynia, are characterized by different patterns of idiopathic pain in the anal and perianal regions that may radiate down the legs or into the buttocks or to the coccygeal region. These conditions are defined by exclusion because they are not referable to any of the common disorders such as anal fistula, abscess, hemorrhoids, and the like. There is some agreement that the underlying problem involves muscle spasm of the levator muscles. In certain cases, perineal EMG values are elevated, and biofeedback directed toward normalizing function in these muscles has been successful.

NONRELAXING PUBORECTALIS MUSCLE. The contraction of the puborectalis muscle forms the acute angle between the rectum and the anal canal and prevents the movement of material out of the rectum to maintain fecal continence. With defecation, the puborectalis muscle must relax, which allows the anorectal angle to become obtuse, thereby allowing for the effortless expulsion of stool. A nonrelaxing puborectalis refers to the failure of the muscle to relax during defecation. In many cases this problem can be treated with biofeedback techniques.

PROLAPSE. Prolapse is a general term meaning to move forward or down or out, and it subsumes several specific terms that end in -cele (e.g., rectocele, cystocele, and enterocele). Rectal prolapse is the term used to describe the condition in which the rectum moves down the anal canal. On the other hand, rectocele is the term used to describe the condition in which the rectum protrudes into the vagina. The severity of the condition is graded numerically; for example, a fourth-degree rectal prolapse refers to the condition in which the rectum protrudes from the anal canal.

RECTAL COMPLIANCE. When the compliant rectum is distended with a balloon or by its normal contents, there is a momentary increase in pressure, which diminishes rapidly as the smooth muscle relaxes to accommodate the increased volume. As the volume of material increases, the ability to accommodate it is reduced, giving rise to the feeling of urgency and the desire to defecate. However, contraction of the voluntary EAS inhibits contraction of the smooth muscle in the rectum, reducing the sense of urgency, which allows defecation to be postponed to a convenient time.

RECTOCELE. The posterior wall of the vagina and the anterior wall of the rectum are in close apposition, and, as a result of certain poorly understood predisposing factors, the rectum may protrude into the vagina, forming a rectocele. The defect may be large or small, apparent only during straining, or present as a chronic condition.

STRETCH RESPONSE. A two-neuron response in which afferent activity generated by the stretching of a muscle enters the spinal cord and synapses directly with the efferent neurons to that same muscle, causing compensatory contraction or shortening of the muscle. Because only a single synapse is involved, the response occurs with a short latency.

REFERENCES

Allen, R. E., Hosker, G. L., Smith, A. R. B., & Warrell, D. W. (1990). Pelvic floor damage and childbirth: A neurophysiological study. *British Journal of Obstetrics and Gynaecology, 97,* 770–779.

Bower, G. H., & Hilgard, E. R. (1981). *Theories of learning* (5th ed.). Englewood Cliffs, NJ: Prentice-Hall.

Buser, W. D., & Miner, P. B. (1986). Delayed rectal sensation with fecal incontinence: Successful treatment using anorectal manometry. *Gastroenterology, 91,* 1186–1191.

Cerulli, M. A., Nikoomanesh, P., & Schuster, M. M. (1979). Progress in biofeedback conditioning for fecal incontinence. *Gastroenterology, 76,* 742–746.

Chiarioni, G., Scattolini, C., Bonfante, F., & Vantini, I. (1993). Liquid stool incontinence with severe urgency: Anorectal function and effective biofeedback treatment. *Gut, 34,* 1576–1580.

Corman, M. L. (1993). *Colon and rectal surgery* (3rd ed.). Philadelphia: Lippincott.

Doleys, D., Schwartz, M. S., & Ciminero, A. (1981). Enuresis and encopresis. In E. J. Mash & L. G. Terdal (Eds.), *Behavioral Assessment of childhood disorders.* New York: Guilford Press.

Enck, P. (1993). Biofeedback training in disordered defecation: A critical review. *Digestive Diseases and Sciences, 38,* 1953–1960.

Enck, P., Kranzle, U., Schwiese, J., Dietz, M., Lubke, M. J., Erckenbrecht, J. F., Wienbeck, M., & Strohmeyer, G. (1988). Biofeedback training in fecal incontinence. *Deutsche Medizinische Wochenschrift, 113,* 1789–1794.

Engel, B. T., Nikoomanesh, P., & Schuster, M. M. (1974). Operant conditioning of rectosphincteric responses in the treatment of fecal incontinence. *New England Journal of Medicine, 290,* 646–649.

Goldenberg, D. A., Hodges, K., Hersh, T., & Jinich, H. (1980). Biofeedback therapy for fecal incontinence. *American Journal of Gastroenterology, 74,* 342-345.

Henry, M. M., & Swash, M. (1985). Fecal incontinence, defecation and colorectal motility. In M. M. Henry & M. Swash (Eds.), *Coloproctology and the pelvic floor: Pathophysiology and management* (pp. 42–47). London: Butterworths.

Iwata, N., Nagashima, M., & Shimotake, T. (1993). Biofeedback therapy for fecal incontinence after surgery for anorectal malformation: Preliminary results. *Journal of Pediatric Surgery, 28,* 863–866.

Kohlenberg, J. R. (1973). Operant conditioning of human anal sphincter pressure. *Journal of Applied Behavioral Analysis, 6,* 201–208.

Latimer, P. R., Campbell, D., & Kasperski, J. (1984). A component analysis of biofeedback in the management of fecal incontinence. *Biofeedback and Self-Regulation, 9,* 311–324.

Loening-Baucke, V. (1990). Efficacy of biofeedback training in improving fecal incontinence and anorectal physiologic function. *Gut, 31,* 395–402.

Lowery, S. P., Srour, J. W., Whitehead, W. E., & Schuster, M. M. (1985). Habit training as treatment of encopresis secondary to chronic constipation. *Journal of Pediatric Gastroenterology and Nutrition, 4,* 397–401.

MacLeod, J. H. (1987). Management of anal incontinence by biofeedback. *Gastroenterology, 93,* 291–294.

Miller, N. E. (1978). Biofeedback and viseral learning. *Annual Review of Psychology, 29,* 373–404.

Miller, N. E., & DiCara, L. V. (1967). Instrumental learning of heart rate changes in curarized rats: Shaping and specificity to discriminative stimuli. *Journal of Comparative and Physiological Psychology, 63,* 12–19.

Millard, R. J., & Oldenburg, B. F. (1983). The symptomatic, urodynamic and psychodynamic results of bladder re-education programs. *Journal of Urology, 130,* 715–719.

Miner P. B., Donnelly, T. C., & Read, N. W. (1990) Investigation of the mode of action of biofeedback in the treatment of fecal incontinence. *Digestive Diseases and Sciences, 35,* 1291–1298.

Moore, K. L. (1992). *Clinically oriented anatomy* (3rd ed.). Baltimore: Williams & Wilkins.

Netter F. H. (1989). *Atlas of human anatomy.* Summit, NJ: CibaGeigy.

Olness, K., McParland, F. A., & Piper, J. (1980). Biofeedback: A new modality in the management of children with fecal soiling. *Behavioral Pediatrics, 96,* 505–509.

Riboli, F. B., Frascio, M., Pitto, G., Reboa, G., & Zanolla, R. (1988). Biofeedback conditioning for fecal incontinence. *Archives of Physical Medicine and Rehabilitation, 69,* 29–31.

Schiller, L. R., Santa Ana, C., Davis, G. R., & Fordtran, J. S. (1979). Fecal incontinence in chronic diarrhea: Report of a case with improvement after training with rectally infused saline. *Gastroenterology, 77,* 571–753.

Schuster, M. M., Hookman, P., Hendrix, T., & Mendeloff, A. (1965). Simultaneous manometric recording of internal and external anal sphincter reflexes. *Bulletin of the Johns Hopkins Hospital, 116,* 79–88.

Tries, J., & Eisman, E. (1995). *Training manual for bowel dysfunction.* Milwaukee, WI: Clinic for Neurophysiological Learning.

Wald, A. (1981a). Biofeedback therapy of fecal incontinence. *Annals of Internal Medicine, 95,* 146–149.

Wald, A. (1981b). Use of biofeedback in treatment of fecal incontinence in patients with meningomyeloccle. *Pediatrics, 68,* 45–49.

Wald, A., & Tunuguntla, A. K. (1984). Anorectal sensorimotor dysfunction in fecal incontinence and diabetes mellitus. *New England Journal of Medicine, 310,* 1282–1287.

Wexner, S. D., & Daily, T. H. (1988). The diagnosis and surgical treatment of chronic constipation. *Contemporary Surgery, 32,* 59–70.

Whitehead, W. E. (1986). Biofeedback and habit training for fecal incontinence associated with myelomeningocele. *Journal of Pediatric Neuroscience, 2,* 27–36.

Whitehead, W. E., Burgio, K. L., & Engel, B. T. (1985). Biofeedback, treatment of fecal incontinence in geriatric patients. *Journal of the American Geriatric Society, 33,* 320–324.

Whitehead, W. E., Orr, W. C. Engel, B. T., & Schuster, M. M. (1981). External anal sphincter response to rectal distension: Learned response or reflex. *Psychophysiology, 19,* 57–62.

Whitehead, W. E., Parker, L. H., Bosmajian, L. S., Morrell, E. D., Middaugh, S., Drescher, V. M., Cataldo, M. F., & Freeman, J. M. (1982). Behavioral treatment of fecal incontinence secondary to spina bifida (Abstract). *Gastroenterology, 82,* 1209.

Whitehead, W. E., Parker, L., Bosmajian, L., Morrell-Corbin, D., Middaugh, S., Garwood, M., Cataldo, M. F., & Freeeman, J. (1986). Treatment of fecal incontinence in children with spina-bifida: Comparison of biofeedback and behavior modification. *Archives of Physical Medicine and Rehabilitation, 67,* 218–224.

Whitehead, W. E., Parker, L. H., Masek, B. J., Cataldo, M. F., & Freeman, J. M. (1981). Biofeedback treatment of fecal incontinence in patients with myelomeningocele. *Developmental Medicine and Child Neurology, 23,* 313–322.

25

Nocturnal or Sleep Enuresis: The Urine Alarm as a Biofeedback Treatment

Mark S. Schwartz

The extensive literature about the successful use of the urine alarm treatment for sleep enuresis[1] dates back more than 60 years. It is a behavioral therapy and the oldest form of biofeedback (Miller, 1981; Schwartz, 1981). This chapter starts with the similarities between the urine alarm treatment for enuresis and other types of biofeedback. The chapter then focuses on information about enuresis and use of the urine alarm treatment.

THE URINE ALARM AS BIOFEEDBACK

The urine alarm treatment involves placing a urine-sensitive detector on the patient's bed or in the underpants. The detector attaches to a device that produces a loud auditory stimulus to awaken the patient when urination occurs. The patient then arises, goes to the bathroom, returns to bed, and resets the instrument. Therapy proceeds over several weeks to a few months until the patient is dry every night for a few consecutive weeks.

This treatment is very successful when appropriate instruments are used, when patients and families cooperate, and when appropriate professional supervision is present. The "urine alarm treatment should not only be considered the treatment of choice, but the evidence from this review suggests that cure rather than management is a realistic goal for a majority of children suffering from nocturnal enuresis" (Houts, Berman, & Abramson, 1994, p. 743). A treatment program has been offered since 1970 at the Mayo Clinic Rochester (Schwartz & Colligan, 1974; May, Colligan, & Schwartz, 1983) with more than 1000 children and adults treated since then.

The similarities between the urine alarm treatment and other biofeedback treatments for other disorders are as follows:

1. *Sleep-interruption concept.* Neurophysiological models consider both nocturnal bruxism and sleep enuresis as disorders of inadequate arousal. Sleep-interruption biofeedback, an experimental treatment for treating nocturnal bruxism, is similar to that for sleep enuresis.

---

[1]The term "nocturnal enuresis" means bedwetting during sleep. As a sleep disorder, one also can call this "sleep enuresis." Contrast this with "diurnal enuresis," which is daytime wetting. This chapter does not discuss diurnal enuresis. For convenience of reading and space, I use the terms "enuresis" and "sleep enuresis" interchangeably in this chapter.

2. *Monitoring and direct feedback of physiological activity.* Electronic instruments indirectly monitor the interaction between the bladder detrusor and sphincter muscles, and the brain. Direct feedback of urination occurs moments after the sphincter(s) opens.

3. *Physiological self-regulation goal.* The goal of therapy is physiological self-regulation of bladder functioning during sleep.

4. *Binary/threshold feedback* happens when physiological activity exceeds the threshold, and urination occurs. Similarly, for bruxism, the activity is masseter or pterygoid muscle tension above a threshold.

5. *Auditory and visual feedback* are used. Practitioners usually use auditory feedback and sometimes add light feedback for patients difficult to arouse from sleep.

6. *Immediate feedback* is important.

7. *Learning principles of shaping, positive reinforcement, and overlearning* are important. Practitioners arrange for positive reinforcement for successive approximations of goals. For example, families praise patients for waking up by themselves, waking up faster, and for less wetting. Overlearning procedures are common after being dry for several consecutive nights. This involves increasing fluid intake near bedtime. This is similar to exposing other patients to increased stress and assessing their use of relaxation skills. It is similar to tensing the external anal sphincter in response to increasing rectal pressures for patients with fecal incontinence.

8. The *need for regular practice* is emphasized by practitioners.

9. *Symptom baseline and daily record keeping* are used.

10. *Cognitive preparation* of patients is important. This includes a "teaching-machine concept."

11. *Booster treatments* to prevent and manage relapse are commonly part of the urine alarm and other biofeedback therapies.

INFORMATION ABOUT SLEEP ENURESIS

Definitions

Sleep enuresis is persistent bedwetting after age 3 or 4 and without organic pathology accounting for the wetting. A useful distinction is between the more common primary enuresis and the less common secondary enuresis. No sustained period of dryness without treatment occurs for the primary type. Secondary enuresis occurs when wetting resumes after a lengthy period, defined as 3–6 months, of sustained dryness without treatment.

Prevalence, Sex Ratio, Frequency, and Spontaneous Remission

Good estimates report about 15–20% wetting at age 5, about 5% at age 10, 2–3% at age 14, and 1–2% in young adulthood. Enuresis is slightly more common in younger males than females. This ratio is up to 2:1 to about age 11, when the ratio becomes more equal, and is up to 6:1 among patients treated at the Mayo Clinic. Most persons coming for treatment wet several times every week, and most wet every night.

When deciding about treatment, clinicians should consider that about 15% of children wetting at each age from 5 to 19 years will become dry within a year without intervention. Thus, there is close to a 45%[2] chance of becoming dry over a 5-year period even

---

[2]Rounded at 50% in the first edition for ease of communication.

without intervention. The urine alarm treatment is often appropriate from about the age of 5.

Treatment Success Rate and Relapse Rate

Published success rates vary but often show 70–90% of persons treated achieving total dryness. However, there are lower published figures. Relapse rates range from 10–50% within a few months after treatment. Long-term follow-up is important, since relapse can occur beyond a year.

Etiology

There are several models for explaining sleep enuresis, none of which is accepted as the best. One or more of the models can usually account for the enuresis of any given individual. The logic for many of the theories is *post hoc ergo propter hoc* or backward reasoning (Houts, 1991). This Latin phrase, which means "after this, therefore because of it," refers to "the fallacy of assuming something has caused an event merely because it preceded it" (*Random House Dictionary*, 1975). This chapter presents the older, less explanatory, and less popular models first.

Genetic and/or Familial

There is consensus that familial and perhaps genetic factors play a role in causing enuresis for many children. When both parents had or have enuresis, there is a higher chance their child also will have enuresis compared to when only one parent had it. In turn, this probability is higher than when neither parent had enuresis (Cohen, 1975). However, the familial model does not explain most enuresis. It also does not dictate the type of treatment. Furthermore, there is evidence inconsistent with a simple genetic model. For example, concordance rates for enuresis are surprisingly lower for monozygotic twins than for dizygotic twins (Hallgren, 1960) according to Houts' (1991) report.

Psychological Factors

The leading theory many years ago was that enuresis was a result of underlying emotional disturbances. Indeed, there is a higher incidence of enuresis among children seen by mental health professionals for reasons other than enuresis (Kolvin, MacKeith, & Meadow, 1973). Among children with enuresis there is a higher incidence of behavior problems. Significant stress at the critical developmental age of about 3 significantly correlates with increased enuresis. However, most children with enuresis do not show abnormal emotional or behavioral problems. For those who do, these problems often stem from the enuresis. Children with sleep enuresis seen in family practice and pediatric clinics are usually without signs of psychopathology (Wagner & Mathews, 1985; Kolvin et al., 1973). Another argument against a primary psychological explanation is that symptom substitution after successful urine alarm therapy is highly unusual (Baker, 1969). Practitioners familiar with the research and empirical outcome literature would not adopt this type of cause nor recommend traditional types of psychotherapy for childhood sleep enuresis (Houts, 1991).

Behavioral–Learning Factors

These models focus on inadequate learning and habit weakness. The learning models include both classical and respondent conditioning. The original theoretical model for the urine alarm treatment is classical conditioning with variations of avoidance conditioning (Lovibond & Coote, 1970). The original formulations may not be entirely accurate considering later data. However, these models are still viable.

Problems with Sleep Depth or Arousal

A popular hypothesis is that sleep enuresis is often a disorder of sleep stage, arousal problems, or both. Advocates point to data that state it is difficult to awaken many children with enuresis. Also, evidence suggests that the arousal threshold may be abnormally high for some of these children (Finley, 1971). They also may be unresponsive to interoceptive stimuli as from a distended bladder with detrusor muscle contractions (DiPerri & Meduri, 1972). Note that depth of sleep is different from arousability from sleep. Arousability is how easily a person awakens from sleep. Depth refers to the stage or level of sleep. Research is not consistent about depth and arousability among children with enuresis.

We now know that sleep enuresis can occur in all stages of sleep although 85–95% occurs in non-rapid eye movement (NREM) sleep (Sharf & Jennings, 1988). Norgaard et al. (1989) artificially filled the bladders of children during sleep to provoke enuresis. There was no relationship to electroencephalographically (EEG) measured sleep stages. Sleep enuresis is more related to the time of night and not specifically to deep sleep. It is instructive to know that it occurs proportionally in each sleep stage at about the same frequency as the time spent in that stage (Sharf & Jennings, 1988).

It should be remembered that younger children are in the deepest stage of sleep, stage IV, longer than are older children and adults. Parents typically do not try to awaken nonenuretic children, especially in the early period of sleep when they usually try to awaken their bedwetting children. When researchers make such comparisons (Boyd, 1960; Kaffman & Elizur, 1977), they report no differences in arousability.

Some children with enuresis may have an arousal problem and may benefit from very loud stimuli. However, no one knows the percentage among all children with enuresis. Sleep depth and arousal problems may not account for most sleep enuresis events. These factors are unlikely to be the sole or primary explanations for most cases. These explanations are now much less popular than they were a few years ago.

Small Bladder Capacity

Small bladder capacity is another common explanation for enuresis. Some estimate this capacity from the functional bladder capacity (FBC). This is the amount of urine in the bladder before voiding and usually measured after drinking a large amount of fluid and then maintaining a maximum postponement of urination. It is not a measure of true bladder capacity as determined by infusing fluid or gas into a bladder until reflex bladder contractions begin. FBC is a less reliable measure. Many children with enuresis have small FBCs (Starfield & Mellits, 1968). Some children become dry at night when they increase their FBCs with urine-holding techniques. However, this is not a sufficient explanation because of the considerable overlap between the FBCs of children with enuresis and those without it. It is also logical that sleeping through the night results in larger FBCs rather than smaller

FBCs being the cause of the wetting. Enuresis may be one component of developmental delay and suggests inadequate cortical inhibition over afferent bladder stimuli. The hypothesis focusing on dysfunctional detrusor activity could account for the smaller FBCs seen among people with sleep enuresis.

Increasing FBCs with retention training or bladder stretching exercises is sometimes a treatment option. Practitioners should consider this when there is evidence of a small FBC, when one cannot use the urine alarm, or when other therapies, including medications, have proven unsuccessful. Some practitioners include it in multicomponent treatment programs (Sharf & Jennings, 1988). However, by itself, it is not enough for most children.

Nocturnal Polyuria

Practitioners evaluating and treating sleep enuresis should be familiar with the hypothesis of *nocturnal polyuria* causing or contributing to bedwetting. This hypothesis maintains that children with sleep enuresis wet because their kidneys do not concentrate their urine during sleep. This results in overproduction of urine beyond the normal capacity of the child's bladder. The lack of urine concentration may be caused by a lack of the normally increased antidiuretic hormone (ADH) vasopressin during sleep. ADH comes from the nerve cells of the hypothalamus and stores in the posterior lobe of the pituitary. It promotes water reabsorption and increases urine concentration in the kidneys.

There is support for the nocturnal polyuria hypothesis (Norgaard, Pedersen, & Djurhuus, 1985; Rittig, Knudsen, Norgaard, Pedersen, & Djurhuus, 1989). People with enuresis often produce excessive volumes of urine at night. This often exceeds their bladder capacities as determined by cystograms. Among subjects without enuresis, Rittig et al. (1989) found significantly more ADH at night compared to the daytime. This difference was greater compared to that among subjects with sleep enuresis. The serum ADH levels did not differ between day and night for subjects with sleep enuresis. This supports the importance of circadian rhythm and ADH release.

The use of synthetic ADH (1-desamino-8-D-arginine vasopressin), Desmopressin, or DDAVP for short, is the treatment based on this theory. Some also refer to this as arginine vasopressin (AVP) (Knudsen et al., 1991). Availability in the United States dates only to October, 1989.

Since DDAVP acts at the level of the kidneys, it concentrates the urine, thereby reducing the amount of urine going to the bladder during sleep. Hence, a dry bed. See Houts (1991) for a good review. One of the limitations of DDAVP is that it does not change the natural circadian release of ADH. Thus, it only works while one uses it.

Dysfunctional Detrusor Activity

If the detrusor muscle surrounding the bladder is unstable during sleep, spontaneous contractions occur that often result in the release of urine. There are organic and functional versions of this view (Houts, 1991). The organic version is neurogenic bladder with two types, detrusor hyperreflexia and detrusor areflexia. The incidence of these is only 1–5% among children with monosymptomatic sleep enuresis (Houts, 1991). This cannot account for the wetting of most people with sleep enuresis, especially those without clear daytime urgency and wetting. However, practitioners should be aware of these conditions. Detrusor hyperreflexia refers to involuntary contractions of the detrusor muscle during much lower than normal bladder pressures. Detrusor areflexia is the absence of contractions of the detrusor muscle even with high urine volume. This results in overflow incontinence and usually daytime wetting.

The functional version of the dysfunctional detrusor hypothesis refers to the oxymoron "nonneurogenic neurogenic bladder." This assumes detrusor hyperreflexia or areflexia without a neurological cause. There is a presumed "lack of normal coordination of muscular responses during voiding" (Houts, 1991, p. 139). Urodynamic studies can detect detrusor–sphincter dysenergia—continued, intermittent contractions of the external sphincter recorded from the pelvic floor muscles. This condition involves a weak stream of urine, starting and stopping the stream, and residual urine in the bladder from incomplete emptying. Children with this pattern usually show other symptoms such as urgency, frequency, repeat urinary tract infections, daytime wetting, and low FBCs. This is not the pattern observed with children with monosymptomatic sleep enuresis.

The available evidence does not support the idea that functional neurogenic bladder problems cause monosymptomatic sleep enuresis (Houts, 1991). However, research and the insights of Houts (1991) suggest a possible link and explanation for how the urine alarm works. Consider the following facts and logic.

Recordings from the pelvic floor presumably including the external urethral sphincter show a silent EMG signal and relaxation after detrusor contractions occur in normal voiding. This allows urine flow. In contrast, contraction of the pelvic floor and external sphincter muscles can stop detrusor contractions and inhibits micturition. When a child with sleep enuresis wets without arousal from sleep, there is preceding relaxation of the pelvic floor (Norgaard, 1989a, 1989b). In contrast, increased pelvic floor activity precedes the arousal and dryness associated with artificial filling of the bladder. This is presumably due to inhibiting detrusor contractions.

Urine Alarm Treatment, ADH, and Dysfunctional Detrusor Activity

The attempts of Houts (1991) to relate research and knowledge about the urine alarm treatment, ADH, and dysfunctional detrusor activity in sleep enuresis deserve special attention. He carefully speculates that "one mechanism of action in urine alarm treatments may be conditioning of pelvic floor inhibitory responses to bladder filling" (p. 146). Houts more carefully speculates that "it is certainly possible that urine alarm treatments alter endogenous ADH release" (p. 146). The logic is that awakening abruptly might lead to increased endogenous ADH. In part, this is because one general physiological response to stress is increased serum vasopressin.

He does not refer to the data and belief of many practitioners that louder and more noxious auditory stimuli lead to better results with the urine alarm. This speculation is consistent with home remedies that rely on punishment, embarrassment, and ridicule. They are undesirable and not very successful for most children. This may be because of their lack of specific effects on ADH. Perhaps, the timing of the noxious stimulus is important.

Selecting Treatment(s)

It is common and proper to start with the urine alarm treatment alone after proper medical evaluation. Some practitioners prefer a multicomponent treatment package that includes the urine alarm (Houts, Peterson, & Whelan, 1986; Sharf & Jennings, 1988). A description of the multicomponent approach is beyond the scope of this chapter. Practitioners using a urine alarm treatment approach often include patient education, overlearning, and counseling tailored to the individual. Multicomponent programs sometimes include retention-control or bladder-stretching exercises.

Within a stepped-care model, practitioners can consider several choices. These are not in order of preference. All assume patient education in the beginning and periodically thereafter.

1. One can defer all treatment for some children. Waiting for spontaneous remission in children of early elementary school ages results in about 45% becoming dry over 5 years. This is the most conservative method and usually not advisable for most school-age children. It is not advisable for adolescents and adults.

2. Consider the urine alarm approach first and add other behavioral approaches including bladder exercises. This is less conservative but starts with the most effective single treatment.

3. Alternatively, consider medications such as imipramine or DDAVP first. Success during and after treatment is lower than desired and less than with the urine alarm. However, this may be more practical for some patients. Then consider bladder exercises for selected children. Follow this with the urine alarm if prior therapies are unsuccessful. This approach is very conservative but leaves the most effective, reliable, and permanent treatment to last. It also could take many months or more than a year to assess the first treatments.

4. Consider starting with bladder exercises, adding the urine alarm and other conditioning treatments, as needed, and later medications if needed. This is a moderately conservative approach—but frustrating for most during the bladder exercise stage.

5. Consider using multiple behavioral treatments together. This is the most aggressive approach but probably too demanding for many patients and families. There is no way to know which method worked and which to repeat if relapse occurs. This drawback exists when combining medication and the alarm, as well. Combination treatments are for adolescents and adults treated for the first time or patients for whom single treatments were unsuccessful.

INSTRUMENTATION[3]

Getting high-quality urine alarm instruments is very important. Wide variability exists in quality, cost, durability, safety, and appearance. I avoid commercial companies offering instruments and service because they are excessively expensive, often use poor quality instruments, and often provide misinformation. I also discourage using department-store models especially without professional supervision. Major problems with these are their frequent poor quality, inadequate volume, and sometimes annoying "false alarms."

Consider the number of patients you will treat and the difficulty arousing patients before buying instruments. Consider the proximity of sleeping adults helping to supervise the treatment. Consider the portability of the instrument and the availability of technical engineering help for repairs.

---

[3]After completing this chapter I learned about another instrument, the SIMTEK Model ET-7. I include this information for the interest of practitioners. The features listed include a 100-db piezo siren alarm, a 10-watt halogen spotlight, 85-db beeper to awaken parents on delayed alarm nights, a 2-line display giving instructions to user, intermittent reinforcement scheduling pattern, and other features. It interfaces with the Coote pad and others. It is an expensive instrument with a cost over $2000 but offers many features. I have no experience with it. The features such as intermittent reinforcement may appeal to some practitioners. For more information, contact SIMTEK, Inc., 804 E. Taft, Sapulpa, OK 74066; (918) 224-7306.

Consider investing a few hundred dollars for a high-quality system that is reliable and reusable for many years. A high-quality and durable system is cost-efficient if one treats several persons per year. The Coote[4] alarm units that my colleagues and I purchased in 1970 (Coote, 1965) still function well. However, for convenience, Mayo Clinic engineering colleagues construct most of the alarms we use. We still purchase the urine-sensitive pads from Ramsey–Coote Instruments in Australia.[5]

A stimulus intensity of 98–100 decibels at 6 inches from the patient and 91 or 92 decibels at 18 inches is probably adequate for arousing most people with enuresis. Some children are difficult to arouse from sleep even with this intensity. They need stimulus intensities of up to about 100 decibels at 18 inches. Therefore, some practitioners prefer louder intensities. Consider having at least one such unit, although most children awaken without this. The alarm should be in a direct line with the patient and not muffled by bed sheets, blankets, or pillows.

Wrist-worn instruments and department store models that attach by Velcro to the bed clothing produce only about 80 decibels at 18 inches. This loudness is before the muffling effects of sheets or blankets are accounted for. One unit attaches to the patient's upper sleeping garment near the shoulder. It produced only 82 decibels at 6 inches in our tests. One report noted 75 decibels in a popular department store device at a distance of 24 inches (Wagner & Mathews, 1985). Unless a supervising adult easily awakens and is quickly available to help awaken the child, one needs a unit loud enough to awaken the supervising adult. This is especially true for younger children, for enuretic events during deeper and unresponsive sleep stages, and for those with arousal problems.

A high-quality urine-sensitive pad on the bed and a loud alarm unit on a night stand are usually fine. Smaller units with the urine-sensitive part in the underwear are often more practical when traveling because of their compact size. These are adequate for limited use even if the stimulus intensity of the auditory signal is low. It may be better to defer the use of a smaller and quieter unit to when treatment reaches the stage when the person is awakening well with a louder auditory signal.

ASSESSMENT

The following is an assessment guide that outlines information to be obtained during an initial interview.

Enuresis

1. Frequency and pattern of wetting.
2. Events associated with wetting and dryness if wetting is less than nearly every night. These events include fatigue, stress, parents' waking the child, sleeping in different beds or places.
3. Duration of dry periods without help or treatment.
4. Fluid restriction or excess in the hours before bedtime.

---

[4]Note that Peter Coote, the long-term head of Ramsey–Coote Instruments, sold the company to John Flynn and Janet Blainey (Flynn), M.S.W. Peter's beloved wife and partner died a few years ago, and Peter retired. Peter died in 1994. They are missed for their many contributions and for their warmth and charms. The address of the company changed to 18 Edward Street, Sandringham, Victoria 3191, Australia.

[5]The cost of the pads is about $200 each plus shipping.

5. Sleep behavior (e.g., restlessness, nightmares).
6. Other information (e.g., time of wetting, size of wet areas, and self-wakings).
7. Arousability at different times of the night.
8. FBC estimated from history or from daytime measurements.
9. Prior treatments:

    a. Examples of types of prior treatments include fluid restriction, medication, urine alarm, punishment, awakenings by adult, positive reinforcement, counseling, dry bed training, retention control, hypnosis, diet, urological procedures, diet, and surgery.

    b. Other information such as results and problems.

Family, Child, Home

1. Health and competence of child and family.
2. Personality, emotional, behavioral, and stress factors.
3. Family relations for conflicts, separation, and divorce.
4. Enuresis in parents and siblings.

Sleeping Arrangements

1. Does the patient sleep alone or share a room or bed? If sharing a room, what is other's age and does other also have enuresis?
2. Location of the adult supervisor in relation to the child.
3. Proximity of bathroom.
4. Temperature of bedroom and bathroom at night.
5. Usual sleeping apparel.

Recent or Expected Life/Family Changes

1. Family moves or trips.
2. Hospitalization of family member.
3. Is the mother pregnant?

THERAPY MANAGEMENT

Practitioners need to make recommendations for many management aspects of the urine alarm treatment (Dische, 1971, 1973; Doleys, Schwartz, & Ciminero, 1981). The following are many of the management topics that can arise.

Fear of the Alarm

Fear of the alarm is uncommon, especially among older children, aged 7 or older. However, sometimes fear occurs with younger children. Sometimes there is a prior fear of loud noises or sirens.

Allow the child to ring the alarm and turn it off several times to reduce and stop any oversensitivity. Do this in the office and during the first few days at home. Consider using instruments with a loudness adjustment if lower volumes can still awaken the child. One can drape the alarm container or move it farther away from the bed.

If an adverse emotional reaction persists beyond several nights, then suspend therapy and consider options. A severe emotional reaction in the professional's office during the initial session suggests the need for therapy before using the urine alarm treatment. If the child is aged 4 or 5, consider deferring therapy 6 months or longer.

Not Awakening to the Alarm

Failure to waken to the alarm is common, especially with auditory stimuli that are not sufficiently loud. Assist the child in awakening and/or use a louder alarm.

Nocturnal Confusion

Nocturnal confusion is common when an alarm awakens children because the alarm often rings during deeper stages of sleep or the person has an arousal problem. Encourage patience, and prepare parents and children for the possible confusion. Tell parents to guide the child into alertness, keep the lights on, stay close to the child, talk, and guide him or her to the bathroom and back to bed if needed. Confusion usually lessens after a few weeks.

Turning the Alarm Off and Going Back to Sleep

Turning the alarm off and going back to sleep is common. A common solution is moving the alarm a few feet away from the child. The need for a louder alarm is more important as the distance from the child increases. The use of a high-intensity light or large-wattage incandescent bulb can help. One can connect the alarm unit to a light that goes on with the alarm but requires separate action to turn it off. For electrical safety, be sure of complete isolation of the electrical current. Devices on the person do not have a switch to turn off. They require disconnecting the circuit by reaching into the wet underpants.

Restlessness in Bed and Being off the Pad

Restlessness in bed is sometimes a problem. Some children move off the urine-sensitive pad or become wrapped up in their top sheet and blanket. Parents can restrict movement by placing bolsters or a rolled-up blanket between the child and a wall. Another option is a smaller bed. Be sure to secure the top sheet. A small percentage of "off pad" wetting should not reduce success.

Skipping Nights

Practitioners usually recommend against skipping nights. However, there is no good theoretical reason or research evidence to support strict admonishments to avoid skipping any nights. However, avoid skipping more than an occasional night. Consider limiting these to times when the patient is ill, occasions when there are house guests, and brief trips. Skipping nights may even be preferable after frequent and regular dry nights.

Fluid Intake Decisions

Fluid intake decisions are the responsibilities of the supervising professional. Whether to increase fluids and how much will depend on several factors. Consider the duration of treatment, the number of self-wakings occurring, the child and parental attitudes about treatment, and the patient's age and physical size.

After 7 or more consecutive dry nights, consider fluid increases beyond the amount the patient was drinking earlier in treatment. Consider this when the treatment period was average or relatively brief such as a few or several weeks. There is more indication for fluid increases when there were very few or no self-wakings and family acceptance of treatment without major problems. Also consider fluid increases for older children and adults.

In contrast, avoid excessively lengthening treatment with fluid increases beyond the amount being consumed earlier in treatment. Consider cautions or contraindication for this (e.g., lengthy treatment of 5 or 6 months, two or more self-wakings per night, or family resistance). Carefully explain to the patient and family the rationale for the desired overlearning effect of fluid increases for lowering relapse rates. Also, discuss the disadvantages. Consider discussing these issues at the start of treatment to avoid surprises and disappointment later.

The amount of fluid to drink at the beginning of treatment and later varies with the child's age and size, subjective tolerance, and FBC. Drinking 8–12 ounces within 30 minutes of bedtime is an acceptable range in the beginning. Schedule the increases when appropriate. Young and Morgan (1972a, 1972b) reported increases to 32 ounces. However, in my experience 32 ounces is often impractical and often resisted. Some children begin frequent wetting with overlearning procedures (Young & Morgan, 1972a). In these cases, stop or modify the overlearning procedures if frequent wetting persists for 1–3 weeks.

Lengthy Treatment Durations

Expect a lengthy treatment for many children. Published research sometimes suggests that treatment for about 6 weeks is usually enough. However, in clinical practice this is more likely to be the shorter end of the range, especially when one considers that treatment should be continued until there are at least 3 consecutive weeks of dry nights with reasonable fluid intake.

Consider other signs of progress in addition to the number of dry nights. One can count the number of bells. One sometimes sees progress in the increased sleep time before an awakening. Sometimes, there is a decrease in the number of bells even with no reduction of the number of dry nights. Thus, calculate the time between bedtime and the first awakening due to either an alarm or a self-waking. This can help increase and maintain patient and family motivation.

Misinformation

There are misconceptions about the urine alarm treatment. Some parents of children with enuresis read or hear misinformation and fear this treatment. One such misconception is that the treatment involves electric shock. Nearly all instruments do not use shock or other painful stimuli. Another misconception is that this treatment leads only to a brief period of dryness, and wetting resumes soon for most children (Rowan, 1974). This is simply untrue for most persons treated. Such misinformation reflects an uninformed bias rather than the evidence.

Another example of misinformation came from the late Lee Salk (1972). He stated that he saw "cases where male youngsters trained this way [bell conditioning] became sexually impotent later in life." I could never find any mention of such an association in the literature on enuresis or impotence. When I called Dr. Salk, about 1975, he stated that he had based his statement on two or three adult males with impotence who had reported treatment with the urine alarm as children. I trust that interpretation of this requires no further comment. Careful research is the only way to explore the remote chance of a relationship.

Electrochemical Burns

With proper instrumentation the potential risk of electrochemical burns does not exist. Several authors reported electrochemical burns or skin ulcers many years ago (Coote, 1965; Borrie & Fenton, 1966; Forrester, 1966; Lovibond & Coote, 1970). There is no documentation of the frequency of this. This electrochemical reaction leads to skin cell death and deep ulceration. Proper instrumentation, now widely available, virtually eliminates the risk of such a problem. In over 1000 patients treated at the Mayo Clinic Rochester, we never saw this. I encourage review of the Australian standards for these instruments (Standards Association of Australia, 1980) before the purchase or building of such instruments. I am unaware of any standards in the United States.

Other Treatments

Pharmacological therapy for sleep enuresis includes imipramine hydrochloride (Tofranil), oxybutynin (Ditropan), or DDAVP. No medication is as effective as the urine alarm treatment. However, medications continue in wide usage and have a proper place in treatment. I discuss them because practitioners need to know about medications when considering options and answering questions, and one needs this information for discussions with physicians. Knowing more about the medications also can help us learn more about the causes of sleep enuresis and the mechanisms of successful treatment.

Imipramine

Imipramine (Tofranil) is still widely used for treating sleep enuresis. Its use for this dates back more than three decades. MacLean (1960) first reported a side effect of imipramine was stopping urine incontinence among some adult psychiatric patients treated with it for depression. A probable mechanism is its noradrenergic stimulation that inhibits the detrusor muscle through beta receptors and contracts the bladder neck through alpha receptors (Rapoport et al., 1980). Imipramine does appear to reduce detrusor reactivity and to increase external urinary sphincter contraction.

   However, there are tolerance effects for at least some people. Continued use results in less effectiveness and relapse usually occurs after stopping the medication. Most published research also does not report this medication as successful as the urine alarm and reports there is a much higher relapse rate with imipramine. Indeed, most people becoming dry with the drug relapse after stopping it.

   There are other reasons why many physicians avoid using imipramine with most children. There is the risk of accidental overdose leading to cardiac failure (Herson, Schmitt, & Rumack, 1979). Blood absorbs imipramine much faster than many other drugs that children take accidently. Therefore, it is more dangerous than drugs that remain in the stomach longer and allow more time for stomach pumping. Furthermore, many parents report that their children had negative side effects such as increased irritability with imipramine. Admittedly, my experience comes from a biased sample. Those children successfully treated with imipramine do not usually seek further treatment.

   In conclusion, imipramine works for many patients probably by reducing detrusor activity and increasing external sphincter contraction. Its effect diminishes for some during use, and it ceases to be effective for most after being discontinued.

Oxybutynin

The probable mechanism for oxybutynin (Ditropan) also is action on the bladder musculature by reducing detrusor spasms and thus increasing bladder capacity. Its use started as an anticholinergic medication to reduce bladder spasms among urinary-incontinent adults. The limited research with oxybutynin and sleep enuresis suggests that it does reduce wetting slightly. However, it is even less effective than imipramine during and after treatment (Lovering, Tallett, & McKendry, 1988; Houts, 1991) even with age adjusted doses. The latter report suggests that less than one-fourth of patients tested reached 2 weeks of dryness during treatment. Most of those reaching dryness relapsed fully within 3 months after treatment.

Desmopressin

A recent addition in the United States (approved for use in October 1989) is DDAVP. The proposed mechanism is urine output reduction from the kidneys during sleep rather than an effect on the bladder muscles. The first controlled studies were more than 15 years ago on children with sleep enuresis. Efficacy studies started in the early 1980s. The push for its use in medical practice is more recent. Administration is with an intranasal spray, usually with a dose of 20–40 micrograms. Its antidiuretic duration is 7–10 hours. DDAVP is very effective for at least 50% of patients while they are using it; patients tolerate it well with rare negative side effects.

However—and there seems always to be a "however"—the drug is expensive, and the relapse rate is very high. The cost is at least $2.20 per night ($65 a month) or about $800 a year for a 40-microgram dose, and many people need higher doses. There is a significant reduction in wet nights during use. Many children become dry every night. However, a summary of 14 studies by Houts (1991) reports a "mean arrest at post treatment" of only 34%. The range was 12–74%. Furthermore, and more disappointing, is the relapse rate, with most studies showing at least about 75% relapse and many reporting more, up to 100% relapsed to baseline. Moffatt, Harlos, Kirshen, and Burd (1993) reviewed 18 random control studies with 689 subjects. Although these studies reported decreases from 10–91% in the mean frequency of wetting, short-term dryness occurred in only about 25% of the subjects. Only one of the studies directly assessed long-term dryness, and only 21% remained dry. Three other studies reported on incidental long-term dryness after stopping DDAVP, and this occurred in less than 6%. This review concludes that "on the basis of current knowledge, DDAVP is inferior to conditioning alarms as a primary therapy" (p. 420).

Therefore, its main value is for short-term use in specific situations such as when traveling and sleeping away from home and when adequate trials of the urine alarm are clearly unsuccessful.

Acupuncture?

There are other reportedly successful treatments for sleep enuresis (Houts, 1991; Sharf & Jennings, 1988). There is a report from mainland China of the successful use of acupuncture (Xu Baoqin, 1991) among 302 cases. Unfortunately, the report is devoid of sufficient details to make a firm judgment. However, the reported success of this and the success of hypnosis (Olness, 1975) support the idea there are many pathways to treating sleep enuresis. This calls for more research to find out the common biological mechanisms that account for the success of such widely disparate treatments.

Record Keeping

Record keeping is usually not a problem. However, there are patients and families who do not keep good records, do not mail them, or do not bring them as instructed. It is helpful to provide a worksheet for the patient and family with spaces for the necessary information for each night. The essential information needed consists of the date, bedtime, time of bell, self-waking time, morning waking time, and fluid intake near bedtime. Some practitioners also suggest estimates of the wet patch size. The amount urinated at self-waking times and after being dry all night without an awakening by either an alarm or self-waking also is sometimes useful.

Relapse

Relapse is the regular resumption of wetting after reaching an adequate criteria of consecutive weeks of dryness. It is one of the major problems in treating sleep enuresis. The cause(s) of relapse is unknown, and definitions of relapse vary. The classification system (Doleys et al., 1981) provides a basis for defining degrees of wetting and relapse.

Studies report the relapse rate as high as 50%. However, the relapse rate depends upon the strictness of the definition. For example, is it a single wet night or a few wet nights per week for a few weeks? It is common for a few wet nights to occur scattered over several weeks or months. Complete and sustained dryness can occur without added intervention. The accuracy of estimates of the relapse rate also depends on the length of the follow-up period. The latter should be for at least 1 year and preferably 2 years. Three therapy procedures reportedly reduce relapse rates: overlearning, intermittent reinforcement, and extending treatment to a criteria of 4 consecutive weeks of dryness.

Overlearning

Overlearning involves increasing the fluid intake near bedtime after the patient has been dry for 7–14 consecutive nights. Consider amounts of 16–24 ounces for the overlearning procedure. The maximum amount is 32 ounces. Lesser amounts are more practical for some children, especially smaller and younger children. Whether to increase fluid intake and how much depends on several factors discussed in the section on fluid intake. Deciding against the overlearning procedure is reasonable if there has been an adequate treatment trial and if fluid intake has been greater than average for the patient.

Increases of fluid intake as soon as patients begin to be dry have a very long history (Mowrer & Mowrer, 1938; Lovibond, 1964). Controlled studies of the early 1970s showed that the practice can significantly reduce the chances of relapse (Young & Morgan, 1972a, 1972b; Taylor & Turner, 1975). An excellent review of overlearning, intermittent reinforcement, and stimulus intensity is found in Morgan (1978).

The process of how fluid increases work is unclear. Fluid increase might increase FBC and increase the inhibitory bladder control during sleep. It also may give patients more chances to control the bladder and brain interaction at higher levels of bladder pressure. Fluid increases also result in more learning trials and increased treatment time if wetting resumes. With very large amounts of fluid, there is often a temporary resumption of wetting. For about 9% of patients (Young & Morgan, 1972a), overlearning results in many wet nights, the persistence of wetting for several weeks, or both. Such a result may require discontinuing the procedure and reducing fluid intake to a more realistic amount.

Added learning trials alone are unlikely to explain fully the lower relapse rate. The process also might increase the patient's confidence in his or her ability to remain dry with increased fluid intake. How increased confidence might influence the reduced relapse rate is unclear. One can speculate about cognitive self-efficacy.

Intermittent Reinforcement

Intermittent reinforcement also can reduce relapse rates although not more so than over-learning. An example of intermittent reinforcement procedures were those by Finley, Wansley, and Blenkarn (1977). His method of providing such a conditioning schedule requires specialized and expensive instrumentation. One programs it to elicit the alarm contingent on about 70% of the wetting episodes. Practitioners will probably continue to choose overlearning or other procedures that do not require special and expensive instruments. This could change if intermittent reinforcement proves to be more effective.

Consider the following added guidelines when relapse occurs:

1. If the original treatment was short, such as a few or several weeks, consider reusing the urine alarm treatment. However, consider a different treatment if the original treatment required several months and especially if relapse occurred soon after the end of treatment.

2. Reassure the patient and family about a few wet nights, especially if sporadic or occurring at times of illness or fatigue. Encourage patience.

3. If there is a history of urinary tract infections (UTIs), consider repeat urine cultures. This is sometimes significant even with no other signs of infection other than the wetting; UTIs are far more common in girls than boys.

4. There are situations when one should encourage retreatment with the urine alarm even if the parent(s) or child resists treatment. An example is when that treatment was very successful before, the initial treatment period was brief, and it was several months or longer ago. Also, consider the patient's age. If the child is approaching or in adolescence or older, consider encouraging retreatment. If there are no other treatment options available, the choice may be between another trial or no treatment. In this type of situation, practitioners need added clinical skills. One may need to apply additional behavioral and learning principles such as positive reinforcement and shaping procedures. One may need extra efforts to establish a therapeutic alliance with the patient and family. Also, consider louder alarms and extra efforts at reducing later relapse. Very close professional supervision of treatment is probably crucial.

5. With multiple relapses, decisions depend on the degree of prior success, the duration of prior treatments, and the durations of the dry periods between treatments. Consider further urological evaluation.

Unsuccessful or Relatively Unsuccessful Treatment Outcomes

Many factors influence results that fall far short of 100% dryness. Consider the following guidelines when this treatment is or appears unsuccessful at a specific point during or after a prolonged treatment.

1. Assess all possible signs of progress. Look for signs of fewer bells, more self-wakings, longer durations of sleep before awakenings occur, and larger urine outputs. Combine the data into 2- to 4-week blocks. Look for trends. There may be progress that casual inspection of the data does not reveal. Discuss these with the patient and family.

2. Reassess patient and family cooperation, awakening to the alarm, instrumentation functioning, signs of lack of maturation, and duration of treatment.

3. Consider urological problems and further medical evaluation.

4. Consider repeating the treatment in several months. Consider using a louder alarm.

5. Consider other therapies (e.g., medication with the urine alarm, medication alone, other behavior therapies).

Other Children at Home

Problems arise when the patient is a child and other children are sleeping in the same room, especially in the same bed as the child in treatment. Encourage the family to rearrange the sleeping location of other children or the patient. This can help avoid disturbing other children and reduce or avoid their negative reactions.

If another child has sleep enuresis, the question arises whether the treatment of one child might adversely affect the other. Thus, will the alarm ringing at times not contingent upon the other child's bladder state detract from this treatment for the other child if needed later. There is no research on this subject, as ethics prevents experimental research. In practice, conservative practitioners suggest that other children, especially younger children with enuresis, sleep in a separate room. They encourage parents to substantially reduce this potential impact on other children. If the other child with enuresis is older than the proposed patient, consider treating the older child first unless there are compelling reasons for doing otherwise.

MEDICAL ASSESSMENT OF ENURESIS

Read medical references on this subject for details of what to assess, and how, when, and why to do so, or discuss this with physician colleagues. Briefly, unless there is indication for urological abnormalities that could be causing or contributing to the wetting, consider a conservative medical and urological evaluation (Burke & Stickler, 1980). The chances of an organic cause for the enuresis, other than in the 5–10% of girls with UTIs, are very small. Some urologists are more concerned with urological abnormalities (Arnold & Ginsburg, 1975).

All patients with enuresis should receive a medical evaluation, but most younger children will not need urological tests. Except a recommended urine culture for girls, one can usually defer other medical tests until after a reasonable treatment trial. Urological consultation is more important before using the urine alarm treatment for adolescents and adults with sleep enuresis who did not have a prior urologic evaluation. Especially consider this if prior treatment with the urine alarm was clearly unsuccessful. Also, consider urological consultation and tests if there are signs of possible urological disease in addition to the enuresis.

CONCLUSION

Sleep enuresis is a biobehavioral problem calling for consideration of biochemical, physiological, and learning theory variables. This chapter discussed many aspects of sleep enuresis. It provides guidelines for assessment, use of the urine alarm treatment, and information about other treatments. The urine alarm treatment for sleep enuresis is a form of biofeedback. It remains the single most effective therapeutic approach by itself or in combination with other treatments.

GLOSSARY

ANTIDIURETIC HORMONE (ADH, VASOPRESSIN). Hormone that promotes water reabsorption and increases urine concentration in the kidneys. Synthesized in the hypothalamus and stored in the pituitary gland (see text).

AVOIDANCE CONDITIONING. A classical conditioning concept in which a behavior increases in frequency to postpone or avoid an aversive stimulus. In this context, the assumption is that brain–bladder sphincter changes occur to maintain dryness because of the aversiveness of the loud alarm.

BINARY/THRESHOLD FEEDBACK. Two states or conditions, for example, on–off, depending on the presence of a specified behavior; in this case, wetting or no wetting, elicits no alarm or alarm.

BLADDER DETRUSOR. Detrusor means "to push down." It is a general term for any body part that pushes down. In the lower urinary system the detrusor refers to the smooth muscle that composes the wall of the bladder, which contracts to expel urine.

BLADDER STRETCHING EXERCISES. (See *retention-control*.) Behavioral technique used during the day and involving instructions and incentives to keep the urinary sphincter(s) tightly closed against bladder pressure to urinate. The intent is to increase at least FBC during the day and thus increase sleep-time dryness. An assumption was that children with nocturnal enuresis have smaller FBCs than those who are dry. Although the mean FBCs are probably different, there is considerable overlap. Some children do improve significantly, but the overall success rate is not impressive, especially compared to the urine alarm system.

BOOSTER TREATMENTS. In the present context, repeated urine alarm treatment for a relapse after a period of dryness that is usually several months but could be 1 year or more.

CLASSICAL CONDITIONING (RESPONDENT CONDITIONING). (See Chapter 1.) A previously neutral or noneliciting stimulus acquires the capacity to elicit a response (CR) as a result of being paired with an unconditioned stimulus (UCS), one that would elicit the response (UCR) naturally. The neutral stimulus thus becomes a conditioned stimulus (CS). A version of it (classical avoidance conditioning) is a major theory for explaining how the urine alarm system works to eliminate wetting.

CYSTOGRAM (CYSTOMETROGRAM, CMG). A urodynamic test to assess bladder function by measuring the bladder pressure/volume relationship. (See Chapter 23 for further discussion.)

1-DESAMINO-8-D-ARGININE VASOPRESSIN (DDAVP, DESMOPRESSIN). Synthetic ADH. It concentrates urine by acting on the distal tubules of the kidneys. During sleep it reduces urine output to the bladder. Initially touted as highly successful for reducing frequency of wetting in children with nocturnal enuresis, more recent research showed less initial success in addition to the extremely high relapse rate already known. Overall, only about 25% of children become totally dry during treatment. Only as many as 20% of those children remain dry, and some studies report much lower follow-up dryness. One advantage is lessened negative side effects. It may be useful for short-term, temporary use for some children (see text).

DETRUSOR AREFLEXIA. Absence of contractions of the detrusor muscle even with high urine volume (see text).

DETRUSOR HYPERREFLEXIA. Involuntary contractions of the detrusor muscle during much lower-than-normal bladder pressures (see text).

DETRUSOR–SPHINCTER DYSENERGIA. Continued, intermittent contractions of the external bladder sphincter (see text).

DRY BED TRAINING. A specific combination of behavioral techniques based on operant conditioning and intended to decrease nocturnal enuresis. It focuses on positive reinforcement of a variety of behaviors associated with being dry. It is an intensive therapy program requiring frequent waking of the child and carefully specified parental and child behaviors. It is sometimes combined with the urine alarm but has been successful without it as well. The success rate is very good, but many professionals and parents consider it too intense, difficult, and impractical to use in many cases.

FALSE ALARMS. The urine alarm rings without urine. Excess perspiration can do it with instruments that are too sensitive. Old-style sandwich-type metal pads could come into contact during sleep and close the circuit, thus triggering the alarm.

FUNCTIONAL BLADDER CAPACITY (FBC). The amount of urine in the bladder before voiding. Usually measured after drinking a large amount of fluid and maximum postponement of urination. Not a measure of true bladder capacity (see text).

IMIPRAMINE HYDROCHLORIDE (TOFRANIL). A tricyclic antidepressant that, in much smaller doses than used for depression, often results in decreasing or eliminating sleep-time wetting. Original use for this was based on the observation of urine retention and continence as a side effect among depressed psychiatric patients taking imipramine. Fewer than half of children become dry during use (about 40%), and the vast majority relapse after stopping the drug. Only about 15% remained dry in follow-ups. It is still widely used, and, when carefully used and monitored, it can be useful and safe. However, safety issues and negative side effects have led to professional disagreements about its use.

INTERMITTENT REINFORCEMENT. (See Chapter 1.) Also called *schedule of reinforcement* except for continuous reinforcement. Intermittent reinforcement of an operant behavior. Four types are variable-ratio, variable-interval, fixed-interval, and fixed-ratio schedules. The number of times a reinforcement follows a specific behavior varies randomly, at a variable interval, at a fixed interval, or at fixed ratio. The variable-ratio schedule is most resistant to extinction. The enuresis alarm does not go on every time the urine contacts the sensor. It goes on intermittently on a schedule.

MONOSYMPTOMATIC SLEEP ENURESIS. Sleep-time enuresis without any other sleep-time symptoms.

NEUROGENIC BLADDER. Two types are *detrusor hyperreflexia* and *detrusor areflexia*.

NOCTURNAL POLYURIA. Increased frequency of urinations during sleep time because of overproduction of urine as a result of the kidneys not concentrating the urine.

NON-RAPID EYE MOVEMENT (NREM) SLEEP. Stages I–IV. Contrast with REM sleep, which is most associated with dreaming.

NORADRENERGIC STIMULATION. Activated by (or secreting) norepinephrine. Norepinephrine is one of the natural catecholamines—a neurohormone. It has mostly alpha-adrenergic activity and some beta-adrenergic activity. It inhibits detrusor muscle activity through beta receptors and contracts the bladder neck through alpha receptors. *Beta receptors* (beta-adrenergic receptor) are adrenergic receptors that respond to norepinephrine and certain blocking agents. *Alpha receptors* (alpha-adrenergic receptor) are adrenergic receptors that respond to epinephrine and certain specific blocking agents. (See *epinephrine, norepinephrine, catecholamines, adrenal medulla,* Chapters 7, 17, 18.)

OVERLEARNING. An operant conditioning learning and teaching method in which one arranges for additional learning trials beyond the initial evidence of learning a specific behavior.

OXYBUTYNIN (DITROPAN). An anticholinergic and analgesic medication developed specifically to reduce spontaneous spasms of the bladder in incontinent adults. It reduces detrusor activity and increases bladder capacity. Very limited use for nocturnal enuresis in children. Much less successful than imipramine, and relapse also is very high.

POSITIVE REINFORCEMENT. A reinforcer that serves to increase the probability of the behavior it follows.

RETENTION-CONTROL. A behavioral technique intended to increase bladder capacity and holding time. The person attempts to hold the urine as long as he or she can and is reinforced for longer times.

SHAPING. An operant (Skinnerian) conditioning learning and teaching method in which one gives positive reinforcers for successive approximations (small steps) of a specified goal behavior.

STAGE IV SLEEP. The "deepest" level of sleep, sometimes called "restorative" sleep. It occurs in the early period of a sleep cycle. It is very difficult to arouse most people from this stage. The amount of time in Stage IV is related to age. Younger children are in this stage longer than older children, who, in turn, are in Stage IV longer than adults.

UTI. Urinary tract infection.

ACKNOWLEDGMENT

I offer my sincere and warm appreciation to my long-time colleague and friend, Robert C. Colligan, Ph.D. He joined with me in 1970 so we could introduce this treatment at the Mayo Clinic. For his continued friendship and partnership I remain very grateful.

REFERENCES

Arnold S. J., & Ginsburg, A. (1975). Understanding and managing enuresis in children. *Postgraduate Medicine, 58*(6), 73–82.

Baker, B. L. (1969). Symptom treatment and symptom substitution in enuresis. *Journal of Abnormal Psychology, 74,* 42–49.

Borrie, P., & Fenton, J. C. B. (1966). Buzzer ulcers. *British Medical Journal, 2,* 151–152.

Boyd, M. M. M. (1960). The depth of sleep in enuretic school-children and in non-enuretic controls. *Journal of Psychosomatic Research, 4,* 274–281.

Burke, E. C., & Stickler, G. B. (1980). Enuresis—Is it being overtreated? *Mayo Clinic Proceedings, 55,* 118–119.

Cohen, M. W. (1975). Enuresis. *Pediatric Clinics of North America, 22,* 545–560.

Coote, M. A. (1965). Apparatus for conditioning treatment of enuresis. *Behaviour Research and Therapy, 2,* 233–238.

DiPerri, R., & Meduri, M. (1972). L'enuresi notturna: Ulteriori elementi in tema di diagnostica strumentale [Nocturnal enuresis: Further principles of instrumental diagnosis]. *Acta Neurologica (Napoli), 27*(1), 22–27.

Dische, S. (1971). Management of enuresis. *British Medical Journal, 2,* 33–36.

Dische, S. (1973). Treatment of enuresis with an enuresis alarm. In I. Kolvin, R. C. MacKeith, & S. R. Meadow (Eds.), *Bladder control and enuresis* (pp. 211–230). Philadelphia: Lippincott.

Doleys, D. M., Schwartz, M. S., & Ciminero, A. R. (1981). Elimination problems: Enuresis and encopresis. In E. J. Mash & L. G. Terdal (Eds.), *Behavioral assessment of childhood disorders* (pp. 679–710). New York: Guilford Press.

Finley, W. W. (1971). An EEG study of the sleep of enuretics at three age levels. *Clinical Encephalography, 2,* 35–39.

Finley, W. W., Wansley, R. A., & Blenkarn, M. M. (1977). Conditioning treatment of enuresis using a 70% intermittent reinforcement schedule. *Behaviour Research and Therapy, 15,* 419–425.

Forrester, R. M. (1966). Buzzer ulcers (Correspondence). *British Medical Journal, 302.*

Hallgren, B. (1960). Nocturnal enuresis in twins. *Acta Psychiatrica et Neurologica Scandinavica, 35,* 73–90.

Herson, V. C., Schmitt, B. D., & Rumack, B. H. (1979). Magical thinking and imipramine poisoning in two school-aged children. *Journal of the American Medical Association, 241,* 1926–1927.

Houts, A. C. (1991). Nocturnal enuresis as a biobehavioral problem. *Behavior Therapy, 22,* 133–151.

Houts, A. C., Berman, J. S., & Abramson, H. (1994). Effectiveness of psychological and pharmacological treatments for nocturnal enuresis. *Journal of Consulting and Clinical Psychology, 62*(4), 737–745.

Houts, A. C., Peterson, J. K., & Whelan, J. P. (1986). Prevention of relapse in full-spectrum home training for primary enuresis: A components analysis. *Behavior Therapy, 17,* 462–469.

Kaffman, M., & Elizur, E. (1977). Infants who become enuretics: A longitudinal study of 161 kibbutz children. *Monographs of the Society for Research in Child Development, 42*(2, Serial No. 170).

Knudsen, U. B., Rittig, S., Norgaard, J. P., Lundemose, J. B., Pedersen, E. B., & Djurhuus, J. C. (1991). Long-term treatment of nocturnal enuresis with desmopressin: A follow-up study. *Urological Research, 19*(4), 237–240.

Kolvin, I., MacKeith, R. C., & Meadow, S. R. (1973). *Bladder control and enuresis.* Philadelphia: Lippincott.

Lovering, J. S., Tallett, S. E., & McKendry, J. B. J. (1988). Oxybutynin efficacy in the treatment of primary enuresis. *Pediatrics, 82,* 104–106.

Lovibond, S. (1964). *Conditioning and enuresis.* New York: Macmillan.

Lovibond. S. H., & Coote, M. A. (1970). Enuresis. In C. G. Costello (Ed.), *Symptoms of psychopathology: A handbook* (373–396). New York: Wiley.

MacLean, R. E. G. (1960). Imipramine hydrochloride (Tofranil) and enuresis. *American Journal of Psychiatry, 117,* 551.

May, H. J., Colligan, R. C., & Schwartz, M. S. (1983). Childhood enuresis: Important points in assessment, trends in treatment. *Postgraduate Medicine, 74*(1), 111–116,119.

Miller, N. E. (1981). Behavioral medicine, biofeedback, and homeostasis: New applications of learning. *Psychiatric Annals, 11,* 31,35–38,45.

Moffatt, M. E. K., Harlos, S., Kirshen, A. J., & Burd, L. (1993). Desmopressin acetate and nocturnal enuresis: How much do we know? *Pediatrics, 92*(3), 420–425.

Morgan, R. T. T. (1978). Relapse and therapeutic response in the conditioning treatment of enuresis: A review of recent findings on intermittent reinforcement, overlearning and stimulus intensity. *Behaviour Research and Therapy, 16,* 273–279.

Mowrer, O. H., & Mowrer, W. M. (1938). Enuresis—A method for its study and treatment. *American Journal of Orthopsychiatry, 8,* 436–459.

Norgaard, J. P. (1989a). Urodynamics in enuretics I: Reservoir function. *Neurourology and Urodynamics, 8,* 199–211.

Norgaard, J. P. (1989b). Urodynamics in enuretics II: A pressure/flow study. *Neurourology and Urodynamics, 8,* 213–217.

Norgaard, J. P., Hansen, J. H., Wildschiotz, G., Sorensen, S., Rittig, S., & Djurhuus, J. C. (1989). Sleep cystometrics in children with nocturnal enuresis. *Journal of Urology, 141,* 1156–1159.

Norgaard, J. P., Pedersen, E. B., & Djurhuus, J. C. (1985). Diurnal anti-diuretic-hormone levels in enuretics. *The Journal of Urology, 134,* 1029–1031.

Olness, K. (1975). The use of self-hypnosis in the treatment of childhood nocturnal enuresis: A report on 40 patients. *Clinical Pediatrics, 14,* 273–279.

Random House college dictionary (rev. ed.). (1975). New York: Random House.

Rapoport, J. L., Mikkelsen, E. J., Zavaldi, A., Nee, L., Gruneau, C., Mendelson, W., & Gillin, J. C. (1980). Childhood enuresis II. Psychopathology, tricyclic concentration in plasma, and antienuretic effect. *Archives of General Psychiatry, 37,* 1146–1152.

Rittig, S., Knudsen, U. B., Norgaard, J. P., Pedersen, E. B., & Djurhuus, J. C. (1989). Abnormal diurnal rhythm of plasma vasopressin and urinary output in patients with enuresis. *American Journal of Physiology, 256,* F664–F671.

Rowan, R. L. (1974). *Bed wetting: A guide for parents.* New York: St. Martin's Press.

Salk, L. (1972). *What every child would like his parents to know.* New York: Warner; David McKay.

Schwartz, M. S. (1981). *The urine alarm treatment for nocturnal enuresis: A biofeedback treatment.* Paper presented at the 1981 annual meeting of the Biofeedback Society of America, Louisville, KY.

Schwartz, M. S., & Colligan, R. C. (1974). A conditioning program for nocturnal enuresis. *Medical Insight, 6*(4), 12–19.

Sharf, M. B., & Jennings, S. W. (1988). Childhood enuresis: Relationship to sleep, etiology, evaluation, and treatment. *Annals of Behavioral Medicine, 10,* 113–120.

Standards Association of Australia. (1980). *Conditioning equipment for the treatment of nocturnal enuresis (bedwetting alarms)* (AS 2394-1980). Sydney, New South Wales: Author.

Starfield, B., & Mellits, E. D. (1968). Increase in functional bladder capacity and improvement in enuresis. *Journal of Pediatrics, 74*(2), 483–487.

Taylor, P. D., & Turner, R. K. (1975). A clinical trial of continuous, intermittent and overlearning "bell and pad" treatments for nocturnal enuresis. *Behaviour Research and Therapy, 13,* 281–293.

Wagner, W. G., & Mathews, R. (1985). The treatment of nocturnal enuresis: A controlled comparison of two models of urine alarm. *Journal of Developmental and Behavioral Pediatrics, 6*(1), 22–26.

Young, G. C., & Morgan, R. T. T. (1972a). Overlearning in the conditioning treatment of enuresis. *Behaviour Research and Therapy, 10,* 147–151.

Young, G. C., & Morgan, R. T. T. (1972b). Overlearning in the conditioning treatment of enuresis: A long term follow-up study. *Behaviour Research and Therapy, 10,* 419–420.

Xu Baoqin (1991). 302 cases of enuresis treated with acupuncture. *Journal of Traditional Chinese Medicine, 11*(2), 121–122.

X

PROFESSIONAL ISSUES, CONSIDERATIONS, AND GUIDELINES

26

Professional Ethical Behavior for Providers of Biofeedback

Sebastian Striefel

Have you ever asked yourself how knowledgeable you are about ethical principles as they apply to what you do in biofeedback and applied psychophysiology? Do you know *The Ethical Principles of Applied Psychophysiology and Biofeedback* (Association for Applied Psychophysiology and Biofeedback, 1990)? Can you define the following terms: privileged communication, informed consent, dual relationship, moral agent, and aspirational ethics? Do you know how to manage and minimize risk in your professional activities? This chapter is written for you if you answered "No" to any of these questions.

The intent of this chapter is to provide the reader with:

1. Basic, but critical, information about the importance of ethical behavior in professional practice today.
2. Decision-making rules.
3. A review of the application of basic ethical principles.
4. A list of references for further reading.
5. A realization that behaving ethically is essential to professional survival, and thereby requires ongoing attention and education. The use of judgment and ethical reasoning is an essential professional practice skill.

DEFINITIONS

To proceed, readers must have definitions of commonly used terms and concepts. Some definitions are in the following section and some are interspersed throughout the chapter.

Ethics, Ethical Principles, and Law

In its simplest form, ethics is doing what is right. It means engaging in those behaviors that are morally correct and in the best interests of those served (e.g., clients[1] and students). As such, "ethical principles" are the agreed upon, ideal, moral standards of conduct set by a professional group (e.g., Association for Applied Psychophysiology and Biofeedback, 1990).

---

[1]The term "client" suggests personal responsibility and self-control; whereas the term "patient" suggests "a one-down position." The reader is free to equate the term client with the term patient, if so desired.

"Laws," as specified in legal statutes, are the minimal standards of conduct that a society accepts. Both laws and ethical principles guide professional behavior; thus, it is critical that professionals be knowledgeable and current in both. Neither provides specific solutions for how to behave in specific situations. Each provides general guidance and is subject to interpretation. Changes in circumstances can result in needed changes in required behavior.

Ethical Dilemmas

The practical difficulty often faced by professionals centers on how to deal with the ethical dilemmas that arise. An ethical dilemma is any controversy that involves conflicting moral principles or responsibilities in which one must choose between two rights (Callahan, 1988; Striefel, 1986). Unfortunately, many providers are not aware of when they encounter an ethical dilemma. As such, it makes sense that most ethical violations occur inadvertently because providers are not aware of how their behavior or lack of behavior may adversely impact their clients (Corey, Corey, & Callanan, 1993; Lakin, 1991). An example of an ethical dilemma is when one is the only biofeedback provider in a geographical area, and a client seeks help for a problem one is not competent to treat. Does one try to provide treatment or let the client suffer because one is not competent in that area of biofeedback? The dilemma is between doing what is best for the client and operating only in areas in which one is competent. There are many potential solutions to such a dilemma, including getting appropriate training, consultation, or supervision. One must recognize that a dilemma exists, however, before one can deal with it. Some ethical dilemmas are inherent in providing service to clients, in conducting research, and in supervising or training others. It is the practitioner's responsibility to understand the characteristics and sources of ethical dilemmas because it is always the therapist who is the accountable party in a treatment relationship (Lakin, 1991). Pope and Vetter (1992) wrote an excellent article on dilemmas encountered by psychologists. Many of the cases discussed apply directly to providers of biofeedback.

Levels of Ethical Functioning

There are two levels of ethical functioning: mandatory or lower-level ethical functioning and aspirational or higher-level ethical functioning (Corey et al., 1993; Striefel, 1989a). In mandatory ethics, one follows the requirements of the law and the ethical principles of the groups to which one belongs. Doing so provides sensible and good protection against professional or legal action against the provider. At the aspirational level of functioning, one goes beyond the minimal to do what is in the best interests of the client, though it requires additional time and effort. It includes thinking about what effects the practitioner's actions will have on the client and can include activities such as reading or seeking consultation. For example, suppose a practitioner is providing services to a client for back injuries from a car accident. The client has filed a lawsuit to receive compensation for the injuries and thus has waived the right to privileged communication in reference to physiological treatment information. If the practitioner receives a court subpoena for the client's files from the opposing attorney, mandatory ethics dictates release of a copy of the files. Aspirational ethics dictates that one not release the files until: (1) the information in the files is reviewed to determine whether there is sensitive information included that is not relevant to the case, (2) consultation with the client and/or his or her attorney takes place, (3) the subpoena is verified as legal, and (4) possibly even a meeting with the judge is set up in his or her chambers to discuss sensitive information that may not be relevant to the case.

Since ethical codes are difficult to enforce, it is desirable for biofeedback practitioners and other professionals to strive to meet the aspirational, rather than the mandatory level of functioning (Striefel, 1989a). When a professional group does not adhere to the highest level of functioning, society restricts professional practice by passing laws to assure a certain level of functioning (Roswell, 1989). In addition, unethical behavior promotes higher costs for professional liability insurance.

ACQUIRING APPROPRIATE ETHICAL BEHAVIOR

Required Adherence

Biofeedback practitioners must adhere to *The Ethical Principles of Applied Psychophysiology and Biofeedback* and to the ethical principles of the other professional groups to which they belong (e.g., the American Psychological Association for psychologists). Relying only on watching one's mentors to learn ethics is long past (Striefel, 1992b). First, applications of ethics are much more complex today than in the past and are changing as new laws, legal procedures, and ethical codes become established. Second, it is difficult to know whether a mentor is modeling the correct ethical behavior.

How does one learn appropriate ethical behavior when each situation requires a different solution, especially since most ethical principles/codes are vague and provide only general guidance? Several behaviors are required for a provider to behave ethically. The keys to appropriate ethical practice are self-analysis, continuing education, written policies and procedures, adherence to general guidelines for ethical conduct, availability of ethical principles and other ethical and legal materials (library), use of supervision and consultation, and good documentation. Clarification of each of these items is in the sections that follow.

Self-Analysis: What Do You Believe?

Every practitioner should seriously consider investing time in self-analysis to determine his or her beliefs. One way to do this is to write a self-disclosure statement that lists areas in which one is competent to practice (Striefel, 1992c). Another method is to read current materials on ethical principles and moral values and write out what you believe and how that corresponds with expected professional behavior. Some broad moral principles on which ethical principles and codes are based include:

- Nonmaleficence: Do no harm.
- Beneficence: Promote the good.
- Autonomy: Foster self-determination and avoid paternalism.
- Justice: Treat clients fairly.
- Fidelity: Be faithful and keep your promises (Corey et al., 1993)

Each provider should decide what these principles and those of the Association of Applied Psychophysiology and Biofeedback (AAPB) mean in daily practice through reading, thought, and discussion with others.

Education and Professional Library

To increase the chance of helping clients and reduce risks of injury to them, providers need continued education in ethics. Reading one book or taking one course in ethics is not sufficient for being current with ethical practice. One should regularly read ethics articles and books and should attend an ethics workshop or other presentations at least once every

3 years, especially in the early years of one's career and periodically thereafter. Most universities offer courses in ethics, and AAPB offers regular workshops and presentations on ethics at its annual meeting and regional workshops.

Having a good personal, professional library is essential. Some materials to consider for inclusion are:

1. *The Ethical Principles of Applied Psychophysiology and Biofeedback* (Association for Applied Psychophysiology and Biofeedback, 1990).
2. The ethical principles of your discipline.
3. The *Standards and Guidelines for Biofeedback Applications in Psychophysiological Self-Regulation* (Amar et al., 1992).
4. A book on risk management (e.g., *Professional Liability and Risk Management* by Bennett, Bryant, VandenBos, & Greenwood, 1990).
5. Relevant state laws (e.g., licensing, reporting of child abuse and neglect, records retention, commitment, and mental health).
6. Some good books on ethics and on law (e.g., *Issues and Ethics in the Helping Professions* by Corey et al., 1993; *The Psychologist's Legal Handbook* by Stromberg et al., 1988; and *The Paper Office* by Zuckerman & Guyett, 1991).

Written Policies and Procedures

Risk management is an essential component of professional practice today (Striefel, 1992b). One can define risk management as having well-developed written policies and procedures in place and to which all staff members adhere (Striefel, 1992b). Further, these are policies and procedures that

1. Reduce the probability of litigation or the filing of ethical complaints (Bennett et al., 1990).
2. Encourage proactive quality control.
3. Reduce the chance of injury or dissatisfaction by those served.
4. Increase proper professional behavior by all staff.
5. Reduce staff stress (Striefel, 1992b).

Striefel (1992b, 1992c, 1993b) emphasized the importance of having available written policies and procedures for guiding professional practice. The advantages of written policies and procedures are the following: (1) the process of writing the policies and procedures requires a practitioner to think about what he or she is and is not doing and about what could or should be done; (2) they provide a mechanism for increasing the probability that all people in the agency engage in certain key practices in the same way; (3) they can be reviewed internally and by external consultants to assure that they meet ethical and "best practices" standards; and (4) if adhered to, they can help reduce the risk of malpractice litigation and the need to deal with ethical complaints. The policies and procedures should cover all aspects of practice, including, but not limited to (1) fees, billing, and collection procedures; (2) confidentiality; (3) informed consent; (4) contacting the therapist during work and personal time; (5) termination and referral; (6) coverage in provider's absence; and (7) records. See Striefel's article (1993b) for more specifics. The article is available from AAPB for a nominal fee.

The policies and procedures also should include copies of all forms used, so they are readily available to staff. Zuckerman and Guyett (1991) wrote an excellent book that includes a variety of forms and procedures that one can readily adapt to a biofeedback practice. The book, entitled *The Paper Office*, includes copies of many forms on a floppy computer disc. Some vendors of biofeedback instruments and supplies have available a set of forms for use in a biofeedback practice.

The agency should include necessary ethical principles in its policies and procedures manual and should seriously consider requiring all staff to sign a statement that they agree, as a condition of employment, to adhere to *The Ethical Principles of Applied Psychophysiology and Biofeedback* and those of their professional discipline. For those using biofeedback but who are not members of recognized health care professions and not licensed by the state in a health care field, consider requiring that they sign a statement that they agree, as a condition of employment, to adhere to the Ethical Principles of AAPB. Such a policy, if enforced, would provide grounds for educating staff, emphasizing the importance of ethical behavior, and replacing unethical staff when needed.

The General Guidelines for Ethical Conduct

There are five general guidelines to know and adhere to in reference to reducing risks and behaving ethically (Striefel, 1993a). These include:

1. *Be sensitive to individual differences.* This sensitivity includes differences in values, gender, culture, race, religion, sexual preference, age, mental status, disabling conditions, ethnicity, and economic status (Striefel, 1993c). It also includes being sensitive to potential ethical dilemmas and warning signs (red flags), for example, the client who has seen several therapists for a specific problem and never followed through with any of them or who has sued previous service providers. The key concept is to be sensitive to the individual needs of the client and to do what is best for him or her.

2. *Be informed.* To be informed means to be knowledgeable and competent in all areas related to the services you provide. Being knowledgeable means to obtain continued training by taking courses, attending workshops, reading, belonging to study groups, and seeking consultation and supervision (Striefel, 1990a). In addition to being competent in ethics and biofeedback, a provider must be competent in (a) relevant state and federal laws, (b) standards of professional practice, (c) business management, (d) medical issues that require consultation, and (e) marketing and maintaining professional relationships. Being informed requires energy, resources and proactive behavior.

3. *Think and act preventively.* Implementation of thinking and acting preventively begins by (a) knowing one's self, (b) planning one's professional activities, (c) writing out policies and procedures for professional practice, (d) reviewing what and how one provides services, (e) maintaining good liability insurance, (f) establishing a professional relationship with a lawyer, and (g) continuing one's education. Readers can readily add to this list from their own experience. Bennett et al. (1990) outline many behaviors one should and should not engage in if someone files a lawsuit or ethical complaint against a provider.

4. *Seek consultation and supervision.* This needs to be done often, especially when one is providing treatment in areas that are new to the practitioner (Striefel, 1990b). Biofeedback practitioners are expected to practice only in areas in which they are competent by training and experience, unless appropriately supervised (Association for Applied Psychophysiology and Biofeedback, 1990). Seeking consultation with appropriate professionals, (e.g., lawyers, medical personnel, or other biofeedback providers) when ethical issues arise can be most helpful in clarifying the issues involved and in reaching a solution that is within the confines of acceptable practice (Striefel, 1992c). A "best practices" approach to providing biofeedback services often requires providers to work with other professionals whose expertise is crucial to achieving client goals. This often includes evaluation or monitoring

by appropriate medical specialists (e.g., neurologists) to rule out tumors for a client with headaches or a physician to monitor and adjust medication dosages for a client who is on medications for high blood pressure and undergoing biofeedback training for that problem.

5. *Document.* The courts have typically ruled that unless one documents something, it did not occur. In addition, it is unethical not to have sufficient documentation for meeting client needs. A client's records should make clear what the provider did, when, why, and how he or she did it, who did it, and where. Good documentation can help a provider in dealing with third-party payers, other professionals serving the client, the client him- or herself, supervisors or supervisees, an ethics committee, the courts, or anyone else who might have a legitimate right to obtain the information about a client. This chapter provides more information on documentation later.

Ethical Decision Making

All biofeedback providers need a model available for making decisions concerning ethical issues. The process is the same as that which one would use if one were providing psychotherapy, counseling, or other types of professional services. The ethical test is a beginning question to ask oneself (Striefel, 1993a). In essence, would another reasonable practitioner in the same situation decide and behave in the same way? If the answer is "No" or "I don't know," then clearly one needs more input via consultation, reading, or other sources. Ethical decision making requires a systematic, replicable approach to problem solving. Figure 26.1 (flowcharts 1–6) provides an outline of major steps and decision points for making ethical decisions. The major steps in this process include:

1. Determine the facts objectively.
2. Analyze the situation to identify the ethical aspects.
3. List all the possible options and probable results.
4. Seek consultation if and as needed.
5. Make an ethical decision.
6. Take action.
7. Evaluate the decision and outcome and take corrective action, if needed (Kentsmith, Miya, & Salladay, 1986; Schwartz & Striefel, 1987).

Additional questions one can ask oneself in making ethical decisions include:

1. How will it make me feel about myself? Will I feel proud of my behavior? Would I feel good if the decision appeared in the newspaper or if my family knew about it?
2. Is it balanced and fair to all concerned in both the short and long term? Does it promote win–win?
3. How will the client feel about the decision in both the short and long term? Will he or she feel proud?
4. Am I providing competent service? Does it meet the standards of common or "best practices"?

One should take seriously the critical process of ethical decision making. This can prevent potential problems from becoming reality by detecting their chance of occurrence and taking preventive action. Repeatedly using a systematic, ethical decision-making process, such as the one outlined in Figure 26.1, should result in learning the process so well that one could use it in new situations almost automatically.

Flowchart 1. Overview of General Problem Situation

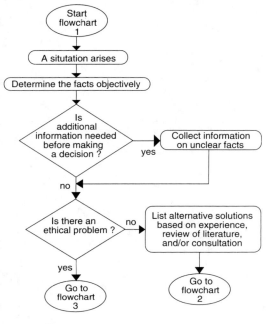

Flowchart 2. Overview of General Problem Situation (cont.)

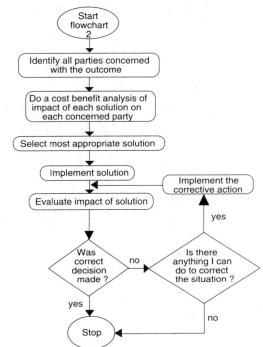

Flowchart 3. Overview of General Problem Situation (cont.)

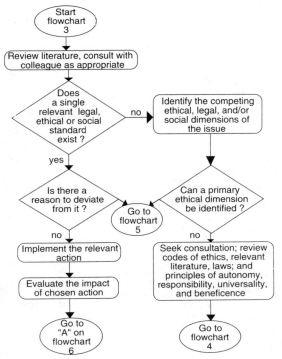

Flowchart 4. Overview of General Problem Situation (cont.)

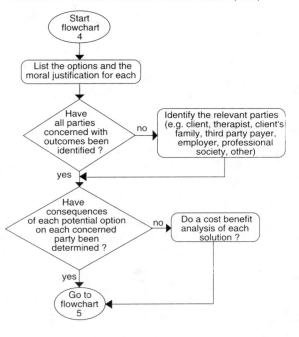

(continued)

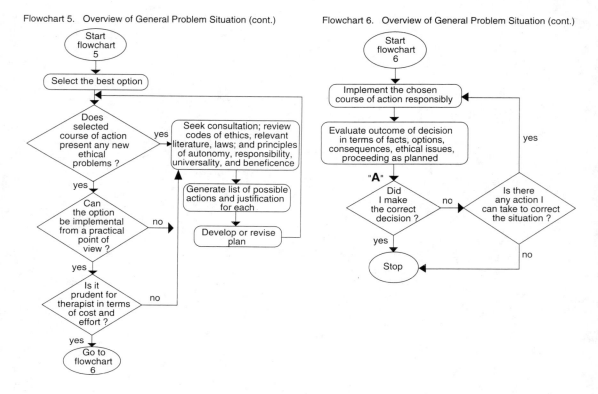

FIGURE 26.1. Flowcharts of the steps in ethical decision making.

ETHICAL PRINCIPLES IN PRACTICE

Several principles and values are useful in guiding professional-practice activities. Many of these principles are part of AAPB's *The Ethical Principles of Applied Psychophysiology and Biofeedback* (1990). Application of these principles and values include items such as: respect, responsibility, competence, and confidentiality.

Respect

In its simplest form one can define respect as holding in high regard, showing consideration for, and avoiding intruding upon or interfering with the lives of others (Guralnik, 1980).

When applied functionally, it means to (Striefel, 1993a):

1. Protect the welfare of those served—first and foremost.
2. Help clients to acquire the self-regulatory skills that will improve the quality of their lives and to choose from available alternatives.
3. Avoid paternalism (assuming one knows better than the client what is best for that person).
4. Avoid undue influence (intentionally or unintentionally influencing a client in an inappropriate way, e.g., coercion).

5. Obtain informed consent on all aspects of assessment, diagnosis, and treatment.
6. Encourage the self-development of client goals.
7. Provide the best service possible within the standards of "best practices" (i.e., being competent).
8. Avoid discriminating against anyone because of gender, race, religion, ethnicity, sexual preference, age, disabilities, or other factors.
9. Accept individual differences of opinion, style, and behavior and be kind and courteous to all.
10. Establish good rapport with each client or refer the client elsewhere.
11. Avoid engaging in potentially problematic dual relationships.
12. Be honest and accurate in all written and oral statements made about biofeedback and other practice areas.
13. Protect clients' rights to privacy, privileged communication, and confidentiality.
14. Keep appropriate records.

Such a list of how to show respect for those served could have many more components. A reader may find expanding the list is both an interesting and useful activity. The failure to show respect for those served can result in many problems for a service provider. For example, clients unhappy with the ways providers interact with them as persons are more likely to initiate action against providers (Bennett et al., 1990). Do you as a provider of biofeedback services show respect for the rights of those you serve?

Responsibility

Practitioners using biofeedback, like other direct service providers, are always responsible for what they do and do not do. In addition, they are also partially responsible for what those whom they supervise do or fail to do. Ethically, practitioners must:

> adhere to the highest standards of their profession. They behave responsibly; accept responsibility for their behavior and the consequences of their behavior; ensure that biofeedback is used appropriately; and strive to educate the public concerning responsible use of biofeedback in treatment, research, and training. (Association for Applied Psychophysiology and Biofeedback, 1990, p. 16)

This statement sounds fairly straight forward. However, actual implementation in daily practice is more complex. In practice, responsible behavior includes (Striefel, 1990a):

1. Protecting the rights and welfare of those served.
2. Advocating for clients.
3. Being competent.
4. Obtaining consultations and supervision, as appropriate.
5. Determining one's own limits.
6. Obtaining additional training when needed.
7. Not trying to treat everyone.
8. Helping to police the behavior of other biofeedback providers.
9. Evaluating the services one provides and taking corrective action as needed.
10. Keeping everyone concerned informed of one's loyalties.
11. Maintaining professional relationships.
12. Not exploiting those served.

13. Respecting clients and their choices.
14. Adhering to relevant laws and ethical principles.
15. Being responsible for one's own behavior and that of those one supervisees (doctrine of respondent superior).
16. Obtaining informed consent.
17. Informing clients of the limits of confidentiality.
18. Avoiding abandoning any client.
19. Guarding against the misuse of one's influence.
20. Complying with the state's licensing law and the Biofeedback Certification Institute of America (BCIA) certification requirements.

A professional cannot blame the client for his or her own lack of responsible behavior.

Informed, sound, and responsible judgment are the basis for responsible practice. One develops the needed skills for responsible practice by reading, attending classes and workshops, obtaining frequent supervision and/or consultation, conducting self-evaluations, through peer reviews, and by knowing one's own areas of competence.

Competence

Striefel (1990c) defined competence:

> as having acquired the training and/or experience required to meet the minimal level of skills necessary for serving clients effectively while adhering to the common standards of practice for providing a particular service or engaging in a particular set of professional activities. (p. 39)

To be competent one must know one's own strengths and limitations. Some ways for determining one's level of competence include: peer review, self-assessment, evaluations of one's impact on clients, and taking exams such as those required for state licensing or BCIA certification.

The most important and meaningful method for determining one's competence is through evaluation of one's impact on clients. If one consistently obtains positive outcomes with specific groups of clients, one is probably competent in that area. If one consistently obtains negative outcomes with a particular type of client, one needs to search further to determine if the negative outcomes are the result of some area of incompetence or other factors (e.g., lack of client compliance). Discussions with the client and other providers of biofeedback service can be useful in clarifying such situations.

To be ethical one must (1) practice only in those areas in which one is competent by training or experience (Association for Applied Psychophysiology and Biofeedback, 1990), (2) obtain training in new areas, and (3) obtain appropriate supervision and/or consultation in applying these new areas to clients. Remaining competent requires continued education and training to both maintain and expand one's areas of practice. It is unethical to exaggerate one's qualifications or skills, and engaging in such behaviors can lead to problems with clients, ethics committees, and can result in malpractice litigation.

It is also important to be alert to signs of fatigue, burnout, and to personal and emotional problems in oneself. When such conditions exist, one is more likely to make mistakes and to behave incompetently. When signs of fatigue occur, one needs to take corrective action by taking a vacation, seeking personal counseling, cutting back on work hours, or engaging in other activities that will alleviate the problem.

Being competent as a supervisor requires more than serving in a supervisory role. Competent supervision requires training, reading, and on-going monitoring and feedback from another competent supervisor/consultant. It is unethical to take on the role of supervision if one is not competent to do so. A competent professional knows what to do, how to do it, when to do it, and when to seek consultation first.

For example, a provider of biofeedback services decided that electroencephalographic (EEG) biofeedback for attention-deficit disorders (ADD) was the "in thing." So, she attended a weekend workshop and started to see such clients. A colleague correctly counseled her to obtain appropriate supervision in working with her first few ADD clients. The colleague also suggested that the provider make clear in the informed consent process that the procedure was experimental and that the provider charge a reduced fee, until such time as she was truly competent. This process reduced the probability of problems for both the provider and the client.

Privacy, Confidentiality, and Privileged Communication

Privacy

Privacy means an individual's right to choose if, when, under what circumstances, and how much one shares his or her beliefs, behavior, or opinions with others (Corey et al., 1993). The U.S. Constitution guarantees the right to a certain level of privacy. One can easily extend the concept of privacy to an individual's physiology. A client has a right to choose whether or not to allow sharing of the recording of his or her physiology with other people. Informed consent, discussed later, is essential before invading this area of one's privacy.

Some practical components of privacy include assuring that (1) one's professional space has a sound barrier so private information from a treatment session can not be overheard in the hall or waiting room, (2) one avoids calling out clients' names in a waiting room, (3) the receptionist does not use client names on the telephone where others can overhear the conversation, (4) the receptionist does not give confidential verbal telephone messages where others can hear them if names are used, (5) therapists only have access to files of their clients or other clients where there is a bona fide need to know, (6) all staff agree to keep client information private, and (7) confidential client records should be kept in locked files not accessible to those who have "no need to know" (e.g., janitors). Many of the components suggested do not exist in common practice; nonetheless, failure to have them in place is a potential violation of a client's right to privacy. If your agency does not include some of these components as a part of its regular procedures, it is in your and your clients' best interest to work with policy makers to implement the needed changes.

It is not sufficient to use the excuse that, "We've always done it this way" or "It's common practice to do it this way in medical settings." Currently, clients are more aware of their rights and violations of those rights. As such, complaints and lawsuits for violations of confidentiality are increasing. For example, violation of confidentiality is the fifth most frequent reason for complaints against psychologists (American Psychological Association, 1993).

Two other terms have their foundation in the concept of privacy; they are confidentiality and privileged communication. Confidentiality is the ethical or moral responsibility of a professional to protect a client from the unauthorized disclosure of information obtained in a treatment relationship (Corey et al., 1993; Striefel, 1989c). It is also more commonly a legal responsibility when licensing laws require those licensed to adhere to a specific code of ethics that includes confidentiality. Privileged communication is a right, defined in legal statutes, that protects a client from having his or her confidential information revealed in a legal proceeding without that person's permission (Striefel, 1989c). There are practical and often complex exceptions to implementation of both confidentiality and privileged communication.

Confidentiality

Clients should be informed, often with written informed consent, of the limits of confidentiality at the onset of treatment (Striefel, 1989c). Some common limits of confidentiality of which clients should be aware include:

1. Certain laws require breaking confidentiality (e.g., all professionals must report suspected and actual child abuse, and some states have a "duty-to-warn" or "protect law" that requires certain professionals to break confidentiality if a client or someone else is in danger of being injured or killed).
2. If a client uses a third-party payer certain information will be revealed.
3. If a client initiates legal action against a provider, that provider has a right to use confidential client information to the extent necessary to defend him- or herself.
4. If services are being provided under court order, confidential information will be shared.
5. If a provider will use collection agencies or a small claims court to collect unpaid bills, the client should be informed of this practice.

Clients also should be aware if the service provider will discuss the client with a supervisor or consultant. If clients are aware of the limits of confidentiality at the onset of services, they can decide whether or not they want to enter treatment under these conditions and how much information to reveal. It is unethical to videotape or audiotape the client without permission. Federal laws exist concerning the confidentiality of information obtained when working with substance-abuse clients or those with AIDS. Information on these laws can be obtained from the State Department of Social Services or from legal centers.

Privileged Communication

All states have privileged communication statutes for lawyers and medical doctors. Some states have privileged communication laws that cover other disciplines, such as psychology and social work. It is up to each provider to find out whether or not such a law covers his or her services. Usually, the licensing law of the specific dicipline includes a privileged communication statute. If covered by law, privileged communication exists when (1) one believes that the provider will not disclose it, (2) the client or potential client makes the communication, and (3) there are no casual third-parties present.

The loss of privileged communication exists when: (1) the law does not cover a relationship, (2) the client initiates legal action against the therapist, (3) when the client files a Workman's Compensation lawsuit, (4) a casual third-party is present, (5) a court orders treatment, and (6) often when there is a risk of suicide or injury to others (Corey et al., 1993; Striefel, 1989c). Other exceptions may exist depending on specific laws in each state.

Two good premises to operate under are (1) "When in doubt, do not give it out," and call your lawyer instead (Stromberg et al., 1988), and (2) if no compelling reason exists, do not give it out, that is, the benefits to the client must outweigh the risks (Striefel, 1989c).

Whenever a practitioner violates a client's confidentiality or reveals privileged communication, documentation is critical. Document the situation, the steps taken, the justifying rationale, consultations sought, the outcome, and anything else pertinent. Practitioners should remember that the client owns the privilege in privileged communication and not the therapist (Striefel, 1989c). The client also can give permission for the practitioner to release information. The client should sign a release-of-information form when agreeing that the practitioner can share certain information with specified other people or agencies.

If a practitioner receives a subpoena for records, he or she should probably take several steps, including, but not limited to:

1. Do not give out the records on the spot. You can take time to determine what action to take.
2. Do not remove or change anything in the client's file (doing so could result in a contempt of court charge).
3. Contact your lawyer to verify that the subpoena is legal and not a look-alike, to clarify whether or not privileged-communication statutes cover your records, and to seek appropriate guidance.
4. Contact the client and his or her lawyer to determine the desirability of compliance.
5. If there are items in the file that do not seem relevant to the case, ask for a session with the judge privately in his or her chambers to determine if some information can be withheld (Corey et al., 1993).

PRACTICE AREAS WITH ETHICAL IMPLICATIONS

This section discusses several major practice areas with ethical implications.

Informed Consent

One area of practice that has taken on increasing importance is that of obtaining informed consent. Informed consent is a process of obtaining a client's permission to engage in various treatments and related activities (Striefel, 1990c). It requires several components.

First, it requires that a client be given all of the information that a reasonable person would want and need to make a decision about how to proceed (Striefel, 1990c). The information should include the advantages and disadvantages of the proposed activities (e.g., assessment or treatment) and those of available alternatives, including taking no action at all (Striefel, 1989c, 1990c). Second, it requires that the client give consent voluntarily without any form of coercion. The third requirement is that the client be competent to make the necessary decision(s). Determining a client's competence can be a simple or complex process and depends on the situation. Generally, one assumes that a client is competent unless there is evidence to the contrary.

A couple of additional terms are useful here. A "moral agent" is a person who can make free choices from the available options and is capable of knowing the difference between right and wrong. One assumes that a moral agent is competent and accountable for his or her behavior.

There are also "moral agents with diminished capacities." This group includes individuals who may or may not be competent to give informed consent. Some of the classes of people who fall in this category are children, individuals with certain disabilities such as mental retardation and mental illness, and people who are not fluent in the language of the service provider (Striefel, 1990c). When working with moral agents who have a diminished capacity, it is a good practice to get informed consent from the appropriate parent, guardian, or advocate in addition to that of the client (Striefel, 1990c).

A fourth consideration is to document the informed consent process. There are several ways to document informed consent. These include writing the information provided to the client and the client's response in the client's file. It is a good idea to have the client sign and date the note. If the informed consent relates to some aspect of practice that is common to many or all clients, then it is probably worthwhile to develop a specific form. Some common areas for informed consent include the limits of confidentiality, fees, and collection procedures.

Other areas of biofeedback and applied psychophysiology where informed consent is important include assessments, treatment approaches, touching the client (e.g., to attach electrodes), type of clothing to wear, release of confidential information, and experimental procedures (Striefel, 1990c). One provider of biofeedback service lost his license to practice for touching a female client's chest without consent. Even with consent, such touching is outside the realm of common practice for most disciplines, and in those cases it is unethical. Two other providers of biofeedback were contacted by their state licensing board for conducting EEG biofeedback with ADD clients. The basis of the complaint against both providers was their failure to make clear that EEG biofeedback is an experimental procedure (at least from the vantage point of the licensing boards in those two states). In one of the cases, the provider was also required to eliminate what the licensing board considered to be exaggerated claims. An honest and accurate informed consent process could have been very helpful in defending the providers of EEG biofeedback against these complaints.

Informed consent is not a one-time process, nor is it a rubber-stamp process (Striefel, 1990c). Informed consent, even if written, is useful only if the consent meets all the requirements previously specified. It is good practice to include some questions to clients to determine whether or not they have understood the information presented to them. For example, after presenting the needed information, one could ask, "In your own words tell me what the advantages and disadvantages are for obtaining biofeedback treatment for your headaches." Or one could consider asking "What other types of treatment are available for treating your headaches and why do you prefer biofeedback instead?" Clients have filed ethical complaints against AAPB members for behaviors such as not obtaining informed consent before touching the client or changing one's fees for a specific client in treatment without first obtaining informed consent. The informed consent process allows a client to decide what he or she wants to do about what the provider proposes (e.g., a client could choose to end treatment rather than pay a higher fee).

The process of informed consent is philosophically in agreement with part of the core of biofeedback. In essence, treatment with biofeedback intends to teach clients to take control of their own physiology and other aspects of their lives. Obtaining informed consent is one way to model for the client that he or she is in fact in charge of the decisions he or she chooses to make. Paternalistic behavior, that is, making decisions about and for clients that they should make for themselves in a sense tells them that the provider sees them as incapable of making decisions.

One final note about informed consent. Clients and research subjects must know that they can refuse to participate in any procedure and that they can withdraw or request changes without any penalty.

Dual Relationships

Although the major concern with dual relationships centers on those of clients and their therapists and other clinical providers, others, such as researchers, teachers, supervisors, and administrators also must be cognizant of potentially problematic dual relationships. A dual relationship occurs whenever a practitioner interacts with a client in more than one role, for example, as therapist and teacher, or as therapist and supervisor (Bennett et al., 1990). It is best to avoid potentially problematic dual relationships. Dual relationships can be of two types, sexual and nonsexual (Bennett et al., 1990). It is best to remember to (1) be only a client's therapist (one role); (2) provide treatment only in your office, not elsewhere (e.g., in a cafe) (Striefel, 1993a); and (3) provide only treatment in your office (e.g., do not socialize with clients there).

Sexual Dual Relationships

The Ethical Principles of Applied Psychophysiology and Biofeedback (Association for Applied Psychophysiology and Biofeedback, 1990) make it clear that it is unethical to engage in any sexual relationship with current clients. Best practice would extend this prohibition to former clients as well (Bennett et al., 1990). In fact, several professional associations (e.g., American Psychological Association, 1992) consider such behavior unethical. In some states, it is a felony to have sexual contact with a current or former client (Corey et al., 1993; Striefel, 1989b). The ethics committee of AAPB has taken action against providers of biofeedback services for engaging in sexual activities with current and/or former clients. Legal action against these same providers has also occurred.

In a recent survey of AAPB members, Percival and Striefel (1994) report that 5% of the membership reported having had sexual contact with clients, and some of these reported that they believed it is ethical! Apparently these individuals did not read the AAPB ethical principles, nor did they attend any recent workshops on ethical conduct. Otherwise they would know that such behavior is always unethical. Excuses such as, "The client initiated it" or "It's okay if it takes place outside of the treatment session" are not accepted by the courts or ethics committees as justifiable reasons (Striefel, 1989c). The provider, not the client, is held accountable by ethics committees for his or her behavior and its consequences (Striefel, 1989c). It is a sign of incompetence not to be aware of the current ethical expectations of one's profession. The 5% figure is about the same as that reported by other mental health professions. It is reassuring that 95% of practitioners know better and avoid such relationships. Hopefully, this will become 100%.

The survey by Percival and Striefel (1994) also reported confusion by the membership on other ethical issues, such as having sexual thoughts about a client or being sexually attracted to a client. It is not unethical to have thoughts and attractions, but it is not ethical to act on them. See Table 26.1 and the Percival and Striefel (1994) article for more examples of ethical issues and possible solutions. Bennett et al. (1990) and Striefel (1986, 1989c) raise several questions that providers of biofeedback should answer honestly for themselves concerning ethical issues related to dual sexual relationships. The topics discussed include touch, sexual attraction, dress and appearance, psychological sexual abuse, and dual relationships between teachers and students, researchers and research subjects, and supervisors and trainees. The reason sexual dual relationships are unethical is that there is a difference in the power of the parties involved, and studies have shown that such a relationship is harmful to clients (Bouhoutsos, Holroyd, Lerman, Forer, & Greenberg, 1983) and students (Kitchner, 1992).

Nonsexual Dual Relationships

Professionals also need to attend to potentially problematic dual relationships of a nonsexual nature. Examples are being a client's business partner, teacher, supervisor, or being close friends with clients, trainees, supervisees, or research subjects. Dual relationships are

TABLE 26.1. Ten Samples of Controversial Ethical Items from the Percival and Striefel Survey of AAPB Members and Possible Ethical Position

1. Giving gifts to those who refer clients to you.	Professionals do not engage in activities which the public might interpret to be a conflict of interest. Fees are based on actual services received or given and not on the referral itself.
2. Refusing to let clients read their charts/notes.	Many states now have laws allowing clients access to their file. Good practice would indicate that client files be maintained on the assumption that client might access them. Public distrust of the providers and of the field of biofeedback is likely to occur if access is not provided within the guidelines of professional practice.
3. Raising the fee during the course of therapy.	Fee disputes are one of the leading causes of malpractice lawsuits and complaints against health care providers. It is prudent not to raise fees during treatment without obtaining informed consent from the client first.
4. Using the same biofeedback instructions for all clients.	Each client's physiology and cognitive style is different; thus, the instructions given to clients receiving biofeedback services should be individualized as needed by each client. Giving the same instructions to all clients could preclude efficient progress.
5. Accepting only male or female clients.	Ethical service providers do not discriminate against anyone purely on the basis of gender. If a provider is not competent to provide services to both males and females, he or she should seek more training.
6. Obtaining only verbal permission to treat client.	It is not unethical to obtain only verbal informed consent before providing treatment to a client. Should a problem arise, however, failure to have documentation can result in difficulties verifying that consent was obtained.
7. Telling clients what they should do.	The goal of biofeedback is self-regulation; thus, paternalism can be problematic in all but rare circumstances. In addition, ethical complaints and malpractice lawsuits have been filed against health care practitioners on the basis of exerting "undue influence." Care should be taken not to use coercion or even give the impression of using coercion.
8. Helping a client file a complaint about a colleague.	Clients have a right to know how to file ethical complaints against unethical providers and to be assisted by providers in doing so. Only by helping "police" other providers can public trust be maintained. Unethical behavior raises the cost of professional liability insurance for everyone.
9. Allowing clients to run up a large unpaid bill.	It is not unethical to allow clients to run up large unpaid bills. However, since attempts to collect large unpaid bills leads to many complaints being filed against providers, it is good practice to establish a payment schedule at the onset of treatment and to maintain it within the guidelines of common practice.
10. Charging a client no fee for therapy.	It is not unethical to provide free (*pro bono*) services to some clients. Providing some free or reduced fee services is one way to help make services available to clients who might not otherwise have access.

Note. From Percival and Striefel (1994, pp. 67–93). Copyright 1994 Plenum Press. Adapted by permission.

problematic because one's professional role places one in a position of power over those served (Bennett et al., 1990). When a professional has more than one role with someone, the chance of a conflict of interest exists, and a professional might make decisions that are not in the best interests of those served. One should enter dual relationships very carefully and only after thorough consideration of the risks and benefits involved. In addition, one must monitor such relationships carefully and might need the assistance of a consultant to deal with any problems that might arise before making a decision to engage in such a relationship.

Supervision

Supervision is an ongoing educational process in which one individual (a supervisor) helps another individual (supervisee) acquire and implement appropriate professional behavior by modeling, monitoring, discussing, and providing feedback on professional activities (Striefel, 1990b). A supervisor has an ethical obligation to do the following (Striefel, 1990b):

1. Assess the skill level of each supervisee regularly.
2. Assist the supervisee in acquiring the needed skills.
3. Assure that the supervisee works with clients only in areas in which he or she is reasonably competent, unless the supervisor is physically present.
4. Provide the level of supervision needed by the specific client and supervisee.
5. Assure that supervisees behave ethically.
6. Supervise only in areas in which he or she is competent.

In addition, a supervisor should meet each client at least once, to assure that the supervisee has conceptualized the problem and treatment needs correctly. In addition, the supervisor should document the supervision.

Supervisors are partially responsible for the behavior of those they supervise (Striefel, 1990b), and clients have a right to know the training status of trainees and who the supervisor is. Ethical supervisors know that it may be fraud to sign insurance forms as the service provider when she or he is only the supervisor and not directly involved in the evaluation and treatment of the client. Ethical supervisors do not agree to a false diagnosis or type of service to collect from the insurance company. Some insurance companies agree that one can sign insurance forms as a supervisor only if the supervisor was in the building where a supervisee conducted the session with a client at the time a client was seen and available at a moment's notice. Read insurance forms and regulations carefully, so you know what is required.

Availability

Once a practitioner accepts a person as a client, he or she has an ethical obligation to be available when needed or must arrange with another competent provider to be available. This availability includes non-office hours and emergency situations. Some clients in physical or psychological pain or who are experiencing an emergency and are unable to reach their service provider or other designated professional initiate actions against the provider based on abandonment. Other examples of risk situations for abandonment occur when one leaves a client alone in a biofeedback session without informed consent and when a professional does not pick up and respond to an important phone message from the client in a timely manner (Striefel, 1992a). Practitioners have an ethical obligation to prepare clients for the practitioner's absence for vacations, emergencies, or other absences, and they need to have a back-up system in place (Striefel, 1992a). A practitioner's procedure for being contacted during non-office hours and for accessing his or her emergency back-up should be part of the informed-consent process. Clients should be given copies of appropriate telephone numbers and procedures (Striefel, 1992a).

Referrals and Termination

There are two referral processes. The first is when someone makes a referral to a professional, and the second is when the professional refers a client elsewhere. There are potential ethical issues related to each of these referral processes.

Incoming Referrals

Justifiable reasons for not accepting a person as a client include:

1. The person's problem is outside the areas of the biofeedback provider's competence.
2. The provider's waiting list is long, and the person needs critical services now.
3. Accepting the person as a client would create a dual relationship or conflict of interest.
4. The person cannot afford the fee charged (most providers do some *pro bono* services).

One must not refuse services to a person purely because of his or her age, gender, race, and so forth. That is, one must not discriminate against a class of people. It is also unethical to accept every client referred as if one were competent to deal with all people and all problems, unless one is universally competent (which is doubtful). Doing so will result in problems sooner or later.

To decide which referrals to accept as clients, a provider needs to know his or her own level of competence. He or she also may need a supervisor/consultant for new application areas and definitely needs to have a systematic process for collecting critical information to decide if the referral is appropriate (Bennett et al., 1990). A process also needs to be in place for getting relevant records from other providers, for getting a signed release for the records, and for giving critical information to potential clients (e.g., fees, collection procedures, parking, etc.).

Outgoing Referrals and Termination

Ethically, it is essential to refer clients elsewhere and/or to terminate services when (1) a client needs a service that the provider of biofeedback cannot provide, even if supervision were available; (2) the provider of biofeedback has become emotionally involved with the client and is unable to be effective (note that ethically, the provider of biofeedback cannot get physically involved); (3) the provider of biofeedback has personal problems that interfere with his or her being able to meet the client's needs; (4) the client is not making progress with the services provided, even after several different approaches were tried, including consultations with other professionals; (5) the client has achieved the goals of treatment; or (6) the provider of biofeedback is moving or will no longer be able to provide services. It is not ethical to keep a client in treatment after he or she clearly and reliably has achieved all the treatment goals.

When making a referral of a client elsewhere, it is common practice to refer a client to a specific provider simply because the provider knows the practitioner to whom he or she makes the referral. Such referrals place the provider at risk of having made a negligent referral, if the practitioner referred to turns out to be incompetent for treating the client's problem or causes harm. It is a better practice to give a client more than one name of competent practitioners whenever possible and let the client choose.

Once the client makes a choice it is useful to have him or her sign a release of information so when the first provider is contacted by the new practitioner, he or she can share information in a timely manner. It is also useful when ending treatment or referring a client to write a summary of the services provided (Bennett et al., 1990). Record in the file the reason for ending treatment or the referral and the details of the process used, information shared (with client consent), and anything else that is important. It is unethical to hold a client's records *in bondage* just because the client did not pay his or her bill (American Psychological Association, 1992).

Abandonment occurs if you as the provider (1) fail to give the client who still needs services the names of other providers before ending your services, (2) end therapy with a client in crisis, (3) fail to recommend to a client before ending therapy that he or she should continue to get therapy elsewhere if you think the person still needs it, and (4) have no emergency or back-up coverage (Bennett et al., 1990). Also consider the possible consequences, and do not end therapy with a client in need just because he or she has not paid the bill.

Ethical Record Keeping

Client files and business records should be thorough and accurate (Bennett et al., 1990). Client records serve many different purposes, including serving as a means for: (1) reviewing client progress, (2) motivating the client, (3) communicating with other service providers, (4) protecting the provider if the client, or someone else on the client's behalf, initiates litigation or files an ethical complaint against the provider, and (5) testifying in court about a client (e.g., worker compensation litigation).

It is essential to maintain a separate file for each client, to protect access to those records, and to release records only with client permission or as required by law or ethical constraints (Bennett et al., 1990). Providers should know their state laws about retention of records, billing and bill collection, and record ownership. A client's records should make clear what services were provided, and when, why (rationale), how, where, and by whom. The provider should make arrangements for the disposition of records if he or she dies, so that other providers who might serve the client can access the information with the client's permission. One usually retains records for at least 3 years, depending on state law, after the last contact with the client and maintains a summary for an additional 12 years (Bennett et al., 1990, American Psychological Association, 1992). Because of the number of years after treatment for which laws allow clients to file lawsuits, it is probably best to keep a good summary forever. New computer technology makes it possible to store 1400 pages of client information on one floppy disc.

Zuckerman and Guyett (1991) and Bennett et al. (1990) provide a listing of the information that one should include in an ethical and legal release-of-records form. Records in a provider's files obtained through a release-of-records form belong to the original agency. Thus it is inappropriate to forward these records to other providers without a proper release. Providers should not falsify anything in a client's file, nor should they falsify any insurance claims. Doing so is unethical and illegal (Bennett et al., 1990). In fact, providers should take care to avoid submitting claims for services that do not meet the third-party payer's requirements. Harrison and King (1993) reported that a provider was found guilty of fraud for submitting a claim to Medicare not because the information provided was inaccurate, although it was accurate, but because the filed claim was without a physician's referral as required by Medicare.

SUMMARY

Service providers must take ethics and its applications seriously. Continuing education is becoming increasingly important as the number of ethical complaints filed against providers increases. Service providers should develop written policies and procedures for guiding their professional behaviors. They also should use on-going consultations and supervision to increase their skills, to resolve problematic issues, and to evaluate the level of risk generated by their practice activities. Service providers must obtain informed consent from all clients. Further, they must assure clients of confidentiality and practice only in those areas in which they are truly competent by education, training, experience, and in accordance with state and certification criteria.

REFERENCES

Amar, P. B., McKee, M. G., Peavey, B. S., Schneider, C. J., Sherman, R. A., & Sterman, M. B. (1992). *Standards and guidelines for biofeedback applications in psychophysiological self-regulation.* Wheatridge, CO: Association for Applied Psychophysiology and Biofeedback.

American Psychological Association. (1992). Ethical principles of psychologists and Code of Conduct. *American Psychologist, 47*(12), 1597–1611.

American Psychological Association. (1993). Report of the ethics committee, 1991 and 1992. *American Psychologist, 48*(7), 811–820.

Association for Applied Psychophysiology and Biofeedback. (1990). The ethical principles of applied psychophysiology and biofeedback. *Biofeedback, 18*(2), 16–19.

Bennett, B. E., Bryant, B. K., VandenBos, G. R., & Greenwood, A. (1990). *Professional liability and risk management.* Washington, DC: American Psychological Association.

Bouhoutsos, J., Holroyd, J., Lerman, H., Forer, B. R., & Greenberg, M. (1983). Sexual intimacies between psychotherapists and patients. *Professional Psychology: Research and Practice, 14*(2), 185–196.

Callahan, J. C. (1988). *Ethical issues in professional life.* New York: Oxford University Press.

Corey, G., Corey, M. S., & Callanan, P. (1993). *Issues and ethics in the helping professions* (4th ed.). Pacific Grove, CA: Brooks/Cole.

Guralnik, D. B. (Ed.). (1980). *Webster's new world dictionary of the American language: Second college edition.* New York: Simon & Schuster.

Harrison, K. J., & King, J. W. (1993, March). Health care fraud: The rising tide of enforcement. *White-Collar Crime Reporter, 7*(3), 1–11.

Kentsmith, D. K., Miya, P. A., & Salladay, S. A. (1986). *Ethics in mental health practice.* New York: Grune & Stratton.

Kitchner, K. S. (1992). Psychologist as teacher and mentor: Affirming ethical values throughout the curriculum. *Professional Psychology: Research and Practice, 23*(3), 190-195.

Lakin, M. (1991). *Coping with ethical dilemmas in psychotherapy.* New York: Pergamon Press.

Percival, G., & Striefel, S. (1994). Ethical beliefs and practices of AAPB members. *Biofeedback and Self-Regulation, 19*(1), 67–93.

Pope, K. S., & Vetter, V. A. (1992). Ethical dilemmas encountered by members of the American Psychological Association: A national survey. *American Psychologist, 47*(3), 397–411.

Roswell, V. A. (1989, Summer). Professional liability: Issues for behavior therapists in the 1980s and 1990s. *Biofeedback, 17*(2), 22–35.

Schwartz, M. S., & Striefel, S. (1987, Fall). A pound of prevention is worth a ton of cure: Biofeedback ethics. *Biofeedback, 15*(3), 4–5.

Striefel, S. (1986, Summer). Ethical conduct in treating the sexually attractive client. *Utah Psychological Association Newsletter*, 2–3.

Striefel, S. (1989a, Winter). A perspective on ethics. *Biofeedback*, *17*(1), 21–22.

Striefel, S. (1989b, Summer). Avoiding sexual misconduct. *Biofeedback*, *17*(2), 35–38.

Striefel, S. (1989c, Fall). Confidentiality vs. privileged communications. *Biofeedback*, *17*(3), 43–46.

Striefel, S. (1990a, Winter). The informed consent process. *Biofeedback*, *18*(1), 51–55.

Striefel, S. (1990b, Summer). The ethics of supervision. *Biofeedback*, *18*(3), 36–37.

Striefel, S. (1990c, December). Responsibility and competence. *Biofeedback*, *18*(4), 39–40.

Striefel, S. (1992a, February). Absences and interruptions of biofeedback therapy. *Biofeedback*, *20*(1), 34–36.

Striefel, S. (1992b, June). Ethics and risk management: An introduction. *Biofeedback*, *20*(2), 44–45.

Striefel, S. (1992c, October). Ethics and risk management: Managing risks. *Biofeedback*, *20*(3), 33–34.

Striefel, S. (1993a, March). *Ethics and risk management in professional practice*. Workshop conducted at 1993 Annual Meeting of the Association for Applied Psychophysiology and Biofeedback, Los Angeles, CA.

Striefel, S. (1993b, February). Ethics and risk management: Written policies and procedures. *Biofeedback*, *21*(1), 42–43.

Striefel, S. (1993c, October). Ethical issues in the biofeedback treatment of people different from yourself: Part 1 an overview. *Biofeedback*, *21*(3), 6–7.

Stromberg, C. D., Haggarty, D. J., Leibenluft, R. F., McMillan, M. H., Mishkin, B., Rubin, B. L., & Trilling, H. R. (1988). *The psychologist's legal handbook*. Washington, DC: Council for the National Register of Health Service Providers in Psychology.

Zuckerman, E. L., & Guyett, I. P. R. (1991). *The paper office*. Pittsburgh: Three Wishes Press.

27

Models of Practice:
The Delivery
of Biofeedback Services

R. Paul Olson

There are two practical considerations related to delivering biofeedback services. The first is the variety of service delivery models. The second is the role of professionals and biofeedback therapists providing services.

MODELS OF PRACTICE

The One-Practitioner Model

This is a major and common model for delivering biofeedback services. In this model, one professional provides all the evaluative and therapy services. Typically, the professionals are mental health professionals, such as psychologists and psychiatrists, and other health professionals such as physical therapists. In this model, the professional treats one patient at a time or works with a small group of patients. The analogues are the individual psychotherapy and group psychotherapy models. Some combine the two models: A patient may be seen individually for intake and evaluation and then treated in a group.

The individual-treatment model allows tailoring evaluation and intervention, but is typically more expensive than the group model, with fewer patients evaluated and treated. The group variant allows providers to treat more patients and is less expensive. However, it provides less attention to each patient.

A third variant of the one-practitioner model is the overlapping model. In this model, one professional uses a staggered and overlapping schedule to treat two patients concurrently in separate offices. During the first part of the session, the professional is in one room reviewing the first patient's home practice and progress. Then, the professional attaches the patient to the biofeedback instruments and leaves the patient alone to receive instrumentation feedback. Preferably, one does this with automated storage of the physiological data. In some cases, the provider instructs the patient in how to adjust the instruments.

Upon leaving the first patient, the professional goes to the second room and repeats the process with the second patient. After starting biofeedback with the second patient, the professional returns to the first patient. The professional then reviews the session, plans homework, and ends the session. The provider then starts an interview with a third patient in the same room. Next, he or she returns to the second room and finishes that session.

Then, the professional starts a fourth patient in the second room. This model requires careful planning and disciplined scheduling. It limits flexibility, and it is difficult to give extra time for patients.

Many factors influence whether a therapist should be in the room with the patient during biofeedback (see Chapter 8). Given certain assumptions, this model can provide important advantages of continuity of care and efficient use of time. One assumes the professional is very competent, highly skilled, and versatile with biofeedback and other therapies. One also assumes the professional can develop effective rapport rapidly with patients.

The cost of services is often higher with this model than with other models. This is a major disadvantage of this model. The higher cost results from many independently licensed professionals who charge higher fees than biofeedback therapists who are not independently licensed. The professional repeats the services for every patient. Thus, another potential disadvantage is the risk of professional burnout. Furthermore, some practitioners lack skills in some therapy procedures, or they have difficulty establishing and maintaining rapid rapport. These factors are also limitations of this model.

The Collaborative Model

In the collaborative form of service delivery, both an independently licensed professional and a biofeedback therapist provide the services. There are four variants of this model.

Staggered-Schedule Model

In this variation, a biofeedback therapist provides services in the staggered or simultaneous schedule of the overlapping model, described above. However, in this version of the model, the two providers rotate rooms and patients about every 30 minutes. The biofeedback therapist attaches one patient to the instruments and conducts a biofeedback therapy session. The other professional reviews the session results, discusses home practice and treatment progress, and provides other interventions with another patient. Either professional may provide some or all services, depending partly on the qualifications of the biofeedback therapist. The analogue for this model would be the services provided by dentists with their dental assistants and hygienists.

Control-Room Model: Overlapping and Group Treatment

In some settings there is a central control room located next to two or more treatment rooms. This arrangement allows both common and tailored audiovisual feedback to each separate room. The instrumentation controls are in the control room. This design allows for one or two professionals to conduct evaluative and therapy sessions simultaneously in two or more rooms.

Evaluation–Therapy Model

A third variation of the collaborative model involves different delegation of services. For example, a licensed, supervising professional conducts the intake, periodic, and final sessions, while the biofeedback therapist conducts all or most of the biofeedback therapy sessions. The first professional obtains a history and decides whether to start therapy, provides a rationale for therapy, and selects the therapy and the procedures. Either professional conducts the baseline psychophysiological stress assessment.

In another variation, a properly trained and credentialed biofeedback therapist provides the intake and initial psychophysiological assessment. The therapist discusses the case with the supervising professional before proceeding with therapy. The supervising professional also may see the patient in the first session, periodically during therapy, and at the end of therapy. This allows the supervising professional to remain in close contact with the patient. It supports the therapist's role and recommendations, encourages compliance with the regimen, and allows better evaluation of progress. Therapist competence, and the relationship, communication, and trust between the professionals are of obvious importance.

Some patients drop out of therapy prematurely. Thus, one disadvantage of this model is that the supervising professional may not have much contact with these patients. The major advantages are the flexibility and lowered costs allowed by the model. If both professionals are competent with biofeedback and other treatment modalities and if they work together well, this can be a very effective model.

Parallel Treatment Model

Some independently licensed health care professionals, including physicians, dentists, and psychologists, are neither interested in conducting biofeedback therapy sessions nor qualified to do so. Yet they may recognize the value and efficacy of biofeedback and other physiological self-regulatory therapies. Such professionals may employ a properly qualified biofeedback therapist who provides the intake, psychophysiological assessment, therapy, and follow-up, while the independently licensed professional provides his or her own specialty services such as psychological assessment, medications, psychotherapy, or dental procedures.

This model allows for both types of intervention simultaneously or sequentially. For example, a patient may receive psychotherapy from one mental health professional and receive relaxation and biofeedback therapies from another professional. Another example is the neurologist, internist, or dentist who requests an evaluation for relaxation and biofeedback therapies by a qualified biofeedback therapist. In this example, the physician or dentist may hold the medical therapy constant during the added assessment and therapy.

Ideally, in this model, the physician, dentist, or psychologist employs a competent biofeedback therapist. Competence and mutual respect help effective communications between the professionals. This may allow the biofeedback therapist to make recommendations regarding who to treat, how to treat, and when to stop treatment. Such an arrangement differs from the employer–employee relationship, in which the employee may only be permitted to follow employer's directions and may be hesitant to make recommendations, and/or may not have decision-making responsibilities.

Using the collaborative models, professionals can provide biofeedback services at lower costs than the one-practitioner model allows. More flexibility in scheduling patients can be another advantage, and there is less risk of the supervising professional developing burnout. The presence of two or more professionals also can provide a greater array of skills and experience. There is still the potential for "burnout" of the biofeedback therapist, and professionals must recognize and help prevent it. Some ways to prevent or lessen "burnout" include:

1. Involving the therapist in the evaluative and decision-making process.
2. Varying job responsibilities.
3. Maintaining high-quality interprofessional communications.
4. Providing support and positive reinforcements.

Professionals often integrate biofeedback with other therapies, such as psychotherapy, family therapy, neurolinguistic programming, systematic desensitization, and hypnosis. A discussion of integrating these is beyond the scope of this chapter.

FUNCTIONS AND RESPONSIBILITIES OF SUPERVISED PARAPROFESSIONALS

The functions and responsibilities of supervised biofeedback therapists depend upon several factors. These include:

- Education, training, and experience.
- Type of setting.
- State regulations.
- Attitudes and experience of the supervising professional.
- Relationship between the supervisor and the supervisee.
- Malpractice insurance guidelines.
- Third-party reimbursement.

One must consider these factors in selecting a model for the delivery of services and when selecting personnel to deliver the services.

The responsibilities of a supervised, qualified biofeedback therapist include at least assisting in the following activities:

- Assessment and evaluation.
- Decisions about patient selection.
- Conducting physiological baselines and psychophysiological stress assessment.
- Providing the therapy rationale and description of therapy.
- Setting therapeutic goals.
- Selecting body sites for feedback.
- Conducting some or all of the biofeedback and other physiological self-regulatory therapy sessions.
- Physiological and symptom data record keeping.
- Evaluation of patient progress.
- Teaching generalization of self-regulatory skills.
- Conducting follow-up evaluation.
- Helping select instrumentation and modalities.
- Maintaining instrumentation and supplies.

Chapter 29 discusses job descriptions, the rationale for job titles, and the responsibilities of supervisory professionals. Before discussing assessment, evaluation, supervision, and program evaluation in this chapter, I briefly discuss the question of therapist qualifications to provide such services.

Who Qualifies as a Biofeedback Therapist?

The question of who qualifies as a biofeedback therapist is complex. The Biofeedback Certification Institute of America (BCIA) provides much of an answer. This certification indicates that the certificant has at least entry-level competency to provide biofeedback and some associated services. Certification is different from licensure provided by individual states. State laws may require that even a professional certified by a national certification agency must still work under the supervision of certain licensed professionals. Professional and ethical considerations and common sense dictate the need for supervision in clinical settings.

Assessment and Supervision

Supervision of professionals who are not state-approved for independent practice is particularly important in the evaluation and assessment phases. This is especially true because many professionals provide biofeedback services to a wide variety of medical, psychological, and dental disorders. Many of these disorders require specified knowledge, training, experience, and state credentials. Professionals unlicensed for independent practice are unlikely to meet all qualifications. Furthermore, some are not members of professional organizations that compel following ethical and professional standards of conduct and practice.

Program Evaluation

Professionals providing biofeedback have a duty to determine which disorders and patient characteristics are predictive of various therapy results. In addition, professionals must continue to assess procedures that are most efficacious and cost-effective for their patients and settings.

For example, analyzing the follow-up results of patients can help improve cost containment. This also can allow services for more patients. A long-term, single-group follow-up study of biofeedback therapy with chronic medical and psychiatric patients (Olson, 1988) reduced patient costs by about 30%. Olson based this on follow-up, self-report data from 93% of 563 consecutive patients treated. Treatment for most of these patients was for headaches and anxiety disorders.

Seven to nine office therapy sessions resulted in no more success than more sessions. At 8-month follow-up, 82% of these patients reported maximum, significant, or moderate improvement. Based on these results, we reduced therapy sessions from 10[1] to 7 sessions. Other clinical settings may show different results.

Such evaluations require time, effort, and finances, but the payoff for practitioners can be worth the investment. For example, conveying such information to referral sources could increase referrals from those who appreciate this responsible approach. Hence, the recommendation for documentation of results and procedures is a good professional practice. It remains important for biofeedback as its development continues with applications for a wide variety of disorders. More discussion of evaluation of professionals and therapy programs is in Chapter 30.

SUMMARY

The responsibilities and functions of professionals providing biofeedback services depend on many important factors. Among them is the model of service delivery. At present, no one model is superior to another; there are advantages and disadvantages associated with each of them. The primary considerations for selection of the model are (1) patient wel-

---

[1]These were the modal number of sessions.

fare; (2) professional qualifications, skills, and experience; (3) practical considerations; and (4) cost-effectiveness. The criteria of efficacy and efficiency are as germane to biofeedback services as they are to other health-related services.

The qualifications of all professionals involved in an evaluation and therapy program are very important regardless of the delivery model. In the collaborative models, the quality of supervision also is very important. Program evaluation is another desirable element of programs using biofeedback. See Chapters 29 and 30 for more discussion of issues related to supervision and program evaluation.

REFERENCE

Olson, R. P. (1988). A long-term, single-group follow-up study of biofeedback therapy with chronic medical and psychiatric patients. *Biofeedback and Self-Regulation, 13*(4), 331–346.

28

Professional Communications

Mark S. Schwartz

Communications about biofeedback involve unique information and considerations. Prudent practitioners take extra care writing reports, session notes, and letters. As Ochs (1990) notes, "A record is a trail of the problem(s), assessments, considerations, interventions, and outcomes of a particular patient's treatment process" (Ochs, 1990, p. 24). I am not attempting to review or duplicate the literature about professional report writing. The focus in this chapter is specifically on writing about clinical biofeedback. It focuses on how practitioners translate session information into clear and useful professional communications.

THE PRESENTATION OF INFORMATION IN PROFESSIONAL COMMUNICATIONS: GENERAL SUGGESTIONS

Professionals and health insurance companies often misunderstand biofeedback. Referral sources are often unfamiliar with biofeedback terminology, rationale, and procedures. Within the same professional setting and different settings, practitioners differ in their communication methods and style and in their terminology. They often record and emphasize different information. This can affect the clarity and value of their communications.

Writing clearly helps us remember what we did. Many other people read what practitioners write, including some persons who are less or not at all familiar with biofeedback. They often do not know biofeedback terminology, procedures, and indeed, what biofeedback means. For example:

1. The supervisor of the therapist directly using the biofeedback reads what the therapist wrote about the sessions.
2. The therapist conducting the biofeedback sessions reads what the supervisor wrote about the session and data.
3. Practitioners in the same setting who are familiar with biofeedback read each other's reports and notes.
4. Other professionals with limited knowledge about biofeedback read notes and reports by practitioners using biofeedback.
5. Referral sources read letters sent to them about patients' treatment using biofeedback.
6. Primary and secondary care referral sources read letters sent to them with quotes from reports discussing biofeedback.

7. Third-party payers read reports and letters that contain biofeedback information.
8. Hospitals review reports and notes containing biofeedback information to assess issues of necessity, quality (efficacy), and economy (reasonableness) (Ochs, 1990).
9. Medical auditing agencies review or assign peer reviewers to read reports and notes containing biofeedback information to assess the necessity, quality, and reasonableness of treatment with biofeedback (Ochs, 1990).

Many practitioners continue working toward standard terminology and ways to write notes and letters. The discussion and examples that follow are not intended to imply that these are the only ways to write such notes and letters. There are multiple proper ways to do such writing. The present examples and guidelines admittedly represent my preferences and style.

Consider the following examples of different descriptions that can occur with the same biofeedback therapy session data. These might be found in patient records, reports to insurance companies, and/or letters to referral sources.

1. His muscle activity started tense, but with biofeedback he reduced the tension to the relaxed range.
2. His muscle activity, recorded from a standard bifrontal placement, started tense with 5–7 microvolts. With biofeedback, he lowered the tension and kept it low after the feedback.
3. His muscle activity, recorded from a standard bifrontal placement, started tense. With his eyes open, the resting muscle activity was mostly 5–7 root mean square (RMS) microvolts (100–200 Hertz bandpass). With his eyes closed, it was mostly over 4 microvolts for several minutes and as low as 3 microvolts at the end of this phase. With biofeedback he lowered his muscle activity further to less than 1 microvolt. He maintained the lower-than-baseline muscle activity after feedback.
4. His muscle activity, recorded from a standard bifrontal placement, started tense. He was sitting up with his back supported against the back of a chair, and his eyes were open. The resting muscle activity was mostly 5–7 RMS microvolts (100–200 Hertz bandpass). With his eyes closed, it was mostly over 4 microvolts for several minutes and as low as 3 microvolts after several minutes. He used visual and then audio biofeedback to reduce the tension further to 2 microvolts in 4 minutes with his eyes open. Then, he rapidly reduced it down to 1 microvolt and sometimes lower during 5 minutes with his eyes closed. After feedback, he maintained the lowered muscle activity, showing mostly about 1 microvolt with his eyes closed and 1–2 microvolts with his eyes open.

The differences among the four examples are obvious. Example 4 provides more information and has better communication value than the others. The first three are correct, but less useful to readers who are trying to understand what occurred. Even example 4 does not provide complete information about potentially useful aspects of the session. For example, the reader may also want to know more about the durations of some phases and breaks and the existence of movement artifacts. Nevertheless, the examples adequately show wide differences.

The following statement summarizes the results of six electromyographic (EMG) biofeedback sessions. It is another extreme example of insufficient and unclear communication.

1. There were six EMG biofeedback sessions given. The patient showed increased ability to relax his frontal and upper back muscles.

The problem with such a statement is that there is not enough information about the sessions, the instruments, and other factors. The next example is comprehensive, and, although acceptable, it is too long for many purposes. However, it is a reasonable example and sometimes is a proper communication.

2. There were six EMG biofeedback-assisted self-regulation sessions. Fifteen-millimeter surface electrodes were on the standard bifrontal site and on a bilateral upper trapezius site about 7 centimeters on either side of about C_7. Monitoring and feedback were in the sitting and standing positions. The sitting position was in a straight, low-backed chair.

Initially, the client's frontal area muscle activity was mostly between 4 and 5 RMS microvolts (100–200 Hertz) while sitting quietly with his eyes open. It was 3–4 microvolts with his eyes closed. Each condition was 4 minutes and recorded in 30-second trials without intertrial intervals. Trials with movement artifacts were reset or omitted. Upper back muscle activity while standing was mostly 5–8 microvolts and 2–3 microvolts while sitting. Audio and visual feedback helped the client reduce the activity from both sites in the initial session to mostly 2–4 microvolts in the frontal area and 4–6 microvolts in the trapezius area. This was not a level considered nontense for resting muscles.

Initially, the client was unable to maintain the slightly reduced muscle activity after the feedback stopped. The postfeedback muscle activity drifted up to prefeedback levels within 2 minutes. In later sessions, he could reduce the activity rapidly from both sites during prefeedback baseline segments. After tensing his muscles mildly or moderately, he could lower the muscle activity rapidly within 30 seconds. He reached the nontense range of 1–2 microvolts and the relaxed range of < 1 microvolt for the duration of 3-minute segments. This showed good self-regulation and contrasted with his difficulty doing so in the initial session. After the intentional tensing in that session, his residual muscle activity was above pretensing trials. In the last two sessions, the client showed good reliability in his abilities to relax before intentional muscle tensing and to relax to the same levels afterwards. He is confident he can better apply these reductions in muscle activity in his daily activities, and I agree.

Now compare descriptions of thermal biofeedback that increase in completeness and communication value.

1. I provided thermal biofeedback.
2. I provided hand temperature biofeedback.
3. I provided hand temperature biofeedback from the right hand.
4. I provided finger temperature biofeedback from the little finger of the right hand.
5. I provided finger temperature biofeedback from the fifth digit, volar surface, third phalange of the right hand.

Let us also consider the following account of a session focused upon finger temperature:

During the baseline with her eyes open for 4 minutes, there was a slight rise of peripheral skin temperature of 2.3° F to 88.5° F. This all occurred in the last 2½ minutes. The temperature probably would have continued to rise with her eyes open. However, I asked her to close her eyes. Time did not permit a longer eyes-open period. With her eyes closed, there was a steady increase in temperature of 2.6° F to 91.1° F in 4 more minutes. This suggests that sitting quietly can reduce vasoconstriction.

Explanation of a serial 13s task and sitting quietly for 3 more minutes before starting the task did not show a decline of temperature. It increased further to 92.2° F in 1½ minutes. Then, it slightly decreased 0.9° F during the 3rd minute just before the task started. This could have been "normal" variation or the beginning of anticipatory arousal. As she began the task, there was a slight drop of temperature to 91.0° F but then a steady rise for 3 minutes to 92.8° F. This suggests the task was not physiologically arousing. Then a decrease began, but there was only a drop of 0.7° in 2 minutes. Perhaps this was "normal" variation or a slow physiological effect. It also might have been due to the cumulative effects of annoyance or frustration working on the task. Of more interest is the steady and signficant drop of 6.2° F after presumably stopping the task and restarting relaxation.

The purpose here is to illustrate the complexity of writing a note that captures the essence of a session. Interpretation is often very difficult and unclear. Was the patient still trying to do the task? Did this result from cumulative stimulation from the task that continued despite the relaxation? Had the patient not done the task, and was she feeling guilty and anxious about the therapist asking her about it? Was she unable to relax after stressful tasks? Was the task not stressful, but was she now thinking of something else that was stressful? Was the drop in temperature part of her usual variations? Therapists ask and try to answer these questions in order to make interpretations that do not leap beyond the data. They may or may not answer the questions even with a careful clinical interview during and after the recording. If one is not comfortable with the answers, then one should be careful about statements in the record.

The purpose here is not to discuss how to answer the questions but rather to illustrate that there are alternative explanations for physiological changes. These explanations are usually not obvious from watching the events in a session. Some patients do not follow the same sequence as the therapist or do not restrict their thoughts to what therapists ask them to think about. A point the writer could have made in the last sample is this: "There was physiological arousal and lability affecting peripheral vascular constriction and dilation."

Therapists discuss and interpret data with patients. This is, after all, patient education and can be therapeutic. This is especially true if it enlightens the patient about the relationships among thoughts, physiological reactivity, and recovery.

Prudent practitioners avoid misinterpreting data. They describe sessions in enough detail and clarity that others reading the description know what took place and the interpretations considered. Describing sessions this way also may promote questioning patients about what they were thinking about during specified phases. It also informs other professionals that the practitioner is being careful with interpretations.

By now, readers are thinking how impractical it is to record such detailed notes. I fully agree! The detailed examples above are intended to provide one extreme of a continuum. Such extensive detail is often impractical and probably unnecessary in routine clinical practice. However, detailed reports are better than those with very limited or no detail. The degree of detail depends on the situation and the professional.

However, thoughtful inclusion of details and interpretations can be educational. It also can enhance one's credibility. A detailed evaluation session, including the first physiological recordings, some details of selected therapy sessions, and a summary of the therapy sessions are often sufficient. One should provide definitions of any terms that are jargon and not clearly understood by others.

INCLUSION OF BIOFEEDBACK EVALUATION AND TREATMENT INFORMATION IN REPORTS AND PEER REVIEWS

The interview evaluation, psychophysiological assessment, and treatment process is complex and involves many topics.[1] There is much information needed in reports and notes. Furthermore, the information differs according to the disorder being assessed and treated. Granted, information needed for reports and session notes about patients with a single, uncomplicated symptom often differs from those about patients with multiple types of symptoms and complicating factors. Moreover, the information needed about patients with tension-type headaches differs considerably from the information about a patient with urinary incontinence. However, the principles, standards, and guidelines for report writing and session notes are the same.

About a decade ago the Peer Review Committee of the Biofeedback Society of America (BSA) developed guidelines for use by practitioners in their communications with third-party payers and peer reviewers (Theiner et al., 1984). It contained examples of proper and improper content, terminology, and phrases. Unfortunately, the BSA (now the Association of Applied Psychophysiology and Biofeedback [AAPB]) did not publish the *Biofeedback Peer Review Manual*. The 1984 document would be a useful starting place. I join with Ochs (1990) in encouraging professional organizations to revisit this topic and develop peer review standards and guidelines.

The outline in Table 28.1 (Theiner et al., 1984) serves as one example of desirable information and a useful sequence for organizing such information. It is not the only outline, but it is a reasonable one to consider. I also include examples of report outlines that I often use. Figure 28.1 contains a word-processing macro for one general evaluation outline that I often use. Figure 28.2 is a sample word-processing macro that forms the foundation for session notes about patients being treated with biofeedback. I trust these may be useful to some readers. I offer these samples for their potential heuristic value.

Practitioners using biofeedback ask for referrals and ask third-party payers to pay for these services. Reviewers make judgments about many aspects of clinical services. It is educational to place ourselves in the position of others less familiar with biofeedback. It is especially useful to imagine ourselves as those people who have questions and doubts about the value and procedures of biofeedback. They often are seeking information and reassurance that the procedures used were proper and cost-effective. Were the reports and notes clear.

Referral sources, reviewers, and third-party payers care about content and clarity. Naive, incomplete, unclear, poorly worded, or careless reports, session notes, and letters detract from a professional's credibility. A self-righteous or defensive attitude on the part of practitioners preparing reports and session notes is unwise, unprofessional, and self-defeating.

---

[1]See Chapters 6 and 7 for discussions of the intake process and baselines. See Chapters 14, 16–25, 32, and 33 for discussions of disorders and information needed in reports.

TABLE 28.1. Proposed Organization of Biofeedback Evaluation and Treatment Information

A. Identifying information
B. Presenting problem(s), disorder(s) and condition(s):
   1.
   2.
   3.
   4.
C. Treatment assessment/rationale:
   1. Assessment techniques:
   2. Rationale for treatment approach:
   3. Assessment results:
      a. Physiological baseline information:
      b. Behavioral/functional baseline information:
D. Treatment goals:
   1.
   2.
   3.
   4.
E. Treatment process:
   1. Biofeedback modalities:
   2. Instrumentation:
   3. Planned/current or prior method(s) to generalize effects:
   4. Other pertinent treatment information:
   5. Summary of physiological session data (attach charts, graphs, etc.):
   6. Summary of behavior/symptom data:
F. Progress to this review point:
G. Services planned:
   1.
   2.
   3.
   4.

Note. From Theiner et al. (1984). Reprinted by permission.

It often is unrewarding financially. Such communications reduce the chances of reimbursement and referrals.

The prudent practitioner places him- or herself in this "devil's advocate" position when reading his or her own written reports. Has one included the essential information, and how well and how clearly did the practitioner present it? Ochs (1990) helped practitioners by noting the problems with reports. Rephrasing his outline slightly and in the form of questions, I offer the items he listed: Was the treatment correct? Was there enough treatment? Was there too much treatment? Were the evaluation conclusions correct? Was the treatment plan adequate? Were the evaluation procedures correct? Was there adequate assessment of efficacy or results?

Ochs (1990) included typical questions asked by review agencies. I offer a slightly modified wording of his questions without changing the substance: Does the available documentation support this treatment for the specific symptom(s) and effects? Is the treatment proper and reasonable? Is the documentation about the biofeedback proper? Does the available documentation show a need for more treatment?

4-xxx-xxx-x
Name _____   **Age** _____

Consultation by: <u>Mark S. Schwartz, Ph.D. [2678]</u>

Referred by: Dr.   **Reasons:** Evaluation of therapy for. . . .

Other MCJ MDs: See reports by Drs. . . .

Presenting problem(s)/symptoms:

Mental status:

History:

Other relevant medical/psychological history:

Medications:

Chemicals:

Stress:

Family/social support:

Self-report measures:

Prior psychological therapies:

Prior relaxation/biofeedback: None

Diagnoses:

Formulation/rationale for treatment:

Recommendations/plan:

1. Needs physiological relaxation. Start conservative relaxation tx.
2. Biofeedback: EMG feedback-assisted self-regulation to. . . . Start with two to three office sessions over about 2 weeks and then review. Consider more office sessions, prn. See separate report.
3. Treatment Goals:
4. Patient-education booklets: *Breathing, Relaxation and Biofeedback, Tension-type Headaches, Caffeine, Anger Management, Insomnia*
5. Start self-report symptom log.
6. Discussed realistic expectations, patient education, relaxation/biofeedback therapies, cognitive-behavioral therapies, time-use management, self-report symptom log, and options.

Prognosis:

[Times: Interview for history = 30 min; Discussion/counseling = 40 min; Report = 20 min.]

FIGURE 28.1. Sample word-processing macro for evaluation report.

Borrowing from Ochs (1990) again, I glean from his remarks that reviewers expect explicit statements and data about the symptoms and condition of the patient before, during, and after treatment. They look for a rationale for estimating the phases of treatment and the length of treatment and for consistency of the measurement systems for symptoms and psychophysiology. For atypical or unusual treatment approaches, they need clear statements about the rationale and methods for assessing changes. Reviewers want information about transfer of training to daily activities and the strengths and limitations of patients. They prefer evaluations and treatment for preexisting and comorbid conditions that could interfere with treatment, compliance, and desired results and expect that practitioners understand and accept factors that could change the treatment plan. Overall, reviewers look for active participation by the practitioner in the treatment.

4-xxx-xxx-x
Name _____ **Age** _____

Interim Information:

Symptoms:
Relaxation and Other Practice and Transfer Information:
Stress:
Problems:

PSYCHOPHYSIOLOGICAL ASSESSMENT/BIOFEEDBACK:

Transducer sites: Standard MCJ psychology psychophysiological assessment with four surface EMG placements recording: bifrontal; bilateral posterior neck; and right and left frontalis-posterior neck (FpN). The two FpN channels provide more sensitive measures of temporalis and occipital tension and provide information on differential bilateral tension. Peripheral skin temperature
from the (L) fifth digit, volar surface, third phalange.

Body positions: Sitting posture w/back and head supported and standing. Others:

Recording conditions: Adaptation (3+ min.), sitting quiet baselines with eyes open and then
closed and basic muscle relax. instructions with eyes closed and then open, mild office stressors
such as math, personal cognitive stress, and making fists, visual and audio feedback introduction
and practice.

Physiological data: EMG μV measured in RMS μV, 100–200 Hertz bandpass.

Bifrontal:

Bilateral posterior neck:

FpN:

Other (e.g., occipital):

SUMMARY: Muscle activity from _____ showed _____ excess tension in the sitting posture. . . .

RECOMMENDATIONS/PLAN:

1. Continue to work on significant reductions of psychophysiological arousals/tension with
   relaxation therapies, biofeedback, and other stress-management procedures including
   cognitive-behavioral therapy. Focus on. . . .
2. . . . .
3. . . . .

[Times: Interview = 15 min; Biofeedback = 25 min; Discussion and plan = 15 min.]

FIGURE 28.2. Sample word-processing macro for evaluation report.

SESSION RECORD KEEPING

Biofeedback treatment records often require detailed and precise descriptions
of the sessions. Practitioners should record any events and conditions that could affect the
patient's physiological functioning and data interpretation.

This section provides a rationale and guidelines for recording selected items. Practitioners do not need all items in every case and session; some information is sometimes
unnecessary. However, most information can be useful, is easy to record, and can help
communications. Therapeutic decisions, comparisons, and communications become more
difficult without some of this information. Each practitioner decides which information is
useful or necessary.

General Information

Time of Day

This is often unnecessary. However, it is useful if one suspects, observes, or learns that the patient's symptoms or ability to regulate his or her physiology varies with the time of day. Computer-based systems provide the time of day automatically.

Patient Waiting Time

It is sometimes useful to record an estimate of the time a patient waited before the physiological recordings started. Prior physical activity, outside temperatures, caffeine or nicotine intake, or stressful events just before the session affect psychophysiological data.

Therapist

The name of the therapist seeing the patient is useful when different therapists provide services for one patient.

Non-Instrument-Related Conditions

Temperature (Indoor/Outdoor)

Indoor temperature should remain nearly constant but sometimes can vary by several degrees. Note the office temperature when such differences might affect therapy sessions. Remember that a significant difference between outdoor temperatures and inside temperatures can affect the data, especially if the patient just came into the office.

Lighting

Lighting can affect relaxation procedures, patient cognitions and comfort, and instrumentation artifact. For electroencephalographic (EEG) monitoring and feedback, notations about the location and type of light, such as fluorescent or incandescent, are useful and sometimes necessary. Remember that flourescent lighting can affect some physiological data such as EMG.

Noise

Noise within the office or outside and nearby may disrupt a session. Whether or not the patient's physiology changes immediately or soon after the noise, note that the noise occurred. Watch for signs of abrupt changes in physiology. This is especially important if it does not return to the prior level rapidly after the noise has ceased. Such information is useful when therapy goals include not reacting to naturally occurring noises or recovering rapidly after the noise.

Type of Chair

Sitting in a recliner or high-backed chair is not similar to most real-life conditions. Therefore, therapists often monitor and provide feedback for patients in different chairs. Record the types of chairs used.

Body Position

Recording body positions also is obvious (e.g., sitting up with head resting back and supported, sitting up with head not supported, full reclining, and standing). One can record these with a shorthand system.

Activity

Notations for this information are more useful for therapists who vary patients' activities during monitoring and feedback. Examples of session activities are resting quietly, reading aloud, reading silently, writing, engaging in conversation, listening to someone else talk, and tensing fists. Other activities include typing, playing an instrument, and talking on the phone. One develops one's own shorthand system.

Instrumentation and Physiological Data

Electrode/Sensor/Thermistor Sites

Temperature Feedback. Therapists vary the location where they place thermistors for recording skin temperature. Variations include hand, digit, side, and phalange. Different sites result in different temperatures, hence the importance of specifying the site. Incidentally, it is more accurate to use the term digit rather than finger. Also consider the terms volar and dorsal for the palm side and back side of the fingers respectively. Abbreviations can be helpful. For example, the abbreviation [R/5D/V/3P] refers to the right hand, fifth digit (little finger), volar surface, third phalange.

Electromyography. Practitioners need to be accurate and clear when recording information about placements of EMG electrodes. However, in routine clinical use, such specificity is often less practical and not always necessary. Consider such terms as: "standard bifrontal," "bilateral masseters," and "bilateral posterior (or cervical) neck." Another individual might misinterpret the location. When precision is important, specify the distance from standard anatomical locations and the exact spacing of the electrodes. One example of the latter is in neuromuscular recruitment. Anatomical drawings are often helpful even when one does not need precision. Specify the type and size of electrodes and the type and brand of conducting cream or gel and its conductivity.

Instrument Checks and Settings

Battery. When using battery-operated instruments, check the batteries before each session, unless they were just charged. This helps avoid conducting a session with weak batteries resulting in meaningless data and a wasted session. A battery check item on a recording form or checklist provides a useful reminder. This is especially useful in an office with multiple therapists using the same instruments.

Electrode–Skin Resistance or Impedance. The importance of determining electrode–skin resistance or impedance depends on several factors including the type of instrumentation, recording site, chance of high resistances, and the purpose of the session. For example, it is sometimes less important for general relaxation than for muscle recruitment in rehabilitation. However, even for relaxation, changes in resistance influence interpretation of microvolt changes. One typically need not include this in communications unless the provider believes that the specific information is important in interpreting the data.

Bandpass. Specifying and communicating the bandpass (e.g., 100–200 Hertz, 100–1000 Hertz) are especially important.

Response Integration Time. Some stand-alone instruments fix the response integration time (RIT), and others permit adjustments. Computer software usually permits several choices with very obvious differences in the visually displayed and audio signals. One need not record a fixed RIT each session. If adjustable, one should check the RIT and consider noting it, unless it is always the same. Notation is important if different therapists use the same instrument. The clinical significance of variations in RIT is unclear. However, one expects significant differences between responses to feedback with very short RITs of about 1 second or less and responses to RITs of about 3 seconds or longer.

Trial Durations, Intertrial Rest Periods, and Breaks. Duration of trials and intertrial rest periods are important. Note breaks between series of trials and the activity during the break such as discussions and topics. Activities may affect physiological data and hence the starting point for the next sequence of trials. Computers automatically record the trial and intertrial durations, but not the breaks. Noting a typical session helps those reading reports to understand the sessions and comparisons between sessions. A sample notation is 15"/0.1 for 15-second trials with 0.1-second intertrial period or recording with no rests.

Scale/Gain. Scale or gain affects the size or degree of change in physiology the instrument feeds back to the patient (similar to the magnification of a microscope). For example, displaying the EMG signal on a range of 1–11 microvolts and 72–82° has less information than 1–5 microvolts and 77–82° F. A patient's ability to regulate his or her physiological activity and interpretation of the data depend partly on the feedback scale. For example, the gain affects the feedback signal. Higher gains "magnify" or amplify physiological signals, and then changes appear larger and clearer. However, if the gain is too high, then tiny fluctuations can be annoying for some patients. Therapists can adjust the gain to fit the patient, task, and stage of progress. In stand-alone instruments, one can specify this such as × 0.1, × 0.3, × 1, × 3, or × 10. This information should be recorded.

Feedback Type. Consider noting the specific type of feedback, graphic displays used, audio range, and threshold information. This helps the therapist remember what he or she used and the patient's reactions. Include this information in communications.

Physiological Data: Artifacts. Accurate interpretation of physiological data requires knowing about artifacts, such as from patient movements (e.g., swallowing, coughing, sneezing, yawning, and talking). Some therapists reset the recordings to stop such trials or drop them from analyses. Sometimes the reduction of movement artifacts across sessions can be considered a therapy goal and a sign of the increased ability of the patient to sit quietly.

THE USE OF STANDARD ABBREVIATIONS AND SYMBOLS

The use of standard abbreviations and symbols helps professionals write notes and reports faster and in much less space. Physicians, nurses, and physical and occupational therapists commonly use standard abbreviations and symbols. Some providers of biofeedback are unfamiliar with many of the standard abbreviations and symbols. Practitioners should be familiar with them when working in settings where others use them. Table 28.2 lists common abbreviations and symbols. A more complete listing is in *The Charles Press Handbook of Current Medical Abbreviations* (1976).

TABLE 28.2. Selected Abbreviations and Symbols for Use in Record Keeping and Interprofessional Communications

Abbrev.	Term	Abbrev.	Term
ā	before (Latin: *ante*)	q.h.	every hour
AMAP	as much as possible	q.2.h	every 2 hours
ANS	autonomic nervous system	q.i.d.	four times a day (Latin: *quater in die*)
BFB	biofeedback		
b.i.d.	twice a day (Latin: *bis in die*)	R	right
BP	blood pressure	RH	right hand
c̄	with (Latin: *cum*)	Rx	drugs, meds., therapy
DBP	diastolic blood pressure	s̄	without (Latin: *sine*)
D/C	discontinue	SBP	systolic blood pressure
Dx	diagnosis	SNS	sympathetic nervous system
EC	eyes closed	SOB	shortness of breath
e.g.	for example	std.	standard
EO	eyes open	Sx	symptoms
est	estimated	therm.	thermal
FB	feedback	t.i.d.	three times a day (Latin: *ter in die*)
freq	frequency	TMJ	temporomandibular joint
f/u	follow-up	Tx	therapy
HA	headache	WNL	within normal limits
HTN	hypertension	w/u	workup
h.s.	at bedtime (Latin: *hora somni*)	×3, ×4	3 times, 4 times (and the like)
Hx	history	×2d, ×3d	for 2 days, for 3 days (and the like)
Hz	Hertz; cycles per second	+	positive, present
L	left	−	negative, absent
LH	left hand	>	greater than
M & N	morning and night	<	less than
meds.	medications	≥	greater than or equal to
N/A	no information available	≤	less than or equal to
N/K	not known	~	approximately
noc.	night	Δ	change
NSC	no significant change	+	slight reaction
N/V	nausea and vomiting	++	noticeable reaction
o.d.	daily, every day, once daily (Latin: *omni die*)	+++	moderate reaction
		++++	pronounced reaction
p̄	after, following (Latin: *post*)	→	results in, or is due to
p.c.	after food (Latin: *post cibum*)	1×	once
p/d	packs per day (cigarettes)	2×	twice
pptd.	precipitated	#	number
p.r.n	as needed (Latin: *pro re nata*)	/	per
pt	patient	'	minute
Px	prognosis	"	second
q̄	each; every (Latin: *quaque*)	↓	decreased, decrease(s)
q̄.d.	every day (Latin: *quaque die*)	↑	increased, increasing

EXAMPLE OF A REPORT OF A COMPLETED PATIENT EVALUATION AND TREATMENT

The following is an example of a final report that could serve for interprofessional communication in the patient's chart. Abbreviations are included intentionally and excessively only to illustrate their use. This report is based on an actual patient's evaluation and treatment.

Ms. K. J., a 23-yr-old medical secretary for 5 yrs, was referred on 3/30/83 by Dr. _____ for eval and Tx of chronic tension HAs dating back 4 yrs, c̄ no change in freq/intensity. The HAs were bifrontal and bitemporal c̄ a little suborbital discomfort. Typically, she was having HAs × 3–4 days/wk but up to 1 wk s̄ a HA and only once as along as 1 mo s̄ a HA. Just prior to Tx the HAs were reported as q.d. for 3–4 wks. The HAs usually began during the day, typically in the AM and early afternoon, and rarely started in the evening. They started more often at work than on weekends and were rarely present upon awakening. Phrenelin helped if taken early in the HA, but she wanted to be independent of meds and prevent the HAs from starting. She chewed gum, often bubble gum, daily, and for 2–3 hrs at a time, usually p̄ lunch. Intake of percolated coffee c̄ caffeine was limited to ~2 8-oz cups in the AM and 1–2 colas/day. Her est. caffeine intake was ~400 mg ± ~50 mg/day.

In the initial physiological recording session, pt showed moderately tense bifrontal muscle activity, mostly ~4.7 integral average μV (100–200 Hz), during resting conditions c̄ EO, and 3.5 μV → 2.4 μV c̄ EO. Mild cognitive stress had minimal impact. Audio FB was associated with ↓ muscle activity → 2–3 μV during and p̄ FB. A R frontal–posterior neck (FpN) recording paralleled the bifrontal results. Her finger temp, from the R 5th digit, volar surface, was initially cool, 78° F, and ↓ to 74° F over the session, suggesting ↑ SNS arousal.

The rationale and Tx procedures were discussed in detail. Audiocassette tapes introducing relaxation and BFB; printed discussion of the goals of therapy, how to schedule relaxations, and the use of relaxation tapes; and taped standardized passive relaxation procedures were provided and discussed. The goals were primarily to develop ↑ physiological self-regulation (e.g., lower and faster lowering of muscle tensions s̄ FB), ↑ freq of applied relaxation of varying durations in a variety of situations, ↑ her confidence in self-regulation, and ↑ awareness and avoidance of excess muscle tension.

Pt was seen for 9 additional office-based sessions, including BFB-assisted portions in 7 sessions. In the first 4 of the BFB sessions, the bifrontal activity was mostly 3–4 μV during the initial resting baseline segments c̄ EO, and > 2 μV c̄ EC. Audio FB from both sites for ~15' ea session was associated with ↓ bifrontal activity to < 3 μV c̄ EO and as low as 2 μV c̄ EC. Similar ↓ were observed from the other site. In the last 2 sessions she was able to ↓ the bifrontal activity to mostly ~2 μV during the resting baseline c̄ her EO and lower c̄ EC.

In the early sessions her finger temps. started in the mid to high 80s and ↓ to the mid to high 70s. At home she reported ↑ finger temps during relaxation from the high 70s to the low 90s. None of the office sessions involved therm. BFB.

A typical session involved resting baseline segments of 4' each c̄ EO and EC, followed by FB segments totaling 10–16" under both conditions, and then p̄ FB segments of ~4 min.

By the 3rd session on 4/18/83, pt was subjectively reporting a 25% ↓ in HA sev and freq and a 75% ↓ in duration. By the 4th session on 4/27/83, she reported a 75% ↓ in sev, freq, & dur compared to pre-Tx. In mid-May she noted much stress at work in the prior 2 wks, but her self-reported Sx records continued to show a ↓ in Sx. By late May, she noted a continued ↓ in HA Sx but first reported "teeth soreness" upon awakening 5–7 mornings. Considerable work stress continued but was expected to ↓ soon when she transferred to another department. On 6/3/83 she noted a clinically significant ↓ in teeth soreness from constant much of the day to only 2–3 hrs/day. A subjective ↓ in HA activity of ~80–85% in sev, freq, and dur was noted, and by mid-June she estimated a 90% ↓ c̄ no teeth soreness for the prior wk. She was relaxing her jaw more freq and had noticed herself drooling during sleep.

Her relaxation practice was reported to be typically 1–2 extended (15'–20') sessions, 10 brief sessions, and 20 minirelaxations each day.

She recorded 5.8 hrs of HA pain/day in the first 13 days & 5.3 hrs/day in the next 14 days. Of these she averaged a total of 0.8 hrs/day of mod and sev pain. In the following 47 days there were 0 hrs of mod or sev pain, hence a 100% ↓, and 2.6 to 4.1 hrs of slight to mild HA/day, c̄ 90% of it slight. The number of mornings on which she awakened with slight or more pain ↓ from 25 mornings (61%) in the first 41 mornings, to only 9 (27%) in the last 33 mornings.

We considered additional monitoring of her nocturnal muscle activity in her home, plus a few more office-based sessions to consolidate her gains, but on 6/27/83 she est a 95% overall ↓ of HA Sx and only 2 slight HA episodes lasting 2–3 hrs each since 6/14/83 and no tooth soreness in nearly 3 wks. She was especially pleased, considering the ↑ stress associated with her upcoming wedding. She wanted to continue on her own. She was dismissed and encouraged to continue per our recommendations and contact us p.r.n.

CONCLUSION

Prudent professionals providing biofeedback services record useful details of sessions and provide clear therapy notes, summaries, and letters. There are advantages for being specific and clear in professional communications. Standard abbreviations speed the record-keeping process and save space in reports.

REFERENCES

Ochs, L. (1990). Rights and responsibilities of report writers: A preliminary personal statement of peer review criteria. *Biofeedback: A Newsmagazine of the Association for Applied Psychophysiology and Biofeedback*, *18*(4), 24–29.

The Charles Press handbook of current medical abbreviations. (1976). Bowie, MD: Charles Press.

Theiner, E. C., Dingus, C. M., Doyle, R., Piercy, D., West, L., Alexander, A., & Schwartz, M. S. (1984). *Proposed biofeedback peer review manual.* Unpublished manuscript, Biofeedback Society of America [now the Association for Applied Psychophysiology and Biofeedback], Wheatridge, CO.

29

Job Descriptions

Mark S. Schwartz

There are several job titles and descriptions among practitioners using bio-feedback. These include some with similar education and training and those working in the same type of settings. Among the more common titles in usage are "biofeed-back therapist," "biofeedback technician," and "certified biofeedback therapist" (CBT). Others include "clinical psychophysiologist," "psychophysiological therapist," "biofeedback trainer," "biofeedback specialist," "biofeedback practitioner," and "stress management specialist."

DEFINITIONS OF BIOFEEDBACK
AND APPLIED PSYCHOPHYSIOLOGY

The definitions of the term "biofeedback" and the added term "applied psycho-physiology" affect job titles and descriptions. In selecting or maintaining a title, does one consider biofeedback narrowly or with all of the added meaning associated with "applied psychophysiology"? Thus, some professionals view the term biofeedback narrowly as mean-ing only specific instrumentation-based procedures. Other professionals still view it as a shorthand term referring to a wide array of evaluative and therapeutic procedures. These include much implied by the broader rubric of applied psychophysiology.

Some writers suggest terms such as "augmented proprioception" and "external psycho-physiological feedback." These terms are technically more accurate but are too cumber-some for routine professional use. Biofeedback still has a broad meaning for many profes-sionals and is still the term with which most professionals and the public are familiar. Common goals among biofeedback and applied psychophysiology therapies include help-ing persons to reduce, stop, and prevent symptoms with physiological self-regulation.

This is not the place to engage in professional polemics on this topic. The term "bio-feedback" has taken on much more meaning than the narrow conceptualization. Many patients referred for biofeedback probably expect that they will receive more than instru-mentation-based therapy. National certification in biofeedback recognizes this, and the writ-ten certification exam covers more than instrumentation.

It is reasonable to continue to use the term biofeedback in its broader sense. The term "applied psychophysiology" will continue to gain favor with some professionals. This term is proper for interprofessional use, for organizations, in publications, and perhaps eventu-ally in journal titles.

IMPLICATIONS OF VARIOUS JOB TITLES

Consider the implications of a job title and the image it conveys. For example, consider the consistency of the title with the functions associated with it. Also, consider the consistency of the title with other health care professionals in other fields. In health care settings, one finds professionals with well-established and respected titles (e.g., "physical therapist," "occupational therapist," "nurse practitioner," and "physician's assistant"). These professionals work under supervision. The degree of independence and responsibilities accorded such individuals depends on several factors including the individuals, the setting, the discipline, the guidelines and regulations in force, and the supervising professionals.

The point is that accepted and respected terms such as "therapist," "assistant," and "practitioner" are all common and all involve supervision. Thus, use of such terms as "biofeedback therapist," "biofeedback assistant," and "biofeedback practitioner" are consistent with common practice. "Technician" is also a common title in health care settings. For example, there are laboratory technicians and X-ray technicians. However, with some exceptions discussed below, most persons providing biofeedback services under supervision are providing far more than only technical services.

I have no strong bias regarding the choice among the terms "therapist," "practitioner," or "assistant." I do not use these titles for myself, preferring to refer to myself as "licensed clinical psychologist who specializes in and is certified in biofeedback." I am hesitant to designate what I think others should use as a title. Several years ago, I conducted a survey of individuals with nondoctoral degrees. All were members of the Biofeedback Society of America (BSA). Most of these worked under supervision and most preferred the title "biofeedback therapist."

Titles such as "clinical psychophysiologist" or "applied psychophysiologist" are consistent with applied psychophysiology. In the first edition, I suggested there were problems using the term "clinical psychophysiologist" for many of the practitioners using biofeedback. Most health professionals who use biofeedback probably do not qualify for such a lofty title. To use such a term, one should probably first qualify as a psychophysiologist (and very few professionals probably do). One can similarly argue legitimately against the term "applied psychophysiologist" for many practitioners. Some professionals with doctoral degrees typically in psychology adopt these titles. It might be a proper designation for selected professionals with carefully identified education and training. However, practitioners without those qualifications still need proper titles. Furthermore, if many adopt these lofty titles, how do the public and other professionals differentiate them from those practitioners referred to as "biofeedback therapists"?

Indeed, how many titles should a field have for its members? It is preferable to keep the number of separate titles to the lowest practical number that fits the functions performed. In the first edition, I suggested two such titles would be sufficient for persons working under supervision in clinical settings. One also could have a designation for someone in a preparatory status (e.g., "student" or "trainee").

Doctoral-level individuals who are educated within a recognized health care discipline and state sanctioned to practice will probably retain their respective licensed titles. Health care professionals with traditional health care disciplines (e.g., nursing and physical therapy) who use biofeedback will probably also retain their respective licensed titles. The more common titles of professionals who use biofeedback include "psychologist," "nurse," "psychiatrist," "physical therapist," "occupational therapist," "clinical social worker," "licensed mental health counselor," and "marriage and family counselor."

As noted above, an important factor in the maturity of a professional field lies in the standardization of proper job titles and the relationship of titles to job functions. A proper and accurate job title also is important for the self-respect of the person holding that title. It also helps other professionals to understand the title and functions and to respect the professionals with those titles. Additionally, it helps in the mobility of the person across employment situations and state lines. National certification helped provide a standard for an entry level of competence including knowledge and basic instrumentation skills.

Standardization of titles and functions is more important for those who prefer to use "biofeedback" in their titles or who need to do so because they have no other discipline or licensed title.

TOWARD A MODEL FOR STANDARDIZATION OF TITLES AND FUNCTIONS

The functions and job descriptions described first are mainly for individuals who work with supervision by other professionals. In some cases both the functions are consistent with much of what other professionals do as well.

Unlike what was presented in the first edition, I am not proposing a specific match of titles and functions. That is the responsibility of professional organizations like the Association of Applied Psychophysiology and Biofeedback (AAPB) and the Biofeedback Certification Institute of America (BCIA), and individual health care settings. The functions presented intend to provide a model and guidance for others to consider; much or all apply to biofeedback therapists. However, some function with the more limited responsibilities of technicians, and others function with more advanced skills and levels of responsibility.

Capabilities and Functions

The BCIA establishes criteria for education, training, and supervised experience for those persons qualifying for certification regardless of their title. However, persons using a title such as "biofeedback therapist" should have more training and a wider range of clinical skills and responsibilities than someone using the title "technician."

One must remember there are no data to support the need for specific qualifications for biofeedback practitioners to achieve therapeutic effectiveness. One bases such criteria on judgment and consensus among professionals. Effectiveness probably depends on a variety of factors including training, supervision, disorders, therapy goals, types of biofeedback, and procedures used.

Practitioners using biofeedback therapies should have the following capabilities, and qualities:

1. Training, knowledge, experience, and skill with a variety of non-instrumentation-based physiological self-regulatory procedures.
2. Training, knowledge, experience, and skill with at least a few biofeedback modalities, including at least electromyographic (EMG), temperature, and electrodermal biofeedback.
3. Training, knowledge, experience, and skill with other modalities such as pulse, breathing, and/or electroencephalographic (EEG) biofeedback.
4. At least fundamental knowledge of behavioral analysis and behavior therapy principles and procedures.

5. Knowledge of at least many of the disorders typically treated in clinical settings.
6. Knowledge of the research literature concerning efficacy, procedures, theoretical issues, and practical issues.
7. Training, knowledge, experience, and skills for providing other applied psychophysiological and behavioral therapies including cognitive-behavioral, relaxed breathing, assertiveness, exposure therapies, and others.
8. Good to excellent interviewing skills.
9. Good to excellent verbal communication skills, in order to provide appropriate cognitive preparation of patients, to create realistic and positive expectations, and communicating with other professionals.
10. Ability to write clear, well-organized, and complete progress notes.
11. Mature attitudes and behavior and the ability to rapidly establish and maintain positive therapeutic relationships and alliances with patients and to relate to them easily in a sensitive and empathetic manner.
12. Ability to be responsible, reliable, well-organized, flexible, and a model of psychophysiological relaxation and self-regulation.
13. Ability to work relatively independently, at least for some sessions or for a short series of sessions.
14. Ability and willingness to demonstrate knowledge in certification examinations through the BCIA.

The functions of practitioners include the following:

1. Conducting routine intake interviews and getting accurate histories and symptom descriptions.
2. Reviewing patients' existing medical, psychological, and/or dental records, and summarizing them for a supervising professional.
3. Answering a variety of questions from patients and professionals about the rationale and procedures involved in biofeedback and associated therapies.
4. Reviewing data with a supervisor, and helping to determine therapy plans and disposition for patients.
5. Helping to locate proper health care professionals for out-of-town patients; preparing or helping to prepare the paper work for such referrals.
6. Providing direct relaxation therapy procedures.
7. Responding to telephone calls and correspondence from patients, and helping each patient as indicated.
8. Providing psychophysiological assessments and biofeedback therapies that include:

   a. Explaining the rationale and therapy procedures clearly.
   b. Selecting proper recording sites.
   c. Properly attaching electrodes and other transducers.
   d. Properly operating instrumentation.
   e. Conducting psychophysiological baselines.
   f. Properly recording physiological data.
   g. Note and accurately record and report behavioral signs of arousal, tension, discomfort, and relaxation.
   h. Providing laboratory stressors for stress profiling.
   i. Shaping desired physiological and cognitive behavior using biological and verbal feedback.

    j. Summarizing, accurately interpreting, and discussing results with patients.
    k. Explaining and instructing patients in self-report record keeping.
    l. Providing and explaining patient education booklets and audiotapes.

9. For symptom logs providing written, tabular, and graphic summaries; providing positive reinforcement and encouragement based on the data; making recommendations for improvements of symptom logs.
10. Providing written, tabular, and graphic summaries of physiological data.
11. Conducting parts of additional therapies, such as assertiveness, cognitive restructuring, systematic desensitization, and other stress management procedures with selected patients.
12. Carrying out short phases of therapy.
13. Maintaining patient files.
14. Maintaining inventory and order supplies.
15. Maintaining biofeedback instruments and arranging for maintenance and repairs.
16. Scheduling patients for return visits.
17. Discussing problems, questions, and therapy issues with the supervisor and other designated professionals.
18. Conducting follow-up of patients, including mail and phone contacts.
19. Answering patients' questions about biofeedback and relaxation.
20. Cooperating and working well with other health professionals.
21. Establishing a supportive and therapeutic relationship with patients.
22. Providing proper answers and suggestions to patients about the following areas:

    a. Difficulties they may experience with relaxation.
    b. Their concern about progress; stressors in their lives; timing and frequency of relaxation; medication (with proper medical/dental consultation).
    c. Caffeine use, other dietary substances, nicotine, and other chemicals that could affect therapy and results.

23. Designing or participating in the design of patient-education materials and data forms.
24. Providing detailed, well-organized, and clear reports, progress notes, and closing summaries.
25. Maintaining continued competence in biofeedback and related fields, by reading and by attending professional meetings and workshops.

Other considerations in developing a job description are the BCIA Task Statements or role delineation for biofeedback practitioners. The BCIA established these as necessary in 1980 (Schwartz, 1981) and updated them in 1990 (Biofeedback Certification Institute of America, 1990). One could formulate much or all of a job description by including the tasks or modifications of them.

Responsibilities of a Supervisor

Fulfilling the above criteria is challenging. Many therapists are responsible for the patients for whom another professional has primary responsibility. Thus, the therapist has major responsibilities, not only for the patient's welfare, but also as an extension of other responsible professionals, including the supervisor and/or the health care institution. Therapists must be flexible and able to analyze situations rapidly and to improvise as may be required by individual patients' needs. Patients need technically proficient therapists who also are sensitive, understanding, supportive, and reassuring.

There also are varying opinions about the responsibilities of the supervising professional. There are supervisors who know little about biofeedback and associated therapies and do not get involved in those aspects of therapy. In contrast, there are supervisory practitioners who are simultaneously providing the same services with other patients and working in tandem with the therapists in the treatment of some or all patients.

There are problems when a supervisor relies on a biofeedback therapist for full knowledge and experience with evaluative and therapy procedures. This is especially true if the supervisor seldom sees the patients. If the supervisor has limited experience with the procedures, then he or she only can provide limited supervision. This leaves therapists on their own.

Several factors influence the need for involvement of the supervising professional including the therapist's qualifications and skills, the patients' disorders, and the complexity of the cases. Supervising professionals see the advantages to being familiar and experienced with the responsibilities of the therapists. They know they should be able to conduct the same therapy when needed.

Beyond the responsibilities listed earlier, the supervising professional has several other important responsibilities and duties. The supervised therapist should not, or need not, be held responsible for these. These other responsibilities include the following:

1. Making final judgments about starting therapies.
2. Writing to referral sources and others about patients' evaluation and therapy.
3. Providing "more authoritative" recommendations to patients and support for what the therapist provided.
4. Reviewing data and guide the therapist about later sessions.
5. Reviewing therapy sessions for completeness and clarity.
6. Providing some therapy sessions to understand selected patients better. This helps increase the patients' confidence and reassurance about the supervising professional's involvement. It also helps the therapist overcome therapy problems.
7. Interviewing and provide more information and reassurance for those patients who are skeptical and hesitant about biofeedback and related therapies.
8. Providing other therapies for patients whose problems and therapies are beyond the scope of practice and competence of the biofeedback therapist.

There are settings in which the supervising practitioner does most of the interviewing, interpretation, therapy, and report writing. Another person does such tasks as attaching sensors, recording physiological data, and giving basic routine instructions. Other functions include administering, scoring, and summarizing self-report forms and similar functions. The term "therapist" does not appear to fit the latter job functions and responsibilities. Since the job title should fit the job functions and responsibilities, the title "biofeedback technician" or similar title may be better for the person performing these functions. Such a person typically has less of the necessary knowledge, credentials, training, and experience. In such cases, a supervising practitioner is more important.

Supervised Professionals, Third-Party Reimbursement, and "Direct" Provision of Services

Can and should third-party reimbursement occur for services provided by someone other than an independently licensed professional? This is a very important question and has major implications for the field of applied psychophysiology and biofeedback. The definition of "direct provider" is also crucial because third-party systems often reimburse independently licensed professionals who are "directly" providing services.

Furthermore, the *Standards and Guidelines for Biofeedback Applications in Psychophysiological Self-Regulation* (Amar et al., 1992) recognize there are providers of biofeedback with demonstrated competence but who do not have a license for independent practice. This document states these persons "must work under the supervision of a licensed professional" (p. 11). The document further specifies that the "supervisor [has] demonstrated knowledge and clinical expertise in psychophysiological self-regulation" (p. 11). If that is not available from the immediate supervisor, someone else must provide it according to these *Standards and Guidelines*. The idealistic intent of the committee that wrote this document and of the AAPB is not in question here. It sounds right and ideally is best. However, in practice, there are many variations from this ideal.

Prudent nonlicensed providers of biofeedback and their supervisors who do not meet the criteria of knowledge and clinical expertise in psychophysiological self-regulation will rectify the situation. Some or many will do this because they know that it is ethically wise. For those who do not, some are at risk if ethical or legal problems arise in their practice.

Some practitioners posit that they can provide services at lower costs if supervised professionals provide some services. There is one potential problem with this rationale put forth by a representative of the Health Insurance Association of America (HIAA) several years ago. The use of such supervised professionals sometimes does not reduce overall health care costs.

The reasoning is that the practice permits the delivery of services to many more patients. Thus, overall costs can be higher for the third-party payer. However, contrasting logic suggests that most of the patients need treatment and continue to seek help in the health care system. It is in the best interest of third-party payers to support the best care for the most people. Many of these people will then be healthier and less frequent users of health care services.

Furthermore, third-party payers should reimburse practitioners who maintain high standards of competence and practice prudently within a stepped-care framework. Practitioners often do this best with the help of supervised professional assistants including qualified and competent biofeedback therapists. This practice is consistent with the use of nurse practitioners, physical therapists, and physicians' assistants. Practitioners using prudent criteria for selecting patients for therapy could contain and lower overall costs to third-party payers. For example, successfully treated patients often do not continue to seek help. With supervised therapists, practitioners often can treat more patients successfully.

The American Psychological Association (APA) supports both the use of and value of nonindependently licensed professionals in the delivery of clinical services, and offers guidelines for such professional conduct under proper supervision. The fees of supervised professionals often are less than for independently licensed and directly reimbursable professionals.

The term "direct" has different connotations for different professionals. It rarely means "face-to-face." For example, the *Random House Dictionary of the English Language* (1969, p. 375) defines the term, as a verb, "to guide by advice, helpful information, instruction. . ."; "to regulate the course of"; "to administer, manage, supervise"; "to give authoritative instructions to"; "to command"; and to "order or ordain (something)."

The American Heritage Dictionary for DOS (1991) defines the word, as a verb, "to manage," "to take charge of with authority," "to aim, guide, or address (something or someone) toward a goal." Synonyms for the word direct, when used as a verb mean "to control the course of (an activity)" and include "operate, conduct, manage, carry on, steer, supervise." When used to mean "to exercise authority or influence over," synonyms are "control and govern." Instead of "to have charge of (the affairs of others)," one can use synonyms such as "run, head, manage, govern, administer, superintend, administrate." The verb direct also means "to show the way to." Synonyms for the latter include "lead, conduct, guide, steer, escort, pilot, usher, route, and shepherd."

If used as an adjective, "direct" is "proceeding or lying in a straight course or line," or "straightforward." These do not mean without the help of others. For example, surgeons provide "direct" services and do so with considerable help of supervised operating room personnel. Supervised professionals conduct some of those services without the surgeon's presence at all times. Physical and occupational therapists in medical settings provide a variety of clinical services without a physician's presence. Physicians direct and supervise these services.

Synonyms for "direct" include "guide" and "order." The *Random House Dictionary* states that "'direct' suggests also giving explanation or advice; the emphasis is not on the authority of the director, but on steps necessary for the accomplishing of a purpose" (1969, p. 375). The term "order" connotes "a personal relationship, in which a person in a superior position imperatively instructs a subordinate (or subordinates) to do something" (1969, p. 375).

Conscientious supervising professionals can supervise others providing therapies using clinical biofeedback while still maintaining a "direct" relationship with the patient and the services. These other professionals should have proper education, training, and credentials as biofeedback therapists.

The definitions of "supervision" and guidelines for it are integral to the issue of direct services acceptable to affected parties. Note that the *Standards and Guidelines* (Amar et al., 1992) state that the "minimum contact for . . . supervisory activities of nonlicensed individuals is one hour per week per halftime employment" (p. 11). Definitions and guidelines need to reflect the many factors and circumstances in clinical settings. The revised seventh draft of the APA *Standards for Providers of Psychological Services* (American Psychological Association, 1985) dropped the prior limit of three *"psychological assistants."* However, it maintains the same concerns and attempts to dissuade misuse by providing that professional psychologists be "sufficiently available to ensure adequate evaluation or assessment, intervention planning, direction, and emergency consultation" (p. 11). This dissuades supervisors from employing and trying to supervise large numbers of unlicensed people.

Those concerned with such relationships might find more structured guidelines more helpful and reassuring. For example, does the independently licensed, supervising professional see each patient at least for part of the intake process? Does the supervising professional assume the responsibility for deciding whether to provide such services? How do supervisors direct the therapy program? Do they meet with the therapists on a regularly scheduled basis to review physiological and symptom data and other clinical factors? Do they assume the responsibility for continuing or stopping therapy? Do they meet with patients for additional aspects of therapy not appropriately provided by the biofeedback therapists?

REFERENCES

Amar, P. B., McKee, M. G., Peavey, B. S., Schneider, C. J., Sherman, R. A., & Sterman, M. B. (1992). *Standards and guidelines for biofeedback applications in psychophysiological self-regulation.* Wheatridge, CO: Association for Applied Psychophysiology and Biofeedback.

The American Heritage dictionary for DOS (college ed.). (1992). Sausalito, CA: Writing Tools Group of Houghton Mifflin.

American Psychological Association. (1985). *Standards for providers of psychological services* (rev. 7th draft). Washington, DC: Author.

Biofeedback Certification Institute of America. (1990). *Blueprint tasks and knowledge statements* (rev. ed.). Wheatridge, CO: Author.

Random House dictionary of the English language (College ed.). (1969). New York: Random House.

Schwartz, M. S. (1981). Biofeedback Certification Institute of America: Blueprint knowledge statements. *Biofeedback and Self-Regulation, 6,* 253–262.

Schwartz, M. S., & Fehmi, L. (1982). *Applications standards and guidelines for providers of biofeedback services.* Wheatridge, CO: Biofeedback Society of America.

XI
QUALITY CONTROL
AND RESEARCH

30

Biofeedback Quality Control: Evaluating the Professionals and the Therapies

J. Suzanne Kroon

Society and consumers demand much from products and services. Consumers do not hesitate to question and challenge the need for and quality of services and goods. Health care practitioners cannot escape from this scrutiny. Consumers are now better shoppers for health care providers and services. Malpractice suits and adjudications reflect the *Zeitgeist*-fostering challenge of the health care providers' professional accountability, competence, and character.

More than a decade ago, Perlin (1982) spoke on the subject of "Legal Regulation of Biofeedback Practice." He reminded the audience that "legal regulation of . . . all professionals . . . increased . . . in recent years." He advised professionals in the biofeedback field to "embark upon a program of voluntary self-regulation in [your] professional practices."

Practitioners of biofeedback must protect their professional futures. We help do this by understanding our legal rights, responsibilities, and limitations. We also do this by maintaining rigorous scientific and clinical standards in our research and clinical treatment programs. Practitioner qualifications, treatment rationale and efficacy, and the duration of the effects of interventions are all subject to legal and public scrutiny. Therefore, we must be careful to check these routinely in our professional practice in addition to the published research. The medical and scientific communities will continue to influence the endurance of the field of biofeedback at least through patient referrals and research funding.

EVALUATING THE PROFESSIONALS

There are still advertisements for "biofeedback instruments" in magazines and mail-order catalogues, and even in comic books. These advertisements "assure" readers that they can learn to "manage life's stresses" and "cure" their ills with a small, "easy-to-operate and fun-to-own" biofeedback gadget for the price of only $49.95 plus tax. Some advertisements state that the instruments will lessen our problems "easily, effectively, in the privacy of our own home or office" in just "minutes per day." The advertisements lead uninformed readers to believe that they can become their own "biofeedback therapist" for a few dollars and in minutes a day. Consider the impact of such advertisements on the public's perception of the qualifications of practitioners who offer biofeedback therapies.

737

Who are the qualified professionals who offer biofeedback therapies? How can the public and others correctly identify them? The diversity of professional titles in the field causes confusion for professionals, referral sources, patients, and third-party payers. In the literature and on office doors, one encounters different titles for those who provide biofeedback therapies. Titles include "biofeedback therapist," "biofeedback technician," "biofeedback trainer," and "biofeedback practitioner." There is more discussion of this issue in Chapter 24.

In addition, the diversity of educational credentials and experiences is confusing for the uninformed. Practitioners hold degrees and licenses in several different health care fields. Some practitioners have educational backgrounds and credentials in fields other than health care.

The recent *Standards and Guidelines for Biofeedback Applications in Psychophysiological Self-Regulation* (Amar et al., 1992, pp. 9–12) by the Association of Applied Psychophysiology and Biofeedback (AAPB) defines acceptable criteria for providers of biofeedback services and recognizes three types of professionals:

1. Licensed health care professionals with demonstrated training and competence in applied psychophysiology and biofeedback. Certification by the Biofeedback Certification Institute of America (BCIA) documents a fundamental level of knowledge and competence.
2. Unlicensed biofeedback therapists who meet the standards for certification defined by the BCIA and who practice only within the limitations of that certification.
3. Educators or applied psychophysiologists who teach or study psychophysiological self-regulation skills in the academic classroom, laboratory, or work place.

A fourth category is also mentioned, the "trainee," who works under direct supervision of a qualified provider. The supervisor assumes full responsibility for the care of the trainee's patients. The AAPB document stresses the importance of adequate supervision of all unlicensed providers. It underscores the importance for all providers to work within the limits of their training and experience.

These standards and guidelines, like the earlier document (Schwartz & Fehmi, 1982), reflect a change in attitude toward the role of biofeedback therapists. Gaardner and Montgomery (1977) suggested that one can cross-train personnel because most biofeedback therapy programs are small and have limited staff. "Thus, receptionists and secretaries can have the training to take over for the primary therapist during illness or vacation" (p. 101). Current knowledge and professional standards strongly question the risks surrounding this advice once considered acceptable by some professionals.

Perlin (1982) lent further support to the firm establishment of professional standards and guidelines for biofeedback providers. He cautioned that naiveté about the ever-changing legal system leaves one particularly vulnerable to lawsuits. Specifically, Perlin encouraged biofeedback providers to understand the legal dimensions of "malpractice" and of "vicarious liability." These involve the legal responsibility a licensed supervisor maintains for work preformed by unlicensed biofeedback providers or trainees.

There is general agreement that biofeedback practitioners should possess interpersonal and clinical skills to foster patients' developing physiological self-regulation. Yet only through national certification examinations and criteria offered through BCIA can professionals establish basic levels of competency in biofeedback.

The more recent *Standards and Guidelines for Biofeedback Applications in Psychophysiological Self-Regulation* (Amar et al., 1992, pp. 12–13) states,

"Licensed professionals and service providers must have demonstrated knowledge in the following areas of Psychophysiological Self-Regulation:

- Definitions and History of Biofeedback
- Relevant Anatomy and Physiology
- Psychophysiology
- Learning Theory and the Application of Principles of Learning Psychophysiology
- Research Methodology
- Theories of Stress
- Instrumentation Terms and Concepts for Various Biofeedback Applications
- Use of Instrumentation
- Assessment of Safety and Accuracy of Instrumentation
- Counseling Skills with Practicum
- Psychological Intake, Assessment and Evaluation Techniques
- Psychophysiological Profiling and Related Assessment Techniques
- Adjunctive Techniques and Cognitive Interventions
- Relationship and Interaction of Medication
- Ethics and Accepted Practices

This document also advocates that "all providers of biofeedback services limit their practice to those areas in which they have skills and expertise. . . . Providers recognize the boundaries of their competence and operate within their level of competence." (pp. 11–12)

EVALUATING THE TREATMENTS

Chapter 27 discusses the major models for delivering biofeedback services—the solo practice, the collaborative model, and variants of both. This section discusses selected roles and work settings of biofeedback providers and their impact upon the quality of treatment.

Professionals developed biofeedback clinics and services in a variety of health care professional settings to meet the needs for and benefits from biofeedback therapies. In contrast with many early practitioners with simple instrumentation, many now have far more advanced microcomputer-interfaced systems. These changes reflect the persistent technical maturation of this field. New members in this field are the fortunate recipients of an abundance of technology and research that did not exist a few years ago.

Nevertheless, newcomers still have their work cut out for them. Educational programs and materials are now far more accessible. There are guidelines established to certify competency in biofeedback therapy through BCIA. Thus, critics are now understandably less tolerant of deficiencies in education, therapy practices, and research methodologies.

Biofeedback Clinic Designs

Three types of professional arrangements are prevalent among biofeedback clinics:

1. A biofeedback therapist working under the supervision of a professional who is state credentialed for independent practice. In this case, the licensed professional also has appropriate education, credentials, and proficiency in biofeedback.
2. A biofeedback therapist working under the direction of a licensed professional who does not have proficiency in biofeedback.

3. A biofeedback therapist working independently within a hospital, clinic, or educational institution. The therapist may or may not have a license as a health care provider and may receive little or no direct professional supervision.

The development of a particular clinic design depends upon the requirements of the professional setting, the budget, and the availability of skilled and otherwise qualified biofeedback providers. One may provide quality biofeedback therapy within any of the above-mentioned arrangements, however, each design has inherent advantages and disadvantages for the staff members involved and for therapies provided. The following discussion is not intended to imply support for any one clinic design over the others.

Therapist Supervised by a Licensed Professional Properly Trained in the Use of Biofeedback

There are clear advantages for the first arrangement. A common example is working with licensed psychologists. It allows for a pooling of knowledge about biofeedback and associated therapies better than the other arrangements. An advantage for the biofeedback therapist is being able to draw upon the supervisor's broad knowledge in evaluation and therapies in addition to biofeedback. This arrangement allows biofeedback therapists to develop more skills in the treatment of patients with specific disorders.

This arrangement may be most valuable for the nonlicensed biofeedback professional in a private practice setting. Health insurance reimbursement may be more predictable when the licensed professional provides close and appropriate supervision. The training, experience, and the skills of the biofeedback therapist determine the extent of the direct supervision required. A prudent supervisor may require that his or her staff show at least basic knowledge and practical skills through the BCIA certification procedures.

Many licensed supervisors favor this arrangement. A significant advantage for them is relief from conducting the routine biofeedback sessions; more time can be devoted to psychotherapy, counseling, program development, and the like.

A possible drawback occurs when the supervisor is supervising an inadequately trained, or otherwise unqualified and nonlicensed therapist. Perlin (1982) cautioned that if a nonlicensed employee is charged with malpractice, then the supervisor may be held legally responsible. The supervisor must remain well informed of the legal responsibilities when supervising a nonlicensed therapist. One needs to exercise considerable caution in hiring, supervising, and assigning duties to these individuals.

Therapist Supervised by a Licensed Professional Not Trained in Biofeedback

A common example of this arrangement is the therapist working with a group of non-psychiatrist physicians or dentists. An advantage of this arrangement is that the therapist has available the professional knowledge and experience of the supervisor. Within specialty clinics, this arrangement also may provide the biofeedback therapist with specific education in medical or dental knowledge, disease processes, and pharmacology that is not often readily available to biofeedback therapists working primarily with nonmedical professionals.

However, this arrangement has some potential disadvantages. A supervisor unskilled in biofeedback may not understand and recognize the limitations of biofeedback interventions or the intricacies of the treatment. One risks inappropriate referrals, and the therapist may feel obliged to try to provide therapy for such patients. The biofeedback therapist may have difficulty telling the supervising physician about inappropriate referrals.

Another disadvantage in this arrangement is that the biofeedback therapist may not have the authority to influence biofeedback program decisions. He or she also may not have opportunities to consult as readily with others who are knowledgeable in biofeedback practices. This arrangement is not one that a newcomer to the biofeedback field may find comfortable or professionally suitable.

Therapist Working Independently within an Institution

A biofeedback therapist, licensed or not, working independently within a hospital, clinic, or other institution may enjoy recognition as an "expert." Some therapists appreciate this arrangement because of the variety of duties and professional independence it allows. However, one easily recognizes the inherent limitations of this arrangement. The unlicensed biofeedback therapist may feel professionally isolated if other professionals in the setting do not recognize and respect the title of "biofeedback therapist." A lack of professional affiliation may, in some facilities, limit medical and other professionals in referring patients for biofeedback therapies.

A biofeedback therapist licensed in a health care field might gain easier acceptance within the institution because there he or she has a more commonly recognized title. Yet working alone often is difficult even for experienced therapists. They must determine whether to accept referrals of patients with disorders unfamiliar to them. Such a therapist may find it disconcerting to have very limited support or input from others well trained in biofeedback.

In summary, the design of biofeedback services varies significantly from one setting to another. However, professionals in each setting can still provide quality treatments. Each arrangement, however, offers biofeedback providers distinct personal and professional advantages and disadvantages.

Evaluating Treatment Efficacy over Time

Published follow-up studies of biofeedback interventions reveal increasing numbers of long-term studies of biofeedback therapies for various disorders. There are a few well-controlled studies published that assess biofeedback therapies across several medical disorders and conditions (see, e.g., Fuller, 1977; Libo & Arnold, 1983; Rosenbaum, Greco, Sternberg, & Singleton, 1981; Olson, 1988; Hatch, Fisher & Rugh, 1987).

The costs in personnel and time for conducting systematic follow-up of patients may be prohibitive for smaller health care groups. Yet no other data can adequately serve to provide support and safeguards for the very future of some of these biofeedback programs. Referral sources, administrators, third-party payers, and patients often ask practitioners to provide evidence of the efficacy and durability of their biofeedback interventions.

There are limitations of staff, time, and finances. Thus, program directors need to be resourceful in developing and conducting follow-up procedures. One suggestion is to develop contacts with nearby colleges or universities. Practitioners can then offer advanced students the chance to gain experience in designing and conducting follow-up studies.

Practitioners may feel frustration reviewing follow-up studies of biofeedback therapies. Ford (1982) reviewed the long-term follow-up literature available on biofeedback therapies for four disorders. He cautioned that the reader cannot easily compare and contrast outcome statistics among studies, because of several inconsistencies encountered:

1. Studies sometimes used different biofeedback modalities for the same disorders.

2. The numbers of treatment sessions often varied widely across studies. Ford found a range of 5 sessions to over 60 sessions. Rosenbaum et al. (1981) included patients with as few as 1 session, and Adler and Adler (1976) included patients with up to 60 sessions.

3. The length of the period of follow-up also varied. The definition of "long-term" ranged from a few months to 5 years.

4. The definition of treatment success also varied. Some studies rated outcomes according to the therapists' judgments of progress, or an independent rating based on the reports of the patient's themselves (Libo & Arnold, 1983).

In addition to these inconsistencies, one may wisely question the effect of the following variables not often defined in the follow-up publications:

5. There are various ways to collect data about symptoms during intake, baselines, treatment, and follow-up. Some older studies started with written self-report measures and yet collected follow-up data via telephone interviews. Cahn and Cram (1980) found low correspondence between follow-up data collected with two separate measurement tools.

6. Clinic populations may differ from one study to another. One must consider the ages, gender, medications, duration of symptoms, severity of symptoms, patient selection, and many other variables.

7. The professional qualifications and personalities of the therapists may have a significant effect on treatment outcome.

Recognizing the need for routinely conducted and well-controlled follow-up studies, Miller (1974) made an innovative recommendation. When a journal accepts a clinical outcome study, the investigator must agree to collect follow-up data for later publication. Except in unique applications, peer-reviewed journals typically require some follow-up, often at least 6 months and sometimes longer. Requiring, long-term follow-up of 2–5 years is an ideal goal, but one with practical problems. In Miller's (1983) presentation to the Biofeedback Society of America (now the AAPB), he re-emphasized the importance of accountable data collection and follow-up. He suggested that follow-up data routinely include such information as:

- Change in satisfaction level of current life.
- Days lost from work since the end of biofeedback treatment.
- Other treatments received since biofeedback treatment ended.
- Changes in medications since the end of biofeedback therapy.

Miller further stated that since the "demands for proof of therapeutic efficacy are increasing . . . several centers should design cooperative studies to secure definitive evidence to convince skeptics and third-party payers." Attempts to do this even for one disorder—headaches—faced many practical complexities and very limited funding.

Researchers and practitioners know the importance of consistently using reliable and valid measurement procedures in evaluation and follow-up. Prudent practitioners select some measures before seeing patients in the intake session. They then continue to use the same measures through the final follow-up contact with the patients.

Measurement Methods

A patient's symptoms, disorder, and condition affect the choice of measurement methods used to identify changes from treatment. One method does not suffice for all.

The value of reliable and systematic measurements in biofeedback applications and research cannot be disputed, however, differences in opinion persist about relying on standardized treatments in clinical settings versus tailored treatments. The difference in opinion is, not surprisingly, between some researchers and clinical practitioners and therapists using biofeedback. Many practitioners and therapists hold that biofeedback therapies must allow the therapist flexibility to tailor the therapy to the individual patient; for example, it must not require that all patients with muscle contraction headaches be treated identically. This refers to using the same feedback displays, the same number of sessions, and the same explanation of the treatment. Some researchers counter that such "free-form" therapy does not lend itself to replication, which is a necessary component of sound behavioral research. This is not the place to debate this topic. The purpose here is to note that, no matter the treatment parameters and tailoring, measurement methods need to remain standard. However, one measurement method does not suffice for all symptoms and disorders. The symptoms and disorder affect the choice of measurement method used to identify changes from treatment.

G. E. Schwartz (1983) called for adopting a research-oriented perspective in the clinical practice of biofeedback. He defines such a perspective as a "general process or attitude involving inquiry, problem solving and constant evaluation on the part of the potential interventionist" (p. 379). He recognized the "middle-ground" between hard-core researchers and hard-core therapists. His position is consistent with that supported in this chapter:

> Since it is unlikely that any one technique will be found 100% effective for all individuals, it behooves the responsible clinician to develop a research-oriented, problem-solving approach to therapy. This requires that the therapist continually monitor his or her own skills in selecting and administering interventions and evaluate their consequences for specific types of patients. (p. 380)

With regard to the responsibility of biofeedback practitioners, G. E. Schwartz (1983) has emphasized that in addition to adequate formal training and continuing education,

> The therapist must come to develop more systematic decision-making skills, and must develop single-subject as well as group-oriented research approaches to evaluating progress in therapy. Systematic procedures can be incorporated into clinics or private practices whereby particular interventions, singularly or in combination, can be continually assessed using evaluation of the feedback provided by the patient. (p. 383)

Measurement methods used before, during, and after therapy include the face-to-face interviews, telephone interviews, written questionnaires, personality assessments, and symptom logs or diaries.

There are several criteria for progress. The original *Applications Standards and Guidelines* (Schwartz & Fehmi, 1982) offers several examples of signs of progress. General criteria for many or most applications include the following: frequency, intensity, and duration of daily symptoms and symptoms occurring during stress and higher-risk situations; medications; hospital visits; self-efficacy thoughts about self-regulation; and changes in life, activities, environment, and family also are general criteria (e.g., returning to work and maintaining normal hours at work).

In addition, practitioners further define specific changes occurring with specific disorders. For example, a positive change in an asthmatic patient is his or her improved reaction to bronchoconstricting agents. A patient with Raynaud's disease may develop a faster recovery after a vasospastic episode. Other examples for several disorders are in Schwartz and Fehmi (1982).

Osgood, Suci, and Tannenbaum (1957) offered suggestions and examples for social scientists seeking to understand, define, and measure the elusive variable called "meaning." They stated that such an index should "be evaluated against the usual criteria for measuring instruments" (p. 11) and should possess the following:

1. *Objectivity.* The method should yield verifiable, reproducible data that are independent of the idiosyncracies of the investigator.
2. *Reliability.* The method should yield the same values with acceptable margins of error duplicating the same conditions.
3. *Validity.* The data should clearly covary with those from some other, independent index of meaning.
4. *Sensitivity.* The method should yield differentiations commensurate with the natural units of the material studied. That is, the method should reflect fine distinctions in meaning as one typically makes in communication.
5. *Comparability.* The method should apply to a wide range of phenomena in the field, making comparisons among different concepts.
6. *Utility.* The method should efficiently yield information pertinent to contemporary theoretical and practical issues. That is, one should avoid cumbersome and laborious methods that prohibit the collection of data at a reasonable rate.

Osgood and his colleagues concluded that the 7-point bipolar scale is the most effective method for measuring subjects' judgments. They based this conclusion on extensive investigations and statistical analyses with various scales. An example of their commonly used scale is presented below:

Extremely Relaxed __ : __ : __ : __ : __ : __ : __ Extremely Tense

The instructions for completing this type of measure are simple. The task is to show the direction and intensity on the 7-point scale (Osgood et al., 1957). Remind patients to place check marks in the middle of the spaces and not on the boundaries or colons between the spaces.

There are numerous reliable and valid objective measures now available for many behavioral and symptom dimensions. For examples and descriptions of many measures of the assessment of pain, see Turk and Melzack (1992). The important point here is to use measures that at least meet Osgood's criteria.

SUMMARY

In summary, professionals are undeniably responsible for collecting and recording accurate and appropriate data during baselines, treatment, and through follow-up. Practitioners using physiological self-regulation therapies need to be familiar with various measurement methods to check the effects of therapy properly.

In addition, clinical and research professionals should adopt standardized methods and formats for collecting, presenting, and publishing data. Rigorous standards of practice affect the future quality of biofeedback and applied psychophysiology and the efficacy and reliability of these interventions.

REFERENCES

Adler, C. S., & Adler, S. M. (1976). Biofeedback-psychotherapy for the treatment of headaches: A five-year follow-up. *Headache, 16*, 189–191.

Amar, P. B., McKee, M. G., Peavey, B. S., Schneider, C. J., Sherman, R. A., & Sterman, M. B. (1992). *Standards and guidelines for biofeedback applications in psychophysiological self-regulation.* Wheatridge, CO: Association for Applied Psychophysiology and Biofeedback.

Cahn, T., & Cram, J. R. (1980). Changing measurement instrument at follow-up: A potential source of error. *Biofeedback and Self-Regulation, 5*, 265–273.

Ford, M. R. (1982). Biofeedback treatment for headaches, Raynaud's disease, essential hypertension, and irritable bowel syndrome: A review of the long-term follow-up literature. *Biofeedback and Self-Regulation, 7*, 521–536.

Fuller, G. D. (1977). *Biofeedback: Methods and procedures in clinical practice.* San Francisco: San Francisco Biofeedback Institute.

Hatch, J. P., Fisher, J. G., & Rugh, J. D. (Eds.). (1987). *Biofeedback: Studies in clinical efficacy.* New York: Plenum Press.

Gaarder, K. R., & Montgomery, P. S. (1977). *Clinical biofeedback: A procedural manual.* Baltimore: Williams & Wilkins.

Libo, L. M., & Arnold, G. E. (1983, March). Factors associated with long-term effectiveness of biofeedback/relaxation therapy. *Proceedings of the Fourteenth Annual Meeting of the Biofeedback Society of America, Denver.* Wheatridge, CO: Association for Applied Psychophysiology and Biofeedback.

Miller, N. E. (1974). Introduction: Current issues and key problems. In *Biofeedback and self-control, 1973.* Chicago: Aldine.

Miller, N. E. (1983, March). *Research models for evaluating clinical efficacy: A three-system approach.* Symposium presented at the Fourteenth annual meeting of the Biofeedback Society of America, Denver, Colorado.

Olson, R. P. (1988). A long-term, single-group follow-up study of biofeedback therapy with chronic medical and psychiatric patients. *Biofeedback and Self-Regulation, 13*(4), 331–346.

Osgood, C. E., Suci, G. J., & Tannenbaum, P. N. (1957). *The measurement of meaning.* Urbana: University of Illinois Press.

Perlin, M. J. (1982, March). *Legal regulation of biofeedback practice: The dawn of a new era.* Paper presented at the Thirteenth Annual Meeting of the Biofeedback Society of America, Chicago.

Rosenbaum, L., Greco, P. S., Sternberg, C., & Singleton, G. L. (1981). Ongoing assessment: Experience of a university biofeedback clinic. *Biofeedback and Self-Regulation, 6*, 103–112.

Schwartz, G. E. (1989). Research and feedback in clinical practice: A commentary on responsible biofeedback therapy. In J. V. Basmajian (Ed.), *Biofeedback: Principles and practice for clinicians* (3rd ed.). Baltimore: Williams & Wilkins.

Schwartz, M. S., & Fehmi, L. (1982). *Application standards and guidelines for providers of biofeedback services.* Wheatridge, CO: Biofeedback Society of America.

Turk, D. C., & Melzack, R. (Eds.). (1992). *Handbook of pain assessment.* New York: Guilford Press.

31

Evaluating Research in Clinical Biofeedback

Mark S. Schwartz

This chapter discusses some questions and issues to consider when evaluating biofeedback research and when discussing therapy procedures and reported results. It also serves to increase awareness when conducting research and when reporting and interpreting clinical results.

High-quality and meaningful research, especially clinical research, is extremely difficult to design and conduct. The topics of research design, methodological considerations, pitfalls in human research, and related topics are covered well in other publications (Barber, 1976; Barlow, Blanchard, Hayes, & Epstein 1977; Green & Shellenberger, 1986a, 1986b; Hersen & Barlow, 1976; Kazdin, 1992; Kewman & Roberts, 1983; Ray, 1979; Ray, Raczynski, Rogers, & Kimball, 1979; Steiner & Dince, 1981, 1983; Taub, 1985; White & Tursky, 1982). Also, the series of papers in the special 1987 issue of *Biofeedback and Self-Regulation* (Furedy, 1987; Shellenberger & Green, 1987; Furedy & Shulhan, 1987; Rosenfeld, 1987; Carlson, 1987) are very useful.

THE GAP BETWEEN CLINICIANS
AND RESEARCHERS: SOME SUGGESTIONS
FOR CLOSING IT

It is unfortunate that clinicians and researchers often appear as adversaries engaged in what appears to be the battle of the Hatfields and the McCoys. As Garmezy and Masten (1986) noted in a related paper, "the slings and arrows of these opposing camps have as yet to be put away as part of an arms reduction package" (p. 501).

Publications and oral presentations are often characterized by premature rejection or exaggeration. Rosenfeld (1987) wrote an eloquent paper expressing his role as mediator and champion of perspective. He reflected upon the position of clinicians, stating that they criticize research results from "stripped-down experimental paradigms" that do not support the specific effects of biofeedback, partially due to the omission of "patient motivational factors."

> Absence of evidence is not evidence of absence; one cannot in the end prove the null hypothesis. That is, a failed half-hearted attempt to find the needle in the haystack does *not* prove that it isn't there. One should really take a good look for it before giving up—if the needle has any value to one, that is. (p. 218; emphasis added)

Exaggeration of clinical results is often the claim of researchers. Practitioners sometimes claim that researchers ask the wrong questions or unimportant questions. Some make accusations of inadequately conducted research and experimenter bias.

In all fairness, these problems are also present in other areas of health care such as psychology (Garmezy & Masten, 1986). That chapter addresses the contributions by psychotherapists and researchers to the science of developmental psychopathology. This follows a brief but poignant discussion of the rationale for and examples of the benefits from a productive alliance rather than an enduring antagonism between the camps.

Researchers and practitioners sometimes do not appreciate their dependency upon one another. "To some extent, the disagreement is semantic [and due to] . . . much misrepresentation—probably due to mutual misunderstanding of the respective positions of the opponents" (Rosenfeld, 1987, p. 217). "Wisdom would dictate a recognition that there were contributions to be made by both talented clinicians *and* researchers" (Garmezy & Masten, 1986, p. 501).

Practitioners are hungry for knowledge about biofeedback, especially when it is relevant to clinical applications. They are hungry for good research and depend on it for answering a myriad of questions and increasing the credibility of clinical procedures. There is no substitute for good research. Again, borrowing from Rosenfeld (1987),

> If biofeedback is to prosper, there must be acceptance by medical and scientific communities. This is ultimately necessary. . . . These . . . communities [ultimately] accept only one kind of evidence, scientific evidence. There [is] some disagreement as to what constitutes scientific evidence. (p. 217)

Researchers need clinicians to help generate the need for questions requiring answers. Without widespread clinical applications there would be far less need for research. Clinicians can often provide researchers with viewpoints and ideas on pertinent research questions and procedures. "Research resulting from such an alliance will foster the common goal of practitioner and [researcher] in improving the effectiveness of . . . therapeutic interventions" (Garmezy & Masten, 1986, p. 501).

Rosenfeld (1987) again helps with his optimism and encouragement. "I believe it is quite possible for clinicians and researchers together to provide scientific evidence" (p. 217). Later, he adds, ". . . researcher and clinician ought to begin talking to each other in advance of doing a study, rather than wasting time in *a posteriori* arguments" (p. 221; emphasis added).

One goal of this chapter is to help increase sophistication and clinical usefulness of research and help consumers of that research. I favor anything that stimulates us all to work closely with one another toward improving the synergistic relationship of research, clinical applications, and reimbursement. Garmezy and Masten (1986) are also helpful in their directness:

> The researcher who is uninformed of the observations depicted in clinical case accounts . . . is at risk for generating unsophisticated, inaccurate, and marginal studies. . . . The clinician equally uninformed about . . . developments in the areas of basic and applied science relevant to the clinical enterprise is at risk for rigidly adhering to a technique or model that can act as a conceptual strait-jacket, containing the therapeutic effort. (p. 501)

Practitioners must be very knowledgeable about research methods and limitations, and those conducting research need to be well versed in clinical procedures and clinical practice. Neither can afford to have narrow or simplistic conceptualizations of biofeedback or other applied psychophysiological therapies. I intend this constructive criticism as informational feedback for those designing and conducting research and for practitioners and others who rely on research to help guide decision making. This does not need to detract from the heuristic value of much research that constitutes steps in the direction of truth.

One can argue that manuscript reviewers, journal editors, book editors, and professional consumers are sufficiently sophisticated and typically are not mislead. Professionals responsible for what professionals and others read appear to take the position of caveat emptor, or "let the buyer beware." There is an assumption that most consumers can properly evaluate research and reviews. This is not the case. There is no question about the increased sophistication of much of the research using biofeedback, however, this is not uniformly the case. With no disrespect intended, it is fair to say practitioners need more sophisticated research.

Journals and professional meetings need to extend their efforts to help consumers understand and evaluate research and to place that research in conceptual and practical contexts. Typically, journal review articles and books that review the literature appear 1 or more years after the research has been published. Letters to the editor about research and issues appear infrequently. Some professionals might applaud seeing journal space devoted to editorial comments and critiques at the time an article is published.

The White and Tursky (1982) book is a good example to follow, in that it provides a useful "round-table" discussion of each chapter. This is a valuable and refreshing book, and one that journal editors and book publishers should consider more often.

We need to reduce the distrust of research that emerges among practitioners. Responsibility for reducing this distrust resides in both camps. I encourage researchers to be mindful of the potential impact on clinical professionals of what they conclude, state, and imply. Everyone should willingly accept data from good research. This is valid regardless of whether the data conflicts with our beliefs or our clinical practices. Practitioners need to remember that it is very difficult to conduct excellent and clinically relevant research. We also must remember that even well-conducted research usually represents only a limited set of conditions.

So what are we all to do? Garmezy and Masten (1986) call for reason when they urge professionals to realize that both clinical relevance and mutual suspiciousness "can be overcome when clinician and scientist share a common regard for the other's area of activity, and a recognition that there are contributions to knowledge each can make to the common enterprise, namely to understand human behavior" (p. 502).

I hope that more researchers will become more aware of and responsive to the needs of their clinical peers. More instances of experienced clinicians and researchers working closely together would be very desirable. Graduate schools and other research settings need to continue incorporating clinical consultations into their educational programs.

It would be encouraging to learn that clinical practitioners were enrolling in research courses specifically focused on biofeedback. Research courses in this field need to become widely available for both current students and practicing clinicians. Such courses would not simply review existing research, but would focus upon issues in conducting research, pitfalls, clinical and conceptual questions, and procedures for capturing the best of experimental control while not compromising the essence of clinical applications. Is this unrealistic or impossible? I do not think so. Researchers and clinicians can work productively together.

This chapter should not be interpreted as an attempt to discredit or minimize the valuable contributions of many researchers. All interested parties should read, study, and try to benefit from the existing literature.

Researchers, clinicians, review authors, journal editors, and this author all have biases. We often have investments in maintaining and supporting our beliefs. However, the above complicating factors need not deter us from pursuing our common goals. We desire and need to understand and make sense of what we read, see, and hear. We want to make useful, competent, and appreciated contributions to patients, colleagues, our shared knowledge base, and our professions. We need careful clinicians who are cautious in their claims and competent in their practices. We also need researchers and authors of reviews who place their views in a realistic perspective.

CONSIDERATIONS IN EVALUATING AND USING RESEARCH RESULTS

The focus of this chapter now turns to questions and factors to consider when reading, evaluating, designing, conducting, writing about, and publishing research. These questions are subsumed under the rubrics of therapists, subjects,[1] therapy, data management, and individual-subject[2] designs. The list is not exhaustive, but it is lengthy enough and broad enough to be of practical and heuristic value.

I also encourage readers to review the emerging literature on the Aptitude × Treatment × Interaction (A × T × I) model of therapy effectiveness (Holloway, Spivey, Zismer, & Withington, 1988; Dance & Neufeld, 1988) discussed briefly in Chapter 3B and the critique by Smith and Sechrest (1992). Briefly, this model proposes that there are interactions of the person and treatment that may account for outcomes. However, in terms of psychotherapy, at least, Smith and Sechrest (1992) are critical of this type of research yielding dependable interactions. They present stringent conditions for this type of research and propose that research that adheres to their criteria "uncover previously 'hidden' mean effects more frequently than interactions" (p. 558). Many readers will also benefit from Maher's (1992) guide to assessing research reports in clinical psychology.

Therapists

Competence

1. Who provided the therapy? Were the therapists and the investigator(s) graduate students or experienced clinicians?

2. What were the education, training, credentials, and experience of the therapists? Did the therapy and research protocol specify the various contingencies that arise in therapy? If so, then the present qualifications of the therapists may become more important. Standardized information about the qualifications of therapists would be of considerable value if available to readers.

3. Some researchers do have good clinical skills, characteristics, and experience. Some have even better skills and training than some clinical therapists. Nevertheless, failure to get a therapeutic effect or replicate one may not reflect a problem with the procedures. Differences may partly be related to different therapists. Thus, do practitioner consumers know enough about the therapists to evaluate the relevance to the practitioner?

---

[1]The term "subjects" also refers to patients and clients who are part of clinical research.

[2]The terms "single-case" or "single-subject" designs are the common terms. (Barlow & Hersen, 1984). I agree with Hawkins' (1989) preference for the term "individual-subject designs" and adopt it for use here. His preference avoids the implications of application only to clinical cases or the use of only one subject in a study. He also steers away from the term, "within-subject" because "it does not discriminate the design from a group design in which subjects in all groups are measured across time . . ." (p. 127).

Investigator/Therapist Confidence and Bias

1. What do we know of the investigators' and therapists' beliefs about the therapy? Did they have confidence in the therapy? Were the therapists required to conduct the research as research assistants or as a part of their clinical practice?

These answers are often unclear, and resolving them is complex and delicate. Investigators or therapists who are not confident in the therapy they are providing may communicate that indirectly to the subjects or patients. This can influence the style and content of the presentations to subjects and the way the therapist provides the therapy.

I am not advocating that only "true believers" conduct therapy research. I know the inherent flaws in this suggestion. However, consumer professionals often want information about the beliefs of authors of the research and reviews. Acknowledging one's confidence and support or one's skepticism about a therapeutic strategy is desirable, appropriate, and honorable. Disguising these beliefs is misleading and fosters misinterpretation.

2. Does the investigator, reviewer, or clinician have a reputation for pushing one viewpoint? Wise consumers interpret research and reviews in the context of the author's other research and the way authors treat others' research and commentaries. Bias is sometimes very subtle. Before making interpretations and drawing conclusions one should learn about the investigator's or reviewer's research program and other publications.

I quickly add that bias is inherently acceptable. An investigator or clinician without biases is probably boring and may be unproductive. The issues are the degree of bias and how the bias interferes with impartiality.

3. Has the investigator, reviewer, or clinician ever reversed his or her position? This can enhance his or her credibility. Did the individual do this based on his or her own or others' research?

Consistency of Behavior and Adherence to Protocols

How do we know that the therapists followed the procedures for all patients in a given condition? Therapists may depart from a standard protocol when a patient/subject varies his or her behavior in certain ways. Are there provisions in the protocol for contingencies that arise during therapy? Did the therapists follow the therapy protocol outline as intended? Did the therapist report the departure to the research investigator?

Rather than implying distrust, these questions recognize a normal and understandable human condition. Therapists and research assistants do not always report to their supervisors all that occurs. They may not regard it as important, or they may expect disapproval from the investigator.

Consistency might be a concern when the content of subjects' questions, comments, and informal talk differs during sessions. Therapists might respond differently to different subjects at different times. Certain of the following factors increase the chance of a therapeutically significant discrepancy between an investigator's plans, what occurred, and what the therapist reported: multiple therapists, the more the bias of the investigator is known to the therapist providing the therapy, or the more the therapist is dependent upon the investigator for support and evaluation, the busier the supervisor, the less supervision, and the less specified protocol with contingencies planned for.

Specific Therapist Characteristics

Is there a description of selected therapist characteristics that could affect the attitudes and behaviors of the patients/subjects? These include age, sex, race, credibility, anxiety, friendliness, and appearance. This is a delicate issue. However, many professionals believe that therapist characteristics influence patient/subject attitudes, behaviors, and outcome. The point here is that many practitioners and researchers reading other's research want and need reports of such information.

Subjects

Subject Preparation for and Understanding of Therapy

1. How prepared for the therapy were the subjects? There is widespread agreement among professionals that patient education is important. It affects patients' attitudes about themselves and the therapy, and it affects compliance. See Chapters 6 and 9 of this book and Schwartz (in press) for discussion of patient education. Some published research offers readers the availability of the patient-education content provided to the subjects. However, most studies report little or no such information. Readers often expect to know what the researchers communicated to the subjects, who told it to them, and with what modalities?

I ask that researchers at least summarize this information in the published paper and make the details of the patient education available. The absence of it raises doubts about the cognitive preparation. This omission makes desirable comparisons among studies and therapy procedures more difficult.

2. What evidence was presented to support the assumption that the subjects understood, accepted, and learned the patient-education content? Providing patient education does not assure adequate understanding, acceptance, learning, and mobilization for therapy. For example, did patients understand, accept, and learn the rationale for therapy and the procedures? Research that gives data about the knowledge understood, accepted, and learned will enjoy a better reception among readers.

Subject Motivation and Expectations

1. In many clinical and experimental situations, one independent variable may have no main therapeutic effect, however, when combined with another independent variable, the interaction leads to dependent variable changes. Rosenfeld (1987) refers to this commonly known observation. He points out that a feedback variable alone may not have an effect except when combined with another variable such as motivation. The feedback, when alone, may have no effect on physiological and symptom changes. He assumes that Green and Shellenberger (1986a, 1986b) agree that "both are necessary, and both must be present simultaneously to effect change" (Rosenfeld, 1987, p. 219).

Thus, practitioners want and need to know about motivational and expectancy variables. Indeed, many of the variables discussed in this chapter may be *necessary* for the "higher-order interactions" to occur. Consider therapist attitudes and confidence, patient education, the absence of other subject problems interfering with therapy, and specific therapy procedures.

Thus, what information is available about the motivation of the subjects toward learning psychophysiological self-regulation and reducing their symptoms? Symptoms are often sufficient motivation, but in some instances the severity or frequency is not enough motivation. There are costs associated with receiving treatment, even in research studies without therapy fees. Such costs include travel, time away from work and other activities, and the like. One must balance the severity and frequency of the symptoms against all the costs that can affect motivation.

2. There is also the issue of "secondary gain." Did the investigator assess the possibility of such variables among the subjects? Can we assume that the motivation of all subjects was enough to reduce their symptoms? Was symptom reduction more motivating than competing factors? Randomization helps control for this variable, but with small samples and individual-subject designs, competing motivations for symptom reduction may compromise the results.

3. Knowing about the subject's expectations about the therapy should be part of most research, especially outcome studies.

Subjects' Attitudes toward Therapists

Did the subjects have confidence and trust in their therapists? What does the research paper tell us about the subjects' attitudes regarding the therapists? These attitudes influence subject behaviors, but published reports often state nothing about these attitudes. Whether or not these attitudes affect outcome, to what degree, and under what conditions are empirical questions. These may be more relevant where therapeutic gains are minimal. In clinical practice, we often assume the importance of this variable. Thus, we want information about it in research reports. Standard methods for assessing attitudes toward therapists would be helpful.

Other Medical and Psychological Problems of Subjects

1. What information is available about the subjects' other medical problems? Papers often include this information, but when the paper does not, the reader and journal reviewer/editor should request it.

2. What information do readers have about personality and psychopathology variables of potential importance (e.g., depression, absorption, locus of control, self-efficacy, anxiety, relaxation-induced anxiety, anger, and interpersonal comfort)?

3. What information do readers have about subjects' time-use management? Examples are procrastination, perfectionism, being overburdened, and time wasters?

Discrepancies between Self-Report Records and Verbal Reports

Were there discrepancies between subjects' self-report symptom records and their verbal reports? Self-report ratings are a valuable source of data, but they have limitations. Many people have difficulty following even simple instructions. Bias can influence their ratings, and their interpretations of ratings also can change over time. Changes in expectation during therapy stages may influence ratings. What did the investigators do to enhance the subjects' understanding of the instructions for symptom ratings? Did the investigators assess and report discrepancies, and did they discuss and resolve them with the subjects? Baseline ratings help control for the effect of discrepancies. Reporting trends during the baseline period provides useful information.

Control of Relevant Variables

Were the experimental and control groups equated or otherwise controlled for potentially relevant variables? Many variables can differ among groups, including baseline and reactive physiological activity, initial responses to feedback, expectancies, understanding, attitudes toward therapy and the therapist, frequency and severity of symptoms, number and intensity of stressors, and use of caffeine and nicotine. One cannot equate groups on all important variables. However, readers still want the information reported and statistical analyses to assess their relative contribution.

Possible Prebaseline Improvement

Some patients show improvement after reassurance about the nonserious nature of their symptoms. Other patients improve when they expect therapy soon. Baselines do not always reflect such changes. Thus, were any of the subjects improving in their symptoms before the baseline period or before starting therapy? Was the baseline period representative of subjects' symptom frequency and severity before the baseline?

Therapy

Therapy Setting

The surroundings can influence the attitudes of subjects toward therapy. Where did the researchers conduct the therapy and how did the subjects perceive it? If one intends to generalize the results to clinical settings, then the surroundings should approximate common clinical environments. Congested or otherwise unprofessional offices are ill suited for therapy. If the therapist uses such an environment, then he or she should consider assessing the subjects' perceptions about the environment.

Specific Procedures

1. Subjects need opportunities to test their self-regulation under conditions that at least approximate those of real life. Patients must apply their psychophysiological self-regulatory skills beyond the professional's office. What were the procedures for transfer of training and generalization of physiological self-regulation? How did the researcher assess this? To make good use of the published research, practitioners need detailed information about this.

Specific questions include whether the researcher conducted baseline and feedback phases with (a) the subject's eyes open and closed, (b) in varied body positions, (c) during and immediately after stressful activity without feedback, and (d) during and immediately after physical activity without feedback.

2. Were the subjects alone or with a therapist during the sessions? Did the research assess whether the subjects preferred and/or did better under either of these conditions?

3. How do readers know that the procedures described were the procedures performed? This is a complex and very sensitive topic, and one not easily answered. How much involvement did the investigator(s) have in the conducting of the research protocol? How closely supervised were the therapists conducting the sessions?

This question does not intend to imply intentional distortions of procedures and data. It is a reminder that distortions can and do occur for a variety of reasons, and that readers should at least be provided some information about the supervision of the therapists. For example, did the investigator observe any of the sessions? This type of question appears suspicious and onerous, yet we all live with a variety of checks and balances in our lives. Practitioners make professional judgments based on research data, and insurance companies make reimbursement judgments based on such data. It is reasonable to expect researchers to provide careful documentation of the specifics of research protocols.

A related question involves deviations from the protocol. What were the provisions in the protocol for various contingencies that occur during therapy sessions? In clinical situations, one does not anticipate all events. Were there clear instructions for what the therapist was to do when such events occurred? Were departures from the protocol documented?

Did the subjects avoid certain activities before therapy sessions? What do we know about what subjects were doing and thinking about during sessions? This is especially useful if the subjects were alone and unobserved during physiological recordings. I realize that journal space is limited. Perhaps journal editorial policy could include procedures to evaluate these questions before accepting a paper for publication, and such information could be made available to interested readers.

Subject Application of Physiological Self-Regulation

How often did the subjects use the self-regulatory procedures in their daily lives? What were the durations? Were they using the procedures at the instructed times during their daily activities? It is not enough for authors to state they instructed the subjects to use the procedures in their daily lives. Documentation and reporting this information are desirable.

Symptom Records and Changes

1. How were the changes in symptoms assessed? Did the investigator or therapist review the self-report symptom forms? What questions did the subjects answer during and after therapy and in later follow-up? Results can differ, depending on the answers to these questions.

2. Research reports should discuss the instructions. How careful were the instructions for the self-report records? Were the records complete? Include information about whether there were data-collection problems and how the investigators managed the problems.

3. There are multiple criteria for significant improvement, not all of which may be present for a specific subject. Were the self-report records analyzed sufficiently to determine whether different subjects improved with different symptom variables? Using one criterion for all subjects does not always reflect significant improvement for some subjects.

4. Were the reported symptomatic changes of clinical significance? What was the operational definition of change of clinical significance? Was there a combination of criteria used? How did the investigators' criteria match the subjects' perception?

Physiological Data and Changes

1. What were the criteria used to determine whether subjects developed physiological self-regulation? Researchers and clinicians sometimes use multiple criteria.

2. Were the physiological data reported in enough detail for the reader to know what occurred in different recording conditions? Summary data are often not enough to give useful information about the psychophysiological activity during different conditions.

Cognitive Factors in Subject Preparation and Therapy

1. How did the researchers cognitively prepare the subjects for biofeedback and other self-regulatory therapies? What were they told? Look for details of the presentations. When lengthy, look for offers for making them available.

2. Recording and reporting the cognitive activity of subjects are useful endeavors. What did the subjects think about during the therapy sessions while using psychophysiological self-regulatory procedures? Did the study discuss the cognitive activity of the subjects?

Use of Cassette Relaxation Tapes

If the research used audio cassette relaxation tapes, then what were the details of the tape? Patients, and presumably research subjects, have different perceptions of and reactions to different factors associated with tape-recorded relaxation procedures, such as content, voice, and tempo. Practitioners should look for information about these variables.

Controls and Assessment

1. Patients and subjects often start health improvement activities other than those specifically recommended and checked by practitioners. Were the effects of caffeine, nicotine, alcohol, and other dietary factors assessed before, during, and after therapy? Examples of other dietary factors are vasoactive amines such as tyramine. These factors influence the therapy results for disorders such as headaches, hypertension, irritable bowel, and anxiety. Prudent clinicians and researchers inquire about such factors, analyze the data, and report it.

2. Were all pertinent medications checked and controlled for throughout the therapy and follow-up stages? Look for sufficient details about medications.

3. Were life events and daily stress assessed before, during, and after therapy? These factors can influence symptoms. Information about their presence, absence, and changes should be documented. Did the analyses control for their possible effects?

4. Aside from biofeedback and other methods of learning physiological self-regulation, what else occurred during the sessions?

5. What information is available about the occurrence and duration of periods of significant symptomatic improvement or remission in the past? For example, patients sometimes have periods of remission or reduction of symptoms during certain times of year (e.g. Raynaud's symptoms during warmer weather, and symptoms during periods of lessened work responsibilities). Long follow-up periods help control for such factors.

Other Research Considerations

1. Look for commonly reported information. This includes the number of sessions, age and sex of subjects, duration and severity of symptoms, randomized assignment to groups, sample sizes, proper statistics, and instrumentation and recording details. Also, look for acceptable criteria for single-case designs.

2. Did the investigator analyze differences between the subjects who were successful and those who were unsuccessful? This takes us to individual-subject experimental research.

Individual-Subject Experimental Research[3]

Individual-subject research should be more commonly conducted and accepted by journals. "One of the most difficult challenges for psychotherapy [biofeedback] research has been to demonstrate convincingly the link between what occurs in the treatment hour and

[3]Single-case research.

patient change" (Jones, Ghannam, Nigg, & Dyer, 1993, p. 381). The relationship between process and outcome is typically unclear with group-comparison designs or controlled clinical trials. Information from individual-subject experimental designs not available from group designs includes the direction, speed, pattern, and final level of effect on each individual (Hawkins, 1989).

A detailed discussion of the single-case research is beyond the scope of this chapter. See the special section of single-case research in psychotherapy in the *Journal of Consulting and Clinical Psychology* (Jones, 1993). There are implications for research in applied psychophysiology and biofeedback.

Hawkins (1989) describes advantages of individual-subject experimental research. It permits comparison of the relative effects of different treatments for each individual. Practitioners receive faster feedback on their efforts using individually graphed data. This feedback to therapists allows more information for therapists and chances to affect contingent changes in their behavior. For some therapists, "the more rapid feedback of data . . . leads to a greater enjoyment of and persistence at the tasks of research, at least for many of us" (p. 128).

As Hawkins (1989) does many times, I too recognize the special contributions of Barlow and Hersen (1984). They emphasize that clinicians need to know for whom, in what manner, and for what duration a procedure is effective. Hawkins (1989) and Barlow and Hersen (1984) assert that individual-subject experimental designs potentially allow more generalization of results to natural settings than does most group research. Practitioners appreciate the researchers using group designs who also report individual data. However, typically this does not involve enough of the unique advantages of individual-subject experimental designs.

Data Management

Data management and mismanagement are serious topics. Data mismanagement is faulty quality control, documentation, or retention of data. Deficiencies in data management, even those appearing as minor,

> increase the risk that errors and omissions will occur and can make them difficult to detect. They can also interfere with data sharing and with secondary analyses of datasets, render archived datasets inaccessible or uninterpretable, make it difficult to confirm that data faithfully correspond to actual results of studies, and prevent replication of statistical results. (Freedland & Carney, 1992, p. 643)

It is serious enough to prompt attention by major scientific organizations, universities, and congressional investigation. There are new regulations and additional proposed federal regulations (Office of Scientific Integrity Review, 1990).

Data mismanagement is not rare in biomedical research. However, there are no systematic studies of it in research fields other than in the realm of investigational drug trials. The full extent of the problem is not known, but there is anecdotal support for data mismanagement at least in less standardized research and in research with less adequate funding (Freedland & Carney, 1992).

The focus here is on "honest error" up to and including what some consider "negligence." This does not include the separate topic of willfully fabricating data and results, an occurrence uncommon in scientific research. Nevertheless, "negligence is clearly unacceptable in scientific research" (Freedland & Carney, 1992, p. 640). However, the line is often unclear between unintentional errors, omissions, and inadequate data management or honest error, compared to negligence or undue carelessness. Freedland and Carney (1992) refer to several references supporting the statement that researchers are accountable for careless practices and unintended deficiencies.

Even researchers well respected by peers can be unable "to reconstruct previously reported analyses of data from clinical databases . . . [and find it] . . . surprisingly difficult to determine which cases and . . . variables . . . [were] used, despite the fact that the original analyses . . . [were] performed with care" (Freedland & Carney, 1992, p. 641). However, these authors point out that except for Food and Drug Administration (FDA) auditing of clinical trials since 1977, "audit worthiness" is a higher standard for data management than required of most research until recently.[4]

For the above reasons, investigators, research assistants, and practitioners need to be conversant with this topic. Reading articles such as Freedland and Carney (1992) is very enlightening. Planning, designing, and conducting research all call for understanding the problems and pitfalls of data management. This is especially true with the use of computer systems. There are many ways that unintentional negligence can occur with data management. Some may view this area as intimidating. However, an awareness of common deficiencies in data management helps prevent such negligence from occurring.

I include a brief summary of common mistakes in data management. The interested reader will refer directly to Freedland and Carney (1992) and other references cited by them (e.g., Marshall, 1990; Office of Scientific Integrity Review, 1990; Racker, 1989). Interested readers also can consult experts including those proficient with computers and interactive data bases and statistical analysis software.

Reasons for data management deficiencies (Freedland & Carney, 1992) include:

1. Unintended side effects of technological progress in computers (e.g., statistical software that ends data management chores).

2. There are problems for computer users checking, documenting, and preserving their work carefully. It can be tedious, time consuming, and complicated. This is more likely to be a problem for documentation and archiving the data for future access, interpretation, and analyses.

3. Some researchers are unable to diagnose subtle flaws in statistical results or adequate documentation. This can be because of inadequate understanding of computer hardware and software. To achieve proficiency with computer programming and statistical packages usually requires considerable time and effort.

Also, data management is often very challenging and can be expensive, and smaller projects often have limited financial resources allocated for this.

Common Deficiencies in Data Management

The following is an attempt to summarize the text of Freedland and Carney (1992). The reader should consult the original for more detailed information.

---

[4]Freedland and Carney (1992) note that during misconduct investigations, the new regulations by the U.S. Public Health Service (PHS) and National Science Foundation provide for data audits by the PHS Office of Scientific Integrity (1990) and the National Science Foundation Office of Inspector General (National Science Foundation, 1988). In addition, there are proposals for routine or random audits by research institutions, funding agencies, and journals. These remain controversial and not yet widely implemented according to Culliton (1988), Institute of Medicine (1989), Rennie (1989), and Stewart and Feder (1987).

Documentation of Data and Computer Programs

One needs accurate and permanent codebook-type information in the data base, such as for variable names and subjects. Some software allows incorporation of this information with the data set. However, some software does not permit permanent documentation, or it stores the information in separate files from the data set. This can result in inadequate documentation of archived data sets. One can lose vital documentation from the original data base. This can happen from exporting data to another software package or exporting data to another computer system. Regardless of how careful the original documentation, translated versions may lack this necessary documentation.

Documentation of Analyses

Programming errors or "bugs" that do not violate software rules or other checks can escape detection by programmers and users of the program. Investigators do not always log essential information and cross-check statistical analyses. Thus, statistical printouts may lack adequate documentation, and checking may involve undetected flaws that are difficult to trace. One needs a hard copy of the statistical analyses. Otherwise, there is no hard evidence confirming the performance of the analyses. A hard copy permits others to review it.

A similar problem directly related to biofeedback involves real-time data acquisition and processing of instrumentation-derived data. With computer-based biofeedback, there is often no hard copy of the data before the analyses. Often there are no notebook records or documentation of the details of sessions. Filtering, composite data, and analytic algorithms alter the original data and can produce untraceable statistical results.

Multiple Data Sets

Limitations of some computer resources dictate dividing data among multiple data sets often linked by advanced data base technologies. One problem is updating and editing downstream datasets that do not automatically update upstream data sets.

Copies of Data Sets

The need for backup for data sets is vital and well known. However, there can be incomplete or unedited copies. Also, copies may not have adequate documentation. Thus, one might analyze the wrong copy or erase the corrected one accidentally. During the original active data-gathering and analysis phases, such problems are unlikely. However, months or years later, one could forget the intricate details of the back-up and data set copies. This would make further use of the data a problem.

Computed Variables and Subsampling

Research sometimes classifies subjects based on variables not within in the data set. An example is classifying subjects based on a composite of their scores on multiple individual measures. Another example is classifying subjects based on individual items within the data set. One needs to save classified and computed scores permanently to prevent losing them. Also, one should update the master copy of the data set.

When reviewing research, some practitioner consumers may wonder about the data management. The only sources of this information are the investigators and verification from journals, the latter of which does not yet exist. Journals could require verification and publish a statement to that effect as part of the policy of the journal. Such verification would be major step forward.

FINAL COMMENTS AND CONCLUSION

I can imagine some readers saying, "No research can possibly satisfy all these criteria." I partially agree. However, I encourage a concerted effort to address the questions and guidelines posed here. Practitioner consumers have a responsibility to ask these questions and the right to expect reasonable responses.

The research "facts" and "truths" of today are often the "myths" of tomorrow. Furthermore, even a well-controlled study probably contains limitations, and other investigators may not replicate it with different samples. As Rosenfeld (1987) summarizes his major point, "We can and must do credible scientific research in the clinical setting" (p. 220). Practitioner consumers often want and need information missing from research reports. Individual-subject experimental designs are desirable and may be necessary. Quality assurance for data management is a major necessity for researchers and practitioner consumers.

This chapter intends to increase understanding of research, reviews, and clinical reports and help increase sophistication and clinical usefulness of research. It intends to remind readers of possible pitfalls and of the needs of practitioner consumers and to stimulate productive discussions.

REFERENCES

Barber, T. X. (1976). *Pitfalls in human research: Ten pivotal points.* New York: Pergamon Press.

Barlow, D. H., Blanchard, E. B., Hayes, S. C., & Epstein, L. H. (1977). Single-case designs and clinical biofeedback experimentation. *Biofeedback and Self-Regulation, 2,* 221–239.

Barlow, D. H., & Hersen, M. (1984). *Single case experimental designs: Strategies for studying behavior change.* New York: Pergamon Press.

Carlson, J. G. (1987). Comments on the Furedy/Shellenberger–Green debate. *Biofeedback and Self-Regulation, 12*(3), 223–226.

Culliton, B. J. (1988, November 4). Random audit of papers proposed. *Science, 242,* 657–658.

Dance, K. A., & Neufeld, R. W. (1988). Aptitude-treatment interaction research in the clinical setting: A review of attempts to dispel the "patient uniformity" myth. *Psychological Bulletin, 104*(2), 192–213.

Freedland, K. E., & Carney, R. M. (1992). Data management and accountability in behavioral and biomedical research. *American Psychologist, 47*(5), 640–645.

Furedy, J. J. (1987). Specific versus placebo effects in biofeedback training: A critical lay perspective. *Biofeedback and Self-Regulation, 12*(3), 169–184.

Furedy, J. J., & Shulhan, D. (1987). Specific versus placebo effects in biofeedback: Some brief back-to-basic considerations. *Biofeedback and Self-Regulation, 12*(3), 211–215.

Garmezy, N., & Masten, A. S. (1986). Stress, competence, and resilience: Common frontiers for therapist and psychopathologist. *Behavior Therapy, 17,* 500–521.

Green, J., & Shellenberger, R. (1986a). Biofeedback research and the ghost in the box: A reply to Roberts. *American Psychologist, 41,* 1003–1005.

Green, J., & Shellenberger, R. (1986b). Clinical biofeedback training and the ghost in the box: A reply to Furedy. *Clinical Biofeedback and Health, 9*(2), 96–105.

Hawkins, R. P. (1989). Developing potent behavior-change technologies: An invitation to cognitive behavior therapist. *The Behavior Therapist, 12*(6), 126–131.

Hersen, M., & Barlow, D. H. (1976). *Single case experimental designs* (2nd ed.). New York: Pergamon Press.

Holloway, R. L., Spivey, R. N., Zismer, D. K., & Withington, A. M. (1988). Aptitude × treatment interactions: Implications for patient education research. *Health Education Quarterly, 15*(3), 241–257.

Institute of Medicine. (1989). *The responsible conduct of research in the health sciences* (Publication No. IOM-89-01). Washington, DC: National Academy Press.

Jones, E. E. (Ed.). (1993). Special section: Single-case research in psychotherapy (7 articles). *Journal of Consulting and Clinical Psychology, 61*(3), 371–430.

Jones, E. E., Ghannam, J., Nigg, J. T., & Dyer, J. F. P. (1993). A paradigm for single-case research: The time-series study of a long-term psychotherapy for depression. *Journal of Consulting and Clinical Psychology, 61*(3), 381–394.

Kazdin, A. E. (Ed.). (1992). *Methodological issues and strategies in clinical research*. Washington, DC: American Psychological Association.

Kewman, D. G., & Roberts, A. H. (1983). An alternative perspective on biofeedback efficacy studies: A reply to Steiner and Dince. *Biofeedback and Self-Regulation, 8*, 487–497.

Maher, B. A. (1992). A reader's, writer's, and reviewer's guide to assessing research reports in clinical psychology. In A. E. Kazdin (Ed.), *Methodological issues and strategies in clinical research*. Washington, DC: American Psychological Association; reprinted from *Journal of Consulting and Clinical Psychology*, 1978, *46*, 835–838.

Marshall, E. (1990). A clash over standards for scientific records [News report]. *Science, 248*, 544–545.

Office of Scientific Integrity Review, Public Health Service. (1990). *Data management in biomedical research*. Washington, DC: Author.

Racker, E. (1989). A view of misconduct in science [Editorial]. *Nature, 339*, 91–93.

Ray, W. J. (Chair). (1979). *Evaluation of clinical biofeedback*. Symposium conducted at the annual meeting of the Biofeedback Society of America. New York: BMA Audio Cassettes. (Audiotape No. 224)

Ray, W. J., Raczynski, J. M., Rogers, T., & Kimball, W. H. (1979). *Evaluation of clinical biofeedback*. New York: Plenum Press.

Rennie, D. (1989). Editors and auditors. *Journal of the American Medical Association, 261*, 2543–2545.

Rosenfeld, J. P. (1987). Can clinical biofeedback be scientifically validated? A follow-up on the Green–Shellenberger–Furedy–Roberts debates. *Biofeedback and Self-Regulation, 12*(3), 217–222.

Schwartz, M. S. (Ed.). (in press). *Patient education: A practitioner's guide*. New York: Guilford Press.

Shellenberger, R., & Green, J. (1987). Specific effects and biofeedback versus biofeedback-assisted self-regulation training. *Biofeedback and Self-Regulation, 12*(3), 185–209.

Smith, B., & Sechrest, L. (1992). Treatment of aptitude × treatment interactions. In A. E. Kazdin (Ed.), *Methodological issues and strategies in clinical research*. Washington, DC: American Psychological Association; reprinted from *Journal of Consulting and Clinical Psychology*, 1991, *59*, 233–244.

Steiner, S. S., & Dince, W. M. (1981). Biofeedback efficacy studies: A critique of critiques. *Biofeedback and Self-Regulation, 6*(3), 275–288.

Steiner, S. S., & Dince, W. M. (1983). A reply on the nature of biofeedback efficacy studies. *Biofeedback and Self-Regulation, 8*, 499–503.

Stewart, W. W., & Feder, N. (1987). The integrity of the scientific literature. *Nature, 325*, 207–214.

Taub, E. (Chair). (1985). *Problems in clinical biofeedback research: Is misapplied scientific "rigor" misleading the public?* Symposium conducted at the annual meeting of the Biofeedback Society of America. Aurora, CO: Meyer Communications Corp. (Audiotape No. BSA 85-22)

White, L., & Tursky, B. (Eds.). (1982). *Clinical biofeedback: Efficacy and mechanisms*. New York: Guilford Press.

XII

PERSPECTIVE: OTHER APPLICATIONS, STATUS, AND THE FUTURE

32

The Biofeedback Journey:
The Biofeedback Odyssey

Mark S. Schwartz

There are many ways to present the last part of this book and the opening and closing chapters. As with other parts and chapters, my goals are to inform, to stimulate, to encourage, and to maintain perspective. I allowed myself some "literary license" in the writing style to lighten some topics that might otherwise be tedious to write and dull to read.

In addition to the symptoms and disorders discussed in earlier chapters, the published literature contains a wide range of other symptoms and disorders for which biofeedback may be at least a part of the treatment package. The chapters that follow provide information for understanding and treating these symptoms and disorders. The intent is also to give impetus to the continued therapeutic evolution of biofeedback and applied psychophysiology. I humbly offer the next few chapters to support the continuation of this journey.

Many of these applications are at the frontier of biofeedback and applied psychophysiology. Many of these frontier applications rely only on case studies or a series of cases. Some applications are emerging from the frontier but still lack studies with the desired experimental rigor. Critics and skeptics may question the justification for including them.

Some historical perspective should help invigorate the rationale for studying individual cases and other applications that appear at the borders of this field. One cannot know if they represent a frontier opening into new and fertile fields, whether they are perched at a precipice, or whether they are at the edge of a wasteland. Those of us who started in this field about 20 years ago viewed all applications as being at the frontier or on a precipice. Now we have research support and widespread clinical applications for many symptoms and disorders. We have to start somewhere, and Neal Miller's (1976) guidance to "be bold in what we try" still applies today. We also must not forget or diminish the other part of his advice, "to be cautious in what we claim." It is with his guiding thought that we embark on these chapters.

Included in these chapters are discussions of symptoms and disorders, descriptions of subjects and patients, types of biofeedback and nonfeedback treatments, treatment information, issues, limitations, and implications. I assume that readers understand there are usually other possible explanations for the results in many reports. Other possible explanations include:

- Nonspecific effects.
- Other therapies or behavioral changes not known by the authors or not reported because they viewed them as insignificant.
- Cognitive changes affecting results.

- Misdiagnosis.
- Spontaneous improvements independent of any intervention.
- Natural progression of the symptoms and disease.
- Exceptions to the rule for the specific symptom and disorder.

When evaluating individual cases and series of cases, we should consider asking the questions raised by Ray et al. (1979). As they state, "even a tentative 'yes' to these questions seems to demand our future efforts toward implementing and researching clinical biofeedback procedures" (p. 90).

- Is it scientifically sound?
- Does it offer an attractive alternative?
- Does it lead the person into conceptualizations and life-styles that are more conducive to health and well-being?

One properly applies different criteria for evaluating the scientific soundness of cases and series of cases than for controlled group studies. One considers the heuristic value, other therapies tried and found unsuccessful, other therapies available, the seriousness or disabling features of the symptoms or disorder, and the expected long-term results without successful therapy. See Chapter 6 on intake decisions and considerations for further discussion of this.

THE BIOFEEDBACK ODYSSEY[1]

Homer's epic poem *The Odyssey* can serve as a metaphor for the past, present, and future of biofeedback and applied psychophysiology.[2] From the Greek epic, an odyssey has come to mean any long series of wanderings, especially when filled with notable experiences, hardships, and the exploration of new terrain. In the dictionary sense of the term "odyssey," the wanderings are sometimes aimless, nomadic, and even disordered. However, just as Homer's Odysseus was ultimately successful in his journey to reach home, the journey of psychophysiological self-regulation with biofeedback will continue to experience many successes along the path to full recognition. The Biofeedback Society of America (BSA) was entering its 20th year, thus completing one full generation of development, when I first delivered similar words (Schwartz, 1988). Twenty years comprise one generation or the average period between the birth of parents and the birth of their offspring.

Thirteen years then remained until the year 2001, the date of the famous book and movie *2001: A Space Odyssey*. However, our field does not seek the universality of something as monolithic as Kubrick's odyssey. Fahrion's (1983) wonderful image from his Presidential Address at the BSA's annual meeting in March 1983 stated, in visionary language,

> Biofeedback, in its cybernetic nature, is like the steering of a ship by a celestial navigator. Future directions of biofeedback depend largely upon the star selected by which the course is set.

The company of diverse, competent, and creative friends continues to enrich this journey. It is likely that these many navigators who set sail upon this sea will choose more

---

[1]Parts of this chapter addressing the journey of this field and the metaphor of the odyssey were taken from my Presidential Address in March 1988.

[2]I reverse the order only to reflect the emphasis in this book. The broader concept is applied psychophysiology.

than one star because of the multidisciplinary nature of biofeedback. Professionals in this field do not and need not feel limited to a single star. The wisdom and experience of many navigators enrich all of us.

The Journey Begins

The Biofeedback Research Society (BRS) was formed in 1969 largely by research psychophysiologists. My professional career at the Mayo Clinic Rochester started only 2 years before that. After 6 years the BRS became the BSA. This is about the same age that children go through the transition from home to school. Similarly the scope of our organization and the field broadened into applied arenas.

The Journey Continued

At age 19, the BSA went through its second transformation into the Association of Applied Psychophysiology and Biofeedback (AAPB). This is the age when many students graduate to institutions of higher learning. This organization returned to some of its roots in psychophysiology at the same interval. The consistency with the journey metaphor struck me, as Odysseus took 20 years to return home.

The Journey of a Family or Separate Journeys

All professionals in this field share some joint responsibility and custody for the young adult we call biofeedback and applied psychophysiology. Some individual professionals proceed on their own journeys and ignore their associates and traveling companions. Some seek their own destinations, their own *Ithicas*, instead of common ones. The AAPB continues as the leading administrative, facilitative, educational, and coordinating organization dedicated to integrating professional disciplines and conceptual frameworks that involve varied scientific and applied areas of psychophysiology and biofeedback. It is the nuclear family for biofeedback.

A Classic Idea from a Great Thinker

Borrowing from the history of the field of behavior therapy and Gordon Paul's vintage[3] question (Paul, 1967), I remind the reader that instead of asking whether biofeedback works, one should ask:

> *What* treatment, by *whom*, is most effective for *this* individual with *that* specific problem, and under *which* set of circumstances? (p. 111)

This idea certainly has enduring excellence and appeal. Middaugh (1990) recognized this and used this idea extremely well in her Presidential Address. She discussed indications for selecting rehabilitation patients when biofeedback would be suitable and useful. Her presentation is one of the best and one of the most understandable, logical, practical, and inspiring of Presidential Addresses. Middaugh's version of Gordon Paul's question is: What does biofeedback contribute to the therapeutic process? With which patients? When carried out in what way? In combination with what other techniques? (p. 193).

She added with emphasis,

---

[3]Lofty meanings of vintage include enduring excellence, appeal, and classic.

> *Does biofeedback work? The answer is "yes,"* if we have a good match between what biofeed-
> back can contribute and what the patient needs; *if* the treatment protocols are well devel-
> oped and carried out correctly; and *if* biofeedback procedures are combined with other
> techniques to fully meet the needs of the patient. (p. 193)

Of course, she added, "This is . . . true of all therapies and has been said before . . ." (Hatch,
1987; Paul, 1967).

One must read the Middaugh (1990) paper to fully appreciate it. I will not attempt
a summary here for it would become nearly as long as the original. Although I cannot do
the paper justice here, I would be remiss if I did not include at least one of her examples of

> the importance of looking beyond simple, overall findings of statistical "difference" or "no
> difference" to a more detailed examination of *which patients* are responding to *what proce-
> dures.* (p. 201)

Middaugh refers to the Whitehead et al. (1986) study of biofeedback versus behavior-
modification treatments for the fecal incontinence associated with spinal cord damage from
spina bifida. She participated in that study during her sabbatical at the National Institute
of Aging (NIA). I paraphrase from her description (p. 201).

Both groups received biofeedback, but for one group the behavior modification
preceeded the biofeedback procedure, allowing for a comparison between behavior modification alone and the combination. One-third of the 33 children became completely continent, and 64% reached at least the 50% criteria. Comparing the two groups showed no
overall difference.

However, biofeedback was statistically superior for nine of the children. These children differed neurologically and in terms of frequency of incontinence. They had low neurological lesions (L_2 or lower) and good rectal sensations. Thus, they had the neurological
capacity for sphincer strengthening and improved sensory–motor coordination. Their incontinence was twice or more a day. Their improvment was presumably the result of improved voluntary control of the external anal sphincter (EAS).

The children with lower rates of incontinence with an average of one or fewer episodes a day had neurological lesions above L2. Thus, they had very poor or no rectal sensations and hyperactive reflexes. Their specific neurological dysfunction did not permit
voluntary control. However, they improved with behavioral management of their bowels
using the defecation reflex.

CONCLUSIONS

These next chapters present several applications and give readers a sense of the scope
of applications on the frontier of the biofeedback field and related emerging areas. They describe many considerations for treating people with various conditions and disorders and derive
implications from reviews of the literature. Inclusion does not imply an expectation that
further research will continue to support the efficacy of all these applications.

These chapters and this book do not purport to cover all applications. One still needs
to consult other sources. One should attend national and state/regional meetings where
biofeedback is a common topic. For emphasis, I repeat that practitioners and researchers
would do well to continue to receive guidance from Neal Miller's words to "be bold in
what we try" and "to be cautious in what we claim" (1976). It is especially with this guiding thought that I proceed with the next chapters.

ACKNOWLEDGMENTS

This is a good place to pay homage to several fine professionals whose foresight gave further impetus to the biofeedback journey. Kenneth R. Gaarder and Penelope S. Montgomery provided the first edition of their useful text, *Clinical Biofeedback: A Procedural Manual*, in 1977. John V. Basmajian gave us the first edition of his classic book, *Biofeedback—Principles and Practice for Clinicians*, in 1979. William J. Ray, James M. Raczynski, Todd Rogers, and William H. Kimball presented an extensive collection of case studies and research guidelines in their book, *Evaluation of Clinical Biofeedback* in 1979. Robert J. Gatchel and Kenneth P. Prince gave us a scholarly and critical appraisal in 1979 with *Clinical Applications of Biofeedback: Appraisal and Status*. David S. Olton and Aaron R. Noonberg gave us their useful text, *Biofeedback: Clinical Applications in Behavioral Medicine*, in 1980. More scholarly and thought-provoking ideas came from Leonard White and Bernard Tursky's book, *Clinical Biofeedback: Efficacy and Mechanisms*, in 1982. Applications and useful commentaries were the focus of *Biofeedback and Family Practice Medicine*, by William H. Rickles, Jack H. Sandweiss, David W. Jacobs, Robert N. Grove, and Eleanor Criswell, in 1983.

REFERENCES

Basmajian, J. V. (Ed.). (1979). *Biofeedback—Principles and practice for clinicians.* Baltimore: Williams & Wilkins.

Fahrion, S. (1983). *Presidential address.* Presented at the 14th annual meeting of the Biofeedback Society of America, Denver.

Gaarder, K. R., & Montgomery, P. S. (1977). *Clinical biofeedback: A procedural manual.* Baltimore: Williams & Wilkins.

Gatchel, R., & Price, K. P. (Eds.). (1979). *Clinical applications of biofeedback: Appraisal and status.* New York: Pergamon Press.

Hatch, J. P. (1987). Guidelines for controlled clinical trials of biofeedback. In J. P. Hatch, J. G. Fisher, & J. D. Rugh (Eds.), *Biofeedback: Studies in clinical efficacy* (pp. 323–373). New York: Plenum Press.

Middaugh, S. J. (1990). On clinical efficacy: Why biofeedback does—and does not—work (Presidential Address). *Biofeedback and Self-Regulation, 15*(3), 191–208.

Miller, N. E. (1976). Fact and fancy about biofeedback and its clinical implications. In *Catalog of selected documents in psychology* (Vol. 6, p. 92). Washington, DC: American Psychological Association.

Olton, D. S., & Noonberg, A. R. (1980). *Biofeedback: Clinical applications in behavioral medicine.* Englewood Cliffs, NJ: Prentice Hall.

Paul, G. L. (1967). Outcome research in psychotherapy. *Journal of Consulting Psychology, 31,* 109–118.

Peper, E., Ancoli, S., & Quinn, M. (Eds.). (1979). *Mind/body integration: Essential readings in biofeedback.* New York: Plenum Press.

Ray, W. J., Raczynski, J. M., Rogers, T., & Kimball, W. H. (1979). *Evaluation of clinical biofeedback.* New York: Plenum Press.

Rickles, W. H., Sandweiss, J. H., Jacobs, D. W., Grove, R. N., & Criswell, E. (Eds.). (1983). *Biofeedback and family practice medicine.* New York: Plenum Press.

Schwartz, G. E., & Beatty, J. (Eds.). (1977). *Biofeedback: Theory and research.* New York: Academic Press.

Schwartz, M. S. (1988). The biofeedback odyssey: Nearing one score and counting (Presidential Address). *Biofeedback and Self-Regulation, 13*(1), 1–7.

White, L., & Tursky, B. (Eds.). (1982). *Clinical biofeedback: Efficacy and mechanisms.* New York: Guilford Press.

Whitehead, W. E., Parker, L., Basmajian, L., Morrill-Corbin, E. D., Middaugh, S., Garwood, M., Cataldo, M. F., & Freeman, J. (1986). Treatment of fecal incontinence in children with spina bifida: Comparison of biofeedback and behavior modification. *Archives of Physical Medicine and Rehabilitation, 67,* 218–224.

33

Irritable Bowel Syndrome

Mark S. Schwartz

Irritable bowel syndrome (IBS) is extremely common, probably the most common set of symptoms presenting to gastroenterologists, and often ranked close to "the common cold as a major cause of time lost from work" ("Irritable Bowel Syndrome," 1992, p. 1).

The reactions to stress and to experiencing emotional distress can exacerbate IBS. The relationship between psychological factors and IBS has much research support. However, this association may be most valid among patients seeking help for their IBS rather than for all people with IBS symptoms (Whitehead, Bosmajian, Zonderman, Costa, & Schuster, 1988; Drossman et al., 1988). Most people with IBS do not seek medical help and in this population, this relationship does not receive the same support (Drossman et al., 1988; Whitehead, 1992a, 1992b). Most of these individuals are psychologically healthy. Some reports show that most community people with IBS believe that psychological stress stimulated their IBS symptoms. However, other reports suggest more modest relationships. Nevertheless, health care professionals face those people who seek help. This group often does show psychological distress and a relationship of this distress to their symptoms.

There is an extensive literature for IBS treated by different forms of biofeedback, multicomponent psychophysiological treatments, and other psychological and applied psychophysiological treatments (Neff & Blanchard, 1987; Blanchard, Schwarz, et al., 1992; Schwarz, Taylor, Scharff, & Blanchard, 1990). The reasoning for these treatments is sound. Most, perhaps nearly all, medical patients with IBS have significant psychological symptoms (Whitehead, Enck, Anthony, & Schuster, 1989). Stress worsens bowel symptoms in about 85% of patients with IBS (Drossman, Sandler, McKee, & Lovits, 1982). The results of medical therapies are often not enough or are disappointing.

DEFINITIONS, INCIDENCE, FEATURES, AND MEDICAL EXAMINATION

The symptoms of IBS include diarrhea, constipation, gas, and abdominal pain. There are reports of 8–19% of the general population with IBS symptoms (Thompson & Heaton, 1980; Drossman et al., 1982; Whitehead, Winget, Fedoravicius, Wooley, & Blackwell, 1982; Whitehead, 1992a, 1992b). The Mayo Clinic Health Letter ("Irritable Bowel Syndrome," 1992) refers to "about one in five adult Americans" with symptoms of IBS although "less than half of these people seek help" (p. 1). Twenty percent to 50% of consultations by gastroenterologists have IBS (Mitchell & Drossman, 1987).

Restrictive criteria for diagnosis (Drossman et al., 1990, p. 165) are:

Continuous or recurrent symptoms for at least three months of:

1. Abdominal pain or discomfort, relieved with defecation, or associated with a change in frequency or consistency of stool; *and*
2. An irregular (varying) pattern of defecation at least 25% of the time (three or more of):
    (i)   Altered stool frequency;
    (ii) Altered stool form (hard or loose/watery stool);
    (iii) Altered stool passage (straining or urgency, feeling of incomplete evacuation);
    (iv) Passage of mucus;
    (v)   Bloating or feeling of abdominal distension.

Other similar criteria are useful to compare ("Functional Gastrointestinal Disorders," 1991):

> Chronic alteration in bowel habit (constipation or diarrhea, or both) associated with abdominal pain. . . . Looser stools at the onset of pain, more frequent stools at the onset of pain, pain relief with defecation, abdominal distension, mucus through the rectum, or a feeling of incomplete evacuation . . . the more of these symptoms present, the more likely the patient has irritable bowel syndrome. (p. 7)

The two sets are very similar. The first emphasizes an irregular and varying pattern of defecation at least 25% of the time, and the second set assumes a similar frequency. The Drossman criteria specify straining or urgency. The Mayo version notes that looser and frequent stools at the onset of pain are criteria for IBS. These symptoms can overlap with other diagnoses.

The symptoms of more serious disease can mimic those of IBS. For example, patients with inflammatory bowel disease (IBD) can have the same symptoms. One must also rule out colon cancer and diverticulosis. Physical examination, laboratory tests, examination of the rectum and a barium enema (BE) are normal parts of a medical work-up, especially if the symptoms have appeared recently. One must rule out colonic disease in patients over age 40 not previously examined. They need either a barium enema or colonoscopy ("Functional Gastrointestinal Disorders," 1991, p. 7). Common and recommended blood tests include a complete blood count (CBC) and erythrocyte sedimentation rate (Drossman et al., 1990). See these and other references for more information and guidance.

There are contraindications and risks for some tests. For example, BEs can "aggravate ulcerative colitis or cause a perforation" in the colon (Larson, 1990, p. 614). Colonoscopy can result in hemorrhage and perforation. However, the risk is very low. Physicians do not recommend it during "an episode of acute diverticulitis, ... [for patients with] vascular disease in the bowel, or are in the midst of an acute phase of colitis" (p. 637).

People with IBS who use and abuse laxatives can develop "*melanosis coli.*" These are deposits of brown or black pigment in the mucus membrane of the colon although not true melanin.

Prudent practitioners tailoring graduated multicomponent treatments to the patient recognize that one must distinguish groups based on the severity and nature of symptoms such as mild, moderate, and severe symptoms (Drossman & Thompson, 1992). About 70% of people with IBS have mild or infrequent symptoms with no disruptions of activities (Drossman & Thompson, 1992). Primary-care physicians typically see these people who have no major functional impairment or psychological disturbance. These patients often can attribute their symptoms to specific stimuli such as food, hormonal changes, or stress. The 25% of patients with moderate symptoms experience periodic disruptions in their activities, often show more psychological distress, and use health care services often. Gastroenterologists often see these people in their local communities. The estimated 5% of IBS patients with severe or intractable symptoms fear a serious underlying disease and gravitate to tertiary medical centers. They are typically not aware of the relationship with their psychological symptoms that are usually present. Their symptoms do not correlate with specific stimuli such as meals, activities, or hormonal changes. The implications and guidelines for adding and tailoring treatment for each level are discussed in a later section.

BIOFEEDBACK AND RELATED THERAPY PROCEDURES

Thermal biofeedback, when used, is usually part of a multicomponent program (Neff & Blanchard, 1987; Blanchard, Schwarz, et al., 1992). This includes patient education for teaching the relationship between psychological stress and bowel symptoms, relaxation, and cognitive stress management. The specific role of thermal biofeedback or other indirect types of biofeedback in the treatment of IBS is unknown. See Chapters 3B and 11 for discussions of how biofeedback, relaxation, and changes in breathing might help.

Use of colonic motility sounds, using an electronic stethoscope, was the first type of biofeedback used for IBS more than 20 years ago (Furman, 1973). Whitehead concludes that the other attempts to use this method (Radnitz & Blanchard, 1988, 1989) were not very successful with small series of cases. He concluded that this method produces "relatively weak treatment effects and the technique is rarely used" (Whitehead, 1992b, p. 69).

Rectal feedback from transducers measuring pressure from a rectal balloon was the basis of reduced contractile activity. However, comparison of this with muscle relaxation and systematic desensitization showed the latter to be better and more practical (Whitehead, 1985). Direct attempts to change colonic motility are not part of current practice.[1]

Relaxation therapy alone shows promise (Blanchard, Greene, Scharff, & Schwarz-McMorris, 1993). Although done with a small series of patients, there were significant improvements compared to symptom monitoring. Methodological limitations preclude confident conclusions. However, this single treatment component is worth considering in a stepped-care approach for some patients.

MEASURES

Self-Report Personality Measures

It is no more important to get self-report personality measures from patients with IBS than it is from patients with many other disorders. The attention to this here is for illustration. Consider the selected personality, behavioral, and symptom measures listed below.[2] They proport to measure dimensions thought useful when trying to understand and treat people with IBS. Research reports have used many of them.

1. Anxiety (e.g., *STAI, BAI, MMPI/MMPI-2*).
2. Anger (e.g., *STAXI, MAI*).

---

[1]Note, however, that physicians use smooth muscle relaxants, such as Bentyl, Levsin, and Librax, to reduce colonic contractions (Cangemi, personal communication, July 11, 1994).

[2]See Chapter 6 for more measures, discussion, and references. See glossary for full names of tests.

3. Illness behaviors (e.g., *IBQ*).
4. Depression (e.g., *BDI, MMPI/MMPI-2*).
5. Other psychosomatic symptoms (e.g., *PSC*).
6. Daily stress (e.g., *DSI*).
7. Multidimensional measures of psychopathology (e.g., *MMPI/MMPI-2*).
8. Symptom measures (e.g., symptom log, *POMS*).
9. Health locus of control (e.g., *MHLC*).
10. Assertiveness (e.g., *Rathus Assertiveness Scale*).
11. Attitudes and beliefs about illness and symptoms.
12. Obsessive and compulsive behaviors.
13. Careful interviewing and questionnaires about parental loss in childhood and sexual abuse.
14. Careful interviewing about psychopathology such as depression and anxiety disorders.

There are many reasons and uses for self-report measures. The following is a summary. Self-report measures can:

1. Document the presence of symptoms and dimensions that need attention.
2. Show changes or lack of changes.
3. Direct practitioners to areas to invest therapeutic time and efforts.
4. Provide data to patients about areas in which to focus therapy.
5. Provide cautions for practitioners to consider avoiding some therapies.
6. Provide cautions for practitioners for approaching relaxation and biofeedback.
7. Confirm or disconfirm impressions from interviews and referral sources.
8. Use in therapy sessions to discuss specific issues, events, attitudes.
9. Provide a basis for referral to other professionals, including referral for considering psychotropic medication and therapy for adult survivors of childhood sexual abuse.

One study suggests that some patients with IBS and an Axis I psychiatric disorder may not do as well with a treatment package (Blanchard, Scharff, et al., 1992). They refer to this treatment as "cognitive-behavioral," but it contained relaxation, thermal biofeedback, home practice, and cognitive stress management therapy. Of their 90 patients, 48 received an Axis I diagnosis based on structured interviews by trained interviewers. Nearly all (96%) were anxiety or mood disorders. The presence of an Axis I diagnosis correlated significantly with treatment results (–.30). Their data suggest that ratings of improvement are worse in this group. However, 14/48 (29%) of these patients reported acceptable improvement (50+%) according to the investigators criteria with the Composite Primary Symptom Reduction Index.

Blanchard, Scharff, et al. (1992) do not give their treatment enough credit. Their statement that "any diagnosable psychopathology would be a poor prognostic indicator for the kinds of treatment used in this study" (p. 649) is unnecessary and not accurate. We do not know enough about the specific anxiety and depression symptoms and diagnoses to accept that statement at face value. Nevertheless, this study helps justify the value of careful interviewing for an anxiety or depression diagnosis. One can agree these patients may need separate therapy before or with the treatment for IBS. However, the study supports the robust nature of the treatment by showing that many patients (29%) with these diagnoses can benefit from this treatment package.

Symptom Measures

A symptom diary or log consists of rating the severity of the common and major IBS symptoms. Points to consider when designing a log of IBS symptoms are:

- Compliance and practicality
- Symptom selection
- Rating system
- Frequency of rating
- Other data (medications, dietary, stress, smoking, activity)
- Consistency with published systems
- Avoidance of relying on global ratings
- Coexisting symptoms and disorders

Tailor the selection of symptoms to the patient in clinical practice. In a standardized program treating many patients and collecting clinical research data, practitioners will probably choose several and include all of them for every patient. However, for an individual patient, one can often select fewer—those symptoms that are present and of most concern. Some of the following symptoms are not specific for IBS (e.g., soiling, nausea, gas), even for those patients with diagnosed IBS. However, including them can sometimes have clinical use.

- Abdominal pain or discomfort
- Abdominal pain or discomfort relieved with bowel movement
- Diarrhea (loose or watery stool)
- Loose stool or more frequent stools at onset of pain
- Urgency
- Soiling
- Constipation or hard stool
- Straining to have the bowel movement
- Feeling of incomplete emptying
- Bloating or feeling abdominal distention
- Passage of mucus
- Bowel gas/flatulence
- Nausea or vomiting

Consider a rating scale with 0 = not present, 1 = mild, 2 = moderate, 3 = severe, and 4 = disabling. Define each term for patients. Some research uses 0 to indicate that the symptom was "not a problem" and 4 to reflect a "debilitating problem." However, this does not appear to allow for the clear nonexistence of the symptom. Furthermore, the term debilitating is a complex one. I respectfully suggest considering another term such as disabling. Certainly IBS can be debilitating (i.e., weakening, devitalizing, or enfeebling). A person might feel that way with severe symptoms yet not report disability in functioning and working. I assume that practitioners also want to know if the symptoms disabled or actually incapacitated the person. Ratings for IBS symptoms could have a 6-point rating scale for consistency with those used for headaches. Consider 0 = no symptoms, 1 = slight or not a problem, 2 = mild intensity, 3 = moderate intensity, 4 = severe, 5 = disabling or incapacitating.

Include medications in the diary, especially those that can cause IBS symptoms and those prescribed to treat some symptoms. Consider including dietary information (e.g., ingestion of caffeine, milk products, or nondigestible carbohydrates such as cabbage and beans) and information on other factors (e.g., stress that could affect IBS symptoms).

Another decision is whether to get these ratings once a day in the evening or multiple times per day. Increased compliance and less data to review and analyze are probable advantages of once-a-day ratings. However, recalling in the evening symptoms that occurred 12 or more hours earlier may be less accurate than obtaining ratings periodically throughout the day. Therefore, consider multiple ratings each day (e.g., early morning, late morning or midday, late afternoon or early evening, and late evening), and tailor the number and specific times to each patient.

Consider the *Composite Primary Symptom Reduction* (CPSR) score developed by the State University of New York (SUNY)–Albany group. One calculates separately a "symptom reduction score" (SRS) for two or three of the primary presenting symptoms. They used abdominal pain, diarrhea, and constipation. To get each SRS score, one subtracts the average symptom rating for a follow-up period from the average rating during a baseline period. The baseline period is 2–4 weeks, and the group typically used 2 weeks for the follow-up period. One then divides this by the baseline average and multiplies this by 100 to get each SRS (e.g., diarrhea reduction score, constipation score, and pain and tenderness score).

Then, one can assess the percentage improvement for the composite of symptoms (e.g., much improved = 75–100%, improved = 50–74%, slightly improved = 20–49%, unimproved = 0–20%, and worse = less than 0% or worse) (Blanchard, Schwarz, & Neff, 1988; Blanchard, Schwarz, et al., 1992). The *CPSR* is the total of the SRSs divided by the number of scores (e.g., 2 or 3). One adds the SRSs and divides this by the number of symptoms.

One can argue that this is a better way to assess improvement. One must have baseline and follow-up periods of equal durations, the time to do the calculations, or a computer program to ease the calculations. One could analyze the differences for each symptom. Ideally, practitioners will get pretreatment baseline data and also follow-up data for at least 1 year. However, getting pretreatment baseline data is not always feasible or is sometimes not prudent in clinical practice. Practitioners often need to adapt from the ideal to the pragmatic (see Chapter 7 for discussion of baselines).

Avoid relying entirely on global ratings. They sometimes markedly overestimate benefit compared to daily symptom data. For example, in one study 71% of the patients who did not improve their symptoms significantly rated themselves as quite competent in learning to overcome IBS symptoms (Blanchard, Schwartz, et al., 1992, p. 188). Global self-improvement ratings at 1-year follow-up showed about 70% improvement among 17 patients compared to about 35% improvement for the CPSR (Schwarz, Blanchard, & Neff, 1986). This difference is substantial. However, inspection of the table (p. 195) of the CPSR and global ratings showed adequate consistency between these two measures for 8 of the 14 subjects. Examples are 95 and 100% CPSR and global respectively, 70 and 75%, 46 and 50%, 100 and 100%, and 94 and 85%. Three subjects markedly overestimated their improvement (i.e., 45% global self-improvement [GSIR] versus only a –27 CPSR or worsening of symptoms; 85% global versus –266 CPSR or worsening, and 30% global versus –7 CPSR. Two others overestimated improvement but much less markedly (i.e., 50% global versus 24 CPSR improvement, 70% global versus 39 CPSR improvement). The clinical conclusion would not be as much of a problem for these two patients as it would be for the other three. One patient markedly underestimated her improvement (0% global versus 68 CPSR).

The lesson here is to use daily ratings whenever possible. Be suspect of global ratings, and do not rely on them. However, one can trust global ratings for some clinical decisions for some patients.

Using the same symptom log as those used in research from major research centers (SUNY–Albany, University of North Carolina at Chapel Hill, and Johns Hopkins) allows more direct comparisons with their data.

Remember that IBS is at least sometimes coexistent with other disorders (e.g., fibro-myalgia syndrome, migraines, chronic fatigue, mood and anxiety disorders). These could affect the specificity of the symptoms, compliance with keeping the log, and the accuracy of the log. This potential complication suggests the need for using less ambiguous symptoms and ratings.

CLINICAL RESPONSE AND OUTCOMES

A multicomponent program of 12 sessions over 8 weeks resulted in clinically significant improvement in some IBS symptoms for at least half of two small samples (11/21 and 9/14) and at follow-ups (Neff & Blanchard, 1987; Schwarz et al., 1986; Blanchard & Schwarz, 1987). The treatment components included education, muscle-relaxation procedures, stress-coping strategies, and three sessions with thermal biofeedback. The stress-coping component was to

> become more aware of their perceptions of and responses to stressful situations . . . . help . . . deal more effectively with stress situations by actively identifying situations that contribute to their symptoms . . . avoiding these situations or developing more effective ways to cope with them. (Neff & Blanchard, 1987, p. 74)

From the same laboratory, investigators conducted "five small-scale replications." They used the same multicomponent treatment program that consistently led to clinical improvement in 40–65% of patients with IBS (Blanchard, Schwarz, Neff, & Gerardi, 1988; p. 187). Clinical improvement means a reduction of symptoms of at least 50%.

However, in a more extensive sample of 91 patients (Blanchard, Schwarz, et al., 1992), there was no difference between their multicomponent package and "an ostensible attention-placebo control" group. Most of both groups improved significantly on several key symptoms. The authors' logical reasoning and data support the contention that the patients in the so-called attention-placebo group converted this into an effective treatment. This study reflects the complexities of treating people with IBS and conducting well-controlled and useful clinical research.

Further complicating interpretation of the results is the chance that this application of the multicomponent approach yielded slightly less successful results than prior applications. The authors raise this possibility themselves. They wrote that, compared to prior studies from that center, this study showed "relatively poor results with the multicomponent treatment. . . . [and there were] relatively high proportions of these treated patients . . . who are . . . symptomatically worse . . ." (Blanchard, Schwarz, et al., 1992, p. 188). They earlier reported only about 18% being worse in follow-up among 45 patients. Compare that to the present 29%. Also, the percentage of patients improving at least 50% is slightly less in this study than in their prior studies. In this study, they report 46% of patients improving (42/91 for the three groups and 28/61 for the two groups treated with multicomponent treatment). Compare that with the nearly 58% (26/45) reported in Blanchard et al. (1988).

One can argue that the improvements in the so-called active treatment groups resulted from expectations and other factors not intended as part of the treatment. However, as Whitehead (1992a) points out, the "maintenance of treatment gains for up to 4 years . . . argues against a placebo effect explaining all the benefits of the multicomponent treatment" (p. 607). The effect lasts a suspiciously long time for a placebo.

How can a person turn an attention-placebo experience into an active treatment? Blanchard, Schwarz, et al. (1992) discuss what their patients reported. For example, they used

> their meditation procedures to "relax" or "to calm" themselves, despite having been told repeatedly during treatment not to relax during the pseudo-meditation training. . . . Others reported adapting the meditative procedures as a distraction technique when faced with stressful circumstances, especially to focus their attention away from GI symptoms. (p. 187)

That group also warmed their hands significantly both within and between sessions as well as or better than the multicomponent group.

We must also consider that some patients make changes in their life-styles without telling their doctor, therapist, or experimenter. Their motivations for these deceptions vary. For example, when people come for treatment, they often read more about their symptoms and discuss their symptoms and treatments with others. They often pay more attention to factors they already knew or suspected would affect their symptoms but had ignored before treatment. They may recall information from articles they read before or while coming for therapy. This is all fine, but practitioners should include these in patient education and evaluations.

Some changes are too subtle even for some patients to realize themselves. For example, their expectations may change. They may notice subtle signs of anxiety, walk more slowly, breathe differently, and relax slightly more often. They may change eating and drinking habits. They may even get medications from another health facility. However, the point here is that an attention-placebo is often not an ineffective experience. It can be an opportunity for many patients to make therapeutic changes. Coming for therapy may become a discriminative stimulus that leads to healthier behaviors.

Identifying the active treatment components, the necessary components, and the sufficient components in a multicomponent treatment of IBS remains unknown. Relaxation is probably one active component (Blanchard et al., 1993). It is imprudent for practitioners to underestimate the potential value of positive expectations (Schwartz, in press). Other applied psychophysiological approaches are probably active and often, although not always, necessary.

We should appreciate the careful expression by Blanchard, Schwarz, et al. (1992, p. 188). Practitioners may rightfully embrace the recommendation for a treatment package similar to the multicomponent treatment for the treatment of IBS. These investigators base this on the replications of their results and the long-term durability of the effects. However, they do not seriously fault other psychological treatments, and they assert that this chronic and often debilitating condition often responds to psychological treatments focused on it.

There is other research support for applied psychophysiological methods resulting in significant improvements of IBS symptoms (see Whitehead, 1992a, for a recent review). One notable example showed that relaxation was more effective than conventional medical treatment for reducing diarrhea, pain, and the number of medical consultations over 3.25 years (Voirol & Hipolito, 1987). This is consistent with the results of Blanchard et al. (1993).

Assertiveness, patient education, and cognitive stress management resulted in significantly more improvement among 11 treated patients compared to a waiting list group of 10 others (Lynch & Zamble, 1989). When those in the waiting group received treatment, they showed significant improvement. Improvements continued 5 months later. One must limit generalization of these results because only 30 of the original 80 patients contacted agreed to participate. Furthermore, nine others dropped out of the study. Lynch and Zamble correctly acknowledge that

> it is possible that . . . persons with certain personality features, patients with illness behavior, and persons with more severe symptoms were over-represented in the sample. . . . are generalizable only to those who (a) are referred to gastroenterologists and (b) accept a psychological treatment rationale. (p. 521)

It is instructive that relaxation and biofeedback were conspicuously and intentionally absent from this treatment program. There are apparently other methods of applied psychophysiology that can help patients with IBS. A critic might raise the possibility that the patient-education and cognitive components are the necessary and perhaps sufficient components (Greene & Blanchard, 1994). These are presumably comparable between the SUNY-Albany and Kingston, Ontario protocols.

Attempts to modify bowel sounds using an electronic stethoscope comprise a more direct biofeedback method. However, the method is rarely, if ever, used in clinical practice. The only published attempt to replicate the original report of success with five patients by Furman (1973) reported equivocal results with their few patients (Radnitz & Blanchard, 1988, 1989).

Another direct biofeedback technique used a rectal balloon to detect contractions from pressure on the balloon. Visual feedback helped 14 of 21 patients with IBS to reduce contractile activity (Bueno-Miranda, Cerulli, & Schuster, 1976). A replication from the same laboratory showed that muscle relaxation and systematic desensitization-type treatments were better than the rectal balloon method (Whitehead, 1985). Based on that study and those by Radnitz and Blanchard (1988, 1989) and personal communications to Whitehead (1992a) about unpublished studies, he ejected rectal pressure feedback to the archives of biofeedback techniques for IBS.

PSYCHOLOGICAL FACTORS

Psychological problems probably are not a cause of IBS symptoms for most people with IBS. However, they may stimulate IBS symptoms in some people, and they may influence the decision to seek medical advice. The disassociation of IBS from usually or commonly being a psychophysiological disorder is a view of recent vintage. See Whitehead (1992a, 1992b, 1993) for recent reviews and discussion. Consistent with that conclusion is a study from England (Thornton, McIntyre, Murray-Lyon, & Gruzelier, 1990). Among 25 outpatients with intractable IBS at a gastroenterology clinic, they found only 4 had a psychiatric disorder. Very few of the other patients reported anxiety. This is a much lower percentage than 53% (48/90) reported by Blanchard, Schwarz, et al. (1992).

Psychological symptoms are often comorbid factors with IBS and often serious enough to warrent treatment whether or not they affect the IBS symptoms. One might not make a psychiatric diagnosis such as a depression or anxiety disorder for most people with IBS. However, this does not mean they are not experiencing significant stress in their lives. Remember, most patients with IBS represent a self-selected group among the population of people with IBS. Also, remember that many of those presenting for help do have psychological symptoms, and most believe that stress starts and worsens their bowel symptoms.

Even among a community sample of people with IBS, psychological stress may trigger or elicit (rather than cause) changes in bowel functioning and, to a slightly lower degree, abdominal pain in many people with IBS (Drossman et al., 1982). Among those meeting bowel dysfunction criteria, about 84% reported psychological factors affected changes in bowel functioning and about 69% reported them affecting abdominal pain. These are impressively large and attention-provoking figures. Even among those not meeting bowel dysfunction criteria, about 68% said stress affected changes in their bowel patterns. Forty-eight percent said it affected their abdominal pain. The specific percentages need some deemphasis because the studies need replications elsewhere and with different populations.

The effect of stress on bowel symptoms also is significant, although less so, in the research from the Whitehead group (Whitehead, Crowell, Robinson, Heller, & Schuster, 1992). They reported on a sample of 39 recruited women who met restrictive criteria for a diagnosis of IBS. The researchers selected the women from a large group of 383 women in the community primarily recruited for nonbowel dysfunction reasons. For those meeting IBS criteria and for the larger group, they assessed "life event stress" every 3 months for 12 months and bowel symptoms.

The correlations between stress and bowel symptoms were modest in both groups. A time-lagged correlation was .33 for the whole sample. Thus, they concluded only "approximately 11% of the variance in bowel symptom reports is attributable to life event stress" (Whitehead et al., 1992, p. 830). This suggests that most people who report stress as the cause of their bowel symptoms could be basing this on infrequent events. They could be misattributing the relationship because of much less frequently perceived associations. The investigators based this on the total of bowel symptoms for all the subjects and across all four visits for which there were data ($N = 343$). They correlated Life Event Scale data (Sarason, Johnson, & Siegel, 1978) for the past 3 months and the frequency of bowel symptoms reported during the subsequent 3 months. They repeated this over four quarterly dates for 1 year. Stress correlated significantly with disability days and health care utilization.

The authors acknowledge the potential for insensitivity of the stress measure. There are potential problems relying on life events reported every 3 months. For example, daily stress might produce transient changes in bowel symptoms missed when asking people to report on the relationship every 3 months. However, the authors point to the consistency of their results with other data from their laboratory when they used a more sensitive method (Haderstorfer, Whitehead, & Schuster, 1989). That method was keeping a symptom log of subjective stress and bowel symptoms four times daily for 1 week. They did this with community women and patients attending an IBS clinic.

Careful readers are cautious interpreting these percentages. The apparent discrepancies mean that different investigators, in different locations, using different criteria and measures, find different results. What first appears on the surface is often not what the core looks like. So, what else is new?

The importance of the lesson is that we must be careful in what we assume about people with IBS. This is especially true if we are in a general medical setting and seeing patients referred for reasons other than IBS. For many of these patients, psychological issues might not be a major aggravating factor. Consider extra caution in patient-education explanations about IBS and when discussing IBS with other health care professionals.

Remote trauma in childhood, such as loss of a parent, sexual or physical abuse, is more associated with IBS among some samples of patients with IBS than among healthy controls or other medical patients with nonfunctional or psychophysiological diseases (Whitehead, 1992a; Drossman, Leserman, et al., 1990; Lowman, Drossman, Cramer, & McKee, 1987, Walker, Katon, Roy-Byrne, Jemelka, & Russo, 1993). "Of 206 patients, 89 (44%) reported a history of sexual or physical abuse in childhood or later in life; all but 1 of the physically abused patients had been sexually abused" (Drossman, Leserman, et al., 1990, p. 828). This group used a standard questionnaire that may have some methodological problems yet probably yields some useful results. Asking questions about sexual abuse in the distant past is very delicate and fraught with complexities (see Chapter 6 for a discussion of evaluating sexual abuse). There are both the potential for misinterpretation of questions and the complex issue of inaccurate memories.

Nevertheless, many of the patients with IBS do report sexual-abuse experiences in their childhood before age 14 (e.g., someone threatened to have sex with them, forced them to touch the sex organs of the other person, or succeeded in having sex with them despite the patient's reluctance). The percentages of these and other occurrences of sexual and physical abuse are typically higher in adulthood in the Drossman, Leserman, et al. (1990) study. Patients are very reluctant to report this, hence practitioners "must actively seek this type of information" (p. 832). These authors acknowledge the preliminary nature of their results. No one yet knows whether this association occurs among people with IBS who do not consult physicians. Thus, the relationship to IBS remains unclear. One must consider that the selection factors that influence some people with IBS to seek help for these symptoms could include the history of abuse.

One reason for the interest in psychological factors associated with IBS (and for other disorders) is an effort to predict outcome from treatments. Such patient selection is not feasible now or in the foreseeable future, however, it is one potential use if the data became sufficiently clear and the treatments sufficiently standard and established.

There are, however, other uses of psychological data. Such data can help practitioners identify early those patients who might need more evaluation and attention in therapy, longer treatment, or other treatments. Furthermore, these data could help develop studies of special treatments for patients with poorer outcome from existing treatments.

Patients with higher trait anxiety, defined by scores of 41 or higher on the Spielberger Trait Anxiety Inventory, do more poorly with the multicomponent treatment than those with scores of 40 or less. This was counter-intuitive. However, the authors suggest that "it could be that the more highly anxious patient is in need of longer, or more intensive treatment" (Blanchard et al., 1988, p. 190). Other research (Blanchard, Radnitz, Schwarz, Neff, & Gerardi, 1987) concludes that a group of 20 successfully treated patients showed significant reductions of depression and state anxiety and more psychological changes than did 12 unsuccessfully treated and 9 patients only monitoring their symptoms. The proverbial "chicken and egg" problem exists here, too, in that one does not know whether symptom reduction lessened anxiety and depression or the reverse. Nevertheless, the authors expressed relief that those failing to reduce their IBS symptoms did not show psychological deterioration. Furthermore, psychological improvements did accompany success with reductions of IBS symptoms. Also noteworthy is the lack of predictive value from a wide array of potential predictors. These include many psychological measures including assertiveness, life events, other psychosomatic symptoms, depression, and standard MMPI scales. In a later study, these investigators again were not able to predict reduction of IBS symptoms from self-report measures of anxiety, depression, psychopathology, and personality (Blanchard, Schwarz, et al., 1992).

PHYSIOLOGICAL REACTIVITY TO STRESS

Of more direct relevance to practitioners using biofeedback is the question of increased or overactive physiological autonomic reactivity (see Chapter 7). Specifically, this usually means sympathetic nervous system (SNS) reactivity to stress among patients with IBS. A common example is cool and sweaty hands. There are several studies reviewed by Payne, Blanchard, Holt, and Schwarz (1992) that support the presence of this reactivity. It is surprising that until very recently the research supporting that belief relied on uncontrolled studies or single physiological responses to single stressor. Agreement now appears clear that

> an adequate study of the psychophysiology of IBS should include multiple physiological responses, measured under multiple environmental stress or conditions. . . . [and comparison with] a normal, non-GI patient control and a GI illness control. . . . to control for the potential effects that coping with a chronic lower GI illness might have on the patients and their SNS. (Payne et al., 1992, p. 294)

The conclusions of this study are that

> IBS patients had lower basal heart rates and the non-patients controls had lower finger-tip temperatures . . . . contrary to the previous body of literature regarding possible . . . SNS arousal states in the IBS patient. [And] . . . IBS patients were not significantly different than the IBD patients or the non-patient controls in their reactivity to stressors. (p. 293)

The reasons for the unexpected results are not clear, especially considering the confidence with which the authors supported the stressful nature of their stressors. The stressors were: mental arithmetic (counting backwards from 100 by 7s) for 2 minutes; negative imagery ("imagine yourself in a stressful situation, one which normally makes you feel tense and uncomfortable") for 2 minutes; and cold pressor for 2–7 minutes. The first two stressors are in common clinical use. It is common for practitioners to use protocols similar to this for stress profiling (see Chapter 7). Note that the IBS subjects came partly from advertising and physician referrals. However, we do not know how many came from each source. Remember, patients seeking medical help for IBS are often different from those in the community. We also know that the 44 IBD patients "were seeking participation in a stress management program" (p. 295). That might reduce the difference from the IBS subjects.

The physiological activity monitored was bifrontal electromyography (EMG), electrodermal activity/skin resistance, heart rate, and index finger temperature. There were no significant clinical changes in several comparisons of stressors versus baselines. It is unexpected and unexplained why the normal controls, friends of the IBS subjects, started with cooler finger temperatures (81° F) and cooled further to the second baseline (80° F) moreso than the IBS subjects.

One cannot make a convincing case for specific SNS reactivity among patients with IBS using these stressors for these periods and in this type of protocol. One could argue that longer exposure to the stressors and more intense stressors would yield more SNS reactivity. However, this must be compared with suitable controls. One implication from this study is that practitioners need to be cautious interpreting SNS physiological baseline data and psychophysiological SNS reactivity to cognitive stimuli. This is true for IBS patients and others (see Chapter 7).

OTHER TREATMENTS TO INCLUDE IN MULTICOMPONENT PROGRAMS

I hope it is patently clear that one should avoid relying exclusively on any single treatment for IBS. If fact, one may risk a malpractice claim to do so. Yes, I used the "M word." To avoid that M word becoming a reality, use another one. "Multicomponent" treatment is prudent and the standard of practice for IBS unless adequate trials of all other credible and proper treatments had been unsuccessful.

Aside from psychological interventions, practitioners encourage people with IBS to focus on eating habits. This is especially true when one suspects specific foods contribute to an individual's symptoms. This includes avoiding specific foods that can increase the risk of IBS symptoms or may elicit these symptoms. Eating on a regular schedule also can help. Overeating, eating too rapidly, or both can increase the risk of IBS symptoms.

If there is constipation, physicians and registered dieticians may recommend gradually adding fiber to the person's diet. My colleagues often start with natural sources (e.g., fruits, vegetables, whole grains, legumes) before trying supplements with psyllium (e.g., Metamucil or Konsyl) that some people tolerate better. Poorly digested fiber and colonic metabolism often lead to gaseousness and bloating (Drossman & Thompson, 1992), but this condition usually subsides over time.

Diarrhea often results from ingesting common irritants to the digestive tract, including nicotine, alcohol, caffeine, spicy foods, concentrated fruit juice (e.g., orange), and raw fruits and vegetables ("Irritable Bowel Syndrome," 1992, pp. 2–3). Bowel stimulation also often stems from fatty foods. A smaller percentage of people get abdominal cramping, gas, and diarrhea from dairy products. This is especially true for those people without the intestinal enzyme, lactase, needed to digest milk sugar. Some dietetic sweeteners, such as sorbitol or fructose, can cause diarrhea. Some medications irritate bowel functioning and may require dose alteration or replacement with alternate medications. Regular aerobic exercises, including walking, are also a frequent recommendation for those people physically able to do them.

Some people present with very restrictive diets. Consider rechallenging and evaluating the effects of suspected dietary substances to avoid unnecessary exaggeration of long-term dietary restriction and possible impairment of nutrition. An elimination diet for diarrhea-dominant IBS can help identify specific sensitivities, but it is a very complex procedure with arguable value.

In a stepped-care model, the above treatments are sometimes not enough. Wise nonmedical practitioners know and accept medications as proper and sometimes necessary for many, although not all patients. There are medications for abdominal pain usually prescribed for periodic symptoms rather than daily use. Similarly, medications including over-the-counter preparations may help prevent or control diarrhea. Some medications irritate bowel functioning and may require dose alteration or replacement with alternate medications. This approach might be all that is available for some patients. For example, a multicomponent psychological and stress management approach may be impractical or resisted.

IMPLICATIONS AND GUIDELINES FOR TREATMENT

The implications and guidelines for multicomponent treatment, the standard of practice for IBS, depend partly on the severity and nature of the symptoms. The graduated approach described by Drossman and Thompson (1992) is an excellent model with many useful recommendations. It is similar to but not exactly the same as a stepped-care model. In the pure stepped-care model, practitioners move through a graduated list or hierarchy of evaluation and treatment procedures. Each step depends on the success of the prior step. This assumes that one can start patients with the first steps.

However, in clinical practice, people present with different degrees of severity, variations of symptoms, and comorbidity with other conditions. The last includes psychological conditions. Patients also hold various beliefs about their primary diagnosis. One can start with different combinations of treatment rather than waiting to observe the outcome of each. Prudent practice usually involves a stepped-care and multicomponent approach and long-term follow-up.

In this composite model for IBS, I borrow from multiple sources. These include the Drossman and Thompson (1992) multicomponent and graduated model, a stepped-care model, and other sources and models. However, the major steps are primarily those of Drossman and Thompson with minor modifications. I combined education and reassurance. I changed the order of some subcomponents and added discussion of each step. Rather than listing them under the three intensity ratings, this design includes all steps and commentary.

This discussion assumes a medical exam for all patients with symptoms that suggest possible IBS. This often includes laboratory tests to rule out serious organic disease. Physicians usually consider either a flexible fiberoptic proctosigmoidoscopy (FlexSig), and barium enema, or fiberoptic colonoscopy if not previously examined or if the patient has not been examined in recent years. These help rule out organic colonic disease in patients over age 40 with symptoms that may be IBS. Physicians particularly consider these tests if the symptoms are new unless the contraindications and risks for colonoscopy or barium enema dictate otherwise for the patient. After making the diagnosis of IBS, the steps and considerations should follow the sequence as set forth below.

Start with Patient Education and Reassurance

Everyone starts here. Use highly credible sources in order to provide patients with information. Use understandable patient education to clearly explain the roles of diet, stress, exercise, and other factors.

Include the view that there may be physiological and psychological factors interacting to elicit their symptoms. Reassure patients about the lack of seriousness, but acknowledge the frustrating and distressing nature of the symptoms for them. Watch for signs of their concerns and fears and consider eliciting these beliefs. Include reassurance before and after medical tests that rule out other causes. Be careful and specific when discussing psychological factors and IBS. Include information about eating habits and regular aerobic exercises, including walking, for those people physically able to do them. Positive expectations should be discussed prudently and realistically. Instructions to make multiple changes, encouragement, and help making the changes can be common elements in successful programs.

Dietary Considerations

This also is for everyone. Practitioners encourage people with IBS to focus on eating habits. (See prior discussion in "Other Treatments to Include in Multicomponent Programs.")

Symptom Monitoring and Modification

Consider adding a symptom log for patients with moderate or severe symptoms. This may be unnecessary for those with milder symptoms. There are variations of the log. Most include at least the time of each bowel movement, the degree of diarrhea, constipation, and pain, and associated factors. One purpose is identifying, eliciting, and intensifying factors such as milk intolerance, caffeine, and stressors. Include information about eating, drinking, medications, and smoking habits. A log serves as another form of patient education, especially when it is used as a source of discussion with a patient.

The above treatments are sometimes not enough, especially for patients with moderate- and severe-intensity symptoms. Thus, consider the next steps. However, the next three steps are not always necessary and are not in order of preference. The sequence and combinations depend on health care specialty, practitioner preferences and skills, patient preferences, and financial considerations. They also depend on availability of time. The order selected is that of Drossman and Thompson (1992) who also imply no specific sequence.

Pharmacotherapy Directed at Specific Symptoms

Consider medications for many, although not all, patients. (See above text under "Other Treatments to Include in Multicomponent Programs.")

Predominant Pain

Physicians often use antispasmodic medications for the pain associated with IBS, especially after a meal. Anticholinergic drugs are commonly used in North America (Drossman & Thompson, 1992).

Predominant Diarrhea

Medications can decrease intestinal transit, enhance absorption of intestinal water and ions, and strengthen rectal sphincter tone. They can reduce diarrhea, urgency, and fecal soiling. Drossman and Thompson (1992) recommend loperamide (Imodium) because it does not cross the blood–brain barrier.

Predominant Constipation

Dietary fiber, coupled with adequate fluid intake, is a long-term treatment of choice for constipation-predominant IBS. Pharmacology, if used at all, is for short-term severe constipation. Physicians usually discourage continued or frequent use of stimulant laxatives. There are several compounds for constipation that are under development or investigation.

Relaxation, Biofeedback, and Behavioral Treatments

Consider the use of a variety of relaxation methods, biofeedback, and other stress management methods for selected and motivated patents. Consider these for some people with moderate or severe symptoms and when one expects or observes that patient education, dietary changes, and medications are not enough.

Although the mechanism(s) are not clear, practitioners assume that reduced anxiety and SNS arousal, and reduced tension in skeletal muscles, are important therapeutic factors. Practitioners assume that increased sense of responsibility and control and improved pain tolerance also are important therapeutic factors. Note that Drossman and Thompson (1992) refer to these procedures as "simple" and combine them under one heading of "relaxation response training, meditation, and autogenic training." Practitioners know that although these at times can be simple, they often are complex and require much more than sometimes implied.

Many practitioners make use of cognitive restructuring separately and as part of biofeedback. Biofeedback for some patients with IBS may be part of the encouraging and cognitive restructuring process rather than needed for the degree of relaxation achieved. For example, practitioners once thought that effective systematic desensitization required deep relaxation. Research showed that the treatment was more robust, that varying degrees of relaxation are usually sufficient, and that cognitive changes can explain symptom improvement for some patients. Tailor the multicomponent treatment to the patient.

Psychological Evaluation

This procedure is easy to justify for many medical patients diagnosed with IBS especially those with moderate to severe symptoms.

Relaxation Therapies

These are easy to properly justify. Various types of relaxation should be used to help people with IBS reduce general muscle tension and reduce autonomic arousal and dysregulation.

Biofeedback-Assisted Relaxation

One can justify biofeedback-assisted relaxation to help reduce autonomic arousal and dysregulation and to enhance patient confidence in selected abilities for physiological self-regulation. For example, thermal biofeedback is a logical and proper component of a treatment program. However, there are limits or boundaries for clinical practice based on the available research. There is not enough evidence to argue persuasively for always needing biofeedback to achieve improvement of IBS. Nevertheless, consider including at least thermal biofeedback. Consider other modalities that involve the autonomic nervous system (ANS). However, practitioners must justify them on logical grounds for specific patients rather than use research justification.

Avoid bowel sound and rectal balloon pressure biofeedback in routine clinical practice. Other types of biofeedback can be part of treating the fecal incontinence that sometimes accompanies the diarrhea-predominant form of IBS. This can help increase awareness of anal canal sensations and strengthen external anal sphincter control (see Chapter 24).

Be cautious monitoring SNS physiological activity especially in the selection of cognitive activities thought stressful and reactive, and in the duration of the stressors. Be cautious interpreting baseline SNS levels and reactivity (see Chapter 7).

Practitioners very knowledgeable and experienced with biofeedback will take issue with statements by Drossman and Thompson (1992) that biofeedback is "relatively expensive." It need be no more expensive than any office-based relaxation therapy or psychotherapy. Practitioners do not need to charge more because they use biofeedback instruments. The proper question to ask is would a form of biofeedback add something useful to the treatment of a specific patient.

Cognitive-Behavioral Therapy

This is appropriate for selected patients with IBS. Therapy should be tailored according to the patient's history, interview, and self-report measures. Consider assertiveness and other anger-management therapy at least for selected patients.

Hypnosis

Hypnosis has some reported effectiveness with IBS. Drossman and Thompson (1992) also separate hypnosis from relaxation and other behavioral approaches and from other psychotherapies. Research usually focuses on it alone and not in combination with behavioral approaches.

Time-Use Management

This is not part of the IBS literature. I include it here as another type of behavioral treatment. It overlaps with the cognitive approach. It addresses the time-wasting effects of procrastination, perfectionism, feeling overburdened, and lacking priorities for self-care, and also involves many other techniques that can reduce the effects of stress. It has implications for IBS and compliance with treatments. See Schwartz and Schwartz (in press) for a patient-education booklet on time-use management that includes multiple components.

Other Therapies

For some patients, the therapies listed above are not enough to reduce stress and physiological arousal. Some need marital therapy, child-management and parenting skills, and/or working through old traumas in their lives including abuse. This is a more expensive way to proceed. In today's health care climate, prudent and conscientious practitioners will reserve this approach for those patients who clearly need it. This approach is for patients with moderate-intensity symptoms and a few with severe symptoms. However, they usually are unresponsive to psychotherapies (Drossman & Thompson, 1992, reporting on Guthrie, Creed, Dawson, & Tomenson, 1991).

Recent research with time-series analysis of sleep disturbance and IBS symptoms the next day indicates that disturbed sleep "is associated with exacerbations of IBS symptoms" the following day (Goldsmith & Levin, 1993, p. 1812). Whether this is a direct or indirect relationship and the mechanism is not known, but the implication is that "therapeutic stategies designed to reduce sleep disruption seem reasonable" (Goldsmith & Levin, 1993, p. 1813).

Intensive Examination and Behavioral Treatment

Drossman and Thompson (1992) understandably refer to "physician-based behavioral techniques" for patients with severe or intractable symptoms. Overall goals include reducing maladaptive illness behaviors in this small but very disabled subset of patients. Including these can help the understanding of all practitioners.

Drossman and Thompson are both physicians, gastroenterologists, and contributors to a premier medical journal. I assume that they would agree that nonphysician practitioners can effectively be part of the team working with these patients. However, inspection of the "behavioral techniques" reveals that these are mostly "physician-based."

The authors focus on intensive medical diagnostic examination with carefully selected procedures "based on objective findings or observation of clinical features over time, or both, rather than in response to patient demands" (p. 1014). They stress avoiding repeated testing. They focus on realistic goals such as "improved function and quality of life rather than complete pain relief or cure" (p. 1014). Treatment decisions based on presented options become more the responsibility of the patient. Physicians, and increasingly primary-care physicians, show an ongoing "commitment to the patient's well-being rather than the treatment of the disease" (p. 1014). Avoid situations that facilitate or reward overfocus on symptoms (e.g., organ recital).

Psychopharmacological Treatment

Some patients with severe or intractable symptoms might benefit from antidepressants or other psychopharmacological treatments (Drossman & Thompson, 1992).

Specific Pain-Management Treatment

When all else is insufficient and the disability continues to be severe, Drossman and Thompson (1992) speculate that an interdisciplinary pain-management program might help as it reportedly helped a group of pelvic pain patients (Kames, Rapkin, Naliboff, Affi, & Ferrer-Brechner, 1990).

GLOSSARY

BARIUM ENEMAS. Barium enemas and X-rays are used in the diagnosis of colon cancer, Crohn's disease, ulcerative colitis, and polyps. A barium enema allows better viewing of the lining of the rectum, colon, and the end of the small bowel (ilium).

COGNITIVE RESTRUCTURING. Usually thought of as one type of cognitive-behavioral therapy in which a person learns new expectancies and new techniques to view himself or herself, others, and events.

COLONIC MOTILITY SOUNDS. Sounds that can be heard with an *electronic stethoscope*. The first type of biofeedback used for IBS, but no longer used.

COLONOSCOPY, FIBEROPTIC. The use of a fiberoptic endoscope, a flexible instrument that transmits light, to allow examination of the colon lining from the anus to the junction (cecum) of the large and small intestines.

COMORBID. Existing together. Indicates that two or more conditions or disorders exist together.

COMPLETE BLOOD COUNT (CBC). Most common and basic blood test. Indications include a screen for possible systemic diseases including suspected hematological (e.g., anemia, leukemia) and infectious diseases. (See Chapters 14 and 15 for a more detailed definition.)

COMPOSITE PRIMARY SYMPTOM REDUCTION INDEX. See *Composite Primary Symptom Reduction.*

COMPOSITE PRIMARY SYMPTOM REDUCTION (CPSR). One calculates separately a *Symptom Reduction Score* (SRS) for two or three of the primary presenting symptoms such as abdominal pain, diarrhea, and constipation. To get each SRS, one subtracts the average symptom rating for a follow-up period from the average rating during a baseline period. The baseline period is 2 to 4 weeks and typically 2 weeks for the follow-up period. Then, one divides this by the baseline average and multiplies by 100 to get the SRS (e.g., Diarrhea Reduction Score). The CPSR is the total of the SRSs divided by the number of scores (e.g., two or three). Developed by the SUNY–Albany group.

CROHN'S DISEASE (ILEITIS OR REGIONAL ENTERITIS). A relatively rare chronic inflammation of the intestine that most commonly affects the lower part of the small intestine (ileum) and often the colon but may also occur in other parts of the entire GI tract. Symptoms include chronic diarrhea, abdominal cramping, pain around the navel or right side of abdomen, low-grade fever, fatigue, anorexia and weight loss, joint pain, and skin lesions.

DISCRIMINATIVE STIMULUS (S^D). A specific condition when reinforcement of a behavior occurs, in comparison to other conditions (stimuli). It is not the common language use of discriminate or distinguish, which focuses on the person discriminating. The S^D refers to properties of the stimulus.

ERYTHROCYTE SEDIMENTATION RATE (SED RATE). Blood test measuring "the rate at which red blood cells settle to the bottom of a container. If the cells settle faster than normal, this can suggest an infection, anemia, inflammation, rheumatoid arthritis, rheumatic fever, or one of several types of cancer" (Larson, 1990, p. 1283).

FLEXIBLE FIBEROPTIC PROCTOSIGMOIDOSCOPY (FLEXSIG). Examining the lower part of the colon (sigmoid) and rectum using a flexible lighted tube. One can see nearly 50% of colorectal cancers or polyps with a FlexSig. Also used in diagnosing Crohn's disease and ulcerative colitis. One can get samples of tissue through this instrument.

GLOBAL RATINGS (Also Subjective Global Estimate; see Chapters 14 and 15). A patient's estimate of his or her symptoms without using a specific rating scale or procedure. Often refers to retrospective estimates (e.g., "I feel 50% better," "The diarrhea is 50% better"). Often not an accurate measure of symptom change, especially compared to using a reliable rating scale.

INFLAMMATORY BOWEL DISEASE (IBD). Inflamatory bowel disorders with overlapping findings but no definite cause. Usually refers to Crohn's disease and ulcerative colitis. The term "colitis" should be applied only to inflammatory disease of the colon. The term "spastic colitis" or "spastic colon" is a misnomer for IBD. It is an old and outdated term for a functional disorder as IBS.

LIFE EXPERIENCE SURVEY. Sarason's (Sarason, Johnson, & Siegel, 1978) modification of the Holmes and Rahe (1967) life experience scale (LES). Uses different life events and a 6-point scale with positive to negative ratings.

MELANOSIS COLI. Deposits of brown or black pigment in the mucous membrane of the colon; not true melanin.

SYMPATHETIC NERVOUS SYSTEM REACTIVITY (SNS REACTIVITY). The SNS is a subdivision of the autonomic nervous system whose fibers arise from the thoracic and lumbar regions of the spinal cord.

SYSTEMATIC DESENSITIZATION. A common and highly successful type of behavioral therapy for fear and phobia responses. There is gradual exposure for very limited periods from the least anxiety-producing to increasingly anxiety-producing. Exposures usually occur with relaxation. Exposure is imagined, with artificial stimuli (e.g., pictures, video; known as in vitro) and/or with real-life stimuli (known as in vivo). (See Chapters 7, 18.)

TESTS/MEASURES, SELF-REPORT.

STAI: State–Trait Anxiety Inventory
BAI: Beck Anxiety Inventory
BDI: Beck Depression Inventory
MMPI/MMPI-2: Minnesota Multiphasic Personality Inventory
STAXI: State–Trait Anger eXpression Inventory
MAI: Multidimensional Anger Inventory
IBQ: Illness Behavior Questionnaire
BDI: Beck Depression Inventory
PSC: Psychosomatic Checklist
DSI: Daily Stress Inventory
POMS: Profile of Mood States
MHLC: Multidimensional Health Locus of Control
Rathus Assertiveness Scale

ULCERATIVE COLITIS. A chronic inflammatory disease in the colon, contrasted with Crohn's, which can be anywhere in the GI tract. Signs and symptoms most often include bloody diarrhea. Others are abdominal pain, urgent bowel movements with pain, fever, weight loss, joint pain, and skin lesions.

ACKNOWLEDGMENT

I am very thankful to gastroenterologist, John R. Cangemi, M.D., of Mayo Clinic Jacksonville, for his review of this chapter. His comments and suggestions were very helpful. This appreciation does not imply his endorsement of the content of this chapter.

REFERENCES

Blanchard, E. B., Greene, B., Scharff, L., & Schwarz-McMorris, S. P. (1993). Relaxation training as a treatment for irritable bowel syndrome. *Biofeedback and Self-Regulation, 18*(3), 125–132.

Blanchard, E. B., Radnitz, C., Schwarz, S. P., Neff, D. F., & Gerardi, M. A. (1987). Psychological changes associated with self-regulatory treatments in irritable bowel syndrome. *Biofeedback and Self-Regulation, 12*(1), 31–37.

Blanchard, E. B., Scharff, L., Payne, A., Schwarz, S. P., Suls, J. M., & Malamood, H. (1992). Prediction of outcome from cognitive-behavioral treatment of irritable bowel syndrome. *Behaviour Research and Therapy, 30*(6), 647–650.

Blanchard, E. B., & Schwarz, S. P. (1987). Adaptation of a multicomponent treatment for irritable bowel syndrome to a small-group format. *Biofeedback and Self-Regulation, 12*(1), 63–69.

Blanchard, E. B., Schwarz, S. P., & Neff, D. F. (1988). Two-year follow up behavioral treatment of irritable bowel syndrome. *Behavior Therapy, 19*, 67–73.

Blanchard, E. B., Schwarz, S. P., Neff, D. F., & Gerardi, M. A. (1988). Prediction of outcome from the self-regulatory treatment of irritable bowel syndrome. *Behaviour Research and Therapy, 26*(2), 187–190.

Blanchard, E. B., Schwarz, S. P., Suls, J. M., Gerardi, M. A., Scharff, L., Greene, B., Taylor, A. E., Berreman, C., & Malamood, H. S. (1992). Two controlled evaluations of multicomponent psychological treatment of irritable bowel syndrome. *Behaviour Research and Therapy, 30*(2), 175–189.

Bueno-Miranda, F., Cerulli, M., & Schuster, M. M. (1976). Operant conditioning of colonic motility in irritable bowel syndrome (IBS) (Abstract). *Gastroenterology, 91*, A867.

Drossman, D. A., Leserman, J., Nachman, G., Li, Z., Gluck, H., Toomey, T. C., & Mitchell, C. M. (1990). Sexual and physical abuse in women with functional or organic gastrointestinal disorders. *Annals of Internal Medicine, 113*, 828–833.

Drossman, D. A., McKee, D. C., Sandler, R. S., Mitchell, M., Cramer, E. M., Lowman, B. C., & Burger, A. L. (1988). Psychosocial factors in the irritable bowel syndrome. *Gastroenterology, 95*, 701–708.

Drossman, D. A., Sandler, R. S., McKee, D. C., & Lovitz, A. J. (1982). Bowel patterns among subjects not seeking health care. *Gastroenterology, 83*, 529–534.

Drossman, D. A., & Thompson, W. G. (1992). The irritable bowel syndrome: Review and a graduated multicomponent treatment approach. *Annals of Internal Medicine, 116*(12, pt 1), 1009–1016.

Drossman, D. A., Thompson, W. G., Talley, N. J., Funch-Jensen, P., Janssens, J., & Whitehead, W. E. (1990). Identification of subgroups of functional gastrointestinal disorders. *Gastroenterology International, 3*(4), 159–172.

Functional gastrointestinal disorders. (1991, Winter). *Mayo Clinical Update, 7*, 7–8.

Furman, S. (1973). Intestinal biofeedback in functional diarrhea: A preliminary report. *Journal of Behavior Therapy and Experimental Psychiatry, 4*, 317–321.

Goldsmith, G., & Levin, J. S. (1993). Effect of sleep quality on symptoms of irritable bowel syndrome. *Digestive Diseases and Sciences, 38*(10), 1809–1814.

Greene, B., & Blanchard, E. B. (1994). Cognitive therapy for irritable bowel syndrome. *Journal of Consulting and Clinical Psychology, 62*(3), 576–582.

Guthrie, E., Creed, F., Dawson, D., & Tomenson, B. (1991). A controlled trial of psychological treatment for the irritable bowel syndrome. *Gastroenterology, 100*, 450–457.

Haderstorfer, B., Whitehead, W. E., & Schuster, M. M. (1989). Intestinal gas production from bacterial fermentation of undigested carbohydrate in irritable bowel syndrome. *American Journal of Gastroenterology, 84*, 375–378.

Irritable bowel syndrome. (1992). *Mayo Clinic Health Letter, 10*(12), 1–2.

Kames, L. D., Rapkin, A. J., Naliboff, B. D., Affi, S., Ferrer-Brechner, T. (1990). Effectiveness of an interdisciplinary pain management program for the treatment of chronic pelvic pain. *Pain, 41*, 41–46.

Larson, D. E. (1990). *Mayo Clinic family health book.* New York: William Morrow.

Lowman, B. C., Drossman, D. A., Cramer, E. M., & McKee, D. C. (1987). Recollection of childhood events in adults with irritable bowel syndrome. *Journal of Clinical Gastroenterology, 9*, 325–330.

Lynch, P. M., & Zamble, E. (1989). A controlled behavioral treatment study of irritable bowel syndrome. *Behavior Therapy, 20*, 509–523.

Mitchell, C. M., & Drossman, D. A. (1987). Survey of the AGA membership relating to patients with functional gastrointestinal disorders. *Gastroenterology, 92*, 1228–1245.

Neff, D. F., & Blanchard, E. B. (1987). A multi-component treatment for irritable bowel syndrome. *Behavior Therapy, 18*, 70–83.

Payne, A., Blanchard, E. B., Holt, C. S., & Schwarz, S. (1992). Physiological reactivity to stressors in irritable bowel syndrome patients, inflammatory bowel disease patients and non-patient controls. *Behaviour Research and Therapy, 30*(3), 293–300.

Radnitz, C. L., & Blanchard, E. B. (1988). Bowel sound biofeedback as a treatment for irritable bowel syndrome. *Biofeedback and Self-Regulation, 13*(2), 169–179.

Radnitz, C. L., & Blanchard, E. B. (1989). A 1- and 2-year follow-up study of bowel sound biofeedback as a treatment for irritable bowel syndrome. *Biofeedback and Self-Regulation, 14*(4), 333–338.

Sarason, J. G., Johnson, J. H., & Siegel, J. M. (1978). Assessing the impact of life changes: Development of the life experiences survey. *Journal of Consulting and Clinical Psychology, 46*, 932–946.

Schwartz, M. S. (Ed.). (in press). *Patient education: A practitioner's guide.* New York: Guilford Press.

Schwartz, M. S., & Schwartz, N. M. (in press). Time use management: A patient education manual. In M. S. Schwartz (Ed.), *Patient education: A practitioner's guide.* New York: Guilford Press.

Schwarz, S. P., Blanchard, E. B., & Neff, D. (1986). Behavior treatment of irritable bowel syndrome: A 1-year follow-up study. *Biofeedback and Self-Regulation, 11*(3), 189–198.

Schwarz, S. P., Taylor, A. E., Scharff, L., & Blanchard, E. B. (1990). Behaviorally treated irritable bowel syndrome patients: A four-year follow-up. *Behaviour Research and Therapy, 28*(4), 331–335.

Thompson, W. G., & Heaton, R. W. (1980). Functional bowel disorders in apparently healthy people. *Gastroenterology, 79*, 283–288.

Thornton, S., McIntyre, P., Murray-Lyon, I., & Gruzelier, J. (1990). Psychological and psychophysiological characteristics in irritable bowel syndrome. *British Journal of Clinical Psychology, 29*, 343–345.

Voirol, M. W., & Hipolito, J. (1987). Relaxation antropoanalytique dans les syndromes de l'intestin irritable: Résultats à 40 mois. *Schweizerische Medizinische Wochenschrift, 117*, 1117–1119.

Walker, E. A., Katon, W. J., Roy-Byrne, P. P., Jemelka, R. P., & Russo, J. (1993). Histories of sexual victimization in patients with irritable bowel syndrome or inflammatory bowel disease. *American Journal of Psychiatry, 150*, 1502–1506.

Whitehead, W. (1985). Psychotherapy and biofeedback in the treatment of irritable bowel syndrome. In N. E. Read (Ed.), *Irritable bowel syndrome* (pp. 245–266). London: Grune & Stratton.

Whitehead, W. E. (1992a). Behavioral medicine approaches to gastrointestinal disorders. *Journal of Consulting and Clinical Psychology, 60*(4), 605–612.

Whitehead, W. E. (1992b). Biofeedback treatment of gastrointestinal disorders. *Biofeedback and Self-Regulation, 17*(1), 59–76.

Whitehead, W. E. (1993). Gut feelings: Stress and the GI tract. In D. Goleman & J. Gurin (Eds.), *Mind/body medicine* (pp. 161–175). New York: Consumer Reports Books.

Whitehead, W. E., Bosmajian, L., Zonderman, A. B., Costa, P. T., & Schuster, M. M. (1988). Symptoms of psychological distress associated with irritable bowel syndrome. *Gastroenterology, 95*, 709–714.

Whitehead, W. E., Crowell, M. D., Robinson, J. C., Heller, B. R., & Schuster, M. M. (1992). Effects of stressful life events on bowel symptoms: Subjects with irritable bowel syndrome compared with subjects without bowel dysfunction. *Gut, 33*, 825–830.

Whitehead, W. E., Enck, P., Anthony, J. C., & Schuster, M. M. (1989). Psychopathology in patients with irritable bowel syndrome. In M. V. Singer & H. Goebell (Eds.), *Nerves and the gastrointestinal tract*. Lancaster, UK: Falk Symposium 50.

Whitehead, W. E., Winget, C., Fedoravicius, A. S., Wooley, S., & Blackwell, B. (1982). Learned illness behavior in patients with irritable bowel syndrome and peptic ulcer. *Digestive Diseases and Sciences, 27*, 202–208.

34

Tinnitus: Nothing Is as Loud as a Sound You Are Trying Not to Hear

Mark S. Schwartz

Subjective tinnitus (ST) is the perception of auditory sensations audible only to the patient. This subjective hearing of sounds without an external source is a problem of surprisingly deafening proportions. Management of tinnitus is a challenge. Most patients report only minor irritation, but some report marked disturbance, including major disruption to their daily lives and sleep. Suicidal thoughts and plans are not common with this condition, but they are also not rare.

Many experts believe that stress, physical tension in cephalic and neck muscles, and cognitive factors are part of the cause or can accentuate the severity of tinnitus and the distress associated with it for many patients with tinnitus (Schleuning, 1991; Rubinstein, 1993; Jakes, Hallam, McKenna, & Hinchcliffe, 1992). This is part of the rationale for using relaxation therapies, biofeedback, and cognitive-behavioral stress management. Rubinstein (1993) provides a recent and extensive review of the proposed relationship between craniomandibular disorders (CMD) and tinnitus. Practitioners assessing and treating patients with tinnitus should read the original report. He studied several very large groups of patients being evaluated for CMD disorders ($N = 376$), others being evaluated for tinnitus (two samples of 102 and 42), and epidemiologic samples ($N = 377$ and 1005). He concluded that there is an association between CMD signs and symptoms and tinnitus. He based this partly on the common association of tinnitus in patients with headaches, fatigue/tenderness in jaw muscles, pain on palpation of masticatory muscles and impaired mandibular mobility compared to epidemiologic samples. Many people with tinnitus report that mandibular movements and bruxism, jaw tenderness/fatigue, and/or pressure on the temporomandibular joints (TMJs) influence and correlate with fluctuations in tinnitus, vertigo, and hyperacusis. Hyperacusis is an "exceptionally acute sense of hearing . . . used to denote a painful sensitiveness to sounds"(*Dorland's Illustrated Medical Dictionary*, 1988, p. 790). Rubinstein's (1993) review and studies support both stomatognathic and biofeedback treatments for reducing or eliminating tinnitus in selected patients.

Increasing physiological self-regulation of striated head muscles and ANS arousal might provide patients with a better sense of control. It also can help them focus their attention away from the tinnitus. However, we do not know whether relaxation and biofeedback have any direct effect on the physiological mechanisms of tinnitus. Paradoxically, audiologic evaluations sometimes show increases in the audio intensity needed to mask the sound even with decreased subjective ratings of severity. For example, Kirsch, Blanchard, and Parnes

(1987) reported three of six subjects were initially in the 35- to 95-decibel range and showed an increase 1 month after treatment. The other three subjects showed either very little or considerable reduction in masking intensity.

Patients often rate noticeable improvement in the ability to manage the stress of tinnitus, and they often report much satisfaction with treatment. This may result from a sense of well-being and better management of associated symptoms. An illustration is a comment from a patient with chronic and disabling subjective tinnitus whom I treated. He reported dramatic and positive changes in his sleep and life after two office visits and a multicomponent behavioral treatment including passive relaxation. He said "the sound is still the same, but it does not bother me the way it did. I now start sleep fast and feel much better during the day."

Research and clinical speculations suggest ways how biofeedback and related procedures might help subjective tinnitus. These include distractor effects, habituation, cognitive changes, sleep improvement, and/or lowered physiological tension and arousal. These are not in any order of preference. The Implications section of this chapter contains a discussion of these.

DESCRIPTION AND SCOPE OF PROBLEM

Some reports suggest that one-third of the United States population report tinnitus and 6% of these (or 2% of the total population) report it as being severe (Kirsch, Blanchard, & Parnes, 1989). Schleuning (1991) refers to 36 million people in the United States complaining of tinnitus. He adds that "almost the entire population has had this symptom at one time or another" (p. 1225). Another report refers to 1% of the adult population as being severely annoyed by tinnitus (Coles, Davis, & Haggard, 1981, as reported by Hallam, Jakes, & Hinchcliffe, 1988). Another publication referred to "up to 20 percent of the United States population" and 8% of British population have subjective tinnitus, and 0.5% report it severe enough to interfere significantly with their normal activities (Podoshin, Ben-David, Fradis, Gerstel, & Felner, 1991). Regardless of which figures one accepts, nearly everyone knows many people who experience tinnitus. There are between about 1.7–3.4 million severe tinnitus sufferers and more than 800,000 severely disabled from it. Although affecting people of any age, most persons with tinnitus are age 40 or older. There is no gender difference. When the tinnitus becomes chronic, it usually lasts forever!

One can classify tinnitus into objective and subjective categories, although this is not a precise classification. Objective tinnitus is sound produced within the head and often heard by the examiner and the patient. There are vascular and mechanical causes of objective tinnitus. Listing or discussing these causes is beyond the scope of this chapter (see Schleuning, 1991, and Marion & Cevette, 1991, for further discussion of the topic). Subjective tinnitus is more common than objective tinnitus. People with subjective tinnitus describe the sounds as "whistling, ringing, roaring, humming, buzzing, static, whooshing, chirping, like running water, among others, or combinations of these noises" (Ince, Greene, Alba, & Zaretsky, 1987, p. 175). There are many presumed causes of subjective tinnitus. These include "otologic, metabolic, neurological, pharmacological, dental, or psychological" (Schleuning, 1991, p. 1228). Other causes include excessive amounts of ear wax (see Schleuning, 1991 for a summary of the causes of subjective tinnitus).

The most common causes of tinnitus are otologic. "More than 90% of patients with tinnitus have some otologic problem. In most instances, the problem is a high-frequency sensorineural hearing loss. This hearing loss is the single most consistent factor in patients with tinnitus" (Schleuning, 1991). Cardiovascular causes are common. Schleuning (1991) reports that "25% of patients who have significant tinnitus are hypertensive" (p. 1229).

Otolaryngologists and other physicians who see these patients often seek help in managing some of these patients from practitioners using applied psychophysiological treatments. The focus here is the biobehavioral management and treatments for subjective tinnitus.

Cognitive-behavioral and relaxation therapies help in the management of subjective tinnitus. These therapies can help patients change their thoughts about their symptoms and help reduce the anxiety and physical tension that often accompany the symptoms. The evidence for reducing the loudness of the tinnitus is not clear, although there is a legitimate rationale for continuing to explore relaxation and biofeedback therapies to reduce the loudness. For example, craniomandibular or temporomandibular disorders (TMD) are probably a common cause or contributing factor to subjective tinnitus (Schleuning, 1991; Rubinstein, 1993). See Chapter 16 for a discussion of the rationale for relaxation and biofeedback therapies for TMD. One can logically extrapolate to treating selected patients with tinnitus for whom the TMD appears to be at least a contributing factor.

For example, I had a female patient aged 40 whose daily tinnitus had started 5 months earlier. She had suffered sensorineural hearing loss in one ear since childhood, and had worn a hearing aid since early adulthood. The government agency for which she worked for many years had undergone a major transition a few months before her symptoms began. Generally she did not tolerate any changes well.

I learned that the patient had a long history of clenching and grinding her teeth dating back to childhood and a major lateral malocclusion untreated by dentists. She had fashioned and used an athletic mouthguard nightly for years to protect the occlusal wear on her teeth but had avoided dentists for years. She observed that her TMJ areas and the sides of her face were more tense during a similar period since the tinnitus started.

I arranged for a dental consultation and proper mouthguard for sleep. In addition, I planned an electromyographic (EMG) biofeedback assessment and biofeedback-assisted relaxation. I also recommended stress management later to help the patient adjust to work changes if needed, although this may not be practical for her. It is not clear whether the increased stress emitted increased daytime and sleeptime bruxing that brought about the tinnitus. The increased stress may have led to both the bruxing and tinnitus independently. However, it was logical and reasonable to focus treatment on reducing the TMD symptoms and to see what happened to the tinnitus symptoms. When I last saw her a few weeks after our first visit, she reported no tinnitus symptoms for about 3 weeks.

Other factors that may accentuate tinnitus severity include depression and anxiety. Many patients with subjective tinnitus report a history of depression and anxiety, and some antidepressant medications help these depressed patients with tinnitus (Schleuning, 1991; Dobie, Sakai, Sullivan, Katon, & Russo, 1993).

Publications about biofeedback and related treatments for tinnitus include both case reports and controlled group-outcome studies. Conclusions are promising but mixed. Several studies and case reports suggest that relaxation and EMG biofeedback can at least reduce the subjective disturbance and annoyance from tinnitus. Some reports suggest that these treatments may reduce the severity or loudness of the tinnitus, although that is much less clear. The methodology flaws in some of the studies are serious. These include lack of control groups, lack of baseline data, and reliance on anecdotal reports. Another serious flaw is using only global measures that probably markedly overestimate improvement. Other studies used insufficient biofeedback, and some studies lack documentation of physiological changes in the biofeedback modalities. Controlled studies typically do not show significant changes in objective measures of tinnitus intensity. Objective audiologic support is typically lacking.

CLINICAL RESPONSE AND OUTCOME

One concludes from the published research that a positive relationship exists between applied psychophysiological therapies and improvements in the subjective well-being of many patients with tinnitus. Applied psychophysiological therapies include relaxation, biofeedback, and cognitive-behavioral therapies. A very comprehensive, extremely well-organized, and thoughtful review is that by Kirsch et al. (1989). Anyone interested in subjective tinnitus should study this review carefully. However, publication of many excellent studies is more recent. I will not reproduce the discussion of the many studies presented so well by Kirsch et al. (1989). They speculate about differences among the results of various studies and the methodology shortcomings of many of them. This includes the lack of sufficient information in many studies. Nevertheless, Kirsch et al. conclude that "improvements can occur on self-reported annoyance, intrusiveness, and coping ability" (p. 63). This review reported about the same state and trait anxiety as for general medical/surgical patients. This argues against the idea that these patients are more anxious than other patients. A more recent study of EMG biofeedback with some useful information is by Podoshin et al. (1991). They also support the use of EMG biofeedback for subjective tinnitus.

Kirsch et al. (1989) also encouraged more investigation of cognitive techniques. More recently, Jakes et al. (1992) reported on a controlled, group-outcome study of cognitive techniques. The value of cognitive therapy received support from this well-controlled group design with 84 subjects. They started with 2 weeks of baseline. They then compared 30 subjects receiving 5 weeks of group cognitive therapy (GCT), subjects in three other treatment groups, and a waiting-list control group. The other treatment groups received a masker therapy, a placebo masker, or a combined group cognitive therapy plus a masker. Follow-up assessment was at 3 months. Measures included the Tinnitus Effects Questionnaire (TEQ) and ratings of the Interference with Daily Activities (IWDA). "Only patients receiving GCT (with or without a masker) were significantly improved over baseline on a tinnitus distress questionnaire" (p. 67), although this "emerged only at the 3-month follow-up assessment" (p. 78).

Hallam (personal communication, February 19, 1993) reports giving patients brief, printed patient information on tinnitus and cognitive therapy for tinnitus. The brief educational information "formed the basis for a discussion in the groups." He now reportedly gives chapters from his book for laypersons, *Living with Tinnitus*, available from the American Tinnitus Association in Portland, Oregon. Another patient-education booklet on the subject of biofeedback, cognitive therapy, and tinnitus is by Schwartz, Green, Rose, and Poole (in press). Part of the value of the Jakes et al. (1992) study is supporting the potential use of cognitive therapies in the treatment package for subjective tinnitus. However, it would be a mistake to conclude from this study that cognitive therapy alone is better than all other treatments. One also cannot conclude that it is better than biofeedback or combinations of comprehensive cognitive, biofeedback, and relaxation treatments.

The research and clinical insights of Podoshin et al. (1991) add other valuable information. For example, they point out potential compliance problems with daily logs of symptoms. They note the potential for countertherapeutic effects when therapists try to monitor some people closely. The Implications section below contains ideas gleaned partly from their report.

A more recent study by Podoshin et al. (1991) also supports the use of biofeedback for tinnitus and claims it was better than a medicine used to treat tinnitus and vertigo.[1] The biofeedback involved 30-minute sessions with bifrontal EMG and visual and auditory feedback from an unspecified instrument. Advantages of the study are the comparisons with other active treatments (medication and acupuncture) and multiple control groups (placebo biofeedback and placebo medication). All the nonbiofeedback groups did not do as well as the biofeedback group of 10 patients (6 male patients, 4 female patients, mean age 56, range 47–66 years). Unfortunately, there is no information about the biofeedback instruments, procedures, and no EMG data presented.

Evaluation of tinnitus with an audiologic procedure for matching the frequency and intensity of the tinnitus with tones did not show a change in pitch presumably in any group (Podoshin et al., 1991). However, this was not clear. Subjective rating provided the basis for improvement that was most significant while resting. The ratings dropped from an average of 2.7 (moderate to severe) to 1.6 (mild to moderate). For the most part, ratings were slightly higher during rest, as expected. This study adds to others supporting the use of EMG biofeedback for tinnitus. It also shows that EMG biofeedback can be better than some other treatments. However, it falls short in the use of biofeedback procedures. Also, the study does not provide the types of data practitioners need and expect to see in published studies using biofeedback.

One of the patients of Podoshin et al. (1991), patient #5, showed a drastic increase in psychosomatic symptom checklist (PSC) score. From pre- to posttreatment, the PSC score increased from 8 to 12. At 3 months, it was 58! There also was much more depression shown in the Beck Depression Inventory (BDI). The score increased from 0 to 4 from pre- to posttreatment, and then up to 28 at 3 months. Subjectively, there was no increase or decrease in the patient's ability to manage her stress at 1 month. However, there was more stress from the tinnitus at 1 month and a higher tinnitus rating. In contrast, there was a marked improvement in audiologic assessment from 65 decibels to "too low to ask." The patient experienced a severe sinus infection, oral surgery, and several severe psychosocial stressors during this period. This example illustrates the complexities of treating and understanding tinnitus.

There are no significant correlations between audiologic measures of intensity and self-reported ratings of disturbance (Kirsch et al., 1987). An important methodology note is that tinnitus intensity can vary. Thus, ratings provide an index over days and weeks, whereas masking measures reflect only one specific moment. Other studies also show little, if any, correlations between audiologic measures of intensity and self-reported ratings of disturbance. In the Kirsch et al. (1987) study, there were substantial drops in frontal EMG from a 5-minute baseline to the last 5 minutes of most of the six relaxation and two EMG feedback sessions. These drops were much more than during session one. The researchers limited the EMG feedback to the bifrontal area, which is not "the best measure of overall muscle relaxation" as Kirsch et al. (1987) would have us believe. There also are not enough data to justify their statement that subjects showed "successful learning of the relaxation techniques, as indicated by the EMG data." In addition, there was no specification of whether or not the therapist was with the subjects during the sessions. Kirsch et al. (1987) reported a 40-minute session with 18 minutes of baseline, relaxation and warming, attachment time,

[1]Cinnarizine (25 milligrams, three times a day) [1-(diphenylmethyl)-4-[(3-phenyl-2-propenyl)piperazine], the calcium channel blocker and antagonist to vasoconstriction in the CNS and blood vessels.

and discussion time. However, we do not know the exact time for feedback, although this is probably not crucial in their study.

The interesting technique of "matching-to-sample feedback" is worth noting as innovative and an example of direct rather than indirect feedback. First reported by Ince and colleagues with 2 cases, they also provided a single group design with 30 patients (Ince et al., 1987). In the Ince et al. (1987) procedure, researchers matched audiometrically produced sounds to each subject's perception of the tinnitus sound and fed back that sound. They determined thresholds for the specific tinnitus sound of each person. They used white noise, narrow-band noise, pure tone sound, or a combination of sounds. Based on each person's description, the experimenter selected a decibel level, a frequency level, and a stimulus. The experimenter presented this to the noninvolved ear or both ears. Each subject guided the adjustment process to help make the stimulus sound as close as possible to the tinnitus sound. The subjects did this by statements such as "make it louder," "make it higher," "make it shriller," or "add some static." The experimenter then slightly reduced the loudness of the stimulus. The goal was to reduce the tinnitus matched to the new loudness level. At the end of each 60 seconds, each subject reported whether the tinnitus reduction matched the external stimulus. If so, there was another reduction of 5 decibels of the external stimulus after a 30-second rest period. This process continued for up to 15 trials or when the tinnitus stopped.

Everyone had 12 or fewer sessions, and the investigators encouraged practice many times a day with the self-regulation method. The authors report that "practice between . . . sessions appeared to be an important variable, and those who practiced the required task as instructed tended to improve more rapidly than those who did not" (p. 180). However, as is usually the case with home practice, "exactly how often the participants did practice and precisely how they practiced between sessions are not known" (p. 180). Furthermore, they intentionally had no tape recording of the audiologic stimuli because there was no way to measure the decibel levels at home to allow feedback about changes.

The Kirsch et al. (1989) review reports that "nearly all subjects demonstrated a marked reduction in tinnitus loudness, with 84 percent reducing the tinnitus by 10–62 dB and several eliminating the tinnitus completely" (p. 61). The review acknowledges their impressive results. However intriguing and promising, the review cautions readers. Global self-reports alone were the basis for assuming generalization outside the office session, and there are no long-term follow-up data. Fatigue or habituation of the auditory system could account for the changes observed in the office.

The matching-to-sample feedback procedures sound like the direct blood pressure feedback procedures (Glasgow, Engel, & D'Lugoff, 1989; Engel, Glasgow, & Gaardner, 1983). One listens to the symptom itself or, for tinnitus, an analogue of the symptom. With that information, one makes internal psychophysiological changes to alter the feedback. There is need for a practical home device to provide the masking stimuli and adjustments in at least the decibel level.

MEASURES

Consider covering at least basic information in an interview and review of the existing recorded history. This includes duration of tinnitus, possible causes (e.g., acoustic trauma, infection, head trauma, and hearing loss), location (right, left, or bilateral), severity, type (e.g., single or multiple sounds, continuous or intermittent sound, or pulsating), quality of sounds, past and present treatments, medications, and the temporal nature of the tinnitus. Also cover the effects on their life and methods the patient uses to manage it. A good audiologic examination should be included.

For a measure of tinnitus disturbance consider using a rating system that separates activity versus rest and sleep conditions (Podoshin et al., 1991). The following is a slight elaboration of this rating system. They used a 0–4 scale; however, the proposed 0–5 scale makes it more comparable to the scale and rating form often used by practitioners treating headaches and other pain symptoms. Some wording changes might also help. Both rating scales are here for interest and consideration.

During Activity
    0 = No tinnitus
    1 = Mild tinnitus without disturbance
    2 = Moderate, which disturbs but does not affect activity
    3 = Severe, which affects activity
    4 = Very severe, which renders activity impossible

During Rest
    0 = No tinnitus
    1 = Mild tinnitus without disturbance
    2 = Moderate, which disturbs but does not affect sleep
    3 = Severe, which affects sleep
    4 = Very severe, which causes severe insomnia and spontaneous arousals

During Activity
    0 = No sound even when thought about
    1 = Slight, barely can hear the sound; ignored or forgotten about often
    2 = Mild, aware all the time but no interference with any activity
    3 = Moderate, disturbing and some interference with activities
    4 = Severe, much interference with activities
    5 = Very severe, incapacitating, makes specific activities impossible

During Rest and at Bedtime
    0 = No tinnitus, even when thought about during rest or trying to sleep
    1 = Slight, barely aware; ignored at times; can rest and sleep well
    2 = Mild, aware all the time, but no interference with rest or sleep
    3 = Moderate, disturbing, and some interference with sleep
    4 = Severe, much interference with sleep
    5 = Very severe, interferences with rest, causes severe insomnia, and spontaneous awakenings from sleep

Consider the TEQ (Hallam et al., 1988; Jakes et al., 1992). There is a 52-item version and a 33-item revised version. The four scores derived from the revised version of the scale are: emotional distress (ED), auditory perceptual difficulties (AP), insomnia (IN), and irrational beliefs (IB). The last claims to measure absolutist, all-or-none thinking, and catastrophic beliefs about tinnitus. Based on studies by Hallam et al. (1988) and Jakes et al. (1992), sensory and perceptual problems only partially overlap with the emotional distress people report. A good discussion of item development and factor analyses is the Hallam et al. (1988) article.[2]

[2]The questionnaires are not yet published or available in the United States. Until there is a publisher of the English version, consider writing to R. S. Hallam, Ph.D., for copies. His address is Psychology Department, University of East London, Romford Road, London E15 4LZ, United Kingdom.

Examples of items in the IN, ED, AP, and IB categories are:

"It takes me longer to get to sleep because of the noises."
"I worry whether I will be able to put up with this problem forever."
"I have more difficulty following a conversation because of the noises."
"Almost all my problems are caused by the noises."

A factor analysis of a German translation of the TEQ showed five factors[3] (Hiller & Goebel, 1992):

1. Cognitive and emotional distress (8 core items, 12 associated items) (27.2% of variance)
2. Intrusiveness (5 core, 3 associated items) (6.7% of variance)
3. Auditory and perceptual difficulties (5 core, 2 associated items) (5.4% of variance)
4. Sleep disturbances (4 core items) (4.9% of variance)
5. Somatic complaints (3 core items) (3.4% of variance)

The distress factor is not the same as that by Hallam's group. This analysis accounts for 40 of the 52 items with very little overlap among the factors or scales. The other items do not correlate significantly with the items in the factors or with each other.

The IWDA (Jakes, Hallam, Rachman, & Hinchcliffe, 1986) is a 23-item checklist also called the Tinnitus Activity Schedule. It purports to measure the number of activities affected by tinnitus. Sample activities are reading newspapers, watching television, relaxing during the day, and dealing calmly with problems. Patients rate each activity on a scale from 0 to 2 or no opportunity[4]: 0 = not at all, 1 = a little, and 2 = a lot. Another measure to consider is the Iowa Tinnitus Handicap Questionnaire (Kuk, Tyler, Russell, & Jordon, 1990).

The TEQ was a key part of two studies of patients with tinnitus seen at a London, England neuro-otology outpatient clinic. Study 1 had 43 female patients and 36 male patients, and Study 2 had 43 female patients and 57 male patients. These resulted in the following conclusions by Hallam et al. (1988). The authors concluded that the ED or mood effect involves depression, anger, irritability, and anxiety. People resent the persistence of the noises, want to escape from them, and worry about their sanity and health. They often develop absolutist beliefs, and their beliefs about tinnitus are mostly independent from the AP and sleep complaints.

Note that among these patients, tinnitus was distressing for the majority. Subjective tinnitus was bilateral in nearly half of the patients in Study 1. The age range was 20–76, with an average of 49. Hallam et al. (1988) reported an average duration of the symptom of 5 years, with a range up to 43 years. Continuous symptoms occurred in more than 80% of the group.

The cognitive model of tinnitus complaints assumes that the attention given to the tinnitus noises is a major contributing factor creating the disturbing effects. If a person views these as threatening or implying future loss, then the result is more likely emotional dis-

---

[3]1. Core items = 3, 13, 17, 21, 27, 43, 44, 47; Associated = 1, 5, 8, 11, 16, 18–20, 28, 37, 39, 41.
  2. Core items = 7, 10, 15, 35, 48; Associated = 5, 20, 34.
  3. Core items = 9, 14, 26, 33, 38; Associated = 2, 50.
  4. Core items = 4, 12, 31, 36.
  5. Core items = 22, 25, 51.

[4]Also available from R. S. Hallam, Ph.D.

tress. Furthermore, attending to the tinnitus interferes with other adaptive activities. This leads to views of the noises being more intrusive and affecting concentration and sleep. It may be that long-term insomnia predating the tinnitus may increase the risk of disturbed sleep after tinnitus starts (Hallam et al., 1988).

IMPLICATIONS, GUIDELINES, AND LIMITS

Intake and Assessment of Subjective Tinnitus

- Include pre- and posttreatment audiologic assessments.
- Consider including patients who suffer from severe tinnitus. Expect that extreme distress and suicidal thoughts characterize some patients.
- Ask questions about sleep problems predating the tinnitus.
- Consider daily self-report records about how bothersome the tinnitus is during activities, rest, and sleep.
- Expect improvement to be less disturbance during rest and sleep rather than during activities.
- Expect improvement from moderate-to-severe range to the mild-to-moderate range.
- Consider periodic sample weeks for getting symptom logs.
- Consider the IWDA questionnaire and the TEQ.
- Some patients will improve at or about five sessions. However, review progress at about five sessions, and consider more sessions if the data justify it.
- Plan on office follow-up rather than relying on phone follow-up.

Interventions

- Consider multiple stress management therapies such as multiple relaxation therapies, biofeedback-assisted muscle and autonomic nervous system relaxation, and cognitive-behavior therapies.
- Consider using bifrontal EMG feedback at least for some patients, but also consider using the frontalis-posterior neck EMG placement to assess temporalis and occipitalis tension better.
- Consider passive relaxation rather than tense–release procedures especially for the cephalic and neck muscles. Why increase tension in these areas unless there is no other way for the patients to relax them?
- Include visual rather than audio feedback that might confound the results. If one must use audio feedback, then consider sounds that the patient selects as pleasant and useful rather than limiting the sounds to a predetermined type. Some of the published reports used clicks.
- Include cognitive-behavior therapy focused at least on the beliefs assessed by the TEQ, other measures, and interviews.
- Consider graduated-exposure procedures. Use relaxation with biofeedback and cognitive procedures while the patient gradually moves in 1- to 5-decibal steps from a state in which an audiologist ideally masks the tinnitus to the least-masked state.
- If there is serious depression, treat it. Include cognitive therapy and address topics in addition to the tinnitus.
- Consider group treatment, however realize that many need individual treatment.
- Assume that some patients are unwilling to accept the idea of learning how to adapt to the tinnitus. They remain focused on finding physical causes and total cures.

- On the other side, assume that many patients do accept the rationale and premises of the behavioral explanations and therapies.
- Consider investing time for patient education.
- Assume that for some patients, the positive effects of treatment may "sink in" after cessation of formal treatment, especially if the treatment is only a few sessions (such as about five).
- Consider using behavioral and cognitive-behavioral techniques such as distraction techniques like those used in cognitive pain management, modifying underlying assumptions, and problem-solving techniques.
- Consider matching-to-sample feedback.
- Consider treatments such as medications, audiologic maskers, and/or surgery.

SPECULATIONS ON HOW BIOFEEDBACK WORKS FOR TINNITUS

Consider that biofeedback and relaxation have "distraction" effects. These treatments help people focus on other body areas, on the feedback stimuli, on breathing, and on other cognitive activities. People may become more adept at distraction as they reduce the tension, arousal, and cognitions associated with focusing on the tinnitus. This may be especially applicable during rest and when trying to start sleep.

Consider possible "habituation" effects after repeated exposure to the tinnitus during relaxation and biofeedback sessions in the office and at home. This alone would not explain improvements in patients with long-term, chronic tinnitus. However, there could be some habituation when one combines a gradual exposure procedure with physiological and cognitive changes. This is one explanation for the effects of exposure therapies for phobias, even for those with long-term phobias.

Cognitive changes include positive expectations and decreased cognitive anxiety including thoughts of helplessness. Successfully challenging and refuting thoughts of the tinnitus being a catastrophe and a disabling condition could be very helpful here as these methods are with some other symptoms. Biofeedback probably functions in feedforward and feedback ways to guide, reinforce, and convince people of their psychophysiological self-regulation and dexterity. It could similarly affect some patients with tinnitus.

Improved sleep could play an important role. For a variety of reasons, many of these patients probably achieve improved sleep. This factor could affect a variety of daytime symptoms including the ability to adjust to the primary symptoms. People with psychophysiological sleep-onset insomnia often benefit from relaxation and cognitive strategies at bedtime. At least for some people, that result is probably the result of changed cognitions at bedtime.

I know of no research that studied sleep efficiency, sleep architecture, and related sleep parameters among tinnitus patients treated with the behavioral interventions discussed here. However, it is a logical speculation that decreased time to sleep onset and reduction of other symptoms associated with sleep deprivation could help. They certainly could result in an increased sense of general well-being, neurocognitive efficiency, and confidence in managing otherwise more distressing symptoms.

The above does not exclude the potential role of reduced physiological muscle tension and arousal. There is not enough direct evidence for accepting the specific role of decreased muscle tension and sympathetic nervous system arousal. For selected patients with evidence of TMD, such as teeth clenching and grinding, this explanation may play an important role.

Other factors also are of potential relevance. During a focused intervention, some patients may make other changes without telling the practitioner or research investigator (e.g., decrease or stop caffeine usage, stop or change medication, or get their ears cleaned). They might change some stressful parts of their life without telling the practitioner. They might get a bedside sound masker, or audio tapes of pleasant sounds, or music that helps them adapt and sleep better. Do not assume that patients will report all these changes. Ask tactfully.

In conclusion, relaxation therapies, EMG biofeedback, and cognitive-behavior therapy can help in the management of subjective tinnitus for some people.

GLOSSARY

AUDIOLOGIC MASKERS. One type of treatment for tinnitus. A small instrument is worn in the ear and produces more acceptable noise than the noise in the ear.

CRANIOMANDIBULAR DISORDERS (CMD). Pertaining to the head and mandible. Sometimes used interchangeably with TMD.

HABITUATION (ADAPTATION). Allows patients to adapt to or adjust to the novel conditions or stimuli such as an office, instrumentation, psychophysiologic recordings, or auditory or visual stimuli. (Also see Chapter 7.)

INTERFERENCE WITH DAILY ACTIVITIES (IWDA) CHECKLIST. A 23-item checklist that measures the number of activities affected by tinnitus. Also called the Tinnitus Activity Schedule. Developed in England by S. C. Jakes, R. S. Hallam, and colleagues.

MATCHING-TO SAMPLE FEEDBACK. Matching audiometric produced sounds to each person's perception of a tinnitus sound and feeding back that sound. Experimental procedure for treating tinnitus. Developed by L. P. Ince and colleagues (1987).

OTOLOGIC. Pertaining to otology, the branch of medicine dealing with medical/surgical treatments of the ear.

STOMATOGNATHIC. Denoting the mouth and jaws together.

SUBJECTIVE TINNITUS (ST). Tinnitus not heard by other people close by. Contrast with objective tinnitus. (See text.)

TEMPOROMANDIBULAR DISORDERS (TMD). Pertaining to disorders involving the temporal and mandibular areas of the head. (Also see Chapter 16.)

TINNITUS EFFECTS QUESTIONNAIRE (TEQ). Self-report questionnaire measure of the effects of tinnitus. There are a 52-item and a 33-item revised versions. Scores include emotional distress, auditory perceptual difficulties, insomnia, and irrational beliefs. Developed in England by R. S. Hallam and S. C. Jakes. (See text.)

ACKNOWLEDGMENT

I am very thankful to otorhinolaryngologist Douglas J. Green, M.D., of Mayo Clinic Jacksonville, for his review of a draft of this chapter. His comments, suggestions, and corrections were very helpful. This appreciation does not imply his endorsement of the content of this chapter.

REFERENCES

Borton, T. E., Moore, W. H. Jr., & Clark, S. R. (1981). Electromyographic feedback treatment for tinnitus aurium. *Journal of Speech and Hearing Disorders, 46*, 39–45.

Dobie, R. A., Sakai, C. S. Sullivan, M. D., Katon, W. J., & Russo, J. (1993). Antidepressant treatment of tinnitus patients: Report of a randomized clinical trial and clinical prediction of benefit. *The American Journal of Otology, 14*(1), 18–23.

Dorland's illustrated medical dictionary (27th ed.). (1988). Philadelphia, PA: W. B. Saunders.

Duckro, P. N., Pollard, C. A., Bray, H. D., & Scheiter, L. (1984). Comprehensive behavioral management of complex tinnitus: A case illustration. *Biofeedback and Self-Regulation, 9*, 459–469.

Elfner, L. F., May, J. G., Moore, J. D., & Mendelson, J. M. (1981). Effects of EMG and thermal training on tinnitus: A case study. *Biofeedback and Self-Regulation, 6*, 517–521.

Engel, B. T., Glasgow, M. S., & Gaardner, K. R. (1983). Behavioral treatment of high blood pressure. II. Follow-up results and treatment recommendations. *Psychosomatic Medicine, 45*(1), 23–39.

Glasgow, M. S., Engel, B. T., & D'Lugoff, B. C. (1989). A controlled study of a standardized behavioral stepped treatment for hypertension. *Psychosomatic Medicine, 51*, 10–26.

Grossan, M. (1976). Treatment of subjective tinnitus with biofeedback. *Ear, Nose, and Throat, 55*, 314–318.

Hallam, R. S., Jakes, S. C., & Hinchcliffe, R. (1988). Cognitive variables in tinnitus annoyance. *British Journal of Clinical Psychology, 27*, 213–222.

Haralambous, G., Wilson, P. H., Platt-Hepworth, S., Tonkin, J. P., Rae Hensley, V., & Kavanagh, D. (1987). EMG biofeedback in the treatment of tinnitus: An experimental evaluation. *Behaviour Research and Therapy, 25*, 49–55.

Hiller, W., & Goebel, G. (1992). A psychometric study of complaints in chronic tinnitus. *Journal of Psychosomatic Research, 36*(4), 337–348.

House, J. W., Miller, L., & House, P.R. (1977). Severe tinnitus: Treatment with biofeedback training. *Transactions of the American Academy of Ophthalmology and Otolaryngology, 84*, 697–703.

Ince, L. P., Greene, R. Y., Alba, A., & Zaretsky, H. H. (1987). A matching-to-sample feedback technique for training self-control of tinnitus. *Health Psychology, 6*(2), 173–182.

Ireland, C. E., Wilson, P. H., Tonkin, J. P., & Platt-Hepworth, S. (1985). An evaluation of relaxation training in the treatment of tinnitus. *Behaviour Research and Therapy, 23*, 423–430.

Jakes, S. C., Hallam, R. S., McKenna, L., & Hinchcliffe, R. (1992). Group cognitive therapy for medical patients: An application to tinnitus. *Cognitive Therapy and Research, 16*(1), 67–82.

Jakes, S. C., Hallam, R. S., Rachman, S., & Hinchcliffe, R. (1986). The effects or reassurance, relaxation training and distraction on chronic tinnitus sufferers. *Behaviour Research and Therapy, 26*, 497–508.

Kirsch, C. A., Blanchard, E. B., & Parnes, S. M. (1987). A multiple-baseline evaluation of the treatment of subjective tinnitus with relaxation training and biofeedback. *Biofeedback and Self-Regulation, 12*, 295–311.

Kirsch, C. A., Blanchard, E. B., & Parnes, S. M. (1989). A review of the efficacy of behavioral techniques in the treatment of subjective tinnitus. *Annals of Behavioral Medicine, 11*(2), 58–65.

Kuk, F. K., Tyler, R. S., Russell, D., & Jordan, H. (1990). The psychometric properties of a tinnitus handicap questionnaire. *Ear and Hearing, 11*, 434–445.

Marion, M. S., & Cevette, M. J. (1991). Tinnitus. *Mayo Clinic Proceedings, 66*, 614–620.

Podoshin, L., Ben-David, Y., Fradis, M., Gerstel, R., & Felner, H. (1991). Idiopathic subjective tinnitus treated by biofeedback, acupuncture and drug therapy. *Ear, Nose and Throat Journal, 70*(5), 284–289.

Rubinstein, G. (1993). Tinnitus and craniomandibular disorders—is there a link? *Swedish Dental Journal Supplement, 95*, 1–45.

Schlwuning, A. J. II. (1991). Management of the patient with tinnitus. *The Medical Clinics of North America: Update in Otolaryngology I, 75*(6), 1225–1237.

Schwartz, M. S., Green, D. J., Rose, D. E., & Poole, A. C. (in press). Tinnitus: ("ear ringing"): Biofeedback and cognitive treatments. In M. S. Schwartz (Ed.), *Patient education: A practitioner's guide*. New York: Guilford Press.

Walsh, W. M., & Gerley, P. P. (1985). Thermal biofeedback and the treatment of tinnitus. *Laryngoscope, 95*, 987–989.

35

Fibromyalgia Syndrome

Mark S. Schwartz

Inclusion of fibromyalgia syndrome (FS) is pertinent here because relaxation therapies with electromyographic (EMG) biofeedback are part of the acceptable treatments for FS. Understanding of this syndrome and treatments remain inadequate. The acceptance of relaxation therapies and biofeedback for fibromyalgia is odd because there are only two studies (Ferraccioli et al., 1987, 1990) and these are very limited and not clear. Why, then, would patient-education literature from the American Rheumatologic Association, chapters in respectable books, and journal articles by respectable authors list biofeedback as one of the major treatments (McCain, 1990, in Fricton & Awad, 1990; Thompson, 1990)? I offer two reasons. First, many practitioners assume that excess muscle tension under voluntary control is part of the problem. Thus, the logic is consistent with the use of relaxation methods with biofeedback. The other reason is other treatments do not reliably yield positive results.

The use of multiple channels of EMG is more logical because of the multiple sites of the symptoms. However, there is no compelling reason, and no evidence yet, that one needs to monitor and feedback from all or most body sites.

DEFINITIONS

A rose by any other name may still be a rose. However, is fibromyalgia by other names still fibromyalgia? There are other names that focus on different aspects of what might be the same disorder or a related but distinct disorder. These other terms include *"fibrositis,"* *"myofascial pain syndrome,"* and *"tension myalgia."* There is abundant literature discussing these (Thompson, 1990; Wolfe et al., 1990). The most widely used term and the term now accepted by the American College of Rheumatology (ACR) is "fibromyalgia syndrome" (FS) (Wolfe et al., 1990).

A brief discussion of the history of the terms is instructive and helps one gain perspective. The term fibrositis was introduced in 1904 by Sir William Gowers and prevailed in the literature of muscle pain syndromes for many years. However, the logic was tenuous, and the assumed inflammation in muscle tissue was dispelled about 40 years later. However, the term had become entrenched in medical practice and acceptable alternatives were not forthcoming (Thompson, 1990). Some professionals mistakenly continue to use this term interchangeably with FS.

People with muscle pain syndromes like fibromyalgia usually present with poor sleep. No discussion of this topic would be adequate without mentioning the seminal work of Harold Moldofsky, M.D., and his colleagues in Toronto (Moldofsky, 1990); he and his group investigated the "alpha–delta sleep" phenomenon in these patients. They preferred the term "alpha EEG NREM sleep anomaly" and referred to FS as a "nonrestorative sleep syndrome." The original proposal to explain the presence of alpha–delta sleep was that emotional distress led to internal arousal and then this sleep anomaly. That hypothesis is no longer tenable as there are many factors that probably can contribute (Moldofsky, 1990; Baumstark & Buckelew, 1992).

One finds the "alpha EEG NREM sleep anomaly" in patients with other diagnoses, so it is nonspecific to FS (Moldofsky, 1990; Baumstark & Buckelew, 1992). However, some research has shown the anomaly to be present much more often during NREM sleep in patients with FS than other disorders studied (e.g., insomnia) (Moldofsky, 1989) or in normals (Moldofsky, Scarisbrick, England, & Smyth, 1975). For example, referring to his early research, Moldofsky (1990) stated that people with FS may show "an average of 60% of NREM sleep occupied by the . . . anomaly" compared to 25% of NREM in insomnia or dysthymia. In addition to multiple tender points, "sleep disturbance, fatigue, [morning] stiffness [>15 minutes] are the cardinal symptoms of fibromyalgia, and each is present in more than 75% of fibromyalgia patients . . . only 56% of patients had all 3 symptoms, and 81% had 2 of the 3" (Wolfe et al., 1990, p. 170).

Although often discussed with myofascial pain syndrome (MPS), there are differences distinguishing FS from MPS (Thompson, 1990). In MPS, the focus is on "trigger points" and a palpable band of tight muscle versus the multiple tender points in FS. Chronic, widespread, systemic-like symptoms are present in FS. Contrast this with the more acute, local nature of symptoms in MPS. However, these distinctions blur when one observes that patients can start with local pain that later becomes widespread.

The similarities of symptoms and the blurring of the distinctions motivated Thompson (1990) to propose the long-used term and diagnosis of "tension myalgia" as a unifying concept. His proposed classification has three divisions: Generalized tension myalgia corresponds to FS, localized tension myalgia corresponds to MPS, and regional tension myalgia fits tension myalgia or the majority of patients with symptoms between the other two divisions. The distinction of primary and secondary FS is out of vogue for the ACR and Thompson (1990) agrees and also avoids such a distinction for tension myalgia. The diagnosis of tension myalgia requires exclusion of other causes of muscle pain (Thompson, 1990, p. 1243). It does not rely on pathognomonic signs of which there are none for FS, MPS, and tension myalgia. In this chapter, I usually use the term FS for convenience and convention. This use does not imply exclusion of the conceptualization of divisions of tension myalgia.

Tension myalgia implies that muscle tension results from spasm, poor posture, overuse, and other factors that are significant in worsening and perhaps causing the symptoms. The lack of EMG confirmation of tension while relaxed, painful muscles are monitored is the same problem also found with many patients with tension headaches. See Chapters 14 and 15 for this discussion. It does not mean that excess tension is never present. It only means that it is not present during rest. Thompson (1990) reports that many patients diagnosed with tension myalgia in his practice have excess muscle tension. He and his colleagues focus on patients misusing their muscles by "habitually co-contracting them, by subjecting them unrelentingly to postural stress, by overusing them, or by a combination of all three factors" (p. 1244). Practitioners can better justify using EMG biofeedback as part of comprehensive treatment when there is EMG evidence of excess muscle tension.

It is very difficult to estimate the incidence of a condition for which there are still disagreements about terminology and definitions. There are estimates of "six million Americans" affected (Baumstark & Buckelew, 1992), although there may be many more. Consider how recently the consensus criteria were defined when thinking about incidence.

Population studies of Scandinavian nonpatients with fibromyalgia suggest fibromyalgia symptoms in 2–4% incidence in the population (Jeffrey Thompson, M.D., personal communication, June 9, 1994). From the lesson of irritable bowel syndrome (IBS; see Chapter 33), there could be a larger array of people with fibromyalgia who rarely consult physicians for these symptoms. For example, a study in Northern England found widespread pain as defined by the ACR90 criteria in 11% of the adults (Jeffrey Thompson, M.D., personal communication, June 9, 1994).

There are often several years between the start of a person's symptoms and a diagnosis. Patients often hear many diagnostic possibilities and hear conflicting opinions. They try different treatments without benefit. All this is enough to add significantly to psychological distress. These patients often learn to be wary of the opinions and advice of health professionals.

MEASURES

Psychological

The measures selected depend on the preference of the practitioner tailoring the assessment. Practitioners should at least consider measures of depression, anxiety, and daily stress. In a more complete evaluation, or if the patient is entering stress management or other form of psychotherapy, practitioners will also consider other measures. These include anger and assertiveness, symptom impact, self-efficacy, attitudes about illness, pain, and related topics, and somatic focus (see Chapter 6 for examples and discussion).

As with many other disorders, there are multiple dimensions to measure. Consider using multiple measures of each when concerned about relying on a single measure of each dimension. Modify interpretation of responses to items when expecting the content of the item to be part of FS. Be very cautious making decisions about the impact on FS by psychological factors.

Pain

Practitioners should consider using pain measures such as the following.

Tender Point Index

Note the tender point index (TPI) is "tender" not "trigger." A qualified professional palpates specified body sites with an estimated pressure such as about 4 kilograms. One can learn to do this by palpating the cork end of a dolorimeter. The sites palpated are the standard sites defined for patients with FS and a few control sites not expected to be tender. See the list of sites later in this chapter.

One scoring system (Wolfe et al., 1990) is a 5-point scale from 0 to 4: 0 = no tenderness or pain, or tenderness with no pain; 1 = mild pain without a grimace, flinch, or withdrawal; 2 = moderate pain with a grimace or flinch; 3 = severe pain and a marked flinch or withdrawal; and 4 = unbearable pain in which the patient is untouchable and withdraws before palpation.

Practitioners may consider another very similar scale by Russell, Fletcher, Michalek, McBroom, and Hester (1991). This scale uses tenderness without a physical response as 1, and tenderness with a physical response such as a wince or withdrawal is 2. The other categories are the same as the Wolfe system.

A flinch is a slight body movement, and a marked flinch is an exaggerated body movement. However, "any indication of pain (moderate or greater) was a better discriminator than pain determinations that called for grimace, flinch, or other manifestations of pain (moderate or greater)" (Wolfe et al., 1990, p. 170).

Dolorimetry

Dolorimetry (DOL) measures the sensations from pressure to pain at the tender soft tissue sites (Wolfe et al., 1990; Russell, 1990). It uses a pressure algometer with a spring-loaded gauge capped with a flat circular rubber or cork stopper about 1.5 centimeters in diameter. One advances the instrument at increments of about 1 kilogram per second and asks the patient to say when it feels painful. The pain threshold is the level when the person shifts from feeling pressure to reporting pain. Properly qualified therapists or doctors do this at several specified body sites and calculate a dolorimeter pain index (DPI). For pain-free people, the threshold is usually above 4 kilograms and less than that for FS patients (Russell, 1990, p. 310).

In a large multicenter sample of 293 patients with FS, the average DOL score for the active sites was 3.4 (SD = 0.07) on a 0–6.5 scale. Compare this to 4.9 (SD = 0.08) for the control patients and a similar score for control sites on the patients with FS. There is no difference between so-called primary FS versus secondary-concomitant FS patients. This distinction is probably unnecessary at the level of diagnosis (Wolfe et al., 1990). Patients with FS often have other rheumatic disorders, and their presence "does not exclude the diagnosis of fibromyalgia" (Wolfe, et al., 1990, p. 171).

Objectivity, reliability, and standardization are all better with the DPI. However, it requires using a device and using numbers with decimals, and it may not be necessary in routine clinical practice. It is in common use in research with FS, but it is not in the comprehensive pain assessment book by Turk and Melzack (1992). Note that Wolfe et al. (1990) concluded that

> palpation of tender points with the thumb was more discriminatory than was dolorimetry. [And] the use of dolorimetry is not recommended in routine clinical practice; it may still be of use in assessing relative severity in research studies and in the medicolegal setting. (p. 171)

Whether using the TPI, DPI, or both, the practitioner should try to get the same measures at regular intervals to assess response to therapy systematically. Also note that the pain threshold can vary throughout the day and from day to day for a given individual (Gudni Thorsteinsson, M.D., personal communication, June, 1994). Therefore multiple measures at different times of the day and over multiple days before, during, and after treatment are required.

Widespread Pain

Widespread pain present for 3 months or longer, is a very useful criterion. It is one of the two criteria of the ACR 1990 Fibromyalgia Classification System. These patients appear to have impairments in their pain modulation systems. They report feeling the full strength of these nociceptive transmissions. Combined with the other criteria of 11 of 18 tender points, widespread pain has very high accuracy (85%). Both sensitivity (88%) and specificity (81%) are good. "Only 1.7 percent of patients with FS who meet the tender point criteria will be misclassified by the widespread pain criteria" (Wolfe et al., 1990, p. 171).

Pain is widespread when the following are all present. Pain is in the left and right side of the body, and pain appears above and below the waist. One also must report axial skeletal pain: pain in areas of the cervical spine, anterior chest, thoracic spine, or low back. Shoulder pain on either side and buttock pain on either side fulfills the side criteria. Low back pain fulfills the lower segment criteria. An example of widespread pain is "right shoulder, left buttock, and thoracic spine" (Wolfe et al., 1990, p. 163).

Tender Points

Text descriptions of tender points are less than ideal. For anatomic figures of the tender points, see Thompson (1990), Wolfe et al. (1990), and Goldenberg (1989). Briefly, there are nine bilateral pairs of sites. These are in the areas of the:

- Occiput: at the suboccipital insertion.
- Sternomastoid/low cervical: on the side of the neck under the lower sternomastoid at the anterior aspect of the intertransverse ligaments of C_{5-7}.
- Trapezius: the midpoint of the upper border of the trapezius.
- Scapula: above the medial border of the scapula at the origins of the supraspinatus muscle.
- Anterior chest at the second rib, near the junction of the second rib to the sternum at or near the second costochondral junction.
- Elbow: outer side of an elbow 2 centimeters distal to lateral epicondyles.
- Gluteal: upper outer quandrant of buttocks in anterior fold.
- Thigh/hip: the side of the upper thigh below the hipbone posterior to the trochanter prominence.
- Knee: the inner side of and slightly higher than kneecap at medial fat pad proximal to the joint line.

See the references such as Wolff et al. (1990) and Goldenberg (1989, 1990) for more technical descriptions.

Self-Report Pain Intensity and Pain Affect Rating Scales

The Visual Analogue Scale (VAS) is a common method for measuring pain intensity in patients with FS. It is usually a 10-centimeter line with the ends labeled as extremes of pain such as from "no pain" to "pain as bad as it could be" (Jensen & Karoly, 1992). Ask patients to mark the line at the point that best indicates their pain intensity. The distance from no pain to their mark is the intensity score, usually measured in millimeters. Administration is easy, although there is an extra scoring step. The scores are ratio data, and there is good construct validity. However, some elderly people and some others have difficulty understanding the task. Careful explanations and patient practice with this method reduce errors.

Versions of this method, graphic rating scales, may be easier for some patients to understand but have some limitations (Jensen & Karoly, 1992). These scales use numbers 0 up to 10 or adjectives such as mild, moderate, and severe. These authors also recommend not using the VAS as the primary or only pain-intensity measure. They describe and illustrate several other self-report scales and procedures.

There are several measures of pain affect (Jensen & Karoly, 1992) worth considering for patients with FS. However, this type of measure is less commonly used with patients with FS. Examples are the Verbal Rating Scale (VRS) and the VAS (Jensen & Karoly, 1992).

Jensen and Karoly (1992) state that "by far the most widely used measure of pain affect is the Affective subscale of the *McGill Pain Questionnaire* (MPQ)" (Melzack, 1975, p. 143) referring to Melzack and Katz (1992). However, it is yet unknown whether measures of pain affect will add anything meaningful to assessing patients with FS.

Morning Stiffness

The criterion of morning stiffness can be part of the sleep log or asked separately. Consider some measure of degree of stiffness such as 0 up to 4 points. Also consider a rating of the duration of stiffness after awakening such as in about 15-minute increments. For other pain measures see Turk and Melzack (1992).

Other Symptoms

Other symptoms are often useful in evaluating patients with FS. Sleep and fatigue are two major symptoms.

Sleep

Measuring sleep quality is crucial because sleep disturbance is one of the central symptoms of FS and present in more than 75% of patients with FS (Wolfe et al., 1990). One can use a sleep log like those used with insomnia patients. Include questions about sleep quality. Ask the patient at least to rate whether he or she awakens tired or nonrefreshed "never," "seldom," "often or usually," or "always."

Fatigue

Consider adding questions about fatigue to the sleep log or pain rating form. One question could assess whether fatigue is seldom or never, often or usually, or always present. Another could assess fatigue one or more times each day on a 0- to 4- or 5-point scale (e.g., within a few minutes after rising from bed, late morning or a few hours after rising from bed, and later afternoon or 8–10 hours after rising from bed).

Disability

Consider assessing and measuring disability. Some suggest using existing measures designed for other disorders. For example, consider the *Sickness Impact Profile* (Bergner, Bobbitt, Pollard, Martin, & Gilson, 1976; Bergner, Bobbitt, Carter, & Gilson, 1981).

Comorbid Disorders

Other symptoms commonly found, indeed often found, among patients with FS are IBS, migraines, and chronic fatigue. One also commonly finds mood disorders such as major depression and anxiety disorders such as panic disorder among patients with FS. Ask questions about these symptoms. Include questions about them in questionnaires and rating forms.

The high comorbidity of several of these disorders is interesting and common. Thus, some professionals speculate about a common or related underlying pathophysiology. One group of investigators coined the term "affective spectrum disorder" (ASD) to signal the potential linkage (Hudson & Pope, 1989, 1990; Hudson, Goldenberg, Pope, Keck, & Schlesinger, 1992). Among 33 women with FS, Hudson et al. (1992) reported 15 of these had current migraines and 3 others had a lifetime diagnosis of migraines, for a total of 55%. IBS was present for 13 patients and 4 more had a lifetime diagnosis of IBS, for a total of 52%. Major depression was present in 6 of the patients and 13 more had nearly lifetime depression, for a total of 58%. Panic disorder with or without agoraphobia was present in 5 of them and 6 more showed these symptoms much longer, for a total of 33%. Symptoms meeting all or nearly all the criteria for CFS were present over a long term and during the study in 23 of the women (70%).

The authors carefully point out that proposing ASD and showing comorbidity of the disorders do not mean that any of these disorders actually causes the other disorders. For example, fibromyalgia is not a cause of major depression. Hudson et al. (1992) raise the possibility of a genetic abnormality, although it does not appear to explain the disorders.

It remains unanswered whether or not these disorders do exist in a "family of psychiatric and medical disorders that share a common physiologic abnormality" (Hudson et al., 1992, p. 363). The authors point out limitations in their data. For example, note that these patients were all from a tertiary medical center. Thus, they might not have reflected the broader array of people with FS and those in primary-care settings. Remember that IBS patients differ markedly between those seen in the community and those seen in medical settings (see Chapter 33).

Part of the argument for linking these disorders is the observation that antidepressant medications from different chemical classes are effective for major depression, panic, migraine, IBS, and FS. Linking disorders that respond to the same treatment is interesting and valuable. However, astute practitioners avoid this pitfall. It is usually an unwarranted leap of logic to work backwards linking disorders this way. For example, the antidepressant imipramine works for depression and nocturnal enuresis for different reasons (see Chapter 25). Nonetheless, the comorbidity begs for explanation and has important implications for clinical practice aside from questions of etiology. For example, even if one is uncomfortable using biofeedback and relaxation for FS based on the limited research, the coexistence of other symptoms and disorders for which there is more published support helps justify using them for a large percentage of patients with FS.

PSYCHOLOGICAL FACTORS

Some professionals believe that stress and reactions to stress influence fibromyalgia symptoms at least with some patients. Whether or not the stress reactions precede or accompany the physical symptoms is not clear. There are some patients with FS who have significant psychological problems (Daily, Bishop, Russell, & Fletcher, 1990; Yunus, Ahles, Aldag, & Masi, 1991; Turk & Flor, 1989). This could aggravate the persistence of FS in some patients. However, it is not a necessary condition for the persistence of symptoms.

To understand the role of psychological factors in the development of and maintenance of FS, one must study patients who have pure FS and no other medical disorders. Other medical disorders commonly coexisting in patients with FS are chronic headaches and dysmenorrhea. For example, about 60 patients of the 103 patients with FS in the Yunus et al. (1991) study also had chronic headaches.

As Yunus et al. (1991) and Turk and Flor (1989) note, there are multidimensional problems in patients with FS. Psychological factors are important for some of these patients. Patients referred to rheumatology clinics may represent a biased sample. There could be more psychological problems among these patients than in the general population of people with FS (Yunus et al., 1991; Merskey, 1989). Nevertheless, this is the subgroup that might need more attention and intervention including psychological treatments.

In one outpatient rheumatology clinic sample of patients with FS, there was a sub-group with significant psychological problems (Yunus et al., 1991). Yunus et al. (1991) defined this subgroup with "simple questions" combined with Minnesota Multiphasic Personality Inventory (MMPI) criteria. Sample questions were: "Do you think you are anxious, tense, or have worries?" "Do you feel depressed, low, or blue?" The MMPI criteria was a T score greater than 69 on four or more of any of the clinical scales.

Using the MMPI criteria alone and using the original norms, there were 24 of 103 (23.3%) in the psychological disturbance group. Using the contemporary norms by Colligan et al. (1984), there were 13 of 103 (12.6%) in this group. About half the FS group had an elevation of 1 or more of scales 1, 2, and 3. However, this is common and expected for patients with chronic pain. It is not a good indication of psychopathology especially without a more fine-grained analysis of the items endorsed in these scales. Older studies in rheumatology clinics using the MMPI also reported subgroups of patients with FS with significant psychological problems. However, in a general internal medicine sample using different measures, Clark et al. (1985) did not find differences between patients with FS compared to control subjects.

Another factor might account for the differences between these studies. There is a potential confounding of the clinical features of FS and MMPI items. Examples of these features are the number of pain sites, the number of tender points, fatigue, poor sleep, and paresthesias. However, the Yunus et al. (1991) study found few significant correlations between the standard MMPI scales and clinical features of FS. The severity of pain was more associated with MMPI profiles with four or more elevations. Using either norms, about half of the group with more abnormal MMPIs showed moderate and severe pain intensity. They showed significantly more intensity than those in the other MMPI groups. The authors therefore concluded that the MMPI could provide "a valid measure of psychological status" in FS patients.

The coexistence of clear and clinically significant depression and anxiety exists but is not typical for patients with FS. For example, among 78 patients studied by Russell et al. (1991) with measures of depression and anxiety, 37.7% had Hamilton Depression Scale scores indicating possible depression (>13) but only 13% had probable depression (>18). The Center for Epidemiologic Studies of Depression Scale (CES-D) (Radloff, 1977) results were similar. Only 9% showed probable depression. Also, only 5%, or 4 patients, had a score indicating probable anxiety (>18). Sixty-eight percent of the patients did not meet criteria for either depression or anxiety.

Measures of daily stress (Brantley, Waggoner, Jones, & Rappaport, 1987) may be useful. Patients with FS report more daily stress than do patients with rheumatoid arthritis and healthy-matched control patients. Patients with more daily stress had more psychological disturbance measured on subscales of the Arthritis Impact Measurement Scale (AIMS) (Meenan, Gertman, Masor, & Dunaiff, 1982). The greater daily stress experienced by patients with FS include a broad spectrum of items beyond illness, income, or education (Daily et al., 1990). The authors note that their results do not clarify "whether stress precedes or follows changes in disease activity and impact" (p. 1384). They point out that FS patients may be hypersensitive and thus overreport daily stress.

CLINICAL RESPONSE AND OUTCOME

It is surprising that there is still only one controlled study of EMG biofeedback for FS (Ferraccioli et al., 1987). They used single-channel frontal EMG with audio feedback and with eyes closed. This is a very modest form of EMG biofeedback for patients with FS. Some version of progressive muscle relaxation was apparently part of the treatment. If this description of the treatment sounds a little vague, it is because the method section provides limited and unclear information. Secondary reports of this study refer to

> 15 patients who underwent 15 sessions of EMG biofeedback over a 5-week observation period . . . [and] . . . a follow-up study, randomizing 12 more patients to . . . EMG-BFT [biofeedback training] or sham biofeedback. (McCain, 1990, p. 299)

Nevertheless, the study reported significant improvements at the end of treatment and at 6-month follow-up. The authors used multiple criteria including number of tender points, pain intensity based on a VAS, and morning stiffness. The authors deserve recognition for their contribution, especially considering the apparently modest treatment and the fact they were treating only patients resistant to prior medical treatment with nonsteroidal anti-inflammatory drugs (NSAIDs).

My interpretation of the original report is that the first 15 patients started with one session attached to the EMG biofeedback instrument and with general suggestions "to obtain muscle relaxation, without any acoustic signal." They then had 15 twice-weekly, 20-minute sessions with progressive muscle relaxation and frontal EMG feedback.

This information is far too nonspecific to draw any understanding of the role of biofeedback. There were six more sessions over the next 80 days. Three of these were weekly right after the prior 15. Two more were fortnightly, and the last session was in the next 2 months. The paper implies that these added sessions presumably included relaxation and biofeedback. Thus, it appears there were 21 treatment sessions after the first baseline session rather than the 15 treatment sessions also reported by the authors.

It is indeed unfortunate that the specific role of biofeedback, and relaxation for that matter, is so unclear. Nevertheless, several of the patients participating did get better compared to their prior treatments and compared to a false EMG biofeedback group. Psychopathological factors, such as depression, resulted in poor outcome.

The same investigators reported a later trial of biofeedback with 10 of 24 female FS patients studied for other purposes (Ferraccioli et al., 1990). The focus of the study was neuroendocrinological. They compared patients with FS and those other chronic pain conditions such as rheumatoid arthritis and low back pain. They studied thyroid-stimulating hormone (TSH), prolactin (PRL), and cortisol profiles. A subset of the FS patients showed no suppression of cortisol to dexamethasone (DXT) and a hyperprolactinemic response to thyroid releasing hormone (TRH). The most common hormone finding was a "blunted TSH response in the absence either of hyperthyroidism or any relationship with cortisol values . . ." (p. 871). TSH comes from the anterior pituitary and stimulates normal hormonal secretions of the thyroid gland.

Ferraccioli et al. (1990) reported that 15 of the 24 women or 62% with FS had one or more abnormal hormone levels using "the strictest critieria" (p. 871) They speculate that patients without these hormone imbalances can benefit from relaxation and EMG biofeedback compared to those with such imbalances. In the three pain conditions studied, the authors conclude there is support for the hypothesis that "chronic pain and stress are important determinants of neuroendocrinologic abnormalities especially at the hypothalamic–pituitary–thyroid axis" (p. 872).

There was no specific information about the biofeedback and relaxation. The relationship between the abnormal hormone levels, FS, and response to biofeedback and relaxation remains unclear. Nevertheless, the neuroendocrinological results have potential implications for practitioners treating with relaxation and biofeedback. Of the 10 patients, there were 7 without neuroendocrinological abnormalities, and 6 of these showed benefit of 50% or more improvement of tender points, MPQ, and VAS with 15 biofeedback sessions and practice. None of the three patients with their defined abnormalities showed benefit from this treatment.

OTHER TREATMENTS

I gleaned most of this section from Thompson (1990). The major treatments for FS and tension myalgia are patient education, reassurance, stopping contributing factors, medications, physical therapies, relaxation, and EMG biofeedback. If all of these are insufficient, practitioners should consider injections and spray and stretch techniques.

Practitioners assess factors such as posture, body mechanics during lifting and other activities, and excess psychological stress. Anatomic factors such as a short leg must also be checked. Patient education includes correcting myths and misattributions about FS. For selected patients, stress management is justifiable. This can help patients manage daily stress, other sources of stress, and adjustment to symptoms. Sleep hygiene and related behavioral methods to improve sleep are prudent and common. Practitioners approach FS patients with a multidisciplinary approach as they do patients with other forms of chronic pain.

Consider oral amitriptyline (Elavil) at bedtime in very low doses (e.g., 10–25 milligrams) or cyclobenzaprine (Flexeril). These medications reduce alpha intrusion into stage IV or delta sleep. This is a condition associated with FS although not specific to it. Alpha–delta sleep disturbance occurs often with FS but also with many other conditions. Nevertheless, some believe that this intrusion of alpha activity into the deep or restorative sleep stage contributes to FS and other disorders. Trials of analgesics or NSAIDs are also common.

Consider low-impact cardiovascular aerobic exercises (e.g., fast walking and bicycling) for selected patients if they can tolerate them. Other therapies include radiant heat, relaxation, stretching, massage, and physical conditioning exercises. If necessary, consider hot packs, high galvanic stimulation, injections, and/or spray and stretch for selected patients.

One paper suggested considering cognitive-behavioral treatment (Bradley, 1989) and described procedures, experimental research designs, and methodology features for such studies. The rationale sounds good. The author suggests five groups. Combine the cognitive-behavioral treatment with medication and aerobic exercise and compare it to a waiting-list group. Compare these groups with an attention-placebo group combined with medication and aerobic exercise. Compare these groups with a medication group, and an exercise group combined with the attention–placebo. His cognitive-behavioral intervention is not strictly cognitive-behavioral. It is a multicomponent treatment including two sessions of relaxation with breathing, warming imagery, and relaxation imagery.

IMPLICATIONS, GUIDELINES, AND LIMITS

For clinical practitioners using relaxation and biofeedback, it may not matter much whether the diagnosis is FS, MPS, or tension myalgia. The roles of relaxation and EMG biofeedback are the same. Consider comprehensive muscle relaxation with biofeedback to enhance general relaxation and for specific body areas involved. I would not limit biofeedback to the frontal area. The logic of using only frontal EMG for these patients escapes me as it probably does many practitioners and patients. However, research is lacking for other areas, and we await more studies.

Many practitioners use multiple muscle sites and simultaneous EMG channels with patients in multiple postures or positions and during multiple office stressor conditions. This may be useful for the regional forms of tension myalgia, although I am unaware of any published research on this subject. I also can see the potential for this more comprehensive approach with patients with other types of tension myalgia, including FS, especially if other and more conservative therapy phases (e.g. medications, increased quality and/or quantity of sleep, exercises, general relaxation) have had insufficient results. Despite its logic, this more comprehensive type of therapy can be time consuming and expensive. Thus, within a stepped-care model, practitioners should consider limiting its use except for selected patients.

Other forms of psychotherapy and stress management are proper for selected patients with significant psychological and stress problems. Tailor treatment to the individual patient. Always treat these patients in close collaboration with physicians in proper specialties.

Consider using relaxation and biofeedback in a stepped-care model. For example, one could use these therapies after stopping other unsuccessful treatments or after a plateau in progress from other treatments. Consider the following sequence that depends on the individual and preferences of the practitioner and patient. A baseline is ideal but often not practical in clinical practice (see Chapter 7). The number of weeks noted are guideline estimates. Treating FS and checking the effects of each treatment take much time. Practitioners will tailor the sequence and content. Insert time between treatments to determine the duration of treatment effects when improvement occurs with a treatment.

Baseline (2–4 weeks).

Patient education and reassurance (at beginning and periodically during treatment).

Medications and adjustment of dosage and type (4–6+ weeks), usually a first-line treatment, but anytime indicated for sleep efficiency, pain relief, and/or mood.

Physical therapy, office-based (6–8 weeks), often early, but can be anytime, for posture, body mechanics, anatomic adjustments, heat, stretching, spray/stretch, etc. Selection depends on patient and effects of treatments.

Exercises for conditioning, non-office-based (4–6+ weeks).

Relaxation and EMG biofeedback (4–8 weeks), often after adequate trials of other treatments; for general relaxation and specific muscles and sets; alone or with some parts of PT program; not a first-line treatment.

Psychological assessment with interview and self-report measures after above, before relaxation, or before all treatments.

Stress management counseling for selected problems (4–6+ weeks). Provide this anytime clearly indicated which is often very early.

Add other treatments usually after the above, if unsuccessful.

Also, consider the treatment algorithm proposed by Thompson (1990) for tension myalgia. It provides a useful model for planning treatment. Practitioners often will combine treatments, and that is often proper. For example, one often combines physical therapy and exercise. I suggest avoiding several office sessions for relaxation without or with biofeedback when starting another treatment such as medication, physical therapy, or exercise.

CONCLUSION

Fibromyalgia syndrome requires multicomponent treatment. Muscle-relaxation therapies and EMG biofeedback are logical and recommended parts of such treatment, although to date there is very little research on this topic.

GLOSSARY

ALPHA–DELTA SLEEP. Anamolous sleep phenomenon, originally described by Hauri & Hawkins (1973), wherein alpha (7.5–11 Hertz) EEG activity occurs in NREM sleep. The occurrence of alpha during delta or slow wave (Stages III and IV) sleep is characteristic and gives this finding its name (Fredrickson & Krueger, 1994). Thought to interfere with restorative nature of the delta sleep stage. The "alpha waves are not regularly accompanied by EMG, respiratory, or other physiological evidence of arousal" (Fredrickson & Krueger, 1994, p. 530). Found in many, but not all, persons with FS and in people with other medical conditions. Also known as "alpha EEG NREM sleep anomaly" (Moldofsky, 1990). Patients with alpha–delta sleep often complain of light and interrupted sleep, feeling unrefreshed and tired upon awakening, daytime fatigue, stiffness, and muscle aching, but not usually of excess daytime sleepiness. Thus, FS is sometimes referred to as a "nonrestorative sleep syndrome." One must differentiate the presence of increased alpha waves during sleep from causes such as from the use of sedative/hypnotics or stimulants that also can produce alpha and background fast activity.

AMITRIPTYLINE (Trade names Elavil and Endep). A tricyclic antidepressant (TCA) drug used in smaller doses for headaches (especially chronic daily headache), episodic tension-type headache, atypical face pain, neck pain, and pain syndromes with sleep disturbance or anxiety. Also used for intermittent migraine and related headaches. Also can help sleep-onset insomnia. Proposed mechanisms include increased synaptic norepinephrine or serotonin, inhibiting 5-HT and norepinephrine reuptake, effects on 5-HT_2 receptors, and decreased beta-receptor density. (Also in Chapters 14 and 15; see *norepinephrine*, Chapter 7.)

AXIAL SKELETAL PAIN. Pain in areas of the cervical spine, anterior chest, thoracic spine, or low back.

CORTISOL. The major natural glucocorticoid hormone released from the adrenal cortex. Regulates aspects of metabolism. (See Chapters 7, 18, 37.)

CYCLOBENZAPRINE (Trade name Flexeril). Relieves skeletal muscle spasm of local origin. Used for a variety of painful musculosketal conditions. Often used with physical therapy, rest, and relaxation.

DEXAMETHASONE (DXT). A synthetic glucocorticoid 25 times more potent than cortisol. Many indications and uses, including as an anti-inflammatory agent. Dexamethasone suppression test is used as a test of hypothalamic–pituitary–adrenocortical function as in the diagnosis of Cushing's syndrome. Also used as a replacement therapy for adrenal insufficiency.

DOLORIMETER. An instrument to measure the severity of tenderness at the soft tissue sites. It uses a pressure algometer with a spring-loaded gauge capped with a flat circular rubber or cork stopper about 1.5 centimeters in diameter. One advances the instrument at increments of about 1 kilogram per second and asks the patient to say when it feels painful. The pain threshold is the level at which the person shifts from feeling pressure to reporting pain.

DYSMENORRHEA. Symptoms, including pain, associated with and during menstruation.

EPICONDYLES. Bony promininces above or on a smooth articular eminence of a bone above its condyle.

FIBROMYALGIA SYNDROME (FS). Constellation of specific symptoms now also called fibromyalgia. (See text.)

FIBROSITIS. Old term still sometimes used. Once used to refer to many pain disorders and was once assumed to include inflammation. Pathological studies dispelled this notion. Different from FS.

HYPERPROLACTINEMIC. Pertaining to, characterized by, or affected by hyperprolactinemia—increased levels of prolactin in the blood. Often associated with microadenoma of the anterior pituitary causing overproduction of the prolactin hormone. Can cause irregularity and cessation of menstruation in women and infertility (hypogonadism) and impotence in men. Associated with amenorrhea and galactorrhea (excess or spontaneous milk flow) in females.

HYPOTHALAMIC–PITUITARY–THYROID AXIS. A term reflecting the interrelationship among the hypothalamus, pituitary, and thyroid glands.

IMIPRAMINE. Anticholinergic medication used for many symptoms including depression and nocturnal enuresis. (See Chapter 25.)

INTERTRANSVERSE LIGAMENTS OF C_{5-7}. Intertransverse ligaments are fibrous bands from one vertebral transverse process to the next. However, they are lacking in the cervical region compared to the lumbar and thoracic regions.

McGILL PAIN QUESTIONNAIRE (MPQ). See Chapter 6.

MMPI/MMPI-2. Minnesota Multiphasic Personality Inventory. (See Chapters 6, 14.)

MYOFASCIAL PAIN SYNDROME (MPS). Common term for muscle strain resulting in tissue damage. Distinguished from FS. In MPS, some (e.g., Dr. Janet Travell) focus on trigger points and a palpable band of tight muscle versus the multiple tender points in FS. (See text.)

NOCICEPTIVE. "Nociceptor is a perpheral nerve organ that receives and transmits painful sensations" (Dox, Melloni, & Eisner, 1979, p. 335). Nociception refers to the body's neurophysiological response to tissue damage. Distinguish nociception from pain, pain behavior, and suffering. "Nociception is the processing of stimuli that are defined as related to the stimulation of nociceptors and capable of being experienced as pain" (Turk & Melzack, 1992, pp. 8–9). Pain is a perceptual process and different from peripheral stimulation, especially as cognitive factors amplify and distort pain experience and suffering.

NONRESTORATIVE SLEEP SYNDROME. Unrefreshing sleep. Associated with disturbance in Stage IV sleep. (See *alpha–delta sleep*.)

NONSTEROIDAL ANTI-INFLAMMATORY DRUGS (NSAID). Aspirin and other salicylates, indomethacin (Indocin), ibuprofen (Advil, Motrin-IB, Nuprin), naproxen, and fenoprofen (Nalfon) are common examples.

OCCIPUT. Area where the neck muscles attach to the back of the head. Lower part of the back of the head.

PATHOGNOMONIC SIGNS. "Specifically distinctive or characteristic of a disease or pathologic condition; a sign or symptom on which a diagnosis can be made" (*Dorland's Illustrated Medical Dictionary*, 1988).

PROGRESSIVE MUSCLE RELAXATION. A very common type of muscle and general relaxation developed by Edmund Jacobson. Starts with tensing and releasing of specific muscle groups and progresses to tensing larger groups, discriminating between tension in selected areas and relaxation in others, and eventually to releasing muscle tension without tensing. The tensing portion is sometimes mistakenly used alone.

PROLACTIN (PRL). Hormone from the anterior lobe of the pituitary. Stimulates milk secretion. Secretion has circadian rhythmicity with increased secretion during specific hours.

PROXIMAL. Nearest the center, midline, point of attachment, or point of origin. Opposite of distal–farthest from a reference point. For example, in limbs, proximal is nearer to the shoulders and hips, and distal is nearest the hands and feet.

SCAPULA. Shoulder blade.

SICKNESS IMPACT PROFILE (SIP). A psychometrically sound and comprehensively tested and revised self-administered or interviewer-administered measure of perceived health status.

SPRAY AND STRETCH (STRETCH AND SPRAY). The use of ethyl chloride to relieve musculoskeletal pain and allow stretching of the muscles. A major part of myofascial therapy as described by Janet G. Travell, M.D., and David G. Simons, M.D. It inactivates myofascial trigger points more quickly than local injections or other methods. Although the spray occurs first, the stretch is the necessary component, and the spray merely eases the stretch.

STERNOMASTOID. Muscles connecting the sternum (breastbone) and the clavicle (collarbone) to the mastoid process of the temporal bone at the nuchal line of the occipital bone (back of the lower part of the ear). Sometimes still called the sternocleidomastoid muscle. Rotates and extends head. Flexes vertebral column.

SUPRASPINATUS MUSCLE. A deep muscle in the upper back and shoulder area under the trapezius. It abducts (draws away) the arm.

TENSION MYALGIA. Common term used to describe many muscle pain disorders. Commonly used at the Mayo Clinics. Implies that muscle tension is caused by spasm, poor posture, overuse, and other factors significant in worsening and perhaps causing muscle pain. Avoids implication of inflammation. Can be divided into three groups: Generalized tension myalgia corresponds to FS, localized tension myalgia corresponds to MPS, and regional tension myalgia fits tension myalgia or most patients with symptoms between the others.

THYROID-STIMULATING HORMONE (TSH). Thyrotropic hormone. Hormone of the anterior pituitary gland. Stimulates growth and function of the thyroid gland.

TRANSDERMAL CLONIDINE. An antihypertensive drug applied to and entering the skin by a patch form or ointment.

TRAPEZIUS MUSCLE. Large triangular muscle of the neck, shoulders, and midback regions. Required to support the shoulders and postural control of the shoulder girdle even standing at rest. Participates with the levator scapulae to raise the shoulders. Participates with other muscles for other movements such as abducting the arm. Has three sets of fibers—upper, middle, and lower. Each set can function separately with other muscles with similar function, or the three sets can work together to rotate the scapula.

TRIGGER POINTS (TrP). One or more hyperirritable spots within the belly of a muscle. So named because, when stimulated, it tends to cause referred pain in distinct distributions. The definition of a TrP, according to Travell and Simons (1983): (1) tender area within a muscle belly; (2) pressure on a TrP causes pain and/or tingling in specific distribution; (3) the muscle shortens, resulting in reduced ROM, and stretching or contracting the muscle causes pain; (4) muscle feels taut at and around the TrP; (5) stimulating the TrP (by snapping it or needling it) often causes muscle contraction: (6) injection of a local anesthetic into the TrP eliminates the local and referred pain.

TROCHANTER PROMINENCE. Major and minor prominences on the upper part of the femur (thigh bone), the bone from the pelvis to the knee and the longest, largest bone in the body.

VISUAL ANALOGUE SCALE (VAS). A straight line, usually 10 centimeters long, with ends labeled as the extremes of pain intensity (e.g., "no pain" to "pain as bad as it could be") or pain affect (e.g., "not bad at all" to "the most unpleasant feeling possible for me"). May have specific points along the line labeled with intensity-denoting adjectives or numbers, called graphic rating scales. Patients indicate which point along the line best represents their pain intensity (and/or pain affect). The distance from the "no pain" (or "not bad at all") end to the mark made by the patient is the pain intensity (or pain affect) score. (Jensen & Karoly, 1992; see Chapters 14 and 15.)

ACKNOWLEDGMENTS

I am very thankful to two physiatrist (pronounced phys-e-at'-rist) colleagues, Jeffrey M. Thompson, M.D., of Mayo Clinic Rochester, and Gudni Thorsteinsson, M.D., of Mayo Clinic Jacksonville, and rheumatologist colleague William W. Ginsberg, M.D., of Mayo Clinic Jacksonville, for their reviews of a draft of this chapter. Their comments, suggestions, and corrections were helpful. This appreciation in no way implies their endorsement of the content of this chapter.

REFERENCES

Baumstark, K. E., & Buckelew, S. P. (1992). Fibromyalgia: Clinical signs, research findings, treatment implications, and future directions. *Annals of Behavioral Medicine, 14*(4), 282–291.

Bergner, M., Bobbitt, R. A., Pollard, W. E., Martin, D. P., & Gilson, B. S. (1976). The Sickness Impact Profile: Conceptual formulation and methodolgy for the development of a health status measures. *International Journal of Health Services, 6*, 393–415.

Bergner, M., Bobbitt, R. A., Carter, W. B., & Gilson, B. S. (1981). The Sickness Impact Profile: Development and final revision of a health status measure. *Medical Care, 19*, 787–805.

Bradley, L. A. (1989). Cognitive-behavioral therapy for primary fibromyalgia. *Journal of Rheumatology, 16*(Supp. 19), 131–136.

Brantley, P. J., Waggoner, C. D., Jones, G. N., & Rappaport, N. B. (1987). A daily stress inventory: Development, reliability, and validity. *Journal of Behavioral Medicine, 10*(1), 61–74.

Clark, S., Campbell, S. M., Forehand, M. E., Tindall, E. A., & Bennett, R. M. (1985). Clinical characteristics of fibrositis: II. A "blinded," controlled study using standard psychological tests. *Arthritis and Rheumatism, 28*, 132–137.

Colligan, R. C., Osborne, D., & Swenson, W. M. (1984). The aging MMPI: Development of contemporary norms. *Mayo Clinic Proceedings, 59*, 377–390.

Daily, P. A., Bishop, G. D., Russell, I. J., & Fletcher, E. M. (1990). Psychological stress and the fibrositis/fibromyalgia syndrome. *Journal of Rheumatology, 17*(10), 1380–1385.

Dorland's illustrated medical dictionary (27th ed.). (1988). Philadelphia: W. B. Saunders.

Dox, I., Melloni, B. J., & Eisner, G. M. (1979). *Melloni's illustrated medical dictionary.* Baltimore: Williams & Wilkins.

Ferraccioli, G., Cavalieri, F., Salaffi, F., Fontana, S., Scita, F., Nolli, M., & Maestri, D. (1990). Neuroendocrinologic findings in primary fibromyalgia (soft tissue chronic pain syndrome) and in other chronic rheumatic conditions (rheumatoid arthritis, low back pain). *Journal of Rheumatology, 17*(70), 869–873.

Ferraccioli, G., Ghirelli, L., Scita, F., Nolli, M., Moozzani, M., Fontana, S., Scorsonelli, M., Tridenti, A., & DeRisio, C. (1987). EMG-biofeedback training in fibromyalgia syndrome. *The Journal of Rheumatology, 14*, 820–825.

Fischer, J., & Corcoran, K. (1994). *Measures for clinical practice: A sourcebook* (2nd ed.). New York: Free Press.

Fredrickson, P. A., & Krueger, B. R. (1994). Insomnia associated with specific polysomnographic findings. In M. H. Kryger, T. Roth, & W. C. Dement (Eds.), *Principles and practice of sleep medicine* (2nd ed., pp. 523–534). Philadelphia: W. B. Saunders.

Fricton, J. R., & Awad, E. A. (Eds.). (1990). *Myofascial pain and fibromyalgia: Advances in pain research and therapy* (Vol. 17). New York: Raven Press.

Goldenberg, D. L. (1989, September 30). Diagnostic and therapeutic challenges of fibromyalgia. *Hospital Practice*, 39–52.

Goldenberg, D. L. (1990). Clinical features of fibromyalgia. In J. R. Fricton & E. A. Awad (Eds.), *Myofascial pain and fibromyalgia: Advances in pain research and therapy* (Vol. 17, pp. 139–146). New York: Raven Press.

Hauri, P., & Hawkins, D. R. (1973). Alpha–delta sleep. *Electroencephalography and Clinical Neurophysiology, 34,* 233–237.

Hudson, J. I., Goldenberg, D. L., Pope, H. G. Jr., Keck, P. E. Jr., & Schlesinger, L. (1992). Comorbidity of fibromyalgia with medical and psychiatric disorders. *American Journal of Medicine, 92,* 363–367.

Hudson, J. I., & Pope, H. G. Jr. (1989). Fibromyalgia and psychopathology: Is fibromyalgia a form of "affective spectrum disorder"? *Journal of Rheumatology, 16*(Suppl. 19), 15–22.

Hudson, J. I., & Pope, H. G. Jr. (1990). Affective spectrum disorder: Does antidepressant response identify a family of disorders with a common pathophysiology? *American Journal of Psychiatry, 147,* 552–564.

Jensen, M. P., & Karoly, P. (1992). Self-report scales and procedures for assessing pain in adults. In D. C. Turk & R. Melzack (Eds.), *Handbook of pain assessment.* New York: Guilford Press.

McCain, G. A. (1990). Management of the fibromyalgia syndrome. In J. R. Fricton & E. A. Awad (Eds.), *Myofascial pain and fibromyalgia: Advances in pain research and therapy* (Vol. 17, pp. 289–303). New York: Raven Press.

Meenan, R. F., Gertman, P. M., Mason, J. H., & Dunaiff, R. (1982). The arthritis impact measurement scales: Further investigation of a health status measure. *Arthritis and Rheumatism, 25,* 1048–1053.

Melzack, R. (1975). The McGill Pain Questionnaire: Major properties and scoring methods. *Pain, 1,* 277–299.

Melzack, R., & Katz, J. (1992). The McGill Pain Questionnaire: Appraisal and current status. In D. C. Turk & R. Melzack (Eds.), *Handbook of pain assessment* (pp. 152–168). New York: Guilford Press.

Merskey, H. (1989). Physical and psychological considerations in the classification of fibromyalgia. *Journal of Rheumatology 16*(Suppl 19), 72–79.

Moldofsky, H. (1989). Sleep and fibrositis syndrome. *Rheumatic Diseases Clinics of North America, 15*(1), 91–103.

Moldofsky, H. (1990). The contribution of sleep-wake physiology to fibromyalgia. In J. R. Fricton & E. A. Awad (Eds.), *Myofascial pain and fibromyalgia: Advances in pain research and therapy* (Vol. 17, pp. 227–240). New York: Raven Press.

Moldofsky, H., Carisbrick, P., England, R., & Smyth, H. (1975). Musculoskeletal symptoms and non-REM sleep disturbance in patients with "fibrositis syndrome" and healthy subjects. *Psychosomatic Medicine, 37*(4), 341–351.

Moldofsky, H., & Scarisbrick, P. (1976). Induction of neuroasthenic musculoskeletal pain syndrome by selective sleep stage deprivation. *Psychosomatic Medicine, 38*(1), 35–44.

Radloff, L. S. (1977). The CES-scale: A self-reported depression scale for research in the general population. *Applied Physiological Measurement, 1,* 385–401.

Russell, I. J. (1990). Treatment of patients with Fibromyalgia Syndrome: Considerations of the whys and wherefores. In J. R. Fricton & E. A. Awad (Eds.), *Myofascial pain and fibromyalgia: Advances in pain research and therapy* (Vol. 17, pp. 305–314). New York: Raven Press.

Russell, I. J., Fletcher, E. M., Michalek, J. E., McBroom, P. C., & Hester, G. G. (1991). Treatment of primary fibrositis/fibromyalgia syndrome with ibuprofen and alprazolam: A double-blind, placebo-controlled study. *Arthritis and Rheumatism, 34*(5), 552–560.

The Sickness Impact Profile: A brief summary of its purpose, uses, and administration. (1978). Unpublished manual, University of Washington, Department of Health Services, Seattle.

Thompson, J. M. (1990). Tension myalgia as a diagnosis at the Mayo Clinic and its relationship to fibrositis, fibromyalgia, and myofascial pain syndrome. *Mayo Clinic Proceedings, 65,* 1237–1248.

Travell, J. G., & Simons, D. G. (1983). *Myofacial pain and dysfunction: The trigger point manual.* Baltimore: Williams & Wilkins.

Turk, D. C., & Flor, H. (1989). Primary fibromyalgia is greater than tender points: Toward a multiaxial taxonomy. *Journal of Rheumatology 16*(Suppl. 19), 80–86.

Turk, D. C., & Melzack, R. (Eds.). (1992). *Handbook of pain assessment*. New York: Guilford Press.

Wolfe, F., Smythe, H. A., Yunus, M. B., Bennett, R. M., Bombardier, C., Goldenberg, D. L., Tugwell, P., Campbell, S. M., Abeles, M., Clark P., Gam, A. G., Farber, S. J., Fiechtner, J. J., Franklin, C. M., Gasstter, R. A., Hamaty, D., Lessard, J., Lichtbroun, A. S., Masi, A. T., McCain, G. A., Reynolds, W. J., Tomano, T. J., Russell, I. J., & Sheon, R. P. (1990). The American College of Rheumatology 1990 criteria for the classification of fibromyalgia: Report of the multicenter criteria committee. *Arthritis and Rheumatism, 33*(2), 160–172.

Yunus, M. B., Ahles, T. A., Aldag, J. C., & Masi, A. T. (1991). Relationship of clinical features with psychological status in primary fibromyalgia. *Arthritis and Rheumatism, 34*(1), 15–21.

36

Treating Special Populations

Mark S. Schwartz

I chose five special populations to highlight the potential for applying treatment procedures to develop physiological self-regulation. The special populations are people with developmental disabilities, older age, schizophrenia, postpolio symptoms, and amputees with phantom-limb pain. These patients are among those some professionals and others might not think are amenable to these treatments. I cannot do justice to the intricacies of treating these people. There is not enough space, and I need to rely mostly on available publications. However, I intend to add something useful and to present enough information to give direction and perspective.

TREATING PEOPLE
WITH DEVELOPMENTAL DISABILITES

Michultka, Poppen, and Blanchard (1988) report the successful treatment of a 29-year-old male patient with severe functional retardation. They used special relaxation procedures called behavioral relaxation training (BRT) (Shilling & Poppen, 1983). The symptoms treated were migraines and frequent tension-type headaches that had been occurring since about age 19. The clinical decision and problems facing the practitioner were whether or not to treat and how to do it. Other reports with groups of developmentally disabled people also support the use of BRT (Lindsay, Baty, Michie, & Richardson, 1989). Biofeedback was not part of the treatment in these reports, however, the authors illustrate the value of relaxation for some of these people, and other studies show the potential value of electromyographic (EMG) biofeedback (Calamari, Geist, & Shahbazian, 1987). Including this case and other references encourages practitioners to adapt relaxation and biofeedback for use with this patient population.

This patient's diagnosis at age 7 was autism attributed to anoxia at birth. At age 26, he achieved a Stanford–Binet IQ below 30. He used one- and two-word phrases and echolalia to express himself. Sometimes, his receptive language allowed him to follow short sequences of commands. However, this was not consistent, and sometimes he did not follow even one-word requests. He had some gross and fine motor skills and could dress and bathe himself.

BRT provided the core of the treatment provided by Denise Michultka and her colleagues at the subject's residential community home (Michultka et al., 1988). There was extensive pretreatment assessment and a baseline for 4 months. The assessment included 15 BRT ratings during "three, 5-minute periods intermittently spaced throughout the 30-minute assessment meeting" (p. 260). The staff checked for complaints of headache and checked the use of medications (Fiorinal, aspirin, and acetaminophen).

Treatment Summary

Readers should read the original article for the details. There were 10 acquisition sessions and 9 sessions assessing learned skills. The former were about 30 minutes and involved demonstrations of each relaxed behavior. The therapist's verbal reinforcements started with a continuous schedule. They were later contingent on longer times for each relaxation behavior. The times were 5, 10, 30, and 60 seconds. Taste reinforcements, twice a session, were for compliance. In the skill sessions, the subject showed that he could do the 10 behaviors and maintain them during about 10 minutes of independent relaxation.

Clinical Response/Results

The mean number of BRT ratings improved gradually. It started with a 15% proficiency rate during the baseline and increased to 80% or more during the last few of the 19 sessions. The subject maintained this during a 3-month follow-up session. The mean number of complaints of headache and his use of analgesic medications declined about 50% at the end of treatment. An informal follow-up with his guardian several months later indicated he no longer complained of headaches or took Fiorinal.

Implications and Limits

Michultka et al. (1988) support the statement that "BRT is a viable method for teaching relaxation to individuals with moderate to severe developmental disabilities" (p. 264). The authors cautiously speculate that their intervention had "a significant effect in decreasing the symptoms of . . . chronic headaches" (p. 264). The use and adaptation of BRT procedures for anxiety in people with severe developmental disabilities have support (Lindsay et al., 1989). These procedures avoid the conceptual awareness needed and so difficult to achieve by people with severe retardation who try to use other forms of relaxation. Thus, it is a major advantage. As Lindsay et al. (1989) describe the sequence:

> The instructor demonstrates the unrelaxed and relaxed states in each area and then helps the person to copy the relaxed behaviors . . . . in a comfortable chair. [They are] . . . asked first to watch the unrelaxed behaviour and then to watch and imitate the relaxed behaviour. . . . with manual guidance if necessary. (pp. 133–134).

There is potential cost-efficiency in using this treatment for this population as a result of minimal professional time and reduced time and expense for management. Further, there is less need for medical attention and tests, and there exists a potential for at least partial home care rather than only residential care.

The limits of the report include a possible bias of the staff reporting complaints of headache and medication use. There are problems with compliance and the length of treatment because of behavioral problems. There were no physiological data because of the subject's motor behavior. The "A–B design" does not allow clear evidence of a treatment effect for the headache symptoms.

Lindsay and his colleagues (1988, 1989) warn of perceived potential abuse of using this "powerful psychological technique" for people who are mentally retarded if it is used solely to keep them quiet and manageable rather than "as a beginning to a treatment program whereby the person is introduced to more adaptive and stimulating opportunities" (Lindsay et al., 1989, p. 139).

TREATING OLDER PEOPLE

The frontier for applications for the elderly involves improving selection and refining treatment procedures. Motivated, creative, and adequately financed developers and settlers will follow the trailblazers in this area.

A common assumption, when I was a young[1] person in this field, was that biofeedback therapies were for young and middle-aged people. It was assumed that older people probably could not learn or relearn psychophysiological self-regulation. Many assumed that biofeedback procedures were too complicated and subtle for older people. Researchers and clinical practitioners eager to show success focused on younger patients. One often assumed that they were more capable of participating in these novel procedures.

In my middle years, changes occurred in reports about biofeedback for older people (Andrasik, 1991). That was about the time the first edition of this book appeared and shortly thereafter. Now, as I near "upper middle age," there is a surge of successful applications for older age groups.

Maria Mannarino spoke for the National Institute on Aging of the National Institutes of Health. She reminded us that in 1990 there are about 52 million Americans aged 65 or older. This is about 22% of the population with 8% at least aged 75 and over 7 million persons aged 80 or older. By the year 2020, the projection is for nearly 29% of us to be aged 65 or older and 4.1% to be aged 80 or older. The latter group will be over 12 million strong. Data from 1983–1984,[2] based on household interviews of civilians not in institutions, indicated for each age group 75 years and over, 75–84 years, and 85 years and over, 35% reported being in excellent or very good health (Mannarino, 1991, p. 392).

The belief in inevitable decline in physical, mental, and sexual functioning with age was accepted as a fact until recently. However, we now know that this inevitable decline is a myth wrote T. Franklin Williams as the Director of the National Institute on Aging (Williams, 1991). These functions do not inevitably decline. Many older persons are functioning very well. For example, in a study of persons without coronary artery disease,

> The cardiac output of people in their 80s was as good as that of people in their 20s . . . . there is great individual variability across the life span . . . . there really is no evidence that cardiac output declines with age. (Williams, 1991, p. 338)

Williams (1991) went on to praise Warner Schaie (1983, 1989) as providing "the most outstanding work on mental functioning across the age span" and as providing "the best longitudinal data on a population followed from age 50 through the 80s" (p. 340). That report shows "no consistent decline in mental function until the middle 80s" (p. 340). Williams (1991) cites evidence that, although there is considerable variability, stability holds for other organ systems as well. There is much research support showing that

---

[1]I do not know when elderly starts in terms of age. There are no agreed upon age criteria for separating young adult, middle age, and elderly. If 40–55 is middle age, as it is according to some, then elderly starts at 56. Well, I am 53, and not ready. My preference is to start elderly as young as age 65. Of course, when I get near age 65, I might adjust that age slightly. Age statistics are often in 10-year blocks from a mid-decade as 45–54, 55–64, 65–74, like the standardization groups for the intelligence and memory measures. For the present discussion, I propose 20–29 as young adult, 30–39 as low middle age or high young adulthood, 40–54 as middle age, and here I add another category "high middle age" as 55–64, older age as 65–74, and elderly as 75+. In 1990, there were over 20 million people age 75+. They are very different from people aged 55–64 and should be treated differently.

[2]Division of Health Interview Statistics, National Center for Health Statistics: Data from the National Health Interview Survey.

older adults have a substantial reserve capacity and are capable of increasing their performance on tests of fluid intelligence as a consequence of guided instruction in problem-solving strategies by an "expert" tutor. (Baltes, Sowarka, & Kliegl, 1989, p. 217)

These investigators at the prestigious Max Planck Institute for Human Development and Education in Berlin, then showed that "older adults are able to generate similar training benefits by themselves without guided instruction in test-relevant cognitive skills by a tutor" (p. 217). Their sample consisted of 72 recruited city-dwelling, elderly adults with an average age of 72 (range 63–90). Their "average educational level (roughly comparable with U.S. information on educational history) was 10.7 years ($SD = 2.0$)" (p. 218). Their reported subjective health was better than average. Older people can learn to solve a variety of tasks and novel problems. They can do this with guided help or without it.

Consider the example involving the neuroendocrine system in response to standard stress tolerance tests cited by Williams (1991).

The circulating level of norepinephrine at rest is about the same for all ages. With the exercise stress test, the norepinephrine level goes far higher in older participants than in younger ones, and . . . stays high. [However], despite this marked rise in norepinephrine, the heart rate in older people does not speed up as much as it does in younger people . . . . true of epinephrine as well: the heart does not respond to the stimulation of these adrenergic circulating hormones. It is believed that these hormones go higher in response to the heart rates's failure to speed up in older persons. This is the body's attempt to try to speed up the heart, but it is not very successful in older people. The cardiac output . . . can increase comparably in both older and younger people in the stress test. Older people accomplish this through a larger stroke volume, despite a slower rate. Thus, if needed, the heart is capable of pumping more blood per beat. (pp. 343–344).

There are many disorders for which there are current interventions involving applied psychophysiology and biofeedback. These include, headaches, neuromuscular rehabilitation, chronic pain, urinary incontinence, fecal incontinence, hypertension, chronic constipation, irritable bowel syndrome (IBS), dysphagia, balance and equilibrium, and diabetes. Mannarino (1991) refers to these and others for which there is at least some existing work and several that need attention such as immune functions.

There are needs to change some biofeedback instrumentation to accommodate to the hearing and visual-acuity changes of older persons (Mannarino, 1991). Additional needs are for new norms for psychophysiological activity, reactivity, and recovery from stress.

Chronic Headaches

Very few available papers existed a few years ago about applications of biofeedback to older people. A decade ago, Blanchard cautioned practitioners about using biofeedback and relaxation for treating elderly patients with very chronic headaches (Blanchard, Andrasik, Evans, & Hillhouse, 1985). This provided a useful challenge to which Abrahamson (1987) graciously responded. She reported a case of a 76-year-old person with hypertension whom she had treated successfully. She also noted that she had successfully treated patients from age 60–76 years with a variety of symptoms. She also reviewed the data of Blanchard et al. (1985) and reflected on her own therapy procedures. She suggested that choosing the thermal biofeedback modality, longer sessions, and other changes in procedural variables may help older patients achieve success.

The State University of New York–Albany group were already examining their own data with a larger sample (Kabela, Blanchard, Appelbaum, & Nicholson, 1989). They examined an uncontrolled series of 16 patients, aged 60–77, with headaches and concluded they could achieve success. Ten of these patients achieved the success criterion of 50% or greater improvement. They accomplished this despite the fact that 5 of them had reported headaches for 40–60 years. Other patients reported headaches for 10–25 years. The successfully treated patients were over age 60, and one was 76.

About the same time, Arena and his colleagues[3] published the first prospective study of muscle relaxation treatment of elderly patients with tension headaches (Arena, Hightower, & Chang, 1988). They reported 70% of their sample significantly improved with eight sessions over 6 weeks.

Soon after that, they published the first prospective study of EMG biofeedback in the treatment of an elderly population with tension headaches (Arena, Hannah, Bruno, & Meador, 1991). They reported a sample of eight patients, with an average age of 65 (range 62–71), who had had at least 30 years of headaches. They adapted their procedures to older patients. Using a standard headache index, four patients improved 53–89%, and three others improved 35–45%. Note that three of the four successfully treated patients were among their older patients including the oldest.

The investigators acknowledge the limits of the uncontrolled small series. Nevertheless, it continued to support the value of using applied psychophysiological procedures with persons in this age range.

Chronic Pain

Middaugh and her colleagues at the Medical University of South Carolina are creating important and useful inroads into the frontier of biofeedback applications to older patients, especially those with chronic musculoskeletal back pain and other chronic pain (Middaugh, Levin, Kee, Barchiesi, & Roberts, 1988; Middaugh, Woods, Kee, Harden, & Peters, 1991; Middaugh, Kee, & Peters, 1992). They compared the results of 59 older patients with 58 younger patients treated in a multidisciplinary chronic-pain rehabilitation program (CPRP). These support the application of biofeedback and relaxation procedures and other interventions for older patients. The average age of the older patients was 63 compared with age 37 for the younger.

The program of Middaugh and colleagues is both inpatient and outpatient and includes a variety of patients. Most of them have musculoskeletal back pain (73% of the older and 83% of the younger). The biofeedback and relaxation involved 8–12 sessions of muscle relaxation, breathing, and EMG biofeedback.

The EMG biofeedback typically focused on the upper trapezius muscles for patients with cervical pain and on the lumbar paraspinous muscles for patients with low back pain. With EMG biofeedback, patients practiced muscle relaxation during various activities. These were sitting, standing, walking, and performing daily activities such as writing and simulated driving. Psychophysiological goals included reaching 93.5° F or higher and 12 breaths per minute or lower for respiration. Goals for EMG included 25 microvolts (peak-to-peak[4]) or less during baselines while sitting or standing, and recovery within 15 seconds.

---

[3]Veterans Affairs Medical Center and Medical College of Georgia in Augusta.

[4]Peak-to-peak microvolts are about three times higher than root mean square and integral average microvolts (see Chapter 4).

Before therapy, only two of the eight older patients with chronic cervical pain could relax the upper trapezius muscles during a sitting baseline. They could not recover to a criterion level of relaxation rapidly after three shoulder shrugs and releases. After therapy, six of the eight older patients met both criteria. The comparable data for the six younger patients was one patient meeting criteria (Middaugh et. al., 1991). The older patients also met criteria for hand temperature and respiration rate. There were no differences between the groups. For the present discussion, the important points are that

> biofeedback/relaxation . . . did not pose special problems for older chronic pain patients . . . compared to younger patients with similiar diagnoses and duration of pain who were receiving treatment in the same multidisciplinary treatment program. Older patients . . . (1) achieved equivalent direction and extent of physiological change, (2) learned the physiological self-regulation skills in a comparable number of training sessions, and (3) reported equivalent improvement in pain report . . . as a whole. (Middaugh et al., 1991, p. 376)

The larger sample reported by Middaugh et al. (1992) lent further support for these conclusions. Both groups showed reduced ratings of maximum pain. One can only speculate about the reasons that only the older sample reported by Middaugh et al. (1991) showed a significant drop in ratings of pain at discharge. One must read the 1991 paper for this discussion and other details of the program. There are actual and other probable differences between older and younger patients and the ways that practitioners treat each group (Middaugh et al., 1991). The 17 older patients, aged 55–78, reduced their use of health care services by 93% and reduced their use of pain-related medications 64% (Middaugh et al., 1988). One expects replications and extensions of their work.

Older people can and do make targeted psychophysiological changes, and they often can do as well as younger patients on changing pain ratings. In contrast to statements by some authors (e.g., Kaplan & Kepes, 1989) who speculate that biofeedback may be "less suitable" for elderly people, biofeedback and relaxation procedures are as proper with them as they are with younger patients.

Constipation

The highly successful use of EMG biofeedback for constipation from paradoxical puborectalis contraction includes mostly older patients. The report by Heymen and Wexner (1993) gives the average age of the 39 patients as 62.6. The oldest patient was 84! See more discussion of this application in Chapter 37. For the present discussion, the conclusion is that practitioners must not exclude older patients from this treatment.

Incontinence

Other examples of successful applications of biofeedback for older patients are for those patients with fecal incontinence (Whitehead, Burgio, & Engel, 1985) and urinary incontinence (McDowell, Burgio, Dombrowski, Locher, & Rodriguez, 1992; Middaugh, Whitehead, Burgio, & Engel, 1989).

The average age of the 18 patients with fecal incontinence selected for treatment was 73. The range was 65–92 years! These patients significantly increased sphincter strength with biofeedback. There was a decrease of incontinence of greater than 75% for 10 of the patients (77%). At 6 months, 60% of the patients maintained their improvement, and 42% did so at 1 year (Whitehead et al., 1985, p. 320).

The criteria for these percentages were continence or soiling less than once per month. Of those unsuccessful, two had severe dementia and one "gross loss of sensation for rectal distension" (p. 323). Five patients maintained continence at 1 year. We may also note that three patients had debilitating and progressive illnesses that probably resulted in the relapses.

Significantly, the 92-year-old male patient initially did very well reducing the incontinence from 3.5 to 0.7 incidents per week. The next oldest patients, aged 81 and 78, did very well after treatment and at both follow-up times. The purpose here is mainly to show the value of this therapy for older patients.

Urinary incontinence from strokes in four patients was the focus of the Middaugh et al. (1989) series. The strokes had occurred 8 months, 2, 4, and 10 years earlier among these patients. Their ages ranged from 61–69 years. All "achieved and maintained continence . . ." (p. 3).

The 27 women and 2 men with urinary incontinence in the McDowell et al. (1992) series had an average age of nearly 75. The age range was 56–90 years. Most ($N = 21$) had a mixed type of urinary incontinence, and 7 had only the urge type. Many of the patients selected and doing well had several other significant health problems including depression, stroke, diabetes, and parkinsonism. The 29 selected patients were among 70 initially referred and evaluated. The others were "ineligible based on their mental status, urologic findings, or more urgent medical problems" (p. 374).

One cannot assess the specific need for biofeedback in this multicomponent treatment study. However, that is not the point of including it here. The point is that the selected patients could participate adequately with the biofeedback procedures and showed excellent results. The average weekly number of accidents dropped from 16.9 to 2.5. Individual patients reduced their accidents an average of 81.6% and 10 of the 29 patients became continent.

Conclusion

Using biofeedback and other applied psychophysiological therapy procedures with older people is no longer a frontier position. It recently progressed into a major development in the heartland. One clearly sees that older age is no longer a criterion for excluding patients.

TRAINING PEOPLE WITH POSTPOLIO SYMPTOMS

Postpolio symptoms affect many thousands of people in the United States. People with these symptoms coined the term "postpolio syndrome" (PPS) (Halstead & Rossi, 1985; Frick & Bruno, 1986; Dalakas, 1990) of which fatigue, pain, muscle weakness, and stress-induced symptoms are among the most common symptoms.

Dalakas (1990) reports that estimates of incidence and prevalence of PPS vary widely. However, a review of several references (Cobb, Mulder, Kurland, Beard, & O'Fallon, 1985; Frick & Bruno, 1986; Windebank et al., 1987; Dalakas, 1990; Agre, Rodriquez, & Tafel, 1991; Berlly, Strauser, & Hall, 1991; Bruno & Frick, 1991) suggests that estimates are that at least about 25% of the survivors of paralytic and nonparalytic poliomyelitis will develop some symptoms known as PPS. (See Windebank, 1995, for important diagnostic and prognostic information.) New symptoms typically develop "28 to 35 years after the acute polio attack" (Delakas, 1990, p. 903). Reported estimates of the number of survivors alive today vary from a few hundred thousand to much higher estimates. Depending on which numbers one accepts, the number of present and potential PPS patients is large. Thus, many practitioners using biofeedback are probably in places in which such patients are seen.

Fatigue that is new and unique for the individual is the most common and probably the most debilitating symptom. Cold limbs are also common but less often reported and usually less debilitating. In people who had polio, fewer than a normal number of motor neurons support many muscles (Dalakas, 1990). There are four effects on neurons by polio. Some are unaffected and some recovered fully after original slight effects. Moderately affected neurons survived but are smaller, and those neurons severely affected did not recover completely. The second set looks normal but "their metabolic machinery and functional endurance may be diminished when stressed later in life" (p. 901).

In a large-scale 1985 survey of 1049 people who had prior polio and current fatigue, 61% reported that emotional stress increased their fatigue (Bruno & Frick, 1987). In a 1990 survey, 82% reported the same (Bruno, Frick, & Cohen, 1991). These data suggest that reducing emotional and physical stress is very important for these patients.

The literature using biofeedback with postpolio symptoms is almost nonexistent. Furthermore, "there are no specific treatments for cold limb syndrome noted in the literature" (Winters, 1991, p. 72; Bruno, Johnson, & Berman, 1985a, 1985b). I found only one report of biofeedback for a postpolio symptom, "postpolio cold limb" (Dietvorst & Eulberg, 1986). They treated a 38-year-old patient who had had poliomyelitis at age 4. She was still suffering from cold reactions in her left foot. She had no other active diseases and took no medications. Starting at age 4, her left leg was cold and mottled in cold ambient temperatures. When the leg became cold, she reported needing 8–12 hours of normal room temperatures to warm it to the same temperature as the unaffected right leg.

Multiple types of relaxation and skin-temperature biofeedback from the left foot resulted in much improvement. There were 13 office sessions over 1 year starting in January. The patient reported that it took longer for her affected foot to get cold when exposed to cold. It became easer for her to warm it after short cold exposures. Peak temperatures became higher with one as high as 91°F.

The presence of "cold and discolored extremities and decreased muscle strength when exposed to mildly cool ambient temperatures" is common among people who had poliomyelitis (Bruno et al., 1985b, p. 865). These vasomotor changes result in a spectrum of reddish violet, to deep, dark blue–violet with frequent reports of "concurrent burning pain and hyperesthesia" that can last for hours (p. 865). The etiology is unclear, but there are implications for practitioners using biofeedback. Bruno et al. (1985b) did not find that cold exposure and cognitive stress (mental arithmetic) produce a vasospastic sympathetic hyperflexia. They suggested impaired constriction of cutaneous vessels in these patients and supported the possibility of

> passive dilatation and engorgement of the cutaneous venous capacitance beds . . . [and] a decrease in sympathetic vasoconstrictor efferent activity following destruction of pre- and post-ganglionic sympathetic neurons by the polio virus. (p. 868)

They went on to say that

> engorgement-induced heat loss and deep tissue cooling may cause post-polios' peripheral motor nerves and muscles to function as if they were always exposed to a reduced ambient temperature. . . . The majority of persons who had polio report impairment of muscle functioning and/or pain with exposure to cold ambient temperatures. . . . They must insulate themselves against the cold . . . [and] only a [few] are so severely affected that they present with cold-related symptoms as their chief complaint. (pp. 868–869)

In understanding the pain sensitivity of postpolio patients, practitioners can consider other reports by Bruno and his colleagues (Bruno et al., 1991). They report MRI evidence for "postencephalitis-like lesions" that suggested to them

> polioencephalitic damage to aging reticular activating system and monoaminergic neurons is responsible for post-polio fatigue, and . . . damage to enkephalin-producing neurons is responsible for hypersensitivity to pain in polio surviviors . . . [and] anti-metabolic action of glucocorticoids on polio-damaged, metabolically vulnerable neurons may be responsible for the fatigue and muscle weakness reported by polio survivors during emotional stress. (p. 1269)

I am unsure why the patient reported by Dietvorst and Eulberg (1986) improved. However, one must commend the authors and hope for other attempts and reports.

For those interested in understanding and treating postpolio symptoms, I suggest reading at least Bruno and Frick (1991), Bruno et al. (1985a, 1985b, 1991), and Windebank (1995). These authors do not discuss biofeedback. However, their work is crucial to understanding the pathophysiology and personalities of many people who still suffer with some sequelae from polio. It also is crucial for understanding people experiencing a return of symptoms, new symptoms, or sequelae of PPS.[5] Being a postpolio survivor myself, I find particular fascination with the work of Bruno, Frick, and others.

There are estimates of over 1.5 million survivors of polio in the United States. Estimates as high as nearly half of these report new PPS symptoms including fatigue, muscle weakness in muscles originally affected or spared, new atrophy, decreased endurance, pain in "biomechanically disadvantaged, deformed, or marginally stable joints" (Dalakas, 1990, p. 902), progressive increase in skeletal deformities, muscle pain, and new bulbar, respiratory, or sleep difficulties (Dalakas, 1990; Bruno & Frick, 1991).

The medical community is now more accepting of the diagnosis of PPS, although desired consensus is still lacking. There are psychological symptoms associated with the premorbid personalities and onset of PPS physical symptoms. This is in addition to the physical symptoms. A multimodal behavioral therapy approach may be useful for many of these patients (Bruno & Frick, 1991).

These authors describe what they call a "compulsive psychophysiological disorder" and distinguish it from "compulsive personality disorder." Their criteria are:

> A. A pervasive pattern of continuous and excessive goal-seeking behavior beginning in childhood or adolescence as indicated by at least four of the following: 1. Marked anxiety generated by and avoidance of any decrease in goal-oriented activities or changes in daily schedule. 2. Refusal to delegate responsibilities or allow others to provide assistance associated with an unusually strong need to be in control. 3. Rigidly and inflexibly judges behavior on the basis of ideals of perfection or "normality." 4. Excessive time-consciousness and Type A behavior. 5. Extreme sensitivity to criticism with the constant expectation of failure and rejection. 6. Inability to identify or express emotions, with the exception of anxiety, anger, and sadness.
>
> B. The association of these behaviors with the exacerbation or maintenance of physical symptoms, such as muscle spasm-induced pain, fatigue, or muscle weakness. (p. 1190)

---

[5]Readers very interested in PPS should consider contacting Richard L. Bruno, Ph.D., and Nancy M. Frick, M. Div., at the Harvest Center, 151 Prospect Ave., Hackensack, NJ 07601. Phone numbers are (201)731-3600 ext. 547 and (210)342-6777.

They also note symptoms such as frequent anxiety, insomnia partly associated with cognitive factors, depression, competitiveness, hard driving, overwork, and a need for control.

Implications

When evaluating and treating patients with a history of polio, a practitioner needs knowledge about the presenting symptoms. This is true whether it is a postpolio cold limb, other postpolio sequelae, or symptoms less directly related to the polio. Remember that

> postpolio syndrome is a clinical diagnosis and essentially a diagnosis of exclusion. . . . Every patient should be carefully examined to exclude any other known medical, neurologic, orthopedic, or psychiatric illnesses that could explain the . . . new symptoms. (Dalakas, 1990, p. 901)

These patients need to

> decrease behaviors that cause physical symptoms, initiate self-care activities, and incorporate stress and time management, energy conservation, work simplification, and a program of relaxation, stretching, and non-fatiguing progressive resistance exercises. (Bruno & Frick, 1991, p. 1191)

This program also tries to get the patients to

> list their treatment goals and keep a daily log of activities, perceived exertion, fatigue, muscle weakness, pain, emotional stress, thoughts, and emotions. (Bruno & Frick, p. 1191)

They use cognitive therapy techniques to

> identify and modify dysfunctional beliefs, fears, and emotions . . . [and] . . . challenge long-held beliefs about self-worth and survival and tolerate the emergence of the powerful fears and long-suppressed emotions generated by the polio experience. (Bruno & Frick, p. 1191, 1192)

TREATING PEOPLE DIAGNOSED AS SCHIZOPHRENIC

People diagnosed as schizophrenic have a variety of symptoms for which tension-reduction treatments might help. However, these people obviously also have a variety of behaviors and other characteristics including psychomotor deficits that interfere with relaxation therapies and biofeedback-assisted procedures. They take medications that can interfere with these treatments. Goals are usually not to treat the underlying problem, that is, whatever is causing the constellation of behaviors called schizophrenia. Goals include changing behaviors such as excess muscle tension that can affect other symptoms and behaviors. These include headaches, muscle spasms, insomnia, general tension, anxiety, and aspects of social behavior.

For early work applying biofeedback to this population one looks to only five studies found by Pharr and Coursey (1989) in their review (Acosta, Yamamoto, & Wilcox, 1978; Nigl & Jackson, 1979; Weiner, 1979; Keating, 1981; Wentworth-Rohr, 1981). Using relaxation and biofeedback with these people is obviously extremely challenging, and few professionals venture into applying and reporting the results of their attempts. The first four reports were with 14 inpatients and 12 outpatients. The Wentworth-Rohr report was with 45 inpatients. A recent single case report (Stein & Nikolic, 1989) showed that a patient diagnosed as undifferentiated schizophrenia could accept and participate in relaxation therapies and biofeedback. The patient derived a clinically significant reduction of anxiety based on self-report measures. The authors described interesting modifications of treatment procedures such as role reversals.

The Pharr and Coursey (1989) report supported the use of EMG feedback for lowering muscle tension. They noted that some people diagnosed as schizophrenic can tolerate EMG biofeedback for 40-minute recording sessions. Using the right forearm extensor muscles and a frontal placement, they compared EMG (root mean square microvolts, 100–200 Hertz bandpass) feedback from a meter and an audio tone. Their patients had seven sessions. These mostly involved a 10-minute baseline, 10 minutes of feedback from the forearm, and 10 minutes of feedback from the frontal area. They added 10 more minutes of postsession recording.

Even with medications such as chlorpromazine, lithium, and anti-Parkinson medications, these patients significantly reduced their muscle tension. The baseline EMG levels were very high: 36 and 30 microvolts in sessions 1 and 2. They were somewhat lower, 22 microvolts, by sessions 6 and 7. They reflected the "integrated absolute levels (microvolts per minute) of muscle tension over 1-minute periods of both sites combined" (p. 234).

The postsession EMG level showed no drop in session 1. However, there were large drops in later sessions. They reported drops to 20 microvolts in sessions 4–6, and then to 15 microvolts in session 7. The variances were very large. The comparison groups received progressive relaxation via an audiotape. A control group listened to audiotaped information on adjustment taken from two psychology texts. Neither of these groups showed improvement.

The value of this study lies in its uniqueness at the time. It provided a controlled study using biofeedback with patients diagnosed with schizophrenia. It showed that many of these patients will participate and reduce muscle tension. There also were some positive global behavior changes in social behavior based on the Nurses Observation Scale for Inpatient Evaluation (NOSIE). These are encouraging, although they need replication and extension.

It is useful to have models within which to plan and develop interventions. The Spaulding, Storms, Goodrich, and Sullivan (1986) paper reviews and offers a useful model and perspective for including relaxation therapies and biofeedback in multimodal treatments of patients with schizophrenia. The model they focus on is the vulnerability–stress model of schizophrenia. In this model,

> persons with schizophrenia may have lower thresholds for disorganization that contribute to vulnerability. Stress increases arousal, which brings many competing responses to the same strength, leading to intrusion of inappropriate responses. Interventions that reduce arousal and lower the strengths of competing responses should reduce psychological deficits. Arousal-reducing, attentional, and cognitive interventions are appropriate for . . . schizophrenic disorders. . . . Remediation . . . may facilitate the effectiveness of neuroleptic medications, social skills training, and family therapy. (p. 560)

These authors proposed that one can teach these patients to manage their own arousal during prodromal and postacute phases. Spaulding et al. (1986) further assert that relaxation techniques are very useful and "a popular modality in service programs for severely disordered psychiatric patients" (p. 565). Referring partly to work by Ford, Stroebel, Strong, and Szarek (1982), they add that "biofeedback may prove to be a useful adjunct to . . . arousal-reduction techniques in schizophrenics" (p. 565).

Treatment Considerations

The work of the late Wentworth-Rohr (1981; personal communication, 1980) provides useful clinical guidelines for using biofeedback with these patients. His experience and clinical wisdom suggested that practitioners should consider showing meticulous attention to the questions and apprehensions of these patients. Devote extra time to be sure of the patient's clear and concrete understanding of the source of the signal. He used EMG, temperature, and electrodermal instruments with a variety of relaxation techniques. He emphasized the need for working with only cooperative patients who are past their overtly psychotic episodes.

Wentworth-Rohr carefully explained relaxation techniques "as taking one's attention and mind and placing them where one wants to." He discouraged free association and any techniques or statements suggesting "letting the mind go blank or empty. . . ." He reminded patients "to maintain their attention (passively) on their body regions, rather than to allow their minds or attention to drift off." He encouraged "recollection of an experience of self-adequacy and a sense of tranquility." If the frontal EMG fell to less than 2 microvolts (100–200 Hertz) and respiration became obviously slow and shallow, he lessened the relaxation depth by instructing patients to recall scenes or images. He apparently was trying to avoid falling asleep or "ego regression."

There were an average of three presenting complaints for those patients for whom biofeedback and behavior therapy were appropriate. The range of complaints was one to five. The average duration was about the same for each complaint. The average number of treatment sessions was 11–12 and the range was 1–32. There were 9 or more sessions for 29 of the 45 patients. It is not clear how many of these sessions were exclusively or mostly for biofeedback, and that is a major limitation. However, Wentworth-Rohr and his colleagues used biofeedback with nearly all the patients in the series, and the case examples focused on biofeedback. Relaxation and biofeedback were core parts of the treatment.

There were significant and lasting improvements in 29 of 46 symptoms. Improvement required nine or more sessions. Follow-up time was an average of 14 months and ranged from 6–46 months. Of the original 45 patients, they could follow 31. Of these, 22 had nine or more sessions. Of these, the six who had 9–11 sessions improved on more problems (14/18, p <.018) than those with more sessions or fewer sessions. Of the 16 with 12–32 sessions, most improved (29/46 problems, p <.077). This compares with poor performance on those with eight or fewer sessions (5/22). They did not control for psychotropic medications. Thirty-five of 45 patients were using such medications.

Other guidelines for working with these patients derive from Liberman, Nuechterlein, and Wallace (1982; as reported by Spaulding et al., 1986). They suggested: eliminating all clutter and other distracting stimuli in the treatment room; dividing the tasks into simple steps; repeating steps often to decrease novelty before moving to new tasks; using graphic charts with clear and simple information to show patients their progress; and using praise for proper and correct responding and mild criticism contingent on improper and error responses.

Implications

- Many patients diagnosed as schizophrenic can participate in treatments involving relaxation and biofeedback modalities.
- Select cooperative patients who are not overtly psychotic.
- Consider patients in the prodromal, postacute, and chronic stages.
- Consider special treatment procedures for these patients.

- Physiological changes occur in the desired direction even with a variety of very potent psychotropic medications.
- New symptoms do not develop. A small percentage, 9% (4/45), of patients may show worsening of symptoms. This is not surprising with this population and unlikely due to treatment.
- Eliminate all clutter and other distracting stimuli in the treatment room such as wires and accessories.
- Divide the tasks into simple steps. Use shortened versions of relaxation procedures.
- Use uncluttered visual displays. For example, display one or two channels rather than more. Keep other information off the screens if possible.
- Repeat steps often before moving to new tasks.
- Use clear and simple graphic charts to show their progress.
- Use only mild comments for incorrect responses.
- Use praise often for proper and correct responses.
- Muscle tension is often much higher in these patients than in most other patients especially those typically seen in medical and psychological settings.
- Consider role reversals when teaching relaxation and using biofeedback. For example, allow the patient to teach the therapist a procedure with and without the biofeedback.
- Significant reduction of psychophysiological tension can start within the first few sessions and between the first few sessions.
- Successful reduction of symptoms and maintenance require nine or more sessions with most of these patients.

The use of biofeedback and related treatments with this population should encourage practitioners to work with these and other severely impaired patients. Their diagnosis and the presence of psychotropic medications should not deter practitioners.

One might need the combination of medication with biofeedback treatments with these patients. It is not yet possible to separate the effects of the nonpharmacological treatments.

TREATING PEOPLE WITH PHANTOM-LIMB PAIN

There is good support for the use of biofeedback for phantom-limb pain symptoms in series of patients treated. Interested readers should read the original articles for detailed discussions (e.g., Sherman, 1980; Sherman, 1989; Sherman, Arena, Sherman, & Ernst, 1989). I offer the following as a summary.

Phantom pain is pain experienced in a body part that no longer exists because of traumatic or surgical amputation. The body part is usually a foot, lower leg, hand, or arm. The phenomenon of pain experienced in body areas that no longer are present is less mysterious after physical explanations are considered. For example, most people with phantom pain also have stump pain. Pure phantom pain is less common. Nerves in the residual limb probably seldom, if ever, become normal. These nerves have limited protection. Poorly fitted prostheses and painful sores create vollies of signals to the brain. According to Sherman, Arena, Sherman, and Ernst (1989), these and other stump problems probably stimulate the brain centers that were formerly reactive to the removed portion of the limb.

Receptor interneurons, formerly associated with the amputated portion of the limb, might detect signals produced by intact nerves from the residual limb. They reach the sensory homunculus along tracks formerly associated with the amputated portion of the limb.

Thus, the brain interprets them as starting from the phantom part. Irritation of the stump increases phantom pain, and resolving the stump problem should help reduce this pain.

Increased muscle tension in the residual limb precedes sensations of cramping phantom pain (Sherman et al., 1989; Sherman, Greffen, Evans, & Grana, 1992). These careful researchers cautiously state that "this evidence can not prove that cramping phantom pain is actually caused by increased muscle tension, but it certainly increases the likelihood that it is the underlying cause" (1992, p. 73). It is less clear but "highly likely that changes in muscle tension are also related to onset of . . . shocking-shooting phantom pain" (p. 73). The detailed discussion of this mechanism is in his 1989 article.

Definitions, Incidence, and Features

Burning and cramping, alone or together, are two very common pain descriptions of phantom pain. Another common one is tingling. Other less common descriptions are shooting, shocking, stabbing, throbbing, and twisting pain. The focus on and distinction between burning and cramping are because Sherman et al. (1989) suggest that skin temperature biofeedback is more for burning pain and EMG biofeedback is more for cramping pain.

Among military veterans with amputations, 80% report significant phantom pain. For the vast majority of amputees, none of the standard treatments provides signficant and lasting benefit according to Sherman and Sherman (1985) and Sherman et al. (1989). Most patients in the series reported by Sherman have unilateral above the knee amputations or below the knee amputations. There are also bilateral, shoulder, at hip, toes, above elbow, and below elbow amputees in the series. Some had the amputations within the past 1–2 years. However, most of the amputations occurred many years before the subjects entered Sherman's studies. Most of those reported are midway in this range or older amputations. The reasons for the amputations often involved war injuries and vehicular accidents, and many also were from vascular problems and diabetes.

Biofeedback

Electromyographic biofeedback from the major muscles of the residual limb is the modality for cramping phantom pain. Skin temperature biofeedback to help increase peripheral blood flow is the modality that Sherman uses for burning pain. Relaxation procedures are part of both treatments.

Clinical Response and Outcome

The contributions of Sherman for understanding and treating phantom pain with biofeedback date back nearly two decades. He first reported the successful treatment and short follow-up for a few cases (Sherman, 1976). He acknowledged probably the first published report was the successful use of relaxation treatment and 6-month follow-up for a single case published 1 year earlier (McKechnie, 1975).

Sherman, Gall, and Gormly's (1979) original treatment, which Sherman continues to use, is surface EMG biofeedback and muscle relaxation. The original series of 16 cases were followed for 1–5 years, and 88% maintained their pain reduction (Sherman et al., 1989).

They assert cautious optimism from their preliminary report of thermal biofeedback for 30 patients with pain presumably related to peripheral vasoconstriction (Sherman et al., 1989). Their rationale for relaxation and thermal biofeedback is straightforward. Decreased blood flow to the residual limb results in phantom pain usually involving burning and sometimes throbbing and tingling sensations. Sherman et al. (1989) state that "several lines of logic and evidence increase the likelihood that changes in blood flow in the peripheral limb are the cause of the change in phantom pain" (p. 270). See their report for the details of this treatment series.

Other Treatments

Muscle relaxation procedures are for both types of phantom pain. The rationale is to decrease muscle tension and help increase blood flow by decreasing vasoconstriction. Sherman et al. (1989) notes that when the pain is due to vasoconstriction, "any method that increases blood flow to the residual limb should attenuate the pain" (p. 272). Medications for achieving this include Nifedipine and nitroglycerine. These are important for patients with extensive peripheral vascular disease who have severe problems with peripheral blood flow (Sherman & Barja, 1989). The other treatments to achieve this are less than ideal, although some patients get at least temporary relief (Sherman & Sherman, 1985; Sherman et al., 1989).

Psychological Factors and Measures

As with other types of chronic pain, psychological factors such as stress and fatigue can worsen phantom pain. However, based on their "detailed reanalysis of the literature" (p. 276) and their experience, Sherman et al. (1989) do not believe that psychological variables cause the pain. Self-report measures used for chronic pain and to assess psychological problems are the same as for other conditions for which psychological factors worsen pain. Use a carefully thought out standard set of measures or tailor the measures to the individual patient.

Implications and Limits

- Carefully assess the descriptions of the phantom limb-pain and factors that might be worsening and relieving it.
- For cramping pain, consider including EMG biofeedback from the muscles in the residual limb.
- For burning pain, consider skin temperature biofeedback from the stump area.
- Consider using muscle-relaxation procedures and other relaxation procedures that can reduce muscle tension and increase blood flow.
- Consider medications for peripheral vasodilation for selected patients.

CONCLUSION

This chapter discussed five special populations to highlight the use and potential for biofeedback and other forms of psychophysiological self-regulation. The research is very encouraging and very supportive for the use of biofeedback for older patients or those with phantom-limb pain. Research is at least encouraging for the use of biofeedback with severe developmental disabilities or schizophrenia. Although very limited literature exists for using biofeedback with persons with PPS, the rationale for considering biofeedback as part of a treatment program for selected patients is discussed.

Most practitioners using biofeedback probably do not see patients with severe developmental disabilities, schizophrenia, postpolio symptoms, or amputees with phantom-limb pain. Nevertheless, for those practitioners interested in these groups and symptoms and for those practitioners who do see these patients, this chapter offers useful information about these groups and practical information to justify using special relaxation therapies and biofeedback.

GLOSSARY

A–B DESIGN. A single-case experimental design in which an intervention or treatment (B) follows a baseline (A).

ADRENERGIC CIRCULATING HORMONES. Includes epinephrine (adrenaline) and norepinephrine (noradrenaline). (See *epinephrine, norepinephrine, adrenal medulla*, Chapters 7, 17, 18.)

ANTIMETABOLIC ACTION OF GLUCOCORTICOIDS. A glucocorticoid is any of the group of corticosteroids that mainly affect carbohydrate, fat, and protein metabolism and have many other effects in the body.

BEHAVIORAL RELAXATION TRAINING (BRT). Special relaxation procedures developed by Poppen and colleagues at Southern Illinois University (Schilling & Poppen, 1983). It involves modeling, prompting, verbal feedback, and positive reinforcement of relaxed and unrelaxed overt behaviors and postures in 10 areas of the body. The goal is to teach relaxed postures associated with reduced muscle tension, but it avoids focusing on internal states and sensations of relaxation that people with severe mental retardation and others with severe disabilities may find very difficult to grasp. BRT is often used with the Behavioral Rating Scale (BRS; Poppen & Maurer, 1982) to help document the relaxation behaviors.

CHLORPROMAZINE. A phenothiazine derivative used as a major tranquilizer.

DYSPHAGIA (APHAGIA). Difficulty swallowing.

ECHOLALIA. Stereotyped repeating of words or phrases of another person.

ENKEPHALIN-PRODUCING NEURONS. Neurons that produce enkephalins, neurotransmitters or neuromodulators in many locations in the brain and spinal cord. Affect pain perception, movement, mood, behavior, and neuroendocrine regulation. Also found in exocrine glands of the GI tract.

HOMUNCULUS, SENSORY. Homunculus literally means "a little man." The sensory and motor homunculus is the proportional representation of various parts of the body in the sensory and motor areas of the cerebral cortex. The homunculus is proportional to the amount of cortical area associated with sensory innervation density of the body areas rather than to the size of the body area. For example, the lips and fingers have a relatively large representation in the sensory homunculus. In the motor homunculus, the fingers, hand, and lips have a relatively larger representation.

HYPERESTHESIA. Increased sensitivity to stimulation such as pain, odors, light, sounds, and touch.

LITHIUM. Lithium salts (lithium carbonate). Commonly used to treat bipolar disorder by attentuating mood swings, especially the manic phase. There are other potential applications.

MONOAMINERGIC NEURONS. Neurons that secrete the monoamine neurotransmitters dopamine, norepinephrine, and serotonin. (See *norepinephrine, catecholamines, adrenal medulla*, Chapters 7, 17, 18.)

NOREPINEPHRINE (NORADRENALINE). A natural neurohormone. One type of *catecholamine*, a body compound having a sympathomimetic action. A powerful vasopressor (constrictor of capillaries and arteries). Others include epinephrine and dopamine. Norepinephrine is released by postganglionic adrenergic nerves and the adrenal medulla (see Chapters 7, 18). Has mostly alpha-adrenergic activity and some beta-adrenergic activity. Pharmaceutical is norepinephrine bitartrate (also called levarterenol bitartrate). (Also see Chapters 7, 14–15, 17, 20.)

PARADOXICAL PUBORECTALIS CONTRACTION. Dyscoordination of the EAS and puborectalis muscles. Tightening of these muscles during attempts to defecate. Causes functional outlet obstruction, also known as dyschezia or difficult or painful evacuation of feces. Other terms for this condition are "anismus" and "pelvic floor outlet obstruction syndrome" (See Chapter 37).

PRE- AND POSTGANGLIONIC SYMPATHETIC NEURONS. The cell bodies of preganglionic neurons are in the CNS. Efferent fibers end in the autonomic ganglia. The cell bodies of the postganglionic neurons are in the autonomic ganglia. They relay impulses beyond the ganglia. The *SNS* is a subdivision of the autonomic nervous system whose fibers arise from the thoracic and upper lumbar regions of the spinal cord.

RECEPTOR INTERNEURONS. Interneurons are between the primary afferent (sensory) neuron and the final motor neuron. Also, neurons whose process is entirely within a specific area and that synapse with neurons extending into that area. Synapse is the junction between nerve cells.

RETICULAR ACTIVATING SYSTEM (RAS). A functional, not a structural (morphological), system receiving afferent sensory impulses from somatic and visceral, and auditory and visual sensory pathways. It relays these impulses to brain structures that activate widely distributed areas of the cerebral cortex. This system controls overall CNS activity, including attentiveness, wakefulness, and sleep. The reticular formation is the network of nuclei and interconnecting fibers in much of the diencephalon, midbrain, pons, and medulla. Alertness and normal mentation require intact interaction between arousal mechanisms of the reticular formation and cognitive functions.

SCHIZOPHRENIA, UNDIFFERENTIATED. Presence of symptoms that meet criteria for schizophrenia but not one of its subtypes.

VASOSPASTIC SYMPATHETIC HYPERREFLEXIA. Hyperreflexia is an exaggeration of reflexes. People who had poliomyelitis can have markedly cold skin, dramatic changes in skin color, burning pain, and hyperesthesia in affected limbs. Vasospastic sympathetic hyperreflexia is one proposed mechanism to explain these reactions to even cool ambient temperatures. The proposal was that damaged descending spinal sympathetic neurons no longer can inhibit vasoconstriction (Kottke & Stillwell, 1951; Bruno, Johnson, & Berman, 1985a, 1985b). Bruno, Johnson, and Berman (1985b) did not support this explanation.

VENOUS CAPACITANCE BEDS. A mass of venous capillaries forming a large reservoir that may be more or less completely filled with blood. Total mass of capillaries and volume capacity. Venous capillaries are minute vessels without a muscular coat. Intermediate structure and location between venules and capillaries . Venous capillaries are also called postcapillary venules and postcapillaries. Postcapillary venules allow lymphocytes to pass from the blood to the lymph.

REFERENCES

Treating People with Developmental Disabilities

Calamari, J. E., Geist, G. O., & Shahbazian, M. J. (1987). Evaluation of multiple component relaxation training with developmentally disabled persons. *Research in Developmental Disabilities, 8*, 55–70.

Lindsay, W. R. (1988). *The assessment and treatment of anxiety and phobia in people with a mental handicap.* Workshop for the British Institute of Mental Handicap.

Lindsay, W. R., Baty, F. J., Michie, A. M., & Richardson, I. (1989). A comparison of anxiety treatments with adults who have moderate and severe mental retardation. *Research in Developmental Disabilities, 10*(2), 129–140.

Michultka, D. M., Poppen, R. L., & Blanchard, E. B. (1988). Relaxation training as a treatment for chronic headaches in an individual having severe developmental disabilities. *Biofeedback and Self-Regulation, 13*(3), 257–266.

Poppen, R., & Maurer, J. P. (1982). Electromyographic analysis of relaxed postures. *Biofeedback and Self-Regulation, 7,* 491–498.

Shilling, D., & Poppen, R. (1983). Behavioral relaxation training and assessment. *Journal of Behavior Therapy and Experimental Psychiatry, 14,* 99–107.

Treating Older People

Abrahamson, C. F. (1987). Response to the challenge: Effective treatment of the elderly through thermal biofeedback combined with progressive relaxation. *Biofeedback and Self-Regulation, 12*(2), 121–125.

Andrasik, F. (1991). Aging and self-regulation: An introduction and overview. *Biofeedback and Self-Regulation, 16*(4), 333–336.

Arena, J. G., Hannah, S. L., Bruno, G. M., & Meador, K. J. (1991). Electromyographic biofeedback training for tension headache in the elderly: A prospective study. *Biofeedback and Self-Regulation, 16*(4), 397–390.

Arena, J. G., Hightower, N. E., & Chang, G. C. (1988). Relaxation therapy for tension headaches in the elderly: A prospective study. *Psychology and Aging, 3,* 96–98.

Baltes, P. B., Sowarka, D., & Kliegl, R. (1989). Cognitive training research on fluid intelligence in old age: What can older adults achieve by themselves? *Psychology and Aging, 4*(2), 217–221.

Blanchard, E. B., Andrasik, F., Evans, D. D., & Hillhouse, J. (1985). Biofeedback and relaxation treatments for headache in the elderly: A caution and a challenge. *Biofeedback and Self-Regulation, 10*(1), 69–73.

Heyman, S., & Wexner, S. (1993, March 25–30). EMG biofeedback retraining for paradoxical puborectalis contractions in patients with chronic constipation. In *Proceedings of the 24th Annual Meeting of the Association for Applied Psychophysiology and Biofeedback, Los Angeles.* Wheatridge, CO: Association for Applied Psychophysiology and Biofeedback.

Kabela, E., Blanchard, E. B., Appelbaum, K. A., & Nicholson, N. (1989). Self-regulatory treatment of headache in the elderly. *Biofeedback and Self-Regulation, 14*(3), 219–228.

Kaplan, R., & Kepes, E. (1989, October 26–29). *Pain problems over 70 and under 40 years.* Paper presented at the Eighth Annual Meeting of the American Pain Society, Phoenix.

Mannarino, M. (1991). The present and future roles of biofeedback in successful aging. *Biofeedback and Self-Regulation, 16*(4), 391–397.

McDowell, J., Burgio, K. L., Dombrowski, M., Locher, J. L., & Rodriguez, R. (1992). An interdisciplinary approach to the assessment and behavioral treatment of urinary incontinence in geriatric outpatients. *Journal of the American Geriatrics Society, 40*(4), 370–374.

Middaugh, S. J., Kee, W. G., & Peters, J. R. (1992, March 19–24). Physiological response of older and younger pain patients to biofeedback-assisted relaxation training. In *Proceedings of the 23rd Annual Meeting of the Association for Applied Psychophysiology and Biofeedback, Colorado Springs.* Wheatridge, CO: Association for Applied Psychophysiology and Biofeedback.

Middaugh, S. J., Levin, R. B., Kee, W. G., Barchiesi, F. D., & Roberts, J. M. (1988). Chronic pain: Its treatment in geriatric and younger patients. *Archives of Physical Medicine and Rehabilitation, 69,* 1021–1026.

Middaugh, S. J., Whitehead, W. E., Burgio, K. L., & Engel, B. T. (1989). Biofeedback in treatment of urinary incontinence in stroke patients. *Biofeedback and Self-Regulation, 14*(1), 3–19.

Middaugh, S. J., Woods, E., Kee, W. G., Harden, R. N., & Peters, J. R. (1991). Biofeedback-assisted relaxation for the aging chronic pain patient. *Biofeedback and Self-Regulation, 16*(4), 361–376.

Schaie, K. W. (1983). The Seattle longitudinal study: A 21-year exploration of psychometric intelligence in adulthood. In K. W. Schaie (Ed.), *Longitudinal studies of adult psychological development* (pp. 64–135). New York: Guilford Press.

Schaie, K. W. (1989). Perceptual speed in adulthood: Cross-sectional and longitudinal studies. *Psychology and Aging, 4,* 443–453.

Whitehead, W. E., Burgio, K. L., & Engel, B. T. (1985). Biofeedback treatment of fecal incontinence in geriatric patients. *Journal of the American Geriatric Society, 33*(5), 320–324.

Williams, T. F. (1991). Health care trends for older people. *Biofeedback and Self-Regulation, 16*(4), 337–347.

Treating People with Postpolio Symptoms

Agre, J. C. Rodriquez, A. A., & Tafel, J. A. (1991). Late effects of polio: Critical review of the literature on neuromuscular function [Review]. *Archives of Physical Medicine and Rehabilitation, 72,* 923–931.

Berlly, M. H., Strauser, W. W., & Hall, K. M. (1991). Fatigue in postpolio syndrome. *Archives of Physical Medicine and Rehabilitation, 72,* 115–118.

Bruno, R. L., & Frick, N. M. (1987). Stress and "type A" behavior as precipitants of post-polio sequelae. *Birth Defects, 23*(4), 145–155.

Bruno, R. L., & Frick, N. M. (1991). The psychology of polio as prelude to post-polio sequelae: Behavior modification and psychotherapy. *Orthopedics, 14*(11), 1185–1193.

Bruno, R. L., Frick, N. M., & Cohen, J. (1991). Polioencephalitis, stress, and the etiology of post-polio sequelae. *Orthopedics, 14*(11), 1269–1276.

Bruno, R. L., Johnson, J. C., & Berman, W. S. (1985a). Motor and sensory functioning with changes in ambient temperature in post-polio subjects: Autonomic and electrophysiological correlates. In L. S. Halstead & D. O. Weichers (Eds.), *Late effects of poliomyelitis* (pp. 95–108). Miami, FL: Symposia Foundation.

Bruno, R. L., Johnson, J. C., & Berman, W. S. (1985b). Vasomotor abnormalities as post-polio sequelae: Functional and clinical implications. *Orthopedics 8*(7), 865–869.

Cobb, M. B., Mulder, D. W., Kurland, L. T., Beard, C. M., & O'Fallon, W. M. (1985). Poliomyelitis in Rochester, MN, 1935–1955: Epidemiology and long-term sequelae: A preliminary report. In L. S. Halstead & D. O. Weichers (Eds.), *Late effects of poliomyelitis* (pp. 121–134). Miami, FL: Symposia Foundation.

Dalakas, M. (1990). Postpolio syndrome. *Current Opinion in Rheumatology, 2,* 901–907.

Dietvorst, T., & Eulberg, M. K. (1986). Self-regulation treatment of post-polio cold limb. *Biofeedback and Self-Regulation, 11*(2), 157–161.

Frick, N. M., & Bruno, R. L. (1986). Post-polio sequelae: Psysiological and psychological overview. Rehabilitation Literature, 47(5–6), 106–111.

Halstead, L. S., & Rossi, C. D. (1985). New problems in old polio patients: Results of a survey of 539 polio survivors. *Othopedics, 8*(7), 845–850.

Kottke, F. J., & Stillwell, G. K. (1951). Studies on increased vasomotor tone in the lower extremities following anterior poliomyelitis. *Archives of Physical Medicine and Rehabilitation, 32,* 401–407.

Windebank, A. J. (1995). Prognosis and differential diagnosis. In L. Halsted & G. Grimby (Eds.), *Postpolio syndrome* (pp. 69–88). Philadelphia: Hanley & Belfus.

Windebank, A. J., Daube, J. R., Litchy, W. J., Codd, M., Chao, E. Y. S., Kurland, L. T., & Iverson, R. (1987). Late sequelae of paralytic poliomyelitis in Olmstead County, Minnesota. *Birth Defects, 23*(4), 27–38.

Winters, R. (1991). Postpolio syndrome. *Journal of the American Academy of Nurse Practitioners, 3*(2), 69–74.

Treating People Diagnosed as Schizophrenic

Acosta, F., Yamanoto, J., & Wilcox, S. (1978). Application of electromyographic feedback to the relaxation of schizophrenic, neurotic and tension headache patients. *Journal of Consulting and Clinical Psychology, 46,* 383–384.

Ford, M., Stroebel, C., Strong, P., & Szarek, B. (1982). Quieting response training: Treatment of psychophysiological disorders in psychiatric inpatients. *Biofeedback and Self-Regulation, 7,* 331–339.

Keating, C. (1981). *Exploration of a combined program of electromyographic biofeedback and progressive relaxation as a treatment approach with schizophrenics.* Unpublished doctoral dissertation, Michigan State University, East Lansing.

Liberman, R. P., Nuechterlein, K., & Wallace, C. (1982). Social skills training and the nature of schizophrenia. In J. Curran & P. Monti (Eds.), *Social skills training* (pp. 5–56). New York: Guilford Press.

Nigl, A., & Jackson, B. (1979). Electromyographic biofeedback as an adjunct to standard psychiatric treatment. *Journal of Clinical Psychology, 44,* 433–436.

Pharr, O. M., & Coursey, R. D. (1989). The use and utility of EMG biofeedback with chronic schizophrenic patients. *Biofeedback and Self-Regulation, 14*(3), 229–245.

Spaulding, W. D., Storms, L., Goodrich, V., & Sullivan, M. (1986). Applications of experimental psychopathology in psychiatric rehabilitation. *Schizophrenia Bulletin, 12*(4), 560–577.

Stein, F., & Nikolic, S. (1989). Teaching stress management techniques to a schizophrenic patient. *The American Journal of Occupational Therapy, 43*(3), 162–169.

Weiner, H. (1979). On altering muscle tension with chronic schizophrenia. *Psychological Reports, 44,* 527–534.

Wentworth-Rohr, I. (1981). Biofeedback for schizophrenia and neurosis. *Frontiers of Psychiatry, Roche Report, 11,* 6–11.

Treating People with Phantom-Limb Pain

McKechnie, R.. J. (1975). Relief from phantom limb pain by relaxation exercises. *Journal of Behavior Therapy and Experimental Psychiatry, 6,* 262–263.

Sherman, R. A. (1976). Case reports of treatment of phantom limb pain with a combination of electromyographic biofeedback and verbal relaxation techniques. *Biofeedback and Self-Regulation, 1,* 353.

Sherman, R. A. (1980). Special review: Published treatments of phantom limb pain. *American Journal of Physical Medicine, 59*(5), 232–244.

Sherman, R. A. (1989). Stump and phantom limb pain. In R. K. Portenoy (Ed.), *Neurologic clinics: Pain.* Philadelphia: W. B. Saunders.

Sherman, R. A., Arena, J. G., Sherman, C. J., & Ernst, J. L. (1989). The mystery of phantom pain: Growing evidence for psychophysiological mechanisms. *Biofeedback and Self-Regulation, 14*(4), 267–280.

Sherman, R. A., & Barja, R. J. (1989). Treatment of post-amputation and phantom limb pain. In K. Foley & R. Payne (Eds.), *Current therapy of pain.* Grand Junction, CO: B. C. Decker.

Sherman, R. A., Gall, N., & Gormly, J. (1979). Treatment of phantom limb pain with muscular relaxation training to disrupt the pain–anxiety–tension cycle. *Pain, 22*(6), 47–55.

Sherman, R. A., Greffin, V. D., Evans, C., & Grana, A. (1992, March 19–24). Temporal relationships between change in phantom pain intensity and change in surface electromyogram of the residual limb. In *Proceedings of 23rd Annual Meeting of the Association for Applied Psychophysiology and Biofeedback, Colorado Springs.* Wheatridge, CO: Association for Applied Psychophysiology and Biofeedback.

Sherman, R. A., & Sherman, C. J. (1985). A comparison of phantom sensations among amputees whose amputations were of civilian and military origins. *Pain, 28,* 285–295.

37

The Frontier: Old and New

Mark S. Schwartz

I offer several examples of biofeedback applications that are in the process of emerging or may soon emerge from the frontier. Some of those included here are older attempts to develop applications, and they continue to linger on the frontier. Some are newer entries on the frontier. I selected these because of their inherent interest, the scope of the disorders and conditions, and for potential heuristic purposes. There are valuable insights to learn from them, and including them helps us remember these bold attempts on the frontier of biofeedback.

Published case studies and research are scant, results are inconsistent, and support for applied psychophysiological procedures is not uniform. Inclusion here does not imply endorsement or a suggestion that these interventions will ever enter the heartland of the field.

However, logic and potential exist for a useful role for applied psychophysiological interventions including biofeedback. The reader should consult published articles for discussions of limitations and procedural and subject selection changes that potentially could lead to successful applications.

CHRONIC CONSTIPATION WITH DYSCHEZIA

Electromyographic (EMG) biofeedback for retraining pelvic floor and external anal sphincter (EAS) musculature is becoming a significant and accepted intervention for the treatment of chronic constipation for selected patients (Bleijenberg & Kuijpers, 1987; Weber, Ducrotte, Touchais, Roussignol, & Denis, 1987; Heyman & Wexner, 1990, 1993; Singles & Cox, 1990; Wexner, Cheape, Jorge, Heymen, & Jagelman, 1992). This application is now available in medical institutions such as the Cleveland Clinics, Mayo Clinics, and the University of Virginia.

This application was only recently on the frontier of practice and is rapidly moving into the heartland. The latest edition of the *Merck Manual* (Berkow & Fletcher, 1992) refers to ". . . biofeedback . . . under investigation" (p. 812) for chronic constipation caused by dysfunction of the pelvic floor and anal sphincters. This condition, "dyschezia," is difficult or painful evacuation of feces due to lack of coordination of the involved muscles. Other terms sometimes used for this condition are "anismus" and "pelvic floor outlet obstruction syndrome."

The rationale for using EMG biofeedback from the EAS involves dyscoordination of the EAS and puborectalis muscles. Thus, affected individuals paradoxically tighten these muscles during attempts to defecate instead of relaxing them to allow normal passage of fecal matter. This causes functional outlet obstruction.

Overuse of laxatives may worsen defecation problems by damaging the nerves and ganglia (the myenteric plexus) needed for movement of fecal material through the colon. Excessive straining can stretch and damage the pudendal nerve responsible for EAS and pelvic floor control. This can lead to more constipation, incontinence, or both. Other rectal problems that can result include rectal prolapse.

Treatment

Treatment should involve a stepped-care approach first trying (1) reassurance; (2) patient education about bowel and sphincter physiology and activity, diet, and nutrition; and (3) dietary changes. For example, daily bowel movements (BM) are not necessary; a BM three times a week is within normal limits for some people. Passing hard stools less than three times a week is one definition of constipation (Larson, 1990).

Briefly, recommendations are to:

- Increase liquid intake to 6–8 glasses a day.
- Increase fiber content of one's diet with more fresh fruits and vegetables.
- Consider adding fiber or bran supplement.
- Add a bulk former with the vegetable fiber psyllium.
- Create a regular time for attempting BMs.
- Never avoid the urge for a BM.
- Exercise daily.
- Occasionally, but not regularly, use mineral oil or milk of magnesia at bedtime.
- Avoid enemas in general and especially those with soap suds.

A need for daily or frequent laxatives is rare, often makes the problem worse, and is dangerous!

One must rule out other medical causes for the constipation (Berkow & Fletcher, 1992, pp. 808–811; Larson, 1990, pp. 633–634). These include:

- Systemic disorders such as debilitating infections, hypothyroidism, hypercalcemia, uremia, or porphyria.
- Colon problems such as megacolon or Hirschsprung's disease, and intestinal obstruction.
- Neurological disorders such as Parkinson's disease, cerebral thrombosis, tumor, and spinal cord injury.
- Medications including those for Parkinson's disease, depression, hypertension, and some cardiac disorders.
- Psychogenic factors such as obsessive–compulsive disorders and eating disorders.

One motility disorder is "colonic inertia" or atypical slow movement of fecal material through the colon (Heyman & Wexner 1993; Berkow & Fletcher, 1992, pp. 811–12). Colonic inertia typically occurs in aged or bedridden patients. However, it sometimes occurs by dulled rectal sensitivity to fecal masses because of frequent lengthy delays in defecation despite the urge or prolonged dependence on laxatives or enemas that often starts in childhood (Berkow & Fletcher, 1992).

A flexible proctosigmoidoscopic examination and a barium X-ray of the esophagus, stomach, and intestine can help rule out colon diseases. Practitioners often get an anorectal physiological evaluation (APE) that can include a colonic transit study, anorectal manometry, cinedefecography (Heyman & Wexner, 1993) or defecatory proctography (Berkow

& Fletcher, 1992), and surface EMG from the pelvic floor or the external anal sphincter. In addition to criteria such as transit time, one looks for increased and paradoxical neuromuscular activity in the puborectalis muscle during the EMG assessment.

Patients learn to schedule consistent times for BMs. General relaxation is often part of treatment in addition to the specific EAS relaxation. Daily sphincter exercises for awareness and control of relaxation and EAS tension are often part of treatment. A daily log of BMs and methods to start a BM are part of the program.

Office biofeedback carries no risks of damaging pelvic floor and EAS muscles. It involves distinguishing between rest, squeeze, and push. A criterion for rest is relaxing pelvic floor muscles to below 2.0 microvolts (100 to 200 Hertz bandpass) according to Heyman and Wexner (1993). Contracting these muscles should reach at least 5.0 microvolts for an average of 10 seconds. Simulating an attempt to defecate while maintaining relaxation of the pelvic floor muscles below 2.0 microvolts are their criteria for a push. The average number of office sessions among the series reported here was 6–8 sessions. The range was 2–13 sessions.

Criteria for success include spontaneous and unassisted BMs and stopping or significantly reducing the use of laxatives, enemas, and digitation. Patients need to discriminate between squeezing, pushing, and resting. They need to push without contracting the puborectalis and EAS muscles.

These reports acknowledge the potential importance of psychological factors. Prudent practitioners consider psychological factors when evaluating patients with chronic constipation. These include obsessive–compulsive features and those with eating disorders. None of the patients reported in these studies of biofeedback for constipation appeared hampered by these factors. Perhaps, they did not exist for these patients.

Reports of Clinical Series

A total of 39 patients by the Cleveland Clinic–Ft. Lauderdale group and another 64 patients by five other groups make up the available literature I found. The success is impressive. Wexner and Heyman and their colleagues report the best success with their criteria and procedures. They reviewed the features of the other studies and limits as they viewed them.

Van Baal, Legvit, and Brummelkanz (1984) treated one case successfully using relaxation biofeedback. Weber et al. (1987) reported 31% success with a heterogeneous group of 24 patients. However, there was limited prebiofeedback assessment for patient selection. Bleijenberg and Kuijpers (1987) reported 70% success with 10 hospitalized patients more similar to the Cleveland Clinic experience. Loening-Baucke (1990) treated 22 children, aged 5–16, with both conventional treatment and EMG-based biofeedback. They reported 77% success with normal defecation. This compared to only 13% among the 19 treated with only conventional treatment. The study by Singles and Cox (1990) with seven patients treated in an average of 5.6 sessions reported a significant decrease or stopping the use of laxatives. They also reported increased BMs unaided by laxatives, enemas, or digital removal. Anxiety and other psychological distress decreased with treatment. Details are not available in this abstract.

I now focus on the largest and most successful series. Heyman and Wexner (1990) started with a report of six patients with long-term chronic constipation caused by paradoxical puborectalis contractions (PPC). Four of these patients showed marked symptomatic improvement with 5–11 office sessions with biofeedback.

Extending the series, Wexner et al. (1992) reported on 18 patients with an average age of nearly 70. The age range was 10–84! The 13 female patients and 5 male patients reported dependence on laxatives or enemas for an average of 27 years. The range was 0.25

to 74 years! After an average of 9 office sessions with biofeedback (range = 2–19 sessions) and follow-up for an average of 9 months (range = 1–17 months), 16 patients (89%) reported success. Only two patients continued use of laxatives once a week or less, and three patients still used enemas. Unassisted evacuation of bowels increased to 7.3 a week from none. The five patients who continued use of assistance also reduced this assistance.

Heyman and Wexner (1993) extended their excellent results and reported on 39 patients (30 female patients and 9 male patients) treated during 3 years from June 1989 through June 1992. All met the criteria of chronic constipation and APE criteria for PPC. The average age was nearly 63 (range = 10–84). Their results with 2–13 office sessions (averge nearly 8) are impressive and presented well. This represents an important contribution.

Thirty-six or 92% showed impressive improvement in unassisted BMs per week from none to an average of 6.4 (range = 1 to 21) ($p < .0001$). Twenty-four (61%) stopped all laxatives, enemas, or digital-assisted BMs. For the 28 patients using laxatives before treatment, laxative use declined from an average 6.8 per week to 1.5 per week. Use of enemas declined from 3.6 to 0.9 per week for 21 patients. The use of digitation declined from 5.3 to 0.8 per week for eight patients. Twelve continued cathartics occasionally. Two of the three patients unsuccessful with this program could distinguish between rest, squeeze, and push. However, they had slow colonic transit times.

Only one patient did not show control of the target muscles. Only four patients quit treatment, and two of these moved away. Including these does not change the significance and reduces the overall success rate down slightly to 84%. The lack of a control group is not a significant problem for interpretation of these results because all these patients first unsuccessfully tried all traditional treatments.

In conclusion, one must agree with Wexner et al. (1992). Among available treatments,

> EMG-based biofeedback appears to have both the highest success rate and the lowest morbidity. . . . can be achieved after inexpensive outpatient therapy . . . . benefit persists for at least 16 months [and] . . . . is the therapy of choice for patients with PPC. (p. 149)

WRITER'S CRAMP

Treating writer's cramp with behavioral and biofeedback techniques has a history of over four decades. It is a rare disorder with unknown prevalence and probably underestimated. One estimate places the prevalence as 69 per million (Nutt, Muenter, Aronson, Kurland, & Melton, 1988). That is roughly about 17,000 to 18,000 in the United States. There are about 4000 cases in the United Kingdom (Marsden & Sheehy, 1990). These estimates are similar as there are about 57 million people in the United Kingdom.

Writer's cramp is very disabling for many persons and typically very resistant to treatment. There are reports of some patients improving with various behavioral techniques. However, many of these reports are very sketchy. Some involve single cases or only a few cases. Many have significant methodology problems. Some provided biofeedback from only one or two muscle sites or from unusual sites, included other behavioral strategies, or provided combinations of treatment including psychotherapy. Much of the older behavioral literature focused mainly on behavioral techniques other than biofeedback.

Despite these problems, this disorder remains the subject of continued research and clinical efforts. A review of EMG biofeedback for writer's cramp concluded that despite results showing some patients improving it reached "its near demise" (Ince, Leon, & Christidis, 1986). Nevertheless, it is a logical approach, and this frontier outpost remains active and viable. Recent attempts with biofeedback provide more details and show more promise especially by Japanese investigators Murabayashi et al. (1992) and Mishima, Kitagawa, Hara, and Nakagawa (1992).

Marsden and Sheehy (1990) have a neurological/genetic focus and cite much evidence supporting the view that writer's cramp is a "focal motor disorder, with a close relation to dystonia" (p. 148). Although they present a very informative and scholarly paper, the authors give scant attention to relaxation and biofeedback. They ignored most of the literature on biofeedback available to that date. They refer to only one paper with six subjects (Bindman & Tibbetts, 1977) and downplay the improvement of three of the six patients.

One must read the original papers to understand the scope and depth of this disorder. I suggest reading at least those by Marsden and Sheehy (1990), Ince et al. (1986), Murabayahsi et al. (1992), and Mishima et al. (1992). I include more information from some of these in part because they are not readily available. Other references of historical interest include Reavley (1975); Uchiyama, Lutterjohan, and Shah (1977); Rowan (1980); Cottraux, Juenet, and Collet (1983); and Rubow (1983).

Etiologies, Features, Aggravating Factors, and Classification

When a person with writer's cramp starts to write or after writing a few words, there is excess gripping of the pen or pencil, and they typically cannot write.

> The hand may pronate, with ulnar deviation of the wrist and elevation of the elbow. Sometimes the thumb and index finger flex, so that they ride up the pen. Less commonly, the index finger or thumb, or both, extend to lift off the pen, which may fall from the grip. . . . Sudden jerks of the hand and arm may cause unintended strokes of the pen, or drive the nib through the paper. Tremor is common. (Marsden & Sheehy, 1990, p. 148)

Injury to the hand or arm immediately before symptom onset occurs in 5–10% of persons with writer's cramp. However, the onset is insidious in most patients. There are hints of inheritance in a small percentage of persons. Spontaneous remission for months or years reportedly occurs in about 5%. However, relapse is also common. For about half of patients, difficulty in writing is the only symptom. For many, there is progression to other manual acts. It is surprising that persons with writer's cramp can write shorthand without difficulty (Marsden & Sheehy, 1990).

There are disagreements about the etiologies of writer's cramp. Some of this disagreement may result from the health care specialties of the investigators and the types of patients who seek their help. There are different classifications of subtypes.

Tremor, paralytic, stiffness or rigid, and dystonic types form one classification (Tanaka & Öumi, 1982). Mishima et al. (1992) distinguish between spastic, tremor, and dystonic.

Marsden and Sheehy (1990) distinguish between a dystonic type versus simple type. In the "dystonic" type, there is involvement of other manual actions from the beginning. Persons with "simple writer's cramp" "can carry out other manual motor tasks normally" (p. 150). They also distinguish a group they call "progressive writer's cramp," which starts as simple writer's cramp. However, these persons develop difficulties with other hand actions such as using eating utensils, shaving, threading a needle, and applying cosmetics. Although not clearly dystonic by their criteria, this group, as with the other two, often show "subtle neurological signs on close examination." Furthermore, "a few, particularly those with younger onset, . . . develop involuntary spontaneous dystonic muscle spasms" (p. 150) of the arm, neck, or other limbs. Thus, the argument for considering writer's cramp as a focal dystonia.

Different researchers may get different results in part because of treating patients with different features. Writer's cramp is probably not a unitary disorder. Patient selection, as for other disorders treated with biofeedback, is probably very important.

For diagnosing this disorder, Mishima et al. (1992) emphasize

> The most basic and important point is that a patient has difficulty in hand movements only when writing . . . . If a patient has difficulty in a voluntary movement, which is clearly different from handwriting, at the beginning of the symptom, he/she should not be diagnosed as writer's cramp. When hand motions such as holding chopsticks and buttoning clothes, which include similar movements to writing, have gradually become disturbed . . . he/she can be diagnosed as writer's cramp. (p. 104)

This sounds like the progressive type described by Marsden and Sheehy (1990).

On the basis of patient's scripts and EMG, types of writer's cramp are then distinguished. Some persons complain of a chronic disturbance but not one severe enough to prevent writing. They only want to preserve ideal writing. These are not candidates for biofeedback according to Mishima et al. (1992). Although not stated, I assume they do not show significant EMG elevations or the other cardinal symptoms. The authors' statement that these people are "fairly neurotic" implies that one should consider other treatment approaches.

Mishima et al. (1992) divide the patients with objective disturbance into three types. In the spastic type, muscle tension related to writing remains very high thus preventing smooth movements. In the tremor type, there is tremulous movement when starting attempts to write. The third is the dystonic type, the most severe and most difficult to treat. There are "bizarre movements . . . such as flexion and/or a torsion of the wrist and an extension of the fingers, which never previously appeared during normal writing" (p. 105).

Some professionals link emotional factors to the cause, persistence, and relapse for some persons with writer's cramp. These emotional factors include anxiety and anger. The assumption is there may be psychological factors involved in many patients, although Marsden and Sheehy (1990) disagree. This link is not clear, and many professionals consider organic factors as primary. Some persons develop other more widespread neurological diseases (Marsden & Sheehy, 1990). However, practitioners often need to consider psychological factors and treat these. For example, relapses reportedly occur during times of increased stress. Secondary gain from the symptom may be a factor complicating treatment in some persons. For example, some persons reportedly drop from treatment despite improvement.

Treatments

Reported treatments tried include an altered grip on writing instruments, altered instruments, anticholinergic medications, beta blockers, muscle relaxants, anxiolytics, and botulinum toxin (Botox). Behavioral stategies tried include aversion techniques with electrified pens, massed practice, relaxation therapies, systematic desensitization, operant shaping procedures, and various combinations of these. Published reports show mixed results. Some medications benefit some persons, but often there are negative side effects or limited duration of benefit. Aversion techniques benefit some patients. However, this is not an acceptable treatment for many patients. As discussed in this section, relaxation and biofeedback help some patients.

For Mishima et al. (1992), evaluation includes surface EMG assessment of multiple muscle sites while holding different writing instruments during different types of writing.

Writing instruments include ball-point pens and different types of pencils. The EMG sites include the upper trapezius, forearm flexors and extensors, and hand muscles such as from the thenar eminence. They provide writing samples before and after treatment. They provided 101 biofeedback sessions over 25 weeks for one 32-year-old male patient and 200 sessions for another 25-year-old male patient! However, these were very difficult cases, classed as dystonic, and both maintained improvement and work 1 year later.

Murabayashi et al. (1992) report slightly better results with 8 "tremor" type patients than with 11 classified as "rigid" or "stiffness" type. However, the variation in percentage is probably not significantly different. Of those classed as tremor type, 2 showed marked improvement, 2 showed moderate improvement, and 2 showed mild improvement. Of the 11 classed as rigid, 1 improved markedly, 3 showed moderate improvement, and 3 mildly improved. There was no mention of response for the one dystonic type. Of the 20 patients, 12 (60%) reported no difficulty writing, and 4 more reported only mild difficulty after treatment.

Although medications started before biofeedback treatment did not have reported benefits, evaluation of this is unclear and most patients continued one or more medications. These included 17 taking minor tranquilizers, 11 using beta blockers mostly for tremor-type symptoms, and 3 using a muscle relaxant. Autogenic relaxation procedures were used by 8 patients mostly with tremor-type symptoms.

Biofeedback involved 10 weekly sessions. Each had 4 minutes of baseline divided into 2 segments and 10 segments of 2 minutes each with EMG feedback from the forearm flexors or extensors. Feedback was audio, and the EMG data were integrated.

Using an arbitrary criterion of at least 10% reduction in muscle tension from the beginning to after treatement, Murabayashi et al., 1992, report 6 of the 8 patients showing marked or moderate improvement. Of the others, there was mostly no decrease in muscle tension. They do not provide information about how they determined the decreases. There were 3 cases with both types showing further improvement among 13 patients followed for 1–46 months. There is no information about categories of improvement. This important cumulative effect sometimes appears in other applications.

The dystonic type is the most severe and most difficult to treat. However, Mishima et al. (1992) reported successfully treating two cases they classified as dystonic. Treatment also may be effective for the spastic type (Mishima et al., 1992). Combining biofeedback with medication, such as a beta blocker, may be effective for the tremor type.

Guidelines for Evaluation and Treatment

Based on the available literature, I offer guidelines for evaluations and therapy procedures.

- Obtain a medical/neurological evaluation.
- Obtain a careful and detailed history and description of the presenting symptoms and other fine motor difficulties.
- Consider classifying patient according to an exiting system such as (1) simple, progressive, dystonic, or (2) spastic, tremor, or dystonic. At least describe the features and progression. One need not dismiss patients with focal dystonia although treatment will be more difficult and probably longer.
- Consider the chance of spontaneous remission if the symptoms are of recent onset and the patient is young. Consider this when planning the length of treatment.
- Consider trials of medications such as anxiolytics and/or beta blockers if indicated and preferred by patient. Obtain writing samples and EMG measurements before, during, and after medication trials. Maintain medications if indicated by improvement.

- Record and feedback from multiple EMG sites. Having an EMG instrument that can record and feedback from five sites would be ideal. Recording from at least two sites simultaneously is the absolute minimum. Consider muscle recording and feedback sites including the upper trapezius, deltoid, biceps, forearm flexors and extensors. Also, consider the muscles in the hand such as the abductor pollicis brevis, or on the thenar eminence.
- Record measurements during different types of writing such as very slow versus normal rate, simple figures and letters versus sentences and paragraphs.
- Demonstrate high muscle tension at least during writing.
- Obtain recordings of the same movements with normals for comparisons.
- Compare muscle activity from various muscles with normal persons engaged in the same activities with the hand.
- Use different writing instruments with different degrees of difficulty, such as ballpoint pen, pencils, and mechanical pencils.
- Use different thicknesses of writing instruments.
- Start biofeedback with muscles that patients can relax more easily, even if not directly involved in writing. Consider starting with shoulders.
- Progress to muscles more involved with writing. Start with simple movements.
- Consider general relaxation for selected patients.
- Be prepared to provide a variety of treatment strategies including behavioral strategies. Relaxation and biofeedback should be among the treatments available.
- Consider relaxation of writing muscles during resting.
- For some patients, consider starting without holding a pen or pencil and then only holding it without an intent to write.
- Allow patients to determine posture for holding pen/pencil unless very odd or posture prevents relaxation of target muscles.
- Progress from easy writing of easier figures, symbols, and letters to more difficult attempts such as single words and sentences.
- Progress from slow writing to faster writing.
- Practice often.
- Use rest periods between writing periods of 1–5+ minutes.
- Include both auditory and visual feedback.
- Include transfer of training procedures.
- Get both short- and long-term follow-up of at least 1 year.
- First focus on treating the secondary movements learned to overcome the primary movements (i.e., involuntary or less voluntary).
- Start with secondary symptoms that are more learned than with primary symptoms under less voluntary control.
- Include deep relaxation of specific muscles during rest.
- Plan gradual relearning with successive approximations in small steps.
- Prepare patients for the chance of a lengthy treatment. Consider continuing treatment "as long as . . . symptoms appear to be . . . controllable" (Mishima et al., 1992, p. 111).

The implications from the literature reviewed are that EMG biofeedback is appropriate as part of the treatment for selected patients with writer's cramp. The decision depends partly on the etiology such as whether the symptoms are part of a progressive neurological disorder. Unless a new medication becomes available that is highly successful, EMG biofeedback will continue to be a viable frontier approach with potential for further development.

HAND AND WRIST DISORDERS OF MUSICIANS

There is a small and promising literature for using EMG biofeedback to help musicians with hand and wrist disorders. These disorders involve overuse and other unique physical stressors associated with playing a musical instrument. Another potential application is part of teaching correct motor skills while an individual is learning to play an instrument. The purpose of this section is only to point to the application of biofeedback for selected patients.

The reason for including this here is the relationship to writer's cramp in some cases. For example, some professionals view some of these cases as occupational cramps and a focal dystonia (Marsden & Sheehy, 1990; Newmark & Hochberg, 1987). As such, one could apply biofeedback procedures to musicians such as guitarists, reed instrument players (e.g., clarinetists, saxaphonists), pianists, and others (Fischer-Williams & Sovine, 1984).

Other biofeedback applications for musicians are found in Morasky, Reynolds, and Sowell (1983), LeVine (1983), LeVine and Irvine (1984), Morasky, Reynolds, and Clarke (1981), Levee, Cohen, and Rickles (1976), and Montes, Bedmar, and Martin (1993).

However, there are other causes (e.g., nerve compression syndromes, overuse, tendon injuries, blisters) that require other approaches (Amadio & Russotti, 1990). It is beyond the intent here to discuss these disorders. The purpose of this section is to point to the application of biofeedback for selected patients. Before one embarks on applying biofeedback to a musician's hand and wrist difficulties, prudent practitioners will be very familiar with organic causes and treatment options. For example, see Hochberg, Leffert, Heller, and Merriman (1983), Amadio and Russotti (1990), Fry (1986), Hoppmann and Patrone (1989), Lockwood (1989), and Mandel (1990).

ASTHMA

Introduction, Rationale, and Role of Relaxation and Biofeedback

Asthma is another potentially fruitful application that Shellenberger, Amar, Schneider, and Stewart (1989) and Shellenberger, Amar, Schneider, and Turner (1994) conclude meets efficacy criteria for biofeedback. They refer to four references (Lehrer, Hockron, McCann, Swartzmann, & Reba, 1986; Peper, 1988; Peper, Smith, & Waddell, 1987; Roland & Peper, 1987). In addition, there is the important work by Kotses et al. (1991). The Lehrer et al. (1986) research is important and supportive of relaxation and biofeedback with asthma. However, the treatment was multimodal and used a very small sample. The authors consider it "tentative until replicated." This section adds others references about asthma and both supportive and qualifying reports.

The extensive literature on psychological aspects of asthma is conspicuously missing from this chapter. However, practitioners and other interested readers should be familiar with that literature, and I include some of those references.

The rationale for general relaxation is to accomplish diminished parasympathetic reactivity and therefore reduced bronchoconstriction of at least the larger upper airways. A shift to slower and diaphragmatic breathing from faster and chest breathing is the primary goal of the Peper group strategy. Both strategies are straightforward. The rationale for trachea-noise feedback is also direct. I will not discuss it because the results are less promising so far. The rationale for facial relaxation is not straightforward and needs some discussion to end or reduce the puzzled looks and head scratching of some readers.

The facial muscles–pulmonary strategy or the proposed "trigeminal–vagal connection" is less obvious. Kotses and his colleagues showed that reduced tension in the facial muscles leads to decreases in air-flow resistance for asthmatic children and healthy adults. Peak expiratory flow rate (PEFR) increased immediately and lasted for several hours after facial relaxation. Moreover, long-term follow-up shows maintenance of these effects (Kotses et al., 1991). One may speculate that voluntary breathing habits also changed during this treatment.

Increases in facial tension somehow result in increased air-flow resistance in PEFR or total respiratory resistance at least in healthy subjects. The question is how this happens? The interesting rationale offered by Kotses and his colleagues has potential for explaining the facial muscle–pulmonary relationship. It also has important implications for explaining how facial and cephalic relaxation may affect other physiological functioning. Their focus is on the trigeminal and vagal nerves.

According to this model, tension in the facial muscles increases afferent activity in trigeminal nerve (TN), the seventh cranial nerve (CN7), known as the facial nerve. Remember that afferent activity is the transmission of nerve activity from sense organs to nerve centers in the brain. This, in turn, "affects efferent vagal activity, a determinant of broncho-motor tone" (Kotses et al., 1991, p. 3).

There are several lines of research consistent with this model according to Kotses and his colleagues. These include cranial nerve anatomy (Carpenter & Sutin, 1983), broncho-motor regulation (Nadel, 1976; Tomori & Widdicombe, 1969), and reflexive connections between afferent vagal activity and facial motor neuron activity in cats (Tanaka & Asahara, 1980). They admit to the speculative nature of this formulation proposing a reflex explanation of the muscular and pulmonary events. Kotses and his colleagues (1991) provide good evidence for a relationship between facial relaxation and desired pulmonary changes.

Definitions, Prevalence, Features, and Medical Examination

Breathing difficulty is the main symptom of asthma. Air forced through narrowed bronchial tubes makes a hoarse whistling sound called wheezing. Coughing, often in clusters, also is very common. This sometimes results in coughing up mucus. Episodes last minutes, hours, and sometimes days, and it can be dangerous.

Asthma prevalence is substantially rising worldwide. The prevalence is over 40 per 1000 and up to 60 per 1000 for females aged 20 and younger. The rise also includes number of hospitalizations and mortality (Ellis, 1993). The direct and indirect costs of asthma in the United States in 1990 were $6.2 billion (Henderson, 1993). Ellis (1993) believes that this staggering figure can become substantially lower.

An updated definition of asthma comes from the 1992 National Asthma Education Report (Ellis, 1993). Asthma is "airway obstruction that is reversible (but not completely reversible in some patients) either spontaneously or with treatment, airway inflammation, and increased airway responsiveness to a variety of stimuli" (p. 52). The obstruction of smaller peripheral airways is irreversible in some patients, especially those with severe disease. This definition notes an inflammatory factor in "virtually every case, even those of mild degree" (Ellis, 1993, p. 52). One implication is the need to treat the inflammation.

See Ellis (1993) for a discussion of asthma therapeutics including the bronchodilators beta$_2$-adrenergic agonists and theophylline, and anti-inflammatory therapies including avoidance, cromolyn sodium, and corticosteroids. "There is world consensus that beta$_2$-agonists delivered via inhalation are the drugs of choice for relief of symptoms of acute exacerbations of asthma and for prevention . . . of exercise-induced bronchoconstriction" (Ellis, 1993, pp. 53–54). However, Ellis notes that "as many as 50% to 60% of adults do not use the MDIs [metered-dose inhalers] correctly. . . . The two most important aspects of proper techniques are slow inhalation and breath holding" (p. 54).

Complicating the use of MDIs are reports of rare paradoxical bronchoconstriction, reports of tolerance from regular rather than prn use, and other negative side effects. For example, there are reports of increased mortality among those regularly using inhaled beta$_2$-agonist bronchodilators, especially fenoterol, t.i.d. or q.i.d.

One unanswered question is whether the drugs are inherently dangerous. Alternatively, do physicians prescribe routine prophylactic use for those patients with worsening disease who are otherwise poorly controlled? These drugs are "still the drugs of choice for relief of acute symptoms of asthma and for prophylaxis of exercise-induced bronchoconstriction" (Ellis, 1993, p. 54).

Conspicuously absent from Ellis (1993) and other articles in this series is any mention of relaxation and biofeedback. Therefore, why include this section in this book? I also asked that question. There are several compelling reasons. Published reports of these treatments for asthma continue. Some practitioners continue to use relaxation and biofeedback at least as adjuncts for treating asthma. Furthermore, an Association for Applied Psychophysiology and Biofeedback (AAPB) document lists asthma as one condition for which these treatments can be effective (Shellenberger et al., 1989, 1994).

In general, the medical field is more comfortable with therapies with which it is more familiar. Most physicians and practitioners typically do not see most of the journals that publish the research on relaxation and biofeedback. They are hesitant to embrace alternative therapies such as relaxation and biofeedback for which they have limited understanding and experience. This should not be discouraging. Remember, these treatments were once not part of accepted medical practice for other disorders for which they are now standard therapies (e.g., tension-type headaches, urinary and fecal incontinence, and Raynaud's disease). If these treatments work and if good research continues to support their value for selected patients, then they will find a respected place.

Biofeedback and Related Procedures

Both general relaxation without biofeedback, and three types of biofeedback are part of the published literature on asthma. I start with a brief discussion of general relaxation and then focus on biofeedback applications.

General Relaxation without Biofeedback Instrumentation

The use of general relaxation without biofeedback instrumentation is a basic part of this literature. Progressive muscle relaxation often results in statistically significant improvements in pulmonary function. However, reviews (e.g., Richter & Dahme, 1982) caution practitioners because, as Lehrer, Sargunaraj, and Hochron (1992) note, "the magnitude of the changes generally falls short of the standard criteria for clinical significance used in evaluating asthma medication" (p. 640). They refer to the 15% increase in air flow cited by Richter and Dahme (1982). Nonetheless, the consistency with which relaxation results in improved air flow, does support its value as "a useful adjunct to medical management, at least for some asthmatics" (Lehrer et al., 1992, p. 640).

Pointing modestly to their own "preliminary data," Lehrer et al. (1992) refer readers to their earlier work (Lehrer et al., 1986). They suggest that patients for whom relaxation might be more helpful are those with predominantly bronchoconstriction or obstruction in the larger, upper airways. This is where the predominant autonomic influence is parasympathetic. This relies partly on the Gellhorn (1958) model of the neurophysiological basis of neuromuscular relaxation. Gellhorn proposes that "both sympathetic and parasympathetic reactivity" diminish with "muscle relaxation throughout the body" (Lehrer et al., 1992, pp. 640–641).

I could not deduce that conclusion from my own review of the esoteric and highly complicated Gellhorn paper. However, I admit to my limitations in understanding most of that paper. I assume that few other practitioners can refer to this paper with confidence. Fortunately, however, we can rely on Lehrer et al. (1992) for an interpretation of Gellhorn (1958). In addition, there are other sources on which to explain the value of relaxation for asthma (Mussell & Hartley, 1988; Kotses et al., 1991).

Biofeedback: Special Instrumentation and Treatment Procedures

Listed below are three types of biofeedback and a summary description of each. These are in order of increasing complexity. Interested readers should read the original articles for details of the procedures and protocols.

EMG Biofeedback-Induced Facial Relaxation. This is standard bifrontal relaxation. It relies on a single source of the feedback signal to achieve relaxation of the head and face muscles. The research is with children with a mean age between 11–12 and an age range of 7–16 years.

Consider the protocol by Kotses et al. (1991).

- Provide patient education with the family present.
- Get daily and weekly recording of asthma symptoms.
- Record PEFR twice daily in the morning and evening using a mini-Wright meter. The child inhales completely. He or she then blows fast and hard through the meter three times, each separated by 1 minute or longer.
- Get periodic measurements of pulmonary functions in the office. This includes forced expiratory volume (FEV_1), forced vital capacity (FVC), PEFR, and forced expiratory flow ($FEF_{25-75\%}$). The frequency of these depend on whether the protocol is purely a clinical one or for research. In research, consider these before and after each office session. Repeat this after office treatment sessions.
- Use at least a standard bifrontal EMG site.
- Use wide-bandpass filtering of about 5–1000 Hertz.
- Use at least auditory feedback with a continuously averaged, signal contingent on decreasing facial tension. Note that Kotses et al. (1991) did not mention relaxation during the session or specifically for home practice. In clinical practice, I see potential for augmenting the office and home procedures with relaxation instructions.
- Include baseline EMG recordings each session before the feedback segment. Kotses used a 4-minute baseline and 16 minutes of feedback for eight sessions.
- Include home practice.
- Provide short-term and long-term follow-up sessions. These include evaluation of pulmonary functions, review of symptom logs, discussions of problems, and repeated questionnaires.

EMG Biofeedback from Accessory Breathing Muscles and Incentive Inspirometer Feedback. This strategy focuses on shifting breathing from chest breathing and breath-holding to slow diaphragmatic breathing. The EMG signals are from the upper back and the shoulder area over the upper-trapezius and right scalene muscles (Peper et al., 1987; Peper & Tibbitts, 1992). Other electrode placements that give good signals reflecting "overall upper thoracic tension" and reflect the tension in accessory breathing muscles also are acceptable.

The second type of feedback used in this approach is with a plastic incentive inspirometer. The cost for an inspirometer is under $20 per patient. The person inhales, and an adjustable marker on the plastic column shows the volume of air inhaled. The patient inhales three times before attempting higher volumes. One records the EMG at the peak of each volume and calculates an average. The goal inhalation volume is 4000 milliliters or as much as each person can achieve if less than 4000. See Chapter 11 for a detailed discussion of breathing and the protocol of Peper and his colleagues.

This protocol includes baseline measures, weekly sessions of about 1.5 hours each for an average of 16 weeks. Follow-up is at 15 months. Mastery at each phase precedes moving to the next phase. After mastering the slow diaphragmatic breathing, patients learn to generalize this during activities such as walking, talking, and bicycling. Then, they proceed with becoming more aware of abdominal versus chest breathing and the volumes of air inhaled. The next phase is desensitization during activities such as purposeful wheezing. Tailor progression through the phases. Each subject completes a self-assessment questionnaire[1] before and after treatment and at follow-up.

Trachea-Noise Feedback. This is more complicated than the other two methods. A microphone on the throat records the intensity of wheezing or tracheal noise that transforms into a visual and auditory feedback. This is not part of current clinical practice. However, if one wants to use trachea-noise biofeedback, contact M. J. Mussell[2] (Mussell, 1986a, 1986b, 1986c; Mussell & Williams, 1986; Mussell & Hartley, 1988) and/or Brian Tiep,[3] (Tiep, Alaniz, & Cordell, 1976; Tiep, Belman, & Tieppe, 1980).

Psychological Factors: Panic and Dyspnea-Fear

The symptoms of panic and fear are often found among people with asthma, as Dirks, Kinsman, Staudenmayer, and their other Denver colleagues repeatedly reported in the late 1970s (Dirks, Kinsman, Staudenmayer, & Kleiger, 1979). As with people with panic disorders, people with asthma often avoid situations that present a potential risk for interrupting or temporarily obstructing their breathing (Yellowlees & Kalucy, 1990). They often report fear or panic with their asthma attacks (Kinsman, Luparello, O'Banion, & Spector, 1973). Anxiety disorders are very common (Yellowlees, Alpers, Bowden, Bryant, & Ruffin, 1987; Yellowlees & Kalucy, 1990), and panic disorder diagnoses occur more often among people with asthma than in the general population (Carr, Lehrer, & Hochron, 1992). The study by Carr et al. (1992) supported a dyspnea-fear theory for people with asthma.

Measures

Pulmonary Measures

These can be confusing for many practitioners and students. See Carr et al. (1992), medical textbooks, and the glossary at the end of this chapter for more information.

---

[1]Available from Erik Peper, Ph.D., Hensill Hall, Room 714, San Francisco State University, 1600 Holloway Avenue, San Francisco, CA 94132.

[2]M. J. Mussell, Department of Information, Faculty of Engineering, Yanagata University, Yonezawa-992, Japan.

[3]Brien Tiep, M.D., Casa Colvina Hospital, 255 E. Bonita, Pomona, CA 91767.

Asthma Symptom Measures

Consider using the Weekly Asthma Diary (Creer, Backiel, Ullman, & Leung, 1986). This provides a daily summary of morning and evening PEFT scores, medications, and self-ratings of asthma severity. Also consider the Report of Asthma Attack/Episode (Creer et al., 1986). This questionnaire describes the perceived precipitant of the asthma episode, the severity, and methods taken to reduce the attack. Some use the self-report Asthma Symptom Checklist (ASC; Kinsman et al., 1973). This provides ratings of frequency and severity of 36 symptoms. There are five main factors of symptoms: panic/fear, bronchoconstriction, hyperventilation, fatigue, and irritability (Brooks, Richards, Bailey, & Martin, 1989).

Clinical Response, Outcome, and Follow-Up

Facial Muscle EMG Feedback

In some children, reduced tension in the facial muscles appears to improve air flow indicated by the FEV_1/FVC (Kotses et al., 1991). Moreover, children maintaining their baseline muscle tension did not improve. Those learning facial relaxation showed better FEV_1/FVC scores compared to the other group during the last 3 months of the follow-up. However, other measures of lung function did not reflect satisfactory improvement. This was presumably because of larger variability within the other measures compared to FEV_1/FVC that had about half the variability.

Home peak flow values stayed stable and did not show the improvement seen in the office measures. The authors speculated about the possible reasons for this discrepancy. For example, the laboratory instruments were more sensitive to pulmonary changes than were the portable instruments. Home recording procedures were more variable.

The anxiety and attitudes about their asthma improved more at follow-up for those reducing facial tension and improving their pulmonary function than for the other children. Note that both groups improved on these indices but not to the same degree. Both groups showed improvements in self-rated severity of asthma, use of prn medications, and frequency of asthma attacks. This was presumably a result of common factors in both groups such as maintaining symptom logs. This provided improved observation of early warning cues for an asthma episode signalling corrective actions.

The authors concluded that pulmonary function improves with biofeedback-induced facial relaxation and home practice. In turn, this improved attitudes about asthma and decreased anxiety. However, it was not enough to result in improvement on all important measures such as asthma severity. Consider this biofeedback protocol as an adjunct to management of asthma.

Inspiratory Feedback and EMG Feedback of Accessory Breathing Muscles

The procedures developed by Peper and his colleagues (Peper & Tibbetts, 1992) appear promising. They originally treated 21 volunteer adults in groups. The average age was 34. There were an average of 16 weekly sessions and follow-up at 15 months for 17 of the subjects. The multicomponent protocol also included hand warming with guided imagery. "At the follow-up all subjects significantly reduced their EMG tension levels while simultaneously increasing their inhalation volumes. [They] reported reductions in their asthma symptoms, medication use, emergency room visits, and breathless episodes" (Peper & Tibbetts, 1992, p. 143).

The number of subjects achieving 4000 milliliters increased from 7 of the 17 subjects assessed before the baseline to 14 subjects after treatment. Eleven maintained this at follow-up. The number of emergency room visits decreased from 1.5 per year for 17 subjects to 0.53 during the 15 months follow-up period. Breathlessness episodes decreased from 2.4 per day to 0.74 per day, and medication use also decreased.

The usual follow-up periods in this literature are much shorter, with an average of about 21 weeks for 12 studies (of a total of 30 studies reviewed) reporting follow-up in the reviews by Cluss (1986) and Dahl, Gustafsson, and Melin (1990).

The authors acknowledge limitations of their study. They did not have a control group, used volunteer subjects, relied on self-reports of clinical improvement, and used a multi-component protocol. However, they correctly point to the reduction of fear and increased confidence in the ability to continue breathing during the start of wheezing. Some learned a sense of control and hope that they did not have before treatment.

Trachea-Noise Feedback

Trachea-noise feedback results are not as positive and robust as the others. However, this strategy does yield "some detectable bronchodilation" (Lehrer et al., 1992) but "only marginal improvement. . . . in reversing full-blown asthma attacks" (p. 641).

Medical and Related Information for Nonmedical Practitioners

Nonmedical practitioners and researchers treating patients with asthma need to know the factors affecting asthma symptoms and the current medical therapies. An excellent recent, brief, and readable reference is by Ellis (1993).

Avoiding Allergens and Irritants

Patients with asthma typically receive information and strong advice to avoid irritants. In a stepped-care model, starting to avoid these first or early in treatment is prudent. Patients need to show reasonable compliance with prescribed avoidance of known or probable irritants. Prudent practitioners need to know about irritants before, during, and after all therapies for asthma. This is as important as checking dietary factors known to increase the risk of symptoms such as IBS, blood pressure, and migraines.

The following is mostly derived from the Mayo Clinic Family Health Book (Larson, 1990), and some is from Ellis (1993). An underlying principle of treatment is that preventing the inflammatory process is the best treatment (Ellis, 1993). Avoiding exposure to specific allergens is sometimes very effective.

- Avoid smoking, smokers, and all types of smoke such as from wood, leaves, and rubbish.
- Avoid dust, paint, paint remover fumes, sawdust, and similar irritants. Remove household items that attract and hold dust if the person is allergic to dust.
- If sensitive to analgesics, then avoid aspirin, ibuprofen,[4] and other nonsteroidal anti-inflamatory drugs (NSAIDs) used for pain. Examples of NSAIDs are indomethacin (Indocin), naproxen (Naprosyn), mefenamic acid (Ponstel), sulindac (Clinoril), and piroxicam (Feldene).

---

[4]Over-the-counter trade names are Advil, Nuprin, and Motrin. Prescription trade names include Rufen.

- Condition the air with air conditioning and filters for dust and pollen control. Avoid an ozone-producing air purifier. Clean humidifiers regularly to avoid molds and other growths.
- Many people need to avoid animals such as cats because of animal dander. This includes furniture and rugs made with animal hair.
- About 4–8% of people with asthma need to avoid foods with *sulfites*. Reactions usually start a few minutes after ingesting foods or drinks with sulfites among people sensitive it. Sulfites are in wine, beer, dehydrated fruits, potatoes, some seafoods, dehydrated soups, maraschino cherries, some soft drinks, and avocado mixtures. Also, avoid restaurants and grocery stores that use sulfites to keep lettuce and fruits looking fresh.

Implications from Relaxation and Biofeedback Research

There are methodology limitations and conflicting research reports about relaxation and biofeedback treatments for asthma. Nevertheless, many children and adults with asthma improve significantly with one or more of these treatments. Practitioners faced with clinical patients may take comfort with the availability of these procedures. Selecting procedures depends at least on practitioner training and experience, and availability of instruments. EMG biofeedback is available to all practitioners, and the inspirometer feedback is easily available. Trachea-noise biofeedback is very specialized and available to only a few practitioners. It is not part of clinical practice.

For EMG facial relaxation, consider at least the bifrontal site, a wide bandpass, and auditory feedback. Consider other EMG sites that improve the measurement of facial, head, and neck muscles. (See Chapters 14 and 15 for discussion of the frontal–posterior neck recording placement.) Including added muscle activity might be an improvement if the Kotses et al. (1991) theory is valid. The proposed facial muscles–pulmonary strategy or trigeminal–vagal connection still needs further research support.

Consider various types of auditory feedback for patient comfort (e.g., avoid using headphones for selected patients who are uncomfortable with them or use headphones that are comfortable). Also, visual feedback can be used, at least for parts of the session.

Consider combining EMG feedback from accessory breathing muscles, facial and head muscles, plus inspiratory feedback. Consider using other forms of breathing feedback, although I found no reports of these with asthma.

Self-management procedures (Kotses et al., 1991) such as self-report symptom logs can help increase chances for children observing changes happening early in asthma attacks. Awareness of early-warning cues might prompt corrective action (Creer, Kotses, & Reynolds, 1989). Multiple self-report and parent-report measures of asthma symptoms as used by the Kotses group are helpful. Plan for at least 1 year of follow-up.

The lack of controlled studies with diaphragmatic breathing limits confidence in this strategy. However, the logic and the straightforward nature of this treatment make it compelling to include in a treatment package.

There are other limitations to the studies discussed in this section. The use of volunteers and self-selected subjects who are not patients raises the question of whether these subjects have more motivation than others. This approach, like so many others, may only be useful for the highly motivated and very compliant patients.

Relying solely on self-reports can be a mistake as Peper and Tibbetts (1992) acknowledge. This includes self-report of clinical improvement, medication use, emergency room visits, and breathlessness episodes.

Comprehensive multicomponent protocols do not allow one to ascribe the contribution of any component. Conspicuously absent so far from this literature are comparative studies. For example, we do not yet know how the diaphragmatic strategy compares with the facial relaxation strategy, or with a combination of both.

One other concern is the potential for exacerbation of symptoms if there is parasympathetic rebound from relaxation. Based on the Gellhorn (1958) model, Lehrer et al. (1992) speculate that "the decreased parasympathetic activity might be expected to produce upper-airway bronchodilation" and "relaxation therapy may actually be found to produce a parasympathetic rebound effect" (p. 641). I include this because of the potential seriousness. However, these authors do not cite any such reported incidents in any of the reports they reviewed. It remains a theoretical potential rather than a risk based on any empirical data.

Asthma is a serious disorder with the demonstrated potential for mortality. Therefore relying only on biofeedback and relaxation is very unwise despite how well the treatment is conducted. At present, all these strategies are adjunctive to medical treatments of asthma.

The disabling and sometimes fatal nature of asthma may stem from a variety of factors. Brief mention of a number of these, thought by some to be important, will suffice to alert and remind practitioners and others of these factors. Be aware that some medical professionals raise questions about the risks of bronchodilator medications that stimulate the beta-sympathetic branch of the autonomic nervous system. Others caution about inadequate medical treatment, especially for asthma's inflammatory element (Lehrer et al., 1992). Be aware of and try to help with family dysfunction and reactions to separation and loss, especially for children. Also, be aware and try to help with poor adherence to medications, poor self-care, and patients disregarding their symptoms.

POSTURE TRAINING FOR IDIOPATHIC SCOLIOSIS

A creative biofeedback application helps some adolescents with idiopathic scoliosis—a lateral curvature of the spine. It uses an ambulatory biofeedback device developed by Dworkin and Miller. This is an example of applications now made possible because of technological advances in computer chips and microprocessors. To appreciate this application, one must read the original article desribing the device, the rationale, and its successful application for 12 female adolescents with progressive idiopathic scoliosis (Dworkin et al., 1985). There is a brief description of it by Miller (1985). These authors also refer to a more extensive study (Birbaumer, Flor, Cevey, Dworkin, & Miller, 1994), with both scoliosis and kyphosis, a forward curvature of the spine.

Scoliosis affects about 2–4% of adolescents. This application is for about 7% of those with the idiopathic or familial type of pathological lateral curvature of the spine for whom the scoliosis is severe enough to produce truncal deformity (Dworkin et al., 1985). Sixty to 80% of people with the idiopathic type are female individuals. The usual nonsurgical treatment is the wearing of a brace every day for 23 hours a day for several years. Although successful, there are many obvious drawbacks (Dworkin et al., 1985). Another technique is paraspinal electrical stimulation via surgical implantation or transcutaneous applications. However, this is not a benign approach and probably not the treatment of choice for many adolescents. The other option is spinal-fusion surgery.

The biofeedback device and treatment work "by enhancing the patient's perceptions of incorrect posture and encouraging her to correct the position of her spine" (Dworkin et al., p. 2497). Biofeedback also provides "activation of specific groups of the patient's muscles to correct scoliotic curvature" and "develops learned muscle control through the patient's own nervous system rather than forcing contraction with extrinsic electric currents" (p. 2497). I predict this feedback device and application will develop as an efficacious biofeedback treatment.

HYPERHIDROSIS

The hallmark of primary (idiopathic, essential) hyperhidrosis is excess perspiration of the palms, soles, and/or axillas accentuated by mental stimuli more than by heat and exercise. It is often a very distressing problem for persons with it. It is socially embarrassing, causes staining and rotting of clothing, can lead to social withdrawal, and interferes with the grasping of objects. It wets papers the person is writing on and runs the ink. It even can result in electric shock. Plantar hyperhidrosis is excessive sweating of the soles of the feet. It leads to bromhidrosis,[5] friction blisters, infection, and rotting of socks and shoes.

White (1986) reviews the major medical treatments such as aluminum chloride topical medication, tanning agents, iontophoresis, systemic anticholinergics, excision of axillary sweat glands, and sympathectomy. One typically starts with a simple, safe, and inexpensive treatment such as aluminum chloride which is often enough for axillary hyperhidrosis. Each treatment approach has limits but some success. He also notes that biofeedback and psychotherapy are worth trying for some patients (White, 1986).

Reports using biofeedback include those of Fotopoulos and Whitney (1978), Harris and Sieveking (1979), Duller and Gentry (1980), Farrar and Hartje (1987), Kawahara and Kikuchi (1992), and Alvarez, Cortes, and Rodriguez (1993).

Kawahara and Kikuchi (1992) treated five individuals (aged 16 to 25) with a chief complaint of hyperhidrosis. The authors used a prototype device called a capsule air-change method. It measures and provides visual feedback of sweating volume from dry nitrogen gas humidity data on the palm. They showed that three subjects could markedly inhibit sweating with feedback. In the first session, these three showed a paradoxical increase of sweat during feedback. One interpretation was that the feedback was stressful to the subjects. Inhibited sweat occurred during feedback in the next three to four sessions. The weekly sessions consisted of four 5-minute trials and 5-minute resting intervals. There were no controls, no self-reported symptom data, and no comparisons with conventional electrodermal biofeedback.

However, the results showing inhibited sweat during feedback from a device measuring sweat is an important finding. Observing increased sweat during feedback in the first session is also of clinical value. Whether this device will become practical for clinical use and whether it has any advantages over the electrodermal modality await future studies.

Farrar and Hartje (1987) reported on their comprehensive treatment program with five medically referred patients with hyperhidrosis. Treatment involved several methods of stress management, counseling, and a structured biofeedback program. The program involved multiple stressors and feedback stages. Feedback focused on skin conductance in addition to frontal EMG and hand temperature. They reported a decrease of skin conductance of 61% and a reduction of symptoms of 75%. Ratings were four times a day. The report did not contain any details about the data, and there were no controls. Combining several treatment components confounds interpretation of the role of biofeedback. However, the paper does support the idea that people with hyperhidrosis can reduce sweat during office procedures and can reduce daily excess sweating.

---

[5]Sweat that becomes foulsmelling from bacterial decomposition.

Alvarez et al. (1993) reported using skin conductance feedback and imagery with 25 recruited subjects who had had at least 10 years of palmer hyperhidrosis. They kept daily, hourly ratings during a 2-week baseline and during treatment. The combined treatment was effective treatment for the five subjects completing this approach. This group had a mean of nearly 18 sessions with some many fewer and some many more. One cannot evaluate the other groups well because of the large number of drop-outs and other methodologically confounding factors. This report does not meet publication standards. However, it is consistent with other reports that showed significant improvement in sweating during office feedback procedures and in reduced self-reported daily symptoms.

Consider a self-report symptom log with time and situation samples. Consider including self-report ratings of daily stressors. Monitor more than one body site in the office and in the self-report log. For example, consider both hands. Consider one hand and one foot, or axillary, one hand, and one foot. Careful placement of electrodes is important to insure reliable data. For example, different degrees of pressure of Velcro-attached electrodes on the fingers can produce different data.

MENOPAUSAL HOT FLUSHES

This usage is another recent and bold application of applied psychophysiological approaches to treat menopausal hot flushes (HFs) successfully. The potential value is substantial for the comfort of many of the millions of women with menopausal HFs. Pharmacotherapy includes estrogen replacement or alpha$_2$-adrenergic agonists. The potential value of applied psychophysiological treatments is especially for those women for whom pharmacotherapy is insufficient or contraindicated. This is still in the frontier but shows much promise for future development.

The clearest demonstration of success used slow and deep diaphragmatic breathing as the only treatment (Freedman & Woodward, 1992b). This followed pilot work many years earlier (Germaine & Freedman, 1984) and careful methodological research to help justify this application and objectively document symptom changes (Freedman, 1989; Freedman & Woodward, 1992a; Freedman, Woodward, & Sabharwal, 1990; Woodward, Grevill, & Freedman, 1991).

Freedman and Woodward (1992b) treated 11 postmenopausal women with 8 sessions of paced respiration. They compared this group with other groups of equal numbers receiving progressive muscle relaxation (PMR) via live instruction or a placebo-control procedure involving alpha-EEG (electroencephalography) feedback with eyes open. Documentation of HF symptom changes was with 24-hour ambulatory recordings of sternal skin conductance level (SCL) beyond 2 micromhos. These investigators showed in prior research that this criterion corresponds very well (86–95%) with patients' reports of HFs. Only the relaxed breathing group showed significant reductions of HF frequency, reduced respiration rate, and increased tidal volumes. The breathing measures supported the role of the breathing procedures. The HFs dropped from about 15 per day to about 10 per day. Respiration during office sessions dropped from about 14 breaths per minute (b/min) to about 10 b/min. Refinements and extensions of the treatment may result in greater improvements.

The hot flush occurs in about 75% of women during menopause. Most have this symptom for at least 1 year and 25–50% for more than 5 years (Berkow & Fletcher, 1992). The episodes usually last from a few seconds to at least several minutes. The term menopause literally means last menstruation. In popular use, it refers to the years of gradual reduction of menstruation. The average age for the last menstruation is 50 to 51 in the United States, but these changes can start from about age 40 to about age 55. However, there are significant individual differences, and many women are asymptomatic. Estimates are that about 25% of women report no physiological changes except the gradual end of menstruation. About 25% of women report very bothersome changes. These include frequent night sweats and embarrassment during the day when the flushes and sweating occur. The other 50% note only slight changes.

There are many emotional and psychological symptoms that accompany the menopause. These include insomnia, fatigue, anxiety, and irritability. Other symptoms include dizziness, paresthesias, palpitations, tachycardia, urinary incontinence, nausea, constipation, diarrhea, myalgias, cold hands and feet, and headaches. One can attribute at least many of these to hormonal changes. However, psychological interventions are proper for many women with emotional problems and psychophysiological symptoms during the years of menopause. The potential role for relaxation and biofeedback, and other applied psychophysiological and stress management interventions for other symptoms is often logical.

The usual indicated pharmacological treatment is estrogen replacement with "the lowest effective dose of estrogen . . . combined with a progesterone, because . . . adding progesterone reduces the risk of endometrial cancer" (Larson, 1990, p. 1069). Another value of estrogen replacement is in preventing osteoporosis. This is especially important for women at higher risk for osteoporosis and includes those with premature menopause. Other medications treat many of the other symptoms that accompany the menopausal stage. However, there are contraindications and adverse reactions for some women.

The rationale for relaxation and biofeedback includes the significantly dramatic changes in respiration that often precede the HF (Woodward, Grevill, et al., 1991). Evidence implicates the activation of the central sympathetic nervous system (SNS) in the onset of HFs. Some women with HFs show a breathing pattern involving higher tidal volumes and lower b/min. These occur with feelings of breathlessness even during quiet rest. Breathing returns to lower tidal volume and higher b/min after the HF.

Other justifications include the emotional stress reactions of many women with HFs and treatment for many of the specific symptoms associated with menopause. Often there is severe interference with sleep. Further justification stems from the effectiveness of relaxation and biofeedback for some of these symptoms associated with other conditions. Furthermore, there are limitations of some pharmacological interventions for some women.

Lee and Taylor (1987) reported an application of relaxation and biofeedback to HFs in one woman. The HFs had occured many times each day for a year. Estrogen therapy was contraindicated because the patient had cancer. Anxiolytic medications were not helpful. Treatment involved four sessions of progressive relaxation and supportive counseling, and EMG biofeedback from the forearm flexors over the 15 weekly sessions. HF frequency dropped from 24–30 per day in the first month (November in New York) to the range of 12–18 in the second month, 6–12 in the third month, and 0–6 per day for the next 3 months. The choice of EMG site is unusual and unexplained, and the abstract presents no details of the treatment and patient. One can only speculate about the biofeedback and the relaxation. However, the patient did show dramatic improvement soon after starting the intervention, and this lasted for at least several months.

ORAL–PHARYNGEAL DYSPHAGIA

"Dysphagia" is difficulty swallowing. There are several organic causes for dysphagia and proper medical and diagnostic examination is necessary. I make no attempt to review the organic medical disorders and treatments. There are specific exercises for patients with neurophysiological deficits (Logemann, 1986; Huckabee, 1992). Review these in other sources such as the *Merck Manual* (Berkow & Fletcher, 1992), *Mayo Clinic Family Health Book* (Larson, 1990), and medical textbooks. Dysphagia is different from "globus" or the sensation of a lump in the throat. Globus is usually thought of as a stress-related phenomenon and treated as such.

Oral–pharyngeal dysphagia commonly occurs after acute and chronic medical and neurological disorders such as cerebral vascular accidents (CVAs), traumatic brain injuries (TBIs), carcinoma, and degenerative neuromuscular diseases. Swallowing problems can severely interfere with the health of these and other patients.

The focus here is the application of biofeedback and other applied psychophysiological strategies for selected patients with dysphagia. One application is after surgery or injury and another is idiopathic anxiety about choking. In recent years, standard therapy by a speech or language pathologist/therapist more often occurs with biofeedback assistance (Huckabee, 1992).

I found only four papers with only three cases using biofeedback for patients diagnosed with dysphagia (Haynes, 1976; Latimer, 1981; Bryant, 1991; Huckabee, 1992). However, I suspect there are more practitioners successfully using biofeedback than may be inferred by the limited literature.

The patient treated by Bryant (1991) illustrates one type of application for dysphagia. This patient had profound dysphagia,

> secondary to neural and tissue damage accompanying surgical resection and radiation treatment of oral and lymphatic carcinoma. . . . [She] had received partial tongue resection, right radical neck dissection, dissection of the right facial nerve, lateral lobectomy of the right parotid gland, ligation of the external carotid artery and marginal mandibulectomy of the right vertical ramus. Following surgeries, she received high dose radiation therapy . . . [and] received total nutrition per naso–gastric tube feedings. (p. 166)

Biofeedback was an adjunct to two of the standard therapies provided. Her swallowing returned to normal with 23 sessions over 10 weeks. One of strategies was the Valsalva or hard-swallow technique. This is to increase strength of the pharyngeal swallow and clear the pharyngeal cavities of residual postswallow pooling. The other stategy was the Mendelsohn maneuver to help opening of the cricopharyngeal sphincter. The patient must be aware of the height of the laryngeal elevation while swallowing and hold that position for several seconds before finishing the swallowing cycle. See Bryant (1991) and Huckabee (1992) for discussions of the procedures and the value of biofeedback in this therapy.

In 1981, Susan Lowery[6] and I used biofeedback as part of multimodal treatment for a 40-year-old female patient with severe dysphagia of 3 months' duration. This followed a 20-year history of her fear of choking and mild dysphagia. Over the preceding 3 months, she had lost 20 pounds, and she weighed 110 pounds (68 inches tall) when we first saw her. Her fear had developed into a severe phobic avoidance of nearly all eating. Her diagnoses did not include anorexia nervosa. She had normal esophageal motility, and her Minnesota Multiphasic Personality Inventory (MMPI) was clearly within normal limits. During resting baselines, there was considerable frontal muscle tension. We observed 10–15 microvolts (integral average, 100–200 Hertz) with her eyes open and 8–9 microvolts with her eyes closed. We also noted excess tension in the sternohyoid region. In 6 days, we provided six office sessions. These included EMG biofeedback from the frontal and sternohyoid areas.

---

[6]I depart here from my practice of not reporting my patients in this book. I do this in part because there are so few reported cases but more because I want to keep alive the memory of Susan Lowery. She worked with me as a biofeedback therapist at the Mayo Clinic Rochester for about 2 years.

We taught the patient passive relaxation procedures and encouraged her to relax before and during meals. She significantly decreased her cigarette smoking from three packs per day and stopped all caffeine. She started a high-calorie, high-nutrition liquid "blender-type" diet and gradually increased solid foods during this period. She showed considerable reduction of frontal and sternohyoid muscle activity with her eyes closed. These became 1.5–3 microvolts before each feedback phase. With her eyes open, there was much less reduction, and she remained tense with 8–12 microvolts.

By the end of the six days, the patient was eating full-sized meals and snacks with a wide variety of foods. The time required to eat decreased as bite sizes increased, and she gained 4 pounds in these 6 days. At that time, she left the hospital and returned to her home town. At 7-week follow-up, she continued increasing the variety of foods eaten, further decreased the time to eat, and had gained an additional 9.5 pounds. She was still using the relaxation procedures and reported no choking sensations over the 7 weeks. She reported some hesitancy to eat some vegetables and was not usually eating with persons outside her family.

We did not know whether biofeedback actually had been necessary. We assumed that it helped her gain control of her swallowing. However, it at least helped this patient to gain confidence in her ability to self-regulate her swallowing. This case illustrates one way that practitioners can apply a biobehavioral treatment with biofeedback. The adjunctive use of biofeedback with other standard therapies including behavioral therapies is a frontier settlement with much potential.

FUNCTIONAL VOICE DISORDERS

Functional voice disorders include hyperfunctional dysphonia. In these disorders, surface laryngeal area EMG biofeedback, videoendoscopic feedback, relaxation, and related techniques show value within a multicomponent treatment. Treatment also includes voice therapy (Aronson, 1990). I present a very brief summary of two reports and list several references. More detailed discussion is within the scope of this chapter but beyond available time.

Sime and Healy (1993) provide a recent report of therapy for a patient with a hyperfunctional voice disorder. The report shows a creative use of EMG biofeedback as an adjunct in a successful combination of therapy techniques. Therapy included voice therapy with visual feedback and cognitive-behavioral therapy.

A 45-year-old man needed to reduce the volume and duration of verbal communication during presentations. He needed to do this to improve his voice quality. Voice therapy with visual feedback from a computer-aided fluency establishment training system (Goebel, 1986) helped significantly but was not enough. The patient continued to strain the respiratory and vocal musculature by "trying to force the expression of too many words, too quickly, with too little expired air to maintain normal phonation" (p. 284).

The EMG electrodes were over the area of the infrahyoid muscles. Feedback showed the patient the excess muscle tension during rest and vocalization. It also showed the slow recovery of muscle tension after he had stopped talking. The EMG biofeedback helped identify the excess tension and reduce some of it. The EMG data also helped the therapist set therapy goals and provided information for the patient and therapists about his progress.

A prior example (Andrews, Warner, & Stewart, 1986) showed successful use of laryngeal EMG biofeedback in five patients with hyperfunctional dysphonia. Feedback was from over the area of the pars recta site of the cricothyroid muscle. This muscle is the most superficial of the intrinsic laryngeal muscles. These treatments were in the context of a voice training program. The study was unable to show a difference in outcome compared to five matched patients receiving general relaxation.

Anyone planning or providing this type of biofeedback would benefit from reading at least these two papers. They provide many useful details. Other references discussing the use of specialized voice feedback and at least laryngeal-area, EMG biofeedback include Prosek, Montgomery, Walden, and Schwartz (1978), McFarlane and Lavorato (1984), Bastian and Nagorsky (1987), D'Antonio, Lotz, Chait, and Netsell (1987), Redenbaugh and Reich (1989), Allen, Bernstein, and Chait (1991), Stemple, Weiler, Whitehead, and Komray (1980), and Watson, Allen, and Allen (1993). Practitioners needing a textbook on voice disorders should consider the classic Aronson (1990).

HERPES

Reports of relaxation, biofeedback, or other applied psychophysiological treatments for reducing genital herpes outbreaks among people with frequent outbreaks are sparse (Longo, Clum, & Yeager, 1988; VanderPlate & Kerrick, 1985; Burnette, Koehn, Kenyon-Jump, Hutton, & Stark, 1991). The last is the first controlled study of relaxation I found. The rationale for considering stress management interventions for recurrent herpes simplex is the presumed link between psychosocial stress and recurrences.

Results of the Burnette et al. (1991) multiple-baseline across-subjects design with eight subjects concluded that modified progressive muscle relaxation "clearly . . . was the effective element in reduction of herpes" (p. 244) for the five improved subjects. The reduction of frequency of outbreaks ranged from 40–93%.

This study is impressive and encouraging for several reasons. It involved unusually long, self-report symptom baselines ranging from 13–30 weeks. The subjects all reported very high baseline frequency averaging between about 2 to nearly 7 days per week. The number of office relaxation therapy sessions was only three for all subjects. These occurred over 3–6 weeks. Follow-up was at least 3 months, during which time patients maintained their self-report symptom log. The subjects reported using relaxation one or more times per day. The median was 5 days a week and ranged from almost 3 days a week to nearly daily. The frequency and severity of herpes episodes decreases naturally over time. However, there are several reasons supporting the role of relaxation. First, these subjects had long histories of 2–14 years. Four subjects reported herpes for longer than 5 years. Furthermore, the subjects recorded lengthy baseline symptom data, and the reductions occurred over a short time.

The available reports are encouraging. This application should remain a frontier outpost for further development and consideration at least for selected patients. However, there are limits to this study. The authors did not report on the use of any medications. Presumably, the subjects were not taking acyclovir (Zovirax). This drug is highly effective for reducing the number of days with symptoms and the severity of herpes simplex types 1 and 2.

There are potential advantages in using relaxation therapies for people with herpes. Consider relaxation therapy for patients who do not respond to oral acyclovir and those few persons for whom the adverse effects continue and are very distressing. Adverse effects include nausea, vomiting, diarrhea, headache, and rash. Consider it for those few people for whom there are contraindications for acyclovir. These include hypersensitivity, people who are severely immunocompromised, and those taking potentially nephrotoxic agents. Other contraindications include intending to become pregnant, being pregnant, or intending to breastfeed. There are similar, although fewer, considerations for the ointment form and the sterile powder form for intravenous use of acylovir.

We do not know the effects of relaxation on milder cases or those for whom stress is less of a factor or is no factor. For example, some recurrence of symptoms stems from physical irritation of the affected area.

The authors encourage more studies with biofeedback to assess relaxation, and to "establish greater confidence in the subject's relaxation ability" (Burnette et al., 1991, p. 246). They suggest considering using relaxation therapies with stressful roleplaying. They also suggest other forms of stress management such as time management tailored to the individual.

I acknowledge the bold and excellent paper by Burnette et al. (1991). However, their psychophysiological self-regulation treatment was meager. That suggests the robust nature of relaxation therapy. It also suggests the potential value of more comprehensive psychophysiological self-regulation with biofeedback and other applied psychophysiological interventions tailored to the patient.

SYNCOPE: STRESS-INDUCED OR VASOVAGAL

Syncope is fainting or a sudden and brief loss of consciousness. It usually occurs from momentary insufficient blood supply to the brain. Vasovagal syncope is one type of fainting episode. Emotional stress and the person's reactions are a common major precipitant. Common symptoms include nausea, weakness, visual blurring, sweating, lightheadedness, and yawning. There are several common examples of situations and stimuli that prompt these behaviors and symptoms. These include the sight of blood, injections, pain, dental procedures, venipuncture, medical paraphernalia, films or pictures of medical diseases, illness, or accidents.

One must establish the correct diagnosis and rule out other causes for the syncope that require medical attention. A variety of cardiovascular and noncardiovascular causes can result in syncope. It has many of the same features of phobic responses, and treatment will often include behavioral approaches used for phobias. However, an important distinction is the syncope itself.

Including only one case on stress-induced syncope does not imply there are no other cases or studies, but, there are very few. However, this one sufficiently illustrates the potential value of relaxation and biofeedback and other clinical approaches.

McGrady and Argueta Bernal (1986) focused their intervention on relaxation procedures, frontal EMG, and hand temperature biofeedback. They also combined this with cognitive-behavioral stress management and graduated exposure within a systematic desensitization model.

A major part of the rationale for the presumed importance of the relaxation and the biofeedback was learning that before fainting "the patient increased muscle tension for several minutes" (p. 24). His wife observed that he "went rigid" and tensed "his whole body." The sequence was stimulus → anxiety → increased muscle tension → sensations of weakness and limb heaviness → nausea and sweating → lightheadedness → syncope.

McGrady and Argueta Bernal noted excess muscle tension during resting baselines in the frontal and cervical neck regions. They noted increased general tension and decreased hand temperature while talking about various stressors. They then reported substantial decreases in resting muscle tension. Tension reached the relaxed range. Hand temperature increases were up to 95°F.

Although the syncopal episodes occurred only two or three times a year, there was daily fear of fainting and anxiety episodes with presyncopal symptoms. At 1-year follow-up there were no reported syncopal incidents. The patient reported that events before treatment would result in presyncopal symptoms or syncopal episodes. With relaxation procedures, these events resulted in asymptomatic reactions or successful management. For example, he could receive a novocaine injection and dental treatment without a problem.

The number of office sessions and the types of biofeedback and relaxation procedures should be tailored for the specific patient. The need for other applied psychophysiological therapies, such as desensitization and cognitive-behavior therapies, also depends on the specific patient. The authors of this case report caution about using the tensing portion of PMR during relaxation because it can result in presyncopal sensations (McGrady & Argueta Bernal, 1986).

Some therapists can successfully treat without the biofeedback. For example, we do not know whether reaching the physiological levels reported was necessary for treatment success. The value of the biofeedback in this case may be in the confidence it provides and reinforces for the patient and therapist. For selected patients, some or all of this treatment package offers a logical and justifiable option for treatment.

SICKLE-CELL CRISES

Another example of a bold attempt to apply biofeedback and applied psychophysiological interventions as adjunctive therapy is by Cozzi, Tryon, and Sedlacek (1987). They reported using six EMG and six thermal biofeedback sessions with eight outpatients with sickle-cell disease who were 10–20 years old. Treatment focused on biofeedback for headaches as a crisis symptom, analgesic use, and anxiety. A follow-up questionnaire at 6 months showed reduced headaches, less pain during these crises, and less use of analgesics. There were no improvements in hospitalizations or emergency room visits compared to the 6-month baseline before treatment.

Two prior reports of applied psychophysiological interventions reported improvement in uncontrolled case studies of sickle-cell disease. These reports involved a few sessions of thermal biofeedback and hypnosis or a combination treatment including hypnosis, relaxation, and cognitive strategies.

A discussion of sickle-cell disease is beyond the scope of this chapter. Briefly, it is a genetic anemic disease producing entrapment or sludging of red blood cells in small blood vessels. This restricts oxygenated blood from getting to parts of the body and results in painful episodes or crises. These include headaches or generalized pain in various parts of the body. Other symptoms include shortness of breath and fever. More serious symptoms include kidney failure, strokes, and other permanent damage to organs.

The frequency and timing of these crises vary individually. Some authorities consider emotional distress a possible factor increasing the risk of symptom crises in people with sickle-cell disease. Emotional distress also may increase the risk of stress-related symptoms accompanying the crises from the disease. This is the rationale for considering applied psychophysiological interventions as adjuncts to treatment. Having the disease is a major stress. This is because of the increased vulnerability to infections and the potentially serious consequences of the disease.

ERYTHROMELALGIA

Erythromelalgia[7] is a very rare disorder.[8] However, if you encounter it in clinical practice, you will want resource information. One must read the references for detailed discussions of the complexity and seriousness of this disorder (Levine & Gustafson, 1987; Michiels & van Joost, 1988, 1990; Kurzrock & Cohen, 1989). This section brings this disorder to the reader's attention, briefly notes the only two reported case studies using biofeedback, and shares treatment ideas.

In some ways, this condition is the opposite of Raynaud's. However, both can coexist in the same person. It involves sudden and intensive spastic dilation of blood vessels or "paroxysmal vasodilation." The symptoms include burning pain, increased skin temperature, and redness. The feet, and less often the hands, are usually the site of the symptoms.

Terminology

The terms for the name of this disorder come from Greek words meaning red (*erythros*), extremities (*melos*), and pain (*algos*). There are three different names for this condition. The original is "erythromelalgia," coined by Mitchell (1878), who described the first 16 cases. This term is acceptable although some writers argue for other terms such as erythermalgia and erythmalgia. It can be idiopathic or secondary to other diseases. The idiopathic form is probably the more common and may have a better prognosis (Babb, Alarçon-Segovia, & Fairbairn, 1964).

Medical Treatments

This disorder is very difficult to treat and is typically refractory. Treatments try a variety of approaches including medications, cold exposure, and elevating the limb(s), but these are not reliably helpful.

Feedback Cases

I know of only two reported cases using biofeedback (Putt, 1978; Cahn & Garber, 1990). Both are worth reviewing because they reported the value of biofeedback. The Eryrhromelalgia Association report three other patients with the primary form who reportedly had some benefit from treatment with biofeedback. However, I think these are not published reports. I unsuccessfully treated a 51-year-old woman who was almost totally disabled by her symptoms. She probably had the secondary type combined with Raynaud's. I mention this to note the origin of my interest and awareness of the complexity and seriousness of the disorder.

The first published case using biofeedback was by a nurse (Putt, 1978). She treated a women using various relaxation procedures in 13 sessions over 11 weeks. She used biofeed-

[7]Optional spellings are "erythermalgia" and "erythmalgia."

[8]Consider contacting the Erythromelalgia Foundation, P.O. Box 218, Duncannon, PA 17020, (717) 834-5330 or 5065, or the Erythromelalgia Association of America, Good Samaritan Hospital and Medical Center, 1015 N.W. 22nd Avenue, Portland, OR 97210. Because of the rareness of this disorder, consider contacting Thom W. Rooke, M.D., at the Mayo Clinic Rochester, MN. He and his colleagues in the Division of Cardiovascular Diseases have extensive medical knowledge and experience with this disorder.

back instruments at least to check skin temperature. The published account does not clearly describe or report direct temperature feedback to the patient, although there was implicit feedback from the therapist. The patient "expressed a fear of allowing her toes to warm because she became uncomfortable at about 32 degrees Centigrade [89.6°F]" (p. 628). This is well within the range of average skin temperatures. She did learn to warm her toe temperatures without symptoms. Medication needs gradually decreased, and for 3 months she was without symptoms. The appearance of her toes and skin improved significantly. She tolerated foot temperatures of about 91–93°F. She then resumed smoking and had a partial relapse a few months later. However, her symptoms and medication use improved again after resuming office and home relaxation during 2 more months of treatment. The importance of this report, very early in the history and maturation of biofeedback, is for its heuristic value. Although we do not know enough of the treatment specifics, we do learn that:

- Warming was the treatment.
- Treatment involved a variety of relaxation procedures.
- Thermal biofeedback played some role.
- There was probable improvement in symptoms and reduced medication.
- There was a probable relapse and improvement after repeated treatment.
- These patients fear warming, and hence practitioners need be careful with this approach.

The other case is by Cahn and Garber (1990). They "hypothesized that the painful symptoms may represent a rebound vasodilation" (p. 51). One therapy goal was avoiding large changes in temperature rather than only avoiding warm temperatures. Another goal was to help the patient gradually warm her extremities without stimulating an attack. The multimodal treatment included thermal feedback, blood volume pulse feedback, respiration feedback, and multiple relaxation techniques. The authors believe that convincing her that "warm was good" was critical. After 1 year, the patient continued to have occasional attacks, but the severity decreased and there were significantly fewer episodes. Her foot temperatures consistently rose to over 90.0°F. Self-report records from June 1988 to July 1989 showed about 40–70 or more attacks per month in the first 3 months. This dropped to 5–10 attacks per month in the last 3 months, an improvement of more than 90%.

Implications

There is a chance that biofeedback might play a useful role in the treatment of some patients with this disorder. Selecting patients with the primary form probably is wiser. Collaboration with physicians knowledgeable about this disorder is obvious.

Biofeedback instruments should include multiple channels of temperature and at least one channel for pulse amplitude or blood volume pulse. Consider a minimum of two channels and preferably four or more temperature channels. This is because of the variability across digits and the need to check both feet and both hands. One should expect many sessions over many months.

Consider providing at least some of this therapy *pro bono* or within a research project. I suggest this because of the embryonic stage of development of this treatment for the disorder and the lengthy nature of treatment.

VISUAL ACCOMMODATION AND OTHER OCULOMOTOR ABNORMALITIES

Applications for oculomotor abnormalities have a long history. An old review (Rotberg & Surwit, 1981) pointed toward the promise of applications in this area. Most of the publications at that time were case studies. Now, there are many experimental studies and replications of successful results for some applications.

Nevertheless, these applications remain mostly in the frontier and some are controversial. Examples of applications with research support are the use of specialized biofeedback instruments and procedures for visual acuity (accommodation), strabismus, nystagmus, and amblyopia. Other applications include blepharospasm,[9] and intraocular pressure (IOP), and glaucoma.

This section does not review the research or discuss these applications. My experience in this area is only with a few patients with blepharospasm. I admit to once being myopic about accommodation of biofeedback applications to visual acuity and other applications for ophthalmic disorders. I avoided aligning my focus on strabismus and typically oscillated about nystagmus. However, I now envision the potential for this application more clearly.

I encourage reading at least Collins et al. (1988), Trachtman (1987), Halperin and Yolton (1986), and Hodes and Howland (1986). They are eye opening and will help readers improve their focus and reduce oscillation.

OTHERS

Other frontier outposts using biofeedback and/or relaxation therapies as part of treatment for medical conditions include dysmenorrhea (Chesney & Tasto, 1975; Dietvorst & Osborne, 1978; Hart, Mathisen, & Prater, 1981; Balick, Elfner, May, & Moore, 1982), cerebral palsy (Finley, 1990; Finley, Niman, Standley, & Ender, 1976; Finley, Niman, Standley, & Wansley, 1977), reflex sympathetic dystrophy, or minor causalgia (Blanchard, 1979; Alioto, 1981), and torticollis (Cleeland, 1973, 1989; Korein & Brudney, 1976; Jahanshahi, Sartory, & Marsden, 1991; Watanabe Nakagawa, Matsuoka, Mishima, & Ohno, 1992).

In addition to hyperhidrosis discussed in this chapter, there also is a literature on applied psychophysiological applications, including relaxation and biofeedback, to various dermatological conditions and disorders (Goodman, 1994; Winchell & Watts, 1988; McMenamy, Katz, & Gipson, 1988; Horne, White, & Varigos, 1989; Haynes, Wilson, Jaffe, & Britton, 1979; Manuso, 1977; Miller, Coger, & Dymond, 1974).

There is successful application of applied psychophysiological treatments such as relaxation therapies for nausea and vomiting as conditioned aversive side effects from cancer chemotherapy (Burish, Shartner, & Lyles, 1981; Shartner, Burish, & Carey, 1985; Carey & Burish, 1988; Burish & Jenkins, 1992). This application enjoys much research support. It should enter the heartland for other functional causes of nausea and vomiting.

The relationship between nausea and immune function is another important subject of research (Bovbjerg et al., 1990; also, see below under "Psychoneuroimmunology"). This

---

[9]Consider contacting the Benign Essential Blepharospasm Research Foundation, Inc., 2929 Calder Avenue, Suite 304, P.O. Box 12468, Beaumont, TX 77726-2468.

research has implications for understanding the hypothesized classical conditioning process cause of anticipatory nausea and vomiting as well as implications for applied psychophysiological interventions for treating these disturbing symptoms.

Other potential applications include as adjuncts to treating hemophilia (Varni, 1981; Lichstein & Eakin, 1985), diabetic ulcers (Shulimson, Lawrence, & Iacono, 1986), and electrical burn-related pain (Bird & Colborne, 1980).

I apologize to these authors and other professionals studying and/or using biofeedback for these conditions and disorders. Mentioning these areas without any discussion does not imply that they are any less important or have any less potential. I simply ran out of time, space, and energy.

FARTHER ALONG THE FRONTIER: ELECTRIFYING, STIRRING, AND VITALIZING?

There are three areas for which I would be remiss if I did not at least briefly mention them. These are applications to (1) psychoneuroimmunology; (2) EEG feedback applications for addictions, attention-deficit/hyperactivity disorder (ADHD), pain, and other behaviors; and (3) new looks at the unconscious and the role of psychophysiology and the unconscious.

Researchers in these areas may object to assigning them to this status, and some may object to mentioning them together. For example, there is respected and inspiring research on psychoneuroimmunology. There is revitalized, stirring, and respected research on "new looks" at the concept of the unconscious. The most recent addition is the prospect of newly proposed EEG applications to addictions and other conditions that represent either a revelation or a revolution. This third area is stimulating, exciting, and arouses passion among some professionals. However, the controversy agitates, inflames, and worries others.

How could I not include these in detail, readers may ask? Well, issues of time, space, and enough knowledge are the answers. I am not prepared to discuss these topics extensively at this time. I could not do them justice and might do more harm than intended or justified. Nevertheless, all are intriguing, exciting, and major parts of the future of applied psychophysiology. At least, they will probably continue to kindle new ideas and inspiration in their ability to illuminate and inspire novel therapeutic applications.

Unconscious

There is new scientific scrutiny of the concept of the "unconscious" by many credible scientists. "The reality of unconscious processes is no longer questionable" (Loftus & Klinger, 1992, p. 761). However, some academic psychologists go beyond skepticism and suggest that the concept "unconscious cognition" does not belong in psychology. See the appendices in Greenwald (1992). He summarizes and discusses his response to scientists who dismiss the possibility of unconscious cognition as well as presents a survey of expert opinion on unconscious cognition.

If one accepts the concept unconscious cognition, then one vital issue and question involves the sophistication of these processes. There are differences among scientists about the sophistication of the unconscious, but there is considerable agreement that in research and theory there are "exciting times . . . ahead for the unconscious" (Loftus & Klinger, 1992, p. 761). One can add to this the excitment also being felt among many clinical practitioners.

Many scientists adopt new terms instead of unconscious. In part, they do this to separate themselves and their research from the "excess baggage that accompanies the very idea of a psychoanalytic unconscious" (Loftus & Klinger, 1992, p. 762). Many of these terms may be found in the series in the *American Psychologist*. For the present discussion, I use the term unconscious for convenience. Also, consider "nonconscious" (Lewicki, Hill, & Czyewska, 1992), or "cognition without attention" and "verbally unreportable cognition" (Greenwald, 1992).

Consider some implications of a new understanding of the unconscious by whatever name one calls it. There are diverse concepts and fields of research, theory, and applications intermeshed with unconscious processes.

The clinical, theoretical, and research implications of unconscious processes, psychophysiological assessment and interventions include many topics. There is much overlap among these. The purpose here is to move toward organizing ideas for the future and to stimulate others. Many readers will already know that some or many of these concepts relate to unconscious processes.

Several concepts and topics involve psychophysiological assessment and therapies, psychotherapies, neuropsychological assessment of memory, and therapies for memory symptoms and disorders. These include:

- People learn psychophysiological perceptions previously outside of their awareness. These include many such as fecal and urinary incontinence, enuresis, nocturnal and diurnal bruxism.
- Practitioners assess and treat cognitive and somatic cue-producing psychophysiological reactivity previously outside of awareness. These include cognitive distraction techniques for pain.
- Practitioners assess and help patients modify event-related potentials (ERPs) for pain control.
- Practitioners assess and treat so-called conversion disorders such as functional amnesia, blindness, deafness, speech, and motoric symptoms.
- Practitioners assess and treat PTSD such as from motor vehicle accidents and sexual assault-induced psychophysiological disorders.
- Psychologists assess memory and provide therapies. This includes priming techniques for
  Combatting amnesia.
  Recovery of old memories such as for childhood sexual and physical abuse.
  Neurocognitive retraining and rehabilitation after head injuries and strokes.
- Practitioners use subliminal and whisper techniques.
- Practitioners use hypnosis therapies.
- A few practitioners and researchers are attempting to use conditioning techniques to help arousal from coma.
- There is research about learning during anesthesia. This is for improved postoperative recovery. This technique uses therapeutic suggestions administered during anesthesia.
- Practitioners use techniques for lie detection and for assessing malingering.
- In psychoneuroimmunology, practitioners and research use therapy techniques to achieve clinically significant changes.

There are many quotes from several sources that I think worthwhile and could include in this section. However, in the interest of space I have chosen two by Greenspan

(1991) which are clinical rather than scientific. However, they convey a sense of the potential role of biofeedback. "Biofeedback helped . . . to reestablish homeostasis and mastery, as well as to trust that a trip to the unconscious was both safe and worthwhile" (p. 11). Referring to a patient he had treated for chronic pain after a traumatic MVA, Greenspan's interpretations included that

> certain symptoms may not be produced by the injury or illness itself, but by the body's unconscious distress response to the initial trauma . . . the trauma triggers earlier unconscious memories, and the associated feelings and physiology [of] being out of control. Information that normally flows through internal . . . circuits can become short-circuited by the electrical activity associated with chronic distress. Relaxing this system and externally linking the unconscious responses of the body to auditory and visual feedback reestablishes this informational circuit, and thereby reestablishes the hierarchy by which the neocortex can specifically and effectively autoregulate. (p. 10)

Psychoneuroimmunology

For immunologically related disorders, there are many inhabitants in the frontier and the promise remains. However, the land is still untamed and replete with obstacles, both within the settlements and surrounding them. Nevertheless, there will continue to be well-meaning and highly motivated inhabitants striving to find the formula to bring this into the heartland. This frontier area remains vibrant. This is because it enjoys a long duration of investments. Also, there is much development in the surrounding territories.[10] Furthermore, there are significant potential and profound benefits that could derive from further development.

For many professionals, this is one of the most exciting potential applications of applied psychophysiology including relaxation and biofeedback. For some practitioners, it is acceptable now as an application for selected patients. However, most researchers and clinicians suggest and use caution at present despite pressured temptation.

Research supports the conclusions that biobehavioral factors and the brain influence the immune system (Gruber et al., 1993; Ader, Felten, & Cohn, 1991; Halley, 1991; O'Leary, 1990; Bovbjerg et al., 1990).

There also is support for the contention that biobehavioral strategies influence measurable immune system changes and are of potential therapeutic importance. For other examples, see Gruber et al. (1993) and Halley (1991). These strategies include relaxation and biofeedback. This chapter does not discuss other applied psychophysiological strategies except when combined with relaxation or biofeedback. Examples of other behavioral interventions that could help the immune system include social support (Kiecolt-Glaser et al., 1985), guided imagery and relaxation (Gruber, Hall, Hersh, & Dubois, 1988), immune system imagery (Rider et al., 1990), music-assisted cell-specific imagery (Rider & Achterberg, 1989), and self-disclosure (Pennebaker, Kiecolt-Glaser, & Glaser, 1988).

Most of the studies reporting relaxation and biofeedback beneficial to the immune system involve various types of normal samples (Peavey, Lawlis, & Goven, 1985; McGrady et al., 1992). However, there also are reports with patient samples (Gruber et al., 1988, 1993).

Gruber et al. (1993) used an applied psychophysiological treatment package with 13 patients who had modified radical mastectomies and were lymph-node negative. This study combined relaxation procedures, guided imagery, and frontal EMG biofeedback in a controlled single crossover design. Seven patients started treatment. The other six patients in a

---

[10]There is much research support for the negative effects of stress and the positive effects of relaxation on immunologic activity.

delayed treatment group eventually also participated in the treatment package. The results suggest that this intervention influenced immune function in immune assays in the desired direction based on multiple pre–post comparisons. It produced "statistically significant effects primarily on T-cell populations including natural killer cells. Antibodies were minimally affected . . ." (p. 14). Specifically, the author's report "that *MLR* is the most responsive index to behavioral interventions. Con-A,[11] a T-cell measure, was second" (p. 16; emphasis added).

Note that "several weeks to months were required for changes to reach statistical significance" (p. 14). This leads to the speculation that "long-term effects of behavioral interventions . . . are cumulative" (p. 15). The investigators provide necessary and ethical cautions for interpreting their data. They also acknowledge the complex and unclear relationship between immune changes and reduced physiological activity. The relationship is not linear. They speculate on potential mechanisms and focus on altered plasma levels of cortisol.

See the reference section for other references in the area of psychoneuroimmunology and applied psychophysiology. This list is illustrative and not exhaustive. I am not prepared to discuss this topic more substantively here. Interested readers will draw their own conclusions about how far out in the frontier this area remains. There are several basic and essential questions and challenges for us to consider.

1. Do biobehavioral and CNS factors change the immune system in both undesired and desired directions?
2. Can one help teach the immune system to make significant changes in desired directions with applied psychophysiological strategies such as relaxation and biofeedback?
3. Do the immunological changes reach clinical significance?
4. Can one elicit immunological changes among patients that reach statistical and clinical significance?
5. Which immunological conditions and diseases respond to applied psychophysiological strategies?
6. Do changes among patients last long enough to affect long-term effects for preventing or reversing immunologically related diseases?
7. Which applied psychophysiological strategies result in immunological changes that reach statistical and clinical significance?

The answer to at least the first two questions is clearly "Yes." The answers to others remain more challenging. See the references for examples of reports and studies that support questions 1, 2, 4, and 7.

One must continue to speculate about the mechanism(s) of change. For example, is it the physiological relaxation? Is it via cognitive changes associated with the relaxation and biofeedback procedures? Is it caused by hormonal changes, reductions in adrenalin, brain catecholamines, plasma levels of cortisol, or other chemical changes? This uncertainty is not different from that present with many interventions including other applications of biofeedback and relaxation, many medications, and psychotherapies.

Major challenges remain in this field. Research must confirm results with more samples of patients and show the clinical significance of the immunological changes beyond statistical significance. Furthermore, research must clarify the active ingredients in the strategies.

---

[11]MLR is mixed lymphocyle responsiveness. Con-A is concanavalin A responsiveness.

These frontier settlements will remain for a long time. There is promise for a role for applied psychophysiology in effecting immunological changes of clinical significance. However, the complexities and challenges are monumental, and prudent practitioners will be very cautious about applications and claims about results.

EEG Feedback Applications to ADHD, Addictions, Pain, and More?

This is the latest area emerging on the frontier. The types of EEG feedback involved differ markedly. Practitioners are developing new terminology to advance into these new territories. New terms include "neurotherapy and neurofeedback" and "alpha–theta feedback." There is now a Brainwave Section of the AAPB and a new organization called the Society for the Study of Neuronal Regulation. I hope researchers and advocates for each of these EEG areas will forgive me for partially subsuming them under one rubric.

I cannot discuss EEG feedback substantively. I humbly admit to insufficient knowledge, understanding, and experience. However, this chapter must include it. No discussion of the status and future of biofeedback would be complete without it.[12] I focus here on three types of EEG and applications. Chapter 20 discusses EEG feedback for ADHD. This includes 12- to 14-Hertz sensorimotor rhythm (SMR) and 4- to 7-Hertz theta activity (Lubar, 1989). EEG feedback for addictions and some other disorders include alpha–theta rhythms (Peniston & Kulkosky, 1989, 1990). The EEG somatosensory evoked potential (SEP), especially the P300 component, is a major focus of the work on pain (Rosenfeld, 1990, 1992). Another potential application for alpha–theta EEG is for PTSD (Peniston & Kulkosky, 1991).

In addition, Tansey (1990a, 1990b, 1990c) reviewed his work on various types of EEG feedback applications including therapy for reducing blood pressure. See his papers for more references. The earlier work with EEG feedback for seizure disorders is not the subject of this section and is reviewed by Lubar (1989).

The applications to ADHD and addictions emit passion and controversy among many researchers and clinical practitioners. The potential application of a different type of EEG feedback to pain (Rosenfeld, 1992) is less controversial at present. In part, this is because the claims are still couched more cautiously.

The bold attempts to treat various conditions and disorders with EEG feedback will remain in the frontier for a while. Indeed, I expect the issue of EEG feedback will be with us for a long time. I do not know whether it will emerge into the heartland or wither in the frontier as did its ancestors.

Aside from urging reading of the published research in this area, I encourage interested readers to read the series of commentaries that started in 1992 in the AAPB *Newsmagazine* (Rosenfeld, 1992; Wuttke, 1992; Ochs, 1992; Fritz, 1992; Peniston, Kulkosky, Fahrion, & Walters, 1992; Wichramasekera, 1993; Cowan, 1993; Ochs, 1993). In the last of this series (Taub & Rosenfeld, 1994) they refer to Taub, Steiner, Smith, Weingarten, and Walton (1994) which is the most recent article I found.

Those interested in addictions may benefit from reading Prochaska, DiClemente, and Norcross (1992). They summarize the research on self-initiated, professionally facilitated changes in addictive behaviors. They discuss the research on five stages that individuals

---

[12]I know several scientists in this field and like and respect several of them. However, this book is not the place to take sides in an area as complex, controversial, and spirited as EEG feedback. There are intense sensitivities and professionals' credibility at stake. Thus, except neurofeedback for ADHD (Chapter 20), I avoided asking anyone to write a section or chapter on this topic. I included the ADHD application to illustrate the application receiving the most attention.

progress through before ending an addiction. These are precontemplation, contemplation, preparation, action, and maintenance. They offer a transtheoretical model that provides an approach to integration of several theories, therapy techniques, and philosophies.

CONCLUSION

This chapter presents several applications and gives readers a sense of the scope of applications. The chapter describes many considerations for treating people with various disorders. Inclusion does not imply an expectation that further research will continue to support the efficacy of all these applications. The chapter does not purport to cover all applications. Read other sources such as Ray et al. (1979), Hatch et al. (1987), Basmajian (1989), and Shellberger et al. (1994) for information and references about other applications.

In the years since the dawn of the term biofeedback, the annual meetings of the Biofeedback Research Society (BRS), Biofeedback Society of America (BSA), and AAPB encountered many speculative ideas and claims about new applications. This field continues to attract advocates of bold and novel ideas. It allows expression to these ideas and allows them to cultivate. It also allows criticism in the spirit of scientific debate. We did not dampen open inquiry and boldness. Had we done so, we would not have the many advances in knowledge and successful applications discussed elsewhere in this book and in this chapter. We must remain open. However, the burden of proof is on the advocates.

For the applications discussed in this and other chapters, the questions facing researchers and clinical practitioners include the following: (1) Does it work? (2) For what symptoms and conditions does it work? (3) What exactly is it that is working? (4) For whom does it work? (5) Is it practical and cost-effective?

GLOSSARY

ABDUCTOR POLLICIS BREVIS. Abductor muscle of the thumb. Inserts at the proximal phalanx of the thumb. Aids in flexion of the thumb.

ALPHA–THETA FEEDBACK. Including and progressing from EEG feedback of alpha activity to theta activity.

AMBLYOPIA. Literally means dull eye. Often called lazy eye. Poor vision in the nondominant eye. Usually results from strabismus, the general term for crossed eyes (esotropia) or otherwise misaligned eyes (exotropia or walleye) such as an eye turning outward or up or down. Also can be caused by a great degree of farsightedness, nearsightedness, or astigmatism in one eye. The stronger eye becomes more dominant as the impaired eye is "turned-off" by the brain.

ANISMUS. See *dyschezia*.

ANORECTAL MANOMETRY. Measurement of pressure from contraction of the muscles of the junction between the anus and rectum. Uses balloons and pressure transducers to measure external anal sphincter (EAS) and internal anal sphincter (IAS) muscles.

ATTENTION-DEFICIT/HYPERACTIVITY DISORDER (ADHD). See Chapter 20.

BAND-PASS FILTERING (Also bandwidth filtering). An electronic device that calculates the frequencies of a specific circuit and curtails or rejects certain other frequencies while allowing others in a specified band or range of frequencies to pass through unmodified. Bandwidth is the range of frequencies (Hertz or cycles per second) recorded. Filters cut off frequencies above and below the range of interest. For example, common EMG band-pass filters allow 100–200 Hertz (narrow), 100–500 Hertz, or 20–1000 Hertz (wide) to pass through. (See Chapter 4 text. Also, see Applications Standards Committee, 1992.)

BLEPHAROSPASM. Involuntary contraction of the orbicularis oculi muscle producing more or less complete closure of the eyelids. Essential type shows no abnormality of the eye or fifth cranial (trigeminal) nerve.

BOTULINUM TOXIN (Trade name Botox). Used to treat patients with focal dystonia, blepharospasm, strabismus, torticollis, and spastic dysphonia. Six distinct types, A–F. Botox is botulium toxin A. It is injected into muscle groups and weakens the strength of involuntary contractions by a presynaptic mechanism. Treatments are often repeated at 3- and 6-month intervals. Requires subspecialized medical training to use.

BROMHIDROSIS. Sweat that becomes foul smelling as a result of bacterial decomposition.

BRONCHOCONSTRICTION. Decreasing the caliber or diameter of a bronchus. The bronchi are the two main breathing tubes from the trachea to the lungs.

BRONCHODILATORS. Drugs that expand (dilate, open) the lumina of the main airways (bronchi) of the lungs. *Beta$_2$-adrenergic agonists* (stimulators) are drugs that have an "affinity for and stimulate physiologic activity at cell receptors normally stimulated by naturally occurring substances" (*Dorland's Illustrated Medical Dictionary*, 1988). In this case, stimulating bronchodilation for persons with bronchospasm. *Theophylline* is another bronchodilator drug.

BRONCHOMOTOR TONE. Bronchomotor means affecting the caliber of the bronchi. The tone or tension of the muscle that affects the caliber of the bronchi.

CAUSALGIA. Burning pain caused by peripheral nerve injury. Often with trophic skin changes. For example, a symptom of reflex sympathetic dystrophy (RSD). (See Chapter 17 for trophic and RSD.)

CINEDEFECOGRAPHY. A dynamic analysis of the anorectum and evacuation process. It is used as part of the diagnosis of certain conditions including paradoxical contractions of the puborectalis and descending perineum. It provides more value in assessing the relative comparison of resting, squeezing, and pushing in an individual patient rather than judging the values of each stage against normal controls. While the patient is in a left lateral decubitus position, the rectum is filled with a premixed semisolid barium sulfate paste. The X-ray table is then tilted upright and the patient sits on a water-filled commode while attempting to evacuate the mixture. The process is fluoroscoped and video recorded. Clinical history is essential for interpreting the cinedefecographic findings and recommending therapy.

COLONIC INERTIA. Atypical slow movement of fecal material through the colon.

CONVERSION DISORDERS. "Pseudoneurological" motor or sensory symptoms or deficits meeting several criteria (American Psychiatric Association, 1994, pp. 452–457). Examples are paralysis, aphasia, blindness, deafness, and seizures.

CORTICOSTEROIDS. Used mainly as anti-inflammatory drugs to treat arthritis, certain skin diseases, insufficiency of the adrenal gland (see Chapters 7, 18), thyroiditis, some cancers, and other disorders.

CORTISOL. The major natural glucocorticoid hormone released from the adrenal cortex. Regulates aspects of metabolism. A type of corticosteroid pharmaceutically called hydrocortisone. (Also, see Chapters 7, 18, 35.)

CRANIAL NERVE 7 (CN7). Facial nerve (nervus facialis). It has two roots. The large motor root supplies the muscles of facial expression, scalp, and others. The smaller root or intermediate nerve (nervus intermedius) is sensory and parasympathetic. Distribution includes the anterior two-thirds of the tongue, soft palate, sublingual glands, and other areas and functions. Parasympathetic nervous system is a subdivision of the autonomic nervous system whose fibers originate from the brainstem and sacral region of spinal cord.

CRICOPHARYNGEAL SPHINCTER. Pertaining to the cricoid cartilage and the pharynx.

CROMOLYN SODIUM. An antiallergy drug that interferes with allergic histamine release.

DEFECATORY PROCTOGRAPHY. Special X-ray examination of abnormalities of the defecatory anatomy.

DIGITATION. Finger-like process.

DYSCHEZIA (ANISMUS, PELVIC FLOOR OUTLET OBSTRUCTION SYNDROME). Difficult or painful evacuation of feces as a result of lack of coordination of the involved muscles.

DYSMENORRHEA. Painful menstruation.

DYSTONIA. Disordered tonicity of muscle. "Sustained abnormal postures and disruptions of ongoing movement resulting from alterations in muscle tone" (Berkow & Fletcher, 1992) Three classes: generalized, segmental, or focal. Focal affects a single body area. Segmental is the rare spread to an adjacent body area. More rarely, dystonia is generalized. Dystonia syndromes include Meige syndrome (blepharospasm–oromandibular), torticollis, spastic dysphonia (laryngeal), occupational (writer's cramp), and symptomatic (with degenerative and metabolic CNS disorders such as Wilson's disease, cerebral palsy, and stroke).

EXTERNAL ANAL SPHINCTER (EAS). See Chapter 24.

$FEF_{25-75\%}$. Mean forced expiratory flow during the middle 50% of the *FVC* (forced vital capacity).

FEV_1 (FORCED EXPIRATORY VOLUME IN 1 SECOND). The volume of air exhaled in the first second of the forceful and maximum exhalation. It is very dependent on effort and much more so than *forced expiratory flow at 50% vital capacity* (FEF_{50}). The latter reflects the rate of airflow in the middle airways. Analyses of FEV_1, FVC, and FEF_{50} logically depend on the patient's height, weight, age, and gender. Some people are bigger "blowhards" than others.

FEV_1/FVC RATIO. The ratio of 1 second of forced expiratory volume to the total volume or FVC. The relationship of obstruction is inversely related to this ratio. Airflow obstruction decreases the normal high rate of airflow during the first second of forced exhalation. This reduces the ratio. The more obstruction, the smaller the FEV_1 and the lower the resulting number from the ratio.

FLEXIBLE (FIBEROPTIC) PROCTOSIGMOIDOSCOPIC EXAMINATION (FLEXSIG). Examining the lower part of the colon (sigmoid) and rectum using a flexible lighted tube. One can see nearly 50% of colorectal cancers or polyps with a FlexSig. Also used in diagnosing Crohn's disease and ulcerative colitis. One can get samples of tissue through this instrument. See Chapter 33.

FOCAL MOTOR DISORDER. Localized at one or more foci.

FVC (FORCED VITAL CAPACITY). The maximum volume of air that one can forcefully clear (exhale) from the lungs from a full inspiration, with no limit to the duration of expiration. It equals the inspiratory capacity plus the expiratory reserve volume. Asthmatic obstruction does not reliably affect it, but it is a figure used in some ratio comparisons. (Also, Chapter 11.)

GLAUCOMA. A group of diseases with the common feature of progressive damage to the optic nerve caused by increased pressure within the eyeball. Two forms are acute and chronic. The chronic form affects about 95% of the people with glaucoma. A leading cause of blindness in the United States. It need not cause severe loss of vision or blindness if detected and treated early. In the chronic form, there is gradual loss of peripheral vision, and it often is undetected for years. There are no early warning signs. Regular eye checkups from age 40 is the only way to diagnosis it early. Eye drops with beta-adrenergic blockers or oral medications can lower the pressure for many persons. If drugs are unsuccessful, laser or other surgery is considered.

HARD SWALLOW TECHNIQUE. To increase strength of the pharyngeal swallow and clear the pharyngeal cavities of residual postswallow pooling.

HEMOPHILIA. Several inherited disorders of specific clotting factors. Most common is hemophilia A (classic). In type B (Christmas disease) a different clotting factor is lacking. The most common hereditary bleeding disorder is von Willebrand's disease.

HIRSCHSPRUNG'S DISEASE (CONGENITAL MEGACOLON). Infants with this disorder develop an abnormally large or dilated colon. Signs include failure to pass meconium (a dark green material) stool, vomiting, abdominal distention, and failure to have a bowel movement. Dehydration, weight loss, diarrhea, and constipation also may occur. Diagnosis is by rectal biopsy. Treatment is surgery and usually successful.

HYPERCALCEMIA. Excess calcium in the blood. Symptoms include fatigue, muscle weakness, depression, anorexia, nausea, and constipation. There are many different major causes (e.g., excess parathyroid hormone as from primary hyperparathyroidism, carcinoma of the parathyroid, hyperthyroidism, and many others). There is usually excess bone resorption and release of Ca into the extracellular fluid (ECF).

HYPERTHYROIDISM. Excessive secretion of hormone by the thyroid gland. It is characterized by increased metabolic rate, goiter, and disturbances in the autonomic nervous system.

HYPOTHYROIDISM, ADULT. See Chapter 17 for detailed definition. (Also see *myxedema*.) Caused by an underactive thyroid gland. The person feels physically and mentally sluggish. Symptoms include constant tiredness, muscle aches, slowed heart rate, constipation, dry and lusterless skin, thickened skin, hoarse voice, hearing loss, puffy face, dry hair, goiter in some people, heavy and prolonged menstrual periods, decreased interest in sex, and/or an inability to stay warm in cool or cold ambient temperatures. Increased weight, if present, is slight. Treatment is usually successful.

INTRAOCULAR PRESSURE (IOP). Pressure from excess fluids within the eye. A sign of certain pathological conditions such as glaucoma.

IONTOPHORESIS. Ion therapy or ionic medication. Introduces ions into the body tissues through the skin for treatment.

LIGATION. The procedure during surgery for tying off blood vessels with a filament to prevent them from bleeding.

MEGACOLON. Giant colon. A congenital or acquired abnormally enlarged colon, often caused by nerve damage. Movement of feces becomes severly impaired. Causes include *Hirschsprung's disease*, severe neurological disorders including Parkinson's disease, and spinal cord injury. Narcotics and some other medications can cause megacolon. Psychogenic megacolon is related to faulty bowel habits, often in mentally retarded children and adults with chronic and severe psychiatric disorders.

MENDELSOHN MANEUVER. Facilitates opening and "stretching" of the cricopharyngeal sphincter by volitionally increasing and maintaining elevation of the larynx. Biofeedback monitoring is from the muscles between the thyroid cartilage and inferior tip of the mandible. The patient holds the swallow for several seconds before completing it.

MIXED LYMPHOCYTE REACTION (MLR). (Also mixed lymphocyte culture, MLC) Lymphocytes are white blood cells (B cells and T cells) produced in bone marrow, lymph nodes, and the spleen. They have a primary role in the body's immune defense system. Uses of the MLR include selecting compatible donors for bone marrow and renal transplantation and typing certain antigens. Also used in diagnosis of immunodeficiency diseases. Antigens produce antibodies in reaction to invaders into the body such as harmful germs and viruses.

MYENTERIC PLEXUS. A plexus is a generic term for a network of lymph vessels, nerves, or veins. The myenteric plexus is part of the enteric plexus in the tunica muscularis. The enteric plexus is autonomic nerve fibers in the digestive tube wall. Contains a variety of types of fibers.

NATURAL KILLER CELLS. These lymphocytes are also called cytotoxic T cells. They also are referred to as large granular lymphocytes because of large granules shown by light microscopy. They kill viruses by first binding to cells infected with a virus and then secreting molecules that are toxic to cells. An early and major part of the immune defense system.

NOCTURNAL AND DIURNAL BRUXISM. Teeth grinding and/or clenching during sleep and/or while awake. (See Chapter 16.)

NYSTAGMUS. Involuntary and constant cyclical movement of the eyeball in any direction. Persons with this may not be aware of it. A symptom with a variety of causes that may be congenital or acquired.

OPERANT SHAPING PROCEDURES. Skinnerian behavioral principle of positively reinforcing small steps, successively approximating a more complex goal behavior. (See *shaping* in Chapter 1.)

PARASYMPATHETIC REACTIVITY. Reactivity of the parasympathetic branch of the autonomic nervous system. Parasympathetic nervous system is a subdivision of the autonomic nervous system whose fibers originate from the brainstem and sacral region of the spinal cord. *Autonomic nervous system* is part of the peripheral nervous system that consists of sympathetic and parasympathetic subdivisions. Innervates cardiac muscle, smooth muscle, and glands. (See Chapters 1 and 7 for more on ANS and reactivity.)

PAROXYSMAL VASODILATION. Intensive spastic dilation of blood vessels.

PARS RECTA SITE OF THE CRICOTHYROID MUSCLE. Pars means division of a larger area, organ, or structure. Fibers of this muscle insert into the lower (caudal) edge (margin) of the thyroid cartilage. This muscle is the most superficial of the intrinsic laryngeal muscles.

PEAK EXPIRATORY FLOW RATE (PEFR). Maximal expiratory flow rate in pulmonary function test, in liters per minute.

PELVIC FLOOR OUTLET OBSTRUCTION SYNDROME. Difficult or painful evacuation of feces because of lack of coordination of the involved muscles. (Same as *anismus* and *dyschezia*.)

PORPHYRIA. A group of inherited metabolic disorders involving pigment metabolism. Abnormal biosynthesis and metabolism of the iron-containing portion of the hemoglobin molecule (heme) from disturbed metabolism of porphyrin. Causes increased production and excretion of porphyrin or precursors. Porphyrin is derived from hemoglobin and form the basis of respiratory pigments.

PSYCHONEUROIMMUNOLOGY. Study of the interrelationships among immunology, the nervous system, and psychology.

PTSD. Posttraumatic stress disorder.

PUBORECTALIS MUSCLE. Pertaining to the pubis (os pubis) and rectum. The pubis is the anterior inferior part of the hip bone (os coxae) on either side. Helps support pelvic viscera and counters intra-abdominal pressure increases. (See Chapter 23.)

PUDENDAL NERVE. A nerve supplying the perineum including the genitalia, the urethral sphincter, and the external anal sphincter. The pudendum (plural is pudenda) is the external genitalia of humans, especially women. (See Chapter 23.)

RECTAL PROLAPSE. A form of pelvic prolapse in which the pelvic floor muscles stretch or slacken, resulting in one or more lower abdominal organs, in this case a portion of the rectal mucosa, sagging into the anal canal and protruding through the anus. More common in elderly women and those who gave birth to several children. (See *pelvic prolapse*, Chapter 23.)

REFLEX SYMPATHETIC DYSTROPHY (RSD). Sympathetically mediated burning sensation or pain and tenderness, usually in a hand or foot and sometimes a kneecap or hip. Other symptoms are thin or shiny skin along with increased sweating and hair growth. It can develop weeks or months after an injury, heart attack, or stroke. In the second phase, usually developing over months, the skin becomes cool and shiny. Contracture may occur. Usually occurs after age 50 in men and women about equally. Loss of minerals in bones is typical and revealed by X-rays. If not treated promptly, irreversible damage can occur. Analgesics, heat and cold, and exercise are common treatments. Corticosteroid drugs are useful for some people. (See Chapter 17.)

SICKLE-CELL DISEASE. A genetic anemic disease producing entrapment or sludging of red blood cells in small blood vessels (see text).

SOMATOSENSORY EVOKED POTENTIAL (SEP). A type of evoked response potential (ERP) or evoked cortical potential triggered by somatosensory stimuli. These stimuli activate corresponding neuroanatomic cortical areas in the sensorimotor area. Special computer analysis of the EEG allows measurement of the latency, duration, and amplitude of selected cortical waveforms such as the P300. (See Chapter 20.)

SPONTANEOUS REMISSION. Signs and symptoms of a disease diminishing or disappearing unaided or without an obvious cause.

STERNOHYOID. Relating to the sternum and hyoid bone. The muscle that depresses the hyoid bone and larynx. The hyoid bone is a horseshoe-shaped bone at the base of the tongue, above the thyroid cartilage.

STRABISMUS. Eye disorder usually involving cross-eye (esotropia), in which an eye turns inward, or walleye (exotropia), when there is outward turning of an eye, and occasionally downward or upward turning of an eye. First seen usually in early childhood. Children do not outgrow strabismus (and *amblyopia*). Prompt treatment is usually considered essential to avoid what ophthalmologists and most optometrists consider will be permanent damage. Early treatment methods include optical, medical, and surgical. For example, if the strabismus occurs only when looking at close objects, then eyeglass correction may help. Medical treatment includes eyedrops. Surgery is for realigning the eye muscles.

SUBLIMINAL TECHNIQUES. Purported learning techniques using stimuli one cannot discriminate or detect. Example is audiotapes with purported subliminal messages.

SULFITES. Salts of sulfurous acid. Present in many food products, especially wine. Also used as preservative and to sanitize foods, especially in salad bars. Most people have no sensitivity to sulfites. If sensitivity is clearly present, be careful eating salads, fresh fruits, potatoes, shellfish, and wine. Check labels for sodium bisulfite, potassium bisulfite, sodium sulfite, sulfur dioxide, and potassium metabisulfite.

SYSTEMATIC DESENSITIZATION. A commonly used and highly successful type of behavioral therapy for fear and phobia responses. There is gradual exposure for very limited periods from the least anxiety-producing to increasingly anxiety-producing. Exposures usually occur with relaxation. Exposure is imagined, with artificial stimuli (e.g., pictures, video; in vitro) and/or with real-life stimuli (in vivo). (See Chapters 7, 18.)

T CELL. A type of lymphocyte or white blood cell and part of the immune system. Activated by the thymus gland. Attacks antigens directly. Makes lymphokines that stimulate macrophages or cells that engulf (phagocytize) bacteria. (Also see *natural killer cells.*)

THENAR EMINENCE. Prominence at the thumb base.

TIDAL VOLUME (V_T). Amount of air inhaled and exhaled in one respiratory cycle. (See Chapter 11.)

TORTICOLLIS (CERVICAL DYSTONIA WRYNECK). Severe twisting of the neck to one side, caused by excess contraction of muscles. Several types and causes. Can be congenital or acquired.

TOTAL RESPIRATORY RESISTANCE. (Total pulmonary resistance) Vascular resistance of pulmonary circulation such as the pulmonary artery and veins and mitral valve.

TRIGEMINAL–VAGAL CONNECTION. The relationship between the trigeminal (5th cranial nerve) and the vagus nerve (10th cranial). The trigeminal nerve is sensory and motor: its sensory function is for the face, teeth, mouth, and nasal cavity; the motor function is for the mastication muscles. The vagus nerve also is both sensory and motor: sensory fibers go to the ear, tongue, pharynx, and larynx; motor fibers go to the pharynx, larynx, esophagus, and parasympathetic and visceral afferent fibers to the thoracic and abdominal viscera. The proposed connection is an attempt to explain how facial/head relaxation could affect breathing and other bodily functions (see *parasympathetic*).

UREMIA. Toxic state from insufficient excretion from and regulation by the kidneys.

VALSALVA MANEUVER. Forcible exhalation effort against a closed glottis. Increases intrathoracic pressure and interferes with venous return to the heart. Also forced exhalation effort against occluded (pinched) nostrils and closed mouth.

VIDEOENDOSCOPIC FEEDBACK. An endoscope allows examination of a hollow cavity or organ. Types include bronchoscope for the trachea and bronchial tree; gastroscopy for the esophagus, stomach, and duodenum; colonoscopy for the colon to the anus; arthroscopy for joints; and cystoscopy for the bladder. Video allows filming of the area examined. Feedback is an experimental procedure for providing direct viewing to the patient.

VISUAL ACUITY. Sharpness of vision.

WHISPER TECHNIQUE. A modified auditory subliminal technique in which the recipient can hear the voice and barely discern or not quite discern the words. Superimposed on other, more clear verbal communication, intended to affect cognitive and psychophysiological functioning. Recently developed by Dr. Thomas Budzynski and colleagues (Budzynski, Reinking, & Mader, 1993).

ACKNOWLEDGMENTS

I am very thankful to allergist Juan C. Guarderas, M.D., and neurologist Kathleen Donovan, M.D., of Mayo Clinic Jacksonville; and Thomas Rooke, M.D., for their reviews of sections of this chapter. Their comments and suggestions were very helpful. This appreciation does not imply their endorsement of the content of this chapter.

REFERENCES

Chronic Constipation with Dyschezia

Berkow, R., & Fletcher, A. J. (1992). *The Merck manual of diagnosis and therapy* (16th ed.). Rayway, NJ: Merck.

Bleijenberg, G., & Kuijpers, H. C. (1987). Treatment of the spastic pelvic floor syndrome with biofeedback. *Diseases of the Colon and Rectum, 30,* 108–111.

Heyman, S., & Wexner, S. (1990). EMG training for paradoxical puborectalis in patients with chronic constipation. *Biofeedback and Self-Regulation, 15,* 64–65.

Heyman, S., & Wexner, S. (1993, March 25–30.). EMG biofeedback retraining for paradoxical puborectalis contractions in patients with chronic constipation. In *Proceedings of the 24th Annual Meeting of the AAPB,* Los Angeles. Wheatridge, CO: Association for Applied Psychophysiology and Biofeedback.

Larson, D. E. (Ed.). (1990). *Mayo Clinic family health book.* New York: William Morrow.

Loening-Baucke, V. (1990). Modulation of abnormal defecation dynamics by biofeedback treatment in chronically constipated children with encopresis. *Journal of Pediatrics, 116,* 214–222.

Singles, J. M., & Cox, D. (1990, March 23–28). Evaluation of a biofeedback-based behavior modification program for the treatment of chronic constipation. In *Proceedings of the 21st Annual Meeting of the AAPB, Washington, DC.* Wheatridge, CO: Association for Applied Psychophysiology and Biofeedback.

Van Baal, J. G., Legvit, P., & Brummelkanz, W. H. (1984). Relaxation biofeedback conditioning as treatment of a disturbed defection reflex. *Diseases of the Colon and Rectum, 27,* 185–194.

Weber, J., Ducrotte, P. H., Touchais, J. Y., Roussingnol, C., & Denis, P. H. (1987). Biofeedback training for constipation in adults and children. *Diseases of the Colon and Rectum, 30,* 844–846.

Wexner, S. D., Cheape, J. D., Jorge, J. M. N., Heymen, S., & Jagelman, D. G. (1992). Prospective assessment of biofeedback for the treatment of paradoxical puborectalis contraction. *Diseases of the Colon and Rectum, 35,* 145–150.

Writer's Cramp

Bindman, E., & Tibbetts, R. W. (1977). Writer's cramp—a rational approach to treatment. *British Journal of Psychiatry, 131,* 143–148.

Cottraux, J., Juenet, C., & Collet, L. (1983). The treatment of writer's cramp with multimodal behavior therapy and biofeedback: A study of 15 cases. *British Journal of Psychiatry, 142,* 180–183.

Ince, L. P., Leon, M. S., & Christidis, D. (1986). EMG biofeedback for handwriting disabilities: A critical examination of the literature. *Journal of Behavior Therapy and Experimental Psychiatry, 17*(2), 95–100.

Marsden, C. D., & Sheehy, M. P. (1990). Writer's cramp. *Trends in Neurosciences, 13*(4), 148–153.

Mishima, N., Kitagawa, K., Hara, T., & Nakagawa, T. (1992). Treatment of writer's cramp with dystonic involuntary movements by biofeedback therapy. In K. Shirakura, I. Saito, & S. Tsutsui (Eds.), *Current Biofeedback Research in Japan* (pp. 103–112). Tokyo: Shinkoh Igadu Shuppan.

Murabayashi, N., Takekoshi, I., Takada, H., Igarashi, M., Nonaka, T., Tsuboi, K., Nakano, K., & Tsutshi, S. (1992). The effects of electromyogram biofeedback on writer's cramp. In K. Shirakura, I. Saito, & S. Tsutsui (Eds.), *Current biofeedback research in Japan* (pp. 93–102). Tokyo: Shinkoh Igadu Shuppan.

Nutt, J. G., Muenter, M. D., Aronson, A., Kurland, L. T., & Melton, L. J. (1988). Epidemiology of focal and generalized dystonia in Rochester, Minnesota. *Movement Disorders, 3*(3), 188–194.

Reavley, W. (1975). The use of biofeedback in the treatment of writer's cramp. *Journal of Behavior Therapy and Experimental Psychiatry, 6,* 335–338.

Rowan, D. C. (1980). *Behavioral approaches in the management of movement disorders.* Paper presented at the First World Congress on Behavior Therapy, Jerusalem, Israel.

Rubow, R. (1989, March 17–22.). EMG biofeedback in the treatment of writer's cramp. In *Proceedings of the 20th Annual Meeting of the Association for Applied Psychophysiology and Biofeedback, San Diego.* Wheatridge, CO: Association for Applied Psychophysiology and Biofeedback.

Tanaka, N., & Oumi, S. (1982). The clinical types of writer's cramp and indication of EMG-biofeedback therapy. *Japanese Journal of Psychosomatic Medicine, 22,* 41–48.

Uchiyama, K., Lutterjohann, M., & Shah, M. D. (1977). Biofeedback-assisted desensitization treatment of writer's cramp. *Journal of Behavior Therapy and Experimental Psychiatry, 8,* 169–171.

Hand and Wrist Disorders of Musicians

Amadio, P. C., & Russotti, G. M. (1990). Evaluation and treatment of hand and wrist disorders in musicians. *Hand Clinics (Hand Injuries in Sports and Performing Arts), 6*(3), 405–416.

Fischer-Williams, M., & Sovine, D. L. (1984, March 23–28). Musicians with occupational hand disorders treated by biofeedback. In *Proceedings of the 15th Annual Meeting of the Biofeedback Society of America, Albuquerque.* Wheatridge, CO: Association for Applied Psychophysiology and Biofeedback.

Fry, H. J. H. (1986). Prevalence of overuse (injury) syndrome in Australian music schools. *British Journal of Industrial Medicine, 44,* 35–40.

Hochberg, F. H., Leffert, R. D., Heller, M. D., & Merriman, L. (1983). Hand difficulties among musicians. *Journal of the American Medical Association, 249*(14), 1869–1872.

Hoppmann, R. A., & Patrone, N. A. (1989). A review of musculoskeletal problems in instrumental musicians. *Seminars in Arthritis and Rheumatism, 19*(2), 117–126.

Levee, J. R., Cohen, M. J., & Rickles, W. H. (1976). Electromyographic biofeedback for relief of tension in the facial and throat muscles of a woodwind musician. *Biofeedback and Self-Regulation, 1*(1), 113–120.

LeVine, W. R. (1983). Behavioral and biofeedback therapy for a functionally impaired musician: A case report. *Biofeedback and Self-Regulation, 8,* 161–168.

LeVine, W. R., & Irvine, J. K. (1984). In vivo EMG biofeedback in violin and viola pedagogy. *Biofeedback and Self-Regulation, 9,* 161–168.

Lockwood, A. H. (1989). Medical problems of musicians. *New England Journal of Medicine, 320,* 221–227.

Mandel, S. (1990). Overuse syndrome in musicians: When playing an instrument hurts. *Postgraduate Medicine, 88*(2), 111–114.

Montes, R., Bedmar, M., Martin, M. (1993). EMG biofeedback of the abductor pollicis brevis in piano performance. *Biofeedback and Self-Regulation, 18*(2), 67–77.

Morasky, R. L., Reynolds, C., & Clarke, G. (1981). Using biofeedback to reduce left arm extensor EMG of string players during musical performance. *Biofeedback and Self-Regulation, 6,* 207–216.

Morasky, R. L., Reynolds, C., & Sowell, L. E. (1983). Generalization of lowered EMG levels during musical performance following biofeedback training. *Biofeedback and Self-Regulation, 8,* 207–216.

Asthma

Brooks, C. M., Richards, J. M., Baily, W. C., & Martin, B. (1989). Subjective symptomatology of asthma in an outpatient population. *Psychosomatic Medicine, 51,* 102–108.

Carpenter, M. B., & Sutin, J. (1983). *Human neuroanatomy* (8th ed.). Baltimore: Williams & Wilkins.

Carr, R. E., Lehrer, P. M., & Hochron, S. M. (1992). Panic symptoms in asthma and panic disorder: A preliminary test of the dyspnea-fear theory. *Behaviour Research and Therapy, 30*(3), 251–261.

Cluss, P. A. (1986). Behavioral interventions as adjunctive treatments for chronic asthma. *Progress in Behavior Modification, 20,* 123–160.

Creer, T. L., Backiel, M., Ullman, S., & Leung, P. (1986). *Living with asthma. Part 1: Manual for teaching parents the self-managment of childhood asthma: Part 2. Manual for teaching children the self-management of asthma* (NIH Publication No. 86-2364). Washington, DC: U.S. Government Printing Office.

Creer, T. L., Kotses, H., & Reynolds, R. V. C. (1989). Living with asthma. Part II: Beyond CARIH. *Journal of Asthma, 26,* 31–52.

Dahl, J., Gustafsson, D., & Melin, L. (1990). Effects of a behavioral treatment program on children with asthma. *Journal of Asthma, 27*(1), 41–46.

Dirks, J. F., Kinsman, R. A., Staudenmayer, H., & Kleiger, J. H. (1979). Panic-fear in asthma: Symptomatology as an index of signal anxiety and personality as an index of ego resources. *Journal of Nervous and Mental Disease, 167*(10), 615–619.

Dorland's illustrated medical dictionary (27th ed.). (1988). Philadelphia: W. B. Saunders.

Ellis, E. (1993, January/February). Advances in asthma therapeutics. *Group Practice Journal,* 51–57.

Gellhorn, E. (1958). The neurophysiological basis of neuromuscular relaxation. *Archives of Internal Medicine, 102,* 393–399.

Henderson, W. R. Jr. (1993, January/February). Current understanding of the pathophysiology of allergic disorders. *Group Practice Journal,* 58–64.

Kinsman, R. A., Luparello, T., O'Banion, K., & Spector, S. (1973). Multidimensional analysis of the subjective symptomatology of asthma. *Psychosomatic Medicine, 35,* 250–267.

Kotses, H., Harver, A., Segreto, J., Glaus, K. D., Creer, T. L., & Young, G. A. (1991). Long-term effects of biofeedback-induced facial relaxation on measures of asthma severity in children. *Biofeedback and Self-Regulation, 16*(1), 1–21.

Lehrer, P. M., Hochron, S. M., McCann, B. S., Swartzman, L., & Reba, P. (1986). Relaxation decreases large-airway but not small-airway asthma. *Journal of Psychosomatic Research, 30,* 13–25.

Lehrer, P. M., Sargunaraj, D., & Hochron, S. (1992). Psychological approaches to the treatment of asthma. *Journal of Consulting and Clinical Psychology, 60*(4), 639–643.

Mussell, M. J. (1986a). A trachea-noise biofeedback device to help reduce bronchospasm in asthmatics. *Journal of Biomedical Engineering, 8,* 341–344.

Mussell, M. J. (1986b). Control of the expired CO_2 level and minute-ventilation during a hyperventilation challenge for asthmatics. *Journal of Biomedical Engineering, 8,* 213–216.

Mussell, M. J. (1986c). *An automatic bronchial hyperventilation challenge, the responses of asthmatics to eucapnic hyperventilation and exercise, and the effects of trachea-noise biofeedback on bronchoconstriction in asthmatics.* Doctoral dissertation, Biomedical Engineering, Sussex University.

Mussell, M. J., & Hartley, J. P. R. (1988). Trachea-noise biofeedback in asthma: A comparison of the effect of trachea-noise biofeedback, a bronchodilator, and no treatment on the rate of recovery from exercise- and eucapnic hyperventilation-induced asthma. *Biofeedback and Self-Regulation, 13*(3), 219–234.

Mussell, M. J., & Williams, G. (1986). Equipment to condition inspired air over a wide temperature and humidity range, for a hyperventilation challenge for asthmatics. *Medical and Biological Engineering and Computing, 24,* 499–505.

Nadel, N. A. (1976). Airways: Autonomic regulation and airway responsiveness. In E. B. Weiss & M. S. Segal (Eds.), *Bronchial asthma: Mechanisms and therapeutics.* Boston: Little, Brown.

Peper, E. (1988). Strategies to reduce the effort of breathing: Electromyographic and inspirometry biofeedback. *Respiratory Psychophysiology* (pp. 113–122). London: Macmillan.

Peper, E., Smith, K., & Waddell, D. (1987). Voluntary wheezing versus diaphragmatic breathing with inhalation (Voldyne) feedback: A clinical intervention in the treatment of asthma. *Clinical Biofeedback and Health, 10*(2), 83–88.

Peper, E., & Tibbitts, V. (1992). Fifteen-month follow-up with asthmatics utilizing EMG/Incentive Inspirometer feedback. *Biofeedback and Self-Regulation, 17*(2), 143–151.

Richter, R., & Dahme, B. (1982). Bronchial asthma in adults: There is little evidence for the effectiveness of behavioral therapy and relaxation. *Journal of Psychosomatic Research, 26,* 533–540.

Roland, M., & Peper, E. (1987). Inhalation volume changes with inspirometer feedback and diaphragmatic breathing coaching. *Clinical Biofeedback and Health, 10*(2), 89–97.

Schwartz, M. S., & Fehmi, L. (1982). *Application standards and guidelines for providers of biofeedback services.* Wheatridge, CO: Association for Applied Psychophysiology and Biofeedback.

Shellenberger, R., Amar, P., Schneider, C., & Stewart, R. (1989). *Clinical efficacy and cost effectiveness of biofeedback therapy: Guidelines for third party reimbursement.* Wheatridge, CO: Association for Applied Psychophysiology and Biofeedback

Shellenberger, R., Amar, P., Schneider, C., & Turner, J. (1994). *Clinical efficacy and cost effectiveness of biofeedback therapy: Guidelines for third party reimbursement* (2nd ed.). Wheatridge, CO: Association for Applied Psychophysiology and Biofeedback.

Tanaka, T., & Asahara, T. (1980). Synaptic activation of vagal afferent on facial motoneurons in the cat. *Brain Research, 212*, 188–192.

Tiep, B. L., Alaniz, J., & Cordell, J. (1976). Respiratory feedback: Two non-invasive approaches in the treatment of patients with chronic obstructive airway disease. *Proceedings of the San Diego Biomedical Symposium, 15*, 371–374.

Tiep, B. L., Belman, M. J., & Trippe, M. (1980). Wheeze-biofeedback in exercise induced bronchospasm. *American Review of Respiratory Disease (Abstract edition), 121*, 200.

Tomori, Z., & Widdcombe, J. G. (1969). Muscular, bronchomotor, and cardiovascular reflexes elicited by mechanical stimulation of the respiratory tract. *Journal of Physiology* (London), *200*, 25–49.

Yellowlees, P. M., Alpers, J. H., Bowden, J. J., Bryant, G. D., & Ruffin, R. E. (1987). Psychiatric morbidity in patients with chronic airflow obstruction. *Medical Journal of Australia, 146*, 305–307.

Yellowlees, P. M., & Kalucy, R. S. (1990). Psychobiological aspects of asthma and the consequent research implications. *Chest, 97*, 628–634.

Posture Training for Idiopathic Scoliosis

Birbaumer, N., Flor, H., Cevey, B., Dworkin, B., & Miller, N. E. (1994). Behavioral treatment of scoliosis and kyphosis. *Journal of Psychosomatic Research, 38*(6), 623–628.

Cevey, B., Birbaumer, N., Dworkin, B., Miller, N. E., Zielke, K., Parsch, K., zu Eulenburg, F., Matzen, K., & Springer, H.-H. (n. d.) *Biofeedback in the treatment of scoliosis and kyphosis.* Unpublished work cited in Miller (1985).

Dworkin, B., Miller, N. E., Dworkin, S., Birbaumer, N., Brines, M. L., Jonas, S., Schwentker, E. P., & Graham, J. J. (1985). Behavioral method for the treatment of idiopathic scoliosis. *Proceedings of the National Academy of Science, 82*, 2493–2497.

Miller, N. E. (1985). Some professional and scientific problems and opportunities for biofeedback. *Biofeedback and Self-Regulation, 10*(1), 3–24.

Hyperhidrosis

Alvarez, L. M., Cortes, J. F., & Rodriguez, D. (1993, March 25–30). Cognitive-behavioral therapy for the treatment of palmar hyperhidrosis. In *Proceedings of the 24th Annual Meeting of the Association for Applied Psychophysiology and Biofeedback, Los Angeles, CA.* Wheatridge, CO: Association for Applied Psychophysiology and Biofeedback.

Duller, P., & Gentry, W. D. (1980). Use of biofeedback in treating chronic hyperhidrosis: A preliminary report. *British Journal of Dermatology, 103*, 143–146.

Farrar, S., & Hartje, J. C. (1987, March 13–18). Hyperhidrosis: A successful methodology for treatment. In *Proceedings of the 18th Annual Meeting of the Biofeedback Society of America, Boston, MA.* Wheatridge, CO: Association for Applied Psychophysiology and Biofeedback.

Fotopoulos, S. S., & Whitney, P. S. (1978). Biofeedback in the treatment of psychophysiological disorders. *Biofeedback and Self-Regulation, 3*(4), 331–361.

Harris, J., & Sieveking, N. (1979). Case study in hyperhidrosis. *American Journal of Clinical Biofeedback, 2*(1), 31.

Kawahara, K., & Kikuchi, T. (1992). A study of palmar sweating biofeedback (A preliminary report). In K. Shirakura, I. Saito, & S. Tsutsui (Eds.), *Current biofeedback research in Japan* (pp. 174–183). Tokyo: Shinkoh Igaku Shuppan.

White, J. W. Jr. (1986). Treatment of primary hyperhidrosis. *Mayo Clinic Proceedings, 61*, 951–956.

Menopausal Hot Flushes

Freedman, R. R. (1989). Laboratory and ambulatory monitoring of menopausal hot flashes. *Psychophysiology, 26,* 573–579.

Freedman, R. R., & Woodward, S. (1992a). Elevated α_2-adrenergic responsiveness in menopausal hot flushes: Pharmacologic and biochemical studies. In P. Lomax & E. Schonbaum (Eds.), *Thermoregulation: The pathophysiological basis of clinical disorders.* Basel: Karger.

Freedman, R. R., & Woodward, S. (1992). Behavioral treatment of menopausal hot flashes: Evaluation by ambulatory monitoring. *American Journal of Obstetrics and Gynecology, 167*(2), 436–439.

Freedman, R. R., Woodward, W., & Sabharwal, S. (1990). α_2-Adrenergic mechanism in menopausal hot flushes. *Obstetrics and Gynecology, 76,* 573–578.

Germaine, L., & Freedman, R. R. (1984). Behavioral treatment of menopausal hot flashes: Evaluation by objective methods. *Journal of Consulting and Clinical Psychology, 52,* 1072–1079.

Lee, C. T., & Taylor, D. N. (1987, March 13–18). Biofeedback, relaxation training and supportive counseling in the treatment of menopausal hot flush. In *Proceedings of the 18th Annual Meeting of the Association for Applied Psychophysiology and Biofeedback, Boston.* Wheatridge, CO: Association for Applied Psychophysiology and Biofeedback.

Woodward, S., Grevill, H., & Freedman, R. R. (1991, March 15–20). Respiratory alterations during menopausal hot flashes. In *Proceedings of the 22nd Annual Meeting of the Association for Applied Psychophysiology and Biofeedback*, Dallas. Wheatridge, CO: Association for Applied Psychophysiology and Biofeedback.

Oral–Pharyngeal Dysphagia

Bryant, M. (1991). Biofeedback in the treatment of a selected dysphagic patient. *Dysphagia, 6,* 140–144.

Haynes, S. N. (1976). Electromyographic biofeedback treatment of a woman with chronic dysphagia. *Biofeedback and Self-Regulation, 1*(1), 121–126.

Huckabee, M. L. (1992). Application of EMG biofeedback in the treatment of oral pharyngeal dysphagia. In *Electromyograph applications in physical therapy* (No. 6). West Chazy, NY: Thought Technology.

Latimer, P. (1981). Biofeedback and self-regulation in the treatment of diffuse esophageal spasm: A single case study. *Biofeedback and Self-Regulation, 6*(2), 181–189.

Logemann, J. A. (Ed.). (1986). Management of the patient with disordered oral feeding. In *Evaluation and treatment of swallowing disorders.* San Diego: College Hill Press.

Functional Voice Disorders

Allen, K. D., Bernstein, B., & Chait, D. H. (1991). EMG biofeedback treatment of pediatric hyperfunctional dysphonia. *Journal of Behavior Therapy and Experimental Psychiatry, 22*(2), 97–101.

Andrews, S., Warner, J., & Stewart, R. (1986). EMG biofeedback and relaxation in the treatment of hyperfunctional dysphonia. *British Journal of Disorders of Communication, 21,* 353–369.

Aronson, A. E. (1990). *Clinical voice disorders* (3rd ed.) New York: Thieme.

Bastian, R. W., & Nagorsky, M. J. (1987). Laryngeal image biofeedback. *Laryngoscope, 97,* 1346–1349.

D'Antonio, L., Lotz, W., Chait, D., & Netsell, R. (1987). Perceptual-physiologic approach to evaluation and treatment of dysphonia. *Annals of Otology, Rhinology, and Laryngolgogy, 96,* 187–190.

Goebel, M. (1986). *A computer-aided fluency establishment trainer (CAFET).* Falls Church, VA: Annadale Fluency Clinic.

McFarlane, S. C., & Lavorato, A. S. (1984). The use of videoendoscopy in the evaluation and treatment of dysphonia. *Journal of Communication Disorders, 9,* 117–126.

Prosek, R. A., Montgomery, A. A., Walden, B. E., & Schwartz, D. M. (1978). EMG biofeedback in the treatment of hyperfunctional voice disorder. *Journal of Speech and Hearing Disorders, 43,* 282–294.

Redenbaugh, M. S., & Reich, A. R. (1989). Surface EMG and related measures in normal and vocally hyperfunctional speakers. *Journal of Speech and Hearing Disorders, 54*(1), 68–73.

Sime, W. E., & Healey, E. C. (1993). An interdisciplinary approach to the treatment of a hyperfunctional voice disorder. *Biofeedback and Self-Regulation, 18*(4), 281–287.

Stemple, J. C., Weiler, E., Whitehead, W., & Komray, R. (1980). Electromyographic feedback training with patients exhibiting a hyperfunctional voice disorders. *The Laryngoscope, 90*, 471–476.

Watson, T. S., Allen, S. J., & Allen, K. D. (1993). Ventricular fold dysphonia: Application of biofeedback technology to a rare voice disorder. *Behavior Therapy, 24*, 439–446.

Herpes

Burnette, M. M., Koehn, K. A., Kenyon-Jump, R., Hutton, K., & Stark, C. (1991). Control of genital herpes recurrences using progressive muscle relaxation. *Behavior Therapy, 22*, 237–247.

Longo, D. J., Clum, G. A., & Yaeger, N. J. (1988). Psychosocial treatment of recurrent genital herpes. *Journal of Consulting and Clinical Psychology, 56*, 61–66.

VanderPlate, C., & Kerrick, G. (1985). Stress reduction of severe recurrent genital herpes virus. *Biofeedback and Self-Regulation, 10*(2), 181–188.

Syncope: Stress-Induced or Vasovagal

McGrady, A. V., & Argueta Bernal, G. A. (1986). Relaxation based treatment of stress induced syncope. *Journal of Behavior Therapy and Experimental Psychiatry, 17*(1), 23–27.

Sickle-Cell Crises

Cozzi, L., Tryon, W. W., & Sedacek, K. (1987). The effectiveness of biofeedback-assisted relaxation in modifying sickle cell crisis. *Biofeedback and Self-Regulation, 12*(1), 51–61.

Thomas, J. E., Koshy, M., Patterson, L., Dorn, L., & Thomas, K. (1984). Management of pain in sickle cell disease using biofeedback therapy: A preliminary study. *Biofeedback and Self-Regulation, 9*, 413–420.

Zeltzer, L. K., Kellerman, J., Dash, J., & Holland, J. P. (1979). Hypnotically induced pain control in sickle cell anemia. *Pediatrics, 69*, 533–535.

Erythromelalgia

Babb, R. R., Alarçon-Segovia, D., & Fairbairn, J. P. (1964). Erythermalgia: Review of 51 cases. *Circulation, 2*, 136–141.

Cahn, T. S., & Garber, A. (1990, March). Biofeedback treatment of erythromelalgia: A case study. In *Proceedings of the 21st Annual Meeting of the Association for Applied Psychophysiology and Biofeedback*, Washington, DC. Wheatridge, CO: Association for Applied Psychophysiology and Biofeedback.

Kurzrock, R., & Cohen, P. R. (1989). Erythromelalgia and myeloproliferative disorders. *Archives of International Medicine, 149*, 105–109.

Levine, A. M., & Gustafson, P. R. (1987). Erythromelalgia: Case report and literature review. *Archives of Physical Medicine and Rehabilitation, 68*, 119–121.

Michiels, J. J., & van Joost, T. (1988). Primary and secondary erythermalgia, a critical review (editorial). *Netherlands Journal of Medicine, 33*, 205–208.

Michiels, J. J., & van Joost, T. (1990). Erythromelalgia and thrombocythemia: A causal relation. *Journal of the Academy of Dermatology, 22*(1), 107–111.

Mitchell, S. W. (1878). On a rare vaso-motor neurosis of the extremities, and on the maladies with which it may be confounded. *American Journal of Medical Science, 76*, 2–36.

Putt, A. M. (1978). Erythromelalgia—a case for biofeedback. *Nursing Clinics of North America, 13*(4), 625–630.

Visual Accommodation and Other Oculomotor Abnormalities

Collins, F. L., Pbert, L. A., Sharp, B., Smith, S., Gil, K. M., & Odom, J. V. (1988). Visual acuity improvement following fading and feedback training—I. Comparison of myopic and emmetropic volunteers. *Behaviour Research and Therapy, 26*(6), 461–466.

Halperin, E., & Yolton, R. L. (1986). Ophthalmic applications of biofeedback. *American Journal of Optometry and Physiological Optics, 63*(12), 985–998.

Hodes, R. L., & Howland, E. W. (1986). Ocular and stabilization feedback: An evaluation of two EMG biofeedback control procedures. *Biofeedback and Self-Regulation, 11*(3), 207–220.

Rotberg, M. H., & Surwit, R. S. (1981). Biofeedback techniques in the treatment of visual and ophthalmologic disorders. *Biofeedback and Self-Regulation, 6*(3), 375–388.

Trachtman, J. N. (1987). Biofeedback of accommodation to reduce myopia: A review. *American Journal of Optometry and Physiological Optics, 64*(8), 639–643.

Dysmenorrhea

Balick, L., Elfner, L., May, J., & Moore, J. (1982). Biofeedback treatment of dysmenorrhea. *Biofeedback and Self-Regulation, 7*, 499–520.

Chesney, M. A., & Tasto, D. L. (1975). The effectiveness of behavior modification with spasmodic and congestive dysmenorrhea. *Behaviour Research and Therapy, 13*(4), 245–253.

Dietvorst, T. F., & Osborne, D. (1978). Biofeedback-assisted relaxation training for primary dysmenorrhea: A case study. *Biofeedback and Self-Regulation, 3*(3), 301–305.

Hart, A. D., Mathisen, K. S., & Prater, J. S. (1981). A comparison of skin temperature and EMG training for primary dysmenorrhea. *Biofeedback and Self-Regulation, 6*(3), 367–373.

Reflex Sympathetic Dystrophy

Alioto, J. T. (1981). Behavioral treatment of reflex sympathetic dystrophy. *Psychosomatics, 22*(6), 539–540.

Blanchard, E. B. (1979). The use of temperature biofeedback in the treatment of chronic pain due to causalgia. *Biofeedback and Self-Regulation, 4*(2), 183–188.

Cerebral Palsy

Finley, W. W. (1990). Biofeedback relaxation training for the Cerebral Palsied child. *California Biofeedback: The Newsletter of the Biofeedback Society of California, 6*(3), 1, 12–13, 24–25.

Finley, W. W., Niman, C., Standley, J., & Ender, P. (1976). Frontal EMG biofeedback training of athetoid cerebral palsy patients: A report of six cases. *Biofeedback and Self-Regulation, 1*, 169–182.

Finley, W. W., Ninan, C., Standley, J., & Wansley, R. A. (1977). Electrophysiologic behavior modification of frontal EMG in cerebral palsied children. *Biofeedback and Self-Regulation, 2*, 59–79.

Torticollis

Cleeland, C. S. (1973). Behavioural technics in the modification of spasmodic torticollis. *Neurology, 23*, 1241–1247.

Cleeland, C. S. (1989). Biofeedback and other behavioral techniques in the treatment of disorders of voluntary movement. In J. V. Basmajian (Ed.), *Biofeedback: Principles and practice for clinicians* (3rd ed., pp. 159–167). Baltimore: Williams & Wilkins.

Jahanshahi, M., Sartory, G., & Marsden, C. D. (1991). EMG biofeedback treatment of torticollis: A controlled outcome study. *Biofeedback and Self-Regulation, 16*(4), 413–448.

Korein, J., & Brudney, J. (1976). Integrated EMG feedback in the management of spasmodic torticollis and focal dystonias: A prospective study of 80 patients. In M. D. Yahr (Ed.), *The basal ganglia* (pp. 385–424). New York: Raven Press.

Watanabe, K., Nakagawa, T., Matsuoka, Y., Mishima, N., & Ohno, Y. (1992). Application of EMG biofeedback to the patients with Spasmodic Torticollis. In K. Shirakura, I. Saito, & S. Tsutsui (Eds.), *Current biofeedback research in Japan* (pp. 85–92). Tokyo: Shinkoh Igaku Shuppan.

Dermatologic Disorders

Eczema

Horne, D. J. de L., White, A. E., & Varigos, G. A. (1989). A preliminary study of psychological therapy in the management of atopic eczema. *British Journal of Medical Psychology, 62,* 241–248.

Manuso, J. S. J. (1977). The use of biofeedback-assisted hand warming training in the treatment of chronic eczematous dermatitis of the hands: A case study. *Journal of Behavior Therapy and Experimental Psychiatry, 8,* 445–446.

McMenamy, C. J., Katz, R. C., & Gipson, M. (1988). Treatment of eczema by EMG biofeedback and relaxation training: A multiple baseline analysis. *Journal of Behavior Therapy and Experimental Psychiatry, 19*(3), 221–227.

Miller, R. M., Coger, R. W., & Dymond, A. M. (1974). Biofeedback skin conductance conditioning in dyshidrotic eczema (Letter to the Editor). *Archives of Dermatology, 109,* 737–738.

Psoriasis

Benoit, L. J., & Harrell, E. H. (1980). Biofeedback and control of skin cell proliferation in psoriasis. *Psychological Reports, 46,* 831–839.

Goodman, M. (1994). An hypothesis explaining the successful treatment of psoriasis and thermal biofeedback: A case report. *Biofeedback and Self-Regulation, 19*(4), 347–352.

Hughes, H. H., England, R., & Goldsmith, D. A. (1981). Biofeedback and psychotherapeutic treatment of psoriasis: A brief report. *Psychological Reports, 48,* 99–102.

Winchell, S. A., & Watts, R. A. (1988). Relaxation therapies in the treatment of psoriasis and possible pathophysiologic mechanisms. *Journal of the American Academy of Dermatology, 18*(1), 101–104.

Atopic Dermatitis/Neurodermatitis

Haynes, S. N., Wilson, C. C., Jaffe, P. G., & Britton, B. T. (1979). Biofeedback treatment of atopic dermatitis: Controlled case studies of eight cases. *Biofeedback and Self-Regulation, 4*(3), 195–209.

Cancer Chemotherapy

Bovbjerg, D. H., Redd, W. H., Maier, L. A., Holland, J. C., Lesko, L. M., Niedzwiecki, D., Rubin, S. C., & Hakes, T. B. (1990). Anticipatory immune suppression and nausea in women receiving cyclic chemotherapy for ovarian cancer. *Journal of Consulting and Clinical Psychology, 58*(2), 153–157.

Burish, T. G., & Jenkins, R. A. (1992). Effectiveness of biofeedback and relaxation training in reducing the side effects of cancer chemotherapy. *Health Psychology, 11*(1), 17–23.

Burish, T. G., Shartner, C. D., & Lyles, J. N. (1981). Effectiveness of multiple muscle-site EMG biofeedback and relaxation training in reducing the aversiveness of cancer chemotherapy. *Biofeedback and Self-Regulation, 6*(4), 523–535.

Carey, M. P., & Burish, T. G. (1988). Etiology and treatment of the psychological side effects associated with cancer chemotherapy: A critical review and discussion. *Psychological Bulletin, 104*(3), 307–325.

Shartner, C. D., Burish, T. G., & Carey, M. P. (1985). Effectiveness of biofeedback with progressive muscle relaxation training in reducing the aversiveness of cancer chemotherapy: A preliminary report. *Japanese Journal of Biofeedback Research, 12,* 33–40.

Diabetic Ulcers

Shulimson, A. D., Lawrence, P. F., & Iacono, C. U. (1986). Diabetic ulcers: The effect of thermal biofeedback-mediated relaxation training on healing. *Biofeedback and Self-Regulation 11*(4), 311–319.

Electrical Burn-Related Pain

Bird, E. L., & Colborne, G. R. (1980). Rehabilitation of an electrical burn patient through biofeedback. *Biofeedback and Self-Regulation, 5*(2), 283–287.

Unconscious

Bruner, J. (1992). Another look at new look 1. *American Psychologist, 47*(6), 780–783.

Budzynski, T., Reinking, R., & Mader, J. (1993). *Cyborium 2010.* Available from Hyper Synch Unlimited, P. O. Box 32028, Sarasota, FL 34239, (813) 366-3063.

Erdelyi, M. H. (1992). Psychodynamics and the unconscious. *American Psychologist, 47*(6), 784–787.

Gaarder, K. (1991). Biofeedback and the unconscious mind. *Biofeedback: Newsmagazine of the Association for Applied Psychophysiology and Biofeedback, 19*(1), 16–17.

Ghoneim, M. M., & Block, R. I. (1992). Learning and consciousness during general anesthesia. *Anesthesiology, 76,* 279–305.

Ghoneim, M. M., Block, R. I., & Fowles, D. C. (1992). No evidence of classical conditioning of electrodermal responses during anesthesia. *Anesthesiology, 76,* 682–688.

Greenspan, K. (1991). Clinical encounters with the unconscious. *Biofeedback: Newsmagazine of the Association for Applied Psychophysiology and Biofeedback, 19*(1), 9–11.

Greenwald, A. G. (1992). New look 3: Unconscious cognition reclaimed. *American Psychologist, 47*(6), 766–779.

Jacoby, L. L., Lindsay, D. S., & Toth, J. P. (1992). Unconscious influences revealed: Attention, awareness, and control. *American Psychologist, 47*(6), 802–809.

Kihlstrom, J. F., Barnhardt, T. M., & Tataryn, D. J. (1992). The psychological unconscious: Found, lost, and regained. *American Psychologist, 47*(6), 788–791.

Klonoff, E. A., & Moore, D. J. (1986). "Conversion reactions" in adolescents: A biofeedback-based operant approach. *Journal of Behavior Therapy and Experimental Psychiatry, 17*(3), 179–184.

Lewicki, P., Hill, T., & Czyzewska, M. (1992). Nonconscious acquisition of information. *American Psychologist, 47*(6), 796–801.

Loftus, E. F., & Klinger, M. R. (1992). Is the unconscious smart or dumb? *American Psychologist, 47*(6), 761–765.

Merikle, P. (1992). Perception without awareness: Critical issues. *American Psychologist, 47*(6), 792–795.

Miller, N. E. (1992). Some examples of psychophysiology and the Unconscious. *Biofeedback and Self-Regulation, 17*(1), 3–16.

Shevrin, H. (1991). Discovering how event-related potentials reveal unconscious processes. *Biofeedback: Newsmagazine of the Association for Applied Psychophysiology and Biofeedback, 19*(1), 12–15.

Weiss, J. (1990). Unconscious mental functioning. *Scientific American, March,* 103–109.

Wickramasekera, I. (1991). The unconscious, somatization, psychophysiological psychotherapy and threat perception: Footnotes to a cartography of the unconscious mind. *Biofeedback: Newsmagazine of the Association for Applied Psychophysiology and Biofeedback, 19*(1), 18–23.

Psychoneuroimmunology

Ader, R., Felten, D. L., & Cohn, N. (Eds.). (1991). *Psychoneuroimmunology.* New York: Academic Press.

Bovbjerg, D. H., Redd, W. H., Maier, L. A., Holland, J. C., Lesko, L. M., Niedzwiechi, D., Rubin, S. C., & Hakes, T. B. (1990). Anticipatory immune suppression and nausea in women receiving cyclic chemotherapy for ovarian cancer. *Journal of Consulting and Clinical Psychology, 58*(2), 153–157.

Gruber, B. L., Hall, N. R., Hersh, S. P., & Dubois, P. (1988). Immune system and psychological changes in metastatic cancer patients while using ritualized, relaxation and guided imagery. *Scandinavian Journal of Behavior Therapy, 17*, 25–46.

Gruber, B. L., Hersh, S. P., Hall, N. R. S., Waletzky, L. R., Kunz, J. F., Carpenter, J. K., Kverno, K. S., & Weiss, S. M. (1993). Immunological responses of breast cancer patients to behavioral interventions. *Biofeedback and Self-Regulation, 18*(1), 1–22.

Halley, F. M. (1991). Self-regulation of the immune system through biobehavioral strategies. *Biofeedback and Self-Regulation, 16*(1), 55–74.

Kiecolt-Glaser, J. K., & Glaser, R. (1988). Methodological issues in behavioral immunology research with humans. *Brain, Behavior, and Immunity, 2*, 67–78.

Kiecolt-Glaser, J. K., Glaser, R., Williger, D., Stout, J., Messick, G., Sheppard, S., Ricker, D., Romisher, S. C., Briner, W., Bonnell, G., & Donnerberg, R. (1985). Psychosocial enhancement of immunocompetence in a geriatric population. *Health Psychology, 4*, 25–41.

Kunz, J. F., Gruber, B. L., Tamarkin, L., Paciotti, G., & Hersh, S. P. (1993, March 25–30). Salivary cytokine immune response in patients with systemic lupus erythematosus: A pilot study. In *Proceedings of the 24th Annual Meeting of the Association for Applied Psychophysiology and Biofeedback, Los Angeles*. Wheatridge, CO: Association for Applied Psychophysiology and Biofeedback.

McGrady, A., Conrad, P., Dickey, D., Garman, D., Farris, E., & Schumann-Brzezinski, C. (1992). The effects of biofeedback-assisted relaxation on cell-mediated immunity, cortisol, and white blood cell count in healthy adult subjects. *Journal of Behavioral Medicine, 15*(4), 343–354.

Peavey, B. S., Lawlis, F., & Goven, A. (1985). Biofeedback-assisted relaxation: Effects on Phagocytic capacity. *Biofeedback and Self-Regulation, 10*(1), 33–47.

Pennebaker, J. W., Kiecolt-Glaser, J. K., & Glaser, R. (1988). Disclosure of traumas and immune function: Health implications for psychotherapy. *Journal of Consulting and Clinical Psychology, 56*, 239–245.

O'Leary, A. (1990). Stress, emotion, and human immune function. *Psychological Bulletin, 108*(3), 363–382.

Rider, M. S., & Achterberg, J. (1989). Effect of music-assisted imagery on neutrophils and lymphocytes. *Biofeedback and Self-Regulation, 14*(3), 247–257.

Rider, M. S., Achterberg, J., Lawlis, G. F., Goven, A., Toledo, R., & Butler, J. R. (1990). Effect of immune system imagery on secretary IgA. *Biofeedback and Self-Regulation, 15*(4), 317–333.

Electroencephalography

Cowan, J. D. (1993). Alpha–theta brainwave biofeedback: The many possible theoretical reasons for its success. *Biofeedback: Newmagazine of the Association for Applied Psychophysiology and Biofeedback, 21*(2), 11–16.

Fritz, G. (1992). Letter to the editor. *Biofeedback: Newmagazine of the Association for Applied Psychophysiology and Biofeedback. 20*(3), 5, 9.

Lubar, J. F. (1989). Electroencephalographic biofeedback and neurological applications. In J. V. Basmajian (Ed.), *Biofeedback: Principles and practice for clinicians*, 3rd ed. (pp. 67–90). Baltimore: Williams & Wilkins.

Ochs, L. (1992). EEG treatments of addictions. *Biofeedback: Newmagazine of the Association for Applied Psychophysiology and Biofeedback, 20*(1), 8–16.

Ochs, L. (1993). Interview with Len Ochs by S. R. Kilgoru. *Biofeedback: Newmagazine of the AAPB, 21*(3), 10–14.

Peniston, E. G., & Kulkosky, P. J. (1989). Alpha–theta brainwave training and beta-endorphin levels in alcoholics. *Alcoholism: Clinical and Experimental Research, 13*, 271–279.

Peniston, E. G., & Kulkosky, P. J. (1990). Alcoholic personality and alpha–theta brainwave training. *Medical Psychotherapy: An International Journal, 3*, 37–55.

Peniston, E. G., & Kulkosky, P. J. (1991). Alpha–theta brainwave neurofeedback for Vietnam veterans with combat-related posttraumatic stress disorder. *Medical Psychotherapy: An International Journal, 4*, 47–60.

Peniston, E. G., Kulkosky, P. J., Fahrion, S. L., & Walters, E. D. (1992). Letter to the editor. *Biofeedback: Newmagazine of the Association for Applied Psychophysiology and Biofeedback, 20*(3), 11.

Prochaska, J. O., DiClemente, C. C., & Norcross, J. C. (1992). In search of how people change: Applications to addictive behaviors. *American Psychologist, 47*(9), 1102–1114.

Rosenfeld, J. P. (1992). "EEG" treatment of addictions: Commentary on Ochs, Peniston, and Kulkosky. *Biofeedback: Newmagazine of the Association for Applied Psychophysiology and Biofeedback, 20*(2), 12–17.

Rosenfeld, J. P. (1990). Applied psychophysiology and biofeedback of event-related potentials (brain waves): Historical perspective, review, and future directions (Research Recognition Award Paper). *Biofeedback and Self-Regulation, 15*(2), 99–119.

Rosenfeld, J. P. (1992). New directions in applied psychophysiology. *Biofeedback and Self-Regulation, 17*(2), 77–87.

Tansey, M. (1990a). EEG for a better BP. *Biofeedback: Newmagazine of the Association for Applied Psychophysiology and Biofeedback, 18*(3), 25–28.

Tansey, M. (1990b). EEG for a better BP. *Biofeedback: Newmagazine of the Association for Applied Psychophysiology and Biofeedback, 18*(4), 37–38.

Tansey, M. (1990c). Righting the rhythms of reason: EEG biofeedback training as a therapeutic modality in a clinical office setting. *Medical Psychotherapy, 3*, 57–68.

Wichramasekera, I. (1993). Observations, speculations, and an experimentally testable hypothesis: On the mechanism of the presumed efficacy of the Peniston and Kulkosky procedure. *Biofeedback: Newmagazine of the Association for Applied Psychophysiology and Biofeedback, 21*(2), 17–20.

Wuttke, M. (1992). Addiction, awakening, and EEG biofeedback. *Biofeedback: Newsmagazine of the Association for Applied Psychophysiology and Biofeedback, 20*(2), 18–22.

Hemophilia

LaBaw, W. L. (1975). Auto-hypnosis in haemophilia. *Haematologia, 9*, 103–110.

Lichstein, K. L., & Eakin, T. L. (1985). Progressive versus self-control relaxation to reduce spontaneous bleeding in hemophiliacs. *Journal of Behavioral Medicine, 8*(2), 149–162.

Varni, J. W. (1981). Self-regulation technologies in the management of chronic arthritic pain in hemophilia. *Behavior Therapy, 12*, 185–194.

Others

American Psychiatric Association. (1994). *Diagnostic and statistical manual of mental disorders* (4th ed.). Washington, DC: Author.

Applications Standards Committee. (1992). *Standards and guidelines for biofeedback applications in psychophysiological self-regulation* (pp. 62–66). Wheatridge, CO: Association for Applied Psychophysiology and Biofeedback.

Basmajian, J. V. (Ed.). (1989). *Biofeedback: Principles and practice for clinicians* (3rd ed.). Baltimore: Williams & Wilkins.

Hatch, J. P., Fisher, J. G., & Rugh, J. D. (1987). *Biofeedback: Studies in clinical efficacy*. New York: Plenum Press.

Piotrowski, C., & Lubin, B. (1990). Assessment practices of health psychologists: Survey of APA division clinicians. *Professional Psychology, Research and Practice, 21*(2), 99–106.

Ray, W. J., Raczynski, J. M., Rogers, T., & Kimball, W. H. (1979). *Evaluation of clinical biofeedback*. New York: Plenum Press.

38

Status of Professionals and Publications and One More Look Forward

Mark S. Schwartz
R. Paul Olson

"How do I leave thee? Let me count the ways."[1]
"Fifty ways to close the cover."[2]

Biofeedback and related areas of applied psychophysiology remain a vigorous, intriguing, complex, challenging, and innovative field. The scope and successes of applications continue to be encouraging and often impressive. Wide recognition and acceptance continue by the public, by health care professions, and third-party payers. These contribute to an exciting, yet partially charted future. These enthusiastic statements do not obscure awareness of the problems in the field or the existance of skeptics and critics. However, our enthusiasm now is not fanciful any more than it was 20 years ago.

STATUS OF PROFESSIONAL DEVELOPMENTS AND TOPICS

The annual educational and scientific meeting of the Association for Applied Psychophysiology and Biofeedback (AAPB) is still the major meeting in this field. The AAPB periodically publishes *Task Force Reports* (Hatch, Fisher, & Rugh, 1987) that review research on biofeedback applications. Other publications (Amar et al., 1992; Shellenberger, Amar, Schneider, & Stewart, 1989) also are of value and worth reading. A revision of the *Task Force Reports* is in the planning stage.

In addition to the national organizations, there are many state and regional societies, several of which hold educational and scientific meetings and workshops for professionals. Several private programs[3] provide comprehensive training.

---

[1]Thanks to Robert Browning for "How do I love thee? Let me count the ways."

[2]I (Schwartz) thank Paul Simon for the song "Fifty Ways to Leave Your Lover" and my wife, Nancy, for the revised idea after I shared "How do I leave thee. . . ." Need I add that neither of the revised quotes bears any relationship to our relationship, and only Browning's original does.

[3]Contact the BCIA for a list of their approved programs. See Chapter 29 for addresses.

Educational opportunities exist in many universities and colleges. A large-scale survey of education and training programs was done by Noonberg (1985) in 1980 and is, by now, outdated. He surveyed 344 American Psychological Association (APA) graduate schools. Of the 191 responding, 111 (58%) were offering biofeedback training including mostly didactic graduate instruction and/or practical experience. Of 95 internships responding from among 175 surveyed, 64 (67%) offered internships.

The Education Committee of the AAPB[4] publishes a list of many academic courses focused on biofeedback (e.g., Rubin, Dietvorst, & Sesney, 1987). This came from 51 programs responding to a survey of graduate and undergraduate courses and internships in 27 states and 2 Canadian provinces. The information includes the sponsoring institution, length and level of the courses, practicum and special features of the courses.

Third-party reimbursement for clinical biofeedback applications increased in the 1980s. However, there is still much variation among the states and third-party payers.

The issue of reimbursement relates to the issue of determining who is a qualified clinical provider of biofeedback therapies. In 1980, the Biofeedback Society of America (BSA) sponsored the formation of the Biofeedback Certification Institute of America (BCIA) incorporated early in 1981. The BCIA is an independent, credible, national organization that credentials professionals in biofeedback and separately in stress management education. The biofeedback credential continues to increase in credibility and recognition. For example, a Preferred Provider Organization (PPO) in Florida reportedly uses the BCIA credential as a criterion for reimbursing biofeedback services (T. Dietvorst, personal communication, 1993).

STATUS OF THE PROFESSIONS, DEGREES, AND PRACTITIONER SETTINGS

Professionals with varied educational degrees from many different health care disciplines use biofeedback in many health care settings. Psychology, with its clinical, counseling, and educational specialties, probably still has the most practitioners. Within medicine, there also are several specialties using biofeedback. These include neurology, psychiatry, physical medicine and rehabilitation, cardiovascular medicine, gastroenterology, urology, obstetrics and gynecology, dermatology, rheumatology, endocrinology, ophthalmology, immunology, otorhinolaryngology, and oncology. Practitioners also include physical therapists, occupational therapists, nurses, social workers, speech pathologists, dentists, chiropractors, mental health counselors, marriage and family counselors, pastoral counselors, and educators.

Practitioners use biofeedback and other forms of applied psychophysiology in many settings. These include public and private inpatient and outpatient programs, mental health centers, Veterans Administration medical centers, and on military bases. Many private practice offices also offer biofeedback services. Public schools and many universities and colleges also include biofeedback courses and applications.

A survey of the assessment practices of 270 responding (of 670 surveyed) members of the American Psychological Association's Health Psychology Division, showed 56% (151) mentioned using biofeedback at least for assessment (Piotrowski & Lubin, 1990). Of these 151, 47 frequently used biofeedback, 31 used biofeedback moderately, and 73 used biofeedback occasionally. The 151 respondants using biofeedback were more than those men-

---

[4]Interested readers can contact the AAPB for the list of institutions. See Chapter 29 for addresses.

tioning any of 20 paper-and-pencil measures except the Minnesota Multiphasic Personality Inventory (MMPI).

STATUS OF PUBLICATIONS

Another sign of the vigor of biofeedback is the published literature. The first bibliography of the biofeedback literature, edited by Butler and Stoyva (1973), contained about 850 references. The second edition, published 5 years later, listed about 2300 references (Butler, 1978). Thousands of additional publications have appeared since 1978 (Hatch & Riley, 1985; Hatch & Saito, 1990; Hatch, 1993). There was a downward trend in worldwide publications in English of journal articles from 1985 through 1991 (Hatch, 1993). There was a dramatic increase in dissertations from 1970 to the peak in 1982. However, there was a steady decline from then through 1991 when there were only nine located.

About 150 journal articles appeared each year from 1987 through 1991. There was no decline during that period. Most journal articles appeared in medical journals, although this has been declining since the mid-1980s. Many factors could account for the downward trend. Hatch (1993) speculated that it could partly "reflect the maturation of the field and a move from simplistic and easily performed research toward more complex and sophisticated issues" (p. 147). During these years, economic and political upheavals worldwide and health care crises dislocated professionals in some countries. The effect reduced funding and changed priorities.

Biofeedback has enjoyed a long history and considerable growth in several foreign countries including Japan and Russia. There is much to learn from becoming familiar with published and translated research from these and other countries. The Japanese, Russians, and others from the former U.S.S.R. are prolific researchers and continue to expand our knowledge about biofeedback applications. They have often attempted trials of biofeedback for conditions and disorders for which there are few published accounts elsewhere. See many examples from the Japanese Society of Biofeedback Research in the edited book by Shirakura, Saito, and Tsutshi (1992). Also, see the publication *Biofeedback: Theory and Practice* by Shtark and Kall (1993). It is in Russian with English abstracts.

Some researchers are reluctant to use the term biofeedback in the titles of their research. This probably reduced the number of articles found,[5] since the computerized bibliographical searches reporting the decline required the use of the term biofeedback. Therefore, it probably missed publications and dissertations that involved biofeedback but did not use that term in their title.

The biofeedback field is in a transition stage. Applications are becoming more specific, and some researchers and practitioners are selecting subjects and patients more carefully for treatment. Practitioners and researchers are considering more cognitive variables as is also occurring in related fields such as behavior therapy. Beliefs do have biological consequences. Expectancy and self-efficacy beliefs do affect treatment and compliance.

We are confident that the biofeedback field will remain vibrant and continue to develop. It is not decaying or moving from the heartland into a remote frontier. The concepts underlying biofeedback will continue to thrive. That is, to improve their health,

---

[5]Some researchers perceive and assert that inclusion of the term biofeedback in their list of publications is less valuable for their academic standing. This was part of the rationale for changing the name of the national professional organization to AAPB. In fact, some would drop the term biofeedback entirely, although there is considerable opposition to this proposal, notwithstanding respect for the proponents. Dropping the term biofeedback is not a view shared by all respected researchers.

humans can alter their psychophysiological activity using increased information about that activity.

Many publications in well-respected journals continue to reveal the diversity and richness of the contributions to this field. These include theoretical, experimental, and applied contributions. One need only look at the topics presented at the AAPB, regional, state, and specialty meetings to appreciate this fact.

Scientific scrutiny tempered the enthusiasm and optimism of many during the early years of biofeedback. Scientific support for applied biofeedback increased despite the critics and the complexities of conducting credible and useful research in this field.

OTHER APPLICATIONS AND INNOVATIONS: STATUS AND THE FRONTIER[6]

The development of biofeedback and related therapies is clear in the wide range of applications discussed in this book. One always assumes that successful applications are for selected patients. Selection factors include the integrity of the nervous system, other viable therapies previously and now available, and avoiding contraindications. Practitioner factors affecting success include skills and attitudes about the therapy and the patient. Patient factors affecting success include understanding, attitudes, motivation, and compliance.

A few common successful applications include those for patients with tension-type headaches, migraine headaches, Raynaud's disease, fecal incontinence,[7] urinary incontinence, nocturnal enuresis, essential hypertension, and temporomandibulor disorders.

Successful applications of therapies aided by biofeedback instrumentation and procedures also include neuromuscular motor-control training and re-education for patients with neuromuscular symptoms and disorders. These include spasmodic torticollis and cerebral palsy, and disorders involving peripheral nerve damage, hemiplegia and paraplegia, incomplete spinal cord lesions, lower-motor neuron lesions. Other examples include rehabilitation after muscle-tendon transfers. See Chapters 21 and 22 for more about these applications and prospects for the future.

Other professionals discuss the frontiers of biofeedback in physical rehabilitation. Trying to cover the status and future of this huge and complicated area is the subject of many articles and chapters (e.g., Wolf & Fischer-Williams, 1987; Basmajian, 1989; Middaugh, 1989; Tries, 1989; Sherman & Arena, 1992).

A frontier does not imply totally uncharted or novel areas for exploration. There are inhabitants in a frontier. There are outposts, and minor and major settlements before it becomes a part of the heartland. Crude or approximate forms of order may exist with a rough infrastructure before there is a thoroughly functioning infrastructure.

Parts of a frontier show promise and eventually develop into rich farmland or cities. Other productive and very promising areas last only a limited time and then prove worth-

---

[6]I (Schwartz) chose the term "frontier" rather than "cutting edge" or "leading edge." The term "cutting edge" connotes accomplished and latest technological advances rather than those with much promise and potential. With my conservative bent, I backed away from cutting edge, although some of the ideas and topics may soon be at the cutting edge, and some professionals probably consider some of these already there. "Leading edge" is a good term that could work, but it connotes concepts as most important, uppermost, matchless, best, and much more. I am a stickler for words, although I hope not in the sense of being a fanatic or nitpicker. I do admit to being a perfectionist and a lover of words. It is the precisionist meaning of stickler to which I try to adhere.

[7]Both fecal and urinary incontinence are secondary to a variety of diseases and conditions.

less like an old gold mine. Still others soon turn out to be full of "fools' gold" with a very short life.

Still other areas show promise for a long time but must await a developer or a *Zeitgeist* to blossom into their potential. Even areas with many trappings of civilization need further cultivation and major renovations to reach their potential. Others reach a zenith but wither and decay without continued nurturance and care. The heartland of today can deteriorate tomorrow as the crowded inner cities of our nation decay. Some, like parts of an inner city awaiting redevelopment, hold promise for rebirth and a second coming.

This metaphor fits the therapeutic applications as they currently exist with biofeedback. For example, within the current heartland of biofeedback are applications for tension-type and migraine headaches, and incontinence. These therapeutic areas were once far out on the frontier.

The current frontier includes applications with few case studies and series of cases. It includes applications with many studies supporting success but for which widespread acceptance and habitation have yet to occur.

Admittedly, we do not know which applications will become successful within the heartland rather than remain on the frontier. Similarly, we do not know which will drop off the edge or decay as potential areas of application. We can only speculate and admit that these are impressions.

Furthermore, biofeedback will evolve into parts of interventions for many symptoms rather than as the only intervention. For some applications, biofeedback will apply to selected patients with specified symptoms and conditions rather than for most persons with those symptoms and conditions.

For many disorders, the technology with which the intervention becomes useful and how practitioners apply it will probably change. There may be other interventions such as pharmacological, that become more successful, practical, and more cost efficient than applied psychophysiological interventions. That would detract from the present predictions or the value of applied psychophysiological interventions, although it would not end their value. For example, pharmacological therapy with Desmopressin (DDAVP) for nocturnal enuresis stops bedwetting in nearly all persons. However, the relapse rate is extremely high, so its use does not end the value of the contingent sleep-interruption conditioning treatment. The latter also is much less expensive than using DDAVP.

Frontier applications for several symptoms and disorders are now useful or promising for selected patients. For many of these, biofeedback shows much potential for becoming an accepted part of the heartland. However, they require more exploration and the help of developers and funding to create the needed infrastructure to bring them fully into the heartland. These include constipation, writer's cramp, posture training for scoliosis, hyperhidrosis, functional voice disorders, dysphagia, menopausal hot flashes, visual disorders, functional and conditioned nausea and vomiting, tinnitus, fibromyalgia, postpolio symptoms, and attention-deficit disorder and attention-deficit/hyperactivity disorder (ADD/ADHD).

A LAST LOOK FORWARD

Within the next few years, we expect continued developments within at least the following areas of biofeedback:

1. Scientific advances will continue to show increased quality of research. These will include comparative studies with other treatments for various disorders and studies studying process variables and analyzing treatment components.

2. Applications will extend to additional medical disorders and more types of populations.

3. Increased professionalism will continue to show itself in several ways.

4. Increasingly sophisticated, sensitive, and reliable office instrumentation, recording techniques, and procedures will become readily available and practical to use.

5. Increasingly sophisticated and practical ambulatory recording and feedback instrumentation will become readily available.

6. Researchers and clinicians will work more closely together and gain more understanding and sensitivity about their interdependence and unique contributions to each other.

7. New and reliable biofeedback modalities will become available for which no current and practical instrumentation exits. These will permit monitoring and feedback about patients' physiological and biochemical events and processes.

8. Multi-institutional studies of the role of biofeedback therapies will take place to help support the efficacy and cost effectiveness of such therapies.

9. There will be more clarification of the disagreements about the active components of biofeedback. These attempts will help reconceptualize the factors affecting outcome. These include information, cognitive factors, and expectancy.

10. Specific applications will continue to emerge and develop. These will focus on specific feedback techniques rather than techniques for reduction of general tension and arousal. These applications will target specific symptoms or clusters of symptoms.

11. Several more areas of application will emerge from the frontier and enter the heartland of widespread professional acceptance.

12. Knowledge and sophistication will increase for selecting patients for specific applications. This will increase the success of these applications and improve cost-efficiency.

WHAT CAN YOU DO?

Most practitioners, researchers, educators, and students know they must continue to read voraciously. One must do this to learn, improve, avoid misinformation, teach accurately, and conduct valuable and useful research. Most also know that they must attend the annual AAPB meeting and regional and state meetings that include applied psychophysiology and biofeedback. Membership in these organizations brings strength to the organizations and to members. We realize the costs can be significant for maintaining memberships and attending meetings. However, there are costs for avoiding these responsibilities. If you cannot join several, then join one. If you cannot attend several meetings, then attend one major meeting per year. Whatever you do and how often you do it, just do it.

We encourage these organizations to continue creative and cost effective methods for providing education to those professionals who cannot otherwise attend. In addition to books and audio- and videotapes, we encourage television conferences and a program for consultants and lecturers.

There is another strong recommendation and request to readers. Please contribute to the Foundation for Education and Research in Biofeedback and Related Sciences[8] (The AAPB Foundation). Help it grow to a major source of funding for research, education, and scholarships. It is the only such organization of its kind. There is probably not enough time for the Foundation to grow to a major source of research and educational support for professionals of our generation. However, many of us can bequeath ample funds for future

[8]Mailing address is 10200 West 44th Ave., Suite 304, Wheatridge, CO, 80033.

generations. For example, in one Life Insurance Trust, one member of AAPB includes a bequest of at least $35,000.

FINALE: CLOSING THE COVER

Researchers and practitioners often do not know for sure when an application or technique represents a frontier opening into fertile fields. They may be standing at the edge of a precipice or future wasteland. Nevertheless, many continue to be passionate, in the sense of ardent and enthusiastic. Many continue to be dynamic, vigorous, assertive and bold, yet flexible. They continue to be pensive, yet warm, engaging, and humorous.

Those of us who started in this field 20–25 years ago viewed all applications in the frontier. Many were potentially near a precipice or wasteland. Now, we have good research support and widespread clinical applications for many symptoms and disorders. We had to start somewhere, and Neal Miller's guidance to "be bold in what we try" is still applicable today. We also must remember and adhere to the other part of his advice "to be cautious in what we claim" (Miller, 1976).

We can and must work together as practitioners, researchers, and educators. We can and must understand our mutual interdependency and join as fellow travelers and good Samaritans.

Be inquisitive, creative, and maintain high standards of professional ethics. Become more involved and support professional membership organizations. Maintain continued competence.

Biofeedback will and must continue as a major and expanding focus within applied psychophysiology, behavioral health, and behavioral medicine. It will and must continue as a major part of health care intervention. As Middaugh (1990) reflects,

> In these days of accountability, how can we justify working with muscles and *not* use EMG monitoring? How can we teach relaxation and *not* monitor physiological changes? (p. 207; emphasis added)

Many of the goals we seek are akin to the top of a high and rugged mountain. However, it is the sides of the mountain that sustain life, not the top. It is the ski slope, not the top that bears the fun. It is the journey that is the adventure, not reaching a place. Enjoy the journey. We thank each reader and others and wish you all a productive, healthy, and exciting journey.

We thank Susan Middaugh (1990) for a quote to close the volume. Significantly, it is the one she used to close her presidential address.

> Biofeedback instrumentation is not only a tool to help us *do*, but a tool to help us *think* about what we are doing, and what our patients and our studies are telling us about why biofeedback does—and does not—work. (p. 207)

REFERENCES

Amar, P. B., McKee, M. G., Peavey, B. S., Schneider, C. J., Sherman, R. A., & Sterman, M. B. (1992). *Standards and guidelines for biofeedback applications in psychophysiological self-regulation.* Wheatridge, CO: Association for Applied Psychophysiology and Biofeedback.

Basmajian, J. V. (Ed.). (1989). *Biofeedback: Principles and practice for clinicians* (3rd ed.). Baltimore: Williams & Wilkins.

Butler, F. (1978). *Biofeedback: A survey of the literature.* New York: Plenum Press.

Butler, F., & Stoyva, J. (1973). *Biofeedback and self-control: A bibliography.* Wheatridge, CO: Biofeedback Society of America.

Hatch, J. P. (1993, March 25–30). Declining rates of publication within the field of biofeedback continue: 1988–1991. In *Proceedings of the 24th annual meeting of the Association for Applied Psychophysiology and Biofeedback, Los Angeles* (pp. 146–149). Wheatridge, CO: Association for Applied Psychophysiology and Biofeedback.

Hatch, J. P., Fisher, J. G., & Rugh, J. D. (Eds.). (1987). *Biofeedback: Studies in clinical efficacy.* New York: Plenum Press.

Hatch, J. P., & Riley, P. (1985). Growth and development of biofeedback: A bibliographic analysis. *Biofeedback and Self-Regulation, 10*(4), 289–299.

Hatch, J. P., & Saito, I. (1990). Growth and development of biofeedback: A bibliographic update. *Biofeedback and Self-Regulation, 15*(1), 37–46.

Middaugh, S. (1989). Biobehavioral techniques. In R. Scully & M. Barnes (Eds.), *Physical therapy* (pp. 986–997). Philadelphia, PA: J. B. Lippincott.

Middaugh, S. J. (1990). On clinical efficacy: Why biofeedback does—and does not—work (Presidential Address). *Biofeedback and Self-Regulation, 15*(3), 191–208.

Miller, N. E. (1976). Fact and fancy about biofeedback and its clinical implications. In *Catalog of selected documents in psychology* (Vol. 6, p. 92). Washington, DC: American Psychological Association.

Noonberg, A. R. (1985). Biofeedback training: Offerings, plans, and some attitudes in graduate schools and internships. *Biofeedback and Self-Regulation, 10*(1), 25–32.

Piotrowski, C., & Lubin, B. (1990). Assessment practices of health psychologists: Survey of APA Division Clinicians. *Professional Psychology, Research and Practice, 21*(2), 99–106.

Rubin, N. J., Dietvorst, T. F., & Sesney, J. W. (1988). Academic courses in biofeedback. *Biofeedback and Self-Regulation, 13*(3), 267–270.

Shellenberger, R., Amar, P., Schneider, C., & Stewart, R. (1989). *Clinical efficacy and cost effectiveness of biofeedback therapy: Guidelines for third party reimbursement.* Wheatridge, CO: Association for Applied Psychophysiology and Biofeedback.

Shellenberger, R., Amar, P., Schneider, C., & Turner, J. (1994). *Clinical efficacy and cost effectiveness of biofeedback therapy: Guidelines for third party reimbursement* (2nd ed.). Wheatridge, CO: Association for Applied Psychophysiology and Biofeedback.

Sherman, R. A., & Arena, J. G. (1992). Biofeedback in the assessment and treatment of low back pain. In J. V. Basmajian & R. Nyberg (Eds.), *Spinal manipulation therapies* (pp. 177–197). Baltimore, MD: Williams & Wilkins.

Shirakura, K., Saito, I., & Tsutsui, S. (Eds.). (1992). *Current biofeedback research in Japan.* Tokyo: Shinkoh Igadu Shuppan.

Shtark, M. B., & Kall, R. (Eds.). (1993). *Biofeedback-2: Theory and practice* (in Russian). Trevose, PA: Futurehealth; and Institute of Medical and Biological Cybernetics, Siberian Department, Russian Academy of Medical Science, Novosibirsk.

Tries, J. (1989). EMG feedback for the treatment of upper-extremity dysfunction: Can it be effective? *Biofeedback and Self-Regulation, 14*, 21–53.

Wolf, S. L., & Fischer-Williams, M. (1987). The use of biofeedback in disorders of motor function. In J. P. Hatch, J. G. Fisher, & J. D. Rugh (Eds.), *Biofeedback: Studies in clinical efficacy* (pp. 153–177). New York: Plenum Press.

Index